Contemporary Authors®
NEW REVISION SERIES

ISSN 0275-7176

Contemporary Authors®

A Bio-Bibliographical Guide to
Current Writers in Fiction, General Nonfiction,
Poetry, Journalism, Drama, Motion Pictures,
Television, and Other Fields

NEW REVISION SERIES
volume 99

GALE GROUP

THOMSON LEARNING

Detroit • New York • San Diego • San Francisco
Boston • New Haven, Conn. • Waterville, Maine
London • Munich

Library of Congress Catalog Card Number 62-52046
ISBN 0-7876-4608-3
ISSN 0275-7176
Printed in the United States of America

10 9 8 7 6 5 4 3 2 1

Contents

Preface

Contemporary Authors (*CA*) provides information on approximately 100,000 writers in a wide range of media, including:

- Current writers of fiction, nonfiction, poetry, and drama whose works have been issued by commercial publishers, risk publishers, or university presses (authors whose books have been published only by known vanity or author-subsidized firms are ordinarily not included)

- Prominent print and broadcast journalists, editors, photojournalists, syndicated cartoonists, graphic novelists, screenwriters, television scriptwriters, and other media people

- Authors who write in languages other than English, provided their works have been published in the United States or translated into English

- Literary greats of the early twentieth century whose works are popular in today's high school and college curriculums and continue to elicit critical attention

A *CA* listing entails no charge or obligation. Authors are included on the basis of the above criteria and their interest to *CA* users. Sources of potential listees include trade periodicals, publishers' catalogs, librarians, and other users.

How to Get the Most out of *CA*: Use the Index

The key to locating an author's most recent entry is the *CA* cumulative index, which is published separately and distributed twice a year. It provides access to *all* entries in *CA* and *Contemporary Authors New Revision Series* (*CANR*). Always consult the latest index to find an author's most recent entry.

For the convenience of users, the *CA* cumulative index also includes references to all entries in these Gale literary series: *Authors and Artists for Young Adults, Authors in the News, Bestsellers, Black Literature Criticism, Black Literature Criticism Supplement, Black Writers, Children's Literature Review, Concise Dictionary of American Literary Biography, Concise Dictionary of British Literary Biography, Contemporary Authors Autobiography Series, Contemporary Authors Bibliographical Series, Contemporary Dramatists, Contemporary Literary Criticism, Contemporary Novelists, Contemporary Poets, Contemporary Popular Writers, Contemporary Southern Writers, Contemporary Women Poets, Dictionary of Literary Biography, Dictionary of Literary Biography Documentary Series, Dictionary of Literary Biography Yearbook, DISCovering Authors, DISCovering Authors: British, DISCovering Authors: Canadian, DISCovering Authors: Modules* (including modules for Dramatists, Most-Studied Authors, Multicultural Authors, Novelists, Poets, and Popular/Genre Authors), *DISCovering Authors 3.0, Drama Criticism, Drama for Students, Feminist Writers, Hispanic Literature Criticism, Hispanic Writers, Junior DISCovering Authors, Major Authors and Illustrators for Children and Young Adults, Major 20th-Century Writers, Native North American Literature, Novels for Students, Poetry Criticism, Poetry for Students, Short Stories for Students, Short Story Criticism, Something about the Author, Something about the Author Autobiography Series, St. James Guide to Children's Writers, St. James Guide to Crime & Mystery Writers, St. James Guide to Fantasy Writers, St. James Guide to Horror, Ghost & Gothic Writers, St. James Guide to Science Fiction Writers, St. James Guide to Young Adult Writers, Twentieth-Century Literary Criticism, 20th Century Romance and Historical Writers, World Literature Criticism,* and *Yesterday's Authors of Books for Children.*

A Sample Index Entry:

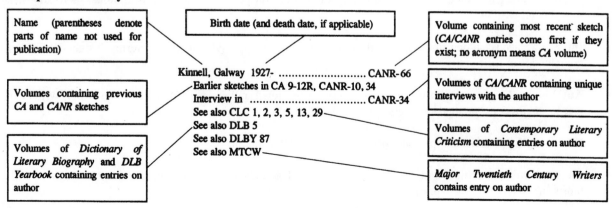

How Are Entries Compiled?

The editors make every effort to secure new information directly from the authors; listees' responses to our questionnaires and query letters provide most of the information featured in *CA*. For deceased writers, or those who fail to reply to requests for data, we consult other reliable biographical sources, such as those indexed in Gale's *Biography and Genealogy Master Index,* and bibliographical sources, including *National Union Catalog, LC MARC,* and *British National Bibliography.* Further details come from published interviews, feature stories, and book reviews, as well as information supplied by the authors' publishers and agents.

An asterisk (*) at the end of a sketch indicates that the listing has been compiled from secondary sources believed to be reliable but has not been personally verified for this edition by the author sketched.

What Kinds of Information Does An Entry Provide?

Sketches in *CA* contain the following biographical and bibliographical information:

- **Entry heading:** the most complete form of author's name, plus any pseudonyms or name variations used for writing

- **Personal information:** author's date and place of birth, family data, ethnicity, educational background, political and religious affiliations, and hobbies and leisure interests

- **Addresses:** author's home, office, or agent's addresses, plus e-mail and fax numbers, as available

- **Career summary:** name of employer, position, and dates held for each career post; resume of other vocational achievements; military service

- **Membership information:** professional, civic, and other association memberships and any official posts held

- **Awards and honors:** military and civic citations, major prizes and nominations, fellowships, grants, and honorary degrees

- **Writings:** a comprehensive, chronological list of titles, publishers, dates of original publication and revised editions, and production information for plays, television scripts, and screenplays

- **Adaptations:** a list of films, plays, and other media which have been adapted from the author's work

- **Work in progress:** current or planned projects, with dates of completion and/or publication, and expected publisher, when known

- **Sidelights:** a biographical portrait of the author's development; information about the critical reception of the author's works; revealing comments, often by the author, on personal interests, aspirations, motivations, and thoughts on writing

- **Interview:** a one-on-one discussion with authors conducted especially for *CA*, offering insight into authors' thoughts about their craft

- **Autobiographical essay:** an original essay written by noted authors for *CA*, a forum in which writers may present themselves, on their own terms, to their audience

- **Photographs:** portraits and personal photographs of notable authors

- **Biographical and critical sources:** a list of books and periodicals in which additional information on an author's life and/or writings appears

- **Obituary Notices** in *CA* provide date and place of birth as well as death information about authors whose full-length sketches appeared in the series before their deaths. The entries also summarize the authors' careers and writings and list other sources of biographical and death information.

Related Titles in the *CA* Series

Contemporary Authors Autobiography Series complements *CA* original and revised volumes with specially commissioned autobiographical essays by important current authors, illustrated with personal photographs they provide. Common topics include their motivations for writing, the people and experiences that shaped their careers, the rewards they derive from their work, and their impressions of the current literary scene.

Contemporary Authors Bibliographical Series surveys writings by and about important American authors since World War II. Each volume concentrates on a specific genre and features approximately ten writers; entries list works written by and about the author and contain a bibliographical essay discussing the merits and deficiencies of major critical and scholarly studies in detail.

Available in Electronic Formats

GaleNet. *CA* is available on a subscription basis through GaleNet, an online information resource that features an easy-to-use end-user interface, powerful search capabilities, and ease of access through the World-Wide Web. For more information, call 1-800-877-GALE.

Licensing. *CA* is available for licensing. The complete database is provided in a fielded format and is deliverable on such media as disk, CD-ROM, or tape. For more information, contact Gale's Business Development Group at 1-800-877-GALE, or visit us on our website at www.galegroup.com/bizdev.

Suggestions Are Welcome

The editors welcome comments and suggestions from users on any aspect of the *CA* series. If readers would like to recommend authors for inclusion in future volumes of the series, they are cordially invited to write the Editors at *Contemporary Authors*, Gale Group, 27500 Drake Rd., Farmington Hills, MI 48331-3535; or call at 1-248-699-4253; or fax at 1-248-699-8054.

Contemporary Authors Product Advisory Board

The editors of *Contemporary Authors* are dedicated to maintaining a high standard of excellence by publishing comprehensive, accurate, and highly readable entries on a wide array of writers. In addition to the quality of the content, the editors take pride in the graphic design of the series, which is intended to be orderly yet inviting, allowing readers to utilize the pages of *CA* easily and with efficiency. Despite the longevity of the *CA* print series, and the success of its format, we are mindful that the vitality of a literary reference product is dependent on its ability to serve its users over time. As literature, and attitudes about literature, constantly evolve, so do the reference needs of students, teachers, scholars, journalists, researchers, and book club members. To be certain that we continue to keep pace with the expectations of our customers, the editors of *CA* listen carefully to their comments regarding the value, utility, and quality of the series. Librarians, who have firsthand knowledge of the needs of library users, are a valuable resource for us. The *Contemporary Authors* Product Advisory Board, made up of school, public, and academic librarians, is a forum to promote focused feedback about *CA* on a regular basis. The five-member advisory board includes the following individuals, whom the editors wish to thank for sharing their expertise:

- **Barbara C. Chumard,** Reference/Adult Services Librarian, Middletown Thrall Library, Middletown, New York.

- **Eva M. Davis,** Teen Services Librarian, Plymouth District Library, Plymouth, Michigan.

- **Adam Janowski, Jr.,** Library Media Specialist, Naples High School Library Media Center, Naples, Florida.

- **Robert Reginald,** Head of Technical Services and Collection Development, California State University, San Bernadino, California.

- **Barbara A. Wencl,** Media Specialist, Como Park High School, St. Paul, Minnesota.

International Advisory Board

Well-represented among the 100,000 author entries published in *Contemporary Authors* are sketches on notable writers from many non-English-speaking countries. The primary criteria for inclusion of such authors has traditionally been the publication of at least one title in English, either as an original work or as a translation. However, the editors of *Contemporary Authors* came to observe that many important international writers were being overlooked due to a strict adherence to our inclusion criteria. In addition, writers who were publishing in languages other than English were not being covered in the traditional sources we used for identifying new listees. Intent on increasing our coverage of international authors, including those who write only in their native language and have not been translated into English, the editors enlisted the aid of a board of advisors, each of whom is an expert on the literature of a particular country or region. Among the countries we focused attention on in 2000 are Mexico, Puerto Rico, Germany, Luxembourg, Belgium, the Netherlands, Norway, Sweden, Denmark, Finland, Taiwan, Singapore, and Japan, as well as England, Scotland, Wales, Ireland, Australia, and New Zealand. The nine-member advisory board includes the following individuals, whom the editors wish to thank for sharing their expertise:

- **Lowell A. Bangerter,** Professor of German, University of Wyoming, Laramie, Wyoming.

- **David William Foster,** Regent's Professor of Spanish, Interdisciplinary Humanities, and Women's Studies, Arizona State University, Tempe, Arizona.

- **Frances Devlin-Glass,** Associate Professor, School of Literary and Communication Studies, Deakin University, Burwood, Victoria, Australia.

- **Hosea Hirata,** Director of the Japanese Program, Associate Professor of Japanese, Tufts University, Medford, Massachusetts.

- **Linda M. Rodríguez Guglielmoni,** Associate Professor, University of Puerto Rico—Mayagüez, Puerto Rico.

- **Sven Hakon Rossel,** Professor and Chair of Scandanvian Studies, University of Vienna, Vienna, Austria.

- **Steven R. Serafin,** Director, Writing Center, Hunter College of the City University of New York, New York City.

- **Ismail S. Talib,** Senior Lecturer, Department of English Language and Literature, National University of Singapore, Singapore.

- **Mark Williams,** Associate Professor, English Department, University of Canterbury, Christchurch, New Zealand.

CA Numbering System and Volume Update Chart

Occasionally questions arise about the *CA* numbering system and which volumes, if any, can be discarded. Despite numbers like " 29-32R," " 97-100" and " 190," the entire *CA* print series consists of only 217 physical volumes with the publication of *CA* Volume 191. The following charts note changes in the numbering system and cover design, and indicate which volumes are essential for the most complete, up-to-date coverage.

CA First Revision
- 1-4R through 41-44R (11 books)
  Cover: Brown with black and gold trim.
  There will be no further First Revision volumes because revised entries are now being handled exclusively through the more efficient *New Revision Series* mentioned below.

CA Original Volumes
- 45-48 through 97-100 (14 books)
  Cover: Brown with black and gold trim.
  101 through 191 (91 books)
  Cover: Blue and black with orange bands.
  The same as previous *CA* original volumes but with a new, simplified numbering system and new cover design.

CA Permanent Series
- *CAP*-1 and *CAP*-2 (2 books)
  Cover: Brown with red and gold trim.
  There will be no further Permanent Series volumes because revised entries are now being handled exclusively through the more efficient *New Revision Series* mentioned below.

CA New Revision Series
- CANR-1 through CANR-99 (99 books)
  Cover: Blue and black with green bands.
  Includes only sketches requiring significant changes; **sketches are taken from any previously published CA, CAP, or CANR volume.**

If You Have:	You May Discard:
CA First Revision Volumes 1-4R through 41-44R and *CA Permanent Series* Volumes 1 and 2	*CA* Original Volumes 1, 2, 3, 4 Volumes 5-6 through 41-44
CA Original Volumes 45-48 through 97-100 and 101 through 191	**NONE:** These volumes will not be superseded by corresponding revised volumes. Individual entries from these and all other volumes appearing in the left column of this chart may be revised and included in the various volumes of the *New Revision Series*.
CA New Revision Series Volumes *CANR*-1 through *CANR*-99	**NONE:** The *New Revision Series* does not replace any single volume of *CA*. Instead, volumes of *CANR* include entries from many previous *CA* series volumes. All *New Revision Series* volumes must be retained for full coverage.

A Sampling of Authors and Media People
Featured in This Volume

Peter Ackroyd

An accomplished, versatile writer, Ackroyd has authored works ranging from poems to novels, criticism to biographies. He first became prominent in literary circles as a biographer of Ezra Pound, T. S. Eliot, and Charles Dickens, but soon won acclaim for his novels, which frequently fictionalize the lives of famous historical personalities such as Oscar Wilde and the poet Thomas Chatterton. In 1985 Ackroyd received both the Whitbread Award and the *Guardian* fiction prize for the novel *Hawksmoor,* and in 1998, the James Tait Black Memorial Prize for Best Biography for *The Life of Thomas More.*

Amit Chaudhuri

Chaudhuri, a novelist born in Calcutta, India, raised in Bombay, and educated in England, has drawn attention from critics for his ability to write with affection about his native land. *A Strange and Sublime Address,* which is comprised of a novella and short stories, met with critical acclaim and won the author the Betty Trask Award (regularly bestowed to first-time novelists under the age of thirty-five). Chaudhuri's lyrical prose often bears the imprint of the visual arts, especially Indian folk art, which the author believes has retained certain aspects of cultural integrity that colonialism sought to abolish. Chaudhuri is also the author of the novels *Afternoon Raag* and 2000's *A New World.*

Seymour M. Hersh

Hersh first gained prominence as an investigative reporter in November, 1969, when he broke the story of the My Lai massacre in Vietnam. Initially refused by several publishers, the series was eventually picked up by the independent Dispatch News Service and earned Hersh a Pulitzer Prize for international reporting as well as several other prestigious awards. He was hired by the *New York Times* in 1972 and, over the next three decades, has received numerous honors for his investigative reporting. Among Hersh's titles are *The Price of Power: Kissinger in the Nixon White House, The Samson Option: Israel's Nuclear Arsenal and American Foreign Policy,* and *Against All Enemies: Gulf War Syndrome; The War between America's Ailing Veterans and Their Government.*

Denis Johnson

Johnson's poems and novels provide candid, slice-of-life perspectives on offbeat subjects. In his first verse collection, *The Man among the Seals,* he included poems about a man imagining an auto mishap and one speculating about the lives of two mice trapped in mousetraps. These and other poems in the volume were prized for their lively structure—rolling rhythms and sometimes jarring line breaks—as well as for their somewhat odd points of view. Johnson's highly praised novels include *Angels* and *Fiskadoro.* He is also the author of *Jesus's Son,* a collection of short fiction consisting of eleven brief, interconnected stories narrated by an unnamed young man who is addicted to drugs and alcohol.

Julia Kristeva

Kristeva is one of the most influential and prolific thinkers of modern France. Trained in linguistics, psychoanalysis, and literary criticism, her cross-disciplinary writings have been praised by colleagues from a wide variety of academic departments. She is most widely known for her contribution to literary theory, such as 1980's *Desire in Language: A Semiotic Approach to Literature and Art* and her 1974 examination of modernist poetry and prose *Revolution in Poetic Language.* In addition to her theoretical works, Kristeva has also published several novels; 1990's *Les Samourais* (translation published as *The Samurai*) is a semi-autobiographical work that incorporates characters representative of several Parisian intellectuals of the mid-1960s.

Richard Matheson

A versatile writer with an affinity for horror, science fiction, fantasy, and suspense, Matheson is the author of the vampire novel *I am Legend,* the science fiction novel *The Shrinking Man,* and the suspenseful novels *A Stir of Echoes, Hell House,* and *Duel.* Matheson, whose fiction finds terror in the most mundane aspects of life, is also noted for the memorable scripts he contributed to the original *Twilight Zone* television show of the 1960s and for his screenplay *The Incredible Shrinking Man,* adapted from his novel. In 1984, he was honored with the World Fantasy Lifetime Achievement Award.

Geoffrey Moorhouse

Moorhouse is best known for his innovative travel writings. An editor and writer affiliated with various English newspapers for nearly two decades, he began publishing book-length accounts of his world travels in the 1960s. Among his works are *Against All Reason,* an investigation into monastic life, *The Fearful Void,* which describes Moorhouse's solitary crossing of the Sahara desert, and *The Boat and the Town* a product of a year the author spent working as a deep-sea fisherman out of Gloucester, Massachusetts. In 1984, Moorhouse received the Thomas Cook Travel Book Award for *To the Frontier: A Journey to the Khyber Pass.*

Alicia Ostriker

Ostriker is the author of numerous books of poetry and several works of feminist literary criticism that examine the relationship between gender and literature. In *Stealing the Language: The Emergence of Women Poets in America,* Ostriker emphasizes her theory that women poets are "challenging and transforming the history of poetry. They constitute a literary movement comparable to romanticism or modernism in our literary past." She is the recipient of many honors, including the William Carlos Williams Prize for the poetry volume *The Imaginary Lover.*

Acknowledgments

Grateful acknowledgment is made to those publishers, photographers, and artists whose work appear with these authors' essays. Following is a list of the copyright holders who have granted us permission to reproduce material in this volume of *CA*. Every effort has been made to trace copyright, but if omissions have been made, please let us know.

Photographs/Art

Peter Ackroyd: Ackroyd, photograph. © Jerry Bauer. Reproduced by permission.

Yehuda Amichai: Amichai, photograph. © Jerry Bauer. Reproduced by permission.

Ira Berkow: Berkow, photograph. © The New York Times. Reproduced by permission.

Glen Cook: Cook, photograph. © 1998 Olan Mills. Reproduced by permission of the author.

Stanley Crouch: Crouch, photograph by Martine Bisagni. Reproduced by permission.

Robert Gale: Gale, photograph. AP/Wide World Photos. Reproduced by permission.

Seymour Hersh: Hersh, photograph. AP/Wide World Photos. Reproduced by permission.

Ted Koppel: Koppel, photograph. AP/Wide World Photos. Reproduced by permission.

Julia Kristeva: Kristeva, photograph. © Jerry Bauer. Reproduced by permission.

Bernard Levy: Levy, photograph. The Library of Congress.

Peter Lovesey: Lovesey, photograph. © Phil Monk. Reproduced by permission.

Shirley MacLaine: MacLaine, photograph. © Archive Photos. Reproduced by permission.

Richard Matheson: Matheson, photograph. Tor Books. Reproduced by permission.

Colum McCann: McCann, photograph. © Jerry Bauer. Reproduced by permission.

Alicia Ostriker: Ostriker, photograph by J. P. Ostriker. Reproduced by permission of Alicia Ostriker.

Mario Puzo: Puzo, photograph. © Jerry Bauer. Reproduced by permission.

Rainer Maria Rilke: Rilke, photograph. Corbis-Bettmann Reproduced by permission.

David Shields: Shields, photograph by Tom Collicott. Reproduced by permission.

Danielle Steel: Steel, photograph. © Ed Kashi/Corbis. Reproduced by permission.

Whit Stillman: Stillman, photograph. The Kobal Collection. Reproduced by permission.

A

ACKROYD, Peter 1949-

PERSONAL: Born October 5, 1949, in London, England; son of Graham and Audrey (Whiteside) Ackroyd. *Education:* Clare College, Cambridge, M.A., 1971; attended Yale University, 1971-73.

ADDRESSES: Home—London, England. *Agent*—Anthony Sheil Associates Ltd., 43 Doughty St., London WC1N 2LF, England.

CAREER: Writer. *Spectator,* literary editor, 1973-77, managing editor, 1977-81; London *Times,* television critic, 1977-81; chief book reviewer, 1986—.

MEMBER: Royal Society of Literature (fellow).

AWARDS, HONORS: Somerset Maugham Award, 1984, for *The Last Testament of Oscar Wilde;* Whitbread Award and fiction prize from *Guardian,* both 1985, for *Hawksmoor;* Heinemann Award for nonfiction, Royal Society of Literature, 1985, for *T. S. Eliot: A Life;* James Tait Black Memorial Prize for Best Biography, University of Edinburgh, 1998, for *The Life of Thomas More.*

WRITINGS:

POETRY

Ouch, Curiously Strong Press (London), 1971.
London Lickpenny (also see below), Ferry Press (London), 1973.
Country Life (also see below), Ferry Press, 1978.

Peter Ackroyd

The Diversions of Purley, and Other Poems (contains poems from *London Lickpenny* and *Country Life*), Hamish Hamilton (London), 1987.

NOVELS

The Great Fire of London, Hamish Hamilton, 1982.
The Last Testament of Oscar Wilde, Harper (New York City), 1983.

Hawksmoor, Hamish Hamilton, 1985, reprinted, Harper, 1986.

Chatterton, Grove (New York City), 1988.

First Light, Viking Penguin (New York City), 1989.

English Music, Knopf (New York City), 1992.

The House of Doctor Dee, Hamish Hamilton, 1993, reprinted, Penguin (New York City), 1994.

Dan Leno and the Limehouse Golem, Sinclair-Stevenson (London), 1994, published as *The Trial of Elizabeth Cree: A Novel of the Limehouse Murders,* Nan A. Talese (New York City), 1995.

Milton in America, Nan A. Talese, 1997.

The Plato Papers: A Prophecy, Nan A. Talese, 2000.

NONFICTION

Notes for a New Culture: An Essay on Modernism, Barnes & Noble (New York City), 1976.

Dressing Up: Transvestism and Drag: The History of an Obsession, Simon & Schuster (New York City), 1979.

Ezra Pound and His World, Scribner (New York City), 1981.

T. S. Eliot: A Life, Simon & Schuster, 1984.

(Editor) *PEN New Fiction,* Quartet Books (London), 1984.

Dickens, Sinclair-Stevenson, 1990, reprinted, HarperPerennial (New York City), 1992.

Introduction to Dickens, Sinclair-Stevenson, 1991, reprinted, Ballantine (New York City), 1992.

Blake, Sinclair-Stevenson (London), 1995.

(Editor) Oscar Wilde, *The Picture of Dorian Gray,* G. K. Hall (Thorndike, ME), 1995.

The Life of Thomas More, Chatto & Windus (London), 1998.

London: The Biography, Chatto & Windus, 2000.

Contributor of short story "The Inheritance" to the anthology *London Tales,* edited by Julian Evans, Hamish Hamilton, 1983. Author of introductions to *Dickens' London: An Imaginative Vision,* Headline (London), 1987, and *Recent Works,* by Frank Auerbach, Marlborough (New York City), 1994. Contributor of book reviews to periodicals, including the *New York Times Book Review.*

SIDELIGHTS: Considered an accomplished, versatile writer, Peter Ackroyd has authored works ranging from poems to novels, criticism to biography. He was published first as a poet. His first book, *London Lickpenny,* prompted a *Times Literary Supplement* reviewer to deem him "a delicate and insistent stylist" whose words

"[make] not only an odd poetry, but a poetry out of the oddness of the world." Ackroyd came to literary prominence, however, as a biographer, and his well-received volumes on literary giants T. S. Eliot and Charles Dickens were complemented by his novels, which frequently fictionalize the lives of famous historical personalities such as Oscar Wilde and Thomas Chatterton. Glen M. Johnson, writing in the *Dictionary of Literary Biography,* explained that "as his career has developed, Ackroyd has sought 'a new way to interanimate' biography and fiction." In addition to fusing history and fiction, his novels also consider the nature of time and art, often involving their protagonists in situations that transcend time and space. Ackroyd once told *Contemporary Authors (CA):* "My own interest isn't so much in writing historical fiction as it is in writing about the nature of history as such. . . . I'm much more interested in playing around with the idea of time."

In 1982 Ackroyd published his first novel, *The Great Fire of London,* which revolves around the film production of Charles Dickens's novel, *Little Dorrit.* Ackroyd's tale presents itself as a continuation of the Dickens novel, which concerns a young girl's trials and tribulations in Victorian England. Beginning with a summary of Dickens's work, *The Great Fire of London* then introduces its own cast of Dickensian characters, including Spenser Spender, a filmmaker who plans the adaptation of *Little Dorrit;* Sir Frederick Lustlambert, a bureaucrat who arranges the film's financing; and Rowan Phillips, a Dickens scholar who has written the film's script. Another important figure is Little Arthur, an adult so named because he ceased growing at age eight. Little Arthur is proprietor of an amusement park near Marshalsea Prison, a key setting in *Little Dorrit.* When Arthur's park closes, he loses his grasp on reality and commits murder. Once apprehended, he is sentenced to Marshalsea Prison, where Spender is filming his adaptation. Spender's insistence on realism eventually sparks the disaster of the novel's title, a raging inferno resulting from a mishap on the film set.

Galen Strawson, in his review of *The Great Fire of London* in the *Times Literary Supplement,* described Ackroyd's novel as an extension of Dickens's *Little Dorrit.* "Ackroyd is clearly intrigued by the idea of past fiction working great changes in present (fictional) reality," Strawson wrote, "and he misses few chances to make further connections and to elaborate the network of coincidences." Strawson was also impressed with Ackroyd's insights into human nature, writing that "he is continually alive . . . to that hidden presence in many people's lives which he calls 'the vast sphere of unremembered wishes,' and to the effects it has on their conscious thoughts and actions."

Ackroyd followed *The Great Fire of London* with *The Last Testament of Oscar Wilde,* a novel purporting to be Wilde's autobiography, written during the final months of the author's life in Paris, where he had fled in self-imposed exile after serving two years in a British prison for indecency. Many critics praised Ackroyd's duplication of Wilde's own writing style and commended the work for its compelling insights into the personality of the notorious Irish writer. Toronto *Globe and Mail* critic William French, for instance, declared that Ackroyd "does an uncanny job of assuming Wilde's persona." Similarly, London *Times* reviewer Mary Cosh, who called Ackroyd's novel "a brilliant testament in its own right," lauded Ackroyd for fashioning a well-rounded portrait of Wilde. Cosh wrote: "Not only does Peter Ackroyd exert a masterly command of language and ideas that credibly evokes Wilde's sharp wit in epigram or paradox, but he captures the raw vulnerability of the man isolated behind his mask."

When *The Last Testament of Oscar Wilde* was published in 1983, Ackroyd was already working on the biography, *T. S. Eliot: A Life.* In researching the poet's life, Ackroyd encountered imposing obstacles: he was forbidden by Eliot's estate from quoting Eliot's correspondence and unpublished verse, and he was allowed only minimum citations of the published poetry. Critics generally agreed, however, that Ackroyd nonetheless produced a worthwhile account of the modernist poet. As A. Walton Litz wrote in the *New York Times Book Review:* "Given all these restrictions, Peter Ackroyd has written as good a biography as we have any right to expect. He has assimilated most of the available evidence and used it judiciously." Rosemary Dinnage, who reviewed *T. S. Eliot* in the *New York Review of Books,* also praised Ackroyd's difficult feat, observing that he "illuminates Eliot's poetry and criticism more acutely than many a ponderous academic volume." And *Newsweek*'s Paul Gray contended that Ackroyd's biography "does more than make the best of a difficult situation; it offers the most detailed portrait yet of an enigmatic and thoroughly peculiar genius." In the end, Ackroyd acknowledged that his inability to quote Eliot's letters or work made for a better book. "I had to be much more inventive about how I brought him to life," he told *CA.*

In searching for a subject for his next biography, which eventually became *Dickens,* Ackroyd told *CA* that he sought "to choose someone who would be a difficult subject, as Eliot was, so I chose the opposite extreme. With Dickens, there have been so many biographies that it's an equal challenge to do something different. It's always the challenge of doing a subject that attracts

me." Unlike the work on Eliot, many other biographies of Dickens existed, so Ackroyd's intent was not to provide the definitive account of the writer's life, but rather to "rescue the character" of Dickens, as Verlyn Klinkenborg wrote in the *Smithsonian,* and thereby "[cross] the boundary between Dickens' fiction and his life." Klinkenborg further asserted that "[Ackroyd] does this not only to show how the novels illuminate the life, but also to understand the transforming powers of Dickens' imagination." Yet James R. Kincaid of the *New York Times Book Review* lamented that *Dickens* utilizes none of the twentieth-century conventions for understanding biography: "post-structuralist suspicions have made no inroads, and even Freud causes no alarm." Despite this, Kincaid allowed that *Dickens* sets itself apart from other biographies on the author and "demands our attention precisely (and only) because it is so open to the strange."

After several more novels, Ackroyd returned to biography with *Blake,* an account of William Blake, the visionary poet and artist who lived from 1757 to 1827. A London native, Blake's life appeared outwardly unremarkable. He was happily married, lived modestly, and worked hard. But many of Blake's contemporaries considered him insane; he spoke of his grandiose visions and hallucinations as if they were commonplace, often astounding acquaintances by relating his conversations with devils and angels. Blake was an engraver by trade whose illustration style was composed of intricate scenes of battling angels and fallen men, and he boldly compared his writing to John Milton's *Paradise Lost.* "Ackroyd does Blake the considerable service of taking his visions as seriously and soberly as he [Blake] did," stated a reviewer in the *Economist,* who added that Blake "has found the gentlest of biographers." In addition, Ackroyd's knowledge of London history serves to accentuate the biography, continued the reviewer, since he is familiar with the places that Blake would have known and which are the most likely locales for some of his prose. Charles Moore of the *Spectator* commented that Blake's eccentricities, one of which he called a "magnificent lack of embarrassment," were in fact the result of what Ackroyd deemed the "peculiar kind of lucidity which springs from those who have nothing left to lose."

Winner of the Whitbread Award, *Hawksmoor* fuses the detective and horror story genres. One of the work's two principal characters is Nicholas Hawksmoor, a police detective trying to solve a series of grisly murders at various eighteenth-century churches in London. Alternating with the account of Hawksmoor's progress are chapters on Victorian architect Nicholas Dyer. Dyer adheres to certain demonic principles and consecrates his churches with human blood sacrifices to please Satanic creatures. Dyer's nemesis is renowned architect Christopher Wren, his superior, who contends that science and rational thought will bring an end to superstition. Hawksmoor is also faithful to rationalism, and when he fails to perceive the connection between the two sets of murders, he finds himself slowly going insane.

Like Ackroyd's earlier novels, *Hawksmoor* impressed critics as a daring, technically innovative work. *Newsweek*'s Peter S. Prescott called it "a fascinating hybrid, a tale of terrors that does double duty as a novel of ideas." Similarly, *Time*'s Christopher Porterfield, who noted that Ackroyd possessed "a gift for historical pastiche," acknowledged "the eerie interplay between the earlier age and our own," and commended *Hawksmoor* as "a fictional architecture that is vivid, provocative, and as clever as . . . the devil." Another of the novel's many enthusiasts was Joyce Carol Oates, who wrote in the *New York Times Book Review* that *Hawksmoor* was "primarily a novel of ideas, a spirited debate between those who believe . . . that 'the highest Passion is Terrour' and those who believe . . . that the new science of rationalism and experimental method will eventually eradicate superstition." Oates deemed Ackroyd a "virtuoso" and lauded *Hawksmoor* as "an unfailingly intelligent work of the imagination."

Ackroyd executed another multiple-narrative story with *Chatterton,* a novel revolving around seventeenth-century poet Thomas Chatterton, who committed suicide when he was seventeen. In Ackroyd's novel, Chatterton appears through an autobiographical document that suggests he may have faked his death. The document is owned by Charles Wychwood, a minor poet obsessed with an old portrait whose subject might have been Chatterton. The painting, however, is dated 1802, thus serving as further indication that Chatterton might not have died in 1770. Another story line concerns the creation of an actual painting, Henry Wallis's *The Death of Chatterton.* But this painting, too, is misleading, for Wallis finished it in 1856, long after Chatterton's death, and relied on another young man, writer George Meredith, to represent Chatterton. Further discrepancies of authenticity and originality abound in the novel—a writer steals plots from second-rate Victorian novels, and an artist's secretary completes his employer's canvases. Even Chatterton confesses to chicanery of a sort, having attributed his own poems to fictitious fifteenth-century clergyman Thomas Rowley.

With *Chatterton,* Ackroyd strengthened his reputation as a unique and compelling storyteller. Dennis Drabelle, in his review for the *Washington Post Book World,*

called Ackroyd's work a "witty, tricky new novel," and "a contrivance of the highest order." Denis Donoghue, writing in the *New York Times Book Review,* was similarly enthusiastic, describing *Chatterton* as "a wonderfully vivid book," and "superb." London *Times* reviewer Victoria Glendinning praised the novel as "agile and entertaining." She added, "In *Chatterton* [Ackroyd] has at least three balls in the air, and [he] keeps them up there."

With the novel *English Music,* critics were divided on the success of Ackroyd's time-twisting and reality-bending plot. An involved story regarding Timothy Harcombe and his spiritualist father's wish that he learn everything possible about English culture—"English music," he calls it—the novel traverses time and a multitude of ideas that wind their way through fantasy and reality. It is a story of the wandering soul that critic Chris Goodrich of the *Los Angeles Times Book Review* compared to James Joyce's *Ulysses,* "though one written very, very small," but concluded that the book "rarely seems more than an academic exercise." Michael Levenson of the *New Republic* summarized the novel's theme: "Life on the margins is the universal norm. The center is an optical illusion."

The interconnectedness of time past, present, and future is also central to Ackroyd's next book, *The House of Doctor Dee,* a historical novel concerning the Elizabethan-era intellectual John Dee, a purported practitioner of black magic and alchemy. Dee alternates narrative duties with Matthew Palmer, the modern-day inheritor of Dee's house in London, whose curiosity sparks an investigation into the house's lurid history. Much of the book's detail concerns the milieu of fifteenth-century London's buildings and history, one of Ackroyd's favorite subjects. *Spectator* reviewer Francis King noted the differing styles of the two narrators—Dee writes in an Elizabethan dialect that reminds King of Ben Jonson, and Matthew writes in a more modern voice—and called the contrast "fascinating." As Matthew learns more about the house's previous owner, paranormal occurrences abound—not the least of which is Matthew's discovery that he is embroiled in an ancient plot concerning an immortal homunculus. Soon Dee and Matthew's paths cross, and as they become aware of each other through visions and research, both are eventually redeemed in "a timeless London," stated Eric Korn of the *Times Literary Supplement,* "for time can be deconstructed by any magician or novelist."

Multiple narratives again are the crux of *Dan Leno and the Limehouse Golem,* published in the United States as *The Trial of Elizabeth Cree: A Novel of the Limehouse*

Murders. In 1881, a seedy district in London suffers a gruesome series of murders that some residents believe is the work of a golem. Exhibiting Ackroyd's penchant for infusing his fiction with historical figures, the suspects include Karl Marx, George Gissing, and Dan Leno, one of the era's popular comedians. But Ackroyd weaves throughout his narrative the pages of a diary that may or may not be written by the murderer him or herself; the diary hints that the killer is actually John Cree, whose wife Elizabeth, a former vaudeville cross-dresser, is hanged for poisoning him during the opening pages of the novel. An air of growing oppression builds throughout the work, as people (both real and fictitious), the squalor of 1880s London, and the tangled storyline weigh increasingly heavily upon the reader's imagination.

Reviewing *The Trial of Elizabeth Cree* for the *Spectator,* David Sexton proclaimed that Ackroyd "manages these parallel narratives expertly. . . . He just loves to feel all London's past coming up behind him." Valerie Martin agreed in the *New York Times Book Review,* noting that the suspects in the work are all "men of ideas . . . obsessed with the need for social reform," and stated that the book is "not so much a novel of ideas as a novel about some men who had ideas." "Mr. Ackroyd's methods are both subtle and outrageous," Martin concluded. "Everything and everyone in [*The Trial of Elizabeth Cree*] is so intimately connected that one reads with a sense of the world becoming progressively smaller and tighter. . . . The tone is agitated and compelling, by turns macabre and inventive, and this novel is a fine addition to Mr. Ackroyd's impressive body of work."

Placing his blind protagonist, English writer John Milton, squarely in the North American colonies in his 1996 novel, *Milton in America,* is "Ackroyd's joke," according to *Times Literary Supplement* reviewer Treve Broughton. Milton perceived the exodus of his countrymen to New England as a kind of purgatory second only to death, and is recorded as referring to America as "a savage desert." In Ackroyd's novel, the fictional Milton finds himself aboard ship and sailing for New England, hence avoiding capture by British authorities for publishing pamphlets critical of the Crown (the real Milton was in fact imprisoned for the same transgression). Among his fellow runaways aboard ship, he becomes what Broughton termed a "hero in exile and visionary of the New World, accepting the adulation of his fellow passengers and generally talking up a storm." A shipwreck ends his dreams of a grandiose landing in Boston; Milton instead finds himself aground in the New England wilderness, where he eventually

founds his own colony. Broughton praised the work for its allusions and creativity, although he commented that the narrative sometimes fails from a lack of "conviction and pace." He also called Ackroyd's Milton "a wonderful creation: as exasperating and exhilarating as we have come to expect of an Ackroyd hero." Citing parallels to Milton's *Paradise Lost,* John Clute viewed the work with a more critical eye. "Blindness governs the telling of the book, and is its final message," Clute stated in *New Statesman.* "Milton's own blindness, as he stumbles into a paradise he will soon be instrumental in losing, is matched by the virtuoso blindness of the text itself, most of which comprises letters, recounted anecdotes, reveries, heresay." *Milton in America,* Clute concluded, "is a hard book to judge."

The Life of Thomas More is Ackroyd's biography of More (1479-1535), the lawyer and statesman who was beheaded for refusing to support Henry VIII's divorce from Catherine of Aragon and subsequent marriage to Anne Boleyn, and who was subsequently declared a saint by the Catholic Church. "Ackroyd makes him a man," wrote Bryce Christensen in *Booklist,* "with all the paradoxes, ironies, and complexities that mortality entails." Ackroyd traces More's life, from his baptism to his execution. Included are descriptions of his upbringing, education, and the people he interacted with, including his friend, the humanist Erasmus.

Andrew Sullivan wrote in the *New York Times Book Review* that Ackroyd sees More "not as an early individualist (as in Robert Bolt's gorgeously anachronistic play, *A Man for All Seasons*), or as an early ultramontane absolutist (in the vein of much nineteenth-century Roman Catholic hagiography), or even as a twisted and conflicted bigot (as in Richard Marius's biography, *Thomas More*). Rather, Ackroyd sees More simply as a particularly sensitive, and elegantly playful, representative of a vibrant, late-medieval, Catholic England." Sullivan claimed that Ackroyd "has an ear and a nose for physicality, and he deploys his expertise in the history of London to illustrate this faith. Rather than condescending to medieval Catholicism, Ackroyd empathetically observes it." A *Kirkus Reviews* contributor called *The Life of Thomas More* "a limpidly written and superbly wrought portrait of a complex hero."

Ackroyd's *The Plato Papers* is set in the year 3700. The fantasy novella includes fifty-five short chapters of meditations, essays, and dialogues. The Plato of the story lives in a utopian London and is also a philosopher and teacher. "The Age of Witspell," has replaced "The Age of Mouldwarp," the scientific period that collapsed in the year 2300. Through his papers, Plato tries to educate Londoners about previous ages and encourages them to learn from history how the past can clarify the present. He works from the scraps of information that have survived into Witspell, and misses the mark when he credits Charles Dickens with writing a fictional work entitled *On the Origins of Species by Means of Natural Selection,* and says that Brother Marx was a comedian who wrote about gender, class, and race. "*The Plato Papers* is a significant comic achievement," wrote Nick Gevers for *infinity plus* online. "But one is always aware in these passages that Plato is the fool whose japes conceal wisdom; every statement he makes about our time is symbolically or spiritually true at the core of its misprision. His scholarly madness is always close to true vision. And so, as Plato is vouchsafed a full and accurate experience of Mouldwarp, in which he can wander its streets and speak with its souls of its benighted, activity-besotted, inwardly blind inhabitants, the novel's tone darkens."

John Sutherland said in the *New York Times Book Review* that the novel reminded him of Walter M. Miller Jr.'s *A Canticle for Leibowitz.* "But the initial impression is surprise. One did not expect this book." Sutherland noted that *The Plato Papers* "is unlike anything else Peter Ackroyd . . . has written." Sutherland wrote that "the most enjoyable section of the book is the opening one, which is replete with jokes—some extremely funny."

Ackroyd told *CA:* "Some of the cadences and the images and the ideas and the perceptions and even the very phrases which occurred in my poetry have recurred in the fiction. It's not as if I've lost the poetry; it's just been transformed into another context.

"I think of myself primarily as a novelist. The other activities are marginal but related—certainly I think my novels and biographies are connected, although not in ways I myself could interpret. I leave that to the critics."

BIOGRAPHICAL/CRITICAL SOURCES:

BOOKS

Contemporary Literary Criticism, Gale, Volume 34, 1985, Volume 52, 1989.

Dictionary of Literary Biography, Volume 155: *Twentieth-Century Literary Biographers,* Gale, 1995.

PERIODICALS

America, January 19, 1985.

Antioch Review, summer, 1985.

Booklist, October 1, 1998, Bryce Christensen, review of *The Life of Thomas More;* January 1, 2000, review of *The Plato Papers,* p. 871.

Books, September-October, 1993, p. 8; summer, 1995, p. 22.

Choice, March, 1999, review of *The Life of Thomas More,* p. 1329.

Christian Science Monitor, February 1, 1985; January 10, 1990, Merle Rubin, review of *First Light,* p. 13; February 25, 1991, Merle Rubin, review of *Dickens,* p. 13; December 10, 1998, Merle Rubin, "Thomas More's Devotion to a Higher Law," p. 16; January 20, 2000, review of *The Plato Papers,* p. 16.

Economist, September 29, 1984; November 11, 1995; December 4, 1999, review of *The Plato Papers,* p. 4.

Globe and Mail (Toronto), January 7, 1984; June 26, 1999, review of *The Plato Papers,* p. D15.

Guardian Weekly, September 12, 1993, p. 28.

Kirkus Reviews, September 15, 1998, review of *The Life of Thomas More;* December 1, 1999, review of *The Plato Papers,* p. 1824.

Library Journal, January, 2000, review of *The Plato Papers,* p. 154.

London Review of Books, November 17, 1983; December 22, 1994, pp. 20-22.

Los Angeles Times Book Review, December 2, 1984; February 14, 1988; October 25, 1992, pp. 3, 11; June 25, 1995, p. 12; January 16, 2000, review of *The Plato Papers,* p. 11.

Maclean's, February 17, 1986.

New Republic, December 17, 1984; January 18, 1993, pp. 29-32.

New Statesman, March 19, 1976; November 30, 1979; January 29, 1982; October 12, 1984; September 27, 1985.

New Statesman and Society, September 9, 1994, p. 39.

Newsweek, November 26, 1984; February 24, 1986.

New Yorker, March 25, 1985; November 23, 1992, pp. 142-143.

New York Review of Books, April 30, 1981; December 20, 1984.

New York Times, August 21, 1995, p. B3.

New York Times Book Review, December 16, 1984; January 19, 1986; January 17, 1988; January 13, 1991, pp. 1, 24; October 11, 1992, Alison Lurie, "Hanging out with Hogarth," p. 7; November 9, 1992, Christopher Lehmann-Haupt, "Books of the

Times; An Entertainment for the Library"; April 16, 1995, p. 7; August 21, 1995, Richard Bernstein, "Books of the Times; The Limehouse Killings and Much, Much More"; April 14, 1996, Penelope Fitzgerald, "Innocence and Experience"; September 14, 1997, review of *Blake,* p. 44; October 25, 1998, Andrew Sullivan, "Public Man, Public Faith"; February 6, 2000, John Sutherland, "After Mouldwarp," p. 7.

New York Times Magazine, December 22, 1991, pp. 27-36.

Observer (London), August 29, 1993, p. 51; September 11, 1994; March 14, 1999, review of *The Life of Thomas More,* p. 14; March 28, 1999, review of *The Plato Papers,* p. 13.

Publishers Weekly, December 25, 1987, pp. 59-60; December 6, 1999, review of *The Plato Papers,* p. 55.

Smithsonian, January, 1993, pp. 131-132.

Spectator, September 29, 1984; September 28, 1985; September 11, 1993, p. 27; September 10, 1994; September 23, 1995, pp. 36-37.

Time, December 3, 1984; February 24, 1986; May 29, 1995, p. 72.

Times (London), April 14, 1983; September 27, 1984; September 26, 1985; February 19, 1987; June 8, 1987; September 3, 1987.

Times Literary Supplement, May 3, 1974; December 7, 1979; August 28, 1981; January 29, 1982; April 15, 1983; September 21, 1984; November 30, 1984; September 27, 1985; September 11, 1987; September 10, 1993, p. 20; September 9, 1994, p. 21; August 30, 1996, p. 23.

Tribune Books (Chicago), November 18, 1984; November 1, 1992, p. 6.

Voice Literary Supplement, December, 1984; December 1992, p. 6.

Wall Street Journal, April 9, 1996, Robert M. Adams, review of *Blake,* p. A16; May 6, 1997, Paul Dean, review of *Milton in America,* P. A20; October 22, 1998, Perez Zagorin, review of *The Life of Thomas More,* p. A20.

Washington Post Book World, December 9, 1984; February 16, 1986; January 24, 1988.

OTHER

Infinity plus, http://www.iplus.zetnet.co.uk/ (August 12, 2000).

*   *   *

ACZEL, Amir D. 1950-

PERSONAL: Born November 6, 1950, in Carmel, Israel; U.S. citizen; son of E. L. (a ship's captain) and Miriam (a homemaker) Aczel; married Debra G., October 4, 1984; children: Miriam. *Education:* University of California at Berkeley, A.B., 1975, M.S., 1976; University of Oregon, Ph.D., 1982. *Avocational interests:* Skiing.

ADDRESSES: Home—Medway, MA. *Office*—Department of Mathematics, Bentley College, Waltham, MA 02452. *E-mail*—aaczel@bentley.edu.

CAREER: University of Alaska, associate professor of mathematics, 1982-88; Bentley College, Waltham, MA, associate professor of mathematics, 1988—.

MEMBER: American Mathematical Society, American Statistical Association, Delta Sigma Pi.

AWARDS, HONORS: Excellence in Teaching Award, University of Oregon, 1980; Professor of the Year Award, Bentley College, 1997.

WRITINGS:

Complete Business Statistics, Irwin (Homewood, IL), 1989, new edition, Irwin/McGraw Hill (Boston, MA), 1999.

Statistics: Concepts and Applications, Irwin (Chicago, IL), 1995.

How to Beat the IRS at Its Own Game: Strategies to Avoid—and Survive—an Audit, Four Walls Eight Windows (New York, NY), 1994, new edition published as *How to Beat the IRS at Its Own Game: Strategies to Avoid—and Fight—an Audit,* 1995.

Fermat's Last Theorem: Unlocking the Secret of an Ancient Mathematical Problem, Four Walls Eight Windows (New York, NY), 1996.

Probability 1: Why There Must Be Intelligent Life in the Universe, Harcourt (New York, NY), 1998.

God's Equation: Einstein, Relativity, and the Expanding Universe, Four Walls Eight Windows (New York, NY), 1999.

Mystery of the Aleph: Mathematics, the Kabbalah, and the Search for Infinity, Four Walls Eight Windows (New York, NY), 2000.

The Riddle of the Compass, Harcourt (New York, NY), 2001.

SIDELIGHTS: Amir D. Aczel is a professor of mathematics who writes about mathematics, physics, and astronomy for general readers. His books blend historical anecdote, character studies, and hard science to explain such concepts as probability theory, Fermat's Last Theorem, and Einstein's cosmological constant, to those who are curious—if unskilled—in higher math. "For one practiced in dealing with numbers, Amir Aczel certainly has a way with words," observed Jeanette Brown in *Astronomy*. Brown added that Aczel's books present "a beautiful marriage of mathematics and prose." In *Discover* magazine, Jeffrey Winters wrote: "At a time when so many popular physics books avoid equations and fudge mathematical explanations, Aczel wants to delve deep into the mathematics. He believes—as Einstein did—it is in fact the underlying mathematics that makes the universe elegant."

Aczel was best known as a theoretical statistician until the mid-1990s when he published *Fermat's Last Theorem: Unlocking the Secret of an Ancient Mathematical Problem,* a study of breakthrough work done on a previously unsolved 300-year-old theorem. The success of that work led to one of Aczel's best-known books, *Probability 1: Why There Must Be Intelligent Life in the Universe.* The book's topic and title were originally proposed by Dr. Carl Sagan, but Sagan died before he could begin the project. Aczel took up the challenge, and his book expands upon the theories proposed by astronomer Frank Drake in 1961. "In essence," wrote *New York Times Book Review* correspondent John Durant, "'Probability 1' is a review of Drake's equation in the light of scientific evidence. Aczel argues convincingly that the number of planets suitable for life is extremely large." He bolsters his arguments with information about recent discoveries of planets orbiting other stars, the latest investigations into the possibility of life on Mars and at least one of Jupiter's moons, and with the facts of biology and evolution on Earth. His final argument, however, is a purely mathematical one: given the size of the universe, the number of stars and galaxies, the probability of *intelligent* extraterrestrial life is one hundred percent.

Critics were mixed in their assessment of *Probability 1.* Durant explained: "Statistics are extremely powerful and important, and Aczel is a very clear and capable exponent of them. But statistics cannot substitute for empirical knowledge about the way the universe behaves." Jeanette Brown, on the other hand, concluded: "Before reading Aczel's book you may find it easy to shrug off his conclusions. After you've finished *Probability 1,* you may find it harder to do so."

In *God's Equation: Einstein, Relativity, and the Expanding Universe,* Aczel demonstrates that the cosmological constant, discovered and then discounted by Albert Einstein, has once again become an important aspect of the general theory of the behavior of the universe. The book not only discusses the physics behind the expanding universe, but also details Einstein's genius and his working methods during his most prolific period as a physicist/astronomer. "*God's Equation* is not just a retelling of breakthroughs in early twentieth century physics," noted Winters. "Aczel makes it a study of the intersection of mathematics and the physical world." *Booklist* correspondent Bryce Christensen called *God's Equation* "one of the most exciting scientific detective stories ever told," and "a marvelous distillation of epoch-making science."

Aczel once told *CA:* "I write to express myself. I am interested in great nonfiction that tells a true story in an exciting, engaging way. I work late into the night, almost every night. I compose entire chapters in my head, then write them down with very few revisions. I use no book outline, but rather let the story tell itself in the most natural way. If a story doesn't flow, it is not worth telling. *Fermat's Last Theorem* had many stories in it, at different levels: the great problem, unsolved for 300 years, the life stories of the mathematicians who contributed to the final proof, and the intrigue—the human drama."

BIOGRAPHICAL/CRITICAL SOURCES:

PERIODICALS

Astronomy, November, 1998, Jeanette Brown, review of *Probability 1: Why There Must Be Intelligent Life in the Universe,* p. 106; March, 2000, review of *God's Equation: Einstein, Relativity, and the Expanding Universe,* p. 104.

Booklist, September 1, 1998, Gilbert Taylor, review of *Probability 1,* p. 44; September 15, 1999, Bryce Christensen, review of *God's Equation,* p. 206; December 1, 1999, Donna Seaman, review of *God's Equation,* p. 676; October 1, 2000, Bryce Christensen, review of *The Mystery of the Aleph: Mathematics, the Kabbalah, and the Search for Infinity,* p. 296.

Discover, November, 1999, Jeffrey Winters, review of *God's Equation,* p. 124.

Economist, July 17, 1999, "New Light on Planets," p. 9.

Library Journal, August, 1999, Harold D. Shane, review of *God's Equation,* p. 131.

New York Times Book Review, November 15, 1998, John Durant, review of *Probability 1,* p. 69.

Publishers Weekly, August 17, 1998, review of *Probability 1,* p. 60; September 13, 1999, review of *God's Equation,* p. 67; August 21, 2000, review of *The Mystery of the Aleph,* p. 61.

ADAMS, Jad 1954-

PERSONAL: Born November 27, 1954, in London, England; son of Andrew and Amy Adams. *Education:* University of Sussex, B.A., 1976; Birkbeck College, University of London, M.A., 1982. *Politics:* "Left." *Religion:* Christian. *Avocational interests:* Antiquity, the theater.

ADDRESSES: Home—London, England. *Agent*—MBA Literary Agents, 45 Fitzroy St., London W1P 5HR, England.

CAREER: Television professional, 1982—, began as researcher, became series producer. Associated with television programs, including *The Dynasty: The Nehru-Gandhi Story* for the BBC and PBS, *The Clintons: A Marriage of Sex, Lies, and Power* for Britain's ITV, and *AIDS: The Unheard Voices* for Britain's Channel 4. London Borough of Lewisham, member of borough council, 1978-86; Nightwatch (charity for the homeless), chair, 1992—.

MEMBER: Royal Historical Society (fellow).

AWARDS, HONORS: Named Young Journalist of the Year, British Press Awards, 1977; Royal Television Society Award for the best international documentary film, 1987, for *AIDS: The Unheard Voices.*

WRITINGS:

AIDS: The HIV Myth, St. Martin's Press (New York, NY), 1989.
Tony Benn: A Biography, Macmillan (London, England), 1992.
Double Indemnity: Murder for Insurance, Headline (London, England), 1994.
(With Phillip Whitehead) *The Dynasty: The Nehru-Gandhi Story,* Penguin (London, England), 1997.
Madder Music, Stronger Wine: The Life of Ernest Dowson, Poet and Decadent, I. B. Tauris Publishers/St. Martin's Press (New York, NY), 2000.

Author of television scripts.

WORK IN PROGRESS: A TV series and novel about fraud in science; biographically based TV series on London's East End for Britain's ITV and the History Channel.

SIDELIGHTS: The work of British writer and television producer Jad Adams has reflected his interest in contemporary social and political issues, as well as his research concerning historical figures. In several cases Adams's projects have included film documentary and prose presentations on shared subjects. After producing the award-winning television documentary *AIDS: The Unheard Voices,* Adams went on to create a book on a similar theme, *AIDS: The HIV Myth.* Similarly, he has written feature articles on various aspects of the life of Lord Kitchener after having produced *Kitchener—The Empire's Flawed Hero* for British television and the A&E network.

Adams's 1997 book *The Dynasty: The Nehru-Gandhi Story* is a companion piece to a documentary film that was seen on PBS in the United States. Written with Phillip Whitehead, it presents four generations of a family made famous by its prominence in Indian politics. Their political dynasty also faced violent political opposition that led to the deaths of both Indira and Rajiv Gandhi.

Among Adams's more widely reviewed work is his biography *Madder Music, Stronger Wine: The Life of Ernest Dowson, Poet and Decadent.* A Victorian poet, Dowson and his unhappy life story are no longer familiar to many, although some lines of his poetry have become highly familiar references. Well known as motion picture titles, the phrases "gone with the wind" and "days of wine and roses" both come from his verse. Adams reminds readers that Dowson was an infamous literary figure in his day and perhaps the prototype of the popular image of the writer so possessed by his work that he is seen scribbling on napkins in dark cafés.

Dowson led a short, tormented life. Both of his parents died at their own hands: his father was killed by an overdose of medication used to treat tuberculosis-related insomnia and his mother committed suicide shortly thereafter. Their son suffered from severe depression and became an alcoholic. It was probably Dowson's sense of mission as a poet that saved him from his own suicidal thoughts. However, one of his most important sources of inspiration was highly controversial, his unrequited love for a preteen waitress. Born into a middle-class family and educated at Oxford, Dowson suffered from obsessions that left him impoverished and homeless when he died of tuberculosis at age thirty-two.

In a review for the *Guardian,* Steven Poole called Adams's book "a loving snapshot" of the Victorian decadent. *Kirkus Reviews* deemed the work to be an "intricately detailed study," but one "strongly informed by the author's own perspective." The reviewer concluded, "While Dowson's relentless Sturm und Drang is sometimes hard to take, Adams's sympathetic portrait of this man offers much for history and literature buffs alike." Writing in the *Independent,* Richard Davenport-Hines called the book "a shrewd, affectionate and readable biography, which will arouse few people to care about his poetry but vividly evokes his self-destructive career in *fin-de-siècle* London." Davenport-Hines also judged that "Adams's handling of Dowson's ruling obsession is deft, tender, and never prurient. He provides fascinating details of the sexual subcultures of Victorian Soho."

Commenting on his interests, motivations, and experiences as a writer, including his interest in becoming a novelist, Adams told *CA:* "I was born and have always lived in London, though I have traveled widely. I have sustained myself by working in journalism. I have always questioned established values, and some of my best work has involved probing fashionable notions in science to test their validity. My film *AIDS: The Unheard Voices* is about the scientists who were questioning whether the human immunodeficiency virus (HIV) had been misidentified as the cause of acquired immunodeficiency syndrome (AIDS). A twelve-part documentary film series *Food: Fad or Fact?* asked what scientific evidence there was to back the dietary advice of 'health educators.' My controversial book *AIDS: The HIV Myth* was a deliberate challenge to the complacency of the 'AIDS establishment' in refusing to countenance any view of AIDS other than the one which ensured their continued preeminence. My biography of Tony Benn, involving a vast amount of research that took four years, presents one of the great European radicals of the twentieth century.

"I have had no success in my chosen field, fiction writing, but I am currently working on a fifth novel. In describing my own work, I once wrote: 'The Adams canon of literature, in fiction as much as nonfiction, has been about failed concepts, failed ambitions, failed relationships, failed ideals.'

"I consider that intellectuals have a moral obligation to be committed in society, so as not to allow the stupid and bigoted to govern by default. I served for eight years as an elected councillor in my area of London. I also campaigned successfully for a change in Britain's antiquated property laws relating to the ownership of apartments. The new law came into effect in November, 1993. I have worked with homeless people in London since 1979 and now head the homelessness society Nightwatch and campaign on local environmental issues."

BIOGRAPHICAL/CRITICAL SOURCES:

PERIODICALS

Kirkus Reviews, August 15, 2000, review of *Madder Music, Stronger Wine: The Life of Ernest Dowson, Poet and Decadent,* p. 1153.
Los Angeles Times, October 30, 2000, Merle Rubin, "The Tragic Story of a Talented and Doomed Poet," p. E4.
New York Times, December 17, 2000, Sherie Posesorski, review of *Madder Music, Stronger Wine.*
Rain Taxi, spring, 2001, Thomas Wiloch, review of *Madder Music, Stronger Wine,* p. 49.
Times (London), July 9, 1992, p. 5.
Washington Post, November 5, 2000, Karl Beckson, "Aesthetes, Decadents, and Avant-gardists Who Livened up the Late Nineteenth Century," p. X8.

OTHER

BooksUnlimited, http://www.booksunlimited.co.uk/ (January 22, 2000), Steven Poole, "The List."
Independent, http://www.independent.co.uk/ (February 9, 2000), Richard Davenport-Hines, "Short, Sad Days of Absinthe and Poetry."

*   *   *

ALI, Tariq 1943-

PERSONAL: Born October 21, 1943, in Lahore, India (now Pakistan); son of Mazhar Ali Khan (a landowner) and Tahira Hyat. *Education:* Punjab University, B.A. (with honors), 1963; also attended Oxford University.

ADDRESSES: Home—27 Drylands Rd., London N8 9HN, England. *Office*—New Left Review, 15 Greek St., London W1, England.

CAREER: Writer and political activist; member of editorial board, *New Left Review;* leading member of Fourth International. Fellow, Transnational Institute, Amsterdam, Netherlands.

WRITINGS:

(Compiler) *The Thoughts of Chairman Harold,* with illustrations by Ralph Steadman, Gnome Press (London, England), 1967.

(Editor) *The New Revolutionaries: A Handbook of the International Radical Left,* Morrow (New York, NY), 1969, published in England as *New Revolutionaries: Left Opposition,* Owen (London, England), 1969.

Pakistan: Military Rule or People's Power?, Morrow (New York, NY), 1970.

The Coming British Revolution, J. Cape (London, England), 1972.

(With Gerry Hedley) *Chile: Lessons of the Coup: Which Way to Workers' Power?,* International Marxist Group (London, England), 1974.

1968 and After: Inside the Revolution, Blond & Briggs (London, England), 1978.

Trotsky for Beginners, Pantheon (New York, NY), 1980.

Can Pakistan Survive?, Penguin (New York, NY), 1983.

(Editor) *What Is Stalinism?,* Penguin (New York, NY), 1984.

(Editor) *The Stalinist Legacy: Its Impact on Twentieth-Century World Politics,* Penguin (New York, NY), 1984.

An Indian Dynasty: The Story of the Nehru-Gandhi Family, Putnam (New York, NY), 1985.

Street Fighting Years: An Autobiography of the Sixties, Collins (London, England), 1987.

Revolution from Above: Where Is the Soviet Union Going?, Hutchinson (London, England), 1988.

(With Howard Brenton) *Moscow Gold,* Nick Hern (London, England), 1990.

Redemption (novel), Chatto & Windus (London, England), 1990.

(Contributor) *21: 21 Picador Authors Celebrate 21 Years of International Writing,* Picador (London, England), 1993.

Shadows of the Pomegranate Tree (novel), Chatto & Windus (London, England), 1992, Verso (New York, NY), 1993.

(With Susan Watkins) *1968—Marching in the Streets,* Free Press (New York, NY), 1998.

(With Brenton) *Ugly Rumours,* Nick Hern (London England), 1998.

Fear of Mirrors (novel), Dufour Editions (Chester Springs, PA), 1998.

The Book of Saladin (novel), Verso (London, England), 1999.

The Stone Woman (novel), Verso (London, England), 2000.

(Editor) *Masters of the Universe?: NATO's Balkan Crusade,* Verso (London, England), 2000.

(With Howard Brenton and Andy de la Tour) *Snogging Ken* ("disposable theater" play); contributor to *New Left Review, Inprecor, New Statesman & Society, Monthly Review,* and *Red Weekly.* Member of editorial board, *Labour Focus on Eastern Europe.*

WORK IN PROGRESS: A fourth historical novel on the Muslim empires of the Middle East.

SIDELIGHTS: Tariq Ali is well known in Great Britain as a political activist, social commentator, historian, filmmaker, and novelist. Born in what is now Pakistan, and educated in India and at Oxford University, Ali embraced leftist politics as a young man. In the late 1960s he was an active radical in London, protesting his country's involvement in the Vietnam War as well as its policies toward the Soviet Union and other socialist nations. More recently he has written books and commentary about the ongoing political struggles in India and Pakistan, while continuing his sometimes-scathing criticism of the British government.

Ali's nonfiction reflects the broad range of his interests. He has published first-hand accounts of life in the Soviet Union and in post-Soviet Russia, memoirs and studies of the student movement in the 1960s, simple explanatory texts on Stalinism and Trotskyism, and modern political histories of India and the Balkan crisis. In a *Monthly Review* piece on Ali's *Revolution from Above: Where Is the Soviet Union Going?,* Daniel Singer noted that the author "manages to pass on to the reader the excitement of a country where serious periodicals sell like hot cakes, where books, films, plays are political events, where people simultaneously discover their past and the art of political debate." Singer added that *Revolution from Above* "deserves to be read by all Western leftists interested in the fate of the Soviet Union. . . . Whether one agrees with [Ali] or not, his chapters raise all the issues the left must tackle: the resistance of bureaucracy, market and planning in a single state, the relevance of memory, the power to be granted to the Soviets, and, finally, Russians' relations with the outside world. Besides, the book is topical despite the furious pace of events."

The 1990s ushered in a new phase in Ali's writing career. He began to publish fiction that also illustrates his views of the world as a leftist, a Muslim, and a historian. Three of his novels, *Shadows of the Pome-*

granate Tree, The Book of Saladin, and *The Stone Woman,* address various aspects of Muslim empire-building in different historical eras. *Shadows of the Pomegranate Tree* centers on the fall of Islam in Spain. *The Book of Saladin* is a fictitious memoir dictated by the great ruler Salah-al-Din, who wrested Jerusalem from Christian control in the twelfth century. This work seeks to dismiss the European stereotype of Saladin as a ruthless and godless conqueror; indeed, *World Literature Today* critic Bruce King emphasized the novel's postcolonial sensibilities, observing that the book is "shaped by modern sensibilities as well as facts" that depict European Crusaders in a distinctly negative light while recounting the story with all the "excitement of an old Hollywood epic." A *Kirkus Reviews* correspondent declared that, in *The Book of Saladin,* "one is carried along by the sheer gallop of the storytelling and dead-on sense of time and place." *The Stone Woman* moves ahead to the end of the nineteenth century and views the decline of the Ottoman Empire through the eyes of one jaded family. A contributor to *Kirkus Reviews* deemed the novel "a richly woven historical tapestry." James Hopkin, in *New Statesman,* praised the "grace and guile" with which Ali constructs the narrative, and commended the novel as "enchanting" and "captivating."

Ali's mainstream novels include *Redemption,* a comic account of political radicals in Eastern Europe attempting to cope with social and economic changes during the 1990s, and *Fear of Mirrors,* a candid portrayal of life in Germany since the nation's reunification. A *Publishers Weekly* contributor considered *Redemption* a "hilarious trip down memory lane" for readers familiar with the radical Left, but added that Ali makes the book surprisingly moving as well as satirical. Of *Fear of Mirrors, Booklist* correspondent David Cline wrote that the work "reveals a keen mind and strong political insight." A *Publishers Weekly* reviewer likewise considered the book "valuable . . . especially for those interested in the current thinking of the European [L]eft."

BIOGRAPHICAL/CRITICAL SOURCES:

PERIODICALS

Booklist, November 15, 1998, David Cline, review of *Fear of Mirrors,* p. 564.
Economist, April 29, 1989, "1,001 Slights," p. 92; August 19, 2000, "A Fictional Clash of Civilisations—On the Edge," p. 76.

Kirkus Reviews, September 15, 1998, review of *Fear of Mirrors;* August 15, 2000, review of *The Stone Woman,* p. 1144.
Monthly Review, October, 1989, Daniel Singer, review of *Revolution from Above: Where Is the Soviet Union Going?,* p. 61.
Nation, June 5, 1989, Boris Kagarlitsky, review of *Revolution from Above: Where Is the Soviet Union Going?,* p. 765.
New Republic, May 27, 1985, Shiva Naipaul, review of *An Indian Dynasty: The Story of the Nehru-Gandhi Family,* p. 26.
New Statesman, January 8, 1999, Jane Jakeman, review of *The Book of Saladin,* p. 55; April 24, 2000, Nina Raine, interview with Tariq Ali, Howard Brenton, and Andy de la Tour, p. 43; September 11, 2000, James Hopkin, review of *The Stone Woman,* p. 56.
New York Times, July 4, 1969.
New York Times Book Review, April 21, 1985, William Borders, review of *An Indian Dynasty: The Story of the Nehru-Gandhi Family,* p. 25.
Publishers Weekly, October 18, 1991, review of *Redemption,* p. 50; October 12, 1998, reviews of *Fear of Mirrors* and *The Book of Saladin,* p. 59; June 26, 2000, review of *The Stone Woman.*
World Literature Today, winter, 2000, Bruce King, review of *The Book of Saladin,* p. 245.*

*   *   *

AMICHAI, Yehuda 1924-2000

PERSONAL: First name sometimes transliterated as "Yehudah"; born 1924, in Germany; immigrated to Palestine in 1936; naturalized Israeli citizen; died, September 25, 2000; children: David, Emanuella.

CAREER: Poet and writer. *Military service:* Served in the British Army in World War II and with Israeli defense forces during the Arab-Israeli war of 1948.

AWARDS, HONORS: Israel's Prize for Poetry, 1982; foreign honorary member, American Academy and Institute of Arts and Letters, 1986.

WRITINGS:

IN ENGLISH

Lo me-'akhshav, Lo mi-kan (novel), [Tel Aviv], 1963, translation by Shlomo Katz published as *Not of This Time, Not of This Place,* Harper (New York City), 1968.

Yehuda Amichai

Selected Poems, translation from the original Hebrew by Assia Gutmann, Cape Goliard Press, 1968, published as *Poems,* introduction by Michael Hamburger, Harper, 1969.

Selected Poems of Yehuda Amichai, translation from the original Hebrew by Gutmann, Harold Schimmel, and Ted Hughes, Penguin (London), 1971.

Songs of Jerusalem and Myself (poetry), translation from the original Hebrew by Schimmel, Harper, 1973.

Travels of a Latter-Day Benjamin of Tudela, translation from the original Hebrew by Ruth Nevo, House of Exile (Toronto), 1976.

Amen (poetry), translation from the original Hebrew by the author and Hughes, Harper, 1977.

On New Year's Day, Next to a House Being Built, Sceptre Press (Knotting, England), 1979.

Time: Poems, Harper, 1979.

(Editor with Allen Mandelbaum) Avoth Yeshurun, *The Syrian-African Rift, and Other Poems,* translation by Harold Schimmel, Jewish Publication Society (Philadelphia), 1980.

Love Poems (also see below), translation from the original Hebrew by Glenda Abramson and Tudor Parfitt, Harper, 1981.

(Editor with Mandelbaum) Dan Pagis, *Points of Departure,* translation from the original Hebrew by Stephen Mitchell, Jewish Publication Society, 1982.

The Great Tranquility: Questions and Answers, translation from the original Hebrew by Abramson and Parfitt, Harper, 1983, reprinted, Sheep Meadow (Riverdale, NY), 1997.

The World Is a Room, and Other Stories, Jewish Publication Society (Philadelphia, PA), 1984.

Travels (bilingual edition), translation from the original Hebrew by Nevo, Sheep Meadow, 1986.

The Selected Poetry of Yehudah Amichai, translation from the original Hebrew by Mitchell and Chana Bloch, Harper, 1986, revised and expanded edition, University of California Press, Berkeley, 1996.

The Early Books of Yehuda Amichai, translation from the original Hebrew by Schimmel, Hughes, and Gutmann, Sheep Meadow, 1988.

Poems of Jerusalem: A Bilingual Edition (also see below), Harper, 1988.

Even a Fist Was Once an Open Palm with Fingers: Recent Poems, selected and translated by Barbara and Benjamin Harshav, HarperCollins (New York City), 1991.

Poems of Jerusalem; and, Love Poems: Bilingual Edition, Sheep Meadow, 1992.

I Am Sitting Here Now, Land Marks Press (Huntington Woods, MI), 1994.

Poems: English and Hebrew, Shoken (Jerusalem), 1994.

Yehuda Amichai, A Life of Poetry, 1948-1994, HarperCollins, 1994.

Exile at Home (poetry), photographs by Frederic Brenner, Harry N. Abrams (New York City), 1998.

Open Closed Open: Poems, translated from the original Hebrew by Bloch and Chana Kronfeld, Harcourt (New York City), 2000.

OTHER

Author of *Akhshav uva-yamim ha-aherim* (poetry; title means "Now and in Other Days"), [Tel Aviv], 1955; *Ba-ginah ha-tsiburit* (poetry; title means "In the Park"), [Jerusalem], 1958-59; *Be-merhak shete tikvot* (poetry), [Tel Aviv], 1958; *Be-ruah ha-nora'ah ha-zot* (stories), Merhavya, 1961; *Masa' le-Ninveh* (play; title means "Journey to Nineveh"), 1962; and *Shirim, 1948-1962* (title means "Poetry, 1948-1962"), [Jerusalem], 1962-63. Also author of *'Akshav ba-ra'ash,* 1968, *Mah she-karah le-Roni bi-Nyu York,* 1968, *Pa 'amonim ve-rakavot,* 1968, *Ve-lo 'al menat li-zekor* (poetry), 1971, *Mi yitneni malon* (title means "Hotel in the Wilderness"), 1972, and *Me-ahore kol zeh mistater osher gadol* (poetry), 1974.

Translator of German works into Hebrew. Amichai's works have been translated into thirty-seven languages, including French, Swedish, Chinese, and Spanish.

SIDELIGHTS: In the later years of his life, Yehuda Amichai came to be recognized as perhaps Israel's finest poet. His poems—written originally in Hebrew—have been translated into thirty-seven languages, and whole volumes have been published in English, French, German, Swedish, Spanish, and Catalan. In an online review for the *East Bay Express,* Stephen Kessler noted that Amichai had "long been one of the planet's preeminent poets. . . . Jewish down to the bones, his humanity is broadly universal, obsessed as Amichai [was] with time and death, war and peace, love and memory, joy and suffering." *New Republic* essayist C. K. Williams found in Amichai "the shrewdest and most solid of poetic intelligences."

Born in Germany in 1924, Amichai left that country at the age of twelve with his family and journeyed to Palestine. During the 1948 Arab-Israeli war, he fought with the Israeli defense forces. The rigors and horrors of his service in this conflict and in World War II inform his poetry, although, to quote Kessler, the political slant is "elusive," addressing the issues of Arab-Israeli relations in metaphorical, rather than ideological, terms. By the mid-1960s Amichai was "already regarded in many circles in Israel as the country's leading poet," to quote Robert Alter in the *New York Times Magazine.* Since then, Amichai's reputation outside of Israel soared—Alter stated that the author "has been accorded international recognition unprecedented for a modern Hebrew poet."

In his novel *Not of This Time, Not of This Place,* Amichai struggled with "the torment of being buried alive in the irrelevant past." The novel's hero is torn between returning to the German town where he grew up and staying in Jerusalem and "immersing himself in a love affair with an outsider who has had no part in it." In his review of the novel for the *New Yorker,* Anthony West explained: "The alternatives are both impossibilities. The past is still going on back in Germany, and it is inescapable in Israel: the knowledge of what men are and what they can do that was acquired in the years of Hitler's 'final solution' cannot be discarded or ignored, and it is no easier to live with when one is in the country of the ex-butchers than it is in that of the ex-victims."

Amos Elon highlighted the theme of struggle for identity in *Not of This Time, Not of This Place:* "Amichai is brought up in Israel, but the question of his identity sits heavily on his mind as much as with his Jewish-American fellow writers. He attempts a synoptic view of modern Jewish existence; its keys are ambivalence and disintegration, rather than clarity, unity or nationalistic simplicities." The treatment of this struggle for identity is different, however, from other novels dealing with Holocaust themes. Alter observed: "The fact of his German childhood, his awareness of kin and earliest friends murdered by the Nazis, clearly determines the broad direction of the sections of his novel set in Germany, and yet the general attempt of the book to make moral contact with the destruction and its perpetrators is eminently that of an Israeli beyond the experience, not of a European Jew actually torn by it."

Leon Wieseltier commented that Amichai's poetry "must compel the attention not only of devotees of modern Hebrew literature, but of anyone concerned with the state of contemporary poetry in general." In a review of *Poems,* Aaron Kramer wrote: "[Amichai] makes us leap from association to association, metaphor to metaphor—arriving finally at the hush of understanding. His sense of disorientation, noncommunication, and despair at times seems too pervasive— perilously close to self-pity. But the volcanic lyricism of this German-born, Israeli poet bursts through again and again. There are many superlative songs of love, war, and loss." Alter wrote: "Amichai's great gift has been his ability to express the concerns of a somberly mature imagination in a style that could seem—sometimes quite deceptively—simplicity itself."

While serving in the British Army, Amichai was influenced by modern English and American poetry, and, according to Alter, Amichai's early work bears a resemblance to the poetry of Dylan Thomas and W. H. Auden. "[German poet Ranier] Rilke," wrote Alter, "is another informing presence for him, occasionally in matters of style—he has written vaguely Rilkesque elegies—but perhaps more as a model for using a language of here and now as an instrument to catch the glimmerings of a metaphysical beyond." Although Amichai's native language was German, he read Hebrew fluently by the time he immigrated to Palestine.

Chad Walsh commented in the *Washington Post Book World:* "A Jewish poet, like a Greek, has the enormous advantage of an immense history and tradition which he can handle with an easy familiarity, and play with as a foil to the homogenized culture that is spreading over the globe like a universal parking lot. This combination of the old and the new speaks very powerfully in Amichai's poetry and makes him, as it were, a contemporary simultaneously of King David the psalmist and Eric Sevareid." Amichai once raised a similar point about the ease with which he handled different cultures and traditions in an interview published in the *American Poetry Review:* "I grew up in a very religious household. . . . So the prayers, the language of prayer itself became a kind of natural language for me. Also, I'm *not* religious anymore, but still it's very natural for me. So I use it. I don't try—like sometimes poets do—to 'enrich' poetry by getting more *cultural* material or more *ethnic* material into it. It comes very naturally."

Other critics have noted that Amichai had a talent for bridging the gap between the personal and the universal. Grace Shulman, writing in the *Nation,* observed: "Yehuda Amichai has a rare ability for transforming the personal, even private, love situation, with all its joys and agonies, into everybody's experience, making his own time and place general." Of the poetry collection *Amen,* Rochelle Ratner wrote: "The most important thing that Amichai teaches us is that the universal can only be approached through one's most personal experience. There is no anger and little guilt in these poems, only a quiet acceptance and a depression which strives to fill itself with love and caring. In many poems, the poet is alone, remembering and regretting, but silence doesn't have to be empty—Amichai knows that."

In *The Selected Poetry of Yehuda Amichai,* a collection bringing together poems published between 1955 and 1985, Amichai's early work is translated by Stephen Mitchell, and his later work by Chana Bloch. In his *New York Times Book Review* assessment of the collection, Edward Hirsch described the Amichai of the 1950s and 1960s as "more formal and metaphysical . . . a tender ironist influenced by W. H. Auden . . . and by such poets as John Donne and George Herbert." In contrast, the Amichai of the 1970s and 1980s, according to Hirsch, is "in some ways a sparer and more informal poet whose colloquial free verse rhythms seem modeled, perhaps, on William Carlos Williams and whose profuse imagery and lightning-flash analogies may be compared to Deep Imagism."

According to Hirsch, one of Amichai's central works is a long autobiographical poem that has been translated into English as both *Travels* and *Travels of the Last Benjamin of Tudela.* Hirsch described the poem as a "miniature Jewish version of Wordsworth's *Prelude,* charting the growth of a poet's soul from the vantage point of middle age." *Travels* traces the poet's life by comparing it to that of major figures from Jewish history. Hirsch wrote that the poem "dramatizes [Amichai's] sense of being poised between his father's life and his son's, his struggle to feel worthy and whole, . . . and his assessment of the way his own life is tied to the fate of Israel." Furthermore, Hirsch stated that Amichai "is a representative man with unusual gifts who in telling his own story also relates the larger story of his people."

Amichai's collection titled *A Life of Poetry 1948-1994,* is a comprehensive work, covering verse written during the Arab-Israeli war through poetry newly and "beautifully translated" by Benjamin and Barbara Harshov, noted a *Publishers Weekly* contributor. While Amichai "historically belongs to the 1948 generation in Israeli literature," wrote Gila Ramras-Rauch for *World Literature Today,* she places Amichai's work "in effect . . . with the Statehood Generation of the 1960s . . . stripping the language of its heavy historical gear and enhancing its accessibility to contemporary readers." Elizabeth Gunderson commented in *Booklist* that Amichai has the ability to "take on the burden of history, but the load rarely strains his work or makes him appear omnipotently beyond the reaches of human skirmishes." With any lifetime oeuvre, critics seem tempted to define periods in an artist's work. However, Ramras-Rauch found this difficult to do in Amichai's case: "From its inception it was not the poetry of a young man. His daring images, his subtle irony, his subdued tone have been his hallmarks for decades. . . . The speaker continues to conduct his ever-present dialogue with the inventory of his life."

Open Closed Open, published in Israel in 1998 and in English translation in 2000, has been described as Amichai's *magnum opus.* The sequence of twenty-five poems was characterized in *Publishers Weekly* as "a searching late book from a writer who acknowledges the high stakes of writing and of life as lived daily." To quote C. K. Williams, the book "comprises a sustained outburst of inspiration, and it has a . . . complicated relation to wisdom and to matters of the spirit." In a work rich in simile and metaphor, Amichai employs the rich spiritual tradition of the Jews—and the modern anxieties of the Jewish state—to comment on the wider human emotions of religious doubt, parental love, and commitment to the world. Kessler observed: "The poignancy of our earthly sojourn, its ephemeral sweetness, the pregnancy of the smallest human gestures, the haunted beauty and richness of the most mundane things and events—none of this is lost on the poet. He dares to tackle cosmic themes in domestic terms." Williams concluded: "To sojourn with Amichai in the vast, rugged, sympathetic domain of his imagination is to be given leave to linger in one of those privileged moments when we are in a confidential and confident engagement with our own spirits, when we know with certainty that such a process of imaginative self-investigation is proper and just, regardless of the substance or the occasion of our thoughts."

BIOGRAPHICAL/CRITICAL SOURCES:

BOOKS

Abramson, Glenda, editor, *The Experienced Soul: Studies in Amichai,* Westview Press (Boulder, CO), 1997.
Abramson, Glenda, *The Writing of Yehuda Amichai: A Thematic Approach,* State University of New York Press (Albany, NY), 1989.
Amichai, Yehuda, *Not of This Time, Not of This Place,* Harper, 1968.
Alter, Robert, *After the Tradition: Essays on Modern Jewish Writing,* Dutton, 1969.
Cohen, Joseph, *Voices of Israel: Essays on and Interviews with Yehuda Amichai, A. B. Yehoshua, T. Carmi, Aharon Appelfeld, and Amos Oz,* State University of New York Press, 1990.
Contemporary Literary Criticism, Gale, Volume 9, 1978, Volume 22, 1982, Volume 57, 1990.
Lapon-Kandelshein, Essi, *To Commemorate the 70th Birthday of Yehuda Amichai: A Bibliography of His Work in Translation,* Institute for the Translation of Hebrew Literature (Ramat Gan, Israel), 1994.

PERIODICALS

American Poetry Review, November/December, 1987.
Booklist, October 1, 1994, p. 230; March 15, 2000, Donna Seaman, review of *Open Closed Open,* p. 1313.
Commentary, May, 1974.
Hudson Review, autumn, 1991.
Kenyon Review, winter, 1988.
Library Journal, July, 1969; July, 1977.
Nation, May 29, 1982.
New Republic, March 3, 1982; July 3, 2000, C. K. Williams, "We Cannot Be Fooled, We Can Be Fooled," p. 29.
New Yorker, May 3, 1969.
New York Times Book Review, August 4, 1965; July 3, 1977; November 13, 1983; August 3, 1986, Edward Hirsch, "In Language Torn from Sleep," p. 14.
New York Times Magazine, June 8, 1986, Robert Alter, "Israel's Master Poet," p. 40.
Publishers Weekly, August 29, 1994, p. 66; March 27, 2000, review of *Open Closed Open,* p. 71.
Tikkun, May-June, 1994, p. 96.
Times Literary Supplement, October 17, 1986.
Village Voice, July 2, 1985; April 14, 1987.
Virginia Quarterly Review, autumn, 1987.
Washington Post Book World, February 15, 1970.
World Literature Today, Spring, 1995, pp. 426-427.

OTHER

East Bay Express Online, http://www.eastbayexpress.com/ (September 24, 2000), Stephen Kessler, "Theology for Atheists."

OBITUARIES:

New Republic, October, 9, 2000, p. 28.
Poetry, December, 2000, p. 232.
Times (London), October, 13, 2000, p. 25.*

*   *   *

AMICHAI, Yehudah
    See AMICHAI, Yehuda

*   *   *

APPACHANA, Anjana 1956-

PERSONAL: Born May 10, 1956, in Mercara, India; naturalized U.S. citizen; daughter of S. T. (an army officer) and Parvathy (a school teacher; maiden name, Parvathy Chinnappa) Appachana; married Rajiv Krishna Sinha (a professor), January 31, 1982; children: Malavika (daughter). *Education:* Delhi University, B.A. (with honors), 1976; Jawaharlal Nehru University, M.A., 1978; Pennsylvania State University, M.F.A., 1988. *Avocational interests:* Reading, music, travel.

ADDRESSES: Home—Tempe, AZ. *Agent*—Victoria Gould Pryor, Arcadia, 31 Lake Place N., Danbury, CT 06810.

CAREER: World Wildlife Fund, New Delhi, India, assistant North region organizer, 1979-80; D.C.M. Data Products, New Delhi, personnel officer, 1981-84; Pennsylvania State University, State College, teaching assistant, 1985-88; Arizona State University, Tempe, faculty associate, 1989, visiting professor, 1998-99; Tempe Preparatory Academy, Tempe, teacher, beginning 2000. Freelance writer; Young Men's Christian Association, creative writing instructor for Writers' Voice, 1998.

AWARDS, HONORS: O. Henry Festival Award, 1989, for the short story "Her Mother"; Hawthorden fellow, 1993 and 1998; National Endowment for the Arts creative writing fellowship, 1995-96; fellow, Millay Colony for the Arts, 1996; member of residency roster, Arizona Commission on the Arts, 1998-2000.

WRITINGS:

Incantations and Other Stories, Virago Press, 1991, Rutgers University Press (New Brunswick, NJ), 1992.
Listening Now (novel), Random House (New York, NY), 1998.

Work represented in anthologies, including *The O. Henry Festival Stories,* Transverse Press, 1989; *Such Devoted Sisters,* Virago Press, 1993; *Oxford Book of Modern Women's Stories,* Oxford University Press (New York, NY), 1994; *The Longman Anthology of Short Fiction,* Longman (New York, NY), 2001; and *The Vintage Book of Indian Writing, 1947-1997,* edited by Salman Rushdie and Elizabeth West. Contributor of stories to periodicals, including *Passport: Magazine of New International Writing, Webster Review, Artful Dodge, Namaste, Calyx: Journal of Art and Literature by Women, The Long Story, Sojourner, Eve's Weekly, Room of One's Own,* and *Illustrated Weekly of India. Incantations and Other Stories* was translated into German.

SIDELIGHTS: Indian-born author Anjana Appachana has had literary success in India, England, the United States, Denmark, and Germany. Her volume of short stories, *Incantations,* received widespread and favorable critical attention, and her works of short fiction have been published in many periodicals and anthologies internationally. Reviewing the volume in the Indian periodical *Hindu,* K. C. Nambiar complimented Appachana for being "an unbiased and perceptive observer of the fast changing face of India's urban scene, especially of the generation of young women in their twenties."

The title story of *Incantations* concerns a twelve-year-old girl named Geeti who is burdened with her newly-wed sister's terrible secret—that she was raped before her marriage by the man who is now her brother-in-law. Mini Shrinivasan in *Business India* labeled the tale "one of the most deeply disturbing stories about contemporary Indian life that one has ever come across." The critic further noted that Geeti's "terror" is "palpable." Another story, titled "Prophecy," is about a college student, Amrita, who is prevented from making her appointment with an abortionist by restrictive college residence officials. Told through the eyes of Amrita's friend, it concludes with her expulsion after she suffers a miscarriage in the presence of college authorities and is sent home to an arranged marriage. "Her Mother," which is the last installment of *Incantations,* is told through the device of a mother in India writing a letter to her rebellious daughter in the United States; in the course of putting her words on paper the mother realizes the isolation she shares with her daughter.

Some reviewers of *Incantations* remarked that Appachana is at her best when she is dealing with the lives and problems of Indian women, but the only character who appears in more than one of the volume's stories is Sharmaji, a male office worker whom Nambiar described as "an engagingly incorrigible shirker of work." Uma Parameswaran in *World Literature Today* offered a favorable opinion of Sharmaji as well, predicting that he "will doubtless appear in many more" of Appachana's tales.

BIOGRAPHICAL/CRITICAL SOURCES:

PERIODICALS

Belles Lettres, winter, 1992-1993, p. 42.
Boston Sunday Globe, May 3, 1998, Edith Milton, "Women with Men: An Old-fashioned Novel of India, Telling Truths as New as Ever," p. E1.
Business India, June 22, 1992, Mini Shrinivasan, review of *Incantations,* p. 227.
Hindu, November 3, 1992, K. C. Nambiar, review of *Incantations,* p. 20; March 7, 1999, "An Imaginative Arena."
Indian Express Magazine, January 17, 1999, Mini Kapoor, review of *Listening Now.*
Indian Review of Books, April 16-May 15, 1999, Lakshmi Holmström, review of *Listening Now,* pp. 5-6.
India Today International, May 25, 1998, p. 24.
Library Journal, March 15, 1998, p. 91.
New York Times Book Review, April 19, 1998, Anderson Tepper, "A Deep and Distant Time," p. 24.

Outlook, January 18, 1999, Meenakshi Mukherjee, "Of Inner Courtyards: Old-fashioned, Yet Nuanced, This Tale of Female Suffering Compels," p. 80.

Publishers Weekly, January 19, 1998, p. 369.

World Literature Today, spring, 1993, Uma Parameswaran, review of *Incantations.*

OTHER

Rediff on the Net, http://www.rediff.co.in/ (August 29, 1999), Ashok Banker, "Room to Breathe."

*   *   *

ARDLEY, Neil (Richard) 1937-

PERSONAL: Born May 26, 1937, in Wallington, Surrey, England; son of Sydney Vivian (a clerk) and Alma Mary (Rutty) Ardley; married Bridget Mary Gantley (a researcher), September 3, 1960; children: Jane Catherine. *Education:* University of Bristol, B.Sc., 1959. *Avocational interests:* Musical composition.

ADDRESSES: Home—Lathkill House, Youlgrave, Derbyshire DE4 1WL, England. *Office*—13a Priory Ave., London W4, England.

CAREER: World Book Encyclopedia, London, England, editor, 1962-66; Hamlyn Publishing Group, London, editor, 1967-68; full-time writer.

MEMBER: Royal Society of Arts (fellow).

AWARDS, HONORS: Science Book Prize and *Times* Educational Senior Information Book Award, both 1989, both for *The Way Things Work.*

WRITINGS:

FOR CHILDREN

(Editor and adapter) *How Birds Behave* (adapted from John Sparks's *Bird Behavior*), Hamlyn Publishing Group, 1969, Grosset, 1971.

Atlas of Space, Macdonald Educational, 1970.

Experiments with Heat, Wolfe Publishing, 1970.

What Do You Know?, Hamlyn Publishing Group, 1972.

(Editor) Elizabeth S. Austin and Oliver L. Austin, *The Look-It-up Book of Birds,* revised edition, Collins, 1973.

The Earth and Beyond, Macmillan, 1974.

Countries and Homes, Macmillan, 1974.

Birds, Sampson Low, 1975, Warwick Press, 1976, revised edition, 1982.

Atoms and Energy, Sampson Low, 1975, Warwick Press, 1976, revised edition, 1982.

Purnell's Find out about Wonders of the World, Purnell Books, 1976.

(Editor) Vaclav Kvapil, *Exploring the Universe,* Hamlyn Publishing Group, 1976.

The Amazing World of Machines, Angus & Robertson, 1977.

Let's Look at Birds, Ward Lock, 1977, Derrydale, 1979.

Man and Space, Macdonald Educational, 1978.

The Scientific World, Pan Books, 1978.

Know Your Underwater Exploration, Rand McNally, 1978, published in England as *Underwater Exploration,* Purnell Books, 1978.

Musical Instruments, Macmillan, 1978, Silver Burdett, 1980.

People and Homes, Macmillan, 1978.

Guide to Birds, Pan Books, 1979.

Purnell's Find out about Birds, Purnell Books, 1979.

Stars, Macdonald Educational, 1980, Silver Burdett, 1981.

Our World of Nature: A First Picture Encyclopedia, Purnell Books, 1981.

(With wife, Bridget Ardley) *One Thousand-One Questions and Answers,* Kingfisher Books, 1981.

Nature, illustrated by Chris Shields, Pan Books, 1981.

Transport on Earth, F. Watts, 1981.

Out into Space, F. Watts, 1981.

Tomorrow's Home, F. Watts, 1981.

At School, Work, and Play, F. Watts, 1981.

Our Future Needs, F. Watts, 1982.

Health and Medicine, F. Watts, 1982.

Future War and Weapons, F. Watts, 1982.

Fact or Fantasy, F. Watts, 1982.

Computers, Warwick Press, 1983.

Working with Water, F. Watts, 1983.

Using the Computer, F. Watts, 1983.

My Favourite Encyclopedia of Science, Hamlyn Publishing Group, 1983.

Hot and Cold, F. Watts, 1983.

Sun and Light, F. Watts, 1983.

First Look at Computers, F. Watts, 1983.

Making Metric Measurements, F. Watts, 1984, published in England as *Making Measurements,* F. Watts, 1984.

Exploring Magnetism, F. Watts, 1984.

Making Things Move, F. Watts, 1984.

Discovering Electricity, F. Watts, 1984.

Air and Flight, F. Watts, 1984.

Sound and Music, F. Watts, 1984.

Simple Chemistry, F. Watts, 1984.

Force and Strength, F. Watts, 1984.

How Things Work, Silver Burdett, 1984.

ZX Spectrum and User Guide, Dorling Kindersley, 1984.

The Science of Energy, Macmillan, 1985.

Music: An Illustrated Encyclopedia, Hamlyn Publishing Group, 1987.

My Own Science Encyclopedia, Hamlyn Publishing Group, 1987.

Exploring the Universe, Macmillan, 1987.

The Inner Planets, Macmillan, 1987.

The Outer Planets, Macmillan, 1987.

(With David Macaulay) *The Way Things Work,* Houghton, 1988.

(With wife, Bridget Ardley) *Skin, Hair, and Teeth,* Macmillan, 1988.

The World of the Atom, F. Watts, 1989.

Music, Knopf, 1989.

(With wife, Bridget Ardley) *India,* Macmillan, 1989.

(With wife, Bridget Ardley) *Greece,* Macmillan, 1989.

Twentieth-Century Science, Wayland, 1989.

(With David West) *The Giant Book of the Human Body,* Hamlyn Publishing Group, 1989.

Bridges, Macmillan, 1989.

Dams, Macmillan, 1989.

Oil Rigs, Macmillan, 1989.

Language and Communications, F. Watts, 1989.

Sound Waves to Music, Gloucester Press, 1990.

Wings and Things, Puffin Books, 1990.

Snap Happy, Puffin Books, 1990.

Tune In, Puffin Books, 1991.

Bits and Chips, Puffin Books, 1991.

Light, Heinemann, 1991, Macmillan, 1992.

The Science Book of Light, Harcourt, 1991.

The Science Book of Water, Harcourt, 1991.

The Science Book of Colour, Harcourt, 1991.

The Science Book of Air, Harcourt, 1991.

The Science Book of Things That Grow, Harcourt, 1991.

The Science Book of Magnets, Harcourt, 1991.

The Science Book of Sound, Harcourt, 1991.

The Science Book of Electricity, Harcourt, 1991.

The Science Book of the Senses, Harcourt, 1992.

The Science Book of Machines, Harcourt, 1992.

The Science Book of Hot and Cold, Harcourt, 1992.

The Science Book of Energy, Harcourt, 1992.

The Science Book of Weather, Harcourt, 1992.

The Science Book of Numbers, Harcourt, 1992.

The Science Book of Motion, Harcourt, 1992.

The Science Book of Gravity, Harcourt, 1992.

Heat, Simon & Schuster, 1992.

101 Great Science Experiments, Dorling Kindersley, 1993.

Dictionary of Science: 2,000 Key Words Arranged Thematically, DK Publishing, 1995.

A Young Person's Guide to Music: A Listener's Guide, DK Publishing, 1995.

How Things Work: 100 Ways Parents and Kids Can Share the Secrets of Technology, Reader's Digest Association, 1995.

Jets, DK Publishing, 1997.

(With David Macaulay) *The New Way Things Work,* Houghton, 1998.

Electricity, Simon & Schuster, 1999.

Music, DK Publishing, 2000.

Science, DK Publishing, 2000.

FOR ADULTS

(Editor) Arrigo Polillo, *Jazz: A Guide to the History and Development of Jazz and Jazz Musicians,* Hamlyn/American, 1969.

Birds of Towns, Almark Publishing, 1975.

Birds of the Country, Almark Publishing, 1975.

Birds of Coasts, Lakes, and Rivers, Almark Publishing, 1976.

(With Brian Hawkes) *Bird-Watching,* Macdonald Educational, 1978.

Bird Life, Sackett & Marshall, 1978.

Birds of Britain and Europe, Ward Lock, 1978.

(With Ian Ridpath) *The Universe,* Silver Burdett, 1978.

Illustrated Guide to Birds and Birdwatching, Kingfisher Books, 1980.

(With Robin Kerrod) *The World of Science,* Macdonald & Co., 1982.

Contributor to *Our World Encyclopedia, Joy of Knowledge Encyclopedia, Collins Music Encyclopedia, Caxton Yearbook, Children's Britannica, The Biographical Dictionary of Scientists (Physicists),* and *The Children's Illustrated Encyclopedia.*

SIDELIGHTS: Neil Ardley is a British writer with over one hundred books to his credit. His far-ranging interests have taken him from nonfiction titles on birding and jazz to all aspects of science. Though he has written titles for an adult audience, the vast majority of his work is aimed at juvenile readers, with numerous titles in Watts's "Action Science" series as well as in Harcourt's "The Science Book of . . ." series. Recognized for his clear and concise informational approach,

Ardley generally focuses on a hands-on technique, employing simple experiments in his books to demonstrate larger scientific truths.

Born in Surrey, England, in 1937, Ardley grew up during World War II and attended the University of Bristol, where he earned a bachelor's degree in science in 1959. From 1962 to 1966 he was an editor of the *World Book Encyclopedia;* then he worked as an editor for a time at a British publishing house before turning to writing full time in 1969. Ardley once commented, "My experience with the *World Book Encyclopedia* gave me an appreciation of the necessity to express ideas clearly and concisely. In my information books, I've tried to link this to a sense of wonder at the marvels of the world."

Ardley has spent over three decades doing precisely that, and his books on topics from building bridges to computers to the why's of weather attest to his own curiosity vis-a-vis the natural world. Sylvia S. Marantz, writing in *School Library Journal,* described as "mind-boggling" the broad range of questions Ardley answers in his 1984 title, *How Things Work.* In this book, Ardley tackles the mechanics of everything from a refrigerator to the human body. "Students can look up a machine, manufacturing operation or even body part in the index," Marantz explained, "and be referred to a clear picture and explanation." In his *Computers,* Ardley took on that complex topic in a "detailed approach to the subject," according to John Brown in a *School Librarian* review. Ardley looks at the history of computers, their applications, and their internal architecture and processes in a "clearly written text with broader scope than most books on the subject written for children," according to Zena Sutherland in the *Bulletin of the Center for Children's Books.* In *The World of the Atom* Ardley turned his nonfiction lens on the building blocks of matter, dealing with concepts such as elements, compounds, crystals, radioactivity, and nuclear energy. Godfrey Hall, writing in *School Librarian,* noted in particular a "fascinating section on solutions" and "an excellent glossary." Hall concluded, "This is the kind of book which would be useful on its own, or as part of the series."

Ardley has written for several series, most prominently the "Action Science" and "The Science Book of . . ." collections. The former series is aimed at primary school students and provides simple experiments to accompany science facts. In *Working with Water,* for example, students can float an egg, make a siphon, or show how water has a skin to it. "Each experiment is described and illustrated very carefully," observed a reviewer for

Junior Bookshelf, "and the last paragraph in each case gives the scientific explanation for the results." The same reviewer pointed out that such experiments entail a "minimum of equipment, are not messy and yet are fascinating with practical applications." In *Hot and Cold* and *Sun and Light,* Ardley continues this winning combination of fact and hands-on projects. "The experiments are, for the most part, written in a clear, easy-to-follow style," noted Gale P. Jackson in a *School Library Journal* review of both volumes. Ardley's *Exploring Magnetism* and *Making Metric Measurements* "will motivate curious students to further investigation," noted Andrea Antico in *School Library Journal,* and *Booklist* contributor Karen Stars Hanley felt that *Making Metric Measurements* would be "a handy source of project ideas and inspiration" for students in the middle grades. Hanley concluded, "As with other titles in the Action Science series, the scientific explanation underlying each experiment is highlighted, and emphasis is placed on sound methodology." A reviewer for *Junior Bookshelf* thought that Ardley's *Making Things Move* for the same series "is a book to interest all children, not just those who are forever experimenting." Denise M. Wilms, reviewing Ardley's *Making Things Move* and *Discovering Electricity* in *Booklist,* wrote that the "strength of these experiments and activities lies in their simplicity: they can be done easily by a child alone or in a group." In *Air and Flight* and *Sound and Music* Ardley provides the same hands-on approach to these subjects. Antico wrote in a *School Library Journal* review that "these readable, colorful books will motivate young scientists." Reviewing several volumes in the series, including *Air and Flight,* Robert H. Cordella noted in *Science Books and Films* that each book "is well written, well illustrated, and well bound."

Another popular effort from Ardley is "The Science Book of . . ." series. These books are similar in format and in projected audience to the "Action Science" series, but they substitute color photographs for the drawings found in the earlier titles. Each title in "The Science Book of . . ." series includes from ten to fourteen experiments on the subject at hand and employ common household items in most cases. Numbered, step-by-step instructions take the young scientist through each experiment or activity, with each step carefully photographed. "All of the volumes begin with appropriate cautions about safety measures, and include special warning symbols for any steps that require caution and/or adult help," noted Susan L. Rogers in a *School Library Journal* review of *The Science Book of Air* and several other titles in the series. Rogers also praised the multi-ethnic mix of youngsters portrayed in the illustrations as well as the fact that the books "demonstrate a useful balance of action and knowledge." A reviewer for *Science Books and Films* also noted the "hands-on" approach to the books in the series, calling the experiments "exciting." Such experiments will, the reviewer concluded, "produce satisfying, tangible results that will spark continuing interest in science." *Booklist* critic Carolyn Phelan, reviewing several titles in the series, including *The Science Book of Air,* felt that "this is one of the more attractive series of science experiment books to appear lately." Phelan also noted that most of the equipment for the experiments in the books would be "readily available in the average household."

Yet another popular series for which Ardley has contributed titles is "The Way It Works" books from Macmillan. These books introduce middle graders to scientific topics from electricity to heat and light. Combining color photos with simple, clear text, the series attempts to make technology comprehensible to young readers. Small boxes on each page also highlight information and provide interesting facts. Leigh Riesenfeld, reviewing Ardley's *Light* in *Appraisal: Science Books for Young People,* felt that it "provided clear answers to some questions that I am frequently asked, for example, What is a Hologram? How does a laser work? What is radar?" Engineering and construction practices are introduced in the "How We Build Series" to which Ardley contributed several volumes, including *Bridges, Dams,* and *Oil Rigs.* Reviewing the entire group of books, Susan Penny wrote in *School Library Journal* that the series was "well-conceived" and the "information is well organized and is presented concisely in nontechnical language." An historical overview introduces each topic, and then the building process itself is described along with science experiments that relate to each step in the construction.

Ardley has also taken his experimental approach to science as a whole with his 1993 *101 Great Science Experiments.* This book includes activities grouped in eleven topical divisions, such as air and gasses, light, color, senses, electricity, and others. "School and public libraries will do parents and children a great favor by adding *101 Great Science Experiments* to their collections," commented James Rettla in *Wilson Library Bulletin.* Denia Hester, reviewing the same title in *Booklist,* declared, "What makes this book special is the clean, simple format with equally simple instructions." Gary A. Griess, reviewing *101 Great Science Experiments* in *Science Books and Films,* felt that "among several books of this type, [Ardley's] ranks high because of the simplicity of the materials it requires, as well as its ease of execution, quality of illustrations, and accuracy of information." Other general reference

science and fact books from Ardley include *Dictionary of Science,* which defines over two thousand chemistry and physics terms, and the award-winning *The Way Things Work* and *The New Way Things Work,* both in collaboration with David Macaulay, the latter being "a sure bet for both adult and juvenile collections," according to *Booklist*'s Stephanie Zvirin.

Ardley is also a musician, both composing music and playing the synthesizer. One of his earliest books for adults was a jazz history and directory. For juveniles, he has also demonstrated his love for music in the 1987 title *Music: An Illustrated Encyclopedia,* as well as in the 1995 book *A Young Person's Guide to Music.* The former title is "an excellent addition to any music shelf and a great gift for any music lover," according to Barbara Jo McKee in *Voice of Youth Advocates.* In *A Young Person's Guide to Music* Ardley focuses on classical music and uses an accompanying CD to illustrate the music discussed. *Booklist*'s Phelan opined that "this book offers music students a wide range of options," from a study of musical instruments to a survey of classical music from ancient through baroque and on to modern. Phelan further commented that the book is a "rich resource for young people who want to understand orchestral music." Tim Moses, reviewing the same title for *Boston Book Review* online, concluded that "this book is an excellent guide to understanding one of mankind's oldest and greatest art forms."

Ardley, in the decades he has been writing children's books, has tackled a wide range of topics. Whether explicating the make-up of the atom, or describing how to build a bridge, or explaining how to play a French horn, he has continually demonstrated that concision and clarity are the best tools in the nonfiction writer's workshop.

BIOGRAPHICAL/CRITICAL SOURCES:

BOOKS

The New Grove Dictionary of Jazz, St. Martin's Press, 1994.

PERIODICALS

Appraisal: Science Books for Young People, winter, 1992, p. 79; winter, 1993, Leigh Riesenfeld, review of *Light,* pp. 87-88; winter-spring, 1996, pp. 8-9.

Booklist, June 1, 1984, Karen Stars Hanley, review of *Making Metric Measurements,* p. 1395; October 1, 1984, Denise M. Wilms, review of *Making Things Move* and *Discovering Electricity,* p. 214; September 1, 1985, p. 637; May 15, 1989, p. 1642; March 1, 1991, Carolyn Phelan, review of *The Science Book of Air* and others, p. 1381; February 1, 1994, Denia Hester, review of *101 Great Science Experiments,* p. 1003; October 15, 1995, p. 414; December 15, 1995, Carolyn Phelan, review of *A Young Person's Guide to Music,* p. 694; December 1, 1998, Stephanie Zvirin, review of *The New Way Things Work,* p. 674.

Bulletin of the Center for Children's Books, June, 1984, Zena Sutherland, review of *Computers,* p. 101.

Chicago Tribune Book World, March 18, 1984, p. 30.

Horn Book Guide, fall, 1991, p. 294; spring, 1992, p. 98; spring, 1993, p. 103; spring, 1994, p. 116; spring, 1996, p. 328; fall, 1996, p. 125.

Junior Bookshelf, December, 1983, review of *Working with Water,* p. 240; March, 1984, review of *Making Things Move,* p. 123; June, 1988, p. 133; June, 1990, p. 139.

New Scientist, November 21, 1992, p. 45C.

Publishers Weekly, October 23, 1995, p. 70.

RQ, summer, 1996, p. 567.

School Librarian, March, 1984, John Brown, review of *Computers,* pp. 267-268; March, 1989, Godfrey Hall, review of *The World of the Atom,* p. 107.

School Library Journal, March, 1984, Gale P. Jackson, review of *Sun and Light* and *Hot and Cold,* p. 153; June, 1984, p. 79; September, 1984, Sylvia S. Marantz, review of *How Things Work,* pp. 75-76; September, 1984, Andrea Antico, review of *Making Measurements* and *Exploring Magnetism,* p. 112; April, 1985, Andrea Antico, review of *Sound and Music* and *Air and Flight,* p. 84; July, 1985, p. 173; March, 1991, Susan Penny, review of *Bridges* and others, p. 198; May, 1991, Susan L. Rogers, review of *The Science Book of Air* and others, pp. 96, 98; August, 1992, p. 150; March, 1993, p. 203; August, 1996, p. 112.

Science Books and Films, March-April, 1986, p. 226; January-February, 1986, Robert H. Cordella, review of *Air and Flight* and others, pp. 162-163; March, 1992, p. 50; April, 1994, Gary A. Griess, review of *101 Great Science Experiments,* p. 79; June-July, 1995, review of "The Science Book of . . ." series, pp. 129-130.

Times Educational Supplement, November 19, 1989, p. 34; November 8, 1991, p. 32; February 7, 1992, p. 34; November 24, 1995, p. 15.

Voice of Youth Advocates, June, 1987, Barbara Jo McKee, review of *Music: An Illustrated Encyclopedia,* p. 95.

Washington Post Book World, May 14, 1989, p. 20.

Wilson Library Bulletin, March, 1994, James Rettla, review of *101 Great Science Experiments,* p. 94.

OTHER

Boston Book Review, http://bookwire.bowker.com/ (March 3, 2000).*

*   *   *

ARMITAGE, Shelley S(ue) 1947-

PERSONAL: Born June 17, 1947, in Fort Worth, TX; daughter of Robert Allen (a banker and farmer) and Dorothy (a banker; maiden name, Dunn) Armitage. *Ethnicity:* "White, non-Hispanic." *Education:* Texas Tech University, B.A., 1969, M.A., 1971; University of New Mexico, Ph.D., 1983.

ADDRESSES: Home—P.O. Box 524, Vega, TX 79092. *Office*—Department of English, University of Texas at El Paso, El Paso, TX 79968; fax 915-747-5981. *E-mail*—armitage@utep.edu.

CAREER: Vega Enterprise, Vega, TX, reporter and columnist, 1961-65; Tarrant County Junior College, Hurst, TX, assistant professor, 1971-74, associate professor of English, 1975-78; University of Asmara, Asmara, Ethiopia, lecturer, 1974; University of Albuquerque, Albuquerque, NM, assistant professor of interdisciplinary studies, 1981-82; West Texas State University, Canyon, associate professor of English, 1982-89; University of Hawaii at Manoa, Honolulu, professor of American studies, 1990-96; University of Texas at El Paso, Roderick Professor, 1995, director of Women Studies Program, 1996—. Universidade Nova de Lisboa, Fulbright scholar, 1990; University of Warsaw, Distinguished Fulbright Professor, 2000; Memphis State University, visiting professor. New Mexico Humanities Council, executive director, 1985. U.S. Olympic Women's Basketball Team, alternate member, 1976.

MEMBER: Modern Language Association of America, American Studies Association, American Association of University Professors, Western Literature Association, Western Writers Association, Phi Beta Kappa.

AWARDS, HONORS: Grants from National Endowment for the Humanities, 1973-74, 1978-79, and 1999; Rockefeller grant, 1985; named distinguished alumna, English department, Texas Tech University, 1992.

WRITINGS:

(Editor, with Thomas Barrow and William Tydeman) *Reading into Photography: Essays on Photographic Criticism,* University of New Mexico Press (Albuquerque, NM), 1983.

John Held, Jr.: Illustrator of the Jazz Age (biography), Syracuse University Press (Syracuse, NY), 1987.

(Editor) Peggy Pond Church, *Wind's Trail: The Early Life of Mary Austin* (biography), Museum of New Mexico Press (Santa Fe, NM), 1990.

Peggy Pond Church (biography), Boise State University (Boise, ID), 1993.

(Editor) *That Dancing Ground of Sky: The Collected Poetry of Peggy Pond Church,* Red Crane Books (Santa Fe, NM), 1993.

Kewpies and Beyond: The World of Rose O'Neill (biography), University Press of Mississippi (Jackson, MS), 1994.

Women Writing Culture, Locust Hill Press, 1995.

Bones Incandescent: The Nature Journals of Peggy Pond Church, Texas Tech University Press (Lubbock, TX), 2001.

Contributor to books, including *The American Self, Badges and Bullets,* and *Multilingual America.* Contributor of more than fifty scholarly articles and poems to magazines, including *Western Humanities Review, Paintbrush, American Transcendental Quarterly, Journal of Popular Culture, Exposure,* and *New Mexico Humanities Review.* Editor of *American Indian Quarterly,* 1974-76.

SIDELIGHTS: Shelley S. Armitage told *CA:* "A writer/photographer friend of mine once told me, 'Whatever you do, don't sell the family farm.' Even though it's hard to know whether anyone would even buy the family farm in today's market, I haven't sold it, and I don't intend to. Despite my university profession taking me to regions in the United States and to Eastern Europe, Portugal, and Eritrea, I keep this eighty-year-old farmhouse and keep returning to the rolling pastureland nearby.

"These very different places—the rolling plains of northwest Texas and the academic centers located in urban areas—keep alive my intellectual curiosities and my 'habit of landscape.' I believe the rhythms of the two in part inspire the form of our inner voice, the facsimile of which makes itself heard on the page.

"Having just completed a literary biography of Peggy Pond Church, which incorporates her personal journals kept on and about the Pajarito Plateau in northern New Mexico, I am particularly fond of what Church said about her own writer's sources. She credited the sound of the Rio Frijoles, located in the Pajarito area, with the sound, rhythm, pacings of her poems. A pianist and a basketball player in the early days of that sport for women, she relates tapping out rhythms which became prosodies, beginning in her childhood years by the river. My own writing about Church attempted a lyric voice, perhaps because I share Church's own metaphoric renderings of place and inner voice.

"So, as Eudora Welty so eloquently reminded us years ago, place effects a kind of focus which resolves itself into point of view. This perspective (rather than a fixed notion of literary point of view) becomes a narrative, a story emanating from a particular place or region.

"My recent nonfiction work—about Tiqua pueblo in El Paso, Texas, women's western lives, African-American cartoonist Jackie Ormes, and the poet Peggy Church—continues a relationship with the various places and regions of these people even as it resonates with my own. I hope to continue to work on breaking through the expectations of genre through stylistic ventures which themselves are rooted in the connections between the metaphors of voice and landscape."

*   *   *

AULETTA, Robert 1940-

PERSONAL: Born March 5, 1940, in Woodside, NY; son of Anthony Andrew (a teamster) and Margaret (a secretary and homemaker; maiden name, Stark) Auletta; married Carol Carey, 1964 (divorced, 1980); married Jeni Breen (a dancer and choreographer), 1985; children: Colleen, Deirdre. *Education:* Queens College of the City University of New York, B.A., 1964; Yale University, M.F.A., 1969. *Politics:* "Utopian socialist." *Religion:* "Born a Catholic and still recovering."

ADDRESSES: Home—484 West 43rd St., New York, NY 10036. *Office*—School of Visual Arts, 209 East 23rd St., New York, NY 10010. *Agent*—Helen Merrill, 295 Lafayette St., Suite 915, New York, NY 10012-2700. *E-mail*—rauletta@compuserve.com.

CAREER: University of Illinois at Urbana-Champaign, Champaign, assistant professor of theater, 1969-74; School of Visual Arts, New York, NY, teacher of theater, 1975—. Yale University, playwright in residence,

1974-77, teacher, 1974-77, visiting lecturer, 1993—; Southern Connecticut State College, teacher, 1974-76; O'Neill Theater Center, Waterford, CT, teacher, 1978-79; Harvard University, teacher of summer playwriting classes, 1984-97; Columbia University, teacher of playwriting, 1986.

AWARDS, HONORS: Peter Pauper Press Award for creative writing, 1964; John Golden fellowship, Leonard Elmster fellowship, at Yale University, 1967-69; Mollie Kazan Award, 1969, for *Red Mountain High;* Rockefeller grant, 1972; playwriting fellowship, Columbia Broadcasting System, 1975-76; Hazan Foundation grant, 1974; citation for one of eight most outstanding plays produced outside of New York City during 1982-83 season, American Theater Critics' Association, for *Rundown;* grants from National Endowment for the Arts, 1982 and 1987; Obie Award, *Village Voice,* 1982, for *Virgins* and *Stops;* Hollywood Drama Logue Award, 1986, for *Sophocles' Ajax;* grant from New York State Foundation for the Arts, 1987.

WRITINGS:

PLAYS

The National Guard (one-act), first produced in New Haven, CT, at Experimental Theater, Yale School of Drama, 1966.

Foreplay—Doorplay, first produced in New Haven, CT, at Yale School of Drama, 1967.

Red Mountain High (two-act), first produced in New Haven, CT, at Studio Theater, Yale School of Drama, 1968.

Coocooshay (two-act), first produced in New York, NY, at New York Shakespeare Festival, December, 1970.

Stops (one-act; first produced in New Haven, CT, at Yale Repertory Theater, February, 1973), published in *Antaeus 66: Plays in One Act,* [New York, NY], 1991.

Walk the Dog, Willie (two-act; first produced in New Haven, CT, at Yale Repertory Theater, February, 1976), Broadway Play Publishing (New York, NY), 1986.

Wednesday Sharp (one-act), first produced in New Haven, CT, at Yale Cabaret, April, 1977.

Guess Work (one-act), first produced in New Haven, CT, at Yale Repertory Theater, October, 1978.

Expo 99 (one-act), first produced in New Haven, CT, at Yale Cabaret, December, 1978.

Joe: A Dramatic Idiocy (one-act), first produced in New York, NY, at Theater for the New City, April, 1980.

Hage: The Sexual History (two-act), first produced in Waterford, CT, at Eugene O'Neill Theater Center, July, 1981.

The Tobogganists (one-act), first produced in New York, NY, at Ensemble Studio Theater, September, 1981.

Virgins (one-act), first produced in New York, NY, at Public School 122, January, 1982.

Rundown (two-act), first produced in Cambridge, MA, at American Repertory Theater, April, 1982, Theater Communications Group, 1981-82.

Days in a Can (one-act), first produced in New York, NY, at West Bank Cabaret, November, 1983.

Birth (one-act), first produced in New York, NY, at Cooper Union, December 12, 1983.

A Bull Refusing to Die in Madrid (one-act), first produced in New York, NY, at West Bank Cabaret, November, 1985.

Diesel Moon, first produced as a staged reading in Cleveland, OH, at Cleveland Playhouse, January, 1986.

(Adaptor) *Sophocles' Ajax* (first produced in Washington, DC, at Kennedy Center, June 7, 1986), published in *Theatre,* fall-winter, 1986.

(With Donald Byrd) *Blue Margaritas,* first produced in New York, NY, at La Mama Experimental Theater Club, 1987.

Speak Easy, first performed by Donald Byrd Dance Company in New York, NY, at Symphony Space, 1988.

Alimony Tales, first performed in New York, NY, at West Bank Theater Bar, 1989.

White Bucks, first performed in New York, NY, at West Bank Cabaret, 1990.

Amazons and Nuclear Ear, first performed in New York, NY, at Harold Clurman Theater, 1990.

Hey, Hey, LBJ (one-act), first performed in Chicago, IL, at Organic Theater, 1992.

Lucifer Distracted (two-act), first performed as a staged reading in Poughkeepsie, NY, at Vassar College, 1992, produced in New York, NY, at National Academy of Dramatic Arts, 1993.

(Adaptor) George Buchner, *Danton's Death,* first performed in Houston, TX, at Alley Theater, 1992.

(Adaptor) Aeschylus, *The Persians,* first performed in Salzburg, Austria, at Salzburg Festival, 1993.

(Adaptor) Aeschylus, *The Oresteia,* first performed in Cambridge, MA, at American Repertory Theater, 1994-95.

(Adaptor) Moliere, *Tartuffe,* first performed in Cambridge, MA, at American Repertory Theater, 1996.

(Adaptor) Johann Wolfgang von Goethe, *Faust, Part One,* first performed in workshop in Los Angeles, at Classical Theater Laboratory, 1996.

Red Train (e-book), Broadway Play Publishing (New York, NY), 2000.

The plays *The National Guard, Red Mountain High, Walk the Dog, Willie,* and *Foreplay—Doorplay* were published in *Yale/Theatre; Stops* was published in *Playwrights for Tomorrow,* Volume 10, Minnesota Press; author's version of Aeschylus's *The Persians* was published by Sun and Moon Press (College Park, MD). Scenes from another play, *Agamemnon,* were published in *Harvard Review.*

OTHER

Contributor of theater articles to periodicals, including *Drama, Parabais,* and *Theater.*

ADAPTATIONS: Two of Auletta's plays have been recorded on videotape: *Danton's Death,* directed by Robert Wilson, and *The Persians,* directed by Peter Sellars. They are held in the permanent archives of the Theater Collections, Lincoln Center Branch, New York Public Library.

WORK IN PROGRESS: The Master, full-length play in one act, "a darkly satirical comedy focusing on all the dedication, determination, and hard work that go into making bad theater"; *Rabbits* and *Roanoke,* two one-act plays "dealing with loss and spiritual breakdown"; *Early On,* a "surreal one-act play which concerns itself with the possibility of redemption."

SIDELIGHTS: Playwright Robert Auletta told *CA:* "When did it all begin, the words, where did they start, come from? Often writers talk about the books around them as they were growing up. That was not the case for me, though. The words that later became part of my life seemed to have had their origin somewhere else. Outside books. Later I located them in books. But it all began in play, I believe, in those endless mid-century days of light and darkness, alive with the myriad somersaults, antics and tricks that children seem able to conjure so easily, Prospero-like, out of the raw elements, and then turn to their wonder and advantage—fall and winter, shadows and movement, the early cold snapping the body to attention with its dangerous voltage, icy with living excitement, tires burning in vacant lots, potatoes blackening in the flames, geese streaking through the sky, and those mysterious elm trees brushing back the wind; and, on the other side of the equinox, the sun, with all its unending gifts, all those wonderful spring-summer mornings, in Flushing, New York.

"But what exactly is this 'play' that I am trying to speak about? No more than the imagination, really, turning, twisting, and teasing the world around you; and the world returning the favor. Later, buildings and automobiles, people and passions became involved; but in the beginning the play that I am concerned with is devoid of these things—just the basic lineaments of geography and nature, solitary and mysterious: just sunlight, a small hill, green and gold and shadows; or an animal, or the thought of an animal hiding in the high grass, with you standing and squinting into this sea of grass and sun, playing warriors and animals, and great battles beginning and ending, and creatures that cannot be described, dancing weirdly about, and the sight of fire filling the darkness, and maybe some mysterious lovely face speaking to you, giving you chills—someone who is everywhere, and all things, and nothing. Nothing at all, really. And looking back at it now, you know that it was the secret, the landscape where this happiness, the happiness of creativity lay, the secret that spoke to you. No, not so much books; we didn't have many of them in the house in those days. And there wasn't any television till later on, to interrupt things.

"Something else quite important happened during this time. At the age of seven I became an altar boy and began serving mass at St. Ann's Catholic Church, just up the street from where I lived on 59th Avenue in Flushing, Queens. This was where the theatre began for me, and the possibility of language first came alive; but the language that entered my mind at that time, that special, magical tongue, capable of so many amazing things, wasn't English; but something entirely different: it was Latin, the Latin of the Catholic mass. It was the ritual of the Mass, and the mystery of that ancient language, that, I believe, prepared me for the theatre."

BIOGRAPHICAL/CRITICAL SOURCES:

BOOKS

McDonald, Marianne, *Ancient Sun, Modern Light: Greek Drama on the Modern Stage,* Columbia University Press (New York, NY), 1992.
Stephens, Michael, *The Dramaturgy of Style: Voices in Short Fiction,* Southern Illinois University Press (Carbondale, IL), 1986.

PERIODICALS

American Theatre, February, 1995, Scott T. Cummings, "Blood Relations," pp. 10-15, 68.
Boston Globe, December 2, 1994, pp. 43, 51.
Boston Phoenix, April 13, 1982.

New York Times, May 2, 1982; March 28, 1985.
Other Stages, January 13-26, 1986.
Theater, fall-winter, 1986, article by W. D. King.

*　　*　　*

AXELROD, Alan 1952-
(Jack Griffin)

PERSONAL: Born August 25, 1952, in New York, NY; son of Samuel George (a buyer) and Helen Josephine (Vlcek) Axelrod. *Education:* Northeastern Illinois University, B.A., 1972; University of Iowa, M.A., 1973, Ph.D., 1979.

ADDRESSES: Home—Atlanta, GA. *Office*—c/o Prentice-Hall, Inc., Englewood Cliffs, NJ 07632.

CAREER: State Historical Society of Iowa, Iowa City, assistant editor, 1977-79; Lake Forest College, Lake Forest, IL, lecturer in English, 1979-80; Furman University, Greenville, SC, assistant professor of English, 1980-82; Henry Francis du Pont Winterthur Museum, Winterthur, DE, assistant editor, beginning 1982; currently freelance writer.

MEMBER: American Studies Fellows, Tennessee Squires.

WRITINGS:

Records of a Chance Meeting (poetry), Ad Hoc Press, 1977.
Charles Brockden Brown: An American Tale, University of Texas Press (Austin, TX), 1983.
(Editor) *Colonial Revival in America,* Norton (New York, NY), 1984.
Art of the Golden West, Abbeville Press (New York, NY), 1990.
(Author of commentary) *Songs of the Wild West,* Simon & Schuster (New York, NY), 1991.
The War between the Spies: A History of Espionage during the American Civil War, Atlantic Monthly Press (New York, NY), 1992.
(With Charles Phillips) *What Every American Should Know about American History: 200 Events That Shaped the Nation,* B. Adams (Holbrook, MA), 1992.

Chronicle of the Indian Wars: From Colonial Times to Wounded Knee, Prentice Hall (Englewood Cliffs, NJ), 1993.
(With Phillips) *My Brother's Face: Portraits of the Civil War in Photographs, Diaries, and Letters,* Chronicle Books (San Francisco, CA), 1993.
The Environmentalists: A Biographical Dictionary from the 17th Century to the Present, Facts on File (New York, NY), 1993.
Dictators and Tyrants: Absolute Rulers and Would-be Rulers in World History, Facts on File (New York, NY), 1995.
(With Phillips) *What Everyone Should Know about the 20th Century: 200 Events That Shaped the World,* B. Adams (Hollbrook, MA), 1995.
(Editor, with Phillips) *Encyclopedia of the American West,* 4 volumes, Macmillan (New York, NY), 1996.
The Complete Idiot's Guide to American History, Alpha Books (Indianapolis, IN), 1996, 2nd edition, 2000.
The Complete Idiot's Guide to Mixing Drinks, Alpha Books (Indianapolis, IN), 1997.
The International Encyclopedia of Secret Societies and Fraternal Orders, Facts on File (New York, NY), 1997.
(With Jim Holtje) *201 Ways to Deal with Difficult People,* McGraw (New York, NY), 1997.
(With Holtje) *201 Ways to Manage Your Time Better,* McGraw (New York, NY), 1997.
(With Holtje) *201 Ways to Say No Gracefully and Effectively,* McGraw (New York, NY), 1997.
The Pocket Idiot's Guide to Bartending, Alpha Books (Indianapolis, IN), 1998.
The Complete Idiot's Guide to the Civil War, Alpha Books (Indianapolis, IN), 1998.
Miss Nomer's Guide to Painfully Incorrect English: Because It's about Time You Stopped Sounding Like an Imbecile, Berkley Books (New York, NY), 1998.
(With Phillips) *The Macmillan Dictionary of Military Biography: The Warriors and Their Wars, 3500 B.C.-Present,* Macmillan, 1998.
(With Christopher De Pree) *The Complete Idiot's Guide to Astronomy,* Alpha Books (Indianapolis, IN), 1998.
Patton on Leadership: Strategic Lessons for Corporate Warfare, Prentice-Hall, 1999.
The Complete Idiot's Guide to Jazz, Alpha Books (Indianapolis, IN), 1999.
Ace Your Midterms & Finals: Fundamentals of Mathematics, McGraw (New York, NY), 1999.
Ace Your Midterms & Finals: Introduction to Physics, McGraw (New York, NY), 1999.
Ace Your Midterms & Finals: Introduction to Psychology, McGraw (New York, NY), 1999.

Ace Your Midterms & Finals: U.S. History, McGraw (New York, NY), 1999.

Ace Your Midterms & Finals: Principles of Economics, McGraw (New York, NY), 1999.

(With Phillips and Kurt Kemper) *Cops, Crooks, and Criminologists: An International Biographical Dictionary of Law Enforcement,* Checkmark Books (New York, NY), 2000.

(Editor) *The Quotable Historian: Words of Wisdom from Winston Churchill, Barbara Tuchman, Edward Gibbon, Julius Caesar, David McCullough, and More,* McGraw (New York, NY), 2000.

American Treaties and Alliances, CQ Press (Washington, DC), 2000.

The Complete Idiot's Guide to the American Revolution, Alpha Books (Indianapolis, IN), 2000.

Elizabeth I, CEO: Strategic Lessons from the Leader Who Built an Empire, Prentice-Hall, 2000.

(With Harry Oster and Walton Rawls) *The Penguin Dictionary of American Folklore,* Penguin (New York, NY), 2000.

Encyclopedia of Historical Treaties and Alliances, Facts on File (New York, NY), 2001.

Also author, under pseudonym Jack Griffin, of *How to Say It at Work,* published by Prentice-Hall. Contributor to periodicals, including *Down Beat, South Carolina Review, American Studies, Palimpsest,* and *Winterthur Portfolio.*

SIDELIGHTS: Alan Axelrod is a prolific author of reference books and how-to guides for business leadership, as well as a plethora of informational volumes on everything from physics to folklore. His contributions to the "Complete Idiot's Guide" series include books on the Civil War, astronomy, jazz, and mixing cocktails, while his more serious and detailed works explore the American West, military history, and secret societies. Few writers of any stripe could keep pace with Axelrod, who has been turning out as many as three or four books per year since the early 1990s.

Two of Axelrod's better-known titles are *Patton on Leadership: Strategic Lessons for Corporate Warfare* and *Elizabeth I, CEO: Strategic Lessons from the Leader Who Built an Empire.* Both of these books examine the lives and philosophies of two outstanding leaders who managed—sometimes with audacity—to achieve dominance over formidable enemies. A reviewer in *Canadian Manager* felt that *Patton on Leadership* "reveals the master at work and shows how to apply his principles in the business world." A *Publishers Weekly* review of *Elizabeth I, CEO* likewise suggested that his-

tory buffs "will enjoy the brief portraits of Queen Elizabeth's governing style in various circumstances." As Axelrod explained to a *Fortune* interviewer, Elizabeth recognized the importance of developing a strong image, and made herself into a "cultural icon that would satisfy a need" among her English subjects. This is a strategy that present-day business leaders could adopt to their own advantage. "They do need to create an image that satisfies the culture of their organization," Axelrod commented.

For some years Axelrod has worked closely with Charles Phillips, and their most notable collaboration is the editing of the four-volume *Encyclopedia of the American West,* as well as *The Macmillan Dictionary of Military Biography.* These works are reference books containing entries on people, events, cultural trends, and places pertinent to the topics. A contributor to *Booklist* commended the *Encyclopedia of the American West* for its "concise, well-written information about persons, places, or things."

Axelrod once told *CA:* "My critical writing is about the New World as a personal and cultural icon and totem: a metaphor. While my scholarly interest is principally in early American literature, the metaphoric function of America first became clear to me (as doubtless it has to any number of undergraduates) in reading *The Great Gatsby.* Fitzgerald's novel does not merely treat the so-called American dream, but rather reveals the New World as a place that demands the production of dreams—extorts them, really—as if the whole solid continent were only the projected imaginings of the men and women who have lived and labored on it. Unfortunately, as Nick Carraway discovers and Jay Gatsby himself fails to discover, metaphor must exist in a world of substance; the pure ether of dreams is fed by the poor earth of greed, lust, and stupidity, suffering the decay time works on all finally substantial things.

"I study the ways in which American writers use the New World as the stuff of metaphor and how these writers manage—or fail to manage—reconciliation between dream and substance. Of course, dreams and the failure of dreams are not peculiar to America. But because the New World existed in the European imagination long before it was explored physically and because its imaginative being has persisted long after its physical exploration, mythic structures evolved about America that have united it permanently and peculiarly to the individual and collective imagination. What is more, the drama of the conflict between imagined metaphor and actual substance, while hardly unknown in the Old

World, is especially intense in America because the New World is as much a place of ineluctable fact as it is the territory of illusion. Its very existence compelled Europeans to revise religion and cosmogony. America was a wilderness that forced upon inhabitants and intruders alike a necessary regard for empirical exigencies. Even after the wilderness was 'settled,' the civilization it bore governed itself by the empirical principles of such philosophers as John Locke, while the national philosophy evolved into 'pragmatism' and the national literature worked itself into 'realism.' Nevertheless, the practical founders of our government were simultaneously Platonists, the pragmatic philosophers Transcendentalists, and the realist writers intensely romantic.

"So American literature, as I study it, is frontier literature—not just the geographical frontier that appears in the works of James Fenimore Cooper or Francis Parkman or even Walt Whitman, but the figurative frontier that informs virtually all of our important literary works. In creating a metaphor from the physical, intellectual, and emotional materials of the New World, our most characteristic writers established their camps on a frontier far more enduring than any geographical demarcation. The point at which dream confronts substance, the American metaphor is a frontier that holds in dramatic dialectic the anxious, hopeful self and the threatening, promising world beyond it.

"This is what excites me about American literature."

BIOGRAPHICAL/CRITICAL SOURCES:

PERIODICALS

Booklist, March 15, 1996, review of *Cops, Crooks, and Criminologists: An International Biographical Dictionary of Law Enforcement,* p. 1312; December 1, 1996, review of *Encyclopedia of the American West,* p. 680; September 1, 1997, review of *International Encyclopedia of Secret Societies and Fraternal Orders,* p. 164; June 1, 1998, review of *The Macmillan Dictionary of Military Biography,* p. 1812; July, 2000, Ted Hipple, review of *Patton on Leadership: Strategic Lessons for Corporate Warfare,* p. 2053.

Canadian Manager, spring, 2000, review of *Patton on Leadership: Strategic Lessons for Corporate Warfare,* p. 30.

Fortune, November 13, 2000, interview, "Just Don't Lock Your Enemies in the Tower: Advice from the Sixteenth Century," p. 458.

Library Journal, June 15, 2000, Dale Farris, review of *Patton on Leadership: Strategic Lessons for Corporate Warfare,* p. 135.

Publishers Weekly, July 10, 2000, review of *Elizabeth I, CEO: Strategic Lessons from the Leader Who Built an Empire,* p. 50.

Sky & Telescope, April, 1999, E. Samuel Palmer, "Respectable Textbook Alternative," p. 80.*

*   *   *

AYER, Eleanor H. 1947-1998

PERSONAL: Born September 6, 1947, in Burlington, VT; died June 5, 1998, in Frederick, CO; daughter of William H. (a plumbing and heating contractor) and Shirley T. (an elementary school teacher; maiden name, Thomas) Hubbard; married John Ayer (a publisher); children: Madison, William. *Education:* Newhouse School of Journalism, Syracuse University, B.S., 1969, M.S., 1970.

CAREER: Editor and freelance writer. Laubach Literacy Foundation, Syracuse, NY, associate editor for *News for You,* 1967-69, associate editor of New Readers Press, 1969-70; *Jackson Hole Guide,* Jackson, WY, assistant editor, 1971; Jende-Hagan (book distribution and publishing company), Frederick, CO, co-founder, editor, and marketing manager, beginning 1972; Pruett Publishing Company, Boulder, CO, production/promotion coordinator, 1972; Shields Publishing Company, Fort Collins, CO, production/promotion coordinator, 1973-74; Renaissance House Publishing Company, Frederick, editor and marketing manager, beginning 1984. Founder and writer for *The American Traveller* (travel guides), beginning 1987.

MEMBER: Society of Children's Book Writers and Illustrators, Rocky Mountain Book Publishers Association, Mountain and Plains Booksellers Association, Colorado Authors' League.

AWARDS, HONORS: Top Hand Awards for young adult nonfiction, Colorado Authors' League, 1991, for *Teen Marriage,* and 1992, for *The Value of Determination;* Notable Children's Trade Book in the Field of Social Studies designation, Children's Book Council/National Council for the Social Studies, 1992, for *Margaret Bourke-White: Photographing the World;* Top Hand Award for specialty writing, Colorado Authors' League, 1992, for *Southwest Traveler: A Guide to the Anasazi and other Ancient Southwest Indians.*

WRITINGS:

FOR YOUNG ADULTS; NONFICTION

Teen Marriage, Rosen (New York, NY), 1978.

Germany, Rourke, 1990.

The Value of Determination, Rosen, 1991.

Berlin ("Cities at War" series), Simon & Schuster (New York, NY), 1992.

Boris Yeltsin: Man of the People, Dillon (New York, NY), 1992.

Margaret Bourke-White: Photographing the World, Dillon, 1992.

Our Flag ("I Know America" series), Millbrook, 1992.

Our National Monuments ("I Know America" series), Millbrook, 1992.

The Anasazi, Walker, 1993.

Everything You Need to Know about Teen Fatherhood, Rosen, 1993.

Teen Suicide: Is It Too Painful to Grow Up?, Twenty-first Century Books/Holt (New York, NY), 1993.

Our Great Rivers and Waterways ("I Know America" series), Millbrook, 1994.

Ruth Bader Ginsburg: Fire and Steel on the Supreme Court, Dillon, 1994.

The United States Holocaust Memorial Museum: America Keeps the Memory Alive, Dillon, 1994.

Everything You Need to Know about Stress, Rosen, 1994.

Everything You Need to Know about Depression, Rosen, 1994.

(With Helen Waterford and Alfons Heck) *Parallel Journeys,* Atheneum (New York City), 1995.

Germany: In the Heartland of Europe ("Exploring Cultures of the World" series), Benchmark (Tarrytown, NY), 1996.

Poland: A Troubled Past, a New Start ("Exploring Cultures of the World" series), Benchmark, 1996.

Adolf Hitler ("The Importance of . . ." series), Lucent (San Diego, CA), 1996.

Homeless Children ("Overview" series), Lucent, 1997.

Colorado ("Celebrate the States" series), Benchmark, 1997.

It's Okay to Say No: Choosing Sexual Abstinence ("Teen Pregnancy Prevention" series), Rosen, 1997.

Lewis Latimer: Creating Bright Ideas, Raintree/Steck-Vaughn (Austin, TX), 1997.

The Survivors ("Holocaust Library"), Lucent, 1998.

Charles Dickens ("The Importance of . . ." series), Lucent, 1998.

Life as a Nazi Soldier ("The Way People Live" series), Lucent, 1998.

In the Ghettos: Teens Who Survived the Ghettos of the Holocaust, Rosen, 1999.

Teen Smoking ("Overview" series), Lucent, 1999.

NONFICTION; "COLORADO CHRONICLES" SERIES; ILLUSTRATED BY JANE KLINE

Famous Colorado Men, Renaissance House (Frederick, CO), 1980.

Famous Colorado Women, Renaissance House, 1981.

Indians of Colorado, Renaissance House, 1981.

Hispanic Colorado, Renaissance House, 1982.

Colorado Wildlife, Renaissance House, 1983.

(Editor) *Colorado Businesses,* Renaissance House, 1984.

(Editor) Suzanne Thumhart, *Colorado Wonders,* Renaissance House, 1986.

Colorado Chronicles Index, Renaissance House, 1986.

NONFICTION; "AMERICAN TRAVELER" SERIES

Colorado Traveler: Hall of Fame: A Gallery of the Rich and Famous, Renaissance House, 1987.

Colorado Traveler; Birds; A Guide to Colorado's Unique Varieties, Renaissance House, 1987.

Colorado Traveler: Parks and Monuments, Renaissance House, 1987.

Colorado Traveler: Colorado Wildflowers: A Guide to Colorado's Unique Varieties, Renaissance House, 1987.

Colorado Traveler: Colorado Wildlife: A Guide to Colorado's Unique Animals, Renaissance House, 1987.

Colorado Traveler: Skiing, Renaissance House, 1987.

Colorado Traveler: Discover Colorado, Renaissance House, 1988.

Arizona Traveler: Birds of Arizona: A Guide to Unique Varieties, Renaissance House, 1988.

Arizona Traveler: Discover Arizona: The Grand Canyon State, Renaissance House, 1988.

Arizona Traveler: Arizona Wildflowers, Renaissance House, 1989.

Arizona Traveler: Indians of Arizona: A Guide to Arizona's Heritage, Renaissance House, 1990.

Southwest Traveler: A Guide to the Anasazi and Other Ancient Southwest Indians, Renaissance House, 1991.

Californian Traveler: Earthquake Country: Traveling California's Fault Lines, Renaissance House, 1992.

California Traveler: Parks and Monuments of California: A Scenic Guide, Renaissance House, 1992.

NONFICTION; "HOLOCAUST" SERIES

A Firestorm Unleashed: January 1942-June 1943,
    Blackbirch (Woodbridge, CT), 1998.
Inferno: July 1943-April 1945, Blackbirch, 1998.
(With Stephen D. Chicoine) *From the Ashes: May 1945
    and After,* Blackbirch, 1998.

FICTION

Green Light on the Tipple, Platte 'N Press, 1978.

OTHER

Also author of revised editions of *Drug Abuse,* 1991,
Sexual Abuse, 1992, and *Family Violence,* 1993, all
published by Rosen; and editor of volumes in the
"American Traveler" series, published by Renaissance
House.

SIDELIGHTS: A woman with varied interests, Eleanor
H. Ayer spent much of her adult career making history
come alive for students. From biographies such as *Ruth
Bader Ginsberg: Fire and Steel on the Supreme Court*
to self-help books for teens to guide books focusing on
her home state of Colorado and other parts of the United
States, Ayer brought a thorough understanding and the
ability to provide food for thought to each of her
subjects. Of special interest to the author was the Holocaust and the Nazi politics that precipitated it, having
been the subject of several of Ayer's books. Among
these is the critically praised 1998 work *The Survivors,*
which discusses the emotional and physical aftereffects
of the Holocaust on those who lived through the horror
of Hitler's attempt to eliminate the Jews.

Born in Burlington, Vermont, in 1947, Ayer attended
Syracuse University. Graduating with a degree in journalism in 1969, she went on to obtain her master's degree the following year before moving to the western
United States to begin her career in writing and
publishing. After working for several different publishers in both Wyoming and Colorado, Ayer joined Renaissance House Publishing Company in 1984, where
she worked on a series of books that included *Indians
of Colorado* and *Colorado Businesses.* Three years later,
in 1987, she decided to break out on her own as a
freelance author of travel guides. *Our National Monuments,* one of her first efforts, discusses twenty-two
monuments, parks, and other historic sites: the events

they commemorate, the history of their construction,
and efforts underway to preserve them. 1994's *Our
Great Rivers and Waterways* continues in the same vein,
with a geographical description of rivers in the United
States and a discussion of the part each of these waterways has played in the nation's history. Both part of the
"I Know America" series, Ayer's books were described
as "concise summaries presented in an attractive format" by *School Library Journal* contributor Sylvia S.
Marantz. Other books reflecting Ayer's fascination with
the U.S.'s historic landscape include *The Anasazi,* a report on the archeological evidence of the Pre-Columbian
culture that once flourished in the American Southwest,
and *Colorado,* a detailed description of the state that
encompasses geography, history, government, and
culture.

Ayer adopted a straightforward approach in her books
directed at teen readers. In 1997's *It's Okay to Say No:
Choosing Sexual Abstinence* she "realistically addresses" the choice to abstain from sexual relationships,
according to *Booklist* contributor Frances Bradburn.
Commenting on Ayer's inclusion of practical advice
from experts, parents, and other teens, Bradburn went
on to note that the author "convincingly presents
[abstinence's] sometimes less immediate benefits." *Everything You Need to Know about Teen Fatherhood* begins with the risks associated with sexual relations, one
of which is pregnancy. Addressing herself to young
men who are about to be fathers, Ayer explains the importance of commitment when deciding to be part of a
child's life. The author "neither preaches or scolds as
she considers the emotions and practical considerations
associated with teen fatherhood," noted Stephanie Zvirin in her favorable *Booklist* appraisal of the work. In
Everything You Need to Know about Stress Ayer alerts
young people to the many subtle and not-so-subtle
sources of pressure and stress in their lives, while in
Teen Smoking she adopts a less supportive attitude, en-
couraging young people to quit smoking through a discussion of peer pressure, a look at the way teens are
manipulated by tobacco advertising, and a list of tips
for breaking the habit. In his review of *Teen Smoking* in
Booklist, reviewer Randy Meyer cited Ayer's work as
"peppered with insightful quotes . . . that humanize the
issue."

Beginning with 1994's *The United States Holocaust
Memorial Museum: America Keeps the Memory Alive,*
Ayer spent a great deal of time researching and writing
about one of the most tragic eras in human history:
German dictator Adolph Hitler's efforts to eliminate the
Jewish race and others through imprisonment and mass
executions. In *The Survivors,* published in 1998, she

uses both primary and secondary source material to describe the efforts of those liberated from Nazi concentration camps in May of 1945 to start a new life: their move to Displaced Persons camps, their often futile efforts to return to home and find family members who had disappeared, and the anti-Semitism they encountered. Citing the book as "exemplary for both its quality of writing and its thorough treatment of the situation," critic Heidi Borton praised *The Survivors* as a "welcome addition" to books for teen readers in her *Voice of Youth Advocates* review. Other books focusing on the Holocaust and its aftermath include *In the Ghettos: Teens Who Survived the Ghettos of the Holocaust, Adolph Hitler,* and *From the Ashes: May 1945 and After.* Ayer also aided in the work of two people who lived to tell about life in Hitler's Germany. *Parallel Journeys* presents the accounts of both Helen Waterford, then a young Jewish woman living in Germany who was captured after fleeing to Holland and sent to Auschwitz, and Alfons Heck, a member of the Hitler Youth who joined the army and fought on the German Front. Praising Ayer's contribution of a historical background through which readers can more easily relate to the co-authors' memoirs, *Voice of Youth Advocates* contributor Judy Silverman added: "It's impossible to praise this book too highly."

BIOGRAPHICAL/CRITICAL SOURCES:

PERIODICALS

Booklist, June 15, 1992, p. 1818; December 1, 1992; October 1, 1993, Stephanie Zvirin, review of *Everything You Need to Know about Teen Fatherhood,* p. 327; May 15, 1995, Hazel Rochman, review of *Parallel Journeys,* p. 1647; September 1, 1997, Frances Bradburn, review of *It's Okay to Say No,* p. 69; October 15, 1997, Hazel Rochman, review of *A Firestorm Unleashed,* p. 396; January 1, 1999, Randy Meyer, review of *Teen Smoking,* p. 884.

Bulletin of the Center for Children's Books, January, 1998, Betsy Hearne, review of *A Firestorm Unleashed,* pp. 162-163.

Kirkus Reviews, January 1, 1993, review of *The Anasazi,* p. 1.

Kliatt, November, 1999, Ann Kramer, review of *Homeless Children,* p. 4.

Publishers Weekly, June 26, 1995, review of *Parallel Journeys,* p. 109.

School Library Journal, October, 1992, p. 124; March, 1993, Pat Katka, review of *Boris Yeltsin,* p. 205; June, 1994, Sylvia S. Marantz, review of *Our Great Rivers and Waterways,* p. 136; April, 1995, Claudia Morrow, review of *Ruth Bader Ginsberg: Fire and Steel on the Supreme Court,* p. 158; September, 1995, Sharon Grover, review of *The United States Holocaust Memorial Museum: America Keeps the Memory Alive,* p. 204; January, 1996, Pat Katka, review of *Adolph Hitler,* pp. 128, 131; August, 1997, Allison Trent Bernstein, review of *Colorado,* pp. 160-161; January, 1998, Edward Sullivan, review of *It's Okay to Say No,* p. 118; February, 1998, Marcia Posner, review of *A Firestorm Unleashed,* p. 134; July, 1998, Marcia Posner, review of *The Survivors,* p. 102; August, 1999, Jack Forman, review of *In the Ghetto,* pp. 165-166.

Science Books and Films, May, 1993, James E. Ayers, review of *The Anasazi,* p. 110.

Voice of Youth Advocates, December, 1992, p. 298; August, 1993, Lana Voss, review of *Boris Yeltsin,* p. 173; August, 1995, Judy Silverman, review of *Parallel Journeys,* p. 178; December, 1998, Heidi Borton, review of *The Survivors,* p. 376; June, 1999, Beth E. Anderson, review of *The Importance of Charles Dickens,* p. 128.*

B

BAL, Mieke (Maria Gertrudis) 1946-

PERSONAL: Born March 14, 1946, in Heemstede, The Netherlands; daughter of Bernhardus Henricus Bal and Suzanne Koster; children: two. *Ethnicity:* "White." *Education:* University of Amsterdam, received degree, 1969; University of Utrecht, Ph.D. (French and general literature), 1977.

ADDRESSES: Home—Stadionweg 44, 1077 SM Amsterdam, The Netherlands; 172 Shepard St., Rochester, NY 14619. *Office*—Amsterdam School for Cultural Analysis, University of Amsterdam, Spuistraat 210, 1012 VT Amsterdam, Netherlands. *E-mail*—mieke.bal@hum.uva.nl.

CAREER: Associated with several universities in the Netherlands; University of Utrecht, co-founder of Women's Studies Program, 1981, director, beginning 1982; University of Rochester, Rochester, NY, professor of comparative literature and art history, Susan B. Anthony Professor of Women's Studies, 1987-91, adjunct visiting professor of visual and cultural studies, 1991—; University of Amsterdam, professor of theory of literature and co-founder and director of the Amsterdam School for Cultural Analysis, Theory, and Interpretation (ASCA), 1991—. Visiting professor at universities, including University of Montreal, 1983, 1984; University of Quebec at Montreal, 1984, 1985; the British Academy, 1984; and University of Toronto, 1987; research associate and visiting lecturer at Harvard University Divinity School, 1985-86. William H. Morton Distinguished Senior Fellow in the Humanities, Dartmouth College; Andrew D. White Professor-at-Large, Cornell University; Ailsa Mellon Bruce Visiting Senior Fellow, National Gallery of Art. Advisor of the Dutch Founda-tion of Scientific Research and National Committee of Emancipation Research (both in the Netherlands). Has appeared in radio presentations. Has served on the editorial board of several publications, including *Style, Semeia, Feminist Inquiry,* and *Signature: A Journal of Theory and Canadian Literature.*

MEMBER: National Committee of Research in Women's Studies.

AWARDS, HONORS: Rockefeller Foundation Residency Program in Humanities, 1985-86; Ford Foundation grant, 1985-86; named Northrop Frye Professor of Theory of Literature, University of Toronto, 1987; Biblical Archeology Society Award, 1991, and Award of Excellence, American Academy of Religion, 1991, both for *Murder and Difference: Gender, Genre, and Scholarship on Sisera's Death;* honorary doctorate, University of Bergen, Norway.

WRITINGS:

NONFICTION

Complexité d'un roman populaire, La Pensee universelle (Paris), 1974.

Narratologie: Essais sur la signification narrative dans quatre romans modernes, Klincksieck (Paris), 1977, revised and translated as *Narratology: Introduction to the Theory of Narrative,* University of Toronto Press (Toronto), 1985, revised and expanded edition, 1997.

De Theorie van vertellen en verhalen, Coutinho (Muiderberg), 1978, revised second edition, 1980, third edition, 1985.

(Editor) *Mensen van papier: Over personages in de literatuur,* Van Gorcum (Assen), 1980.

(With Jan van Luxemburg and Willem Weststeijn) *Inleiding in de literatuurwetenschap,* Coutinho, 1981, seventh edition, 1992.

(Editor) *Literaire genres en hun gebruik,* Coutinho, 1981.

(With Fokkelien van Dijk and Grietje van Ginneken) *En Sara in haar tent lachte: Patriarchaat en verzet in bijbelverhalen,* HES (Utrecht, Netherlands), 1984.

Femmes imaginaires: L'Ancien Testament au risque d'une narratologie critique, Nizet (Paris), 1986, selections translated, revised, and published in the United States as *Lethal Love: Feminist Literary Readings of Biblical Love Stories,* Indiana University Press (Bloomington, IN), 1987.

(With Luxemburg and Weststeijn) *Over literatuur,* Coutinho, 1987.

Het Rembrandt Effect: Visies op kijken, HES, 1987.

Death and Dissymmetry: The Politics of Coherence in the Book of Judges, University of Chicago Press (Chicago), 1988.

Murder and Difference: Gender, Genre, and Scholarship on Sisera's Death, Indiana University Press, 1988, second edition, 1992.

Verkrachting verbeeld: Seksueel geweld in cultuur gebracht, HES, 1988.

(Editor) *Anti-Covenant: Counter-reading Women's Lives in the Hebrew Bible,* Almond Press (Sheffield, England), 1989.

On Storytelling: Essays in Narratology, edited by David Jobling, Polebridge Press (Sonoma, CA), 1991.

Reading "Rembrandt": Beyond the Word-Image Opposition: The Northrop Frye Lectures in Literary Theory, Cambridge University Press (Cambridge, England), 1991, second edition, 1994.

On Meaning-making: Essays in Semiotics, Polebridge Press, 1994.

(Editor, with Inge E. Boer) *The Point of Theory: Practices of Cultural Analysis,* Continuum (New York), 1994.

Double Exposures: The Subject of Cultural Analysis, Routledge (New York City), 1996.

Images proustiennes, ou comment lire visuellement, XYZ Editeur (Montreal), 1997, translated by Anna-Louise Milne as *The Mottled Screen: Reading Proust Visually,* Stanford University Press, 1997.

The Practice of Cultural Analysis: Exposing Interdisciplinary Interpretation, Stanford University Press, 1999.

Quoting Caravaggio: Contemporary Art, Preposterous History, University of Chicago Press, 1999.

CONTRIBUTOR

Actes de la journee de travail sur Madame Bovary, E.N.S. (Paris), 1973.

Moderne Encyclopedie van de wereldliteratuur, Volume 3, De Haan (Haarlem, Netherlands), 1980, Volume 10, 1984.

Feministische Theologie, edited by C. Halkes, Studium General (Nijmegen, Netherlands), 1982.

Flaubert: La Dimension du texte, edited by P. M. Wetherhill, Manchester University Press (Manchester, England), 1982.

Over verhalen gesproken, edited by J. Hoogteijling and F. C. de Rover, Wolters-Noordhoff (Gröningen, Netherlands), 1982.

Pragmatics and Stylistics, edited by W. van Peer and J. Renkema, Acco (Leuven/Amersfoort, Netherlands), 1984.

Le Donne e i segni: Scrittura, linguaggio, identita nel segno della differenza famminile, edited by Patrizi Magli, Il Lavoro editoriale (Ancona, Italy), 1985.

Colette: Nouvelles approches critiques, edited by Bernard Bray, Nizet, 1986.

De Macht van de tekens: Opstellen over maatschappij, edited by Aart van Zoest, HES, 1986.

The Female Body in Western Culture: Semiotic Perspectives, edited by Susan Suleiman, Harvard University Press (Cambridge, MA), 1986.

Ik zing mijn lied voor al wie met mij gaat: Vrouwen in de volksliteratuur, edited by Ria Lemaire, HES, 1986.

Linguistics and the Study of Literature, edited by T. D'haen, Rodopi (Amsterdam, Netherlands), 1986.

Semiotique et analyse textuelle: Description, paraphrase, metalangage, edited by Maryse Souchard, College Saint Boniface (Winnipeg, Manitoba, Canada), 1987.

Feministisch gelesen, Volumes 1 and 2, edited by Renate Jost, Mieke Korenhof, and Eva Renate Schmidt, Kreuz Verlag (Stuttgart, Germany), 1988.

Also contributor of articles to periodicals, including *Rapports, Neophiologus, Revue des Langues Vivantes, Forum der Letteren, Romaneske, Le Français dans le monde, Poetique, Litterature, Spektator, NRC-Handelsblad, Zagadnienia Rodzajow Literackich, Hollands Maandblad, Lalies, Poetics Today, Degres, Tijdschrift voor vrouwenstudies, V/S Versus, Arethusa, Amsterdaemmer Beitraege zur neueren Germanistik, Schrift, Style, Studies in Twentieth-century Literature, Semiotica, Australian Journal of French Studies, Semiotiek, Dispositio, Diacritics,* and *Recherches semiotiques/Semiotic Inquiry.*

SIDELIGHTS: Dutch academician Mieke Bal has written and edited a number of books in the fields of semiotics, literary theory, and women's studies. Some of her best-known works deal with the portrayal of female characters in the Bible. Her volumes have seen print in many European countries, including France, Germany, and her native country of the Netherlands. Since becoming a professor of comparative literature and women's studies at the University of Rochester in New York, Bal has published many of her books in English. Notable among them are *Lethal Love: Feminist Literary Readings of Biblical Love Stories, Murder and Difference: Gender, Genre, and Scholarship on Sisera's Death, Death and Dissymmetry: The Politics of Coherence in the Book of Judges,* and, edited with Inge E. Boer, *The Point of Theory: Practices of Cultural Analysis.* Bal has also contributed numerous articles to both books and periodicals, and has been active in women's studies conferences.

One of Bal's earliest works to appear in English, *Lethal Love,* is a revised version of a book initially published in France as *Femmes Imaginaires: L'Ancien Testament au risque d'une narratologie critique.* As Monica Furlong noted in the *Times Literary Supplement,* the author's theme in this volume "is that the authors of the Old Testament see women as 'victimizers.'" Bal examines Biblical women such as Eve, Delilah, Ruth, and Bathsheba to illustrate her point, utilizing both semiotics and psychoanalysis in her discussion.

Another book by Bal, *Murder and Difference: Gender, Genre, and Scholarship on Sisera's Death,* discusses, as its subtitle indicates, the Old Testament story of the death of Sisera. As Bal points out, there are two separate accounts in the Book of Judges of this event in which Sisera, an enemy general, is murdered by an Israelite woman named Jael. One is, in the words of Janice Fiamengo in *Canadian Literature,* "a prose narrative which emphasizes Jael's treachery in breaking the laws of hospitality"; the other, "an ecstatic lyric celebrating Jael's power and the erotic pleasure of the murder." Bal argues that the former is a more masculine form of expression, while the latter is more feminine; furthermore, the masculine style has been preferred by those in authority for many centuries. Fiamengo had high praise for *Murder and Difference:* "Bal's serious scholarship is an excellent example of how disciplines can be transformed from within."

Death and Dissymmetry also provides readers with an examination of the Old Testament book of Judges. One of the highlights of the volume is Bal's analysis of the women involved in the story of Samson: Yael, Abimelech's mother, and Delilah. A *Christian Century* reviewer lauded Bal's "considerable skill" in "unearth-[ing] meanings" in the Biblical material.

In *The Point of Theory,* Bal and co-editor Boer gather together essays that argue for the necessity of having a theory by which to approach and assimilate knowledge. As Roger Cardinal explained in the *Times Literary Supplement,* the contributors' "collective example attests to the genuine point of articulating theory at the outset of a given investigation, arguing—with impressive consistency despite their diverse backgrounds— that before searching for meanings, one must first acquire a conceptual container, even if that container has later to be modified or superseded." Cardinal went on to report that the volume "does home in on two principal areas, history and art history," for its analysis, and concluded that while "a collection of this kind is necessarily kaleidoscopic . . . most of the contributors express themselves lucidly and clearly."

Bal's *Quoting Caravaggio: Contemporary Art, Preposterous History* explores the way some modern artists, including Andres Serrano and Carrie Mae Weems, "quote" the great Italian Baroque painter Caravaggio in pieces of modern art. Bal sees the quotation of Old Masters by modern artists as a process of entanglement that has consequences for both the contemporary and historical pieces. "Caravaggio is probably the most attractive of the Old Masters to the young artists who find themselves being invited to pick a partner from among the illustrious dead in order to demonstrate that museums aren't merely cemeteries," observed Nicholas Penny in the *London Review of Books.* Penny added: "Mieke Bal introduces us to some contemporary artists who have made use of Caravaggio or have claimed a relationship with him." In the *New Republic,* Andrew Butterfield maintained that Bal "chooses to interpret Caravaggio not only in light of contemporary art, but as if he were an artist living today." Butterfield found Bal's premise "overstated and unconvincing." He added: "Quotation and imitation have been common features throughout twentieth-century art . . . and they have not had the impact on the originals that she claims." Conversely, a critic for *Art Gnomiz* magazine found *Quoting Caravaggio* to be "a rigorous, rewarding work . . . a brilliant critical exposition of contemporary artistic representation and practice."

BIOGRAPHICAL/CRITICAL SOURCES:

PERIODICALS

Canadian Literature, fall/winter, 1994, pp. 232-234.
Choice, June, 1986, p. 1536; October, 1992, p. 286.

Christian Century, February 1, 1989, p. 148.
London Review of Books, August 10, 2000, Nicholas Penny, "Models and Props," pp. 27-29.
Modern Fiction Studies, autumn, 1987, pp. 535-544.
New Republic, January 17, 2000, Andrew Butterfield, review of *Quoting Caravaggio: Contemporary Art, Preposterous History,* p. 25.
Times Literary Supplement, November 6, 1987, p. 1232; July 15, 1994, p. 20.

OTHER

Art Gnomiz, http://www.gnomiz.it/nexus/arte00/caravagg.htm/ (November 6, 2000), review of *Quoting Caravaggio: Contemporary Art, Preposterous History.**

*   *   *

BARBOUR, Karen 1956-

PERSONAL: Born October 29, 1956, in San Francisco, CA; daughter of Donald C. (a physician) and Nancy B. Barbour; married Hermann Lederle (an artist), 1981. *Education:* University of California, Davis, B.A., 1976; San Francisco Art Institute, M.F.A., 1980.

ADDRESSES: Home and office—51 Warren St., 5th Floor, New York, NY 10007.

CAREER: Freelance illustrator, author, animator, and painter.

AWARDS, HONORS: Certificate of Excellence, American Institute of Graphic Arts Book Show, and Parents' Choice Award, Parents' Choice Foundation, both 1987, both for *Little Nino's Pizzeria.*

WRITINGS:

FOR CHILDREN; SELF-ILLUSTRATED

Little Nino's Pizzeria, Harcourt (San Diego, CA), 1987.
Nancy, Harcourt (San Diego, CA), 1989.
Mister Bow Tie, Harcourt (San Diego, CA), 1991.

ILLUSTRATOR

Helen Barolini, *Festa: Recipes and Recollections of Italy,* Harcourt (San Diego, CA), 1988.

Arnold Adoff, *Flamboyan,* Harcourt (San Diego, CA), 1988.
James Berry, *When I Dance: Poems,* Harcourt (San Diego, CA), 1991.
Anna Kate Winsey, *Toby Is My Best Friend,* Silver Burdett (Morristown, NJ), 1992.
Adoff, *Street Music: City Poems,* HarperCollins (New York, NY), 1995.
Jane Yolen, *A Sip of Aesop,* Blue Sky Press (New York, NY), 1995.
Eric Metaxas, *Princess Scargo and the Birthday Pumpkin: The Native American Legend,* Rabbit Ears (New York, NY), 1996.
Lee Bennett Hopkins, editor, *Marvelous Math: A Book of Poems,* Simon & Schuster (New York, NY), 1997.
Juan Felipe Herrere, *Laughing out Loud, I Fly: Poems in English and Spanish,* HarperCollins (New York, NY), 1998.
Eve Bunting, *I Have an Olive Tree,* HarperCollins (New York, NY), 1999.

SIDELIGHTS: The work of artist Karen Barbour has graced the pages of a number of well-received children's books, including *I Have an Olive Tree* by Eve Bunting and *A Sip of Aesop* by Jane Yolen. In addition to working with other picture-book authors, Barbour has created several original works, including *Nancy* and *Mister Bow Tie,* the latter a story about a homeless man who is befriended by a young girl and her family. In *Nancy* a newcomer extends a hand of friendship as a way to break into an established clique of four best friends in her new neighborhood and finds that creativity is the key to acceptance. "Ms. Barbour has a real fix on what it is to be young," observed *New York Times Book Review* contributor Christina Olson in praise of *Nancy.* "While the story . . . has its appeal, it is the raucous artwork that grabs readers' attention and holds it," added Ilene Cooper in her *Booklist* appraisal. Cooper also noted Barbour's uninhibited use of wavy lines, polka dots, and fun, vibrant colors.

Born in San Francisco in 1956, Barbour attended both the University of California and the San Francisco Art Institute, earning her master of fine arts degree in 1980. Her first picture-book effort, *Little Nino's Pizzeria,* proved to be a success, winning her both a commendation from the American Institute of Graphic Arts and a Parents' Choice Foundation award. Published in 1987, *Little Nino's Pizzeria* sparked the interest of book publishers looking for talented artists to enhance the work of established authors. Barbour's move to New York City put her in proximity to a number of these publishers, and she was quick to gain illustration assignments. Her first illustration job—an Italian cookbook titled *Festa*—was published in 1988; moving from there to picture books was a short step to a successful career.

When I Dance, a collection of poems by James Berry, meshes the sounds of English with those of Berry's native Caribbean, and critics remarked that Barbour's artwork adds to the overall effect with its use of folk-style motifs. Also praised by reviewers are Barbour's bright and fanciful paintings for Lee Bennett Hopkins' *Marvelous Math: A Book of Poems. School Library Journal* contributor Lee Bock called them "lively illustrations [that] dance and play around the poems." In yet another poetry collection, Arnold Adoff's *Street Music: City Poems,* Barbour's whimsical artwork brings to life the hustle and bustle of crowded city streets. "Graceful, stylized forms fill the pages with pattern and texture against vibrant background colors," noted *Horn Book* reviewer Nancy Vasilakis. Similarly, a *Publishers Weekly* critic said Barbour's pictures "vibrate a jazzy fluidity and rhythm."

Barbour's artwork for *I Have an Olive Tree,* a picture book by Eve Bunting, was praised for both its historical accuracy and its overall technique. Noting that the illustrations "have the flavor of Greek folk art," a *Horn Book* reviewer commended in particular Barbour's use of a "multi-hued palette and curving lines." A *Publishers Weekly* contributor called the book "visually arresting," while *Booklist* reviewer Hazel Rochman explained that the artist's flat, bright paintings, with their heavy, black lines, "combine folk art and magic realism to show the circles of connection that sweep across time and place."

BIOGRAPHICAL/CRITICAL SOURCES:

PERIODICALS

Booklist, October 1, 1989, Ilene Cooper, review of *Nancy,* p. 343; February 1, 1995, Carolyn Phelan, review of *Street Music: City Poems,* p. 1005; May 15, 1999, Hazel Rochman, review of *I Have an Olive Tree,* p. 1702; March 15, 2000, review of *Laughing out Loud, I Fly,* p. 1342.
Horn Book, July-August, 1991, Mary M. Burns, review of *When I Dance,* p. 469; May-June, 1995, Nancy Vasilakis, review of *Street Music: City Poems,* p. 337; July, 1999, review of *I Have an Olive Tree,* p. 452.

Kirkus Reviews, August 15, 1991, review of *Mister Bow Tie,* p. 1086.
New York Times Book Review, November 26, 1989, Christina Olson, review of *Nancy,* p. 23; November 10, 1991, Dinitia Smith, review of *Mister Bow Tie,* p. 52.
Publishers Weekly, September 6, 1991, review of *Mister Bow Tie,* p. 103; April 19, 1993, video review of *Princess Scargo and the Birthday Pumpkin,* p. 29; December 19, 1994, review of *Street Music: City Poems,* p. 54; August 7, 1995, review of *A Sip of Aesop,* p. 460; May 24, 1999, review of *I Have an Olive Tree,* p. 78.
School Library Journal, November, 1989, Karen Litton, review of *Nancy,* p. 74; September, 1995, JoAnn Rees, review of *A Sip of Aesop,* p. 198; October, 1997, Lee Bock, review of *Marvelous Math,* p. 118.*

*   *   *

BAUER, Tricia

PERSONAL: Born in Baltimore, MD; married Bill Bozzone (a writer); children: Lia. *Education:* Attended Lake Erie College; Goddard College, studied in graduate writing program.

ADDRESSES: Home—West Redding, CT. *Office*—Rosen Publishing Group, Inc., 25 West 26th St., New York, NY 10010.

CAREER: Writer. Rosen Publishing Group, Inc., New York, NY, director of special markets for children's books.

MEMBER: Poets and Writers.

AWARDS, HONORS: "Discover Great New Writers" citation, Barnes & Noble, 1997, for *Boondocking.*

WRITINGS:

Working Women and Other Stories (short stories), Bridge Works (Bridgehampton, NY), 1995.
Boondocking (novel), Bridge Works (Bridgehampton, NY), 1997.
Hollywood and Hardwood (novel), Bridge Works (Bridgehampton, NY), 1999.
Shelterbelt (novel), St. Martin's Press (New York, NY), 2000.

Contributor of fiction and poetry to anthologies, including *The Next Parish Over,* edited by Patricia Monaghan, New Rivers Press (St. Paul, MN), 1993, and *Eating Our Hearts Out,* edited by Leslea Newman, Crossing Press (Trumansburg, NY), 1993. Contributor of fiction and poetry to periodicals, including *Western Humanities Review, Calyx, American Literary Review, Carolina Quarterly, American Voice, Black Warrior Review,* and *Massachusetts Review;* contributor of travel features to *New York Times* and *International Herald Tribune* (Paris).

SIDELIGHTS: Tricia Bauer's fiction offers "abrupt revelations of life's possibilities as well as its pain," to quote Ellen Pall in the *New York Times Book Review.* The Connecticut-based author of stories and novels is most at home examining close relationships, such as those between husband and wife, mothers and children, or troubled extended families. Bauer's work is rooted in the blue-collar and the mundane, but it explores the challenges of life that shape personalities and the sense of self. Her characters, according to a *Kirkus Reviews* contributor, are "good people moving through a prosaic yet curiously charged landscape, giving new shading to the concepts of home and family."

Bauer's first book, *Working Women and Other Stories,* consists of a series of tales in which characters ultimately seek more than mere financial gain from their employment. As they move away from their childhood homes and into first jobs or career changes, they make discoveries about themselves that alter notions of what they ultimately might become. Her debut novel, *Boondocking,* is also about leaving home, but from a different perspective. In *Boondocking,* Clayton and Sylvia Vaeth take to the road in a trailer in order to protect their infant granddaughter, Rita, from her drug-addled father. The Vaeths spend more than a decade traveling the country, pursued by Rita's father, until an ultimate reckoning occurs. *Christian Science Monitor* critic Merle Rubin found the work to be a "vivid, believable account" that offers "a closer look at the many ways in which trailer-life affects [The Vaeths'] sense of themselves and their perception of the world."

Bauer has said that *Hollywood and Hardwood* is her most autobiographical novel. The multiple-voiced narrative centers around a married couple named Lou and Renata as they struggle to make their way in the entertainment industry. Lou and Renata meet in Vermont at a summer stock theater and fall deeply in love. The strength of their bond is tested again and again as Lou finds—and loses—success as a stage and screenwriter,

and Renata strives to overcome her blue-collar background and land important roles. A *Kirkus Reviews* writer cited the work for its "vignettes that excel in sensitivity as they explore the charms and costs of artistic ambition." In *Booklist,* Mary Carroll commended *Hollywood and Hardwood* for being "low on glitz and long on character." Carroll also noted that the novel would appeal to readers who want a serious examination of a milieu that is often rendered in broader strokes in pop fiction. *January Magazine* correspondent Linda Richards found the novel "convincing in many ways," concluding that *Hollywood and Hardwood* "remains a masterful work. Bauer's spare and eloquent language is a delight."

Shelterbelt offers another thematic departure for Bauer. In this novel, a pregnant teenager named Jade must come to terms with her brother's mysterious death and her family's dissolution in its aftermath. Wandering first to Connecticut and then to San Francisco, Jade seeks solace in the deeds of her pioneer ancestors and her own burgeoning sense of independence. A *Publishers Weekly* reviewer deemed the book "winsome but wandering," concluding that the author's "verve and grace . . . [manage] to make Jade's plight compelling."

BIOGRAPHICAL/CRITICAL SOURCES:

PERIODICALS

Booklist, March 15, 1999, Mary Carroll, review of *Hollywood and Hardwood,* p. 1288.
Christian Science Monitor, November 24, 1997, Merle Rubin, review of *Boondocking.*
Kirkus Reviews, June 15, 1997, review of *Boondocking;* January 15, 1999, review of *Hollywood and Hardwood.*
Library Journal, March 1, 1999, Vicki J. Cecil, review of *Hollywood and Hardwood,* p. 108.
New York Times Book Review, September 24, 1995, Ellen Pall, review of *Working Women and Other Stories;* January 11, 1998, Andrea Higbie, review of *Boondocking,* p. 14.
Publishers Weekly, February 22, 1999, review of *Hollywood and Hardwood,* p. 63; September 11, 2000, review of *Shelterbelt,* p. 69.

OTHER

January Magazine, http://www.januarymagazine.com/ fiction/hardwood/ (January, 1999), Linda Richards, review of *Hollywood and Hardwood.*

Newbeats.com, http://www.newbeats.com/tricia.html (November 6, 2000), David Chiu, review of *Hollywood and Hardwood.*

*   *   *

BEATY, Shirley MacLean
See MacLAINE, Shirley

*   *   *

BECKERMAN, Ilene 1935-

PERSONAL: Known by her family as "Gingy"; born June 15, 1935, in New York, NY; married and divorced twice; children: Isabelle Beckerman Edelman, Lillie Beckerman Bryen, Michael, Joseph, Julie. *Education:* Simmons College, degree in communications.

ADDRESSES: Home—New Jersey. *Office*—c/o 35 Mill St., Bernardsville, NJ 07921. *Agent*—(public speaking) Arlynn Greenbaum, Authors Unlimited, 31 East 32nd St., New York, NY 10016.

CAREER: MDB & A (advertising agency), Bernardsville, NJ, past vice president; currently retired. Author and illustrator; public speaker. After college held various jobs at Harvard University.

WRITINGS:

(And illustrator) *Love, Loss, and What I Wore* (memoir), Algonquin Books of Chapel Hill (Chapel Hill, NC), 1995.
(And illustrator) *What We Do for Love,* Algonquin Books of Chapel Hill (Chapel Hill, NC), 1997.
(And illustrator) *Mother of the Bride: The Dream, the Reality, the Search for a Perfect Dress,* Algonquin Books of Chapel Hill (Chapel Hill, NC), 2000.

Contributor to periodicals, including *Los Angeles Times, Victoria,* and *New York Times.*

SIDELIGHTS: Ilene Beckerman began a second career as a writer when she was sixty. The former advertising agency executive has since written and illustrated three books that are based on her personal experiences. Her treatment of events, including the most painful and difficult of times, includes a strong dose of humor. Two of the books, *Love, Loss, and What I Wore* and *Mother of the Bride: The Dream, the Reality, the Search for a Perfect Dress,* focus on the role that clothes, and their selection, have played in her life. Characteristically, she joked with Sylvia Slaughter in the *Olympian,* "I might feel like Grandma Moses—she didn't start until she was ancient either—but I try not to look like her." In a more serious vein, Beckerman once told *CA:* "Other than touching, writing is the most intimate way of relating to another person."

Beckerman's first book was the memoir *Love, Loss, and What I Wore.* Written for family reading, she did not originally expect to publish the book that details memories from the 1950s and 1960s and their links to different outfits. The book was published in 1995 and was translated into German, Japanese, Portuguese, and French.

The author used a similarly light-hearted approach in *What We do for Love.* In part, the book examines the familiar experiences of courtship: the first infatuation, love letters, breakups and make-overs, and marriage vows. It also, however, reveals the darker chapters in Beckerman's life, including the often disappointing, unsavory experiences she has had with boyfriends and husbands. After two marriages—the first to an older professor, the second to an advertising executive—ended, Beckerman finally finds true love late in life.

Commenting on the connection between *What We Do for Love* and *Love, Loss, and What I Wore,* Alexandra Jacobs wrote in *Entertainment Weekly* that Beckerman has now produced a "wry, rueful catalog of the very paramours those rags helped her land." Jacobs commented that the light tone is made possible by the book's happy ending. A *Publishers Weekly* reviewer found that Beckerman continues to make use of her "keen observational skills," but that in her second book, "she probes deeper, laying bare the details of the series of relationships she has had with men over the years. Humor works as a disarming foil."

In *Mother of the Bride* Beckerman jokes about the rigors of preparing for a daughter's wedding, an experience she faced three times. Beckerman's daughter wants a big, traditional wedding in which every detail is important. To escape some of this nightmare, Beckerman hires a wedding consultant, but she is still on call for shopping trips to buy a wedding dress. The author advises mothers that their dress will not really be noticed and asserts that it doesn't really matter if everything is perfect. Serious notes include Beckerman remembering the absence of her own mother, who died when she was young, when buying her own wedding dress off the rack. And the book's humor does not hide the author's fear that she is losing her daughter.

In the *Olympian,* Beckerman said that she had "spent sleepless nights just trying to decide whether we should use brown or blue ink on the invitations." Slaughter noted that the author was "only half kidding, one of the trademarks" of her writing. In *Publishers Weekly,* a reviewer found that "With an enticing mix of wry sophistication and loving naïveté, Beckerman succinctly expresses motherhood's enduring push-and-pull. . . . [She] breathes fresh vitality into this familiar rite of passage."

In addition to writing, Beckerman now also appears as a public speaker. Her program invites the audience to share their clothes-related memories and to bring the clothes themselves as illustration.

BIOGRAPHICAL/CRITICAL SOURCES:

PERIODICALS

Entertainment Weekly, February 13, 1998, Alexandra Jacobs, review of *What We Do for Love,* p. 66.
Olympian, July 30, 2000, Sylvia Slaughter, "Mother of Three Passes on Humor of Weddings."
Publishers Weekly, December 7, 1998, review of sound recording of *What We Do for Love,* p. 28; March 27, 2000, review of *Mother of the Bride: The Dream, the Reality, the Search for a Perfect Dress,* p. 66.

*   *   *

BENEDICT, Helen 1952-

PERSONAL: Born November 5, 1952, in London, England; daughter of Burton (a professor of anthropology) and Marion (a writer; maiden name, Steuber) Benedict; married Stephen O'Connor (a writer and teacher), May 10, 1980; children: Simon, Emma. *Education:* University of Sussex, B.A., 1975; University of California at Berkeley, M.A., 1979.

ADDRESSES: Home—New York, NY. *Office*—Graduate School of Journalism, Columbia University, New York, NY 10027. *Agent*—Richard Parks Literary Agency, 138 East 16th St., #5B, New York, NY 10003. *E-mail*—hb22@columbia.edu.

CAREER: New Wings, Novato, CA, managing editor, 1979; *Independent and Gazette,* Richmond, CA, reporter and feature writer, 1980-81; Columbia University, New York, NY, professor of journalism, 1986—; writer. Director of Delacorte Center's Magazine Career Institute, 1986; visiting lecturer at University of California at Berkeley, 1991.

MEMBER: PEN, Author's Guild, Association for Education in Journalism and Mass Communication.

AWARDS, HONORS: Fellowships from Virginia Center for the Creative Arts, 1986, 1998, 2000, 2001, MacDowell Colony for Writers and Artists, 1987, and Cummington Community and School of the Arts, 1988, 1989, and 1990; awards for "best book of the year for teenagers" from New York Library and for "best book for young adults" from American Library Association, both 1988, and citation as one of "best books of the decade" from *Booklist,* 1989, all for *Safe, Strong, and Streetwise;* special mention in *Pushcart Prize,* 1988-89, for story "A World like This"; grants from Columbia Graduate School of Journalism, 1989, and Gannett Foundation's National Research and Publications Program for Journalists in Education, 1989; Lowell Mellett special citation, 1994, for *Virgin of Vamp: How the Press Covers Sex Crimes;* New York Public Library best book selection, 1997, for *Bad Angel.*

WRITINGS:

NONFICTION

(With others) *Women Making History: Conversations with Fifteen New Yorkers,* New York City Commission on the Status of Women (New York, NY), 1985.
Recovery: How to Survive Sexual Assault, Doubleday (New York, NY), 1985, updated edition, Columbia University Press (New York, NY), 1994.
Safe, Strong, and Streetwise (for young adults), Little, Brown (Boston, MA), 1987.
Portraits in Print: A Collection of Profiles and the Stories behind Them, Columbia University Press (New York, NY), 1991.
Virgin or Vamp: How the Press Covers Sex Crimes, Oxford University Press (New York, NY), 1992.

FICTION

A World like This (novel), Dutton (New York, NY), 1990.

Bad Angel (novel), Dutton (New York, NY), 1996.
The Sailor's Wife (novel), Zoland, 2001.

Work represented in anthologies, including *Fiction Writer's Market,* Writer's Digest Books, 1984; and *Conversations with Bernard Malamud,* edited by Lawrence Lasher, University of Mississippi Press, 1991. Contributor to periodicals, including *Antioch Review, Columbia Journalism Review, Fordham Law Review, Glamour, Ms., New York Times Book Review, New York Woman, Ontario Review, San Francisco Examiner, San Francisco Review of Books, Soho News, Washington Post Book World, Working Woman, Women's Review of Books, Nation, Poets and Writers Magazine,* and *Writer's Digest.*

WORK IN PROGRESS: A novel; more nonfiction.

SIDELIGHTS: Helen Benedict is a professor of journalism who has received attention for her writings on rape and sex crimes. Among her earliest works is *Recovery: How to Survive Sexual Assault,* which she derived from extensive interviews with rape victims. Benedict told *CA* that she still "receives letters in reaction to this book to this day." She followed *Recovery* with *Safe, Strong, and Streetwise,* in which she advises young adults on safety and well-being.

Benedict is perhaps best known for *Virgin or Vamp: How the Press Covers Sex Crimes.* In this book she exposes the sexism that she perceives as inherent in the coverage of sex crimes against women. She denotes the manner in which female victims are seemingly cast as either unrealistically innocent or sexually reckless. Benedict reported to *CA* that *Virgin or Vamp* "has broken new ground: no other book has been written about how the press covers sex crimes, even though these crimes are such popular fodder for the press." A critic for the *New York Times Book Review* proclaimed that *Virgin or Vamp* "makes a powerful case for reform in the way the daily press approaches its coverage of sex crimes." *Columbia Journalism Review* correspondent Susan Rieger wrote: "On its surface, *Virgin or Vamp* is an exercise in press criticism. In its heart, it's a book with a mission. While its 'first and foremost' purpose is to look at the ways newspapers perpetuate the myths and stereotypes surrounding rapes and other violent crimes against women, its 'purpose' is 'ultimately to show reporters and editors how to cover sex crimes without further harming the victims.'" Rieger concluded that the work "makes an airtight case. It's not only the Senate Judiciary Committee and the Navy brass who 'just don't get it.' As Benedict makes very clear, most of the media haven't a clue."

In 1990 Benedict produced her first novel, *A World like This,* which she described to *CA* as the story of "a teenager in prison and what happens to her upon her release." Set in England in the mid-1970s, the story follows a troubled heroine named Brandy as she commits a frivolous crime and winds up in a Borstal, a prison for young offenders. The opening of the novel concerns Brandy's stay in the prison and her relationship with a guard who becomes her lover. Once released, Brandy has not been rehabilitated or redeemed by her experience, but she still compares it favorably to the poverty-stricken outside world from which she came. "The ironic subject of *A World like This* is the impossibility of maintaining goodness and innocence in a grim world that has little use for either," noted Bill Kent in the *New York Times Book Review.* Kent further stated that the novel "offers such a brutally unsentimental view of England's underclass that, like Brandy, we begin to long for the cruel simplicity of the Borstal."

Benedict's other novels also feature young female protagonists in challenging situations. In *Bad Angel,* a Dominican-American teenager takes her rage out on her infant and in turn is beaten by her own mother. *The Sailor's Wife,* once again set in the 1970s, explores the difficult decisions a young American wife must make after her hasty marriage to a traditional Greek merchant marine. *New York Times Book Review* contributor Katherine Ramsland called *Bad Angel* "an authentic account of hardship and faith in a violent, poverty-stricken . . . neighborhood." In his *New York Times Book Review* piece on *The Sailor's Wife,* Peter Bricklebank praised Benedict for "an intelligent look at belonging, duty and independence."

Benedict is also author of *Portraits in Print,* which includes profiles on such writers as Joseph Brodsky, Bernard Malamud, and Susan Sontag. Accompanying these profiles, which appeared earlier in various magazines, are discussions of what Benedict considers "the ethical dilemmas inherent in interviewing people about their private lives."

Benedict told *CA:* "I came to my current specialization as a press critic on a path that is natural to journalists. Unlike academic scholars, journalists tend not to specialize early in their career but to generalize until their experience and research lead them to particular subjects. I thus began my career writing about almost anything, but soon developed two main focuses: crime victims, particularly women; and literature.

"My interest in victims began, in a sense, as early as my childhood. I lived for several years in Mauritius and the Seychelles, islands full of poverty and disease. On returning home to England, where I grew up, I was much affected by the contrast between the haves and the have-nots and developed an early, passionate intolerance of injustice. This same passion later drove me to choose journalism as a career.

"My interest in literature, meanwhile, was almost a birthright. I grew up in the midst of London's literary world, wrote a 'novel' at the age of eight, a book about how to raise children at age nine, and another 'novel' at eleven. Journalism seemed the perfect career to combine my love of writing with my passion for justice.

"Once I reached college I majored in developmental psychology and, as part of my training, went to work as a volunteer in a prison for minor girls. Being only twenty-one and more interested in the downtrodden than the authorities, I befriended and studied the inmates and was appalled to discover that seventy percent of them had been raped by relatives. The tragedy of their plight led to my lifelong interest in rape and its victims, to my decision to become a journalist, and to my books on related subjects.

"At the University of California, Berkeley, I continued my interest in rape by interviewing victims about whether they should be named by the press. I also published magazine and newspaper pieces about rape.

"In 1979 I went to work as a feature writer for the *Independent and Gazette* in California, where I was able to write dozens of articles on rape, battered women, child prostitutes, and related subjects, as well as many pieces on authors and the literary world.

"Finally deciding I was more suited to long-form journalism than to newspaper writing, I left the *Gazette* and moved to New York City to free-lance. After five years of writing on the subject of rape, I wrote *Recovery*. My next book, *Safe, Strong, and Streetwise,* appeared shortly after I was hired at Columbia University to teach magazine journalism. Teaching gave me the freedom to think more and write for money less, and thus I was able to finally combine my literary bent with my work in the prison and my interviews with rape victims by writing the novel, *A World like This.* A year later I published *Portraits in Print.*

"As my experience teaching journalism grew, my two fields of specialization—literature and sex crimes—began to fuse. I found myself increasingly using a liter-

ary approach to journalism in the way I edited and analyzed newspaper and magazine stories with my students. I also found myself increasingly interested in the language used about sex crimes. I thus conceived of *Virgin or Vamp.*"

BIOGRAPHICAL/CRITICAL SOURCES:

PERIODICALS

Booklist, March 15, 1996, Mary Carroll, review of Bad Angel, p. 1238.
Columbia Journalism Review, October 15, 1992, Susan Rieger, "Raped Again?"
Library Journal, November 15, 2000, Jo Manning, review of *The Sailor's Wife,* p. 324.
Michigan Law Review, May, 1993.
Nation, October 11, 1993, Leora Tanenbaum, review of *Virgin or Vamp: How the Press Covers Sex Crimes,* p. 397.
New York Times Book Review, April 8, 1990, Bill Kent, "Borstal Girl," p. 29; November 22, 1992, Bill Kovach, "Writing about Rape"; April 14, 1996, Katherine Ramsland, review of *Bad Angel;* January 21, 2001, Peter Bricklebank, review of *The Sailor's Wife.*
Publishers Weekly, January 15, 1996, review of *Bad Angel,* p. 442; August 14, 2000, review of *The Sailor's Wife,* p. 324.

OTHER

Previewport, http://www.previewport.com/ (June 29, 2001).

*   *   *

BERKOW, Ira 1940-

PERSONAL: Born January 7, 1940, in Chicago, IL; son of Harold and Shirley (Halperin) Berkow; married. *Education:* Miami University (Oxford, Ohio), B.A., 1963; Northwestern University, M.S.J., 1965.

ADDRESSES: Office—New York Times, 229 West 43rd St., New York, NY 10036.

CAREER: Minneapolis Tribune, Minneapolis, MN, sports reporter and book reviewer, 1965-67; Newspaper Enterprise Association, New York City, sports colum-

Ira Berkow

nist, 1967-76, senior editor, 1974-76; freelance writer, 1976-81; *New York Times,* New York City, sports feature writer and columnist, 1981—, senior writer, 1997—.

MEMBER: Authors Guild, Baseball Writers of America, PEN.

AWARDS, HONORS: Rockin' Steady was named among "best books" by American Library Association, 1974; *DuSable Panthers* was named among "best books" by New York Public Library, 1977; Cable ACE Award nomination for best sports documentary, 1983, for *Champions of American Sports;* Edgar Award finalist, 1988, for *The Man Who Robbed the Pierre;* Pulitzer Prize finalist, 1988, for distinguished commentary.

WRITINGS:

Oscar Robertson: The Golden Year, Prentice-Hall (Englewood Cliffs, NJ), 1971.
(With Walt Frazier) *Rockin' Steady: A Guide to Basketball and Cool,* Prentice-Hall, 1974.

Beyond the Dream: Occasional Heroes of Sports, Atheneum (New York City), 1975.
The DuSable Panthers: The Greatest, Blackest, Saddest Team from the Meanest Street in Chicago, Atheneum, 1977.
Maxwell Street: Survival in a Bazaar, Doubleday (New York City), 1978.
(With Rod Carew) *Carew,* Simon & Schuster (New York City), 1979.
The Man Who Robbed the Pierre: The Story of Bobby Comfort, Lion Books, 1980, Atheneum, 1987.
Red: A Biography of Red Smith, Times Books (New York City), 1986, McGraw (New York City), 1987.
Pitchers Do Get Lonely, and Other Sports Stories, Atheneum, 1988.
(Editor and author of introduction) Hank Greenberg, *Hank Greenberg: The Story of My Life,* Times Books, 1989, Triumph Books (Chicago, IL), 2001.
Hank Greenberg: Hall-of-Fame Slugger, Jewish Publication Society (Philadelphia, PA), 1991.
(Contributor) Jackie Mason, *How to Talk Jewish,* St. Martin's (New York City), 1991.
To the Hoop: The Seasons of a Basketball Life, Basic Books (New York City), 1997.
(Author of foreword) *Red Smith on Baseball: The Game's Greatest Writer on the Game's Greatest Years,* I. R. Dee (Chicago, IL), 2000.
Court Vision: Unexpected Views on the Lure of Basketball, Morrow (New York City), 2000.

One of Berkow's *New York Times* columns was included in the anthology *Best American Sports Writing of the Century* (Houghton Mifflin, Boston/New York City, 1999), edited by David Alderstam.

ADAPTATIONS: The film rights to *The Man Who Robbed the Pierre: The Story of Bobby Comfort* have been purchased by DreamWorks.

SIDELIGHTS: Ira Berkow is a Pulitzer Prize-nominated sports columnist for the *New York Times* whose pieces appear under the banner "Sports of the Times." Berkow began his association with the *New York Times* in March of 1981, overlapping for a few months with his friend and mentor, the notable columnist Red Smith. Like Smith, Berkow infuses his work with humor, as well as with the belief that fundamental truths about life can be found on the basketball court and the baseball diamond. Or, as one *Publishers Weekly* correspondent put it, Berkow "revels in the chance to make as many connections as possible between the life of the game and the game of life."

Berkow had written half a dozen books before he joined the staff of the *New York Times,* among them a true crime story entitled *The Man Who Robbed the Pierre: The Story of Bobby Comfort.* Despite the demands of column writing for one of the biggest newspapers in the country, Berkow has continued to publish books in the ensuing decades, beginning with *Red: A Biography of Red Smith.* Although they only spent a mere nine months working as colleagues at the *Times,* Berkow and Smith had known one another for years—a casual friendship initiated by Berkow when he was still an aspiring collegian. Some reviewers found Berkow's affection for Smith to be an enriching part of the biography. In the *New York Times,* for instance, Peter Golenbock declared that Berkow "has, in fact, written a thoroughly enjoyable, lively book. . . . Through Mr. Berkow's characterization, I came to admire Red, the person. Mr. Berkow showed him to be a gentle man who didn't feel the need to downgrade his competitors to make himself look good." *New York Times Book Review* correspondent Wilfrid Sheed deemed *Red* a "skillful biography," in part due to Berkow's understanding of the demands of sportswriting. Sheed concluded: "In a field where two good outings out of three may be considered a hot streak, it may take a peer to appreciate and convey the worth of a man who, in his prime, routinely turned in five, six, seven, if they'd let him, gems a week."

To the Hoop: The Seasons of a Basketball Life is a semi-memoir in which Berkow examines "a lifetime's worth of ball games, teammates . . . and opponents," to quote Charley Rosen in the *New York Times Book Review.* Berkow recalls his formative years in Chicago, playing basketball in his neighborhood, and then acquaints the reader with the lessons he has learned from high school, college, and pickup basketball—including games with pro teammates. In his *New York Times* piece on *To the Hoop,* Avery Corman suggested that the book itself "has the ramshackle quality of a pickup game, . . . combining memoir, character sketches, a personal odyssey of family life, and sports reporting." *Booklist* contributor Wes Lukowsky appreciated the manner in which his love of basketball has forced Berkow to confront "the aging process honestly, with humor and grace." Lukowsky styled the work "a fine book by a fine writer and a wise man."

Berkow's *Court Vision: Unexpected Views on the Lure of Basketball* consists of a series of interviews with celebrities from many walks of life on the subject of basketball. *Library Journal* correspondent William O. Scheeren lauded the book as "perceptive" and "of interest to all basketball fans," but also added that readers "do not have to be rabid fans to enjoy this work."

BIOGRAPHICAL/CRITICAL SOURCES:

PERIODICALS

Booklist, April 15, 1997, Wes Lukowsky, review of *To the Hoop: The Seasons of a Basketball Life,* p. 1362; May 15, 2000, Wes Lukowsky, review of *Court Vision: Unexpected Views on the Lure of Basketball,* p. 1720.

Library Journal, June 1, 2000, William O. Scheeren, review of *Court Vision: Unexpected Views on the Lure of Basketball,* p. 140.

New York Times, May 28, 1986, Peter Golenbock, "Swift of Sports," p. C20; July 29, 1997, Avery Corman, "Shooting and Scoring, Sometimes."

New York Times Book Review, June 8, 1986, Wilfrid Sheed, "A Pretty Nice Way to Make a Living," p. 1; June 8, 1997, Charley Rosen, "The Basketball Diaries," p. 28.

Publishers Weekly, April 24, 2000, review of *Court Vision: Unexpected Views on the Lure of Basketball,* p. 74.

*   *   *

BLAKE, Raymond B. 1958-

PERSONAL: Born October 6, 1958, in Pushthrough, Newfoundland, Canada; son of Benedict (a fisherman) and Minnie (a homemaker; maiden name, Garland) Blake; married Wanda J. Anderson (a fund-raising director), August 6, 1983; children: Robert Alexander, Benedict David. *Education:* Memorial University of Newfoundland, B.A. (with honors) and B.Ed., both 1979; York University, M.A., 1983, Ph.D., 1991. *Religion:* Anglican.

ADDRESSES: Home—2515 Margaret Pl., Regina, Saskatchewan S4V 1Z4, Canada. *Office*—Saskatchewan Institute of Public Policy, University of Regina, Regina, Saskatchewan S4S 0A2, Canada; fax 306-585-5780. *E-mail*—raymond.blake@uregina.ca.

CAREER: Teacher of social studies and history at a collegiate institute in St. Anthony, Newfoundland, Canada, 1979-83 and 1984-86; *Canadian Historical Review,* bibliographer, 1988-91, proofreader, 1991; Brock University, St. Catharines, Ontario, Canada, faculty member, 1991; York University, Downsview, Ontario, Canada, faculty member, 1991-92; University of Alberta, Edmonton, Alberta, Canada, visiting assistant professor of history, 1992-93; St. Thomas University, Fredericton, New Brunswick, Canada, assistant professor of history, 1993-94; Mount Allison University, Sackville, New Brunswick, Canada, professor of Canadian studies, beginning 1994, Winthrop Pickard Bell fellow at Centre for Canadian Studies, 1994-95, director of the center, beginning 1995; University of Regina, Regina, Saskatchewan, Canada, associate professor of history and director of Saskatchewan Institute of Public Policy.

MEMBER: Association of Canadian Studies, Canadian Historical Association, Council for Canadian Unity.

AWARDS, HONORS: Grants from Canadian Union of Education Workers, 1992, Department of the Secretary of State in Canada, 1993, and Social Science and Humanities Research Council of Canada, 1994-2001; Paul Pari Award, Mount Allison University, 1996 and 1998.

WRITINGS:

Canadians at Last: Canada Integrates Newfoundland as a Province, University of Toronto Press (Toronto, Ontario, Canada), 1994.

(Editor, with Jeff Keshen, and contributor) *A History of Social Welfare in Canada: Selected Readings,* Copp Clark Longman (Toronto, Ontario, Canada), 1995.

(Editor with others) *The Welfare State in Canada: Past, Present, and Future,* Irwin Publishing (Toronto, Ontario, Canada), 1997.

(Editor with others) *Canada and World Order: Facing the New Millennium,* Irwin Publishing (Toronto, Ontario, Canada), 2000.

From Fishermen to Fish: Canada's Fisheries Policy, Canadian Institute for International Affairs (Toronto, Ontario, Canada), 2000.

Contributor to books, including *Twentieth-Century Newfoundland: Explorations,* edited by Peter Neary and J. K. Hiller, Breakwater Books (St. John's, Newfoundland, Canada), 1994; *Fighting the Good Fight: Canada and the Second World War,* edited by Neary and J. L. Granatstein, Copp Clark Longman (Toronto, Ontario, Canada), 1995; *How Deep in the Ocean?: Essays on the History, Sociology, Archaeology, and Ecology of the Canadian East Coast Fishery,* edited by James E. Candow and Carol Corbin, Louisbourg Institute and University College of Cape Breton (Sydney, Nova Scotia, Canada), 1997; and *Canadian Annual Review of Politics and Public Affairs, 1991,* edited by David Leyton-Brown, University of Toronto Press (Toronto, Ontario,

Canada), 1998.. Contributor of articles and reviews to history and Canadian studies journals, including *American Review of Canadian Studies.*

SIDELIGHTS: Raymond B. Blake once told *CA:* "I treat research and writing as a job, just like any other I've had. Writing a book takes determination and good time management, mixed with a fair measure of luck. Although I am more productive at some times than at others, I think writer's block might be grossly exaggerated. All workers have their good times and their bad, but if I worked on an assembly line, I could not leave whenever I felt uninspired! Even when things are not going well, I remain at my computer. To start a book is easy; to finish it requires discipline.

"I write about Canadian history and hope to contribute to the understanding of the nation experience of Canada."

*　　*　　*

BLOOM, Amy 1953-

PERSONAL: Born June 18, 1953, in New York, NY; daughter of Murray (a journalist and author) and Sydelle (a writer, teacher, and group therapist) Bloom; married Donald Moon (a professor), August 21, 1977; children: Alexander (stepson), Caitlin, Sarah. *Education:* Wesleyan University, B.A., 1975; Smith College, M.S.W., 1978.

ADDRESSES: Agent—Phyllis Wender, Rosenstone/Wender, 3 East 48th St., New York, NY 10017.

CAREER: Private practice of psychotherapy, Middletown, CT, 1981—; writer.

AWARDS, HONORS: National Book Award nomination, 1993, for *Come to Me;* O. Henry Award, 1994, for the story "Semper Fidelis"; nomination for National Book Critics Circle Award, 2000, for *A Blind Man Can See How Much I Love You.*

WRITINGS:

Come to Me (short stories), HarperCollins (New York, NY), 1993.

Love Invents Us (novel), Random House (New York, NY), 1996.

A Blind Man Can See How Much I Love You (short stories), Random House (New York, NY), 2000.

Work represented in anthologies, including *Best American Short Stories, 1991,* edited by Alice Adams, Houghton Mifflin (Boston, MA), 1991; *Best American Short Stories, 1992,* edited by Robert Stone and Katrina Kenison, Houghton Mifflin (Boston, MA), 1992; *Here Lies My Heart: Essays on Why We Marry, Why We Don't, and What We Find There,* Beacon Press (Boston, MA), 1999; *Best American Short Stories, 2000,* edited by E. L. Doctorow, 2000; and *The Secret Self: A Century of Short Stories by Women.* Contributor to periodicals, including *New Yorker, Antaeus, Story, Mirabella, Self, Vogue,* and *Atlantic Monthly.*

WORK IN PROGRESS: A nonfiction book about gender; another collection of stories.

SIDELIGHTS: Amy Bloom demonstrates her knowledge of the human condition in stories and novels that celebrate "the human need to connect, no matter how awkwardly, how painfully, or how late," to quote Susan Balee in the *Philadelphia Inquirer.* A practicing psychotherapist who began writing short stories in her spare time, Bloom creates characters who must face life's most difficult moments—ill health, the death of a spouse, lover, or child, the working-through of family trauma. As Dottie Enrico put it in *USA Today,* "One gets the sense that Bloom embraces life's disappointments and imperfections and does her best, through her writing, to create a world in which people prevail over those disappointments with honesty and acceptance." Consistently praised for the precision and verisimilitude of her observations, Bloom displays "a compelling emotional intelligence at work," according to John Martin in the *Bloomsbury Review. Austin Chronicle* contributor Marion Winik wrote: "Her easygoing empathy for . . . situations and the characters who inhabit them make her stories an epiphany to read—and her unfailing wit makes them a pleasure."

Bloom received a National Book Award nomination for her first book, *Come to Me,* a collection of twelve short stories. In *Come to Me,* the author delves into the emotional states and mental illnesses of her characters, ranging from Rose, a schizophrenic woman whose family tries to come to terms with her illness in "Silver Water," to an adulterous pianist whose story is related in "The Sight of You." "Although her stories may be full of tragic implications, Ms. Bloom's characters possess extraordinary dignity that lifts them beyond pity," Barbara Kaplan Lane noted in the *New York Times.* "Those whom circumstances might otherwise define as victims or villains reveal heroic potential in the author's skillful, empathic hands." "What Bloom manages to do in story after story is vary her voice . . . alternate the point of view, change the cadence," declared Ruth Coughlin in the *Detroit News.* "But throughout—always, always—she is able to maintain an extraordinarily high level of emotion and a piercingly sharp intelligence." According to *New York Times Book Review* contributor Anne Whitehouse, Bloom "has created engaging, candid and unorthodox characters, and has vividly revealed their inner lives." Coughlin called *Come to Me* "a remarkable collection, an exhilarating display of a talent both large and luminous." Likewise, Elizabeth Benedict, reviewing the collection in the *Los Angeles Times Book Review,* concluded: "*Come to Me* is so rich, moving and gracefully written, it's hard to believe [Bloom] hasn't been doing this all her life."

Bloom's first novel, *Love Invents Us,* emerges in part from a story that appeared in the collection *Come to Me.* The larger novel format enables the author to develop her characters in greater detail and explore their lives over a longer span of time, without losing what Donna Seaman described in the *Chicago Tribune* as "her arresting economy and pointed poignancy." In the novel, the protagonist Elizabeth Taube tells her story in her own words, the story of an unattractive, awkward child searching for love and affection long denied. Her urban Jewish parents are cold and distant, her classmates hostile and cruel. "To compensate for this agonizing combination of indifference and malice," wrote Gary Krist in the *Washington Post,* "Elizabeth is forced to find warmth wherever she can." Not surprisingly, the lonely child does not always make the wisest choices.

Among Elizabeth's discoveries is Mr. Klein, the furrier from the story "Light Breaks Where No Sun Shines," who encourages her to model his furs in her underwear in the back room of his shop and gives Elizabeth the esteem-building praise and warmth that was missing from her life. Another discovery is Mrs. Hill, an elderly, disabled member of a black church who engages Elizabeth's services as a companion and caretaker, and whose genuine interest in the young woman provides a parent-substitute that inspires Elizabeth's "loyalty unto death," as Winik commented in the *Los Angeles Times.* A more "unhealthy" discovery, according to Krist, is English teacher Max Stone, "a pitiful character, a married father tortured by his scandalous desire for a girl who could be his daughter."

These encounters prepare Elizabeth for her own true love, who turns out to be a black high school basketball player. With Huddie Lester, Krist wrote, "Elizabeth gets her first glimpse of a passion unmuddied by complexities and shame, and it's in these scenes that *Love Invents Us* truly comes into its own." Seaman commented: "Elizabeth narrates . . . in a voice as notable for its matter-of-factness in the face of trauma as for its nimble wit, a style that makes each complex scene shimmer."

If the first part of the novel represents discovery, then the second acknowledges loss. Huddie's father exiles him to Alabama, and Mrs. Hill dies. Max, who has become less a lover and more a friend, is afflicted by a series of tragedies that ruin his ability to proffer the love that Elizabeth continues to seek. Huddie's long-delayed return proves anticlimactic. As Winik reported, "it seems the characters are helpless against the assaults of destiny." The final part of the book suggests reconciliation. Winik maintained that "things are turning out . . . not perfectly, but hopefully, with . . . the suggestion, if not the assurance, of a happy ending."

Bloom's critics were full of praise for this first novel. Winik wrote: "It is a quiet book . . . you almost don't notice how brave it is." Seaman concluded: "Bloom's precise, sensual and heartbreaking tale reminds us that the most exquisite of pleasures can be wedded to the most searing of sorrows" and "we are both scarred and strengthened by the ordeal." Krist summarized: "Although her book is not flawless . . . its intelligence and passion never flag." The reviewer concluded that Bloom has shown her readers "that while love may take many different and surprising forms, there's never enough of it to go around."

Death looms large in many of the stories collected in *A Blind Man Can See How Much I Love You*. Characters suffer from breast cancer, Parkinson's disease, and the loss of children. *Santa Monica Mirror* correspondent Kate Cooney deemed the work "a catalog of characters in the midst of the hard stuff of life." Cooney added: "We don't often think about paradise as a destination we have to row toward but Bloom shows us time and again that the pleasure and pain of life are intrinsically intertwined." Bloom details her characters' behavior in the face of life-altering experiences, noting the tendency to behave badly and then feel guilty in response to dire circumstance. "Exotic intimacies color the sharply wrought stories in Amy Bloom's fine new collection. And they reveal themselves hauntingly as these tales unfold," stated Janet Maslin in the *New York Times*. "In a set of stories whose characters find them-

selves bridging various chasms—medical, sexual, racial—and casually breaking assorted taboos, Ms. Bloom writes warmly and astutely, with arresting precision, about the various adjustments that they make." John Martin observed: "This is not a brand of storytelling easily imitated or duplicated. It requires a writer of sure abilities and deep intuition." In an online review for *NewCityNet*, Shelly Ridenour concluded: "These stories are the backbone of modern, nontraditional family life: families broken and disjointed and pieced together, proving that blood may be thicker than water, but it's still not as strong as hope—or blind determination. Truly, a work of real literary entertainment."

Bloom grew up in Long Island, New York, and spent a great deal of her time in her local library. After earning a degree in government and theater, she received her master's degree in social work and went into private practice. "I became a therapist because I am not judgmental," Bloom explained to Lane. "People have always liked to tell me their stories. Even when I was seventeen, taking the Long Island Railroad to a summer job, the conductor sat down to tell me his life story."

BIOGRAPHICAL/CRITICAL SOURCES:

PERIODICALS

Austin Chronicle, August 25, 2000, Marion Winik, "A Blind Man Can See What a Good Writer Amy Bloom Is."

Belles Lettres, winter, 1993, p. 28.

Bloomsbury Review, September-October, 2000, John Martin, review of *A Blind Man Can See How Much I Love You,* p. 23.

Booklist, December 15, 1996, p. 708.

Chicago Tribune, January 26, 1997.

Detroit News, August 4, 1993, p. 3F.

Harper's Bazaar, January, 1997, p. 54.

Hudson Review, winter, 1994, pp. 770-771.

Library Journal, January, 1994, p. 200; December, 1996, p. 141.

Los Angeles Times Book Review, June 13, 1993, pp. 3, 12; January 12, 1997, p. 8.

New Statesman and Society, April 15, 1994, p. 38.

New York Times, June 20, 1993, section CN, p. 14; August 16, 1993, p. C18; July 24, 2000, Janet Maslin, "How Do I Love Thee? Count the Unusual Ways."

New York Times Book Review, July 18, 1993, p. 16; January 19, 1997, p. 23; September 10, 2000, Joan Smith, "Role Reversals," p. 24.

People, February 24, 1997, p. 32.

Philadelphia Inquirer, July 30, 2000, Susan Balee, review of *A Blind Man Can See How Much I Love You.*

Publishers Weekly, June 5, 2000, review of *A Blind Man Can See How Much I Love You,* p. 69.

Santa Monica Mirror, September 13-19, 2000, Kate Cooney, "The Life Stories of Amy Bloom."

Studies in Short Fiction, fall, 1994, p. 694.

USA Today, September 8, 2000, Dottie Enrico, "'Blind Man' Opens Eyes to Female Psyche."

U.S. News and World Report, January 27, 1997, p. 69.

Voice Literary Supplement, December, 1993, p. 10.

Washington Post Book World, February 23, 1997, p. 3.

OTHER

NewCityNet, http://www.weeklywire.com/ (August 8, 2000), Shelly Ridenour, "'Blind' Leading."

NYPOST.com, http://www.nypost.com/books/10279.htm/ (November 7, 2000), Nan Goldberg, review of *A Blind Man Can See How Much I Love You.*

*   *   *

BLOOMFIELD, Maxwell H(erron III) 1931-

PERSONAL: Born August 17, 1931, in Galveston, TX; son of Maxwell Herron and Violet Clemons (Turner) Bloomfield; married Helen Lorraine Anderson, September 11, 1965. *Education:* Rice University, B.A., 1952; Harvard University, LL.B., 1957; Tulane University, Ph. D., 1962. *Politics:* Democrat. *Religion:* Roman Catholic.

ADDRESSES: Home—1913 Saratoga Dr., Adelphi, MD 20783. *Office*—c/o Department of History, Catholic University of America, Washington, DC 20064.

CAREER: Tulane University, New Orleans, LA, lecturer in history, 1961-62; Ohio State University, Columbus, instructor in history, 1962-66; Catholic University of America, Washington, DC, assistant professor, 1966-68, associate professor, 1968-74, professor of history, 1974-98, professor emeritus, 1998—, chair of department, 1977-80. University of Virginia, visiting professor, 1973. Member of the Bar of the state of Texas. *Military service:* U.S. Army, 1952-54.

MEMBER: American Historical Association, American Society for Legal History, American Catholic Historical Association, Organization of American Historians, Phi Beta Kappa.

AWARDS, HONORS: Fellow of American Bar Foundation, 1968-69, and Project '87, 1981; grant from American Bar Association, 1979-80.

WRITINGS:

Alarms and Diversions: The American Mind through American Magazines, 1900-1914, Mouton, 1967.

American Lawyers in a Changing Society, 1776-1876, Harvard University Press (Cambridge, MA), 1976.

(With Carl S. Smith and John P. McWilliams) *Law and American Literature: A Collection of Essays,* Knopf (New York, NY), 1983.

Peaceful Revolution: Constitutional Change and American Culture from Progressivism to the New Deal, Harvard University Press (Cambridge, MA), 2000.

Contributor to history journals. Member of editorial board, *Maryland History,* 1974-75, *Capitol Studies,* 1979-80, and *Legal Studies Forum,* 1985-96.

SIDELIGHTS: In his book, *Peaceful Revolution: Constitutional Change and American Culture from Progressivism to the New Deal,* Maxwell H. Bloomfield examines the role of American popular culture in promoting the idealistic message of the U.S. Constitution. Specifically focusing on the first three decades of the twentieth century, Bloomfield's study ranges from the muckraking novels of Upton Sinclair to the propaganda films produced by early women suffragists. Time and again, Bloomfield argues, America's popular culture has rekindled the public's faith in orderly political change according to constitutional guidelines. The critic for *Kirkus Reviews* found *Peaceful Revolution* to be "a significant contribution to the history of 20th-century popular and political culture."

BIOGRAPHICAL/CRITICAL SOURCES:

PERIODICALS

American Historical Review, February, 1977.

Kirkus Reviews, July 1, 2000, review of *Peaceful Revolution: Constitutional Change and American Culture from Progressivism to the New Deal,* p. 928.

New England Quarterly, December, 1969; December, 1976.

William and Mary Quarterly, April, 1977.

BLUM, William (Henry) 1933-

PERSONAL: Born March 6, 1933, in Brooklyn, NY; son of Isadore (a factory worker) and Ruth (maiden name, Katz) Blum; married Adelheid Zoefel (a translator); children: Alexander. *Education:* City College (now City College of the City University of New York), B.B.A., 1955. *Politics:* Socialist.

ADDRESSES: Home—5100 Connecticut Ave. NW #707, Washington, DC 20008. *E-mail*—bblum6@aol.com.

CAREER: Accountant in New York, NY, 1955-60; International Business Machines Corp., New York, NY, computer systems analyst and programmer, 1960-64; U.S. State Department, Washington, DC, computer systems analyst and programmer, 1964-67; *Washington Free Press,* Washington, DC, founder, editor, and columnist, 1967-69; freelance journalist in the United States, South America, and Europe, 1970-76; Radio Station KPFA, Berkeley, CA, business manager and news writer, 1976-80; *Daily Californian,* Berkeley, CA, general manager and writer, 1981-82; writer, 1982—.

MEMBER: National Writers Union.

WRITINGS:

The CIA: A Forgotten History—U.S. Global Interventions since World War II, Zed (London, England), 1986.
Killing Hope: U.S. Military and CIA Interventions since World War II, Common Courage Press (Monroe, ME), 1995.
Rogue State: A Guide to the World's Only Superpower, Common Courage Press (Monroe, ME), 2000.
West-Bloc Dissident: A Cold War Memoir, Soft Skull Press (New York, NY), 2001.

Contributor of articles to periodicals, including *Covert Action Quarterly, In These Times, Los Angeles Times, National Catholic Reporter, People's Almanac, Progressive, San Francisco Chronicle,* and *Z magazine.*

SIDELIGHTS: William Blum told *CA:* "My political writing is aimed principally at dispelling the myths—particularly the anti-Communism and anti-socialism myths—that all Americans are raised to believe. This is a formidable task, for I have to do battle with no less than a lifetime of indoctrination of my potential audience."

In his magazine articles and books such as *Killing Hope: U.S. Military and CIA Interventions since World War II* and *Rogue State: A Guide to the World's Only Superpower,* Blum seeks to provide American readers with a new portrait of the United States. In lieu of the image of America as a champion of democracy, human rights, and morality, Blum describes a "rogue state" that orchestrates assassinations, promotes terrorism, and subverts other governments in the name of self-interest. He has documented literally hundreds of instances in which the CIA and other U.S. agencies have actively—if quietly—promoted torture, the loss of life, or the use of weapons of mass destruction.

Blum spent three years working in the U.S. State Department before resigning in protest over the Vietnam War. He remained in Washington, D.C., and was one of the founders of the *Washington Free Press,* the first alternative newspaper in the nation's capital. He has been a freelance journalist in the United States, Europe, and South America. In addition to his firsthand reportage, he has been diligent in pursuing newspaper accounts and congressional testimony that support his thesis. According to Donald Gutierrez in the *Bloomsbury Review,* Blum's "evidence and argumentation generally support his major idea; that the nation most dangerous and oppressive to other nations in the past 50 years has been America."

In his review of *Rogue State,* Gutierrez called the work "invaluable." The critic added: "Ignited by a powerful introduction, Blum's book provides a sizable amount of striking data and discussion arguing that the U.S. is hardly the beacon of democracy, freedom, and justice it proffers itself to be, to itself and to the rest of the world. Blum presents this point forcefully." *Booklist* correspondent Mary Carroll likewise found *Rogue State* to be "a useful counterweight to naive celebrations of our corporate global future." Gutierrez concluded: "If only a tenth of these charges were true, they still would demonstrate major felonious hypocrisy on the part of the American government. . . . *Rogue State* is a guide to ample and convincing evidence that the United States, citadel of global democratic idealism, has for more than 50 years been—and remains—the most terrifying military force in the world."

BIOGRAPHICAL/CRITICAL SOURCES:

PERIODICALS

Bloomsbury Review, September/October, 2000, Donald Gutierrez, "Scanning the Global Horizon," p. 10.

Booklist, June 1, 2000, Mary Carroll, review of *Rogue State: A Guide to the World's Only Superpower,* p. 1809.

OTHER

William Blum's Web Site, http://www.members.aol.com/superogue/homepage.htm/ (April 26, 2001).

*   *   *

BLUMENTHAL, Eileen (Flinder) 1948-

PERSONAL: Born January 12, 1948, in New York, NY; daughter of Philip and Diane (Flinder) Blumenthal. *Education:* Brown University, B.A. and M.A., both 1968; Yale University, M.A., 1972, M.Phil., 1974, Ph. D., 1977.

ADDRESSES: Office—Mason Gross School of the Arts, Rutgers University, New Brunswick, NJ 08903.

CAREER: St. Louis-Chaminade Education Center (now Chaminade College of Honolulu), Honolulu, Hawaii, instructor in English, 1968-69; Chapman College, Orange, CA, visiting instructor with World Campus Afloat, 1969-70; Queensborough Community College of the City University of New York, Bayside, NY, instructor in theatre, 1970-71; Wesleyan University, Middletown, CT, visiting instructor in theatre, 1976-77; Rutgers University, New Brunswick, NJ, 1977—, began as assistant professor, currently professor of theatre arts.

WRITINGS:

Joseph Chaikin: Exploring as the Boundaries of Theatre, Cambridge University Press (New York City), 1984.
Julie Taymor, Playing with Fire: Theater, Opera, Film, Abrams (New York City), 1995, revised edition, 1999.

Contributor to journals and newspapers. Theatre critic for *Soho Weekly News* and *Village Voice,* 1978—.

SIDELIGHTS: Eileen Blumenthal's book, *Julie Taymor, Playing with Fire: Theater, Opera, Film,* is a look at the career of a prolific director and designer in the American theater. Best known for her adaptation of Disney's film, *The Lion King,* as a Broadway stage play, Taymor has long been known for her expertise in designing masks and puppets for use on stage. Blumenthal's account of Taymor's work explains the sources for her designs in Japanese and Indonesian theatre. Taymor's "success is a testament to a wide-ranging, inquiring mind and a dynamic personality, which this book captures admirably," according to Patrick J. Smith in *Opera News.* In his review of the book for *Library Journal,* Robert W. Melton found that "it is easily the most accessible introduction to Taymor available."

Blumenthal once told *CA:* "I have a strong interest in Asian (Balinese, Cambodian, and Japanese) performance traditions, especially dance and theater, using them as a lens to focus on cultures in extreme transition. I have some competence in French and Indonesian languages, and I have traveled extensively in Asia and Europe, as well as Latin America and Africa. Another interest is the Western avant-garde."

BIOGRAPHICAL/CRITICAL SOURCES:

PERIODICALS

American Theatre, April, 1996, review of *Julie Taymor, Playing with Fire,* p. 30.
Choice, February, 1996, review of *Julie Taymor, Playing with Fire,* p. 960.
Library Journal, March 1, 2000, Robert W. Melton, review of *Julie Taymor, Playing with Fire,* p. 92.
New York Times Book Review, March 3, 1996, Arnold Aronson, review of *Julie Taymor, Playing with Fire,* p. 19.
Opera News, January 20, 1996, Patrick J. Smith, review of *Julie Taymor, Playing with Fire,* p. 43.*

*   *   *

BOGNER, Norman 1935-

PERSONAL: Born November 13, 1935, in New York, NY; son of Manny (a businessman) and Rose (Schwartz) Bogner; married Felice Gordon (a fashion designer), November 15, 1959; children: Jonathan Scott, Nicholas Sean. *Education:* Attended University of Alabama, 1953-54, New York University and New School for Social Research, 1958-59; University of Syracuse, B.A. (cum laude), 1957.

ADDRESSES: Home—Santa Monica, CA. *Agent*—c/o Forge, 175 Fifth Ave., New York, NY 10010.

CAREER: Writer. Jonathan Cape Ltd. (publishers), London, England, editor, 1960-61, editorial manager, 1962-63; ABC Television Ltd., Teddington, England, story editor for *Armchair Theatre*, 1963-65.

WRITINGS:

In Spells No Longer Bound, J. Cape (London), 1961.
Spanish Fever, Longmans, Green (London), 1963, reprinted, New English Library (London), 1978.
Divorce, Deutsch (London), 1966, published as *Seventh Avenue*, Coward (New York City), 1967.
The Madonna Complex, Coward, 1968, revised edition, Forge (New York City), 2000.
Making Love, W. H. Allen (London), 1971.
The Hunting Animal, Morrow (New York City), 1974.
Snowman, Dell (New York City), 1978.
Arena, Delacorte, 1979.
California Dreamers, Simon & Schuster (New York City), 1981.
To Die in Provence, Forge, 1998.
Honor Thy Wife, Forge, 1999.

Also author of stage plays, *Boys and Girls Come out to Play, The Waiters,* and *The Man from Esher,* television play, *The Match,* and screenplay, *Privilege.* Contributor to *Now & Then. The Madonna Complex* has been translated into German.

SIDELIGHTS: Norman Bogner's novels combine such elements as family intrigue, crime, and sexual escapades into thrilling page-turner plots. His books have sold over 28 million copies worldwide.

Bogner wrote his first novel, *In Spells No Longer Bound,* after he gave up a university teaching fellowship and left New York for Europe. According to Susan R. Cox in the *Fort Lauderdale Sun-Sentinel,* he completed the novel in Spain and then got a job in a department store in England, "before leaving his precious manuscript in the front office of the only London publishing house he'd heard of." They published the novel and asked him to stay on as editor. By the mid-1960s, Bogner had turned to freelance writing.

In *The Madonna Complex,* Bogner presents the story of an obsessed billionaire and the woman he wishes to possess. Teddy Franklin is accustomed to getting his

way in business, but when he meets United Nations translator Barbara Hickman, he finds that he cannot have everything he desires. Their tumultuous relationship ends in the Canadian wilderness where Teddy, fleeing the police, must rely upon Barbara to save him. A *Kirkus Reviews* critic dubbed the story "a gussied-up Jacqueline Susann novel," while a reviewer for *Publishers Weekly* called it "engrossing if melodramatic."

In *To Die in Provence,* a psychotic serial killer is terrorizing the idyllic French countryside. When French police officer Michel Danton is called in to investigate, he begins to suspect an American ex-porn star and his wealthy girlfriend. According to *Publishers Weekly,* the novel's strongest features include "a richly detailed setting, psychologically accurate character portrayals, and an attractive and engaging hero." Alice DiNizo in *Library Journal* found the killer's character to be "well delineated albeit repugnant," while David Pitt in *Booklist* explained that "Bogner wins us over with a tightly constructed plot and those endlessly fascinating, full-bodied characters."

Bogner's *Honor Thy Wife* is an "intricately plotted novel of family intrigue and ungovernable desire," as a critic for *Publishers Weekly* described it. Lawyer Terry Brett loved and lost Allison Desmond during the 1960s; now she returns to his life with their unexpected son. Brett soon finds himself with two wives, a high-profile lawsuit involving a professional basketball player, and complications rising from the deceptions he has practiced. Carol J. Bissett in *Library Journal* called *Honor Thy Wife* a "soap opera of a story, filled with familial confusion and heartache." The *Publishers Weekly* critic noted that "all the threads are satisfyingly tied up in the novel's last half."

BIOGRAPHICAL/CRITICAL SOURCES:

BOOKS

Authors in the News, Volume II, Gale (Detroit), 1976.

PERIODICALS

Best Sellers, November 1, 1968; February 1, 1971.
Booklist, August, 1998, David Pitt, review of *To Die in Provence,* p. 1972; June 1, 2000, Karen Harris, review of *To Die in Provence,* p. 1925.
Fort Lauderdale Sun-Sentinel, April 23, 1975.

Kirkus Reviews, August 1, 1998, review of *To Die in Provence;* July 1, 2000, review of *The Madonna Complex,* p. 900.

Library Journal, August, 1998, Alice DiNizo, review of *To Die in Provence,* p. 128; June 15, 1999, Carol J. Bissett, review of *Honor Thy Wife,* p. 105.

New York Times, February 2, 1967.

New York Times Book Review, March 12, 1967; December 8, 1968.

Publishers Weekly, July 13, 1998, review of *To Die in Provence,* p. 61; July 12, 1999, review of *Honor Thy Wife,* p. 78; July 17, 2000, review of *The Madonna Complex,* p. 177.

Times Literary Supplement, July 24, 1969.

Toronto Sun, August 9, 1998, review of *To Die in Provence.* *

*　　*　　*

BOYD, Brian (David) 1952-

PERSONAL: Born July 30, 1952, in Belfast, Northern Ireland; son of David Boyd and Jean Abernethy; married Janet Eden, 1974 (divorced, 1980); partner of Bronwen Nicholson (an editor); stepchildren: Cassandra, Thomasin, Alexandra. *Education:* University of Canterbury, B.A., 1972, M.A. (with honors), 1974; University of Toronto, Ph.D., 1979.

ADDRESSES: Home—55 Marsden Ave., Auckland 4, New Zealand. *Office*—Department of English, University of Auckland, Private Bag 92019, Auckland 1, New Zealand. *Agent*—Georges Borchardt, 136 East 57th St., New York City 10022. *E-mail*—b.boyd@auckland.ac.nz.

CAREER: Victoria University, Wellington, New Zealand, junior lecturer, 1974; University of Auckland, Auckland, New Zealand, postdoctoral fellow, 1979-80, lecturer, 1980-85, senior lecturer, 1986-91, associate professor, 1992—. Consultant, New York Public Library, New York City.

MEMBER: PEN, Modern Language Association.

AWARDS, HONORS: Claude McCarthy fellowship, New Zealand University Grants Committee, 1981-82; Thomas Carter Essay Prize, *Shenandoah,* 1989, for a chapter of *Vladimir Nabokov: The Russian Years;* Goodman Fielder Wattie Book awards, third prize, 1991, second prize, 1992; Robert and Suzanne Weiss fellow, Amherst College, 1992.

WRITINGS:

Nabokov's Ada: The Place of Consciousness (criticism), Ardis, 1985.

Vladimir Nabokov (biography), Princeton University Press (Princeton, NJ), Volume 1: *The Russian Years,* 1990, Volume 2: *The American Years,* 1991.

Nabokov's Pale Fire: The Magic of Artistic Discovery, Princeton University Press, 1999.

(Author of introduction) Vladimir Nabokov, *Speak, Memory: An Autobiography Revisited,* Knopf (New York City), 1999.

(Editor and author of annotations and introductions; with Robert Martin Pyle) *Nabokov's Butterflies: Unpublished and Uncorrected Writings by Vladimir Nabokov,* translated from the Russian by Dmitri Nabokov (Vladimir Nabokov's son), Beacon, 2000.

Editor of three-volume Library of America collection published in 1996: *Nabokov: Novels and Memoirs, 1941-1951, Nabokov: Novels 1955-1962,* and *Nabokov: Novels 1969-1974;* contributor to periodicals, including *Shenandoah, Scripsi, Southern Review, Islands, Landfall, Times Literary Supplement,* and *New York Times.*

Boyd's work has been translated into French, German, Japanese, Russian, and Spanish.

WORK IN PROGRESS: Editing *Nabokov: Oeuvres Romanesques Completes; Progressing by Contraries: Shakespeare's Pivot Characters,* a book of criticism; biography of philosopher Karl Popper.

SIDELIGHTS: Brian Boyd is the author of a critically praised, two-volume biography of Vladimir Nabokov, the celebrated writer whose works include the novels *Lolita* and *Pale Fire. Vladimir Nabokov: The Russian Years* traces the first half of Nabokov's life, ending as Nabokov leaves Paris for America in 1940, while the second volume, *Vladimir Nabokov: The American Years,* is concerned with the remaining years of Nabokov's life, which he split between the United States and Switzerland. *New York Times Book Review* contributor Sergei Davydov trumpeted the arrival of the first volume, calling it "superb" and praising Boyd for bringing "back to life a most remarkable man, who valued literature above all else." Walter Kendrick, also writing in the *New York Times Book Review,* called the second volume "a truly monumental achievement."

Reviewers of Boyd's biography stressed the importance of Nabokov's art. Michael Dirda wrote in the *Washington Post Book World* that Nabokov had "the most brilliant English prose style of his time" and that he had written "a handful of masterpieces of which *Lolita* and *Pale Fire* are merely the best known." Critics marked Boyd the meritorious biographer of a remarkable literary figure. Davydov, for instance, ended his review with the words, "We will not need another biography of Nabokov for the foreseeable future," and Kendrick stated, "Nabokov has found, at last, a biographer worthy of him." Jay Parini commended Boyd in the *Los Angeles Times Book Review:* "Prof. Boyd . . . has done his homework with almost superhuman diligence, tracking his subject to the far ends of the Earth, and it shows." Parini concluded, "*Vladimir Nabokov: The Russian Years* is an exquisitely written book that will not be superseded for a very long time." "In every respect then," Dirda remarked, "this is yet another of those masterly literary biographies of recent years, eligible to sit at the right hand of Richard Ellmann's *James Joyce,*" which won a National Book Award in 1960.

In 1899 Nabokov was born in St. Petersburg, Russia, to a wealthy aristocratic family. His childhood has been called idyllic and furnished him with "memories of a perfect boyhood amid fauna and flora, books and butterflies, loving parents and first love," as Davydov wrote. Nabokov learned Russian, French, and English as a child, and by the time he was fifteen "he had read more of the great works in his three languages than most native speakers of them read in a lifetime," Davydov summarized. Nabokov's father, a parliamentary leader who would be killed while protecting a former Russian colleague from an assassin in 1922, sent his family to the Crimea after the Bolshevik Revolution in 1917, the first of many exiles imposed on Nabokov throughout his life. He attended Cambridge University, then moved to Germany, where his family had settled. When he was twenty-five, he married Vera Slonim, the woman who would give Boyd access to Nabokov's papers after the author's death. During his years in Germany, Nabokov "emerged as the best among the younger generation of emigré Russian writers," Kendrick appraised. In 1937, Nabokov fled Nazi Germany with his Jewish wife and their son, Dmitri. He lived in Paris until 1940, when he once again left his residence behind for America, where he was unknown.

In *Vladimir Nabokov: The American Years,* Boyd describes Nabokov's life in America, where he taught literature at Stanford University, Wellesley College, and Cornell University. Butterfly collecting, a passion Nabokov had developed in his youth, occupied much of his time throughout his life, and he spent many summers pursuing that interest in the American West. In the twenty-one years Nabokov lived in America, he never owned a house. Instead, he and his family lived in sublets and motels until 1961, when they took up residence in a hotel in Montreux, Switzerland, where they remained until Nabokov's death in 1977. In 1960, Nabokov had become independently wealthy due to the huge success of his novel *Lolita,* enabling him to give up his teaching career and focus on his writing in relative seclusion. In the last eighteen years of his life he published a book virtually every year; his last, *Look at the Harlequins!,* came out in 1974.

Nabokov also published an autobiography, *Speak, Memory,* which, years later, was republished with an introduction by Boyd. *Speak, Memory: An Autobiography Revisited*'s 1999 release came five centuries after Nabokov wrote his account of his life and marked the one hundredth anniversary of Nabokov's birth. Random House's Web site posted some of Boyd's comments on the acclaimed author's autobiography: "*Speak, Memory* is the one Nabokov work outside his finest novels—*The Gift, Lolita, Pale Fire, Ada*—that is a masterpiece on their level. . . . [It is] the most artistic of autobiographies. . . . [It] fuses truth to detail with perfection of form, the exact with the evocative, and acute awareness of time with intimations of timelessness."

Boyd's interest in Nabokov started at an early age: He read *Pale Fire* three times when he was seventeen. Around the age of forty-seven, Boyd published an study of that work, *Nabokov's Pale Fire: The Magic of Artistic Discovery,* in which he "skillfully peels away the layers of [that] novel in a feast of literary detective work," observed *Library Journal* contributor Ronald Ratliff. In *Nabokov's Pale Fire,* Boyd refutes some people's contentions that *Pale Fire* is merely a satire of the literary life.

Boyd collaborated with butterfly expert Robert Martin Pyle to edit, annotate, and introduce *Nabokov's Butterflies: Unpublished and Uncorrected Writings by Vladimir Nabokov,* a 2000 publication that contains some text translated from the Russian by Nabokov's son, Dmitri. *Nabokov's Butterflies* is "a fascinating volume" that brings to light "Nabokov's obsession with butterflies," praised Jay Parini in *Guardian. Nabokov's Butterflies* contains segments of Nabokov's diaries, correspondence, interviews, poems, stories, novels, drawings, and autobiography, as well as scientific writing.

Reviewers such as *New York Times Book Review* contributor Laurie Adlerstein noted that *Nabokov's Butterflies,* particularly the portions of heavily scientific writings by Nabokov, would be tiring if read through completely. A *Publishers Weekly* critic maintained that the "gigantic compendium of butterfly-relevant Nabokoviana" contains more text than even a "Nabokov-obsessed taxonomist would want to read"; nevertheless, asserted the critic, "devotees will delight to browse in and scholars will want to own [it]." "Even Nabokov . . . might tire of a collection noting every time a moth flits by a lamp in Nabokov's writings," suggested Adlerstein, who also faulted the manner in which Boyd and Pyle excerpted some of Nabokov's longer works of fiction. Parini, however, found relief in their editorial decision to truncate some of Boyd's more scientific text and applauded Boyd and Pyle's inclusion of multiple forms of Boyd's writing.

"In his shrewd introduction [to *Nabokov's Butterflies*] Boyd teases out the connections between the writer and the lepidopterist," observed Parini, explaining: "One comes to understand Vladimir Nabokov as novelist more completely and precisely by understanding that science gave this canny author 'a sense of reality that should not be confused with modern (or "postmodern") epistemological nihilism.'" "I had not realized the extent to which Nabokov's fiction depended on his attention to the natural world," revealed Parini, who concluded: "Nabokov offered, in his magnificent fiction, a complete taxonomy of the human spirit. He might not have been so meticulous and thorough were it not for the parallel interest in lepidoptery, so many on view here." In contrast, Adlerstein said *Nabokov's Butterflies* juxtaposes science and art, but cannot integrate them."

Discussing the importance of *Nabokov's Butterflies* in *Spectator*, John Fowles commented, "We can't begin to enter Nabokov's world, or worlds, unless we realize that, like every great writer of fiction, he had a vital sense of humour. This scholarly book (an outstanding triumph for Anglo-American publishing) constantly hints at or suggests this. It is expertly edited and annotated. . . . [I]t gives an unbelievably rich portrait of a genius. . . . Nobody who has not read this book can call himself a true natural historian."

Boyd once told *CA*: "Biography offers a writer a rare combination: to undertake exhaustive scholarly research on a figure of major intellectual importance and yet to excite an audience far beyond academia. Although Nabokov was highly regarded—in the 1960s he was often considered the best writer alive—many have thought of him as primarily an astonishing stylist, a verbal magician. I wanted to suggest that there was much more

to him than that: that he had a coherent and highly individual philosophy that shaped his style, his structures, his strategies, and that there was meaning in his magic."

BIOGRAPHICAL/CRITICAL SOURCES:

BOOKS

Boyd, Brian, *Vladimir Nabokov: The Russian Years,* Princeton University Press, 1990.

PERIODICALS

Examiner and Chronicle (San Francisco), October 7, 1990.
Globe and Mail (Toronto), October 20, 1990; September 28, 1991, p. C7.
Guardian, March 25, 2000, Jay Parini, "The Wings of Desire."
Library Journal, October 15, 1999, Ronald Ratliff, review of *Nabokov's Pale Fire,* p. 70.
Los Angeles Times Book Review, November 11, 1990, Jay Parini, review of *Vladimir Nabokov: The Russian Years,* pp. 1, 8.
New York Times Book Review, October 14, 1990, pp. 3, 26-27; September 22, 1991, pp. 1, 22-23; May 7, 2000, Laurie Adlerstein, review of *Nabokov's Butterflies.*
Publishers Weekly, March 13, 2000, review of *Nabokov's Butterflies,* p. 74.
Spectator, April 15, 2000, John Fowles, "The High Ridges of Knowledge," pp. 36-37.
Times, November 17, 1990; January 9, 1992, p. 10.
Tribune Books (Chicago), November 25, 1990, p. 1, 4.
Washington Post Book World, October 21, 1990, Michael Dirda, review of *Vladimir Nabokov: The Russian Years,* pp. 1, 11.*

*   *   *

BRADLEY, John Ed(mund Jr.) 1958-

PERSONAL: Born August 12, 1958, in Opelousas, LA; son of John Edmund (a coach and teacher) and Virval Marie (a teacher; maiden name, Fontenot) Bradley. *Education:* Louisiana State University, B.A., 1980. *Religion:* Catholic.

ADDRESSES: Home—2035 Delmar St., Opelousas, LA 70570-4715.

CAREER: Washington Post, Washington, DC, staff writer, 1983-87; writer.

AWARDS, HONORS: Pulitzer Prize nomination, Columbia University Graduate School of Journalism, 1985, for sports writing; stories have been selected for inclusion in *Best Sports Stories,* 1985 and 1986.

WRITINGS:

NOVELS

Tupelo Nights, Atlantic Monthly Press, 1988.
The Best There Ever Was, Atlantic Monthly Press, 1990.
Love & Obits, Holt (New York, NY), 1992.
Smoke, Holt (New York, NY), 1994.
My Juliet, Doubleday (New York, NY), 2000.

OTHER

Also author of short stories; contributing writer, *Washington Post,* 1988-89; contributing editor, *Esquire,* 1991—; contributing writer, *Sports Illustrated,* 1993—.

Bradley's works have been published in France, Japan, Sweden, and Holland.

SIDELIGHTS: John Ed Bradley, an American journalist and novelist, received a Pulitzer Prize nomination in 1985 for his sports writing at the *Washington Post.* As an undergraduate at Louisiana State University, he was an all-star football player, a distinction he shares with John Girlie, the narrator of his first novel, *Tupelo Nights.* Upon graduating, Girlie must decide whether to accept an offer to turn professional or to return to his hometown of Old Field, Louisiana, to take care of his emotionally distraught mother, a former model and beauty queen whose husband mysteriously vanished when John was nine. Girlie goes back to Old Field and tries to make everything "right and simple," as *New York Times Book Review* contributor Jayne Anne Phillips explained. The novel delineates the struggles Girlie encounters: dealing with his troubled mother's sexual advances; working nights cleaning toilets; chumming with his friend Charley, a former seminarian who drinks, does drugs, and digs graves at night; and falling in love with an older woman whose husband deserted her when their three-month-old baby died. In the end, Girlie leaves Old Field and its people behind to escape his mother's suffocating love, while realizing that he is duplicating his father's disappearance. Phillips quoted one of Girlie's beliefs: "[I]n this world it is possible to leave at any moment and never return, to go away and begin again, and dying is not the only way."

Tupelo Nights received favorable reviews, with many critics comparing Bradley's prose to Ernest Hemingway's. Joseph Olshan wrote in the *Chicago Tribune:* "Bradley vividly evokes the neon-lighted bars of Old Field and its baroque cemeteries, recreating a stifling small town loneliness. These rapturous images are welcome in the pruning age of minimalism." *Los Angeles Times Book Review* contributor Carter Coleman commented that *Tupelo Nights* "is a moving work, tender, heartfelt and as lonesome as the bayou on a misty night." Harry Crews, writing in the *Washington Post,* called the novel "tender and filled with the joy of being alive and a reverence for the struggle of failed human beings trying to find their way in the world." Crews ended: "Anyone who reads this extraordinary first novel will return to it again in memory and dreams. It lingers in the mind as only the best fiction does."

Bradley's second novel, *The Best There Ever Was,* elicited mixed responses from critics. *Chicago Tribune* reviewer Douglas Seibold admitted the novel didn't reach the standards set by Bradley's first novel: "Writers are at least as susceptible to the sophomore slump as athletes, and in *The Best There Ever Was,* Bradley appears to have succumbed in trying to diverge from the sort of material he handled so well in his debut." Coach Harold Gravely, the novel's protagonist, led a college football team to a Sugar Bowl victory thirty years ago but hasn't had a winning season in nearly a decade, and the university is pressuring him for his resignation. When he is diagnosed with lung cancer, Gravely successfully uses his illness to evoke the sympathy of the board of supervisors, which makes him coach for life. Marianne Gingher confessed in *Washington Post* that "Coach Gravely's game is one I could have missed." Bill Kent, however, wrote in *New York Times Book Review* that *The Best There Ever Was* "is a noble achievement, a compassionate, unsentimental attempt to find meaning in an older generation's failure to live out its dreams."

Love & Obits, Bradley's third novel, examines the predicament of Joseph Burke, a reporter for the fictional *Washington Herald.* After his affair with the wife of a U.S. senator is publicized in gossip columns, Burke is demoted to writing obituaries for the paper, "a job reserved for those the *Herald*'s corporate attorney will not fire outright, afraid to risk the ire of the union," commented *Chicago Tribune* reviewer Christopher

Zenowich. Although some critics again maintained that their expectations were not met by the novel, Zenowich, after quoting Bradley's description of the obituary desk's increased busyness in winter, wrote, "This is beautifully balanced, emotionally poignant prose." *New York Times Book Review* contributor David Murray called *Love & Obits* a "charmingly funny, offbeat novel." In the *Los Angeles Times Book Review*, Tim Appelo remarked that though he found the book "disappointing" in light of the author's earlier works, "Bradley's imagination is so strong and strange he often strikes notes resonant of the greatest, scariest newspaper novel ever written, Nathanael West's *Miss Lonelyhearts*. He shares a bit of West's despairing hilarity, his bent for sinister slapstick."

Published in 1994, Bradley's next novel, *Smoke,* tells of a small Southern town and a couple of its inhabitants who dream of vengeance against the national chain superstore that they believe is driving some of the local shops out of business. "The novel's triumph," according to a *Publishers Weekly* reviewer, is Bradley's portrait of the billionaire owner of the superstore chain. *Booklist* contributor Joe Collins felt the novel was "occasionally amusing," but complained that it was "long [and] repetitious" and contained "big gooey dollops of sentimentality." Collins believed that *Smoke* would have been better as a short story. However, the *Publishers Weekly* critic who enjoyed Bradley's "colorful" cast praised: "Occasional clichés and moments of treacle do not spoil this otherwise delightful homespun narrative."

With *My Juliet,* Bradley gives readers a "moody, sadly comic novel" filled with "murder, sex and family secrets," described *Publishers Weekly*. This story, his fifth novel, is set in New Orleans and follows Sonny, a thirty-something, going-nowhere portrait-painter, and the object of his obsession, Juliet, the girlfriend who dumped him years earlier. Juliet, who was working in California as an actress in adult films, returns to her wealthy New Orleans home and re-enters Sonny's life. "Witty dialogue and lush scenery" outweigh the novel's somewhat seedy side, asserted the *Publishers Weekly* critic, calling *My Juliet* "a wild suspenseful and ultimately bittersweet read."

BIOGRAPHICAL/CRITICAL SOURCES:

BOOKS

Contemporary Literary Criticism, Volume 55, Gale (Detroit, MI), 1989, pp. 31-34.
Contemporary Novelists, sixth edition, St. James (Detroit, MI), 1996.

PERIODICALS

Booklist, Joe Collins, review of *Smoke,* April 1, 1994, p. 1422.
Chicago Tribune, April 11, 1988; September 14, 1990.
Globe and Mail (Toronto), June 18, 1988.
Kirkus Reviews, March 1, 1994, p. 226.
Kliatt, March, 1996, p. 5.
Library Journal, February 1, 1994, Charles Michaud, review of *Smoke,* p. 110; March 1, 2000, review of *My Juliet,* p. S4.
Los Angeles Times Book Review, July 10, 1988, pp. 3, 8; February 9, 1992, pp. 3, 7; July 3, 1994, p. 5.
Newsweek, September 17, 1990, p. 59.
New York Times, April 9, 1988.
New York Times Book Review, June 19, 1988, p. 10; November 18, 1990, p. 36; February 9, 1992, p. 18; June 26, 1994, Sharon Oard Warner, review of *Smoke,* p. 28; November 26, 1995, p. 32.
Publishers Weekly, February 21, 1994, review of *Smoke,* p. 233; July 3, 2000, review of *My Juliet,* p. 47.
Times Literary Supplement, November 25, 1988, p. 1306.
Tribune Books (Chicago), February 16, 1992, p. 4.
Washington Post, April 26, 1988; September 18, 1990.
Washington Post Book World, May 15, 1994, p. 4.*

*   *   *

BRENDON, Piers (George Rundle) 1940-

PERSONAL: Born December 21, 1940, in Cornwall, England; son of George (a writer) and Frances (a journalist; maiden name, Cook) Brendon; married Vyvyen Davis (a teacher), 1968; children: George, Oliver. *Ethnicity:* "Caucasian." *Education:* Magdalene College, Cambridge, M.A., 1965, Ph.D., 1970. *Politics:* Labour.

ADDRESSES: Home—4B Millington Rd., Cambridge, England CB3 9HP.

CAREER: Cambridgeshire College of Arts and Technology, Cambridge, England, lecturer in history, 1966-79, head of department, 1977-79; writer, 1979—. Occasional lecturer and broadcaster. Cambridge University, keeper of the Archives Center and fellow of Churchill College, 1995-2001.

WRITINGS:

(Editor, with William Shaw) *Reading They've Liked,* Macmillan (London, England), 1967.

(Editor, with Shaw) *Reading Matters,* Macmillan (London, England), 1969.

(Editor, with Shaw) *By What Authority?,* Macmillan (London, England), 1972.

Hurrell Froude and the Oxford Movement, Merrimack Book Services (Topsfield, MA), 1974.

Hawker of Morwenstow: Portrait of a Victorian Eccentric, J. Cape (London, England), 1975.

Eminent Edwardians, Secker & Warburg (London, England), 1979, Houghton Mifflin (Boston, MA), 1980.

(With Rex Bloomstein) *Auschwitz and the Allies* (television documentary), British Broadcasting Corp. (BBC-TV), 1981.

The Life and Death of the Press Barons, Secker & Warburg (London, England), 1982, Atheneum (New York, NY), 1983.

Winston Churchill: A Biography, Harper (New York, NY), 1984, published in England as *Winston Churchill: A Brief Life,* Secker & Warburg (London, England), 1984.

(With Bloomstein) *Human Rights* (television documentary), Thames Television, 1984.

Ike: His Life and Times, Harper (New York, NY), 1986, published in England as *Ike: The Life and Times of Dwight D. Eisenhower,* Secker & Warburg (London, England), 1986.

Our Own Dear Queen, Secker & Warburg (London, England), 1986, David & Charles (North Pomfret, VT), 1987.

Thomas Cook: 150 Years of Popular Tourism, Secker & Warburg (London, England), 1991.

(With Phillip Whitehead) *The Windsors: A Dynasty Revealed,* Hodder & Stoughton (London, England), 1995, revised edition, Pimlico, 2001.

The Motoring Century: The Story of the Royal Automobile Club, Bloomsbury, 1997.

The Dark Valley: A Panorama of the 1930s, Knopf (New York, NY), 2000.

Author (with others) of other television documentary scripts. Script consultant, *The Windsors* (four-part documentary), and *The Churchills* (three-part documentary). Contributor of reviews to numerous periodicals, including the London *Times, New York Times, Observer, Mail on Sunday,* and *Columbia Journalism Review.*

WORK IN PROGRESS: A History of the Decline and Fall of the British Empire, publication by J. Cape (London, England) expected in 2006.

SIDELIGHTS: With *The Life and Death of the Press Barons,* "Piers Brendon has revived, with elegance and distinction, the discipline of digestible history which gave writers like Barbara Tuchman their early success: a 'tissue of innumerable biographies,' only lightly drawn together with generalizations, strongly spiced by anecdote, and written in a style that combines bravura with allusiveness," stated Roy Foster in the *Times Literary Supplement.* "This is a more substantial achievement than it may sound; the subjects for such an approach need to be carefully selected, the terrain well mapped, and the material produced with a sustained flourish," the critic continued. *The Life and Death of the Press Barons* is a "witty study of the press lords of England and America," summarized *Washington Post Book World* contributor Bernard A. Weisberger. The critic added that the work contains "some 250 of the funniest and shrewdest pages of business and cultural history that you are likely to find between covers in any given year." Tracing the careers and idiosyncrasies of executives such as Joseph Pulitzer, Horace Greeley, William Randolph Hearst, and James Gordon Bennett, the author "offers routine cautions on the growth of conglomerates and other sober matters," observed *New York Times* reviewer Walter Goodman. Goodman further noted that the main pleasures of the book "lie in the portraits of the men who made the papers." Although these anecdotes constitute a major portion of the book, "the range of sources behind *The Life and Death of the Press Barons* is eclectic and interesting, and some of the best material . . . comes from unpublished sources," Foster maintained. "What emerges is on one level a gallery of eccentrics, and on another a series of studies in the tactics of power."

Brendon narrows his focus to a single individual in *Winston Churchill: A Biography.* Because many in-depth studies of the former British prime minister have been written, "Brendon has wisely settled for a 'brief life,' which is in effect a brilliant sketch for a portrait," remarked *Times Literary Supplement* contributor C. M. Woodhouse. Despite its brevity, "*Winston Churchill* is nonetheless a brilliant *tour de force,*" wrote Joe Mysak in the *National Review,* "even if it is not quite Winston Churchill. Recounting ninety years at breakneck speed, especially ninety years as densely packed as Churchill's, inevitably produces distortion." The critic explained that the author "is not seduced by the minutiae of experience, and he is not tedious," but "he is better at telling what his subject did than what he was like."

London *Times* contributor Woodrow Wyatt, however, claimed that "small blemishes apart, a reader who does not want to know too much about Churchill can safely begin here." By using a variety of anecdotes, "Brendon builds a convincing picture of the great man," Woodhouse commented. "His judgment is good and his style succinct. His view of Churchill is entirely without hagiography . . . [exposing] the warts and all." "Most important of all," judged Mysak, "Mr. Brendon demonstrates that Churchill was one of those relics, those dinosaurs, who fought all his life for duty, honor, and country."

The author's aim in *Ike: His Life and Times,* "as with his previously acclaimed study of Winston Churchill, was to write a succinct and readable biography and this he has achieved admirably," Edward Hamilton maintained in the *Spectator.* Brendon's study of former U.S. president Dwight D. Eisenhower "is fluently written, witty and never loses sight of the subject," the critic added. "If sometimes the judgments are too sweeping, the tone too flippant in the desire for the memorable phrase, all can be forgiven. This is a tour-de-force and should confirm Brendon as one of the best writers of history at work today." *New York Times Book Review* contributor Townsend Hoopes similarly called *Ike* a "witty [and] perceptive" analysis that reveals "the author's moral penetration and his concentration on gathering evidence to show Eisenhower's chronic vacillation and remarkably opaque moral standards." While the critic faulted Brendon for the occasional oversimplification, he concluded: "This is a telling analysis that is bound to have an impact on the current debate over Eisenhower's proper place in history."

Guy Halverson wrote in the *Christian Science Monitor* that Brendon's biography "is especially useful . . . [in] demythologiz[ing] the Eisenhower-as-instant-hero viewpoint that has arisen in recent years." Fred Greenstein explained in a *Washington Post Book World* article that "there are two quite separable kinds of Eisenhower revisionism" that have improved the former president's rating over previous assessments. "Brendon has read [this] new scholarship on Eisenhower and delved into the archives," the critic elaborated. "He is familiar with the seeming contradictions" of Eisenhower's presidential career, and his challenges to the new theories "lead him to raise important questions." Greenstein added that, "although Brendon is unable to do full justice to his subject or his own commendable aims, he provides an original account of an historical actor about whom much more remains to be said." "As the author convincingly demonstrates," wrote Hamilton, "Eisenhower was a highly complex man whom it was all too easy to take at his own apparent estimation. . . . Brendon calls him 'one of the most enigmatic characters ever to occupy the White House' and admits there will never be a last word on him. Meanwhile however, Piers Brendon's book will do just fine."

In *The Dark Valley: A Panorama of the 1930s,* Brendon offers "a sweeping picture of how politics shaped the fate of ordinary people between the Wall Street crash and the onset of World War II," according to Mark Mazower in the *New York Times Book Review.* The 800-page book serves as an overview of the 1930s from an international perspective, covering events in Japan, China, and the Soviet Union, as well the major powers of Europe and the United States. Character sketches describe the important politicians of the era as Brendon ties the desperate economic times to a rise in fascism and a general retreat from liberalism. As Mazower put it, the author "is concerned to convey the very texture of life: the sense of place, jokes, food and fashion can all be found in this account. But beyond this lies a grander goal—to learn the lessons of the 1930's, above all how to ensure that economic crisis never again jeopardizes political stability."

Reviewers have praised both the scope of *The Dark Valley* and the author's writing style. *Christian Science Monitor* contributor Richard A. Nenneman praised the work as a "superlative attempt to re-create the world that passed away in 1939." Nenneman added that Brendon "has written a history that even a general reader will have trouble putting down." Calling the book "a dazzling display of scholarship," *History Today* reviewer Robert Pearce noted that Brendon "brings the past vividly to life . . . with riveting narrative and a plethora of brilliant anecdotes and superbly evocative quotations. *The Dark Valley* shows just how compelling history can be." Although he disagreed with Brendon's analysis, Mark Mazower also concluded that the author "has read widely and synthesizes complex research in a readable and pleasing way." Likewise, a *Publishers Weekly* reviewer concluded: "[Brendon's] writing is superlative, his vocabulary precise and extensive; he displays remarkable talent for the revealing phrase and the polished anecdote."

Brendon once told *CA:* "Were I to fill in this section properly, it would consist of a paean of nihilistic hatred and Swiftian vituperation directed at almost every aspect of public life I can think of, from Mrs. Thatcher to dumping nuclear waste in the seas, from racialism to killing whales, from sports and sportspersons to the drivel excreted by the media. In short, the only optimistic features on my horizon are private ones—family, friends, and work."

BIOGRAPHICAL/CRITICAL SOURCES:

PERIODICALS

Booklist, January 15, 1995, review of *The Windsors: A Dynasty Revealed,* p. 892.

Christian Science Monitor, June 24, 1983; October 3, 1986, Guy Halverson, review of *Ike: His Life and Times;* October 5, 2000, Richard A. Nenneman, "A Bleak Decade Brought to Light," p. 15.

Foreign Affairs, November-December, 2000, Stanley Hoffman, review of *The Dark Valley: A Panorama of the 1930s,* p. 170.

History Today, October, 2000, Robert Pearce, review of *The Dark Valley,* p. 54.

Illustrated London News, autumn, 1992, review of *Thomas Cook: 150 Years of Popular Tourism,* p. 98.

National Review, November 2, 1984, Joe Mysak, review of *Winston Churchill: A Biography.*

New Scientist, April 12, 1997, review of *The Motoring Century: The Story of the Royal Automobile Club,* p. 44.

New Statesman, May 30, 1997, review of *The Motoring Century,* p. 51.

New York Times, April 7, 1983, Walter Goodman, review of *The Life and Death of the Press Barons.*

New York Times Book Review, April 20, 1980; November 30, 1986, Townsend Hoopes, review of *Ike;* December 24, 2000, Mark Mazower, "Hard Times."

Observer, January 13, 1991.

Publishers Weekly, December 19, 1994, review of *The Windsors,* p. 39; September 4, 2000, review of *The Dark Valley,* p. 92.

Spectator, January 10, 1987, Edward Hamilton, review of *Ike.*

Time, October 23, 2000, R. Z. Sheppard, review of *The Dark Valley,* p. 90.

Times (London), April 5, 1984, Woodrow Wyatt, review of *Winston Churchill;* November 13, 1986.

Times Educational Supplement, May 10, 1996, review of *Eminent Edwardians,* p. 7.

Times Literary Supplement, February 18, 1983, Roy Foster, review of *The Life and Death of the Press Barons;* April 13, 1984, C. M. Woodhouse, review of *Winston Churchill;* January 25, 1991; July 18, 1997, review of *The Motoring Century,* p. 7.

Washington Post Book World, April 24, 1983, Bernard A. Weisberger, review of *The Life and Death of the Press Barons;* September 7, 1986, Fred Greenstein, review of *Ike.*

*   *   *

BROOKES, Tim 1953-

PERSONAL: Born June 24, 1953, in London, England; son of Colin (a teacher and social worker) and Margaret (a social worker and artist) Brookes; married Barbara Boutsikaris (a counselor), June 25, 1994; children: two daughters. *Education:* Pembroke College, Oxford, M.A., 1977. *Politics:* "Armchair socialist." *Religion:* "Armchair Buddhist." *Avocational interests:* Cricket, tennis, soccer, music, gardening.

ADDRESSES: Office—Department of English, 315 Old Mill, University of Vermont, Burlington, VT 05405. *Agent*—Henry Dunow, Harold Ober Associates, 425 Madison Ave., New York, NY 10017. *E-mail*—tbrookes@zoo.uvm.edu.

CAREER: University of Vermont, Burlington, instructor in English, 1974-94; writer. Regular commentator for "Sunday Weekend Edition," National Public Radio, beginning in 1989; worked variously as a soccer coach, singer/guitarist, and as a journalist for an alternative weekly in Vermont, a local daily, a rock station, an entertainment newsletter, and the public radio program guide-cum-magazine.

MEMBER: Chittenden County Cricket Club.

AWARDS, HONORS: Best feature award, New England Press Association, 1984; four awards from Gannett.

WRITINGS:

Catching My Breath: An Asthmatic Explores His Illness, Times Books (New York City), 1994.

(With others) *The Blair Handbook: Instructor's Edition,* Blair Press/Prentice-Hall (Englewood Cliffs, NJ), 1994.

Signs of Life: A Memoir of Dying and Discovery, Times Books, 1997.

A Hell of a Place to Lose a Cow: An American Hitchhiking Odyssey, National Geographic Society (Washington, DC), 2000.

Contributor to periodicals, including *Atlantic, Boston Globe,* and *New York Times Magazine.*

SIDELIGHTS: After suffering from an unusually severe asthma attack, radio commentator and journalist Tim Brookes decided to investigate the subject in 1994's *Catching My Breath: An Asthmatic Explores His Illness.* A native of England, Brookes spent several years moving back and forth between the United States and his homeland after earning a degree from Oxford University. He finally settled in Vermont and eventually became a regular contributor of articles and essays to such national publications as the *New York Times Magazine.* He also began working as a commentator for National Public Radio.

Brookes begins *Catching My Breath* with a detailed description of asthma, a breathing disorder which causes normal lung activity to malfunction and triggers a severe reduction in breathing ability within seconds. An attack can be fatal if an epinephrine-based chemical inhalant—or in Brookes's case, an injection of epinephrine—is not administered immediately. Next, the author chronicles the medical and social history of asthma, the various theories and attempted remedies, and what it is like to live permanently with a condition that has no cure. As Brookes explains in the book, many facets of the affliction remain a mystery to modern medical science. Brookes recounts being told by a doctor that "symptom control" is the most that can achieved in treating asthma, and the writer reflects that "controlling symptoms is in a way the opposite of self-understanding."

In writing *Catching My Breath,* Brookes gained knowledge of and a new perspective on his affliction by reading, questioning doctors, and investigating alternative therapies. His research included watching a lung operation in a hospital and accompanying a medical team to a New York City shelter for welfare families. Asthma, Brookes explains, is affected by environmental conditions such as air quality, ventilation systems, and stress, and is more common among the poor. In *Catching My Breath,* Brookes describes asthma as a burdensome companion that has attached itself to him for life, but the writer's "plot is his growing realization that he and asthma are actually quite well matched," observed *New York Times Book Review* critic Arthur W. Frank. "Asthma makes Mr. Brookes into the person he wants his ideal physician to be. . . . His rare combination of popular science, social criticism and memoir uses his own alteration through suffering to reconceive social health."

Brookes drew on his mother's illness and eventual death from cancer in *Signs of Life.* Besides providing a detailed account of his mother's battle against the disease, and the reactions of her family to it, Brookes's book also outlines the history of the hospice movement, a therapeutic approach to treating cancer patients with dignity. According to the *Publishers Weekly* critic, "Brookes brings his mother's strong, independent spirit to life." "Brookes's honest appraisal of hospice care," wrote Karen McNally Bensing in *Library Journal,* "brings much-needed balance to the debate over care of the dying."

In *A Hell of a Place to Lose a Cow: An American Hitchhiking Odyssey,* Brookes recounts a cross-country journey from the East Coast to the West Coast, and back again to his home in Vermont. Along the way he accepts rides from a variety of Americans and, based on their conversations, comments on contemporary society. Although a *Kirkus Reviews* critic noted that Brookes's "political sensibility can become cloying," he nonetheless rated the book "a frequently charming narrative epic." GraceAnne A. DeCandido in *Booklist* praised Brookes's book for displaying a "cheerful lack of anxiety and a disarming lack of pretense."

Brookes told *CA:* "I always wanted to be able to put 'Writer' under 'Occupation' in my passport, and consequently I spent a decade and a half in Britain, then the United States, then back in Britain, writing poetry, then short fiction, then long fiction, before I finally ground to a halt in the middle of a novel in 1983, facing the overwhelming evidence that I could fake a good imitation, but that I wasn't saying anything worth reading.

"By then I was in the United States, and both my part-time college teaching job and the small inheritance from my grandfather that had paid for part of an M.F.A. degree had run out. I turned to writing journalism—reviews, essays, features, hard news, up to nine pieces a week—for an alternative weekly in Vermont, then for a local daily, a rock station, an entertainment newsletter, and the public radio program guide-cum-magazine.

"By 1991 I was publishing in more visible outlets, including the *Atlantic* and the *New York Times Magazine,* and had been a regular commentator for National Public Radio for two years. But my life was as fragmented, impoverished and hectic as ever—so much so, in fact, that I had an asthma attack that might have killed me. This, and a kind referral from a fellow struggling author, led directly to *Catching My Breath,* which somehow managed to use a full range of the voices I'd been gathering during this decade of apprenticeship. It also taught me that I write best when I'm angry or afraid."

BIOGRAPHICAL/CRITICAL SOURCES:

BOOKS

Brookes, Tim, *Catching My Breath: An Asthmatic Explores His Illness,* Times Books, 1994.

PERIODICALS

Booklist, February 1, 1997, William Beatty, review of *Signs of Life,* p. 911; July, 2000, GraceAnne A. DeCandido, review of *A Hell of a Place to Lose a Cow,* p. 2000.

Choice, January, 1998, review of *Signs of Life,* p. 851.

Kirkus Reviews, May 1, 1994, review of *Catching My Breath,* p. 601; January 1, 1997, review of *Signs of Life;* June 15, 2000, review of *A Hell of a Place to Lose a Cow,* p. 852.

Library Journal, July, 1994, review of *Catching My Breath,* p. 120; February 1, 1997, Karen McNally Bensing, review of *Signs of Life,* p. 99.

New York Times Book Review, September 25, 1994, review of *Catching My Breath,* p. 23.

Publishers Weekly, May 9, 1994, review of *Catching My Breath,* p. 58; January 6, 1997, review of *Signs of Life,* p. 55.

OTHER

Tim Brookes's Home Page, http://www.uvm.edu/ (August 29, 2000).*

*   *   *

BRUNVAND, Jan Harold 1933-

PERSONAL: Born March 23, 1933, in Cadillac, MI; son of Harold N. (a civil engineer) and Ruth (Jorgensen) Brunvand; married Judith Darlene Ast (a librarian), June 10, 1956; children: Erik, Amy, Dana, Karen. *Education:* Michigan State University, B.A., 1955, M.A., 1957; attended University of Oslo, 1956-57; Indiana University, Ph.D., 1961.

ADDRESSES: Home—1031 First Ave., Salt Lake City, UT 84103. *Office*—Department of English, University of Utah, Salt Lake City, UT 84112. *E-mail*—jan. brunvand@m.cc.utah.edu.

CAREER: University of Idaho, Moscow, assistant professor of English, 1961-65; Southern Illinois University at Edwardsville, associate professor of English, 1965-66; University of Utah, Salt Lake City, associate professor, 1966-71, professor of English and folklore, 1971—, currently professor emeritus. Indiana University, visiting assistant professor, summer, 1965. Member of Utah Folk Arts advisory panel, 1976—. Guest on morning programs and talk shows, including *Late Night with David Letterman. Military service:* U.S. Army, Signal Corps, 1962-63.

MEMBER: International Society for Contemporary Legend Research, American Association of University Professors, American Folklore Society (fellow; president, 1985), California Folklore Society.

AWARDS, HONORS: Fulbright scholar in Norway, 1956-57; Fulbright grant for Romania, 1970-71; Guggenheim fellow, 1970-71; fellow in Romania, International Research and Exchanges Board, 1973-74, 1981; fellow of Committee for the Scientific Investigation of Claims of the Paranormal.

WRITINGS:

A Dictionary of Proverbs and Proverbial Phrases from Books Published by Indiana Authors before 1890, Indiana University Press (Bloomington, IN), 1961.

The Study of American Folklore: An Introduction, with instructor's manual, Norton (New York, NY), 1968, 4th edition, 1998.

A Guide for Collectors of Folklore in Utah, University of Utah Press (Salt Lake City, UT), 1971.

Norwegian Settlers in Alberta, National Museum of Man (Ottawa, Ontario, Canada), 1974.

Folklore: A Study and Research Guide, St. Martin's Press (New York, NY), 1976.

(Editor) *Readings in American Folklore,* Norton (New York, NY), 1979.

Folktale (sound recording), Everett/Edwards (De Land, FL), 1979.

School Folklore (sound recording), Everett/Edwards (De Land, FL), 1979.

The Vanishing Hitchhiker: American Urban Legends and Their Meanings, Norton (New York, NY), 1981.

The Choking Doberman and Other "New" Urban Legends, Norton (New York, NY), 1984.

The Mexican Pet: More "New" Urban Legends and Some Old Favorites, Norton (New York, NY), 1986.

Curses! Broiled Again! The Hottest Urban Legends Going, Norton (New York, NY), 1989.

The Taming of the Shrew: A Comparative Study of Oral and Literary Versions, Garland Publishing (New York, NY), 1991.

The Baby Train and Other Lusty Urban Legends, Norton (New York, NY), 1993.

(Author of introduction and commentary) *The Big Book of Urban Legends,* Paradox Press (New York, NY), 1994.

(Editor) *American Folklore: An Encyclopedia,* Garland Publishing (New York, NY), 1996.

Too Good to Be True: The Colossal Book of Urban Legends, Norton (New York, NY), 1999.

The Truth Never Stands in the Way of a Good Story, University of Illinois Press (Urbana, IL), 2000.

Encyclopedia of Urban Legends, American Bibliographic Center-Clio Press (Santa Barbara, CA), 2001.

Contributor to books, including *The Western Folklore Conference: Selected Papers* (monograph), edited by Austin E. Fife and J. Golden Taylor, Utah State University Press (Logan, UT), 1964; *Popular Culture and Curricula,* edited by Ray B. Browne and Ronald J. Ambrosetti, Bowling Green University (Bowling Green, OH), 1970; *American Folk Legend: A Symposium,* edited by Wayland D. Hand, University of California Press (Berkeley, CA), 1971; *Folklore Today: Festschrift for Richard W. Dorson,* edited by Glassie, Linda Degh, and Felix J. Olinas, Indiana University Press (Bloomington, IN), 1976; and *Subject and Strategy: A Rhetoric Reader,* 2nd edition, edited by Paul Escholz and Alfred Rosa, St. Martin's Press (New York, NY), 1981. Author of column, "Urban Legends," distributed by United Features Syndicate, 1987-92. Contributor of over a hundred articles and reviews to folklore journals and to newspapers. *Midwest Folklore,* assistant editor, 1959-60, book review editor, 1961-64; *Journal of American Folklore,* associate editor, 1963-67 and 1973-76, book review editor, 1967-73, editor, 1976-80.

WORK IN PROGRESS: More research and investigation into urban legends.

SIDELIGHTS: Jan Harold Brunvand, professor emeritus of English and folklore at the University of Utah, has written numerous books on what he calls "urban legends." Urban legends, though often sworn to be true by their tellers, are largely unsubstantiated modern-day stories that criss-cross the globe mainly by word of mouth. Brunvand has made a name for himself by compiling, researching, and, in most cases, debunking these tales. In *Skeptic* magazine, a reviewer cited Brunvand for "almost singlehandedly pioneering an entirely new field of study." *Library Journal* correspondent Richard K. Burns likewise styled Brunvand "the dean of urban folklore" and commended him for producing "impressive scholarship."

Some of the stories Brunvand has investigated include one about a woman tourist in Mexico who, upon finding a cute little dog, sneaked the dog back to the United States only to be told by her veterinarian that the dog was actually a sewer rat. Another legend involves a cat that exploded after being placed in the microwave oven by an owner who wanted to dry it off. According to Brunvand, some of these legends are grounded in the past, and they often take slightly different forms as they move from region to region. No matter what their origin or form, however, they are pure fiction. Nevertheless, it is not uncommon for these stories to be picked up by the media and printed or reported as truth, mak-

ing them seem all the more valid. As the author put it in a *CNN.com* interview, "These are stories told with some conviction as if they are true, attributed to a friend or a friend of a friend, that are too coincidental or bizarre to be literally true."

Brunvand's books relate many known urban legends, providing some explanation as to what they mean and why they have arisen. In a conversation with *U.S. News and World Report* contributor Alvin P. Sanoff, Brunvand maintained that such tales "fill a need people have to tell each other stories, to know the latest that's going on. . . . These stories are the folklore of the mostly educated, white middle class. . . . In an urbanized society, these stories provide a common bond. They are a means by which strangers can easily communicate with one another." In a *Time* review, Donald Morrison observed: "Why do such stories survive, even flourish, in an age of science and cynicism? Many of them, says Brunvand, serve as cautionary tales, sermonettes on the evils of, say, parking in deserted lanes or buying cheap imported goods. Others are inspired by suspicion of change—of microwave ovens or fast-food restaurants. Writes Brunvand: 'Whatever is new and puzzling or scary, but which eventually becomes familiar, may turn up in modern folklore.'" Some of these legends are even viewed as part of ongoing racial or cultural stereotyping, like stories involving Southeast Asian immigrants to the United States capturing and eating people's pets.

Although *Times Literary Supplement* critic Mark Abley noted that Brunvand's first collection on urban legends, *The Vanishing Hitchhiker: American Urban Legends and Their Meanings,* is weak in terms of explaining the implications and the significance of urban legends, *New York Times* reviewer Christopher Lehmann-Haupt claimed that Brunvand's third collection, *The Mexican Pet: More "New" Urban Legends and Some Old Favorites,* "offers enough material to suggest a number of conclusions." According to Lehmann-Haupt, "Brunvand includes new versions of beliefs and stories discussed in his earlier books, so that we may judge for ourselves how apocryphal stories evolve. He also attempts here to establish the provenance of several legends, particularly those that have been circulated by the media. . . . *The Mexican Pet* is enlightening in several respects. By seeing new permutations of old stories, we become convinced that what we once took as gospel is indeed nothing more than plausible fabrication." *New York Times Book Review* contributor Gahan Wilson, in a review of *The Baby Train and Other Lusty Urban Legends,* cautioned against dismissing these stories completely, arguing that their purpose is to "remind us that life is wonderful and mysterious after all." Wilson concluded that Brunvand is "a bona fide scholar" on a "sincere, if slightly wacky, educational mission." In another *New York Times Book Review* piece on *The Mexican Pet,* Scott Simon declared: "It is the charm of Mr. Brunvand's scholarship and presentation that he delivers the sad news of the falsehood of these stories without being professorially reproachful toward those of us who have relayed them. . . . He manages to shave the veneer of veracity from these tales while letting the stories stand as accurate anecdotes about the anxieties of our times."

Brunvand told *CNN.com* that he sees no end to fabulous tales of technology gone awry. "There have been lots of them already," he stated. "For example, they involve cell phones, computers, ATMs, modern warfare, airplane travel, microwave ovens. I expect there will continue to be new legends about new technological advances. If not, I am out of business!"

BIOGRAPHICAL/CRITICAL SOURCES:

BOOKS

Brunvand, Jan Harold, *The Vanishing Hitchhiker: American Urban Legends and Their Meanings,* Norton (New York, NY), 1981.

PERIODICALS

Booklist, August, 1996, review of *American Folklore: An Encyclopedia,* p. 1920.
Choice, May, 1969; May, 1982.
Columbia Journalism Review, March, 1982.
Detroit Free Press, July 6, 1984.
Journal of American Folklore, January, 1969; July, 1978; October, 1978.
Library Journal, April 1, 2000, Richard K. Burns, review of *The Truth Never Stands in the Way of a Good Story,* p. 109; July, 1999, Richard K. Burns, review of *Too Good To Be True: The Colossal Book of Urban Legends,* p. 103.
New York Times, July 21, 1986, Christopher Lehmann-Haupt, review of *The Mexican Pet: More "New" Urban Legends and Some Old Favorites,* p. C18.
New York Times Book Review, July 6, 1986, Scott Simon, "Did You Hear about the Naked Skier?," p. 8; May 30, 1993, Gahan Wilson, "The Poodle in the Microwave."

Skeptic, winter, 2000, "Urban Legends Too Good to Be True," p. 12.
Skeptical Inquirer, July, 2000, Kendrick Frazier, review of *The Truth Never Stands in the Way of a Good Story,* p. 57.
Smithsonian, November, 1992.
Time, November 9, 1981.
Times Literary Supplement, August 13, 1982, Mark Abley, review of *The Vanishing Hitchhiker: American Urban Legends and Their Meanings.*
Tribune Books (Chicago), July 17, 1986.
U.S. News and World Report, September 22, 1986, article by Alvin P. Sanoff.

OTHER

CNN.com, http://www.cnn.com/ (September 22, 1999), "Jan Harold Brunvand."

*   *   *

BRUST, Steven K. (Zoltan) 1955-

PERSONAL: Born November 23, 1955, in St. Paul, MN; son of William Z. (a professor) and Jean (Tilsen) Brust; married (separated); children: Corwin Edward, Aliera Jean and Carolyn Rocza (twins), Antonia Eileen. *Education:* Attended University of Minnesota—Twin Cities. *Politics:* "Trotskyist." *Religion:* "Materialist." *Avocational interests:* Cooking, poker, Middle-Eastern drumming.

ADDRESSES: Home—3248 Portland Avenue S., Minneapolis, MN 55407. *E-mail*—kzb@dreamcafe.com. *Agent*—Valerie Smith, Route 44-55, RD Box 160, Modena, NY 12548.

CAREER: Employed as systems programmer, 1976-86, for various companies, including Network Systems, New Brighton, MN, 1983-86; full-time writer, 1986—. Former actor for local community theater; rock 'n' roll drummer; drummer for Middle-Eastern and Oriental dancers; folk guitarist, banjoist, singer, and songwriter.

MEMBER: Science Fiction Writers of America, Interstate Writers Workshop, Minnesota Science Fiction Society (executive vice president), Pre-Joycean Fellowship.

WRITINGS:

SCIENCE FICTION AND FANTASY NOVELS

To Reign in Hell, Steel Dragon, 1984.
Brokedown Palace, Ace Books, 1985.

The Sun, the Moon, and the Stars, Armadillo Press, 1987.

Cowboy Feng's Space Bar and Grille, Ace Books, 1990.

The Phoenix Guards, Tor Books, 1991.

(With Megan Lindholm) *The Gypsy,* Tor Books, 1992.

Agyar, Tor Books, 1992.

Athyra, Ace Books, 1993.

Five Hundred Years After (sequel to *The Phoenix Guards*), Tor Books, 1994.

ORCA, Ace Books, 1996.

(With Emma Bull) *Freedom and Necessity,* Tor Books, 1997.

"VLAD TALTOS" SERIES

Jhereg, Ace Books, 1983.

Yendi, Ace Books, 1984.

Teckla, Ace Books, 1986.

Taltos, Ace Books, 1988.

Phoenix, Ace Books, 1990.

Dragon, Tor Books, 1998.

The Book of Jhereg (contains *Jhereg, Yendi,* and *Teckla*), Ace Books, 1999.

OTHER

Work represented in anthologies, including *Liavek Anthology,* 1985.

SIDELIGHTS: In the realms of science fiction and fantasy, Steven K. Brust's fans have become accustomed to discovering exciting and strange, yet believable, new worlds. "It is very easy to cheat when writing fantasy—to say, 'This is magic, it just works,'" Brust once commented. "But if one is able to avoid this trap, one has the power to work real magic with the story. For me, magic must be either an alternate set of physical laws, used to express something about how we view our tools, or else a metaphor for Mystery, or the Unknown, or whatever."

Brust's own Hungarian ancestry is evident in many of his books, especially his popular five-book series that chronicles the adventures of Vlad Taltos, a warlock and hired assassin educated by a swordsman and a sorceress, who carries out assignments on behalf of the Dragonlords of the Dragaeran Empire. In *Jhereg* (1983), the first book in the series, young Vlad is left to fend for himself when his father dies. The young man quickly discovers that his early education comes in handy when he has to rely on his own cunning and wit to survive

among the powerful Dragaerans. In his *Booklist* review, Roland Green notes that "the book features intelligent world building" and "good handling of the assassin character."

Brust uses flashbacks to establish the chronology and setting of *Yendi* (1984), the second book in the series, which is actually a prequel. Here, readers discover how Vlad has risen through the ranks from his start as a small-time mobster to his current status as a major criminal. *Yendi* also chronicles the romance and courtship of Vlad and Cawti, the Dagger of the Jhereq, who would become his wife. Roland Green, again writing in *Booklist,* says that *Yendi* "is as intelligent, witty, and generally well written as its predecessor."

The third book in the series, *Teckla* (1986), picks up where the first, *Jhereg,* left off. This time, Vlad becomes involved in a revolution against the Dragaeran Empire along with the Teckla, the Empire's lowest class of citizens. During the rebellion, Vlad finds himself in the role of Cawti's protector, which only exacerbates their rocky relationship. The chronology of the series shifts again as the fourth novel, *Taltos* (1988), goes back to Vlad's early life. Writing about *Taltos* in *Voice of Youth Advocates,* Carolyn Caywood states, "This is one of the four novels of *Taltos* which will be of interest to the fantasy fan who discovers any one of them."

Phoenix, the fifth book in the series, finds Vlad embroiled once again in revolution and upheaval. This novel, which *Voice of Youth Advocates* reviewer Caywood describes as "more somber and more straightforward" than Brust's previous efforts, finds Vlad questioning his life-long beliefs and occupation. Caywood adds that some fans may be disappointed by the introspective nature of this book, but that "readers who are willing to follow the author's lead will discover that his conclusion has added depth to the entire series."

The Dragaeran Empire is not the only fantasy world that Brust envisions in rebellion and turmoil. *To Reign in Hell,* published just after *Jhereg* in 1984, takes place in Heaven where some of the angels are in the midst of their own revolution. "There are many fantasy novels that are thinly disguised Christian metaphors," Brust once stated. "So I wrote *To Reign in Hell,* which is a Christian metaphor that is really a thinly disguised fantasy novel." *Voice of Youth Advocates* reviewer Janet R. Mura applauds *To Reign in Hell* and declares that Brust "has created an engaging story with consummate skill and ability."

Another of Brust's tales derived from Hungarian folklore is *Brokedown Palace* (1985), a story of magic and determination set in a crumbling palace on the banks of the river of Faerie. The plot deals with four brothers who share power in the land of Fenario. Writing in *Voice of Youth Advocates,* Jean Kaufman remarks, "The author creates a land where magic is expected if not really loved." Kaufman goes on to refer to the book as "a sophisticated and rewarding fantasy."

In *The Sun, the Moon, and the Stars* (1987), a retelling of a Hungarian folktale in the idiom of modern fantasy, Brust again writes about brothers. This time, there are three, and they are on a quest to return the sun, moon, and stars to the sky, thereby bringing light to the world. Interestingly, Brust uses the folktale in this case as the framework for a novel depicting the struggle of five young artists to achieve the impossible. A reviewer for *Library Journal* explains how the author utilized his "Fantasist" conventions and generated a book that is "recommended for general fiction and fantasy collections."

With *Cowboy Feng's Space Bar and Grille* (1990), in which a fiendish paranoiac named the Physician decides to destroy his native planet in order to stop the spread of a deadly illness called Hags Disease, Brust proves that he can write science fiction as well as fantasy. The setting is Feng's, a bar and grille that features Jewish cooking, a dance floor, and the ability to travel through time and space. A contributor in *Publishers Weekly* notes that "Brust's fantasy landscape seems truer than the backdrops of many realistic novels" and, in *Voice of Youth Advocates,* Mary R. Voors calls the work "a compelling and humorous science fiction novel."

The Phoenix Guards (1991) is set in Dragaera, the same world that was home to Vlad Taltos in Brust's earlier books. Though a *Publishers Weekly* reviewer notes that this book "shares the wit and exuberance of the *Taltos* books," don't expect to find Vlad here; it is a thousand years earlier. Even its sequel, *Five Hundred Years After* (1994), is set too early for Vlad to make an appearance. "Full of flamboyant action and arch dialogue, this latest adventure in Brust's popular 'Dragaeran' novels pits sword against sorcery in classic swashbuckling style," according to a critic for *Library Journal.*

In *The Gypsy* (1992) a collaborative effort between Brust and Megan Lindholm, a sinister being called Fair Lady reaches out from a parallel universe seeking to extend her shadowy dominion through magic, corrup-

tion, and murder. Opposing her is a cast of magical archetypes fronted by the Gypsy. A reviewer in *Publishers Weekly* calls the book "a powerful and memorable fantasy" and Scott Winnett, writing in *Locus,* notes that it is "an exciting fantasy/mystery crossover," referring to Brust and Lindholm's work as "one of the best jobs yet combining these contrasting genres. The marriage of the two genres is near-perfect."

Brust created something of a puzzle in *Agyar* (1992), an impressively wrought modern vampire/redemption yarn. The novel is presented as a bunch of bits and pieces, like a diary, written by John Agyar, an amateur with time on his hands and an old Royal typewriter, in the abandoned house where he is staying. The pieces of the puzzle are shaped by the author's first-person point of view; the clues lie more in what he doesn't say than what he does. Agyar's secret is pretty obvious, but Brust tantalizes, holding off on a firm confirmation for much of the novel. Eventually the puzzle pieces fall together, as events come to a head. *Locus* reviewer Carolyn Cushman considers *Agyar* "a different vampire novel, a striking contemporary dark fantasy." *Kirkus Reviews* notes that the work is "compact, understated, and highly persuasive. Brust accomplishes with a wry turn of phrase or a small flourish what others never achieve despite hundreds of gory spatters." *Washington Post Book World* reviewer Robert K. J. Killheffer refers to *Agyar* as "good, fast-moving, intelligent fun."

Brust collaborated with Emma Bull for his next book, *Freedom and Necessity* (1997). The story, which a *Publishers Weekly* critic describes as a "romantic mystery-adventure," unfolds in nineteenth-century England after a young man gets a letter from his cousin two months after his supposed death. Writing in *Booklist,* reviewer Roland Green calls *Freedom and Necessity* "an exceptional page-turner" that "deserves a place in every self-respecting fantasy collection."

In his next book, *Dragon* (1998), Brust brings back Vlad Taltos, his most popular protagonist. A prequel to *Yendi* and a sequel to *Jhereg, Dragon* recounts Vlad's early career as an assassin. When Vlad accepts an assignment to search for a stolen sword, his actions start a war between two dragonlords, and Vlad becomes a soldier in one of the dragonlord's armies. *Booklist*'s Green complains that in *Dragon,* "Brust's writing style has changed noticeably," but he concedes that "Vlad's devotees will not be put off by anything so petty as stylistic dissonance." Writing for *Library Journal,* reviewer Jackie Cassada states that *Dragon* "belongs in libraries" where the Vlad Taltos series is popular. A *Publishers*

Weekly reviewer praises *Dragon* and the skill with which Brust incorporates his literary influences into the story: "As always, Brust invests Vlad with the panache of a Dumas musketeer and the colloquial voice of one of Roger Zelazny's Amber heroes. This is a rousing adventure with enough humor, action, and sneaky plot twists to please newcomers as well as longtime fans."

"There appears to be a split in literature between work with strong story values and nothing else, and work that has depth and power but no story values," Brust has said. "The stuff I enjoy reading most can be read as simple entertainment, but rewards more intense reading as well. Since I try to write the sort of stories I like to read, that is what I attempt to do in my own work. Science fiction is a category that allows and even encourages this, WHICH IS ONE OF THE REASONS I WRITE IT."

BIOGRAPHICAL/CRITICAL SOURCES:

PERIODICALS

Analog: Science Fiction/Science Fact, September, 1987, p. 159; December, 1992, p. 161; June, 1993, p. 160.

Booklist, July, 1983, Roland Green, review of *Jhereg,* p. 1387; September 15, 1984, R. Green, review of *Yendi,* p. 108; February 15, 1986, p. 851; April 1, 1987, p. 1180; March, 1988, p. 1098; November 1, 1990, p. 504; August, 1991, pp. 2108, 2110; June 15, 1992, p. 1811; March 1, 1994, pp. 1185, 1188; March 15, 1997, R. Green, review of *Freedom and Necessity,* p. 1231; September 15, 1998, R. Green, review of *Dragon,* p. 205.

Bookwatch, June, 1993, p. 2.

Kirkus Reviews, March 1, 1987, p. 338; September 1, 1991, p. 1121; May 15, 1992, p. 641; December 15, 1992, review of *Agyar,* p. 1517; February 15, 1994, p. 179.

Kliatt, April, 1990, p. 22; November, 1993, p. 14; July, 1994, p. 13.

Library Journal, March 15, 1987, review of *The Sun, the Moon, and the Stars,* p. 93; September 15, 1991, p. 117; February 15, 1993, p. 196; March 15, 1994, review of *Five Hundred Years After,* p. 104. November 15, 1998, Jackie Cassada, review of *Dragon,* p. 95; August, 1999, Jackie Cassada, review of *Jhereg,* p. 148.

Locus, July, 1991, p. 33; October, 1991, p. 44; July, 1992, p. 47; September, 1992, Scott Winnett, review of *The Gypsy,* p. 37; April, 1993, p. 46; August, 1993, p. 44; February, 1994, Carolyn Cushman, review of *Agyar,* p. 75; March, 1994, p. 35; April, 1994, p. 47; May, 1994, p. 47.

Magazine of Fantasy and Science Fiction, December, 1987, p. 35; April, 1999, Michelle West, review of *Dragon,* p. 36.

Publishers Weekly, March 4, 1983, p. 97; June 1, 1984, p. 63; November 22, 1985, p. 50; March 27, 1987, p. 36; December 8, 1989, review of *Cowboy Feng's Space Bar and Grille,* p. 50; August 2, 1991, review of *The Phoenix Guards,* p. 66; May 25, 1992, review of *The Gypsy,* p. 43; February 14, 1994, p. 83; January 27, 1997, review of *Freedom and Necessity,* p. 77; October 19, 1998, review of *Dragon,* p. 60.

Science Fiction Chronicle, December, 1987, p. 46; July, 1990, p. 37; June, 1992, p. 33; December, 1992, p. 38; February, 1994, p. 28; June, 1994, p. 39.

Voice of Youth Advocates, June, 1986, Jean Kaufman, review of *Brokedown Palace,* p. 86; February, 1986, Janet R. Mura, *To Reign in Hell,* p. 393; August, 1988, Carolyn Caywood, review of *Taltos,* p. 137; June, 1990, Mary R. Voors, review of *Cowboy Feng's Space Bar and Grille,* p. 113; December, 1990, p. 269; February, 1991, C. Caywood, review of *Phoenix,* p. 361; April, 1991, p. 10; April, 1992, p. 40; December, 1992, p. 320; February, 1993, p. 345; August, 1994, p. 154; April, 1999, Nancy K. Wallace, review of *Dragon,* p. 45.

Washington Post Book World, May 2, 1993, Robert K. J. Killheffer, review of *Agyar,* p. 8.

OTHER

The Dream Café, http://www.dreamcafe.com/ (May 10, 2001).

*　　　*　　　*

BRYANT, James C(ecil), Jr. 1931-

PERSONAL: Born October 21, 1931, in Lake Wales, FL; son of James Cecil and Mary Lou (McCranie) Bryant; married Marion Lois Carnett, June 19, 1955; children: David, Albert. *Ethnicity:* "Scotch-Irish." *Education:* Stetson University, B.A., 1954; Southern Baptist Theological Seminary, B.D., 1958; University of Miami, M.A., 1961; University of Kentucky, Ph.D., 1967; Brooklyn Center, Long Island University, graduate study.

ADDRESSES: Home—1470 Leafmore Pl., Decatur, GA 30033. *Office*—President's Office, Mercer University, Macon, GA 31207. *E-mail*—bryant_jc@mercer.edu.

CAREER: Ordained minister of Baptist Church, 1952; pastor in Miami, FL, 1958-63, Corinth, KY, 1963-67, Quincy, FL, 1968-69, and Atlanta, GA, 1975-1992; Florida State University, Tallahassee, assistant professor of English, 1967-73, taught at Overseas Study Center in Florence, Italy, 1969-70; Mercer University, Atlanta, GA, associate professor, 1973-76, head of Humanities Division, 1973-76, professor of English, 1976-92; Mercer University, Macon, GA, currently university historian and special assistant to the president. Atlanta Baptist History Committee, chair, 1980—; Atlanta Union Mission, member of advisory board; Old Guard of the Gate City Guard, member, 1990—; Yaarab Shrine Temple, member. *Military service:* U.S. Naval Reserve, 1948-52.

MEMBER: American Association of University Professors, College English Association, Modern Language Association of America, Renaissance Society of America, Council of Authors and Journalists (chair, board of trustees, 1984-90), German-American Society (member of board of directors, 1976), South Atlantic Modern Language Association, Southeastern Renaissance Conference, Georgia Baptist Historical Society (president, 1990-93), Georgia Writers, Inc. (founding member, 1994; member of advisory board, 1998—), Atlanta Historical Society, Atlanta Writers Club (second vice president, 1974-75; president, 1975-76), Atlanta Press Club, Rotary Club (member of board of directors, 1977), Scottish Rite Masons (KCCH), Sons of the American Revolution (treasurer and vice president, 1971, 1972, 1973), Lake Toxaway Country Club (North Carolina), Landings at Trillium (North Carolina), Oglethorpe Club (Savannah, GA), Chatham Club (Savannah), Capital City Club (historian), Druid Hills Golf Club (historian).

AWARDS, HONORS: Florida Heritage Award from Colonial Dames, 1972, for *Indian Springs: The Story of a Pioneer Church;* Dixie Council of Authors and Journalists, award for fiction, 1973, award for biography, 1975, for *The Morningside Man: A Biography of James Pickett Wesberry,* Special Award, 1983; fellow of International Biographical Institute, Cambridge University, 1986; Franklin M. Garret Award in Atlanta History, 1998, for a history of the Fox Theater.

WRITINGS:

New Columbus and the Baptist Church, privately printed, 1965.
Indian Springs: The Story of a Pioneer Church, Florida State University Press (Tallahassee, FL), 1972.

Smooth Runs the Water, Broadman (Nashville, TN), 1973.
The Morningside Man: A Biography of James Pickett Wesberry, Morningside Baptist Church (Atlanta, GA), 1975.
(With Charlie Brown) *Charlie Brown Remembers Atlanta: Memoirs of a Public Man as Told to James C. Bryant,* R. L. Bryan Co. (Columbia, SC), 1982.
Tudor Drama and Religious Controversy, Mercer University Press (Macon, GA), 1984.
The Atlanta Baptist Association, Atlanta Baptist Association (Atlanta, GA), 1984.
Mountain Island in Owen County, Kentucky: The Settlers and Their Churches, Owen County Historical Society, 1986.
James McDonald: Pioneer Missionary to East Florida, Florida Baptist Historical Society (DeLand, FL), 1986.
Capital City Club: The First One Hundred Years, 1883-1983, The Club (Atlanta, GA), 1991.
A Gift for Giving: The Story of Lamar Rich Plunkett, Mercer University Press (Macon, GA), 1993.
Druid Hills Golf Club: The Story and the People, 1912-1997, [Atlanta, GA], 1998.
The Miradov Room: Memories of an Era, 1939-1998, [Atlanta, GA], 1999.

Also contributor to periodicals, including *Atlanta Journal-Constitution, American Literature, English Studies, Event, Guideposts, Renaissance Papers, Viewpoints, Savannah, Scottish Rite Journal,* and *United Daughters of the Confederacy.* Literary specialist, *Youth in Action,* 1972-73; editor, *Basharat,* 1977—.

WORK IN PROGRESS: Mercer University History, a five-year project.

*   *   *

BURCHFIELD, R(obert) W(illiam) 1923-

PERSONAL: Born January 27, 1923, in Wanganui, New Zealand; immigrated to England, 1949; son of Frederick (an electrician) and Mary (Blair) Burchfield; married Ethel May Yates, July 2, 1949 (divorced, 1976); married Elizabeth Austen Knight, November 5, 1976; children: (first marriage) Jennifer Catherine, Jonathan Robert, Elizabeth Jane. *Education:* Attended Wanganui Technical College, 1934-39; Victoria University of Wellington, M.A., 1948; Oxford University, Magdalen College, B.A., 1951, M.A., 1955. *Religion:* Protestant.

Avocational interests: Rugby (member of New Zealand Army team in Italy, 1945), travel in the United States, Europe, New Zealand, and the Far East.

ADDRESSES: Home—The Barn, 14 The Green, Sutton Courtenay, Oxfordshire OX14 4AE, England.

CAREER: Oxford University, Oxford, England: Magdalen College, junior lecturer in English language and literature, 1952-53; Christ Church, lecturer in English language and literature, 1953-57; St. Peter's College, lecturer, 1955-63, fellow and tutor in English language and literature, 1963-79, senior research fellow, 1979-1990, fellow emeritus, 1990—. Oxford University Press, chief editor of "Oxford English Dictionaries," 1971-84. *Military service:* Royal New Zealand Artillery, 1941-46; served in Italy; became sergeant.

MEMBER: Early English Text Society (honorary secretary, 1955-68; member of council, 1968-80), American Academy of Arts and Sciences (foreign honorary member).

AWARDS, HONORS: Rhodes scholarship, 1949-51; Commander, Order of the British Empire, 1975; D.Litt. from University of Liverpool, 1978, and Victoria University of Wellington, 1983; City of Wanganui, New Zealand, Freedom Prize, 1986; Shakespeare Prize, FVS Foundation, Hamburg, Germany, 1994.

WRITINGS:

(With C. T. Onions and G. W. S. Friedrichsen) *The Oxford Dictionary of English Etymology,* Oxford University Press (New York, NY), 1966.
(Editor) *A Supplement to the Oxford English Dictionary,* Oxford University Press (New York, NY), Volume 1: *A-G,* 1972, Volume 2: *H-N,* 1976, Volume 3: *O-Scz,* 1982, Volume 4: *Se-Z,* 1986.
The Quality of Spoken English on BBC Radio, 1979.
The Spoken Word, BBC Publications, 1981.
The Spoken Language as an Art Form, 1981.
(Editor) William Cobbett, *A Grammar of the English Language,* Oxford University Press (New York, NY), 1984.
The English Language, Oxford University Press (New York, NY), 1985.
(Editor) *The New Zealand Pocket Oxford Dictionary,* Oxford University Press (New York, NY), 1986.
Studies in Lexicography, Oxford University Press (New York, NY), 1987.

Unlocking the English Language, Faber (London, England), 1989.
Points of View: Aspects of Present-Day English, Oxford University Press (New York, NY), 1992.
The Cambridge History of the English Language, Volume V: *English in Britain and Overseas,* 1994.
(Editor) H. W. Fowler, *The New Fowler's Modern English Usage,* third edition, Oxford University Press (New York, NY), 1996.
Contributor to *Medium Aevum, Essays and Studies, Notes and Queries,* and other journals. Co-editor, *Notes and Queries,* 1959-62.

SIDELIGHTS: With the printing of the fourth and final volume of *A Supplement to the Oxford English Dictionary,* lexicographer R. W. Burchfield's twenty-nine-year effort to update the reference publication ended. The length of the project was due, in part, to the Oxford convention of tracing every new English word back to its first published use—an exhausting task considering the more than 62,000 new entries in the book. "Volume four was the most wonderful book of all because it took me to the end," Burchfield is quoted as saying in *Newsweek.* "I've been running at the speed of electricity just to get there in thirty years."

Peter Ackroyd admitted that such an undertaking is not without its flaws. "Dictionaries may be established upon the idea of 'true meaning,' but this is just as much an illusion as 'correct English,'" he wrote in his London *Times* review. "Every time a word is used, its meaning is changed; every sentence which is uttered at the same time modifies syntax." However, Ackroyd viewed the supplement as "a project of a different kind—a monument of scholarship rather than of semiology, and one that provides a permanent record of the language of our time." Burchfield's augmentation is the last of the Oxford dictionaries to be printed in the old-fashioned hot-metal process; future editions will be stored on accessible databases. Ackroyd noted that *A Supplement to the Oxford English Dictionary* "brings to a conclusion an enterprise that will be remembered as long as the language itself survives."

Fowler's Modern English Usage was first published in 1926 and revised in 1965 by Ernest Cowers. Erik Wensberg said in the *Wall Street Journal* that Burchfield's third edition, *The New Fowler's Modern English Usage,* "pulls a much-loved and slightly eccentric work out of the charm of the past and into the whirlwind of today's language." Burchfield uses modern words in his advice on usage, word choice, grammar, style, and syntax. He also includes information about the differences in

American and British usage. A *Booklist* reviewer pointed out that Burchfield "provides new usage for words such as gender (Fowler said it was only a grammatical term)."

James Bowman wrote in *National Review* that "in Burchfield's world it is all right to know the old rules (and most of them he sets out under their appropriate entries), just so long as we pretend that we don't know or care much about them." Bowman concluded by saying that "ultimately, neither elegance nor error are to be wished away by no-fault grammarians such as Burchfield. I imagine him as a well-meaning decolonizer who leaves behind him a humane and enlightened constitution even though he knows that corrupt and bloodthirsty natives will tear it up within a week of his departure. At least he has done his bit. His hands are clean. But neither has he made life any better, or shown anyone how to write well."

Christopher Lehmann-Haupt wrote in the *New York Times Book Review* that "at first, a sampling of this reviewer's pet peeves seemed reassuring. Under the entry 'I,' Mr. Burchfield writes: 'Between you and I must be condemned at once. Anyone who uses it now lives in a grammarless cavern in which no distinction is recognized between a grammatical object and a subject.' Elsewhere, for example in his comments on 'black English,' on 'chair, chairperson,' on 'split infinitive,' and on 'hopefully' as a 'sentence adverb,' his tolerance of change seems both reasoned and admirable. But the more you sample, the more you are troubled by the degree to which tolerance lapses into passive acceptance in the face of regrettable change."

An *Economist* reviewer wrote that Burchfield's book "has a far stronger claim to be called a 'dictionary of usage' than Fowler had. . . . In sum, there is good reason for both books. The 1926 Fowler is already a period piece, though no one has ever gone wrong by taking its advice. The same, no doubt, will in time be true of 'Burchfield'—as, perhaps, by 2097 the publisher of its latest revision will dare to call it."

BIOGRAPHICAL/CRITICAL SOURCES:

PERIODICALS

Booklist, March 1, 1997, review of *The New Fowler's Modern English Usage,* p. 1195.
Chicago Tribune, June 22, 1986.
Economist, February 1, 1997, review of *The New Fowler's Modern English Usage,* p. 87.
Incorporated Linguist, summer, 1984.
Library Journal, March 15, 1997, Neal Wyatt, review of *The New Fowler's Modern English Usage,* p. 57.
Los Angeles Times Book Review, March 17, 1985.
National Review, February 10, 1997, James Bowman, review of *The New Fowler's Modern English Usage,* p. 52.
Newsweek, June 2, 1986.
New York, December 23, 1996, Christopher Bonanos, review of *The New Fowler's Modern English Usage,* p. 190.
New Yorker, December 23, 1996, John Updike, review of *The New Fowler's Modern English Usage,* p. 142.
New York Times Book Review, December 26, 1996, Christopher Lehmann-Haupt, "To Praise Fowler and to Bury Him."
Rising Generation (Tokyo), January 1, 1973; February 1, 1973; March 1, 1973.
Times (London), January 24, 1985; July 16, 1987; October 28, 1996.
Times Literary Supplement, March 22, 1985; May 9, 1986; July 17, 1987.
Wall Street Journal, December 2, 1996, Erik Wensberg, review of *The New Fowler's Modern English Usage,* p. A18.*

C

CARROL, Shana
See NEWCOMB, Kerry

*   *   *

CHANG, Raymond 1939-

PERSONAL: Born March 6, 1939, in Hong Kong; naturalized U.S. citizen; son of Junsheng (a banker) and Jufen (a homemaker; maiden name, Li) Chang; married Margaret A. Scrogin (a librarian and writer), August 3, 1968; children: Elizabeth Hope. *Ethnicity:* "Chinese." *Education:* University of London, B.S. (with first class honors), 1962; Yale University, M.S., 1963, Ph.D., 1966.

ADDRESSES: Home—146 Forest Rd., Williamstown, MA 01267. *Office*—Department of Chemistry, Williams College, Williamstown, MA 01267. *E-mail*—raymond. chang@williams.edu.

CAREER: Washington University, St. Louis, MO, post-doctoral research fellow, 1966-67; Hunter College of the City University of New York, New York, NY, assistant professor of chemistry, 1967-68; Williams College, Williamstown, MA, assistant professor, 1968-73, associate professor, 1974-78, professor of chemistry, 1978—, Halford R. Clark Professor of Natural Sciences, 1989—, chair of department, 1993-95. University of California, Lawrence Radiation Laboratory, visiting scientist at Laboratory of Chemical Biodynamics, 1972-73; Stanford University, visiting professor, 1977-78; Amherst College, visiting scientist, 1981. American Chemical Society, member of examination committees for physical chemistry, 1979-83, and general chemistry, 1983-85; Olympiad Examinations Task Force, member, 1989-91.

MEMBER: American Chemical Society, American Association for the Advancement of Science, Sigma Xi.

AWARDS, HONORS: Speaking of Chinese was included on the New York Public Library's list of Books for the Teen Age, 1980, 1981, and 1982; Parents' Choice Honor Book award, 1990, for *In the Eye of War,* and 1999, for *Da Wei's Treasure;* outstanding children's book citation, *Parenting,* 1994, for *The Cricket Warrior;* Selectors' Choice, *Elementary School Library Collection,* 2000, for *The Beggar's Magic.*

WRITINGS:

WITH WIFE, MARGARET A. CHANG

Speaking of Chinese, Norton (New York, NY), 1978, 3rd edition, 2001.
In the Eye of War, Margaret K. McElderry Books/Macmillan (New York, NY), 1990.
The Cricket Warrior, illustrated by Warwick Hutton, Margaret K. McElderry Books/Macmillan (New York, NY), 1994.
The Beggar's Magic, illustrated by David Johnson, Margaret K. McElderry Books/Simon & Schuster (New York, NY), 1997.
Da Wei's Treasure, illustrated by Lori McElrath-Eslick, Margaret K. McElderry Books/Simon & Schuster (New York, NY), 1999.

OTHER

Basic Principles of Spectroscopy, McGraw-Hill (New York, NY), 1971.
Physical Chemistry with Applications to Biological Systems, 2nd edition, Macmillan (New York, NY), 1981.

General Chemistry, Random House (New York, NY), 1986.

(With W. Tikkanen) *The Top Fifty Industrial Chemicals,* Random House (New York, NY), 1988.

(With Jerry S. Faughn and Jon Turk) *Physical Science,* Saunders College Publishing (Philadelphia, PA), 1995.

Chemistry, 6th edition, W. C. Brown/McGraw-Hill (Dubuque, IA), 1998.

(With M. Ashour-Abdalla) *CyberChem: A CD-ROM for General Chemistry,* W. C. Brown/McGraw-Hill (Dubuque, IA), 1998.

Essential Chemistry, 2nd edition, W. C. Brown/McGraw-Hill (Dubuque, IA), 2000.

Physical Chemistry for the Chemical and Biological Sciences, University Science Books (Sausalito, CA), 2000.

Contributor of about forty articles to chemistry journals. Member of editorial board, *Chemical Educator.*

WORK IN PROGRESS: Chemistry books.

SIDELIGHTS: Raymond Chang's wife, Margaret A. Chang, told *CA:* "Chang's family moved to Hong Kong from their home in Shanghai to escape the 1937 Japanese invasion of China. Chang was born in the British Crown Colony, the youngest son of a family that already included nine children. Not long after the Japanese marched into Hong Kong on Christmas Day, 1941, the Changs moved back to Shanghai, where they lived under Japanese occupation. In 1949 they returned to Hong Kong, leaving Shanghai for good.

"Because of his family's background and the many relocations, Chang became fluent in several Chinese dialects. At home he heard his mother's dialect, Western Mandarin. He talked with his playmates in Shanghainese, while in school they all learned Peking Mandarin, the national standard for spoken language. In Hong Kong he had to learn a completely different spoken language, the Cantonese dialect of southern China. Fortunately for him, the same written language unites all of China.

"At the age of seventeen, Chang followed his sister to London for what he thought would be a few years of study in the West. He did not return to Hong Kong for seventeen years, and then it was only for a brief visit. On the boat that took him to England, Chang soon realized that the English he had learned as a Chinese schoolboy was inadequate for everyday communication and totally useless for reading the dinner menu, which was all in French! Once in London, he set about improving his English and now speaks so fluently that most people assume he was born in the United States.

"After a couple of years in preparatory school, Chang entered the University of London to study chemistry, and he graduated with first class honors. Partly because three of his sisters had married and moved to the United States, he decided to continue his education in America. He earned his Ph.D., married an American, and moved to a scenic corner of New England to become a chemistry professor at Williams College.

"Since for many years he was the only Asian on the faculty, Chang often went outside his field of chemistry to explain Chinese language and culture to curious students. For several years he taught a popular winter study course, a one-month introduction to Chinese language and calligraphy. When he tried to gather background materials for his course, he found no book on the Chinese language that was written for the general reader, the layman without a background in linguistics or Sinology.

"Though he was already the author of two chemistry books, he asked me to help him write a popular introduction to the Chinese language, one that people interested in China could read in bed without a pencil. *Speaking of Chinese* was the result. Chang drew on his boyhood experiences to select the proverbs, describe Chinese grammar, and write the calligraphy used in the text.

"In 1982 Chang led a group of Williams College students and alumni on a winter study tour of the People's Republic of China. It was his first trip home in more than thirty years. In Shanghai, he was amazed by the vast numbers of people, all so healthy and well-clothed. His old neighborhood looked far more crowded than he remembered. His childhood home, shabby but still standing, housed three families.

"Like many Chinese professionals who have returned to their native land for a visit, he found the territory familiar, but he knew that the country of his childhood was no longer his."

Chang drew on the memory of his years in Shanghai when he and his wife wrote *In the Eye of War,* a novel for children about a Chinese family in occupied

Shanghai. Also with his wife he wrote *The Cricket Warrior,* a retelling of a favorite childhood story. Two other picture books followed. *The Beggar's Magic* was drawn from the same collection of Chinese folk tales as *The Cricket Warrior. Da Wei's Treasure* was adapted from a story Chang's mother told her family in Shanghai.

BIOGRAPHICAL/CRITICAL SOURCES:

PERIODICALS

Focus on Asian Studies, autumn, 1978, review of *Speaking of Chinese,* p. 40.
Horn Book, June, 1979, review of *Speaking of Chinese.*
Scientific American, December, 1978, review of *Speaking of Chinese.*

* * *

CHAUDHURI, Amit 1962-

PERSONAL: Born May 15, 1962, in Calcutta, India; son of Nages Chandra (a corporate executive) and Bijoya (a homemaker and singer; maiden name, Nandi Majumdar) Chaudhuri; married Rinka Khastgir, December 12, 1991. *Education:* University of London, B.A. (with honors), 1986; Balliol College, Oxford, D.Phil., 1993. *Religion:* Hindu. *Avocational interests:* North Indian classical music (vocal).

ADDRESSES: Home—6 Sunny Park, Flat 10, 8th Floor, Calcutta, India 700019. *Agent*—Derek Johns, A. P. Watt Ltd., 20 John St., London W1, England. *E-mail*—amitchaudhuri@hotmail.com.

CAREER: Writer. Oxford University, Oxford, England creative arts fellow at Wolfson College, 1992-95; Cambridge University, Cambridge, England, Leverhulme fellow in English, 1997-99.

AWARDS, HONORS: Betty Trask Award, Society of Authors, 1991, for *A Strange and Sublime Address;* K. Blundell Trust award, 1993, for writing a second novel; Commonwealth Writers' Prize for Best First Book (Eurasia), for *A Strange and Sublime Address;* Encore Prize, Society of Authors, 1994, for *Afternoon Raag;* book award for fiction, *Los Angeles Times,* 2000, for *Freedom Song;* Arts Council writing award.

WRITINGS:

A Strange and Sublime Address (novella and short stories; also see below), Heinemann (London, England), 1991.
Afternoon Raag (novel; also see below), Heinemann (London, England), 1993.
Freedom Song (novel; also see below), Picador (London, England), 1998.
A Strange and Sublime Address [and] *Afternoon Raag* [and] *Freedom Song,* Knopf (New York, NY), 1999.
A New World (novel), Knopf (New York, NY), 2000.

Work represented in anthologies, including *The Oxford Companion to Twentieth-century Poetry,* Oxford University Press (New York, NY). Contributor to periodicals, including *New Yorker, Granta, New Republic, London Review of Books, Times Literary Supplement,* and *London.*

SIDELIGHTS: Amit Chaudhuri, who was born in Calcutta, India, raised in Bombay, and received university education in England, has drawn attention from critics for his ability to write with affection about his native land. *A Strange and Sublime Address,* which met with critical acclaim and won Chaudhuri the Betty Trask Award (regularly bestowed to first-time novelists under the age of thirty-five), is comprised of a novella and short stories. The 35,000-word novella tells of Sandeep, a ten-year-old boy living a lonely life in Bombay, who visits his uncle for the holidays in Calcutta. Although Chaudhuri reportedly denies that the novella is narrowly autobiographical, *Times of India* reviewer Mandira Sen observed that it does bear the imprint of the author's own life. "As a child, growing up in Bombay, [Chaudhuri] too visited relatives in Calcutta," Sen commented. However, the critic pointed out that Chaudhuri is primarily "interested in interweaving what he perceives as culture and place, to put it together, rather the way a painting is." Throughout *A Strange and Sublime Address,* Chaudhuri's lyrical prose bears the imprint of the visual arts. As reported in *Times of India,* Chaudhuri acknowledges that painting has shaped his work. The author has been especially influenced by Indian folk art, which he believes has retained certain aspects of cultural integrity that colonialism sought to abolish.

Sensibility itself is at the heart of Chaudhuri's novella. *A Strange and Sublime Address* evokes Sandeep's childhood, painting a panoramic picture of everyday life within his large family. "The days drift into each other, the children play ceaselessly, are caught, oiled, and bathed by one of the aunts. Mealtimes are leisurely affairs, each moment spent savouring the sensual delights of food," remarked Kaveri Ponnapa in *Times of India.* The reviewer added that this accumulated detail, expressed in Chaudhuri's imagistic prose, conjures the "enigmatic city" of Calcutta. In *Vogue,* John Lanchester noted that the "most original, most dramatic, and most impressive feature" of the novella is "that nothing whatsoever happen[s] in it—nothing *at all.* . . . The evocation of the routine . . . strikes me still as an extraordinary thing to have brought off." The stories in *A Strange and Sublime Address,* which were considered "slight" by Mark Wormald in *Times Literary Supplement,* impressed Ponnapa in *Times of India.* The critic found the tales "seamless, atmospheric, and rich in imagery" and stated that Chaudhuri "excels in transfixing a single, evanescent incident."

Afternoon Raag, Chaudhuri's second novel, is, according to critics, like its predecessor—filled with rich, textured language and devoid of conventional plot. Here Chaudhuri's narrator, an Indian man attending Oxford University, tries unsuccessfully to strike up a relationship with two female students. The book conveys such sentiments as a longing for home and a distinct sensitivity to detail. In *Afternoon Raag,* Chaudhuri describes "the abidingness of an English interior" and a foreign student's attachment to a room as "one's first friend . . . a relationship that is natural and unthinking, its air and light what one shares with one's thoughts." Like Amitav Ghosh and Sunetra Gupta, two of Chaudhuri's Indian literary contemporaries, Chaudhuri demonstrates—in the words of Aamer Hussein of the *Times Literary Supplement*—"an untainted pride in his culture and an unambiguous attitude to the hazards and vagaries of the migrant's situation."

BIOGRAPHICAL/CRITICAL SOURCES:

BOOKS

Chaudhuri, Amit, *Afternoon Raag,* Heinemann (London, England), 1993.

PERIODICALS

Guardian (London), June 29, 1993.
London Review of Books, August 19, 1993.
Observer (London), June 13, 1993, p. 62.
Times (London), August 22, 1993.

Times Literary Supplement, August 23, 1991, Mark Wormald, review of *A Strange and Sublime Address,* p. 21; June 18, 1993, Aamer Hussein, review of *Afternoon Raag,* p. 23.
Times of India, September 23, 1991, Mandira Sen and Kaveri Ponnapa, reviews of *A Strange and Sublime Address.*
Vogue, July, 1991, John Lanchester, review of *A Strange and Sublime Address.*

*   *   *

COLLINS, David R(aymond) 1940-

PERSONAL: Born February 29, 1940, in Marshalltown, IA; son of Raymond A. (an educator) and Mary Elizabeth (a secretary; maiden name, Brecht) Collins. *Education:* Western Illinois University, B.S., 1962, M.S., 1966. *Politics:* Democrat. *Religion:* Roman Catholic. *Avocational interests:* Lecturing, reading, tennis, bridge, people.

ADDRESSES: Home—3403 45th St., Moline, IL 61265. *E-mail*—kimseuss@aol.com.

CAREER: Woodrow Wilson Junior High School, Moline, IL, English teacher, 1962-83; Moline Senior High School, Moline, English teacher, 1983-97. Friends of the Moline Public Library, president, 1965-67; Moline Library Board, member, 1990-93; Rock Island County Historical Society Board, member, 1998—; Comm University Board, member, 1998—; Quest College Board, member, 1999—.

MEMBER: National Education Association (life member), Children's Reading Roundtable, Society of Children's Book Writers and Illustrators (charter member), Authors Guild, Authors League of America, Juvenile Forum (president, 1975—), Writers' Studio (president, 1968-72), Mississippi Valley Writers Conference (founder; director, 1974—), Illinois Education Association, Illinois Congress of Parents and Teachers (life member), Illinois State Historical Society (life member), Blackhawk Division of Teachers of English (president, 1967-68), Quad City Writers Club, Quad City Arts Council, Midwest Writing Center (president, 1999—), Phi Delta Kappa, Kappa Delta Pi, Delta Sigma Pi.

AWARDS, HONORS: Outstanding Juvenile Writer Award, Indiana University, 1970; Judson College Writing Award, 1971; Writer of the Year Awards, Writers'

Studio, 1971, and Quad City Writers Club, 1972; Alumni Achievement Award, Western Illinois University, 1973; Outstanding Illinois Educator Award, 1976; Junior Literary Guild Award, 1981; Midwest Writing Award, 1982; Gold Key Award, 1983; Catholic Press Writing Award, 1983; National Catholic Book Award, 1984, for *Thomas Merton: Monk with a Mission;* Veterans of Foreign Wars Teacher of the Year Award, 1987-88; Distinguished Alumni Award, Western Illinois University, 1993; Cornelia Meigs Literary Award, 1990; Louise Messer Young Authors Prize, 1994; American Legion Illinois Teacher of the Year, 1994.

WRITINGS:

FOR CHILDREN

Great American Nurses, Messner, 1971.

Walt Disney's Surprise Christmas Present, illustrated by Vance Locke, Broadman (Nashville, TN), 1971.

Football Running Backs: Three Ground Gainers, Garrard (Champaign, IL), 1976.

Illinois Women: Born to Serve, DeSaulniers, 1976.

A Spirit of Giving, illustrated by Susan Hall, Broadman (Nashville, TN), 1978.

The Wonderful Story of Jesus, illustrated by Don Kueker and Bill Hoyer, Concordia, 1980.

(With Evelyn Witter) *Notable Illinois Women,* Quest, 1982.

The Special Guest, Broadman (Nashville, TN), 1984.

Not Only Dreamers, Brethren (Elgin, IL), 1986.

The Greatest Life Ever Lived, Brethren (Elgin, IL), 1991.

Attack on Fort McHenry, Rigby Educational, 1995.

(With Rich Johnson and Bessie Pierce) *Moline: City of Mills,* Arcadia (Charleston, SC), 1998.

(With Rich Johnson, Bessie Pierce, and Bj Elsner) *Rock Island: All-American City,* Arcadia (Charleston, SC), 1999.

Bettendorf: "Iowa's Most Exciting City," Arcadia (Charleston, SC), 2000.

Davenport: Jewel of the Mississippi, Arcadia (Charleston, SC), 2000.

FOR CHILDREN; FICTION

Kim Soo and His Tortoise, illustrated by Alix Cohen, Lion, 1970.

Joshua Poole Hated School, illustrated by Cliff Johnston, Broadman (Nashville, TN), 1976.

If I Could, I Would, illustrated by Kelly Oechsli, Garrard, 1979.

Joshua Poole and Sunrise, illustrated by Cliff Johnston, Broadman (Nashville, TN), 1980.

The One Bad Thing about Birthdays, illustrated by David Wiesner, Harcourt (New York, NY), 1981.

Joshua Poole and the Special Flowers, illustrated by Cliff Johnston, Broadman (Nashville, TN), 1981.

Ride a Red Dinosaur, illustrated by Larry Nolte, Milliken (St. Louis, MO), 1987.

Probo's Amazing Trunk, Modern Curriculum (Cleveland, OH), 1987.

Ara's Amazing Spinning Wheel, Modern Curriculum (Cleveland, OH), 1987.

Ursi's Amazing Fur Coat, illustrated by Ed Beyer, Modern Curriculum (Cleveland, OH), 1987.

Leo's Amazing Paws and Jaws, illustrated by Jim Theodore, Modern Curriculum (Cleveland, OH), 1987.

Ceb's Amazing Tail, Modern Curriculum (Cleveland, OH), 1987.

Hali's Amazing Wings, Modern Curriculum (Cleveland, OH), 1987.

The Wisest Answer, illustrated by Deborah G. Wilson, Milliken (St. Louis, MO), 1988.

Grandfather Woo Comes to School, Milliken (St. Louis, MO), 1988.

FOR CHILDREN; BIOGRAPHY

Linda Richards: First American Trained Nurse, Garrard, 1973.

Harry S. Truman: People's President, Garrard, 1975.

Abraham Lincoln, Mott Media (Milford, MI), 1976.

George Washington Carver, Mott Media (Milford, MI), 1977.

Charles Lindbergh: Hero Pilot, Garrard, 1978.

George Meany: Mr. Labor, St. Anthony Messenger, 1981.

Dorothy Day: Catholic Worker, St. Anthony Messenger, 1981.

Thomas Merton: Monk with a Mission, St. Anthony Messenger, 1982.

Francis Scott Key, Mott Media (Milford, MI), 1982.

Johnny Appleseed, illustrated by Joe Van Severen, Mott Media (Milford, MI), 1983.

Florence Nightingale, Mott Media (Milford, MI), 1983.

The Long-legged Schoolteacher: Lyndon Baines Johnson, from the Texas Hill Country to the White House, Eakin (Austin, TX), 1985.

Country Artist: The Story of Beatrix Potter, illustrated by Karen Ritz, Carolrhoda (Minneapolis, MN), 1988.

To the Point: The Story of E. B. White, illustrated by Amy Johnson, Carolrhoda (Minneapolis, MN), 1988.

Harry S. Truman: Our 33rd President, Garrett Educational (Ada, OK), 1988.

Grover Cleveland: Our 22nd and 24th President, Garrett Educational (Ada, OK), 1988.

Woodrow Wilson: Our 28th President, Garrett Educational (Ada, OK), 1989.

Zachary Taylor: Our 12th President, Garrett Educational (Ada, OK), 1989.

Noah Webster—God's Master of Words, Mott Media (Milford, MI), 1989.

Jane Addams, Warner, 1989.

Clara Barton, Warner, 1989.

James Buchanan: Our 15th President, Garrett Educational (Ada, OK), 1990.

William McKinley: Our 25th President, Garrett Educational (Ada, OK), 1990.

Gerald Ford: Our 38th President, Garrett Educational (Ada, OK), 1990.

Pioneer Plowman: A Story about John Deere, illustrated by Steve Michaels, Carolrhoda (Minneapolis, MN), 1990.

Tales for Hard Times: A Story about Charles Dickens, illustrated by David Mataya, Carolrhoda (Minneapolis, MN), 1991.

J. R. R. Tolkien—Master of Fantasy, illustrated by William Heagy, Lerner (Minneapolis, MN), 1991.

Lee Iacocca—Chrysler's Good Fortune, Garrett Educational (Ada, OK), 1992.

Philip Knight—Running with Nike, Garrett Educational (Ada, OK), 1992.

Black Rage: The Story of Malcolm X, Dillon (New York, NY), 1992.

M-A-R-K T-W-A-I-N! A Story about Samuel Clemens, Carolrhoda (Minneapolis, MN), 1993.

Tad Lincoln: White House Wildcat, Discovery Enterprises, 1994.

Shattered Dreams: The Story of Mary Todd Lincoln, Morgan Reynolds (Greensboro, NC), 1994.

Arthur Ashe: Against the Wind, Dillon (New York, NY), 1994.

Eng and Chang: The Original Siamese Twins, Dillon (New York, NY), 1994.

William Jefferson Clinton: Our 42nd President, Garrett Educational (Ada, OK), 1995.

Farmworker's Friend: A Story about Caesar Chavez, Carolrhoda (Minneapolis, MN), 1995.

Casimir Pulaski: Soldier on Horseback, illustrated by Larry Nolte, Pelican (Gretna, LA), 1995.

You're Never Alone: The Thomas Merton Story, Pauline Books and Media (Boston, MA), 1996.

Got a Penny? The Dorothy Day Story, Pauline Books and Media (Boston, MA), 1997.

Beyond the Clouds: A Story about Christa Mcauliffe, Pauline Books and Media (Boston, MA), 1997.

Bix Beiderbecke: Jazz Age Genius, Morgan Reynolds, 1998.

Tiger Woods: Golf Superstar, illustrated by Larry Nolte, Pelican, 1998.

Magnificent Failure: The Story of Father Solanus Casey, Pauline Books and Media (Boston, MA), 1998.

Write a Book for Me: The Story of Marguerite Henry, Morgan Reynolds, 1999.

Tiger Woods: Golfing Champion, illustrated by Larry Nolte, Pelican, 1999.

Clara Barton: Angel of the Battlefield, Barbour, 1999.

Washington Irving: Storyteller for a New Nation, Morgan Reynolds, 2000.

(With Kris Bergren) *Ishi: The Last of His People,* illustrated by Kelly Welch, Morgan Reynolds, 2000.

Shooting Star: A Story about Michael Jordan, Eakin, 2000.

Servant to the Slaves: The Story of Henriette Delille, Pauline Books and Media (Boston, MA), 2000.

Huey P. Long: Mr. Louisiana, Pelican, 2001.

Dr. Shinichi Suzuki: Teaching Music from the Heart, Morgan Reynolds, 2001.

OTHER

Also contributor to periodicals, including *Catholic Boy, Catholic Miss, Child Life, Highlights for Children, Junior Discoveries, Modern Woodman, Plays,* and *Vista.*

WORK IN PROGRESS: A biography of John Paul Jones; an adult novel; completion of a series of four books about the Quad Cities.

SIDELIGHTS: David R. Collins is the author of nearly one hundred titles for young readers, books that both "entertain and educate," in the words of the author. Collins has written mostly in the field of biography and has tackled subjects ranging from President Harry S. Truman to basketball superstar Michael Jordan and tennis great Arthur Ashe. His books have looked at famous social activists from Caesar Chavez to Malcolm X, and from phenomena such as the Siamese twins Chang and Eng to literary greats such as Charles Dickens and Washington Irving.

Collins, a long-time English teacher, has a healthy respect for words and for his audience. "Children are curious," Collins once commented. "Their minds [are] open and flexible. A child is eager to enjoy new adventures. Anyone choosing to write for young readers faces an exciting challenge and a great responsibility. He must remember that his words and ideas may have a lasting effect on his reader's imagination, personality, even his entire character. Young readers deserve the best in reading."

Collins grew up in "a world of books and readers," as he once commented, and early on "entertained thoughts about becoming an author." He also had dreams of becoming a professional football player, but by the time he reached high school he realized that his physical stature was more in tune with that of a jockey than a pulling guard. He decided to go into teaching instead, as his father and older brother had, though he continued working on the school newspaper even in college. After beginning his teaching career, he found that his time for personal writing was greatly curtailed. "I was busy working with my students on their own writing skills." It was one of Collins's students who actually got him started writing again. A seventh grader challenged him on a writing assignment he had given the class. The young student dared Collins to do the assignment himself, and the teacher took up the challenge. "I had motivated the group by telling them how 'fun' and 'exciting' the writing project would be," Collins said. "I discovered it was WORK and TEDIOUS, but the challenge spurred me on. Soon I was submitting manuscripts regularly, and regularly getting rejected. (Once I even received a match taped to my manuscript!) But I persisted." Persistence has paid off for Collins; eventually, one of his manuscripts was accepted and this led to a writing career that has spanned several decades and has produced nearly one hundred titles with more on the way.

Though Collins has written some fiction for young readers, as well as science books, his focus has been on biography. "People fascinate me," Collins further noted. "Always have. Therefore, my interest in biography grows even stronger. I love researching my subjects, uncovering new and interesting material. I've written about people from A to Z, from Appleseed to Zachary Taylor." One of Collins's earliest titles was *Walt Disney's Surprise Christmas Present*, which deals with a little-known moment in Disney's youth in Missouri and dramatizes the events of a Christmas when the young boy's artistic aspirations were encouraged by a loving and supportive family. A reviewer for *Library Journal* called the book "quick-moving," but also characterized it as "slight and sentimental."

This was the first of many books Collins has written on artists and writers. *To the Point*, his biography of the

author of *Charlotte's Web*, E. B. White, "outlines [White's] life accurately enough," wrote a critic for *Kirkus Reviews*, but "is pedestrian in style." Beatrix Potter, the creator of the beloved "Peter Rabbit" books, has also been profiled in *Country Artist*, a book written in an "easy-to-read format," according to *School Library Journal* critic Patricia Homer. *Tales for Hard Times* follows the life and career of Charles Dickens. "The text reads smoothly and quickly," noted Eldon Younce in *School Library Journal*, "as it describes how Dickens managed to leave his poverty-stricken past behind, but not to forget it."

More famous writers come under the Collins lens in *M-A-R-K T-W-A-I-N! A Story about Samuel Clemens, Write a Book for Me: The Story of Marguerite Henry,* and *Washington Irving: Storyteller for a New Nation.* In the first title, Collins writes in an "anecdotal style" that "will appeal to readers," according to *School Library Journal* contributor Sandy Kirkpatrick, who nonetheless found the "absence of documentation" to be an "unfortunate weakness." *Booklist* critic Kay Weisman found this Mark Twain biography to be "a lively book that may well draw readers to . . . Clemens' work." Newbery Award winner Marguerite Henry is profiled in *Write a Book for Me.* "Readers looking for facts about this beloved writer's life may find this account of interest," noted Kitty Flynn in *Horn Book Guide.* Reviewing the same title in *Booklist,* Carolyn Phelan felt that while the book is "not a penetrating study of the woman or writer, [it] provides intriguing insights into the inspiration and research behind" many of her works. In *Washington Irving: Storyteller for a New Nation* Collins provides a "thorough" look at Irving's life, according to Renee Steinberg in *School Library Journal.* Writing in *Booklist,* Phelan felt that "Collins' succinct biography gives a sense of Irving's personality as well as his personal history and personal accomplishments."

Collins has also profiled a wide range of political and historical personages in his brief biographies. United States presidents Zachary Taylor, Woodrow Wilson, Harry Truman, and Bill Clinton have all been subjects, while Abe Lincoln is represented also by his mischievous son in *Tad Lincoln: White House Wildcat* and by his widow in *Shattered Dreams: The Story of Mary Todd Lincoln.* "Brisk writing drives this sympathetic portrait of a vivacious woman who was probably unfairly criticized in her own day," observed a contributor for *Kirkus Reviews* of the Mary Todd Lincoln biography. "*Shattered Dreams* is highly readable and well-researched," according to Carrie Eldridge in *Voice of Youth Advocates.* "Place it into the hands of reluctant readers and put it on Hilo reading lists. But give it to your good readers too."

Social activists and thinkers also find a place in Collins's lengthy list of biographical subjects. In *Black Rage: The Story of Malcolm X* Collins attempts in the space of about one hundred pages to trace the life and career of this man who converted his anger into a political movement and was silenced by an assassin's bullet at age forty. "A book this short cannot hope to do justice to a man as complex as Malcolm X," commented *Booklist* reviewer Sheilamae O'Hara, "but Collins does a careful and evenhanded job of introducing one of the twentieth century's most influential black activists." Caesar Chavez, who dedicated his life to winning better conditions for Mexican farm workers in the United States, is portrayed in *Farmworker's Friend*. April Judge, reviewing the title in *Booklist,* found that "aspects of Chavez' personal life are smoothly blended with his continued struggles to improve the plight of his fellow man."

Additionally, names from history—recent and more distant—find their way into Collins's wide-ranging canon. Charles Lindbergh, the first man to fly solo across the Atlantic Ocean, is profiled in a biography of the same name. "The author covers the salient points in Lindbergh's life, makes very clear the role he played in aviation and science, and projects a feeling for both the man and his times," noted Ralph Adams Brown in a *School Library Journal* review of *Charles Lindbergh: Hero Pilot*. A Polish patriot who fought for the Americans in the Revolutionary War is the subject of *Casimir Pulaski: Soldier on Horseback,* a "thorough biography," according to Peter D. Sieruta in *Horn Book Guide*. "Collins' text flows smoothly and will interest history buffs," wrote Weisman in another *Booklist* review. The first famous Siamese twins are the focus of *Eng and Chang*. Born in Thailand in the early nineteenth century, the twins, who were actually ethnically Chinese, gained U.S. citizenship in 1839. Famous for their condition, the two refused to be separated, eventually married sisters, and had a score of children between them. "Collins presents a lively portrait of these unique brothers who traveled throughout the world," wrote Pat Katka in *School Library Journal*.

Sports figures are also a favorite subject for Collins. With his *Arthur Ashe: Against the Wind* he details the life of that famous tennis star who overcame the color barrier to become one of the best-loved players in the game. Following the course of Ashe's career from his childhood in segregated Virginia to UCLA to pro tennis and to his tragic death from AIDS in 1993, "Collins portrays this champion in a fine sports journalism style," declared Anne O'Malley in a *Booklist* review. O'Malley further dubbed the book a "sure winner in school and

public libraries." Janice C. Hayes, writing in *School Library Journal*, felt that Collins's "clearly written, sensitive . . . biography accurately describes" Ashe's life, and that readers "will find Collins's book interesting, informative, and readable." Collins takes on another sports star in *Tiger Woods: Golf Superstar,* a book that "vividly portrays a young man who is remarkable not just for his athletic ability and his intelligence, but for his positive attitude and demeanor," as Jackie Hechtkopf noted in *School Library Journal*. Hechtkopf further commented, "Even libraries that already have material on Tiger Woods should find space for this one." Collins returned to the same subject with another title that is for older readers, *Tiger Woods: Golfing Champion*. This second book includes a brief history of golf, employs dialogue in some parts, and is overall a "livelier" title than the first, according to Janice C. Hayes in *School Library Journal*.

After teaching full-time for thirty-five years, Collins retired in 1997 and has since devoted all his time to writing and speaking in schools. "Why did I decide to write for children?" Collins once commented. "Probably because some of my best childhood adventures were discovered in books. . . . I owe a tremendous debt to the realm of children's literature. Perhaps if I can offer something worthwhile to young readers, part of that debt will be repaid. What advice would I give student writers? First of all, READ. Read whatever and whenever you can. In your own writing, DARE TO BE DIFFERENT. . . . If you are serious about writing, THINK as a writer. The people you meet might become characters in your writing, their adventures could become plots, the places you visit could become settings. Do I like being an author? No, I don't. I LOVE being an author."

BIOGRAPHICAL/CRITICAL SOURCES:

PERIODICALS

Booklist, May 1, 1989, p. 1545; October 15, 1992, Sheilamae O'Hara, review of *Black Rage,* pp. 420-421; March 1, 1994, Kay Weisman, review of *M-A-R-K T-W-A-I-N!,* p. 1256; February 1, 1995, Anne O'Malley, review of *Arthur Ashe,* p. 997; February 15, 1996, Kay Weisman, review of *Casimir Pulaski,* p. 1011; December 15, 1996, April Judge, review of *Farmworker's Friend,* p. 722; July, 1998, p. 1870; March 15, 1999, Carolyn Phelan, review of *Write a Book for Me,* p. 1325; April 1, 2000, Carolyn Phelan, review of *Washington Irving,* p. 1456.

Bulletin of the Center for Children's Books, September, 1981, p. 7; May, 1992, p. 232.

Horn Book Guide, spring, 1993, p. 137; spring, 1995, p. 149; fall, 1995, p. 381; fall, 1996, Peter D. Sieruta, review of *Casimir Pulaski,* p. 371; spring, 1997, p. 156; fall, 1998, p. 412; fall, 1999, Kitty Flynn, review of *Write a Book for Me,* p. 378.

Kirkus Reviews, April 1, 1989, review of *To the Point,* p. 544; March 15, 1992, p. 392; August 15, 1994, review of *Shattered Dreams,* p. 1124; February 15, 1999, p. 298.

Library Journal, October 15, 1971, review of *Walt Disney's Surprise Christmas Present,* p. 3484.

Publishers Weekly, April 14, 1989, p. 68; May 12, 1989, p. 293.

School Library Journal, September, 1975, pp. 74-75; May, 1976, p. 80; November, 1978, Ralph Adams Brown, review of *Charles Lindbergh,* p. 42; December, 1979, p. 94; August, 1989, Patricia Homer, review of *Country Artist,* p. 146; March, 1991, Eldon Younce, review of *Tales for Hard Times,* p. 201; March, 1994, Sandy Kirkpatrick, review of *M-A-R-K T-W-A-I-N!,* p. 227; February, 1995, Pat Katka, review of *Eng and Chang,* p. 105; March, 1995, Janice C. Hayes, review of *Arthur Ashe,* p. 209; January, 1999, p. 137; June, 1999, Jackie Hechtkopf, review of *Tiger Woods: Golf Superstar,* p. 112; September, 1999, p. 230; January, 2000, Janice C. Hayes, review of *Tiger Woods: Golfing Champion,* p. 140; May, 2000, Renee Steinberg, review of *Washington Irving,* p. 179.

Voice of Youth Advocates, May, 1992, p. 302; August, 1992, p. 183; December, 1994, Carrie Eldridge, review of *Shattered Dreams,* p. 296.

*   *   *

COOK, Glen (Charles) 1944-

PERSONAL: Born July 9, 1944, in New York, NY; son of Charles Albert (a civil servant) and Louella Mabel (Handy) Cook; married Carol Ann Fritz, June 14, 1971; children: three sons. *Education:* Attended University of Missouri, 1962-65. *Avocational interests:* Stamp collecting.

ADDRESSES: Home—4106 Flora Place, St. Louis, MO 63110. *Agent*—Russell Galen, Scovil-Chichak-Galen Literary Agency, 381 Park Ave. South, Suite 1020, New York, NY 10016.

CAREER: General Motors Corp., St. Louis, MO, auto assembler at Fisher Body Plant, 1965-67, munitions in-

Glen Cook

spector at Chevrolet Army Plant, 1967-70, material controller, 1970-74, worker in grinding, plastic, and rework, 1974-98; retired, 1998—. Also worked as cook, restaurant manager, janitor, baker's helper, waiter, busboy, fruit packer, clerk, and forklift driver. *Military service:* Served eight years in U.S. Navy and Navy Reserve.

WRITINGS:

(Under pseudonym Greg Stevens) *The Swap Academy,* Publisher's Export Corp. (San Diego, CA), 1970.

SCIENCE FICTION AND FANTASY NOVELS

The Heirs of Babylon, Signet Books (New York City), 1972.

The Swordbearer, Timescape (New York City), 1982.

Passage at Arms, Warner Books (New York City), 1985.

A Matter of Time, Ace Books (New York City), 1985.

The Dragon Never Sleeps, Warner Books, 1988.

The Tower of Fear, Tor (New York City), 1989.
Sung in Blood, NESFA Press (Cambridge, MA), 1990.

"STARFISHERS" TRILOGY

Shadowline, Warner Books, 1982.
Starfishers, Warner Books, 1982.
Stars' End, Warner Books, 1982.

"DARKWAR" TRILOGY

Doomstalker, Warner Books, 1985.
Warlock, Warner Books, 1985.
Ceremony, Warner Books, 1986.

"BLACK COMPANY" SERIES

The Black Company (also see below), Tor Books, 1984, reprinted, 1997.
Shadows Linger (also see below), Tor Books, 1984, reprinted, 1992.
The White Rose (also see below), Tor Books, 1985, reprinted, 1997.
Annals of the Black Company (omnibus; includes *The Black Company, Shadows Linger,* and *The White Rose),* Nelson Doubleday (New York City), 1986.
Shadow Games, Tor, 1989.
The Silver Spike, Tor, 1989.
Dreams of Steel, Tor, 1990.
Bleak Seasons, Tor, 1996.
She Is the Darkness, Tor, 1997.
Water Sleeps, Tor, 1999.
Soldiers Live, Tor, 2000.

"DREAD EMPIRE" SERIES

Shadow of All Night Falling, Berkley (New York City), 1979.
October's Baby, Berkley, 1980.
All Darkness Met, Berkley, 1980.
The Fire in His Hands, Pocket (New York City), 1984.
With Mercy toward None, Baen (New York City), 1985.
Reap the East Wind, Tor, 1987.
All Ill Fate Marshalling, Tor, 1988.

"GARRETT" SERIES

Sweet Silver Blues (also see below), New American Library (New York City), 1987.
Cold Copper Tears (also see below), New American Library, 1988.

Bitter Gold Hearts (also see below), New American Library, 1988.
The Garrett Files (includes *Sweet Silver Blues, Bitter Gold Hearts,* and *Cold Copper Tears),* Science Fiction Book Club, 1988.
Old Tin Sorrows, New American Library, 1989.
Dread Brass Shadows, Roc (New York City), 1990.
Red Iron Nights, Roc, 1991.
Deadly Quicksilver Lies, Roc, 1993.
Petty Pewter Gods, Roc, 1996.
Faded Steel Heat, Roc, 2000.
Angry Lead Skies, Roc, 2002.

OTHER

Work represented in anthologies, including *Clarion,* edited by Robin Scott Wilson, New American Library, 1971. Contributor to periodicals.

SIDELIGHTS: Glen Cook is "the working man's fantasy writer," according to Gary Westfahl in *St. James Guide to Fantasy Writers.* A factory worker himself, Cook usually focuses his attention on the common people in his fantasy worlds, rather than the upper classes. The soldiers in his popular "Black Company" series, for example, are unhappy mercenaries, fighting because they are bound to do so; his hard-boiled private eye character, Garrett, is constantly dealing with problems caused by cruel, indifferent leaders; and "even the princes and wizards of the Dread Empire novels are usually Poor Boys Made Good—children of peasants or pig farmers who rise by merit to high positions—not persons To The Manor Born," according to Westfahl. *Library Journal* correspondent Jackie Cassada likewise noted Cook's "singular talent for combining gritty realism and high fantasy." Whatever his aims, Cook has established himself as one of the best-selling authors of *noir* fantasy, as attested to by the many Web pages devoted to his work, as well as ongoing sales of his paperbacks.

One of Cook's first popular creations was the "Dread Empire" series, set in a fantasy world with warring regions similar to Europe, China, and the Middle East. Another major series is the "Black Company," which describes a group of heartless adventurers who fight first for the dark and evil Lady, then join the employ of her enemy. "Befitting its title, the mood in this series is brutal and dark: the heroes routinely slaughter other men, while the villains routinely slaughter women and children as well," noted Westfahl. "Yet Cook is clearly more comfortable dealing with the manipulated underlings of wars and intrigues, not their manipulators; and the Company physician Croaker, outwardly as cruel as his comrades but inwardly troubled by their activities, is an effective and involving narrator."

The "Black Company" series has proven popular with fantasy fans who like books that are darker and more caustic—and not necessarily resolved by happy or moralistic endings. The world of the Black Company is "strongly flavored with elements of South and Southeast Asia," to quote a *Publishers Weekly* reviewer, and that Eastern flavor extends to the author's treatment of myths, religion, and the details of war. *Booklist* correspondent Roland Green stated: "The religion and folklore, in particular, have an authentic, multilayered flavor." Another *Publishers Weekly* reviewer likewise found parallels with old novels about the British Raj, but that reviewer concluded that a Black Company novel "offers virtually anything a fantasy reader could ask for."

Westfahl rates the "Garrett" series as Cook's most significant achievement. It features a hardboiled detective who solves mysteries involving fantasy creatures. "Considering this premise, one might dismiss the books as little more than humorous incongruity, a combination of divergent forms—fantasy and detective fiction—for satiric effect," mused the critic. "However, despite a light tone reminiscent of Raymond Chandler, Cook tells these stories with both lively imagination and surprising conviction, and the apparently disparate elements blend together with remarkable success. On reflection, this is perhaps not surprising: after all, Chandler's Marlowe was always a knight-errant in disguise, and his shadowy and mysterious Los Angeles was always a displaced fantasy world. . . . Cook's Garrett series demands attention as an important—and, in its way, quite serious—contribution to modern fantasy." *Kliatt* reviewer Gail E. Roberts compared Cook not only to Raymond Chandler, but to Dashiell Hammett as well. Writing about one Garrett book, *Petty Pewter Gods,* Jan E. V. W. Hanson remarked in *Voice of Youth Advocates* that it is a "sometimes funny and clever," and speculated that "fans of Raymond Chandler or Douglas Adams might enjoy this."

BIOGRAPHICAL/CRITICAL SOURCES:

BOOKS

St. James Guide to Fantasy Writers, St. James Press (Detroit), 1996.

PERIODICALS

Booklist, September 15, 1997, Roland Green, review of *She Is the Darkness,* p. 216; February 1, 1999, Roland Green, review of *Water Sleeps,* p. 966.

Kirkus Reviews, February 1, 1996, p. 181; January 15, 1999, review of *Water Sleeps;* June 15, 2000, review of *Soldiers Live,* pp. 841-42.
Kliatt, March, 1996, p. 14.
Library Journal, March 15, 1999, Jackie Cassada, review of *Water Sleeps,* p. 112; July, 2000, Jackie Cassada, review of *Soldiers Live,* p. 146.
Locus, April, 1994, pp. 33, 48.
Publishers Weekly, March 4, 1996, review of *Bleak Seasons,* p. 59; September 22, 1997, review of *She Is the Darkness,* p. 74; February 8, 1999, review of *Water Sleeps,* p. 199.
Science Fiction Chronicle, May, 1996, p. 57.
Voice of Youth Advocates, April, 1996, p. 36.

*   *   *

COSE, Ellis Jonathan 1951-

PERSONAL: Born February 20, 1951, in Chicago, IL; son of Raney and Jetta (Cameron) Cose; married Lee Llambelis, May, 1992. *Ethnicity:* "Black." *Education:* University of Illinois at Chicago Circle, B.A., 1972; George Washington University, M.A., 1978.

ADDRESSES: Office—*Newsweek* Magazine, 251 West 57th St., New York, NY 10019. *Agent*—Michael Cungdon, Don Cungdon Associates, 156 5th Ave., New York, NY 10010; fax: 212-663-9785.

CAREER: Chicago Sun-Times, Chicago, IL, columnist, editor, and national correspondent, 1970-77; Joint Center for Political Studies, Washington, DC, senior fellow and director of energy policy studies, 1977-79; *Detroit Free Press,* Detroit, MI, editorial writer and columnist, 1979-81; Gannett Center for Media, Columbia University, New York City, fellow, 1987; *New York Daily News,* New York City, editorial page editor, 1991-93; *Newsweek,* New York City, contributing editor, 1993—. Member of environmental advisory committee of U.S. Department of Energy, 1978-79; resident fellow at National Academy of Sciences and National Research Council, 1981-82; *USA Today,* special writer, 1982-83, contributor and essayist, 1996—; Institute for Journalism Education, University of California at Berkeley, president and chief executive officer, 1983-86; *Time,* contributor and press critic, 1988-90. Has appeared on nationally televised programs on major American networks and has been interviewed for British, Brazilian, and Canadian television.

MEMBER: National Association of Black Journalists.

AWARDS, HONORS: Newswriting award, Illinois United Press International, 1973; Stick-o-Type Award,

Chicago Newspaper Guild, 1975; Lincoln University National Unity awards for Best Political Reporting, 1975 and 1977; Outstanding Young Citizen of Chicago Jaycees, 1977; shared National Association of Black Journalists Award with three colleagues, 1997, for *Newsweek* cover package, "Black Like Who?"; University of Missouri Honor Medal for Distinguished Service in Journalism, 1997. Fellowships and grants from the Ford Foundation, Andrew Mellon Foundation, Rockefeller Foundation, and Aspen Institute for Humanistic Studies.

WRITINGS:

Energy and the Urban Crisis, Joint Center for Political Studies (Washington, DC), 1978.
(Editor) *Energy and Equity: Some Social Concerns,* Joint Center for Political Studies (Washington, DC), 1979.
Decentralizing Energy Decisions: The Rebirth of Community Power, Westview Press (Boulder, CO), 1983.
The Quiet Crisis, Institute for Journalism Education, 1987.
The Press, Morrow (New York, NY), 1989.
A Nation of Strangers: Prejudice, Politics, and the Populating of America, Morrow (New York, NY), 1992.
The Rage of a Privileged Class, HarperCollins (New York, NY), 1993.
A Man's World: How Real Is Male Privilege—and How High Is Its Price?, HarperCollins (New York, NY), 1995.
Color-Blind: Seeing beyond Race in a Race-obsessed World, HarperCollins (New York, NY), 1997.
(Editor) *The Darden Dilemma: Twelve Black Writers on Justice, Race, and Conflicting Loyalties,* HarperPerennial (New York, NY), 1997.
The Best Defense, HarperCollins (New York, NY), 1998.
(With Christina Dodd) *A Knight to Remember,* Harper (New York, NY), 1999.

Also designer/director of study, *The Quiet Crisis: Minority Journalists and Newsroom Opportunity,* 1985, and author of *Employment and Journalism,* 1986. Former columnist for periodicals, including *Chicago Sun-Times* and *Time.*

SIDELIGHTS: A desire to promote understanding across the color line helped lead Ellis Jonathan Cose to a career as a journalist and writer on public policy issues. Asked in an interview why he became a writer, Cose commented, "I was a sort of creature of the late 1960s."

The West Side of Chicago, where Cose grew up in one of the city's public housing developments, was marked by violent riots in the aftermath of the assassinations of activists Malcolm X and Martin Luther King, Jr. "Out of the riots, I saw so much destruction, so much devastation," Cose said. "At least part of it was due to the fact that people didn't understand each other well enough."

If he started writing as a way to bridge differences, Cose stayed in it because he "enjoyed writing and the process of discovery," he said. Writing was a rewarding career for Cose from early on in his life: he had his first column, writing about Chicago communities, in the *Chicago Sun-Times* when he was nineteen years old. He continued working for the paper while studying psychology at the University of Illinois in Chicago. His column's subject matter began to include national politics, and the *Sun-Times* assigned Cose to cover Jimmy Carter's 1976 presidential campaign. The campaign took Cose outside Chicago and exposed him to new issues. In the wake of the energy crisis, Cose became interested in the way energy policy affected lower-class citizens. Several of his books cover the subject, including *Energy and the Urban Crisis.*

Cose continued to move back and forth between journalism and work in the public sector. After a stint in print journalism in the first years of the 1980s, he went to California to run the Institute for Journalism Education. He left the position to write *The Press,* which profiled the personalities and the companies that run major U.S. newspapers, including Katharine Graham of the *Washington Post* and Al Neuharth, head of the Gannett newspaper chain that owns *USA Today.*

Moving from journalism education to writing books and working in magazines, Cose has focused more recently on issues of race and class. In *The Rage of a Privileged Class,* Cose looks at members of the American black middle class and examines multiple aspects of the prejudice many of these educated, competent professionals face and the anger they feel as a result. "Mr. Cose has gathered numerous provocative and often poignant stories to illuminate the questions at the heart of the book," commented Arnold Rampersad in his *New York Times* book review. The stories cover a range of incidents, Rampersad added, moving from outright contempt to more subtle questions of power and authority between blacks and whites.

Cose's stated purpose in writing this best-seller was "to spur interracial dialogue," Rampersad noted. According to this reviewer, the author was moved to begin work on *The Rage of a Privileged Class* after attending a conference for black executives in the mid-1980s, where he heard many attendees comment upon how they were treated differently than their white counterparts.

"A journalist rather than a scholar, Mr. Cose seems nevertheless to be familiar with most of the serious studies relevant to his topic," Rampersad continued; "He takes pains to be fair to all concerned." "Certainly he accomplishes his goal of capturing and scrutinizing the mixture of pride and despair, privilege and hurt, equanimity and anger that disfigures the lives of middle-class blacks," Rampersad affirmed. "This is a disciplined, graceful exposition of a neglected aspect of the subject of race in America."

Published in 1995, *A Man's World: How Real Is Male Privilege—and How High Is Its Price?* "listens in on the Beleaguered Male," stated Amy Alexander in her *Knight-Ridder/Tribune News Service* examination of this book. According to Alexander, Cose has picked up on an undercurrent of men's anxiety and uneasiness in today's confusing times: "They share an overall feeling that much is amiss with their world, and that they are losing control over how to right it." Alexander describes Cose as saying that, for thirty years, since the beginnings of the feminist movement, "the public has been preoccupied with the condition of women in America." In addition, Alexander says, Cose points out the conflict that has arisen between people today expecting equal pay and equal rights for men and women and the fact that their personal interactions and philosophies don't always coincide with this legal ideal. "I think there will always be conflict between the sexes," Cose grants, but he holds the belief that most men and women want to understand and get along with each other.

"Mr. Cose . . . is a great one for posing difficult questions; like most observers of the American scene, he is a little bit weaker when it comes to working out the answers," observed Stephen L. Carter in his *New York Times Book Review* assessment of *A Man's World*. Cose argues that most men "exercise little power over anybody—most men, like most people, are simply struggling to get by," Carter continued. He commented favorably on the quality of Cose's prose and the organization of his arguments, but faulted the book's lack of footnotes to back up its statistics. "And after portraying through his interviews all the confusion that men suffer, and after analyzing his data to show the difficulties in issues widely thought to be simple, Mr. Cose leaves the reader hanging," Carter maintained. "Nevertheless, Mr. Cose's energy is daunting and his is a welcome voice of moderation."

Of *Color-Blind: Seeing beyond Race in a Race-obsessed World*, Alan Wolfe insisted in the *New York Times Book Review* that Cose "has written a book this country desperately needs, one with genuine healing potential. And he has done so without modifying his belief that significant racial injustice persists in the United States." Many people believe that the issue of race is a determining and divisive factor in America. "*Color-Blind* wades into all the racial hot spots," Wolfe continued, including affirmative action and black separatism. "Mr. Cose approaches each the same way, by talking to people and reporting what they have to say, comparing American experiences with those in South Africa and Brazil and reflecting on his own experience." Although Cose proposes a program for making the United States a more race-neutral nation, Wolfe felt that the book "would have ended on a stronger note if Mr. Cose instead had tried to distill the essence of his advice into moral language."

The Best Defense, a courtroom drama, is Cose's first fictional outing and, simultaneously, an exploration of some of the complex racial issues that Cose discussed in his previous works of nonfiction. The main character is a black, female lawyer who defends a white Manhattan businessman, John Wisocki, against murder charges in the shooting death of a younger Hispanic colleague. During a corporate downsizing, Wisocki is replaced in his job at a computer company by the colleague. The suspenseful case revolves around the question of whether the killing was accidental or instead was Wisocki's way of seeking revenge against the company's affirmative action policies.

BIOGRAPHICAL/CRITICAL SOURCES:

PERIODICALS

Commonweal, February 25, 1994, Don Wycliff, review of *The Rage of a Privileged Class.*

Knight-Ridder/Tribune News Service, July 7, 1995, Amy Alexander, "Author Ellis Cose Examines Men's Sense of Bewilderment," p. 707.

New York Times Book Review, January 9, 1994, Arnold Rampersad, review of *The Rage of a Privileged Class;* June 25, 1995, Steven L. Carter, review of *A Man's World: How Real Is Male Privilege—and How High Is Its Price?;* February 9, 1997, Alan Wolfe, review of *Color Blind: Seeing beyond Race in a Race-obsessed World.*

Publishers Weekly, March 23, 1992, Will Nixon, "Ellis Cose: Writing a History of Immigration, He Discovered a Deep Vein of Nativism in America's Past" (interview), p. 47.*

CROOK, J(oseph) Mordaunt 1937-

PERSONAL: Born February 27, 1937, in London, England; son of Austin Mordaunt (a civil servant) and Irene (Woolfenden) Crook; married Margaret Mulholland, July 4, 1964 (divorced, 1975); married Susan Mayor, July 9, 1975. *Education:* Brasenose College, Oxford, D.Phil., 1961, M.A., 1962.

ADDRESSES: Home—55 Gloucester Ave., London NW1 4BA, England.

CAREER: Institute of Historical Research, London, England, research fellow, 1961-62; University of London, Bedford College, London, research fellow, 1962-63; University of Leicester, Leicester, England, lecturer in history, 1963-65; University of London, lecturer in history at Bedford College, 1965-75, reader in architectural history, 1975-81, professor at Royal Holloway and Bedford New College, 1981-99, professor emeritus, 1999—, director of Victorian Studies Centre, 1990-99. Warburg Institute, research fellow, 1970-71; Oxford University, Slade Professor of Fine Arts, 1979-80; Cambridge University, visiting fellow at Gonville and Caius College, 1984-85; University of London, public orator, 1988-90. Department of the Environment, member of Historic Buildings Council, 1974-80.

MEMBER: British Academy (fellow), Society of Architectural Historians (member of executive committee, 1964-75), Victorian Society (member of executive committee, 1970-75), Georgian Group (member of executive committee, 1970-75), Society of Antiquaries, Worshipful Company of Goldsmiths (freeman and liveryman).

AWARDS, HONORS: Hitchcock Medal for *History of the King's Works, 1782-1851.*

WRITINGS:

The Greek Revival, Country Life Books (Feltham, England), 1968.

(Editor) Charles L. Eastlake, *A History of the Gothic Revival,* Humanities (Atlantic Highlands, NJ), 1970, revised edition, 1978.

Victorian Architecture: A Visual Anthology, Johnson, 1971.

The British Museum, Praeger (New York, NY), 1972.

The Greek Revival: Neo-Classical Attitudes in British Architecture, 1760-1870, John Murray (London, England), 1972, revised edition, 1995.

(Editor) R. Kerr, *The Gentleman's House,* Johnson, 1972.

(Editor) J. T. Emmett, *Six Essays,* Johnson, 1972.

(With M. H. Port) *History of the King's Works: 1782-1851,* H.M.S.O., 1973.

The Reform Club, Reform Club (London, England), 1973.

(With H. M. Colvin, J. Newman, and J. Summerson) *History of the King's Works, 1660-1782,* H.M.S.O., 1975.

(Editor, with Howard Colvin and Terry Friedman) *Architectural Drawings from Lowther Castle Westmorland,* Society of Architectural Historians of Great Britain (London, England), 1980.

William Burges and the High Victorian Dream, University of Chicago Press (Chicago, IL), 1981.

(Editor of exhibition catalog entries) *The Strange Genius of William Burges, "Art-Architect," 1827-1881,* National Museum of Wales (Cardiff, Wales), 1982.

(With C. A. Lennox-Boyd) *Axel Haig and the Victorian Vision of the Middle Ages,* Allen & Unwin (Boston, MA), 1984.

The Dilemma of Style: Architectural Ideas from the Picturesque to the Post-Modern, University of Chicago Press (Chicago, IL), 1987.

The Rise of the Nouveaux Riches: Style and Status in Victorian and Edwardian Architecture, John Murray (London, England), 1999.

Contributor to *Sir William Chambers, Knight of the Polar Star,* by John Harris, A. Zwemmer (London, England), 1970; and *Thomas Harrison in Lancaster,* Visual Arts Centre, University of Lancaster (Lancaster, England), 1978. Contributor to *Architectural Review, Country Life, Connoisseur, R.I.B.A. Journal, Times Literary Supplement,* and *Burlington.* Editor, *Architectural History,* 1967-75.

SIDELIGHTS: The Rise of the Nouveaux Riches: Style and Status in Victorian and Edwardian Architecture by J. Mordaunt Crook describes how the newly wealthy Englishmen who made vast fortunes in industry and international finance in the nineteenth and early twentieth centuries converted some of their extraordinary riches into architecture. In addition to being an architectural history, *The Rise of the Nouveaux Riches* is also a sociological study, as Crook points out how these men improved their positions in society and essentially reinvented the British ruling class and shifted its balance of power. In the book, Crook, a leading British architectural historian, explains how the newly affluent Victorians and Edwardians expressed their ideals and established and celebrated themselves through the homes they bought or built. He compares the styles of architecture and decoration that were favored by the *nouveaux riches* with the styles preferred by the existing aristocrats whose "old money" and advantages had been inherited from affluent forefathers. According to the book, the new millionaires opted for the Classical style of architecture, as opposed to the Gothic, Tudor, and Jacobean revival styles selected by the aristocracy.

In *Literary Review*, critic Hugh Massingberd described *The Rise of the Nouveaux Riches* as an "engrossing, eye-opening study" and a rare find—"an academic work that is a joy to read." In Crook's view, the architecture of *nouveaux-riches* homes was generally second-rate, Massingberd went on to explain. This reviewer noted how Crook attributes this to the new millionaires' overriding concern with finding architects to simply carry out their instructions, which prevailed over their sense of aesthetics and good taste. "Much fun is had with the details of nouveau taste," this reviewer wrote of the examples of excess that Crook shares in the work. Massingberd deemed *The Rise of the Nouveaux Riches* as Crook's "masterpiece, an instructive and entertaining tour de force which makes one look at the reshaping of the aristocracy through 'loadsamoney' and at the social history of architecture in a new way."

A reviewer for *Publishers Weekly* found *The Rise of the Nouveaux Riches* disappointing, lacking enough detail about the history of the wealthy families and their homes. This commentator did consider the book "attractive reading" but disliked its use of small, black-and-white photos to illustrate the homes.

David Cannadine proclaimed Crook's work "a clever, scholarly, witty and abundantly illustrated book" in his review in the *New York Times Book Review*. In addition, Cannadine asserted that the book addresses questions about where and how the *nouveaux riches* lived, how they spent their money, and whether they lived up to their wealth "with impressive authority and elegant erudition."

BIOGRAPHICAL/CRITICAL SOURCES:

PERIODICALS

Literary Review, October 7, 1999, Hugh Massingberd, "Some Ugly Brutes."

New York Times Book Review, February 6, 2000, David Cannadine, "There Goes the Neighborhood."

Publishers Weekly, November 29, 1999, review of *The Rise of the Nouveaux Riches: Style and Status in Victorian and Edwardian Architecture*, p. 63.

Telegraph, May 31, 1999, John Gross, "Ormolu, and Oodles of It."

*   *   *

CROUCH, Stanley 1945-

PERSONAL: Born December 14, 1945, in Los Angeles, CA.

ADDRESSES: Office—c/o *New Republic*, 1220 Nineteenth St. NW, Washington, DC 20036.

CAREER: Playwright and actor under Jayne Cortez, in Studio Watts company, 1965-67; drummer with pianist Raymond King, 1966; drummer and bandleader with various groups, including Quartet and Black Music Infinity, 1967—; Claremont College, Claremont, CA, instructor in drama, literature, and jazz history, 1969-75; writer. Appears on television and radio.

WRITINGS:

Ain't No Ambulances for No Nigguhs Tonight (poems), R. W. Baron, 1972.

Notes of a Hanging Judge: Essays and Reviews, 1979-1989, Oxford University Press (New York City), 1990.

The All-American Skin Game; or, The Decoy of Race: The Long and the Short of It, 1990-1994, Pantheon (New York City), 1995.

Always in Pursuit: Fresh American Perspectives, 1995-1997, Pantheon, 1998.

Don't the Moon Look Lonesome: A Novel in Blues and Swing, Pantheon, 2000.

(With others) *The Reading Room: Writing of the Moment*, edited by Barbara Probst, Great Marsh (New York City), 2000.

(Contributor) Jill Nelson, editor, *Police Brutality*, Norton, 2000.

Works represented in anthologies, including *Black Fire*, 1968; *We Speak as Liberators: Young Black Poets*, 1970; and *Black Spirits*, 1972. Staff writer and jazz critic for *Village Voice*, 1979-88; columnist for *Los An-*

Stanley Crouch

geles Free Press, Cricket, New York Daily News, and *SoHo Weekly News;* contributing editor for *New Republic,* 1990—; contributor to periodicals, including *New Yorker, New York Times,* and *Esquire.* Composer of various musical pieces, including "Future Sallie's Time," "Chicago for Bobby Seale," "The Confessions of Father None," "Flying through Wire," "Attica in Black September," and "Noteworthy Lady"; albums include *Now Is Another Time* and *Past Spirits.*

SIDELIGHTS: Stanley Crouch has performed in many roles, among them musician, jazz critic, social critic, poet, essayist, and novelist. The first book Crouch published was a volume of poetry entitled *Ain't No Ambulances for No Nigguhs Tonight.* In *Library Journal,* Sandford Dorbin maintained that the publication is "God-intoxicated" and "worddrunk." Dorbin also called Crouch "wildly uneven, as you would expect a natural poet to be." Following the 1972 collection, Crouch applied his style outside the bounds of poetry and music, discussing a variety of topics in a bold manner. "Armed with an elephant's memory and a passionate knowledge of and engagement with art (blues and jazz especially, though not exclusively) and history (American, though not exclusively), Crouch delights in slaying the dragons of convention—particularly those that guard the sometimes-insular world of black intellectuals," wrote Amy Alexander in *Salon.*

"There's a fine line between lyricism and luster. At least, there is for Stanley Crouch, the iconoclastic culture critic. . . . Few writers . . . juxtapose their best and worst qualities as blithely as Crouch. He has a gift for courageous phrases—tightly alliterated and rhythmically risky—that ring in the ear like a great horn line. The downside is that he doesn't always distinguish real insight from glib turns of phrase," stated a *Boston Phoenix* review of Couch's "everything-but-the-kitchen-sink collection" of writings, *The All-American Skin Game, or, The Decoy of Race: The Long and the Short of It, 1990-1994* (1995). In a *Booklist* assessment of the same volume, Bonnie Smothers remarked that Crouch "talks a lot of interesting stuff" but "is not an easy person to relate to because he is one of those 'in-your-face' thinkers whose very smugness seems meant to alienate and provoke" And Alexander commented, "Crouch's troublemaking reputation was made with his first essay collection, 1990's *Notes of a Hanging Judge,* which smacked the slumbering genre of race and cultural criticism out of its 30-year torpor."

In his 1990 omnibus, *Notes of a Hanging Judge,* Crouch explores a variety of subjects ranging from feminism, black power, and the Third World to boxing, popular culture, and the movies of Spike Lee. Like Ralph Ellison and Albert Murray, two other writers with roots in jazz, Crouch uses music, according to *American Spectator* contributor Martha Bayles, "as a vantage point to scrutinize the rest of the world." With his essays, Crouch "sets himself apart from and above the tides of current opinion," according to Deirdre English in the *New York Times Book Review.* The author is a severe critic of political and cultural leaders who view black Americans as the helpless victims of racist oppression. The "hanging judge" in his book title is the freebooter Henry Morgan, "who sent many of his former pirate buddies to the gallows, certain that they deserved what they got." Crouch, who was once a black nationalist, blames the excesses of the movement and its prominent leaders for the collapse of the civil rights struggle. He scorns black proponents of separatism, anti-Semitism, and what he sees as selfish opportunism. He considers jazz to be the musical expression of a traditional "heroic optimism" among black Americans, and he praises the historic willingness of blacks "to take the field, to do battle, and to struggle up from the sink holes of self-pity." His prescription for African American progress rejects the idea of African innocence or superiority and proclaims the need for personal responsibility, education, and reasoned debate. With these recommendations, according to English, Crouch "comes off less like a hanging judge than a knowing and anxious father figure."

Crouch is severely critical of prominent figures such as Malcolm X, the "chief black heckler of the civil rights movement," and Kwame Toure (Stokely Carmichael), "the ghost of Pan-African nationalism past." He also attacks other notables, including novelist Toni Morrison and filmmaker Spike Lee. Morrison won a Pulitzer Prize for her novel, *Beloved,* but is dismissed by Crouch as a writer of "portentous melodrama." Spike Lee is characterized as a "middle-class would-be street Negro" whose acclaimed and controversial film, *Do the Right Thing,* is a "rancid fairy tale." According to Bayles, Crouch finds Lee's "attachment to 1960s-style militance . . . the sentimental indulgence of a privileged youth ill-informed about the real problems of the black poor."

Though some critics denounced what they considered to be Crouch's personal attacks on various figures, many praised *Notes of a Hanging Judge* as insightful and refreshing. "It's rare to find both verbal virtuosity and rational coherence in the same person," noted Bayles. "For this reason alone, it's worth reading *Notes of a Hanging Judge.*" *Nation* contributor Gene Seymour observed that, while one may disagree with the author, "you have to appreciate the fact that, like any good jazz player, Crouch never repeats himself or does the predictable." Seymour also noted that Crouch's "willingness to call upon a wide range of references gives his collection a supple, almost buoyant texture." Writing in *Washington Post Book World,* David Nicholson commented, "From politics to art to jazz to the blues to literature, Crouch covers the waterfront. Throughout, he is not only provocative but perceptive and, on more than one occasion, wise. In the end it must be said that this is the kind of book you want not merely to read, but to ponder."

In 1998 readers were given another collection of Crouch's writings, *Always in Pursuit: Fresh American Perspectives, 1995-1997.* In the essays, speeches and reviews which were culled from many sources, Crouch presents "the same themes" as in previous writings, observed Bonnie Smothers in a *Booklist* review. "If a reader can push beyond Stanley's narrowly held opinions, there's gold to be mined from his hyperbolic riffs and rants. . . . Many pieces are entertaining, though disturbing." A *Kirkus Reviews* critic who referred to Crouch as a "jazz guru and social/cultural critic" was impressed with Crouch's discussion of Albert Murray, Christopher Darden, and various jazz figures, but found Crouch's words on other topics to be troublesome: "Crouch sustains whole stretches of fine, sometimes expert material, but overall this 'intellectual medley' is wildly erratic, and its best verses rarely transcend its verbiage." In contrast, a *Publishers Weekly* reviewer

claimed, "Crouch's fluid style, clearly influenced by the blues and jazz he loves, keeps his prose interesting."

Crouch's fiction debut came in 2000 with the publication of *Don't the Moon Look Lonesome: A Novel in Blues and Swing. Library Journal* contributor Ellen Flexman praised the novel—the story of an interracial couple of jazz musicians struggling with "race, art, success, and family," calling it a "stylish love story," and applauding the author's ability to make his prose evoke "a blues band or a gospel choir."

In 2000 Crouch's writing was published, along with the work of others, in *The Reading Room: Writing of the Moment,* edited by Barbara Probst; and in *Police Brutality,* edited by Jill Nelson. Vanessa Bush in *Booklist* described *Policy Brutality* as "a compelling reader on the enduring evil of police brutality in a democratic society and its tacit social acceptance." As well as contributing to anthologies and various periodicals such as *New Yorker* and *Esquire,* Crouch has been a columnist for *Los Angeles Free Press, Cricket, New York Daily News,* and *SoHo Weekly News.* In addition, he has been contributing editor for *New Republic.*

BIOGRAPHICAL/CRITICAL SOURCES:

BOOKS

Crouch, Stanley, *Notes of a Hanging Judge: Essays and Reviews, 1979-1989,* Oxford University Press, 1990.

PERIODICALS

American Spectator, September, 1990, pp. 35-36.

Booklist, Bonnie Smothers, review of *The All-American Skin Game,* October 15, 1995, p. 370; Smothers, review of *Always in Pursuit,* December 1, 1997, p. 586; Ellen Flexman, review of *Don't the Moon Look Lonesome,* April 1, 2000, p. 129; Vanessa Bush, review of *Police Brutality,* May 15, 2000, p. 1707.

Boston Phoenix, "From the Pulpit: Stanley Crouch Offers Doses of Hectoring and Passion," April 4-11, 1996.

Kirkus Reviews, review of *Always in Pursuit,* December 1, 1997.

Library Journal, April 1, 1972, p. 1328.

Nation, May 21, 1990, pp. 710-712.

New York Times Book Review, Deirdre English, "Nobody's Victim," March 11, 1990, p. 9.

Publishers Weekly, review of *The All-American Skin Game,* September 11, 1995, p. 67; review of *Always in Pursuit,* November 24, 1997, p. 58.

Time, April 9, 1990, p. 92.

Washington Post Book World, April 8, 1990, p. 5.

OTHER

Salon, http://www.salon.com/ (July 16, 2000), Amy Alexander, article including discussion of *Notes of a Hanging Judge* and *The All-American Skin Game.**

*   *   *

CURNOW, (Thomas) Allen (Monro) 1911-
(Whim-Wham)

PERSONAL: Born June 17, 1911, in Timaru, New Zealand; son of Tremayne Monro (an Anglican clergyman) and Jessamine Towler (Gambling) Curnow; married Elizabeth Jaumaud Le Cren, 1936 (divorced, 1965); married Jenifer Mary Tole, August 31, 1965; children: Wystan Tremayne Le Cren, Belinda Elizabeth Allen Curnow Morley, Timothy Charles Monro. *Ethnicity:* "Caucasian." *Education:* Attended St. John's College, Auckland, New Zealand, 1931-33; University of New Zealand, B.A., 1933.

ADDRESSES: Home—62 Tohunga Cres., Parnell, Auckland, New Zealand. *Agent*—Curtis Brown Ltd., P.O. Box 19, Paddington 2021, Australia. *E-mail*—curnow@extra.co.nz.

CAREER: Press, Christchurch, New Zealand, reporter, 1936-40, subeditor, 1941-48, drama critic, 1945-47; *News Chronicle,* London, England, reporter and subeditor, 1949; University of Auckland, Auckland, New Zealand, senior lecturer, 1951-66, associate professor of English, 1967-76. Upstate New York Poetry Circuit, guest poet, 1966; has given poetry readings at University of Cincinnati and University of Pennsylvania, 1966, Library of Congress, 1966, 1974, and in England, Canada, and Australia.

AWARDS, HONORS: Travel award, New Zealand State Literary Fund, 1949; Carnegie grant, 1950; Jessie Mackay Memorial Prize, New Zealand branch of International PEN and State Literary Fund, 1957, for *Poems,*

1949-1957, and 1962, for *A Small Room with Large Windows: Selected Poems;* New Zealand Book Award, 1958, 1963, 1975, 1980, 1983, and 1987; Fulbright fellowship, 1961; Institute of Contemporary Arts fellowship, Washington, DC, 1961; Whittall Fund Award, Library of Congress, 1966 and 1974; Litt.D., University of Auckland, 1966, and University of Canterbury, 1975; New Zealand Poetry Award, 1975, for *Collected Poems, 1933-1973,* 1979, for *An Incorrigible Music: A Sequence of Poems,* and 1983, for *You Will Know When You Get There: Poems, 1979-1981;* Katherine Mansfield memorial fellowship, 1983; Commander, Order of the British Empire, 1986; Dillons Commonwealth Poetry Prize, for *Continuum: New and Later Poems,* 1989; Queen's Gold Medal for Poetry, 1989; Order of New Zealand, 1990; A. W. Reed Lifetime Achievement Award, 2000.

WRITINGS:

POETRY COLLECTIONS

Valley of Decision, [Auckland, New Zealand], 1933.

Enemies: Poems, 1934-36, Caxton Press (Christchurch, New Zealand), 1937.

Not in Narrow Seas, Caxton Press (Christchurch, New Zealand), 1939.

Island and Time, Caxton Press (Christchurch, New Zealand), 1941.

(With A. R. D. Fairburn, Denis Glover, and R. A. K. Mason) *Recent Poems,* Caxton Press (Christchurch, New Zealand), 1941.

(Under pseudonym Whim-Wham) *Verses, 1941-1942,* Caxton Press (Christchurch, New Zealand), 1942.

Sailing or Drowning, Progressive Publishing Society (Wellington, New Zealand), 1943.

(Editor) *A Book of New Zealand Verse, 1923-1945,* Caxton Press (Christchurch, New Zealand), 1945, revised edition, 1951.

Jack without Magic, Caxton Press (Christchurch, New Zealand), 1946.

At Dead Low Water, and Sonnets, Caxton Press (Christchurch, New Zealand), 1949.

Poems, 1949-1957, Mermaid Press (Wellington, New Zealand), 1957.

(Under pseudonym Whim-Wham) *The Best of Whim-Wham,* Paul's Book Arcade, 1959.

(Editor) *The Penguin Book of New Zealand Verse,* Penguin (Harmondsworth, England), 1960.

A Small Room with Large Windows: Selected Poems, Oxford University Press (London, England), 1962.

(Under pseudonym Whim-Wham) *Whim-Wham Land,* Blackwood & Janet Paul (Auckland, New Zealand), 1967.

Trees, Effigies, Moving Objects: A Sequence of Poems, Catspaw Press (Wellington, New Zealand), 1972.

An Abominable Temper, and Other Poems, Catspaw Press (Wellington, New Zealand), 1973.

Collected Poems, 1933-1973, A. H. & A. W. Reed (Australia), 1974.

An Incorrigible Music: A Sequence of Poems, Auckland University Press (Auckland, New Zealand), 1979.

You Will Know When You Get There: Poems, 1979-81, Auckland University Press (Auckland, New Zealand), 1982.

The Loop in Lone Kauri Road: Poems, 1983-1985, Auckland University Press (Auckland, New Zealand), 1986.

Continuum: New and Later Poems, 1972-1988, Auckland University Press (Auckland, New Zealand), 1988.

Selected Poems, 1940-1989, Viking (London, England), 1990.

Early Days Yet: New and Collected Poems, 1941-1997, Carcanet Press (Manchester, England), 1997.

The Bells of Saint Babel's: Poems, 1997-2000, Auckland University Press (Auckland, New Zealand), 2001.

PLAYS

The Axe: A Verse Tragedy (produced in Christchurch, New Zealand, at Little Theatre, Canterbury University College, 1948), Caxton Press (Christchurch, New Zealand), 1949.

Moon Section, produced in Auckland, New Zealand, at Auckland Festival, 1959.

Doctor Pom, produced in Auckland, New Zealand, 1964.

Four Plays (contains *The Axe,* revised version, and three radio plays, all produced by New Zealand Broadcasting Corporation: *The Overseas Expert,* broadcast 1961, *The Duke's Miracle,* broadcast 1967, and *Resident of Nowhere,* broadcast 1969), A. H. & A. W. Reed (Australia), 1972.

Il Miracolo del Duca (Italian translation of *The Duke's Miracle* by Italo Verri), Casa Editrice 'Liberty house' di Lucio Scardino, Ferrara (Italy), 1994.

OTHER

Look Back Harder: Critical Writings, 1935-84, Auckland University Press (Auckland, New Zealand), 1987.

Work represented in anthologies, including *Poems from New Writing,* John Lehmann (London, England), 1946; *An Anthology of New Zealand Verse,* Oxford University Press (New York, NY), 1956; *A Garland for Dylan Thomas,* Clark & Way, (New York, NY), 1963; and *Seven Centuries of Poetry in English,* Oxford University Press (New York, NY), 1987. Contributor to periodicals, including *Meanjin Quarterly, Poetry, New World Writing, Times Literary Supplement, London, Partisan Review, Verse,* and *London Review of Books.*

WORK IN PROGRESS: Satirical pieces and more poems.

SIDELIGHTS: Allen Curnow is, according to the essayist for *Contemporary Poets,* "a central figure in modern New Zealand poetry. His *A Book of New Zealand Verse, 1923-1945,* a selection of poems supported by an impressive introduction, made apparent for the first time that New Zealand's modern poets had produced the beginnings of a distinct tradition. The period of colonial literature was over—this was Curnow's point, demonstrated by the fact that the poets were no longer romanticizing their environment with an eye to, or with the eyes of, English readers, but coming to terms with it as it was." Speaking of Curnow's own poems, the essayist especially praised those found in the collection *An Incorrigible Music: A Sequence of Poems,* in which "Curnow juxtaposes images of coastal New Zealand with modern urban Italy and a Borgia murder with that of the Italian statesman Aldo Moro (exactly 500 years later). The mind and the poetic skills are cast out wide to bring together these various realities, each of them a means of confronting death in a new way. Curnow has never written better."

Curnow once told *CA:* "My first very youthful poems came from a personal religious crisis during studies for the Anglican ministry and the social crisis of the 1930s depression. A few of the poems which followed touched on New Zealand life and history: a poet's attempt to solve questions about where he was, the language and tradition being almost everywhere, and his country rather inconveniently but ineluctably *somewhere.* There was 'The Unhistoric Story' about Cook's first southern voyage, 'The Victim' about a Dutch crewman killed in a clash with the Maori when Abel Tasman made the first European discovery of New Zealand (in 1642), and 'Landfall in Unknown Seas,' written on commission by the New Zealand government to celebrate the 300th anniversary of Tasman's voyage. There was also a sonnet, 'The Skeleton of the Great Moa' about New Zealand's giant extinct bird. It pleases me that all these works have continued to be quoted, nearly forty years after their first appearance—not only in literary works, but occasionally in historical and even scientific studies. It pleased me less when one or two younger writers chose to regard me as a banner-bearer for some kind of hole-and-corner poetic nationalism. The truth was that for a few years my island nation served me the way Yeats said his 'System' served him—it 'gave me metaphors for poetry.'

"Like some other New Zealand authors," Curnow recalled, "I was to find dramatic writing (especially for the stage) a somewhat frustrating exercise in a country without dramatic tradition or well-established theater. Since 1970 I have persisted with poems about the troublesome question of how to be in two (or more) places at once, i.e., Auckland, New Zealand, and Washington, D.C. A title like 'Trees, Effigies, Moving Objects,' for instance, is an excuse for arranging in perspective a giant kauri tree, the Washington Memorial, a roadside effigy of the Virgin at Paraparaumu, and Nebuchadnezzar's golden idol. Can I perhaps unite a memory of the Duomo in Florence, by way of the assassin's dagger which killed Giuliano de'Medici in 1478, with my own rusty fishing knife and a *kahawai* landed at Kare Kare, and the chemistry of a garden poison for snails? This may sound far-fetched, but isn't it one of the tasks of a poet to transform the far-fetched into the self-evident?"

Curnow added, "Extended trips to Italy, France, and the United Kingdom (1974, 1978, 1983) must have helped to 'universalise' (if the word isn't too pretentious) my later writing, but not to obscure where it all begins, in a life and a home in the South-West Pacific."

BIOGRAPHICAL/CRITICAL SOURCES:

BOOKS

Contemporary Poets, 6th edition, St. James Press (Detroit, MI), 1996.

Roddick, Alan, *Allen Curnow,* Oxford University Press (New York, NY), 1980.

PERIODICALS

Islands, autumn, 1975.

Landfall, autumn, 1963; spring, 1983; spring, 1989; spring, 1990.

Observer (London), October 16, 1983.

Poetry Review, Volume 78, number 1, 1988.

Quadrant, September, 2000, Max Richards, "Allen Curnow, New Zealand's Major Poet."

Scripsi (Melbourne, Australia), spring, 1983.

Times Literary Supplement, July 31, 1987, p. 823; June 1, 1989, p. 593.

Verse, Volume 8, number 2, 1991, Michael Hulse, "Allen Curnow at Eighty: A Celebration."

D

de LANGE, N. R. M.
See de LANGE, Nicholas (Robert Michael)

* * *

de LANGE, Nicholas (Robert Michael) 1944-
(N. R. M. de Lange)

PERSONAL: Born August 7, 1944, in Nottingham, England; son of George David and Elaine (Jacobus) de Lange. *Education:* Christ Church, Oxford, B.A., 1966, M.A., 1969, D.Phil., 1970.

ADDRESSES: Office—Faculty of Oriental Studies, Cambridge University, Sidgwick Ave., Cambridge CB3 9DA, England.

CAREER: University of Southampton, Southampton, England, Parkes Library fellow, 1969-71; Cambridge University, Cambridge, England, lecturer in Rabbinics, 1971—.

WRITINGS:

A Woman in Israel, Ecumenical Society of the Blessed Virgin Mary, 1975.
Origin and the Jews: Studies in Jewish-Christian Relations in Third-Century Palestine, Cambridge University Press (New York City), 1976.
Apocrypha: Jewish Literature of the Hellenistic Age, Viking (New York City), 1978.
Atlas of the Jewish World, Facts on File (New York City), 1984.

Judaism, Oxford University Press (New York City), 1986.
Reflections on Translating, Judaic Studies Program, University of Cincinnati (Cincinnati), 1993.
The Illustrated History of the Jewish People, Harcourt (New York City), 1997.
An Introduction to Judaism, Cambridge University Press (New York City), 2000.
(Editor) *Hebrew Scholarship and the Medieval World,* Cambridge University Press (New York City), 2001.

Sometimes publishes under the name N. R. M. de Lange.

TRANSLATOR

Amos Oz, *My Michael,* Knopf, 1972.
Oz, *Elsewhere, Perhaps,* Harcourt (New York City), 1973.
Oz, *Touch the Water Touch the Wind,* Harcourt (New York City), 1974.
Oz, *Unto Death,* Harcourt (New York City), 1975.
Oz, *The Hill of Evil Counsel,* Harcourt (New York City), 1978.
Oz, *Where Jackals Howl and Other Stories,* Harcourt (New York City), 1981.
Oz, *Black Box,* Harcourt (New York City), 1988.
Oz, *To Know a Woman,* Harcourt (San Diego), 1991.
Oz, *My Michael,* Vintage (New York City), 1992.
Oz, *Fima,* Harcourt (New York City), 1993.
Oz, *Under This Blazing Light,* Press Syndicate of the University of Cambridge (New York City), 1995.
Oz, *Don't Call It Night,* Harcourt (San Diego), 1996.
Greek Jewish Texts from the Cairo Genizah, J. C. B. Mohr (Tübingen, Germany), 1996.

Oz, *Panther in the Basement,* Harcourt (New York City), 1997.

Abraham B. Yehoshua, *A Journey to the End of the Millennium,* Doubleday (New York City), 1999.

CONTRIBUTOR

J. A. Michener, editor, *Firstfruits,* Jewish Publication Society, 1973.

H. Crouzel and others, editors, *Origeniana,* Universita di Bari, 1975.

Jacob Sonntag, editor, *New Writing from Israel,* Corgi, 1976.

(Author of introduction) Peter Levy, translator, *The Psalms,* Penguin (Hardmondsworth), 1976.

Elliott Anderson, editor, *Contemporary Israeli Literature,* Jewish Publication Society, 1977.

P. D. A. Garnsey and C. R. Whittaker, editors, *Imperialism in the Ancient World,* Cambridge University Press, 1978.

Emanuel Litvinoff, editor, *Jewish Short Stories,* Penguin, 1979.

J. A. Emerton and S. C. Reif, editors, *Interpreting the Hebrew Bible,* Cambridge University Press, 1982.

A. Stacpoole, editor, *Mary's Place in Christian Dialogue,* St. Paul Publication, 1982.

(Translator and author of introduction and notes, with Marguerite Harl) *Origene: Philoclie 1-20 et la lettre a Africanus,* Editions du Cerf, 1983.

M. Vegetti, editor, *Orialita, Scrittura, Spettacolo,* Boringheri (Turin), 1983.

Also contributor to *Tradition, Transition, and Transmission,* edited by B. D. Fox, 1983. Contributor to *Encyclopedia Judaica, Macmillan's Encyclopedia, Encyclopedia Judaica,* and *Dictionary of Philosophy.* Contributor of more than one hundred articles, translations, and reviews to theology journals and other periodicals, including *Commentary* and *Harper's.*

SIDELIGHTS: Nicholas de Lange, a reader in Hebrew and Jewish Studies at Cambridge University, is also a translator of the works of Amos Oz and others, editor of a number of collections, and author of books on culture and history. De Lange produced a collection of essays by eight international scholars that cover a history spanning more than 2,000 years in *The Illustrated History of the Jewish People.* Periods covered stretch back from the earliest tribes, kingdoms, and wars to modern times. Contributor Oded Irshai documents the cultural interactions between the Jewish, Islamic, and Christian peoples. Michael R. Marrus writes about the Holocaust,

and Derek J. Penslar describes modern-day Israel. The book contains 150 illustrations and sixteen maps. A *Publishers Weekly* contributor commented that "where new data or interpretations have come to light, myth is transformed by political, religious, or sociological insight." Andrew B. Wertheimer noted in *Library Journal* that while *The Illustrated History of the Jewish People* "does provide a well-illustrated, balanced format to encourage historical exploration," it lacks a glossary of terms used by the essayists.

In *An Introduction to Judaism* de Lange discusses Jewish history and philosophy, books, customs and rituals, the place of the family in Jewish society, and laws that relate to birth, marriage, death, and mourning. He also writes of the future of Judaism. *Booklist* reviewer George Cohen wrote that the book "is intended for students of religion and others who seek an introduction to the faith." While *Library Journal* reviewer Naomi E. Hafter deemed the book's chronological table, which ends with the 1973 Yom Kippur War, "a shortcoming," a contributor to *Publishers Weekly* commented that de Lange "has clearly satisfied his objective, offering an overall introduction to Judaism that will be useful to both Jewish and non-Jewish readers."

De Lange told *CA:* "I am interested in texts and translations, texts as translations, translations as texts. The most influential translation of all time was the translation of the Bible from Hebrew into Greek. I have written about this event in *Apocrypha.* But the Hebrew Bible was also in a sense a translation; a translation into words of the experiences and yearnings of an amazing people, and of their deepest reflections on the nature of human life. This text, through its translations into other languages, has become the foundation of Western thought. I am fascinated by the Bible and its influence. In my work on Origen, the first great Christian interpreter of the Bible, I have concentrated on his relationship to this text. Each generation needs to relate to the past in its own way—to make its own translations. We live in an age which is not particularly religious, but which is obsessed with history. We are constantly reinterpreting the texts which make up our history, translating them into our own language. All writing, perhaps all thought, is translation. Reading is an act of translation, too.

"Most readers are unaware of this question of translation and the problems it raises. Even in the narrowest sense of the word—translation of a text from one language into another—the meaning of translation is too little understood. People think they have read an author if they have read his works in translation. What they have read is the work of a translator—a reader who is also a writer. Because of the barriers of language, readers need translators. But they do not appreciate them. The translator is noticed only when he manifestly fails, when he intrudes between reader and author. There are many fine translators: their writings are read, but their names are hardly known.

"I first took up the challenge of translation seriously in 1970, when I started translating the writings of Amos Oz. We met in Oxford and became friends. All our translations are produced in collaboration. He reads, I listen and write; I read, he listens and comments. I believe this process is the most satisfactory way of translating. When translating dead authors I have often longed to hear their voices, to ask them questions. I do not know if my translations of Amos Oz are good translations, but at least I know that they are faithful to the author's intentions. I used to think, as many people think, that translation consists of exchanging one word for another, like changing money. I have learned through experience that a faithful translation is not necessarily a literal one. A translator's loyalty is not to words. He has to be faithful to his author, to himself, to his readers. He has to interpret ideas, longings, moods. He has to absorb them, make them his own, and pass them on. The words help, but sometimes they get in the way.

"Amos Oz is a skillful writer (to my mind he is the best living writer of Hebrew prose). Although there is a great deal of local color in his books, their themes are universal themes, and I think he has important things to say to English readers. These factors help me as a translator. But I believe that Oz and I also have a common philosophy, a philosophy of translation in its widest sense. His characters struggle to express themselves in words; they are aware of the inadequacy of language and of its magic. They quote the Hebrew Bible and interpret it in their own way. They wrestle with the burden of their past and try to find its meaning for the present.

"This is the way I see my own task, too."

BIOGRAPHICAL/CRITICAL SOURCES:

PERIODICALS

Booklist, January 1, 2000, George Cohen, review of *An Introduction to Judaism*, p. 837.

Library Journal, October 15, 1997, Andrew B. Wertheimer, review of *The Illustrated History of the Jewish People*, p. 74; January, 2000, Naomi E. Hafter, review of *An Introduction to Judaism*, p. 119.

Publishers Weekly, September 29, 1997, review of *The Illustrated History of the Jewish People*, p. 73; February 14, 2000, review of *An Introduction to Judaism*, p. 191.*

*   *   *

DELONG, Lea Rosson 1947-

PERSONAL: Born June 13, 1947, in Ferriday, LA; daughter of Aaron Kenneth (a civil engineer) and Patsy Ruth (a homemaker; maiden name, Smith) Rosson; married Harris Coggeshall DeLong (a marketing representative), September 1, 1979; children: Timothy Rosson, Catherine Rosson. *Education:* Cottey College, A.A., 1969; University of Oklahoma, B.A., 1971; University of Kansas, M.A., 1973, Ph.D., 1983.

ADDRESSES: Home—Des Moines, IA. *Office*—Department of Art, Drake University, 25th St. and University Ave., Des Moines, IA 50311. *E-mail*—lrldrg@aol.com.

CAREER: University of Kansas, Lawrence, assistant curator of Spencer Museum of Art, 1974-76; Drake University, Des Moines, IA, instructor, 1976-80, assistant professor, 1980-83, associate professor, 1983-90, adjunct associate professor of art, beginning 1990; Des Moines Art Center, Des Moines, adjunct curator, 1989-91, research curator, 1998-2000.

MEMBER: College Art Association of America.

WRITINGS:

(With Gregg Narber) *New Deal Mural Projects in Iowa*, Drake University (Des Moines, IA), 1983.

Nature's Forms/Nature's Forces: The Art of Alexandre Hogue, University of Oklahoma Press (Norman, OK), 1985.

New Deal Art of the Upper Midwest, Sioux City Art Center (Sioux City, IA), 1988.

Experience Art: A Young People's Guide to the Des Moines Art Center Collection, Des Moines Art Center (Des Moines, IA), 1991.

Shifting Visions: O'Keeffe, Guston, Richter, Des Moines Art Center (Des Moines, IA), 1999.

Christian Petersen, Sculptor, Iowa State University Press (Ames, IA), 2000.

Contributor to *Chemistry Imagined: Reflections of Science,* Smithsonian Institution Press (Washington, DC), 1993. Contributor to *Woman's Art Journal.*

*   *   *

DeVORKIN, David H(yam) 1944-

PERSONAL: Born January 6, 1944, in Los Angeles, CA; son of Howard (a chemical engineer) and Judith (a teacher; maiden name, Schoenberg) DeVorkin; married Kunie Fujiki (a systems analyst), June 2, 1970; children: Hannah Fujiki. *Education:* University of California, Los Angeles, A.B., 1966; San Diego State College (now University), M.S., 1968; Yale University, M.Phil., 1970; University of Leicester, Ph.D., 1978.

ADDRESSES: Office—Department of Space Science, National Air and Space Museum, Smithsonian Institution, Washington, DC 20560. *E-mail*—David. DeVorkin@nasm.si.edu.

CAREER: Central Connecticut State College, New Britain, assistant professor of astronomy, 1970-76, associate professor of astronomy, 1979; American Institute of Physics Center for History of Physics, consultant research associate, 1977-78; National Air and Space Museum, Washington, DC, associate curator, 1980-84, curator, 1984—, Space Science and Exploration Department chairman, 1984-86.

MEMBER: History of Science Society, International Astronomical Union, American Astronomical Society (former chair of history division), Royal Astronomical Society, Astronomical Society of the Pacific.

WRITINGS:

(Editor with A. G. D. Philip) *In Memory of Helen Norris Russell,* Dudley Observatory, 1977.
The History of Modern Astronomy and Astrophysics: A Selected, Annotated Bibliography, Garland Publishing, 1982.
Practical Astronomy: Lectures on Time, Place, and Space, Smithsonian Institution Press, 1986.
Race to the Stratosphere: Manned Scientific Ballooning in the United States, Springer-Verlag (New York City), 1989.
Science with a Vengeance: How the Military Created the U.S. Space Sciences after World War II, Springer-Verlag, 1992.

(Editor) *The American Astronomical Society's First Century,* American Astronomical Society (Washington, DC), 1999.
Henry Norris Russell: Dean of American Astronomers, Princeton University Press (Princeton, NJ), 2000.

SIDELIGHTS: David H. DeVorkin, curator of the Smithsonian Institution's National Air and Space Museum, has written a number of books on astronomy, physics, and space science. Among his most acclaimed works are *Race to the Stratosphere: Manned Scientific Ballooning in the United States, Science with a Vengeance: How the Military Created the U.S. Space Sciences after World War II,* and *Henry Norris Russell: Dean of American Astronomers.*

In *Race to the Stratosphere* DeVorkin documents the first balloon flights to be conducted by Americans for scientific purposes. These flights occurred throughout the 1930s under the auspices of various government agencies. Besides studying cosmic rays, a new area for scientific investigation at the time, these flights also broke altitude records for manned ascents. Following World War II balloon flights continued to be used by the military to study conditions in the upper atmosphere. According to Robert Seidel in *Science,* "By weaving patronage, politics, physics and aerostatics together in his narrative, DeVorkin makes what had previously been regarded as a sideshow in the history of American science an exemplar of the interactions of science and American society."

Science with a Vengeance traces how the American military developed the nation's space program through their experiments with rockets captured from Nazi Germany at the end of World War II. The Nazis had perfected two rockets—the V1 and V2—which were capable of flying long distances and delivering a payload of high explosives. The V2, in particular, was a true rocket capable of traveling in earth's upper atmosphere. Capturing sixty-two V2 rockets at war's end, the American military experimented with their capabilities both for military and scientific purposes. From their research, enormous advances were made in studying cosmic rays and ultraviolet rays, and in using spacecraft for photographic research. DeVorkin's account, Alex Roland explained in *Science,* is "a straightforward description of the research that was done and how it was accomplished." Roland went on to call *Science with a Vengeance* "an important book" and "a richly detailed case study."

DeVorkin presents the life story of the "Dean of American Astronomers" in his *Henry Norris Russell.* The first biography to be written on the pioneering astronomer,

DeVorkin's book combines an account of Russell's personal life with an analysis of his scientific work and the impact he had on the field of astronomy. In addition to his studies into the evolution of stars and the beginnings of the solar system, Russell also is remembered for the Hertzsprung-Russell diagram, still used by those in the field of stellar astrophysics. Russell played a crucial role in turning American astronomy from "an observation-based discipline to an active, theory-driven science," as James Olson explained in *Library Journal.* Olson found DeVorkin's biography to be "very scholarly" and "very readable." The critic for *Publishers Weekly* noted that "it's easy to see why people in the relevant fields . . . will want this very informative volume."

DeVorkin once told *CA:* "My early interest in astronomy was stimulated by my father, who worked on rocket propulsion chemistry after World War II and often talked about astronomy, rockets (especially V2 rockets), and science fiction with me. I became an amateur astronomer and telescope builder and worked through UCLA as a research assistant, planetarium guide and lecturer, and guitar instructor. I became interested in the history of modern astronomy while an observer at Lick and Yerkes observatories and especially after graduate work at Yale. I switched formally to history in 1974 while teaching astronomy at CCSC, and completed a thesis on the symbiotic relationship of schemes of spectral classification and stellar evolution in the late nineteenth and twentieth centuries. My interests have always been on the history of recent astrophysics, and coming to the National Air and Space Museum has given me a chance to study what science has done with captured German V2 rockets. The 'V' stands for 'vengeance weapon,' and so it is a study of 'science with a vengeance.'"

BIOGRAPHICAL/CRITICAL SOURCES:

PERIODICALS

Choice, March, 1993, review of *Science with a Vengeance,* p. 1178.
Library Journal, July, 2000, James Olson, review of *Henry Norris Russell,* p. 132.
National Forum, summer, 1992, review of *Race to the Stratosphere,* p. 40.
Physics Today, July, 1993, Bruce Hevly, review of *Science with a Vengeance,* p. 77; February, 2000, Morton S. Roberts, review of *The American Astronomical Society's First Century,* p. 56.

Publishers Weekly, July 17, 2000, review of *Henry Norris Russell,* p. 188.
Science, September 22, 1989, Robert Seidel, review of *Race to the Stratosphere,* p. 1401; April 30, 1993, Alex Roland, review of *Science with a Vengeance,* p. 703.
Sky and Telescope, July, 1993, review of *Science with a Vengeance,* p. 61.
Town and Country, July, 1994, review of *Science with a Vengeance,* p. 628.*

*   *   *

DEXTER, N. C.
   See DEXTER, (Norman) Colin

*   *   *

DEXTER, (Norman) Colin 1930-
   (N. C. Dexter)

PERSONAL: Born September 29, 1930, in Stamford, England; son of Alfred (a taxi driver) and Dorothy (Towns) Dexter; married Dorothy Cooper (a physiotherapist), March 31, 1956; children: Sally, Jeremy. *Education:* Christ's College, Cambridge, B.A., 1953, M.A., 1958. *Politics:* Socialist ("lapsed"). *Religion:* Methodist ("lapsed").

ADDRESSES: Home—56 Banbury Rd., Oxford OX2 7RG, England.

CAREER: Wyggeston School, Leicester, England, assistant classics master, 1954-57; Loughborough Grammar School, Loughborough, England, sixth form classics master, 1957-59; Corby Grammar School, Corby, England, senior classics master, 1959-66; Oxford Local Examination Board, Oxford, England, assistant secretary, 1966-76, senior assistant secretary, 1976-87. *Military service:* Royal Corps of Signals, 1949-50.

MEMBER: Crime Writers Association, Detection Club.

AWARDS, HONORS: M.A., Oxford University, 1966; Silver Dagger Award, Crime Writers Association, 1979, for *Service of All the Dead,* and 1981, for *The Dead of Jericho;* Gold Dagger Award, Crime Writers Association, 1989, for *The Wench Is Dead,* and 1992, for *The Way through the Woods;* M.A., Leicester University,

1996; Medal of Merit, Lotus Club, 1996; Cartier Diamond Dagger, Crime Writers Association, 1997, for outstanding services to crime literature.

WRITINGS:

"INSPECTOR MORSE" MYSTERIES

Last Bus to Woodstock, St. Martin's Press (New York City), 1975.

Last Seen Wearing (also see below), St. Martin's Press, 1976.

The Silent World of Nicholas Quinn, St. Martin's Press, 1977.

Service of All the Dead, Macmillan (London), 1979, St. Martin's Press, 1980.

The Dead of Jericho, St. Martin's Press, 1981.

The Riddle of the Third Mile (also see below), Macmillan, 1983.

The Secret of Annexe 3 (also see below), Macmillan, 1986, St. Martin's Press, 1987.

The Wench Is Dead, Macmillan, 1989, St. Martin's Press, 1990.

The Jewel That Was Ours, Macmillan, 1991, Crown (New York City), 1992.

The Way through the Woods, Macmillan, 1992, Crown, 1993.

Morse's Greatest Mystery and Other Stories (contains "As Good as Gold," "Morse's Greatest Mystery," "Evans Tries an O-Level," "Dead as a Dodo," "At the Lulu-Bar Motel," "Neighbourhood Watch," "A Case of Mis-Identity," "The Inside Story," "Monty's Revolver," "The Carpet-Bagger," and "Last Call"), Macmillan, 1993.

The Daughters of Cain, Macmillan, 1994, Crown, 1995.

Death Is Now My Neighbour, Macmillan, 1996, Crown, 1997.

The Remorseful Day: The Final Inspector Morse Novel, Crown, 1999.

OTHER

(Under name N. C. Dexter, with E. G. Rayner) *Liberal Studies: An Outline Course,* 2 volumes, Macmillan, 1964, revised edition, 1966.

(Under name N. C. Dexter, with Rayner) *Guide to Contemporary Politics,* Pergamon (London), 1966.

Work represented in several anthologies, including *Murder Ink,* edited by Dilys Winn, Workman, 1977; *Winter's Crimes 9,* edited by George Hardinge, St. Martin's Press, 1978; *Winter's Crimes 13,* edited by Hardinge, St. Martin's Press, 1982; and *Winter's Crimes 21,* edited by Hilary Hale, Macmillan, 1989.

ADAPTATIONS: Stories based on Dexter's Inspector Morse character were adapted for television and aired on the PBS program *Mystery! Inspector Morse: Driven to Distraction* by Anthony Minghella is a screenplay based on characters created by Dexter and published by University of Cambridge, 1994. Several of Dexter's novels have also been recorded and released as audio books.

SIDELIGHTS: "To most readers of Colin Dexter's books," wrote *Dictionary of Literary Biography* contributor Bernard Benstock, "his major accomplishment is the creation of his particular detective hero, Detective Chief Inspector Morse of the Thames Valley Constabulary of Kidlington, Oxon." Inspector Morse is an irascible figure, fond of beer and tobacco, but nonetheless held in awe by his associate, Detective Sergeant Lewis. "At times," Benstock revealed, "his seediness is similar to the seediness of a Graham Greene character, his bluster and swagger similar to John Mortimer's Rumpole of the Bailey, but always there is an element of the pathetic to counterbalance the braggadocio. Morse's vulnerable and remarkable character unfolds serially from book to book, so that eventually there are no mysteries about him—except for his given name."

Dexter introduced Inspector Morse in 1975 in *Last Bus to Woodstock,* which established many of the central characteristics of Dexter's work. "*Last Bus to Woodstock* concerns the brutal murder (and possible sex-murder) of a scantily clad female hitchhiker, whose companion at the bus stop fails to identify herself," wrote Benstock. "Several young women are likely possibilities for the companion, but Morse is frustrated by their refusal to be honest with him." Morse finds himself sidetracked after having identified the wrong person as the murderer. "The grisly deaths of a husband and wife, each of whom had confessed to the murder," Benstock continued, "bring matters to a head, and Morse apprehends the woman murderer—an attractive young woman he had admired, who confesses that she has fallen in love with him—as she is taken away to stand trial." Dexter treats each of the Morse mysteries as a puzzle, complete with misleading clues, red herrings, and false trails. "Once you choose the wrong word," explained a *Virginia Quarterly Review* contributor, "the whole puzzle can be filled incorrectly."

Morse's irritability is balanced by his companion in mystery-solving, Detective Sergeant Lewis. Cushing Strout, writing in *Armchair Detective,* compared the relationship between Lewis and Morse to that of Arthur Conan Doyle's Sherlock Holmes and John Watson, calling Dexter's work "the best contemporary English example of adapting and updating Doyle's technique." Like Holmes, Strout continued, "Morse is a bachelor," but, "in spite of his generally cynical expectations about human nature and the world, unlike Holmes he is always romantically vulnerable (in spite of disappointing experience) to being smitten by love at first sight for some attractive and intelligent, but quite inappropriate woman." In contrast to Morse, Strout continued, Sergeant Lewis "is working class, a family man, and a competent policeman in a routine way. He has a refreshing common sense that Morse often sorely lacks, and the two men (like Holmes and Watson in this respect) know how to tease each other."

Dexter, Strout explained, "has collated his novels under the heading of 'what may be termed (though it sounds a bit posh) the exploitation of reader-mystification.'" This is a traditional attribute of English detective fiction: the ability to mislead the reader, who is trying to identify the culprit. The classic mystery novel, as set forth by one of the earliest practitioners of the genre, G. K. Chesterton, should present the reader with all the clues available to the detective, but in such a way that the reader fails to make the connection with the criminal until after the detective uncovers the guilty party. "Inferior writers," Strout continued, "tend to cast suspicion on so many characters that it is . . . like hiding one card amid the rest of the deck, rather than performing the much more difficult classic trick, wherein the 'money card' is one of only three cards." "Dexter," the critic concluded, "keeps shifting the pieces, like a conjuror misdirecting the audience by giving a specious explanation of his trick, until they finally make a coherent and credible picture with the lagniappe of a last surprise." In a review of *The Daughters of Cain* for the *New York Times Book Review,* Marilyn Stasio advised readers "to get out their pencils, timetables and aspirin."

As the series progresses, Dexter also begins to play highly literate games with his readers, ranging from apparently gratis references to literature, such as James Joyce's *Ulysses* in *The Riddle of the Third Mile* and Sophocles' Oedipus trilogy of plays in *The Dead of Jericho.* He also uses inscriptions and epigraphs at the beginning of each chapter like a chorus in a Greek play to comment on the story's action and the state of Morse's mind. "The basic norm in the Dexter novels," Benstock declared, "is best characterized by the epigraph to chapter 14 of *The Riddle of the Third Mile:* 'Preliminary investigations are now in full swing, and Morse appears unconcerned about the contradictory evidence that emerges.'"

Morse demonstrates many of his best points in the Gold Dagger award-winning novel, *The Wench Is Dead.* Critics have compared the book to Josephine Tey's classic detective novel *The Daughter of Time,* in which her detective, Alan Grant, immobilized in hospital with a fractured spine, tries to solve a historical mystery—the disappearance of young Edward V and his brother Richard of York in the Tower of London during the reign of Richard III. Morse is hospitalized with a bleeding ulcer, and to ease his boredom he reopens a Victorian murder case that took place in Oxford: the death by drowning of a female passenger on a canal boat in the mid-nineteenth century. Morse's wits and temper, wrote Stasio in the *New York Times Book Review,* "tug the reader into the detective's hospital bed to share his single-minded pursuit of the truth."

Dexter ended the Inspector Morse series in 1999 with his final case, *The Remorseful Day: The Final Inspector Morse Novel.* Morse is called in to re-investigate the two-year-old murder of a local nurse, a woman with whom he was once romantically involved. In the course of the investigation, Morse's long-time health problems come to the fore, leading to a final ending not only to the story but to the Morse series. "This finale to a grand series," noted the critic for *Publishers Weekly,* "presents a moving elegy to one of mystery fiction's most celebrated and popular characters." Reviewing the novel for *Booklist,* Bill Ott described it as "an audaciously clever and surprisingly moving finale."

Dexter's Inspector Morse novels have established him as a pivotal figure in modern English detective fiction. Throughout the series, Benstock states, "the comic vies with the grotesque, pathos with the tragic, within an effective evocation of the mundane. The surface realities of ordinary life consistently color the criminal situations without impinging on the careful artifice of the usual murders and the bumbling but brilliant methods of investigation undertaken almost in spite of himself by Chief Inspector E. Morse." According to the essayist for the *St. James Guide to Crime and Mystery Writers,* Dexter "has established himself in the forefront of British writers with some of the cleverest and most complicated plots, delighting a vast and ever growing band of devoted readers." Michael Leapman, writing in *New Statesman,* called Morse "one of the great detectives of English fiction."

BIOGRAPHICAL/CRITICAL SOURCES:

BOOKS

Contemporary Popular Writers, St. James Press (Detroit), 1997.

Dictionary of Literary Biography, Volume 87: *British Mystery and Thriller Writers since 1940, First Series,* Gale (Detroit), 1989.

St. James Guide to Crime and Mystery Writers, 4th edition, St. James Press, 1996.

PERIODICALS

Armchair Detective, winter, 1989, pp. 76-77; fall, 1990, p. 497; summer, 1993, review of *The Jewel That Was Ours,* p. 45; summer, 1994, p. 272; summer, 1995, review of *The Daughters of Cain,* p. 342; fall, 1995, pp. 434-437.

Booklist, March 1, 1995, Emily Melton, review of *The Daughters of Cain,* p. 1139; October 1, 1995, Emily Melton, review of *Morse's Greatest Mystery,* p. 212; December 1, 1996, Bill Ott, review of *Death Is Now My Neighbor,* p. 619; December 1, 1999, Bill Ott, review of *The Remorseful Day,* p. 660.

Books, November, 1994, review of *The Daughters of Cain,* p. 16.

Entertainment Weekly, April 23, 1993, Gene Lyons, review of *The Way through the Woods,* p. 50; April 4, 1997, Nikki Amdur, review of *Death Is Now My Neighbor,* p. 79; December 12, 1997, Tom De Haven, review of *The Way through the Wood,* p. 78.

Insight on the News, May 22, 1995, Elizabeth M. Cosin, review of *Daughters of Cain,* p. 25.

Kirkus Reviews, March 1, 1995, review of *The Daughters of Cain,* p. 270.

Library Journal, February 1, 2000, Fred M. Gervat, review of *The Remorseful Day,* p. 121.

Listener, July 8, 1976; June 30, 1977.

Los Angeles Times Book Review, April 9, 1995, review of *The Daughters of Cain,* p. 12.

New Republic, March 4, 1978.

New Statesman, September 20, 1996, Boyd Tonkin, "Watching the Detectives," p. 45; October 25, 1999, Michael Leapman, "Clotted Heart" and review of *The Remorseful Day,* p. 54; November 20, 2000, Andrew Billen, "Requiem for a Cop," p. 47.

New York Times Book Review, May 20, 1990, p. 53; April 4, 1993; April 16, 1995, review of *The Daughters of Cain,* p. 29; March 2, 1997, review of *Death Is Now My Neighbor,* p. 20.

People Weekly, May 8, 1995, Cynthia Sanz, review of *The Daughters of Cain,* p. 46.

Publishers Weekly, March 8, 1993, review of *The Way through the Woods,* p. 71; March 13, 1995, review of *The Daughters of Cain,* p. 63; October 9, 1995, review of *Morse's Greatest Mystery,* p. 79; December 30, 1996, review of *Death Is Now My Neighbor,* p. 57; January 24, 2000, review of *The Remorseful Day,* p. 296.

South China Morning Post, September 16, 1999, "Crime Writer Closes Book on Inspector Morse."

Time, April 26, 1993, p. 65, William A. Henry III, review of *The Way through the Woods,* p. 65.

Times Literary Supplement, September 26, 1975; April 23, 1976; August 26, 1977; June 5, 1981; October 25, 1991, p. 21; October 23, 1992, p. 22; December 23, 1994, review of *The Daughters of Cain,* p. 21.

Virginia Quarterly Review, autumn, 1992, p. 131.

Wall Street Journal, April 27, 1995, review of *The Daughters of Cain,* p. A12; March 28, 1997, review of *Death Is Now My Neighbor,* p. A14.

Washington Post Book World, December 20, 1987, p. 8.*

*   *   *

DICKSON, Mora (Hope-Robertson) 1918-

PERSONAL: Born April 20, 1918, in Glasgow, Scotland; daughter of Laurence and Mora (Sloan) Hope-Robertson; married Alexander Graeme Dickson, August 30, 1951. *Education:* Edinburgh College of Art, Diploma of Art, 1941; Byam Shaw School of Drawing and Painting, London, England, certificate, 1950. *Religion:* Christian.

ADDRESSES: Home—19 Blenheim Rd., London W4, England. *Office*—c/o Blackwell Publishing, 108 Cowley Rd., Oxford OX4 1JF, England.

CAREER: Writer and artist, c. 1962—. Founder, with husband, of Community Service Volunteers and Voluntary Service Overseas.

WRITINGS:

Baghdad and Beyond, Rand McNally (Chicago, IL), 1962.

New Nigerians, Rand McNally, 1963.

A Season in Sarawak, Rand McNally, 1964.

A World Elsewhere: Voluntary Service Overseas, Rand McNally, 1965.

Israeli Interlude, Dobson, 1965.

Count Us In, Dobson, 1966.

Longhouse in Sarawak, Gollancz (London), 1971.

Beloved Partner, Gollancz, 1974.

The Inseparable Grief, Epworth, 1975.

A Chance to Serve, Dobson, 1976.

Asian Assignment, Dobson, 1979.

The Powerful Bond, Dobson, 1980.
The Aunts, St. Andrews Press, 1981.

Also author of *Teacher Extraordinary,* 1986, and *Nannie,* 1988.

SIDELIGHTS: British author Mora Dickson has written a number of books based on her travels throughout the world on behalf of governmental development programs. She and her husband, Alexander Dickson, have worked as volunteers with several organizations, including UNESCO. She is also co-founder with her husband of Community Service Volunteers and Voluntary Service Overseas, two organizations which involve British young people in service to their own and foreign communities. She has lived and worked in Nigeria, Iraq, and Sarawak and has travelled extensively throughout Asia, the Pacific, and the United States.

Dickson writes about her volunteer organization in *A World Elsewhere: Voluntary Service Overseas.* Based on correspondence she has received from young people who have participated in the program, Dickson's account tells of the volunteers' work as teachers and recreational directors in a number of foreign countries with traditionally friendly ties to England. B. J. Brewster in the *Library Journal* praised the book's "well-chosen selections" from volunteer letters and Dickson's own "excellent woodcut illustrations." The critic for the *Times Literary Supplement* found *A World Elsewhere* to be "a success story and it makes exciting reading."

In *Baghdad and Beyond* Dickson writes of her life in Iraq in the mid-1950s when her husband was serving with a UNESCO technical mission. Although the critic for the *Times Literary Supplement* believed that "Dickson is no writer," he did find that "she is a most persuasive artist, and the book is richly illustrated with her own drawings." The reviewer for *Kirkus* noted that Dickson's "book is strongly and pleasantly flavored with her personality." He particularly admired her "native talent for observation and for self-mocking cheerfulness."

In 1957 Dickson and her husband visited Sarawak, an island now part of Malaysia, to investigate various developmental programs then underway. Their visit inspired them to establish Voluntary Service Overseas. Dickson's account of the visit, and of the experiences of the first teenaged volunteers to work in Sarawak, is contained in *A Season in Sarawak.* Paul Bixler, reviewing the title for *Library Journal,* noted that "the coura-

geous Mrs. Dickson tells of her own experiences among the people of the rough Sarawak backcountry as a kind of long introduction" to the story of Voluntary Service Oversea. When focusing on the young volunteer workers, "Dickson writes perceptively," Bixler stated. The *Times Literary Supplement* critic found that Dickson's "account of [the Voluntary Service Overseas group's] successful beginning given here is absorbing," while Dickson's woodcut illustrations "are altogether charming and make her book a pleasure to read."

BIOGRAPHICAL/CRITICAL SOURCES:

PERIODICALS

Best Sellers, May 15, 1965, review of *A World Elsewhere,* p. 97.
Booklist, June 1, 1962, review of *Baghdad and Beyond,* p. 679.
Choice, January, 1968, review of *Israeli Interlude,* p. 1301.
Commonweal, May 28, 1965, E. M. Greaves, review of *A World Elsewhere,* p. 333.
Kirkus, February 15, 1962, review of *Baghdad and Beyond,* p. 206.
Library Journal, June 15, 1962, David Dorman, review of *Baghdad and Beyond,* p. 2378; January 15, 1964, Paul Bixler, review of *A Season in Sarawak,* p. 238; April 15, 1965, B. K. Brewster, review of *A World Elsewhere,* p. 1924.
Times Literary Supplement, November 24, 1961, review of *Baghdad and Beyond,* p. 841; December 28, 1962, review of *A Season in Sarawak,* p. 1007; November 26, 1964, review of *A World Elsewhere,* p. 1082; June 30, 1966, review of *Israeli Interlude,* p. 578.*

*   *   *

DINER, Hasia R(ena) 1946-

PERSONAL: Born October 7, 1946, in Milwaukee, WI; daughter of Morris (a teacher) and Ita (Eichenbaum) Schwartzman; married Steven Diner (a college professor), July 12, 1970; children: Shira Miriam, Eli. *Education:* University of Wisconsin at Madison, B.A., 1968; University of Chicago, M.A.T., 1970; University of Illinois at Chicago Circle, Ph.D., 1975. *Religion:* Jewish.

ADDRESSES: Home—4 Washington Square Village, 8-L, New York, NY 10012. *Office*—Skirball Department of Hebrew and Judaic Studies, Department of History, New York University, 51 Washington Square South, New York, NY 10003. *E-mail*—hrd@is4.nyu.edu.

CAREER: University of Maryland, College Park, instructor in history, beginning 1975; Radcliffe College, Bunting Institute, Cambridge, MA, research associate, 1978-80; Washington Semester in the Arts and Humanities, American University, Washington, DC, 1980-84; University of Maryland, Department of American Studies, professor of history, 1984-96; New York University, New York City, Paul S. and Sylvia Steinberg Professor of American Jewish History, 1996—. Instructor at Federal City College, 1975-76; visiting assistant professor, George Washington University, 1976-77, and Goucher College, 1977-78. Director of employment discrimination counseling, Women's Legal Defense Fund, 1975. Visiting lecturer at numerous universities and conferences. Consultant to films and public history projects, including *They Came for Good: A History of the Jewish People in America, The Life and Times of Hank Greenberg, Hollywoodmania, Jews and Blacks in the Civil Rights Movement,* and *The Irish in America.*

MEMBER: American Historical Association, Organization of American Historians, American Studies Association, Association for Jewish Studies, Immigration History Society, Association for Religion in Intellectual Life (member of board), American Academy of Jewish Research (fellow), National Capitol Labor Historians, American Jewish Committee, Chesapeake Area Women Historians.

AWARDS, HONORS: One of twenty living women historians included in book *American Women Historians, 1700-1900s,* Greenwood Press, 1998.

WRITINGS:

(Contributor) Arthur Schlesinger and Roger Bruns, editors, *Congress Investigates,* Chelsea House (New York City), 1975.

In the Almost Promised Land: American Jews and Blacks, 1915-1935, Greenwood Press (Westport, CT), 1977, reprinted, Johns Hopkins University Press (Baltimore, MD), 1995.

Women in Urban Society: An Annotated Bibliography, Gale (Detroit, MI), 1979.

Erin's Daughters in America: Irish Immigrant Women in the Nineteenth Century, Johns Hopkins University Press, 1984.

A Time for Gathering: The Second Migration, 1820-1880, Volume 2 of "The Jewish People in America," Johns Hopkins University Press, 1992.

(Contributor) *Abba Hillel Silver and American Zionism,* F. Cass (London), 1997.

(Contributor) *Struggles in the Promised Land: Toward a History of Black-Jewish Relations in the United States,* Oxford University Press (New York City), 1997.

Jews in America (young adult), Oxford University Press, 1998.

(Contributor) *African Americans and Jews in the Twentieth Century: Studies in Convergence and Conflict,* University of Missouri Press (Columbia, MO), 1998.

(Contributor) *An Emotional History of the United States,* New York University Press (New York City), 1998.

(Contributor) Louis Wirth, *The Ghetto,* Transaction Publishers (New Brunswick, NJ), 1998.

(Contributor) *Migration Theory: Talking across the Disciplines,* Routledge (New York City), 2000.

The Lower East Side Memories: The Jewish Place in America, Princeton University Press (Princeton, NJ), 2000.

(Editor, with Jeffrey Shandler and Beth S. Wenger) *Remembering the Lower East Side,* Indiana University Press (Bloomington, IN), 2000.

Memories of Hunger: Immigrant Foodways and the Construction of Ethnic Identities, Harvard University Press (Cambridge, MA), 2001.

Member of editorial committee, *Association for Jewish Studies Newsletter;* manuscript referee, *Jewish Social Studies, Journal of American Ethnic History, Radical History Review, Journal of American History,* and *Journal of Women's History.* Contributor to scholarly journals, including *Journal of American Ethnic History, Shofar, CommonQuest, Studies in Contemporary Jewry,* and *Journal of Israeli History.*

SIDELIGHTS: Hasia R. Diner is the Paul and Sylvia Steinberg Professor of American Jewish History at New York University, a specialist in immigration history, Jewish history, and the history of Jewish relations with other ethnic and racial minorities in America. Diner's *Lower East Side Memories: A Jewish Place in America* explores the transformation of New York City's Lower East Side from an actual neighborhood populated by poor Jewish immigrants from Eastern Europe into a mythical community celebrated for its ethnic and religious solidarity and its colorful traditions. In her book, Diner explores the ways in which nostalgia—principally in literature and film—shapes current day perceptions of the Lower East Side of the past. Paul Berman explained in the *New York Times Book Review:* "The old Jewish neighborhood . . . entered into a curious new phase, of which . . . Diner . . . has now made herself the historian. The neighborhood declined in real life while it rose in legend. Jews poured out and books poured in; instead of crowds of people, crowds of memory. The neighborhood was simultaneously abandoned and sacralized."

Lower East Side Memories received warm comments from most critics. A *Kirkus Reviews* commentator called the book "a provocative account of how the Lower East Side of New York became a mythical citation in the American Jewish narrative." The critic added: "Admirably researched, this offers a perceptive revisionist analysis of American Jewry's most distinctive former address." A reviewer for *Publishers Weekly* likewise noted: "Diner's research and conclusions are both convincing and original." Berman concluded: "In her wanderings around the old East Side, Diner, the inspired historian, has found her way to a particular intersection that no one else has located quite so precisely. She has stumbled on the exact place where cultural identity, historical myth and geographical location run together, in a tangle of traffic and honking horns—a strangely emotional place."

BIOGRAPHICAL/CRITICAL SOURCES:

PERIODICALS

Booklist, July, 1999, Ellen Mandel, review of *Jews in America,* p. 1932.
Kirkus Reviews, August 1, 2000, review of *Lower East Side Memories: A Jewish Place in America,* p. 1093.
New York Review of Books, December 2, 1999, David Brion Davis, "Jews and Blacks in America," p. 57.
New York Times Book Review, November 12, 2000, Paul Berman, "Tell Me What Street Compares with Mott Street."
Publishers Weekly, July 31, 2000, review of *Lower East Side Memories: A Jewish Place in America,* p. 84.

OTHER

Religious Studies in Secondary Schools, http://www.rsiss.org/bkdiner/ (October 2, 2000), Sonja Spear, review of *Jews in America.**

*   *   *

DOBYNS, Stephen 1941-

PERSONAL: Born February 19, 1941, in Orange, NJ; son of Lester L. (an Episcopal minister) and Barbara (Johnston) Dobyns; married; three children. *Education:* Attended Shimer College, 1959-60; Wayne State University, B.A., 1964; University of Iowa, M.F.A., 1967. *Politics:* Democrat. *Religion:* None.

ADDRESSES: Home—32 Warwick Rd., Watertown, MA 02172.

CAREER: State University of New York College at Brockport, instructor in English, 1968-69; *Detroit News,* Detroit, MI, reporter, 1969-71; writer, 1971—. Visiting lecturer in creative writing, University of New Hampshire, 1973-75, University of Iowa, 1977-78, and Boston University, 1978-79. Member of staff, Goddard College, 1978-80, and Warren Wilson College, 1981.

AWARDS, HONORS: Concurring Beasts was a Lamont Poetry Selection for 1971; MacDowell Colony fellowships, 1972 and 1976; Yaddo Colony fellowships, 1972, 1973, 1977, 1981 and 1982; National Endowment for the Arts fellowships, 1974 and 1981; Guggenheim fellowship, 1983; National Poetry Series winner, 1984, for *Black Dog, Red Dog.*

WRITINGS:

POETRY

Concurring Beasts, Atheneum (New York City), 1972.
Griffon, Atheneum, 1976.
Heat Death, Atheneum, 1980.
The Balthus Poems, Atheneum, 1982.
Black Dog, Red Dog, Holt (New York City), 1984.
Cemetery Nights, Viking (New York City), 1987.
A Boat off the Coast, Viking, 1987.
Body Traffic: Poems, Viking, 1990.
Velocities: New and Selected Poems, 1966-1992, Viking, 1994.
Common Carnage, Penguin Poets (New York City), 1996.
Best Words, Best Order: Essays on Poetry, St. Martin's (New York City), 1996.
Pallbearers Envying the One Who Rides, Penguin Poets, 1999.

NOVELS

A Man of Little Evils, Atheneum, 1973.
Saratoga Longshot, Atheneum, 1976.
Saratoga Swimmer, Atheneum, 1981.
Dancer with One Leg, Dutton (New York City), 1983.
Saratoga Headhunter, Viking, 1985.

Cold Dog Soup, Viking, 1985.

Saratoga Snapper, Viking, 1986.

Saratoga Bestiary, Viking, 1988.

The Two Deaths of Senora Puccini, Viking, 1988.

Saratoga Hexameter, Viking, 1990.

The House on Alexandrine, Wayne State University Press (Detroit), 1990.

After Shocks, Near Escapes, Viking, 1991.

The Wrestler's Cruel Study: A Novel, W. W. Norton (New York City), 1993.

Saratoga Haunting, Viking, 1993.

Saratoga Backtalk, W. W. Norton, 1994.

Saratoga Trifecta, Penguin (New York City), 1995.

Saratoga Fleshpot, W. W. Norton, 1995.

The Church of Dead Girls, Metropolitan Books (New York City), 1997.

Saratoga Strongbox: A Charlie Bradshaw Mystery, Viking, 1998.

Boy in the Water, Metropolitan Books, 1999.

SHORT STORIES

Eating Naked, Metropolitan Books, 2000.

OTHER

Contributor of poems to periodicals, including *New Yorker, Nation,* and *Poetry.*

ADAPTATIONS: The Church of Dead Girls has been optioned by Home Box Office (HBO) for a feature film.

SIDELIGHTS: In a letter to *CA,* Stephen Dobyns expressed his thoughts on writing both novels and poetry: "Although I sometimes write fiction, I do it only as a diversion. I consider myself entirely a poet, am concerned with it twenty-four hours a day, feel that it requires that attention if one is to be successful, feel there is no subject which cannot be best treated by poetry, feel that myself and any poet is always at the beginning of his craft." Dobyns is one of a select few modern writers who has enjoyed critical success for his poetry as well as popular success with his fiction. His "Saratoga" series of detective novels sell briskly, as do his psychological thrillers such as *The Church of Dead Girls.* At the same time, his accessible poetry "blends philosophical musings with daft, deft metaphors and a cheeky vernacular . . . to rib us into thought," according to Bill Christophersen in *Poetry.* Calling Dobyns "a compelling writer whose voice speaks directly . . . to

readers of all kinds," Bill Ott in *Booklist* added: "Using plain but always precise language, he plumbs the reservoirs of emotion lurking beneath the events of everyday life."

Poetry critic Ralph J. Mills, Jr. suggested that Dobyns's verse contains "wit, intelligence and surrealist obliquity . . . [and] these dimensions of his work are sustained throughout. . . . Dobyns's combination of humor and the bizarre or sinister displays itself most obviously—and to considerable effect—in his socio-political poems, where the odd, seemingly irrational constructions match with terrifying rightness the absurdity and violence of our public life, our foreign wars." Assessing Dobyns's Lamont poetry selection, *Concurring Beasts, Saturday Review* contributor Robert D. Spector wrote: "Dobyns looks warily at the chaotic world, dislikes what he sees, and responds to its disorder in crisply controlled verse keyed to a sardonic wit one scale above cynicism." In the *New York Times Rook Review,* Andy Brumer praised *Black Dog, Red Dog,* the 1984 National Poetry Series winner: "While many of the poems have the illusion of an almost documentary objectivity, they reveal instead the soulful confessions of one individual in turmoil. . . . This is a harrowing book, not meant to please but to instruct."

In a *New York Times Book Review* piece about *Velocities: New and Selected Poems,* Anthony Libby noted that Dobyns displays "a . . . traditional style of masculinity, somewhat cool or repressed, angry, torn by constant awareness that 'we are the creatures that love and slaughter.' . . . Bullets pock his poetry of social commentary, which is marked more by horror than by ideology." The critic concluded that much of Dobyns's verse "has a somber, eccentric beauty not quite like anything else around these days." Elsewhere in the *New York Times Book Review,* David Kirby explained the role of humor in Dobyns's work: "Life can be pretty grisly in Mr. Dobyns's poems. But life isn't a tragedy in which we are fatally mired. Instead, it is a farce we view from a certain remove—not much of one, but it is as though we were watching on a movie screen." A *Publishers Weekly* reviewer, in a piece on *Common Carnage,* likewise stated that what distinguishes Dobyns's poetry "is the peculiar, edgy way he cuts his own darkness with a humor that is rooted in curiosity."

Dobyns has also drawn favorable attention for his novels, most of which are of the crime fiction genre. *Washington Post Book World* columnist Jean M. White cited Dobyns's fiction for its "slyly quiet humor and tender feeling." In a *Washington Post Book World* review of

Dancer with One Leg, Lawrence Block wrote of Dobyns: "His writing is honest, toughminded, and as uncompromising as his unforgettable hero. There's not a false sentence anywhere, not a moment where interest flags." Comparing Dobyns to Vladimir Nabokov in a *Washington Post* review of *Cold Dog Soup,* Carol E. Rinzler concluded: "[Dobyns] possesses a sensibility that is worth capturing in the amber of fiction, thoughtful but not devoid of sentiment, intelligent but not sterile."

Dobyns is best known for his "Saratoga" series, a group of crime novels set in Saratoga Springs, New York, featuring a self-doubting detective named Charlie Bradshaw and his hedonistic sidekick, Victor Plotz. Many of the plots center around corruption in the horse racing industry, as Saratoga is a prominent stop on the thoroughbred racing schedule. Dobyns was among a group of detective writers who began to see their protagonists as mortals rather than stereotypes—Charlie Bradshaw has undergone a divorce, a great deal of self-recrimination, and a turbulent descent into middle age. In an interview with *Booklist,* Dobyns explained: "I don't like mystery heroes who are too perfect—characters who never have problems, or if they do, conquer them easily, and who have great secondary knowledge of subjects like wine or German shepherds. I wanted to write about a character who caught colds, who had problems with his car, whose marriage was falling apart—someone, in other words, who seemed far more realistic to me." Of Victor Plotz, who narrates several of the novels himself, Dobyns noted: "I'm sure he resembles many of my own darker qualities. . . . Working from his point of view is fun. Victor's jokes are a pleasure to write."

New York Times Book Review correspondent Ann Arensberg declared: "Stephen Dobyns's mystery novels have two major assets that accumulate high rates of interest from book to book: his setting, Saratoga Springs, and his private detective, Charlie Bradshaw. . . . Unlike most fictional detectives, who give the same flawless performance over and over again in a world outside time, Charlie is allowed by his creator to suffer changes and even to age. He is mortal, like us, and his struggles and successes matter."

Dobyns is equally acclaimed for his darker psychological thrillers. In *After Shocks, Near Escapes,* he describes in harrowing detail the lasting effects of a devastating earthquake on one young Chilean girl and her extended family. The novel's narrator, Lucy Recabarren, looks back from a troubled adulthood to the events surrounding the earthquake, which forever altered her naïve certainties about existence. "Populating a historical catastrophe with fictional characters, [Dobyns] examines not so much the earthquakes in their past as the futures they project for themselves after the great disaster," Ron Loewinsohn observed in the *New York Times Book Review.* The critic added: "Stephen Dobyns is a writer with an impressive range. . . . He is mostly interested in the quake as a very provocative organizing metaphor: the ground we stand on, the present moment, is *always* unstable, always shaky."

The author explores this theme further in his well-received *The Church of the Dead Girls.* A series of grisly murders in a small town provokes a level of paranoia and vigilante justice that might have seemed inconceivable to the heretofore complacent and "civilized" townspeople. "This chiller is about the awful power of fear," maintained a *Publishers Weekly* reviewer. "When the people of Aurelius go looking for a monster, monsters are all they can see." *Booklist* contributor Joanne Wilkinson praised the book as a "dark, cerebral thriller" in which Dobyns is "not as interested in the pathology of the serial killer . . . as he is in the pathology that exists within us all."

The pathology of community is again dissected in *Boy in the Water,* a thriller set at a private academy in New Hampshire. Seeking release from the guilt he feels over the death of his wife and daughter in a house fire, Jim Hawthorne takes a job as headmaster at Bishop's Hill Academy, a school known for its wealthy but troubled student population. Despite his best efforts, Hawthorne finds that the staff and many of the students are conspiring against him—with deadly results. In his *Booklist* review of *Boy in the Water,* Bill Ott wrote: "This one adds elements of gothic horror to the mix, and the result is absolutely compelling. . . . Dobyns not only scares us with what is out there but also with what we find (or don't find) within ourselves."

The Wrestler's Cruel Study finds Dobyns in a more experimental vein. Pairing Nietzschian and Gnostic philosophies with professional wrestling and a tale of self-transformation, the story follows the adventures of a wrestler named Marduk the Magnificent as he searches for his abducted girlfriend. According to Sven Birkerts in the *New York Times Book Review,* the novel is "utterly preposterous, and quite serious . . . Indeed, such is Mr. Dobyns's cunning that right when we think his novel has slipped into terminal silliness, he pulls us upright with some arresting metaphysical insight. And just when we are persuaded that the work is in fact a worthy meditation on good and evil, a banana peel appears underfoot and sends us sprawling." A *Kirkus Reviews* critic deemed the work "stunningly imaginative, so liberating in its sense of possibilities in life and art, and so much fun."

Dobyns's first collection of short stories, *Eating Naked,* plumbs the depths of human frailty through meditations on failed marriages, bizarre deaths, and dysfunctional families. *Booklist* correspondent Michele Leber felt that the short story format allows Dobyns "a show of ingenuity, even exuberance," as he "takes an idea, from the mundane to the bizarre, and runs with it." In the *New Fiction Forum,* Roger Boylan observed that the author "balances compassion, believability, and poignancy" in his tales. Boylan concluded: "These are finely-crafted, jarring stories that leave the reader with a sense of apprehension at the sheer craziness of what passes for everyday life. Dobyns at his best gives us a real chill when he lifts the curtain on what lies beyond."

BIOGRAPHICAL/CRITICAL SOURCES:

BOOKS

Stitt, Peter, *Uncertainty and Plentitude: Five Contemporary Poets,* University of Iowa Press (Iowa City, IA), 1997.

PERIODICALS

Booklist, April 15, 1997, Joanne Wilkinson, review of *The Church of Dead Girls,* p. 1400; July, 1997, Bill Ott, "The *Booklist* Interview: Stephen Dobyns," p. 1798; April 15, 1999, Bill Ott, review of *Boy in the Water,* p. 1472; April 1, 2000, Michele Leber, review of *Eating Naked,* p. 1432.
Library Journal, June 15, 1973; March 1, 1976; January 1, 1977.
New Fiction Forum, summer, 2000, Roger Boylan, "The Naked and the Dead," pp. 31-33.
New York Times, April 19, 1985; December 2, 1988, John Gross, "Detectives Fighting Crime and Time," p. C29.
New York Times Book Review, September 23, 1984; September 29, 1985; December 23, 1990, David Kirby, "Life's Goofy Splendors"; July 21, 1991, Ron Loewinsohn, "Life on the Richter Scale"; July 4, 1993, Ann Arensberg, "The Body under Jacko's Pool Hall"; August 15, 1993, Sven Birkerts, "Don't Mess with Marduk the Magnificent"; January 15,

1995, Anthony Libby, "One Gives Us 'Happiness'; The Other, 'Gluttony'"; June 22, 1997, David Walton, review of *The Church of Dead Girls,* p. 20; September 19, 1999, Erik Burns, review of *Boy in the Water,* p. 21.
Poetry, September, 1997, Bill Christophersen, review of *Common Carnage,* p. 347.
Publishers Weekly, February 26, 1996, review of *Common Carnage,* p. 101; April 28, 1997, review of *The Church of Dead Girls,* p. 48; March 6, 2000, review of *Eating Naked,* p. 80.
Saturday Review, March 11, 1972.
Times Literary Supplement, July 29, 1977.
Washington Post, December 3, 1985.
Washington Post Book World, December 20, 1981; September 5, 1982; May 15, 1983; May 19, 1985.*

*   *   *

DOCKSTADER, Frederick J. 1919-1998

PERSONAL: Born February 3, 1919, in Los Angeles, CA; died, March 21, 1998; son of Frederick and Dorothy (Wilson) Dockstader; married Alice Elizabeth Warren (an architect), December 25, 1952. *Education:* Arizona State College, B.A., 1940, M.A., 1941; Western Reserve University (now Case Western Reserve University), Ph.D., 1951.

ADDRESSES: Home—165 West 66th St., New York, NY 10023. *Office*—Museum of the American Indian, Heye Foundation, Broadway at 155th St., New York, NY 10032.

CAREER: Cranbrook Institute of Science, Bloomfield Hills, MI, research associate, 1942-50, staff ethnologist, 1950-52; Dartmouth College, Hanover, NH, faculty member and museum curator, 1952-55; Museum of the American Indian, Heye Foundation, New York, NY, associate director, 1955-60, director, beginning 1960. Practicing silversmith. U.S. Department of the Interior, Indian Arts and Crafts Board, commissioner, 1955-67, chair, 1965-67. Adjunct professor, Columbia University, 1964-66.

MEMBER: Cranbrook Institute of Science (fellow), Rochester Museum of Arts and Sciences (fellow), American Anthropological Association (fellow), American Association of Museums, Society for American Archaeology, New York State Museum Association (treasurer), New York City Museums Council (former president), Cosmos Club (Washington, DC), Century Club (New York, NY).

AWARDS, HONORS: Lotos Club award, 1972.

WRITINGS:

Kachina and the White Man, Cranbrook Institute of Science (Bloomfield Hills, MI), 1954.

(Editor, with Alice W. Dockstader) *The American Indian in Graduate Studies: A Bibliography of Theses and Dissertations,* Museum of the American Indian, 1955, 2nd revised edition, 1974.

Indian Art in America: The Arts and Crafts of the North American Indian, New York Graphic Society (New York, NY), 1962, 3rd revised edition, 1968.

Indian Art in Middle America: Pre-Columbian and Contemporary Arts and Crafts of Mexico, Central America, and the Caribbean, New York Graphic Society (New York, NY), 1964.

Indian Art in South America: Pre-Columbian and Contemporary Arts and Crafts, New York Graphic Society (New York, NY), 1967.

(With Ferdinand Anton) *Pre-Columbian Art and Later Indian Tribal Arts,* Abrams (New York, NY), 1968.

(With Lewis Krevolin) *Naked Clay: Unadorned Pottery of the American Indian,* Museum of the American Indian, 1972.

(Compiler) *Books about Indians,* 2nd revised edition, Museum of the American Indian, 1972.

Indian Art of the Americas, Museum of the American Indian, 1973.

Masterworks from the Museum of the American Indian, Heye Foundation, Metropolitan Museum of Art (New York, NY), 1973.

Collecting American Indian Arts and Crafts, Crown (New York, NY), 1973.

Weaving Arts of the North American Indian, Crowell (New York, NY), 1978, revised, IconEditions (New York, NY), 1993.

(Editor) *Oscar Howe: A Retrospective Exhibition: Catalogue raisonné* (Catalogue), Thomas Gilcrease Museum Association (Tulsa, OK), 1982.

The Song of the Loom: New Traditions in Navajo Weaving, Hudson Hills Press (New York, NY), 1987.

SIDELIGHTS: Frederick J. Dockstader lived much of his early life on Navajo and Hopi reservations. He once told *CA* that his areas of interest covered all the Americas, and his "primary concern is the ability of aboriginal man to maintain his culture vis-a-vis encroaching Western civilization." Dockstader's books documented the arts and crafts of Native American peoples throughout North and South America.

In *Indian Art in America, Indian Art in Middle America,* and *Indian Art in South America,* Dockstader presented highly-illustrated introductions to Native American art.

Drawing for his illustrations on the collection of the Museum of the American Indian, of which he served as director, Dockstader wrote explanatory material for each volume which F. L. Cinquemani of *Library Journal* called "simple and clear" and "of interest to the beginning collector as well as to the student."

All three volumes garnered critical acclaim for the high quality of Dockstader's writing and the wealth of illustrations presented. Speaking of *Indian Art in America,* Oliver La Farge in the *New York Herald Tribune Lively Arts* labeled the volume "the handsomest and most comprehensive book yet published on the esthetic values of the products . . . of the North American Indians." Mary Gormly, in her *Library Journal* review of *Indian Art in South America,* noted that the "250 superb photographs . . . with accompanying commentaries on style, origin, and significance present a most thorough survey of the arts of an important but largely unknown area."

Dockstader was active in the designing and working of silver for most of his life, and taught the craft for many years in Michigan and New Hampshire. His work was exhibited in a great many museums and won prizes at the Cranbrook Art Academy, the Cleveland Institute of Art, and other exhibits.

BIOGRAPHICAL/CRITICAL SOURCES:

PERIODICALS

Booklist, September 1, 1961, review of *Indian Art in America,* p. 17.

Chicago Sunday Tribune, April 30, 1961, G. I. Quimby, review of *Indian Art in America,* p. 6.

Choice, April, 1968, review of *Indian Art in South America,* p. 187; June, 1969, review of *Pre-Columbian Art and Later Indian Tribal Arts,* p. 498.

Kirkus, April 1, 1961, review of *Indian Art in America,* p. 352.

Library Journal, July, 1961, Lee Ash, review of *Indian Art in America,* p. 2460; January 1, 1965, F. L. Cinquemani, review of *Indian Art in Middle America,* p. 107; February 15, 1968, review of *Indian Art in South America,* p. 743; September 15, 1968, Lee Ash, review of *Pre-Columbian Art and Later Indian Tribal Arts,* p. 3121.

Nation, July 22, 1968, D'Arcy McNickle, review of *Indian Art in South America,* p. 54.

Natural History, June, 1965, M. D. Coe, review of *Indian Art in Middle America,* p. 9; May, 1968, T. C. Patterson, review of *Indian Art in South America,* p. 71.

New York Herald Tribune Lively Arts, April 30, 1961, Oliver La Farge, review of *Indian Art in America,* p. 27.

New York Times Book Review, April 30, 1961, R. B. Inverarity, review of *Indian Art in America,* p. 7; December 6, 1964, John Canaday, review of *Indian Art in Middle America,* p. 76; December 1, 1968, John Canaday, review of *Pre-Columbian Art and Later Indian Tribal Arts,* p. 6.

San Francisco Chronicle, July 30, 1961, review of *Indian Art in America,* p. 22.

Scientific American, June, 1965, review of *Indian Art in Middle America,* p. 145.

Spectator, November 24, 1961, Geoffrey Grigson, review of *Indian Art in America,* p. 792.

Times Literary Supplement, January 21, 1965, review of *Indian Art in Middle America,* p. 51.

OBITUARIES:

PERIODICALS

New York Times, March 24, 1998, p. D23.*

* * *

DODD, Wayne (Donald) 1930-
(Donald Wayne)

PERSONAL: Born September 23, 1930, in Clarita, OK; son of Homer D. and Maggie M. (Potts) Dodd; married Betty Coshow, June 7, 1958 (divorced November 12, 1980); married Joyce Barlow (an artist and designer), June 27, 1981; children: Elizabeth, Hudson. *Education:* University of Oklahoma, B.A., 1955, M.A., 1957, Ph. D., 1963.

ADDRESSES: Home—11292 Peach Ridge Rd., Athens, OH 45701. *Office*—c/o Ohio Review, 344 Scott Quad, Ohio University, Athens, OH 45701.

CAREER: Poet, editor, and educator. University of Colorado, Boulder, instructor, 1960-64, assistant professor of English, 1964-68; Ohio University, Athens, associate professor, 1968-73, professor of English, 1973-94, Edwin and Ruth Kennedy Distinguished Professor of Poetry, 1994-2001, professor emeritus, 2001—. Fellow, Center for Advanced Studies, Wesleyan University, 1964; summer faculty fellow, University of Colorado, 1966. *Military service:* U.S. Navy, 1948-52.

MEMBER: Associated Writing Programs, Phi Beta Kappa.

AWARDS, HONORS: American Council of Learned Societies fellow, 1964-65; Award for Editorial Excellence, Ohioana Foundation, 1979; fellowships from Ohio Arts Council, 1980, 1989, and 1998; National Endowment for the Arts fellowship in poetry, 1982; Krout Award for Lifetime Achievement in Poetry, Ohioana Library Foundation, 1991; fellowship from National Park Service, 1993; Pulitzer Prize nomination, 1994, for *Of Desire and Disorder;* Rockefeller Foundation fellowship, 1995; National Book Award nomination, 1998, for *The Blue Salvages;* and Ohio Governor's Award for the Arts, 2001.

WRITINGS:

POETRY

We Will Wear White Roses, Best Cellar Press, 1974.

Made in America, Croissant, 1975.

The Names You Gave It, Louisiana State University Press (Baton Rouge, LA), 1980.

The General Mule Poems, Juniper Press Books, 1981.

Sometimes Music Rises, University of Georgia Press (Athens, GA), 1986.

Echoes of the Unspoken, University of Georgia Press (Athens, GA), 1990.

Of Desire and Disorder, Carnegie Mellon University Press, 1994.

The Blue Salvages, Carnegie Mellon University Press, 1998.

OTHER

(Under pseudonym Donald Wayne) *The Adventures of Little White Possum* (juvenile), Putnam (New York, NY), 1970.

A Time of Hunting (novel), Seabury Press, 1975.

(Editor) *Poets on the Line,* Ohio Review (Athens, OH), 1987.

Toward the End of the Century: Essays into Poetry, University of Iowa Press (Iowa City, IA), 1992.

(Editor) *Art and Nature: Essays by Contemporary Writers,* Ohio Review (Athens, OH), 1993.
(Editor) *Mentors,* Ohio Review (Athens, OH), 1994.

Contributor of poems to several anthologies, including *The New Breadloaf Anthology of American Poetry,* and *A Book of Luminous Things: An Anthology of World Poetry.* Contributor of poems, reviews, and articles to over forty periodicals and journals, including *American Scholar, Boulevard, Denver Quarterly, Georgia Review, Gettysburg Review, Iowa Review, Kayak, Missouri Review, Southern Review,* and *Nation.* Editor, *Ohio Review,* 1971-2001.

SIDELIGHTS: Wayne Dodd is, according to Kevin Walzer in the *Southern Humanities Review,* "a fine poet who, as editor of the *Ohio Review,* has been an influential figure in American poetry during the past two decades."

Dodd's *Toward the End of the Century: Essays into Poetry* explores the nature and purpose of contemporary poetry. Dodd does not write in the pure essay form but rather in what the critic for *Publishers Weekly* called "fragmentary, disjointed thoughts." Scott Minar, writing in the *Antioch Review,* found Dodd's approach to be "both essays about poetry and essays becoming poetry." Throughout the book, Dodd argues that free verse has become the best poetic form for contemporary poets to use and defines the role of poetry as embodying "the complexity of experience and the world," as Walzer explained. In making his argument, Dodd draws on arguments from a diverse range of fields. The *Publishers Weekly* critic pointed out that "the most valuable aspect of these essays is Dodd's ability to combine the thoughts of poets, mathematicians, and scientists in interesting ways." Minar concluded that "these essays are profoundly insightful, moving, and brilliant."

BIOGRAPHICAL/CRITICAL SOURCES:

PERIODICALS

Antioch Review, summer, 1994, Scott Minar, review of *Toward the End of the Century,* p. 537.
Kliatt, September, 1994, review of *Of Desire and Disorder,* p. 26.
Publishers Weekly, September 7, 1992, review of *Toward the End of the Century,* p. 90.
Reference and Research Book News, February, 1993, review of *Toward the End of the Century,* p. 35.

Southern Humanities Review, spring, 1994, review of *Toward the End of the Century,* pp. 199-204.

*   *   *

DOMHOFF, G(eorge) William 1936-

PERSONAL: Born August 6, 1936, in Youngstown, OH; son of George William and Helen Susanne (Cornett) Domhoff; married Judith Clare Boman (a nursery school teacher), August 20, 1961 (divorced, July, 1975); children: Lynne Starr, Lori Susanne, William Packard, Joel James. *Education:* Duke University, B.A., 1958; Kent State University, M.A., 1959; University of Miami, Coral Gables, FL, Ph.D., 1962.

ADDRESSES: Office—Cowell College, University of California, Santa Cruz, CA 95060.

CAREER: Los Angeles State College, Los Angeles, CA, assistant professor of psychology, 1962-65; University of California, Cowell College, Santa Cruz, assistant professor, 1965-69, associate professor of psychology, beginning 1969, currently professor of psychology and sociology. Harbor commissioner, Santa Cruz Port District, 1977-78.

WRITINGS:

Who Rules America?, Prentice-Hall (Englewood Cliffs, NJ), 1967, 3rd edition published as *Who Rules America? Power and Politics in the Year 2000,* Mayfield (Mountain View, CA), 1998.
C. Wright Mills and the Power Elite, Beacon Press (Boston, MA), 1968.
The Higher Circles: The Governing Class in America, Random House (New York, NY), 1970.
Fat Cats and Democrats: The Role of the Big Rich in the Party of the Common Man, Prentice-Hall (Englewood Cliffs, NJ), 1972.
The Bohemian Grove and Other Retreats: A Study in Ruling-Class Cohesiveness, Harper (New York, NY), 1974.
Who Really Rules?: New Haven and Community Power Reexamined, Transaction Books (New York, NY), 1978.
The Powers That Be: Processes of Ruling-Class Domination in America, Random House (New York, NY), 1978.
(Editor) *Power Structure Research,* Sage Publications (Newbury Park, CA), 1980.

(With Richard L. Zweigenhaft) *Jews in the Protestant Establishment,* Praeger (New York, NY), 1982.

Who Rules America Now?: A view for the '80s, Prentice-Hall (Englewood Cliffs, NJ), 1983.

The Mystique of Dreams: A Search for Utopia through Senoi Dream Theory, University of California Press (Berkeley, CA), 1985.

(Editor, with Thomas R. Dye) *Power Elites and Organizations,* Sage Publications (Beverly Hills, CA), 1987.

The Power Elite and the State: How Policy is Made in America, Aldine de Gruyter (New York, NY), 1990.

(With R. L. Zweigenhaft) *Blacks in the White Establishment?: A Study of Race and Class in America,* Yale University Press (New Haven, CT), 1991.

Finding Meaning in Dreams: A Quantitative Approach, Plenum Press (New York, NY), 1996.

State Autonomy or Class Dominance?: Case Studies on Policy Making in America, Aldine de Gruyter, 1996.

(With R. L. Zweigenhaft) *Diversity in the Power Elite: Have Women and Minorities Reached the Top?,* Yale University Press (New Haven, CT), 1998.

SIDELIGHTS: G. William Domhoff has written a number of academic studies of American political life. In these books, he argues that a governing class exists which controls many of the country's leading institutions. Among his best known titles are *Who Rules America?, Fat Cats and Democrats, The Bohemian Grove and Other Retreats,* and *Diversity in the Power Elite.*

Who Rules America? introduces Domhoff's basic argument by documenting those who run some of the leading businesses, colleges, foundations, and governmental bodies in America. He maintains that these people, all members of wealthy families, constitute a social class with its own agenda. John Lustig in the *Library Journal* claimed that, in *Who Rules America?,* Domhoff "has written a challenging book which . . . deserves a place on the library shelf." While R. L. Heilbroner in the *New York Review of Books* found that Domhoff's thesis failed to "specify exactly what is meant by the 'control' that the upper class wields," he nonetheless believed that "Domhoff's book is lean and precise and . . . marshals its facts carefully."

Domhoff analyzed the leaders of the Democratic Party and the big-money contributors they answer to in his book *Fat Cats and Democrats.* Using campaign records, questionnaires, and interviews with party leaders, Domhoff documents the party's largest contributors and shows how they control Democrat policies. W. V. Shan-

non in the *New York Times Book Review* criticized Domhoff for his "hyped-up style" and "far-reaching generalizations." But Gore Vidal, writing in the *New York Review of Books,* found that "Domhoff has seen and measured the tip of an iceberg which most of the other passengers on the U.S. *Titanic* have not noticed."

In *The Bohemian Grove and Other Retreats* Domhoff looks at three of the most exclusive social clubs in the United States: the Bohemian Club, the Rancheros Visitadores, and the Round-up Riders of the Rockies. Most of the book chronicles the activities at the Bohemian Grove, a country retreat used by the Bohemian Club for summer outings, during a two-week retreat by some of the club's most wealthy members. "The subject is a fascinating one," admitted J. R. Coyne in the *National Review.* "But Domhoff misses it all. There's no texture here, no life, no fabric." Donald Goddard, in his review for the *New York Times Book Review,* felt that "only an academic would feel it worthwhile to 'prove' the self-evident proposition that the custodians of America's wealth . . . generally stick together." But D. J. McColman in the *Library Journal* praised the book for Domhoff's "delineation of various social linkages among powerful personages."

Domhoff's *Diversity in the Power Elite,* co-written with Richard L. Zweigenhaft, examines the racial, ethnic, religious, and gender makeup of America's upper class. Finding that minorities are under-represented among the nation's elite institutions, Domhoff nonetheless argues that their presence in these institutions may stall more fundamental change "by creating the illusion of participation," as Martin Oppenheimer noted in the *Monthly Review.* Oppenheimer called *Diversity in the Power Elite* "meticulous" and "thoroughly documented."

BIOGRAPHICAL/CRITICAL SOURCES:

PERIODICALS

American Sociology Review, June, 1968, N. W. Polsby, review of *Who Rules America?,* p. 476.

Annals of the American Academy, May, 1968, A. A. Berle, review of *Who Rules America?,* p. 201.

Book World, September 27, 1970, Bernard Weisberger, review of *The Higher Circles,* p. 4.

Choice, April, 1968, review of *Who Rules America?,* p. 262.

Christian Century, November 15, 1967, review of *Who Rules America?,* p. 1466; August 5, 1970, review of *The Higher Circles,* p. 944.

Commonweal, October 11, 1968, William Schechner, review of *Who Rules America?,* p. 67.

Library Journal, November 15, 1967, John Lustig, review of *Who Rules America?,* p. 4164; June 1, 1972, Hindy Schachter, review of *Fat Cats and Democrats,* p. 2103; April 1, 1974, D. J. McColman, review of *The Bohemian Grove and Other Retreats,* p. 1049.

Monthly Review, September, 1999, Martin Oppenheimer, review of *Diversity in the Power Elite,* p. 56.

Nation, November 4, 1968, V. K. Dibble, review of *Who Rules America?,* p. 470.

National Review, December 20, 1974, J. R. Coyne, review of *The Bohemian Grove and Other Retreats,* p. 1476.

New Republic, April 27, 1974, Peter Barnes, review of *The Bohemian Grove and Other Retreats,* p. 24.

New York Review of Books, January 4, 1968, R. L. Heilbroner, review of *Who Rules America?,* p. 18; August 10, 1972, Gore Vidal, review of *Fat Cats and Democrats,* p. 8.

New York Times Book Review, October 15, 1972, W. V. Shannon, review of *Fat Cats and Democrats,* p. 38; May 5, 1974, Donald Goddard, review of *The Bohemian Grove and Other Retreats,* p. 52.

Political Science Quarterly, summer, 1997, Edward W. Lehman, review of *State Autonomy or Class Dominance?,* p. 317.*

* * *

DONALDSON, Stephen R(eeder) 1947-
(Reed Stephens)

PERSONAL: Born May 13, 1947, in Cleveland, OH; son of James R. (an orthopedic surgeon and medical missionary) and Mary Ruth (a prosthetist and occupational therapist; maiden name, Reeder) Donaldson; first marriage ended in divorce; married, 1980 (wife's name, Stephanie). *Education:* College of Wooster, B.A., 1968; Kent State University, M.A., 1971.

ADDRESSES: Office—41 Broadway, New York, NY 10003.

CAREER: Writer. Akron City Hospital, Akron, OH, assistant dispatcher, 1968-70; Kent State University, Kent, OH, teaching fellow, 1971; Tapp-Gentz Associates, West Chester, PA, acquisitions editor, 1973-74; Ghost Ranch Writers Workshops, NM, instructor, 1973-77; University of New Mexico, teaching assistant in literature after 1982.

MEMBER: International Association for the Fantastic in the Arts, United States Karate Alliance, American Contract Bridge League, Duke City Bridge Club.

AWARDS, HONORS: British Fantasy Award, 1978, for *The Chronicles of Thomas Covenant: The Unbeliever;* John W. Campbell Award, World Science Fiction Convention, 1979, for best new writer; Balrog awards for best novel, 1981, for *The Wounded Land,* and 1983, and for best collection, 1985, for *Daughter of Regals and Other Tales;* Saturn Award for best fantasy novel, 1983; Book of the Year awards, Science Fiction Book Club, 1987, for *The Mirror of Her Dreams,* and 1988, for *A Man Rides Through.*

WRITINGS:

FANTASY

The Chronicles of Thomas Covenant: The Unbeliever (Volume I: *Lord Foul's Bane,* Volume II: *The Illearth War,* Volume III: *The Power That Preserves*), Holt (New York, NY), 1977.

The Second Chronicles of Thomas Covenant: The Unbeliever (Volume I: *The Wounded Land,* 1980, Volume II: *The One Tree,* 1982, Volume III: *White Gold Wielder,* 1983), Ballantine (New York, NY).

Gilden-Fire, Underwood-Miller (San Francisco, CA), 1982.

Daughters of Regals and Other Tales (includes the novella *Gilden-Fire*), Del Rey, 1984.

Mordant's Need (Volume I: *The Mirror of Her Dreams,* 1986, Volume II: *A Man Rides Through,* 1987), Ballantine (New York, NY).

(Editor) *Strange Dreams: Unforgettable Fantasy Stories,* Bantam (New York, NY), 1993.

"THE GAP CYCLE" SERIES; SCIENCE FICTION

The Gap into Conflict: The Real Story, Bantam (New York, NY), 1990.

The Gap into Vision: Forbidden Knowledge, Bantam (New York, NY), 1991.

The Gap into Power: A Dark and Hungry God Arises, Bantam (New York, NY), 1992.

The Gap into Madness: Chaos and Order, Bantam (New York, NY), 1994.

The Gap into Ruin: This Day All Gods Die, Bantam (New York, NY), 1996.

UNDER PSEUDONYM REED STEPHENS

The Man Who Killed His Brother, Ballantine (New York, NY), 1980.

The Man Who Risked His Partner, Ballantine (New York, NY), 1984.

The Man Who Tried to Get Away, Ballantine (New York, NY), 1990.

OTHER

(Contributor) Judy-Lynn del Rey, editor, *Stellar #4,* Ballantine (New York, NY), 1978.

(Contributor) Terry Carr, *The Year's Best Fantasy,* Berkley Publishing (New York, NY), 1979.

Reave the Just and Other Tales, Bantam/Spectra (New York, NY), 1999.

Also contributor to science fiction magazines; both "Thomas Covenant" series have been translated for publication in other languages; author's papers are housed in the Department of Special Collections of the Kent State University Libraries.

ADAPTATIONS: White Gold Wielder is available as a recording from Camden, 1983.

SIDELIGHTS: Stephen R. Donaldson is the author of a number of lengthy, complexly plotted sagas in the science-fiction/fantasy genre that have earned him both critical praise and a devoted readership. Yet he struggled for many years as a writer, unable even to find a publisher who would work with him, before his books landed on the bestseller lists. Donaldson is perhaps best known for his *The Chronicles of Thomas Covenant: The Unbeliever,* which appeared in 1977. It sold millions, and was likened to one of the most famous trilogies in fantasy fiction, J.R.R. Tolkien's *Lord of the Rings.*

Like all of Donaldson's subsequent novels, the "Thomas Covenant" story drew readers into a plot in which forces of good and evil battled to destroy one another; always, the author's anti-hero protagonists struggle with ethical dilemmas that echo eternal religious themes while cruelty and violence run amok. "The moral import of his fantasies is their very heart and soul," remarked fellow fantasy writer Brian Stableford in an essay about Donaldson for the *St. James Guide to Fantasy*

Writers. "Few other writers in the genre are capable of reaching such a terrible pitch of indignation and horror at the contemplation of the human capacity for abusing others."

Born in Cleveland, Ohio, in 1947, Donaldson was the son of Presbyterian missionaries, and at the age of three he left the Midwest with his parents to settle permanently in India. In the city of Miraj, Donaldson's orthopedic surgeon father treated victims of leprosy who had lost their extremities; his mother worked at the same hospital as a prosthetist and occupational therapist.

The exotic Asian locale, meanwhile, offered the young Donaldson the kind of adventures most children only read about in books; on one occasion, he was kept home from school because a deadly tiger was on the prowl. "India is both a mysterious and exotic place," Donaldson told Robert Dahlin in a *Publishers Weekly* interview. "And a very grim place of human misery. I grew up with wild physical beauty, strange cultural evidence of magical or spiritual events. There was a snake charmer on every corner."

A bookworm who devoured whatever English-language titles were available to him in Miraj, Donaldson became enamored with fantasy and adventure literature at an early age, reading everything from the "Hardy Boys" mystery series to the African escapade tales of Joseph Conrad; the *Chronicles of Narnia* by C.S. Lewis was also a particular favorite. Returning to Ohio at the age of sixteen, Donaldson enrolled at its College of Wooster, a small, private liberal-arts school. There, he learned that his years in India did not seem to count for much: "In my wing of the dorm, we had five National Merit scholars, five professional musicians and a guy who had already written eight novels," he told *People* writer John Neary. "I was the only person who didn't have something immense to offer the world." One Sunday, Donaldson attended church services, contemplating his future, and found a solution. "Something in my mind leapt the gap between being addicted to reading stories and wanting to write them," he explained to Neary.

After graduating in 1968, Donaldson went on to study English at Kent State University, earning his master's degree three years later. The following year, he sat in a church pew once again, listening to his father tell a congregation about the years in India and his work treating sufferers of leprosy. A chronic infectious disease that brought on devastating physical disfigurement, leprosy was once so feared that its victims were often sent to die in special colonies on remote islands, to which only religious missionaries would venture as aid workers. In more modern times, the disease has proved treatable, but on that day in church, Donaldson's father was discussing the psychological trauma that leprosy sufferers still experienced. Donaldson began to think about writing a novel with a protagonist, a contemporary husband and father, who contracts the disease. From this came the Thomas Covenant character, hero of the first six of Donaldson's novels.

In the fall of 1972, Donaldson began writing the first novel in the fantasy series. Married and living in New England, he worked for a Pennsylvania publisher for a year, but spent the next four years involved in the Covenant project. His wife, a social worker, supported him both financially and emotionally, but he became dejected as his pile of rejection slips from publishers grew. The industry professionals who critiqued Donaldson's submissions voiced doubts about the potential appeal of the title character: Thomas Covenant is a successful novelist devastated by the diagnosis of leprosy; a head injury lands him in another universe where, instead of social ostracism, he is hailed as a messiah-like savior sent to keep Lord Foul from destroying The Land, as the fictional world is known.

Fully aware of the folly of his situation, Donaldson even lied to neighbors about what he did for a living. "I just immersed myself in my work," he told Dahlin in a *Publishers Weekly* interview. "It's difficult to find words to describe how bad I felt." He collected a total of 47 rejection slips from American publishers before trying, one more time, to interest Ballantine, publishers of the wildly popular fantasy novels from English medieval scholar J.R.R. Tolkien (1892-1973), *The Hobbit* and *The Lord of the Rings.* Donaldson once admitted that his perseverance was curious. As he once told Jean W. Ross, "good writers usually aren't that unlucky; bad writers usually don't try that hard."

But at Ballantine the second time around, Donaldson's manuscript luckily landed on the desk of famed editor Lester del Rey, who believed it held promise. Del Rey worked intensely with the neophyte author to edit the lengthy saga for publication. Published in 1977, the three-volume *Chronicles of Thomas Covenant: The Unbeliever* appeared in hardcover as a Science Fiction Book Club selection, an unusual achievement in the fantasy-fiction genre for a first-time author, but one that spoke highly of del Rey's belief in Donaldson's saga.

Lord Foul's Bane, the first book in "The Chronicles of Thomas Covenant," introduces the afflicted, unhappy writer and his sudden transcendence into another realm.

Soon after Covenant regains consciousness and realizes he is in a puzzling new world called The Land, he is mistaken for one of its mythical heroes, Berke Halfhand. He also encounters Lord Foul, a powerful, destructive figure who is determined to ruin The Land and kill off its populace by unleashing environmental toxins. Though he was an outcast in his previous life, Covenant is hailed by denizens of The Land as their long-awaited savior, the hero with the power to foil Lord Foul.

In the first volume, Donaldson creates a complex, intricate realm with a long history, highly stratified social organization, and series of alliances and enmities among its many life forms. The narrative and cast are expanded across the other two volumes, *The Illearth War* and *The Power That Preserves.* Covenant discovers early on that he possesses magical powers, but the realization does not heighten his sense of self-esteem to any degree. He emerges as an anti-hero, an unlikely messiah uncomfortable with his role, an embittered man still plagued by the cynicism and pessimism that marked his earthly existence. He begins to call himself "the Unbeliever," and at times even doubts that the fantastical adventures are occurring outside of his own imagination. In the end, he is offered a choice between the two worlds.

"The real surprise of the tale," wrote John Calvin Batchelor in a review of the trilogy for the *Village Voice,* "comes not when Foul is unexpectedly undone, but rather when Covenant is returned by the Creator to Earth to die of an allergic reaction." Other assessments were positive, though some faulted the first-time author's ornate prose style—a criticism that would follow Donaldson throughout his career. A *Publishers Weekly* review declared that the work possesses "riches and excitements a plenty for the fantasy minded," while Judith Yamomoto declared that the trilogy "shows promise and makes absorbing reading" in her *Library Journal* review.

The "Covenant" series quickly reached the two-million sales mark in paperback, was translated into several other languages, and earned Donaldson comparisons to Tolkien. In the United Kingdom, the three-part series won the British Science Fiction Society's top award for 1978. A surge in popularity in the works of Tolkien—related to the posthumous publication in 1977 of his *Silmarillion* manuscript—coincided with Donaldson's debut as an author, and the two authors seemed to share a readership. When asked about the influence of Tolkien upon his work, Donaldson told Ross that "there are obviously many details in Covenant which purportedly show the influence of Tolkien. But almost without exception those details were consciously chosen because what I could gain by them was worth the risk that my readers might think I was imitating Tolkien."

Despite the professional and financial rewards that Donaldson had finally achieved, success also brought unexpected changes to his life. As he explained to Dahlin in the *Publishers Weekly* interview, his wife had become "so used to taking care of me that when she didn't have to anymore, she saw me going away from her"; their marriage ended in divorce. Eager to immerse himself in writing another series—he had spent the years between 1972 and 1976 creating the Covenant trilogy—Donaldson was instead cajoled by Lester del Rey to write a second trilogy. The author was initially reluctant to do so, but then began to think that perhaps there were more complex moral issues left unexplored in the first series, whose battles between good and evil were conducted in a physical arena with a great deal of violent, bloody action.

The Second Chronicles of Thomas Covenant: The Unbeliever, which began with the publication of *The Wounded Land* in 1980, returns Covenant to The Land a few millennia later; Lord Foul has been resurrected and again threatens it. Accompanying Covenant this time is Dr. Linden Avery, a female physician plagued by a guilty conscience related to the untimely death of her parents. In the second volume, 1982's *The One Tree,* the pair set out on a granite ship to an island called the One Tree Land; a delegation of giants and Elohim, considered holders of "Earth Power," come along. Here Covenant and Linden fall in love, adding a romantic twist to the series and centering some of the plot development around issues of love and trust, as Donaldson wanted to do for this second series. Throughout this novel and Volume III, *White Gold Wielder,* which appeared in 1983, Covenant suffers from a poison venom that Lord Foul used against him. Once again, the reluctant hero utilizes his powers to save The Land, which has been afflicted with a Foul-induced plague.

Reviews for this second Covenant trilogy were mixed. "As one burrows deeper into the inflated text it soon becomes apparent that the rules, not to mention the standards, of good fiction are violated repeatedly on every page," decreed Timothy Robert Sullivan in a *Washington Post Book World* review of *White Gold Wielder.* Still, the second trilogy was equally popular among Donaldson's fans. As Stableford noted in the *St. James Guide to Fantasy Writers* essay, both series "demonstrated that vast numbers of readers were not only pre-

pared to immerse themselves in the plight of a man with a particularly horrible disease, but were avid to do so. . . . They were enthusiastic to participate in his quest, which was explicitly stated to be a hard battle against his own unbelief, primarily directed against an enemy which personified the determination of others to despise him."

By now Donaldson had spent over a decade writing draft upon draft of his fantastical, allegorical tales, which drew heavily upon religious themes in their explorations of timeless moral quandaries. As he told Ross, "Science fiction and fantasy try to answer the question 'What does it mean to be human?' by altering the context (the world) in order to test real conceptions of humanness against alien definitions of reality or alien conceptions of humanness against normal or familiar ones." Donaldson continued: "Science fiction, in fact, takes an explicitly speculative approach to the great theme of literature. Fantasy, on the other hand, does the same thing by delving explicitly into the human imagination. (I don't mean to be confusing about this. Imagination is, of course, the tool of all creative vision. In fantasy, imagination is the subject as well as the tool.) It follows—naturally—that I consider science fiction and fantasy (but especially fantasy) to be the fundamental form of literature. Lacking the imaginative immediacy of fantasy (or the rational rigor of science fiction), 'mainstream fiction' is a bastardized art form, 'a genre apart.'"

During the early 1980s, Donaldson concentrated on two other series of fantasy novels. The first volume of "Mordant's Need," titled *The Mirror of Her Dreams,* was published by Ballantine in 1986. His unlikely hero this time is a heroine, Terisa Morgan. A wealthy New Yorker with a conflicted relationship with her parents, Terisa possesses a great deal of material wealth but little self-esteem. She is so insecure that inside her home is a room completely walled in mirrors, to prove to herself her very existence. An *Alice in Wonderland*-type encounter with an unusual mirror transports her to the land of Mordant. Her emissary is Geraden, an inept sorcerer who was attempting to follow an edict to bring a strong male warrior to help Mordant through a particularly trying time of political instability.

The denizens of Mordant exhibit disbelief when the bumbling Geraden presents Terisa, a meek and anxious young woman, as their savior. King Joyse, ruler of the tenuously united kingdom, seems dismissive of her as well, though many in Mordant think that the monarch might be suffering from dementia. In the second and concluding volume of the saga, *A Man Rides Through,* the king continues to be obsessed with playing a game called hopboard, similar to chess, while his empire disintegrates. Terisa, finding herself in the middle of political battle, realizes that in Mordant she possesses special powers that can indeed help its people. A romance develops between her and Geraden, King Joyse is not at all deranged, and the army of High King Festten is defeated; Mordant rejoices.

Susan Shwartz, reviewing the first volume of the Mordant series for the *New York Times,* wrote favorably of Donaldson's maturation as a writer. The 1986 tome, Shwartz noted, "demonstrates steady growth. Though he has replaced the tortuous, almost impenetrable, language that proved such heavy going in the Chronicles with the leaner, suppler prose of his novellas, Mr. Donaldson still focuses on outcasts."

Donaldson, who retreated to New Mexico to write after his flush with success, spent the latter half of the 1980s working on a third saga, *The Gap Cycle.* The first volume of this space opera, *The Real Story,* was published by Bantam in 1990. A trio of characters—a villain, a victim, and a rescuer—are introduced, but over the course of the series they often exchange roles as plot and character developments warrant. Nick Succorso and Angus Thermopyle are space pirates who despise one another; Morn Hyland is a female law-enforcement official for the United Mining Companies. Thermopyle kidnaps Hyland, setting in motion a series of space chases, unlikely alliances, and fantastical inventions. An evil force called Amnion hopes to achieve complete control over the galaxy. A review of this first volume by Faren C. Miller in *Locus* compared Donaldson's effort to the seventeenth-century dramas of the English stage. "Like those early masters, he esteems nothing better than villainy writ so large, and so charged with anguish, it calls for pity as well as horror," Miller observed.

In the second volume in the series, *The Gap into Vision: Forbidden Knowledge,* Morn and Nick must flee to one of the galaxy's forbidden zones. Amnion and its agents remain determined to take over the realm. The plot reveals that Morn is haunted by a terrible secret—she once suffered from something called "Gap Sickness," which caused her to wreck a vessel that belonged to her family. A more ominous secret is also disclosed: Morn is expecting a child, the result of a liaison with Angus.

In the 1992 entrant to the series, *The Gap into Power: A Dark and Hungry God Arises,* Nick—less of a hero than before—considers trading Morn to Amnion; mean-

while, Angus has been brainwashed and is now a far more honorable person. Both men arrive at a trading post, Billingate, with plans to sabotage it. A *Publishers Weekly* review of this volume found Donaldson's plot beyond intricate, and conceded that "through it all runs Donaldson's trademark sadism, betrayal, amorality and purposeless cruelty."

The plot of the Donaldson's fourth volume, 1994's *The Gap into Madness: Chaos and Order,* takes the reader further into Amnion's devious plan to mutate Earth's inhabitants into a race of aliens. Both the United Mining Police and agents of Amnion are desperately trying to locate people whose blood contains antibodies that will become the basis for a drug to prevent the alienization. Morn's son, Davies, begins to take on a more integral role in the action, while Nick and a scientist develop the immunity drug. Aliens from Amnion pursue a space ship with Davies aboard, but UMC personnel are also on the trail in an attempt to rescue Morn.

In the concluding volume, *The Gap into Ruin: This Day All Gods Die,* Donaldson ties up the complex story and its related subplots. A showdown in Earth's orbit takes place between Morn's forces and an Amnion faction. A review of the final novel in the series from *Publishers Weekly* termed it "a crowd-pleasing story told on a grand scale, SF adventure with a genuinely galactic feel."

Donaldson has also written several other shorter works, as well as a few detective novels. In 1984, a volume of stories titled *Daughters of Regals and Other Tales* was issued by the Del Rey imprint. Included in it was *Gilden-Fire,* an outtake from the second volume of the first "Thomas Covenant" series, *The Illearth War,* that had to be excised because of length and plot considerations. *Daughters of Regals* also contained several unusual shorter works from the writer, such as "Animal Lover," the tale of a scientist with plans to create an army of genetically modified, weapons-proficient creatures.

Another story in the collection, "The Conqueror Worm," tracks the speedy disintegration of an already-faltering marriage when an enormous centipede appears in the home; Donaldson has said that this story was perhaps the most difficult writing experience of his career. A *Publishers Weekly* assessment of the volume compared *Daughters of Regals* to the work of Donaldson's "Thomas Covenant" series, and concluded that overall, the pieces "demonstrate that his intense style and offbeat approach can be quite effective in other realms."

Under the pseudonym Reed Stephens, Donaldson has also written a series of detective novels. The first, *The Man Who Killed His Brother,* was issued by Ballantine in 1980, and introduces another unlikely hero, Mick Axbrewder. A heavy drinker nicknamed "Brew," Mick is approached by his ex-wife, Ginny, a private investigator. Brew's thirteen-year-old niece has vanished, and Ginny and others fear that a serial killer is at work. A *Publishers Weekly* review observed that while the plot of this amateur detective story offers no surprises, the author "fits the pieces together neatly."

In the second Reed Stephens book, 1984's *The Man Who Risked His Partner,* a sobered Brew and a devastated Ginny—who has lost her hand in an accident—again join forces when a banker hires them, fearing he is the target of a local organized crime ring. *The Man Who Tried to Get Away,* a third in the series, appeared in 1990.

Donaldson is also the author of the 1998 collection, *Reave the Just and Other Tales,* his first since 1984's *Daughters of Regals.* The work contains a number of short stories and novellas, many of them previously published in anthologies or magazines, and garnered its creator the customary critical plaudits. Writing for *Booklist,* Roberta Johnson noted that though a few of the stories were characteristically bleak, like Donaldson's longer works, the tales in *Reave the Just* were "more often exciting, moving and even comic."

The writer may return to his Thomas Covenant hero for one final trilogy. As he once told Ross, "I do have some ideas I like for a new large fantasy. But I have trouble dealing with all the expectation surrounding such a project—other people's as well as my own. My publishers (and maybe my readers) expect me to change the clothes and the names and a few other details and serve up Covenant again," Donaldson said. "I, on the other hand, expect myself to do both 'totally different' and 'better' than Covenant. This exerts a lot of pressure (it's one of the problems that comes with success) and I still have to learn to deal with it."

BIOGRAPHICAL/CRITICAL SOURCES:

BOOKS

Contemporary Literary Criticism, Volume 46, Gale, 1988.

Contemporary Popular Writers, St. James Press, 1997.

St. James Guide to Fantasy Writers, first edition, edited by David Pringle, St. James Press, 1996.

St. James Guide to Science Fiction Writers, fourth edition, St. James Press, 1996.

PERIODICALS

Booklist, April 15, 1994, p. 1484; December 1, 1998, Roberta Johnson, review of *Reave the Just and Other Tales,* p. 655.

Fantasy Review, November, 1986, p. 28.

Galileo, January, 1978.

Kirkus Reviews, February 15, 1996, p. 265; November 15, 1998, review of *Reave the Just and Other Tales,* p. 1637.

Library Journal, October 15, 1977, Judith Yamomoto, review of *The Chronicles of Thomas Covenant,* pp. 2184-2185.

Locus, December, 1990, Faren C. Miller, review of *The Gap into Conflict: The Real Story,* p. 17; June, 1994, p. 27.

Los Angeles Times, January 29, 1978.

Los Angeles Times Book Review, May 1, 1983.

Magazine of Fantasy and Science Fiction, February, 1979.

Montreal Star, December 13, 1977.

New York Times, November 30, 1986, Susan Shwartz, review of *Mirror of Her Dreams,* section 7, p. 16.

New York Times Book Review, February 18, 1979; August 14, 1983.

People, July 26, 1982, John Neary, "Both Sales and Sagas Are Fantastic for Stephen Donaldson and His Leper Hero," p. 58.

Publishers Weekly, August 15, 1977, review of *The Chronicles of Thomas Covenant,* p. 56; June 27, 1980, Robert Dahlin, interview with Stephen R. Donaldson, p. 12; October 31, 1980, review of *The Man Who Killed His Brother,* p. 83; February 19, 1982, p. 62; March 2, 1984, review of *Daughters of Regals,* p. 86; November 16, 1990, p. 48; May 3, 1991, p. 66; September 28, 1992, review of *The Gap into Power: A Dark and Hungry God Arises,* p. 69; March 4, 1996, review of *The Gap into Ruin: This Day All Gods Die,* p. 58; December 14, 1998, review of *Reave the Just and Other Tales,* p. 61.

San Francisco Examiner, October 5, 1977.

Science Fiction and Fantasy Book Review, May, 1982; November, 1983, p. 24-25.

Science Fiction Review, September-October, 1978; November, 1982; May 1983.

Village Voice, October 10, 1977, John Calvin Batchelor, "Tolkien Again: Lord Foul and Friends Infest a Morbid but Moneyed Land," pp. 79-80.

Voice of Youth Advocates, June, 1988, p. 95; June, 1993, pp. 100-101; October, 1996, Diane G. Yates, review of *The Gap into Ruin: This Day All Gods Die,* p. 216; August, 1999, D. Yates, review of *Reave the Just and Other Tales,* p. 190.

Washington Post, August 12, 1980; August 21, 1980.

Washington Post Book World, December 11, 1977; June 26, 1983, Timothy Robert Sullivan, review of *White Gold Wielder,* p. 10; November 23, 1986, p. 9.*

*   *   *

DORF, Fran 1953-

PERSONAL: Born December 27, 1953, in Philadelphia, PA; daughter of Edward (in sales) and Beatrice (a secretary) Freeman; married Robert L. Dorf (a business executive), January 21, 1978; children: Rachel, Michael (deceased). *Education:* Boston University, B.S., 1975; New York University, M.S., 1985.

ADDRESSES: Office—c/o Penguin Putnam, Author Mail, 375 Hudson Street, New York, NY 10014.

CAREER: Esquire, New York City, merchandising manager, 1976-77; International Playtex, Stanford, CT, promotion manager, 1978-81; writer.

WRITINGS:

A Reasonable Madness (Literary Guild selection), Carol Publishing Group (New York City), 1991, reprinted, Vivisphere (Poughkeepsie, NY), 2000.
Flight (Literary Guild selection), New American Library/Dutton (New York City), 1992, reprinted, Vivisphere, 2000.
Saving Elijah, Putnam (New York City), 2000.

WORK IN PROGRESS: Another novel.

ADAPTATIONS: Saving Elijah has been optioned for a motion picture by Sydney Pollack.

SIDELIGHTS: Fran Dorf's novels blend psychological suspense, supernatural twists, and elements of the thriller in order to plumb such topics as parental grief, brain damage, and psychotherapy. On her Web site, the author tells readers: "I'm interested in what's underneath the surface of life, whether it's psychological, parapsychological, supernatural, or divine. . . . What I'm more concerned with are the angels and monsters *inside* people's heads rather than those that can be seen in a group encounter." Having earned a master's degree in psychology—and then having turned to creative writing as a career—Dorf peoples her novels with characters that struggle both inwardly and outwardly to understand the demons shaping their lives.

Saving Elijah, Dorf's third novel, concerns a desperate mother's attempts to save her dying son. The author herself lost a son in 1994, and some of the novel's most poignant moments occur in a pediatric intensive care unit, which Dorf describes in detail. The story's heroine, Dinah Galligan, makes a Faustian bargain with an evil and seductive ghost from her past. In exchange for Elijah's recovery, Dinah must allow the ghost to occupy her body at will. "*Saving Elijah* may not strike you as your idea of light summer reading," noted Patricia Wynn Brown on the Web site *Columbia AlivewireD.* "But once you experience this well-written and compelling story, you will be strangely uplifted and better able to face life's complications head on." *BookBrowser* correspondent Harriet Klausner commended *Saving Elijah* as a "taut psychological thriller . . . a fabulous tale that should make Fran Dorf a household name." Observing that the novel "crackles with suspense, dark humor, and provocative questions," a *Publishers Weekly* reviewer concluded: "Dorf has created a compelling page-turner that turns a family tragedy into a spellbinding novel."

Commenting on the writing process on her Web site, Dorf declared: "People often suppose that fiction comes directly from the writers' experience. It *does,* of course, but not necessarily in the way that assumption implies, even fiction labeled 'autobiographical.' Fiction is a soup—a big, boiling, bubbling pot whose ingredients might include almost anything, anything seen, heard, felt, read, imagined, experienced, or dreamed. And just as each human being is a distinct and unique creation within the universe, fiction—indeed, each *individual* fiction—is unique to its creator and its moment, in process and method, skill, and scope, as much as it is in sources."

BIOGRAPHICAL/CRITICAL SOURCES:

PERIODICALS

Booklist, June 1, 2000, Ellie Barta-Moran, review of *Saving Elijah,* p. 1852.
Publishers Weekly, April 24, 2000, review of *Saving Elijah,* p. 56.

OTHER

BookBrowser, http://www.bookbrowser.com/ (June 2, 2000), Harriet Klausner, review of *Saving Elijah.*

Columbia AlivewireD, http://www.alivewired.com/ (July 20, 2000), Patricia Wynn Brown, "Good Grief."

Fran Dorf Web Site, http://www.frandorf.com/ (October 2, 2000).*

* * *

DORO, Edward 1908-1987

PERSONAL: Born February 3, 1908, in Dickinson, ND; died January, 1987. *Education:* University of Southern California, B.A., 1930; University of Pennsylvania, M.A., 1931; attended University of Paris, 1932-33; University of California, Berkeley, M.L.S., 1957.

CAREER: Yale University Library, New Haven, CT, senior assistant in rare books, 1958-59; Northwestern University Library, Evanston, IL, curator of rare books, 1959-62; New School for Social Research (now New School University), New York, NY, teacher of literature, 1962-63; Museum of Fine Arts, Houston, TX, lecturer and librarian, 1963-65; Franconia College, Franconia, NH, instructor in creative writing and college librarian, 1965-67; John F. Kennedy University, Martinez, CA, professor of humanities and university librarian, 1967-69; Monterey Institute of Foreign Studies, Monterey, CA, professor of humanities, 1969-73. Poet reader for Library of Congress Archives of American Poets, 1962.

MEMBER: American Library Association (life member).

AWARDS, HONORS: Russell Loines Memorial Award, National Institute of Arts and Letters, 1933, for *The Boar and Shibboleth;* Guggenheim fellowship in poetry, 1936; L.H.D., Sussex Institute of Technology, 1971.

WRITINGS:

POEMS

Alms for Oblivion, Casa Editorial Hispano-Americana (Paris, France), 1931.

The Boar and Shibboleth, Knopf (New York, NY), 1932.

Shiloh: Fragments on a Famous Theme, Putnam (New York, NY), 1936.

Mr. Zenith & Other Poems, Bookman Press (New York, NY), 1942.

Parisian Interlude, Doan (Evanston, IL), 1960.

The Furtherance, Franconia College Press (Franconia, NH), 1966.

OTHER

Also author of plays *The Prophet from Izmir,* 1972, and *The Spanish Locket,* 1974. Poetry anthologized in *Great Poems of the English Language, Twentieth-Century American Poetry, Bartlett's Quotations,* and other collections.

SIDELIGHTS: Edward Doro published several collections of poetry, including *The Boar and Shibboleth, Shiloh: Fragments on a Famous Theme,* and *Mr. Zenith & Other Poems.* Doro's poetry was marked by a visionary quality. The poems in his book *The Boar and Shibboleth,* for example, were described by E. L. Walton in the *New York Times* as a "riotous world of fancy and strange apparitions," although Walton found that Doro exhibited "an amazing command of technique and of various manners." William Rose Benet, writing of the same book for the *Saturday Review of Literature,* wrote: "I urge all lovers of [the] fabulous, . . . all seekers for magic in verse, all who desire their poetry slightly mad, to seek out this wellspring without delay and drink of its illuminating waters."

In *Shiloh: Fragments on a Famous Theme* Doro wrote a verse account of the life of Jesus in which the Savior does not die on the cross but is taken away into the mountains by his followers. *Shiloh*'s "chief distinction lies . . . ," wrote the reviewer for *Books,* "in the authenticity of background and setting, and the beauty of descriptive passages." While R. P. Blackmur in *Poetry* believed that "a good half of Mr. Doro's rhymes are either dangling, inept of sense, or disfigurements of sense," the critic for the *Times Literary Supplement* found that the book "is intensely conceived and is full of flashes of mystical insight."

Doro's *Mr. Zenith & Other Poems* features a mystical dialogue between Zenith and four characters who are aspects of him. Dudley Fitts, writing in the *Saturday Review of Literature,* noted that the poem "has its deft moments." R. E. Roberts, in another review of the book for the *Saturday Review of Literature,* believed that "the poem has many remarkable passages, and displays Mr. Doro's gift for the arresting phrase."

BIOGRAPHICAL/CRITICAL SOURCES:

PERIODICALS

Booklist, February, 1934, review of *The Boar and Shibboleth,* p. 175.

Books, February 14, 1937, review of *Shiloh,* p. 14.

Los Angeles Times, October 22, 1933, R. T. Thompson, review of *The Boar and Shibboleth,* p. 5.

Nation, December 27, 1933, E. L. Watson, review of *The Boar and Shibboleth,* p. 739.

New York Times, December 17, 1933, E. L. Walton, review of *The Boar and Shibboleth,* p. 8; April 11, 1937, E. L. Walton, review of *Shiloh,* p. 8.

Poetry, May, 1937, R. P. Blackmur, review of *Shiloh,* p. 166; August, 1943, Milton Hindus, review of *Mr. Zenith & Other Poems,* p. 286.

Saturday Review of Literature, November 4, 1933, William Rose Benet, review of *The Boar and Shibbeloth,* p. 241; July 24, 1943, R. E. Roberts, review of *Mr. Zenith & Other Poems,* p. 7; August 28, 1943, Dudley Fitts, review of *Mr. Zenith & Other Poems,* p. 9.

Times Literary Supplement, March 13, 1937, review of *Shiloh,* p. 190.*

* * *

DREWE, Robert (Duncan) 1943-

PERSONAL: Born January 9, 1943, in Melbourne, Australia; son of Royce Burrell (a business executive) and Dorothy (a homemaker; maiden name, Watson) Drewe; married Sandra Symons (a magazine editor), March 21, 1970; married Candida Baker; children: (previous marriage) James, Benjamin, Amy, Jack, Laura.

ADDRESSES: Home—Sydney, Australia. *Office*—c/o Pan Macmillan, Author Mail, Level 18, St. Martin's Tower, 31 Market Street, Sydney, New South Wales, 2000, Australia.

CAREER: West Australian, Perth, Australia, cadet reporter, 1961-64; *Age,* Melbourne, Australia, reporter, 1964-65, head of the Sydney bureau, 1965-70; *Australian,* Sydney, Australia, daily columnist, 1970-73, features editor, 1971-72, literary editor, 1972-74; *Bulletin,* Sydney, special writer, 1975-76, contributing editor, 1980-82; *Mode,* Sydney, columnist, 1981-82; *Sydney City Monthly,* Sydney, columnist, 1981-83; Fraser Publishing Co., Surry Hills, New South Wales, Australia,

consultant and editorial director, 1983—; *Who Weekly,* film critic, 1992-94. Writer in residence at University of Western Australia, 1976, 1979, and at La Trobe University, Melbourne, 1986; member of literature board, Australian Council, 1989-92; judge at various literary competitions in Australia. Honorary foundation member of Center for Studies in Australian Literature.

MEMBER: PEN, Australian Society of Authors, Australian Journalists Association.

AWARDS, HONORS: Australian Council fellowships, 1974, 1977, 1978, 1982, and 1985; Walkley National Awards for journalism, 1976 and 1981; grant from United States government, 1978, for *The Savage Crows;* NBC Banjo Award, 1987; Commonwealth Literary Prize, 1990; Australia Creative fellow, 1993-96; Vance Palmer Prize, 1997, for *The Drowner.*

WRITINGS:

(Co-author) *The Seven Cities of Australia,* John Ferguson, 1976.

The Savage Crows (novel), Collins, 1976.

A Cry in the Jungle Bar (novel), Collins, 1981.

The Bodysurfers (stories; includes "Baby Oil" and "The Silver Medallist"), Fraser Publishing, 1983, Faber, 1984.

(Co-author) *Bondi,* Fraser Publishing, 1984.

Cartoons (novel), Fraser Publishing, 1985.

Fortune (novel), Picador, 1987.

The Bay of Contented Men (stories; includes "Radiant Heat," "Life of a Barbarian," and "All the Boys"), Picador, 1991.

Our Sunshine, Pan Macmillan (Sydney, Australia), 1991.

(Editor) *The Picador Book of the Beach,* Picador, 1993.

The Drowner, St. Martin's Press (New York City), 1997.

The Shark Net: Memories and Murder, Viking (New York City), 2000.

Also editor of *The Penguin Book of the City,* 1997. Contributor to periodicals.

ADAPTATIONS: Various tales from *The Bodysurfers* have been staged, adapted for radio and television, and filmed.

SIDELIGHTS: Robert Drewe is an Australian writer who has earned critical recognition for his novels and short stories. His first novel, *The Savage Crows,* concerns the folly of an Australian author, Stephen Crisp, who feels personal guilt because of Australia's allegedly genocidal practices against Tasmanian aborigines. Self-reproach over both a failed marriage and an unfulfilling relationship with a promiscuous bisexual has left Crisp emotionally distraught. He therefore departs from Sydney, the place of so many of his personal disappointments, and determines to chart his country's treatment of its natives. Interspersed with accounts of Crisp's life and work are excerpts—fabricated by Drewe—of actual government mediator George Augustus Robinson's journals, which detail his discomfort in serving on behalf of the Australian government in dealings with the Tasmanian aborigines. But Robinson's allegedly conciliatory actions only undermined the natives' already tenuous hold in the region, and his patronizing view of the aborigines ultimately created a climate that prompted their elimination from the area. Frank Pike, in a *Times Literary Supplement* appraisal of *The Savage Crows,* described Drewe as "a social documentarist," and Rosemary Dinnage, in her *New Statesman* review, noted that Drewe manages to depict both "sleazy, suburban present-day Australia and . . . a savage, beautiful space/time hinterland."

A Cry in the Jungle Bar is the story of a rough-and-tumble Australian working in the Philippines as an authority on water buffalo. This hero, Dick Cullen, joins his colleagues on a hedonistic tour of the region's bars, brothels, and drug houses. In one such place, a particularly seedy brothel, Cullen falls victim to violence. Bloody and filthy, he reels to the perimeter of a jungle, where he ponders his degenerate existence.

The Bodysurfers comprises a collection of stories that frequently share characters—various members of architect David Lang's family—and an ocean shoreline setting. Jim Crace, writing in the *Times Literary Supplement,* commented that *The Bodysurfers* is "a remarkably seductive and exuberant collection which manages, in its portrayal of human relationships, to be both mordant in tone and playful in manner."

Another of Drewe's publications, *The Bay of Contented Men,* is a collection of emotionally charged tales. Among the stories in this volume are "Radiant Heat," where the hero begins to suspect that his aging mother's mind is degenerating; "Life of a Barbarian," in which a businessman comes to dread his family life; and "All the Boys," in which architect David Lang, frequent protagonist in the earlier *Bodysurfers,* fondly recalls the period preceding the decline of his marriage. *Times Literary Supplement* reviewer David Montrose, in his as-

sessment of *The Bay of Contented Men,* observed that Drewe "exhibits a considerable talent for evoking edgy atmospheres, writing eloquently but never obtrusively."

Drewe won wide acclaim for his novel, *The Drowner,* a bestseller in Australia and winner of the Vance Palmer Prize. The story is set in the 1880s and tells of engineer Will Dance, who meets Angelica Lloyd in Bath, England, and journeys with her to western Australia to work on a water pipeline from the coastal city of Perth to the goldmines of the interior. The harsh terrain of the Australian desert, a typhoid outbreak in a goldmining boomtown, and Will's efforts to complete the pipeline complicate his troubled romance with Angelica. Sheila M. Riley in *Library Journal* called the novel "beautifully written," while the critic for *Publishers Weekly* believed that "the desert mining town . . . comes fully to life, invigorated by crisp and moving portrayals of Drewe's minor characters and the monotonous beauty of the hostile . . . countryside." A contributor for *Kirkus Reviews* found the book "clever, informative, [and] exquisite in sensibility." Murray Waldren, in an article for the *Literary Liaisons* Web site, concluded that *The Drowner* was Drewe's "best book by far."

In *The Shark Net: Memories and Murder,* Drewe turned from fiction to write an autobiographical account of his 1950s childhood in western Australia and his eventual realization that he had lived close to serial killer Eric Cooke, who terrorized the city of Perth. Cooke killed one of Drewe's young friends, and the author even spoke to him once at his father's workplace. Mixing fictionalized scenes with real memories, Drewe creates what Michael Fitzgerald in *Time* called a "readable memoir" written with "crispness and clarity." Fitzgerald continued, "Don't be deceived by the apparent nonchalance of his style. . . . *The Shark Net* is . . . skillfully engineered." A critic for *Publishers Weekly* noted that the story balances "Drewe's lonely childhood" with "his account of the senseless and random murders, which at times is deeply affecting." David Pitt, reviewing the book for *Booklist,* claimed that "Drewe is a careful, precise writer, and his ability to create vivid pictures with only a handful of words is virtually unmatched." And Jim Burns wrote in *Library Journal,* "In his recounting of his formative years, Drewe succeeds in reminding us that the dark side is always near."

Speaking to Waldren about the joys and disappointments of writing, Drewe maintained: "You know, the only real satisfaction from writing is the one you get when it's over. . . . The most disappointing thing is always the huge gap between your intentions and ambitions and what you finally come up with. Whether its writing novels or plays or films, the difficulty is always getting it within the limitations and boundaries of the form."

Drewe once told *CA:* "I am interested in getting to the essence of my country in my fiction. This has necessitated wide traveling inside and outside the country—to China; India and the neighboring South; East Asian and Pacific regions; the United States, where I lived for two years; and Europe."

BIOGRAPHICAL/CRITICAL SOURCES:

PERIODICALS

Australian Book Review, October, 1996, review of *The Drowner,* p. 9; September, 1997, review of *The Penguin Book of the City,* p. 28; May, 1998, review of *The Drowner,* p. 44.
Booklist, June 1, 2000, David Pitt, review of *The Shark Net,* p. 1835.
Books, summer, 1998, review of *The Drowner,* p. R2.
Kirkus Reviews, August 1, 1997, review of *The Drowner,* p. 1131.
Library Journal, October 1, 1997, Sheila M. Riley, review of *The Drowner,* p. 120; June 1, 2000, Jim Burns, review of *The Shark Net,* p. 160.
New Statesman, August 26, 1977, Rosemary Dinnage, review of *The Savage Crows;* December 19, 1997, review of *The Drowner,* p. 87; July 24, 1998, review of *Our Sunshine,* p. 48.
Newsweek, October 29, 1984.
Observer, July 10, 1994, review of *The Picador Book of the Beach,* p. 21.
Publishers Weekly, September 8, 1997, review of *The Drowner,* p. 57; June 19, 2000, review of *The Shark Net,* p. 71.
Time, March 13, 2000, Michael Fitzgerald, "Deadly Twists of Fate: In *The Shark Net,* Robert Drewe Weaves Together a Coming-of-Age Memoir and a True-Crime Story," p. 67.
Times Literary Supplement, September 9, 1977, Frank Pike, review of *The Savage Crows,* p. 1069; April 11, 1980, p. 416; August 24, 1984, Jim Crace, review of *The Bodysurfers,* p. 935; November 27, 1987, p. 1309; December 3, 1987, p. 1367; September 6, 1991, David Montrose, review of *The Bay of Contented Men,* p. 21; September 23, 1994, review of *The Picador Book of the Beach,* p. 24; July 4, 1997, review of *The Drowner,* p. 23; July 17, 1998, review of *Our Sunshine,* p. 23.

Woman's Journal, July, 1994, review of *The Picador Book of the Beach,* p. 14.
World Literature Today, winter, 1991, p. 185.

OTHER

Literary Liaisons, http://www.ozemail.com.au/~waldrenm/ (September 11, 2000).*

*   *   *

DUDLEY, Donald Reynolds 1910-1972

PERSONAL: Born March 3, 1910, in Smethwick, Staffordshire, England; died August 31, 1972; married Eryl Margaret Griffith, September 17, 1938; children: Susan Margaret, Mary Elizabeth. *Education:* St. John's College, Cambridge, B.A., M.A., 1932; Yale University, graduate study, 1932-33.

CAREER: Cambridge University, Cambridge, England, fellow at St. John's College, 1935-37; University of Reading, Reading, England, lecturer in Latin, 1937-44; Oxford University, Oxford, England, Fereday fellow at St. John's College, 1938-41; University of Birmingham, Birmingham, England, director of extramural studies, 1944-55, professor of Latin, beginning 1955, dean of faculty of arts, 1958-61. King Edward's Foundation, member of governing body. Bailiff, 1963-64.

WRITINGS:

A History of Cynicism: From Diogenes to the 6th Century A.D., Methuen (London, England), 1937.
The Civilization of Rome, Mentor Press (London, England), 1960, revised edition, New American Library (New York, NY), 1962.
(With Graham Webster) *The Rebellion of Boudicca,* Routledge & Kegan Paul (London, England), 1962.
The Roman Conquest of Britain, A.D. 43-57, Dufour (London, England), 1965, revised edition, Pan Books (London, England), 1973.
(Editor and contributor) *Lucretius,* Basic Books (New York, NY), 1965.
(Editor, with T. A. Dorey) *Roman Drama,* Basic Books (New York, NY), 1965.
(Translator) *The Annals of Tacitus: A New Translation,* New American Library (New York, NY), 1966.

(Editor, translator, and author of commentary) *Urbs Roma: A Source Book of Classical Texts on the City and Its Monuments,* Phaidon, 1967.

The World of Tacitus, Secker & Warburg (London, England), 1968, Little, Brown (Boston, MA), 1969.

(Editor, with D. M. Lang) *The Penguin Companion to Literature,* Volume 4: *Classical, Byzantine, Oriental, African,* McGraw (New York, NY), 1969, revised edition, 1971.

(Editor) *Virgil,* Basic Books (New York, NY), 1969.

The Romans: 850 B.C.—A.D. 337, Knopf (New York, NY), 1970, published as *Roman Society,* Penguin (London, England), 1975.

(With T. A. Dorey) *Rome against Carthage,* Secker & Warburg (London, England), 1971, Doubleday (New York, NY), 1972.

(Editor) *Silver Latin,* Routledge & Kegan Paul (London, England), 1972.

Editor, with T. A. Dorey, of the series "Studies in Latin Literature and Its Influence," Routledge & Kegan Paul (London, England). Contributor of articles on Roman history to professional journals.

SIDELIGHTS: Donald Reynolds Dudley wrote a number of historical studies of ancient Rome, including *The World of Tacitus* and *The Romans: 850 B.C.—A.D. 337.* With T. A. Dorey, he wrote *Rome against Carthage,* a study of the Punic Wars. *The World of Tacitus* is a study of the renowned Roman historian's life, focusing on his beliefs and attitudes toward the major elements of his society. "Dudley's book," wrote J. S. Margon in the *New York Times Book Review,* "is designed as an aid and companion to readers of Tacitus in Latin or in translation." According to T. M. Robinson in *Library Journal,* while *The World of Tacitus* is definitely a scholarly work, "the pungency of its style and intrinsic interest of its subject will make it fascinating reading for the layman." Dudley's "experienced eye," concluded Steve Roday in the *Christian Science Monitor,* "has taken in the many ebbs and tides of Tacitian scholarship, [and] the modern reader . . . is always directed through a fine, regular expository style."

In *The Romans: 850 B.C.—A.D. 337* Dudley presents an extensive overview of Roman society, including its art, philosophy, politics, geography, literature and major figures. A critic for the *Virginia Quarterly Review* called *The Romans* "a truly masterful book, synthesizing an immense amount of diverse material so skillfully. . . . It is highly recommended." A reviewer for the *Times Literary Supplement* also found words of praise for Dudley's effort, claiming that "few scholars could have done it better than Professor Dudley has done."

Dudley teamed with T. A. Dorey for *Rome against Carthage,* a history of the bloody rivalry between the two budding empires that resulted in three major wars and the eventual destruction of Carthage. Dudley and Dorey cover the political background to the conflict, the major participants on both sides, and the primary military campaigns. A *Times Literary Supplement* critic called *Rome against Carthage* "an excellent and up-to-date survey." A *Choice* reviewer cited the authors for having "produced a work which combines style and humor without being overwhelmed by their material."

BIOGRAPHICAL/CRITICAL SOURCES:

PERIODICALS

American Historical Review, July, 1966, L. L. Howe, review of *The Roman Conquest of Britain, A.D. 43-57,* p. 1303.

Choice, November, 1969, review of *The World of Tacitus,* p. 1281; June, 1972, review of *Rome against Carthage,* p. 558.

Christian Science Monitor, August 28, 1969, Steve Roday, review of *The World of Tacitus,* p. 13.

Classical World, May, 1963, Michael Woloch, review of *The Rebellion of Boudicca,* p. 262; April, 1966, S. L. Dyson, review of *The Roman Conquest of Britain, A.D. 43-57,* p. 285; September, 1969, H. W. Benario, review of *The World of Tacitus,* p. 21.

Encounter, October, 1971, R. F. Willetts, review of *Rome against Carthage,* p. 61.

Library Journal, April 15, 1966, W. S. Debenham, review of *The Roman Conquest of Britain, A.D. 43-57,* p. 2058; April 15, 1969, T. M. Robinson, review of *The World of Tacitus,* p. 1628.

New York Times Book Review, October 12, 1969, J. S. Margon, review of *The World of Tacitus,* p. 46.

Times Literary Supplement, December 7, 1963, review of *The Rebellion of Boudicca,* p. 946; December 5, 1968, review of *The World of Tacitus,* p. 1387; January 22, 1971, review of *The Romans,* p. 90; September 10, 1971, review of *Rome against Carthage,* p. 1083.

Virginia Quarterly Review, summer, 1971, review of *The Romans,* p. cxxvii.*

*   *   *

DURANT, David N(orton) 1925-

PERSONAL: Born July 29, 1925, in Nottingham, England; son of Edward (an agent) and Winifred (Pratt) Durant; married Christabel Wright, March 15, 1951; children: Nicholas, Jonathan, Andrew. *Education:*

Thames Nautical Training College, H.M.S., 1942. *Religion:* Agnostic.

ADDRESSES: Home—Old Hall, Bleasby, Nottingham NG14 7FU, England. *Agent*—David Higham Associates Ltd., 5-8 Lower John St., Golden Sq., London W1R 4HA, England.

CAREER: Durant & Son Ltd., Nottingham, England, founder and president, 1950-72; freelance writer, 1970—. Lecturer at Attingham Summer School, University of Nottingham, University of Manchester, University of Sheffield, and in the United States, including Harvard University and the Smithsonian Institution. Member of council of Nottingham Building Preservation Trust; architectural history consultant to Allied Breweries. *Military service:* British Merchant Marine, 1942-50.

MEMBER: Society of Authors, English Speaking Union.

WRITINGS:

Bess of Hardwick: Portrait of an Elizabethan Dynast, Atheneum (New York, NY), 1978, revised edition, Peter Owen, 1999.
Arbella Stuart, Weidenfeld & Nicolson (London), 1978.
Raleigh's Lost Colony, Atheneum (New York, NY), 1981.
Living in the Past: An Insider's Social History of Historic Houses, Aurum Press (London), 1988.
The Handbook of British Architectural Styles, Barrie & Jenkins (London), 1992.
Life in the Country House: A Historical Dictionary, J. Murray (London), 1996.
Where Queen Elizabeth Slept and What the Butler Saw: Historical Terms from the Sixteenth Century to the Present, St. Martin's (New York, NY), 1997.

Contributor to *Country Life* and *History Today.*

SIDELIGHTS: David N. Durant has written many books related to English history. His *Bess of Hardwick: Portrait of an Elizabethan Dynast* is the story of a powerful woman who fashioned her own brand of success in the male-dominated world of Tudor England. During her lifetime, which spanned some eighty years, Bess made four shrewd marriages. In this way, she amassed huge property holdings for herself. She oversaw the construction of Hardwick Hall in Derbyshire, an imposing castle that still stands today. Among her other achievements, Bess of Hardwick acted as jailer to Mary Queen of Scots. Bess took as her model her queen, Elizabeth I, to whom she was unfailingly loyal. "One woman gained power by multiple marriages, the other by never marrying at all," noted Helen Hackett in her *Times Literary Supplement* review of *Bess of Hardwick.* She commented that "more comparison of their negotiations of the constraints of their age would be intriguing," but praised Durant's book as "rich in meticulously researched detail." Of particular interest, in Hackett's view, are Durant's observations on daily life in Elizabethan times and the ways in which political alliances were forged. For example, when Bess married the Earl of Shrewsbury, their bond was reinforced by the marriages of his son Gilbert to her twelve-year-old daughter, and of her son Henry to Shrewsbury's eight-year-old daughter. *Library Journal* contributor Bennett D. Hill noted the broad appeal of *Bess of Hardwick,* stating: "Popular audiences will enjoy this interesting book. . . . [It] is a sound, well written, if not scholarly, study."

Durant was again involved with the history of the Elizabethan era with his book, *Raleigh's Lost Colony,* which documented the failed attempt, led by Sir Walter Raleigh, to establish an English colony on Roanoke Island. Identifying Durant as a historian who "simplifies, narrates, and enlivens the scholar's analysis," a reviewer for *Choice* praised *Raleigh's Lost Colony* as "evocative."

Durant once told *CA:* "I always had a compulsion to write books, but the urgent necessity of earning a living intervened between reality and ambition. Now in my early fifties, I have started on a career that has matured over thirty years. I aim to produce easy to read, clear historical biographies, as a contrast to the academics, who appear mainly unable to write understandable English. I hate inefficiency and suffer from finding myself inefficient. I hate carelessness and consequently suffer again. I find writing is a very humbling trade. I am humbled twice a day on the average—it is said to be good for the soul. Nevertheless I am enjoying life for about the first time."

BIOGRAPHICAL/CRITICAL SOURCES:

PERIODICALS

Booklist, March 15, 1993, review of *The Handbook of British Architectural Styles,* p. 1302; September 1, 1997, review of *Where Queen Elizabeth Slept and What the Butler Saw,* p. 172.

Choice, November, 1981, review of *Raleigh's Lost Colony,* p. 434.

Contemporary Review, December, 1996, review of *Life in the Country House: A Historical Dictionary,* p. 335; May, 1999, review of *Bess of Hardwick: Portrait of an Elizabethan Dynast,* p. 276.

Library Journal, February 1, 1978, Bennett D. Hill, review of *Bess of Hardwick: Portrait of an Elizabethan Dynast,* p. 358; June 15, 1997, review of *Where Queen Elizabeth Slept and What the Butler Saw,* p. 82; March 1, 2000, Michael Rogers, review of *Bess of Hardwick: Portrait of an Elizabethan Dynast,* p. 129.

Observer, September 1, 1996, review of *Life in the Country House: A Historical Dictionary,* p. 15.

Times Literary Supplement, June 26, 1981, Peter Marshall, review of *Raleigh's Lost Colony,* p. 734; September 3, 1999, Robin Buss, review of *Bess of Hardwick: Portrait of an Elizabethan Dynast,* p. 32.*

*   *   *

DUTTON, Paul Edward 1952-

PERSONAL: Born December 8, 1952, in London, Ontario, Canada; son of Charles E. (in business) and Frances (in business; maiden name, Neely) Dutton; married Barbara Jane Regier (in business), May 25, 1974; children: Laura, Kate. *Education:* University of Western Ontario, B.A., 1976; University of Toronto, M.A., 1977, Ph.D., 1981; Pontifical Institute of Mediaeval Studies, Toronto, Ontario, Canada, M.S.L., 1979, M.S.D., 1988.

ADDRESSES: Home—Port Coquittan, British Columbia, Canada. *Office*—Department of History, Simon Fraser University, Burnaby, British Columbia V5A 1S6, Canada. *E-mail*—dutton@sfu.ca.

CAREER: Simon Fraser University, Burnaby, British Columbia, Canada, professor of medieval history, 1983—.

WRITINGS:

The *"Glosae super Platonem" of Bernard of Chartres* (critical edition), Pontifical Institute of Mediaeval Studies (Toronto, Ontario, Canada), 1991.

(Editor) *Carolingian Civilization: A Reader,* Broadview Press (Peterborough, Ontario, Canada), 1993.

The Politics of Dreaming in the Carolingian Empire, University of Nebraska Press (Lincoln, NE), 1994.

(Editor) *Charlemagne's Courtier: The Complete Einhard,* Broadview Press (Peterborough, Ontario, Canada), 1998.

(With Edouard Jeauneau) *The Autograph of Eriugena,* Brepols (Turnhout, Belgium), 1996.

(With Herbert L. Kessler) *The Poetry and Paintings of the First Bible of Charles the Bald,* University of Michigan Press (Ann Arbor, MI), 1997.

E

ELSHTAIN, Jean Bethke 1941-

PERSONAL: Born January 1, 1941, in Windsor, CO; daughter of Paul George (an educator) and Helen (a community activist and homemaker; maiden name, Lind) Bethke; married Errol L. Elshtain (a public health official), September 5, 1965; children: Sheri, Heidi, Jenny, Eric. *Education:* Colorado State University, B.A., 1963; attended University of Wisconsin (now University of Wisconsin at Madison), 1963-64; University of Colorado, M.A., 1965; Brandeis University, Ph.D., 1973.

ADDRESSES: Office—Divinity School, University of Chicago, 1025 East 58th St., Chicago, IL 60637.

CAREER: Colorado State University, Fort Collins, instructor in history, 1964-65; Northeastern University, Boston, MA, lecturer in political science, 1972-73; University of Massachusetts at Amherst, instructor, 1973, assistant professor, 1973-76, associate professor, 1976-80, professor of political science, beginning 1980; University of Chicago, Chicago, IL, Laura Spelman Rockefeller Professor of Social and Political Ethics at Divinity School. Yale University, visiting professor, 1980-81; Harvard University, visiting professor, 1994; Institute for Advanced Study, Princeton, NJ, member of board of trustees. PEW Forum on Religious and Public Life, co-chair; National Commission on Civic Renewal, member.

MEMBER: International Political Science Association, International Association for Philosophy of Law and Social Philosophy, American Political Science Association (vice president, 1999-2000), American Academy of Arts and Sciences, Conference for the Study of Political Thought, Women's Caucus for Political Science, Council on Civil Society (chair).

AWARDS, HONORS: Woodrow Wilson fellowship, 1963-64; MacDowell Colony fellowship, summer, 1981; citations for outstanding academic book, *Choice,* c. 1982, for *Public Man, Private Woman: Women in Social and Political Thought,* and c. 1998, for *New Wine and Old Bottles: International Politics and Ethical Discourse;* "notable book" citation, *New York Times,* 1995, for *Democracy on Trial;* Theologos Award, American Theological Booksellers Association, 2000, for *Who Are We? Critical Reflections and Hopeful Possibilities;* Lilly fellow at National Humanities Center, 2000-01; Guggenheim fellow.

WRITINGS:

Public Man, Private Woman: Women in Social and Political Thought, Princeton University Press (Princeton, NJ), 1981.
(Editor and contributor) *The Family in Political Thought,* University of Massachusetts Press (Amherst, MA), 1982.
Intimacy and Cultural Form, 1983.
Meditations on Modern Political Thought: Masculine/Feminine Themes from Luther to Arendt, Praeger (New York, NY), 1986.
Women and War, Basic Books (New York, NY), 1987, 2nd edition with new epilogue, University of Chicago Press (Chicago, IL), 1995.
(Editor, with David Blankenhorn and Steven Bayme) *Rebuilding the Nest: A New Commitment to the American Family,* Family Service America (Milwaukee, WI), 1990.

(Editor, with Sheila Tobias) *Women, Militarism, and War: Essays in History, Politics, and Social Theory,* Rowman & Littlefield (Savage, MD), 1990.

Power Trips and Other Journeys: Essays in Feminism as Civic Discourse, University of Wisconsin Press (Madison, WI), 1990.

(With others) *But Was It Just? Reflections on the Morality of the Persian Gulf War,* Doubleday (New York, NY), 1992.

(Editor) *Just War Theory,* New York University Press (New York, NY), 1992.

Democracy on Trial, Anansi (Concord, Ontario, Canada), 1993, Basic Books (New York, NY), 1995.

(Editor, with J. Timothy Cloyd) *Politics and the Human Body: Assault on Dignity,* Vanderbilt University Press (Nashville, TN), 1995.

Augustine and the Limits of Politics, University of Notre Dame Press (South Bend, IN), 1995.

(Editor, with David Popenoe and Blankenhorn) *Promises to Keep: Decline and Renewal of Marriage in America,* Rowman & Littlefield (Lanham, MD), 1996.

Democratic Authority at Century's End, University of Oregon Books (Eugene, OR), 1997.

Real Politics: At the Center of Everyday Life, Johns Hopkins University Press (Baltimore, MD), 1997.

New Wine and Old Bottles: International Politics and Ethical Discourse, University of Notre Dame Press (South Bend, IN), 1998.

Who Are We? Critical Reflections and Hopeful Possibilities, Eerdmans (Grand Rapids, MI), 2000.

(With Azizah Y. al-Hibri and Charles C. Haynes) *Religion in American Public Life: Living with Our Deepest Differences,* Norton (New York, NY), 2001.

Jane Addams and the Dream of American Democracy, Basic Books (New York, NY), 2001.

(Editor) *The Jane Addams Reader,* Basic Books (New York, NY), 2001.

Contributor to books, including *Studies in Socialist Pedagogy,* edited by Theodore M. Norton and Bertell Ollman, Monthly Review Press (New York, NY), 1978; *Liberalism and the Modern Policy,* edited by Michael J. Gargas McGrath, Dekker (New York, NY), 1978; *The Prism of Sex: Toward an Equitable Pursuit of Knowledge,* edited by Julia Sherman and Evelyn T. Beck, University of Wisconsin Press (Madison, WI), 1980; *Women and Public Policy,* edited by Irene Diamond, Longman (New York, NY), 1982; and *Great American Reformers.* Contributor of more than seventy articles and reviews to political science journals and popular magazines, including *Commonweal, Dissent, Quest, Nation, Newsday,* and *Progressive.* Member of editorial board, *Women and Politics.* Elshtain's books have been translated into Czech, Italian, and Japanese.

SIDELIGHTS: Jean Bethke Elshtain is a scholar whose work incorporates ethics, political science, philosophy, and religion. She is deeply concerned with social trends and the unintended consequences of democracy in an era marked by the cult of the individual. An ethical thinker who draws upon theological sources, she was one of the first scholars to declare a crisis in the American family and, by extension, the American community. Through her books, lectures, and essays, Elshtain "champions a civic philosophy that attends to the dignity of everyday life as a democratic imperative of the first order," according to Patrick H. Samway in *America. New York Times Book Review* correspondent Judith Shulevitz stated that one of the most important features of Elshtain's work "is how prescient she has turned out to be; her political perspective, which seemed old-fashioned in its day, is the conventional wisdom now."

Elshtain trained as a political scientist, but her more recent academic appointments have encompassed both that discipline and ethics. Moreover, she is known beyond academia for her critiques of radical political movements that ignore limits and are trends in modern society which undermine respect for the dignity of human beings. "Jean Bethke Elshtain is a rare asset in the increasingly specialized world of academia," commented Patrick J. Deneen in *Commonweal.* "Not only has she resisted the widespread academic tendency toward self-imposed irrelevance, but she has succeeded—where few have been able—in appealing to an educated audience whose names don't inevitably begin with the title Dr. or Professor. . . . Elshtain casts her net widely in the fields of politics, philosophy, and literature, in social commentary and feminist critique, and comes up with a rich and compelling catch." Shulevitz made a similar observation when she called Elshtain "a public intellectual with a knack for wiggling out of the categories she's been shoehorned into."

Among Elshtain's better known works is *Democracy on Trial,* in which she argues that democratic institutions in America have been severely weakened by the loss of the civic dimension of rights. She mourns the lack of distinction between public and private life, warning that when politics is everywhere, it is in fact nowhere. This theme also informs *Real Politics: At the Center of Everyday Life,* a collection of her essays on political and social topics. In a *Christian Century* review of the latter title, Glenn Tinder wrote: "Jean Bethke Elshtain dislikes ideologies and all grand theories because they replace the concrete and quotidian with sweeping abstractions. . . . Elshtain is concerned with the indispensable part language plays in realizing a rich daily life, and with its coarsening and depletion under the impact of such forces as war, commerce and bureaucracy." Tinder concluded: "Elshtain is one of the most attractive political theorists now writing. Amid ideological extremes and inanities, she is invariably sensible. . . . In the universe of academic discourse, her wit and informality make her a bright and shining light."

Elshtain once told *CA:* "My work is iconoclastic, challenging received 'truths' from the history of political thought and within contemporary political and social thought, including feminism. I am concerned with the way innovative ideas become hardened into deadening dogmas. One of my chief concerns is children, the way they are viewed and the way they are treated. It seems to me that much of the political ferment of our recent past concentrated almost exclusively on promoting a certain kind of 'individual liberation' that rapidly turned into self-serving individualism. Within this frame of reference, concern for others gets derogatively labeled 'self-abnegation.' We have lost a sense of community and of the dignity of caring and being of service. I would restore this without, at the same time, restoring the unjust constraints that previously prevented persons, especially women, from expressing their own sense of self. This is a complex task, but one that is worthwhile and important. I attribute this ethical and moral dimension of my work to having been reared in a family in which such imperatives were central and in which responsibility for self *and* others was seen as necessarily intertwined.

"These concerns lead me to be demanding but mindful of human limitations. Thus, I am spared, at least most of the time, from trafficking in moralistic heavy-handedness by a deeply rooted sense of irony and a recognition that there is much to laugh about and at—most often oneself."

BIOGRAPHICAL/CRITICAL SOURCES:

PERIODICALS

America, September 20, 1997, Patrick H. Samway, review of *Real Politics: At the Center of Everyday Life,* p. 30.

American Political Science Review, June, 1997, review of *Augustine and the Limits of Politics,* p. 432.

Annals of the American Academy of Political and Social Science, March, 1996, review of *Democracy on Trial,* p. 220.

Armed Forces and Society, summer, 1993, review of *Just War Theory,* p. 637.

Booklist, November 15, 1994, review of *Democracy on Trial,* p. 560.

Books and Culture, May, 1997, review of *Augustine and the Limits of Politics,* p. 30.

Books in Canada, February, 1996, review of *Democracy on Trial,* p. 30.

Choice, September, 1993, review of *Women, Militarism, and War: Essays in History, Politics, and Social Theory,* p. 63; May, 1995, review of *Democracy on Trial,* p. 1524; November, 1995, review of *Augustine and the Limits of Politics,* p. 473; February, 1998, review of *Real Politics,* p. 1057; April, 1999, review of *New Wine and Old Bottles: International Politics and Ethical Discourse,* p. 1530.

Christian Century, May 24, 1995, review of *Democracy on Trial,* p. 570; April 23, 1997, review of *Augustine and the Limits of Politics,* p. 421; January 21, 1998, Glenn Tinder, review of *Real Politics,* p. 62.

Christian Science Monitor, February 10, 1995, review of *Democracy on Trial,* p. 11.

Commonweal, February 10, 1995, review of *Democracy on Trial,* p. 18; May 22, 1998, Patrick J. Deneen, review of *Real Politics,* p. 27.

Ethics, January, 1994, review of *Just War Theory,* p. 423; July, 1999, review of *Real Politics,* p. 943.

International Philosophical Quarterly, March, 1998, review of *Augustine and the Limits of Politics,* p. 95.

Journal of Church and State, autumn, 1999, review of *New Wine and Old Bottles,* p. 828.

Journal of Politics, February, 1996, review of *Democracy on Trial,* p. 262; February, 1999, review of *Real Politics,* p. 254.

Kirkus Reviews, November 1, 1994, review of *Democracy on Trial,* p. 1454; September 15, 1997, review of *Real Politics,* p. 1431.

Library Journal, November 1, 1997, review of *Real Politics,* p. 102.

New York Times Book Review, January 22, 1995, John Gray, "Does Democracy Have a Future?," p. 1; December 14, 1997, Judith Shulevitz, "Prematurely Correct," p. 18; September 10, 2000, John T. Noonan Jr., "Sins of the Marketplace," p. 28.

Publishers Weekly, December 5, 1994, review of *Democracy on Trial,* p. 63.

Quarterly Journal of Speech, November, 1997, review of *Augustine and the Limits of Politics,* p. 488.

Reason, April, 1995, review of *Democracy on Trial,* p. 55.

Review of Politics, spring, 1997, review of *Augustine and the Limits of Politics,* p. 365.

Signs, spring, 1993, review of *Power Trips and Other Journeys: Essays in Feminism as Civic Discourse,* p. 693.

Society, May-June, 1997, Peter Dennis Bathory, "Augustine through a Modern Prism," p. 73.

Theological Studies, June, 1997, review of *Augustine and the Limits of Politics,* p. 389.

U.S. Catholic, June, 1998, "Private Lives, Public Matters," p. 30.

Virginia Quarterly Review, spring, 1998, review of *Real Politics,* p. 61.

World and I, June, 1995, review of *Democracy on Trial,* p. 342.

*   *   *

ERICKSON, Peter (Brown) 1945-

PERSONAL: Born August 11, 1945, in Worcester, MA; son of Irving Peter (a public high school math teacher) and Elinor (a public high school English teacher; maiden name, Brown) Erickson; married Tay Gavin (an artist), June 30, 1968 (died October 23, 1998); children: Andrew Sven, Ingrid Adriana, Benjamin Peter. *Education:* Amherst College, B.A. (magna cum laude), 1967; graduate study at Center for Contemporary Cultural Studies, University of Birmingham, Birmingham, England, 1967-68; University of California at Santa Cruz, Ph.D., 1975; Simmons College, M.S.L.S., 1984.

ADDRESSES: Home—81 Buxton Hill Rd., Williamstown, MA 01267. *Office*—Clark Art Institute, 225 South St., P.O. Box 8, Williamstown, MA 01267. *E-mail*—Peter.Erickson@clarkart.edu.

CAREER: Williams College, Williamstown, MA, assistant professor of English, 1976-81; Kent fellow and visiting assistant professor at Wesleyan University, 1981-83; Clark Art Institute, Williamstown, MA, research librarian, 1985—.

MEMBER: Modern Language Association, Shakespeare Association of America, Renaissance Society of America.

WRITINGS:

Patriarchal Structures in Shakespeare's Drama, University of California Press (Berkeley, CA), 1985.

(Editor, with Coppélia Kahn, and contributor) *Shakespeare's "Rough Magic": Renaissance Essays in Honor of C. L. Barber,* University of Delaware Press (Newark, DE), 1985.

(Contributor) Jean E. Howard and Marion F. O'Connor, editors, *Shakespeare Reproduced: The Text in History and Ideology,* Methuen (New York, NY), 1987.

(Contributor) Marianne Novy, editor, *Women's Re-Visions of Shakespeare,* University of Illinois Press (Urbana, IL), 1989.

Rewriting Shakespeare, Rewriting Ourselves, University of California Press (Berkeley, CA), 1991.

(Contributor) Henry Louis Gates, Jr. and K. A. Appiah, editors, *Toni Morrison: Critical Perspectives Past and Present,* Amistad (New York, NY), 1993.

(Author of afterword) Marianne Novy, editor, *Cross-Cultural Performances: Differences in Women's Re-Visions of Shakespeare,* University of Illinois Press (Urbana, IL), 1993.

(Contributor) Tracy Mishkin, editor, *Literary Influence and African-American Writers,* Garland Publishing (New York, NY), 1996.

(Editor and author of introduction) Harry Berger, Jr., *Making Trifles of Terrors: Redistributing Complicities in Shakespeare,* Stanford University Press (Stanford, CA), 1997.

(Contributor) Felicia Hardison Londré, editor, *Love's Labour's Lost: Critical Essays,* Garland Publishing (New York, NY), 1997.

(Contributor) Marianne Novy, editor, *Transforming Shakespeare: Contemporary Women's Re-Visions in Literature and Performance,* St. Martin's Press (New York, NY), 1999.

(Editor, with Clark Hulse, and contributor) *Early Modern Visual Culture: Representation, Race, and Empire in Renaissance England,* University of Pennsylvania Press (Philadelphia, PA), 2000.

(Contributor) Arthur F. Kinney, editor, *New Critical Essays on Hamlet,* Routledge (New York, NY), 2001.

(Contributor) Philip C. Kolin, editor, *New Critical Essays on Othello,* Routledge (New York, NY), 2001.

Contributor of articles to *Shakespearean Criticism, Contemporary Literary Criticism, Dictionary of Literary Biography,* and *Women's Studies Encyclopedia.* Contributor of numerous articles and reviews to periodicals, including *PMLA, Transition, Women's Studies, Chronicle of Higher Education, Kenyon Review, Criticism, Shakespeare and the Classroom, Shakespeare Quarterly,* and *Callaloo.*

SIDELIGHTS: Peter Erickson told *CA:* "Though I have published primarily as a Shakespearean, I have maintained the pattern of working in two different historical periods—in Renaissance literature and in contemporary twentieth-century literature, the latter exemplified by my essays on June Jordan, Toni Morrison, and Adrienne Rich. Because of my commitment to this second area, my investment in Shakespeare is not total; I see Shakespeare's work from outside as well as inside, and this double vision places his work in a qualified perspective. Full-strength feminist criticism of Shakespeare can be made to appear negative when it is cut off from its larger context, its contribution to the feminist revaluation of the tradition as a whole. The constructive spirit of the project of re-vision can emerge fully only if we reject narrow period specialization as the exclusive definition of what constitutes the professionally legitimate and instead acknowledge responsibility to the entire range of cultural heritage, including the present.

"My first book on Shakespeare was written almost entirely within the tradition of American feminist psychoanalytic criticism as it existed at the end of the 1970s. My second book is situated in a much wider theoretical frame of reference that takes into account both the changes within feminist Shakespeare criticism brought about by the entry of significant new critics such as Margaret Ferguson and Jean Howard, and the development outside of feminist criticism of the major critical currents of new historicism in the United States and cultural materialism in England. In particular I focus on the creative tensions between feminist criticism and new historicism. My goal is less to achieve an impossible, ideal synthesis or reconciliation than to examine some of the conceptual elements necessary for a distinctively feminist historicism.

"A chief difference between feminist and new historicist approaches is that the critical spirit of the former is more conducive to the intellectual demands of political engagement, which the latter tended to suppress, shy away from, or leave less than fully developed. Two forms that this engagement takes in feminist criticism are canon revision and identity politics, and both involve alertness to the contemporary political implications of our scholarship.

"I pursue identity politics, a concept for which I am indebted to Adrienne Rich's foreword to *Blood, Bread, and Poetry* (1986), in order to extend the abstract notion of the 'critic in history' by giving it a high degree of specificity. Rather than treating contemporary critics as a unified collective body, I emphasize our differences and I consider my own situation with regard to gender, race, class, sexual orientation, and ethnic and national identity, as these multiple facets bear on literary interpretation. Placing my male gender in this larger context as one component in a whole set of specific cultural locations, I now address my role as a male feminist critic. While there are dangers in a male feminist position, I believe an even greater danger for male critics is the avoidance or abjuration of direct involvement with feminist issues. My goal is to explore the difficulties of male feminism while remaining committed to—rather than abandoning—my position as a male feminist critic.

"Looking back, I can see that my work has participated in a major development in Shakespeare and Renaissance studies over the last two decades of the twentieth century—namely, the shift from a focus on gender in the 1980s to a focus on race in the 1990s. My first book was published in 1985 during the initial phase of feminist Shakespeare criticism, while my second book in 1991 reflects the turn toward race.

"Yet this second book proved to be a turning point in ways I did not anticipate. Although the book achieved its goal of combining the two areas of Shakespeare and contemporary African-American literature in which I had previously worked separately, this move was less a resolution than a starting point because the implications of my argument were not yet fully worked out. I made the connection between Shakespeare and race not by considering Shakespeare's responses to race, but rather indirectly by examining black writers' responses to Shakespeare. I do not mean to discount the latter formulation since it led to the explicit political analysis in my subsequent essay 'Multiculturalism and the Problem of Liberalism' in 1992.

"However, this method had the effect of deferring the theme of race to a much later historical moment, and therefore a gap remained in the overall approach. The next step required to bring the argument full circle would be locating the issue of race within the early modern period itself. In a very real sense, the book was completed only two years after its publication in an essay that squarely addressed the issue of race in the context of the Renaissance. Two key elements in this 1993 essay, entitled 'Representations of Blacks and Blackness in the Renaissance,' were the inclusion of visual images and the attention to white identity.

"I have continued to expand both elements in my ongoing writing on race. Both helped to shape the collection *Early Modern Visual Culture: Representation, Race, and Empire in Renaissance England,* which appeared in 2000, thus marking the start of the new century."

BIOGRAPHICAL/CRITICAL SOURCES:

PERIODICALS

Criticism, winter, 1993, review of *Rewriting Shakespeare, Rewriting Ourselves,* p. 137.
Renaissance Quarterly, summer, 1993, review of *Rewriting Shakespeare, Rewriting Ourselves,* p. 423.
Shakespeare and the Classroom, fall, 1998, pp. 53-56.

F-G

FARROW, John
See FERGUSON, Trevor

*   *   *

FERGUSON, Trevor 1947-
(John Farrow)

PERSONAL: Born November 11, 1947, in Seaforth, Ontario, Canada; son of Percy A. (a reverend) and M. V. Joycee (a teacher; maiden name, Sanderson) Ferguson; married Lynne Hill (an educator), 1985.

ADDRESSES: Home—Hudson, Quebec, Canada. *Agent*—Anne McDermid and Assoc., 92 Willcocks St., Toronto, Ontario M5S 1C8, Canada. *E-mail*—trevorferguson@compuserve.com.

CAREER: Author.

MEMBER: Writers' Union of Canada (chair, 1990-91).

AWARDS, HONORS: Hugh MacLennan Award for Fiction, Quebec Writers' Federation, 1996.

WRITINGS:

High Water Chants, Macmillan (Toronto), 1977.
Onyx John, McClelland and Stewart (Toronto), 1985.
The Kinkajou, Macmillan, 1989.
The True Life Adventures of Sparrow Drinkwater, HarperCollins (Toronto), 1993.

The Fire Line, HarperCollins, 1995.
The Timekeeper, HarperPerennial (Toronto), 1995.

UNDER PSEUDONYM JOHN FARROW

City of Ice, Random House (New York City), 1999.
Ice Lake, Random House, 2001.

ADAPTATIONS: City of Ice was being adapted by Alliance/Atlantis as a feature film.

WORK IN PROGRESS: Long, Long, Short, Long, a play commissioned by infinitheatre, Montreal; *Bright Shining as the Sun,* a novel.

SIDELIGHTS: Trevor Ferguson is a Canadian author whose six literary novels received outstanding reviews but sold less than a thousand copies each. Ferguson, who lives with his wife Lynne near Montreal, continued to write and teach writing but could not attain commercial success. In 1997 he decided to try something different—a mystery thriller. He wrote *City of Ice* under the pseudonym John Farrow, and the book was successfully marketed, not only in Canada, but also in the United States, Japan, Great Britain, and eleven other countries. Bill Ott wrote in *American Libraries* that "a new crime-fiction star has been born."

The story is set in winter in Montreal, but *Maclean's* reviewer Anthony Wilson-Smith called it "international in overall scope." The protagonist, police detective Emile Cinq-Mars was described by Wilson-Smith as "tough, complex, antisocial, smug, and not always likable. . . . He confronts disparate characters, from rogue cops and homeless indigents to bikers and interlopers from the RCMP, CIA and ex-KGB types gone over to the Russian Mafia." Ferguson based his character's name on real-life Montreal policeman Jacques Cinq-Mars, who displayed some of the same traits as his fictional namesake. Wilson-Smith said that "not all characters and plot devices work. . . . But overall, Ferguson, who admires the morally complex thrillers of John le Carré and Martin Cruz Smith (*Gorky Park*), achieves much the same high ground."

Ott wrote in *Booklist* that the author "uses his setting to establish a landscape of danger, the frigid atmosphere (lethal in itself) mirroring the all-encompassing peril that surrounds the hero." A *Publishers Weekly* reviewer said he "artfully depicts French-English working relationships as well as immigrant groups on the fringes of Canadian culture, including the arrogant, well-meaning Americans." Two *Library Journal* contributors commented on *City of Ice.* A. J. Anderson said the novel "works with an odd, idiosyncratic magic" and the plot "has more facets than a fly's eye." Jo Ann Vicarel said the author "has produced a noir novel of depth and perception." Peter Khoury, reviewing the novel in the *New York Times Book Review,* called it a "deft thriller" that "explores the question of how far those who are supposedly on the right side of the law should go in pursuing justice."

BIOGRAPHICAL/CRITICAL SOURCES:

PERIODICALS

American Libraries, February, 2000, Bill Ott, "Quick Bibs," p. 66.
Booklist, April 15, 1999, Bill Ott, review of *City of Ice,* p. 1478.
Globe and Mail (Toronto), March 27, 1999, review of *City of Ice,* p. D14.
Kirkus Reviews, March 1, 1999, review of *City of Ice,* p. 316.
Library Journal, April 15, 1999, A. J. Anderson, review of *City of Ice,* p. 143; November 15, 1999, Jo Ann Vicarel, review of *City of Ice,* p. 132.
Maclean's, May 3, 1999, Anthony Wilson-Smith, "Written to Sell: It's No Mystery What Is Popular with the Public," p. 62.
New York Times Book Review, September 12, 1999, Peter Khoury, review of *City of Ice,* p. 27.
Publishers Weekly, March 22, 1999, review of *City of Ice,* p. 68.

FINN, David 1921-

PERSONAL: Born August 30, 1921, in New York, NY; son of Jonathan (a writer) and Sadie (Borgenicht) Finn; married Laura Zeisler (a travel agent), October 20, 1945; children: Kathy Finn Bloomgarden, Dena Finn Merriam, Peter, Amy Finn Binder. *Education:* City College (now of the City University of New York), B.S., 1943. *Avocational interests:* Collecting contemporary sculpture.

ADDRESSES: Home—New Rochelle, NY. *Office*—Ruder Finn, Inc., 301 East 57th St., New York, NY 10022.

CAREER: Ruder Finn, Inc. (public relations firm), New York, NY, cofounder, 1948, partner, 1948-56, president, 1956-68, chair of board of directors, 1968—. New York University, adjunct associate professor. Jewish Museum, vice chair of board of directors; Cedar Crest College, past chair of board of directors; member of board of directors of National Trust for the Humanities, American Forum for Global Education, MacDowell Colony, Jewish Theological Seminary of America, New Hope Foundation, American Crafts Council, American Friends of Hebrew University, Victor Gruen Center for Environmental Planning, Institute for Advanced Studies in the Humanities, Franklin Book Programs, Inc., Artists for the Environment Foundation, American College in Switzerland, and International Center of Photography; Institute for the Future, past member of board of directors; International Business Institute, member of advisory council; member of advisory board of Council for the Study of Mankind, Bernard M. Baruch College of the City University of New York, New York City Office of Cultural Affairs, and Manpower Opportunities in Israel; Parsons School of Design, member of board of overseers; City College of the City University of New York, member of board of visitors. *Military service:* U.S. Army Air Forces, 1944; became first lieutenant.

MEMBER: Academy of American Poets (member of board of directors), American Academy of Arts and Sciences (member of board of directors).

WRITINGS:

Public Relations and Management, Reinhold (New York, NY), 1956.
The Corporate Oligarch, Simon & Schuster (New York, NY), 1969.

The Business-Media Relationship: Countering Misconceptions and Distrust, AMACOM (New York, NY), 1981.

The Corporate Oligarch, University Press of America (Lanham, MD), 1983.

How to Visit a Museum, Abrams (New York, NY), 1985.

How to Look at Sculpture: Text and Photographs, Abrams (New York, NY), 1989.

How to Look at Photographs: Reflections on the Art of Seeing, Abrams (New York, NY), 1994.

(With Judith A. Jedlicka) *The Art of Leadership: Building Business-Arts Alliances,* Abbeville Press (New York, NY), 1998.

How to Look at Everything, Abrams (New York, NY), 2000.

(And photographer) *20th-Century American Sculpture in the White House Garden,* Abrams (New York, NY), 2000.

(And photographer) *Hope: A Monument to Raoul Wallenberg,* Overlook Press (New York, NY), 2001.

Contributor of paintings to books, including *Byzantium,* by William Butler Yeats, Black Swan Books (Redding Ridge, CT), 1983; and *Evocations of Four Quartets: Paintings,* Black Swan Books (Redding Ridge, CT), 1990. Contributor to *Handbook of Public Relations.* Contributor to professional journals and popular magazines, including *Harper's* and *Saturday Review.*

PHOTOGRAPHER

Gustav Vigeland, *Embrace of Life,* Abrams (New York, NY), 1969.

Henry Moore, *As the Eye Moves,* Abrams (New York, NY), 1971.

Frederick Hartt, *Donatello, Prophet of Modern Vision,* Abrams (New York, NY), 1973.

Hart, *Michaelangelo's Three Pietas: Photographic Study,* Abrams (New York, NY), 1976.

Henry Moore: Sculpture and Environment, Abrams (New York, NY), 1977.

Oceanic Images, Abrams (New York, NY), 1978.

H. Peter Stern and David Collens, *Sculpture at Storm King,* Abbeville Press (New York, NY), 1980.

(With daughter, Amy Binder) *The Busch-Reisinger Museum, Harvard University,* Abbeville Press (New York, NY), 1980.

The Florence Baptistery Doors, Viking (New York, NY), 1980.

New Rochelle: Portrait of a City, Abbeville Press (New York, NY), 1981.

Canova, Abbeville Press (New York, NY), 1983.

Greek Monumental Bronze Sculpture, Vendome Press (New York, NY), 1983.

John Beardsley, *A Landscape for Modern Sculpture: Storm King Art Center,* Abbeville Press (New York, NY), 1985.

Meyer Schapiro, *The Romanesque Sculpture of Moissac,* Braziller (New York, NY), 1985.

Richard P. Brettell, *An Impressionist Legacy: The Collection of Sara Lee Corporation,* Abbeville Press (New York, NY), 1986.

Stephen Spender, *In Irina's Garden, with Henry Moore's Sculpture,* Thames & Hudson (New York, NY), 1986.

Charles Avery, *Giambologna: The Complete Sculpture,* Moyer Bell (Mount Kisco, NY), 1987.

A Grace of Sense: The Sculpture of Joan Sovern, Black Swan Books (Redding Ridge, CT), 1988.

Vision of Harmony: The Sculpture of Saul Baizerman, Black Swan Books (Redding Ridge, CT), 1989.

Janis C. Conner, *Rediscoveries in American Sculpture: Studio Works, 1893-1939,* University of Texas Press (Austin, TX), 1989.

Bruno Lucchesi: Sculptor of the Human Spirit, Hudson Hills Press (New York, NY), 1989.

Alfred Kazin, *Our New York,* Harper (New York, NY), 1990.

Walter J. Boyne, *Art in Flight: The Sculpture of John Safer,* Hudson Hills Press (New York, NY), 1991.

Marie Busco, *Rodin and His Contemporaries: The Iris and B. Gerald Cantor Collection,* Cross River Press (New York, NY), 1991.

Marilyn E. Weigold, *Opportunitas: The History of Pace University,* Pace University Press (New York, NY), 1991.

Lika Mutal, Abrams (New York, NY), 1996.

Evelyn Silber, *Gaudier-Brzeska: Life and Art,* Thames & Hudson (New York, NY), 1996.

Dena Merriam, *Stanley Bleifeld,* Madison Books (Lanham, MD), 1996.

Avery, *Bernini: Genius of the Baroque,* Bulfinch (Boston, MA), 1997.

William Weaver, *A Legacy of Excellence: The Story of Villa i Tatti,* Abrams (New York, NY), 1997.

Merriam and Eleanor Munro, *Carole A. Fuerman: Sculpture,* National Book Network (Lanham, MD), 1999.

SIDELIGHTS: After spending many decades at the helm of an international public relations firm, David Finn developed a highly successful secondary career as an artist and photographer of sculpture. Finn has traveled widely in order to photograph the world's most important sculptures, and his pictures, collected into books, convey the spirit of the three-dimensional works. He is also the author of several "how to" books for general readers, including *How to Visit a Museum* and *How to Look at Everything.* According to a reviewer in *Petersen's Photographic,* Finn feels that those who look at the world more creatively "can experience life more fully."

One of the many books to which Finn has contributed photographs is *Our New York* by Alfred Kazin. In that work, Kazin ruminates about growing up in Brooklyn and residing in Manhattan, while Finn captures images of the city, its parks, sculptures, monuments, people, museums, and skyline. *New York Times* columnist Herbert Mitgang called the book "a paean to the sidewalks of New York, a love song to New Yorkers and an effort to meter the bounce and energy that electrify the skyscraper canyons." *New York Times Book Review* contributor Anatole Broyard noted that *Our New York* succeeds in producing a cogent portrait of the city: "The inanimate parts of New York, the buildings that are not actively rotting or seething with restless humanity, the skyscrapers and modern museums, the bridges, grids and profiles against the sky, are soothingly abstract." Broyard added, "Most of the faces photographed by Mr. Finn are carefully wiped clean of expression, for to show something is to invite anything. . . . Sometimes, though, Mr. Finn's faces betray a kind of amnesiac grieving over their lost expressions; they look like memories, or prisons, or feelings."

BIOGRAPHICAL/CRITICAL SOURCES:

PERIODICALS

Library Journal, February 15, 1998, Jack Perry Brown, review of *Bernini: Genius of the Baroque,* p. 137; September 1, 2000, Jennifer L. S. Moldwin, review of *How to Look at Everything,* pp. 201-202.

New York Times, June 14, 1981, Lynne Ames, "Revolution about Westchester," Section 11, p. 2; January 8, 1990, Herbert Mitgang, "Seeing New York as Nurturer of Mind and Spirit," section C, p. 18.

New York Times Book Review, January 14, 1990, Anatole Broyard, "An Uneasy Walker in the City," p. 9.

Petersen's Photographic, September, 2000, review of *How to Look at Everything,* p. 16.

Publishers Weekly, May 27, 1996, review of *Lika Mutal,* p. 60; March 31, 1997, review of *A Legacy of Excellence: The Story of Villa i Tatti,* p. 53.

GALE, Robert L(ee) 1919-

PERSONAL: Born December 27, 1919, in Des Moines, IA; son of Erie Lee (a sales manager) and Miriam (Fisher) Gale; married Maureen Dowd, November 18, 1944; children: John, James, Christine. *Education:* Dartmouth College, B.A., 1942; Columbia University, M.A., 1947, Ph.D., 1952.

ADDRESSES: Home—131 Techview Ter., Pittsburgh, PA 15213.

CAREER: University of Delaware, Newark, DE, instructor, 1949-52; University of Mississippi, University, MS, assistant professor, 1952-56, associate professor, 1956-59; University of Pittsburgh, Pittsburgh, PA, assistant professor of English, 1959-60, associate professor, 1960-65, professor of American literature, 1965-87. Fulbright professor at Oriental Institute, Naples, Italy, 1956-58, and University of Helsinki, 1975. *Henry James Review,* member of editorial board. *Military service:* U.S. Army, Counter Intelligence Corps, 1942-46; became second lieutenant.

MEMBER: Modern Language Association of America, Phi Beta Kappa.

WRITINGS:

The Caught Image: Figurative Language in the Fiction of Henry James, University of North Carolina Press, 1964.

Thomas Crawford, American Sculptor, University of Pittsburgh Press, 1964.

Barron's Simplified Approach to Thoreau's "Walden," Barron's, 1965.

Plots and Characters in the Fiction of Henry James, Archon, 1965.

Barron's Simplified Approach to Ralph Waldo Emerson and Transcendentalism, Barron's, 1966.

Barron's Simplified Approach to Crane's "The Red Badge of Courage," Barron's, 1966.

Barron's Simplified Approach to "The Grapes of Wrath" by John Steinbeck, Barron's, 1966.

A Critical Study Guide to James' "The American," Littlefield, 1966.

A Critical Study Guide to James' "The Ambassadors," Littlefield, 1967, published as *Pennant Key-indexed Study Guide to Henry James' "The Ambassadors,"* Educational Research Associates, 1967.

Robert L. Gale

A Critical Study Guide to James' "The Turn of the Screw," Littlefield, 1968.

A Critical Study Guide to Dreiser's "Sister Carrie," Littlefield, 1968.

Plots and Characters in the Fiction and Sketches of Nathaniel Hawthorne, Archon, 1968.

Barron's Simplified Approach to Edgar Allan Poe, Barron's, 1969.

Plots and Characters in the Fiction and Narrative Poetry of Herman Melville, Archon, 1969.

Richard Henry Dana, Jr., Twayne (Boston, MA), 1969.

Barron's Simplified Approach to Edith Wharton's "Ethan Frome," Barron's, 1969.

Plots and Characters in the Fiction and Poetry of Edgar Allan Poe, Archon, 1970.

Francis Parkman, Twayne (Boston, MA), 1973.

Plots and Characters in the Works of Mark Twain, two volumes, Archon, 1973.

Charles Warren Stoddard, Boise State University (Boise, ID), 1977.

John Hay, G. K. Hall (Boston, MA), 1978.

Charles Marion Russell, Boise State University (Boise, ID), 1979.

Luke Short, G. K. Hall (Boston, MA), 1981.

Will Henry/Clay Fisher, Boise State University (Boise, ID), 1982.

Will Henry/Clay Fisher (Henry W. Allen), G. K. Hall (Boston, MA), 1984.

Louis L'Amour, G. K. Hall (Boston, MA), 1985, revised edition, 1992.

A Henry James Encyclopedia, Greenwood Press (Westport, CT), 1989.

Matt Braun, Boise State University (Boise, ID), 1990.

A Nathaniel Hawthorne Encyclopedia, Greenwood Press (Westport, CT), 1991.

The Gay Nineties in America, Greenwood Press (Westport, CT), 1992.

A Cultural Encyclopedia of the 1850s in America, Greenwood Press (Westport, CT), 1993.

A Herman Melville Encyclopedia, Greenwood Press (Westport, CT), 1995.

(Editor) *Dictionary of Literary Biography,* Volume 186: *Nineteenth-Century American Western Writers,* Gale (Detroit, MI), 1997.

An F. Scott Fitzgerald Encyclopedia, Greenwood Press (Westport, CT), 1998.

A Sarah Orne Jewett Companion, Greenwood Press (Westport, CT), 1999.

A Dashiell Hammett Companion, Greenwood Press (Westport, CT), 2000.

An Ambrose Bierce Companion, Greenwood Press (Westport, CT), 2001.

A Lafcadio Hearn Companion, Greenwood Press (Westport, CT), 2001.

Editor of "Plots and Characters" series, Archon, 1976-81. Contributor to books, including *Eight American Authors,* edited by James Woodress, Norton, 1971; *Academic American Encyclopedia,* twenty volumes, Arete, 1980; *Fifty Western Writers,* by Richard W. Etulain and Fred Erisman, Greenwood Press, 1982; and *American National Biography,* edited by John A. Garraty, twenty-four volumes, Oxford University Press, 2000. Also contributor to *American Literary Scholarship: An Annual,* Duke University Press, 1970, 1977-85.

WORK IN PROGRESS: A Ross Macdonald Companion, for Greenwood Press.

SIDELIGHTS: Robert L. Gale has written extensively about American writers of the nineteenth and twentieth centuries. His *An F. Scott Fitzgerald Encyclopedia* details "all Fitzgerald's works and named fictional characters; and biographical sketches of his family, friends, and associates," as Mary Ellen Quinn described it in *Booklist.* The result is "an extensive guide to Fitzgerald," according to Charles Nash in the *Library Journal.* Nash found, too, that "though the work is designed to be informational rather than interpretative, Gale's most interesting entries are those that do flirt with judgment." Quinn recommended *An F. Scott Fitzgerald Encyclopedia* for "high-school, public, and academic libraries."

In *A Sarah Orne Jewett Companion,* Gale provides a reader's guide to the works of Jewett, a writer from the late nineteenth century. Covering all twenty of Jewett's books as well as her prolific contributions to periodicals, Gale's guide contains plot summaries, a listing of all major and minor characters, brief biographies of Jewett's family and literary friends, and sources for further study. M. L. Robertson in *Choice* found that, although Gale's book might be less useful for new readers of Jewett's work, "certainly plot summaries can alert more experienced readers to forgotten or as yet unread works."

Gale once told *CA:* "Given the current proliferation of recherche and—let us hope—ephemeral literary criticism, I believe that more basic and informative writing such as I conscientiously attempt will continue to be welcomed by mainstream readers."

BIOGRAPHICAL/CRITICAL SOURCES:

PERIODICALS

Booklist, February 1, 1999, Mary Ellen Quinn, review of *An F. Scott Fitzgerald Encyclopedia,* p. 996.
Choice, January, 2000, M. L. Robertson, review of *A Sarah Orne Jewett Companion,* p. 930.
Journal of American History, March, 1995, review of *A Cultural Encyclopedia of the 1850s in America,* p. 1901.
Library Journal, August, 1998, Charles Nash, review of *An F. Scott Fitzgerald Encyclopedia,* p. 76; May 1, 2001, Peter Dollard, review of *An Ambrose Bierce Companion,* p. 70.
Wilson Library Bulletin, January, 1993, James Rettig, review of *The Gay Nineties in America,* p. 107; March, 1994, James Rettig, review of *A Cultural Encyclopedia of the 1850s in America,* p. 88.

*   *   *

GAVRON, Daniel 1935-

PERSONAL: Born December 7, 1935, in London, England; son of Nathan (a patent attorney) and Lily (Ettman) Gavron; married Angela Jacobs (a teacher of blind children), September 20, 1957; children: Etan, Ilana, Assaf. *Education:* Attended School of Oriental and African Studies, London, 1955-59. *Politics:* Social Democrat. *Religion:* "Jewish-Agnostic."

ADDRESSES: Home—Motza Elite, Jerusalem, Israel. *Agent*—c/o Rowman & Littlefield, 4720 Boston Way, Lanham, MD 20706.

CAREER: Regional Tourist Office, Arad, Israel, tourist officer, 1961-63; Kaiser Engineers, Sdom, Israel, secretary, 1963-67; University of the Negev, Beersheba, Israel, public relations officer, 1967-71; Israel National Radio, Jerusalem, news editor and senior reporter, 1971-80, head of English News, 1980-82; *Jerusalem Post,* Jerusalem, Israel, night editor and feature writer, 1982—. Founding editor, *Palestine-Israel Journal.* Founder-settler of Arad, new town in the Negev, chairman of Arad Settlers Committee, 1963; former leader in Habonim youth movement and former kibbutz member. *Military service:* Israel Defense Forces (Reserves), 1961—.

WRITINGS:

NONFICTION

Walking through Israel (nonfiction), Houghton Mifflin (Boston), 1980.
Israel after Begin (nonfiction), Houghton Mifflin, 1984.
Saul Adler, Pioneer of Tropical Medicine: A Biography, Balaban International (Glenside, PA), 1997.
The Kibbutz: Awakening from Utopia, Rowman & Littlefield, 2000.

NOVELS

The End of Days, Jewish Publication Society (Philadelphia), 1970.
Pilgrims, Creative Arts Book Company (Berkeley, CA), 2000.

OTHER

Contributor to a number of journals, including *Commentary.*

WORK IN PROGRESS: The Other Foot, a contemporary Israeli thriller; *An Israel Social History.*

SIDELIGHTS: Daniel Gavron was born in London, but left England in 1961 to start a new life on a kibbutz in Israel. The kibbutz movement began in the early twentieth century as a means of building an Israeli state. Living communally, members worked on farms or in light industry to provide products for export and for their own needs. Kibbutz members built entire communities, providing homes for newcomers and establishing a sense of solidarity and purpose among themselves. Originally conceived as a socialist experiment in cooperative work, the kibbutz experiment has gone through many changes but continues in the present era. Gavron's ten years on the kibbutz and his background as a journalist uniquely qualified him to write *The Kibbutz: Awakening from Utopia,* a review of this social experiment. In it, he takes his readers on a tour of ten settlements, from Degania, the original kibbutz, to Tammuz, a modern urban commune. He shows the widely varying ways in which communities handle their finances, child-care, work assignments, and other aspects of life. He illustrates how changing political currents, emigration, an increasing emphasis on privatization, and other forces have altered the original vision of the kibbutz. "The subtitle is apt: the story of the kibbutz is evolving," commented a contributor to *Kirkus Reviews.* "Still, with only three percent of [Israel's] population, the kibbutzim are responsible for seven percent of Israel's exports, ten percent of its industrial output, and forty percent of its agriculture. The egalitarian tradition isn't dead; it is maturing. Revealing and educational, Gavron's snapshot is a valuable account of a unique social movement."

BIOGRAPHICAL/CRITICAL SOURCES:

PERIODICALS

Booklist, July, 2000, Vanessa Bush, review of *The Kibbutz: Awakening from Utopia,* p. 1980.
Kirkus Reviews, June 15, 2000, review of *The Kibbutz: Awakening from Utopia,* p. 856.
Library Journal, July, 2000, Sanford R. Silverburg, review of *The Kibbutz: Awakening from Utopia,* p. 119.
Los Angeles Times Book Review, November 9, 1980.*

*   *   *

GENTRY, Peter
    See NEWCOMB, Kerry

*   *   *

GERSTLER, Amy 1956-

PERSONAL: Born October 24, 1956, in San Diego, CA. *Education:* Received B.A. from Pitzer College.

ADDRESSES: Home—530 South Barrington, #108, Los Angeles, CA 90049. *Office*—c/o Viking Penguin, 375 Hudson St., New York, NY 10014.

CAREER: Poet, fiction writer, and journalist. Visiting professor of creative writing, University of California at Irvine, 1996. Performer of text-works and collaborator on installations in museums, including Museum of Contemporary Art, Santa Monica Museum of Art, Whitney Museum, and Josh Baer Gallery.

AWARDS, HONORS: Second-place citation, *Mademoiselle* fiction contest, 1987; National Book Critics Circle Award, 1991, for *Bitter Angel.*

WRITINGS:

Yonder (poems), Little Caesar Press, 1981.
Christy's Alpine Inn (poems), Sherwood Press, 1982.
White Marriage/Recovery (poems), Illuminati (Los Angeles), 1984.
Early Heaven (poems), Ouija Madness Press, 1984.
Martine's Mouth (fiction), Illuminati, 1985.
The True Bride (poems), Lapis Press (Santa Monica, CA), 1986.
Primitive Man (fiction), Hanuman Books (New York City), 1987.
(With Alexis Smith) *Past Lives* (artists book), Santa Monica Museum of Art (Santa Monica, CA), 1989.
Bitter Angel (poems), North Point Press (San Francisco, CA), 1990, reprinted, Carnegie Mellon University Press (Pittsburgh, PA), 1997.
Nerve Storm (poems), Viking-Penguin (New York City), 1993.
Crown of Weeds (poems), Penguin (New York City), 1997.
Medicine (poems), Penguin, 2000.

Contributor of articles to periodicals, including *Art Forum* and *Los Angeles Times.*

SIDELIGHTS: Known for witty, complex poetry that reflects such themes as redemption, suffering, and survival, Amy Gerstler won the 1991 National Book Critics Circle Award for the collection *Bitter Angel.* Though Gerstler has penned several poetry volumes, including *Yonder, Early Heaven, Christy's Alpine Inn,* and 1993's *Nerve Storm,* she is best known for *Bitter Angel,* which garnered significant critical acclaim. Gerstler has also received praise for *White Marriage/Recovery,* which *Los Angeles Times Book Review* contributor Jonathan

Kirsch deemed "an odd but utterly beguiling bit of small-press ephemera." The critic called the writing "spare, almost encoded, but richly evocative."

In *Bitter Angel* Gerstler introduces a variety of narrators, including a saint, ghost, clairvoyant, father, child, and lover. Her characters are often outsiders who, according to *Publishers Weekly,* "share a kind of grace" because of their disenfranchisement. Gerstler also evokes the surreal, supernatural, and ironic, using various poetic forms and vernacular speech. Sexuality is another of Gerstler's themes, as Eileen Myles observed in the *Voice Literary Supplement:* "Actually, it's not sex she's talking about but desire, even lust, which cohabits with unlikely traits: modesty, a longing for disembodiment, death, disintegration, and a queer reverence for sainthood and suffering."

Bitter Angel was enthusiastically received by reviewers, who praised Gerstler's originality. A *Publishers Weekly* critic commented that Gerstler "balances classical allusion with bold experimentation in voice, form and content." The result is a "tension" that lends an "urgent, honest edge" to her work. According to Myles, Gerstler's poetry is "extremely rich. But not cluttered and not loud." The reviewer added that "the supernatural, the sexy mundane, the out-of-sight are simply her materials, employed as they might be in a piece of religious art."

"In Gerstler," wrote David Shapiro in *American Poetry Review,* "we see how effective a quiet ruminative and contemplative poem can be. . . . On the other hand, Gerstler has a series of complex, humorous prose poems which can be as immediate and imagistic as a germ: 'A few germs float up the baby's nose while the mother reads, making the infant sneeze.'" According to *American Book Review* contributor Sarah Gorham, the poems in *Bitter Angel* "strip down all basic assumptions about beauty and truth and holiness, and begin a struggle for redemption from the gutter. . . . Because of this, the drive for ascension in Gerstler's work becomes that much more valiant, and comic." And Michael Dirda, writing in *Washington Post Book World,* noted that although some of the poet's juxtapositions appeared "improbable," "all objections are overruled by Gerstler's sheer acrobatic brilliance."

Gerstler followed *Bitter Angel* with *Nerve Storm,* where she "continues her intense, and often savage, pursuit of redemption," according to a *Publishers Weekly* reviewer. Pat Monaghan, writing in *Booklist,* called Gerstler's

realm one of "hallucinatory moments in normal, even crass, circumstances." In one poem, a cow announces that "Prior to this promotion / I was the town drunk." Although disappointed with some of the poems in *Nerve Storm,* the *Publishers Weekly* reviewer noted that Gerstler's "best poems are relentless, soul-searching, surreal and wonderfully inexplicable."

The poems in *Medicine* explore the medical and metaphysical through prayers, laments, and lists that "channel great lyric eruptions," to quote Donna Seaman in *Booklist.* Included in the volume is a poem in which Gerstler confronts a woman in a coma and another in which she prays over an infant, mindful of the suffering it will face in its life. Another poem, "A Non-Christian on Sunday," describes a quiet but slightly unsettling world in the absence of church-goers. *Library Journal* reviewer Ann K. van Buren cited the volume for its "entertaining verbal swordplay as well as socially significant compositions." A *Publishers Weekly* correspondent noted that the best poems in the work "always have a distinctive spin, run through her abiding interests, the intersections of self, soul sickness and cultural drek." The critic concluded: "This is a vibrant and passionate collection of poems."

BIOGRAPHICAL/CRITICAL SOURCES:

BOOKS

Gerstler, Amy, *Bitter Angel,* North Point Press (San Francisco, CA), 1990.
Gerstler, Amy, *Nerve Storm,* Viking-Penguin (New York City), 1993.

PERIODICALS

American Book Review, January-March, 1991, pp. 27, 29.
American Poetry Review, January-February, 1991, pp. 37-47.
Booklist, October 1, 1993; June 1, 2000, Sonna Seaman, review of *Medicine,* p. 1839.
Library Journal, September 1, 2000, Ann K. van Buren, review of *Medicine,* p. 214.
Los Angeles Times Book Review, April 8, 1984, p. 6.
New York Times, December 14, 1990.
Publishers Weekly, December 22, 1989, pp. 4-5; October 18, 1993, p. 69; June 5, 2000, review of *Medicine,* p. 90.

Voice Literary Supplement, February, 1990, pp. 7-8.
Washington Post Book World, March 3, 1991, pp. 6-7.*

*　　*　　*

GIFF, Patricia Reilly 1935-

PERSONAL: Born April 26, 1935, in Brooklyn, NY; daughter of William J. and Alice Tiernan (Moeller) Reilly; married James A. Giff, January 31, 1959; children: James, William, Alice. *Education:* Marymount College, B.A., 1956; St. John's University, M.A., 1958; Hofstra University, professional diploma in reading, 1975. *Religion:* Roman Catholic.

ADDRESSES: Home—15 Fresh Meadow Rd., Weston, CT 06883. *Agent*—George Nicholson, Sterling Lord Literistic, 65 Bleecker St., New York, NY, 10012.

CAREER: Public school teacher in New York City, 1956-60; Elmont Public Schools, Elmont, NY, teacher, 1964-84. Freelance writer, 1979—. The Dinosaur's Paw (children's book store), Fairfield, CT, cofounder and partner, 1994—.

MEMBER: Society of Children's Book Writers and Illustrators, Authors Guild.

AWARDS, HONORS: Honorary D.H.L., Hofstra University, 1990; Newbery Honor award, American Library Association, 1997, for *Lily's Crossing.*

WRITINGS:

FOR CHILDREN

Fourth-Grade Celebrity (also see below), illustrated by Leslie Morrill, Delacorte (New York, NY), 1979.
The Girl Who Knew It All (also see below), illustrated by Morrill, Delacorte (New York, NY), 1979.
Today Was a Terrible Day, illustrated by Susanna Natti, Viking (New York, NY), 1980.
Next Year I'll Be Special, illustrated by Marylin Hafner, Dutton (New York, NY), 1980.
Left-handed Shortstop: A Novel, illustrated by Morrill, Delacorte (New York, NY), 1980.
Have You Seen Hyacinth Macaw?: A Mystery, illustrated by Anthony Kramer, Delacorte (New York, NY), 1981.

The Winter Worm Business: A Novel, illustrated by Morrill, Delacorte (New York, NY), 1981.
The Gift of the Pirate Queen, illustrated by Jenny Rutherford, Delacorte (New York, NY), 1982.
Suspect, illustrated by Stephen Marchesi, Dutton (New York, NY), 1982.
Loretta P. Sweeny, Where Are You?: A Mystery, illustrated by Kramer, Delacorte (New York, NY), 1983.
Kidnap in San Juan, Dell (New York, NY), 1983.
The Almost Awful Play, illustrated by Natti, Viking (New York, NY), 1984.
Rat Teeth, illustrated by Morrill, Delacorte (New York, NY), 1984.
Watch Out, Ronald Morgan, illustrated by Natti, Viking (New York, NY), 1985.
Love, from the Fifth Grade Celebrity, Delacorte (New York, NY), 1986.
Mother Teresa: A Sister to the Poor (nonfiction), illustrated by Ted Lewin, Viking (New York, NY), 1986.
Happy Birthday, Ronald Morgan, illustrated by Natti, Viking (New York, NY), 1986.
Laura Ingalls Wilder: Growing Up in the Little House (nonfiction), illustrated by Eileen McKeating, Viking (New York, NY), 1987.
Tootsie Tanner Why Don't You Talk? An Abby Jones Junior Detective Mystery, illustrated by Kramer, Delacorte (New York, NY), 1987.
Columbus Circle, Dell, 1988.
Ronald Morgan Goes to Bat, illustrated by Natti, Viking (New York, NY), 1988.
I Love Saturday, illustrated by Frank Remkiewicz, Viking (New York, NY), 1989.
Poopsie Pomerantz, Pick Up Your Feet, Delacorte (New York, NY), 1989.
Matthew Jackson Meets the Wall, Delacorte (New York, NY), 1990.
The War Began at Supper: Letters to Miss Loria, Delacorte (New York, NY), 1991.
Diana: Twentieth-Century Princess (nonfiction), illustrated by Michele Laporte, Viking (New York, NY), 1991.
Show Time at the Polk Street School: Plays You Can Do Yourself or in the Classroom, illustrated by Blanche Sims, Delacorte (New York, NY), 1992.
Shark in School, illustrated by Sims, Delacorte (New York, NY), 1994.
Ronald Morgan Goes to Camp, illustrated by Natti, Viking (New York, NY), 1995.
Good Luck, Ronald Morgan, illustrated by Natti, Viking (New York, NY), 1996.
Lily's Crossing, Delacorte (New York, NY), 1997.
Katie Cobb Two, Viking (New York, NY), 1999.
Louisa May Alcott (nonfiction), Viking (New York, NY), 1999.

Nory Ryan's Song, Delacorte (New York, NY), 2000.

Fourth-Grade Celebrity and The Girl Who Knew It All, Dell, 2000.

Edith Stein: Sister Teresa Benedicta of the Cross, Holiday House (New York, NY), 2001.

All the Way Home, Delacorte (New York, NY), 2001.

"KIDS OF THE POLK STREET SCHOOL" SERIES

The Beast in Ms. Rooney's Room, illustrated by Blanche Sims, Delacorte (New York, NY), 1984.

The Candy Corn Contest, illustrated by Sims, Delacorte (New York, NY), 1984.

December Secrets, illustrated by Sims, Delacorte (New York, NY), 1984.

Lazy Lions, Lucky Lambs, illustrated by Sims, Delacorte (New York, NY), 1985.

Say "Cheese", illustrated by Sims, Delacorte (New York, NY), 1985.

Purple Climbing Days, illustrated by Sims, Delacorte (New York, NY), 1985.

In the Dinosaur's Paw, illustrated by Sims, Delacorte (New York, NY), 1985.

Snaggle Doodles, illustrated by Sims, Delacorte (New York, NY), 1985.

The Valentine Star, illustrated by Sims, Delacorte (New York, NY), 1985.

Sunny-Side Up, illustrated by Sims, Delacorte (New York, NY), 1986.

Fish Face, illustrated by Sims, Delacorte (New York, NY), 1986.

Pickle Puss, illustrated by Sims, Delacorte (New York, NY), 1986.

"NEW KIDS AT THE POLK STREET SCHOOL" SERIES

The Kids of the Polk Street School, Dell, 1988.

B-E-S-T Friends, Dell, 1988.

If the Shoe Fits, Dell, 1988.

Watch Out! Man-eating Snake, Dell, 1988.

All about Stacy, Dell, 1988.

Fancy Feet, Dell, 1988.

Stacy Says Good-Bye, Dell, 1989.

Spectacular Stone Soup, Dell, 1989.

Beast and the Halloween Horror, Dell, 1990.

Emily Arrow Promises to Do Better This Year, Dell, 1990.

Monster Rabbit Runs Amuk!, Dell, 1990.

Wake up Emily, It's Mother Day, Dell, 1991.

"POLKA DOT, PRIVATE EYE" SERIES

The Mystery of the Blue Ring, Dell, 1987.

The Powder Puff Puzzle, Dell, 1987.

The Riddle of the Red Purse, Dell, 1987.

The Secret at the Polk Street School, Dell, 1987.

The Case of the Cool-Itch Kid, Dell, 1989.

Garbage Juice for Breakfast, Dell, 1989.

The Clue at the Zoo, Dell, 1990.

The Trail of the Screaming Teenager, Dell, 1990.

"LINCOLN LIONS BAND" SERIES

Meet the Lincoln Lions Band, illustrated by Emily Arnold McCully, Dell, 1992.

Yankee Doodle Drumsticks, illustrated by McCully, Dell, 1992.

The Jingle Bells Jam, illustrated by McCully, Dell, 1992.

The Rootin' Tootin' Bugle Boy, illustrated by McCully, Dell, 1992.

The Great Shamrock Disaster, illustrated by McCully, Dell, 1993.

"POLK STREET SPECIAL" SERIES

Write up a Storm with the Polk Street School, Dell, 1993.

Turkey Trouble, Dell, 1994.

Count Your Money with the Polk Street School, illustrated by Blanche Sims, Dell, 1994.

Postcard Pest, illustrated by Sims, Dell, 1994.

Look out, Washington, D.C.!, illustrated by Sims, Dell, 1995.

Pet Parade, illustrated by Sims, Dell, 1996.

Green Thumbs, Everyone, illustrated by Sims, Dell, 1996.

Oh Boy, Boston!, illustrated by Sims, Dell, 1997.

Next Stop, New York City! The Polk Street Kids on Tour, illustrated by Sims, Dell, 1997.

Let's Go, Philadelphia!, illustrated by Sims, Dell, 1998.

"BALLET SLIPPERS" SERIES

Dance with Rosie, illustrated by Julie Durrell, Viking (New York, NY), 1996.

Rosie's Nutcracker Dreams, illustrated by Durrell, Viking (New York, NY), 1996.

Starring Rosie, illustrated by Durrell, Viking (New York, NY), 1997.

A Glass Slipper for Rosie, illustrated by Durrell, Viking (New York, NY), 1997.

Not-So-Perfect Rosie, illustrated by Durrell, Viking (New York, NY), 1997.

Rosie's Big City Ballet, illustrated by Durrell, Viking (New York, NY), 1998.

"FRIENDS AND AMIGOS" SERIES

Good Dog, Bonita, illustrated by DyAnne DiSalvo-Ryan, Gareth Stevens (Milwaukee, WI), 1998.

Adios, Anna, illustrated by DiSalvo-Ryan, Gareth Stevens (Milwaukee, WI), 1998.

Happy Birthday, Anna, Sorpresa!, illustrated by DiSalvo-Ryan, Gareth Stevens (Milwaukee, WI), 1998.

Ho, Ho, Benjamin, Feliz Navidad, illustrated by DiSalvo-Ryan, Gareth Stevens (Milwaukee, WI), 1998.

It's a Fiesta, Benjamin, illustrated by DiSalvo-Ryan, Gareth Stevens (Milwaukee, WI), 1998.

Say Hola, Sarah, illustrated by DiSalvo-Ryan, Gareth Stevens (Milwaukee, WI), 1998.

"THE ADVENTURES OF MINNIE AND MAX" SERIES

Kidnap at the Catfish Café, illustrated by Lynne Cravath, Viking (New York, NY), 1998.

Mary Moon Is Missing, illustrated by Lynne Cravath, Viking (New York, NY), 1998.

OTHER

Advent: Molly Maguire, Viking (New York, NY), 1991.

ADAPTATIONS: Several of Giff's books, including *Happy Birthday, Ronald Morgan, Today Was a Terrible Day,* and *The Almost Awful Play,* have been recorded on audio cassette and released by Live Oak Media. Many of Giff's books have been translated into Spanish.

SIDELIGHTS: A prolific author, Patricia Reilly Giff specializes in writing humorous books for middle-grader readers. In both her novels and her multi-book series, Giff explores situations that are readily familiar to young people: putting on a class play, having a pet, and getting along with family and friends. Giff's background

as a teacher and reading consultant has given her a unique perspective on her readers. Although she did not begin writing until her early forties, Giff always had a clear idea of her objectives. She once commented, "I had worked with so many children who had terrible problems that I wanted to say things that would make them laugh. I wanted to tell them they were special. . . . I wish I had started sooner."

Born in Brooklyn, New York, in 1935, Giff recalled her childhood as an adventure in reading. As she once commented, "While the rest of the kids were playing hide and seek, I sat under the cherry tree reading. On winter evenings I shared an armchair with my father while he read *Hiawatha* and *Evangeline* to me. I read the stories of my mother's childhood and every book in our little library in St. Albans. I wanted to write. Always."

After graduating from high school, Giff enrolled at Marymount College, where she studied the classic authors of English literature, such as Keats, Poe, Pope, and Dryden. Intimidated by such masterworks, she changed her major from English to business, "and then to history, where I listened to a marvelous man named Mullee spin tales about the past. I fell into teaching because my beloved dean, who had no idea I wanted to write, saw that it was a good place for me." Teaching would be her main focus for close to two decades, her time too full of work and family to grant a place to writing. Married with three children, a master's degree in history, and a professional diploma in reading, Giff rounded the corner to age forty when it hit her: "I hadn't written a story; I hadn't even tried."

Determined to pursue her childhood dream, she said, "I dragged myself out of bed in the early morning darkness to spend an hour or two at my typewriter before I had to leave for school. Slowly and painfully, I began to write." Her first published book, *Fourth Grade Celebrity,* appeared in 1979, and its success convinced Giff to dedicate herself to her craft. Along with a number of Giff's books for school-age readers, *Fourth Grade Celebrity* has been through a number of printings, a reflection of its author's ability to connect with the interests of young people. In many of her series, Giff teams with an accomplished illustrator who uses a light, humorous touch to bring to life each of the author's likeable, realistic characters.

Several of Giff's series books have featured the popular students of her fictional Polk Street School. In 1992's *Show Time at the Polk Street School* pivotal teacher Ms.

Rooney decides to have her students stage plays. Three play scripts, along with the student's efforts to make them come to life, are included in the volume, which serves as "a solid introduction for aspiring thespians," according to a *Kirkus Reviews* contributor. Bring-your-pet-to-school week becomes the focus of *Pet Parade,* as student Beast looks for another pet to take to Ms. Rooney's class because his own dog, Kissie Poo, does nothing well except sleep. In *Next Stop, New York City!* and *Look out, Washington, D.C.!* the Polk Street School gang descends on some of the nation's largest cities, with humorous chaos the expected result. Serving as both a story and a tour guide of sorts, the books feature maps of their subject cities, as well as phone numbers of the most favorite tourist attractions for kids.

In the "Ballet Slippers" series, Giff introduces young readers to Rosie O'Meara, an aspiring dancer whose enthusiasm for ballet sometimes gets her into trouble. In *Starring Rosie,* although unhappy about finding herself cast as the evil witch rather than the star in *Sleeping Beauty,* Rosie rebounds, offers to find a boy to play the handsome prince, and then must make good on her promise. But finding a boy willing to wear tights on stage in front of all his friends proves to be no easy task in what *School Library Journal* contributor Eva Mitnick characterized as a "breezy and fun" read. *A Glass Slipper for Rosie* finds the young dancer involved in another class production, although disappointment follows when she realizes her grandfather may not be in town to see the show. Calling the book a "delightful addition to the series," *School Library Journal* critic Janet M. Bair praised *A Glass Slipper for Rosie* as "a well-rounded story about family and friends."

In addition to seeing many of her popular stories translated into Spanish for Hispanic students, Giff has also written a series that incorporates children from Spanish-speaking cultures. In *Ho, Ho, Benjamin, Feliz Navidad* a young boy shares the holiday season with his homesick Ecuadorian neighbor and learns about Christmas celebrations in other countries. *Adios, Anna,* another installment in Giff's "Friends and Amigos" series, finds Sarah Cole dejected after her best friend, Anna Ortiz, goes away for summer vacation. Deciding to occupy her time by trying to learn to speak Spanish, Sarah borrows Anna's house key to use one of her books and then mislays the key. "Children are sure to enjoy Sarah's funny adventures as they also learn some Spanish," commented *School Library Journal* reviewer Maria Redburn, who also praised Giff's inclusion of basic Spanish vocabulary words. Sarah appears again in *Say Hola, Sarah.* Here her progress in learning Spanish is being aided by Anna, although she is frustrated at how

slowly she is advancing in another book that includes short lessons in the language.

In the late 1990s, with over sixty books for young readers to her credit, Giff changed gears somewhat by penning *Lily's Crossing,* a coming-of-age story for older readers. In the poignant story, which takes place during the summer of 1944 as World War II rages across Europe, fifteen-year-old Lily is left behind with her grandmother as her widowed father joins the army to fight the Nazi threat overseas. The novel draws on Giff's own memories of the war years and took four years to complete. "When I sat down to write the book," Giff told a *Publishers Weekly* interviewer, "I wanted to see what I remembered. I made a list of everything I could think of—posters I had seen, the banner in our church with names of who was missing and who was dead. I was surprised by how much I remember." While grounded in her own life, the story's protagonist, Lily, is not modeled after Giff, as many readers might think. The character just "took over" at one point, the author explained in her interview. Praising the work as "a fine piece of historical fiction that evokes a time and place without taking advantage of its characters' emotional lives," *Bulletin of the Center for Children's Books* contributor Janice M. Del Negro noted that *Lily's Crossing* "coalesces [plot and characters] into an emotional whole that is fully satisfying."

Since she began her career as a children's author in the late 1970s, Giff has enjoyed the writing process more and more, particularly when it involves a young audience. "Writing became one of the most important parts of my life, a part that now I couldn't do without," she once recalled. "I hope to say to all the children I've loved that they are special . . . that all of us are special . . . important just because we are ourselves." In 1994 she and several members of her family started a hometown bookstore entirely devoted to children's books. Giff views her new enterprise, named The Dinosaur's Paw, as "a community that brings children and books together."

BIOGRAPHICAL/CRITICAL SOURCES:

BOOKS

Holtze, Sally Holmes, editor, *Fifth Book of Junior Authors,* H. W. Wilson, 1983, pp. 132-133.

PERIODICALS

Booklist, January 15, 1993, Kay Weisman, review of *Meet the Lincoln Lions Band,* p. 907; July, 1994, Stephanie Zvirin, review of *Shark in School,*

p. 1947; December 1, 1994, Carolyn Phelan, review of *Turkey Trouble*, pp. 680-681; June 1, 1995, Kay Weisman, review of *Look out, Washington, D.C.!*, p. 1770; July, 1995, Julie Yates Walton, reviews of *Ronald Morgan Goes to Camp*, p. 1878; September 1, 1996, Carolyn Phelan, review of *Dance with Rosie* and *Rosie's Nutcracker Dreams*, p. 125; September 15, 1996, Susan Dove Lempke, review of *Pet Parade*, p. 238; December 15, 1996, Carolyn Phelan, review of *Starring Rosie*, p. 726; May 1, 1997, Carolyn Phelan, review of *Not-So-Perfect Rosie*, p. 1493; October 1, 1997, Carolyn Phelan, review of *A Glass Slipper for Rosie*, p. 329; October 15, 1999, Barbara Baskin, review of *Lily's Crossing*, p. 467.

Bulletin of the Center for Children's Books, May, 1984; September, 1984; March, 1985; April, 1986; January, 1992, review of *Diana: Twentieth-Century Princess*, p. 125; July-August, 1995, review of *Look out, Washington, D.C.!*, pp. 383-384; October, 1996, review of *Good Luck, Ronald Morgan*, p. 59; April, 1997, Janice M. Del Negro, review of *Lily's Crossing*, pp. 282-283.

Horn Book, July-August, 1993, Maeve Visser Knoth, review of *Next Year I'll Be Special*, p. 442; September-October, 1994, Maeve Visser Knoth, review of *Shark in School*, p. 611; March-April, 1997, Mary M. Burns, review of *Lily's Crossing*, p. 198.

Kirkus Reviews, November 15, 1992, review of *Show Time at Polk Street*, p. 1442; September 1, 1993, review of *Next Year I'll Be Special*, p. 1143; September 15, 1994, p. 1271; October 15, 1998, review of *Kidnap at the Catfish Café*, p. 1531.

New York Times Book Review, September 2, 1984; May 18, 1997, Jane Langton, review of *Lily's Crossing*, p. 24.

Publishers Weekly, November 2, 1992, review of *Meet the Lincoln Lions Band* and *Yankee Doodle Drumsticks*, p. 71; July 5, 1993, review of *Next Year I'll Be Special*, p. 72; April 18, 1994, Sally Lodge, "The Author as Bookseller: Patricia Reilly Giff's Career Comes Full Circle," p. 26; October 7, 1996, review of *Dance with Rosie*, p. 76; January 20, 1997, review of *Lily's Crossing*, p. 403; April 27, 1998, "On the Road with Patricia Reilly Giff," p. 29; May 4, 1998, review of *Love, from the Fifth Grade*, p. 216; November 9, 1998, review of *Kidnap at the Catfish Café*, p. 77; December 13, 1999, review of *Kidnap at the Catfish Café*, p. 32; July 24, 2000, review of *Nory Ryan's Song*, p. 94.

School Library Journal, January, 1992, April L. Judge, review of *Diana: Twentieth-Century Princess*, p. 102; September, 1994, Mary Ann Bursk, review of *Shark in School*, p. 184; June, 1995, Pamela K. Bomboy, review of *Ronald Morgan Goes to Camp*, p. 80; October, 1995, Maria Redburn, review of *Ho, Ho, Benjamin, Feliz Navidad*, p. 37, and *Adios Anna*, p. 38; March, 1996, Eunice Weech, review of *Say Hola, Sarah*, p. 174; August, 1996, Anne Parker, review of *Pet Parade*, p. 122; September 1, 1996, pp. 125, 130; March, 1997, Eva Mitnick, review of *Starring Rosie*, p. 152; October, 1997, Suzanne Hawley, review of *Next Stop, New York City!*, pp. 95-96; December, 1997, Janet M. Bair, review of *A Glass Slipper for Rosie*, p. 90; January, 1999, Janie Schomberg, review of *Mary Moon*, p. 88.*

*   *   *

GISCOMBE, C. S. 1950-

PERSONAL: Born November 30, 1950, in Dayton, OH; son of Cecil S. (a physician) and Daisy (a teacher; maiden name, Smith) Giscombe; married Katharine E. Wright (a teacher and zoo curator), August 10, 1975; children: Madeline Wright. *Education:* State University of New York at Albany, B.A., 1973; Cornell University, M.F.A., 1975. *Politics:* "Left wing."

ADDRESSES: Office—Department of English, Pennsylvania State University, 116 Burrowes Hall, State College, PA 16804.

CAREER: Syracuse University, Syracuse, NY, assistant professor of English, 1977; Cornell University, Ithaca, NY, editor of *Epoch*, 1978-98, lecturer in English, beginning 1980; Illinois State University, Normal, IL, professor of English, 1989-98; Pennsylvania State University, State College, PA, professor of English, 1998—.

MEMBER: Poets and Writers.

AWARDS, HONORS: Poetry fellow of Creative Artists Public Service (CAPS), 1981-82, and National Endowment for the Arts, 1986-87; editor's grant from Coordinating Council of Literary Magazines, 1987; poetry fellow of New York Foundation for the Arts, 1988; Carl Sandburg Award for Poetry, 1998; fellowships from Fund for Poetry and Illinois Arts Council; Fulbright Research Award from the Council for the International Exchange of Scholars.

WRITINGS:

Postcards (poetry), Ithaca House (Ithaca, NY), 1977.
Here (poetry), Dalkey Archive Press (Normal, IL), 1994.

Giscome Road (poetry), Dalkey Archive Press (Normal, IL), 1998.

Into and out of Dislocation (travel memoir), Farrar, Straus/North Point Press (New York, NY), 2000.

Two Sections from "Practical Geography: Five Poems," Diaeresis Books (Boca Raton, FL), 2000.

Inland (poetry), Leroy Books (San Francisco, CA), 2001.

Also author of the unpublished work "Archie Underground" (for children). Contributor of poetry and prose to periodicals, including *New American Writing, Callaloo, O-Blek, Iowa Review,* and *Hudson Review.* Editor, *American Book Review;* contributing editor, *Cross-Cultural Poetics.*

WORK IN PROGRESS: A poetry book about the Midwest, tentatively titled "Prairie Style"; a prose book about trains, train travel, train metaphors, and other forms of public transport; a book of "cross-genre" essays on poetics, race, geography, and film culture, tentatively titled "Back Burner."

SIDELIGHTS: C. S. Giscombe told *CA:* "I'm struck again and again by the role geography plays in my writing. I mean, language tends to occur to me in terms of place, of location." Giscombe is a recognized figure in the African-American poetic avant-garde. He received the Carl Sandburg Award for Poetry in 1998 and was commended in *Publishers Weekly* for his "powerful, understated meditation on place, ancestry and time" in his poetry collection *Here.* The same *Publishers Weekly* critic noted that Giscombe reveals the African-American experience effectively "because he so well evokes his individual consciousness."

In the mid-1990s Giscombe became fascinated with the legend of John Robert Giscombe, a noted Jamaican adventurer who traveled through British Columbia in search of gold. C. S. Giscombe and his family set out for Canada to retrace John Giscombe's steps, and the poet charted his personal explorations in *Into and out of Dislocation.* "'The book is about travel, race, family as metaphor, and physicality,'" Giscombe declared, in an article in the *Digital Collegian.* "'It is written for an educated audience with a sense of metaphor.'"

Reviewers found much to praise in the pages of *Into and out of Dislocation.* "Giscombe meditates on the meanings of borders and race and family," declared Bonnie Smothers in *Booklist.* "His is an engaging albeit erudite study." A *Publishers Weekly* reviewer wrote:

"Giscombe's evocation of Canada, during both John's time and the present, is deeply affecting. . . . His . . . style provides many reflective gems, especially on the issues of race and culture."

BIOGRAPHICAL/CRITICAL SOURCES:

PERIODICALS

Booklist, April 15, 2000, Bonnie Smothers, review of *Into and out of Dislocation,* p. 1515.

Library Journal, April 1, 1999, review of *Giscome Road,* p. 95.

Publishers Weekly, October 31, 1994, review of *Here,* p. 56; May 25, 1998, review of *Giscome Road,* p. 87; April 24, 2000, review of *Into and out of Dislocation,* p. 75.

Virginia Quarterly Review, winter, 1999, review of *Giscome Road,* p. 29.

OTHER

Digital Collegian, http://www.collegian.psu.edu/archive/ (February 25, 2000), Lindsay Bennett, "Local Author to Publish Book after Historic Trip."

*   *   *

GOLDBERG, Natalie

PERSONAL: Born in the United States of America.; divorced; companion of Michelle Huff (a lawyer).

ADDRESSES: Home—Northern New Mexico and St. Paul, MN. *Agent*—c/o Bantam Books, 1540 Broadway, New York, NY 10036.

CAREER: Writer and teacher of writing.

WRITINGS:

Chicken and in Love (poems), Holy Cow Press (Minneapolis, MN), 1980.

Writing down the Bones: Freeing the Writer Within (nonfiction), Shambhala (Boston, MA) 1986, abridged version released on audio cassette by Shambhala (Boston, MA), 1990.

Wild Mind: Living the Writer's Life (nonfiction), Bantam (New York, NY), 1990.

Long Quiet Highway: Waking up in America (nonfiction), Bantam (New York, NY), 1993.

Banana Rose (novel), Bantam (New York, NY), 1995.

Living Color: A Writer Paints Her World (autobiography; self-illustrated), Bantam (New York, NY), 1997.

Thunder and Lightning: Cracking Open the Writer's Craft (nonfiction), Bantam (New York, NY), 2000.

Contributor of articles to periodicals, including *Writer's Digest.*

SIDELIGHTS: Natalie Goldberg is a teacher of writing and conductor of numerous writing workshops, who shares her love of writing and seeks to inspire and instruct aspiring writers in her books, *Writing down the Bones: Freeing the Writer Within, Wild Mind: Living the Writer's Life,* and *Thunder and Lightning: Cracking Open the Writer's Craft.* Interwoven among Goldberg's instructions are autobiographical portions that reveal her own methods and struggles as a writer, as well as other more spiritual aspects of her life, especially the effect that Goldberg's study of Zen Buddhism has had on her life.

Laced with quotations from Zen masters, *Writing down the Bones,* Goldberg's 1986 writer's guide, encourages others to look within themselves to find their own creative voice. This volume met with mixed reviews from critics such as *Sewanee Review*'s George Garrett, who stated: "Not much practical advice for dealing with publishers or the big bad world here; but there are some helpful thoughts about creative flexibility and process. Most of what she says has to do with poetry, but it is more or less transferable wisdom." Goldberg, however, received praise for her 1990 book, *Wild Mind: Living the Writer's Life,* in which she shares more personal, intimate glimpses of her own life than in *Writing down the Bones,* and demonstrates to reluctant writers how she integrates writing into her busy life. *Bloomsbury Review* contributor Kay Marie Porterfield found *Wild Mind* a "cause for celebration," and felt that Goldberg "provides both novice and seasoned writers with inspiration and insight into the process of writing from the heart."

In her 1993 publication, *Long Quiet Highway: Waking up in America,* Goldberg reveals more details of her life as a woman, writer, and teacher, with special emphasis on feminism and meditation. At the heart of *Long Quiet Highway,* in particular, is Goldberg's relationship with Zen master Katagiri Roshi, whose life and teachings changed Goldberg's view of life and of writing. Although highly personal in nature, *Long Quiet Highway* is rife with insight for writers and other artists. Critically well-received, *Long Quiet Highway* elicited praise from Mark Gerson, writing in *Quill and Quire:* "From the classrooms of her suburban childhood to her painful acceptance of Roshi's death, Goldberg writes from the heart of her experience, with an honest simplicity that is compelling." *Bloomsbury Review* contributor Judith K. Mahrer also applauded *Long Quiet Highway,* proclaiming: "I was deeply touched by this book. I felt I had been privileged to share, in very special ways, in the life of someone who has worked diligently to make sense of her life and to give it meaning. . . . Unlike her two earlier books, this is not a book on writing technique, though writing is one of the major themes. This book is really about waking up and living a conscious life."

Goldberg issued *Banana Rose,* her first novel, in 1995. The novel is set in the 1960s and opens in Taos, New Mexico, where Goldberg lives. Nell Schwartz, a frustrated artist from Brooklyn, New York, has come to Taos to live in a commune. She renames herself Banana Rose, and soon falls in love with Gauguin, a Minnesotan musician whose real name is George Howard. The two leave the commune for an adobe hut with no indoor plumbing, where they spend time making love, preparing vegetarian meals, and smoking marijuana with their friends, who have names such as Happiness and Neon. But, as the magic of their lives meets reality, their friends return to the more conventional world one by one. Banana Rose and Gauguin, too, leave Taos for Minneapolis, and quickly assimilate into the average American lifestyle, marrying, taking jobs, and reclaiming their original names. Ultimately, they divorce. Older and wiser, Nell moves back to New Mexico, where her artistic creativity blossoms.

Goldberg's depiction of the New Mexico landscape impressed reviewer Georgia Jones-Davis, who remarked in the *Los Angeles Times* that the author "allows [New Mexico's] raw, panoramic splendor to function like a living, breathing character in the story. . . . The spiritual quality of the place, the colors of the earth and sky, the smell of rain, the forked lightning, the shadows on Taos Mountain—none of this is lost on her characters." Commenting on the novel as a whole, Jones-Davis added: "*Banana Rose* is a problematic yet touching novel, awkward in places, poetic and amazingly powerful in others."

In addition to writing and teaching, Goldberg has been an avid painter since the 1970s, although she has always considered this art subordinate to her writing. She gave up painting for a time during the writing of *Banana Rose,* then came back to it after she realized that painting was "a deep source" of her writing. "When I cut out painting, I cut off that underground stream of mayhem, joy, nonsense, absurdity," she writes in *Living Color: A Writer Paints Her World,* which contains auto-biographical essays accompanied by her fanciful, cartoon-like paintings. This book shows that painting "is the secondary art that feeds and nurtures her primary creative work," related Donn Fry in the *Seattle Times.* Fry expressed disappointment that "Goldberg never probes too deeply into the connection between visual and verbal images," but concluded, "Goldberg's easy candor and engaging art ultimately outweigh these concerns." *Booklist*'s Donna Seaman found the work "lovely and inspiring" in its illustration, in words and pictures, of Goldberg's life and art.

Goldberg returned to the art for which she is best known, providing guidance to writers, in *Thunder and Lightning: Cracking Open the Writer's Craft.* Reviewing this work for *Booklist,* James O'Laughlin remarked that for admirers of Goldberg's previous works, *Thunder and Lightning* would be of much interest, showing once again the writer's "commitment to 'writing practice.'" Similarly, a reviewer for *Publishers Weekly* notes that Goldberg delves into her own experiences as a writer to guide others through the tough process of creation, writing "as someone who has been there and back." In a profile of Goldberg for the *Advocate,* Victoria Price reported that this book "takes on the tough practicalities of the writing life." She quoted Goldberg as saying, "What I want to tell people is that it's great that you want to write, but get real about it. Writing is pleasurable—at the beginning, anyway. But it's also hard, like a marriage or any kind of relationship. You fall madly in love, and then you move in. It's hard, but you stay in it, hopefully."

BIOGRAPHICAL/CRITICAL SOURCES:

PERIODICALS

Advocate, August 29, 2000, p. 65.

Bloomsbury Review, March, 1991, p. 16; March-April, 1993, pp. 12, 22.

Booklist, September 1, 1997, p. 48; August, 2000, James O'Laughlin, review of *Thunder and Lightning: Cracking Open the Writer's Craft,* p. 2098; November 15, 2000, Nancy Spillman, review of *Long Quiet Highway: A Memoir on Zen in America and the Writing Life,* p. 656..

Library Journal, March 1, 2000, p. S10.

Los Angeles Times, January 31, 1995, p. E5.

Los Angeles Times Book Review, February 21, 1993, p. 6.

New York Times Book Review, April 16, 1995, p. 16.

Publishers Weekly, December 28, 1992, p. 52; January 9, 1995, p. 54; January 23, 1995, p. 44; June 5, 2000, review of *Long Quiet Highway: A Memoir on Zen in America and the Writing Life,* p. 63; July 31, 2000, review of *Thunder and Lightning: Cracking Open the Writer's Craft,* p. 87.

Quill and Quire, July, 1993, p. 53.

Seattle Times, October 2, 1997.

Sewanee Review, Summer, 1988, pp. 516-525.

Women's Review of Books, July-August, 1987, pp. 11-12.*

*   *   *

GOLDSTEIN, Rebecca 1950-

PERSONAL: Born February 23, 1950, in White Plains, NY; daughter of Bezalel Newberger (a cantor) and Loretta Newberger (a homemaker); married Sheldon Goldstein (a physicist); children: Yael Tamar, Danielle Elizabeth. *Education:* Barnard College, B.A., 1972; Princeton University, Ph.D., 1976. *Religion:* Jewish.

ADDRESSES: Office—c/o Viking Penguin, 375 Hudson St., New York, NY 10014.

CAREER: Novelist. Barnard College, professor of philosophy, 1976-86; Columbia University, adjunct assistant professor of writing, 1994—.

AWARDS, HONORS: MacArthur Foundation fellowship, 1996.

WRITINGS:

NOVELS

The Mind-Body Problem, Random House (New York, NY), 1983.

The Late-Summer Passion of a Woman of Mind, Farrar, Straus (New York, NY), 1989.

The Dark Sister, Viking (New York, NY), 1991.

Strange Attractors (short stories), Viking (New York, NY), 1993.

Mazel, Viking (New York, NY), 1995.

Properties of Light: A Novel of Love, Betrayal, and Quantum Physics, Houghton (Boston, MA), 2000.

ADAPTATIONS: Godlstein's short stories have been included in *Chanuka Lights,* an audiocassette produced by the National Public Radio, 1995.

SIDELIGHTS: In response to a query from the *New York Times Book Review,* Rebecca Goldstein commented: "Writing my first novel recalled for me the pleasures of playing hooky in high school, the only extracurricular activity in which I participated. I was using the purloined time in a way agreeable to the strange kid that I was—at the public library, laboring over heavy tomes of philosophy."

Goldstein's early interest in philosophy has since led to a career as a professor and has also become a continuing theme of her novels. Goldstein's much-reviewed first book, *The Mind-Body Problem,* sets forth the dilemma that occupies protagonists in her subsequent works as well, how to incorporate the demands of the body into a life dominated by the concerns of the mind.

The Mind-Body Problem is a comic novel in which the protagonist, Renee, is a graduate student in philosophy whose insecurity about her own intellectual capabilities leads her to marry a man generally acknowledged to be a genius. Their troubled relationship is at the center of this academic satire, and inspired Caroline Seebohm of the *New York Times Book Review* to remark: "The first 50 or so pages of *The Mind-Body Problem* are so clever and funny that I had to put the book down and go to the fridge to cool off." Reviewers found that the academic backdrop of the book allowed Goldstein various plot possibilities. Diane Cole of *Ms.* wrote that "Goldstein succeeds brilliantly in smuggling into her novel short courses on everything from the history of mathematics to the trouble with Talmudic logic," while John Nicholson of the London *Times* noted that Goldstein "assaults the pretensions and insensitivity of academe with a bludgeon." Despite her contention that "This is a terrific first novel. Also ultimately disappointing," Anne F. Wittels of the *Los Angeles Times* concluded: "Goldstein is intelligent and perceptive, bawdy and witty—an articulate writer of great talent."

Goldstein followed *The Mind-Body Problem* with *The Late-Summer Passion of a Woman of Mind,* the story of a forty-six-year-old professor whose personal experiences and training in philosophy have taught her to disdain emotional attachments of any kind. Through this character, reviewers noted, Goldstein surveys the academic milieu and forms extreme, and often funny, opinions on its behavior and morals. When one student manages to break through Professor Mueller's armor, setting free her repressed past, Goldstein's writing, according to Michiko Kakutani of the *New York Times,* "takes on a pleasing emotional chiaroscuro, a deepening and darkening of ambition." Critic Robert Cohen of the *New York Times Book Review* found that there was a certain "predictability" to the book that resulted from the "stereotypes that are applied to [Mueller's] profession." Ron Grossman of the *Chicago Tribune* also remarked on the predictable plot of the novel, but noted that "it is, in fact, testimony to Goldstein's talents that a reader isn't tempted to set the book down despite its foregone conclusion."

The *New York Times's* Kakutani wrote of Goldstein's third novel, *The Dark Sister,* "one has the exhilarating sense . . . of reading a writer who has just discovered the full possibilities of her talent." Other reviewers also remarked on the ambitious scope of *The Dark Sister,* which is not only a satire of heavy-handed feminist fiction and an examination of relationships between women, but contains a novel within the novel that explores psychological and philosophical themes through the personae of William and Henry James, the celebrated nineteenth-century philosopher and his novelist brother. The novel's complex structure found favor with some reviewers, while others were less enthusiastic. Ann Thwaite of the *Washington Post Book World* noted positively that "seeking the truth is of course never straightforward and *The Dark Sister* is not a book for lovers of the simple and straightforward." Margaret Cannon, on the other hand, writing in the Toronto *Globe & Mail,* felt that "the plot of *The Dark Sister* is simple yet demanding" and she disliked use of multiple narrators: "the dilemma for . . . Goldstein is simply that she doesn't know who's writing." Nevertheless, Kakutani concluded that Goldstein's "writing . . . is clever, observant and nimble. And while the alarming conclusion of *The Dark Sister* feels a bit truncated and abrupt, the schematism that bogged down her last novel is nowhere to be seen."

Mazel, while more straightforward that some of Goldstein's work, nevertheless explores philosophical questions. The central character is Sasha Saunders, whom Goldstein had introduced in the short story collection *Strange Attractors.* A rabbi's daughter from an Orthodox community in Poland, Sasha escaped the traditions of her upbringing by becoming an actress in a Yiddish theater group, and the horrors of the Holocaust by coming to the United States. She is an intelligent, sardonic woman who believes that "mazel"—Yiddish for "luck"—has been the driving force in her life. In her old age, she is contentedly retired in New York City, and her daughter, Chloe, and granddaughter, Phoebe, have both become college professors. But Sasha and Chloe are taken aback when Phoebe embraces Orthodoxy. The book includes a satiric portrait of modern Orthodox life in American suburbia and an affectionate one of Sasha's childhood community.

Lore Dickstein, writing in the *New York Times Book Review,* found the skewering of suburban life "full of flash and brilliance," but thought the flashback to Sasha's early years "dosed with saccharine nostalgia." Dickstein elaborated, "All this potted history and faux-Yiddish folklore overwhelms a novel already weighed down by innumerable homespun homilies on the nature of luck, chance and rational choice." But *Booklist*'s Donna Seaman praised *Mazel* as "ebullient" and "folktale-like"; it "celebrates the passion of the old Jewish ways, the resiliency of women, and our capacity for joy," she wrote. A *Publishers Weekly* reviewer also had a positive reaction, calling the novel Goldstein's "most accessible and beguiling" and "one that discriminating readers won't want to miss."

Properties of Light: A Novel of Love, Betrayal, and Quantum Physics, deals with the love affair of two brilliant physicists, Justin Childs and Dana Mallach, whose father, Samuel, is also an accomplished physicist but is angry with fellow scientists who failed to appreciate his work. While Justin and Dana develop a passionate romance, Samuel joins them in a scientific project aimed at reconciling quantum mechanics and the theory of relativity. Complications and betrayals ensue, however, with destructive consequences. The story "gives Ms. Goldstein a chance to explore her perennial themes about the dichotomies between mind and body, intellect and passion, logos and eros," observed Kakutani in the *New York Times.* But Kakutani found Goldstein's explorations of her characters' work and their emotions both wanting: "Though it's impossible not to admire Ms. Goldstein's efforts to write a Gothic suspense story that's also a novel of ideas, her characters remain too two-dimensional and her storytelling too ponderous for the reader to ever become fully engaged." A *Publishers Weekly* reviewer, however, felt that Goldstein "gracefully deconstructs our contradictory impulses." "Though the rarefied air the characters breathe can be stifling," the reviewer wrote, "at its best the novel is bewitchingly ethereal." Similarly, a reviewer for *Booklist* appreciated Goldstein's writing style, calling the work a "thrillingly lucent tragedy."

BIOGRAPHICAL/CRITICAL SOURCES:

PERIODICALS

Booklist, September 15, 1995, p. 141; August, 2000, Donna Seaman, review of *Properties of Light,* p. 2112.
Chicago Tribune, April 13, 1989.
Globe & Mail (Toronto), August 31, 1991, p. C7.
Los Angeles Times, November 1, 1983.
Ms., January, 1984, pp. 14-15.
New York Times, April 18, 1989; August 6, 1991; August 29, 2000.
New York Times Book Review, September 25, 1983, p. 14; March 17, 1985; May 7, 1989; October 29, 1995.
Publishers Weekly, August 7, 1995, p. 441; June 19, 2000, review of *Properties of Light,* p. 57.
Tikkun, January, 2001, review of *Properties of Light,* p. 60.
Times (London), February 21, 1985.
Washington Post Book World, July 14, 1991.*

*   *   *

GONZALEZ, Anibal 1956-

PERSONAL: Born August 25, 1956, in San German, Puerto Rico; son of Anibal Gonzalez Irizarry (a television news anchor) and Ruth Perez de Gonzales (a homemaker); married Priscilla Melendez (a professor of Spanish), June 30, 1990. *Education:* University of Puerto Rico, B.A. (magna cum laude), 1977; Yale University, Ph.D., 1982.

ADDRESSES: Home—State College, PA. *Office*—Department of Spanish, Italian, and Portuguese, Pennsylvania State University, 352 North Burrowes Bldg., University Park, PA 16802-6203.

CAREER: University of Texas at Austin, assistant professor, 1982-87, associate professor of Spanish, 1987-90; Michigan State University, East Lansing, associate professor, 1990-93, professor of Spanish, 1993; Pennsylvania State University, University Park, Edwin Erle Sparks Professor of Spanish, 1994—. Vanderbilt University, visiting assistant professor, 1987. Michigan State University Press, member of editorial board, 1993-94.

MEMBER: Instituto Internacional de Literatura Iberoamericana, Asociacion Internacional de Hispanistas, Modern Language Association of America.

AWARDS, HONORS: Grants from Institute of Latin American Studies and Mellon Foundation, 1985, 1988.

WRITINGS:

La cronica modernista hispanoamericana, Jose Porrua Turanzas (Madrid, Spain), 1983.
La novela modernista hispanoamericana, Editorial Gredos (Madrid, Spain), 1987.
Journalism and the Development of Spanish American Narrative, Cambridge University Press (New York, NY), 1993.
(Translator and author of prologue) Jorge Luis Borges, *Un ensayo autobiográfico,* epilogue by María Kodama, Galaxia Gutenberg/Círculo de Lectores/ Emecé, 1999.

Contributor to books. General editor, "Cambridge Latin American and Iberian Studies" series, Cambridge University Press (New York, NY), 1995-97; general editor, Bucknell Studies in Latin American Literature and Theory, Bucknell University Press, 1998—. Contributor of about fifty articles and reviews to scholarly journals. *Revista de Estudios Hispanicos,* member of editorial board, 1987—, guest editor, 1990; member of editorial board of *Latin American Literary Review,* 1985—, *Chasqui,* 1991-95, and *Centennial Review,* 1992-94.

WORK IN PROGRESS: "Abuses and Admonitions: Ethics and Writing in Modern Spanish American Narrative," a study of the role of ethics in contemporary Spanish American narrative; research on the return to love and sentimental themes in Spanish American narrative after the 1970s.

*   *   *

GOODWIN, Eugene D.
  See KAYE, Marvin (Nathan)

*   *   *

GREALY, Lucy 1963-

PERSONAL: Born in 1963, in Dublin, Ireland; immigrated to the United States: daughter of a television network employee (father) and a journalist. *Education:* Sarah Lawrence College, B.A.; University of Iowa, M.F.A.

ADDRESSES: Home—New York, NY. *Office*—c/o Houghton Mifflin, 2 Park St., Boston, MA 02107.

CAREER: Writer. Worked through a temporary employment agency in London, England; Fine Arts Work Center, Provincetown, MA, fellow, 1993. Instructor at Amherst College, Sarah Lawrence College, Bennington College, and the University of Iowa.

AWARDS, HONORS: National Magazine Award, c. 1994, for an excerpt from *Autobiography of a Face* published as "Mirrorings: To Gaze upon My Reconstructed Face" in *Harper's,* February, 1993; *Times Literary Supplement* Poetry Prize, Sonora Review Poetry Prize; two Academy of American Poets Prizes; Whiting Writer's Award.

WRITINGS:

Autobiography of a Face (autobiography), Houghton (Boston, MA), 1994, published as *In the Mind's Eye,* Century (London, England), 1994.
As Seen on TV: Provocations, St. Martin's (New York, NY), 2000.

Also author of *Everyday Alibis,* a book of poetry, and of a novel. Contributor to *Best American Essays, 1994.* Contributor of poetry and articles to periodicals, including *Paris Review* and *Times Literary Supplement.*

WORK IN PROGRESS: A novel.

SIDELIGHTS: Lucy Grealy dazzled critics in 1994 with her first book, *Autobiography of a Face,* and she has continued to earn respect and awards for her poetry and essays. *Autobiography of a Face,* which was published in England under the title *In the Mind's Eye,* is a personal memoir. In it, Grealy recounts the difficulties she experienced after the age of nine when half of her jaw was removed due to cancer. Originally from Dublin, Ireland, Grealy and her family were living in a suburb of New York City when she was diagnosed with a tumor in the early 1970s. She and her family were told that the cancer, known as Ewing's Sarcoma, was a rare strain and potentially fatal. The surgery to remove the jaw was followed by two and one-half years of chemotherapy. Of her weekly medical visits, she writes: "The two large syringes were filled with chemicals so caustic to the vein that each had to be administered very slowly. The whole process took about four minutes; I had to remain utterly still. Dry retching began in the first fifteen seconds, then the throb behind my eyes gave everything a yellow-green aura, and the bone-deep pain of alternating extreme hot and cold flashes made me tremble, yet still I had to sit motionless and not move my arm."

A *Times Literary Supplement* reviewer observed that Grealy "succeeds brilliantly in evoking the feelings of a young girl caught up in a painful world she does not fully understand, and which makes little effort to understand her." In *Autobiography of a Face,* Grealy recounts the years of hostility and humiliation she encountered from the world because of her unusual appearance. Even as an adult, she writes of crossing the street to avoid oncoming children, remembering her own difficult school days and knowing youngsters may still be equally vicious. Grealy explains how her outward appearance eventually caused her to feel flawed inwardly but also discusses the coping mechanisms she developed. While growing up, Grealy found refuge first in horses, and later in books and writing. She recalls that, as a college student, "I became forthright and honest in the way that only the truly self-confident are, who do not expect to be rejected, and in the way of those like me, who do not even dare to ask acceptance from others and therefore expect no rejection."

After college, Grealy lived in a number of locales, including London and Germany, then decided to undergo a radical form of reconstructive surgery because, as she explained, "I didn't feel I could pass up yet another chance to 'fix' my face, which I confusedly thought concurrent with 'fixing' my self, my soul, my life." Grealy describes these final surgical procedures and the effect they had on her life. *New York Times Book Review* critic A. G. Mojtabai declared that "both book and life are unforgettable." Mojtabai surmised that "some readers will be disappointed that the author's new face is never described; I was not." Mojtabai explained that "long before the final operation, the text created a face for this reader, sculptured it down to the deeper-than-bone depths of character, a face that is taut, bright-eyed, fierce with intelligence and feeling—complete." Margo Jefferson, critiquing Grealy's work for the *New York Times,* observed that "so many memoirs make you feel that you've been sealed up inside a wall with a monomaniac. A really good one, like *Autobiography of a Face,* makes you feel there is more to ask and learn. You are not just seeing the writer; you are not trying to see yourself. You are seeing the world in a different way."

In 2000, a collection of short pieces by Grealy was published under the title *As Seen on TV: Provocations.*

Rooted in the author's experiences and reflections on such subjects as death, disease, and tango lessons, the articles are in some ways more like short stories than formal essays, declared a writer for *Kirkus Reviews.* They are stories that take the reader "for a ride along streams of consciousness that glide from relatively calm reflections on poetry and prose to the rapids of a ride in a New York City taxi." Readers of *Autobiography of a Face* will recognize Grealy's twin sister, Sara, and her brother Sean, as well as the stable of horses that figured prominently in the earlier book. Grealy's train of thought frequently moves from personal details to universal subjects: a description of a gathering of some drag-queen friends leads to a meditation on the concept of femininity, and some remarks on television's talking horse, Mr. Ed, open the door to a discussion of Christ on the cross. As the *Kirkus Reviews* commentator put it, "The ostensible subjects of the various chapters are mere launch pads for hard-won, clear-headed thoughts on what it means to be alive." It is a "funny, imaginative, and intelligent collection. . . . Relaxed, honest, and illuminating," concluded the reviewer.

BIOGRAPHICAL/CRITICAL SOURCES:

BOOKS

Grealy, Lucy, *Autobiography of a Face,* Houghton (Boston, MA), 1994.

PERIODICALS

American Scholar, winter, 1996, review of *Autobiography of a Face,* p. 142.
Antioch Review, spring, 1995, p. 249.
Belles Lettres, spring, 1995, review of *Autobiography of a Face,* p. 9.
Booklist, September 1, 1994, review of *Autobiography of a Face,* p. 9; January 15, 1995, review of *Autobiography of a Face,* p. 852.
English Journal, September, 1995, review of *Autobiography of a Face,* p. 120.
Entertainment Weekly, November 4, 1994, review of *Autobiography of a Face,* p. 69.
Harper's, February, 1993, pp. 66-75.
Kirkus Reviews, June 15, 1994, review of *Autobiography of a Face,* pp. 819-820; July 1, 2000, review of *As Seen on TV: Provocations,* p. 934.
Kliatt, November, 1995, review of *Autobiography of a Face,* p. 24; September, 1997, review of *Autobiography of a Face,* p. 4.

Library Journal, July, 1994, review of *Autobiography of a Face,* p. 120; January, 1995, review of *Autobiography of a Face,* p. 49.

Ms., November, 1994, review of *Autobiography of a Face,* p. 74.

New Age, winter, 1995, review of *Autobiography of a Face,* p. 71.

New York Times, September 28, 1994, review of *Autobiography of a Face,* p. C19.

New York Times Book Review, September 25, 1994, review of *Autobiography of a Face,* pp. 11-12; December 4, 1994, review of *Autobiography of a Face,* p. 66; August 20, 1995, review of *Autobiography of a Face,* p. 24; December 3, 1995, review of *Autobiography of a Face,* p. 86.

Off Our Backs, April, 1995, review of *Autobiography of a Face,* p. 11.

Publishers Weekly, June 27, 1994, review of *Autobiography of a Face,* p. 61; November 7, 1994, review of *Autobiography of a Face,* p. 42.

Reference & Research Book News, March, 1995, review of *Autobiography of a Face,* p. 52.

Sewanee Review, October, 1995, review of *Autobiography of a Face,* p. 640.

Times Literary Supplement, June 17, 1994, review of *In the Mind's Eye,* p. 31.

Village Voice, December 14, 1994, review of *Autobiography of a Face,* p. 85.

Virginia Quarterly Review, spring, 1995, review of *Autobiography of a Face,* p. 54.

Women's Review of Books, March, 1995, review of *Autobiography of a Face,* p. 16.*

*   *   *

GREGOR, A(nthony) James 1929-

PERSONAL: Born April 2, 1929, in New York, NY; son of Antonio (a factory worker) and Mary (Gazzini) Gimigliano. *Education:* Columbia University, B.A., 1952, M.A., 1959, Ph.D., 1961.

ADDRESSES: Home—75 Parnassus Rd., Berkeley, CA 94708. *Office*—Department of Political Science, University of California, Berkeley, CA 94720.

CAREER: University of Hawaii, Honolulu, assistant professor of philosophy, 1961-63; University of Kentucky, Lexington, associate professor of philosophy, 1964-66; University of Texas at Austin, associate professor of philosophy, 1966-67; University of California at Berkeley, professor of political science, 1967—. Adjunct professor at U.S. Department of State, School of Professional Studies, 1968—. *Military service:* U.S. Army, 1946-48.

MEMBER: Institut International de Sociologie, American Philosophical Association, American Political Science Association, American Sociological Association.

AWARDS, HONORS: Guggenheim fellow, 1974.

WRITINGS:

A Survey of Marxism, Random House (New York City), 1965.

Contemporary Radical Ideologies, Random House, 1968.

The Ideology of Fascism, Free Press (New York City), 1969.

An Introduction to Metapolitics, Free Press, 1971.

The Interpretations of Fascism, General Learning Press, 1974.

The Fascist Persuasion in Radical Politics, Princeton University Press (Princeton, NJ), 1974.

Sergio Panunzio: Il Sindacalismo edil fondamento razionale del fascismo, G. Volpe (Roma), 1978.

The Young Mussolini and the Origins of Fascism, University of California Press (Berkeley), 1979.

Italian Fascism and Developmental Dictatorship, Princeton University Press, 1979.

The Taiwan Relations Act and the Defense of the of China, Institute of International Studies, University of California Press, 1980.

(With Maria Chang and Andrew B. Zimmerman) *Ideology and Development, Sun Yat-sen and the History of Taiwan,* Institute of East Asian Studies (Berkeley, CA), 1981.

(Editor) *The U.S. and the Philippines: A Challenge to a Relationship,* Heritage Foundation (Washington, DC), 1983.

(With Chang) *The Republic of China and U.S. Policy: A Study in Rights,* Ethics and Public Policy Center (Washington, DC), 1983.

The Iron Triangle: A U.S. Security Policy for Asia, Hoover Institution Press (Stanford, CA), 1984.

Crisis in the Philippines: A Threat to U.S. Interests, Ethics and Public Policy Center, 1984.

The China Connection: U.S. Policy and the People's Republic of China, Hoover Institution Press, 1986.

The Philippine Bases: U.S. Security at Risk, Ethics and Public Policy Center, 1987.

Arming the Dragon: U.S. Security Ties with the People's Republic of China, Ethics and Public Policy Center, 1988.

In the Shadow of Giants: The Major Powers and the Security of Southeast Asia, Hoover Institution Press, 1989.

Land of the Morning Calm: Korea and American Security, Ethics and Public Policy Center, 1990.

Marxism, China, and Development: Reflections on Reality, Transaction Publishers (New Brunswick, NJ), 1994, revised as *Marxism, China, and Development: Reflections on Theory and Reality,* Transaction Publishers, 1999.

Interpretations of Fascism, Transaction Publishers, 1997.

Phoenix: Fascism in Our Time, Transaction Publishers, 1999.

A Place in the Sun: Marxism and Fascism in China's Revolution, Westview Press (Boulder, CO), 2000.

The Faces of Janus: Marxism and Fascism in the Twentieth Century, Yale University Press (New Haven, CT), 2000.

Author of monographs. Contributor to journals.

SIDELIGHTS: James A. Gregor is a political scientist with special expertise on fascism and on the politics of the Far East. In his book, *The Faces of Janus: Marxism and Fascism in the Twentieth Century,* Gregor explores the relationship of fascism and communism, concluding that they naturally feed into and out of each other. He shows how fascism had its beginning in communism, and how elements of fascism are integral to communism. He proposes that because of this, the breakup of the Soviet empire will naturally dispose the former Soviet states to move toward fascist governments. "The real political spectrum Gregor sees is democratic and non-democratic," commented Harry V. Willems in a *Library Journal* review of *The Faces of Janus.* In *Phoenix: Fascism in Our Time,* Gregor identifies various fascist governments throughout history and provides an understanding of the current features of fascism as well as the socioeconomic and political conditions that foster it. *Interpretations of Fascism* is another of Gregor's works that is considered a seminal resource on the subject.

Gregor's understanding of politics in Southeast Asia and China is demonstrated in numerous books, including *Land of the Morning Calm: Korea and American Security, The Republic of China and U.S. Policy: A Study in Human Rights,* and *Arming the Dragon: U.S. Security Ties with the People's Republic of China.* In *Land of the Morning Calm,* he examines the improve-

ments that have occurred in Korea despite the North's acceptance of Stalinism. Strategically located, Korea could play a significant role in the future of the region, and with this in mind, Gregor discusses its economic and political past and future and the implications of U.S. foreign policy in Korea. Gregor and co-author Maria Chang take a look at another strategic stronghold, the island of Taiwan, in *The Republic of China and U.S. Policy.* In this book, they study Taiwan's history and its future, concluding that the island has provided an admirable model for undeveloped countries seeking to cope with Westernization.

BIOGRAPHICAL/CRITICAL SOURCES:

PERIODICALS

Library Journal, Harry V. Willems, review of *The Faces of Janus: Marxism and Fascism in the Twentieth Century,* March 1, 2000, p. 110.

Journal of Politics, May, 1997, review of *Marxism, China, and Development,* p. 635.

National Review, June 15, 1984, Chilton Williamson, Jr., review of *The Republic of China and U.S. Policy: A Study in Human Rights,* p. 58.

*   *   *

GRIFFIN, Jack
See AXELROD, Alan

*   *   *

GROSE, Peter (Bolton) 1934-

PERSONAL: Born October 27, 1934, in Evanston, IL; son of Clyde Leclare (a historian) and Carolyn (a teacher; maiden name, Trowbridge) Grose; married Claudia Kerr (an education administrator), September 11, 1965; children: Carolyn Bronia, Stephanie Kim. *Education:* Yale University, B.A., 1957; Pembroke College, Oxford University, M.A., 1959.

ADDRESSES: Office—c/o International Security Program, Belfer Center for Science and International Affairs, John F. Kennedy School of Government, Harvard University, 79 John F. Kennedy St., Cambridge, MA 02138; fax: 617-496-4403.

CAREER: Associated Press, London correspondent, 1959-60, and from the Congo and West Africa, 1961-62; *New York Times,* New York City, correspondent in

Paris, France, 1963, chief correspondent in Saigon, South Vietnam, 1964-65, chief of Moscow bureau, 1965-67, diplomatic correspondent in Washington, DC, 1967-70, chief of Jerusalem bureau, 1970-72, member of editorial board, 1972-76, chief of United Nations bureau, 1976-77; United States Department of State, Policy Planning Staff, Washington, DC, deputy director, 1977-78; Columbia University, New York City, research associate and international affairs fellow with the Rockefeller Foundation, 1978-80, research associate with the Middle East Institute, 1978-81; Seven Springs Center, Mt. Kisco, NY, director of studies, 1981-82; Council on Foreign Relations, New York City, senior fellow, 1982, and director of Middle East studies, 1982-84; Belfer Center for Science and International Affairs (BCSIA), research fellow for the International Security Program; Harvard University, John F. Kennedy School of Government, fellow. Associated with Horace Mann School; Vineyard Haven Yacht Club, governor.

MEMBER: Century Association, Pembroke College Foundation (president, 1986-90), United Oxford and Cambridge University Club.

AWARDS, HONORS: Morris J. Kaplan Memorial Award for a book on Israel; Jewish Book Council, and Present Tense Award for social and political analysis, American Jewish Committee, both 1984, both for *Israel in the Mind of America;* honorary fellow of Pembroke College, 1987.

WRITINGS:

The Next Steps toward Peace between Israel and Its Neighbors, Seven Springs Center (Mt. Kisco, NY), 1980.
The United States, NATO, and Israeli-Arab Peace, Seven Springs Center (Mt. Kisco, NY), 1981.
Israel in the Mind of America, Knopf (New York, NY), 1983.
A Changing Israel, Vintage Books (New York, NY), 1985.
Gentleman Spy: The Life of Allen Dulles, Houghton Mifflin (Boston, MA), 1994.
Continuing the Inquiry: The Council on Foreign Relations from 1921 to 1996, Council on Foreign Relations (New York, NY), 1996.
Operation Rollback: America's Secret War behind the Iron Curtain, Houghton Mifflin (Boston, MA), 2000.

Managing editor of the journal *Foreign Affairs,* 1984-89, executive editor, 1989-93. Contributor of articles and reviews to periodicals, including *Boston Globe, Washington Post,* and *New York Times.*

SIDELIGHTS: Peter Grose is a journalist who specializes in foreign affairs. Among his writings is a biography of Allen Dulles, a former director of the United States Central Intelligence Agency (CIA). Dulles headed the CIA when Presidents Eisenhower and Kennedy were in office. Following "the Bay of Pigs fiasco," stated a *Kirkus Reviews* critic, Dulles left his post on President Kennedy's order. Published in 1994, Grose's "compelling biography" of Dulles's life, *Gentleman Spy: The Life of Allen Dulles,* "demystifies the master spy," praised the *Kirkus Reviews* critic, who said, "Grose's outstanding study . . . gives readers insight into both a period of history and the development of the CIA."

In 1996, readers were first presented Grose's *Continuing the Inquiry: The Council on Foreign Relations from 1921 to 1996.* "This sprightly work tells the story of the Council on Foreign Relations, established in the aftermath of the First World War and now in its 75th year," stated David C. Hendrickson in a *Foreign Affairs* review. Hendrickson asserted: "Anniversaries are moments not only for celebration but also for reflection. Grose has provided a fond recital of past accomplishments, recalled long-forgotten quarrels, and sketched a handsome outline of institutional history. If the brevity of his account is such as to pique, rather than satisfy, the curiosity of the historian, one must acknowledge that the occasion would have been ill served by a lengthy tome. What Grose does capture is the spirit of the undertaking: the sense of its founders, as well as its renovators, that America has a continuing need to be drawn out of its parochialisms."

In *Operation Rollback: America's Secret War behind the Iron Curtain,* a 2000 publication "[b]ased in part on recently declassified documents," noted Andrew Nagorski in *Newsweek International,* Grose "offer[s] compelling evidence that the United States wasted no time in launching covert operations against the Soviet Union after World War II." "[M]ost of [the United States'] early attempts at 'Rollback' of the Iron Curtain failed miserably," relayed Nagorski, who described *Operation Rollback* as a "scrupulously researched" work and wrote, "Grose transforms the potentially dry bureaucratic battles over Soviet policy into a rip-roaring yarn, complete with a colorful cast of characters both in the back corridors of power and in the field." Calling Grose "an astute analyst" and *Operation Rollback* a "well-researched and contextualized work," Gilbert Taylor maintained in *Booklist* that the book "is a shadowy corner of the cold war that intelligence buffs will eye intently."

Among Grose's earlier publications are books culled from his experiences in Israel and on the U.S. diplomatic front. Grose spent much of his career in various positions with the *New York Times,* including three years as a diplomatic correspondent in Washington and then a two-year stint as head of the paper's Jerusalem bureau; in 1977 he resigned to take a policy planning position at the U.S. State Department. In 1984 he became managing editor of *Foreign Affairs,* obtaining executive director status in 1989. Grose has also been affiliated with the Seven Springs Center of Mt. Kisco, New York; in the early 1980s he served as its director of studies, and the center has published two of his books—*The Next Steps toward Peace between Israel and Its Neighbors,* a 1980 work, and *The United States, NATO, and Israeli-Arab Peace,* published the following year.

Grose's 1983 book, *Israel in the Mind of America,* was hailed as an interesting examination of the complex relationship between two nations whose histories are intricately tied to one another. In researching the work, Grose was able to look into archival materials in Israel that had only recently been declassified. The volume begins with a retrospective of the long history of Jewish immigration to America, an influx that dates from the 1700s. Until about 1880, most of these immigrants were of Western European ancestry, and established prosperous, assimilated communities in many American cities. Yet Grose points out that when waves of Russian and Polish Jews—fleeing pogroms back home—arrived on American shores in the last decades of the nineteenth century, many members of the existing Jewish-American community viewed these newcomers with apprehension. This attitude, in turn, helped spawn support for Zionism, a movement that called for the establishment of a separate Jewish homeland; American Jews had not embraced this mid-nineteenth-century idea until their poorer, less-educated Eastern European cousins started moving into U.S. cities in record numbers.

In *Israel in the Mind of America,* Grose explains that American Jews were not in complete agreement on the issue of Zionism; some feared that their loyalties to the United States would be divided should a separate Jewish state come into existence; others saw a Jewish homeland as a place where democratic American ideals could find a true home. Grose presents both sides of the issue in sections on the pillars of the Jewish community in the United States throughout these decades and the differing views these leaders held. Other chapters discuss anti-Semitic sentiment in America during these years, and Grose chronicles both official and unofficial actions and attitudes of the primarily east coast, patrician establishment that set U.S. policy.

Israel in the Mind of America looks at the series of events that helped launch the State of Israel after World War II. Grose details the behind-the-scenes machinations at the United Nations in the late 1940s over the vote that would allow Palestine to be partitioned into separate Arab and Jewish sections. The official support given by the United States toward this fledgling Israeli state was long considered to be altruistic in aim and a response to the influence of the Jewish American community. According to some critics, Grose's chronicle of the vote trading, lobbying, and pressure tactics used by prominent Americans to garner the necessary caucus weakens the United States' declaration of magnanimity.

Israel in the Mind of America won praise from reviewers for its insights into the complex set of issues that have guided U.S.-Israeli relations; however, Leon Wieseltier of the *Washington Post Book World* found fault with some of Grose's assertions, stating, "His knowledge of Jewish history, and of the history of Zionism, is not deep," but granted that "Grose's study of the reception of Zionism by the American foreign policy establishment is quite illuminating." *New Republic* writer David S. Landes concluded that *Israel in the Mind of America* "as a whole is a well-told and fascinating story." *New York Times Book Review* writer Henry F. Graff remarked, "Grose confidently negotiates the history of the politics and diplomacy with a ready eye for quotation and anecdote. He is able to evoke in a paragraph or two the essence and foibles of the many principal actors, giving the book the quality of a pageant."

Grose again returned to the subject of Israel for his 1985 volume, *A Changing Israel.* The work came about as the result of a study conducted by the Council on Foreign Relations, an organization with which Grose was once affiliated as a senior fellow. *A Changing Israel* looks at the nation during the 1970s and 1980s and identifies four major changes that altered the country's political composition and bode even more transformations for the future. The first is the divisiveness among an array of citizens with differing devotional attitudes—conservative, Orthodox Jews versus the more liberal, Reformed Jews. This matter of religious observance, however, is overshadowed by a runaway inflation that made life difficult for every Israeli and threatened the very survival of the country's economy. Grose also analyzes the increasing Arab birthrate, projecting a more equitable, binational Israel. Finally, Grose argues that the change in direction of Israeli foreign policy—moving from one of defense to one of offense, especially with the country's 1982 invasion of Lebanon, served to sever some of the unconditional support that the Israeli government and military received from its people—and not just those who have made Israel their home. *Washington Post Book World* writer J. Robert Moskin found

A Changing Israel "short enough, clear enough and right often enough to offer a reader a quick once-over of the state of Israel today."

BIOGRAPHICAL/CRITICAL SOURCES:

PERIODICALS

America, September 23, 1995.

Booklist, March 15, 2000, Gilbert Taylor, review of *Operation Rollback,* p. 1298.

Business Week, December 19, 1994.

Foreign Affairs, January-February, 1997, David C. Hendrickson, review of *Continuing the Inquiry,* p. 159.

Kirkus Reviews, review of *Gentleman Spy,* October 1, 1994.

Library Journal, November 15, 1983, p. 2157.

Los Angeles Times Book Review, December 4, 1983, p. 12.

New Republic, December 31, 1983, David S. Landes, review of *Israel in the Mind of America,* pp. 26-32.

Newsweek International, May 8, 2000, Andrew Nagorski, "Rolling Back the Iron Curtain," p. 66.

New York Times Book Review, December 25, 1983, pp. 4, 21; December 9, 1984; March 17, 1985, p. 27.

Publishers Weekly, October 7, 1983; September 24, 1984; January 18, 1985, p. 71.

Washington Monthly, November, 1994, pp. 50-53.

Washington Post, May 21, 2000.

Washington Post Book World, February 19, 1984, p. 10; October 28, 1984, p. 12; March 17, 1985, p. 11.*

*　　*　　*

GUTCHEON, Beth R(ichardson) 1945-
(Beth Richardson)

PERSONAL: Surname rhymes with "escutcheon"; born March 18, 1945, in Sewickley, PA; daughter of Frank Elmer and Rosemound (Fitch) Richardson; married Jeffrey Gutcheon (an architect and piano player), March 18, 1968; children: David Stray. *Education:* Radcliffe College, B.A., 1967.

ADDRESSES: Office—c/o HarperTrade, 10 East 53rd St., New York, NY 10022.

CAREER: Little, Brown, Inc., Boston, MA, editorial assistant, 1967-68; Hit Factory (recording studio), New York, NY, manager, 1969; writer; lecturer on making patchwork quilts and on graphic design in fabric. Has exhibited art pieces in the United States, Canada, Europe, and Japan. Member of Information and Education Committee of Planned Parenthood of New York, NY, 1971-74.

AWARDS, HONORS: The Children of Theatre Street was nominated for an Academy Award as Best Documentary Feature of 1977.

WRITINGS:

The Perfect Patchwork Primer, McKay (New York, NY), 1973.

Abortion: A Woman's Guide, Abelard, 1973.

(With husband, Jeffrey Gutcheon) *The Quilt Design Workbook,* Rawson Associates, 1975.

The Children of Theatre Street (filmscript), Peppercorn-Wormser, 1977.

The New Girls (novel), Putnam (New York, NY), 1979.

Still Missing (novel), Putnam (New York, NY), 1981.

Without a Trace (filmscript; based on *Still Missing*), 20th Century-Fox, 1983.

Domestic Pleasures (novel), Villard Books (New York, NY), 1991.

The Good Fight (filmscript), Hearst Entertainment Productions, 1992.

Saying Grace (novel), Harper (New York, NY), 1995.

Five Fortunes (novel), Cliff Street Books (New York, NY), 1998.

More than You Know (novel), Morrow (New York, NY), 2000.

Contributor to periodicals, including *New York Times Magazine, American Craft, Fiberarts,* and *Ms.*

SIDELIGHTS: Beth R. Gutcheon once told *CA:* "I've been lucky enough to develop two parallel careers, one as a maker and teacher of abstract and graphic art, the other as a writer. They balance each other well in my life and in fact are not as different as they seem to be. The making of the art pieces happens in some inaccessible and non-verbal cave of the brain, as does the first casting about for the substance of a piece of writing; both require the maker to sit still and shut up for long periods of time. The teaching of design requires me to find ways to express visual concepts verbally, and simply and clearly, so that I can communicate them to students who may have gifts as designers, but who almost never have any art education or a familiarity with the academic vocabulary of their craft. Similarly it seems to me that the principle challenge of writing fiction is to figure out how to render the sights and smells and nuances of what I imagine, in words. Imagining a story seems to me not so hard—I think everyone has great stories to tell if they just tell you about why it is their Uncle Albert hasn't spoken to his sister for twenty years. The problem is not the story but how to get it out of my brain and into yours without boring you to death."

According to Susan Isaacs, writing in the *New York Times Book Review,* Gutcheon is very successful at getting the story of *The New Girls,* which concerns life in a prep school during the early 1960s, into her readers' brains. Gutcheon, Isaacs remarked, "is such a gifted storyteller that she can even make a person named Muffin Bundle our close friend by involving us in the details of her life. . . . Her characters are intelligent, brave, witty, insipid, charming, noble and dumb. . . . They are human and real." An *Atlantic* reviewer added that Gutcheon "is blessed with encyclopedic recall of a privileged adolescence, and with a deft way of switching tone from the comic to the touching." Overall, the reviewer concluded, her book is "light of heart and serious of mind."

Gutcheon followed *The New Girls* with *Still Missing,* a tale of how a six-year-old boy's disappearance affects his mother. Susan, the mother, is determined to pursue every lead in the search for her son, Alex. *New York Times Book Review* contributor Nora Johnson credited Gutcheon with maintaining "an intense emotional pitch" throughout the novel, "without ever letting Susan slip from our sympathies by believing too much or too little in the likelihood of Alex's reappearance." Gutcheon adapted the book into the film *Without a Trace,* directed by Stanley R. Jaffe and starring Kate Nelligan as Susan. Gutcheon's other ventures into film include *The Children of Theatre Street,* an Academy Award-nominated documentary about Russia's Kirov School of Ballet, and the made-for-television movie *The Good Fight.*

Gutcheon's 1991 novel, *Domestic Pleasures,* is a study of complex relationships among affluent Manhattanites. Martha is an illustrator, divorced, with a teenage son; rather surprisingly, she falls in love with Charlie, the lawyer who represented her husband in the divorce proceedings, and who now, after the ex-husband's death in a plane crash, is handling his estate. Charlie, also divorced, has a teenage daughter. He and Martha find that numerous present and former relationships complicate their love affair. "This state-of-the-art story of love's leftovers . . . rings true," related Anne Tolstoi Wallach in the *New York Times Book Review,* while a *Publishers*

Weekly critic praised Gutcheon's "witty dialogue" and "canny observations." Wallach complained that Gutcheon "tends to sacrifice depth for breadth," introducing too many characters and situations, but she allowed that "there is still a world of entertainment in *Domestic Pleasures.*"

Saying Grace deals with a woman whose well-ordered life falls apart—and with how she copes. Rue Shaw, the head of a private school in California, loses her job, husband, and daughter in short order. This was all a bit too much for *Booklist* reviewer Joanne Wilkinson, who described the book as "sinking under the weight of all that turmoil." A *Publishers Weekly* commentator thought the novel focused too much on the stoic Rue's viewpoint, and that it would have been valuable to see the novel's action through the eyes of its interesting supporting characters. "This quiet novel fails to deliver sufficient emotional impact," the critic concluded.

Gutcheon's next effort, *Five Fortunes,* explores the lives of five women who meet at a health spa: Jill, college student and rape survivor, and her mother, Amy, a wealthy New Yorker; Carter, a private detective from Los Angeles; Laura, a politician and recent widow from Idaho; and Rae, a former fan-dancer whose husband has an advanced case of Alzheimer's disease. The women bond during their stay at the spa and have their fortunes told by a local palm reader; the story follows them through the many life changes they go through in the following year. Gutcheon's non-stereotypical characterizations bring freshness to what might be considered a stereotypical structure, according to *Library Journal*'s Cynthia Johnson, who asserted that "the reader cannot help wanting to know what happens next." A *Publishers Weekly* reviewer also found this "fast-paced story" compelling, while a *Kirkus Reviews* critic called it "both a page-turner and a day-brightener."

More than You Know is a far different type of story, set in coastal Maine and detailing how a nineteenth-century murder affected a Depression-era love affair between relatives of, respectively, the victim and the principal suspects. The lovers, Hannah and Conary, even claim to have seen ghosts. The story is told from Hannah's perspective of decades later, as an old woman. Megan Harlan, writing in the *New York Times Book Review,* thought Gutcheon's interweaving of the nineteenth- and twentieth-century stories "creates real suspense"; she also noted that Gutcheon "evinces, with stark and elemental resonance, the way love and hatred shape lives." A *Publishers Weekly* commentator asserted that Gutcheon "combine[s] a humdinger of a ghost tale with a haunting story of young love," and applauded her "sophisticated prose," "narrative skill," and true-to-life depiction of the Maine seaside setting. A *Kirkus Reviews* critic, though, derided the novel's "schematic plot" and "unconvincing characters," adding that "both undo a potentially haunting love story." But *Library Journal* contributor Beth E. Andersen praised the "deliciously suspenseful foreboding" found in the close of each chapter, and *Booklist*'s GraceAnne A. DeCandido dubbed the novel "unputdownable."

Gutcheon believes that fiction is more than entertainment. In *Library Journal,* she explained: "For me [fiction] is the ultimate social document. It's a threshing operation, by which we separate the significant details from those that did not, after all, fuse into a mesh of cause and effect; it's the way we sort out what really happened, to ourselves and to each other, and what it meant, as opposed to what we thought it meant at the time. Fiction is the truth in a form we can make some emotional use of."

BIOGRAPHICAL/CRITICAL SOURCES:

PERIODICALS

Atlantic, November, 1979.
Booklist, May 15, 1995, Joanne Wilkinson, review of *Saying Grace,* p. 1631; May 15, 1998, Grace Fill, review of *Five Fortunes,* p. 1595; February 15, 2000, GraceAnne A. DeCandido, review of *More than You Know,* p. 1080.
Kirkus Reviews, February 15, 2000, p. 193.
Library Journal, June 15, 1979; April 15, 1998, Cynthia Johnson, review of *Five Fortunes,* p. 112; January, 2000, Beth E. Andersen, review of *More than You Know,* p. 159.
New York Times, December 21, 1977.
New York Times Book Review, October 14, 1979; August 30, 1981, Nora Johnson, "Foreign Settings and Domestic Scenes," p. 10; July 7, 1991, Anne Tostoi Wallach, "How Many in the Bed?"; May 7, 2000, Megan Harlan, "Possessed in Maine."
Publishers Weekly, April 12, 1991, Sybil Steinberg, review of *Domestic Pleasures,* p. 45; May 8, 1995, p. 287; April 6, 1998, p. 59; March 8, 1999, John F. Baker, "A Move to Morrow," p. 16; February 7, 2000, p. 59.*

*   *   *

GUTTRIDGE, Leonard F(rancis) 1918-

PERSONAL: Born August 27, 1918, in Wales; came to the United States in 1947; married Jean Stoddart (a secretary), August 25, 1956; children: Bruce, Vivien. *Education:* Attended school in Cardiff, Wales. *Politics:*

"Moderate by Welsh standards, leftish on the American scale." *Religion:* "Of the open mind."

ADDRESSES: Office—c/o Berkley Publishers, 375 Hudson St., New York, NY 10014.

CAREER: Indian Embassy, Washington, DC, librarian, 1950-61; writer, 1961—. *Military service:* Royal Air Force, 1939-45; served in North Africa; became sergeant.

MEMBER: Royal Air Force Association.

WRITINGS:

(With Jay D. Smith) *Jack Teagarden: Story of a Jazz Maverick,* Cassell (London, England), 1960, Da Capo Press (New York, NY), 1976.
(With Jay D. Smith) *The Commodores: The U.S. Navy in the Age of Sail,* introduction by James C. Bradford, Harper (New York, NY), 1969.
(With George S. McGovern) *The Great Coalfield War,* Houghton (Boston, MA), 1972.
Icebound: The Jeannette *Expedition's Quest for the North Pole,* Naval Institute Press (Annapolis, MD), 1986.
Mutiny: A History of Naval Insurrection, Naval Institute Press (Annapolis, MD), 1992.
Ghosts of Cape Sabine: The Harrowing True Story of the Greely Expedition, Putnam (New York, NY), 2000.

Contributor of stories and articles to magazines in England and the United States, including, *Saga, Stag,* and *Melody Maker.*

WORK IN PROGRESS: Research on new findings concerning Abraham Lincoln's assassination, with Ray A. Neff.

SIDELIGHTS: Leonard F. Guttridge has written two books on disastrous expeditions to the Arctic. *Icebound: The Jeannette Expedition's Quest for the North Pole* recreates an 1879 trek financed by newspaper publisher James Gordon Bennett. Bennett had previously backed the Stanley-Livingstone expedition to Africa, and he hoped to boost newspaper circulation with reportage about another adventure. He paid for the *Jeannette,* the ship to be used, while the U.S. Navy provided five officers to pilot her. The *Jeannette* sailed north through the Aleutian islands, but the voyage ended tragically with her few survivors clinging to the ice. Naval and congressional inquiries covered up the facts, in Guttridge's opinion. An *Atlantic* reviewer, however, felt that the only crime committed by the navy was its willingness to cooperate "with the gaudy and basically irresponsible Bennett." Nevertheless, the critic called the book a "meticulous" and "well-written" account of the doomed expedition.

Another ill-fated dash to the Arctic is recounted in *Ghosts of Cape Sabine: The Harrowing True Story of the Greely Expedition.* The Greely Expedition was organized by William Henry Howgate, a rogue officer in the Army Signal Corps who convinced the United States to take part in an international venture to set up scientific stations in the Arctic. The Army, Navy, Congress, and the press all had a hand in the venture, which was to be led by Howgate's friend, Lieutenant Adolphus Greely of the Signal Corps. Greely and his party were dropped off at Lady Franklin Bay in August of 1881, equipped with extensive provisions and enough supplies to build excellent housing. They were to be restocked annually from a supply ship. But no ship was ever sent. The party struggled to reach civilization, but in the end there were few survivors. Horrible stories suggesting that some of Greely's party had resorted to cannibalism began to surface. *Atlantic Monthly* reviewer Phoebe-Lou Adams said the work is "as fascinating and exciting as any adventure novel, even though the reader knows the outcome from page one."

Guttridge once told *CA:* "No matter how often produced under compulsions of necessity, my writing output has always reflected my interests. My principal instinctive addiction has been to jazz—ever since I heard Duke Ellington records via the British Broadcasting Corporation on a neighbor's radio in 1934. I like many forms of music, but defy anyone to play me something, anything, more thrilling than the V-Disc 'Uncle Sam Blues' with its marvelous Lips Page vocal.

"I am addicted, too, to suspense stories and movies. I saw Hitchcock's 'Secret Agent' the day before I enlisted in the Royal Air Force, and disagree with those who do not list it among his best. I wrote some crime stories, managed to sell one to the last of the real pulps, *Popular Detective,* before the breed vanished.

"Power struggles of whatever description—between individuals in a mutually tight spot—intrigue me, and my love of the same took over in *The Commodores* so ef-

fectively that one reviewer called the book '*Executive Suite* on the high seas.' I maintain, indeed insist, that the best and most inexhaustible source for such dramatic staples as human conflict and the ironies of fate is true history, conscientiously researched.

"My Welsh origins, I suppose, have determined my interest in fantasy. And they may also, given that country's historic association with coal, have led me to the story I wrote with Senator McGovern of this country's most dramatic labor war."

BIOGRAPHICAL/CRITICAL SOURCES:

PERIODICALS

Atlantic Monthly, October, 1986, review of *Icebound: The Jeannette Expedition's Quest for the North Pole,* p. 104; February, 2000, Phoebe-Lou Adams, review of *Ghosts of Cape Sabine: The Harrowing True Story of the Greely Expedition,* p. 105.
Library Journal, September 1, 1992, review of *Mutiny: A History of Naval Insurrection,* p. 189.
New York Times Book Review, February 20, 2000, Roland Huntford, review of *Ghosts of Cape Sabine: The Harrowing True Story of the Greely Expedition,* p. 11.*

*   *   *

GWYNN, Robin D(avid) 1942-

PERSONAL: Born June 5, 1942, in Newtonmore, Scotland; son of John David (a civil engineer) and Grace Lawless (a historian; maiden name, Lee) Gwynn; married Margaret Diana Rodger (a librarian), February 15, 1971; children: Jennifer Lee, David Morton. *Ethnicity:* "European." *Education:* Pembroke College, Cambridge, B.A., 1964, Certificate in Education, 1965, M.A., 1968; University of London, Ph.D., 1976. *Religion:* Anglican.

ADDRESSES: Home—23 Clyde Rd., Napier, New Zealand; fax 06-835-2412. *E-mail*—gwynn@paradise. net.nz.

CAREER: Trent Park College of Education, London, England, part-time lecturer in history, 1965-66; University of London, Goldsmith's College, London, part-time lecturer in history, 1966-67; Massey University, Palmerston North, New Zealand, lecturer, 1969-75, senior lecturer, 1976-86, reader in history, 1987-96. Candidate for Alliance Party in New Zealand general elections, 1996 and 1999. Director of British Huguenot Heritage Year, 1984-85; chair of Palmpex '82 National Philatelic Exhibition; jury chair, Tarapex '86 and Royal 100 National Philatelic Exhibitions; chair of seven national philatelic literature exhibitions, 1989-2001. Palmerston North Christian Home Trust, began as vice president, became president, 1974-81; New Zealand Philatelic Confederation, began as vice president, became president, 1988-92.

MEMBER: Royal Philatelic Society of New Zealand (president).

AWARDS, HONORS: Leverhulme fellow, 1984-85.

WRITINGS:

A Calendar of the Letter Books of the French Church of London from the Civil War to the Restoration, 1643-1659, Scolar Press, 1979.
Huguenot Heritage: The History and Contribution of the Huguenots in Britain, Routledge & Kegan Paul, 1985, revised edition, Sussex Academic Press, 2001.
Collecting New Zealand Stamps, Heinemann Reed, 1988.
Minutes of the Consistory of the French Church of London, Threadneedle Street, 1679-1692, Huguenot Society of Great Britain and Ireland, 1994.
The Huguenots of London, Alpha Press, 1998.
The Denial of Democracy, Cosmos Publications, 1998.

Contributor to history and philatelic journals.

WORK IN PROGRESS: Research on Huguenot refugees, especially in Britain, on New Zealand philately, and on mail salvaged from shipwrecks.

SIDELIGHTS: Robin D. Gwynn once told *CA:* "Although I am not myself of Huguenot descent, I embarked on the study of the Huguenots through a family connection. As a university student at Trinity College in Dublin, my mother was encouraged to work on the Huguenots in Ireland. She subsequently wrote the standard work on that subject and became the first official researcher appointed by the Huguenot Society. She died in 1964, shortly before my final examinations. When I was asked if I wanted to write a doctoral thesis, I embarked on a project my mother would probably have undertaken had she lived: a history of the Huguenots in Britain. I did not know it would take twenty years to complete!

"By the end of that time I had sufficient knowledge to be invited from New Zealand to act as director of Huguenot Heritage Year in Britain. This was a memorable experience involving many aspects outside my normal academic environment, such as publicity, radio and television work, some twenty-eight museum exhibitions, English Tourist Board trails, and special church services culminating in one which filled St. Paul's Cathedral.

"The interest that the celebration evoked—still very much alive fifteen years later—was itself a commentary on the significance of the Huguenots in British history. Not only do they provide an outstanding example of the successful assimilation of a large alien minority, but these French Protestants shared a steely resolve that made them particularly valuable immigrants. They made specific contributions to a wide variety of art, crafts, banking and mercantile pursuits, professions, and religious denominations. With such a broad subject the last word can never be said, but the interest is unending."

BIOGRAPHICAL/CRITICAL SOURCES:

PERIODICALS

Observer, March 3, 1985.
Times Literary Supplement, October 11, 1985.

H

HADDAD, Gladys 1930-

PERSONAL: Born September 12, 1930, in Cleveland, OH; daughter of Fred (in construction industry) and Rose (a homemaker; maiden name, Amor) Haddad. *Education:* Allegheny College, B.A., 1952; Lake Erie College, B.F.A., 1974; Case Western Reserve University, M.A., 1961, Ph.D., 1980. *Religion:* Episcopalian.

ADDRESSES: Home—1640 South Belvoir Blvd., Cleveland, OH 44121. *Office*—Interdisciplinary Centers and Programs, Case Western Reserve University, Cleveland, OH 44106-1120; fax: 216-368-5241. *E-mail*—gmh3@po.cwru.edu.

CAREER: Schoolteacher in Lyndhurst, OH, 1952-60, and Cleveland Heights, OH, 1960-63; Lake Erie College, Painesville, OH, professor of American studies and administrator, also academic dean and executive assistant to the president, 1963-89; Case Western Reserve University, Cleveland, OH, director of Western Reserve Studies symposium, 1985—, professor of American studies and administrator, 1990—. Western Reserve Historical Society, administrator, 1989—.

MEMBER: American Studies Association, Ohio Historical Society, Western Reserve Architectural Historians (member of board of directors), Ohio Humanities Council, Women Historians of Greater Cleveland, Lake County (OH) Historical Society, Fortnightly Musical Club (vice president).

AWARDS, HONORS: Award from American Association for State and Local History, 1988; Achievement Award from *Northern Ohio Live,* 1991; Silver "Telly" (documentary), 1994, for *Samuel Mather: Vision, Leadership, Generosity.*

WRITINGS:

(Editor, with Harry F. Lupold) *Ohio's Western Reserve: A Regional Reader,* Kent State University Press, 1988.

(Editor, with David R. Anderson) *Anthology of Western Reserve Literature,* Kent State University Press, 1992.

Laukhuff's Book Store of Cleveland: An Epilogue, Northern Ohio Bibliophilic Society, 1997.

Author of several video documentaries: *Samuel Mather: Vision, Leadership, Generosity,* 1994; *Samuel and Flora Stone Mather: Partners in Philanthropy,* 1995; and *Flora Stone Mather: A Legacy of Stewardship,* 1997. Editor, *Western Reserve Studies: A Journal of Regional History and Culture.*

WORK IN PROGRESS: Flora Stone Mather—Her Life, Her Legacy: A Biography.

SIDELIGHTS: Gladys Haddad told *CA:* "I am a regionalist of Northeastern Ohio's Western Reserve, where I study its literature, history, and art. My professional life (teaching, writing, and speaking) is all centered in this area." She added: "I have directed the annual Western Reserve Studies Symposium since 1985, when I founded it to encourage scholarship about the region."

* * *

HAILEY, J. P.
See HALL, Parnell

HALL, Parnell 1944-
(J. P. Hailey)

PERSONAL: Born October 31, 1944, in Culver City, CA; son of James and Frances (Benn) Hall; married Lynn Mandel, 1975; children: Justin, Toby. *Education:* Marlboro College, B.A., 1968.

ADDRESSES: Home—New York, NY. *Agent*—Donald Maass, Donald Maass Literary Agency, 160 West 95th St., Suite 1B, New York, NY 10025. *E-mail*—parnellh@ pipeline.com.

CAREER: Marlboro Theater Company, actor, 1968, 1970-74; Windsor Mountain School, Lenox, MA, teacher, 1974-75, Berkshire Community College, Pittsfield, MA, teacher, 1975; Stockbridge School, Stockbridge, MA, teacher, 1975-76; screenwriter, 1977-84; Claims Investigation Bureau, Mount Vernon, NY, private detective, 1985-87; novelist, 1987—. Appeared in the films *Hercules in New York,* 1969, and *A New Leaf.*

MEMBER: International Association of Crime Writers, Private Eye Writers of America (vice president, 1993-94; president, 1995-96), Mystery Writers of America, American Crime Writers, Sisters in Crime.

AWARDS, HONORS: Edgar Award nomination for best first novel, Mystery Writers of America, 1988, for *Detective;* Private Eye Writers of America, Shamus Award nomination for best first private eye novel, 1988, *Detective,* and Shamus Award nomination for best private eye novel, 1996, for *Movie.*

WRITINGS:

MYSTERY NOVELS; "STANLEY HASTINGS" SERIES

Detective, Donald I. Fine (New York, NY), 1987.
Murder, Donald I. Fine (New York, NY), 1988.
Favor, Donald I. Fine (New York, NY), 1988.
Strangler, Donald I. Fine (New York, NY), 1989.
Client, Donald I. Fine (New York, NY), 1990.
Juror, Donald I. Fine (New York, NY), 1990.
Shot, Donald I. Fine (New York, NY), 1991.
Actor, Mysterious Press (New York, NY), 1993.
Blackmail, Mysterious Press (New York, NY), 1994.
Movie, Mysterious Press (New York, NY), 1995.
Trial, Mysterious Press (New York, NY), 1996.
Scam, Mysterious Press (New York, NY), 1997.

Suspense, Mysterious Press (New York, NY), 1998.
Cozy, Carroll & Graf (New York, NY), 2001.

MYSTERY NOVELS; "PUZZLE LADY" SERIES

A Clue for the Puzzle Lady, Bantam (New York, NY), 1999.
Last Puzzle and Testament, Bantam (New York, NY), 2000.
Puzzled to Death, Bantam (New York, NY), 2001.

MYSTERY NOVELS; "STEVE WINSLOW" SERIES; UNDER PSEUDONYM J. P. HAILEY

The Baxter Trust, Donald I. Fine (New York, NY), 1988.
The Anonymous Client, Donald I. Fine (New York, NY), 1989.
The Underground Man, Donald I. Fine (New York, NY), 1990.
The Naked Typist, Donald I. Fine (New York, NY), 1990.
The Wrong Gun, Donald I. Fine (New York, NY), 1992.

OTHER

Author of the screenplay *C.H.U.D.*

WORK IN PROGRESS: A Puzzle in a Pear Tree, a novel for the "Puzzle Lady" series, completion expected in 2002.

SIDELIGHTS: Perhaps best known for his mystery novels featuring Manhattan private detective Stanley Hastings, Parnell Hall also authors the "Steve Winslow" series of novels, about an iconoclastic lawyer, under the pseudonym J. P. Hailey, and has begun a series focusing on a hard-drinking, middle-aged sleuth known as the "puzzle lady." Hastings, as reviewers have frequently pointed out, is one of the more likable and less hard-boiled private eyes in fiction. Although a licensed detective, this frustrated playwright and happily married family man makes his living as an "ambulance chaser" for a personal-injury lawyer, signing up clients and taking their statements. The criminal cases that come his way, often accidentally, cause him to rely on his "street smarts," his wit, and the overcoming of his realistic fears as he fumbles his way toward solutions. Hall, according to reviewer Marvin Lachman in *Armchair Detective,* based Hastings's character on some of his own experiences as an aspiring writer and New York City dweller.

In Hall's debut novel, *Detective,* Hastings finds his first client murdered and tracks down the killer at his own expense. Lachman found the puzzle element of the novel to be "rather ordinary," although its writing makes it "an often amusing, fast-paced first novel with considerable suspense." In a review of Hall's second novel, *Murder,* a *Publishers Weekly* writer looked back on *Detective* as a "notable debut." *Murder* involves a neighbor of Hastings who has been blackmailed into working as a prostitute; when she is killed, Hastings comes under suspicion and solves the crime in order to clear his own name. As in *Detective,* Hastings collaborates with Police Sergeant MacAuliff, whom author Hall uses as a foil for his protagonist and a source of witty observations on police procedure.

In his third published adventure, *Favor,* Hastings is sent to Atlantic City to investigate MacAuliff's sleazy son-in-law as a favor for that police sergeant. He infiltrates the mob using what a *Publishers Weekly* critic called "a hilarious, albeit unbelievable, modus operandi" and plunges into "a web of intrigue that is pure entertainment for the reader." For *Booklist*'s Robertson, *Favor* was a "spirited, well-made" entry in "a very funny, very smart mystery series." A *Library Journal* reviewer felt that after a slow beginning, the novel moves along in a way that is both enjoyably comical and believably real.

Hastings's fourth volume, *Strangler,* finds him accused by an unpleasant police sergeant (not MacAuliff) of committing a series of murders by strangulation. His clearing of his own name results in what a *Library Journal* reviewer called "a great addition to the series." Wrote *Booklist* contributor Robertson, "It's great fun to meet a sleuth with very few answers." Hastings, that reviewer explained, "reaffirms one's belief in the power of relentless mediocrity."

With his next assignment, in *Client,* Hastings follows a client's wife to a motel, falls asleep on his stakeout, and finds himself framed for her murder. This prompted *Booklist*'s Stuart Miller to call Hastings "delightfully inept," and the case "yet another highly readable mystery starring one of the most unusual private eyes ever to take on a case." For *Library Journal, Client* represented "continued high quality" in the series, marked by a swift, humorous style.

Juror finds Hastings performing jury duty on a case which he admits is boring. The murder in question is that of a fellow juror, a woman whom Hastings had been driving to the courtroom each morning. The novel provides an occasion for observations on jury trials and on murder investigations which a *Publishers Weekly* critic found to be the book's strong points; the same critic also cited the plot for lacking "dispositive clues" which would enable the reader to solve the case. *Kliatt* contributor Rita M. Fontinha, however, found *Juror* "suspenseful to the end, and great fun too," and *Armchair Detective* critic Jon L. Breen declared it "hugely enjoyable" for its "terrific stunt payoff" and its observations on the jury system.

Hall's next Hastings title, *Shot,* finds Hastings working for a wealthy woman to investigate her own boyfriend; the boyfriend is then found dead and once again, Hastings is a suspect. The plot, a *Publishers Weekly* reviewer warned, contains an "all-encompassing red herring" but is enlivened by two climaxes—one comic and one serious—and "vivid looks at Manhattan's seamier side." In *Chicago's Tribune Books,* reviewer Kevin Moore commented that Hastings's ordinariness and the other characters' believability, although well rendered, make the tale less exciting. For Marilyn Stasio, however, *Shot* provided evidence that Hall's series is "forever fresh."

In *Actor,* Hastings accepts a friend's invitation to perform in a Connecticut theater group; the stabbing death of the stage manager provides the crime, and the setting affords an opportunity for observations about the denizens of the theatrical profession. Wrote Stasio, "Mr. Hall knows the theatrical drill to which he hilariously subjects Stanley." The protagonist, Stasio asserted, "wins our vote for Best Performance by an Actor on the Verge of a Nervous Breakdown." A *Kirkus Reviews* critic found the novel amusing, but weak on detection, and "middling for the series." But in the opinion of a *Publishers Weekly* critic, the novel, despite a slow start, deserved a "standing ovation."

Blackmail concerns an attractive female client who hires Hastings to pay off a blackmailer for pornographic pictures in which the client does not even appear. The client then turns up dead, as does another individual, and an elaborate sting is gradually uncovered by Hastings with the aid of his wife, Alice. *Booklist* writer Wes Lukowsky found this "an intelligent, unusual spin on the tough-guy detective," and calls the dialogue "the best this side of George V. Higgins." *Publishers Weekly* praised the characterization, pace, and dialogue, but noted that the plot is too complex for most readers. A *Kirkus Reviews* writer, claiming that Hall's novels often start with great ideas, found this one to be a winner from beginning to end: "Every page quivers with comic frustration, and the result is an absolute joy."

Hastings's tenth published adventure, *Movie,* gives him the opportunity to observe the world of filmmaking, as a screenplay of his is accepted by a producer. Murder enters when a homeless man is killed near the set, and then a sound technician is also found dead. A *Kirkus Reviews* contributor felt the plot does not meet the level of the witty banter in the book, but that "anyone who can relax and ignore the mystery is guaranteed a good time." A *Publishers Weekly* critic, disappointed by this volume, felt the tedium of the fictitious movie shoot infected the novel itself. However, Lukowsky called this book "an entertaining entry in an underappreciated series."

Hastings's next book appearance, in *Trial,* finds him once again on his professional turf as an ambulance-chaser for a lawyer. His employer is defending a man accused of murdering his wife; the defendant has an apparently good alibi concerning a poker game, but Hastings has doubts, and then one of the poker players is killed. The novel ends with a surprise, and *Booklist* contributor George Needham called it "lots of fun." For a *Publishers Weekly* reviewer, the novel was well paced and balanced, containing a complex alibi with "a lot of very sharp turns in the courtroom." A *Kirkus Reviews* contributor remarked that the novel's climactic scene is "memorable, though far-fetched," and that the series itself is "rollicking."

Hastings moves on to an "intricate and fiendishly funny case," in the words of a *Publishers Weekly* reviewer, in his next book, *Scam.* In this installment of the series an investment banker hires the private detective to collect information about a woman he met in a singles bar. A series of dead bodies impinge on the investigation, and once again Hastings is framed for murder. Wrote the *Publishers Weekly* reviewer, "smart dialogue, clever plotting and a perfectly executed reverse scam . . . result in sparkling entertainment." The novel also won plaudits from a *Kirkus Reviews* critic, who commended Hall for taking "slender material" and weaving it into "a gossamer web of riddles by turns puzzling, suspenseful, and hilarious." According to Stasio, *Scam* showed that "what Mr. Hall does to the private-eye formula is very funny, but it isn't frivolous. His puzzles, for all their manic nonsense, are fiendish constructions of sound logic."

Hastings's thirteenth outing, *Suspense,* brings him good luck as well, in the opinion of a *Publishers Weekly* reviewer. Here, a bestselling suspense novelist's wife hires Hastings to uncover the source of harassing phone calls—and the calls lead to murder. The case gives Hastings an opening to offer comically wise observations on the publishing industry with its agents, editors, and would-be writers. David Pitt of *Booklist* pointed out the self-referential nature of this comedy in this "very clever" novel about the suspense genre; for example, the characters frequently state that the case on which Hastings is working would make a bad novel. For Pitt, this experiment worked, because *Suspense* is "first-class fun from start to finish."

Hall introduced Cora Felton in *A Clue for the Puzzle Lady.* Cora, the "puzzle lady," lives in Bakerhaven, a charming suburban town in Connecticut, where her neighbors frown on her heavy drinking but bask in her fame as a creator of nationally syndicated crossword puzzles without realizing that her niece Sherry ghostwrites the puzzles. Cora gets to work on a different kind of puzzle, though, when crossword-puzzle clues start turning up on dead bodies. A *Publishers Weekly* reviewer welcomed the character of Cora, describing her as "a true original" and "Miss Marple as a promiscuous lush." The reviewer also commended the supporting characters, the dialogue, and the plot. *Booklist* contributor GraceAnne A. DeCandido noted that some of the book's elements seemed overly familiar, but added, "Hall works with them in such deft ways, with such spiffy dialogue, that we are immediately seduced."

Cora and Sherry return in *Last Puzzle and Testament,* in which a strange woman named Emma Hurley dies and leaves a will granting her substantial wealth to whichever one of her heirs can solve a complicated puzzle—with Cora in charge of the judging. But soon, someone starts killing the players, and Cora and her niece must shift into crime-solving mode. "The second puzzle for Cora Felton . . . is even better than her clever debut," noted a *Publishers Weekly* critic, while DeCandido, again reviewing for *Booklist,* predicted that "this novel's puzzles within puzzles will charm and so will its attractive cast."

Hall once told *CA:* "I began writing my first novel, *Detective,* in 1985, when I was working as a private investigator in New York City. The firm I worked for serviced negligence lawyers, the type who advertised for clients on TV. I interviewed the accident victims, usually those who had fallen on the city sidewalk, and photographed the casts on their arms and legs, and the cracks in the pavement that had tripped them. While this was real detective work, it was not the type I was used to reading about in mystery novels, and it occurred to me how ill equipped I would be if I had to solve a murder. So that's how I began my novel. The detective is in his office, and the client is telling him, 'You have to help me, someone's trying to kill me.' This is where the P.I. says, 'There, there, citizen,' straps on his gun, and goes out to fight the bad guys. Stanley Hastings says, 'Are you kidding? I don't have a gun, I have a camera. I take pictures of cracks in the sidewalk.' When the man is killed, Stanley is devastated, and spends the rest of the book trying to make up for the fact he could not help him because he was not 'a real detective.'"

BIOGRAPHICAL/CRITICAL SOURCES:

PERIODICALS

Armchair Detective, winter, 1992, pp. 58-59; spring, 1996, pp. 174-175.

Booklist, January 15, 1988, p. 830; September 15, 1988, p. 123; July, 1989, p. 1871; March 15, 1990, p. 1418; March 15, 1994, p. 1330; March 15, 1995, p. 1311; January 1 & 15, 1996, pp. 795-796; December 1, 1997, David Pitt, review of *Suspense,* p. 611; October 1, 1999, GraceAnne A. DeCandido, review of *A Clue for the Puzzle Lady,* p. 346; July, 2000, DeCandido, review of *Last Puzzle and Testament,* p. 2013.

Kirkus Reviews, December 15, 1987, p. 1701; March 1, 1993, p. 262; January 1, 1994, p. 20; February 1, 1995, p. 109; December 1, 1995, p. 1670; February 15, 1997, p. 258; November 1, 1997, review of *Suspense,* p. 1608; October 1, 1999, review of *A Clue for the Puzzle Lady,* p. 1527.

Kliatt, September, 1993, p. 10.

Library Journal, September 1, 1988, pp. 185-186; May 1, 1989, p. 101; April 1, 1990, p. 140; November 1, 1999, review of *A Clue for the Puzzle Lady,* p. 128.

New York Times Book Review, July 15, 1990, p. 26; February 7, 1993, p. 28; May 30, 1993, p. 13; April 27, 1997, Marilyn Stasio, review of *Scam,* p. 36; December 12, 1999, for *A Clue for the Puzzle Lady,* p. 41.

Publishers Weekly, December 18, 1987, p. 57; August 19, 1988, pp. 60-61; October 5, 1990, p. 92; April 26, 1991, p. 49; March 8, 1993, p. 70; January 10, 1994, p. 47; January 30, 1995, p. 88; December 11, 1995, p. 59; January 27, 1997, p. 80; October 20, 1997, review of *Suspense,* p. 57; October 25, 1999, review of *A Clue for the Puzzle Lady,* p. 54; August 14, 2000, review of *Last Puzzle and Testament,* p. 332.

Tribune Books (Chicago), July 2, 1989, pp. 4-5; July 7, 1991, p. 6.

HARDESTY, Nancy A(nn) 1941-

PERSONAL: Born August 22, 1941, in Lima, OH; daughter of Byron Tapscott (a tool and die maker) and Ruth Lucille (a bank clerk; maiden name, Parr) Hardesty. *Education:* Wheaton College, Wheaton, IL, A.B., 1963; Northwestern University, M.S.J., 1964; University of Chicago, Ph.D., 1976. *Politics:* Democrat. *Religion:* Episcopalian, Universal Fellowship of Metropolitan Community Churches.

ADDRESSES: Home—7 Woodridge Dr., Greenville, SC 29611-2015.

CAREER: Lima News, Lima, Ohio, reporter, 1961-63; *Christian Century,* Chicago, IL, editorial assistant, 1964-65; *Eternity,* Philadelphia, PA, assistant editor, 1966-69; Trinity College, Deerfield, IL, assistant professor of English and sports information director, 1969-73; Emory University, Candler School of Theology, Atlanta, GA, assistant professor of American church history, 1976-80; Central Gwinnett High School, Lawrenceville, GA, English teacher, 1980-1982; freelance writer/editor, 1982-88; Clemson University, Clemson, SC, visiting assistant/associate professor of religion, 1988-96, associate professor of religion, 1996-99, professor of religion, 1999—. Founding member, Evangelical and Ecumenical Women's Caucus, Daughters of Sarah.

WRITINGS:

(With Letha Scanzoni) *All We're Meant to Be: A Biblical Approach to Women's Liberation,* Word Books, 1974, revised edition, Abingdon, 1986, 3rd edition, Eerdmans, 1992.

Great Women of Faith, Baker Book, 1980.

Women Called to Witness, Abingdon, 1984, revised edition, University of Tennessee Press, 1999.

Inclusive Language in the Church, John Knox, 1987.

The Memory Book, Presbyterian Publishing House, 1989.

"Your Daughters Shall Prophesy": Revivalism and Feminism in the Age of Finney, Carlson, 1991.

Contributor to *The Cross and the Flag,* Robert G. Clouse and others, editors, Creation House, 1972; *It's O.K. to Be Single,* Gary R. Collins, editor, Word Books, 1976; *Women and the Word,* Helen Gray Crotwell, editor, Fortress, 1978; *Women of Spirit,* Rosemary Ruether and Eleanor McLaughlin, editors, Simon & Schuster,

1979; *Solo Flight,* Jim Towns, editor, Tyndale, 1980; *Sanctification and Liberation,* Theodore Runyon, editor, Abingdon, 1981; *Women in New Worlds,* Hilah F. Thomas and Rosemary Skinner Keller, editors, Abingdon, 1981; *Religion in South Carolina,* Charles H. Lippy, editor, University of South Carolina Press, 1993; *Spirituality and Social Responsibility: Vocational Vision of Women in the United Methodist Tradition,* Rosemary Keller, editor, Abingdon, 1993; *Rattling Those Dry Bones: Women Changing the Church,* June Steffensen Hagen, editor, Luramedia, 1995; *In Our Own Voices: Four Centuries of Women and Religion in America,* Rosemary Keller and Rosemary Ruether, editors, Harper San Francisco, 1995; *The Changing Shape of Protestantism in the South,* Marion Aldridge and Kevin Lewis, editors, Mercer University Press, 1996.

WORK IN PROGRESS: A history of gender and religion in the twentieth century; a history of faith healing in the holiness-Pentecostal tradition.

SIDELIGHTS: Nancy A. Hardesty told *CA:* "I have been reared, educated and employed within a conservative, 'evangelical' Christian context. There I have seen first-hand the discrimination practiced against women and have felt the frustration when such oppression is buttressed with biblical and religious arguments. I decided to fight back. My goal is to learn more about Christian women of the past, their work and their beliefs, and then to communicate their inspiring stories to people today."

*   *   *

HARRIS, Charlaine 1951-

PERSONAL: Born November 25, 1951, in Tunica, MS; daughter of Robert Ashley (a principal) and Jean (a librarian; maiden name, Balentine) Harris; married Hal Schulz (a chemical engineer), August 5, 1978; children: two sons, one daughter. *Education:* Southwestern at Memphis, B.A., 1973. *Avocational interests:* Animals, gardening, cooking, unsolved murder cases.

ADDRESSES: Home—1185 Sheppard Rd. N.E., Orangeburg, SC 29115.

CAREER: Bolivar Commercial, Cleveland, MS, offset darkroom operator, 1973-74; Clarksdale Press Register, Clarksdale, MS, typesetter, 1974-76; Delta Design Group, Greenville, MS, typesetter, 1975-77; Federal Express Corp., Memphis, TN, typesetter, 1977-78; writer.

MEMBER: Mystery Writers of America, American Crime Writers League, Sisters in Crime, Arkansas Mystery Writers Alliance, Mensa.

WRITINGS:

NOVELS

"AURORA TEAGARDEN" MYSTERIES

A Bone to Pick, Walker (New York, NY), 1992.
Three Bedrooms, One Corpse, Scribner (New York, NY), 1994.
The Julius House, Scribner (New York, NY), 1995.
Dead over Heels, Scribner (New York, NY), 1996.
A Fool and His Honey, St. Martin's (New York, NY), 1999.

"LILY BAIRD" MYSTERIES

Shakespeare's Landlord, St. Martin's (New York, NY), 1996.
Shakespeare's Champion, St. Martin's (New York, NY), 1997.
Shakespeare's Christmas, St. Martin's (New York, NY), 1998.
Shakespeare's Trollop, St. Martin's (New York, NY), 2000.

OTHER

Sweet and Deadly, Houghton (Boston), 1980.
A Secret Rage, Houghton (Boston), 1984.
Real Murders, Walker (New York, NY), 1990.

SIDELIGHTS: Charlaine Harris's first novel, *Sweet and Deadly,* concerns the efforts of a journalist to solve the murder of her parents in a small Southern town. "In this small, self-contained world, everyone seems to know everything about the neighbors," declared a *Washington Post* reviewer. The critic praised Harris's handling of racial issues and summed up *Sweet and Deadly* as "more than a well-plotted mystery."

Harris began a successful mystery series with *A Bone to Pick,* featuring Aurora Teagarden, a librarian and amateur detective who returns to her home town in Georgia. The sequel, entitled *Three Bedrooms, One Corpse,* finds

Aurora assisting her mother, a realtor, by showing a house, only to discover the corpse of another realtor inside. A subplot finds Aurora romantically torn between a dependable minister and a mysterious, possibly dangerous businessman. A *Publishers Weekly* reviewer called *Three Bedrooms, One Corpse* a "high-spirited" mystery. In *The Julius House,* Aurora has married and moved into a home which, years before, was the scene of a mysterious disappearance. The past reaches out and she is soon drawn into another mystery, one in which "the author's brisk, upbeat style keeps tension simmering under the everyday surface," according to a *Publishers Weekly* critic. Many critics felt the series reached a new level with *A Fool and His Honey,* which featured an abandoned baby, a mystery drug, and yet another murder. *Booklist* reviewer John Rowen noted that after starting out in a "cozy" style, "Harris ambushes the reader with a stunning ending that carries the impact of Sherlock Holmes falling into the Reichenbach Falls." A *Publishers Weekly* commentator praised the author's "skill and panache."

Harris created a unique new character in Lily Bard, a cleaning lady with a top-flight education and a horrible past. A savage attack years ago has left Lily physically and emotionally scarred, wary of people, and obsessed with self-defense. She lives in the tiny town of Shakespeare, Arkansas. In the debut novel, *Shakespeare's Landlord,* Lily witnesses the disposal of a dead body. Through careful questioning of her clients, Lily begins to unravel the mystery, but she is also being stalked by someone who wants to do her harm. *Shakespeare's Landlord* is a "finely tuned, colorful and suspenseful tale, filled with vigorous and unique characters," according to *Publishers Weekly.* Lily's adventures continue in *Shakespeare's Champion, Shakespeare's Christmas,* and *Shakespeare's Trollop.* The series is praised by several reviewers for its tight plotting and brisk pace, but a *Publishers Weekly* contributor pointed out that "Lily has such an engaging voice, full of pain and redemption, that the collecting of clues and the unfolding of the crime take a back seat to her personal story." Concluded Stuart Miller in *Booklist:* "Lily Bard is one of the best-drawn and most compelling characters in contemporary mystery fiction—complex, smart, streetwise, tough. . . . Harris has reached a new high."

Harris told *CA:* "I have always identified myself as a writer internally, though the evidence didn't appear until last year. I have never wanted to do anything else in my life. I have written at least since I was nine years old. The necessity of earning a bare living kept me from writing full time until I was twenty-seven, which was probably a very good thing. I read about eight books per week, both in and out of my genre.

"I chose to write in the mystery genre because I have always enjoyed mysteries myself. It is a multi-level genre, providing not only an intellectual puzzle, but also a study of life and death, however lightly treated. The mystery is also one of the few truly American art forms."

BIOGRAPHICAL/CRITICAL SOURCES:

PERIODICALS

Armchair Detective, spring, 1995, review of *The Julius House,* p. 211.
Booklist, November 1, 1992, review of *A Bone to Pick,* p. 491; July, 1996, Stuart Miller, review of *Shakespeare's Landlord,* p. 1808; September 15, 1998, review of *Shakespeare's Christmas,* p. 204; September 1, 1999, John Rowen, review of *A Fool and His Honey,* p. 72; May 1, 2000, GraceAnne A. DeCandido, review of *Shakespeare's Trollop,* p. 1599.
Kirkus Reviews, February 15, 1994, review of *Three Bedrooms, One Corpse,* p. 176; December 15, 1994, review of *The Julius House,* p. 1523; June 15, 1996, review of *Shakespeare's Landlord,* p. 860; September 1, 1996, review of *Dead over Heels,* p. 1277; December 1, 1997, review of *Shakespeare's Champion,* p. 1739; October 1, 1998, review of *Shakespeare's Christmas,* p. 1416; August 15, 1999, review of *A Fool and His Honey,* p. 1263; July 1, 2000, review of *Shakespeare's Trollop,* p. 921.
Library Journal, March 1, 1994, review of *Three Bedrooms, One Corpse,* p. 122; January, 1995, review of *The Julius House,* p. 142; October 15, 1996, review of *Shakespeare's Landlord,* p. 112; November 1, 1998, Rex E. Klett, review of *Shakespeare's Christmas,* pp. 127-128; August, 1999, Rex E. Klett, review of *A Fool and His Honey,* p. 145.
Publishers Weekly, September 28, 1992, review of *A Bone to Pick,* p. 67; February 21, 1994, review of *Three Bedrooms, One Corpse,* p. 237; January 9, 1995, review of *The Julius House,* p. 58; June 24, 1996, review of *Shakespeare's Landlord,* p. 48; September 2, 1996, review of *Dead over Heels,* p. 116; October 6, 1997, review of *Shakespeare's Champion,* p. 77; September 7, 1998, review of *Shakespeare's Christmas,* p. 88; August 23, 1999, review of *A Fool and His Honey,* p. 51; July 3, 2000, review of *Shakespeare's Trollop,* p. 52.
Washington Post Book World, July 19, 1981; December 20, 1998, review of *Shakespeare's Christmas,* p. 4.

OTHER

BookBrowser, http://www.bookbrowser.com/(January 24, 1998), Harriet Klausner, review of *Shakespeare's Champion.**

HARRISON-CHURCH, Ronald James 1915-1998

PERSONAL: Born July 26, 1915, in Wimbledon, England; died November 30, 1998; son of James Walter (a schoolmaster) and Jessie May (Fennymore) Church; married Dorothy Violet Harrison (a biology teacher), August 2, 1944; children: Julia Rosalind, Christopher Julian. *Education:* London School of Economics and Political Science, London, B.S., 1936, Ph.D., 1943; Institute of Education, London, diploma in education, 1939; attended University of Paris.

CAREER: University of London, London School of Economics and Political Science, London, England, assistant lecturer, 1944-47, lecturer, 1947-58, reader, 1958-64, professor of geography, 1964-77. University of Wisconsin—Madison, visiting professor, 1956; Indiana University—Bloomington, visiting professor, 1965; University of Tel Aviv, visiting professor, 1972-73; Haifa University, visiting professor, 1972-73; lecturer at Universities of Chicago, Minnesota, Kansas, Kansas City, and Cincinnati, at Syracuse University, and at universities in Brazil, France, Belgium, and Germany. Lecturer and broadcaster in French for the French and African services of British Broadcasting Corp.

AWARDS, HONORS: Back Award from Royal Geographical Society, 1957, for contributions to the economic geography of West Africa.

WRITINGS:

Modern Colonization, Hutchinson, 1951.
West Africa: A Study of the Environment and Man's Use of It, Longmans, Green, 1957, Wiley (New York, NY), 1959, 7th edition, 1974.
Environment and Policies in West Africa, Van Nostrand (New York, NY), 1963, revised edition, 1974.
(With J. I. Clarke, P. J. H. Clarke, and H. J. R. Henderson) *Africa and the Islands,* Wiley (New York, NY), 1964, 3rd edition, Longmans, Green, 1971, Wiley (New York, NY), 1972.
(With Peter Hall, G. R. P. Lawrence, W. R. Mead, and Alice Mutton) *An Advanced Geography of Northern and Western Europe,* Hulton Educational Publications, 1967, 2nd edition, 1973.
Looking at France, Lippincott (Philadelphia, PA), 1970, 2nd edition, 1974.

Contributor to *Africa South of the Sahara;* also contributor to *Encyclopaedia Britannica* and *Chambers's Encyclopaedia.* Contributor to professional journals.

SIDELIGHTS: Ronald James Harrison-Church pursued geography throughout his career, with a particular emphasis on West African issues. His doctoral studies focused on road systems in Africa. Harrison-Church was interested in studying the impacts of the transition from colonialism in general, thus representing a sector of geography called political geography. Between the 1950s and 1970s, he traveled extensively to serve in academic lecture positions in various locations around the world. In the late 1970s he retired due to health issues but continued to lecture with his wife (a botanist) on cruise ships. Harrison-Church visited every country in West Africa except Portuguese Guinea, and traveled in many other African countries, as well as in Europe, Asia, and the Americas.

OBITUARIES:

PERIODICALS

Times (London), December 29, 1998.*

*   *   *

HECHT, Michael L. 1949-

PERSONAL: Born March 15, 1949, in New York, NY; son of Sigmund (in sales) and Mary (a bookkeeper; maiden name, Perlmutter) Hecht; children: J. Rebecca Hecht Kayo, James Jared. *Education:* Queens College of the City University of New York, B.A., 1971, M.A., 1973; University of Illinois at Urbana-Champaign, Ph. D., 1976.

ADDRESSES: Home—2102 East Alameda Dr., Tempe, AZ 85282. *Office*—Department of Communication, Arizona State University, Tempe, AZ 85287-1205.

CAREER: University of Illinois at Urbana-Champaign, Urbana, instructor in communication, 1975-76; University of Montana, Missoula, assistant professor of communication, 1976-78; California State University, Northridge, assistant professor of communication, 1978-79; University of Southern California, Los Angeles, assistant professor of communication, 1979-83; Arizona State University, Tempe, assistant professor, 1983-85, associate professor, 1985-89, professor of communication, 1989-97; Penn State University, professor and department head, 1997—. Xerox Corp., Systemix Division, data analyst and project manager, 1979-81.

Executive producer of the drug prevention videotape *Killing Time,* 1990; producer and writer of the videotape *Homelessness: Everybody's Problem,* 1993; producer of the public access cable production *Kids Broadcasting System News.* City of Fountain Valley, member of gifted education advisory board, 1981-83; Tri-City Community Behavioral Health, member of citizens' advisory board, 1984-90; community youth baseball and basketball coach.

MEMBER: International Communication Association, International Network for the Study of Personal Relationships, World Communication Association, Speech Communication Association, Society for Intercultural Education, Training, and Research, Western Speech Communication Association (chair of Interpersonal Interest Group, 1984-85).

AWARDS, HONORS: Access Producers Achievement Award, Dickenson Cablesystems, 1982, for *Kids Broadcasting System News;* scholar, Speech Communication Association, 1990; Silver Medal, Questar Competition, and finalist, International Film and Video Festival of New York, both 1991, for *Killing Time;* Article of the Year Award, Society for Intercultural Education, Training, and Research, 1991, for "A Mexican American Perspective on Interethnic Communication"; grants from National Institute on Drug Abuse, U.S. Department of Education, Pinal Hispanic Council, and Center for Substance Abuse Treatment.

WRITINGS:

(Editor, with J. A. DeVito, and contributor) *The Nonverbal Communication Reader,* Waveland, 1989.
(Editor, with S. Petronio, J. K. Alberts, and J. L. Buley, and contributor) *Contemporary Perspectives on Interpersonal Communication,* Brown & Benchmark, 1993.
(With M. J. Collier and S. Ribeau) *African American Communication,* Sage Publications (Newbury Park, CA), 1993.
(Editor) *Communicating Prejudice,* Sage Publications (Newbury Park, CA), 1998.
(Contributor) *Adolescent Relationships and Drug Abuse,* Erlbaum (New York, NY), 2000.

Work represented in anthologies, including *Small Group Communication: A Reader,* edited by R. S. Cathcart and L. A. Samovar, W. C. Brown, 1988; *Handbook of Intercultural Communication,* edited by M. K. Asanti and W.

B. Gudykunst, Sage Publications (newbury Park, CA), 1989; and *Communication and Relationship Maintenance,* edited by D. J. Canary and L. Stafford, Academic Press, 1994. Contributor of more than forty articles to communication and social science journals. Member of editorial board, *Communication Education,* 1985-90, *Communication Reports,* 1986-91, *Management Communication Quarterly,* 1989-91, *Western Journal of Speech Communication,* 1990-93, *Journal of Social and Personal Relations,* 1990—, and *Communication Monographs,* 1992—.

WORK IN PROGRESS: Research on African-American communication, Jewish-American identity, romantic love, and communication, and drug resistance strategies.

SIDELIGHTS: Michael L. Hecht told *CA:* "I write about a variety of topics involving communication and social relationships. This work is guided by the desire to understand the people in the world around me. I started writing about communication in graduate school, encouraged by mentors like Joseph DeVito, and found I enjoyed the creative process.

"When I first began to write about communication, I focused on the people around me, mostly college students. I soon found that I could not get a rich understanding of the world through the eyes of such a narrow spectrum of our society. As a result, my work has enlarged across different ethnic and age groups, as well as across geographical regions. I want to describe how people interpret their social relationships and interactions: what makes communication and relationships work, what obstacles present themselves and how people deal with them, what links people and what keeps them apart."

*   *   *

HERMAN, Barbara 1945-

PERSONAL: Born May 9, 1945, in New York, NY; daughter of Robert and Ruth Herman; married Miles Morgan, 1974; children: Daniel. *Education:* Cornell University, B.A., 1966; Harvard University, M.A., 1967, Ph.D., 1976.

ADDRESSES: Home—468 North Flores St., Los Angeles, CA 90048. *Office*—Department of Philosophy, University of California, Los Angeles, CA 90024.

CAREER: Massachusetts Institute of Technology, Cambridge, assistant professor of philosophy, 1973-80; University of Southern California, Los Angeles, visiting assistant professor, 1980-81, assistant professor, 1981-84, associate professor, 1984-92, professor of philosophy and law, 1992-94; University of California, Los Angeles, Griffin Professor of Philosophy, 1994—, and department head. Princeton University, visiting associate professor, 1987. California Council for the Humanities, member, 1991-93; Charlotte Newcombe Fellowship Program, member of philosophy panel, 1992—; American Academy of Pediatrics, member of Bioethics Committee, 1989-91. Editor, *Pacific Philosophical Quarterly,* 1982-92; associate editor, *Ethics,* 1992—.

MEMBER: American Philosophical Association.

AWARDS, HONORS: Guggenheim fellow, 1985-86; Perkins fellow, Princeton University, 1987; fellow, National Endowment for the Humanities, 1992.

WRITINGS:

Morality and Rationality: A Study of Kant's Ethics, Garland Publishing (New York City), 1990.
(Contributor) Amelie Rorty and Owen Flanagan, editors, *Identity, Character, and Morality,* MIT Press (Cambridge, MA), 1990.
(Contributor) John Deigh, editor, *Ethics and Personality,* University of Chicago Press (Chicago, IL), 1992.
The Practice of Moral Judgment, Harvard University Press (Cambridge), 1993.
(Contributor) Louise Antony and Charlotte Witt, editors, *A Mind of One's Own,* Westview (Boulder, CO), 1993.
(Contributor) D. Heyd, editor, *Toleration: An Elusive Virtue,* Princeton University Press (Princeton, NJ), 1995.
(Editor with Andrews Reath and Christine M. Korsgaard) *Reclaiming the History of Ethics: Essays for John Rawls,* Cambridge University Press (New York City), 1997.
(Editor) John Rawls, *Lectures on the History of Moral Philosophy,* Harvard University Press, 2000.

Contributor to philosophy journals, including *Ethics* and *Philosophical Review.*

BIOGRAPHICAL/CRITICAL SOURCES:

PERIODICALS

Kirkus Reviews, August 15, 2000, review of *Lectures on the History of Moral Philosophy,* p. 1177.*

HERSH, Seymour M. 1937-

PERSONAL: Born April 8, 1937, in Chicago, IL; son of Isadore and Dorothy (Margolis) Hersh; married Elizabeth Sarah Klein (a physician), May 31, 1964; children: Matthew, Melissa, Joshua. *Education:* University of Chicago, B.A., 1958, graduate study, 1959.

ADDRESSES: Home—3214 Newark St. N.W., Washington, DC 20008-3345. *Office*—Suite 320, 1211 Connecticut Ave. NW, Ste. 320, Washington, DC 20036.

CAREER: City News Bureau, Chicago, IL, police reporter, 1959-60; United Press International, correspondent in Pierre, SD, 1962-63; Associated Press, correspondent in Chicago and Washington, DC, 1963-67; *New York Times,* reporter in Washington, DC bureau, 1972-75 and 1979, in New York City, 1975-78; writer, 1979—. Press secretary to Senator Eugene J. McCarthy during presidential campaign, 1968. Correspondent, *New Yorker* magazine, 1993—.

AWARDS, HONORS: George Polk Award, Worth Bingham prize, Sigma Delta Chi distinguished service award, and Pulitzer Prize for international reporting, all 1970, all for stories on the My Lai massacre; *My Lai Four* was named one of the best nonfiction books of the year by *Time,* 1970; Front Page Award, Scripps-Howard service award, and George Polk Award, all 1973, all for stories on bombing in Cambodia; Sidney Hillman Award and George Polk Award, both 1974, both for stories on CIA domestic spying; John Peter Zenger Freedom of the Press award and Drew Pearson Prize, both 1975, for stories on CIA involvement in Chile; George Polk Award and Sigma Delta Chi distinguished service award, both 1981, for *New York Times Magazine* articles on the role of ex-CIA men in training Libyan terrorists; *Los Angeles Times* book prize in biography, National Book Critics Circle Award in general nonfiction, Sydney Hillman Award, and Investigative Reporters and Editors (IRE) Award, all 1983, all for *The Price of Power; IRE Award, 1996, for The Samson Option.*

WRITINGS:

Chemical and Biological Warfare: America's Hidden Arsenal, Bobbs-Merrill, 1968.
My Lai Four: A Report on the Massacre and Its Aftermath, Random House, 1970.
Cover-Up: The Army's Secret Investigation of the Massacre of My Lai Four, Random House, 1972.

Seymour M. Hersh

The Price of Power: Kissinger in the Nixon White House, Summit, 1983.

"The Target Is Destroyed": What Really Happed to Flight 007 and What America Knew about It, Random House, 1986.

The Samson Option: Israel's Nuclear Arsenal and American Foreign Policy, Random House, 1991.

The Dark Side of Camelot, Little, Brown, 1997.

Against All Enemies: Gulf War Syndrome; The War between America's Ailing Veterans and Their Government, Ballantine, 1999.

Also author of television documentary *Buying the Bomb,* first produced on Public Broadcasting Service (PBS-TV), March 5, 1985.

SIDELIGHTS: Seymour M. Hersh first gained prominence as an investigative reporter in November, 1969 when he broke the story of the My Lai massacre in Vietnam. Initially refused by several publishers, the series was eventually picked up by the independent Dispatch News Service and earned Hersh a Pulitzer Prize for international reporting as well as several other prestigious awards. With these credentials, which were bolstered by his two critically acclaimed books on the

massacre and its cover-up, Hersh was able to land a full-time reporting job at the *New York Times.* According to *Washington Post* contributor Richard Lee, he soon became their "ace investigative reporter . . . , virtually a world unto himself at the paper, breaking important stories about the CIA's domestic intelligence activities, the secret bombing of North Vietnam, and Kissinger's wiretapping of his closest aides at the State Department."

In 1977, Summit Books editor Jim Silberman approached Hersh about doing a whole book on Henry Kissinger, but, convinced that the story was "old" news, Hersh initially declined, Silberman persisted, finally convincing Hersh that an outsider's viewpoint was needed to balance the "official" memoirs that were then appearing in such abundance. Shortly thereafter, Hersh left the *Times*—which did not then grant leaves of absence—and devoted himself wholeheartedly to the project, traveling all over the world to interview those who had worked with Kissinger in his role as national security adviser. The result was *The Price of Power: Kissinger in the Nixon White House,* a massive book almost four years in the making that made headlines for its controversial portrayal of a power-hungry Kissinger.

Originally conceived as a study of Kissinger, the book soon shifted focus to include Richard Nixon. "It started out as the foreign policy of Kissinger," Hersh told Lee. "It became Kissinger and Nixon. It started out, let's get a look at the policy, and gradually developed," Hersh explained. Suspecting that the duplicity uncovered in the Watergate scandal was also a factor in foreign affairs, Hersh set out "to prove that Kissinger and Nixon were two peas in a pod, and the pod was in the sewer," according to *Village Voice* reviewer Eliot Fremont-Smith. *Newsweek* reviewer Peter S. Prescott believed "the purpose of [Hersh's] book is to document Kissinger's excesses, and what he believes they cost our country—in terms of human life and the nation's honor and security." In his interview with Richard Lee, Hersh described his goal this way: "This is a book about how people and personalities shape policy incredibly more than you think. Personalities, prejudices, and people. . . . It says some very, very important decisions are made for reasons that stagger the imagination."

Working from information he collected during almost a thousand interviews, from archives made available under the Freedom of Information Act, and from both Kissinger's and Nixon's memoirs, Hersh compiles a long list of sins. One of the most damaging allegations is that Kissinger worked both sides of the street in the

1968 campaign, "feeding secret information about the Paris peace talks to the Nixon campaign after offering the Humphrey forces Nelson Rockefeller's derogatory files on Nixon," in *Newsweek* reporter Jonathan Alter's words. In this way, Kissinger was able to ingratiate himself with both parties, thus assuring himself an appointment regardless of who won.

Such double dealing was a way of life for Kissinger, according to Hersh, who argues that the foreign policy that emerged under Nixon's administration was the product of two deeply flawed personalities. "Nixon had a consuming need for flattery and Kissinger a consuming need to provide it," he writes in *The Price of Power*. At times their collusion may have brought the world dangerously close to nuclear war. As evidence, Hersh offers the case of the president's "madman" theory, explained by Walter LeFeber in the *Washington Post Book World*: "State and CIA knew the [Vietnam] war could not be won. But Nixon disagreed. He and Kissinger quickly settled in 1969 'on the one overriding principle that would guide Vietnam policy for the next four years: South Vietnam must remain non-Communist forever.' They would accomplish the impossible by bombing relentlessly. 'Tell those sons of bitches,' Nixon instructed Kissinger, 'that the President is a madman and you don't know how to deal with him.' The 'madman's' first step in Indochina was secret massive bombings of Cambodia, where the North Vietnamese had bases."

Unwilling to restrict his criticisms to the secret Cambodian bombings or other recognized blunders, Hersh also faults what many consider Kissinger and Nixon's foreign policy successes—the SALT treaty with the Soviets, the Berlin agreement, and the opening of China to name a few. Writing in the *Nation*, Alan Wolfe described *The Price of Power* as "a blood-hound tracking Kissinger, sniffing his every statement, following his every move, and at pauses in the action, waiting, just waiting, for him to take the next step. It will long serve as the official record of the major foreign policy atrocities of the Nixon years." And yet, Wolfe surmises that "Hersh's relentlessness . . . ultimately weakens his prosecutorial style, if not his case. Like a college debater, he is determined to take the opposite position no matter how ridiculous. . . . You have to hate Kissinger an awful lot to sympathize with the right-wing critique of SALT I or to adopt the China Lobby position on recognition of Peking. Hersh does, and there is no reason for it, political or literary. An evil man who did no good would be unworthy of the epic treatment Hersh gives Kissinger."

While asserting that many of Hersh's charges are "valid," *New York Times Book Review* contributor Stanley Hoffmann took exception to the author's sources. "While many of them chose to remain anonymous . . . , a large number are named. They are, on the whole, losers of bureaucratic battles or men who resigned from the N[ational] S[ecurity] C[ouncil] staff because of political or moral differences with Government policy or Mr. Kissinger's long-time opponents. . . . Many of these informants are honorable men, but it would be surprising if what emerged from their anecdotes and complaints amounted to the whole story." *Times Literary Supplement* reviewer Adam Watson expressed a similar view: "Since Kissinger made a large number of bitter personal enemies and trod on a great many toes, and since American officials are often ready to pass judgment on their political bosses, it was not difficult for someone as diligent and as skilled in defamatory investigation as Hersh to assemble a very formidable battery of disgruntled and critical comment. He fires this mass of testimony by hostile witnesses at the reader against a background of narrative designed to show that Kissinger was petty, jealous, vain, a lickspittle, a liar and a cheat. . . . But soon the long and very detailed litany of allegation and suggestion becomes wearisome, in the same way as the succession of sexual escapades in pornographic fiction. Indeed, the book, for all its guise of seriousness, is political pornography, which excites some readers until they are sated and fills others with accumulating disgust."

New York Times reviewer Christopher Lehmann-Haupt, on the other hand, asserted, "this is a book that doesn't just gossip and tattle, but reconstructs four years of American foreign policy in far greater detail than Mr. Nixon did in his own official memoirs, and almost rivals the exhaustiveness of Mr. Kissinger's two volumes. . . . This is a book that through its factual density avoids the typically hectoring tone of the investigative reporter or the ideologue with an axe to grind. Indeed, Mr. Hersh manages to sound like a historian, a morally objective one at that." *Newsweek*'s Peter S. Prescott concluded that "on balance . . . Hersh proves his case many times over." And *Chicago Tribune Book World* contributor Harry Ashmore said that while "publication was greeted with instant charges of partisan character assassination, . . . my own reading yields no suspicion of personal malice. 'The Price of Power' is unique among exposes of this kind in its sparing use of anonymous sources and its identification of obviously subjective judgments, in footnotes and end papers."

While Hersh's uncovering of My Lai was considered groundbreaking, his 1991 book *The Samson Option: Israel's Nuclear Arsenal and American Foreign Policy,* "is less startling," said an *Economist* reviewer, "for an obvious reason: Israel's possession of nuclear weapons is one of the worst-kept secrets in the world." As early as 1970 the *Times* had reported on Israel's growing arsenal of bombs and missiles; that news was further developed in a 1986 piece produced for Britain's *Sunday Times.*

Still, Hersh's whose "reputation for meticulous research and accuracy" merits *The Samson Option* some serious attention, according to Maclean's contributor William Lowther. Not only does the book "purport to expose the Israeli nuclear program, but it also sheds new light on the notorious Jonathan Jay Pollard spy case" and alleges that a leading British journalist—who once received photographs of a weapons facility from Mordechai Vanunu, an expatriate Israeli defense worker—was an undercover agent of Mossad, the Israeli secret service agency. In allegations Davies and publisher Robert Maxwell denied, Hersh writes that the two conspired to betray Vanunu: "Lured to Rome by a pretty Mossad agent," Lowther related, "Vanunu was kidnapped, drugged and returned to Israel, where he was sentenced to 18 years in prison." (Publisher Maxwell was discovered drowned near his yacht off the Canary Islands soon after the publication of *The Samson Option.*)

For an investigator like Hersh, suggested Lawrence Freedman in a *New York Times Book Review* piece, "the story of the Israeli bomb must have appeared as a ripening plum just waiting to be picked." With this work "he seizes the opportunity, and manages in a readable and fascinating account to convey a keen sense of the dynamic propelling Israel's nuclear program."

An altogether different kind of reaction greeted Hersh's 1997 book *The Dark Side of Camelot.* In this volume Hersh portrays President John F. Kennedy as a chief executive whose tenure was marked by numerous indiscretions. The book covers various topics: JFK's alleged liaisons with prostitutes and mistresses, the attempted assassination of Cuba's Fidel Castro, and the Kennedy administration's links to organized crime.

The release of *Camelot* set off a firestorm of controversy. There was a lengthy *New York Times* article accusing Hersh of falling prey to a set of forged documents supposedly detailing a hush-money payoff to alleged Kennedy mistress Marilyn Monroe. That was followed by features in *New Yorker* and *Vanity Fair* also portraying Hersh as duped—even though, as Jacob Weisberg pointed out in an online *Slate* article, the author never

mentioned the documents in his book. *Time* magazine checked in with a JFK cover story asking "how believable is [Hersh's] new book?" The author also endured what Weisberg called "a two-day grilling" on NBC's *Today Show* "that seemed like payback for the time and money NBC had wasted on a documentary it abandoned because of suspicions about the forged papers."

Then there were the reviews of *Camelot,* which leaned toward the negative. "Some of the backlash can be ascribed to accumulated resentment against Hersh, widely regarded as talented but surly," noted Michael Rust. Writing for *Insight on the News,* Rust continued: "Still, reviewers have often painted the book as nothing more than a collection of highbrow gossip."

This is not true, Rust asserted. "There is much useful information in [Camelot] and it is hard to imagine future chroniclers of the New Frontier ignoring the work. Hersh has produced a readable if not always convincing chronicle of Kennedy misdeeds. His goal, he makes clear at the beginning, is to show that character flaws have real consequences." Likewise, Weisberg declared that while Hersh "does hyperventilate from time to time," the author "still manages to present his case in roughly the way a fair-minded historian or journalist should. He includes enough contrary evidence that readers can disagree with his conclusions without doing their own research elsewhere."

BIOGRAPHICAL/CRITICAL SOURCES:

BOOKS

Authors in the News, Volume 1, Gale (Detroit, MI), 1976;

PERIODICALS

Bloomsbury Review, January-February, 2000, Donald K. Gutierrez, review of *Against All Enemies,* p. 3.
Chicago Tribune Book World, April 2, 1972; June 19, 1983.
Detroit Free Press, February 23, 1975.
Economist, October 26, 1991, review of *The Samson Option,* p. 111.
Foreign Affairs, May-June, 1998, David C. Hendrickson, review of *The Dark Side of Camelot,* p. 140.
Insight on the News, January 26, 1998, Michael Rust, review of *The Dark Side of Camelot,* p. 36.

Maclean's, November 18, 1991, William Lowther, review of *The Samson Option,* p. 81.

Michigan Daily, August 13, 1983.

Nation, July 23, 1983; December 9 1991, Alexander Cockburn, ". . . And Egg on the Face of the Tiger," p. 73.

National Review, August 19, 1983; December 22, 1997, William F. Buckley, Jr., "How to Handle Hersh?," p. 74.

New Republic, August 1, 1983.

Newsweek, June 13, 1983; June 20, 1983.

New York Times, May 6, 1970; June 9, 1983.

New York Times Book Review, June 14, 1970; March 26, 1972; July 3, 1983; September 9, 1986, Christopher Lehmann-Haupt, review of *The Target Is Destroyed;* November 17, 1991, Lawrence Freedman, "What Do They Have, and When Did We Know It?"

People, October 6, 1986, Montgomery Brower, "Reporter Seymour Hersh Unravels the Tragic Mystery of Flight 007," p. 57.

Saturday Review, May 30, 1970; April 1, 1972.

Time, November 17, 1997, Alan Brinkley, review of *The Dark Side of Camelot,* p. 50.

Times Literary Supplement, October 28, 1983.

Village Voice, June 21, 1983.

Washington Post, April 27, 1982.

Washington Post Book World, June 12, 1983.

OTHER

Slate, http://slate.msn.com/, (November 13, 1997), Jacob Weisberg, "JFK TKO-Seymour Hersh's Book is Better than the Critics Say It Is." *

*   *   *

HEYES, (Nancy) Eileen 1956-

PERSONAL: Born August 10, 1956, in Los Angeles, CA; daughter of William, Jr. (an engineer) and Helen Gwendolyn Califf (a registered nurse) Heyes; married Rob Waters (an editor), April 6, 1986; children: Jeremy Warren, Christopher Benton. *Education:* California State University, Long Beach, B.A. (with honors), 1980. *Politics:* Independent. *Avocational interests:* Raising children, gardening, running.

ADDRESSES: Home—Raleigh, NC. *Office*—c/o Millbrook Press, 2 Old New Milford Rd., P.O. Box 335, Brookfield, CT 06804-0335. *E-mail*—HeyesWaters@ mindspring.com.

CAREER: Los Angeles Times, Costa Mesa, CA, copy editor, 1979-81; *Aptos Post,* Aptos, CA, news editor, 1981-82; *Desert Sun,* Palm Springs, CA, staff writer, 1982; *Orange County Register,* Santa Ana, CA, copy editor, 1982-84; *Los Angeles Times,* Los Angeles, CA, electronic publishing copy editor, 1984-86, features section copy editor, 1986-90, copy editor of San Fernando Valley and Ventura County editions, 1991-93, business section copy editor, 1993-94; *News & Observer,* Raleigh, NC, copy editor, 1994—, children's book review columnist, 1995—. Freelance writer, 1990—.

MEMBER: Society of Children's Book Writers and Illustrators, Authors Guild.

AWARDS, HONORS: Citations in "Books for the Teen Age," New York Public Library, for *Children of the Swastika: The Hitler Youth* and *Adolf Hitler; Children of the Swastika* was selected as a "children's book of the year" by Child Study Council.

WRITINGS:

Children of the Swastika: The Hitler Youth (young adult), Millbrook Press (Brookfield, CT), 1993.

Adolf Hitler (young adult), Millbrook Press (Brookfield, CT), 1994.

Tobacco U.S.A.: The Industry behind the Smoke Curtain (young adult), Twenty-first Century, 1999.

Contributor of articles to magazines and newspapers, including *Los Angeles Times, Seattle Times,* and *Publishers Weekly.*

WORK IN PROGRESS: Two picture books; a young adult novel set in postwar East Germany; a middle-grade mystery series set in Depression-era New York.

SIDELIGHTS: Eileen Heyes once told *CA: "Children of the Swastika: The Hitler Youth* came to be written almost by accident. I was researching the Hitler Youth for a historical novel about a girl who grew up in Nazi Germany and after the war must face up to what she has been a part of. It quickly became apparent to me just how sinister the Hitler Youth was, and how calculated. It very deliberately took everything that is good and right about teenagers—the idealism, the competitive spirit, the desire to change the world—and twisted it. Here was something with a message that was universal, and I found little children's literature on the subject."

Heyes later added: "After I finished writing *Children of the Swastika,* Millbrook Press asked me to write a biography of Hitler for young adults, and I did.

"*Tobacco U.S.A.: The Industry behind the Smoke Curtain* sprouted (pun intended!) from a conversation with my publisher at Millbrook. After we'd discussed and discarded several book ideas, I noted that I was living in North Carolina and suggested, 'How about something on tobacco?' She liked the idea, and what had been merely an interesting topic for me became an obsession for the next year. I wanted to write a book that could not have been written by any other writer living anywhere else. I spent hours in tobacco fields, listening to farmers. I walked along with an auctioneer as the cured tobacco was sold to cigarette companies' agents. I interviewed a cancer survivor, an anti-tobacco lobbyist, a teenage activist. The result, I hope, is an agenda-free book that brings clarity to a very complex issue, so that young readers are better equipped to understand what they read in the newspaper and to make their own informed decisions.

"I feel a kinship with teenagers because they are at an age where life's major issues are coming into focus. It's scary, it's exhilarating, it's the most vulnerable time in our lives. The hurts and the discoveries of teen years last forever.

"I want my books to raise at least as many questions as they answer. From questions, truth emerges. From mistakes, good judgment develops. Young readers need these things more than they need any particular worldview stuffed into their heads."

BIOGRAPHICAL/CRITICAL SOURCES:

PERIODICALS

Booklist, February 15, 1993; March 1, 1993, p. 1221; December 15, 1999.
Book Report, May-June, 1993; January-February, 1995.
Children's Book Review, winter, 1993.
Kirkus Reviews, January 1, 1993, p. 61.
School Library Journal, November, 1994; January, 2000.
Voice of Youth Advocates, June, 1993.

*   *   *

HOFF, Joan 1937-
(Joan Hoff-Wilson)

PERSONAL: Born June 27, 1937, in Butte, MT; married in 1961. *Education:* University of Montana, B.A., 1957; Cornell University, M.A., 1959; University of California at Berkeley, Ph.D., 1966.

ADDRESSES: Office—Ohio University Contemporary History Institute, 102 Brown House, Athens, OH 45701-2979. *E-mail*—hoffj@oak.cats.ohiou.edu.

CAREER: California State University at Sacramento, assistant professor of U.S. diplomatic history, 1967-70; Arizona State University, Tempe, associate professor, 1970-76, professor of U.S. foreign relations, 1976-81; Indiana University at Bloomington, professor of history and foreign relations, 1981-95; Center for the Study of the Presidency, New York City, president and chief executive officer, 1995-97; Ohio University at Athens, professor of history and director of Contemporary History Institute, 1997—. Visiting scholar, Harvard Law School 1976-77, Brookings Institute, 1979, Woodrow Wilson International Center for Scholars, 1980, and University College, Dublin, 1992-93. Cofounder and editor, *Journal of Women's History,* 1989-96.

MEMBER: Organization of American Historians, American Historical Association, Conference on Peace Research in History, Coordinating Committee on Women in the Historical Profession (president, 1978-80), Society of Historians of American Foreign Relations.

AWARDS, HONORS: Grant from Penrose Fund, American Philosophical Society, 1968; Stuart L. Bernath Book Prize from Society of Historians of American Foreign Relations, 1972, for *American Business and Foreign Policy, 1920-1933;* National Endowment for the Humanities fellowship, 1973-74, grant, 1975-77; fellow of Radcliffe Institute, 1976-77; Berkshire Article Award, Berkshire Conference of Women Historians, 1977; Guggenheim fellowship, 1981-82; Fulbright fellowships, 1986 and 1992-93; certificate for editorial excellence from Council of Editors of Learned Journals, 1990, for *Journal of Women's History.*

WRITINGS:

American Business and Foreign Policy, 1920-1933, University Press of Kentucky (Lexington, KY), 1971.
(Editor) *The Twenties: The Critical Issues,* Little, Brown (Boston, MA), 1971.
Ideology and Economics: U.S. Relations with the Soviet Union, 1918-1933, University of Missouri Press (Columbia, MO), 1974.
(Editor) *Report on the West Coast Women's Studies Conference,* Know, Inc. (Pittsburgh, PA), 1974.

Herbert Hoover: Forgotten Progressive, Little, Brown (Boston, MA), 1975.

(With Albie Sachs) *Sexism and the Law: A Study of Male Beliefs and Legal Bias in Britain and the United States,* Martin Robertson, 1978, Free Press (New York, NY), 1979.

(Editor, with Ellis W. Hawley and Robert Zieger) *Herbert Hoover as Secretary of Commerce, 1921-1928: Studies in New Era Thought and Practice,* University of Iowa Press (Iowa City, IA), 1981.

(Editor, under name Joan Hoff-Wilson, with Marjorie Lightman) *Without Precedent: The Life and Career of Eleanor Roosevelt,* Indiana University Press (Bloomington, IN), 1984.

(Editor, under name Joan Hoff-Wilson) *Rights of Passage: The Past and Future of the ERA,* Indiana University Press (Bloomington, IN), 1986.

Wellington's Marriage: A Soldier's Wife, Weidenfeld & Nicolson (London, England), 1987.

(Editor, with Susan Gubar) *For Adult Users Only: The Dilemma of Violent Pornography,* Indiana University Press (Bloomington, IN), 1989.

Law, Gender, and Injustice: A Legal History of U.S. Women, New York University (New York, NY), 1991.

Watergate Revisited, East Carolina University (Greenville, NC), 1993.

Nixon Reconsidered, Basic Books (New York, NY), 1994.

(Editor, with Moureen Coulter) *Voices of Irish Women: Past and Present,* Indiana University Press (Bloomington, IN), 1995.

(Editor, with Robert Ferrell) *Dictionary of American History, Supplement H,* Scribner (New York, NY), 1996.

(With Marian Yeates) *The Cooper's Wife Is Missing: The Trials of Bridget Cleary,* Basic Books (New York, NY), 2000.

Editor, *Presidential Studies Quarterly,* 1996—. Contributor to periodicals, including *Human Rights.*

SIDELIGHTS: Historian Joan Hoff has wide-ranging interests as an editor and author. She has written books on the history of the Soviet Union, on the legal status of women in the twentieth century, and on two Republican presidents, Herbert Hoover and Richard M. Nixon. As director of Ohio University's Contemporary History Institute, and as founding editor of the prestigious *Journal of Women's History,* Hoff is in a position to shape the scholarly study of modern issues in America and abroad. In a profile of Hoff released on the Ohio University Web site, she noted her preferences as a teacher and writer. "The history I'm interested in is not usually popular or in the mainstream," she commented. "I bring to all my work a strong materialist interpretation because my books on politics are driven by economics."

In the late 1980s Hoff was invited to interview Richard Nixon on the subject of his presidency. She spent long hours with the former president and also conducted research and interviews with Nixon's associates, in an effort to judge Nixon without the bias engendered by the Watergate scandal. Her appraisal, published in 1994 as *Nixon Reconsidered,* offers a detailed assessment of Nixon's domestic and foreign policies, concluding that he was stronger on the domestic front and sadly lacking in foreign policy, especially toward Southeast Asia and the Third World. In the *New York Times Book Review,* Richard Norton Smith wrote: "Ms. Hoff's basic contention—that Nixon's claim to favorable historical treatment rests on his domestic policies rather than his more widely praised foreign expertise—is not new. . . . What sets this book apart is its exhaustive research and the provocative intellectual framework within which the Nixon Presidency is assessed." In a *Booklist* review of *Nixon Reconsidered,* Gilbert Taylor concluded: "Harsh though she can be, Hoff maintains scrupulous fairness in arguing for 'restrained rehabilitation.'"

The Cooper's Wife Is Missing: The Trials of Bridget Cleary, which Hoff co-authored with Marian Yeates, is a scholarly account of the late-nineteenth-century murder of Bridget Cleary, an Irishwoman who was purported to have been possessed by fairies. Cleary's torture-murder at the hands of her husband and family is considered the last death for witchcraft in Europe's history. Hoff and Yeates examine the broad implications of the celebrated event and the subsequent trials of those implicated in the murder, revealing the cultural, social, and political fallout that literally shaped the history of Ireland. *Publishers Weekly* correspondent Dermot McEvoy noted that the authors "have captured the political climate of the last half of the 19th century as few writers have." In a separate *Publishers Weekly* review of the work, a critic concluded that it "brings new clarity and perspective to an important moment in Irish history."

BIOGRAPHICAL/CRITICAL SOURCES:

PERIODICALS

American Historical Review, February, 1974, p. 246; October, 1975, p. 1056; October, 1976, p. 800; April, 1985, p. 510.

Booklist, August, 1994, Gilbert Taylor, review of *Nixon Reconsidered,* p. 2081; September 15, 2000, Mary Carroll, review of *The Cooper's Wife Is Missing: The Ritual Murder of Bridget Cleary,* p. 193.

Historian, spring, 1996, Mitchell K. Hall, review of *Nixon Reconsidered,* p. 645.

History, October, 1985, p. 471.

Journal of American History, March, 1985, p. 896.

Journal of Interdisciplinary History, summer, 1996, James L. Baughman, review of *Nixon Reconsidered,* p. 172.

New Republic, February 19, 1990, Alan Wolfe, review of *For Adult Users Only: The Dilemma of Violent Pornography,* pp. 27-31.

New York Review of Books, July 14, 1994, Theodore Draper, review of *Nixon Reconsidered,* p. 26.

New York Times Book Review, August 17, 1975, p. 19; October 30, 1994, Richard Norton Smith, "The Nixon Watch Continues," p. 9; October 8, 2000, David Willis McCullough, "The Fairy Defense."

Publishers Weekly, June 27, 1994, review of *Nixon Reconsidered,* p. 64; August 7, 2000, Dermot McEvoy, "The 'Fairy' Tale of Another Bridget," p. 20; August 7, 2000, review of *The Cooper's Wife Is Missing: The Ritual Murder of Bridget Cleary,* p. 87.

Times Literary Supplement, November 19, 1987, p. 1256.

Yale Review, April, 1992, Sara Suleri, review of *For Adult Users Only: The Dilemma of Violent Pornography,* p. 197.

OTHER

Forum, http://www-as.phy.ohiou.edu/forum/(spring, 1998), "Joan Hoff Joins History Department."

Ohio University Website, http://www.ohiou.edu/ (October 18, 2000).*

*　　　*　　　*

HOFF-WILSON, Joan
　　See WILSON, Joan Hoff

*　　　*　　　*

HONDERICH, Ted 1933-

PERSONAL: Born January 30, 1933, in Baden, Ontario, Canada; son of John William (a pamphleteer and printer) and Rae Laura (a teacher; maiden name Armstrong) Honderich; married third wife, Jane O'Grady, 1989; children: Kiaran, John Ruan. *Education:* University of Toronto, B.A., 1959; University of London, Ph.D., 1969. *Politics:* Socialist. *Religion:* None.

ADDRESSES: Home—4 Keats Grove, Hampstead, London NW3 2RT, England. *E-mail*—t.honderich@ucl.ac. uk.

CAREER: Previously lecturer at University of Sussex, Sussex, England; University of London, University College, London, England, 1964, began as lecturer and reader in department of philosophy, professor of philosophy, currently Grote Professor Emeritus of the Philosophy of Mind and Logic. Visiting professor at Yale University and City University of New York, 1970-71.

WRITINGS:

Punishment: The Supposed Justifications, Harcourt, 1969, revised edition, Penguin (New York, NY), 1971, Polity Press, 1989.

(Editor) *Essays on Freedom of Action,* Routledge & Kegan Paul, 1973.

(Editor) *Social Ends and Political Means,* Routledge & Kegan Paul, 1976.

Three Essays on Political Violence, Basil Blackwell, 1977, revised and expanded edition published as *Violence for Equality: Inquiries in Political Philosophy, Incorporating Three Essays on Political Violence,* Penguin (New York, NY), 1980.

(Editor) *Philosophy as It Is,* Penguin (New York, NY), 1979.

(Editor) *Morality and Objectivity,* Routledge & Kegan Paul, 1984.

(Editor) *Philosophy through Its Past,* Penguin (New York, NY), 1984.

A Theory of Determinism: The Mind, Neuroscience, and Life-Hopes, Oxford University Press (Oxford, England), 1988.

Mind and Brain, originally published as part of *A Theory of Determinism: Th Mind, Neuroscience, and Life-Hopes,* Oxford University Press (Oxford, England), 1990.

Conservatism, Hamish Hamilton, 1990.

How Free Are You?: The Determinism Problem, Oxford University Press (Oxford, England), 1993.

(Editor) *The Oxford Companion to Philosophy,* Oxford University Press (Oxford, England), 1995.

(Editor) *The Philosophers: Introducing Great Western Thinkers,* Oxford University Press (Oxford, England), 1999.

Philosopher: A Kind of Life, Routledge, 2000.

Contributor of articles to books and periodicals. Editor, *International Library of Philosophy and Scientific Method, The Arguments of the Philosophers,* and *The Problems of Philosophy.*

WORK IN PROGRESS: Current interests include the philosophy of mind—relation of mind to brain.

SIDELIGHTS: Philosopher Ted Honderich is a respected voice in his field, having written or edited several volumes on philosophy and its practitioners. His 1980 study, *Violence for Equality: Inquiries in Political Philosophy,* was labeled a "courageous swim against the current" of political thought by reviewer Laurie Taylor in the London *Times.* A series of essays, the book examines the targets of violence in Britain and the feasibility of fomenting social change or "rectify[ing] social imbalances" through violent acts. The work also considers the moral dilemmas of determining which circumstances justify the use of illegal force to end miseries that remain unchecked by conventional government action.

Among Honderich's more generally accessible works is *The Oxford Companion to Philosophy,* for which he served as editor. Comprised of nearly two thousand entries from more than two hundred contributors, the book is intended to be both a complete reference work and a volume that general readers will find "amiable" and "diverting." Critics differed, however, on how well Honderich succeeded in this aim. Ward Jones, in the *Times Literary Supplement,* wrote that "This combination of goals pulls the *Companion* in opposite directions." Jones appreciated the more entertaining elements in the book, but argued that they detracted from its scholarly rigor and placed more emphasis on personalities than on the actual subject of philosophy. "Its entertainment value exceeds its reference value," Ward concluded. *New Statesman and Society* reviewer Richard Kearney pointed out that the *Companion* covered ancient, medieval, and non-Western philosophies admirably, but betrayed marked bias in its treatment of more modern subjects. Kearney pointed out that Honderich's volume ignored interesting work on imagination by such phenomenologists as Husserl, Sartre, Fink, Ricoeur, and Bachelard, and failed to mention such major figures in French philosophy as Foucault, Kristeva, Lyotard, Deleuze, and several others. Yet the critic pointed out that the book's treatment of the analytical thinkers is "invariably respectful, even reverential." This bias, however, did not detract from the opinion of *Booklist*'s reviewer, who admired the *Companion*'s "wide variety of interesting, idiosyncratic articles" and highly recommended the book.

Honderich told *CA* that he considers his major work to be *A Theory of Determinism: The Mind, Neuroscience, and Life-Hopes,* published in 1988. This book, widely reviewed in academic circles, presents a thesis on the relationships between mental events and the physiological workings of the brain.

BIOGRAPHICAL/CRITICAL SOURCES:

PERIODICALS

Booklist, October 1, 1995, p. 353.
Ethics, October 1990, p. 216.
Inquiry, March 1989, p. 29.
Library Journal, May 15, 1999, p. 99.
Mind, October 1989, p. 642.
New Statesman and Society, July 6, 1990, p. 381; October 20, 1995, p. 37.
Philosophical Quarterly, July 1990, p. 381; April 1991, p. 256.
Philosophical Review, October 1991, p. 648.
Philosophy, January 1989, p. 109.
Publishers Weekly, January 1, 2001, Leslie Armour, review of *Philosopher: A Kind of Life,* p. 76.
Review of Politics, fall 1991, p. 733.
Times (London), March 1, 1980.
Times Literary Supplement, February 21, 1986; November 4, 1988; November 3, 1995.

OTHER

Ted Honderich Web site, http://www.ucl.ac.uk/~uctytho (June 28, 2001).*

*　　*　　*

HOPKINS, Keith 1934-

PERSONAL: Born June 20, 1934, in London, England; son of Albert Thomas (in business) and Helene (a homemaker; maiden name, Venn) Hopkins; married Juliet Phelps Brown (a psychologist), August 8, 1963; children: Rachel, Edmund, Benjamin. *Education:* King's College, Cambridge, received B.A.; M.A., 1961.

ADDRESSES: Home—46 Laurier Rd., London NW5 1SJ, England. *Office*—Kings College, Cambridge University, Cambridge CB2 1ST, England. *Agent*—A. P. Watt Ltd., 26/28 Bedford Row, London WC1R 4HL, England.

CAREER: University of London, London School of Economics and Political Science, London, England, 1963-71, began as lecturer, became senior lecturer in sociology; Brunel University, Uxbridge, England, professor of sociology, 1971—. Fellow of King's College, Cambridge, 1963-67; member of Institute for Advanced Study, Princeton, NJ, 1969-70, 1974-75, and 1983.

WRITINGS:

(Editor) *Hong Kong: The Industrial Colony,* Oxford University Press (New York, NY), 1971.
Sociological Studies in Roman History, Cambridge University Press (New York, NY), Volume I: *Conquerors and Slaves,* 1978, Volume II: *Death and Renewal,* 1983.
(Editor, with C. R. Whittaker and P. Garnsey) *Trade in the Ancient Economy,* University of California Press (Berkeley, CA), 1983.
A World Full of Gods: The Strange Triumph of Christianity, Free Press (New York, NY), 2000, published as *A World Full of Gods: Pagans, Jews, and Christians in the Roman Empire,* Weidenfeld & Nicolson (London, England), 2000.

SIDELIGHTS: Keith Hopkins takes a lively look at the ascent of Christianity in his book, *A World Full of Gods: The Strange Triumph of Christianity.* Several reviewers noted that while the author's material is familiar, his approach to it is unique. He puts forth the theory that early Christianity was divided into many sects, some fiercely opposed, and that a seemingly unified Christianity was only accomplished after years of competition between factions. Hopkins creates commentary using devices such as a dialog between two time-travelers and a description of the filming of a television documentary on the Dead Sea Scrolls. The author has stated that he used this experimental style in the hopes of more vividly evoking the thoughts and feelings of people living in various ages and societies.

A *Kirkus Reviews* contributor praised the "dazzling panache" with which Hopkins pursued his inquiry and found the author's narrative full of "daring, imaginative stuff." Less enthusiastic was a reviewer for *Economist,* who found Hopkins's fictional television documentary device a "gimcrack," albeit one with a "solid, structured and interesting argument" as its foundation. The reviewer allowed that Hopkins presented his case with "force and life," and credited him with doing "a real service" by presenting the ideas behind many obscure but important texts. Yet in the end, that reviewer found

Hopkins's historical liberties unacceptable, particularly an invented deathbed meditation by St. Augustine in which the saint expressed grave doubts about the faith he had worked so hard to spread. "The pugnacious saint wrote no such thing," reported the *Economist*'s writer. "It's no novelty for historians to put words in their characters' mouths. But in the bad old days they used words that the character concerned might well have used, not ones that he probably hadn't."

Hopkins "breaks every rule of historiography," asserted a *Publishers Weekly* reviewer. That writer felt that Hopkins's book ultimately failed to do what its author intended, "yet this is nevertheless a magnificent, rollicking failure, one that has readers laughing out loud in one paragraph and feeling dizzy in the next, struck by an insight so powerful that it demands reconsideration of what seemed secure knowledge the moment before. . . . The view from the top is disappointing, but it remains an exhilarating climb."

BIOGRAPHICAL/CRITICAL SOURCES:

PERIODICALS

Economist, March 18, 2000, review of *A World Full of Gods: Pagans, Jews, and Christians in the Roman Empire,* p. 10.
Helios, Volume IX, 1982.
Kirkus Reviews, July 1, 2000, review of *A World Full of Gods: The Strange Triumph of Christianity,* p. 937.
Publishers Weekly, June 26, 2000, review of *A World Full of Gods: The Strange Triumph of Christianity,* p. 69.
Times Literary Supplement, December 21, 1979; February 24, 1984.*

*   *   *

HORNE, Gerald 1949-

PERSONAL: Born January 3, 1949, in St. Louis, MO; son of Jerry (a truck driver) and Flora (a maid) Horne. *Education:* Princeton University, B.A., 1970; University of California at Berkeley, J.D., 1973; Columbia University, Ph.D., 1982. *Politics:* Peace and Freedom Party.

ADDRESSES: Home—972 West Campus Point Ln., Goleta, CA 93117. *Office*—CB 5250, University of North Carolina, Chapel Hill, NC 27599-5250.

CAREER: Writer, lawyer, and journalist. Former executive director of National Conference of Black Lawyers; conducted human rights investigations in West Bank/Gaza and Philippines. Chair of Peace and Freedom Party.

WRITINGS:

Black and Red: W. E. B. Du Bois and the Afro-American Response to the Cold War, 1944-1963, State University of New York Press (Albany, NY), 1985.

Communist Front? The Civil Rights Congress, 1946-1956, Fairleigh Dickinson University Press (East Brunswick, NJ), 1988.

Studies in Black: Progressive Views and Reviews of the African American Experience, Kendall/Hunt (Dubuque, IA), 1992.

Reversing Discrimination: The Case for Affirmative Action, International Publishers (New York, NY), 1992.

Black Liberation/Red Scare: Ben Davis and the Communist Party, University of Delaware Press (Newark, DE), 1993.

Race for the Planet: The US and the New World Order, Kendall/Hunt (Dubuque, IA), 1994.

(Editor, with Mary Young) *Testaments of Courage: Selections from Men's Slave Narratives,* Franklin Watts (New York, NY), 1995.

The Fire This Time: The Watts Uprising and the 1960s, University Press of Virginia (Charlottesville, VA), 1995.

Powell v. Alabama: The Scottsboro Boys and American Justice, Franklin Watts (New York, NY), 1997.

(Editor, with Young) *W. E. B. Du Bois: An Encyclopedia,* Greenwood Press (Westport, CT), 2000.

Race Woman: The Lives of Shirley Graham Du Bois, New York University Press (New York, NY), 2000.

From the Barrel of a Gun: The United States and the War against Zimbabwe, 1965-1980, University of North Carolina Press (Chapel Hill, NC), 2001.

Class Struggle in Hollywood, 1930-1950: Moguls, Mobsters, Stars, Reds, and Trade Unionists, University of Texas Press (Austin, TX), 2001.

Also contributor to *Thinking and Rethinking U.S. History,* Council on Interracial Books for Children, 1988.

SIDELIGHTS: Gerald Horne has written many books that examine aspects of American history from a leftist political perspective, especially those aspects that concern black Americans. In *Black Liberation/Red Scare: Ben Davis and the Communist Party,* he presents the life and world of Ben Davis, a black Communist politician who worked hard to improve conditions for the underclass. Davis was born in 1903, raised in an affluent home and, after taking a law degree at Harvard, he seemed poised to assume his place among the black bourgeoisie. His life changed considerably in the 1930s, when he became part of the defense team for Angelo Herndon, a Communist organizer who was indicted and tried under a conspiracy statute that had once been used to punish those taking part in slave uprisings. Though the trial was lost, Davis quickly became involved in other critical cases, such as the trial of the "Scottsboro Boys"—black youth who were falsely accused, convicted, and sentenced to death for the rape of two white women. For his own safety during this trial, Davis was brought to New York City, where he became a popular figure. He became passionately committed to the Communist party, believing it to be the means by which the black race could truly throw off the lingering burden of slavery and oppression. Horne's book details Davis's life and accomplishments.

In *The Fire This Time: The Watts Uprising and the 1960s,* Horne uses the 1965 riot in Los Angeles's Watts neighborhood "to fashion a careful, painstakingly detailed, and ambitious study of the cultural meaning of the 1960s and the urban politics of Los Angeles," advised Herman Gray in *The Annals of the American Academy of Political and Social Science.* Gray held Horne's book up as a "model of careful scholarship," thanks to its in-depth research and "rich interpretive framework." Gray concluded: "Horne's voice—passionate, clear, and critical—is never far from the story, guiding, criticizing, and interpreting, in short, ensuring that the rebellion's central dynamics, contours, contradictions, tragedies, triumphs, and participants are brought to life and critically engaged."

Horne turned his attention to a unique life in *Race Woman: The Lives of Shirley Graham Du Bois,* a biography of the widow of famed scholar and civil rights leader, W. E. B. Du Bois. Though best known as the caretaker of W. E. B. Du Bois in his declining years, Shirley Graham Du Bois had a notable career in her own right. Raised in somewhat privileged circumstances, Shirley enjoyed a good education in music and the arts. As a young woman she attended various colleges and traveled widely. During the Depression, she staged a massive opera, *Tom Tom,* which boasted a cast of some 500 performers. She became involved with W. E. B. Du Bois when he was under attack from anti-Communist forces during the middle years of the twentieth century, and after his death she continued to travel, finally becoming a citizen of Tanzania. She died in

China in 1977. A reviewer for *Publishers Weekly* called Horne's book "eloquent and rich with telling anecdotes" about world-famous people, and concluded that while *Race Woman* "may not completely unravel the enigma of Shirley Graham Du Bois . . . it gets closer to her heart and soul than any previous attempt."

BIOGRAPHICAL/CRITICAL SOURCES:

PERIODICALS

American Academy of Political and Social Science Annals, January, 1997, Herman Gray, review of *The Fire This Time: The Watts Uprising and the 1960s,* p. 202.

American Humanities Review, December, 1995, review of *Black Liberation/Red Scare: Ben Davis and the Communist Party,* p. 1712.

Black Scholar, summer, 1994, review of *Black Liberation/Red Scare: Ben Davis and the Communist Party,* p. 75.

Booklist, April 15, 1997, Hazel Rochman, review of *Powell v. Alabama: The Scottsboro Boys and American Justice,* p. 1415.

Bookwatch, November, 1992, review of *Reversing Discrimination,* p. 5.

Choice, January, 1995, review of *Black Liberation/Red Scare: Ben Davis and the Communist Party,* p. 859; February, 1996, p. 1010.

History: Reviews of New Books, spring, 1996, review of *The Fire This Time: The Watts Uprising and the 1960s,* p. 112.

Horn Book Guide, fall, 1997, review of *Powell v. Alabama,* p. 324.

Kirkus Reviews, July 1, 2000, review of *Race Woman: The Lives of Shirley Graham Du Bois,* p. 937.

Library Journal, August, 1993, review of *Black and Red,* p. 123.

Monthly Review, March, 1995, W. H. Locke Anderson, review of *Black Liberation/Red Scare: Ben Davis and the Communist Party: Ben Davis and the Communist Party,* p. 57.

Pacific Historical Review, February, 1997, review of *The Fire This Time: The Watts Uprising and the 1960s,* p. 99.

Publishers Weekly, August 7, 2000, review of *Race Woman: The Lives of Shirley Graham Du Bois,* p. 83.

School Library Journal, June, 1997, review of *Powell v. Alabama,* p. 138.

Science & Society, summer, 1997, review of *Black Liberation/Red Scare,* p. 284.*

HUSSMAN, Lawrence Eugene, Jr. 1932-

PERSONAL: Born March 20, 1932, in Dayton, OH; son of Lawrence Eugene and Genevieve Hussman; married wife, Anne, June 13, 1959 (divorced, 1985); children: Stephen, Sarah. *Education:* University of Dayton, B.A., 1954; University of Michigan, M.A., 1957, Ph.D., 1964. *Politics:* Democrat. *Avocational interests:* Travel, fishing.

ADDRESSES: Home—2865 Gramercy Pl., Fairborn, OH 45324. *Office*—Department of English, Wright State University, Colonel Glenn Highway, Dayton, OH 45435.

CAREER: University of Portland, Portland, OR, instructor, 1961-63, assistant professor of English, 1963-65; Wright State University, Dayton, Ohio, assistant professor, 1965-67, associate professor, 1968-79, professor of English and chairman of department, 1980-93. Fulbright professor, University of Warsaw, 1993-94; visiting professor, University of Aberta, Lisbon, 1995-96; Fulbright professor, University of Lublin (Poland), 2000-01. *Military service:* U.S. Army, 1954-56.

MEMBER: Modern Language Association of America.

AWARDS, HONORS: Grant from the National Endowment for the Humanities.

WRITINGS:

Dreiser and His Fiction: A Twentieth-Century Quest, University of Pennsylvania Press (Philadelphia, PA), 1983.

(Editor) Marguerite Tjader, *Love That Will Not Let Me Go: My Time with Theodore Dreiser,* Peter Lang (New York, NY), 1998.

Harbingers of a Century: The Novels of Frank Norris, Peter Lang (New York, NY), 1999.

Contributor to literature journals.

WORK IN PROGRESS: Secrets of the University; Desire and Disillusionment in the American Novel.

SIDELIGHTS: Lawrence Eugene Hussman, Jr., told *CA* that his book, *Harbingers of a Century: The Novels of Frank Norris,* is "about Norris's development from naturalist to mystic and from Darwinian to love-ethic advocate." Norris, a California writer active around the turn of the twentieth century, is sometimes considered a throwback to the writers of the nineteenth century. In *Harbingers of a Century,* Hussman argues that Norris's work, which often presented themes of desire and disillusionment, provided an important transition into the twentieth century and modernism. Hussman argues that Norris's fiction should be grouped with the materialist philosophers. He illuminates Norris's development of an existential ethic based on love for "another" and compassion for "the other." He also provides commentary on previous critical analysis of Norris's work. Each chapter is devoted to one of Norris's books, a common approach, but Shawn St. Jean commented in a *Dreiser Studies* review, "Hussman considerably freshens this somewhat dated approach through constant comparisons of the main work under consideration to Norris' other novels and to a wide range of works by American authors of the nineteenth and twentieth centuries. . . . One observes Hussman's thesis evolving along with Norris' career, maturing from the general to the specific, in a manner that never induces readerly lethargy, a common side-effect of many thesis-driven critical books."

Hussman brought new light to the biography of American novelist Theodore Dreiser when he edited the memoirs of Marguerite Tjader, one of the most significant of Dreiser's many lovers. Tjader, a novelist in her own right, was a fiercely independent woman who was able to maintain a long-standing relationship with Dreiser despite many conflicting interests. Tjader always maintained a certain respect for and consideration of Dreiser's long-suffering wife, Helen. Donna Campbell, a reviewer for *Dreiser Studies,* characterized Tjader as having "a strongly-held and strongly-willed idealism," and stated that Hussman's "excellent notes and introduction meticulously detail the biographical framework and significance of Tjader's work."

BIOGRAPHICAL/CRITICAL SOURCES:

PERIODICALS

American Literature, May, 1984, review of *Dreiser and His Fiction: A Twentieth-Century Quest,* p. 284.
Antioch Review, fall, 1984, review of *Dreiser and His Fiction: A Twentieth-Century Quest,* p. 504.
Choice, October, 1983, review of *Dreiser and His Fiction: A Twentieth-Century Quest,* p. 277.
Dreiser Studies, spring, 1999, Donna Campbell, review of *Love That Will Not Let Me Go: My Time with Theodore Dreiser;* fall, 1999, Shawn St. Jean, review of *Harbingers of a Century: The Novels of Frank Norris,* pp. 58-61.

Modern Fiction Studies, summer, 1984, review of *Dreiser and His Fiction: A Twentieth-Century Quest,* p. 304.*

* * *

HUXLEY, Aldous (Leonard) 1894-1963

PERSONAL: Born July 26, 1894, in Godalming, Surrey, England; died November 22, 1963, in Hollywood, CA; son of Leonard and Julia (Arnold) Huxley; married Maria Nys, 1919 (died, 1955); married Laura Archera, 1956; children: Matthew. *Education:* Balliol College, Oxford, B.A., 1916. *Avocational interests:* Painting, walking, playing piano, "riding in fast cars."

CAREER: Eton College, Eton, England, schoolmaster, 1917-19; staff member of *Athenaeum* and *Westminster Gazette,* 1919-24; writer.

MEMBER: Athenaeum Club.

AWARDS, HONORS: Award of Merit and Gold Medal, American Academy of Arts and Letters, 1959; D.Litt., University of California, 1959.

WRITINGS:

NOVELS

Crome Yellow, Chatto & Windus (London, England), 1921, Doran (New York, NY), 1922, reprinted, Chatto & Windus (London, England), 1963, Harper (New York, NY), 1965.
(Translator) R. de Gourmont, *A Virgin Heart,* N. L. Brown, 1921.
Antic Hay (also see below), Doran, 1923.
Those Barren Leaves, Doran, 1925, reprinted, Avon (New York, NY), 1964.
Point Counter Point, Doubleday (Garden City, NY), 1928, reprinted, Harper (New York, NY), 1969.
Brave New World (also see below), Doubleday (Garden City, NY), 1932, reprinted, Bantam (New York, NY), 1960, edited and with an introduction by Harold Bloom, published as *Aldous Huxley's Brave New World,* Chelsea House (New York, NY), 1995.
Eyeless in Gaza, Harper (New York, NY), 1936, reprinted, Bantam (New York, NY), 1968.
After Many a Summer Dies the Swan, Harper (New York, NY), 1939, reprinted, 1965.

Time Must Have a Stop, Harper (New York, NY), 1944.

Ape and Essence, Harper (New York, NY), 1948.

The Genius and the Goddess, Harper (New York, NY), 1955.

Antic Hay and The Gioconda Smile (also see below), Harper (New York, NY), 1957.

Brave New World [and] *Brave New World Revisited* (also see below), Harper (New York, NY), 1960.

Island, Harper (New York, NY), 1962.

SHORT STORIES

Limbo: Six Stories and a Play, Doran, 1920.

Mortal Coils: Five Stories (also see below), Doran, 1922, reprinted, Chatto & Windus (London, England), 1968.

Little Mexican and Other Stories, Chatto & Windus (London, England), 1924, reprinted, 1959.

Young Archimedes and Other Stories, Doran, 1924.

Two or Three Graces: Four Stories, Doran, 1925, reprinted, Chatto & Windus (London, England), 1963.

Brief Candles, Doubleday (Garden City, NY), 1930, reprinted, Chatto & Windus (London, England), 1970.

The Gioconda Smile, Chatto & Windus (London, England), 1938.

Collected Short Stories, Harper (New York, NY), 1957.

The Crows of Pearblossom, Random House (New York, NY), 1968.

POETRY

The Burning Wheel, B. H. Blackwell (London, England), 1916.

The Defeat of Youth and Other Poems, Longmans, Green (London, England), 1918.

Leda and Other Poems, Doran, 1920.

Selected Poems, Appleton, 1925.

Arabia Infelix and Other Poems, Fountain Press, 1929.

Apennine, Slide Mountain Press, 1930.

The Cicadas and Other Poems, Doubleday (Garden City, NY), 1931.

The Collected Poetry of Aldous Huxley, edited by Donald Watt, Harper (New York, NY), 1971.

PLAYS

Francis Sheridan's The Discovery, Adapted for the Modern Stage, Chatto & Windus (London, England), 1924, Doran, 1925.

The World of Light: A Comedy in Three Acts, Doubleday (Garden City, NY), 1931.

The Gioconda Smile (adapted from Huxley's short story), Harper (New York, NY), 1948, also published as *Mortal Coils,* Harper, 1948.

Now More than Ever, University of Texas Press (Austin, TX), 2000.

NONFICTION

Along the Road: Notes and Essays of a Tourist, Doran, 1925, reprinted, Books for Libraries Press, 1971.

Jesting Pilate: An Intellectual Holiday, Doran, 1926, reprinted, Greenwood (Westport, CT), 1974, published in England as *Jesting Pilate: The Diary of a Journey,* Chatto & Windus (London, England), 1957.

Essays New and Old, Chatto & Windus (London, England), 1926, Doran, 1927, reprinted, Ayer, 1968.

Proper Studies: The Proper Study of Mankind Is Man, Chatto & Windus (London, England), 1927, Doubleday (Garden City, NY), 1928, reprinted, Chatto & Windus, 1957.

Do What You Will (essays), Doubleday (Garden City, NY), 1929, reprinted, Chatto & Windus (London, England), 1970.

Holy Face and Other Essays, Fleuron, 1929.

Vulgarity in Literature: Digressions from a Theme, Chatto & Windus (London, England), 1930, Haskell House, 1966.

Music at Night and Other Essays, Chatto & Windus (London, England), 1930, Doubleday (Garden City, NY), 1931, reprinted, Books for Libraries Press, 1970.

On the Margin: Notes and Essays, Doran, 1932, reprinted, Chatto & Windus (London, England), 1971.

Beyond the Mexique Bay: A Traveller's Journal, Harper (New York, NY), 1934, reprinted, Greenwood (Westport, CT), 1975.

1936 . . . Peace?, Friends Peace Committee (London, England), 1936.

The Olive Tree and Other Essays, Chatto & Windus (London, England), 1936, Harper (New York, NY), 1937, reprinted, Books for Libraries Press, 1971.

What Are You Going to Do about It? The Case for Constructive Peace, Chatto & Windus (London, England), 1936.

An Encyclopedia of Pacifism, Harper (New York, NY), 1937, reprinted, Garland (New York, NY), 1972.

Ends and Means: An Inquiry in the Nature of Ideals and Into the Methods Employed for Their Realization, Harper (New York, NY), 1937, reprinted, Greenwood (Westport, CT), 1969.

The Most Agreeable Vice, [Los Angeles, CA], 1938.

Words and Their Meanings, Ward Ritchie Press, 1940.

Grey Eminence: A Study in Religion and Politics, Harper (New York, NY), 1941, reprinted, 1975.

The Art of Seeing, Harper (New York, NY), 1942, reprinted, Chatto & Windus (London, England), 1964.

The Perennial Philosophy, Harper (New York, NY), 1945, reprinted, Books for Libraries Press, 1972.

Science, Liberty, and Peace, Harper (New York, NY), 1946.

(With Sir John Russell) *Food and People,* [London, England], 1949.

Prisons, with the "Carceri" Etchings by G. B. Piranesi, Grey Falcon Press, 1949.

Themes and Variations, Harper (New York, NY), 1950.

(With Stuart Gilbert) *Joyce, the Artificer: Two Studies of Joyce's Method,* Chiswick (London, England), 1952.

The Devils of London, Harper (New York, NY), 1952.

(With J. A. Kings) *A Day in Windsor,* Britannicus Liber (London, England), 1953.

The French of Paris, Harper (New York, NY), 1954.

The Doors of Perception, Harper (New York, NY), 1954, reprinted, 1970.

Heaven and Hell, Harper (New York, NY), 1956, reprinted, 1971.

Tomorrow and Tomorrow and Tomorrow and Other Essays, Harper (New York, NY), 1956, published in England as *Adonis and the Alphabet and Other Essays,* Chatto & Windus (London, England), 1956.

A Writer's Prospect—III: Censorship and Spoken Literature, [London, England], 1956.

Brave New World Revisited, Harper (New York, NY), 1958.

Collected Essays, Harper (New York, NY), 1959.

On Art and Artists: Literature, Painting, Architecture, Music, Harper (New York, NY), 1960.

Selected Essays, Chatto & Windus (London, England), 1961.

The Politics of Ecology: The Question of Survival, Center for the Study of Democratic Institutions (Santa Barbara, CA), 1963.

Literature and Science (also see below), Harper (New York, NY), 1963.

New Fashioned Christmas, Hart Press, 1968.

America and the Future, Pemberton Press, 1970.

The Human Situation: Lectures at Santa Barbara, 1959, edited by Piero Ferrucci, Harper (New York, NY), 1977.

The Basic Philosophy of Aldous Huxley, American Institute of Psychology, 1984.

Between the Wars: Essays and Letters, Ivan R. Dee (Chicago, IL), 1994.

The Hidden Huxley: Contempt and Compassion for the Masses, 1920-36, Faber (Boston, MA), 1994.

Aldous Huxley's Hearst Essays, Garland (New York, NY), 1994.

Complete Essays, Ivan R. Dee (Chicago, IL), 2000.

COLLECTIONS

Texts and Pretexts: An Anthology with Commentaries, Chatto & Windus (London, England), 1932, Harper (New York, NY), 1933, reprinted, Norton (New York, NY), 1962.

Rotunda: A Selection from the Works of Aldous Huxley, Chatto & Windus (London, England), 1932.

Retrospect: An Omnibus of His Fiction and Non-Fiction over Three Decades, Harper (New York, NY), 1947, reprinted, Peter Smith, 1971.

The Letters of Aldous Huxley, Chatto & Windus (London, England), 1969, Harper (New York, NY), 1970.

Great Short Works of Aldous Huxley, Harper (New York, NY), 1969.

Collected Works, Chatto & Windus (London, England), 1970.

The Wisdom of the Ages, two volumes, Found Class Reprints, 1989.

OTHER

Jonah, Gotham (New York, NY), 1977.

Moksha, edited by Michael Horowitz and Cynthia Palmer, Houghton (Boston, MA), 1977.

(With Christopher Isherwood) *Jacob's Hands,* St. Martin's Press (New York, NY), 1998.

Author of screenplay *Woman's Vengeance,* based on his own novel *The Gioconda Smile,* 1947, and, with others, of screenplays *Pride and Prejudice,* 1940, *Jane Eyre,* 1944, and *Madame Curie.*

Contributor to numerous periodicals, including *Life, Playboy, Encounter,* and *Daedalus.*

A collection of Huxley's original manuscripts is housed at the University of California, Berkeley.

*ADAPTATIONS:*Several of Huxley's novels have been adapted for the stage and for film.

SIDELIGHTS: When Aldous Huxley was sixteen he was stricken with a disease of the eyes, which left him temporarily blind and permanently disrupted his plan to enter the medical profession. Yet his scientific training remained a major force in all his future endeavors. He became a renowned and prolific man of letters, writing essays, fiction, and poetry, as well as criticism of painting, music, and literature, all of it touched by his scientific and analytic processes of thought and sense of detail.

Huxley's oeuvre is often seen as falling into two periods: his early work, much of it social satire, is arch and occasionally condescending; his later work, essentially mystical, is prophetic but in places self-righteous. The first period includes novels like *Crome Yellow* and *Antic Hay,* witty and sardonic dissections of British society, particularly its artists and aristocrats. It also includes the well-known *Brave New World,* which Andre Maurois once called "an exercise in pessimistic prognostication, a terrifying Utopia." The later period is marked by the publication in 1936 of the novel, *Eyeless in Gaza,* which concerns the transformation of Anthony Beavis from cynic to mystic. A similar theme is explored in the novel, *Time Must Have a Stop,* as well as Huxley's later essays (especially *The Perennial Philosophy*) and his last novel, *Island.*

At the chronological center of his career, Huxley balanced these two thrusts and produced the novel, *Point Counter Point,* which many critics regard as his most accomplished work of fiction. In it he confronted all of contemporary man's ideals—religion and false mysticism, science, art, sex, politics—and the disillusionment that their inadequacy invokes. In *Point Counter Point,* Huxley achieved for the first time what he called the "musicalization of fiction." He shifted and juxtaposed moods, scenes, and characters, and he modulated themes, creating through these variations a verbal counterpoint. As the character Philip Quarles puts it: "He shows several people falling in love, or dying, or praying in different ways—dissimilars solving the same problem." In this fashion, each of the characters (who are all representative of an idea or type) is enhanced and more clearly illuminated than he would be through a conventional presentation of events. Moreover, this breaking down of the story, relating the plot gradually and in pieces, parallels Huxley's theme: people who live for ideas and absolutes will be fragmented, unfulfilled human beings. He suggests that the world must be seen as a whole and accepted as it is, just as the novel, while being studied part by part from within, must be grasped in its entirety if any of the characters are to have significance.

As well as representing ideals, the characters in *Point Counter Point* are based on real people, for the book is a *roman à clef.* The most attractive of them is Mark Rampion, the whole man, who strongly resembles D. H. Lawrence, Huxley's lifelong friend. In turn, Rampion's friend Philip Quarles is suggestive of Huxley himself, a novelist concerned with point of view and a man whose problem is "to transform a detached intellectual scepticism into a way of harmonious all-round living."

In his search for such transformation, Aldous Huxley went through many stages of mystical belief. His biographers and critics often cite his experiments with such hallucinogenic drugs as mescaline and lysergic acid (which he labeled "psychodelic") as a means of discovering new dimensions of the human psyche. But Huxley's brother Julian best explained his mystic inclinations in *Aldous Huxley: A Memorial Volume.* Julian Huxley said that Aldous was equally fascinated by the hard facts of scientific discovery and by the facts of mystical experience. But, he added, the more science discovers and "the more comprehension it gives us of the mechanisms of existence, the more clearly does the mystery of existence itself stand out." That is, the more human beings may comprehend operative details, the more mysterious will seem the process itself. Hence, Aldous Huxley's mysticism was founded upon scientific training and his search for spiritual truth based on the urge, as Julian put it, "to achieve self-transcendence while yet remaining a committed social being."

Remarkably, new Huxley writings are still being published some forty years after his death in 1963. A screenplay, *Jacob's Hands,* co-authored with Christopher Isherwood, was put into print in 1998, after actress Sharon Stone helped to track down the manuscript. A similar set of circumstances led to the publication of *Now More than Ever,* a stage play that was never produced. These items may be "more of a historical curiosity," as J. Sara Paulk put it in *Library Journal,* but they do speak to the ongoing power and persuasion of Huxley's major works. Reprints of Huxley's essays, as in the volume *Between the Wars: Essays and Letters,* reveal one of the twentieth century's "premier dystopian writers," to quote Tracy Lee Simmons in the *National Review.* Simmons characterized Huxley as "often wrong, always fascinating, when right, dead right, almost in spite of himself."

BIOGRAPHICAL/CRITICAL SOURCES:

BOOKS

Atkins, John, *Aldous Huxley,* Orion Press (Columbus, OH), 1968.

Baker, Robert S., *Brave New World: History, Science, and Dystopia,* Twayne (Boston, MA), 1990.

Bedford, Sybille, *Aldous Huxley: A Biography,* Knopf (New York, NY), 1974.

Birnbaum, Milton, *Aldous Huxley's Quest for Values,* University of Tennessee Press (Knoxville, TN), 1971.

Bowering, Peter, *Aldous Huxley: A Study of the Major Novels,* Athlone (London, England), 1968.

Brander, Laurence, *Aldous Huxley: A Critical Study,* Bucknell University Press (Cranbury, NJ), 1970.

Brook, Jocelyn, *Aldous Huxley,* Longmans, Green (London, England), 1954.

Calder, Jenni, *Huxley and Orwell: 'Brave New World' and '1984,'* Arnold, 1976.

Clark, Ronald W., *The Huxleys,* McGraw (New York, NY), 1968.

Contemporary Literary Criticism, Gale (Detroit, MI), Volume 1, 1973, Volume 3, 1975, Volume 4, 1975, Volume 5, 1976, Volume 8, 1978, Volume 11, 1979, Volume 18, 1981, Volume 35, 1985.

Dasgupta, Sanjukta, *The Novels of Huxley and Hemingway: A Study in Two Planes of Reality,* Prestige (New Delhi, India), 1996.

Deery, Jane, *Aldous Huxley and the Mysticism of Science,* St. Martin's Press (New York, NY), 1996.

Dictionary of Literary Biography, Gale (Detroit, MI), 1990 Volume 36: *British Novelists, 1890-1929: Modernists,* Gale (Detroit, MI), 1985, Volume 100: *Modern British Essayists, Second Series.*

Dunaway, David King, *Aldous Huxley Recollected: An Oral History,* AltaMira Press, 1998.

Firchow, Peter, *Aldous Huxley: A Satirist and Novelist,* University of Minnesota Press (Minneapolis, MN), 1972.

Firchow, Peter Edgerly, *The Ends of Utopia: A Study of Aldous Huxley's 'Brave New World,'* Bucknell University Press (Cranbury, NJ), 1984.

Greenblatt, Stephen J., *Three Modern Satirists: Waugh, Orwell, and Huxley,* Yale University Press (New Haven, CT), 1965.

Holmes, Charles M., *Aldous Huxley and the Way to Reality,* Indiana University Press (Bloomington, IN), 1970.

Huxley, Julian, *Aldous Huxley: A Memorial Volume,* Harper (New York, NY), 1965.

Huxley, Laura Archera, *This Timeless Moment: A Personal View of Aldous Huxley,* Farrar, Straus (New York, NY), 1968.

Izzo, David Garrett, *Aldous Huxley and W.H. Auden: On Language,* Locust Hill Press, 1998.

Kuehn, Robert E., editor, *Aldous Huxley: A Collection of Critical Essays,* Prentice-Hall (Englewood Cliffs, NJ), 1974.

Meckier, Jerome, editor, *Critical Essays on Aldous Huxley,* G. K. Hall (Boston, MA), 1996.

Meckier, Jerome, *Aldous Huxley: Satire and Structure,* Barnes & Noble (New York, NY), 1969.

Nugel, Bernfried, *Now More than Ever: Proceedings of the Aldous Huxley Centenary Symposium, Munster, 1994,* P. Lang (New York, NY), 1996.

Schulz, Clair, *Aldous Huxley, 1894-1963: A Centenary Catalog,* Decline and Fall (Stevens Point, WI), 1994.

Thody, Peter, *Huxley: A Biographical Introduction,* Scribner (New York, NY), 1973.

Woodcock, George, *Dawn and the Darkest Hour: A Study of Aldous Huxley,* Viking (New York, NY), 1972.

PERIODICALS

Atlantic, January, 1975.

Booklist, July, 1994, Alice Joyce, review of *Between the Wars: Essays and Letters,* p. 1916.

Books and Bookmen, March, 1971.

Choice, November, 1970.

Commonweal, March 28, 1975.

Economist, December 20, 1969.

Esquire, April, 1975.

Library Journal, July, 2000, J. Sara Paulk, review of *Now More than Ever,* p. 91.

Nation, June 8, 1970.

National Review, January 31, 1975; October 10, 1994, Tracy Lee Simmons, review of *Between the Wars: Essays and Letters,* p. 81.

New Leader, November, 1968.

New Republic, May 16, 1970; November 16, 1974.

New Statesman, November 28, 1969.

Newsweek, May 4, 1970; December 9, 1974.

New Yorker, July 18, 1970; February 17, 1975.

New York Times Book Review, September 20, 1998, William Ferguson, review of *Jacob's Hands,* p. 24.

Publishers Weekly, June 6, 1994, review of *Between the Wars: Essays and Letters,* p. 53; July 27, 1998, review of *Jacob's Hands,* p. 53.

Review America, February 22, 1975.

Saturday Review, May 2, 1970.

Saturday Review/World, November 16, 1974.

Time, December 2, 1974.

Times Literary Supplement, December 18, 1969; February 17, 1984.

Washington Post Book World, May 31, 1970; June 16, 1985.

OTHER

Aldous Huxley-somaweb, http://www.primenet.com/~matthew/huxley/ (December 5, 2000), "Huxley Links."

Huxley Hotlinks, http://www.huxley.net/hotlinks.htm/ (December 5, 2000), "Aldous Husley's Life and Work."*

I-J

ISADORA, Rachel 1953(?)-

PERSONAL: Born c. 1953, in New York, NY; married Robert Maiorano (a ballet dancer and writer), September 7, 1977 (divorced, May, 1982); married James Turner; children: (second marriage) Gillian Heather. *Education:* Attended American School of Ballet.

ADDRESSES: Office—c/o William Morrow and Co., 1350 Avenue of the Americas, New York, NY 10019.

CAREER: Dancer with Boston Ballet Company, Boston, MA; freelance author and illustrator of children's books.

AWARDS, HONORS: Children's Book of the Year awards, Child Study Association, 1976, for *Max,* 1985, for *I Hear* and *I See,* and 1986, for *Flossie and the Fox* and *Cutlass in the Snow;* Children's Choice award, International Reading Association and Children's Book Council, 1976, Children's Book Showcase award, Children's Book Council, 1977, American Library Association (ALA) notable book citation, and Reading Rainbow selection, all for *Max;* ALA notable book citation, 1979, for *Seeing Is Believing; Boston Globe-Horn Book* honor book for illustration citation, 1979, Best Book for Spring award, *School Library Journal,* 1979, and Caldecott Honor Book award, ALA, 1980, all for *Ben's Trumpet; A Little Interlude* was included in American Institute of Graphic Arts Book Show, 1981; Best Book award, School Library Journal, and ALA notable book citation, both 1982, both for *The White Stallion;* Children's Book award, New York Public Library, 1983, for *City Seen from A to Z;* Outstanding Science Trade Book citation, National Science Teachers Association and Children's Book Council, 1985, for *I Touch; Horn Book* honor list citation, 1987, for *Flossie and the Fox;* ALA notable book, 1991, for *At the Crossroads;* Junior Literary Guild citation, for *Willaby.*

WRITINGS:

FOR CHILDREN; SELF-ILLUSTRATED

Max, Macmillan, 1976.
The Potters' Kitchen, Greenwillow, 1977.
Willaby, Macmillan, 1977.
(With Robert Maiorano) *Backstage,* Greenwillow, 1978.
Ben's Trumpet, Greenwillow, 1979.
My Ballet Class, Greenwillow, 1980.
No, Agatha!, Greenwillow, 1980.
Jesse and Abe, Greenwillow, 1981.
(Reteller) *The Nutcracker,* Macmillan, 1981.
City Seen from A to Z, Greenwillow, 1983.
Opening Night, Greenwillow, 1984.
I Hear, Greenwillow, 1985.
I See, Greenwillow, 1985.
I Touch, Greenwillow, 1985.
The Pirates of Bedford Street, Greenwillow, 1988.
(Adaptor) *The Princess and the Frog* (based on *The Frog King* and *Iron Heinrich* by Wilhelm and Jacob Grimm), Greenwillow, 1989.
(Adaptor) *Swan Lake: A Ballet Story* (based on the ballet by Pyotr Ilich Tchaikovsky), Putnam, 1989.
Friends, Greenwillow, 1990.
Babies, Greenwillow, 1990.
At the Crossroads, Greenwillow, 1991.
Over the Green Hills, Greenwillow, 1992.
Lili at Ballet, Greenwillow, 1993.
(Adaptor) *Firebird,* Putnam, 1994.

My Ballet Diary, Penguin Putnam, 1995.

Lili on Stage, Penguin Putnam, 1995.

(Adaptor) *The Steadfast Tin Soldier* (based on the story by Hans Christian Andersen), Penguin Putnam, 1996.

(Adaptor) *The Little Match Girl* (based on the story by Hans Christian Andersen), Penguin Putnam, 1996.

Lili Backstage, Penguin Putnam, 1997.

Young Mozart, Penguin, 1997.

(Adaptor) *The Little Mermaid* (based on the story by Hans Christian Andersen), Penguin Putnam, 1998.

Isadora Dances, Viking Penguin, 1998.

A South African Night, HarperCollins, 1998.

Caribbean Dreams, Putnam, 1998.

Listen to the City, Putnam, 1999.

ABC Pop!, Viking Penguin, 1999.

Sophie Skates, Penguin Putnam, 1999.

123 Pop!, Penguin Putnam, 2000.

Bring on the Beat, Putnam, 2001.

Nick Plays Baseball, Putnam, 2001.

Peekaboo Morning, in press, 2002.

FOR CHILDREN; ILLUSTRATOR

Robert Maiorano, *Francisco,* Macmillan, 1978.

Elizabeth Shub, *Seeing Is Believing,* Greenwillow, 1979.

Maiorano, *A Little Interlude,* Coward, McCann & Geoghegan, 1980.

Shub, *The White Stallion,* Greenwillow, 1982.

Shub, *Cutlass in the Snow,* Greenwillow, 1986.

Patricia C. McKissack, *Flossie and the Fox,* Dial, 1986.

Ruth Young, *Golden Bear,* Viking, 1990.

Sandol Stoddard, editor, *Prayers, Praises, and Thanksgivings,* Dial, 1992.

Reeve Lindbergh, *Grandfather's Lovesong,* Viking, 1993.

OTHER

Also author of *Fulton Fish Market,* Putnam.

ADAPTATIONS: Ben's Trumpet has been adapted into both a videocassette and a filmstrip with audiocassette.

SIDELIGHTS: After a short-lived career as a professional dancer, Rachel Isadora turned to children's book illustration and writing, fashioning a career notable both for its achievements and variety. From such award-winning titles as *Max* and *Ben's Trumpet,* to biographies, to retellings of fairy tales and ballet stories, to the "Lili" series of tales of a little girl's association with the world of ballet, and to distant corners of the world such as South Africa and the Caribbean, Isadora has turned a painterly eye and an artist's perception to retrieve lasting images and playful voices. Recipient of a Caldecott Honor award as well as numerous "notable book" and "honor book" citations, Isadora features people of various races, nationalities, and ages in her works and draws and paints in many styles, from black and white to soft pastel washes to bright icons of pop art. Often her illustrations complement simple texts about such characters as novice ballerinas, hopeful musicians, and promising artists. "Work like this is a dancer's fantasy," she once commented. "Because ballet is so demanding, dancers' stage careers are short. They can only dream of going on and on forever. With art, I can go on and on, and for me it's the only work that compares in intensity and joy."

Isadora began dancing as a toddler, after wandering into her older sister's dance class. By age eleven she was performing professionally and also studying at the American School of Ballet on a scholarship. Throughout the years, though, she was troubled by extreme shyness. While in class, for instance, she wouldn't practice new movements until she could rehearse in an empty studio. She struggled, too, with the great pressures that came from training professionally. To release tension, she began drawing. "Ballet was very real to me: my world," she revealed to Elaine Edelman in a *Publishers Weekly* interview. "To escape it, I drew—so that became my fantasy world. I could express my thoughts in it, I could even express my anger. I couldn't do that as a dancer."

Seven years of study finally culminated in an offer to dance with the New York City Ballet; however, instead of accepting, Isadora broke down. "I went into my room," she told Edelman, "and didn't come out for three months." A few years later she joined the Boston Ballet Company, but a foot injury ended her brief career, and she was forced to establish herself in another vocation. So she loaded a paper bag with her sketches—all "odds and ends on bits of paper," she once commented—and took them to New York, hoping to obtain work as an illustrator. Her venture proved successful, for almost immediately she was assigned to work on her first book.

Both written and illustrated by Isadora, *Max* received considerable attention. Winner of the 1976 Child Study Association Children's Book of the Year award, the story revolves around the title character, a young baseball player who one day joins his sister at her ballet class. Clad in his uniform, the boy exercises along with the young ballerinas and soon realizes that ballet training could improve his athletic skills. He then becomes a regular pupil. Many reviewers praised Isadora for the nonsexist message they found in *Max* that ballet can be enjoyed by all. They also commended the author for her black-and-white illustrations, finding them graceful, lively, and lifelike. The dancers are "poised but fetchingly unpolished," decided a reviewer for *Publishers Weekly.*

In 1979 Isadora incorporated music and dance in what is one of her best-known works, *Ben's Trumpet.* Winner of the 1980 Caldecott Honor award, the book is set during the 1920s Jazz Age and centers on Ben, a young boy who lives in the ghetto. Ben longs to play the lively music that emanates from a neighborhood club, but he cannot afford to buy a trumpet. His dream comes true, though, when a seasoned jazz musician not only gives the youngster an instrument, but also teaches him to play. *Ben's Trumpet* is a "poignant, spare story," observed Marjorie Lewis in *School Library Journal.* Reviewers also lauded Isadora for the story's inventive artwork, which is reminiscent of the art deco style popular during the 1920s and 1930s. Bold outlines, dancing silhouettes, keyboards, and zigzag lines cover the pages of the book, forming a pictorial image of the music. "Jazz rhythms visually interpreted in black and white fairly explode," proclaimed Mary M. Burns in *Horn Book,* while Linda Kauffman Peterson, writing in *Newbery and Caldecott Medal and Honor Books,* declared that the drawings possess a "swinging, throbbing beat."

Isadora returned to the world of ballet in subsequent books, many of which have been praised for their realistic portrayals of dancers' movements. Among these are 1978's *Backstage,* which Isadora wrote with her first husband, ballet dancer Robert Maiorano. The story describes a young girl's trek through the theater to meet her mother, who is rehearsing for the famous ballet *The Nutcracker. Opening Night* features a nervous and excited young dancer who is braving her first performance. The book traces her steps from the time she walks backstage, to her first leap in front of the audience, to the moment she finds roses in her dressing room after the production. Yet another book, *My Ballet Class,* portrays young ballerinas of all nationalities, who are depicted laughing, cluttering the dressing room floor, putting on their tights and ballet slippers, and stretching out and practicing. The dancers are sketched "with fluid agility," judged *Booklist* reviewer Barbara Elleman. "Facial expressions and body movements are surely and thoughtfully captured."

Lili at Ballet is also about dance class, but centers on one young girl who dreams of becoming a serious ballerina. It outlines the practical aspects of learning ballet, such as clothing, exercises, and some of the classic steps. A *Kirkus Reviews* contributor praised Isadora's illustrations for "nicely capturing [the dancers'] poise and grace." Deborah Stevenson, writing in *Bulletin of the Center for Children's Books,* noted that "actual young dancers may want more sweat and less gossamer," but she also felt that *Lili at Ballet* "is a nice Nutcrackery treat for armchair Giselles." "Isadora's own background in ballet is evident in the abundance and precision of her illustrations and in her understanding of the enthusiasm of the young dancer," concluded *Horn Book* reviewer Hanna B. Zeiger. Isadora has followed the adventures of her young ballerina through several more picture books. In *Lili on Stage,* Lili performs in *The Nutcracker* ballet as a party guest in act one. Once home, she dreams of her next performance. "The book's charm lies partly in the subject, but mainly in the simplicity and realism of both text and illustrations," wrote Carolyn Phelan in a *Booklist* review. Zeiger noted in *Horn Book* that the "watercolor illustrations are like confections and will be a delightful reminder for children who have seen the ballet performed." Lili next leads the reader to the excitement that goes on behind the curtains in *Lili Backstage,* a book that captures the "excitement of putting on a show," according to *Booklist*'s Hazel Rochman. "For the stagestruck," Rochman further commented, "even the technical names will be magical, and they will pore over the graphic details of professionals at work."

Isadora did for professional skating with *Sophie Skates* what she has done for ballet with her "Lili" books. Eight-year-old Sophie desperately wants to become a professional skater and religiously practices five mornings a week and three afternoons after school. Now she is preparing for a competition and is back at the rink for a further lesson. "The story line gracefully shares space with watercolor sidebars that give behind-the-scenes background," noted a reviewer for *Publishers Weekly.* "A winning score for Isadora once again," the same reviewer concluded. *Booklist* contributor Susan Dove Lempke felt that *Sophie Skates* "provides an excellent balance between information . . . and a profile of a believable little Asian American girl living the exhausting, exhilarating life many little girls dream of." "Young skaters—armchair or otherwise—will glide through this one," commented a contributor to *Horn Book.*

The real lives of artists are explored in two biographies for young readers, *Young Mozart* and *Isadora Dances.* Reviewing the former title, a writer for *Publishers Weekly* commented, "Biographies for the very young can be a tricky business. In this absorbing account of the great composer's life, Isadora adroitly navigates the potential hazards." The same reviewer also commented on Isadora's "serene watercolors," which "provide an almost impressionistic backdrop to the unfolding events." Writing in *Booklist,* Rochman called *Young Mozart* an "upbeat picture-book biography," as well as a "handsome introduction" to the subject. Isadora presents the same sort of introduction for the American dancer Isadora Duncan in *Isadora Dances,* "another highly accessible biography," according to a contributor to *Publishers Weekly.* In a *Booklist* review, Rochman suggested that "dance lovers . . . will feel the excitement and joyful freedom of Duncan's expressive style."

Isadora explores themes unrelated to music or the ballet in other books, such as *Willaby* and *The Pirates of Bedford Street,* two narratives about young artists. Among her more distinctive "non-music" works, though, is 1983's *City Seen from A to Z.* An urban alphabet book, *City* is a collection of street scenes—all drawn in gray, black, and white—depicting the moods, settings, and ethnic diversity of New York. Black, Asian, and Jewish people populate the pages, caught in such activities as window shopping, relaxing in the sun, and strolling through city streets. Isadora also incorporates an element of surprise into many of her scenes: "L," for example, points to the picture of a ferocious lion ironed onto the back of a young boy's T-shirt, while "Z" stands for the chalk-drawn zoo that two children have sketched on the sidewalk. She also portrays elderly people sharing ice cream with their grandchildren or minding them at the beach. "Young and old people of different cultures and individual tastes all seem snugly at home," wrote Leonard S. Marcus in the *New York Times Book Review.* And Beryl Lieff Benderly concluded in the *Washington Post Book World* that "Isadora's elegant, perceptive pictures capture small realities of city life."

The sounds of the city are evoked in the 1999 title, *Listen to the City,* rendered in pop art that captures "the sights and sounds of the city," according to a *Horn Book* reviewer. "In keeping with the Lichtenstein look, the text is limited to painted onomatopoeic words and brief utterances enclosed in dialogue bubbles," noted the same writer. Grace Oliff called *Listen to the City* an "exuberant picture book" in *School Library Journal.* "The use of rich primary colors, coupled with the unique design of the pages, sometimes juxtaposing images in oddly angled segments, captures the energy of urban life," Oliff further observed. With *ABC Pop!* and *123 Pop!,* Isadora also utilized pop art imagery in a novel manner to produce an alphabet and a counting book respectively. Reviewing the former title, *Horn*

Book contributor Lolly Robinson noted, "Isadora has created a striking alphabet book in homage to the pop art she admired as a child. . . . But the pacing is pure Isadora, revealing a vitality that harks back to *Ben's Trumpet* and *City Seen from A to Z.*" Also reviewing *ABC Pop!,* *Booklist* critic Michael Cart felt that "Isadora's artfully energetic book will appeal to eyes of all ages." Writing about Isadora's *123 Pop!,* *Booklist* reviewer Gillian Engberg found it to be a "sophisticated, playful introduction to numbers," while Robinson noted in another *Horn Book* review that the artist "manages to maintain her spontaneous style with vibrant gestural lines, surprising color choices, and unexpected whimsical touches."

Isadora has also gone farther afield with three picture books about South Africa: *At the Crossroads, Over the Green Hills,* and *A South African Night.* In the first title, an ALA notable book, South African children gather to welcome home their fathers, who have been away for several months working in the mines. The second, *Over the Green Hills,* "is a loving portrait of the Transkei and its people," according to a critic for *Junior Bookshelf.* *A South African Night* is a "simply written picture book [that] focuses on the transition from day to night" in Kruger National Park, according to Gebregeorgis Yohannes in *School Library Journal.* Yohannes further observed that "Isadora's vibrant watercolor illustrations are evocative of both the human bustle and the wild untamed life force of the animals." More exotic locations are served up in *Caribbean Dreams,* an "evocative" book, according to *Booklist*'s Ilene Cooper, and one that "captures the mood of an island and the spirit of children." A writer for *Publishers Weekly* called this same book a "simple, rhythmic paean to the Caribbean."

BIOGRAPHICAL/CRITICAL SOURCES:

BOOKS

Children's Literature Review, Volume 7, Gale (Detroit, MI), 1984, pp. 102-109.

Holtze, Sally Holmes, editor, *Fifth Book of Junior Authors and Illustrators,* H. W. Wilson, 1983, pp. 159-160.

Peterson, Linda Kauffman, and Marilyn Leathers Solt, *Newbery and Caldecott Medal and Honor Books: An Annotated Bibliography,* G. K. Hall, 1982, p. 372.

St. James Guide to Children's Writers, fifth edition, St. James Press (Detroit, MI), 1999.

PERIODICALS

Booklist, January 15, 1980, Barbara Elleman, review of *My Ballet Class,* p. 720; November 15, 1995, Carolyn Phelan, review of *Lili on Stage,* March 15, 1997, Hazel Rochman, review of *Lili Backstage,* p. 1247; May 1, 1997, Hazel Rochman, review of *Young Mozart,* p. 1500; February 15, 1998, p. 1019; March 15, 1998, Hazel Rochman, review of *Isadora Dances,* p. 1246; November 1, 1998, Ilene Cooper, review of *Caribbean Dreams,* p. 503; July, 1999, Michael Cart, review of *ABC Pop!,* p. 1949; December 1, 1999, Susan Dove Lempke, review of *Sophie Skates,* p. 711; May 1, 2000, Gillian Engberg, review of *123 Pop!,* p. 1672; June 1, 2000, p. 1909; September 1, 2000, Stephanie Zvirin, review of *Sophie Skates,* p. 118; March 1, 2001, Stephanie Zvirin, review of *Isadora Dances,* p. 1280.

Bulletin of the Center for Children's Books, April, 1993, Deborah Stevenson, review of *Lili at Ballet,* p. 253; September, 1997, p. 14; April, 1998, p. 82; July, 1998, p. 386; June, 1999, p. 354.

Horn Book, June, 1979, Mary M. Burns, review of *Ben's Trumpet,* pp. 293-294; May-June, 1993, Hanna B. Zeiger, review of *Lili at Ballet,* p. 318; January-February, 1996, Hanna B. Zeiger, review of *Lili on Stage,* p. 98; July-August, 1997, p. 443; May-June, 1999, Lolly Robinson, review of *ABC Pop!,* p. 315; January-February, 2000, review of *Sophie Skates,* p. 66; March-April, 2000, review of *Listen to the City,* p. 186; May-June, 2000, Lolly Robinson, review of *123 Pop!,* p. 294.

Junior Bookshelf, August, 1993, review of *Over the Green Hills,* pp. 127-128.

Kirkus Reviews, May 15, 1991, p. 672; January 1, 1993, review of *Lili at Ballet,* p. 61; April 1, 1997, p. 558; January 15, 1998, p. 113; April 1, 1998, p. 496; October 1, 1998, p. 1460; May 1, 1999, p. 722.

New York Times Book Review, May 22, 1983, Leonard S. Marcus, review of *City Seen from A to Z,* p. 39; November 11, 1984, p. 55; January 15, 1995, p. 25; July 20, 1997, p. 22.

Publishers Weekly, August 2, 1976, review of *Max,* p. 114; February 27, 1981, Elaine Edelman, "Rachel Isadora and Robert Maiorano," pp. 66-67; October 10, 1994, p. 70; February 13, 1995, p. 79; March 31, 1997, review of *Young Mozart,* p. 73; March 2, 1998, review of *Isadora Dances,* p. 67; October 26, 1998, review of *Caribbean Dreams,* p. 65; October 11, 1999, review of *Sophie Skates,* p. 74; January 1, 2001, review of *Nick Plays Baseball,* p. 92.

School Library Journal, February, 1979, Marjorie Lewis, review of *Ben's Trumpet,* p. 43; June, 1991, p. 80; March, 1998, p. 196; August, 1998, Gebregeorgis Yohannes, review of *A South African Night,* p. 140; April, 1999, p. 99; June, 1999, p. 116; August, 1999, p. 39; November, 1999, p. 143; May, 2000, Grace Oliff, review of *Listen to the City,* p. 144; June, 2000, p. 133; April, 2001, Adele Greenlee, review of *Nick Plays Baseball,* p. 131.

Teacher Librarian, May, 1999, p. 47.

Washington Post Book World, May 8, 1983, Beryl Lieff Benderly, "This Is the Way the World Works," pp. 16-17.*

*   *   *

JAMES, David 1955-

PERSONAL: Born 1955, in Detroit, MI; son of Lindon (a gas company serviceman) and Sharon (a secretary; maiden name, Kyle) James; married Debra Marie Ketterer (a nurse), December 30, 1977; children: Collin David, Nathan Lindon, Leah Helene. *Education:* Western Michigan University, B.A., 1977; Central Michigan University, M.A., 1979; Wayne State University, Ed.D., 1998.

ADDRESSES: Home—P.O. Box 721, Linden, MI 48451. *Office*—Dean's Office, Oakland Community College, 7350 Cooley Lake, Waterford, MI 48327.

CAREER: St. Clair Community College, Port Huron, MI, instructor in English, 1979-80; Siena Heights College, Adrian, MI, director of admissions, 1980-86; University of Michigan-Flint, Flint, MI, director of admissions, 1986-96; Oakland Community College, Waterford, MI, dean of Academic and Student Services, 1996—.

AWARDS, HONORS: Poetry grant from Michigan Council for the Arts, 1983.

WRITINGS:

A Heart out of This World (poetry), Carnegie-Mellon University Press, 1984.
Do Not Give Dogs What Is Holy (poetry), March Street Press, 1994.

Contributor of poems, stories, and one-act plays to magazines, including *Mid-American Review, Quarterly West, Parting Gifts, Driftwood Review, Rattle, American Literary Review, Poetry Now, Paris Review, Slant, Main Street Poetry Journal, Sou'wester,* and *Cimarron Review.*

SIDELIGHTS: David James told *CA:* "I've been writing for over twenty-five years now; it looks like I'm in it for the long haul. I try not to censor my thoughts, but allow my frazzled brain to connect wherever and to whatever it wants to."

*   *   *

JENKINS, Beverly 1951-

PERSONAL: Born February 15, 1951, in Detroit, MI; daughter of Cornelius Hunter (a retired teacher) and Delores Hunter (a retired administrative assistant); married Mark Jenkins; children: Melaina, Jonathan. *Ethnicity:* "African American." *Education:* Studied English literature at Michigan State University.

ADDRESSES: Home—Belleville, MI. *Agent*—c/o HarperCollins/Avon Books, 10 East 53rd St., 20th Fl., New York, NY 10022.

CAREER: Writer. Worked for the Michigan State University graduate library, 1974-80; started theater company at Michigan State University; read poetry in library shows, East Lansing, MI; has worked as a librarian in Belleville, MI.

MEMBER: Romance Writers Association.

AWARDS, HONORS: Night Song was named a Waldenbooks Bestseller, 1994.

WRITINGS:

ROMANCE NOVELS

Night Song, Avon (New York, NY), 1994.
Vivid, Avon (New York, NY), 1995.
Indigo, Avon (New York, NY), 1996.
Topaz, Avon (New York, NY), 1997.
Throughout the Storm, Avon (New York, NY), 1998.
The Taming of Jesse Rose, Avon (New York, NY), 1999.
Always and Forever, Avon (New York, NY), 2000.

SIDELIGHTS: Staking out new territory in the genre of romance fiction, Beverly Jenkins has tapped a massive audience with her stories set in the late nineteenth century that feature all-black casts. Her novels have been heralded for presenting black life in a positive light, as well as for providing a vivid sense of place and time thanks to her extensive use of historical details. "My mission in life has turned into bringing that history back to life," Jenkins said in a telephone interview with *CA* about her focus on the black experience. "We're a very, very proud race. And America could not be America without the African-American patches in the American history quilt."

Jenkins's novels go beyond "traditional" black issues and frequently shatter stereotypes about the black experience. "Romance is a necessary part of life, but so many books about black people are studies in survival," she told a contributor in *People.* "Not everything has to be about the civil rights movement." Her novels have prompted many grateful letters from fans, who often laud her positive treatment of blacks. As she noted in her interview, "Black women are so grateful and so appreciative to have positive stories that reflect not only the positive relationships between black men and black women, but highlight the history." Jenkins's historical research has won her a degree of respect not often accorded romance writers; her novels have become required reading in some college courses and a topic for book clubs more interested in history than romance.

Jenkins's roots as a storyteller derive from her early years growing up in Detroit. Her father was a high school teacher and her mother an administrative assistant; both parents instilled a strong appreciation of learning in their seven children. "Education has always been very, very important," noted Jenkins about her family. "It made me like an addict," she added in *People* in reference to the bounty of books in her childhood home. "I had to have so much print every day. One summer, I'd read nothing but Zane Grey. Or Isaac Asimov. Every day."

A bright student, Jenkins got her first taste of writing as editor of the school newspaper while a fourth grader at Jones Elementary School in Detroit. She gives a lot of credit to her elementary school teachers for setting her on the right path toward her writing career. Her reading prowess and talent for speaking before a crowd resulted in frequent appearances as a narrator for school plays. Jenkins wore many hats in her school productions, often serving as announcer, choir member, and dancer. Her love of performing has continued through the years, and reading from her works to audiences of her fans is one of her greatest thrills today.

While Jenkins read many romance novels as a youth, her greatest love was westerns by authors such as Grey and Louis L'Amour. This love was fueled by her grandfather, who was a big fan the genre and of "shoot-'em-up" western movies. One of Jenkins's great treats as a child was watching old John Wayne movies with her grandfather on weekends. From her mother, Jenkins gained an appreciation of history, especially of the black experience that textbooks in her school virtually ignored. She lamented the fact that few people knew anything about black history during the period between the end of slavery and the civil rights movements that began in the mid-twentieth century. "History books have a tendency to say we didn't exist," she told *People.* "It's always black folks came to America, black folks were slaves, black folks were freed in 1865. Then we disappeared. History picks us up again rioting in Watts in 1965. But what happened for those 100 years?" She expanded on this for Kelley L. Carter in the *Detroit Free Press,* saying, "We knew we were here. We built colleges, we built churches, we raised families. So I think that's my mission. To retell that 19th-century history, the bittersweet story that it was."

Jenkins took her interest in books to Michigan State University, where she majored in English literature. While a student there, she met her future husband, Mark Jenkins, who later became a fervent supporter of her quest to become a writer. Although she didn't graduate from Michigan State, she remained there as librarian in the graduate library for six years starting in 1974. She also helped start a theater company at the school. Jenkins's writing during this time consisted mostly of poetry, and she and a friend often read their material at poetry shows in East Lansing.

With urging from her husband, Jenkins began writing her first romance novel in the 1980s. Her setting for her first book was an 1880s settlement in the Midwest, where many blacks relocated after the Civil War. While containing the usual passion and sexual fireworks of romance fiction, Jenkins's story also offered extensive historical passages that chronicled life on the plantation, the black migration to the North, and the hardships faced by blacks staking out a new life in a new territory. "I have a tendency to write the history first," noted Jenkins in *People.* "So I have to give them large love scenes to reward the readers."

It took Jenkins thirteen years to finish writing her first novel, and finding a publisher proved difficult. "Publishers didn't believe there was a market," Jenkins remembered in *People.* "Like advertisers, they believed black people didn't have the money to buy these things." After four years of trying to get her book published, Jenkins finally hooked up with Avon Books in

1994, thanks to the efforts of agent Vivian Stephens. Avon recognized the potential of her first novel and printed 78,000 copies, an especially high number for romance fiction. Titled *Night Song,* Jenkins's inaugural effort proved a tremendous success and became a Waldenbooks bestseller for the year. It was also chosen as an alternate book of the month by the Doubleday Book Club and Literary Guild. "It's unusual for a first novel to be chosen, but we thought we could sell it," commented Arlene Friedman, editorial director of the Doubleday Book Club, about *Night Song* in *People.* "And we liked the authentic historical background with the romance." Called "totally captivating" by a reviewer in *Affaire de Coeur, Night Song* was one of the first romance novels to display black characters on its cover. When the book was signed, Jenkins even got involved in the search for a model for the cover, tracking down someone she had seen in *Essence* magazine.

The success of *Night Song* allowed Jenkins to quit her job as a librarian and focus on writing full time. Proving that her first novel was not beginner's luck, she struck gold again with *Vivid,* published in 1995. Set in the rugged countryside of western Michigan in 1876, this book shattered a number of stereotypes about blacks. Its main character was a black female doctor who had to overcome prejudices against blacks as well as those against women practicing medicine. As in *Night Song,* Jenkins wove extensive history throughout her story and even included a bibliography of suggested readings at the back of the book. Marcia Abramson gave *Vivid* four stars in her review in the *Detroit Free Press,* and sales of the book were brisk. "Though *Vivid* is only her second novel, Jenkins' writing is as impressive as the scholarship bibliography at the back of the book," noted Abramson.

In *Indigo,* published in 1996, Jenkins focused on the brewing romance between a member of a unique elite class of pre-Civil War blacks and a former slave who nurtures him after he is injured. Set against a backdrop of the underground movement to free slaves, the story explored new ground by delving into prejudice not just against blacks but between blacks of different classes. "As usual, Ms. Jenkins has created wonderful, sensitive, caring people. . . . The history is tactfully presented to give the reader a better understanding of the injustices of slavery," said a reviewer in *Rendezvous.*

In September of 1997 Jenkins published her fourth romance novel, a western titled *Topaz.* Dedicated to her grandfather and set in Oklahoma, which was still Indian Territory in the 1880s, it concerns a woman investigative reporter who enters into a marriage of convenience with a lawman. Her seventh novel, *Always and Forever,* a story of mail-order brides making the journey from Illinois to a frontier settlement in Kansas developed by black men who served in the Civil War, is a companion piece that details "what happened before, during and after the events in *Topaz,*" related Gwendolyn E. Osborne in *Black Issues Book Review.* The book includes an attraction-of-opposites romance between the starchy woman banker and the former Texas peace officer who are in charge of the group of brides. "In true Jenkins style, *Always and Forever* provides valuable glimpses into little-known aspects of black life in post-Civil War America," Osborne reported.

Jenkins's output of one book a year may be considered low by romance standards, but her books require her to spend approximately a year on research. She also must fit her writing and research into a busy schedule of what in her interview she called "typical small-town kind of stuff," especially activities with her children that range from Brownies to band boosters. Jenkins feels the well of her creativity runs deep and expects to keep churning out the books for many years to come. "There's so much African-American history that has not been highlighted," she said. "I could be writing for the next twenty-five years and still not touch all the material that's there." A science fiction buff, Jenkins would eventually like to write a science fiction romance—one that emphasizes the science fiction aspect, with the romance in the background. She has no regrets regarding her choice of genre, even though romances are not always considered "serious" literature. "I enjoy being a popular writer," she claimed. "I don't need anybody to tell me that this is art and that is not. It's in the eyes of the reader."

BIOGRAPHICAL/CRITICAL SOURCES:

BOOKS

Contemporary Black Biography, Volume 14, Gale (Detroit, MI), 1997.

PERIODICALS

Affaire de Coeur, July, 1994, review of *Night Song,* p. 40; November, 1995, p. 39.
Black Issues Book Review, September, 2000, Gwendolyn E. Osborne, review of *Always and Forever,* p. 24.

Detroit Free Press, November 22, 1995; December 6, 1995; November 13, 1996, p. 44; September 15, 2000, Kelley L. Carter, "Heartfelt Stories," section C, pp. 1-2.
People, February 13, 1995, pp. 153-155.
Rendezvous, September, 1996, review of *Indigo,* p. 22.
Tallahassee Democrat, December 10, 1995.*

For a previous interview given by Jenkins, please see *Contemporary Authors* volume 156, pp. 237-39.

*   *   *

JENSEN, Paul M(orris) 1944-

PERSONAL: Born January 11, 1944, in Greenport, NY; son of Christian (a mariner) and Emily (a teacher; maiden name, Morris) Jensen. *Education:* State University of New York at Albany, B.A., 1965; Columbia University, M.F.A., 1966; further graduate study at State University of New York at Buffalo, 1969, and New York University, 1973, 1974.

ADDRESSES: Home—31 East St., Oneonta, NY 13820. *Office*—Department of Communication Arts, State University of New York College, Oneonta, NY 13820. *E-mail*—jensenpm@snyoneva.cc.oneonta.edu.

CAREER: High school teacher of English, 1966-67; State University of New York College at Oneonta, instructor, 1967-70, assistant professor, beginning 1970, currently professor of film.

WRITINGS:

The Cinema of Fritz Lang, A. S. Barnes (San Diego, CA), 1969.
Boris Karloff and His Films, A. S. Barnes (San Diego, CA), 1974.
The Men Who Made the Monsters, Twayne (New York, NY), 1996.
Hitchcock Becomes "Hitchcock," Midnight Marquee Press, 2000.

Contributor to books, including *The Sound Film,* edited by Arthur Lennig, Walter Snyder (Troy, NY), 1969; *The Hollywood Screenwriter,* edited by Richard Corliss, Avon (New York, NY), 1972; *The Classic Cinema: Essays in Criticism,* edited by Stanley J. Solomon, Harcourt (New York, NY), 1973; *Masterworks of the Ger-*

man *Cinema,* Harper (New York, NY), 1974; and *Boris Karloff,* edited by Gary Svehla and Susan Svehla, Midnight Marquee Press, 1996. Contributor to periodicals, including *Variety, Phantasm, Video Watchdog, Scarlet Street, Films in Review, Film Heritage,* and *Film Comment.*

WORK IN PROGRESS: Research on the life and career of Merian C. Cooper.

SIDELIGHTS: Paul M. Jensen informed *CA* that he appeared as an interview subject in documentary films that accompanied the Universal Studios DVD releases of the films *Frankenstein, The Mummy, The Invisible Man, Bride of Frankenstein,* the 1943 film *The Phantom of the Opera,* and *Creature from the Black Lagoon.* He added: "I also wrote and recorded the film-long secondary audio track commentary for the DVD release of *The Mummy.*"

*   *   *

JEROME, John 1932-

PERSONAL: Born November 7, 1932, in Tulsa, OK; son of Ralph and Gwendolyn (Stewart) Jerome; married Nancy Sellman, December 20, 1952 (divorced, 1965); married Chris McCall (a writer), September 3, 1966; children: (first marriage) Kathleen, Martin Stewart, Julia. *Education:* North Texas State College (now University), B.A., 1955.

ADDRESSES: Home—Franconia, NH. *Agent*—c/o Random House, Author Mail, 299 Park Ave., New York, NY 10171-0002.

CAREER: Sports Car Digest, Odessa, TX, editor, 1959-62; *Car and Driver Magazine,* New York, NY, managing editor, 1962-64; Campbell-Ewald Co., Detroit, MI, advertising copywriter, 1964-65; *Skiing Magazine,* New York, NY, editor, 1965-67; columnist for *Esquire* magazine; freelance writer and editor.

WRITINGS:

Sports Illustrated Skiing, Lippincott (Philadelphia, PA), 1971, revised edition published as *Skiing,* Lippincott (Philadelphia, PA), 1971.
The Death of the Automobile, W.W. Norton (New York, NY), 1972.

Truck: On Rebuilding a Worn-out Pickup, and Other Post-Technological Adventures, Houghton (Boston, MA), 1977.
On Mountains: Thinking about Terrain, Harcourt (New York, NY), 1978.
The Sweet Spot in Time, Summit, 1980.
Staying with It, Viking (New York, NY), 1984.
Staying Supple, Bantam (New York, NY), 1987.
Stone Work: Reflections on Serious Play and Other Aspects of Country Life, Viking (New York, NY), 1989.
The Writing Trade: A Year in the Life, Cahners Publishing, 1991.
The Man on the Medal: The Life and Times of America's First Great Ski Racer, photographs by Dick and Miggs Durrance, Durrance Enterprise (Aspen, CO), 1995.
Blue Rooms: Ripples: Rivers, Pools, and Other Waters, Holt (New York, NY), 1997.
The Elements of Effort: Reflections on the Art and Science of Running, Breakaway Books (New York, NY), 1997.
On Turning Sixty-five: Notes from the Field, Random House (New York, NY), 2000.

SIDELIGHTS: John Jerome has built a successful writing career with subjects as varied as physical fitness, truck repair, wall-building, and growing old. Christopher Lehmann-Haupt of the *New York Times* has written extensive reviews of a number of Jerome's works. "You understand automotive mechanics?" he asked in one critique. ". . . I don't understand them. Never did. And I loved John Jerome's *Truck.*" He continued, "It doesn't really matter to your appreciation of *Truck* whether you even care to understand automobiles. The book is not so much about automotive mechanics as it is about mind and matter. . . . You find out a lot about the way the human mind works."

On Mountains is another example of Jerome's philosophical-technical approach to his subject matter. As Lehmann-Haupt, commenting once again in the *New York Times,* wrote, "[Jerome's] passages . . . are lucid verbal diagrams that sometimes verge on poetry. And when he can relate himself directly to his subject . . . his pages are almost exciting." *Time* writer Peter Stoler, on the other hand, noted that "*On Mountains* wittily bypasses the customary because-it-is-there rationale to examine the fascination and terror of peaks and promontories. . . . Even those who have never left sea level will enjoy the author's lofty musings." A *New York Times Book Review* critic echoed Stoler's opinion of *On Mountains,* saying that "it is true that many others have covered this high ground before, but I am unaware of an up-to-date book on mountains that so summarizes the subject as clearly as does this one. . . . While the trails are still too snowy or slick, this is the book to read, preparing for your own delectable mountain this summer."

Jerome's interest in physical fitness is reflected in his *One Sweet Spot in Time* and *Staying with It,* the latter an account of his own attempts to become a competitive swimmer at the age of forty-seven. As Jerome writes in *Staying with It,* he wanted to find out how increased training balanced out with an increase in age. Lehmann-Haupt admired the way Jerome "alternates between specific activity and reflection on it," asserting that "[t]he payoff is a delight." The critic continued, "The narrative spine and solid information in *Staying with It* combine to give Mr. Jerome both the chance and the space to ramble comfortably."

Lehmann-Haupt also reviewed Jerome's 1989 volume, *Stone Work,* a reflective account of the details of moving a stone wall. "The object," according to the critic, ". . . is for Mr. Jerome to get outside his head." As Jerome tears down the old wall, he muses, "It would be an exhausting business, almost a parody of human effort. Tear down the old wall, haul it to the new site, stack it back up again stone by stone. Stone is another word for total: stone-broke, stone cold, stone-deaf. Moving a wall would be stone work—hyperwork, Ur-work, mindless, brutalizing toil." But Jerome soon lapses into reflections on the meaning of what he is doing—and on his own family ghosts. Lehmann-Haupt noted that the book also "resolves itself into a Thoreauvian meditation on the seasons" and commented that *Stone Work* "is Mr. Jerome's most intelligent and skillfully written book to date."

In 1991 Jerome mused on the freelance writing profession in *The Writing Trade: A Year in the Life,* which a *Publishers Weekly* critic called "a wise and knowing guide through a full turn of seasons, on the loop and at the keyboard." He returned to the subject of physical fitness in his 1997 book *Elements of Effort: Reflections on the Art and Science of Running.* The essays in this volume revolve around the seasons, as Jerome reflects on life while running. Wes Lukowsky said in *Booklist* that it is "doubtful" that the book will become a classic, but that "it will certainly be a favorite among those who find the experience of running as rewarding spiritually as physically."

Jerome's ruminations on various bodies of water are collected in his 1997 book *Blue Rooms: Ripples, Rivers, Pools, and Other Waters. New York Times* reviewer Carolyn T. Hughes called this work an "odd mixture of memoir, travelogue and scientific analysis." Mixing new material with essays that had appeared elsewhere, Jerome "paints a glistening picture of his life in water," according to a *Publishers Weekly* reviewer. Reflecting on favorite swimming spots from his childhood, he also remembers and philosophizes about his family and life and in general. The *Publishers Weekly* reviewer noted that "Jerome proves that water carries memory and insight as surely as it carries sound."

The year before his sixty-fifth birthday, Jerome decided to keep a journal of his reflections on aging. It was published in 2000 as *On Turning Sixty-five: Notes from the Field.* After rereading Henry David Thoreau, Jerome, with what GraceAnne A. DeCandido in *Booklist* called "surprising grace and no small measure of cantankerousness," shares the positive and negative effects of growing older. He is distressed, for example, when he and his wife find that they no longer have the strength for long stretches of canoeing. Jerome dwells especially on what he calls "draw[ing] the line between fighting and accepting." A critic for *Publishers Weekly* said that although Jerome "offers no insights on age and death, his talent for conveying his experience with an evolved, observant awareness makes this capably written relevant for anyone facing 65."

BIOGRAPHICAL/CRITICAL SOURCES:

BOOKS

Jerome, John, *On Turning Sixty-five: Notes from the Field,* Random House (New York, NY), 2000.

Jerome, John, *Staying with It,* Viking (New York, NY), 1984.

Jerome, John, *Stone Work: Reflections on Serious Play and Other Aspects of Country Life,* Viking (New York, NY), 1989.

PERIODICALS

Booklist, November 1, 1997, Wes Lukowsky, review of *Elements of Effort,* p. 447; April 1, 2000, GraceAnne A. DeCandido, review of *On Turning Sixty-five,* p. 1419.

National Review, March 3, 1978; September, 1, 1978.

New York Times, November 20, 1972; February 21, 1977; June 19, 1984, Christopher Lehmann-Haupt, review of *Staying with It,* p. C28; July 3, 1989,

Christopher Lehmann-Haupt, review of *Stone Work*, section 1, p. 17; December 14, 1997, Carolyn T. Hughes, review of *Blue Rooms.*

New York Times Book Review, April 16, 1978.

Publishers Weekly, November 15, 1991, review of *The Writing Trade,* pp. 58-59; May 5, 1997, review of *Blue Rooms,* p. 190; April 24, 2000, review of *On Turning Sixty-five,* p. 68

Time, April 10, 1978.

Washington Post Book World, November 12, 1972.*

*   *   *

JOHNSON, Denis 1949-

PERSONAL: Born 1949, in Munich, West Germany (now Germany).

ADDRESSES: Home—Good Grief, ID. *Office*—c/o Robert Cornfield, 145 West 79th St., New York, NY 10024.

CAREER: Writer, journalist. Taught one semester at the Iowa Writers' Workshop, University of Iowa, 1992.

AWARDS, HONORS: National Poetry Series Award; American Institute of Arts and Letters, Sue Kaufman Award for Fiction, for *Angels;* Whiting Writers' Award from the Whiting Foundation, 1986, for works demonstrating "exceptionally promising emerging talent"; *The Name of the World* listed as one of *Salon*'s ten best fiction books of 2000; grants from Arizona Arts Commission, Massachusetts Arts Council, John Guggenheim Foundation, and National Endowment for the Arts.

WRITINGS:

The Man among the Seals (poetry), Stone Wall Press (Iowa City, IA), 1969.

Inner Weather (poetry), Graywolf (Port Townsend, WA), 1976.

The Incognito Lounge, and Other Poems (poetry), Random House (New York, NY), 1982.

Angels (novel), Knopf (New York, NY), 1983.

Fiskadoro (novel), Knopf (New York, NY), 1985.

The Stars at Noon (novel), Knopf (New York, NY), 1986.

(Author of text) Mark Klett, *Traces of Eden: Travels in the Desert Southwest* (photography), Beaverbooks, 1986.

The Veil (poetry), Knopf (New York, NY), 1987.

Resuscitation of a Hanged Man (novel), Farrar, Straus (New York, NY), 1991.

Jesus' Son (short stories), Farrar, Straus (New York, NY), 1992.

The Throne of the Third Heaven of the Nations Millennium General Assembly: Poems Collected and New (poetry), Harper (New York, NY), 1995.

Already Dead: A California Gothic (novel), Harper (New York, NY), 1997.

The Name of the World (novel), Harper (New York, NY), 2000.

Hellhound on My Trail (play), produced in San Francisco, CA, 2000.

Seek: Reports from the Edges of America & Beyond, Harper (New York, NY), 2001.

ADAPTATIONS: Jesus' Son was adapted into a film by Elizabeth Cuthrell, David Urrutia, and Oren Moverman, directed by Alison Maclean, and released by Lions Gate in 1999.

SIDELIGHTS: Denis Johnson's poems and novels provide candid, slice-of-life perspectives on offbeat subjects. In his first verse collection, *The Man among the Seals,* he included poems about a man imagining an auto mishap and one speculating about the lives of two mice trapped in mousetraps. These and other poems in the volume were prized for their lively structure—rolling rhythms and sometimes jarring line breaks—as well as for their somewhat odd points of view. A critic in *Virginia Quarterly Review* called *The Man among the Seals* "an astonishing first book" and praised the poems as "dramatically satisfying and whole." The reviewer also marveled at Johnson's accomplished writing—he was only twenty when the book appeared—and declared that the poems seemed those "of a mature writer in mid-career."

In his second collection, *Inner Weather,* "Johnson forgoes some of his stylistic experimentation," related Joe Nordgren in the *Dictionary of Literary Biography: American Poets Since World War II, Third Series.* Because of this, "his poetic structure more consistency complements his poems' sense and themes," Nordgren added. Most of the fifteen poems in this collection are about ordinary people in despair. "While dramatizing daily events and searching for ways to allow his subjects to project themselves, he accounts for the less than perfect, the less than dazzling aspects of life that people gloss over so as to avoid blame or guilt," Nordgren observed.

Johnson next published *The Incognito Lounge, and Other Poems,* which strengthened his reputation as a chronicler of the unusual aspects of American culture.

His characters are sad, lonely, often on the margins of society, denizens of seedy bars and greasy-spoon diners. The title poem, according to Nordgren, is "a frightening—at times surreal—descent into the refuse of fallen lives." Yet Johnson does not look down on these characters, and he recognizes that they are capable of redemption, Nordgren added. Alan Williamson, critiquing the collection in the *New York Times Book Review,* declared that Johnson is "good at American voices" and added that he convincingly "suffers over the anomie he describes." A commentator for *Antioch Review* was even more impressed, calling *The Incognito Lounge* "a welcome antidote to any number of literary and spiritual malaises." The critic cited "the scalding wit of the poems" and contended that *The Incognito Lounge* was among "the most appealing and exciting books" of 1982.

Johnson's body of poetic work, including later collections *The Veil* and *The Throne of the Third Heaven of the Nations Millennium General Assembly: Poems Collected and New,* shows his poems to be "distinguished by its stylistic vitality and emotional honesty, indicating his intense engagement with language and experience," in Nordgren's opinion. "Forgiveness and surviving memories and mistakes of the past are his dominant themes, since it is impossible to live, in his words, as a 'fallen person.'"

Johnson followed *The Incognito Lounge* with his first novel, *Angels,* which tells of two desperate characters—Jamie and Bill—and their decline into crime. Jamie and Bill meet on a bus leaving Oakland, California, where Jamie had just left her unfaithful husband. Heading east with her two children, Jamie befriends Bill, a thrice-divorced ex-convict with whom she becomes romantically involved. In Pittsburgh, the lovers part, with Bill heading for Chicago. Jamie eventually travels there too, to find Bill, but she is raped during her search. After the lovers rejoin, they travel to Phoenix, Bill's hometown. There Jamie succumbs to drug addiction and Bill resumes his criminal activities. Near the book's end, drugged-out Jamie is committed to an asylum. Bill, who had murdered a prison guard, awaits execution.

Angels earned critical praise for Johnson's evocation of American life's grimmer aspects. *Newsweek's* Peter S. Prescott called Johnson "an accurate and unsentimental observer of people and events" and commended his skill at making readers "know his characters rather better than we might want—to the point of forgiveness." Prescott called *Angels* "a beautiful book." Speer Morgan, writing in *Saturday Review,* also cited Johnson's ability in eliciting readers' "empathy with [the novel's] characters." Morgan deemed *Angels* "a fine first novel."

In his second novel, *Fiskadoro,* Johnson wrote of life after a nuclear holocaust. Set in the near future, *Fiskadoro* presents a world of mutants, primitive fisherman and traders. Among these survivors are Grandmother Wright, a one-hundred-year-old woman—half Chinese—who has lost her ability to speak; A. T. Cheung, a ragtime clarinetist who is preoccupied with history; and Fiskadoro, Cheung's protégé, who lacks memory and thus seems the most likely candidate to contend with the future.

Some critics were exuberant in recommending *Fiskadoro* as a compelling tale of survival and acceptance. *Newsweek's* Prescott, who called *Fiskadoro* "a remarkable novel," wrote that its "principal theme concerns the problems of learning what has been lost and the role memory plays in survival." Similarly, Bruce Van Wyngarden wrote in *Saturday Review* that *Fiskadoro* presents "a world where knowledge is a shattered mirror and no one has more than a couple of pieces." Van Wyngarden deemed Johnson's second novel "a world of bewitching power." Stephen Dobyns in the *Washington Post Book World,* described *Fiskadoro* as "beautifully written and constantly entertaining" and called Johnson "a wonderful story-teller."

Johnson's next novel, *The Stars at Noon,* failed to elicit the praise accorded his previous books, however. Set in 1984 in Managua, Nicaragua, the story revolves around the activities of its self-destructive narrator—a "North American female prostitute-drifter with a press card, which has been revoked"—and her lover, referred to only as "the Englishman," who is on the run after passing Costa Rican industrial secrets to the Sandinistas. "Johnson apparently means for this novel to address a modern condition marked by cynicism and despair," wrote John Gabree in the *Washington Post.* The critic added that the "narrator is so bent on her own corruption it is impossible to tell where the boundaries of good and evil lie, or whether there is any good at all. . . . All that is being played out in these pages are the final twitches of a dying soul." Michiko Kakutani declared in the *New York Times* that *The Stars at Noon* successfully "conjures up a hellish vision of Managua and the outlying country through dozens of details and heat-glazed images," but found that "we never really care whether or not [the protagonist] betrays her lover, and we certainly never care what eventually happens to her. Mr. Johnson's shimmering descriptions of Central America provide us with moments of relief, but in the end, his narrator's tiresome voice drags the novel down, submerging the magic of his prose."

Critics have noted a variety of influences on Johnson's work, particularly his fiction—one critic compares

Fiskadoro to both Samuel Beckett's work and reggae music. In the *New York Times Book Review,* Johnson acknowledged an eccentric assortment of influences ranging from the writings of Robert Stone and Flannery O'Connor to the songs of Bob Dylan and the music of Eric Clapton and Jimi Hendrix. Johnson added: "Other influences come and go, but those I admire the most and those I admired the earliest . . . have something to say in every line I write."

Jesus' Son, Johnson's first collection of short fiction, consists of eleven brief, interconnected stories narrated by an unnamed young man who is addicted to drugs and alcohol. The book's title comes from Lou Reed's song "Heroin" ("When I'm rushing on my run / And I feel just like Jesus' son"), and addiction of one sort or another figures prominently in each of the stories. Indeed, drugs and alcohol are virtually the only constants in the narrator's life; the settings of the stories vary (rural Iowa, Seattle, Phoenix), as do the man's friends, and the reader learns nothing about his past. He reveals himself exclusively through his words and his various incarnations: a hitchhiker, a barfly, the owner of a $60 car with no brakes. Those around him are an assortment of lowlifes and losers, inhabitants of a bleak and often violent American demimonde. The most striking feature of these stories, however, is the incantatory, almost dreamlike, quality of the narrator's voice. Although almost every story recounts some gruesome or sensational incident—a horrific car accident, a bizarre emergency room case, a pointless shooting—the narrator's voice remains eerily matter-of-fact throughout.

Jesus' Son received numerous positive reviews. *New York Times* critic Michiko Kakutani lauded Johnson's "dazzling gift for poetic language, his natural instinct for metaphor and wordplay." *Nation* reviewer Marianne Wiggins found that "reading these stories is like reading ticker tape from the subconscious." And Todd Grimson, a *Los Angeles Times Book Review* contributor, noted, "Denis Johnson writes as though he inhabits a waking dream." Jack Miles concluded a long *Atlantic Monthly* review of the collection with these words: "Denis Johnson's path as a writer . . . is as untypical as his vision, but *Jesus' Son* may eventually be read not just as a moment in his evolution but as a distinctive turn in the history of the form. He is doing something deeply new in these stories, and the formal novelty brings us into a new intimacy with the violence that is rising around us in this country like the killing waters of a flood." Interestingly, Johnson, himself a recovered drug and alcohol addict, was at first reluctant to publish the collection, even though most of the stories had already appeared in various periodicals. He considered the work

too autobiographical, too personal. As he remarked to a *Washington Post* interviewer in 1993, "The reason I wasn't publishing them is I didn't want people to say, 'Oh, look at this guy!' But I don't think we really have the right to make decisions like that. Authors should think of themselves as dead."

The response of some critics to Johnson's next novel, *Already Dead: A California Gothic,* was not nearly as positive. The book seemed to perplex, even to annoy, several reviewers. Set in rural northern California, this complex, labyrinthine "gothic" (which features trolls, spirits, and all manner of New Age devotees) centers on Nelson Fairchild, Jr., an alcoholic marijuana farmer who stands to inherit a substantial fortune. Nelson has a great many problems, including being targeted by hit men, but his main concern is how to get rid of his estranged wife. Nelson's dying father, a devout Catholic who will not tolerate divorce, plans to leave his fortune to this estranged wife, hoping thereby to sustain his son's marriage. Nelson, however, has other plans, and sets out to find someone to kill his wife. In Carl Van Ness, he finds the perfect candidate, for Van Ness, a violent criminal bent on self-destruction, is, for all intents and purposes, "already dead."

But the plot of *Already Dead* defies easy summarization or encapsulation. David Gates, writing in the *New York Times Book Review,* found the plot engulfed in "murk," but noted, "That's not a knock, necessarily. Johnson is a wonderful writer, and murk is one of the things he does best—even if it sometimes swamps the proceedings entirely." Gates, who considered the entire novel "a little over the top," went on to observe, "Johnson's characters, even the nonviolent ones, are so convincingly scary it's uncomfortable to be in their company." In a *New York* magazine review of the novel, Luc Sante wrote, "The narrative does not describe an arc so much as some kind of fractal meander." After wondering whether Johnson realized "how unbearable his protagonist is," or whether the book merely suffered from "a case of absent editor," Sante remained perplexed: "[B]ecause Johnson is such a splendid writer, and so tricky and idiosyncratic and non-Euclidian, . . . there may be something else afoot. *Maybe it's all a test.*"

The short novel *The Name of the World* focuses on a university professor's efforts to get on with his life following the deaths of his wife and daughter in an automobile accident. For the first few years after the tragedy, the professor, Michael Reed, is existing rather than living; then an unconventional young woman—a cellist and a stripper who nevertheless reminds Reed of his lost loved ones—comes along to shake him up. An *Economist* reviewer noted that the plot "would seem slight, unless it happened to you" and dubbed the book "a triumph of tone," filled with offbeat observations. *New York Times Book Review* commentator Robert Stone thought that sometimes the novel's "transitions are rocky, and the view can be dim. At other times, Johnson's unique lyricism lights up his book's interior world." Stone found the character of the cellist-stripper, Flower Cannon, "improbably believable, one of the book's finer creations," but Richard Eder, writing in the daily *New York Times,* deemed Reed's relationship with her "arbitrary and gestural, a necromancy that is incantation and very little magic." Eder contended that even though parts of the book were strong, Johnson's writing eventually turned into "poetic curdle." *Newsweek* critic David Gates, however, considered *The Name of the World* "a haunting novella," while a *Publishers Weekly* contributor remarked that it "manages to be both lyrical and raw." The *Economist* reviewer concluded, "Deft, moving, and wonderfully odd, this is a slim novel in physical size only."

In *Seek: Reports from the Edges of America & Beyond,* Johnson collected eleven essays written over a twenty-year period. They explore a diverse cross-section of people all searching for something to believe in and for a life that stands apart from the values of mainstream America. The people he writes about include Christian bikers, hippies, and right-wing militiamen. Although always present in his anecdotes, Johnson only refers to himself in the third person or as a separate character, a technique that creates "an askew, out-of-body point of view," in the opinion of a *Publishers Weekly* reviewer. While this strains his credibility as a reporter, it "adds sincerity to his plight as a human," noted the writer, who concluded that *Seek* is "intriguing and insightful."

BIOGRAPHICAL/CRITICAL SOURCES:

BOOKS

Contemporary Literary Criticism, Volume 52, Gale (Detroit, MI), 1989.
Contemporary Novelists, sixth edition, St. James Press (Detroit, MI), 1996.
Dictionary of Literary Biography, Volume 120: *American Poets since World War II, Third Series,* Gale (Detroit, MI), 1992.

PERIODICALS

American Book Review, January-February, 1983, p. 18; May-June 1985, pp. 15-16.

Antioch Review, spring, 1983.
Atlantic Monthly, June, 1993, Jack Miles, review of *Jesus' Son,* pp. 121-127.
Boston Review, October/November, 1993, review of *Jesus' Son,* pp. 30-31; February/March, 1996, pp. 31-33.
Chicago Tribune Book World, October 30, 1983.
Commonweal, August 9, 1985, pp. 444-45; August 13, 1993, review of *Jesus' Son,* p. 23.
Economist (US), July 15, 2000, "Six New Novels," p. 12.
Entertainment Weekly, August 15, 1997, review of *Already Dead: A California Gothic,* p. 68; May 11, 2001, review of *Seek: Reports from the Edges of America & Beyond,* p. 74.
Globe and Mail (Toronto), September 13, 1986.
Georgia Review, winter, 1982, Peter Stitt, "A Remarkable Diversity," pp. 911-22.
Harper's, August, 1999, Vince Passaro, review of *Jesus' Son,* p. 80.
Iowa Review, spring, 1982, pp. 246-50.
Library Journal, May 1, 1995; August, 1997, p. 130; September 1, 2000, Marc Kloszewski, review of *The Name of the World,* p. 249.
London Review of Books, June 20, 1984, pp. 19-20.
Los Angeles Times, September 28, 1983; November 7, 1986.
Los Angeles Times Book Review, May 5, 1985; February 28, 1993, Todd Grimson, review of *Jesus' Son,* p. 3.
Nation, February 15, 1993, Marianne Wiggins, review of *Jesus' Son,* pp. 208-209; June 25, 2001, David L. Ulin, review of *Seek: Reports from the Edges of America & Beyond,* p. 25.
Newsweek, September 19, 1983; July 8, 1985; July 31, 2000, David Gates, "What's in a Name? Denis Johnson's Topsy-turvy Novella Pulls with G-Force," p. 64 .
New York, August 4, 1997, Luc Sante, review of *Already Dead: A California Gothic,* pp. 57-58.
New Yorker, July 15, 1983, pp. 83-85.
New York Times, September 10, 1983; September 14, 1983, p. 14; May 1, 1985, p. C23; September 13, 1986; October 31, 1986; December 11, 1992, Michiko Kakutani, review of *Jesus' Son,* p. C31; July 14, 2000, Richard Eder, "The Ever-widening Circles of Grief."
New York Times Book Review, October 10, 1982; October 2, 1983; May 13, 1984; May 26, 1985; September 28, 1986, p. 7; October 18, 1987, p. 46; December 27, 1992, p. 5; August 31, 1997, David Gates, review of *Already Dead: A California Gothic,* p. 5; July 9, 2000, Robert Stone, "In Transit."

People Weekly, October 13, 1997, p. 39.

Poetry, May, 1997, p. 90.

Publishers Weekly, July 7, 1997, p. 49; May 15, 2000, review of *The Name of the World,* p. 86; May 7, 2001, review of *Seek: Reports from the Edges of America & Beyond,* p. 235.

Review of Contemporary Fiction, spring, 2001, Irving Malin, review of *The Name of the World,* p. 201.

Saturday Review, October, 1983, May/June, 1985.

Sewanee Review, summer, 1983, pp. 457-473.

Time, August 11, 1997, review of *Already Dead: A California Gothic,* p. 77.

Times (London), April 19, 1984.

Times Literary Supplement, April 4, 1984; May 4, 1984, p. 486; May 24, 1985.

Variety, September 4, 2000, Dennis Harvey, review of *Hellhound on My Trail,* p. 32.

Village Voice, June 4, 1985; October 28, 1986, p. 51.

Virginia Quarterly Review, winter, 1971.

Washington Post, November 1, 1986; February 3, 1993, p. C1.

Washington Post Book World, June 30, 1985; February 21, 1993, p. 9.

OTHER

Salon, http://www.salon.com/ (June 25, 2001), "Denis Johnson's 'Hippies'"; Laura Miller, review of *The Name of the World.**

*   *   *

JOHNSON, Edwin Clark 1945-
(Toby Johnson)

PERSONAL: Born August 4, 1945, in San Antonio, TX; son of Edwin Magruder (a wholesale florist) and Lois (a wholesale florist; maiden name, Clark) Johnson; companion to Clifton (Kip) Dollar (an innkeeper), since March 16, 1984. *Education:* St. Louis University, B.A., 1968; California Institute of Integral Studies, M.A., 1976, Ph.D., 1978. *Religion:* "Northern California Jungian Buddhist." *Avocational interests:* Gay activism, comparative religion.

ADDRESSES: Home—P.O. Box 2762, Wimberley, TX 78676. *Agent*—James Cypher, 616 Wolcott Ave., Beacon, NY 12508-4247. *E-mail*—tobyjohnso@aol.com.

CAREER: Servite friar, 1968-70; Mann Ranch Seminars, Ukiah, CA, senior staff member, 1972-74; Mount Zion Hospital, San Francisco, CA, psychiatric technician at Crisis Clinic, 1975-77; Tenderloin Clinic, San Francisco, CA, staff counselor, 1976-79; Urban and Rural Systems Association, San Francisco, CA, research associate, 1979-81; Southern Dharma Foundation, Hot Springs, NC, staff member, 1981; *Calendar,* San Antonio, TX, contributing editor, 1981-86; psychotherapist in private practice, San Antonio, TX, 1982-88; Liberty Books, Austin, TX, co-owner, 1989-94; bed and breakfast operator, with Clifton Dollar, 1997-2001. Member of services coordinating committee of San Francisco Mental Health Services; spokesperson for Gay Mental Health Task Force; member of Red Cross AIDS Task Force, San Antonio, TX.

MEMBER: SAGA (San Antonio Gay Alliance; co-chairman, 1982-84), Reality Club, Phi Beta Kappa, Alpha Sigma Nu.

AWARDS, HONORS: Lambda Literary Award for science fiction, 1990, and nomination to Gay Science Fiction Hall of Fame, 1999, both for *Secret Matter.* Lambda Literary Award, 2000, and *Foreword* magazine nomination for best gay/lesbian nonfiction, both for *Gay Spirituality.*

WRITINGS:

(With Toby Marotta) *The Politics of Homosexuality,* Houghton Mifflin (Boston, MA), 1981.

(With Toby Marotta) *Sons of Harvard: Gay Men from the Class of 1967,* Morrow (New York, NY), 1982.

(Under name Edwin Clark Johnson) *The Myth of the Great Secret: A Search for Spiritual Meaning in the Face of Emptiness,* Morrow (New York, NY), 1982.

In Search of God in the Sexual Underworld: A Mystical Journey, Morrow (New York, NY), 1983.

(Under name Toby Johnson) *Plague: A Novel about Healing,* Alyson (Boston, MA), 1987.

(Under name Toby Johnson) *Secret Matter,* Lavender Press (South Norwalk, CT), 1990.

Getting Life in Perspective, Lavender Press (South Norwalk, CT), 1991.

(Under name Toby Johnson) *The Myth of the Great Secret: An Appreciation of Joseph Cambpell,* Celestial Arts (Berkeley, CA), 1992.

(Under name Toby Johnson) *Gay Spirituality: The Role of Gay Identity in the Transformation of Human Consciousness,* Alyson (Los Angeles, CA), 2000.

Editor, *White Crane: A Journal of Gay Men's Spirituality.* Contributor to periodicals.

WORK IN PROGRESS: Two Spirits, a novel about Navajo spirituality, in collaboration with Walter L. Williams. *Gay Perspective: What Our Homosexuality Tells Us about Life, the Universe, and God.*

SIDELIGHTS: Edwin Clark Johnson, best known under the name Toby Johnson, addresses spiritual issues for gay people in his writings. At times Johnson uses science fiction or suspense novels to illustrate the various levels of spirituality in modern society. Other times he engages the reader directly in ethical or religious debate through works of nonfiction. In the novel, *Secret Matter,* for instance, Johnson explores homosexual identity and relationships by creating a race of aliens who interact with humans. *Plague: A Novel about Healing* is a thriller in which an AIDS educator must thwart a sinister plot to withhold a cure for the deadly illness. The book raises awareness not only on the subject of AIDS but also on spiritual aspects of healing.

Johnson is also the author of *Gay Spirituality: The Role of Gay Identity in the Transformation of Human Consciousness.* Himself a former Catholic monk, Johnson examines how the gay culture has ushered in 'a new age in spiritual transformation incorporating world religions, modern mythology, and social change,' to quote Jeff Ingram in *Library Journal.* A *Publishers Weekly* reviewer felt that *Gay Spirituality* "consists of putting a gay spin on many traditionally religious themes."

"Religion and spirituality have been the major driving forces in my life," Johnson told *CA.* "As a young man, I spent some seven years deeply involved with Catholic monastic life. *The Myth of the Great Secret* is the story of my exposure to world religions, Jungian thought, the work of Joseph Campbell, and modern (countercultural and 'new age') thought, and the way it changed my understanding of the spiritual quest.

"After leaving religious life in 1969 I moved to San Francisco. I spent the seventies very involved with 'California consciousness' and especially with the efforts of sexual liberation.

"During that time I worked in a psychiatric emergency clinic while I completed my graduate studies. After receiving a Ph.D. in counseling psychology I worked in an avant-garde mental health clinic in San Francisco's Tenderloin district.

"That job introduced me to Toby Marotta, a Harvard-trained social scientist doing research on homosexual lifestyles in the Tenderloin. We became friends and,

later, business partners. We worked together on two books, *The Politics of Homosexuality,* and *Sons of Harvard: Gay Men from the Class of 1967.* We took a job for the federal government, to study juvenile prostitution.

"Later, I worked as a psychotherapist in my hometown, San Antonio. My work was primarily concerned with assisting individuals to deal with the traumatic changes in their lives as a result of exposure to HIV, the AIDS-related virus, and with helping political and social institutions cope with this health crisis. *Plague: A Novel about Healing* is a novel about AIDS and attitudinal healing.

"In the 1990s, my long-term partner, Kip Dollar, and I owned the lesbian and gay bookstore in Austin, Texas, and then moved to the country to run a small bed and breakfast business, first outside Denver and then back in Texas, midway between San Antonio and Austin. Johnson & Dollar were the first male couple registered as "Domestic Partners" in Travis County, Austin, Texas, October 11, 1993.

Johnson continued: "For all that I write about problems (loss of religious certainty; teenage prostitution) and disasters (AIDS; nuclear accident), I am confident and optimistic that humankind will continue to mature and that we'll make it past the turbulence of the present day. I believe coping with historical crises is one of the major functions of spirituality and mysticism."

More recently, Johnson told *CA:* "My primary motivation is to contribute to the evolution of consciousness, specifically by explaining both the nature of religion and the nature of homosexuality. Gay people have always been religious leaders, from primitive shamans and witch doctors to American Indian berdache healers, to monks, priests, and bishops. That organized religion is so blinded and confused by sexuality and homosexuality is evidence of a need for a modern psychologically sophisticated and demythologized spirituality.

"I've written several autobiographical accounts of my spiritual/psychological experience and three novels that dramatize important issues in gay men's spirituality— all shot through with the wisdom I learned from Joseph Campbell. Following Campbell, I believe storytelling is one of the most potent ways to communicate wisdom. My . . . recent work, *Gay Spirituality: The Role of Gay Identity in the Transformation of Human Consciousness,* summarizes the wisdom I learned from Campbell and from my perspective as a modern, self-aware gay man."

BIOGRAPHICAL/CRITICAL SOURCES:

PERIODICALS

Library Journal, August, 2000, Jeff Ingram, review of *Gay Spirituality: The Role of Gay Identity in the Transformation of Human Consciousness,* p. 111.
Los Angeles Times, September 6, 1983.
Publishers Weekly, July 10, 2000, review of *Gay Spirituality: The Role of Gay Identity in the Transformation of Human Consciousness,* p. 60.

OTHER

White Crane Journal, http://www.whitecranejournal.com/ (December 6, 2000), "The Mystical Gay Novels of Toby Johnson."*

*   *   *

JOHNSON, Toby
    See JOHNSON, Edwin Clark

*   *   *

JONES, Geoffrey (Gareth) 1952-

PERSONAL: Born July 8, 1952, in Birmingham, England; son of Cyril Gareth and Alice May Jones. *Education:* Corpus Christi College, Cambridge, B.A., 1974, Ph.D., 1978. *Avocational interests:* Wine, Chinese astrology, travel.

ADDRESSES: Home—Flat 1, 32 Leinster Gardens, London W2 3AN, England. *Office*—295 Morgan Hall, Harvard Business School, Soldiers Field, Boston, MA 02163; and Department of Economics, University of Reading, P.O. Box 218, Whiteknights, Reading RG6 2AA, England; fax 617-496-5994. *E-mail*—gjones@hbs.edu.

CAREER: Cambridge University, Cambridge, England, research fellow at Corpus Christi College, 1977-79; University of London, London School of Economics and Political Science, London, England, research officer in business history unit, 1979-81, lecturer in economic history, 1981—. University of Reading, professor of business history, 1988—; Harvard University, Thomas Henry Carroll-Ford Foundation Visiting professor of Business Administration at Harvard Business School, 2000—.

MEMBER: Association of International Business, European Business History Association (president, 1997-99), Association of Business Historians (president, 1992-93 and 2000-01), Business History Conference (president-elect, 2000-01), Economic History Society, Royal Historical Society (fellow).

AWARDS, HONORS: Newcomen Prize, 1985, for article "The Gramophone Company: An Anglo-American Multinational, 1898-1931," and 1996; Harold F. Williamson Jr. Prize, 1994.

WRITINGS:

The State and the Emergence of the British Oil Industry, Macmillan (New York, NY), 1981.
British Multinationals: Origins, Management, and Performance, Gower (Brookfield, VT), 1986.
The History of the British Bank of the Middle East, Cambridge University Press (Cambridge, England), Volume I: *Banking and Empire in Iran,* 1986, Volume II: *Banking and Oil,* 1987.
(With F. Bostock) *Planning and Power in Iran,* Frank Cass (London, England), 1989.
British Multinational Banking, 1830-1990, Clarendon Press (Oxford, England), 1993.
The Evolution of International Business, Routledge (London, England), 1996.
Merchants to Multinationals, Oxford University Press (Oxford, England), 2000.

Contributor to business and economic journals.

EDITOR

(With Peter Hertner) *Multinationals: Theory and History,* Gower (Brookfield, VT), 1986.
(With R. Davenport-Hines) *British Business in Asia since 1860,* Cambridge University Press (New York, NY), 1989.
Banks as Multinationals, Routledge (London, England), 1990.
(With Harm Schroeter) *The Rise of Multinationals in Continental Europe,* Edward Elgar, 1993.

(With Richard Tedlow) *The Rise and Fall of Mass Marketing,* Routledge (London, England), 1993.

(With Nicholas J. Morgan) *Adding Value: Brands and Marketing in Food and Drink,* Routledge (London, England), 1994.

The Trader Multinationals, Routledge (London, England), 1998.

Editor of *Business History.*

WORK IN PROGRESS: The History of Unilever, 1965-1990, completion expected in 2003.

SIDELIGHTS: Geoffrey Jones once told *CA:* "I enjoy writing in the area of business history, which has grown in recent years from a preoccupation with writing in-depth studies of single companies to pursuing a more holistic vision to understand the role and performance of business in our society, past and present. An important development in recent years has been the recognition that the business and history of individual countries, even important ones such as the United States and Japan, cannot be studied in isolation. International and cross-cultural comparisons are challenging but offer the way forward to real understanding. I hope to encourage this approach further in my own writings and through my role as a journal editor."

*　　*　　*

JOYAUX, Julia
     See KRISTEVA, Julia

K

KARBO, Karen (Lee) 1956(?)-

PERSONAL: Born c. 1956, in Detroit, MI; daughter of Richard and Joan Karbo; married Kelley Baker (a filmmaker), 1988. *Education:* University of Southern California, BA, 1977, MA, 1980.

ADDRESSES: Office—P. O. Box 8322, Portland, OR 97207. *Agent*—Sally Wofford Girand, Elaine Markson Agency, 44 Greenwich Ave., New York, NY 10011.

CAREER: Writer. Held various jobs, including dog groomer and agent's assistant, in Los Angeles, CA, 1974-82.

WRITINGS:

NOVELS

Trespassers Welcome Here, Putnam (New York, NY), 1989.
The Diamond Lane, Putnam (New York, NY), 1991.
Motherhood Made a Man out of Me, Bloomsbury, 2000.

OTHER

(With Gabrielle Reece) *Big Girl in the Middle* (biography), Crown (New York, NY), 1997.

Also author of *Nipple Confusion.* Contributor to *Nike Is a Goddess: The History of Women in Sports.* Contributor to periodicals, including *Esquire, Los Angeles Times, Vogue, New Republic, Entertainment Weekly, New York Times Book Review,* and *Voice Literary Supplement.* Contributing editor, *Conde Nast Sports for Women.*

SIDELIGHTS: Karen Karbo is known for her comic novels. Her first book, *Trespassers Welcome Here,* recounts the experiences of various Soviet emigrés adapting to life in southern California. The book revolves around four women, dubbed the Lenin sisters by Karbo, who share an affiliation with the Slavic language department of a local university. Valeria is a Russian language instructor reduced to teaching a course titled "Russian with an Emphasis in Sports Vocabulary" to football players. Tanya, who had worked as an actress in the Soviet Union, has dreams of becoming a big Hollywood star. Selling some contraband that she smuggled in from Russia, Tanya purchases an answering machine that will hopefully record a call inviting her to star in a film. Rounding out the book are tales about Bella Bogga, a woman obsessed with the glamorous trappings of life in California, and Marina, a KGB informer who is married to an American.

Critical reaction to Karbo's first novel was positive. Nancy Wigston, a reviewer for the *Globe and Mail,* called *Trespassers Welcome Here* an "engaging first novel" and termed the book "memorable." Commenting on the book's easy charm, *Washington Post* contributor Melissa Greene called Karbo's novel "light and touching." In addition to praising the author's skill with Russian dialects and personalities, *New York Times Book Review* contributor Elin Schoen Brockman called Karbo "a very funny writer" and noted that "what is amazing about her humor is not merely its abundance but its range—from near slapstick to dry wit." Brockman added that *Trespassers Welcome Here* constituted "a smashing debut."

Karbo's next novel, *The Diamond Lane,* chronicles the wayward dreaming and deal-making to which numerous Californians fall prey. The story revolves around two sisters, Mouse and Mimi. Mimi works as a producer's assistant, attends a community college course entitled "How to Write a Blockbuster," and awaits her big break in the film industry. Mouse is a documentary filmmaker who has spent the last sixteen years in Africa with her boyfriend, Tony. She is reluctantly called back to Hollywood when her mother is injured in a bizarre restaurant accident. Through the fate of a bad telephone connection, Mimi is under the impression that Mouse and Tony are engaged. Mouse arrives home to a mother and sister eager for her impending nuptials. Yielding to familial pressure, Mouse agrees to marry Tony, then determines to film their ceremony for a documentary, *Wedding March.* In the meantime, Tony has teamed up with Mimi's "Blockbuster" instructor and sometime boyfriend, Ralph, to write a screenplay about the couple's life in Africa. The interest of a major producer prompts the two men to commercialize their script—a decision that has the proposed film concluding with Mouse, naked and brandishing an automatic weapon, astride an elephant.

When *The Diamond Lane* was published it was compared to Julia Phillips's *You'll Never Eat Lunch in This Town Again,* a novel that, like Karbo's, makes fun of Hollywood—and more directly the film industry's business ethics. Describing her own book to Laurel Graeber in the *New York Times Book Review,* Karbo stated: "I think of it as *You'll Never Eat Lunch in This Town in the First Place. . . .* And the characters are people who would love to have lunch." *The Diamond Lane* was partially inspired by Karbo's own attempts at a screenwriting career in Hollywood, an experience she found frustrating and demeaning. As she related to Graeber, "It's depressing when you try to sell your soul and nobody wants it." Robert Ward, writing in the *New York Times Book Review,* described Karbo's second novel as "wonderfully comic." Ward judged that special skills are required to make a novel like *The Diamond Lane* work: "The trick is to keep things moving full tilt, but also to keep things real—and Ms. Karbo has done her job brilliantly. Not only is the plot ingenious, but the writing remains deft all the way through." Karbo credits the novel's comic tone to her own outlook which, as she told Graeber, is that "life is hopelessly tragic and hilarious."

Karbo again won praise from reviewers with her novel, *Motherhood Made a Man out of Me,* which a *Publishers Weekly* reviewer called a "sassy, satirical" book full of "tongue-in-cheek riffs on sports and modern life."

The narrator and principle character, Brooke, is an independent movie producer who gives up her career as an independent movie producer for motherhood. Stunned by how completely her baby, Stella, obliterates her former way of life, Brooke begins to refer to herself as Brooke Stellamom instead of using her real surname. When Brooke's friend Mary Rose reveals that she is also pregnant, Brooke lets loose with all she has learned about motherhood "in the form of zinging one-liners and elbow-in-the-side chucklers." Brooke and Mary Rose's devotion to professional basketball is also central to the book's climax. *Booklist* contributor Ellie Barta-Moran found *Motherhood Made a Man out of Me* to be full of "insight and humor" as well as being "fast-paced and delightful."

Karbo teamed up with model and sports star Gabrielle Reece to write *Big Girl in the Middle,* Reece's autobiography. A major player in professional women's volleyball, Reece is a "striking physical presence" as well as the owner of "a sharp, probing mind," according to Michael Silver in *Sports Illustrated.* As a child, Reece was taunted about her height—which at maturity is six feet, three inches—and had problems with her family life as well. The book reveals the ways in which her tribulations made her a stronger person, driven to challenge herself. "Reece's struggles with team chemistry, motivation and leadership are intriguing," commented Silver. *Library Journal* commentator Kathryn Ruffle called *Big Girl in the Middle* "an inspiration to tall girls and young female athletes."

BIOGRAPHICAL/CRITICAL SOURCES:

PERIODICALS

Booklist, September 1, 1998, Sue-Ellen Beauregard, review of *Nike Is a Goddess: The History of Women in Sports,* p. 54; June 1, 2000, Ellie Barta-Moran, review of *Motherhood Made a Man out of Me,* p. 1858.

Globe and Mail (Toronto), July 29, 1989.

Library Journal, July, 1997, Kathryn Ruffle, review of *Big Girl in the Middle,* p. 91.

New York Times Book Review, May 21, 1989, p. 11; September 2, 1990, p. 10; May 19, 1991, p. 9; November 14, 1993, review of *The Diamond Lane,* p. 72.

Observer, December 6, 1992, review of *The Diamond Lane,* p. 57.

Publishers Weekly, May 17, 1993, review of *The Diamond Lane,* p. 76; May 26, 1997, review of *Big Girl in the Middle,* p. 73; May 22, 2000, review of *Motherhood Made a Man out of Me,* p. 74.

Rapport, March 3, 1992, review of *The Diamond Lane,* p. 27.

Sports Illustrated, August 25, 1997, Michael Silver, review of *Big Girl in the Middle,* 20.

Times Literary Supplement, December 11, 1992, review of *The Diamond Lane,* p. 20.

Washington Post Book World, April 2, 1989, p. 6.*

*　　*　　*

KAYE, Marvin (Nathan) 1938-
(Eugene D. Goodwin, Joseph Lavinson, Saralee Terry)

PERSONAL: Born March 10, 1938, in Philadelphia, PA; son of Morris (a television and radio repairman) and Theresa (Buroski) Kaye; married Saralee Bransdorf, August 4, 1963; children: Terry Ellen. *Education:* Pennsylvania State University, B.A. (liberal arts), 1960, M.A. (theatre and English literature), 1962; University of Denver, graduate study, 1960.

ADDRESSES: Agent—c/o St. Martin's Press, 175 Fifth Avenue, New York, NY 10010.

CAREER: Grit (newspaper), Williamsport, PA, reporter, 1963-65, then New York correspondent, 1966—; *Business Travel* (magazine), New York City, assistant managing editor, 1965; *Toys* (magazine), New York City, senior editor, 1966-70; full-time writer, 1970—. Light Opera of Manhattan, public relations director, 1973; New School for Social Research (now New School University), faculty member, 1974-75; adjunct associate professor of creative writing, New York University, 1976—; The Open Book (New York theatre company), co-founder and artistic director, 1976—. Also has worked as a senior editor for Harcourt, Brace Jovanovich; written, acted in, and directed plays; done film work; and sung in *The Hoboken Chicken Emergency,* a comic operetta based on a book by Daniel Pinkwater.

MEMBER: Authors Guild, Authors League of America, Mystery Writers of America (member of awards committee, 1977), Sons of the Desert (treasurer, 1973-75; president, 1977—), Illustrious Order of Dragon Killers, the Wolfe Pack (chairman, awards committee, 1991—).

WRITINGS:

The Histrionic Holmes: An Analysis and Dissertation on the Impersonatory Genius of Sherlock Homes, with Technical Notes and a Compendium of His Performances, illustrated by Tom Walker, Luther Norris (Culver City, CA), 1971.

A Lively Game of Death, Saturday Review (New York City), 1972.

A Toy Is Born, Stein & Day (New York City), 1973, revised edition published as *The Story of Monopoly, Silly Putty, Bingo, Twister, Frisbee, Scrabble, Et Cetera,* 1977.

The Stein & Day Handbook of Magic, illustrated by Al Kilgore, Stein & Day, 1973, reprinted, 1983.

The Grand Ole Opry Murders, Saturday Review, 1974.

The Handbook of Mental Magic, illustrated by Kilgore, Stein & Day, 1975.

Bullets for Macbeth (mystery), Dutton (New York City), 1976.

Catalog of Magic, illustrated by Kilgore, Doubleday (Garden City, NY), 1977.

My Son, the Druggist, Doubleday, 1977.

The Laurel and Hardy Murders: A Hilary Quayle Mystery Novel, Dutton, 1977.

(With Parke Godwin) *The Masters of Solitude* (science fiction), Doubleday, 1978.

My Brother, the Druggist, Doubleday, 1979.

The Incredible Umbrella (humorous fiction), Doubleday, 1979.

The Possession of Immanuel Wolf, and Other Improbable Tales, Doubleday, 1981.

The Amorous Umbrella (sequel to *The Incredible Umbrella;* humorous fiction), Doubleday, 1981.

The Soap Opera Slaughters, Doubleday, 1982.

(With Godwin) *Wintermind* (science fiction), Doubleday, 1982.

(With Godwin) *A Cold Blue Light* ("Aubrey House" horror/ghost novel series), Berkley (New York City), 1983.

Ghosts of Night and Morning ("Aubrey House" horror/ghost novel series), Berkley, 1987.

Fantastique, St. Martin's (New York City), 1992.

EDITOR

Fiends and Creatures (anthology), Popular Library (New York City), 1975.

(With Brother Theodore; and contributor) *Brother Theodore's Chamber of Horrors* (anthology), Pinnacle Books (New York City), 1975.

"Weird Tales," the Magazine that Never Dies, Doubleday, 1988.

Lovers and Other Monsters, Doubleday, 1992.

Sweet Revenge: Ten Plays of Bloody Murder, Fireside Theatre (New York City), 1992.

The Game is Afoot: Parodies, Pastiches, and Ponderings of Sherlock Holmes, St. Martin's, 1994.

(And selector) *Angels of Darkness: Tales of Troubled and Troubling Women,* introduction by Paula Volsky, Guild American, 1995.

The Resurrected Homes: New Cases from the Notes of John H. Watson, M.D., introduction and rubrics by J. Adrian Fillmore, St. Martin's, 1996.

Don't Open This Book!, Doubleday Direct (New York City), 1997.

(With John Betancourt) *The Best of Weird Tales, 1923 (The First Year),* Bleak House (Berkeley House, NJ), 1997.

The Confidential Casebook of Sherlock Holmes, St. Martin's, 1998.

Also editor of *Frantic Comedy,* Fireside Theatre.

SELECTOR; EXCEPT AS NOTED

(With Saralee Kaye) *Ghosts: A Treasury of Chilling Tales Old & New,* Doubleday, 1981.

(With S. Kaye) *Masterpieces of Terror and the Supernatural: A Treasury of Spellbinding Tales Old and New,* Doubleday, 1985.

(With S. Kaye) *Devils and Demons: A Treasury of Fiendish Tales Old & New,* Doubleday, 1987.

Witches and Warlocks: Tales of Blackmagic Old and New, Guild America (Garden City, NY), 1989, published as *The Penguin Book of Witches and Warlocks: Tales of Blackmagic Old and New,* Penguin (New York City), 1991.

Thirteen Plays of Ghosts and the Supernatural, with an introduction by Jose Ferrer, Doubleday (Garden City, NY), 1990.

(With S. Kaye) *Haunted America: Star-spangled Supernatural,* Guild America, 1990.

Masterpieces of Terror and the Unknown, Doubleday, 1993.

(Compilor) *Readers Theatre: What It Is and How to Stage It, and Four Award-winning Scripts,* preface by Mary Stuart, Wildside (Newark, NJ), 1995.

OTHER

Also the author of plays, including *Bertrand Russell's Guided Tour of Intellectual Rubbish* and *A Cold Blue Light* (based on his novel of the same name). Contributor of short stories, under pseudonyms Eugene D. Goodwin and Joseph Lavinson, and verse, under pseudonym Saralee Terry, to periodicals, including *Amazing/Fantastic Stories, Fantasy Macabre, Fantasy Tales, Playthings,* and *Thrust Science Fiction.* Author of column, "Marvin Kaye's Nth Dimension," *Science Fiction Chronicle;* guest-columnist, *Long Life.* Contributing editor of *Mass Retailing Merchandiser, Galileo,* and business publications in the toy-hobby field.

Kaye's books have been published in Canada, France, Great Britain, Germany, Holland, and Spain.

SIDELIGHTS: Marvin Kaye's work is extremely varied, as it includes singing in a comical operetta; writing, directing, and acting in plays; selecting and editing various volumes; and writing comic, horror, mystery, and science fiction. Two horror novels comprise Kaye's "Aubrey House" series, which "most fruitfully explore[s]" the "borderline between the supernatural and the rationally-explicable," noted Darrell Schweitzer in the *St. James Guide to Horror, Ghost and Gothic Writers,* specifying: "In addition to making much use of the concept of a haunted house as a psychic 'battery' (which retains the emotional residue, but not necessarily intelligence of its former inhabitants), both books feature sciences of out-of-body travel. Kaye seems to be well up on contemporary research on the subject." The very bloody *A Cold Blue Light,* written with Parke Goodwin, "is a lyrical haunted-house story in the tradition of Shirley Jackson's *The Haunting of Hill House,*" described Schweitzer, adding: "In the sequel, *Ghosts of Night and Morning.* . . . Kaye, without his collaborator Godwin, is more inclined toward clever plot twists and atmospherics. The tone is different from the first book. . . . seem[ing] almost, at time, to be a particularly convoluted mystery novel. . . . [with] less awe and wonder, but, certainly, plenty of suspense."

When creating another horror novel, *Fantastique,* Kaye pulled from his theatrical experiences "and on Hector Berlioz's *Symphonie Fantastique,* in which the composer imagines that he has murdered his beloved and gone to Hell," reported Schweitzer. "Musical parallels permeate the book and dictate much of its structure. . . . Fortunately," added Schweitzer, "he is a sufficiently capable novelist to keep the book working on many levels at once, so even the musically illiterate will find *Fantastique* worth reading. . . . [It] is a vivid, explosive, demanding novel, quite unlike anything else published in the horror field at the time. . . . a genuine original, not part of a predictable demographic curve."

In addition to Kaye's horror novels, Schweitzer commented on the authors short fiction and anthologies: "Kaye's short fiction tends to be whimsical rather than horrific. . . . Kaye's anthologies are thoroughly researched compilations of new and old ghostly and horrific material, very solidly done." *Masterpieces of Terror and the Unknown* "features both new and old stories (mostly the latter) with an emphasis on terror, which Kaye distinguishes from horror on the basis that terror 'is rooted in cosmic fear of the unknown' and succeeds without the gore and violence on which horror thrives," stated *Booklist* contributor Ray Olson. "Readers may question the choice of certain works, bristle at Kaye's self-promotional references in several of the introductions and dismiss some of the older tales as dated," cautioned a *Publishers Weekly* critic who nevertheless recommended the work as enjoyable for people interested in the genre.

During the 1990s, Kaye edited several unique Sherlock Holmes anthologies: *The Game is Afoot: Parodies, Pastiches and Ponderings of Sherlock Holmes, The Resurrected Homes: New Cases from the Notes of John H. Watson, M.D.,* and *The Confidential Casebook of Sherlock Holmes* all give Sherlock Holmes fans new material to devour. Although unsatisfied with the volumes' organization, a *Publishers Weekly* critic recommended "the best efforts of the best writers" found in *The Game is Afoot,* a collection of original and reprinted "good-natured lampoons, clever spoofs and somewhat academic examinations of Sherlock Holmes's cases." *The Resurrected Homes* is "a must-read for Baker Street fans," according to *Booklist* contributor Margaret Flanagan, who judged the book to be "a clever. . . . entertaining and inventive collection." For the book, Kaye had modern authors mimic what Dashiell Hammett supposedly did: write, on commission, a narrative to interpret notes that doctor John H. Watson left. A *Publishers Weekly* reviewer congratulated the "stout effort," indicating that, in general, the volume contains stories which are "well-crafted. . . . [and] adroitly capture the feel of their models." *The Confidential Casebook of Sherlock Holmes* is "a sparkling collection," described Rex E. Klett in *Library Journal,* of fifteen new mysteries, written by various authors, that are solved by the detective. Despite falling short of the "classics," these stories, praised *Entertainment Weekly* contributor Caren Weiner, are "irresistibly entertaining . . . true to the spirit of the originals."

Kaye once told *CA:* "A thorough training in theatre as an actor, director, and playwright is my principal background and passion. My chief interests in writing are drama and philosophy.

"As a writing instructor, I am constantly appalled by the professional writers who spread the noxious doctrine that *all* you need do is sit in a book-lined chamber and write, write, write and someday someone will find you, a doctrine postulated on the mystique of 'talent.' I maintain that writing is mostly disciplined, thoughtful hard work, training oneself to hew to a regular schedule, and finding out ways to sell and bring one's work before the public. Writing is a profession and it is a business.

"Instead of talent, I look for a psychological need in my students. If they cannot conceive of themselves as successful writers, they will probably not become so. I have constantly encountered sensitive souls who handle the language with intuitive brilliance. But they are so stultified with fear of defining themselves as creative people that they never set goals and work purposefully to achieve them. Those who do may not have as much 'talent,' but if they want to express themselves in this agonizing business, there is probably much more in their psyches than the run-of-the-mill writing professor ever sees.

"Dare people to fly in the face of criticism, and stick to it, and chances are they will eventually succeed—not without pain, but that's part of the dues we pay when we overexcite our brains, as all creators do. Once a famous New York writing teacher told one of my students her book-in-progress showed no talent for novel writing. She was decimated, crucified on the 'talent' mystery altar. I told her to keep at it, and the hell with adverse criticism that doesn't show how to improve one's technique. A month later she sold the same book to Simon & Schuster for more money than I've ever earned—a Literary Guild alternate!"

BIOGRAPHICAL/CRITICAL SOURCES:

BOOKS

St. James Guide to Horror, Ghost and Gothic Writers, St. James Press (Detroit), 1998.

PERIODICALS

Booklist, June 1, 1994; March 1, 1996.
Entertainment Weekly, March 6, 1998.
Library Journal, January, 1988.
Publishers Weekly, February 21, 1994; May 16, 1999; March 4, 1996.
Science Fiction Chronicle, November, 1992.*

KAYSEN, Susanna 1948-

PERSONAL: Born November 11, 1948, in Cambridge, MA.

ADDRESSES: Home—Cambridge, MA. *Agent*—Jonathan Matson, Harold Matson Co., Inc., 276 Fifth Ave., New York, NY 10001.

CAREER: Writer. Has worked as a freelance editor and proofreader.

WRITINGS:

Asa, as I Knew Him, Vintage Books (New York, NY), 1987.
Far Afield, Vintage Books (New York, NY), 1990.
Girl, Interrupted, Turtle Bay Books (New York, NY), 1993.
The Camera My Mother Gave Me, Knopf (New York, NY), 2001.

ADAPTATIONS: Girl, Interrupted was adapted by Lisa Loomer, Anna Hamilton Phelan, and James Mangold into a film, directed by Mangold, starring Winona Ryder and Angelina Jolie, and released by Columbia Pictures in 1999; *Girl, Interrupted* was also adapted as an audiobook by Random Audio, 1999.

SIDELIGHTS: Susanna Kaysen is the author of books that are in varying degrees related to her personal experiences. Kaysen worked as a freelance editor and proofreader until an introduction to an agent set her career in motion. The novel that caught the agent's attention, *Asa, as I Knew Him,* was published in 1987 and received solid reviews. Kaysen followed up the success of her first book three years later with a second novel, *Far Afield.* Kaysen's third book, *Girl, Interrupted,* won both accolades for her and media attention for the book.

Asa, as I Knew Him is the story of a woman's relationship with a man who is very different than her. The narrator, Dinah Sachs, works for a Massachusetts literary journal. Her married lover, Asa Thayer, is the journal's editor, and Dinah, a Jew, is fascinated by his coolly self-centered patrician persona. In the early part of the novel, Dinah recounts her view of the relationship and her and Asa's differing attitudes toward passion and spirituality. Dinah and Asa's relationship is doomed to fail, and *Asa, as I Knew Him* begins to focus on Asa's

youth. Dinah invents or supposes an early crisis in Asa's life that explains, for her, his detachment from the vagaries of romance, and she sets this quasi-fictional account to paper. This secondary story reconstructs Asa's teenaged friendship with another Jew, Reuben Sola, upon whom Asa appears fixated. Dinah writes about the youths' charmed existence in Cambridge, Massachusetts.

Asa, as I Knew Him received positive attention from reviewers, although some perceived Kaysen's generalities about Jewish and Protestant personalities as stereotypical. Laurel Graeber remarked in the *New York Times Book Review,* "It is a tribute to Ms. Kaysen's considerable talent that when she leaves ethnic generalities for the particularities of character, we easily believe in all her inventions." *Los Angeles Times* reviewer Jonathan Kirsch wrote that he "was struck by Kaysen's unusual perspective and her marvelous powers of observation in evoking the agonies and ecstasies of adolescent sexuality." Kirsch wrote that, though *Asa, as I Knew Him* is her first published work of fiction, Kaysen's "prose is so stylish, so confident and so finely crafted that we recognize immediately that we are reading the work of an accomplished writer. And, as an observer of the politics of love and sexual passion, she is already a master."

Kaysen's second novel, *Far Afield,* is based on her experiences accompanying her former husband to the Faeroe Islands, a Danish protectorate in the North Atlantic Ocean. Kaysen recounts the hardships faced by Jonathan Brand, an anthropologist doing research as he lives in a remote and baffling rural landscape. Much of the novel concerns Jonathan's discoveries about himself and his work: prior to his departure from Harvard University, Jonathan had been as isolated from the real world as the remote Faeroese. *Far Afield* is a story of self-discovery from an academic point of view. Its protagonist is the product of an elitist and rigidly intellectual development that, he begins to realize, has hindered his ability to participate fully in life. *New York Times Book Review* critic Sally Lee lauded Kaysen's "confident and polished prose" and Phoebe-Lou Adams, writing in *Atlantic Monthly,* identified *Far Afield* as "a novel distinguished for intelligence, psychological insight, and splendid writing."

Kaysen's third book, *Girl, Interrupted,* is a memoir of her two-year stay in the McLean Psychiatric Hospital, which began when she was seventeen. The book is composed of short vignettes of Kaysen's life inside McLean, with its system of privileges and penalties, and portraits of her fellow inmates—young women in similar circumstances who were battling not to lose control of their lives. "In a strange way we were free . . . ," Kaysen writes. "Our privacy, our liberty, our dignity: all of this was gone and we were stripped down to the bare bone of our selves." Kaysen also writes of her roommate, who had been admitted after having a nervous breakdown in a movie theater, of another young woman who decorated her room with chicken carcasses, and of a boy who told preposterous stories about his father's being involved with dangerous Central Intelligence Agency (CIA) operations—stories that later proved to be true.

Interspersed with these slices of reality are Kaysen's own medical records, which she obtained with the help of a lawyer. The records show that Kaysen had been diagnosed with what was termed a borderline personality disorder, which is usually characterized by a confusion about life choices. In an interview with Missy Daniel in *Publishers Weekly,* the author said that she had not looked at the documents until she was nearly finished writing her own recollections, believing that reading the official version might alter her memories. After reading them, however, she decided to incorporate the doctors' words among the vignettes "because the contrast between their language and my language was interesting. Their record provided a viewpoint on the experience that I couldn't provide." In reflecting on the task of setting this experience on paper, Kaysen remarked that *Girl, Interrupted* "wasn't a pleasure to write. . . . It wasn't agony, but I had to get back to that stuff, and it put me in a terrible frame of mind." She added, "I felt very far from my old self, and that was a source of pain, too. The memories of being eighteen were so awful. Thank heaven I survived it."

Girl, Interrupted received praise from critics. "I came to her book expecting another *Cuckoo's Nest* diatribe against psychiatric coercion," noted Alan A. Stone in the *Boston Review.* "Instead I discovered an elliptical meditation on the experience, with layers of irony, humor, and compassion, for the keepers as well as the kept." A reviewer in the *New Yorker* wrote that Kaysen's own meditations "form a trenchant counterpoint to the copies of her medical records." A *Newsweek* contributor remarked that the volume "dodges all the obvious pitfalls of such a book: . . . madness confers no privileged insights and [Kaysen] peddles no hard-won wisdom." Similarly, *Time* reviewer Andrea Sachs related that "Kaysen concentrates on describing what life in a psychiatric ward is really like. That approach gives *Girl, Interrupted* its feeling of universality and makes Kaysen seem like Everypatient to a grateful readership." Writing in the *New York Times Book Review,* Susan

Cheever observed that "Kaysen describes the claustrophobia of incarceration with a simplicity and grace that let the horror show through," concluding that "Kaysen's compelling and heartbreaking story shows how thin the line is between those society deems mad and those it deems sane."

BIOGRAPHICAL/CRITICAL SOURCES:

BOOKS

Kaysen, Susanna, *Girl, Interrupted,* Turtle Bay Books (New York, NY), 1993.

PERIODICALS

Atlantic Monthly, November, 1990, Phoebe-Lou Adams, review of *Far Afield,* p. 172.
Booklist, March 15, 2000, Whitney Scott, review of audiobook version of *Girl, Interrupted,* p. 1397.
Boston Review, summer, 2000, Alan A. Stone, "Split Personality," pp. 48-50.
Library Journal, August, 2000, Pam Kingsbury, review of audiobook version of *Girl, Interrupted,* p. 179.
Los Angeles Times, April 30, 1987, Jonathan Kirsch, review of *Asa, as I Knew Him,* section 5, pp. 1, 16.
Nation, January 24, 2000, Stuart Klawans, "Y2K: The Prequel," p. 35.
Newsweek, July 5, 1993, review of *Girl, Interrupted,* p. 56.
New Yorker, July 5, 1993, review of *Girl, Interrupted,* p. 101.
New York Times Book Review, May 3, 1987, Laurel Graeber, review of *Asa, as I Knew Him,* p. 44; November 4, 1990, Sally Lee, review of *Far Afield,* p. 24; June 20, 1993, Susan Cheever, review of *Girl, Interrupted,* pp. 1, 24-25.
Publishers Weekly, March 20, 1987, p. 75; August 31, 1990, p. 59; June 14, 1993, Missy Daniel, interview with Susanna Kaysen, pp. 51-52.
Time, July 11, 1994, Andrea Sachs, review of *Girl, Interrupted,* p. 60.*

*   *   *

KELLER, Evelyn Fox 1936-

PERSONAL: Born March 20, 1936, in New York, NY; daughter of Albert and Rachel Fox; children: Jeffrey, Sarah. *Education:* Brandeis University, B.A. (magna cum laude), 1957; Radcliffe College, M.A., 1959; Harvard University, Ph.D., 1963.

ADDRESSES: Office—Massachusetts Institute of Technology, ES1-263B, 77 Massachusetts Ave., Cambridge, MA 02139-4307.

CAREER: New York University, New York, NY, instructor in physics, 1962-63, assistant research scientist, 1963-66, associate professor of mathematical biology, 1970-72; Cornell University Medical College, New York, NY, assistant professor, 1963-69; State University of New York College at Purchase, Purchase, NY, associate professor in division of natural science, 1972-82, chair of mathematics board of study, 1972-74; Northeastern University, Boston, MA, professor of humanities and mathematics, 1982-88; University of California, Berkeley, CA, professor of rhetoric, women's studies, and history of science, 1988-92; Massachusetts Institute of Technology (MIT), Cambridge, MA, professor of history and philosophy of science, 1992—. Special lecturer in mathematical biology at University of Maryland, 1974; MIT Program in Science, Technology, and Society, visiting fellow, 1979-80, visiting scholar, 1980-84, visiting professor, 1985-86; visiting professor at Northeastern University, 1981-82, and Northwestern University, 1985; member of Institute for Advanced Study, Princeton, 1987-88. Gordon Conference on Theoretical Biology, vice chairperson, 1973, chairperson, 1974; organizer and coordinator of Boston Area Colloquium on Feminist Theory, 1982—. Guest lecturer and consultant at institutions including Rutgers University, Columbia University, Harvard University, Brandeis University, and University of California, Santa Cruz.

MEMBER: American Association for the Advancement of Science, Phi Beta Kappa, Sigma Xi.

AWARDS, HONORS: National Science Foundation, fellowship, 1957-61, visiting professorship for women, 1985; Mina Shaughnessy Scholars Award from Fund for the Improvement of Postsecondary Education, 1981-82; Mellon fellowship from Wellesley College Center for Research on Women, 1984; Rockefeller humanities fellowship, 1985-86; distinguished publication award from Association for Women in Psychology, 1986; senior fellow of Society for the Humanities, Cornell University, 1986-87; recipient of MacArthur Foundation fellowship; American Association of University Women Achievement Award, 1990. Honorary degrees include L.H.D., Mt. Holyoke College, 1991, doctorate, University of Amsterdam, 1993, doctorate of humane science, Simmons College, 1995, and doctorate of humane letters, Rensselaer Polytechnic Institute, 1995.

WRITINGS:

A Feeling for the Organism: The Life and Work of Barbara McClintock, W. H. Freeman (New York, NY), 1983.

Reflections on Gender and Science, Yale University Press (New Haven, CT), 1985.

(Editor, with Mary Jacobus and Sally Shuttleworth, and contributor) *Women, Science, and the Body,* Methuen (New York, NY), 1988.

(With others) *Three Cultures: Fifteen Lectures on the Confrontation of Academic Cultures,* Universitaire Pers (Rotterdam, the Netherlands), 1989.

(Editor, with Mary Jacobus and Sally Shuttleworth) *Body/Politics: Women and the Discourses of Science,* Routledge (New York, NY), 1990.

(Editor, with Marianne Hirsch) *Conflicts in Feminism,* Routledge (New York, NY), 1990.

Secrets of Life, Secrets of Death: Essays on Language, Gender, and Science, Routledge (New York, NY), 1992.

(Editor, with Elisabeth A. Lloyd) *Keywords in Evolutionary Biology,* Harvard University Press (Cambridge, MA), 1992.

Refiguring Life: Metaphors of Twentieth-Century Biology, Columbia University Press (New York, NY), 1995.

(Editor, with Helen E. Longino) *Feminism and Science,* Oxford University Press (New York, NY), 1996.

The Century of the Gene, Harvard University Press (Cambridge, MA), 2000.

Contributor to books, including *Working It Out: Twenty-three Women Writers, Artists, Scientists, and Scholars Talk about Their Lives and Work,* Pantheon (New York, NY), 1977; *Discovering Reality: Feminist Perspectives on Epistemology, Metaphysics, Methodology, and Philosophy of Science,* by Sandra Harding and Merrill B. Hintikka, Reidel, 1983; *Nineteen Eighty-four: Science between Utopia and Dystopia,* Reidel, 1984; *Competition among Women: A Feminist Analysis,* Feminist Press (Old Westbury, NY), 1987; and *Hermeneutics and Psychoanalysis,* Rutgers University Press (New Brunswick, NJ).

Also contributor of numerous articles to professional journals, including *Science, Nature, Journal of Theoretical Biology, American Journal of Physics,* and *International Journal of Women's Studies,* and of reviews to periodicals, including *Change* and *New York Times Book Review.* Editor of "Feminist Theory" series for Northeastern University Press; adviser to Harvard University Press. American editor of *Fundamenta Scientiae;* member of editorial board of *Woman's Review of Books, Hypatia,* and *Biology and Philosophy.*

SIDELIGHTS: Evelyn Fox Keller, the recipient of a MacArthur Foundation fellowship ("genius grant"), is a philosopher and historian of science who has addressed such issues as gender and ideology in science, genetic determinism, and the philosophy of evolutionary biology. Keller's work defies easy summary, but she has earned a sizable audience in the scholarly community, especially in the fields of women's studies and the history of science. As Bruce S. Lieberman put it in the *New York Times Book Review,* "The points that Ms. Keller ably makes are important to scientists and historians of science alike."

"Evelyn Fox Keller's biography of Barbara McClintock is a welcome and useful addition to the growing literature on the recent history of . . . women's achievements in science," judged Margaret W. Rossiter in the *New York Times Book Review.* McClintock, recipient of the 1983 Nobel Prize for medicine and several other recent prizes and honorary degrees, was largely ignored when, in the early 1950s, she first presented her observations about the mobility or transposition of genes on chromosomes. In *A Feeling for the Organism: The Life and Work of Barbara McClintock,* Keller outlines several factors that may have contributed to the initial rejection of McClintock's ideas. These include the antifeminist nature of genetic research in that era, the unpopularity of McClintock's subject of study (maize rather than bacteria), and McClintock's colleagues' bewilderment at her unprecedented conclusions.

"The strength of Keller's fine book," asserted Stephen Jay Gould in the *New York Review of Books,* "lies in her successful attempt to . . . [provide] a rare and deep understanding of a troubling, fascinating, and general tale in the history of science—initial rejection (or, more frustratingly, simple incomprehension) of great insights." Expressing a thought echoed by other reviewers, David Graber noted in the *Los Angeles Times Book Review* that McClintock "was, one suspects, not the easiest of subjects for Keller. How does one write of a person whose whole life has been devoted to work even the specialists did not understand?" He commended Keller, who was "trained in the history, philosophy and psychology of science," as "particularly qualified for the task of explicating Barbara McClintock." *A Feeling for the Organism,* he concluded, "must of necessity be as much genetics as biography, and Keller accomplishes the dual task with intellectual power of her own."

In her second book, *Reflections on Gender and Science,* "Keller analyzes the pervasiveness of gender ideology, investigates how it became established and how it still shapes the course of scientific theory and experimentation, and speculates what science might be like if it were gender free," according to Evelyn Shaw in the *New York Times Book Review.* Shaw commended Keller's use of "a wide range of scientific and other literature to bolster her . . . arguments about how the hugely invasive precepts of gender have deformed our concepts of science, kept women from entering the disciplines and undoubtedly shaped the direction of scientific research." After tracing the history of women's exclusion from scientific pursuits, Keller "pleads for a gender-free science, a pluralistic science, one in which many voices can be heard, one that integrates many visions. The methods of achieving this ideal state," Shaw added, "remain illusory." Keller's book "is more an invitation to think than a conclusion," observed Ian Hacking in the *New Republic.* Hacking further noted that, "in general, Keller enters a wise plea for tolerance, cooperation, mutual respect, and more sharing of resources among more competing ideas."

In *The Century of the Gene,* Keller suggests that, "while the gene served 20th-century science well, recent discoveries about the complexity of gene action undermine its position as the unifying concept in biology," to quote Anne Magurran in the *New York Times Book Review.* Keller challenges the current usage of the word "gene," showing that it has become overwhelmed by contradictory concepts. In the *Library Journal,* Gregg Sapp observed that Keller "puts this philosophical problem in a broad context," successfully arguing for "a new vocabulary for the field." In Keller's view, an understanding of how genes work, even a complete encoding of the human genome, does not adequately explain many aspects of basic biology or evolution. *Booklist* correspondent Olson Ray commended Keller for her search for "new terms and concepts . . . needed to supplement and probably retire the gene." Ray concluded: "Though damned demanding, this is top-drawer science reading."

BIOGRAPHICAL/CRITICAL SOURCES:

PERIODICALS

Booklist, October 1, 2000, Olson Ray, review of *The Century of the Gene,* p. 308.

Commonweal, November 3, 2000, Austin L. Hughes, "Questioning the Hype," p. 34.

Library Journal, August, 2000, Gregg Sapp, review of *The Century of the Gene,* p. 148.

Los Angeles Times Book Review, November 6, 1983.

Nation, November 19, 1983.

New Republic, July 15, 1985; July 22, 1985.

New York Review of Books, March 29, 1984.

New York Times Book Review, October 2, 1983; April 21, 1985, Evelyn Shaw, "Science & Technology: Can We Rename Nature?," p. 36; July 14, 1996, Bruce S. Lieberman, review of *Refiguring Life: Metaphors of Twentieth-Century Biology;* December 10, 2000, Anne Magurran, "Backseat Drivers."

Publishers Weekly, September 25, 2000, review of *The Century of the Gene.*

*   *   *

KENDALL, Elizabeth B(emis) 1947-

PERSONAL: Born April 7, 1947, in St. Louis, MO; daughter of Henry C. (a commodity broker) and Elizabeth (Conant) Kendall. *Education:* Radcliffe College, B.A. (cum laude), 1969; Harvard University, M.A.T., 1971. *Politics:* Democrat.

ADDRESSES: Home—400 West 43rd St., Apt. 2L, New York, NY 10036. *Agent*—Maxine Groffsky, 2 Fifth Ave., New York, NY 10011.

CAREER: High school teacher of English in Brookline, MA, 1971-72; substitute teacher in Newton, MA, 1972-73; freelance writer. Member of Manhattan Plaza dance committee; consultant to Ford Foundation.

WRITINGS:

Where She Danced: American Dancing, 1880-1930, Knopf (New York, NY), 1979, published as *Where She Danced: The Birth of American Art-Dance,* University of California Press (Berkeley, CA), 1984.

Dancing, Ford Foundation (New York, NY), 1983.

American Daughter: Discovering My Mother, Random House (New York, NY), 2000.

Also author of *The Runaway Bride,* 1990; also author of television scripts for WNET-TV, including "Dance in America: Pilobolus," 1977, and "Trailblazers of Modern Dance," 1977. Contributor to dance magazines and newspapers.

SIDELIGHTS: Elizabeth B. Kendall presented readers with a double memoir in her book, *American Daughter: Discovering My Mother;* the book is both a remembrance of the author's mother and an autobiography. Kendall's family belonged to the privileged upper middle class in St. Louis, Missouri. Her family was well-educated, with her mother having attended Vassar and her father graduating from Harvard. But the aristocratic society that produced Kendall's parents was destined to fall apart during the years of the Great Depression and World War II. Kendall's book describes the decline of the family's fortunes and the very different ways in which her parents coped with the changes that were forced upon them. Her mother, a serious, socially conscious woman, tried to create new opportunities for herself and other women in these pre-feminist years. Her father, on the other hand, retreated into the solitary hobby of falcony. The bond between Kendall and her mother was unusually close; therefore, the tragedy of her mother's death in an automobile accident was a crushing blow to the author. In her book, she created "a loving tribute to a woman who transcended the stereotypical role of housewife as well as a fascinating record of a mid-twentieth-century American woman's life," stated a *Publishers Weekly* reviewer.

Several commentators noted that while it is an affecting personal story, *American Daughter* is also something more. Cynde Bloom commented in *Library Journal* that by reflecting family life in many small towns in America during the 1950s and 1960s, "Kendall has provided a retrospective on that place and time." A *Kirkus Reviews* contributor elaborated: "With fierce insight, and yet without abandoning the memoir's basic posture, Kendall examines the particulars and generalities of her and her mother's characters—representative women of two generations on the brink of radical change. . . . [She] achieves the alchemical: part family chronicle, part social history, and wholly transcendent intellectual memoir."

Kendall once told *CA:* "I began dancing late, after having been very well-educated in the English language. Dance is very healthy for writers: it removes one's mind completely from words, yet it is a complete discipline itself. Ultimately the wordless language feeds back into the prose. I usually take a dance class every day."

BIOGRAPHICAL/CRITICAL SOURCES:

PERIODICALS

Kirkus Reviews, March 15, 2000, review of *American Daughter: Discovering My Mother,* p. 359.

Library Journal, May 1, 2000, Cynde Bloom, review of *American Daughter: Discovering My Mother,* p. 126.

Publishers Weekly, April 3, 2000, review of *American Daughter: Discovering My Mother,* p. 68.*

* * *

KER WILSON, Barbara 1929-

PERSONAL: Born September 24, 1929, in Sunderland, County Durham, England; daughter of William and Margaret Ker Wilson; married Peter Richard Tahourdin (a composer), December 15, 1956; children: Julia, Sarah. *Education:* Attended North London Collegiate School, 1938-48. *Religion:* Christian.

ADDRESSES: Home—Moreton Bay, Australia. *Agent*— c/o University of Queensland Press, Staff House Rd., P.O. Box 6042, St. Lucia, Queensland 4067, Australia.

CAREER: Oxford University Press, London, England, junior children's editor, 1949-54; Bodley Head, London, managing editor in children's books section, 1954-57; William Collins, London, managing editor, 1958-61; Angus & Robertson, Sydney, Australia, children's books editor, 1965-73; Hodder & Stoughton, Sydney, children's books editor, 1973-76; *Readers Digest* Condensed Books, Sydney, editor, 1978-84; editor for University of Queensland Press.

MEMBER: Australian Society of Authors.

WRITINGS:

FICTION; FOR CHILDREN

Path-through-the-Woods, illustrated by Charles Stewart, Constable, 1957, Criterion, 1958.
The Wonderful Cornet, illustrated by Raymond Briggs, Hamish Hamilton, 1958.
The Lovely Summer, illustrated by Marina Hoffer, Dodd, 1960.
Last Year's Broken Toys, Constable, 1962, published as *In Love and War,* World, 1963.
Ann and Peter in Paris (and in London), two volumes, illustrated by Harry and Ilse Toothill, Muller, 1963-65.
A Story to Tell: Thirty Tales for Little Children, illustrated by Sheila Sancha, J. Garnet Miller, 1964.
Beloved of the Gods, Constable, 1965, published as *In the Shadow of Vesuvius,* World, 1965.

A Family Likeness, illustrated by Astra Lacis Dick, Constable, 1967, published as *The Biscuit-Tin Family,* World, 1968.
Hiccups and Other Stories: Thirty Tales for Little Children, illustrated by Richard Kennedy, J. Garnet Miller, 1971.
The Willow Pattern Story, illustrated by Lucienne Fontannaz, Angus & Robertson, 1978.
(With Jacques Cadry) *The Persian Carpet Story,* illustrated by Nyorie Bungey, Methuen, 1981.
Kelly the Sleepy Koala, illustrated by Lorraine Itannay, Golden, 1983.
Molly, Golden, 1983.
Kevin the Kookaburra, illustrated by Sue Price, Golden, 1983.
Acacia Terrace, illustrated by David Fielding, Ashton Scholastic, 1988.

RETELLER; FOR CHILDREN

Scottish Folk Tales and Legends, illustrated by Joan Kiddell-Monroe, Oxford University Press, Walck, 1954, published as *Fairy Tales from Scotland,* Oxford University Press, 1999.
Fairy Tales of Germany, illustrated by Gertrude Mittelmann, Dutton, 1959.
Fairy Tales of Ireland, illustrated by G. W. Miller, Dutton, 1959.
Fairy Tales of Russia, illustrated by Jacqueline Athram, Dutton, 1959.
Fairy Tales of England, illustrated by J. S. Goodall, Dutton, 1960.
Fairy Tales of France, illustrated by William McLaren, Dutton, 1960.
Fairy Tales of India, illustrated by Rene Mackensie, Dutton, 1960.
Fairy Tales of Mexico, illustrated by G. W. Miller, Dutton, 1960.
Fairy Tales of Persia, illustrated by G. W. Miller, Dutton, 1961.
Legends of the Round Table, illustrated by Marra Calati, Hamlyn, 1966.
Greek Fairy Tales, illustrated by Harry Toothill, Muller, 1966, Follett, 1968.
Animal Folk Tales, illustrated by Mirko Hanak, Hamlyn, 1968, Grosset & Dunlap, 1971.
Tales Told to Kabbarli: Aboriginal Legends Collected by Daisy Bates, illustrated by Harold Thomas, Angus & Robertson, 1972.
The Magic Fishbones and Other Fabulous Tales of Asia, illustrated by Susanne Dolesch, Angus & Robertson, 1974.

The Magic Bird and Other Fabulous Tales from Europe, illustrated by S. Dolesch, Angus & Robertson, 1976.

The Turtle and the Island: Folk Tales from Papua New Guinea, edited by Donald S. Stokes, illustrated by Tony Oliver, Hodder & Stoughton, 1978.

Wishbones: A Folk Tale from China, illustrated by Meilo So, Macmillan, 1993.

OTHER; FOR CHILDREN

Look at Books (nonfiction), illustrated by John Woodcock, Hamish Hamilton, 1960.

(Compiler) *The Second Young Eve,* Blackie, 1962.

(Editor) Bernhardt Gottlieb, *What a Girl (and Boy) Should Know about Sex,* two volumes, Constable, 1962.

(Editor) *Australian Kaleidoscope,* illustrated by Margery Gill, Collins, 1968, Meredith Press, 1969.

Australia, Wonderland down Under (nonfiction), Dodd Mead, 1969.

(Compiler) *A Handful of Ghosts: Thirteen Eerie Tales by Australian Authors,* Hodder & Stoughton, 1976.

(Editor and author of notes) *Alitji: In the Dreamtime* (Aboriginal Pitjantjatjara version of Lewis Carroll's *Alice's Adventures in Wonderland*), adapted and translated by Nancy Sheppard, illustrated by Byron Sewell, Adelaide University Press, 1976.

Just for a Joyride (reader), Holt Rinehart, 1977.

(Editor) *Illustrated Treasury of Australian Stories and Verses for Children,* Nelson, 1987.

(Compiler) *Brief Encounters: Short Stories,* University of Queensland Press, 1992.

(Compiler) *Hands Up!: Who Enjoyed Their Schooldays,* University of Queensland Press, 1994.

NOVELS; FOR ADULTS

Jane Austen in Australia, Secker & Warburg, 1984, published as *Antipodes Jane,* Viking (New York, NY), 1985.

The Quade Inheritance, Secker & Warburg, 1988, St. Martin's Press (New York, NY), 1989.

NONFICTION; FOR ADULTS

Writing for Children, Boardman, 1960, Watts, 1961.

Noel Streatfeild: A Monograph, Bodley Head, 1961, Walck, 1964.

ADAPTATIONS: A Story to Tell: Thirty Tales for Little Children has been adapted for radio and television.

SIDELIGHTS: Barbara Ker Wilson has blended a career as an editor and a writer both in her native England and in her adopted country of Australia. Writing mainly for a juvenile audience, she has produced picture books, young adult novels, retellings of myths and folk tales from around the world, and a miscellany of story collections. Writing for adults, she has produced two popular novels, also read by teens: the speculative history *Jane Austen in Australia,* published in the United States as *Antipodes Jane,* and the historical romance *The Quade Inheritance.* As an editor, she has worked for the publishers Bodley Head and William Collins in England, as well as for Angus & Robertson, Hodder & Stoughton, *Reader's Digest,* and the University of Queensland Press in Australia; she has served as children's editor at most of these houses. From both sides of the editorial desk, Ker Wilson has produced a long list of publications. "Like a number of publisher's editors who are also authors, I am never sure which facet of this double career should come first," she once commented. "As a writer, my primary interest is to tell a story, and time and again I find myself returning to the refreshing vigor of the world's oldest stories, folk tales—the springboard for all fiction, including the most sophisticated modern novel. As a publisher's editor, it is often very satisfactory to be able to suggest ideas which are not right for my own style of authorship to other writers, and see them used successfully."

Born in Sunderland, County Durham, England, in 1929, Ker Wilson grew up during the depression in a family that was in the shipbuilding industry. Luckier than other families, the Ker Wilson's maintained employment during those difficult years, though her father worked at a reduced salary. Growing up near the sea a few hours from Norway, Ker Wilson formed an early love for distant horizons and the charm and fantasy of imagined worlds. "From an early age I was always within hearing of stories and poetry," the author wrote in the *Something about the Author Autobiography Series* (SAAS). "My mother and my aunts read me bedtimes stories, and my father, who had spent his boyhood in India, loved to recite Rudyard Kipling's *Just So Stories.*" Another favorite childhood activity was visiting the toy shop managed by an uncle on Wednesday, which was early closing day. Then she would have the doll houses, the entire play land, to herself. "I was free to explore this magic territory, alone," she noted.

All this changed in 1939. The family moved to a London suburb when Ker Wilson's father became a chief research assistant for an aircraft company. "It seemed almost as though we had moved to a foreign country," Ker Wilson commented in *SAAS*. But there were benefits to this relocation: London, with all its museums and galleries, was only a subway trip away. Ker Wilson and her older half-sister attended the North London Collegiate School for Girls, where scholarship was emphasized and expectations were high. Graduates assumed careers in law, medicine, science, and the arts. Ker Wilson soon became editor of the school magazine. Working on the magazine suited her literary bent. "I knew that I wanted to write from an early age," the author once commented. She had begun writing as early as primary school, when she composed plays and had them performed at the school. "My father wrote erudite scholarly works on engineering science, and I used to accompany him on visits to his publishers, from time to time. This is how I became interested in publishing, as well, from an early age."

Soon events from the larger world intruded; England went to war in 1939 and the Blitz began the following year. The Ker Wilsons slept in an air raid shelter in their garden and spent much of their school time below ground as well. "The worst years of the war in England were 1940-43," Ker Wilson wrote. "The air-raid siren sounded by day as well as by night, and at school we spent quite a lot of our time in the huge air-raid shelter below the new building." At home, after a night spent in the air-raid shelter, the family would emerge to find the lawn "littered with pieces of shrapnel from the thunderous gunfire." The war had a profound influence on Ker Wilson, as she noted in *SAAS:* "To spend one's childhood in a time of war, amid bombing raids and with the very real threat of invasion from across the English Channel, gave those growing years an extra dimension which contained an undeniable element of excitement, but, more importantly, somehow emphasized one's significance as a human being." As a result, she felt "an uplifting awareness of people united in a common cause, with the absolute conviction that we were striving against the power of evil." She would draw upon this inspiration later in her novel *Last Year's Broken Toys.*

After the war, and failing to gain a scholarship to study English or history, Ker Wilson went to a secretarial college. "But now I was determined to carve out a career in book publishing—as well as to become a published writer myself," she wrote. She first took a position at Oxford University Press, ultimately becoming a junior editor in the children's book section. During these years she also became familiar with all aspects of the publishing business, from editing to typography and book design. She also joined the ranks of published

writers, contributing *Scottish Folk Tales and Legends* to the Oxford University Press "Myths and Legends" series. Next, she moved on as managing editor of the children's book list at Bodley Head. From Bodley Head, Ker Wilson went to William Collins, where she was the managing editor of the children's division. But by 1961, with two daughters and a distinguished publishing career, Ker Wilson decided to leave Collins and get on with her own writing.

Her first novel for teenagers, *Path-through-the-Woods,* was published in 1958 and gave her the confidence to strike out on her own as a writer. The novel deals, on one level, with the position of women in society. The story behind a patchwork quilt, the novel is a series of vignettes from Victorian life with a young girl breaking tradition to become a pioneering female doctor. A contributor to the *St. James Guide to Children's Writers* noted that the "middle-class atmosphere is well conveyed" in this novel. Ker Wilson also wrote many titles on fairy tales from around the world before turning her hand to a second novel. Also dealing with the social issue of women's rights, *The Lovely Summer* appeared in 1960. Here Ker Wilson focuses on suffragettes and the enfranchisement of women. The "lovely summer" of the title was the summer of 1914, when World War I began. "This is a convincing and readable book," noted the *St. James Guide to Children's Writers* writer.

Moving to a house in Surrey, Ker Wilson published several more volumes in the next few years: *Beloved of the Gods, Last Year's Broken Toys,* and *A Story to Tell: Thirty Tales for Little Children.* Ancient Rome and the destruction of Pompeii is at the center of *Beloved of the Gods,* while Ker Wilson's own experiences in World War II inform *Last Year's Broken Toys,* an episodic novel with dozens of characters but with the war itself taking center stage. *A Story to Tell* was written for her children and has become a popular standard for radio broadcasts and television adaptations.

Moving to Australia in 1965, Ker Wilson found new inspiration in her adopted country. She quickly saw that there were few books available on the shelves for children with stories told from an Australian or Aboriginal point of view. She began writing such books herself. *A Family Likeness* is a dual tale, looking at the lives of a contemporary Australian girl, Debbie, and her nineteenth-century ancestors during the Australian gold rush. "The starting off point for this story occurred," Ker Wilson recalled, "when I visited a friend who told me that the small looking-glass in my bedroom had been used by her great-great-grandmother in a tent on the goldfields." Another popular story collection also followed, *Hiccups and Other Stories: Thirty Tales for Little Children.*

Soon, however, Ker Wilson found herself back in publishing, as an editor for Angus & Robertson, to produce a children's list of international quality that also focused on Australian and Asian themes. Further work in publishing took Ker Wilson from Adelaide to Sydney to work with Hodder & Stoughton and then *Reader's Digest* in the Condensed Books division. After what she thought would be a final retirement from editing in 1984, she took up writing again full time, but returned to publishing for one last stint. This time she worked for the University of Queensland Press in the young adult and newly formed children's sections.

Throughout these years, Ker Wilson was pursuing the dual career of writer and editor, retelling folk tales from around the world and compiling story collections. One of her most popular children's titles has been *Acacia Terrace,* a history of one corner of Sydney. Built in 1860, this neighborhood has undergone many changes over the years. Ker Wilson tells the story of this neighborhood through its buildings and the people who lived there. "Will the saga close with its demolition, or is there a chance for it to be restored?" asked Susan Wolfe in a *Wilson Library Bulletin* review of the book. "Listen to an old house's memories—a story waiting to be heard." Shirley Wilton, writing in *School Library Journal,* felt that it "is refreshing to have this glimpse of Australia and its history."

Working as compiler and editor, Ker Wilson assembled a potpourri of Australian tales and poetry for *Illustrated Treasury of Australian Stories and Verses for Children,* an "excellent anthology" that offers "a valuable perspective on Australian culture," according to Belle Alderman in *Booklist.* Jeanette Larson commented in *School Library Journal* that "overall the collection offers a good balance of material not readily available in other sources." Two of her popular retellings in picture book format are *The Turtle and the Island* and *Wishbones.* The first is the story of how Papua New Guinea was brought up from the bottom of the ocean by an ambitious turtle and also how the native people of the island came to live there. Adapted from a Papuan myth, the story is "a classic type of creation myth," according to Sonja Bolle, writing in the *Los Angeles Times Book Review.* With *Wishbones* Ker Wilson retells a folk tale from China that is something of a Cinderella motif. Betsy Hearne, reviewing the book in *Bulletin of the Center for Children's Books,* noted Ker Wilson's "ironic twist at the end," while *School Library Journal* critic John Philbrook felt the book was a "clever retelling."

Ker Wilson has also written two novels for adults that have proven popular with adult audiences. Her *Antipodes Jane* tells the what-if story of Jane Austen down under when she accompanies her uncle and aunt (accused of shoplifting); it is also the tale of a lost love in Australia. Mixing some fact with a great deal of historical fiction (Austen was never in Australia), Ker Wilson came up with a "vastly entertaining" story, according to John Espey in the *Los Angeles Times Book Review.* A writer for *Kirkus Reviews* felt that though this "fictional fling" might be "irritating to Janites," Ker Wilson nonetheless "has produced an amusing and even illuminating view of Australia's colonial beginnings." *Times Literary Supplement* contributor Lindsay Duguid, reviewing the English publication of the same book, titled *Jane Austen in Australia,* concluded that the novel "offers some rewarding contrasts; incongruity is part of its appeal."

Ker Wilson's *The Quade Inheritance* began life as an attempt at a spoof gothic, but it emerged as a straight historical story set in 1860s England, with reverberations both in Australia and America. The story of the acquisition and continued possession of a perfect country house over several centuries, "this captivating gothic . . . throbs with the singleminded malevolence of a possessive gentlewoman," character Imogen Quade, according to a reviewer for *Publishers Weekly.* Reviewing the same novel in *School Library Journal,* Keddy Outlaw noted that the book was written in a "crisp literary style, with certain gothic overtones and vivid detail," and it "moves through the lives of its characters with compelling sureness."

Whether retelling folk tales and myths from around the world, writing children's novels and short stories, dealing with more adult themes in novels and nonfiction, or compiling the work of others, Ker Wilson has always maintained an editor's eye for detail and audience. She has combined the skills of able editor and creative writer in her fifty books for both children and adults, but children's books remain closest to her heart. "Both as a children's writer and as an editor, I see children's literature as a great force for international understanding," she once said. "My work with children's writing has taken me all over the world, and I have seen this branch of literature grow and develop significantly in extent and depth."

BIOGRAPHICAL/CRITICAL SOURCES:

BOOKS

Something about the Author Autobiography Series, Volume 18, Gale (Detroit, MI), 1994, pp. 165-184.

St. James Guide to Children's Books, fifth edition, St. James (Detroit, MI), 1999.

PERIODICALS

Booklist, October 19, 1988, Belle Alderman, review of *The Illustrated Treasury of Australian Stories and Verses for Children,* p. 423; April 15, 1989, p. 1435; February 15, 1990, p. 90; January 15, 1991, p. 1033.

Bulletin of the Center for Children's Books, February, 1994, Betsy Hearne, review of *Wishbones,* p. 204.

Kirkus Reviews, April 15, 1985, review of *Antipodes Jane,* p. 350; September 15, 1990, p. 1334.

Los Angeles Times Book Review, July 21, 1985, John Espey, review of *Antipodes Jane,* pp. 1, 6; January 27, 1991, Sonja Bolle, review of *The Turtle and the Island,* p. 8.

Magpies, May, 1994, p. 27; July, 1994, p. 24; September, 1999, p. 20; November, 1999, p. 29.

New York Times Book Review, July 21, 1985, p. 12.

Observer, November 25, 1990, p. 6.

Publishers Weekly, April 5, 1985, p. 65; March 3, 1989, review of *The Quade Inheritance,* p. 87; September 13, 1993, p. 128.

School Library Journal, April, 1988, Jeanette Larson, review of *The Illustrated Treasury of Australian Stories and Verses for Children,* p. 111; September, 1989, Keddy Outlaw, review of *The Quade Inheritance,* p. 286; March, 1990, Shirley Wilton, review of *Acacia Terrace,* p. 233; January, 1991, p. 87; March, 1994, John Philbrook, review of *Wishbones,* p. 219.

Spectator, January 19, 1985, p. 23.

Times Educational Supplement, November 2, 1990, p. R4; September 10, 1993, p. 11.

Times Literary Supplement, October 26, 1984, Lindsay Duguid, review of *Jane Austen in Australia,* p. 1224.

Wilson Library Bulletin, September, 1990, Susan Wolfe, review of *Acacia Terrace,* p. 4.

*   *   *

KIMMEL, Michael S(cott) 1951-

PERSONAL: Born February 26, 1951, in New York, NY; son of Edwin H. and Barbara Diamond (Michtom) Kimmel. *Education:* Vassar College, B.A., 1972; Brown University, M.A., 1974; University of California, Berkeley, Ph.D., 1981.

ADDRESSES: Office—State University of New York, S-401, Social and Behavioral Sciences, Stony Brook, NY 11794-4356. *E-mail*—Michael.Kimmel@sunysb.edu.

CAREER: Bryant College, Smithfield, RI, instructor in sociology, 1973; State University of New York College at Oneonta, instructor in sociology, 1973-74; University of California at Berkeley, instructor in sociology, 1974-76; University of California at Santa Cruz, visiting lecturer, 1977-81; Rutgers University, New Brunswick, NJ, assistant professor of sociology, 1982-86; State University of New York at Stony Brook, professor of sociology, 1987—. Contributing editor of *San Francisco Review of Books,* 1977-85; corresponding editor of *Theory and Society,* 1979-84; book review editor of *Society,* 1981; book editor of *Changing Men,* 1983—.

MEMBER: American Sociology Association, California Anti-sexist Men's Political Caucus, Institute for International Studies (fellow), Chancellor's Patent Fund (fellow), William A. Clark Memorial Library (fellow).

AWARDS, HONORS: Recipient of grants from the Spencer Foundation; fellowship from University of California at Berkeley, 1978-79.

WRITINGS:

Absolutism and Its Discontent: State and Society in Seventeenth-Century France and England, Transaction Books (New Brunswick, NJ), 1988.

(Author of introduction) *Mundus Foppensis* [and] *The Levellers,* William A. Clark Memorial Library (University of California at Los Angeles, CA), 1988.

(Compiler, with Michael A. Messner) *Men's Lives,* Macmillan (New York, NY), 1989.

Revolution: A Sociological Interpretation, Temple University Press (Philadelphia, PA), 1990.

Manhood in America: A Cultural History, Free Press (New York, NY), 1996.

The Gendered Society, Oxford University Press (New York, NY), 2000.

(With Amy Aronson) *The Gendered Society Reader,* Oxford University Press (New York, NY), 2000.

EDITOR

Changing Men: New Directions in Research on Men and Masculinity, Sage (Newbury Park, CA), 1987.

Love Letters between a Certain Late Nobleman and the Famous Mr. Wilson, Haworth (New York, NY), 1990.

Men Confront Pornography, Crown (New York, NY), 1990.

(With Thomas E. Mosmiller) *Against the Tide: "Pro-Feminist" Men in the United States, 1776-1990, a Documentary History,* Beacon (Boston, MA), 1992.

The Politics of Manhood: Profeminist Men Respond to the Mythopoetic Men's Movement (and Mythopoetic Leaders Answer), Temple University Press (Philadelphia, PA), 1995.

(With Charles Stephen) *Social and Political Theory: Classical Readings,* Allyn and Bacon (Boston, MA), 1998.

(And author of introduction) Martin P. Levine, *Gay Macho: The Life and Death of the Homosexual Clone,* New York University Press (New York, NY), 1998.

(With Amy Aronson) Charlotte Perkins Gilman, *Women and Economics: A Study of the Economic Relations between Men and Women as a Factor in Social Evolution,* University of California Press (Berkeley, CA), 1998.

Contributor of articles and reviews to periodicals, including *New York Times Book Review, Los Angeles Times, Washington Post,* and *Harvard Business Review.* Author of foreword of *Boyhood, Growing Up Male: A Multicultural Anthology,* edited by Franklin Abbott, 1998. Interviewed for the PBS documentary *No Safe Place: Violence Against Women,* produced by KUED, Salt Lake City, UT.

SIDELIGHTS: Michael S. Kimmel is a sociologist who has published various volumes on male culture. Notable among his writings is *Manhood in America: A Cultural History,* which explores the ways that notions of masculinity have influenced, and have been influenced by, American culture. In this volume Kimmel argues that men have long been motivated by the desire or need to prove their masculinity. He traces the ways in which the American concept of masculinity, influenced by social and economic changes and pressure, have evolved. He also speculates on the ways in which notions—and representations—of masculinity might further change in the near future. "Kimmel has culled every testosterone tract of the last two centuries in order to find out not what men did, but what they were advised to do," Sam Fussell noted in his *Washington Post Book Review* critique of *Manhood in America.*

Natalie Coulter, reviewing the book for *H-Net Review* online, noted that Kimmel's history begins in the late eighteenth and early nineteenth centuries, when Kimmel believes the Self-Made Man evolved. "According to him," wrote Coulter, "the Self-Made Man was 'a

model of accumulated wealth and status.' As a model, the Self-Made Man has shaped the construction of masculinity in American culture up until the present era."

Nation reviewer Fred Pfeil called Kimmel, a "conspicuously well-intentioned white guy" who "as a cultural analyst is not always up to scratch. He is at his best when dealing with the appeal of baseball and boxing in the late nineteenth century as sublimated echoes of an artisanal assertiveness and self-respect no longer available at the office or factory. . . . But when it comes to either high or popular art, his touch is much less sure. . . . He lumbers through the movies of the fifties without a nod toward the anguished vulnerability and sexual ambiguity of Marlon Brando or James Dean, nor a glance at the elegant corrosions of director Douglas Stirk. And when it comes to rock and roll's display of masculinities, he's just hopeless." Pfeil said "the larger and more symptomatic problem behind *Manhood*'s sprawl is Kimmel's failure to take on the full weight, variety, and complexity of the power relations at work in the construction of white hetero masculinity from the revolutionary period through the present day."

Kimmel tackled gender issues once again in the anthology, *Men's Lives,* which he compiled with Michael Messner. In this anthology, Kimmel and Messner included essays organized around issues men face at different stages of their lives, including early-life issues such as elementary school and boy scouts, and later-life issues, including sports, health, and family issues. In a review of this book for *Sex Roles,* John M. Robertson praised the collection for its depth, noting that articles included in the anthology explored these issues from various vantage points.

Kimmel and Amy Aronson edited the 1998 edition of *Women and Economics: A Study of the Economic Relations between Men and Women as a Factor in Social Evolution.* The book, originally published in 1898, is author Charlotte Perkins Gilman's study of economics and women's dependence on men. Gilman felt that because of this dependence, the sexual relationship was also an economic relationship. She carried this theory further, saying that economics is the basis for all class inequities. Gilman was an intellectual and lecturer who became less notable during the conservatism of the 1920s.

Ann J. Lane reviewed the book for *Industrial and Labor Relations Review.* Lane praised the authors' introduction that ties in Gilman's subsequent writings. Lane disagreed with their view of not considering Gilman a socialist. "I do," said Lane, "and more to the point, she did. She was strongly opposed to Marx's notions of class struggle and the necessity for violence, relying instead on a belief in moral suasion." Lane said that in discussing Gilman's *Herland,* for which Gilman is most well known, that Kimmel and Aronson interpret Gilman's message to her readers as a proposal to consider the way in which society could develop with no men in it. "I believe," wrote Lane, that "Gilman wrote *Herland* as a way of inviting readers to recognize the potential for and meaning of genuine autonomy for women, rather than to judge or condemn men." Lane noted that Gilman is again an important figure with a society and newsletter dedicated to her. Her books are being reprinted, and sociologists and economists are adding their voices, although Lane felt that the field of economics has not yet recognized her contribution. "Perhaps this edition, appearing at this time, will enlarge her audience," said Lane.

Kimmel wrote *The Gendered Society* as a text for his sociology students, including research on how gender affects marriage, the family, parenting, work, and school. He proposes that men and women, rather than being from different planets and being opposite sexes, are "neighboring sexes." He writes that there are more variations within the sexes than between the sexes. A *Publishers Weekly* reviewer said that "although Kimmel's emphasis is frequently on the necessity of transforming masculinity . . . he is scrupulous in maintaining balance and comprehensiveness."

BIOGRAPHICAL/CRITICAL SOURCES:

PERIODICALS

Dissent, fall 1992, pp. 539-41.
Gender and Society, September, 1993, Peter J. Stein, review of *Men's Lives,* p. 462.
Industrial and Labor Relations Review, January, 2000, Ann J. Lane, review of *Women and Economics,* p. 326.
Nation, November 17, 1997, Fred Pfeil, review of *Manhood in America,* p. 30.
Publishers Weekly, February 21, 2000, review of *The Gendered Society,* p. 79.
Sex Roles: A Journal of Research, September, 1995, John M. Robertson, review of *Men's Lives,* p. 459.
Voice Literary Supplement, April 1990, pp. 16-17.
Washington Post Book World, November 5, 1995, Sam Fussell, review of *Manhood in America,* pp. 1, 14.

OTHER

H-Net Review, http://www.h-nt.msu.edu/ (June 4, 2000).
PBS, No Safe Place: Violence against Women, http://www.pbs.org/ (August 14, 2000).*

*   *   *

KIPPENHAHN, Rudolf 1926-

PERSONAL: Born May 24, 1926, in Baerringen, Czechoslovakia; son of Rudolf and Alma (Belz) Kippenhahn; married Johanna Rasper; children: Ruth Kippenhahn Lehmann, Eva, Karin. *Education:* University of Bamberg, Ph.D., 1951.

ADDRESSES: Home—Rheinlandstrasse 10b, 8000 Munich 40, Germany. *Office*—Institute for Astrophysics, Max-Planck-Institute for Physics and Astrophysics, Karl-Schwarzschildstrasse 1, 8046 Garching near Munich, West Germany.

CAREER: Bamberg Observatory, Bamberg, West Germany, scientific assistant, 1951-57; Max-Planck-Institute for Physics and Astrophysics, Institute for Astrophysics, Munich, West Germany, staff member, 1957-65, member of directorate, 1963—, director, 1975—. Professor of astronomy and astrophysics at the University of Göttingen Observatory, 1965-75; honorary professor at Munich University, 1975—.

MEMBER: International Astronomical Union, Society of German Scientists and Physicians (member of scientific council), German Academy of Naturforscher Leopoldina, Goettingen Scientific Society, Braunschweigische Scientific Society, Bavarian Academy of Science, Royal Astronomical Society (associate).

AWARDS, HONORS: Carus Medal from German Academy of Naturforscher Leopoldina, 1973; Carus Prize from city of Schweinfurt, 1974; Verdienstkreuz 1. Klasse des Verdienstordens from Federal Republic of Germany, 1984; Lorenz-Oken-Medal, 1986.

WRITINGS:

(With Claus Moellenhoff) *Elementare Plasmaphysik,* Bibliographisches Institut (Mannheim), 1965.

(Editor with J. Rahe and W. Strohmeier) *The Interaction of Variable Stars with Their Environment: Proceedings of the IAU-Colloquium No. 42, Bamberg, September 6-9, 1977,* Remeis-Sternwarte Bamberg, Astronomisches Institut der Universitaet Erlangen-Nuernberg (Bamberg), 1977.

Hundert Milliarden Sonnen: Geburt, Leben und Tod der Sterne, Piper (Munich), 1980, translation by Jean Steinberg published as *100 Billion Suns: The Birth, Life, and Death of the Stars,* Basic (New York City), 1983, reprinted with new foreword, Princeton University Press (Princeton, NJ), 1993.

Licht vom Rande der Welt: Das Universum und sein Anfang, Deutsche Verlagsanstalt (Stuttgart), 1984, translation by Storm Dunlop published as *Light from the Depths of Time,* Springer-Verlag (New York City), 1987.

Unheimliche Welten: Planeten, Monde und Kometen, Deutsche Verlagsanstalt, 1987, translation published as *Inhospitable Worlds: Planets, Moons, and Comets,* W. H. Freeman (New York City), 1990, translation by Dunlop published as *Bound to the Sun: The Story of Plants, Moons, and Comets,* W. H. Freeman, 1990.

(With A. Weigert) *Stellar Structure and Evolution,* Astronomy and Astrophysics Library, Springer-Verlag (New York City, 1990, revised third printing, 1994.

Der Stern, von dem wir leben, Deutsche Verlagsanstalt, 1990, translation by Dunlop published as *Discovering the Secrets of the Sun,* Wiley (New York City), 1994.

Code Breaking: A History and Exploration, translated by Ewald Osers in collaboration with Kippenhahn, Overlook (Woodstock, NY), 1999.

Associated with *Physical Processes in Comets, Stars, and Active Galaxies: Proceedings of a Workshop Held at Ringberg Castle, Tegernsee, May 26-27, 1986* (festschrift for Kippenhahn and Hermann Ulrich Schmidt on the occasion of their sixtieth birthdays), edited by W. Hillebrandt, E. Meyer-Hofmeister, and H.-C. Thomas, Springer-Verlag (New York City), 1987.

SIDELIGHTS: Among the publications by Rudolf Kippenhahn, a German astrophysicist, is *Discovering the Secrets of the Sun,* originally published as *Der Stern, von dem wir leben.* In the work Kippenhahn "emphasizes some of the central areas of solar physics. . . . [including] the behavior of plasmas . . . magnetohydrodynamics . . . and acoustic and gravity waves within the Sun," related Robert F. Howard, praising in his *Sky & Telescope* review: "The author covers

these difficult topics in a very readable book that contains no equations. . . . Kippenhahn's explanations are always clear and easy to absorb." An *Astronomy* critic noted that the text "assumes some basic understanding of physics," but contended that "Kippenhahn's engaging explanations" will facilitate layperson's recall of the basic information the learned as a highschooler or college student. Although Howard had small issues with the book's translation by Storm Dunlop, as well as with some "[minor] scientific slips," he recommended *Discovering the Secrets of the Sun* as an enjoyable, "very good book."

Code Breaking: A History and Exploration covers "all major and some minor encrypting methods," from those used in the past by Leionidas to those employed by Internet users, summarized J. Mayer in a *Choice* review promoting the work as a "fascinating, clever . . . informative. . . . thoroughly satisfying book." According to Joe Collins' *Booklist* assessment, Kippenhahn presented his information "in a straightforward but provocative style." However, *Library Journal* contributor Dayne Sherman felt Kippenhahn burdened his text with "stodgy technical jargon." In contrast, Mayer determined that occasionally "tedious" explanations were needed for better understanding of information presented later in the book. While Sherman asserted that *Code Breaking* was "neither a good story nor hard science," Collins declared it "the definitive look at the subject" and maintained "[Kippenhahn] enlivens it with fascinating stories."

BIOGRAPHICAL/CRITICAL SOURCES:

PERIODICALS

Astronomy, October, 1983, p. 31; January, 1988, p. 43; April, 1995, p. 96.

Booklist, March 1, 1999, p. 1148.

Choice, November, 1999, p. 562.

Library Journal, April 15, 1999, p. 141.

New York Times Book Review, August 21, 1983; July 6, 1986, p. 24.

Publishers Weekly, April 29, 1983, p. 42.

Science '83, December, 1983, p. 114.

Sky & Telescope, August, 1984, p. 134; September, 1987, p. 262; January, 1992, p. 46; November, 1994, p. 52.*

KOJA, Kathe 1960-

PERSONAL: Born 1960; married Rick Lieder (an artist); children: one son.

ADDRESSES: Home—Detroit, MI, metropolitan area. *Office*—c/o Farrar, Straus, Giroux, 19 Union Sq. W., New York, NY 10003.

CAREER: Writer.

AWARDS, HONORS: Locus Award for Best First Novel, and Bram Stoker Award for Best First Horror Novel, Horror Writers of America, both 1992, both for *The Cipher.*

WRITINGS:

The Cipher, Abyss (New York, NY), 1991.
Bad Brains, Abyss (New York, NY), 1992.
Skin, Delacorte (New York, NY), 1993.
Strange Angels, Delacorte (New York, NY), 1994.
Kink, Holt (New York, NY), 1996.
Extremities (short stories), Four Walls Eight Windows (New York, NY), 1998.
Straydog, Farrar Straus (New York, NY), 2002.

SIDELIGHTS: Kathe Koja, a Michigan novelist living in metropolitan Detroit, is viewed by critics as bringing new blood to the horror genre. "Koja is that rare writer who has not only cultivated a distinctly original approach to horror fiction, but whose unique style is a natural outgrowth of her horror themes. . . . Most of her characters are painters or sculptors on the avant-garde fringe. They live bohemian lives. . . . Forever striving to perfect their artistic self-expression, they are constantly at war with themselves and their colleagues. A fine line separates their creativity from insanity, and their self-absorption and obsessive devotion to their artistic vision frequently pushes them across that line," described Stefan Dziemianowicz in the *St. James Guide to Horror, Ghost, and Gothic Writers,* adding: "Koja has perfected a sensual narrative style that projects the intense emotions of these characters. . . . At moments of horror, when her characters lose control over their situations, Koja boosts the energy of her prose and bombards the reader with streams of images that are almost too incoherent to be absorbed at once. In general, though, her narratives approximate the states of mind of her frustrated, temperamental artists, steadily simmering

by always threatening to boil over. . . . In Koja's fiction any endowment that sets one apart from others is potentially alienating, and those who appear most gifted are often those most cursed."

"Most horror writing is about working through the fear of death, rot, and decay," wrote Richard Gehr in the *Voice Literary Supplement.* "Koja's pitiful heroes, on the other hand, are transformed by it, turning into something even uglier and weirder than the everyday mutants they were before." Koja updates her horror by drawing upon her familiarity with the counter-culture of the 1980s and 1990s. As Edward Bryant explained in a *Locus* review, she "appears to know what's happening down there on the street-level frontiers of guerrilla culture and she's unafraid to pass it on." Yet, even though it is set in the world of urban grunge, "her fiction is both tough and tender, strong streaks of romance reined in by a hard-edged sensibility that rarely flinches," commented Bryant in another *Locus* review.

Published in 1991, *The Cipher* is Koja's first novel and the first in Dell's Abyss horror series. In the *Bloomsbury Review,* Edward Bryant termed it "a brilliantly crafted portrait of disintegrating reality in a grungy contemporary city much like Detroit." The novel follows Nicholas Reid, a video-store clerk and aspiring poet, and his lover, Nakota. The two discover a black hole of sorts in a storeroom in Nicholas's run-down apartment building. The "Funhole," as they call it, intrigues and obsesses them; there appears to be no bottom, and light does not enter it. Things that go in the Funhole disappear or come back changed. A video made by suspending a camera inside the hole yields a tape that is seen differently by different viewers. Eventually, Nicholas's obsession with the hole forces him to spend day and night by its side. This constant proximity to the hole changes him, and his changes affect those around him. "For Nicholas himself, the hole is a phenomenon that forces him to face his miserable, aimless life," noted a *Publishers Weekly* reviewer.

"Koja tells her story with extraordinarily precise language, often lyrical, sometimes brutally direct," Bryant wrote in *Locus.* "There is humor here, but it is designed to saw at your ribs until you wince." "The fear Koja taps into in *The Cipher,*" according to Gehr in the *Voice Literary Supplement,* "is less that of the body dying and rotting (as in [traditional] horror) than an infinity spent contemplating the absence of that which we imagine will complete us." Bryant concluded, "*The Cipher* is an adventurous work for similarly adventurous readers."

Koja followed *The Cipher* with the 1992 publication of *Bad Brains.* Like her previous work, this novel is concerned with transformation and mental anguish. The main character, a painter named Austen, slips and falls in a convenience store parking lot, receiving a head wound. Not only does his injury cause seizures, Austen is plagued by strange hallucinations, including a recurring image of a mucous-like slime creature. Hoping to move ahead of his problems, he embarks on a journey to Texas. His problems follow him, however, and the book climaxes in violence.

With *Skin,* announced a *Kirkus Reviews* critic, "a strong stylist" created "a savage hymn to industrial culture . . . whose breakthrough originality is unique but will leave many fighting off its overload." The 1993 publication tells the story of Tess Bajac, an artist/welder who creates sculptures made from metal scraps, and Bibi Bloss, a performance artist whose work is her own tattooed, scarified, and pierced body. The book follows their relationship and their individual and joint efforts to find expression through mechanized steel and pierced, cut skin. The author of *Skin* shows "considerable talent for evoking atmosphere, but," faulted a *Publishers Weekly* reviewer, "her style . . . distances the characters from the reader and hampers the novel's already minimal movement."

When assessing *Skin,* reviewers theorized on Koja's focus in the novel. As Faren Miller pointed out in *Locus,* "[Koja's] real subject is obsession: the passion to create an artwork, a new self, something *transcendent.* And the horror of it is how people will keep striving till they break." "For all the breathless sensation of out-of-control art and visceral squirming of human flesh transformed by knives, needles, and manic machines," commented Bryant in *Locus,* "the center here is ineluctably human. Tess and Bibi's relationship (as well as each's relationship with the other characters) carries both the fragility and toughness of flesh rather than the cold alloy of machinery." As Miller recognized: "*Skin* is also passionate, deeply informed, and genuine, particularly as it portrays the artist from the inside out."

Koja delivered her fourth novel, *Strange Angels,* in 1994. As with her previous books, the confluence of artistry and madness plays a central role. The book's protagonist is a frustrated photographer named Grant whose girlfriend works as an art therapist. Through her, Grant is introduced to the drawings of a mentally ill man named Robin, whose anguished, twisted art gives the photographer hope for his own struggling talent. Grant convinces Robin to leave therapy and cease his medication, which, while heightening his artistic output, only exacerbates his mental condition. Robin persists in

a fixation with seraphim, and this, coupled with other signs, convinces Grant that Robin is being transformed into an angel. Reviews were mixed for this novel. A *Publishers Weekly* critic denounced the work, calling the characters "one-dimensional monomaniacs" and believing that the author "whines unremittingly in a single-pitched, overwrought stream of consciousness that will probably alienate most readers." A *Kirkus Reviews* contributor praised parts of the book as "sensitive" while labeling the work "gratuitously bizarre" as a whole.

Although "a brilliant stylist" who writes "unembellished sensory impression" which "perfectly express . . . emotional devastation," Koja, in *Kink,* maintained a *Publishers Weekly* reviewer, falls short of previous work. "In this stab at transgressive mainstream fiction" involving a love triangle, Koja's usual character types seem like "self absorbed bores," contended the disappointed critic. *Kink* is an "anticlimactic . . . unsubtle" story with "long breathless clauses strung together in a stream-of-consciousness style," declared *New York Times Book Review* contributor Karen Angel, who faulted the book's overused symbols, damaging "silly central conceit," and the major characters "ultimate realization." Comments in *Publishers Weekly* for Koja's next publication, *Extremities,* were similarly unflattering. The critic called the collection of seventeen stories "daring but unsatisfing," indicating that Koja's "gift for sensory description" was used ineffectively. According to the *Publishers Weekly* reviewer, too much of the text "seemed designed merely to shock" and "such gratuitous grotesquerie" failed to be "provocative" and occasionally created "unintentional comic effect."

In *Washington Post Book World* contributor Paul Di Filippo's view, Koja uses her prose to surgically reveal her vision of horror. "Koja is intent on undercutting and discarding all the unthought and unfelt scaffolding and properties of her chosen form and resurrecting it bright and bloody." She is also uncovering the character of counter-culture art. "Koja is both creating the kind of radical new art she advocates and simultaneously detailing the methods and penalties attendant on such creation," wrote Di Filippo. "A clever trick, by any standards."

BIOGRAPHICAL/CRITICAL SOURCES:

BOOKS

St. James Guide to Horror, Ghost, and Gothic Writers, first edition, St. James (Detroit, MI), 1998.

PERIODICALS

Bloomsbury Review, December, 1991, Edward Bryant, review of *The Cipher,* p. 27.
Kirkus Reviews, February 1, 1993, p. 86; March 15, 1994, p. 325.
Locus, January, 1991, p. 21; December, 1992, pp. 17-18; April, 1993, p. 21.
New York Times Book Review, January 19, 1997, Karen Angel, review of *Kink.*
Publishers Weekly, January 11, 1991, p. 98; February 15, 1993; April 4, 1994, p. 59; April 29, 1996; September 14, 1998.
Voice Literary Supplement, July/August, 1992, Richard Gehr, review of *The Cipher,* p. 5.
Washington Post Book World, March 28, 1993, p. 9.*

*   *   *

KONVITZ, Milton Ridvas 1908-

PERSONAL: Born March 12, 1908, in Safad, Palestine (now Israel); son of Joseph (a rabbi) and Welia (Wilowsky-Ridvas) Konvitz; married Mary Traub (a teacher), 1942; children: Josef. *Education:* New York University, B.S., 1928, M.A., 1930, J.D., 1930; Cornell University, Ph.D., 1933. *Religion:* Jewish.

ADDRESSES: Home—150 Norwood Ave., Oakhurst, NJ 07753-1604.

CAREER: Admitted to New Jersey Bar, 1932. Law practice with John Milton, Jersey City, NJ, 1933-35; Newark Housing Authority, Newark, NJ, general counsel, 1938-43; New Jersey State Housing Authority, general counsel, 1943-45; NAACP Legal Defense and Education Fund, assistant general counsel, 1943-46; Cornell University, Ithaca, NY, professor of industrial and labor relations at School of Industrial and Labor Relations, 1946-73, professor of law at Law School, 1956-73, professor emeritus, 1973—. New York University, lecturer, 1938-46; New School for Social Research, faculty member, 1944-46; Salzburg Seminar in American Studies (Austria), faculty member, 1952; Institute for Advanced Study, Princeton, NJ, member, 1959-60; Center for Advanced Study in the Behavioral Sciences, Palo Alto, CA, fellow, 1964-65; Hebrew University of Jerusalem, visiting professor, 1970. National War Labor Relations Board, public representative for Region 2, 1943-46; Liberian Codification of Laws Project, director, 1952-80; Wage Stabilization Board, hearing commissioner and member of Enforcement Commission, 1952-53; Workers Defense League, member of advisory board.

MEMBER: American Academy of Arts and Sciences (fellow), American Civil Liberties Union (member of national advisory board), Phi Beta Kappa, Coif.

AWARDS, HONORS: Ford Foundation fellow, 1952-53; Guggenheim fellow, 1953-54; fellow, Fund for the Republic, 1955, Center for Advanced Behavioral Sciences, 1964-65, and National Endowment for the Humanities, 1975-76; Distinguished Alumni Award, Washington Square College, New York University, 1964; Mordecai ben David Award, Yeshiva University, 1965; Morris J. Kaplun International Prize, Hebrew University of Jerusalem, 1969; decorated commander and grand band, Star of Africa of Liberia; honorary degrees include Litt. D., Rutgers University, 1954, and Dropsie University, 1975; D.C.L., University of Liberia, 1962; L.H.D., Hebrew Union College, 1966, and Yeshiva University, 1972; LL.D., Syracuse University, 1971, and Jewish Theological Seminary, 1972.

WRITINGS:

On the Nature of Value: The Philosophy of Samuel Alexander, Kings Crown Press, 1946.
The Alien and the Asiatic in American Law, Cornell University Press (Ithaca, NY), 1946.
The Constitution and Civil Rights, Cornell University Press (Ithaca, NY), 1947, reprinted, Octagon (New York, NY), 1977.
(Translator, with others) *Latin-American Legal Philosophy,* Harvard University (Cambridge, MA), 1948.
Civil Rights in Immigration, Cornell University Press (Ithaca, NY), 1953.
Fundamental Liberties of a Free People: Religion, Speech, Press, Assembly, Cornell University Press (Ithaca, NY), 1957.
A Century of Civil Rights, Columbia University Press (New York, NY), 1961.
Expanding Liberties: Freedom's Gains in Postwar America, Viking (New York, NY), 1966.
Religious Liberty and Conscience, Viking (New York, NY), 1968.
(Compiler) *The Recognition of Ralph Waldo Emerson: Selected Criticisms since 1837,* University of Michigan Press (Ann Arbor, MI), 1972.
Judaism and the American Idea, Cornell University Press (Ithaca, NY), 1978.
Torah and Constitution: Essays in American Jewish Thought, Syracuse University Press (Syracuse, NY), 1998.
Fundamental Rights: History of a Constitutional Doctrine, Transaction Publishers (New Brunswick, NJ), 2000.

Nine American Jewish Thinkers, Transaction Publishers (New Brunswick, NJ), 2000.

EDITOR

(With Sidney Hooke) *Freedom and Experience: Essays Presented to H. M. Kallen,* Cornell University Press (Ithaca, NY), 1947, reprinted, Cooper Square (Totowa, NJ), 1975.

Essays in Political Theory Presented to George Sabine, Cornell University Press (Ithaca, NY), 1948.

Alexander Pekelis, *Law and Social Action,* Cornell University Press (Ithaca, NY), 1950.

Bill of Rights Reader: Leading Constitutional Cases, Cornell University Press (Ithaca, NY), 1952, 5th edition, 1973.

Edmond E. Day, *Education for Freedom and Responsibility,* Cornell University Press (Ithaca, NY), 1952, reprinted, Arno (New York, NY), 1978.

Liberian Code of Laws, five volumes, Cornell University Press (Ithaca, NY), 1957-60, revised edition, two volumes, 1973-78.

(With Clinton Rossiter) *Aspects of Liberty: Essays Presented to Robert E. Cushman,* Cornell University Press (Ithaca, NY), 1958.

(With Gail Kennedy) *The American Pragmatists: Selected Writings,* Meridian, 1960.

(With Stephen E. Whicher) *Emerson: A Collection of Critical Essays,* Prentice-Hall (Englewood Cliffs, NJ), 1962.

First Amendment Freedoms: Selected Cases on Freedom of Religion, Speech, Press, Assembly, Cornell University Press (Ithaca, NY), 1963.

Opinions of the Attorney General of the Republic of Liberia, September, 1964-August, 1968, Cornell University Press (Ithaca, NY), 1969.

Judaism and Human Rights, Viking (New York, NY), 1972.

The Legacy of Horace M. Kallen, Associated University Presses (Cranbury, NJ), 1987.

Member of editorial board, *Encyclopedia Judaica.* Editor of *Industrial and Labor Relations,* five volumes, between 1947 and 1952, and *Liberian Law Reports;* chair of editorial board, *Midstream;* member of editorial board, *New Leader* and *Judaism;* co-chair of editorial advisory board, *Journal of Law and Religion.*

BIOGRAPHICAL/CRITICAL SOURCES:

PERIODICALS

Library Journal, September 1, 2000, Naomi E. Hafter, review of *Nine American Jewish Thinkers,* p. 215.

Saturday Review, February 8, 1969.

KOPPEL, Ted 1940-

PERSONAL: Born February 8, 1940, in Lancashire, England; immigrated to United States, 1953, naturalized citizen 1963; married Grace Anne Dorney (an attorney); children: four. *Education:* Syracuse University, B.A., and Stanford University, M.A.

ADDRESSES: Office—Nightline, 1717 Desales Street N.W., Washington, DC 20036-4401.

CAREER: Radio station WMCA, New York City, news correspondent and writer, 1963; American Broadcasting Co., (ABC News) radio correspondent, 1963-67, 1967-71, began as head of Miami bureau, became head of Hong Kong bureau, diplomatic correspondent, 1971-76 and 1977-79, anchorman of Saturday television news, 1976-77, host of television news show, *Nightline,* Washington, DC, 1980—. Freelance writer, 1976-77.

AWARDS, HONORS: DuPont-Columbia award, 1979, for *World News Tonight* series, "Second to None?"; seven other DuPont-Columbia awards; National Press Foundation, Sol Taishoff award for excellence in broadcasting, 1984; Academy of Television Arts and Sciences, eighteen Emmy awards; seven Overseas Press Club awards; three George Foster Peabody awards; two George Polk awards for national television reporting; two Ohio State University awards; two Society of Professional Journalism awards; numerous others.

WRITINGS:

(Compiler) *The Wit and Wisdom of Adlai Stevenson,* Hawthorn (New York City), 1965.

(With Marvin L. Kalb) *In the National Interest* (novel), Simon & Schuster (New York City), 1977.

(With Kyle Gibson) *Nightline: History in the Making and the Making of Television,* Times Books (New York City), 1996.

Off Camera: Private Thoughts Made Public, Knopf (New York City), 2000.

SIDELIGHTS: In November, 1979, the Iranian siege on the American embassy in Teheran commanded national attention, prompting ABC to feature a series of late-night television updates, *America Held Hostage,* often hosted by Ted Koppel. These live nightly specials soon brought Koppel recognition from millions of viewers who appreciated his informed, direct interviewing style.

Ted Koppel

By March, 1980, the television specials had evolved into *Nightline,* a half-hour, late-night, live news show featuring Koppel's special brand of television journalism. *Newsweek* called the show "global in perspective, intimate in presentation and always rivetingly spontaneous." In 1996, when *Nightline* had achieved the status of an institution, Richard Zoglin wrote in *Time* that it had "become the most important news broadcast on television." Featuring debates and town hall meetings as well as interviews and news analysis, the show has "not only report[ed] on but often become a participant in major news events," Zoglin observed. *Nightline* has received praise from many quarters for its handling of serious and diverse topics and for Koppel's refusal to use scripted questions or to be supplied in advance—as some television interviewers are—with interviewees' answers.

Koppel had been with ABC for sixteen years before he became widely known for his coverage of the hostage crisis. He joined ABC News as a radio correspondent in 1963, covering controversial topics such as the Vietnam War and civil rights. After heading the network's Miami and Hong Kong bureaus, he became diplomatic correspondent in 1971, and traveled to China for President

Nixon's 1972 visit. It was as diplomatic correspondent that Koppel began covering, from the State Department, the Iranian crisis. Howard Rosenberg declared in *Washington Journalism Review* that "as occasional anchor of *America Held Hostage,* Koppel showed a new dimension as a facile, pugnacious interviewer." The same article called Koppel "sure-footed, feisty, and phraseworthy," and cited television critic Tom Shales: "What makes *Nightline* click is Koppel's bulls-eye interviewing style. . . . a succession of jabs, rejoinders, and judicious-to-delicious interruptions: Koppel *a cappella.*" *Newsweek* praised Koppel as an "outspoken commentator . . . equipped with a quick and eclectic memory" and admired "his unflappable temperament and on-camera presence."

Koppel took a leave of absence from his position as diplomatic correspondent in 1976 while his wife attended law school. He assumed household duties, cared for their four children, and anchored ABC-TV's Saturday night news. During this time he also collaborated with Marvin Kalb, a diplomatic correspondent for rival network CBS-TV News, on the novel, *In the National Interest.* Both Koppel and Kalb had previously accompanied then U.S. Secretary of State Henry Kissinger on his diplomatic negotiations in the Middle East, and their novel portrays a similar Mideast shuttle diplomacy junket.

The novel's protagonist, Darius Kane, is, like Kalb and Koppel, a foreign correspondent for a major television network. The character covers diplomatic negotiations in the Middle East that are threatened when the secretary of state's wife is kidnapped and then mysteriously released. The book "flavorfully moves through assassinations, chase scenes, White House backbiting, secret agentry—all standard meat in the Washington fiction stewpot, but in this case sauced with three-and-a-half-star pungency by two veteran cooks," wrote Les Whitten in the *Washington Post.* As correspondent Kane searches out the story, continued Whitten, "he rounds out to a hard-working, more than a little self-important, loyal, funny, brave newsman who devotedly cares about chasing down the truth. . . . We see the squalor and the splendor of reporting, and exactly why America can neither be comfortable with it, nor safe without it." Darius Kane's final dilemma reflects a major theme of the book, as Richard R. Lingeman explained in the *New York Times Book Review:* "Ultimately, when he gets his story, he faces the classic conflict between the imperatives of freedom of the press and the national interest."

One of the novel's main characters, Secretary of State Vandenberg, is in part patterned after Henry Kissinger. In the *New York Times Book Review* Kissinger offered some remarks about *In the National Interest* and its fictional secretary of state: "It is fascinating to me, and great fun, to see how these two particularly able journalists visualize highstakes diplomacy on the inside. . . . But overall, I am afraid that in seeking balance Kalb and Koppel have let their literary imagination run wild in the interests of an (admittedly) exciting plot and characterization." Kissinger noted that the unfavorable portrayal of Vandenberg's professional ethics, "raises profound issues of the way public officials are treated in our democracy," but then good-humoredly qualified the statement, adding, "any two authors who have spent 33 days cooped up in an airplane shuttling through the Middle East must be excused for any minor shortcomings, such as the incredible description of a Secretary of State who is fallible."

Koppel collaborated with Kyle Gibson, a *Nightline* producer, to tell the story of the program in *Nightline: History in the Making and the Making of Television.* (Koppel stated in the introduction that while he was interviewed extensively for the book and contributed to it, Gibson was the actual author; *New York Times* reviewer Walter Goodman speculated that the statement could have been "in a spirit of gallantry or in the interests of accuracy or in an effort to distance himself from a project with a promotional taint.") The book highlights some of *Nightline*'s most important broadcasts: a debate over apartheid between South African foreign minister Pik Botha and anti-apartheid leader Bishop Desmond Tutu in 1985; Koppel's grilling of Democratic presidential candidate Michael Dukakis in 1988; an interview in which baseball executive Al Campanis disparaged blacks' management skills; coverage of the 1989 massacre of protesters in Beijing's Tiananmen Square and the bombing of the Oklahoma City federal building in 1995; and programs featuring famed figures including televangelists Jim and Tammy Faye Bakker, U.S. presidents Bill Clinton, Jimmy Carter, and George Bush, and controversial Philippines leader Ferdinand Marcos. The volume also chronicles some of the show's less praiseworthy moments. For example, Koppel says he came to regret his handling of a 1984 interview with Geraldine Ferraro, the first major-party female vice presidential candidate; in hindsight, he thinks he exhibited a sexist attitude. He also says Democratic Party official Mandy Grunwald put him "on the defensive"—a rare occurrence—in a 1992 interview about Clinton.

New York Times Book Review critic Judith Newman applauded the book, calling it "a gripping and often hilarious behind-the-scenes account of a newscast that has transformed this country's idea of the television interview." *Time*'s Zoglin enthused that "for anyone who cares about TV news, the book is fascinating," although he also found that it "has its self-indulgent excesses." Some other reviewers likewise derided the volume as self-indulgent. Goodman, writing in the daily *New York Times,* wished "for a book that read less like a set of Sunday-supplement handouts from network publicity," and he deemed the blow-by-blow accounts of putting on the show "intermittently interesting and increasingly irritating." *Entertainment Weekly* commentator Ken Tucker thought that some of the contents "seem selected primarily to make Koppel look good" and was bothered that the book referred to Koppel in the third person, even though that was ostensibly because of Gibson's authorship. "Ken Tucker thinks it comes off as silly and self-important of Koppel to have agreed to tell his story this way," he remarked.

Goodman and *New Leader* contributor Herbert Dorfman both noted the absence of any mention of the O.J. Simpson case, in which Simpson was accused of murdering his ex-wife and her friend, although *Nightline* devoted dozens of episodes to it. "Isn't some reflection called for on the program's indulgence in Simpsoniana?" Goodman asked. Similarly, Dorfman wondered, "What does Koppel think about his massive treatment of the Simpson story?" and reported that the book had "nothing about the trial, its racial implications or the media circus *Nightline* participated in. If it was done against his better judgment, wouldn't this book be the place to inform us?" Dorfman also expressed disappointment that the book "reveals little about Koppel the man," but related that it makes clear Koppel's role in *Nightline*'s success: "The program is unique because it has pioneered an open style that is exciting when it works. And what makes it work, we increasingly recognize as we read, is Ted Koppel's no-nonsense disposition and direct control."

BIOGRAPHICAL/CRITICAL SOURCES:

PERIODICALS

Entertainment Weekly, June 14, 1996, p. 52.
New Leader, June 3, 1996, p. 18.
Newsweek, February 16, 1981.
New York Times, July 8, 1996.
New York Times Book Review, November 13, 1977; June 23, 1996.
Time, June 17, 1996.
TV Guide, April 18, 1981.
Washington Journalism Review, March, 1981.
Washington Post, November 15, 1977.*

KRISTEVA, Julia 1941-
(Julia Joyaux)

PERSONAL: Born June 24, 1941, in Sliven, Bulgaria; emigrated to France, 1965; married Phillippe Sollers (an editor and novelist); children: one son. *Education:* Attended French schools in Bulgaria; Universite de Sofia, Bulgaria, diplomee, 1963; studied at Academie des Sciences en Litterature comparee, Sofia, and l'Ecole practique des Hautes-Etudes, France; University of Paris VII, Ph.D., 1973.

ADDRESSES: Office—Universite de Paris VII—Denis Diderot, UFR de Sciences des Textes et Documents, 34-44, 2e etage, 2, place Jussieu, 75251 Paris, France.

CAREER: Writer, educator, linguist, psychoanalyst, and literary theorist. Worked as a journalist in Bulgaria; Laboratoire d'anthropologie sociale, research assistant to Claude Levi-Strauss, 1967-73; University of Paris VII—Denis Diderot, instructor, 1972, professor of linguistics, 1973-99, professeur classe exceptionelle, 1999—, director of doctoral program. Established private psychoanalytic practice, Paris, 1978. Visiting professor, Columbia University, 1974—, and University of Toronto, 1992.

MEMBER: Société psychanalytique de Paris, American Academy of Arts and Sciences.

AWARDS, HONORS: Chevalier des Arts et des Lettres, 1987; Chevalier de l'Ordre national du Mérite, 1991; Chevalier de la legion d'honneur, 1997; honorary degrees from Western Ontario University, 1995, Victoria Univeristy, 1997, Harvard University, 1999, University of Belgium, 2000, University of Bayreuth, 2000, and the University of Toronto, 2000.

WRITINGS:

NONFICTION

Semeiotike, recherce pour une semanalyse, Le Seuil (Paris, France), 1969, abridged translation published in *Desire in Language: A Semiotic Approach to Literature and Art,* Columbia University Press (New York, NY), 1980.

(Editor, with Thomas Sebeok) *Approaches to Semiotics, Volume One,* Mouton (The Hague), 1969.

Julia Kristeva

(As Julia Joyaux) *Le langage, cet inconnu, une initiation a la linguistique,* Le Seuil (Paris, France), 1969, as Julia Kristeva, 1981, translated as *Language: The Unknown: An Initiation into Linguistics,* Columbia University Press (New York, NY), 1989.

Le texte du roman: approache sémiologique d'une stucture discursive transformationnelle, Mouton (The Hague), 1970.

(Editor, with Josette Rey Debove and Donna Jean Umiker) *Essays in Semiotics: Essais de Sémiotique,* Mouton (The Hague), 1971.

(Editor) *Épistémologie de la linguistique. Hommage à Emile Benveniste,* Didier (Paris, France), 1971.

La révolution du langage poétique, l'avant-garde à la fin du XIXe siècle, Lautréamont et Mallarmé, Le Seuil (Paris, France), 1974, abridged translation by Margaret Waller published as *Revolution in Poetic Language,* Columbia University Press (New York, NY), 1984.

Des Chinoises, Editions des femmes (Paris, France), 1974, translation by Anita Barrow published as *About Chinese Women,* Urizen (New York, NY), 1977.

(Editor, with Jean-Claude Milner and Nicolas Ruwet) *Langue, discours, société: pour Emile Benveniste,* Le Seuil (Paris, France), 1975.

(With others) *La traversée des signes,* Le Seuil (Paris, France), 1975.

Polylogue, Le Seuil (Paris, France), 1977, translation by Thomas Gora, Alice Jardine, and Leon Roudiez published in *Desire in Language: A Semiotic Approach to Literature and Art,* Columbia University Press (New York, NY), 1980.

(With Jean Michel Ribettes) *Folle Vérité, verite et vraisemblance du texte psychotique,* Le Seuil (Paris, France), 1980.

Pouvoirs de l'horreur, Essai sur l'abjection, Le Seuil (Paris, France), 1980, translation by Roudiez published as *Powers of Horror: An Essay on Abjection,* Columbia University Press (New York, NY), 1982.

Histoires d'amour, Denoel (Paris), 1983, translation by Roudiez published as *Tales of Love,* Columbia University Press (New York, NY), 1987.

Au commencement était l'amour, psychanalyse et foi, Hachette (Paris, France), 1985, translation by Arthur Goldhammer published as *In the Beginning Was Love: Psychoanalysis and Faith,* Columbia University Press (New York, NY), 1987.

A Kristeva Reader, edited by Toril Moi, Columbia University Press (New York, NY), 1986.

Soleil noir: dépression et mélancolie, Gallimard (Paris, France), 1987, translation by Roudiez published as *Black Sun: Depression and Melancholia,* Columbia University Press (New York, NY), 1989.

Etrangers à nous-mêmes, Fayard (Paris, France), 1988, translation by Roudiez published as *Strangers to Ourselves,* Columbia University Press (New York, NY), 1991.

Lettre ouverte à Harlem Désir, Rivages (Paris, France), 1990, translation published as *Nations without Nationalism,* Columbia University Press (New York, NY), 1993.

Les nouvelles maladies de l'ame, Fayard (Paris, France), 1993, translation by Ross Guberman published as *New Maladies of the Soul,* Columbia University Press (New York, NY), 1995.

Le temps sensible, Proust et l'expérience littéraire, Gallimard (Paris, France), 1994, translation published as *Time and Sense: Proust and the Experience of Literature,* Columbia University Press (New York, NY), 1996.

Julia Kristeva, Interviews, edited by Ross Guberman, Columbia University Press (New York, NY), 1996.

Sens et non-sens de la révolte: Discours Direct, Fayard (Paris, France), 1996, translation by Jeanine Herman published as *The Sense and Non-Sense of Revolt,* Columbia University Press (New York, NY), 2000.

The Portable Kristeva, edited by Kelly Oliver, Columbia University Press (New York, NY), 1997.

La révolte intime: (Discours direct), Fayard (Paris, France), 1997.

L'avenir d'une révolte, Calmann-Levy (Paris, France), 1998.

Le féminin et le sacré, Stock (Paris, France), 1998, translation by Catherine Clément published as *Feminine and the Sacred,* Columbia University Press (New York, NY), 2001.

Visions capitales, Reunion des musees nationaux (Paris, France), 1998.

Contre la dépression nationale: Entretien avec Phillippe Petit, Textuel (Paris, France), 1998.

Proust: questions d'identité, Legenda (Oxford, England), 1998.

Le génie féminin: La Vie, la folie, les mots: Hannah Arendt, Melanie Klein, Colette, three volumes, Fayard (Paris, France), 2000.

Crisis of the European Subject, translation by Susan Fairfield, Other Press (New York, NY), 2000.

Jardin des Tuileries: sculptures modernes et contemporaines: Installation conçue par Alain Kirili, 1997-2000, Patrimoine (Paris, France), 2001.

Hannah Arendt—or, Life Is a Narrative, University of Toronto Press (Toronto, Canada), in press.

Contributor to periodicals, including *Critique, Langages, Langues francaises, L'Infiniti, Partisan Review, Revue francais de psychanalyse,* and *Signs.* Member of editorial board, *Tel quel,* 1971—.

NOVELS

Les Samourais, Fayard (Paris, France), 1990, translation published as *The Samurai,* Columbia University Press (New York, NY), 1992.

Le vieil homme et les loups, Fayard (Paris, France), 1991, translation published as *The Old Man and the Wolves,* Columbia University Press (New York, NY), 1994.

Possessions, translation by Barbara Bray, Columbia University Press (New York, NY), 1998.

SIDELIGHTS: Julia Kristeva is one of the most influential and prolific thinkers of modern France. Trained in linguistics, psychoanalysis, and literary criticism, her cross-disciplinary writings have been praised by colleagues from a wide variety of academic departments. While her commitment to social change has caused her to be embraced by many as a feminist writer, Kristeva's relationship to feminism has been one of ambivalence. She is most widely known for her contribution to literary theory, such as 1980's *Desire in Language: A Semi-*

otic Approach to Literature and Art and her 1974 examination of modernist poetry and prose entitled *La Revolution du langage Poetique, l'avant-garde a la fin du XIXe siecle, Lautréamont et Mallarmé,* published in translation in 1984 as *Revolution in Poetic Language.* In addition to her theoretical works, Kristeva has also published several novels; 1990's *Les Samourais* (translation published as *The Samurai*) is a semi-autobiographical work that incorporates characters representative of several Parisian intellectuals of the mid-1960s.

Born in communist Bulgaria in 1941, Kristeva attended French-language Catholic schools before embarking on a career as a journalist in her early twenties. In 1966, after the death of Nikita Kruschev heralded a new wave of Soviet repression in her native country, twenty-five-year-old Kristeva moved to Paris to continue her academic career. While pursuing an advanced degree in linguistics at the University of Paris, she published several essays in linguistic philosophy and contributed to *Tel quel,* a journal edited by Phillippe Sollers, who would later become her husband. Meanwhile, her renown grew both as a writer and scholar and she became accepted as a part of the heady intellectual circle of the period; she would soon be attending lectures by Jacques Lacan while working as a laboratory assistant for anthropologist Claude Levi-Strauss. While politically they would shift to the right over the next three decades, Kristeva's later writings would continue to be imbued with much of the revolutionary fervor Paris exhibited during this era, as well as by the Freudian and Lacanian psychoanalytic theory that captured her interest. Indeed, *New Maladies of the Soul,* an essay collection published in translation in 1995, includes a defense of psychoanalysis written in answer to the rising tide of anti-Freudian scholarship since undertaken in the field.

Kristeva bases her theoretical work on two components of all linguistic operation: the semiotic—that which expresses objective meaning—and the symbolic—the rhythmic, illogical element. What she terms "poetic language" is the intertwining of the semiotic and symbolic, transforming and reshaping one another while providing multiple meanings to their spoken form. Both writers and readers participate in this dialogue between the semiotic and symbolic, making poetic language subjective, versatile, open to myriad interpretations. Though most feminist theorists have considered Kristeva's ideas regarding the semiotic component of language to be valuable in their own women-centered critique, some have also criticized what they perceive as her tendency to stress the written works of men in her studies while ignoring those of women.

Kristeva's area of involvement has shifted more recently from linguistics to psychoanalysis. Her psychoanalytic works include *Powers of Horror: An Essay on Abjection, Tales of Love* and *Black Sun: Depression and Melancholia,* the last being an examination of female depression. All have been marked by her attempt to expand and amplify the Freudian and Lacanian views of early childhood development. Many of Kristeva's critics have deemed her derivation of a maternally based ethics a move away from feminism, a stance that would seem justified after the mid-1980s when Kristeva took a marked stance in opposition to the aims of the women's movement.

Despite the demands of her nonfiction, her teaching, and her frequent trips abroad as a visiting professor at Columbia University, Kristeva has found time to write fiction. Two of her novels, *The Old Man and the Wolves* and *Possessions* are set in the fictional Santa Varvara, an Eastern European resort city where corruption and violence are rife. In the case of *Possessions,* a successful translator is found decapitated after a dinner party and one of her friends, Stephanie Delacour, conducts her own investigation into the grisly murder. *New York Times Book Review* correspondent Mark Edmundson styled *Possessions* "an intellectual detective story" that reflects Kristeva's favorite nonfictional themes: "depression, language, the struggles between the sexes, horror, psychoanalysis, and motherhood." In a *Booklist* review, Brad Hooper deemed *Possessions* a "compelling psychological thriller," adding that the "cerebral" work ". . . is as much about the ways of living as it is about the ways of dying."

BIOGRAPHICAL/CRITICAL SOURCES:

BOOKS

Fletcher, John, and Andrew Benjamin, editors, *Abjection, Melancholia, and Love: The Work of Julia Kristeva,* Routledge (New York City), 1990.
Lechte, John, *Julia Kristeva,* Routledge, 1990.

PERIODICALS

Booklist, February 15, 1998, Brad Hooper, review of *Possessions,* p. 982.
Choice, October, 1995, p. 286.
Discourse: A Review of the Liberal Arts, fall-winter, 1990-91, Suzanne Clark and Kathleen Hulley, "An Interview with Julia Kristeva: Cultural Strangeness and the Subject in Crisis," pp. 149-80.

Hypatia, Volume 3, number 3, 1989.

Library Journal, May 1, 2000, David Valencia, review of *The Sense and Non-Sense of Revolt: The Powers and Limits of Psychoanalysis,* p. 138.

London Review of Books, May 24, 1990, pp. 6-8; January 26, 1995, p. 17.

New York Times Book Review, November 15, 1992, Wendy Steiner, "The Bulldozer of Desire," p. 9; April 5, 1998, Mark Edmundson, "Headless Body in Lawless Burg," p. 35.

Observer, December 6, 1992, p. 57.

Publishers Weekly, January 26, 1998, review of *Possessions,* p. 71.

Romantic Review, January, 1982.

Spectator, November 19, 1994.

Times Literary Supplement, December 4, 1992, p. 20.

Women's Review of Books, January, 1996, p. 19.

Yale-French Studies, Volume 62, 1981.

*   *   *

KUHLKEN, Ken(neth Wayne) 1945-

PERSONAL: Born September 4, 1945, in San Diego, CA; son of Charles Wayne (in business) and Ada (a teacher; maiden name, Garfield) Kuhlken; married Laura Lucille Steinhoff, October 7, 1967; children: Darcy, Cody. *Education:* San Diego State University, B.A., 1968, M.A., 1971; University of Iowa, M.F.A., 1977. *Religion:* Christian.

ADDRESSES: Home—San Diego, CA. *Agent*—Don Gastwirth, 265 College St., Ste. 10-N, New Haven, CT 06510. *E-mail*—kkuhlken@mail.sdsu.edu.

CAREER: High school teacher of English in La Mesa, CA, 1971-73, and Athens, Greece, 1973-74; Department of Public Welfare, El Cajon, CA, welfare eligibility worker, 1974-78; San Diego State University, San Diego, CA, instructor in creative writing, 1978-79; University of Arizona, Tucson, visiting assistant professor of creative writing, 1979-81; California State University, Chico, assistant and associate professor of English, 1981-86; San Diego State University, academic advisor, 1987-2000; Christian Heritage College, associate professor of English, 1997-2000. Printer; operated import business.

WRITINGS:

Midheaven, Viking, 1980.
The Loud Adios, St. Martin's, 1991.

The Venus Deal, St. Martin's, 1992.
The Angel Gang, St. Martin's, 1994.

Contributor of stories to magazines, including *Esquire, Fault, Virginia Quarterly Review,* and *Pacific Poetry and Fiction Review.*

WORK IN PROGRESS: Novels *The Fat Lady* and *The Virgin of Agua Dulce,* and a memoir set in Southern California in the 1960s.

SIDELIGHTS: Ken Kuhlken wrote: "I began writing fiction late, compared to some, at age twenty-five. I have done forty-some other jobs, but writing is the only one that gives me much satisfaction. I traveled a lot as a youth, but am currently slowing down. Grandma was important to my career, also my friend Eric, who died young, but in a couple years gave me confidence, knowledge that there was more to be written about than is often recognized, that the world is a microcosm of the WORLD. Eric (as did Grandma) made me think that I was smart and unique, God bless them.

"I used to be a rock, folk, and blues musician, but a bad one. I like to read, like to try to do things well, like cars, boats, trains, things which move on the surface of the earth. Baseball, women, and Mexico fascinate me, as do Christian churches and the people who find sanctuary in them, so I'll be writing about all that for a while yet.

"I believe in families, Jesus, responsibility, moderation, tolerance, freedom, but find the attempt to make all these concepts work together a challenge."

*   *   *

KYLE, Keith 1925-

PERSONAL: Born August 4, 1925, in Dorset, England; son of William Ernest (a real estate agent) and Elspeth Mary (a schoolteacher; maiden name, Maule) Kyle; married Susan Mary Harpur (a television researcher), September 29, 1962; children: Tarquin David Harpur, Crispin Marcel Keith. *Education:* Magdalen College, Oxford, M.A., 1950. *Politics:* Liberal Democrat. *Religion:* Humanist.

ADDRESSES: Home—25 Oppidans Rd., London NW3 3AG, England. *Office*—Royal Institute of International Affairs, Chatham House, 10 St. James's Sq., London SW1 4LE, England.

CAREER: English-Speaking Union, London, England, secretary of programs and publications department, 1951; British Broadcasting Corporation (BBC) radio, London, producer, 1951-53; *Economist,* Washington, DC, chief U.S. correspondent, 1953-58, political and parliamentary correspondent, London, 1958-60; BBC television, London, reporter and newscaster in Nairobi, Kenya, 1960-64, and London, 1964-82; Royal Institute of International Affairs, London, head of meetings department, 1972-86, special assistant to director, 1987-90, research fellow, 1990-94. Visiting professor of history, University of Ulster, 1993-99. Parliamentary candidate, Labour party, 1966 and 1974, Social Democratic party, 1983; Institute of Politics, Harvard University School of Government, fellow, 1967-68; British-Irish Association, councillor, 1972-86; member of Foreign Secretary's Commission on the Anniversary of the United States Declaration of Independence, 1975-76; Minority Rights Group, councillor, 1980-90; St. Antony's College, Oxford, senior associate member, 1987-89. *Military service:* British and Indian armies, 1943-47, served in Royal Artillery; became captain; received Burma Star.

MEMBER: Royal Institute of International Affairs, Liberal Democrat party, Oxford Union Society, Reform Club.

AWARDS, HONORS: Best Political Correspondent Award (television), 1971; fellowship at Institute of Politics, John F. Kennedy School of Government, 1967-68.

WRITINGS:

Cyprus (nonfiction), Minority Rights Group, 1984, revised edition, 1992.
Suez (nonfiction), St. Martin's (New York, NY), 1991.
(Editor, with Joel Peters) *Whither Israel?: The Domestic Challenge,* St. Martin's (New York, NY), 1993, updated edition, 1994.
The Politics of the Independence of Kenya, St. Martin's (New York, NY), 1999.

Also author of *Cyprus: In Search of Peace,* 1998. Author of London column, *New York Post,* 1958-61; author of international affairs column, *Listener,* 1969-74; contributor to *London Review of Books,* 1979—.

SIDELIGHTS: Keith Kyle is a British journalist who reported on the Suez Crisis, a 1956 confrontation involving British, French, and Israeli forces and the Egyp-

tian government regarding control of the strategic Suez Canal. Kyle's 1991 publication, *Suez,* offers a historical analysis of the individual personalities, as well as the international forces, that were involved. *Suez,* which *Times Literary Supplement* contributor Anthony Howard called "the definitive work" on the crisis, is the result of research carried out over the course of thirty-five years. Kyle was able to incorporate new information into his discussion when formerly classified documents were made available to the public in accordance with Britain's Thirty-Year Rule. The resulting work, according to *New York Times Book Review* contributor Gaddis Smith, reveals "a fascinating interplay of international forces" and offers "an understanding of a major historical root" of later events in the Middle East.

The Suez Crisis began when Egyptian President Gamal Abdul Nasser, having endured repeated skirmishes with Israel, desired an arms buildup. Because the United States was slow to sell weapons to Nasser, he turned to the more compliant Soviet Union. Angered by this move, the British and American governments withdrew promised dam-construction funds. Nasser responded with a legal though provocative act: nationalization of the Suez Canal, a waterway which connects the Mediterranean and Red Seas, enabling ships to circumvent Africa. Though located in Egypt, the canal had been under British control since 1882.

Though U.S. President Dwight D. Eisenhower was in favor of peaceful negotiations with Nasser to ensure western passage through the canal, Britain and France each had reasons to take more aggressive measures. Britain saw its previous control of the canal as a symbol of its power, and France viewed Nasser as a supporter of Arab uprisings in French-controlled Algeria. With French and British support, Israel, which had been invaded by Egypt in 1948 and had been denied passage through the canal, invaded Egypt. When Nasser rejected a British and French ultimatum which required him to surrender the canal and accept their control for the duration of the crisis, troops from those two countries invaded Egypt. Their alleged motive was to end the conflict between Egypt and Israel, but many believe that their actual intention was to force Nasser out of power. Eisenhower strongly resented Britain's masking its true intentions and feared their plot would result in unification of the Arabs and other former colonies against the West, which would give the Soviet Union substantial control in the Middle East. By threatening economic sanctions, Eisenhower, along with the United Nations, forced Britain to withdraw its troops. The Egyptians retained control of the canal.

In the six-hundred-page *Suez,* Kyle produced "a book that, in its comprehensive command, its overall balance and its narrative sweep, easily surpasses all other accounts" of this historical event, commented *Times Literary Supplement* contributor Anthony Howard. The author examines political and diplomatic policies that led to the crisis and speculates why British Prime Minister Anthony Eden used violence, which the author considered unnecessary and inconsistent with Eden's reputation as a diplomat. The author reserves his strongest criticism, however, for the French and British political leaders who believed their collusion would be successful and remain a secret. Praising the depth and accuracy of Kyle's work, *London Times* contributor John Grigg observed, "For narrative vitality, analytic force and shrewdness of judgment, personal and political, [*Suez*] is hard to match."

Kyle brought his experience as a journalist to bear on the stormy history of African independence in his book, *The Politics of the Independence of Kenya.* Kenya's independence from Great Britain was achieved on December 12, 1963, after several years of struggle. Kyle acted as a reporter from Nairobi from 1961 to 1964, for the British Broadcasting Company's television service and for several publications based in the United States and England. The events he investigated first-hand are now considered some of the most significant in the history of Africa. Realizing that this would be so, Kyle took copious notes, archived documents, and conducted and recorded many interviews. As John Reader reported in the *London Review of Books*, Kyle "planned to publish a book on Kenya's Independence soon after the events, but the project was shelved for more than thirty years—fortunately, as it turns out, for by then relevant British government documents had become available . . . along with important personal archives and paper which had been deposited in the Rhodes House library in Oxford." Reader also noted that the long wait for Kyle's book also yielded numerous interviews with prominent figures of the time who were unwilling to openly express their views in the heat of the moment. Predicting that *The Politics of the Independence of Kenya* would find few readers beyond "the specialist field for whom it will be required reading,"

Reader went on to say: "This is a pity, for there is real drama in it, and Kyle's lucid prose brings an invaluable measure of accessibility to this combination of scholarship and personal recollection. And this is no mean achievement. The book is packed with detail, but its narrative style allows the long-term implications of specific policies and the importance—or otherwise—of particular individuals and events to emerge cumulatively."

Kyle told *CA:* "Suez was my first international crisis as a journalist. I particularly enjoyed revisiting the scene as a historian, after thirty years and the release in several countries of the appropriate documents."

BIOGRAPHICAL/CRITICAL SOURCES:

PERIODICALS

American Historical Review, October, 1992, review of *Suez,* p. 1184.
Choice, March, 1994, review of *Whither Israel?: The Domestic Challenge,* p. 1214.
Foreign Affairs, March-April, 1994, William B. Quandt, review of *Whither Israel? The Domestic Challenge,* p. 168.
Journal of Peace Research, November, 1995, review of *Suez,* p. 496.
London Review of Books, March 16, 2000, John Reader, review of *The Politics of the Independence of Kenya,* pp. 31-34.
Middle East Journal, summer, 1992, review of *Suez,* p. 510; winter, 1995, review of *Whither Israel?: The Domestic Challenge,* p. 170.
New York Times Book Review, August 18, 1991, pp.7-8.
Political Science Quarterly, summer, 1994, review of *Suez,* p. 361.
Times Literary Supplement, May 24, 1991, p. 24; February 24, 1995, review of *Whither Israel?: The Domestic Challenge,* p. 28.
Times (London), June 29, 1991, p. 20.*

L

LARSON, Janet Karsten 1945-

PERSONAL: Born June 9, 1945, in South Bend, IN; daughter of Walter John (a mechanical engineer in aeronautics) and Virginia (a musician; maiden name, Ahlbrand) Karsten; married John David Larson (a Lutheran minister), June 14, 1970 (divorced, 1983). *Ethnicity:* "Caucasian." *Education:* Valparaiso University, B.A., 1967; Northwestern University, M.A., 1968, Ph. D., 1975. *Politics:* "Left of the Democratic Party." *Religion:* Lutheran.

ADDRESSES: Office—Department of English, Newark Campus, Rutgers University, Newark, NJ 07102.

CAREER: Chicago City College, Chicago, IL, instructor in English, 1968-69; Northwestern University, Evanston, IL, instructor in English, 1973-74; *Christian Century,* Chicago, IL, associate editor, 1975-78; Rutgers University, Newark Campus, Newark, NJ, assistant professor, 1978-84, associate professor of English, 1984—, director of composition for University College, 1978-85, deputy department chair, 1987-91, co-coordinator of Rutgers/Newark Gender, Race, and Class Curriculum Project, 1989-91, faculty fellow, Center for Historical Analysis, 1995-96. Lutheran Academy for Scholarship, member of honorary board.

MEMBER: American Academy of Religion, Conference on Christianity and Literature, Northeast Victorian Studies Association.

AWARDS, HONORS: Associated Church Press Award, best feature article on a social issue in religious journalism, 1977, for "Redeeming the Time and the Land"; humanities grant, New Jersey Department of Higher Education, 1988-91; fellow, National Endowment for the Humanities, 1990-91, and Institute for the Advanced Study of Religion, Divinity School, University of Chicago, 1990-91; Eccles fellow in humanities, Humanities Center, University of Utah, 1992-93; fellow, Newberry Library, 1993.

WRITINGS:

Dickens and the Broken Scripture, University of Georgia Press (Athens, GA), 1985.

Contributor to books, including *Critical Essays on Charles Dickens's "Bleak House,"* edited by Elliott L. Gilbert, G. K. Hall (Boston, MA), 1989; *Victorian Sages and Cultural Discourse: Renegotiating Gender and Power,* edited by Thais Morgan, Rutgers University Press (New Brunswick, NJ), 1990; and *Oliver Twist* (critical edition), edited by Fred Kaplan, Norton (New York, NY), 1993. Contributor of numerous articles and reviews to periodicals, including *Dickens Studies Annual, Dickens Quarterly, Victorian Studies, Nineteenth-Century Fiction, Religion and Literature, Modern Drama, Modern Philology, Eco-Justice Quarterly,* and *Lutheran Women.* Editor at large, *Christian Century,* 1978-95; member of editorial board, *Cross Currents,* 1990—; member of editorial advisory board, *Christianity and Literature,* 1989—.

WORK IN PROGRESS: The Victorian Woman's Bible: Interpretation and Cultural Discourse in Anglo-American Women's Letters, for Cambridge University Press (New York, NY); *Traveling Spiritualities: Victorian Women's Religious Encounters Abroad,* a biographical and cultural study of trans-cultural religious experiences and exchanges and their representation in travel-related writings by Florence Nightingale, Mary Carpenter, Mary Kingsley, Agnes Smith Lewis, and Frances Ellen Colenso; *Confessions of a Victorian Saint: Florence Nightingale's Turns and Returns to Spiritual Autobiography,* a "life-in-discourse tracking Nightingale's spiritual formation along with the development of her social religious ideas and her public and imperial personae through the corpus of her autobiographical writing, 1845-1878"; essays.

SIDELIGHTS: Janet Karsten Larson told *CA:* "Writing in and outside the academy in a variety of venues and forms continues to be important to me because of the range of my interests; my wariness (rooted in my generation's resistance to conformity) of the constraints that the politics of academic literary criticism place on what one can write; the increasingly profit-oriented agendas of American university presses (not to say of universities like my own); and my sense that so much on the market in literary-critical writing, as driven by competition and fashion as any other market today, and turned in upon itself, is irrelevant to pressing human problems. Remembering St. Paul, I am in the academy but not entirely of it; and I feel compelled to ponder the 'answerability' of all my work (Mikhail Bakhtin's term), asking hard questions about whose interests, questions, and values it serves.

"The difference between my 1975 Northwestern dissertation on the language of *Little Dorrit* and my 1985 Dickens book, which engages Bakhtinian and deconstructionist theory to interpret biblical allusion in six novels (and their illustration) across Dickens's career, registers the sea-change in literary theory from the mid-1970s to the mid-1980s. Better than the old theoretical frameworks, the new ones helped me complicate simplistic scholarly appreciations of the 'Christian' Dickens (based on vague notions of Christian theology as well) and gave me language in which to write about the internal tensions in Dickens's fiction that bear on his varied uses of biblical discourse. While this book also made its contribution to the theory of allusion, perhaps it is chiefly an old-fashioned commitment to writing as accurately as possible about the text in hand, taking in the creative imagination's wayward diversions from any one critical-theory line, that has so far preserved the Dickens book from literary-theory obsolescence as intellectual fashions have marched on.

"Since then my line of academic writing has shifted to women's studies and interdisciplinary approaches. My current work brings women's history, feminist theology and biblical criticism, religious studies, and cultural discourse theory to the analysis of (mostly British nineteenth-century) women's writing in a broad range of genres. This new phase, while selectively appropriating materialist theories, contains a feminist ethical core and resists the academy's reigning narrative of modern secularization. My current major projects are all studies of groups. University presses no longer welcome single-author books, as I discovered when my Nightingale manuscript was first rejected on these grounds without even being read. Long in the making, my book in progress on Victorian women's biblical and social interpretation treats dozens of writers, thinkers, and activists in their English and American contexts as well as in relation to their interpretive traditions, stretching back through the Romantics and the era of Revolution, the Enlightenment, and the English civil war, to the Reformation. Although this book is slated for the Cambridge University Press Victorian cultural studies series, in its treatment of biblical and women's texts it exceeds a strictly materialist approach and positions its subjects within a variety of theoretical frames, including Ricoeur's hermeneutics, appropriate to their individual accomplishments, the tensions in their writings, their ways of using scripture as both written text and cultural text, and the complexity of the Victorian scene to which *they* were answerable.

"The manuscript I've begun on Victorian female spiritual travelers, another group book, insists on taking seriously what women aimed to say even in the face of the problematic politics one cannot ignore in their work. At this point in my discipline, it seems only too easy to show, for instance, that Mary Kingsley and Nightingale are imperialist or patriarchal in their gaze. It's a far more interesting challenge to articulate and weigh their more-than-ideological dimensions in relation to such problems. These women's responses to beauty on their travels, albeit often in terms constructed by their home culture, allow me as well, in the words of Rutgers colleague George Levine, to 'reclaim the aesthetic' dimension of literary study—after all, a major reason I sought a graduate degree in literature rather than in political science (my other college major). In this project, I am also indebted to work being done on spiritual autobiographies of place by members of the American Academy of Religion, a wonderfully diverse, intellectually engaged, and communally oriented professional organization which, for me, has displaced the Modern Language Association.

"No question that academic writing and research engage creative energies: but it's necessary to me to write poetry too, to record with precision my responses to the world; and satire, to give publicly instructive form to my discontents; and, as a member of several watchdog community organizations, letters to the editor on the 'development' glut in my town. Periodically too I plunge back into the investigative reporting I've done for the *Christian Century.* A long personal history with journalism that goes back to my junior high school newspaper days in Ohio, deepened and radicalized by the political consciousness-raising of the late 1960s and early 1970s, disposes me to believe that writing about current issues—prisoners' and other human rights, the death penalty, the disenfranchisement of small-scale coffee farmers in the 'global economy,' ecological justice, race and gender in contemporary film—can and does matter more than academic 'Rad writing' that preaches to the choir in an idiom that only the choir can understand while aggrandizing the scholar, adding to the quotient of cynicism in the world, and obscuring the subject rather than seeking to teach the public through essays and books.

"I love the psychological and religious wisdom, the social and historical reach, and the gorgeous writing of Peter Carey's novel *Oscar and Lucinda,* with all its Victorian literature and culture allusions. But I also enormously admire the legal detective work in William F. Pepper's *Orders to Kill,* an account of the accumulating evidence for the U.S. government conspiracy, with the help of the Mafia, to assassinate Dr. Martin Luther King, Jr., in 1968, an act of state-sponsored terrorism, resulting in the deaths of more than one person, that changed the course of American political and social history. Pepper's book should be read by every American who cares about the past and the vicissitudes of progressive leadership in this country. I can't say the same about much academic literary criticism, including even my own.

"In light of many ambivalences about the university as my place in life, I feel fortunate indeed that my job requires me to be a teacher of literature—a broad field of study that includes autobiographies of civil rights movement leaders and the *Life and Religious Experience of Jarena Lee* (1836), the first African Methodist Episcopal female preacher, as well as the Bible as literature and *Jane Eyre*—at the most diverse campus in the country. Newark and environs comprise a magnet for immigrants and home to black culture. I cherish classroom encounters with these students, who teach me much every day and immensely complicate my perspective as a white, Anglo-Saxon, Protestant woman of privilege. University administrations may be hell-bent on commercializing and virtualizing their institutions out of existence, but to date the students themselves are still turning up, for all their obsession with business degrees and computers still responding to beauty, still looking for knowledge that counts, that helps them understand their world and where they are headed. My historical research helps me teach them about the past—the shadows behind them cast on the present, the courageous human beings on whose ground they stand, the social movements that have kept belief in liberty and justice alive in their (adopted) country. My literary research and writing help me teach them about the powers of language and story to fabricate, create, unravel, and reveal realities that extend far beyond the printed word and computer scroll. My students must make up their own minds, and be able to change them, but I want them to know that the world does not have to belong to the spin doctors, marketing magi, and masters of the bottom line. If the point is not just to interpret the world but to change it, it is still indispensable to *do* interpretation, and reinterpretation, with all the knowledge, skills, and sensitivities one can command. This is what I write about and hope I'm best at by now, what I teach and profess."

*   *   *

LARSON, Jean Russell 1930-

PERSONAL: Born July 25, 1930, in Marshalltown, IA; daughter of Charles Reed and Myrtle (Koester) Russell; married Richard Larson (deceased); married Harold Parks (deceased); children: (first marriage) M. Kathleen McCord, Richard Jr., David Larson, Rosemarie, William, Michael; (second marriage) Patrick, Daniel. *Education:* Attended Winthrop College (Rock Hill, SC), 1948-49; Buena Vista University, B.A. (English); Iowa State University, M.A. (English). *Politics:* Democrat. *Religion:* Roman Catholic. *Avocational interests:* Genealogy, environment, animal welfare, protection of wildlife, classical music.

ADDRESSES: E-mail—Reed@marshallnet.com.

CAREER: Educator and author. Former college instructor. County Red Cross, secretary. Former member of County Central Democrat Committee, Democrat State Platform Committee, County Coalition for Social Justice (chair), Health and Nutrition Board, United Nations Year of the Child committee (county chair), Catholic Peace Movement, and St. Henry Library (chair).

AWARDS, HONORS: Notable Book designation, American Library Association; Lewis Carroll Shelf Award; William Allen White award nominee.

WRITINGS:

Palace in Bagdad: Seven Tales from Arabia, illustrated by Marianne Yamaguchi, Scribner's (New York, NY), 1966.

The Silkspinners, illustrated by Uri Shulevitz, Scribner's (New York, NY), 1967.

Jack Tar, illustrated by Mercer Mayer, Macrae Smith (Philadelphia, PA), 1970.

The Glass Mountain and Other Arabian Tales, illustrated by Donald E. Cooke, Macrae Smith (Philadelphia, PA), 1971.

(Reteller) *The Fish Bride and Other Gypsy Tales,* illustrated by Michael Larson, Shoe String Press, 1999.

Contributor to *Scholastic News* and *Junior Great Books.* Poetry published in *Massachusetts Review, Michigan Quarterly,* and *Literary Review.*

WORK IN PROGRESS: A collection of folk tales.

SIDELIGHTS: Former college professor Jean Russell Larson once explained: "When I stopped teaching, I decided to rewrite all the folk tales I grew up with. *The Fish Bride and Other Gypsy Tales* is the first of these collections.

"People from many parts of the world passed through Iowa and many settled here. My own storytelling family included Norwegians, Irish, Dutch, and some of the first settlers of Connecticut. I believe the preservation of folk tales is important, because those stories are culture-bearing and values-laden."

BIOGRAPHICAL/CRITICAL SOURCES:

PERIODICALS

Booklist, November 1, 1972, review of *The Glass Mountain,* p. 245; November 1, 2000, John Peters, review of *The Fish Bride and Other Gypsy Tales,* p. 533.

Horn Book Magazine, November, 2000, Mary M. Burns, review of *The Fish Bride and Other Gypsy Tales,* p. 765.

Kirkus Review, May 1, 1972, p. 540; August 15, 2000, review of *The Fish Bride and Other Gypsy Tales,* p. 1199.

Library Journal, May 15, 1972, p. 1914.

School Library Journal, September, 2000, Ginny Gustin, review of *The Fish Bride and Other Gypsy Tales,* p. 251.

*   *   *

LAVINSON, Joseph
   See KAYE, Marvin (Nathan)

*   *   *

LEAR, Peter
   See LOVESEY, Peter (Harmer)

*   *   *

LEE, (William) David 1944-

PERSONAL: Born August 13, 1944, in Matador, TX; son of Chant D. and Ruth (maiden name, Rushing; present surname, Carr) Lee; married Jan Miller (a teacher), August 13, 1971; children: Jon Dee, Jodee Duree. *Ethnicity:* "Irish-Texan." *Education:* Colorado State University, B.A., 1967; Idaho State University, M.A., 1970, University of Utah, Ph.D., 1973. *Politics:* Independent. *Religion:* "Deist." *Avocational interests:* Hiking, "wandering back roads and trails."

ADDRESSES: Home—988 Larkspur, St. George, UT 84790. *Office*—Department of Language, Literature, and Humanities, Southern Utah University, Cedar City, UT 84720. *E-mail*—lee_d@suu.edu.

CAREER: Lobo Lodge, Chama, NM, cowhand, 1964-67; Southern Utah University, Cedar City, instructor, 1971-73, assistant professor, 1973-76, associate professor, 1976-79, professor of English, 1979—, chairperson of English department, 1973-82, and head of Department of Language, Literature, and Humanities. National Foundation for Advancement in the Arts, member of board of directors; Utah Endowment for the Arts, served as member of advisory panel and peer group panel; Southern Utah Writers Conference, member of board of directors; member of Utah Arts Council and Utah Academy. Also played with semiprofessional baseball teams, including the Post Texas Blue Stars and the South Plains Texas League Hubbers; also worked as a hog farmer and as a laborer in a cotton mill. *Military service:* U.S. Army, 1967-69; became sergeant; received Spirit of America Honor Medal.

MEMBER: Writers at Work (member of board of advisers).

AWARDS, HONORS: Elliston Award, University of Cincinnati, 1978; first prize for serious poetry, Utah Creative Writing Contests, 1983, for "The Muffler and the Law"; first place award for book-length poetry manuscript, Utah Arts Council, 1988, for *Days Work;* Western States Book Award in Poetry, 1995, for *My Town;* Mountains and Plains States Booksellers Award in Poetry, 1996; named poet laureate of Utah; Utah Governor's Award, lifetime achievement in the arts; grants from National Endowment for the Arts and National Endowment for the Humanities.

WRITINGS:

The Porcine Legacy (poetry), Copper Canyon Press (Port Townsend, WA), 1978.
Driving and Drinking (long poem), Copper Canyon Press (Port Townsend, WA), 1979, 2nd edition, 1982.
Shadow Weaver (poetry), Jawbone (Waldron Island, WA), 1984.
The Porcine Canticles (poetry), Copper Canyon Press (Port Townsend, WA), 1984.
Days Work, Copper Canyon Press (Port Townsend, WA), 1990.
Paragonah Canyon—Autumn, illustrated by Arlene Braithwaite, Brooding Heron Press (Waldron Island, WA), 1990.
My Town (poems), Copper Canyon Press (Port Townsend, WA), 1995.
(With William Kolefkorn) *Covenants: Poems,* Spoon River Poetry Press (Granite Falls, MN), 1996.
Wayburne Pig, Brooding Heron Press (Waldron Island, WA), 1997.
News from Down to the Cafe: New Poems, Copper Canyon Press (Port Townsend, WA), 1999.
A Legacy of Shadows: Selected Poems, Copper Canyon Press (Port Townsend, WA), 1999.

Creator of "David Lee: A Listener's Guide," a series of audio and text publications, Copper Canyon Press, 1999. Work represented in anthologies, including *Anthology of Magazine Verse and Yearbook of American Poetry,* edited by Alan F. Pater, Monitor Book, 1981; *The Southwest: A Contemporary Anthology,* Red Earth Press; *Seven Poets;* and *Writing Poems,* edited by Robert Wallace. Contributor to magazines, including *West Coast Poetry Review, Kayak, Midwest Quarterly, Chowder Review, Willow Springs, Elkhorn Review,* and *Western Humanities Review.*

ADAPTATIONS: Lee and his works are the subject of a television documentary, *The Pig Poet,* broadcast by Public Broadcasting Service.

WORK IN PROGRESS: These Shadowlike Generations; Southwest studies.

SIDELIGHTS: David Lee once told *CA:* "My first interest is my family. I'm a full-time husband and father. I am also a teacher, a part-time pig farmer, constant scribbler, and long distance runner. I write about whatever catches my mind's eye. I've been called an eclectic reader, I suppose I'm an eclectic writer. I'm interested in the concentration and distillation of language and experience. I've also been told I have the cleanest mind in all of Utah: I change it daily. My writing reflects that change. I do not write to express a philosophy; I write to try and recreate the dance of the mind."

BIOGRAPHICAL/CRITICAL SOURCES:

PERIODICALS

Booklist, August, 1999, review of *A Legacy of Shadows* and *News from Down to the Cafe,* p. 2014.
Kirkus Reviews, November 1, 1999, review of *News from Down to the Cafe,* p. 1679.
Publishers Weekly, June 28, 1999, review of *A Legacy of Shadows* and *News from Down to the Cafe,* p. 73.

OTHER

Copper Canyon Press, http://www.coppercanyonpress.org/ (October 19, 2000).*

*   *   *

LEEDY, Loreen (Janelle) 1959-

PERSONAL: Born June 15, 1959, in Wilmington, DE; daughter of James Allwyn (an auditor) and Grace Anne (Williams) Leedy. *Education:* Attended Indiana University—Bloomington, 1978-79; University of Delaware, B.A. (cum laude), 1981.

ADDRESSES: Home—P.O. Box 3362, Winter Park, FL 32790. *E-mail*—me@loreenleedy.com.

CAREER: Craftsperson, specializing in jewelry, 1982-84; writer and illustrator, 1984—. Speaker for schools and conventions. Work included in exhibitions, including Florida Illustrators: Art from Children's Books, 1997-99, and Art of the Picture Book, Martin County Council for the Arts, Stuart, FL, 2000.

MEMBER: Authors Guild, Society of Children's Book Writers and Illustrators.

AWARDS, HONORS: Parents' Choice Award for Illustration, 1987, for *Big, Small, Short, Tall;* Parents' Choice Award in Learning and Doing, 1989, for *The Dragon Halloween Party;* Ezra Jack Keats Award for excellence in the arts, 1989; Best Books Award, *Parents Magazine,* 1990, for *The Furry News: How to Make a Newspaper,* and 1992, for *The Monster Money Book; Fraction Action* included in the Society of Illustrators' Original Art show, New York City, 1994; art depicting sea turtles, from *Tracks in the Sand,* shown at the Greensburgh Nature Center in Scarsdale, NY.

WRITINGS:

SELF-ILLUSTRATED CHILDREN'S BOOKS

A Number of Dragons, Holiday House (New York, NY), 1985.

The Dragon ABC Hunt, Holiday House (New York, NY), 1986.

The Dragon Halloween Party, Holiday House (New York, NY), 1986.

Big, Small, Short, Tall, Holiday House (New York, NY), 1987.

The Bunny Play, Holiday House (New York, NY), 1988.

A Dragon Christmas: Things to Make and Do, Holiday House (New York, NY), 1988.

Pingo the Plaid Panda, Holiday House (New York, NY), 1988.

The Potato Party and Other Troll Tales, Holiday House (New York, NY), 1989.

A Dragon Thanksgiving Feast: Things to Make and Do, Holiday House (New York, NY), 1990.

The Furry News: How to Make a Newspaper, Holiday House (New York, NY), 1990.

The Great Trash Bash, Holiday House (New York, NY), 1991.

Messages in the Mailbox: How to Write a Letter, Holiday House (New York, NY), 1991.

Blast off to Earth! A Look at Geography, Holiday House (New York, NY), 1992.

The Monster Money Book, Holiday House (New York, NY), 1992.

Postcards from Pluto: A Tour of the Solar System, Holiday House (New York, NY), 1993.

The Race, Scott, Foresman (Glenview, IL), 1993.

Tracks in the Sand, Doubleday (New York, NY), 1993.

The Edible Pyramid: Good Eating Every Day, Holiday House (New York, NY), 1994.

Fraction Action, Holiday House (New York, NY), 1994.

Who's Who in My Family?, Holiday House (New York, NY), 1995.

2 X 2 = BOO! A Set of Spooky Multiplication Stories, Holiday House (New York, NY), 1995.

How Humans Make Friends, Holiday House (New York, NY), 1996.

Mission Addition, Holiday House (New York, NY), 197.

Measuring Penny, Henry Holt, 1997.

Celebrate the Fifty States!, Holiday House (New York, NY), 1999.

Mapping Penny's World, Henry Holt, 2000.

Subtraction Action, Holiday House (New York, NY), 2000.

(With Pat Street) *There's a Frog in My Throat,* Winslow Press, 2001.

ILLUSTRATOR

David A. Adler, *The Dinosaur Princess and Other Prehistoric Riddles,* Holiday House (New York, NY), 1988.

Tom Birdseye, *Waiting for Baby,* Holiday House (New York, NY), 1991.

SIDELIGHTS: Loreen Leedy once told *CA:* "Reading, writing, and making art have been important to me throughout my lifetime. The picture book is a unique art form in which the words and art work together to tell the story or convey information. When developing a book, I go back and forth between the text and the illustrations to create a unified whole. My books generally incorporate humor to engage the young reader and include information children are learning in school.

"I choose a subject such as measuring, then think of characters and a setting where the story can take place. For *Measuring Penny,* I used a little girl with a homework assignment to measure 'something,' and dogs because they come in so many sizes and shapes. The story takes place at school, at home, and in the park.

"For *Celebrate the Fifty States!,* the characters are kids from across the United States who are showing what is distinctive about their state. The illustrations include maps, the state bird and flower, products, and famous people and places. I had to do a tremendous amount of research to complete this book.

"The biggest change for me in recent years is that I now use my computer to draw and paint the artwork for my books. It took time to learn how, but it gives me many more creative possibilities. For *Mapping Penny's World,* I took photographs of trees, flowers, and bushes to scan into the computer and add to the art. I can also scan objects such as coins, sticks, and fabric, which are part of the artwork for *Celebrate the Fifty States!*"

BIOGRAPHICAL/CRITICAL SOURCES:

PERIODICALS

Central Florida Family, October, 2000.
Delaware Today, October, 1986.

OTHER

Loreen Leedy Web site, http://www.loreenleedy.com/ (June 14, 2001).

*　　*　　*

LELAND, Christopher Towne 1951-

PERSONAL: Born October 17, 1951, in Tulsa, OK; son of Benjamin Towne (an engineer) and Julia E. (a librarian; maiden name, Sanford) Leland. *Education:* Pomona College, B.A., 1973; University of California, San Diego, M.A., 1980, Ph.D., 1982.

ADDRESSES: Home—Detroit, MI. *Office*—Department of English, Wayne State University, 51 West Warren Ave., Detroit, MI 48214.

CAREER: Montclair State College, Upper Montclair, NJ, member of adjunct faculty, 1980; Pomona College, Claremont, CA, visiting lecturer in composition, creative writing, and literature, 1982; University of California, San Diego, La Jolla, visiting lecturer in composition, creative writing, and literature, 1983; Harvard University, Cambridge, MA, Briggs-Copeland Lecturer,

1983-88; Bennington College, Bennington, VT, member of the faculty, 1988-90; Wayne State University, Detroit, MI, professor of English, 1990—.

MEMBER: Modern Language Association of America, Associated Writing Programs, Poets and Writers.

AWARDS, HONORS: Rotary fellowship for Argentina, 1974; Fulbright fellowship for Argentina, 1979; finalist, PEN Hemingway Award for first novel, 1982, for *Mean Time;* Fulbright junior researcher fellowship, Argentina, 1984; fellowship in fiction, Massachusetts Artists Foundation, 1986; American Specialist Lectureship, United States Information Agency, Argentina, 1986; Certificate of Excellence in Teaching, Danforth Center for Teaching and Learning, Harvard University, and Shane Stevens fellowship in fiction, Bread Loaf Writers' Conference, both 1987; Fulbright American Republics Research fellowship, Argentina and Uruguay, 1989; grants from Wayne State University, 1992-93 and 2000; Fulbright teaching fellowship for Spain, 1996; Board of Governors Distinguished Faculty Award, Wayne State University, 1997; President's Award for Excellence in Teaching, Wayne State University, 1999.

WRITINGS:

Mean Time, Random House (New York, NY), 1982.
The Last Happy Men: The Generation of 1922, Fiction, and the Argentine Reality, Syracuse University Press (New York, NY), 1986.
Mrs. Randall, Houghton (Boston, MA), 1987.
(Translator) *Open Door: Short Stories by Luisa Valenzuela,* North Point Press, 1988.
The Book of Marvels, Scribner (New York, NY), 1990.
The Professor of Aesthetics, Zoland Books, 1994.
Letting Loose, Zoland Books, 1996.
The Art of Compelling Fiction: How to Write a Page-Turner, Story Press, 1998.

WORK IN PROGRESS: Grace: A Novel; Youth: A Novel; The Office Stories by Roberto Mariani (translation); *Fleshly History: Re-evaluating American Sexualities,* a nonfiction book.

SIDELIGHTS: In his first novel, *Mean Time,* Christopher Leland relates the story of Dewey Monroe, a man jailed at age twenty for killing a friend who accused his wife of casual infidelity. After serving ten years of "mean time" in a southwestern prison, Dewey returns home to discover that his wife is, indeed, having an affair with the latest hired hand. Dewey "sets about the business of fitting his . . . unfaithful wife, Carrie, and her current lover, a dark-complected snake-handling fugitive from a Western carnival named Ale, into his plan for revenge," Alan Cheuse observed in the *New York Times Book Review*.

Although Leland's tale of small town repression, infidelity, and violence is not an unusual one, critics noted that the author distinguishes *Mean Time* with powerful writing and the skillful capturing of time and place. "The dust and the townspeople make so claustrophobic an atmosphere you feel it, taste it," Caroline Thompson wrote in the *Los Angeles Times Book Review*. "The evocation of this place is Leland's greatest achievement. He's sucked the town right out of the Southwest and plunked it down between these covers. . . . The auspiciously high level of craftsmanship makes *Mean Time* an especially impressive beginning [for Leland]." Cheuse concurred, calling *Mean Time* "a compelling neo-Faulknerian drama of back country retribution." Despite its well-used plot, the reviewer concluded, the book is "a wickedly lyrical and engrossing first novel, and works some interesting changes in an old theme."

BIOGRAPHICAL/CRITICAL SOURCES:

PERIODICALS

Library Journal, October 1, 1982.
Los Angeles Times Book Review, November 28, 1982, Caroline Thompson, review of *Mean Time*.
New York Times Book Review, January 16, 1983, Alan Cheuse, review of *Mean Time*.

*   *   *

LEONG, Russell (C.) 1950-
(Wallace Lin)

PERSONAL: Born September 7, 1950, in San Francisco, CA; son of Charles Lai (a journalist) and Mollie Joe (a businessperson; maiden name, Chun) Leong. *Education:* San Francisco State College (now University), B.A., 1972; graduate study at National Taiwan University, 1973-74; University of California at Los Angeles, M.F.A., 1990. *Politics:* Democrat. *Religion:* Buddhist.

ADDRESSES: Home—3924 Tracy St., Los Angeles, CA 90027. *Office*—Asian American Studies Center, 3230 Campbell Hall, University of California, Los Angeles, CA 90024.

CAREER: Pacifica Public Radio, editor of *KPFA Folio*, 1975-76; University of California at Los Angeles, publications head for resource development and publications at Asian American Studies Center. Rockefeller American Generations Fellowship Program, coordinator, 1991-93. Editor and director of video documentaries *Morning Begins Here*, Rife International Film Festival, 1985; and *Why Is Preparing a Fish a Political Act?: Poetry of Janice Mirikitani*, Manhattan Cable, 1991.

WRITINGS:

(Editor, with Jean Pang Yip) Him Mark Lai, *A History Reclaimed: An Annotated Bibliography of Chinese Language Materials on the Chinese of America*, Asian American Studies Center, University of California (Los Angeles, CA), 1986.
(Editor, with G. Nomura, R. Endo, and S. Sumida; and contributor) *Frontiers of Asian American Studies: Writing, Research, and Criticism*, Washington State University Press (Detroit, MI), 1989.
(Editor and author of introduction) *Moving the Image: Independent Asian Pacific American Media Arts, 1970-1990*, Visual Communications, 1991.
The Country of Dreams and Dust (poems), West End (Minneapolis, MN), 1993.
Asian American Sexualities: Dimensions of the Gay and Lesbian Experience, Routledge (New York, NY), 1996.
Phoenix Eyes and Other Stories, University of Washington Press (Seattle, WA), 2000.

Also editor, with Edward T. Chang, *Los Angeles— Struggle toward Multiethnic Community: Asian America, African America, and Latino Perspectives*, 1995. Author of foreword, *On a Bed of Rice: An Asian American Erotic Feast*, edited by Geraldine Kudaka, Anchor Books (New York, NY), 1995. Work represented in anthologies (sometimes under the pseudonym Wallace Lin), including *Aiiieeeee! An Anthology of Asian American Writers*, edited by Frank Chin and others, Howard University Press (Washington, DC), 1974; *Charlie Chan Is Dead: An Anthology of Contemporary Asian American Fiction*, edited by Jessica Hagedorn, Viking Penguin (New York, NY), 1993; and *Asian American Literature Mosaic*, edited by Shawn Wong, HarperCollins (New York, NY). Contributor of poems, articles, stories, and reviews to periodicals, including *New England Review*, *Tricycle: The Buddhist Review*, *Positions: East Asia Cultures Critique*, and *In Focus*. Editor, *Amerasia Journal*, 1977—.

WORK IN PROGRESS: A novel.

SIDELIGHTS: Russell Leong is an editor, poet, and novelist whose work reflects dimensions of the Asian-American experience. He recalled to *CA* that his first writing consisted of "strokes written in opaque Chinese ink . . . done unthinkingly as a child: I scrawled ideograms, odd words and sentences—graffiti in English and Chinese—onto wooden school desks. The place: San Francisco Chinatown; the time: a few years after the Second World War. Educated in local Chinese- and American-language schools, I was a member of the community-based Kearny Street Writers Workshop, which spawned Asian American writers, poets, and filmmakers in the 1970s. These poets—Chinese, Filipino, and Japanese Americans—linked their writings with social activism around issues such as ethnic studies, fair housing, Native Americans and Alcatraz Island, and international liberation movements in the Americas and Asia."

Leong identifies himself primarily as a poet. One of his major works in that genre is "Unfolding Flowers, Matchless Flames," a seven-part poem about the Los Angeles riots and Buddhism. Leong commented: "This poem, utilizing the metaphor of fire as both a destructive and redeeming force, reveals linkages between the Vietnam War, the Iraq conflict, and the Los Angeles riots against a landscape of personal life, loss, and Buddhistic beliefs." Another significant work is the sixteen-part poem, "The Country of Dreams and Dust," which in Leong's words "begins and ends with water: from the Canton Delta to the drained swimming pool of a Los Angeles tract house in Little Saigon. The title is a Taoist/Buddhist term (*cheng meng*) which refers to the intertwined realities of the spiritual and secular worlds, which are indivisible in my writings."

Leong contributed to a groundbreaking work when he wrote the foreword to *On a Bed of Rice: An Asian American Erotic Feast*. This anthology, which encompasses themes of marriage, interracial love, and sexual awareness, is one of the first to go beyond commonly-held stereotypes of Asian-American sexuality. Leong contributed to racial understanding in a more tangible sense when he co-edited, with Edward T. Chang, *Los Angeles—Struggle toward Multiethnic Community: Asian American, African America, and Latino Perspectives*. This collection brings together more than two dozen essays from the *Amerasia Journal* to consider the challenges facing the peaceful evolution of a multiracial community in Los Angeles.

Leong's short fiction is collected in *Phoenix Eyes and Other Stories*, published in 2000. The fourteen stories cover themes varying from the struggles faced by immigrants to the life story of an international gigolo. The work is considered ironic and "impressionistic" by a *Publishers Weekly* reviewer, who summarized: "Some of [the stories in *Phoenix Eyes*] are slight, but the best of them exploit the stresses of sexual desire and family relationships, and probe the cultural forces shaping the immigrant experience."

Leong further told *CA:* "Writers who have influenced my thinking include the twentieth-century Chinese writers Lu Hsun and others of the May 4, 1919, literary movement, Asian American playwright Frank Chin, and many others. Their acute and painful sense of history, memory, community, and culture, translated through their fiction or poetry, inspire. I have relied upon the critical eyes of Ethiopian film essayist Teshome Gabriel and Filipino writer N. V. M. Gonzalez, and upon Sam Hamill's thoughtful commentaries and translations. My Vietnamese *Sifu*, or master monk, Thich Minh Ton, has taught me much about the nature of human relations and of divergent forms of Buddhism in contemporary life.

"Mao Zedong's Yenan essays, early Theravada Pali Buddhist texts, songs of the iconoclastic bards of Bengal, Italian novelist Italo Calvino's *Invisible Cities*, Yasunari Kawabata's 'palm-of-the-hand stories,' Frantz Fanon's writings, and Sun Tzu's war strategies rest dustless on my shelf. Poems etched onto the walls of the Angel Island Immigration Station in San Francisco Bay, gravestones of anonymous workers in Chinese American cemeteries which spell *wu-ming* (without name), and multicolored tags of Los Angeles neighborhood graffiti are enduring influences. The fresh ideas of each generation of students also stir thought.

"My poems tend toward the longer narrative. Brevity, on the other hand, characterizes my short stories. I strive for clarity of vision and language in my work, be it poem, story, or novel. I see the writer, beyond immediate family, as a migrant who carries his words from country to country. The words themselves, to paraphrase Calvino, should be light in weight, so as not to sink heedlessly into the sea."

BIOGRAPHICAL/CRITICAL SOURCES:

PERIODICALS

Afterimage, October, 1992, review of *Moving the Image: Independent Asian-Pacific American Media Arts, 1970-1990*, p. 14.

Amerasia Journal, Volume 1, 1995, review of *The Country of Dreams and Dust,* p. 181.

Antioch Review, winter, 1995, review of *The Country of Dreams and Dust,* p. 121.

Choice, October, 1992, review of *Moving the Image: Independent Asian-Pacific American Media Arts, 1970-1990,* p. 309.

Hungry Mind Review, fall, 1992, review of *Moving the Image: Independent Asian-Pacific American Media Arts, 1970-1990,* p. 45.

Kenyon Review, winter, 1995, review of *The Country of Dreams and Dust,* p. 150.

Multicultural Review, October, 1992, review of *Moving the Image: Independent Asian-Pacific American Media Arts, 1970-1990,* p. 71.

Publishers Weekly, October 16, 1995, review of *Asian American Sexualities,* p. 56; June 19, 2000, review of *Phoenix Eyes and Other Stories,* p. 61.

Small Press Review, spring, 1994, review of *The Country of Dreams and Dust,* p. 109.

Tricycle: The Buddhist Review, review of *The Country of Dreams and Dust,* p. 107.*

*   *   *

LETTS, Billie 1938-

PERSONAL: Born May 30, 1938, in Tulsa, OK; daughter of Bill and Virginia (a secretary; maiden name, Barnes) Gipson; married Dennis Letts (a professor of English); children: Shawn, Tracy (son). *Education:* Attended Northeastern State College (now Northeastern Oklahoma State University), 1956-58; Southeast Missouri State College (now University), B.A., 1969; Southeastern Oklahoma State University, M.A., 1974.

ADDRESSES: Home—Durant, OK. *Agent*—Elaine Markson, Elaine Markson Literary Agency, Inc., 44 Greenwich Ave., New York, NY 10011.

CAREER: Teacher and novelist.

MEMBER: Writers Guild of America, Authors Guild, Oklahoma Federation of Writers.

AWARDS, HONORS: Walker Percy Award, 1993; Oklahoma Book Awards, 1995, for *Where the Heart Is,* and 1998, for *The Honk and Holler Opening Soon.*

WRITINGS:

Where the Heart Is (novel), Warner Books (New York, NY), 1995.

The Honk and Holler Opening Soon (novel), Warner Books (New York, NY), 1998.

Contributor of stories to magazines, including *Good Housekeeping* and *North American Review.*

ADAPTATIONS: Where the Heart Is was adapted as a feature film.

WORK IN PROGRESS: A novel, completion expected in 2001.

BIOGRAPHICAL/CRITICAL SOURCES:

BOOKS

Griffis, Molly Levite, *You've Got Mail, Billie Letts,* Eakin Publications (Austin, TX), 1999.

PERIODICALS

Booklist, September 1, 1995, Kathleen Hughes, review of *Where the Heart Is,* p. 41. May 1, 1998, Donna Seaman, review of *The Honk and Holler Opening Soon,* p. 1487; August, 1999, review of *Where the Heart Is,* p. 2025.

Chicago Tribune, August 12, 1998, review of *The Honk and Holler Opening Soon.*

Kirkus Reviews, May 15, 1998, review of *The Honk and Holler Opening Soon.*

Library Journal, July, 1995, Barbara E. Kemp, review of *Where the Heart Is,* p. 121; June 1, 1998, Kimberly G. Allen, review of *The Honk and Holler Opening Soon,* p. 154; November 15, 1998, review of *The Honk and Holler Opening Soon,* p. 124.

New York Times Book Review, August 6, 1995, Dwight Garner, review of *Where the Heart Is,* p. 20.

People Weekly, February 22, 1999, Peter Ames Carlin and Carlton Stowers, "Never Too Late: At 60, Small-Town Novelist Billie Letts Knows Success Was Worth Waiting For," p. 101.

Publishers Weekly, May 15, 1995, review of *Where the Heart Is,* p. 55; May 11, 1998, review of *The Honk and Holler Opening Soon,* p. 50.

School Library Journal, April, 1996, Pamela B. Rearden, review of *Where the Heart Is,* p. 168; January, 1999, Carol Clark, review of *The Honk and Holler Opening Soon,* p. 160.

Southern Living, August, 1998, Carly L. Price, review of *The Honk and Holler Opening Soon,* p. 48.

*   *   *

LEVINE, Suzanne Jill 1946-

PERSONAL: Born October 21, 1946, in New York, NY; daughter of Meyer and Elaine (Berger) Levine. *Education:* Vassar College, B.A., 1967; Columbia University, M.A., 1969; New York University, Ph.D., 1976.

ADDRESSES: Home—120 Hixon Rd., Santa Barbara, CA 93108. *Office*—Department of Spanish and Portuguese, University of California, Santa Barbara, Santa Barbara, CA 93106.

CAREER: Tufts University, Medford, MA, assistant professor of Latin American literature and literary translation, 1977-84; University of Washington, Seattle, associate professor, 1984-88; University of California, Santa Barbara, Santa Barbara, professor of Spanish and Portuguese, 1988—. University of California Interdisciplinary Humanities Center fellow, spring, 1989; University of California Regents fellow, summer, 1989. Lecturer on literary translation, New York University, Hunter College and Graduate Center of the City University of New York, Yale University, and numerous other universities throughout the United States, Europe and Latin America. Free-lance translator and writer. Judge, National Book Awards, 1978, and jurist, Letras de Oro Literary Translation Prize, University of Miami, 1987-89. Consultant to numerous publishers, including E.P. Dutton, Harper & Row, Brooklyn College Press, Wildman Press, and Adler & Adler.

MEMBER: American Literary Translators Association (member of executive council, 1981-84), PEN, International Board of Translators, Instituto Internacional de Literatura Iberoamericana.

AWARDS, HONORS: Mellon fellowship, Wellesley College, 1979; National Endowment for the Arts fellowship grant for literary translation, 1981, 1986; University of Washington Graduate School Research Fund summer grant, 1985; Guggenheim fellowship, 1996; PEN American Award for Career Achievement in Hispanic Studies, 1996; several grants and fellowships from National Endowment for the Arts and National Endowment for the Humanities.

SIDELIGHTS: Suzanne Jill Levine once told *CA:* "Translation—an activity caught between the scholarly and the creative, between technique and intuition—is a route, a voyage if you like, through which a writer/translator may seek to reconcile fragments: fragments of texts, of language, of oneself. More than a moment of interpretation, translation is an act of passage." This act has brought Levine acclaim; several critics praised her translations of Latin American literature. Reviewing *Selected Stories* by Adolfo Bioy Casares for *Americas,* Barbara Mujica observed, "Levine has done a brilliant job of capturing in English Bioy's unique combination of archaic linguistic elegance and street language. The

author's devastating understatements, his subtle irony and wit, and even his shrewdly chosen cliches come across beautifully." James Polk, critiquing the same collection in the *New York Times Book Review,* pronounced it "finely translated." A *Publishers Weekly* reviewer described Levine and Carol Maier's translation of Severo Sarduy's *Christ on the Rue Jacob* as "perfectly" executed. Mujica, even when asserting, in another article for *Americas,* that Levine's work on Manuel Puig's *Tropical Night Falling* produced "a flawed translation" that "seems rather hastily done," remarked that "Levine is certainly one of America's most highly respected translators who has given us ample proof of her capabilities elsewhere." In an interview for *Americas* upon the publication of *The Subversive Scribe: Translating Latin American Fiction,* Edward Taylor, Jr., quoted Levine as saying, "Translation is really a mode of writing. . . . It's an incredibly creative activity." Taylor related that "Levine's translations are often produced in close collaboration—'closelaboration,' as [Guillermo] Cabrera Infante termed their partnership—with authors, in a process akin to co-creation." Taylor reported on the factors that gave Levine an affinity for certain writers: With Cabrera Infante, it was their shared love of wordplay; with Manuel Puig, it was a common interest in Hollywood films of the 1930s and 1940s.

Levine has been not only Puig's translator, but also his friend, and, in *Manuel Puig and the Spider Woman: His Life and Fictions,* his biographer. The biography's title refers to Puig's most famous work, the novel *Kiss of the Spider Woman,* in which an incarcerated gay man recites the plots of movies to his cellmate, a political prisoner. The Oscar-winning 1985 film based on the novel brought new attention to Puig late in his life—he died in 1990—and the book was subsequently adapted into a Broadway musical. In her biography, Levine explains how the movies gave Puig, as a youth, a sense of what life was like beyond the confines of the small Argentine town where he was born in 1932, plus how, in his adulthood, film informed his writings. She also details his adventures once he left his hometown and journeyed all over the world; the development of his political consciousness, including his distaste for Juan Peron's oppressive governance of Argentina; and the influence of his homosexuality on his career.

Writing in the *New York Times Book Review,* Mario Vargas Llosa lauded Levine's book as "well-researched and carefully documented." It is "filled with anecdotes, some amusing . . . others moving, even tragic, all of them drawing a lively, convincing profile," he commented. A *Publishers Weekly* reviewer praised Levine's "splendid job of delineating Puig's cultural influences" and felt she makes a strong case that "Puig was as obsessed with politics as he was with popular culture and the imagination." *Booklist* contributor Brad Hooper applauded the biography's "great psychological depth." Vargas Llosa disagreed with Levine on one point: "I ask myself if Puig's writing has the literary transcendence attributed to it by Levine and other critics. I'm afraid it doesn't; I believe it is more ingenious and brilliant than profound, more artificial than innovative, and too dependent on the fashions and myths of its time to ever achieve the permanence of great literary works." Still, he enthused about Levine's skills as a biographer. "This fascinating book is indispensable for anyone interested in Puig's work," he asserted, adding that it is "a book in which rigor and readability walk arm in arm."

BIOGRAPHICAL/CRITICAL SOURCES:

PERIODICALS

Americas, March/April, 1992, Barbara Mujica, review of *Tropical Night Falling,* p. 60; September/ October, 1994, Edward F. Taylor, Jr., "Versions & Subversions," p. 44; May/June, 1995, Mujica, review of *Selected Stories,* p. 61.

Booklist, July, 1995, Brad Hooper, review of *Christ on the Rue Jacob,* p. 1854; May 1, 2000, Hooper, review of *Manuel Puig and the Spider Woman: His Life and Fictions,* p. 1640.

Library Journal, September 1, 1998, Michael Rogers, review of *Infante's Inferno,* p. 224; May 15, 2000, David W. Henderson, review of *Manuel Puig and the Spider Woman: His Life and Fictions,* p. 94.

New York Times, October 6, 1999, Richard Bernstein, "So Close, Borges's Worlds of Reality and Invention"; August 13, 2000, Mario Vargas Llosa, review of *Manuel Puig and the Spider Woman: His Life and Fictions.*

New York Times Book Review, November 10, 1991 Robert Houston, "Nidia Has a Crush on the Doorman"; November 29, 1992, Daniel Balderston, "Fantastic Voyages"; November 6, 1994, James Polk, "Silly and Misguided about Love"; August 13, 2000, Mario Vargas Llosa, "Saved by Rita Hayworth."

Publishers Weekly, November 2, 1990, review of *Larva: Midsummer Night's Babel,* p. 63; August 23, 1991, review of *Tropical Night Falling,* p. 47; May 15, 1995, review of *Christ on the Rue Jacob,* p. 69; May 1, 2000, review of *Manuel Puig and the Spider Woman: His Life and Fictions,* p. 65.

OTHER

Center for Book Culture, http://www.centerforbookculture.org/ (June 22, 2001), Suzanne Jill Levine, "Reading Manuel Puig: A Biographer's View."*

LÉVY, Bernard Henri 1949-

PERSONAL: Born May 11, 1949, in Beni Saf, Algeria; son of Andre and Ginett Lévy; children: Justine, Antonin.

ADDRESSES: Office—Grasset & Fasquelle, 61 rue des Sts.-Peres, Paris 75006, France.

CAREER: Writer. Editor at Grasset & Fasquelle (publishers) in Paris, France. Former adviser to government of Bangladesh and to François Mitterand.

AWARDS, HONORS: Prix d'Honneur, 1977, for *Barbarism with a Human Face;* Prix Medicis, 1984, for *Le Diable en tête.*

WRITINGS:

Bangladesh: Nationalisme dans le révolution, F. Maspero, 1973.

La Barbarie à visage humain, Grasset (Paris, France), 1977, translation by George Holoch published as *Barbarism with a Human Face,* Harper (New York, NY), 1979.

La Testament de Dieu, Grasset (Paris, France), 1979, translation by George Holoch published as *The Testament of God,* Harper (New York, NY), 1980.

L'Idéologie française, Grasset (Paris, France), 1981.

Questions de principe, Denoel (Paris, France), 1983.

Le Diable en tête, Grasset (Paris, France), 1984.

Impressions d'Asie, photography by Guy Bouchet, Grasset (Paris, France), 1985.

Les Indes rouges, L.G.F., 1985.

Eloge des intellectuels, Grasset (Paris, France), 1987.

Les derniers jours de Charles Baudelaire, Grasset (Paris, France), 1988.

Frank Stella, les années 80, Editions de la Difference (Paris, France), 1990.

César: les bronzes, Editions de la Difference (Paris, France), 1991.

Les aventures de la liberté: une histoire, Grasset (Paris, France), 1991, translation by Richard Veasey published as *Adventures on the Freedom Road: The French Intellectuals in the Twentieth Century,* Harvill (London, England), 1995.

Le judgement dernier: théâtre, Grasset (Paris, France), 1992.

Piero della Francesca, Editions de la Difference (Paris, France), 1992.

Bernard Henri Lévy

(With Francoise Giroud) *Les Hommes et les femmes,* Olivier Orban (Paris, France), 1993, translation by Richard Miller published as *Women and Men: A Philosophical Conversation,* Little, Brown (Boston, MA), 1995.

Le pureté dangereuse, Grasset (Paris, France), 1994.

(Editor) *The Rules of the Game,* [Paris, France], 1998, reprinted as *What Good Are Intellectuals?: 44 Writers Share Their Thoughts,* Algora (New York, NY), 2000.

Comédie, Grasset (Paris, France), 1997.

Le siècle de Sartre: Enquête philosophique, Grasset (Paris, France), 2000.

Contributor to periodicals, including *Le Nouvel Observateur* and *L'Express,* and to compilations, including *Antishemiyut ha-yom,* 1984.

SIDELIGHTS: Bernard Henri Lévy is probably the most celebrated of the several "New Philosophers" who moved to the forefront of radical French thought in the mid-1970s. Lévy's philosophy, a peculiar combination of romanticized pessimism and quasi-biblical monotheism, has sparked controversy in intellectual circles and endeared him to a generation disillusioned by the failings of Marxist socialism. His popularity, however, is also largely dependent on his charisma and photogenic appearance, which have gained him constant attention from the French press. Some critics, noting Lévy's penchant for publicity, claim that his aims are essentially self-serving, but even these detractors concede that he has been instrumental in sustaining French intellectualism as a provocative force in Western thought.

Lévy first received extensive media attention in 1979 as the author of *Barbarism with a Human Face,* a vehement denunciation of Marxist tenets. During his college years Lévy had been active in the leftist movement and had participated in the student/proletariat strike that paralyzed Paris in May, 1968. But in the ensuing years, as the promise of a workers' revolution faded and he perceived weaknesses in practiced socialism, Lévy began to doubt Marxism's viability as a panacea for society's ills. A reading of *The Gulag Archipelago,* Alexander Solzhenitsyn's harrowing account of Stalinist repression and his own experiences in the grueling Soviet labor camps, confirmed Lévy's growing belief that Marxism was not only ineffective but destructive, and in *Barbarism with a Human Face* he produced an incendiary condemnation of his own previously held principles.

"I am the bastard child of an unholy union between fascism and Stalinism," Lévy proclaimed in *Barbarism with a Human Face.* In the book he recalls his earlier faith in Marxism and notes how that faith has since been replaced by informed disillusion. He writes, "Like everyone else I believed in a new and joyful 'liberation'; now . . . I live with the shadows of my past hopes." Lévy added that his book was intended for those leftists who maintained faith in Marxism despite its history as a repressive tool: "To my sorrow, I am addressing the left here," he declared; "my target is the left in its passion for delusion and ignorance."

Much of *Barbarism with a Human Face* is devoted to an explication of Marxism's allegedly intrinsic corruption. Lévy describes theoretical Marxism—which hypothesizes that capitalism leads to a workers' revolution which, in turn, results in a classless society—as the opiate of the naive intellectual, and he calls applied Marxism a barbaric system that inevitably spawns a massive "reactionary machine" for destroying all opposition to itself. According to Lévy, theoretical Marxism's notion of progress—which culminates in a classless society and the end of the state—is applied Marxism's greatest weapon, for it justifies the repression and eradication of anyone deemed subversive and thus regressive. Lévy believes that applied Marxism can never actually result in the end of the state, for Marxists—like the rest of humanity—are motivated by power and material gain, not by the promise of a classless society that would ultimately undermine their own authority. For this reason Lévy claims that Marxism and capitalism are similar, not opposite, and that both are futile, devastating systems.

In *Barbarism with a Human Face,* Lévy seeks to expose Marxism as a flawed, inherently corrupt system. There is no hope for Marxist society, Lévy declares, because the desire for power and wealth compels Marxist leaders to compromise their alleged goal of social equality. Individuals must therefore derive self-worth by opposing Marxist—and capitalist—systems. He advocates resistance through ethical pessimism, which calls for individuals to write ethical treatises even though such works will ultimately fail to effect social change. For Lévy—as for his compatriot predecessor Albert Camus—resistance is hopeless, but it is also the only ethical response to repression.

Upon publication, *Barbarism with a Human Face* proved surprisingly popular with the French public, and the book eventually sold more than one hundred thousand copies. Lévy became a prominent figure in the French press and on television, where his rock-star visage and intensity made him particularly appealing on talk shows. Reaction from the left was predictably negative: Lévy was branded a brash apostate and his book was deemed propaganda. More often, however, the book was considered enlightening, though controversial, and Lévy was acclaimed as a rejuvenating force in French philosophy.

When an English translation was published in 1979, American and British critics were sharply divided on the merits of *Barbarism with a Human Face.* Some reviewers hailed it as a masterful polemic and praised Lévy as a refreshing voice in Western philosophy, while others decried the work as derivative sophistry and dismissed Lévy as a fraud. Among the most praiseworthy assessments was that of Martin Peretz, who wrote in the *New Republic* that Lévy's arguments "exposed the callousness of [leftist] politics and the superficiality of the philosophical rationalizations that underpin that philosophy." Peretz commended Lévy as a polemicist and lauded *Barbarism with a Human Face* as "one of those rare works which changes the mind of an entire generation." Also impressed was *Commentary* reviewer Roger Kaplan, who cited the "cold and lucid elegance" of Lévy's prose and acknowledged the book as a necessary and provocative argument against Marxism. Kaplan described *Barbarism with a Human Face* as "bril-

liantly suggestive," and he credited Lévy for "saying out loud what was rapidly becoming a widespread rumor."

Lévy's detractors, however, complained that his style was excessively rhetorical and that his criticisms of Marxism were too often uncompelling and even wrongheaded. In the *Village Voice,* Richard Yeselson decried the "vacuous petulance" of Lévy's perspective and accused him of being illogical and ignorant. "Lévy's formulations . . . make no sense," Yeselson charged. "Lévy's understanding of the dynamics of class struggle is confused as well." Yeselson added that Lévy's moralism resulted in inaccurate appraisals of both Marxism and human nature, and he claimed that Lévy's credibility was severely undermined by such devastating blunders. Equally vehement was Norman Birnbaum, who wrote in *Nation* that Lévy's arguments were sabotaged by ambition that exceeded knowledge. "Lévy wants to think big," Birnbaum alleged. He accused Lévy of posturing instead of offering credible arguments, and denigrated Lévy's philosophical method as embarrassing. Among the more balanced appraisals of *Barbarism with a Human Face* was that provided by philosophy scholar William Barrett, who was a founder of the Marxist organ, *Partisan Review.* In the *New York Times Books Review,* Barrett contended that Lévy's work was more provocative than profound. "Read . . . as a serious essay on politics and political philosophy," wrote Barrett, "it is disappointing." He added, however, that Lévy's book might be better appreciated as a "personal manifesto," and he acknowledged Lévy as a dazzling stylist. "There is no doubt of Lévy's brilliance, nor of the power of his eloquence," Barrett declared. But he lamented Lévy's slapdash method and complained that the work was impressive but rarely persuasive. "The ideas are too sweeping and unqualified," Barrett charged, "and they are dealt with more rhetorically than analytically."

Lévy courted further critical controversy with *The Testament of God,* in which he advocated an "atheistic spirituality." Monotheism, Lévy claimed, was humanity's only viable, hopeful alternative to totalitarianism, and ethics derived from the Judaic tradition, particularly as evidenced in the Old Testament, afforded humanity a code of conduct—or system of belief—that allowed for constructive living in an age of terror and despair. Lévy called monotheism "the thought of resistance of our age," and he termed the Bible the "book of resistance." God, or at least the notion of a deity, has been "rehabilitated," Lévy pronounced.

American and British reviewers accorded *The Testament of God* mixed notices. Dismayed readers cited

Lévy's largely rhetorical method, and some critics even questioned his intelligence. Thomas Sheehan, for instance, wrote in the *New York Review of Books* that "little can be said about Lévy's position because so little of it is ever argued." Sheehan noted errors regarding the origins of *The Iliad* and *The Odyssey,* both of which Lévy was unaware had been written centuries after the events recounted, and the setting of *Antigone,* which Lévy mistakenly placed in fifth-century Athens instead of second millennium Thebes. And François Bondy complained in *Encounter* that Lévy's essential premise was derivative. "In many cases," Bondy declared, "what he is trying to say already has a long critical tradition. . . . and he comes to certain well-known suspicions and conclusions as if they were both daring and original." But critics also observed that *The Testament of God* was compelling and important. In *Theology Today,* Gabriel Vahanian described Lévy's book as "blunt, pithy, and iconoclastic," and he found Lévy's biblical exegesis admirable. "Read [*The Testament of God*]," Vahanian contended, "and you will not relegate the Bible to its specialists." Roger Kaplan found Lévy's work more problematic, decrying his seeming reluctance to pursue themes but praising his efforts to avoid the blunders of the French left. "The enemies of bourgeois order almost completely dominated the Parisian intellectual and cultural scene for many years," Kaplan alleged in the *Wall Street Journal.* "It is from the morass which they created that Mr. Lévy and others are now painfully extricating themselves." And even Bondy conceded that Lévy's work was "sound and noteworthy."

Lévy followed *The Testament of God* with *L'Idéologie française,* a harsh indictment of French society as inevitably fascist and bigoted. In *L'Idéologie française,* Lévy explores incidents of notorious anti-Semitism, including the Dreyfus affair, in which a Jewish officer was framed for treason, and the entire Vichy period, in which a puppet government persecuted Jews during the German occupation in World War II. These events, Lévy argues, were not examples of aberrant behavior but were manifestations of a perpetual bigotry still thriving in contemporary France.

Since its publication in 1981, *L'Idéologie française* has received criticism in English publications despite the absence of an English-language edition. Like some readers of Lévy's previous volumes, critics of *L'Idéologie française* decried its allegedly reckless arguments and sweeping generalizations. Raymond Aron, for instance, complained in *Encounter* that *L'Idéologie française* contained "an overblown style, cut-and-dried verdicts on the merits and demerits of both the living and the

dead . . . and the use of quotations torn from their context and arbitrarily interpreted." But in the *Times Literary Supplement,* Douglas Johnson noted that an awareness of Lévy's flaws, or idiosyncracies, should not obscure the validity of his polemic. "Things are never so simple as Lévy claims," Johnson acknowledged. "And yet when all his mistakes are pointed out, and all the defects of his reasoning allowed for, one wonders whether there is not something in his argument after all. It remains true that France has shown enthusiasm for racial persecution, and this cannot always be explained away in terms of foolishness."

Adventures on the Freedom Road: The French Intellectuals in the Twentieth Century is based on a television series. Lévy expanded on available footage and interviews in writing the book. Paul Ryan noted in *New Statesman & Society* that this "is not a detailed analysis of 20th-century French thought but a wickedly entertaining summary of actions, errors, and quarrels among the (predominantly male) high echelons of France's classes bavardes . . . Very few reputations emerge unscathed in this catalogue of great writers seduced by the totalitarian temptations of communism and facism." Ryan wrote that this work "features a dazzling cast of characters—from Artaud and Breton to Sartre and Camus and beyond—who laid creative writing aside and took up their pens to write 'for the good of the cause.'" "*Adventures on the Freedom Road* is a powerful book, written in a seductive, personal style and skillfully translated and edited by Richard Veasey," said Stephen Goode in *Insight on the News.* "There may be too many French writers discussed whose names mean little to contemporary readers, but the cautionary tale about the mischief intellectuals can do will come across to readers of any nationality."

Lévy wrote *Women and Men: A Philosophical Conversation* with Françoise Giroud, a feminist journalist and former government minister. The original, in French, was a huge hit, with 80,000 copies sold in the first week. It is written as a conversation in which the authors discuss sex, love, failed love, sexual behavior, and the impact of AIDS. They strengthen their arguments with quotes from politicians, philosophers, and literary figures, such as Anais Nin, Goethe, Joyce, Balzac, Proust, and Sartre. Giroud feels men are suffering as women have grown stronger, and that the situation is worse in the United States than in France. Lévy makes the point that men are really only interested in the difference between women and men. He believes in fidelity, and doubts that we have even had a sexual revolution. "And on and on they circle each other," wrote *Booklist* reviewer Bonnie Smothers, who called the authors "two appealing, extremely well-read people who punctuate their ideas with a wide variety of intriguing references." A *Publishers Weekly* contributor said "sparks fly. . . . Alternately insightful and pretentious, their witty talks sparkle."

Times Literary Supplement reviewer George Steiner said the structure of Lévy's *Le siécle de Sartre: Enquete philosophique* "is anti-systematic, counter-chronological. What we have is a garland, often winding back on itself, of essays on cardinal aspects of Sartre's kaleidoscopic life and genius. Within this labyrinth, there are excursions, at times voluminous, on ancillary topics. . . . The prose is breathless; names and allusions cascade down the page." Lévy elaborates on the role of women in Sartre's life, including Simone de Beauvoir, who had a primary influence on Sartre's creativity. "Lévy speculates on the masturbatory, voyeuristic tenor of Sartre's sexuality," commented Steiner, who felt that Lévy argues the merits of Sartre's *Chemins de la liberte* but gives little attention to Sartre as a dramatist. Steiner wrote that "there are father figures to be slain. Lévy probes more deeply than any previous recorder into Sartre's debts to Gide and to Bergson. . . . Celine is seminal." Steiner called *Le siécle de Sartre* "a tyrannosaurus of a book. It breathes proud fire, challenges all comers, maps a vast polemic terrain, yet, at the same time, manoeuvres with darting lightness and even elegance."

BIOGRAPHICAL/CRITICAL SOURCES:

BOOKS

Almanac of Famous People, sixth edition, Gale (Detroit, MI), 1998.
Contemporary Issues Criticism, Volume 1, Gale (Detroit, MI), 1982.
Encyclopedia of World Biography, second edition, seventeen volumes, Gale (Detroit, MI), 1998.

PERIODICALS

Booklist, January 15, 1995, Bonnie Smothers, review of *Women and Men,* p. 876.
Chicago Review, winter, 1981.
Christian Century, January 28, 1981.
Commentary, February, 1978.
Critic, April 1, 1981.
Encounter, August, 1979; May, 1981; June, 1981.

Insight on the News, January 29, 1996, Stephen Goode, review of *Adventures on the Freedom Road,* p. 30.
Maclean's, February 19, 1979.
Nation, June 2, 1979.
New Republic, April 7, 1979.
New Statesman & Society, November 10, 1995, Paul Ryan, review of *Adventures on the Freedom Road,* p. 38.
New York Review of Books, January 24, 1980.
New York Times, April 2, 1987.
New York Times Book Review, February 11, 1979.
Publishers Weekly, November 28, 1994, review of *Women and Men,* p. 48.
Theology Today, April, 1981.
Time, September 12, 1977.
Times Literary Supplement, July 31, 1981; May 19, 2000, George Steiner, "The Last Philosopher?," p. 3.
Village Voice, February 26, 1979.
Wall Street Journal, October 1, 1980.
Washington Post Book World, February 18, 1979.*

*   *   *

LÉVY, Bernard-Henri
    See LÉVY, Bernard Henri

*   *   *

LIDDY, James (Daniel Reeves) 1934-

PERSONAL: Born July 1, 1934, in Dublin, Ireland; son of James (a doctor) and Clare (Reeves) Liddy. *Ethnicity:* "Irish." *Education:* National University of Ireland, University College, Dublin, M.A., 1959. *Politics:* Fine Gael. *Religion:* Roman Catholic.

ADDRESSES: Home—1924 East Park Pl., Apt. E, Milwaukee, WI 53211. *Office*—Department of English, University of Wisconsin—Milwaukee, P.O. Box 413, Milwaukee, WI 53201.

CAREER: Called to the Bar at King's Inns, Dublin, 1959. San Francisco State College (now University), San Francisco, CA, faculty member, 1967-69; State University of New York at Binghamton, faculty member, 1969; Denison University, Granville, OH, faculty member, 1971-72; University of Wisconsin—Parkside, faculty member, 1972-73; National University of Ireland, University College, Galway, faculty member, 1973-74; University of Wisconsin—Milwaukee, faculty member, 1976-88, professor of English, 1988—. Poet in residence at San Francisco State University, 1967-68, and at Harpur College; visiting professor at State University of New York, Lewis and Clark College, Dennison University, and University College of Galway. Gorey Arts Festival, literature director.

MEMBER: Modern Language Association of America, Associated Writing Programs, Aosdana.

WRITINGS:

Esau, My Kingdom for a Drink: Homage to James Joyce on His Eightieth Birthday (poetry booklet), Dolmen Press (Dublin, Ireland), 1962.

(Contributor) Donald Carroll, editor, *New Poets of Ireland,* Alan Swallow, 1963.

In a Blue Smoke (poems), Dolmen Press (Dublin, Ireland), 1964, Dufour (Chester Springs, PA), 1968.

Blue Mountain (poems), Dufour (Chester Springs, PA), 1968.

(With Jim Chapson and Thomas Hill) *Blue House: Poems in the Chinese Manner,* White Rabbit (Santa Barbara, CA), 1968.

A Life of Stephen Dedalus (poetry booklet), White Rabbit (Santa Barbara, CA), 1969.

A Munster Song of Love and War (poetry booklet), White Rabbit (Santa Barbara, CA), 1971.

(Editor) *Nine Queen Bees,* White Rabbit (Santa Barbara, CA), 1971.

Baudelaire's Bar Flowers (poems), Capra (Santa Barbara, CA), 1974.

Corca Bascin (poems), Dolmen Press (Dublin, Ireland), 1977.

Comyn's Lay (poems), Hit & Run Press (Berkeley, CA), 1978.

Chamber Pot Music (poems), Hit & Run Press (Berkeley, CA), 1982.

At the Grave of Father Sweetman (poems), Malton Press, 1984.

Young Men Go out Walking (novel), Wolfhound Press, 1986.

A White Thought in a White Shade: New and Selected Poems, Kerr's Pink Press (Dublin, Ireland), 1987.

In the Slovak Bowling Alley (poems), Blue Canary Press (Milwaukee, WI), 1990.

(Contributor) *Notes towards a Video of Avondale House,* International University Press, 1991.

Collected Poems, Creighton University Press (Omaha, NE), 1994.

Epitaphery (poems), White Rabbit (Santa Barbara, CA), 1998.

Gold Set Dancing (poems), Salmon Publishing (Cliffs of Moher, Ireland), 2000.

Also author of *Patrick Kavanagh,* 1973; and *Art Is Not for Grown-ups,* 1990. Contributor to *New York Times, Dublin Magazine, Irish Times,* and *Milwaukee Journal.* Former editor of *Arena.*

SIDELIGHTS: James Liddy, a native of Ireland, gave up practicing law in 1966 to become a full-time writer and editor. Since then he has traveled widely in the United States and the United Kingdom, giving poetry readings and teaching English and creative writing. "If you are an Irish poet of my generation," he told the *Milwaukee Journal,* "you simply had to have divine figures, like Yeats and Joyce. And there's Patrick Kavanagh. You definitely have to go for style." *Milwaukee Journal* book editor Leslie Cross feels that despite these national influences, Liddy's idiom "is distinctly his own and definitely contemporary, with a lusty candor that must endear him to his students."

Liddy once told *CA:* "I believe that literature is the religion and politics of the imagination. Therefore a writer never grows too old. He only gets tired on fame—he gets his adolescence back from obscurity."

BIOGRAPHICAL/CRITICAL SOURCES:

BOOKS

Authors in the News, Volume II, Gale (Detroit, MI), 1976.

PERIODICALS

Milwaukee Journal, February 8, 1976.
Poetry, December, 1971.
Times Literary Supplement, July 28, 1978.

OTHER

Creighton University Press, http://www.mockingbird. creighton.edu/ (October 19, 2000).
Irish Writers Online, http://www.homepage.tinet.ie/ (October 19, 2000).
Salmon Publishing Ireland, http://www.salmonpoetry. com/ (October 19, 2000).

LIEBMAN, Ron(ald S.) 1943-

PERSONAL: Born October 11, 1943, in Baltimore, MD; son of Harry Martin and Marta (Altgenug) Liebman; married Simma Weintraub (a travel agent and graphic artist), January 8, 1982; children: Shana, Margot. *Education:* Western Maryland College, B.A., 1966; University of Maryland, J.D., 1969.

ADDRESSES: Home—Washington, DC. *Office*—Patton, Boggs & Blow, 2550 M St. N.W., Washington, DC 20037. *Agent*—Esther Newberg, International Creative Management, 40 West 57th St., New York, NY 10019.

CAREER: U.S. District Court, Baltimore, MD, law clerk to Chief Judge R. Dorsey Watkins, 1969-70; Melnicove, Kaufman & Weiner (law firm), Baltimore, associate, 1970-72; U.S. Department of Justice, Baltimore, assistant U.S. attorney, 1972-78; Sachs, Greenebaum & Taylor (law firm), Washington, DC, partner, 1978-82; Patton, Boggs & Blow (law firm), Washington, DC, partner, 1982—.

MEMBER: American Bar Association, Maryland Bar Association, District of Columbia Bar Association.

WRITINGS:

Grand Jury (novel), Ballantine (New York, NY), 1983.
(Editor, with Scott N. Stone) *Testimonial Privileges: A Treatise,* McGraw (New York, NY), 1983.
Shark Tales: True (and Amazing) Stories from America's Lawyers, Simon & Schuster (New York, NY), 2000.

WORK IN PROGRESS: A novel.

SIDELIGHTS: Ron Leibman first came into the public eye as part of the legal team that prosecuted former vice president Spiro T. Agnew. In 1983 he published a novel set in the world of law, *Grand Jury.* In his book, *Shark Tales: True (and Amazing) Stories from America's Lawyers,* Leibman brings together a collection of real-life anecdotes in which lawyers illustrate how incredibly stupid their clients can be. Moronic replies to cross-examinations, incredible rationalizations for illegal actions, and a wide spectrum of bad behavior and cloudy thinking are all illustrated in *Shark Tales.* Lawyers are skewered in the book, too. For example, numerous anecdotes describe the clash of trendy ideals with the lure of making big money, commonly experi-enced by law students in the 1960s. Leibman makes "no pretension to literary greatness," but *Shark Tales* is "pretty nicely done all the same," according to a writer for *Kirkus Reviews.* And yet that reviewer was not entirely pleased with *Shark Tales,* commenting: "The only downside to the book is the depressing view of the damnable human condition that the anecdotes, as a whole, offer. . . . Some of these tales inspire downright Nietzschean pessimism—but others yield a good yuck or two." A reviewer for *Publishers Weekly* took a more lighthearted view of *Shark Tales,* praising the "dozens of amusing or surprising examples of human behavior from a network of lawyer friends and contacts" presented in the book. Reading *Shark Tales* is "the equivalent of a pleasant bar-stool visit with some good legal yarn spinners," concluded the reviewer.

Leibman once told *CA:* "The work of a trial lawyer and a writer seems, for me at least, to fit together nicely. Any good trial lawyer needs to understand people and the situations and predicaments in which they often find themselves. Obviously, so does a fiction writer. While the trial lawyer deals in fact and the novelist in imagination, both have an audience, and both must be able to communicate, to tell a story. Whether one is a juror or a reader, most people will agree that there is nothing like a good story."

BIOGRAPHICAL/CRITICAL SOURCES:

PERIODICALS

American Bar Association Journal, March, 1984.
International Herald Tribune, January 24, 1984.
Kirkus Reviews, June 15, 2000, review of *Shark Tales: True (and Amazing) Stories from America's Lawyers,* p. 860.
Philadelphia, January, 1984.
Philadelphia Inquirer, January 3, 1984.
Publishers Weekly, November 11, 1983; August 7, 2000, review of *Shark Tales: True (and Amazing) Stories from America's Lawyers,* p. 83.
USA Today, December, 1983.
Washington Post, December 27, 1983.*

* * *

LIN, Wallace
See LEONG, Russell (C.)

LIPPY, Charles H(oward) 1943-

PERSONAL: Born December 2, 1943, in Binghamton, NY; son of Charles Augustus (an engineer) and Natalie (a homemaker; maiden name, Setzer) Lippy. *Education:* Dickinson College, B.A. (magna cum laude), 1965; Union Theological Seminary, M.Div. (magna cum laude), 1968; Princeton University, M.A., 1970, Ph.D., 1972. *Politics:* Democrat. *Religion:* United Methodist.

ADDRESSES: Home—711 Hurricane Creek Rd., Chattanooga, TN 37421. *Office*—Department of Philosophy and Religion, University of Tennessee, 615 McCallie Ave., Chattanooga, TN 37403.

CAREER: Oberlin College, Oberlin, OH, assistant professor of religion, 1972-74; Miami University, Oxford, OH, visiting assistant professor of religion and American studies, 1974-75; West Virginia Wesleyan College, Buckhannon, assistant professor of Bible, religion, and humanities, 1975-76; Clemson University, Clemson, SC, assistant professor, 1976-80, associate professor, 1980-85, professor of religion, 1985-94, professor of history, 1985-88, acting head of department, 1988-89, director of Program in Philosophy and Religion, 1987-88; University of Tennessee at Chattanooga, LeRoy A. Martin Distinguished Professor of Religious Studies, 1994—. University of North Carolina at Chapel Hill, visiting scholar, 1984; Emory University, visiting professor, 1990-91, visiting research scholar, 2000-01; Lutheran Theological Southern Seminary, member of advisory council of Center for Religion in the South, 1990-95. Southeastern Commission for the Study of Religion, member of executive board, 1988-92, chair, 1991-92. Clemson School of Continuing Education for Clergy, director, 1981-86; Clemson Congregations in Touch, president, 1986-87, member of executive committee, 1989-90, director of Lay Academy, 1990; AID Upstate, member of board of directors, 1988-90, 1991-94, president, 1989; Anderson-Pickens-Oconee AIDS Task Force, convener, 1990-94; Southeast Tennessee Ryan White AIDS Care Consortium, member, 1996—, vice chair, 2001—; Alpha Chi Rho Educational Foundation, member of board of trustees, 1987-2000.

MEMBER: American Academy of Religion (vice president of Southeastern Region, 1989-90; regional president, 1990-91), American Society of Church History, American Studies Association, Organization of American Historians, College Fraternity Editors Association (member of board of directors, 1981-87; vice president, 1984-85; president, 1985-86), South Carolina Academy of Religion (vice president, 1980-81; president, 1981-82), Chattanooga Regional Historical Association, Phi Beta Kappa, Omicron Delta Kappa, Pi Gamma Mu, Pi Delta Epsilon, Alpha Psi Omega, Phi Mu Alpha, Alpha Chi Rho (national editor, 1975-87; national chaplain, 1976-87; national vice president, 1985-87; national president, 1987-89), Clemson Faculty Forum Club (vice president, 1986-87; president, 1987-88, 1993-94), Clemson Bridge Club (president, 1980, 1988), Chattanooga Duplicate Bridge Club.

AWARDS, HONORS: Grants from National Endowment for the Humanities, 1975, 1978, 1983 and 1986; *A Bibliography of Religion in the South* was cited as an outstanding academic book of 1987 by *Choice;* Fulbright fellow in India, 1988; *Encyclopedia of the American Religious Experience* was cited as an outstanding reference work for 1988 by American Library Association; *Twentieth-Century Shapers of American Popular Religion* was named an outstanding academic book of 1989 by *Choice;* Louisville Institute Summer Stipend, 1998.

WRITINGS:

Seasonable Revolutionary: The Mind of Charles Chauncy, Nelson-Hall (Chicago, IL), 1981.

A Bibliography of Religion in the South, Mercer University Press (Macon, GA), 1985.

(Editor and contributor) *Religious Periodicals of the United States: Academic and Scholarly Journals,* Greenwood Press (Westport, CT), 1986.

(Editor, with Peter W. Williams, and contributor) *Encyclopedia of the American Religious Experience,* three volumes, Scribner (New York, NY), 1988.

(Editor and contributor) *Twentieth-Century Shapers of American Popular Religion,* Greenwood Press (Westport, CT), 1989.

The Christadelphians in North America, Edwin Mellen (Lewiston, NY), 1989.

(With Robert Choquette and Stafford Poole) *Christianity Comes to the Americas, 1492-1776,* Paragon House (New York, NY), 1992.

Religion in South Carolina, University of South Carolina Press (Columbia, SC), 1993.

(With Choquette and Poole) *Christianity Comes to the Americas,* Paragon House (New York, NY), 1993.

Being Religious, American Style: A History of Popular Religion in the United States, Greenwood Press (Westport, CT), 1994.

(Editor, with P. Mark Fackler) *Popular Religious Magazines of the United States,* Greenwood Press (Westport, CT), 1995.

Modern American Popular Religion, 1996.

(With Robert H. Krapohl) *The Evangelicals: A Historical, Thematic, and Biographical Guide,* Greenwood Press (Westport, CT), 1999.

Pluralism Comes of Age: American Religious Culture in the Twentieth Century, M. E. Sharpe (Armonk, NY), 2000.

Also author of *Popular Religion in Modern America: A Critical Assessment and Annotated Bibliography,* Greenwood Press (Westport, CT). Work represented in anthologies, including *The Apocalyptic Vision in America: Interdisciplinary Essays in Myth and Culture,* edited by Louis P. Zamora, Bowling Green University (Bowling Green, OH), 1982; and *Notes and Sketches from along the Susquehanna,* edited by John Goodell and John L. Topolewski, Academy Books (Rutland, VT), 1984. Contributor to periodicals, including *Magazine of History, Journal of Church and State, Eighteenth-Century Life, Theology Today, Religion in Life,* and *Journal of Popular Culture.*

SIDELIGHTS: Charles H. Lippy has won critical praise for his work on the history and contemporary status of religion in the United States. In *Being Religious, American Style,* he uses religious periodicals, novels, diaries, tracts, and other materials to illustrate how ordinary American people have approached religion, principally in the twentieth century. His focus is on private life rather than institutions and public worship. In *Modern American Popular Religion,* he provides an annotated bibliography of sources for the study of popular religion and modern religious life. Included are sections on evangelicalism and fundamentalism, media ministries, and the religious aspects of self-help and recovery programs.

With *The Evangelicals: A Historical, Thematic, and Biographical Guide,* Lippy and coauthor Robert H. Krapohl illuminate various aspects of American religious life by heightening awareness of the country's evangelical heritage. Pentecostalism, Revivalism, Charismatics, and Fundamentalism are all explored, with an analysis of the people, instructions, and culture of each.

Lippy demonstrates the enriching qualities of religious diversity in *Pluralism Comes of Age: American Religious Culture in the Twentieth Century.* With a historical account of American religious life in all its forms, he "displays the wide and wild diversity of American religious expression," declared Steve Young in a *Library Journal* review. While observing that more per-

sonal accounts would have been beneficial to the text, Young nevertheless deemed the book "useful as a general overview and guide to the literature of the field," and wished it were "twice as long." *Booklist* reviewer Steven Schroeder advised that *Pluralism Comes of Age* is "an accessible introduction to religious diversity in the U.S."

Lippy once told *CA:* "I hope my work has increased awareness of the subtle and delicate interaction of religion and other cultural forces."

BIOGRAPHICAL/CRITICAL SOURCES:

PERIODICALS

American Reference Books Annual, 1997, review of *Modern American Popular Religion,* p. 533.

American Studies International, October, 1996, review of *Encyclopedia of the American Religious Experience, Volumes 1-3,* p. 9.

Americas: A Quarterly Review of Inter-American Cultural History, July, 1993, review of *Christianity Comes to the Americas, 1492-1776,* p. 124.

Booklist, September 1, 1995, review of *Popular Religious Magazines of the United States,* p. 109; June 1, 2000, Steven Schroeder, review of *Pluralism Comes of Age: American Religious Culture in the Twentieth Century,* p. 1804.

Catholic Historical Review, July, 1998, review of *Being Religious, American Style: A History of Popular Religion in the United States,* p. 575.

Choice, March, 1995, review of *Being Religious, American Style,* p. 1140; September, 1996, review of *Modern American Popular Religion,* p. 102.

Church History, September, 1995, review of *Religion in South Carolina,* p. 529; review of *Being Religious, American Style,* p. 548; September, 1997, review of *Modern American Popular Religion,* p. 680.

Historian, winter, 1993, review of *Christianity Comes to the Americas, 1492-1776,* p. 394.

Interpretation: A Journal of Bible History, July, 1996, review of *Being Religious, American Style,* p. 333.

Journal of American History, March, 1993, review of *Christianity Comes to the Americas, 1492-1776,* p. 1573.

Journal of Popular Culture, fall, 1994, review of *Being Religious, American Style,* p. 223.

Journal of Southern History, February, 1995, review of *Religion in South Carolina,* p. 190.

Library Journal, August, 1994, review of *Being Religious, American Style,* p. 92; August, 2000, Steve Young, review of *Pluralism Comes of Age: American Religious Culture in the Twentieth Century,* p. 112.

Reference and Research Book News, June, 1996, review of *Modern American Popular Religion,* p. 5.

Religious Studies Review, January, 1997, review of *Christianity Comes to the Americas, 1492-1776,* p. 91, review of *Being Religious, American Style,* p. 93.

* * *

LLOYD, Craig 1940-

PERSONAL: Born February 13, 1940, in Port Chester, NY; son of John William (a college professor) and Ruth (Craig) Lloyd; married Caryl Ann Lefstad (a college teacher), April 2, 1966; children: John Craig. *Education:* Middlebury College, B.A. (cum laude), 1963; University of Iowa, M.A., 1964, Ph.D., 1970; also studied at London School of Economics and Political Science, 1960-61.

ADDRESSES: Home—1313 17th Ave., Columbus, GA 31901. *Office*—Department of History, Columbus College, Columbus, GA 31907.

CAREER: Columbus College, Columbus, GA, assistant professor of American history, 1971—. Assistant professor of history, University of Iowa, summers, 1971, 1974.

MEMBER: Organization of American Historians.

WRITINGS:

Aggressive Introvert: Herbert Hoover and Public Relations Management, 1912-1932, Ohio State University Press (Columbus, OH), 1973.

Eugene Bullard: Black Expatriate in Jazz-Age Paris, University of Georgia Press (Athens, GA), 2000.

WORK IN PROGRESS: Research on author David Henshaw.

SIDELIGHTS: Craig Lloyd told the story of the first African-American fighter pilot in *Eugene Bullard: Black Expatriate in Jazz-Age Paris.* Eugene Bullard was born in poverty-stricken Columbus, Georgia, near the end of the nineteenth century. Despite his family's humble circumstances, he was raised to believe that he was destined for a remarkable life, and so he was. When he was six years old, an angry lynch mob forced his family to flee Columbus. The next years saw him wandering from one southern state to the next until finally, at the age of nineteen, Bullard stowed away on a ship bound for Germany, hoping to reach France, the setting of many of his childhood dreams. He spent some time in Great Britain, where he worked as a boxer and a vaudevillian; when World War I broke out, he enlisted in the French Foreign Legion. His heroism in combat won him a Croix de Guerre, and he went on to become a fighter pilot. When the war concluded, he took up a glamourous life in Jazz Age Paris, where he owned a nightclub and performed as a jazz drummer. His friends included such luminaries as Josephine Baker and the Prince of Wales. He remained in France, whose citizens embraced him warmly; during World War II, his heroism continued as he worked for the underground resistance movement. A writer for *Kirkus Reviews* commented that so many famous people walk through the pages of *Eugene Bullard* that the real subject seems to be "something of an afterthought in his own biography," and complained that while Bullard's life was certainly noteworthy, "none of it comes through with any clarity or cogency in this effort." A more favorable assessment came from Dave Szatmary in *Library Journal,* who declared that Lloyd "provides a solid monograph for scholars that will serve as the definitive biography of a remarkable man in search of freedom."

Lloyd once told *CA:* "The most important American historians influencing my general views on American history have been dissenters from the traditional 'Whig history' approach to historical issues—men as diverse as William A. Williams, Richard Hofstadter, and Christopher Lasch."

BIOGRAPHICAL/CRITICAL SOURCES:

PERIODICALS

Booklist, August, 2000, Vernon Ford, review of *Eugene Bullard: Black Expatriot in Jazz-Age Paris,* p. 2106.

Kirkus Reviews, July 1, 2000, review of *Eugene Bullard: Black Expatriate in Jazz-Age Paris,* p. 939.

Library Journal, August, 2000, Dave Szatmary, review of *Eugene Bullard: Black Expatriate in Jazz-Age Paris,* p. 126.

Publishers Weekly, July 31, 2000, "August Publication," p. 89.*

LONGACRE, Edward G(eorge) 1946-

PERSONAL: Born December 22, 1946, in Camden, NJ; son of Edgar Thorp (a laboratory technician) and Evelyn (Weisser) Longacre. *Education:* La Salle College, B.A., 1969; University of Nebraska, M.A., 1974; Temple University, Ph.D. *Politics:* Independent. *Religion:* Roman Catholic. *Avocational interests:* Playing tennis and basketball, raising cocker spaniels.

ADDRESSES: Agent—c/o Combined Publishing Inc., 476 West Elm St., P.O. Box 307, Conshohocken, PA 19428.

CAREER: University of Nebraska, Lincoln, instructor in English and history of film, 1972-74; Temple University, Philadelphia, PA, teaching assistant in American military history, 1974-78; Headquarters Strategic Air Command, Offutt Air Force Base, NE, staff historian, 1980—.

WRITINGS:

From Union Stars to Top Hat: A Biography of the Extraordinary General James Harrison Wilson, Stackpole (Harrisburg, PA), 1972.
Mounted Raids of the Civil War, A. S. Barnes (San Diego, CA), 1975.
The Man behind the Guns: A Biography of General Henry Jackson Hunt, Chief of Artillery, Army of the Potomac, A. S. Barnes (San Diego, CA), 1977.
(Editor) *From Antietem to Fort Fisher: The Civil War Letters of Edward King Wightman, 1862-1865,* Fairleigh Dickinson University Press (East Brunswick, NJ), 1985.
The Cavalry at Gettysburg: A Tactical Account of Mounted Operations during the Civil War's Pivotal Campaign, June 9-July 14, 1863, University of Nebraska Press (Lincoln, NE), 1986.
To Gettysburg and Beyond: The Twelfth New Jersey Volunteer Infantry, II Corps, Army of the Potomac, 1862-1865, Longstreet House (Hightstown, NJ), 1988.
Jersey Cavaliers: A History of the First New Jersey Volunteer Cavalry, 1861-1865, Longstreet House (Highstown, NJ), 1992.
Mounted Raids of the Civil War, University of Nebraska Press (Lincoln, NE), 1994.
General John Buford, Combined Books (Conshohocken, PA), 1995.
Pickett, Leader of the Charge: A Biography of General George E. Pickett, C.S.A., White Mane (Shippensburg, PA), 1995.
Grant's Cavalryman: The Life and Wars of General James H. Wilson, Stackpole (Mechanicsburg, PA), 1996.
Army of Amateurs: General Benjamin F. Butler and the Army of the James, 1863-1865, Stackpole (Mechanicsburg, PA), 1997.
Custer and His Wolverines: The Michigan Cavalry Brigade, 1861-1865, Combined Publishing (Conshohocken, PA), 1997.
Joshua Chamberlain: The Soldier and the Man, Combined Publishing (Conshohocken, PA), 1999.
Lincoln's Cavalrymen: A History of the Mounted Forces of the Army of the Potomac, 1861-1865, Stackpole (Mechanicsburg, PA), 2000.
General William Dorsey Pender: A Military Biography, Stackpole (Mechanicsburg, PA), 2001.

Also editor of *The Historical Times Illustrated Encyclopedia of the Civil War,* 1986. Contributor to history journals and reference works.

WORK IN PROGRESS: The Early Morning of War: The Campaign of First Bull Run, June-July 1861; The First Victim: A Biography of General Irvin McDowell; Politician-General: A Biography of John A. McClernand of Illinois.

SIDELIGHTS: Edward G. Longacre once told *CA:* "As one who for several years worked exclusively in the novel and the short story, and only fairly recently as a professional historian, I maintain interests in both fiction and nonfiction writing. In my career field I divide my time and attention between popular and scholarly history. Therefore I'm aware of the desirability of rendering historical data as accurately as possible and in detail sufficient to facilitate appreciation of its complex nature, while also infusing it with the color, drama and immediacy of quality fiction. This will heighten the interest of the reader as well as add to his store of facts; only in this manner can history be brought alive.

"Within my quarter of historiography, my major interest is to uncover previously unpublished first-person sources of inherent documentary value. It is by studying the unvarnished personal records of participants in various epochs—the letters or the diary, for instance, of a Civil War soldier or of his family at home—that one best appreciates the interests, motivations, aspirations, hopes and phobias of those who made history. The historian's challenge is to present these revelations in a context that heightens both our perception of the contemporary setting and our appreciation of the continuity of human experience."

Since 1985, Longacre has been occupied writing histories of various aspects of the American Civil War—books as varied as biographies of well-known generals to chronicles of specific regiments. A *Publishers Weekly* reviewer noted that Longacre is "well known in Civil War circles," and that is not surprising, given the breadth of his knowledge of that conflict and its soldiers. In *Booklist,* Roland Green commended Longacre for books that provide "abundant scholarly direction for those who wish to pursue further study."

One of Longacre's better known books is *Pickett, Leader of the Charge: A Biography of General George E. Pickett, C.S.A.* The work is the first comprehensive biography of the ill-fated George Pickett in more than a quarter of a century. Green, once again writing in *Booklist,* found Longacre's writing "impeccable" and his research completed with "a thoroughness that will stand the test of time." A *Publishers Weekly* correspondent likewise deemed the work "a useful addition to the literature on Confederate command in the Civil War."

Lincoln's Cavalrymen: A History of the Mounted Forces of the Army of the Potomac is the first volume of a projected two-volume survey of cavalry in the Civil War. The first installment charts the evolution of Union cavalry units, some of which were composed of ill-trained amateurs, into superb fighting forces by the end of the war. In the *Library Journal,* John Carver Edwards noted: "This exhaustively researched tome offers fascinating insights." A *Publishers Weekly* contributor also stated that Longacre "succeeds brilliantly in showing us a crucial, much-tested force."

In an online interview with the Military Book Club, Longacre said that he has five known Civil War ancestors, and four of them fought for the Confederacy. Nevertheless, he admitted that he favors the Union emotionally—though not to the point of bias in his work. "I'm Yankee born and bred," he said. "If I had to fight in the Civil War, there's no doubt which side I'd fight on. I would like to think that I would fight for emancipation as much as for the deliverance of the country."

BIOGRAPHICAL/CRITICAL SOURCES:

PERIODICALS

Booklist, February 15, 1996, Roland Green, review of *Pickett, Leader of the Charge: A Biography of General George E. Pickett, C.S.A.,* p. 986; August, 2000, Roland Green, review of *Lincoln's Cavalrymen: A History of the Mounted Forces of the Army of the Potomac,* p. 2106.

Journal of Southern History, February, 1997, William Garrett Piston, review of *Pickett, Leader of the Charge: A Biography of General George E. Pickett, C.S.A.,* p. 175; February, 1998, William M. Ferraro, review of *Grant's Cavalryman: The Life and Wars of General James H. Wilson,* p. 151.

Library Journal, August, 2000, John Carver Edwards, review of *Lincoln's Cavalrymen: A History of the Mounted Forces of the Army of the Potomac,* p. 126.

Publishers Weekly, July 17, 2000, review of *Lincoln's Cavalrymen: A History of the Mounted Forces of the Army of the Potomac,* p. 189.

OTHER

Military Book Club, http://www.militarybookclub.com/ (July, 1999), Philip White, interview with Longacre.*

*　　*　　*

LOVEMAN, Brian E(lliot) 1944-

PERSONAL: Born in 1944 in Los Angeles, CA; son of Bernard J. and Rosalie Loveman; married Sharon Ann Siem; children: Taryn, Mara, Carly, Ryan, Ben. *Education:* University of California, Berkeley, A.B., 1965; Indiana University, M.A., 1969, Ph.D., 1973.

ADDRESSES: Office—Department of Political Science, San Diego State University, San Diego, CA 92182. *E-mail*—loveman@mail.sdsu.edu.

CAREER: U.S. Peace Corps, Washington, DC, community development volunteer in southern Chile, 1965-67; San Diego State University, San Diego, CA, assistant professor, 1973-76, associate professor, 1976-79, professor of Latin American politics, 1979—, chairman of Latin American studies program and co-director of Latin American Studies Center, 1979-81. Visiting assistant professor at University of California, San Diego, summer, 1974. Solana Beach School Board, trustee, 1983-89, president of board of trustees, 1996. Conducted field research in Mexico, Central America, and Chile. Speaker at national seminars and meetings. Research consultant, U.S. Department of Agriculture's Economic Research Service and International Development Research Center, Indiana University at Bloomington.

MEMBER: Phi Beta Kappa, Phi Kappa Phi.

AWARDS, HONORS: Woodrow Wilson fellow, 1965, 1971-72.

WRITINGS:

El campesino chileno le escribe a su excelensia (title means "The Chilean Peasant Writes to His Excellency,"), Instituto de Capacitacion e Investigacion en Reforma Agraria, 1971.

El mito de la marginalidad: Participacion y represion del campesinado chileno (title means "The Myth of Marginality: Participation and Repression of the Chilean Peasantry"), Instituto de Capacitacion e Investigacion en Reforma Agraria, 1971.

Antecedentes para el estudio del movimiento campesino chileno: Pliegos de peticiones, huelgas y sindicatos agricolas, 1932-1966 (title means "Data for the Study of The Chilean Rural Labor Movement: Labor Petitions, Strikes, and Agricultural Unions"), two volumes, Instituto de Capacitacion e Investigacion en Reforma Agraria, 1971.

Struggle in the Countryside: Politics and Rural Labor in Chile, 1919-1973, Indiana University Press, 1976.

Struggle in the Countryside: A Documentary Supplement, International Development Research Center, Indiana University, 1976.

(Editor with Thomas M. Davies, Jr., and contributor) *The Politics of Antipolitics: The Military in Latin America,* University of Nebraska Press (Lincoln), 1978, third edition, 1997.

Chile: The Legacy of Hispanic Capitalism, Oxford University Press (New York, NY), 1979, third edition, 2001.

(Author of introduction and case studies with Thomas M. Davies, Jr.) *Che Guevara on Guerrilla Warfare,* University of Nebraska Press, 1985, third edition, Scholarly Resources (Wilmington, DE), 1997.

Organizaciones privadas para el desarrollo y cooperación internacional: Chile 1973-1990, EFDES (Santiago, Chile), 1990.

The Constitution of Tyranny: Regimes of Exception in Spanish America, University of Pittsburgh Press (Pittsburgh), 1993.

For la Patria: Politics and the Armed Forces in Latin America, Scholarly Resources, 1999.

(With Elizabeth Lira) *Las suaves cenizas del olvido: via chilena de reconciliation politica, 1814-1932,* LOM Ediciones (Santiago, Chile), 1999, second edition, 2000.

(With Elizabeth Lira) *Las ardientes cenizas del olvido, Vía chilena de reconciliación política, 1932-1994,* DIBAM-LOM (Santiago, Chile), 2000.

(With Elizabeth Lira) *Las acusaciones constitucionales en Chile. Una perspectiva histórica,* FLASCO-LOM (Santiago, Chile), 2000.

(Editor) Vicente Perez Rosales, *Times Gone By,* translated by John Polt, Oxford University Press (New York, NY), 2001.

Contributor to books, including *Chile: Politics and Society,* edited by Arturo Valenzuela and J. Samuel Valenzuela, Transaction Books, 1976; *Foreign Investment in U.S. Real Estate,* Economic Research Service, U.S. Department of Agriculture, 1976; *Political Participation in Latin America,* edited by John Booth and Mitchell Seligson, Volume 2, Holmes & Meier, 1979; *International Handbook of Industrial Relations,* edited by Albert Blum, Greenwood Press, 1981; *Research Guide to Andean History,* Duke University Press, 1981; and *Public Policy and Social Institutions,* edited by Harrell Rodgers, Jr., JAI Press, 1984. Contributor to *Handbook of Contemporary Development in World Industrial Relations* and *Andean Research Guide.* Contributor of about thirty articles and reviews to Latin American studies, public administration, journalism, political science, and history journals in the United States, Europe, and Latin America.

SIDELIGHTS: Brian E. Loveman has written extensively about Latin American guerrilla movements, the region's peaceful transition to democracy, and the institutional mechanisms that fostered the dictatorships of the past. Among his books are *Che Guevara on Guerrilla Warfare,* which he wrote with Thomas M. Davies, Jr., and which presents the communist revolutionary's theoretical perspective on the subject, *The Constitution of Tyranny: Regimes of Exception in Spanish America,* which examines the propensity for dictatorship in Latin America, and *For la Patria: Politics and the Armed Forces in Latin America,* a look at the role of the military in Latin American politics. His *Chile: The Legacy of Hispanic Capitalism* has been the most widely read history of Chile in English since its publication in 1976. The third edition brings the history to the end of 2000.

In *The Constitution of Tyranny* Loveman presents his case that Latin American societies have a pervasive mindset that justifies political repression. This mindset, based on the acceptance of military takeover whenever a civilian government fails, results in periodic dictatorship. "This is a powerful indictment," wrote Kenneth Maxwell in *Foreign Affairs,* "buttressed by comprehensive research and lucid presentation."

Loveman's *For la Patria: Politics and the Armed Forces in Latin America* argues that, even with the spread of democracy in the region, the armed forces of

Latin American countries still harbor a strong tradition of having a justifiable role in political life. This belief, Loveman claims, will eventually lead to conflict with the new democratic governments. J. A. Rhodes, reviewing the book for *Choice,* found that "Loveman makes a strong case" and presents a "clear analysis of the role of the military in Latin American public life."

BIOGRAPHICAL/CRITICAL SOURCES:

PERIODICALS

American Historical Review, February, 1986, Leon G. Campbell, review of *Che Guevara on Guerrilla Warfare,* p. 225.
Annals of the American Academy of Political and Social Science, May, 1995, Rosario Espinal, review of *The Constitution of Tyranny,* p. 194.
Choice, November, 1999, J. A. Rhodes, review of *For la Patria,* p. 613.
Foreign Affairs, September-October, 1994, Kenneth Maxwell, review of *The Constitution of Tyranny,* p. 159.

OTHER

Brian Loveman's Homepage, http://www.rohan.sdsu.edu/dept/polsciwb/loveman.html (June 21, 2001).

* * *

LOVESEY, Peter (Harmer) 1936-
(Peter Lear)

PERSONAL: Born September 10, 1936, in Whitton, Middlesex, England; son of Richard Lear (a bank official) and Amy (Strank) Lovesey; married Jacqueline Ruth Lewis, May 30, 1959; children: Kathleen Ruth, Philip Lear. *Education:* University of Reading, B.A. (honors), 1958.

ADDRESSES: Agent—Vanessa Holt Limited, 59 Crescent Road, Leigh-on-Sea, Essex SS9 2PF, England.

CAREER: Writer. Thurrock Technical College, Essex, England, senior lecturer, 1961-69; Hammersmith College for Further Education, London, head of general education department, 1969-75. *Military service:* Royal Air Force, 1958-61; served as education officer; became flying officer.

Peter Lovesey

AWARDS, HONORS: Macmillan/Panther First Crime Novel award, 1970, for *Wobble to Death;* Crime Writers' Association Silver Dagger Awards, 1977, 1995, 1996, and Gold Dagger Award, 1983, for *The False Inspector Dew;* Veuve Clicquot/Crime Writers Association Short Story Award, 1985; Grand Prix de Litterature Policiere, 1985; Prix du Roman d'Aventures, 1987; finalist for Best Novel award, Mystery Writers of America, 1988, for *Rough Cider,* and 1996, for *The Summons;* Ellery Queen Readers award, 1991; Anthony Award, 1991; Mystery Writers of America Golden Mysteries Short Story prize, 1995; Crime Writers' Association/Macallan Silver Dagger awards, 1995, for *The Summons,* and 1996, for *Bloodhounds;* Crime Writers' Association Cartier Diamond Dagger Award, 2000, for lifetime achievement.

WRITINGS:

CRIME NOVELS

The False Inspector Dew, Pantheon (New York, NY), 1982.
Keystone, Pantheon (New York, NY), 1983.

Rough Cider, Bodley Head (London, England), 1986, Mysterious Press (New York, NY), 1987.

Bertie and the Tinman, Mysterious Press (New York, NY), 1988.

The Black Cabinet: Stories Based on True Crimes, Carroll & Graf (New York, NY), 1989.

On the Edge, Mysterious Press (New York, NY), 1989.

Bertie and the Seven Bodies, Mysterious Press (New York, NY), 1990.

Bertie and the Crime of Passion, Little, Brown (Boston, MA), 1993.

The Reaper, Soho Press (New York, NY), 2001.

"SERGEANT CRIBB" MYSTERY SERIES

Wobble to Death, Dodd (New York, NY), 1970.

The Detective Wore Silk Drawers, Dodd (New York, NY), 1971.

Abracadaver, Dodd (New York, NY), 1972.

Mad Hatter's Holiday: A Novel of Murder in Victorian Brighton, Dodd (New York, NY), 1973.

Invitation to a Dynamite Party, Macmillan (London, England), 1974, published as *The Tick of Death,* Dodd (New York, NY), 1974.

A Case of Spirits, Dodd (New York, NY), 1975.

Swing, Swing Together, Dodd (New York, NY), 1976.

Waxwork, Pantheon (New York, NY), 1978.

"PETER DIAMOND" MYSTERY SERIES

The Summons, Mysterious Press (New York, NY), 1995.

Bloodhounds, Warner Books (New York, NY), 1996.

Upon a Dark Night, Mysterious Press (New York, NY), 1997.

The Vault, Soho Press (New York, NY), 2000.

The Last Detective, Doubleday (New York, NY), 1991.

Diamond Solitaire, Mysterious Press (New York, NY), 1992.

STORY COLLECTIONS

Butchers and Other Stories of Crime, Macmillan (London, England), 1985, Mysterious Press (New York, NY), 1987.

The Staring Man and Other Stories, Eurographica (Helsinki), 1989.

The Crime of Miss Oyster Brown and Other Stories, Little, Brown (London, England), 1994.

Do Not Exceed the Stated Dose (novellas and stories), Crippen Landru (Norfolk, VA), 1998.

NONFICTION

The Kings of Distance: A Study of Five Great Runners, Eyre & Spottiswoode (London, England), 1968, published as *Five Kings of Distance,* St. Martin's (New York, NY), 1981.

(With Tom McNab) *The Guide to British Track and Field Literature 1275-1968,* Athletics Arena (London, England), 1969.

The Official Centenary History of the Amateur Athletic Association, Guinness Superlatives (London, England), 1979.

OTHER

(Under pseudonym Peter Lear) *Goldengirl,* Cassell (London, England), 1977, Doubleday (New York, NY), 1978.

(Under pseudonym Peter Lear) *Spider Girl,* Viking (New York, NY), 1980.

(Under pseudonym Peter Lear) *The Secret of Spandau,* M. Joseph (London, England), 1986.

Contributor to over 80 anthologies, including *Winter's Crimes 5,* edited by Virginia Whitaker, St. Martin's (New York, NY), 1973; *Murder Ink: The Mystery Reader's Companion,* edited by Dilys Winn, Workman (New York, NY), 1977; *Winter's Crimes 10,* edited by Hilary Watson, St. Martin's (New York, NY), 1978; *Mystery Guild Anthology,* edited by John Waite, Constable (London, England), 1980; *Best Detective Stories of the Year 1981,* edited by Edward D. Hoch, Dutton (New York, NY), 1981; *Winter's Crimes 14,* edited by Watson, St. Martin's (New York, NY), 1982; *Top Crime,* edited by Josh Pachter, St. Martin's (New York, NY), 1983; *Winter's Crimes 15,* edited by George Hardinge, St. Martin's (New York, NY), 1983; *The Best of Winter's Crimes,* edited by Hardinge, St. Martin's (New York, NY), 1986; *John Creasey's Crime Collection, 1986,* edited by Harris, St. Martin's (New York, NY), 1986; *The Year's Best Mystery and Suspense Stories, 1986,* edited by Hoch, Walker (New York, NY), 1986; *The New Adventures of Sherlock Holmes,* edited by Martin H. Greenberg and Carol-Lynn Waugh, Carroll & Graf (New York, NY), 1987; *John Creasey's Crime Collection, 1988,* edited by Harris, St. Martin's (New York, NY), 1988; *Crime at Christmas: A Seasonal Box of Murderous Delights,* edited by Jack Adrian, Equation, 1988; *A Classic English Crime,* edited by Tim Heald, Pavilion (London, England), 1990; *One Hundred Great Detectives,* edited by Maxim Jakubowski, Xanadu (London, England), 1991; *Royal Crimes,* edited by Jakubowski and Greenberg, Signet (New York, NY), 1994; *Perfectly Criminal,* edited by Martin Edwards, Severn House (London, England), 1996; *Murder on Deck: Shipboard and Shoreline Mystery Stories,* edited by Rosemary Herbert, Oxford University Press (New York, NY), 1998; *Scenes of Crime,* edited by Edwards, Constable (London, England), 2000; and *Criminal Records,* edited by Otto Penzler, Orion (London, England), 2000.

Also author with wife, Jacqueline Ruth Lovesey, of "Sergeant Cribb" teleplays for Granada television and PBS's *Mystery!* program, including *The Last Trumpet, Murder, Old Boy? Something Old, Something New, The Horizontal Witness,* and *The Choir That Wouldn't Sing.* Contributor to periodicals, including *Armchair Detective, Ellery Queen's Mystery Magazine, Harper's,* and *Company.*

ADAPTATIONS: Peter Lovesey's *Goldengirl,* written under the pseudonym Peter Lear, was filmed by Avco Embassy Pictures Corp. in 1979. It starred James Coburn and Susan Anton; ten other Lovesey novels are under option for feature films.

SIDELIGHTS: When Peter Lovesey won the 2000 Crime Writers' Association Cartier Diamond Dagger Award, he became firmly established as one of the most respected and admired mystery writers working today. Other Diamond Dagger Award-winners include P. D. James, John le Carre, Dick Francis, and Ed McBain. Lovesey joined their ranks by virtue of his literate thrillers—some of them set in Victorian England. In a career spanning more than thirty years, Lovesey has written novels of detective fiction as well as thrillers, short story collections, and plays. He is best known for his "Sergeant Cribb" and "Peter Diamond" series, and his work jumps continents and decades, from the 1880s to the present. According to Josh Rubins in the *New York Times Book Review,* Lovesey "has continued to stretch his talents" while earning the title "reigning master of the historical crime novel."

All of Lovesey's fiction is remarkable for its vivid yet offbeat historical details—Ralph Spurrier, writing in the *St. James Guide to Crime & Mystery Writers,* noted that readers "revel in the author's obvious love for the etiquette, finery, and hypocrisy of the Victorian times." Lovesey portrays a clear understanding of the psychology of the societies he depicts. As James Hurt pointed out in the *Dictionary of Literary Biography,* "[Lovesey's] are modern novels about the past, not attempts to resuscitate past forms." More recently, the

author's Peter Diamond novels have proven that Lovesey is just as comfortable with the modern police procedural as he is with history-mysteries. In *Booklist,* Emily Melton called the writer "always appealing" and "one of the mystery genre's brightest and best." A *Kirkus Reviews* critic declared that Lovesey's novels contain "everything the cerebral puzzle-addict craves, from tempting red herrings to literary arcana to deliciously plotted surprises."

Lovesey's interest in sport led him to write his prize-winning first novel, *Wobble to Death.* He told Diana Cooper-Clark in the *Armchair Detective:* "At this time, I didn't regard myself as an authority or expert on the Victorian period. But I had become interested in Victorian sport as a school boy because I wasn't a very good athlete and would have liked to have been. I was flat-footed and butter-fingered and couldn't really perform very well in any team game, so I tried to take up the more individual sports, like high jumping." While researching the life of a Native American athlete, he found a description of the Victorian "wobble," a walking endurance contest. Later, while "perusing the personals columns of the [London] *Times* as Sherlock Holmes used to do," he stated, he discovered an advertisement for a crime novel contest. *Wobble to Death* was the result.

Wobble to Death is the first of a series of novels featuring Detective Sergeant Cribb and his assistant, Constable Thackeray. Critics have praised these books for their authentic evocation of Victorian atmosphere and restrained characterization. Lovesey explained to Cooper-Clark: "I was looking in *Wobble to Death* for a realistic Victorian detective. I was conscious that the great detectives were super figures, the omniscient Sherlock Holmes, the sophisticated Lord Peter Wimsey, and even Hercule Poirot, with the little grey cells. These were not really for me. I wanted somebody who would have to struggle to solve a crime and have to work against the limitations of the period."

Marcel Berlins of the London *Times* wrote: "Peter Lovesey has written eight [Sergeant Cribb] detective novels set in late Victorian times, and not one has fallen short on factual accuracy or ratiocinative skill. . . . Mr. Lovesey's strength is to place those subdued characters into a meticulously researched historical reality, and produce a supremely satisfying novel of detection." All eight novels featuring Cribb and Thackeray proved popular with the reading public. They were adapted and broadcast in America on PBS's *Mystery!* program, and Lovesey later collaborated with his wife Jacqueline to produce six new "Sergeant Cribb" stories for the series.

"For my own pleasure. . ." Lovesey said, "I vary the voices, forms, and styles of the novels, even within the series." He certainly has not limited himself to his Cribb tales. He has also published four collections of short stories, including *Do Not Exceed the Stated Dose,* a volume that contains both stories and short novels. Writing shorter fiction fulfills two goals for Lovesey: the sheer enjoyment of writing stories and, Lovesey said, "the opportunity to take risks and try new things that may be used later in novels."

Yet Lovesey keeps returning to the detective novel. He left the Victorian period for *The False Inspector Dew,* bringing his evocative talents to a 1920s transatlantic cruise. A reviewer for the London *Times* reported: "Lovesey has researched his setting not merely just enough to have plenty of local colour to push in when there's some excuse, but so thoroughly that he had at his fingertips a dozen facts to choose from at any instant." This, along with a gripping story line, the reviewer added, is part of "the charge that powers his book." Hurt further applauded the novel, declaring it to be "one of the best mysteries ever written, one that opens up new possibilities for the genre."

Lovesey continued to experiment with places and time periods. *Keystone,* a mystery set in Hollywood in 1915, appeared next. It involves the Keystone Cops and many other silent film actors, such as Fatty Arbuckle, Mabel Normand, and Mack Sennett. Hurt found in this novel "historically accurate" characterizations and "[f]ascinating technical details of early moviemaking," mixed with a deeper message: that Keystone comedy masks the violence of America about to embark on World War I. In *Rough Cider,* a novel of psychological suspense, and *On the Edge,* in which two ex-WAAF plotters turn into murderesses, Spurrier saw a "much tougher centre . . . than anything the author produced before." Of the latter novel, Spurrier noted, "The setting, style, and feel of the writing is richly authentic and the cliche 'page-turning' is perfectly apt."

Lovesey again returned to the Victorian era with his "Bertie" books. This time, the author features a rather unusual detective—Albert Edward, Prince of Wales, Queen Victoria's son and heir, who later became Edward VII of England. In the first book, *Bertie and the Tinman,* Bertie, as he is known to his intimates, tells the story of the apparent suicide of his favorite jockey, Fred Archer, popularly known as the Tinman. Doubting that Archer was suicidal, the Prince becomes suspicious and launches a personal investigation that takes him all over Victorian London, from the coarsest fleshpots to the

most elegant salons. "The rueful, candid voice [Lovesey] gives to the fleshy prince rings true," declared *Time* magazine contributor William A. Henry III, and "the details of the horse-racing and music-hall worlds are vivid, and much of the tale is sweetly funny." "This is an affectionate look at Prince Albert, a likable chap even with his pomposities and one-sided view of life," reported Newgate Callendar in the *New York Times Book Review.* "And the race-track scenes and backgrounds crackle with authenticity. There is a great deal of humor in the book, even a strong dash of P. G. Wodehouse. *Bertie and the Tinman* is a delightful romp."

Most recently, Lovesey has started yet another series, the Peter Diamond books, which have contemporary settings—generally in and around the city of Bath, England. *The Last Detective* introduces Diamond, a middle-aged, overweight, and cantankerous police inspector who, while not amiss to using computers and lab analysis to solve murders, nevertheless does his best work as an old-fashioned puzzle-solver. "Diamond is a believably flawed soul, sexist and impulsive, yet essentially good-hearted," observed a *Publishers Weekly* reviewer. Rubins felt that *The Last Detective* provided "a bravura performance from a veteran showman: slyly paced, marbled with surprise and, in the end, strangely affecting."

Subsequent Diamond novels have adhered to the formula of *The Last Detective.* Interestingly enough, Lovesey has not forgotten his interest in the past, as some Diamond plots include allusions to Jane Austen and Mary Shelley, while others involve suspicious antiques dealers, history professors, or bibliophiles. In *The Vault,* for instance, Diamond investigates the discovery of a partial skeleton, unearthed from a vault underneath the house in which Shelley wrote *Frankenstein.* A *Publishers Weekly* correspondent maintained that the plot of *The Vault* "crackles with wit and urbanity, snappy dialogue and deeper, fouler doings whispering from the wings."

Lovesey sees his movements through time as evidence of his having "evolved by stages." Recently Lovesey has experienced another evolution, from the written word and the page to the spoken word and the stage. In 1994, Lovesey, along with other British mystery writers Liza Cody and Michael Z. Lewin, toured eight American cities, performing a program filled with skits, dramatic readings, sound effects, and audience participation. Lovesey said in an *Armchair Detective* interview of the performance, "In this show we're still concerned with the craft of writing. There's a serious element even in something which appears to have entertainment value and laughter."

Lovesey and his critics recognize the great gift of this ability to entertain. Hurt credited Lovesey's development of "rich comic characterizations within a traditional puzzle framework" which "humaniz[es] a too often sterile form" as Lovesey's chief contribution to the genre of British mystery writing. Hurt continued: "At his best (and he is often at his best) Lovesey has brought a comic lightness to the mystery novel that has expanded its possibilities in new and unexpected ways." It is likely that Lovesey would agree with this analysis. "The aim of all my writing is to entertain and involve the reader," he said. "If successful, then I can be subversive, suggesting ironies, springing surprises, and now and then chilling the blood."

Lovesey once told *CA:* "My first published work was sports journalism, a long series of pieces, mostly unpaid, on the history of track and field. I chose to write on sports because I wanted to participate, however remotely. I had discovered early in life that I was not cut out to be an athlete; I was pathetically inept at every kind of sport. So I cornered the market in track and field history. One magazine gave me the by-line 'The World's Foremost Authority on the History of Athletics'; in fact, I was the world's *only* authority. But eventually I had enough material for a book. *The Kings of Distance* was published in England in 1968 (1981 in the U.S.).

"I was drawn to mystery writing by the lure of money. In 1969 Macmillan and Panther Books announced a first crime novel competition with a thousand pound first prize. I was then a teacher, earning a salary of less than this. Using a Victorian long distance race as the background, I wrote *Wobble to Death,* won the prize, and was launched as a writer of historical mysteries. Seven more followed, featuring the detectives Sergeant Cribb and Constable Thackeray. They were all adapted for the TV series 'Sergeant Cribb,' made by Granada, and seen in America in the *Mystery!* series on PBS. A further six episodes were scripted by my wife Jacqueline and me.

"I was reluctant to write only historical mysteries, so I tried a modern thriller, *Goldengirl,* under the pen name Peter Lear. This was about a gifted American woman athlete's exploitation by various individuals as she tries to win a unique triple at the Olympics. It was filmed by Avco Embassy, starring Susan Anton and James Coburn, directed by Joseph Sargent.

"I was encouraged to venture out of the Victorian period in my mystery writing, and wrote several one-off novels set in more recent times. In recent years I have tended to alternate between Victorian and contemporary settings. The Victorian series features Bertie, the Prince of Wales, writing his detective memoirs and revealing to perceptive readers more than he intends. The modern novels are about a police sleuth, Peter Diamond, embattled against forensic scientists and computer operators, and, amazingly, coming out the winner."

BIOGRAPHICAL/CRITICAL SOURCES:

BOOKS

Barnes, Melvin, *Murder in Print: A Guide to Two Centuries of Crime Fiction,* Barn Owl Books (Berkeley, CA), 1986.
Benstock, Bernard, editor, *Art in Crime Writing,* St. Martin's Press (New York, NY), 1983.
Burack, Sylvia K., *Writing Mystery and Crime Fiction,* The Writer (Cincinnati, OH), 1985.
Carr, John C., *The Craft of Crime: Conversations with Crime Writers,* Houghton (Boston, MA), 1983.
Cooper-Clark, Diana, *Designs of Darkness: Interviews with Detective Novelists,* Bowling Green State University Popular Press (Bowling Green, OH), 1983.
Dictionary of Literary Biography, Volume 87: *British Mystery and Thriller Writers since 1940,* Gale (Detroit, MI), 1989.
Dove, George N., and Earl F. Bargainner, *Cops and Constables: American and British Fictional Policemen,* Bowling Green State University Popular Press (Bowling Green, OH), 1986.
Keating, H. R. F., *Crime and Mystery: The One Hundred Best Books,* Carroll Graf (New York, NY), 1987.
St. James Guide to Crime Mystery Writers, fourth edition, St. James Press (Detroit, MI), 1996.

PERIODICALS

Armchair Detective, summer, 1981, interview with Peter Lovesey; summer, 1984, review of *Dr. Crippen and the Real Inspector Dew;* spring, 1995, Charles L. P. Silet, "Murder in Motion: An Interview with Liza Cody, Michael Z. Lewin, and Peter Lovesey"; winter, 1997, Kathryn Kennison, review of *Bloodhounds.*
Book & Magazine Collector, December, 1988, Martyn Goodger, "The Detective Novels of Peter Lovesey."

Booklist, September 1, 1991, Peter Robertson, review of *The Last Detective;* March, 1, 1998, Emily Melton, review of *Do Not Exceed the Stated Dose,* p. 1097; August, 2000, Connie Fletcher, review of *The Vault,* p. 2121.

Bookseller, February 14, 1997, "The Friendly Art of Murder."

Crime Time, summer, 2000, Adrian Muller, interview with Peter Lovesey.

Kirkus Reviews, April 1, 1993, review of *Diamond Solitaire,* p. 968; August 1, 2000, review of *The Vault,* p. 1078.

New Republic, March 3, 1982.

Newsweek, July 3, 1978; April 5, 1982.

New York Times, June 15, 1979; October 14, 1983, Anatole Broyard, review of *Keystone,* p. C29.

New York Times Book Review, October 25, 1970; October 15, 1972; February 15, 1976; May 28, 1978; October 3, 1982; March 12, 1989, p. 24; January 20, 1990, p. 35; October 20, 1991, Josh Rubins, "Who Slew Snoo?," p. 40; October 24, 1993, p. 28; January 8, 1995, p. 26; October 8, 1995, Carol Peace Robins, review of *The Summons,* p. 26; April 19, 1998, Marilyn Stasio, review of *Upon a Dark Night;* October 8, 2000, Marilyn Stasio, review of *The Vault,* p. 32.

Publishers Weekly, October 25, 1985; January 6, 1989, p. 92; February 9, 1998, review of *Upon a Dark Night,* p. 76; August 7, 2000, review of *The Vault,* p. 78.

Publishing News, May 26, 2000, Mike Ripley, "A Diamond Winner with Many Jewels to His Crown."

Saturday Review, October 28, 1972.

Spectator, March 28, 1970; April 10, 1982.

Time, April 17, 1978, review of *Waxwork.*

Times (London), March 1, 1980; March 18, 1982; December 31, 1987; October 17, 1991, Marcel Berlins, review of *The Last Detective;* June 24, 2000, Marcel Berlins, review of *The Reaper.*

Times Literary Supplement, April 9, 1970; June 25, 1982; September 20, 1991, Julian Symons, review of *The Last Detective;* February 5, 1999, Patricia Craig, review of *The Vault.*

Wall Street Journal, November 1, 1991, Tom Nolan, review of *The Last Detective;* May 18, 1998, Tom Nolan, review of *Upon a Dark Night.*

Washington Post Book World, September 17, 1972; May 16, 1982; March 20, 1988; October 20, 1992, Richard Lipez, review of *The Last Detective.*

OTHER

TW Books, http://www.twbooks.co.uk/ (April 17, 2000), interview with Lovesey.

LOY, Rosetta 1931-

PERSONAL: Born May 15, 1931, in Rome, Italy; daughter of Angelo (an engineer) and Evelina (Di Ginolamo) Provera; married Giuseppe Loy (in management), April 30, 1955; children: Anna, Benedetta, Margherita, Angelo. *Education:* Degree from Instituto dell' Assuntione, 1950. *Religion:* Catholic.

ADDRESSES: Home—Via di IV Peperino 1, 00188 Rome, Italy. *Agent*—Giovanna Cau, via M. Adelaide 8, Rome, Italy 00197.

CAREER: Writer. Also worked as a publicist, 1975—.

AWARDS, HONORS: Premio Viareggio, opera primo, 1974, for *La bicicletta;* Premio Viareggio, Premio Rapallo, and Campiello Prize, all 1988, and Premio Montalcino, 1990, for *Le strade di polvere.*

WRITINGS:

La bicicletta, Einaudi (Torino), 1974.
La porta dell'acqua, Einaudi (Torino), 1976.
L'estate di Letuque, Rizzoli (Milan), 1982.
All'insaputa della notte, Garzanti (Milan), 1984, second edition published with preface by Cesare Garboli, 1990.
Le strade di polvere, Einaudi (Torino), 1987, translation by William Weaver published as *The Dust Roads of Monferrato,* Knopf (New York, NY), 1991.
Sogni d'inverno, A. Mondadori (Milan), 1992.
Cioccolata da Hanselmann, Rizzoli (Milan), 1995.
La Parola Ebreo, Einaudi (Torino), 1997.
First Words: A Memoir, Metropolitan, 2000.

SIDELIGHTS: Italian novelist Rosetta Loy gained recognition in 1991 with *The Dust Roads of Monferrato,* the translated edition of her 1987 award-winning saga, *Le strade di polvere.* The book chronicles four generations of an Italian landowning family, following them to the brink of the modern age. Loy's novel is filled with the many births, deaths, good fortune, and catastrophes of an epic tale, played out through the lives of various family members. *The Dust Roads of Monferrato* begins in the late eighteenth century when the newly wealthy patriarch builds a grand house on his farmland. The novel then follows his descendants through various upheavals. The story concludes as the youngest daughter marries an industrialist and leaves the family estate behind. The multigenerational scope of the work and Loy's narrative skill were generally praised by reviewers. *Times Literary Supplement* critic Tim Parks, however, found fault with William Weaver's translation, declaring it "far less exhilarating than reading the original," but urging the reader to enjoy "the fine narrative that it is."

Loy related her own life story in *First Words: A Memoir.* Born in 1931, the author grew up in a comfortable world, the daughter of a prosperous Catholic family. She had friends, vacations at the seashore, and in every way lived an orderly, happy life. But her protected world began to crumble as the Nazis advanced through Europe. *First Words* covers the years between 1936 and 1943. During that time the family moved back and forth between German-occupied Rome and the countryside. Her father shut down his engineering business rather than collaborate with the Nazis; this was more than many in Loy's social circle did, for although most of her parents' peers were personally horrified by the Nazis' actions, they felt powerless to put up much resistance. From an adult perspective, Loy bitterly condemns Pope Pius XII, who issued no public statements against the Nazis. Some say his silence was meant to ward off even more persecution against priests, nuns, and Jews, but Loy accuses the former pontiff of lending support to Hitler and issues a "scathing denunciation" against him, in the words of a *Publishers Weekly* reviewer, who concluded that *First Words* is "a powerful act of atonement" for the guilt Loy still claims to feel on behalf of the Roman Catholic Church. "This memoir stands out as an intimate and honest record of the Italian Jews' deprivations and humiliations," declared George Cohen in *Booklist.* And a writer for *Kirkus Reviews* advised, "Though there is little in Loy's memoir that can't be found in a dozen other Holocaust autobiographies, the author's elegant and spare prose distinguishes her from the others."

BIOGRAPHICAL/CRITICAL SOURCES:

PERIODICALS

Booklist, July, 2000, George Cohen, review of *First Words: A Memoir,* p. 1996.
Kirkus Reviews, review of *First Words: A Memoir,* p. 876.
Publishers Weekly, June 12, 2000, review of *First Words: A Memoir,* p. 59.
Times Literary Supplement, November 9, 1990, p. 1215.
World Literature Today, autumn, 1993, review of *Sogni d'inverno,* p. 802; spring, 1996, review of *Cioccolata da Hanselmann,* p. 378.

LYONS, Nick 1932-

PERSONAL: Born June 5, 1932, in New York, NY; married Mari Blumenau (a painter), September 1, 1957; children: Paul, Charles, Jennifer, Anthony. *Education:* University of Pennsylvania, B.S., 1953; Bard College, graduate study, 1956-57; University of Michigan, M.A., 1959, Ph.D., 1963. *Avocational interests:* Angling, travel, literary criticism.

ADDRESSES: Home—342 West 84th St., New York, NY 10024.

CAREER: Hunter College of the City University of New York, New York, NY, faculty member, 1961-88, became professor of English; Crown Publishers, New York, NY, executive editor, 1964-74; Nick Lyons Books (now Lyons Press), New York, NY, founder and president, 1978-99. *Military service:* U.S. Army, 1953-54.

WRITINGS:

(Editor) *Jones Very: Selected Poems,* Rutgers University Press (New Brunswick, NJ), 1966.
(Editor) *Fisherman's Bounty,* Crown (New York, NY), 1970.
The Seasonable Angler: The Adventures and Misadventures of an Angling Addict, Funk & Wagnalls (New York, NY), 1970.
Fishing Widows, Crown (New York, NY), 1974.
The Sony Vision, Crown (New York, NY), 1976.
Bright Rivers, Lippincott (Philadelphia, PA), 1977.
Locked Jaws, Crown (New York, NY), 1979.
Trout River, conception and photographs by Larry Madison, Abrams (New York, NY), 1988.
Confessions of a Flyfishing Addict, Simon & Schuster (New York, NY), 1989.
Spring Creek, illustrated by wife, Mari Lyons, Atlantic Monthly Press (New York, NY), 1992.
A Flyfisher's World, illustrated by M. Lyons, Atlantic Monthly Press (New York, NY), 1996.
(Editor) *In Praise of Wild Trout,* illustrated by Alan James Robinson, Lyons Press (New York, NY), 1998.
(Compiler) *The Quotable Fisherman,* illustrated by Robinson, Lyons Press (New York, NY), 1998.
My Secret Fishing Life, illustrated by M. Lyons, Atlantic Monthly Press (New York, NY), 1999.
(Editor) Ernest Hemingway, *Hemingway on Fishing,* Lyons Press (New York, NY), 2000.
Full Creel: A Nick Lyons Reader, illustrated by M. Lyons, Atlantic Monthly Press (New York, NY), 2000.

Columnist, *Fly Fisherman.* Contributor of articles, stories, poems, and essays to magazines, including *Harper's, Yale Review, Field & Stream, Sports Afield, Outdoor Life, Playbill, Outside, Men's Journal,* and *Quarterly Review of Literature.*

SIDELIGHTS: "Within the pond of those who write about fly-fishing, [Nick] Lyons is one of the bigger fish," a *Publishers Weekly* critic observed in 1999. Indeed, Lyons has been a prolific writer and editor of books and magazine pieces about the sport for three decades. He also is a highly skilled one, in the opinion of numerous reviewers. *Spring Creek,* an account of trout fishing on a Western river (illustrated, like several of Lyons's books, by his wife, Mari), is "a luminous memoir of a month spent in fly-fishing paradise," remarked Jack Friedman in *People. Outdoor Life* contributor Craig Nova called *Spring Creek* "a memorable description of a body of water that makes you feel like you intimately know a river you've never seen."

That made *Spring Creek* "a hard act to follow," wrote Nova, but he had equal praise for the later *A Flyfisher's World,* which "delivers the same grace." This book, also illustrated with drawings by the author's wife, is a collection of essays chronicling Lyons's experiences tracking many types of fish in a diverse group of places, including Montana, the Florida Keys, France, and upstate New York. Christopher Lehmann-Haupt commented in the *New York Times* that the book's components form "the autobiography of a fisherman," and he was impressed with Lyons's ability to "tease a graceful essay out of the most commonplace fishing ritual: the ride to and from the stream ('In the Car'), the encounter with the local equipment shop ('Country Hardware Store'), the moment as a beginner you discover that a fish really can be fooled by an artificial fly ('Au Sable Apocalypse')." A *Publishers Weekly* reviewer dubbed Lyons's writing style "quiet and intimate" and the book "elegant." John Rowen, critiquing the book for *New York State Conservationist,* praised Lyons for "humorous and touching recollections" of fishing with many companions. Nova summed up *A Flyfisher's World* as "a kind of angling autobiography in which honesty, wisdom and lack of snobbery . . . get all mixed up with the joy of catching fish. And joy is the operative word here, since no one, as far as I can tell, likes to catch fish as much as Nick Lyons."

Subsequent collections include *My Secret Fishing Life* and *Full Creel: A Nick Lyons Reader.* The former, a

Publishers Weekly critic remarked, is Lyons's "most introspective book yet." Lyons, noting that his fellow academics failed to understand his love of fishing and desire to write about it, demonstrates here "how the various loves and obsessions of a life interlock," the critic explained. Rowen, writing in *Booklist,* described *My Secret Fishing Life* as an "engaging memoir." *Full Creel,* with many essays focusing on Lyons's family and fishing buddies, is, according to Rowen—again reviewing for *Booklist*—a skillfully assembled collection and "a fine testament to the career of one of our best outdoors writers." A *Publishers Weekly* commentator concluded of *Full Creel* that "Lyons has plenty to say and he says it with such humility, good humor and perspective that even non-anglers have good reason to fish here."

BIOGRAPHICAL/CRITICAL SOURCES:

PERIODICALS

Booklist, April 1, 1999, John Rowen, review of *My Secret Fishing Life,* p. 1377; August, 2000, John Rowen, review of *Full Creel,* p. 2097; September 1, 2000, John Rowen, review of *Hemingway on Fishing,* p. 50.
Library Journal, June 6, 1999, Will Hepfer, review of *My Secret Fishing Life,* p. 12.
New York State Conservationist, December, 1997, John Rowen, review of *A Flyfisher's World,* p. 30.
New York Times, September 22, 1976; January 16, 1977; December 16, 1977; November 14, 1979; June 24, 1996, Christopher Lehmann-Haupt, review of *A Flyfisher's World,* p. C16.
New York Times Book Review, June 6, 1999, Jeff MacGregor, review of "Fishing," p. 12.
Outdoor Life, July, 1996, Craig Nova, review of *A Flyfisher's World,* p. 20.
People, November 30, 1992, Jack Friedman, review of *Spring Creek,* p. 35; June 17, 1996, William Plummer, review of *A Flyfisher's World,* p. 34.
Publishers Weekly, January 16, 1987, p. 20; May 5, 1989, p. 74; October 12, 1992, review of *Spring Creek,* p. 63; April 8, 1996, review of *A Flyfisher's World,* p. 47; March 22, 1999, review of *My Secret Life Fishing,* p. 79; August 21, 2000, review of *Full Creel,* p. 58.
Saturday Evening Post, December 25, 1976.

M

MacLAINE, Shirley 1934-

PERSONAL: Born Shirley MacLean Beaty, April 24, 1934, in Richmond, VA; daughter of Ira O. (a real estate agent) and Kathlyn (MacLean) Beaty; married Steve Parker (a businessman), September 17, 1954 (divorced, 1977; one source says 1983); children: Stephanie Sachiko. *Education:* Attended high school in Washington, DC. *Politics:* Democrat.

ADDRESSES: Home—Los Angeles, CA, and New York, NY. *Office*—c/o Author Mail, Simon & Schuster/Pocket Books, 1230 Avenue of the Americas, New York, NY 10020.

CAREER: Chorus dancer and singer, 1950-53; stage actress in Broadway plays and revues, including *Me and Juliet,* 1953, *The Pajama Game,* 1954, *A Gypsy in My Soul,* 1976, and *Shirley MacLaine on Broadway,* 1984. Made screen debut in 1954; subsequent films include *Around the World in 80 Days, Some Came Running, Ask Any Girl, Can-Can, The Apartment, My Geisha, The Children's Hour, Two for the Seesaw, Irma la douce, What a Way to Go, Two Mules for Sister Sara, The Yellow Rolls-Royce, John Goldfarb Please Come Home, Sweet Charity, The Bliss of Mrs. Blossom, Desperate Characters, The Turning Point, Being There, Loving Couples, A Change of Seasons, Terms of Endearment, Cannonball Run II, Madame Sousatzka, Steel Magnolias,* and *Postcards from the Edge.* Starred in television series *Shirley's World,* 1971; also appeared in television productions of *Amelia, If They Could See Me Now, Gypsy in My Soul,* and in movie adaptation of her book *Out on a Limb.* Delegate to Democratic National Convention, 1968, 1972; member of platform committee, 1972, co-chairperson of McGovern-Shriver National Advisory Committee, 1972. Proprietor of "Higher Self" spiritual seminars, 1987.

Shirley MacLaine

AWARDS, HONORS: International Stardom Award, Hollywood Foreign Press Association, 1954; Academy Award nomination for best actress, American Academy of Motion Picture Arts and Sciences, 1958, for *Some*

Came Running, 1960, for *The Apartment,* 1963, for *Irma la douce,* and 1977, for *The Turning Point;* Foreign Press award for best actress, 1958, 1961, 1963, 1988; Silver Bear award for best actress, International Berlin Film Festival, 1959, for *Ask Any Girl,* and 1971, for *Desperate Characters;* best actress award from Venice Film Festival and British Film Academy, both 1960, both for *The Apartment,* and 1988, for *Madame Sousatzka;* Golden Globe Award, Foreign Press Association, 1964, for *Irma la douce,* and 1988, for *Madame Sousatzka;* best actress award, Italian Film Festival, 1964; Star of the Year Award from Theater Owners of America, 1967; recipient of Emmy awards from Academy of Television Arts and Sciences, including 1974, for *If They Could See Me Now;* named female musical star of the year from Las Vegas Entertainment Awards, 1976; Academy Award for best actress, American Academy of Motion Picture Arts and Sciences, 1984, for *Terms of Endearment.*

WRITINGS:

Don't Fall off the Mountain (autobiography), Norton (New York City), 1970.
(Editor) *McGovern: The Man and His Beliefs,* Norton, 1972.
(Editor and author of introduction) *The New Celebrity Cookbook,* Price, Stern (Los Angeles), 1973.
You Can Get There from Here (memoirs), Norton, 1975.
Out on a Limb (memoirs), Bantam (New York City), 1983.
Dancing in the Light (memoirs), Bantam, 1987.
It's All in the Playing (memoirs), Bantam, 1987.
Going Within: A Guide for Inner Transformation, Bantam, 1989.
Dance While You Can (memoirs), Bantam, 1991.
My Lucky Stars: A Hollywood Memoir, Bantam, 1995.
The Camino: A Journey of the Spirit, Pocket Books (New York City), 2000.

OTHER

Author of narration for *The Other Half of the Sky: A China Memoir,* a film documentary for Public Broadcasting Service, 1975. Also author of video *Shirley MacLaine's Inner Workout.*

SIDELIGHTS: An actress who has moved audiences to laughter and tears, an entertainer who has amazed fans with her seemingly nonstop energy, an author who has outraged critics with tales of New Age spiritualism—

Shirley MacLaine has worn so many hats that she is all but undefinable. Born Shirley MacLean Beaty in Richmond, Virginia (her younger brother would also alter his name and achieve fame as Warren Beatty), she knew early on that she was meant for the stage and screen, and in her youth she took ballet lessons and prepared for her debut. Her first opportunity came in 1950 when, while still in high school, MacLaine won a place in the chorus of a revival of *Oklahoma!* A variety of stage work followed. The 1954 Broadway musical *The Pajama Game* introduced MacLaine to the public in the manner from which legends are made. When the second lead, Carol Haney, broke her ankle, MacLaine, a nineteen-year-old chorus girl and Haney's understudy, went on in her place and was declared an overnight sensation. A Hollywood producer was in the *Pajama Game* audience one night and immediately signed MacLaine for her first movie role, in the Alfred Hitchcock black comedy *The Trouble with Harry.* In a raft of subsequent film roles, MacLaine has played a wide range of characters—a princess in *Around the World in 80 Days,* a prostitute in *Irma la douce,* a nun in *Two Mules for Sister Sara,* a naive dance-hall girl in *Sweet Charity.* To some critics, MacLaine's best acting in the earlier years came in her role as a frustrated urban wife in a little-seen film called *Desperate Characters.*

As she was establishing her career on the screen, MacLaine also took time to pursue her political interests. MacLaine "frolicked at the fringe of President Kennedy's Camelot," related William A. Henry III in a *Time* cover story on the actress. "Then the civil rights movement confronted the racism that she remembered from her Southern girlhood, and she shipped off to Issaquena County, Mississippi, to stay with black families, facing insults and threats on the street. She joined in the Viet Nam War protest, and noisily campaigned for Robert Kennedy in 1968, and, full time for 18 months, for George McGovern four years later."

After a relatively long absence from the big screen, MacLaine reemerged in films in 1977 as an ex-ballet dancer fighting her old rival for the soul of her daughter in *The Turning Point.* MacLaine earned her fourth Academy Award nomination for that role, but the Oscar would again elude her. MacLaine followed *The Turning Point* with the critically acclaimed satire *Being There.* Then there was another lengthy absence from the screen ("Every four years or so, I find a script," she told *Parade* magazine's James Brady in 1988), until, in 1983, MacLaine signed on to play the lead in James Brooks's film of the Larry McMurtry novel *Terms of Endearment.*

As Aurora Greenway, described by the actress as "an impossible, demanding, smothering, self-indulgent woman who made me laugh a lot," MacLaine shared scenes with Jack Nicholson and Debra Winger in this contemporary tear-jerker. MacLaine received raves for her portrayal of one woman's life of heartbreak and humor. "To many people the character was unsympathetic—monstrous or, worse, ridiculous," noted Henry. "[Winger's] cancer-ridden daughter . . . would get most of the sympathy, and [Nicholson's] breezy, boozy ex-astronaut would get most of the laughs. Even more perilous for an actress past 40, Aurora had to age, painfully, gracelessly. Unlike stars who demand that the camera flatter them, the vibrant MacLaine made herself look ravaged, the neglected ruin of a beauty."

While *Terms of Endearment* was widely publicized for its quality and audience appeal, almost as much publicity resulted from the rumors of unrest on the set, particularly in the pairing of the outspoken MacLaine and the equally feisty Winger. Director Brooks attempted to dispell such gossip, telling *People* reporter Scot Haller that following one emotional scene, the two performers "didn't do 20 minutes on how wonderful each other was. It's easy to do dear-darling-hug-hug, but they weren't like that. They were real with each other." Both MacLaine and Winger were nominated for the Academy Award in the best actress category for *Terms of Endearment*. This time, MacLaine did take home the statuette.

The Oscar was just one triumph for MacLaine in 1984, though. That same year she opened on Broadway in a song-and-dance tour de force, garnered a *Time* cover story, and saw one of her books, *Out on a Limb*, reach the top of the bestseller lists. It was also the year MacLaine turned fifty, prompting her to tell Haller that she considers age just a number to ignore. "When I saw the invitations for my [birthday] party . . . I realized how dissociated I am from the meaning of time," she said. "To me, the moment is the only time there is now. The present." While MacLaine professes her loyalty to the present, many of her fans (and most of her critics) associate her with the past. To hear the actress tell it, she goes back far beyond the *Pajama Game* days. As MacLaine detailed to Henry in the *Time* story, she had spent past lives as "a former prostitute, my own daughter's daughter, and a male court jester who was beheaded by Louis XV of France."

Reincarnation, trance channeling, and other spiritual matters of the New Age sciences make up the bulk of MacLaine's successful nonfiction books. Autobiographical in nature, such works as *Don't Fall off the Mountain, You Can Get There from Here, Out on a Limb,*

Dancing in the Light, It's All in the Playing, and *Going Within: A Guide for Inner Transformation* have divided readers, who make these books hot properties, and critics, who almost unanimously dismiss MacLaine's claims as naive and unproven. In a *Playboy* interview, the actress/author explained to David Rensin that "you never really die. If you really read Martin Luther King's writing—and I went to his library in Atlanta and did, the handwritten stuff—you'd see he was quoting Thoreau, Gandhi. And I've read Gandhi and Sadat, and all they talk about is that they don't die. So their knowledge makes them fearless and makes them contribute in an altruistic way. That's real leadership."

She added she also believes "the world is in a transitional period. We're slowly gliding into a new dimension, actually vibrating on a higher frequency. . . . I've been checking out these things that have been happening to other people—for example, flashes of intense heat that bathed me in perspiration at the most incongruous moments in the middle of cold weather; a sense of clairvoyant imagery that turns out to be true the next day; ESP, knowing someone who just walked into a room somewhere is trying to reach you and you pick up the phone and call and he was." Those, said MacLaine, "are the little clues that you get along the way. Those who are not going with this harmonious flow of the body's subatomic structure vibrating to a higher frequency are getting sick. Dis-eased." Expounding on the realities of healing crystals, *deja vu,* and Eastern philosophy, MacLaine declared in a *People* interview with Frank Deford: "I don't believe in accidents anymore. I don't mean there's a grand design, with our lives all planned for us. But I've seen too many coincidences, and I'm sure that people who float in and out of our lives are there for reasons."

By 1987, after the string of bestseller books (one of which, *Out on a Limb,* was adapted into a television miniseries, supposedly on the advice of one of the souls trance-channeled through the author), MacLaine embarked on yet another career. She began a series of spiritual consciousness-raising seminars in which, according to Barbara Kantrowitz in a *Newsweek* story, "the message is always the same: tune into your higher self *or else.*" The "Higher Self" seminar Kantrowitz attended in Florida was "part cosmic pep rally, part seance-in-a-circus tent. Posted on bulletin boards outside the ballroom in Orlando were business cards of psychic counseling services, a brochure describing a cosmic Japanese barley diet and ads for healing crystals." At one point, "MacLaine told the group to climb into an imaginary crystal tank filled with a golden liquid. There, they were to 'blend' with their perfect soul mate."

MacLaine used her brand of motivation for her 1988 book *Going Within*. The volume covers meditation and visualization for the novice soul-seeker. As the book's publicist said in a *Publishers Weekly* article, "It's not just for New Age junkies, but for everyday people who want to reduce stress and understand the contrary forces around them. [MacLaine's] reaching for a much broader audience." *Newsweek* critic David Gates found *Going Within* amusing, if rather hard wading at times. "But the stories are worth the wade—especially the one about the man whose speciality is channeling famous artists. 'I am Toulouse,' he announces in a French accent. 'Toulouse-Lautrec?' MacLaine asks. 'But of course,' he says. (He doesn't actually speak French because simply doing accents 'doesn't tax the medium's energies as much as forcing through a foreign language.')"

MacLaine also has found an audience, and more respect from some reviewers, for books that detail her present life rather than her past lives and spiritual journeys. *Dance While You Can* explores MacLaine's relationships with her parents and her daughter, detailing among other things her mother's thwarted acting ambitions and her father's pride in her writing career. *My Lucky Stars: A Hollywood Memoir* offers plenty of backstage gossip, including MacLaine's revelation that the rumors about problems between her and Debra Winger on the set of *Terms of Endearment* were based on fact. MacLaine also discusses her love affairs with such stars as Robert Mitchum, Danny Kaye, and Yves Montand, and her friendship with Frank Sinatra and his hard-living, fun-loving "Rat Pack," a group that included Dean Martin, Sammy Davis Jr., and Peter Lawford. "The book's best portrait is of Mitchum, an elusive, evasive poetic soul trapped in a hard-drinking barroom brawler's body," commented L.S. Klepp in *Entertainment Weekly*, adding that MacLaine "also presents a sharp-focus picture of Frank Sinatra as the world's touchiest man." Writes MacLaine: "Frank was nice to me, but he muscled others," sometimes to the point of punching out walls—and people. *People* contributor Marjorie Rosen called *My Lucky Stars* "juicy" and filled with "robust, ribald stories." The book also led Rosen to remark, "Shirley MacLaine has been holding out on us. In best-sellers like *Out on a Limb* and *Dancing in the Light,* the New Age Scheherezade has spun improbable tales of her past lives. Turns out her current life can hold its own against anything she may have seen in ancient Atlantis."

MacLaine was back to past-life chronicles, while simultaneously describing a impressive present-life trek, in *The Camino: A Journey of the Spirit.* MacLaine, in her sixties, walked the 500-mile Santiago do Compostela Camino, a route in Spain that has attracted pilgrims since the Middle Ages. There are famous cathedrals all along the way, and the Camino is said to be a place of spiritual energy because of its position directly beneath the Milky Way. MacLaine's book deals in part with the actual physical trip: she walked ten hours a day, slept in dirty, cramped rooms, and encountered a variety of eccentric traveling companions. It also tells of past-life visions she had while on the Camino. One of her incarnations, she says, was a Gypsy woman who was the lover of Charlemagne; what's more, she claims that Charlemagne was reincarnated as Olof Palme, the Swedish prime minister who was assassinated in 1986 and who, MacLaine reveals, was her lover in this life. (In *Out on a Limb,* MacLaine had fictionalized her relationship with Palme, disguising him as a member of the British Parliament.) She also sees herself again in Atlantis, as an androgynous being splitting into man and woman. "In fact, she was Adam and Eve!" exclaimed *Booklist* critic Ilene Cooper, who allowed that "there is no doubt [MacLaine] believes in her own visions" and that she is "a capable writer." A *Publishers Weekly* reviewer asserted that *The Camino* "is a likely candidate for best-sellerdom as well as for ridicule in some quarters."

MacLaine, who said she began writing to fill down time on movie sets, told *Publishers Weekly* interviewer Bill Goldstein that "writing has sustained me. . . . I can't imagine living without some internal life like this, without the belief that we are tied to something bigger than we are." She also informed Goldstein that she has received support even from those who find her beliefs bizarre: "A lot of people might think this is nuts, what I've been writing, but they love the fact that I'm doing it." Just as she has not feared putting her beliefs in the public eye, she has not been deterred by advancing age. In the *Time* cover story, MacLaine averred, "Talent is sweat and knowing yourself, and I feel that mine is increasing with the years." To William A. Henry, the performer's core identity has changed over those same years, from actress, to spiritualist, to writer. MacLaine's style, he observed, "is chatty and at times endearingly naive; her theme is that of the wide-eyed innocent discovering the wonders of the world. She never sounds jaded." MacLaine offered her own description in James Brady's *Parade* interview. "An actor has many lives and many people within him. I *know* there are lots of people inside me." MacLaine concluded with the observation: "No one ever said I'm dull."

BIOGRAPHICAL/CRITICAL SOURCES:

BOOKS

MacLaine, Shirley, *Dance While You Can,* Bantam (New York City), 1991.

MacLaine, Shirley, *Dancing in the Light,* Bantam, 1986.

MacLaine, Shirley, *Don't Fall off the Mountain,* Norton (New York City), 1970.

MacLaine, Shirley, *It's All in the Playing,* Bantam, 1987.

MacLaine, Shirley, *My Lucky Stars: A Hollywood Memoir,* Bantam, 1995.

MacLaine, Shirley, *Out on a Limb,* Bantam, 1983.

Spada, James, *Shirley and Warren,* Collier (New York City), 1985.

PERIODICALS

Booklist, May 15, 1995, Ilene Cooper, review of *My Lucky Stars,* p. 1610; April 1, 2000, Ilene Cooper, review of *The Camino,* p. 1411.

Chicago Tribune, June 26, 1983; April 23, 1984; March 26, 1989.

Entertainment Weekly, May 12, 1995, L. S. Klepp, review of *My Lucky Stars,* p. 54.

Esquire, June, 1975; September, 1975.

Los Angeles Times, July 19, 1987; October 20, 1988.

Los Angeles Times Book Review, August 24, 1983.

Ms., December, 1985; July-August, 1987.

Newsweek, July 27, 1987; April 24, 1989.

New York Times, April 1, 1984.

New York Times Book Review, September 18, 1983.

Parade, December 18, 1988.

People, July 18, 1983; January 26, 1984; February 6, 1984; April 30, 1984; April 17, 1995, Marjorie Rosen, "Darts and Flowers," p. 117.

Playboy, September, 1984.

Publishers Weekly, March 18, 1983; February 3, 1989; August 8, 1991, Bill Goldstein, Write While You can," p. 12; April 17, 2000, review of *The Camino,* p. 61.

Time, March 7, 1977; May 14, 1984; October 14, 1985.

Washington Post, June 21, 1983.*

*   *   *

MARTY, Myron A. 1932-

PERSONAL: Born April 10, 1932, in West Point, NE; son of Emil A. (a teacher) and Louise (Wuerdemann) Marty; married Shirley Lee Plunk, July 31, 1954; children: Miriam Lee, Timothy David, Elizabeth Jane, Jason Charles. *Education:* Concordia Teachers College, B.S.Ed., 1954; Washington University, St. Louis, MO, M.A.Ed., 1960; St. Louis University, M.A., 1965; Ph.D., 1967. *Politics:* Democrat. *Religion:* Lutheran.

ADDRESSES: Home—2028 Elm Circle, West Des Moines, IA 50265. *Office*—Department of History, Drake University,2507 University Ave., Des Moines, IA, 50311-4505; fax 515-271-1870. *E-mail*—myron. marty@drake.edu.

CAREER: Elementary teacher in Fort Wayne, IN, 1954-57; teacher of history in secondary schools, St. Louis, MO, 1957-65; Florissant Valley Community College, St. Louis, assistant professor, 1966-69, associate professor, 1969-72, professor, 1972-80, David L. Underwood Lecturer, 1976, chair of Social Science Division, 1967-75; National Endowment for the Humanities, Division of Education Programs, Washington, DC, member of National Board of Consultants, 1977-80, deputy director, 1980-84, acting director, 1981-82; Drake University, Des Moines, IA, dean of College of Arts and Sciences, 1984-94, director of School of Fine Arts, 1986-94, Ann G. and Sigurd E. Anderson University Professor and professor of history, 1994—, Luther W. Stalnaker Lecturer, 1996. Washington University, St. Louis, summer instructor, 1968; University of Missouri at St. Louis, adjunct professor, 1976; Frank Lloyd Wright School of Architecture, visiting professional staff member, 1998—. Educational Testing Service, member of Committee of Examiners for the History-Social Sciences Exam of the College-Level Examination Program, 1967-76, chair, 1970-74; College Entrance Examination Board, member of American History Discipline Committee, 1974-76; U.S. Commission on Civil Rights, member of Missouri State Advisory Committee, 1974-79; North Central Association of Colleges and Schools, consultant/evaluator for Commission on Institutions of Higher Education, 1977-80, member of executive board, 1977-80, member of Centennial Planning Committee, 1991-95; National Commission on Social Studies in the Schools, member, 1986-90, member of executive committee, 1986-88. Presenter and panelist at professional meetings, including the Smithsonian Institution's Symposium on Frank Lloyd Wright, 1998, a Taliesin Conference in Pittsburgh, PA, 1997, and the annual meeting of the Frank Lloyd Wright Building Conservancy, 1999. Member of Frank Lloyd Wright Foundation and Lincoln Museum.

MEMBER: Organization of American Historians (member of executive board, 1985-88; member of Task Force on History in Community Colleges, 1994-97), Society for History Education, National Council for History Education, State Historical Society of Iowa, National Trust for Historic Preservation, Communal Studies Association, Federation of Intentional Community.

AWARDS, HONORS: University fellow, St. Louis University, 1965-66; fellow, National Endowment for the

Humanities, 1972-73; Newberry Library fellow, 1979; award from Community College Humanities Association, 1986, for contributions to the humanities.

WRITINGS:

Faiths in Conflict: Christianity and Communism, Concordia (St. Louis, MO), 1966.

Lutherans and Roman Catholicism: The Changing Conflict, 1917-1963, University of Notre Dame Press (Notre Dame, IN), 1968.

(With H. Theodore Finkelston) *Retracing Our Steps: Studies in Documents from the American Past,* two volumes, Canfield Press, 1972.

(Editor and contributor) *Responding to New Missions: New Directions for Community Colleges,* Jossey-Bass (San Francisco, CA), 1978.

(With David Kyvig) *Your Family History: A Handbook for Research and Writing,* Harlan Davidson (Arlington Heights, IL), 1978.

(With Kyvig) *Nearby History: Exploring the Past around You,* American Association for State and Local History (Nashville, TN), 1982, 2nd edition, AltaMira Press, 2000.

Daily Life in the United States, 1960-1990: Decades of Discord, Greenwood Press (Westport, CT), 1997.

(With Shirley Marty) *Frank Lloyd Wright's Taliesin Fellowship,* Truman State University Press, 1999.

Consulting editor for "Nearby History" series, American Association for State and Local History (Nashville, TN)/AltaMira Press, and "Exploring Community History" series. Contributor of articles and more than 300 reviews to magazines and newspapers, including *Christian Century, History Teacher, Social Studies, History News, Public Historian, Teaching History, AHA Newsletter, Community College Humanities Review, Social Education,* and *St. Louis Post Dispatch.*

*   *   *

MATHESON, Richard (Burton) 1926-
  (Logan Swanson)

PERSONAL: Born February 20, 1926, in Allendale, NJ; son of Bertolf (a tile floor installer) and Fanny (Mathieson) Matheson; married Ruth Ann Woodson, July 1, 1952; children: Richard, Alison, Christian, Bettina. *Education:* University of Missouri, B.A., 1949. *Avocational interests:* Musical composition, theater, amateur acting.

Richard Matheson

ADDRESSES: Home—Calabasas, CA. *Office*—P.O. Box 81, Woodland Hills, CA 91365. *Agent*—Don Congdon Associates, 156 Fifth Ave., Suite 625, New York, NY 10010.

CAREER: Television and film writer, novelist, short story writer, and playwright.

MEMBER: Writers Guild, Dramatists Guild.

AWARDS, HONORS: Hugo Award from World Science Fiction Convention, 1958, for best screenplay, *The Incredible Shrinking Man;* guest of honor at World Science Fiction Convention, 1958 and 1976; Writers Guild awards for television writing, 1960 and 1974; World Fantasy Award for best novel, 1976, for *Bid Time Return;* World Fantasy Life Achievement Award, 1984; Bram Stoker Award, 1990; "Grand Master" designation from World Horror Convention; Golden Spur Award from Western Writers of America for *Journal of the Gun Years.*

WRITINGS:

FANTASY NOVELS

I Am Legend, Fawcett (New York City), 1954, published as *The Omega Man: I Am Legend,* Berkley Publishing (New York City), 1971.

The Shrinking Man (also see below), Fawcett, 1956.

A Stir of Echoes, Lippincott (Philadelphia, PA), 1958.

Hell House (also see below), Viking (New York City), 1971.

Bid Time Return (also see below), Viking, 1975, published as *Somewhere in Time* (also see below), Ballantine (New York City), 1980.

What Dreams May Come (also see below), Putnam (New York City), 1978.

(Under pseudonym Logan Swanson) *Earthbound,* Playboy (New York City), 1982, revised edition published under name Richard Matheson, Tor, 1994.

(Editor with Martin Harry Greenberg and Charles G. Waugh) *The Twilight Zone: The Original Stories,* Avon (New York City), 1985.

Through Channels, Footsteps Press (Roundtop, NY), 1989.

Somewhere in Time [and] What Dreams May Come: Two Novels of Love and Fantasy, Dream/Press (Los Angeles, CA), 1991.

7 Steps to Midnight, Forge (New York City), 1993.

Now You See It . . . , Tor, 1995.

Also author of *I Am Legend, Book 2.*

OTHER NOVELS

Someone Is Bleeding (suspense), Lion Books, 1953.

Fury on Sunday, Lion Books, 1953.

Ride the Nightmare (suspense), Ballantine, 1959.

The Beardless Warriors, Little, Brown (Boston), 1960.

Journal of the Gun Years: Being Choice Selections from the Authentic Never-Before-Printed Diary of the Famous Gunfighter-Lawman Clay Halser! Whose Deeds of Daring Made His Name a By-Word of Terror in the Southwest between the Years of 1866 and 1876, M. Evans (New York City), 1991.

The Gunfight, M. Evans, 1993.

Shadow on the Sun, M. Evans, 1994.

The Memoirs of Wild Bill Hickock, Jove (New York City), 1995.

Passion Play, Cemetery Dance, 2000.

Hunger and Thirst, Gauntlet Press, 2000.

NONFICTION

The Path: Metaphysics for the '90s, Capra Press (Santa Barbara, CA), 1993, published as *The Path: A New Look at Reality,* Tor, 1999.

(Editor with Ricia Mainhardt) *Robert Bloch: Appreciations of the Master,* Tor, 1995.

Mediums Rare, Cemetery Dance, 2000.

SHORT-STORY COLLECTIONS

Born of Man and Woman: Tales of Science Fiction and Fantasy, Chamberlain Press (Philadelphia, PA), 1954, abridged edition published as *Third from the Sun,* Bantam, 1970.

The Shores of Space, Bantam, 1957.

Shock: Thirteen Tales to Thrill and Terrify, Dell (New York City), 1961, published as *Shock I,* Berkley Publishing, 1979.

Shock II, Dell, 1964.

Shock III, Dell, 1966.

Shock Waves, Dell, 1970.

By the Gun: Six from Richard Matheson, M. Evans, 1993.

SCREENPLAYS

The Incredible Shrinking Man (adapted from Matheson's novel *The Shrinking Man*), Universal, 1957.

(With Lewis Meltzer) *The Beat Generation,* Metro-Goldwyn-Mayer, 1959.

The House of Usher (adapted from Edgar Allan Poe's short story "The Fall of the House of Usher"), American International, 1960.

The Pit and the Pendulum (adapted from Poe's short story), American International, 1961.

Master of the World (adapted from Jules Verne's novels *Master of the World* and *Robur, the Conqueror*), American International, 1961.

Tales of Terror (adapted from Poe's short stories "Facts in the Case of M. Valdemar," "Morella," "The Black Cat," and "The Cask of Amontillado"), American International, 1962.

(With Charles Beaumont and George Baxt), *Burn, Witch, Burn* (adapted from Fritz Lieber's novel *Conjure Wife*), American International, 1962.

The Raven (adapted from Poe's poem), American International, 1963.

The Comedy of Terrors, American International, 1964.

Die! Die! My Darling! (adapted from Anne Blaisdell novel *Nightmare*), Columbia, 1965.

The Young Warriors (adapted from Matheson's novel *The Beardless Warriors*), Universal, 1967.

The Devil's Bride (adapted from Dennis Wheatley's novel *The Devil Rides Out*), Twentieth Century-Fox, 1968.

De Sade, American International, 1969.

Legend of Hell House (adapted from Matheson's novel *Hell House*), Twentieth Century-Fox, 1973.

Somewhere in Time (adapted from Matheson's novel *Bid Time Return*), Universal, 1980.

(With George Clayton Johnson and Josh Rogan) *Twilight Zone—The Movie* (includes "Kick the Can"; "It's a *Good* Life"; and "Nightmare at 20,000 Feet"), Warner Brothers, 1983.

(With Carl Gottlieb and Guerdon Trueblood) *Jaws 3D,* Universal, 1983.

(With son Richard Christian Matheson) *Loose Cannons,* 1990.

TELEPLAYS

Duel (adapted from Matheson's short story), ABC-TV, 1971.

Ghost Story, NBC-TV, 1972.

The Night Stalker, ABC-TV, 1972.

The Night Strangler, ABC-TV, 1973.

Dying Room Only, ABC-TV, 1973.

Scream of the Wolf, ABC-TV, 1973.

Dracula (adapted from Bram Stoker's novel), CBS-TV, 1974.

Trilogy of Terror, ABC-TV, 1974.

The Stranger Within, ABC-TV, 1974.

The Morning After, ABC-TV, 1974.

Dead of Night, ABC-TV, 1975.

The Strange Possession of Mrs. Oliver, NBC-TV, 1977.

The Martian Chronicles (mini-series; adapted from the novel by Ray Bradbury), NBC-TV, 1980.

Author of scripts for numerous television programs, including *Lawman, Twilight Zone, Star Trek, Night Gallery, Alfred Hitchcock Theater, Have Gun—Will Carry, Girl from U.N.C.L.E.,* and *Chrysler Playhouse.*

OTHER

Contributor of poems and short stories to newspapers and magazines, including *Brooklyn Eagle, Playboy, Blue Book, Galaxy,* and *Magazine of Fantasy and Science Fiction.*

ADAPTATIONS: I Am Legend was filmed as *The Last Man on Earth* in 1964 and as *The Omega Man* in 1971; *What Dreams May Come* was adapted into a film, screenplay adaptation by Ron Bass, directed by Vincent Ward, PolyGram Filmed Entertainment, 1998; *A Stir of Echoes* was adapted into a film directed by David Koepp, Artisan Entertainment, 1999.

SIDELIGHTS: Richard Matheson is a versatile writer with an affinity for horror, science fiction, fantasy, and suspense. One *New York Times* critic remarked that Matheson "rivals [Cornell] Woolrich as a portrayer of the noonday devil—the primal panic that lurks in the everyday and daylit." The suspenseful *A Stir of Echoes, Hell House, Duel,* and scripts for the original *Twilight Zone* television show bear out the critic's remarks. *The Shrinking Man* and *I Am Legend,* meanwhile, are evidence of Matheson's mastery of science fiction, and his novels *Bid Time Return* and *What Dreams May Come* show his flair for fantasy and even romance. "Perhaps no author living is as responsible for chilling a generation with tantalizing nightmare visions born of Golden Age television," declared Albert J. Parisi in the *New York Times Book Review.* Parisi added, "Most important, he has given to speculative fiction a raw nerve of introspective truth found in contemporary American literature."

One remarkable quality of Matheson's career is his ability to find terror in the most mundane aspects of life. He imbues ordinary objects with malice, finds evil spirits in old houses and summer cottages, and suggests that his characters' worst enemies are paranoia and loss of control. According to Stefan Dziemianowicz in the *St. James Guide to Horror, Ghost, and Gothic Writers,* the key to Matheson's fiction is a straightforward prose "devoid of the portentous descriptions many horror writers use to create atmosphere. The almost clinical quality of his writing actually adds gravity to his horrors by giving them a solid and seemingly irrefutable basis in reality, no matter how outlandish they seem at first." Dziemianowicz further noted, "To read the fiction of Richard Matheson is to enter a world in which the ordinary unexpectedly shows its dark side and the familiar objects of daily life suddenly develop teeth and claws."

Among Matheson's most famous novels is *I Am Legend,* which concerns the plight of the sole individual who has been spared a virus that transforms its victims into vampires. Each evening the hero is attacked by the bloodsuckers, who are determined to eliminate his presence from earth. He thwarts their efforts by hunting and killing the creatures while they lie dormant away from the fatal sunlight. *I Am Legend* has been filmed with Vincent Price as *The Last Man on Earth* and with Charlton Heston as *The Omega Man*. Matheson did not like either film adaptation, but he did like the "homage" to his concept that informs the classic horror film *Night of the Living Dead*.

Another early Matheson novel that found its way onto film is *The Shrinking Man*. The novel's hero, Scott Carey, finds himself shrinking inexplicably after passing through a strange cloud of gas. As he grows smaller and smaller, he leaves behind the familiar world and enters, at last, an atomic realm where even the building blocks of existence are to him as large as planets. In the *Dictionary of Literary Biography*, Roberta Sharp noted that Matheson's theme in this work bespeaks his interest in "the questions of man's place in the universe and man's fate after death." The filmed adaptation of the novel, *The Incredible Shrinking Man*, won Matheson a coveted Hugo Award for best science fiction film of 1958.

Matheson's novel *The Beardless Warriors* is similarly noted for its effective and compelling evocation of horror, but Matheson's intentions here are entirely realistic. Set during World War II, the story concerns a squad of raw, teenaged recruits engaged in a particularly bloody assault on a German town. William Wise of the *New York Times Book Review* commented, "If some of the author's descriptions of death and destruction are too strong for the squeamish, he can hardly be held to account. He has not invented infantry warfare—he has merely written about it in a plain, honest and compelling way." A critic for the *New York Herald Tribune Book Review* found the combat scenes "too much of a hell." Daniel Talbot in the *Saturday Review* found the book "well told, unpretentious, and continually absorbing." Talbot added, "Mr. Matheson writes his story simply and solidly, the dialogue is exact, the characters believable and pitiable, the circumstances chilling and horrible. Especially effective are Mr. Matheson's descriptions of combat."

Matheson's 1971 thriller, *Hell House*, combines the modern and gothic in a conventional ghost story. A mystic, a medium, and a physicist-parapsychologist are commissioned by a dying man to spend a week in a haunted house and search for proof of life after death. The house contains the spirit of a fiend "who can summon, generally speaking, innumerable mental and physical phenomena to aid in his complete destruction of anyone who dares to threaten his reign of horror," according to Benjamin Przekop in *Best Sellers*. *Hell House*

"is an artfully written piece of fiction," Przekop concluded, "totally absorbing in its progression, brutally compelling in its conclusion; a book well worth one long, scary night's reading, if just for the 'Hell' of it." *Hell House* was also adapted for a 1973 film entitled *Legend of Hell House*.

In his award-winning 1975 novel, *Bid Time Return*, Matheson creates a fantasy of love and time travel. Richard Collier, a thirty-six-year-old writer suffering from a brain tumor, falls in love with Elise, an actress who lived in the nineteenth century. To find her, he immerses himself in the history and ambience of the period and makes his rendezvous with Elise at San Diego's Hotel del Coronado. However, the reader cannot be certain that Collier actually wills himself into the past; the dying writer might only have been lost in delirium. "Whether it be teleportation or delirium, Richard Matheson fashions his hero's wanderings into a fine, atmospheric trip," wrote a critic for the *New York Times Book Review*. *Somewhere in Time*, the film version of the novel, featured Christopher Reeve and Jane Seymour. Speaking of the film version in *Entertainment Weekly*, Matheson said: "The critics lambasted it, but now everybody tells me, 'I love that film.' There's a fan club dedicated to it."

What Dreams May Come is another fantasy-love story, but it is centered this time around the idea of life after death. Chris Nielson, fatally injured in an auto accident, views his own death and funeral, tries to contact his grieving wife, and eventually adjusts himself to life in Paradise. His wife's suicide, though, could destroy his dream of their life together in the hereafter, and Nielson embarks on a Dantesque journey to rescue his wife from eternal damnation. Observed the critic for the *West Coast Review of Books*: "Author Matheson bases this novel on the studies by Elisabeth Kuebler-Ross and Raymond Moody regarding the human experience of death and the after-life and it's quite a trip what with astral shells, etheric doubles, concentric spheres of existence and all sorts of auras to pass through on the way to wonderful 'Summerland' where a glorified 'all mental' body disports itself free of all earthly encumbrances." The film version of *What Dreams May Come* featured Robin Williams and Annabella Sciorra.

Among Matheson's other horror novels is *Earthbound*, wherein a ghost assumes a physical presence by absorbing ectoplasm from her male lovers. The hero of the novel is a screenwriter who arrives with his wife to rekindle their marriage at the site of their honeymoon more than twenty years earlier. The screenwriter meets the ghost and enters into an exhausting, highly sexual relationship with her. After learning that his new lover is a ghost—essentially, a succubus—the hero is compelled to resist her before she consumes him. A *Kirkus Reviews* critic proclaimed *Earthbound* "chilling."

Matheson's equally bizarre short stories—amassed in various collections—include "Through Channels," in which a television provides a link to another dimension; and "The Doll That Does Everything," in which an apparent toy is revealed as a monster. Another of Matheson's accomplished horror writings is "Nightmare at 20,000 Feet," a famous episode from the *Twilight Zone* television program. Here, an airplane passenger becomes increasingly deranged as he comes to believe that a creature is dismantling the plane as it speeds through a storm. The television episode, with an especially memorable performance from William Shatner, was remade with an equally chilling performance by John Lithgow, in the 1983 film *Twilight Zone—The Movie.*

Matheson has also published suspense novels, including *Now You See It,* in which a magician paralyzed by stroke nonetheless falls into all manner of mayhem and murder involving family and friends. The magician, Emil Delacorte, finds that his son is targeted for death by the son's wife and his agent, who are conducting a love affair. A *Kirkus Review* critic noted that "the plot accelerates through a series of false-bottom murders." That same critic, while dismissing *Now You See It* as "a bizarre misfire," conceded that "the telling is sprightly." In *Booklist,* Dennis Winters acclaimed the novel as "a luminous tour de force of terror."

Matheson's teleplays have often concentrated on the eerie and unsettling. Notable among these writings is *Duel,* which he based on personal experience. As he told *CA,* "It happened the day President Kennedy was assassinated. I was playing golf with a friend of mine. We stopped playing and were driving back through this narrow canyon, both of us in a state of great anguish over what had happened. This truck driver tailgated us through the entire canyon. Partially we were terrified, and partially infuriated, turning our rage about the Kennedy assassination into rage at the truck driver. The story idea occurred to me and I jotted it down on the back of an envelope. I wrote the story seven years later and sold it to *Playboy;* then Universal bought it and I made a script out of it. That was one of the very few things in all the years I've been out here that I've really been totally satisfied with."

Duel, which marked the directorial debut of Steven Spielberg, features Dennis Weaver in a life-and-death struggle with the "noonday devil," represented here as a slow-moving oil tanker whose driver engages the hero in a deadly cat-and-mouse game. The suspense builds as the hero comes to understand the danger that confronts him as the rig seems to purposely stalk him across an arid, remote part of Southern California. The protagonist eventually comes to respond in kind to the trucker's dangerous maneuvers. In the ensuing duel, only one driver survives.

Matheson has been largely concerned with the occult and tales of fright in his film scripts. He was Hollywood's dean of Edgar Allan Poe adapters in the early 1960s with films such as *The House of Usher* and *The Raven,* though he told *CA* that his Poe scripts hardly fulfilled any profound desires. "*The House of Usher* was just a one-shot assignment that worked out so well they had me do others," he commented, adding, "I like Poe's poetry; I'm not crazy about his stories. And, really, except for *The House of Usher* and a few moments in *Tales of Terror,* an anthology-type film, it was hardly Edgar Allan Poe. Especially *The Raven*—all I had was the poem, so obviously I had to make up all of it out of my head. By then I was tired of Poe, so I made it a satire."

One lesser-known highlight of Matheson's career is his work as an author of Westerns. His story collection *By the Gun* gathers tales he wrote for magazines in the 1950s; a *Publishers Weekly* reviewer commended the work for its "spare prose and restrained use of action." *Gunfight,* a novel first published in 1993, explores how violence spirals out of control when an infatuated girl begins to spread rumors about a retired Texas Ranger. Another *Publishers Weekly* critic found this book to be "an absorbing parable about the terrible effects of gossip and the tragedy of a peaceable man driven to violence."

Matheson is one of four modern writers who have been honored with a "Grand Master" designation by the World Horror Convention. The other three are Anne Rice, Robert Bloch, and Stephen King. In fact, King has noted that Matheson is the author "who influenced me most as a writer." Reflecting on his life's work in the *New York Times Book Review,* Matheson stated, "I've been very fortunate throughout my career. And I've been lucky enough to have worked with some great and talented people. . . . I was just part of the whole phenomenon coming together. They were exciting times that bubbled over with energy for all those involved."

Matheson told *CA,* "The first book I ever borrowed from the library, when I was about seven years old, was called *Pinocchio in Africa,* which no one's ever heard of but me. I always was fascinated by fantasy, and, I suppose, horror, too. I did a good bit of that in my early years. I had stories and poems published in the *Brooklyn Eagle* when I was about eight years old. I've written a lot of poetry, but I haven't tried to do anything with it.

"I think it's pretty well established that the person who's going to make it as a writer is not hanging around writers asking them how to write. He's off by himself, writing. I've said many times that the perfect description of a writer is someone who cannot not write. The person who really has this compulsion doesn't care what people think. When you want to write, it doesn't matter what anyone tells you, you'll do it anyway. Even if everyone tells you you're terrible, that you have no talent whatever. I don't think there is any advice to be given to would-be writers, because once they're asking you for advice, they're already going in the wrong direction."

BIOGRAPHICAL/CRITICAL SOURCES:

BOOKS

Authors and Artists for Young Adults, Volume 31, Gale (Detroit), 2000.
Contemporary Literary Criticism, Volume 37, Gale, 1986.
Dictionary of Literary Biography, Gale, Volume 8: *Twentieth-Century American Science-Fiction Writers,* 1981, Volume 44: *American Screenwriters, Second Series,* Gale, 1986.
Rathbun, Mark, and Graeme Flanagan, *Richard Matheson—He Is Legend: An Illustrated Bio-Bibliography,* Rathbun (Chico, CA), 1984.
Science Fiction and Fantasy Literature: A Checklist (two volumes), Gale, 1979.
St. James Guide to Horror, Ghost, & Gothic Writers, St. James (Detroit), 1998, pp. 393-395.
Twentieth-Century Science-Fiction Writers, third edition, St. James, 1991, pp. 533-534.

PERIODICALS

Best Sellers, August 15, 1971, Benjamin Przekop, review of *Hell House.*
Booklist, February 15, 1995, Dennis Winters, review of *Now You See It . . . ,* p. 1060; October 15, 1995, p. 386.
Chicago Sunday Tribune, August 21, 1960.

Entertainment Weekly, May 20, 1994, pp. 49-50; October 23, 1998, "Grand Illusionist," p. 8.
Kirkus Reviews, June 1, 1994; December 1, 1994.
Library Journal, April 15, 1994, p. 116; June 15, 1994, p. 96.
Locus, February, 1995, p. 57.
New York Herald Tribune Book Review, September 4, 1960.
New York Times, March 2, 1958.
New York Times Book Review, August 28, 1960; August 29, 1971; March 30, 1975; April 10, 1994, Albert J. Parisi, "New Jersey Q&A: Richard Matheson; An Influential Writer Returns to Fantasy."
Publishers Weekly, March 15, 1993, review of *Gunfight,* p. 70; January 24, 1994, review of *By the Gun,* p. 51; April 25, 1994, p. 59; June 20, 1994, p. 95; December 12, 1994, review of *Now You See It . . .,* p. 49; July 31, 2000, review of *Mediums Rare,* p. 88.
Saturday Review, August 20, 1960, Daniel Talbot, review of *The Beardless Warriors.*
School Library Journal, June, 1994, p. 160.
Science Fiction Chronicle, February, 1995, p. 37.
Variety, November 17, 1971; May 16, 1994, p. 34.
Washington Post, August 19, 1971.
West Coast Review of Books, November, 1978, review of *What Dreams May Come.*
Wilson Library Bulletin, May, 1995, p. 36.

OTHER

Stir of Echoes, http://www.stirofechoes.com/ (October 19, 2000).
Tor Books Web site, http://www.tor.com/ (October 19, 2000).

*   *   *

McCANN, Colum 1965-

PERSONAL: Born 1965, in Ireland; raised in Deansgrange, South County Dublin, Ireland; married Allison Hawke, c. 1993. *Education:* Attended Clonkeen College; Dublin Institute of Technology Rathmines, degree in communications; graduate studies at University of Texas at Austin.

ADDRESSES: Agent—c/o Metropolitan Books/Henry Holt & Co., Inc., 115 West 18th St., New York, NY 10011.

Colum McCann

CAREER: Writer and freelance journalist. Worked for various newspapers, including the *Herald, Evening Press,* and *Connaught Telegraph* in Ireland, and with the United Press in New York City; *Evening Press,* youth correspondent, 1984-85; worked variously as a taxi driver in Cape Cod, MA, bartender, bicycle mechanic, volunteer for a program in rural Texas for troubled urban youths, and apartment manager. Toured America on a bicycle for two years.

AWARDS, HONORS: Hennessy/*Sunday Tribune* Awards, best first fiction and best new writer, 1991, for the short story "Tresses"; Rooney Prize for Irish Literature, 1994.

WRITINGS:

Fishing the Sloe-Black River (short stories), [England], c. 1993.
Songdogs (novel), Metropolitan Books (New York, NY), 1995.
This Side of Brightness (novel), Metropolitan Books (New York, NY), 1998.

Everything in This Country Must (stories), Holt (New York, NY), 2000.

Author of short story, "Tresses," published in the *Sunday Tribune.* Contributor to books, including *Ireland in Exile.* Contributor to periodicals, including *Observer* (London).

ADAPTATIONS: The stories "Fishing the Sloe-Black River," "Smoke," and "Blue in the Face" have been adapted for film.

SIDELIGHTS: Colum McCann is an Irish writer whose debut novel is *Songdogs,* a work *Times Literary Supplement* writer John Tague characterized as "an exciting book, because it vibrates with the energy of a new writer finding his voice." McCann's story takes place over a seven-day period when a young man, Conor Lyons, returns home to County Mayo, Ireland, to visit his father. Lyons has been away several years on an arduous trek with the ultimate goal of finding out what happened to his beautiful and mysterious mother, who disappeared when he was twelve.

In *Songdogs* McCann tells the story of Lyons' recent journey in flashback as the young man attempts to sort out and clean up the eccentric, unwashed and unhealthy life into which his father has sunk. The son's travels parallel the path that his father had once traversed decades before: the elder, Irish-born Lyons had been an itinerant photographer, whose adventures took him through the Spanish Civil War in the 1930s across the Atlantic to Mexico, where he met his wife, and finally to America in the 1950s. The author recreates this first journey in the text by recounting Conor's scrutiny of his father's archive of images. The key to his mother's disappearance lies in the Lyons' disintegrating marriage, some apparently risque photographs that scandalized the rural Irish community, and an incident of disturbing abasement. "It's a nice paradox that the novel's satisfying structure encloses stories of loss, compromise, and unsolved mystery," wrote Hermione Lee in the *New Yorker.*

Other critics responded equally favorably to *Songdogs,* and although *New York Times Book Review* contributor Scott Veale noted that "a first-novelish quality seeps in occasionally," he concluded that "for the most part Mr. McCann's hand is strong and sure. The halting interplay between father and son, in particular, is delicately portrayed." Reviewing what he termed "this hugely inventive debut" for the *Observer,* Tim Adams asserted that "if there is a fault in this book it is that of stasis, paragraphs develop images, then leave them hanging. But stasis is also *Songdogs*'s central metaphor." Lee concurred: "This comedy of torpidity is finely done. And, for all its sadnesses, *Songdogs* reads like a celebration."

"It's always a joy when a second novel lives up to the promise of a writer's debut," remarked a *Publishers Weekly* contributor in 1998, "but this outstanding follow-up to *Songdogs* is a triumph." The reviewer was referring to *This Side of Brightness,* a novel spanning four decades during the first half of the twentieth century. In 1916 New York City, a group of men known as "sandhogs" undertake the arduous and treacherous task of tunnelling underneath the East River to lay the groundwork for the city's fledgling subway system. The job brings together a mosaic of Polish, Irish, Italian, and African-American laborers, who establish strong bonds based on mutual respect: "There is democracy beneath the river," one character states. "In the darkness every man's blood runs the same color."

The story follows Nathan Walker, a black man transplanted from Georgia who joins the company. In the early pages of the book, Walker and three colleagues are caught up in tragedy when a blow-out occurs in the tunnel they are digging (McCann based this scene on an actual incident). While Walker survives, his Irish co-worker and friend, Con O'Leary, is killed. Walker takes it upon himself to look after O'Leary's young, pregnant widow. When the child, Eleanor, is born, the three characters stay in touch over the years—to the point where Walker marries Eleanor.

The legacy of Nathan and Eleanor's mixed-race marriage is one of both love and grief. As a *World of Hibernia* reviewer related, "Their son, Clarence, . . . is killed 'resisting arrest' after he himself killed both the man who ran over his mother in a car crash and a policeman who tried to apprehend him." Clarence's wife, Louisa, "slips into alcoholism and heroin addiction." Their son, Clarence Nathan, "in direct contrast to his grandfather," works the girders high above the city. He witnesses the death by train accident of his eighty-nine-year-old grandfather in the very tunnel Nathan Walker risked his life digging so many years earlier. "It is then that Clarence Nathan seeks refuge underground, becoming 'Treefrog.'"

To *Booklist* writer Bonnie Smothers, "it's not surprising to find [McCann] tackling the peculiar, unexplored and violent nexus" between the persecuted Irish and African-American populations. Likewise, the *BookPage* reviewer cited the author for addressing "the big issues of race, love and time with a literary majesty that completely befits the nature and scope of this family epic."

In 2000 McCann released *Everything in This Country Must,* two stories and a novella centered on "The Troubles" as experienced by three teenagers in modern-day Northern Ireland. The title story is told from the point of view of a fifteen-year-old Irish farm girl as she and her father try to rescue their draft horse, which is trapped in a flooded river. Their efforts prove in vain; and when British soldiers appear on the scene to help, it becomes clear that the father would rather lose the beloved horse than acknowledge the hated British. The girl then knows that the horse must die, "because everything in this country must." This story and the two others, declared Smothers in *Booklist,* "are beautifully, poetically written, but the suffering is so palpable that reading about these characters is painful."

"I think the idea of place is very important to language," McCann told Peter Costanzo for *Title Page.* Speaking of his work on *This Side of Brightness,* McCann continued: "The language in it is much more pared down than the language of, say, the West of Ireland. It's a different landscape, a stark world of light and dark, people living underground. And so the geography demands a different type of word use. Ultimately, though, it is a test of the imagination to match place, time, language and human stories together—to weave them into some proper tapestry."

BIOGRAPHICAL/CRITICAL SOURCES:

PERIODICALS

Booklist, March 1, 1998, Bonnie Smothers, review of *This Side of Brightness;* January 1, 1999, review of *This Side of Brightness,* p. 778; March 15, 2000, Bonnie Smothers, review of *Everything in This Country Must,* p. 1330; August 18, 2000.
Kirkus Reviews, February 15, 1998, review of *This Side of Brightness.*
Library Journal, August, 1995, p. 118; March 15, 1998, Barbara Hoffert, review of *This Side of Brightness,* p. 94; January, 2000, Brian Kenney, review of *Everything in This Country Must,* p. 161.
New Yorker, November 6, 1995, p. 174.
New York Times Book Review, November 5, 1995, p. 24; March 19, 2000, Charles Taylor, review of *Everything in This Country Must,* p. 15.

Observer, July 9, 1995, p. 15.

Publishers Weekly, August 7, 1995, p. 441; January 5, 1998, review of *This Side of Brightness,* p. 57; January 31, 2000, review of *Everything in This Country Must,* p. 80.

Times Literary Supplement, September 22, 1995, p. 23.

World of Hibernia, summer, 1998, review of *This Side of Brightness,* p. 175.

OTHER

BookPage, http://www.bookpage.com/ (August 18, 2000), review of *This Side of Brightness.*

Title Page, http://www.titlepage.com/ (August 18, 2000), Peter Costanzo, interview with Colum McCann.*

*   *   *

McCONNELL, Terrance C(allihan) 1948-

PERSONAL: Born December 19, 1948, in Zanesville, OH; son of Richard Lee (a potter) and Rosemary (a secretary; maiden name, Callihan) McConnell; married Marilyn Anne Lee (a pharmacist), June 13, 1970. *Education:* Wittenberg University, B.A. (summa cum laude), 1971; University of Minnesota, Ph.D., 1975. *Politics:* Democrat. *Avocational interests:* Running, reading.

ADDRESSES: Home—3603 Redfield Dr., Greensboro, NC 27410-2829. *Office*—Department of Philosophy, University of North Carolina at Greensboro, Greensboro, NC 27402-6170; fax 336-334-4720. *E-mail*—tcmcconn@uncg.edu.

CAREER: University of Minnesota—Twin Cities, Minneapolis, instructor in philosophy, 1974-75; Carleton College, Northfield, MN, visiting assistant professor of philosophy, 1975-76; University of North Carolina at Greensboro, assistant professor, 1976-80, associate professor, 1980-87, professor of philosophy, 1987—. St. Olaf College, assistant professor, 1975-76; Duke University, visiting associate professor, 1987. Moses Cone Health Care System, member of ethics committee, 1991—.

MEMBER: American Philosophical Association, American Society of Law, Medicine, and Ethics, American Society of Legal and Political Philosophy, Institute of Society, Ethics, and the Life Sciences, North Carolina Philosophical Society.

AWARDS, HONORS: Fellow of National Endowment for the Humanities, 1989-90 and 1995-96.

WRITINGS:

(Contributor) James B. Wilbur, editor, *The Life Sciences and Human Values: Proceedings of the Thirteenth Conference on Value Inquiry,* State University of New York College at Geneseo, 1979.

Moral Issues in Health Care, Wadsworth Publishing (Belmont, CA), 1982, 2nd edition published as *Moral Issues in Health Care: An Introduction to Medical Ethics,* 1997.

Gratitude, Temple University Press (Philadelphia, PA), 1993.

(Contributor) H. E. Mason, editor, *Moral Dilemmas and Moral Theory,* Oxford University Press (New York, NY), 1996.

Inalienable Rights: The Limits of Consent in Medicine and the Law, Oxford University Press (New York, NY), 2000.

Contributor of articles and reviews to philosophy and medical journals, including *Journal of Medical Ethics, Archives of Internal Medicine, Social Theory and Practice, History of Philosophy Quarterly,* and *Journal of Value Inquiry.* Guest editor, *Philosophical Studies,* 1986, and *Law and Philosophy,* 1995; member of editorial board, *Public Affairs Quarterly,* 1987-90.

WORK IN PROGRESS: Moral Freedom and Government by Consent.

SIDELIGHTS: Terrance C. McConnell once told *CA:* "My book, *Moral Issues in Health Care,* was written as a result of having taught a course in medical ethics for several years. Since the course was well received, I thought writing the book was a good idea. In the book I attempt to survey most of the major issues in medical ethics, explaining the various positions on the issues and the objections that have been advanced against them. Most of the time (though not always) my treatment of the issues is neutral rather than partisan."

BIOGRAPHICAL/CRITICAL SOURCES:

PERIODICALS

Australasian Journal of Philosophy, Volume LVI, number 1, 1977.

Canadian Journal of Philosophy, Volume IV, number 4, 1975; Volume VIII, number 2, 1978.
Ethics, Volume XCI, number 4, 1981.
Ratio, Volume XXII, number 1, 1980.

* * *

McDANIEL, Gerald G(reen) 1945-

PERSONAL: Born October 9, 1945, in Wichita Falls, TX; son of S. C. (a carpenter) and Inez (a homemaker; maiden name, Glasgow) McDaniel. *Education:* Midwestern University (now Midwestern State University), B.A., 1966, M.A., 1968; University of Texas at Austin, Ph.D., 1976. *Politics:* Liberal Democrat. *Religion:* Episcopalian.

ADDRESSES: Home—1410 Sunset, Abilene, TX 79605. *Office*—Department of English, McMurry College, South 14th and Sayles Blvd., Abilene, TX 79697.

CAREER: East Texas State University, Commerce, instructor in English, 1968-71; McMurry College, Abilene, TX, assistant professor, 1976-79, associate professor, 1979-85, professor of English, 1985—. *Greenville Herald-Banner,* wire editor, 1969-72. Texas Democratic Convention, delegate, 1982-86; Taylor County Historical Commission, member, 1983—.

MEMBER: Conference of College Teachers of English, South Central Modern Language Association, West Texas Historical Association, Sigma Tau Delta.

AWARDS, HONORS: Fellow of National Endowment for the Humanities, summer, 1983; Outstanding Faculty Award from McMurry College, 1985.

WRITINGS:

The Women and the Clouds (one-act play), first produced in Abilene, TX, at the Backdoor Theater, August, 1979.
Daughters of Zion (play), first produced in Denton, TX, at North Texas State University, April 21, 1985.
(With John L. Waltman) *Leigh Hunt: A Comprehensive Bibliography,* Garland Publishing (New York, NY), 1985.
Aindreas the Messenger (novel), VanMeter Publishing (Jeffersonville, IN), 2000.

Also author of *Soldier's Joy and Other Sad Songs* and *Phone Manners.* Work represented in anthologies, including *Texas Anthology,* Sam Houston State University Press (Huntsville, TX), 1979.

WORK IN PROGRESS: Additional volumes in a projected four-book series about the fictional Aindreas Rivers, the messenger.

SIDELIGHTS: "My writing falls generally into the regional literature genre," Gerald G. McDaniel once told *CA,* "although I think that it presents more than local color. The major literary figures who have influenced me most in my writing of fiction are William Faulkner, Flannery O'Connor, and Thomas Wolfe. My fiction always manifests a consciousness of the southern evangelical background and traditional southern music.

"My main intellectual interests, other than my doctoral specialization, nineteenth-century British literature, are Texas and southern history and culture, especially religious culture and traditional music. In 1983 I studied with Louis D. Rubin, Jr., at Chapel Hill and augmented my understanding of these areas.

"My travel experience outside the United States is very limited, although in the summer of 1979 I did tour France and Spain in the preparation of a multi-media presentation called 'In Search of the Lost Generation.' Within the United States my travel has been focused on battlefields of the American Civil War."

BIOGRAPHICAL/CRITICAL SOURCES:

PERIODICALS

Publishers Weekly, March 27, 2000, review of *Aindreas: The Messenger,* p. 51.*

* * *

McEACHIN, James 1930-

PERSONAL: Born May 20, 1930, in Pennert, NC.

ADDRESSES: Home—P.O. Box 5166, Sherman Oaks, CA, 91413. *E-mail*—mockinbrd@aol.com.

CAREER: Firefighter, policeman, music producer, actor, and writer. Appeared in television and feature films, including *Up Tight,* 1968; *The Undefeated,* 1969; *The Lawyer,* 1970; *Play Misty for Me,* 1971; *That Certain Summer,* 1972; *Short Walk to Daylight,* 1972; *The Judge and Jake Wyler,* 1972; *The Groundstar Conspiracy,* 1972; *Fuzz,* 1972; *Buck and the Preacher,* 1972; *The Alpha Caper,* 1973; *Christina,* 1974; *This Man Stands Alone,* 1979; *Honeyboy,* 1982; *Sudden Impact,* 1983; *2010,* 1984; *Perry Mason: The Case of the Notorious Nun,* 1986; *Diary of a Perfect Murder,* 1986; *Perry Mason: The Case of the Avenging Ace,* 1988; *Guess Who's Coming for Christmas?,* 1990; *Perry Mason: The Case of the Fatal Framing,* 1992; and *Perry Mason Mystery: The Case of the Jealous Jokester,* 1995. Has appeared in numerous television series, including *Hill Street Blues, Matlock, Diagnosis Murder, Dragnet, Emergency, Quincy, Six Million Dollar Man, Murder She Wrote, St. Elsewhere, I'll Fly Away, City of Angels,* and *All in the Family.* Played title role in the NBC series *Tenafly,* 1973-74. *First Monday,* CBS, cast as supreme court justice, 2001—. *Military service:* Served in the Korean war.

MEMBER: Academy of Motion Pictures Arts and Sciences.

AWARDS, HONORS: Benjamin Franklin Award, Publishers Marketing Association, 1998, for *Farewell to the Mockingbirds;* Distinguished Achievement Award, Morgan State University, 2001; honored by the Maryland House of Delegates, February 2, 2001, for "exemplary sacrifice and services in the defense of the United States of America and outstanding contributions in the performing arts and humanities."

WRITINGS:

NOVELS

Tell Me a Tale: A Novel of the Old South, Lyford Books, 1996.
Farewell to the Mockingbirds, Rharl Publishing Group (Encino, CA), 1997.
The Heroin Factor, Rharl Publishing Group (Encino, CA), 1999.
Say Goodnight to the Boys in Blue, Rharl Publishing Group (Encino, CA), 2000.
The Great Canis Lupus, Rharl Publishing Group (Encino, CA), 2001.

SIDELIGHTS: James McEachin has long worked as a film and television actor, playing more than two hundred roles over more than thirty years, including a recurring one as Lieutenant Brock in nearly twenty *Perry Mason* television movies in the 1980s and 1990s. He is currently featured as a supreme court justice in the new CBS drama, *First Monday.* But he has described himself as first and foremost a storyteller. After being severely wounded in the Korean war "dismissed his dream of a military career," as he once told *CA,* he left his home in New Jersey to recover in Los Angeles, where he began a new career as a music producer, actor, and writer. He said he seeks to bring "a wryness and laughter," plus details from his life experiences, to all of his work. He has written five novels, which range from a tale of post-Civil War Southern life to modern crime thrillers and often deal with racial issues.

McEachin summarized his first novel, *Tell Me a Tale: A Novel of the Old South,* for *CA* as "a trip back into the lives of a small community, Red Springs, North Carolina. Set in the years following the Civil War, it depicts an intimate portrayal of slavery, offering a picture of the innocence of a young boy with a spirit that triumphs over evil men who live small, petty and empty lives." Red Springs is an "unreconstructed" town, clinging to prewar traditions. The young boy, Moses, tells his story of abandonment by his white plantation-owning father, a disastrous fire at the plantation, and the good fortune to have his "Uncle Ben," a distinguished, well-thought-of man, as a beacon through life's tribulations. A writer for *Kirkus Reviews* called *Tell Me a Tale* "a subtle and richly textured first novel. . . . Clearly, McEachin is a man who can wear many hats: a sophisticated debut performance in print."

McEachin's second novel, *Farewell to the Mocking Birds,* is the story of the 24th Infantry Regiment (Colored), also called Company K, during World War I. As white troops were sent off to France, Company K was stationed near Houston, Texas, at a base known for its miserable conditions. A race riot broke out, largely led by Houston police, and many black soldiers were arrested, wounded, and even killed. In response to the riots, the company sergeant led the troops into Houston to rescue their imprisoned comrades. The subsequent court-martial and trial left more than one hundred black soldiers charged with capital crimes; many of them were executed. Reviewing *Farewell to the Mockingbirds* for *Publishers Weekly,* William D. Bushnell called it "a tragic commentary made even more compelling by his astute portrayal of the soldiers . . . and officers involved. He brings the fate of Company K hauntingly to life."

With *The Heroin Factor,* McEachin moved his setting to 1990s Los Angeles, where Wyatt McKnight, a police detective assigned to the narcotics squad, investigates the murder of another officer, Verneau LeCoultre. McKnight, who is black, had little use for LeCoultre, a racist who had a drinking problem and may have been addicted to drugs, as well, because a package of heroin is found with his body. The investigation takes McKnight and a visiting German police officer through many dangers and complications, leading them to a bizarre English aristocrat who cultivates poppies to make heroin. A *Publishers Weekly* reviewer called *The Heroin Factor* "offbeat but never off-kilter" and "not so much a mystery-thriller as an unusual, nearly unresolvable case history." *Booklist* contributor Vernon Ford found it "compelling" and applauded the "three-dimensional" portrayal of McKnight.

Say Goodnight to the Boys in Blue is another crime story, this time set in 1950 in the small, sleepy town of Elton Head, New Jersey, where most of the police officers are eccentric and dishonest. On a winter night, a bigoted white tavern keeper beats a black alcoholic to death. The police on the night shift let him go free, an action that disgusts the shift's lone uncorrupted cop, young, idealistic Danny Carlsson. Over the course of the night, Carlsson works to see that justice is served. The book has "McEachin's most original and strangest plot yet" and is "a delightfully loony and suspenseful story," stated a *Publishers Weekly* critic.

The Great Canis Lupis, in the tradition of Jack London's *Call of the Wild,* is a fantasy adventure exploring the life of a masterful wolf. The story, set from the 1800s to 1927, is told by a grandfather, who weaves a tale for his grandson about a black cowboy who finds himself in China and becomes embroiled in the lives of a group of old-timers who thing they are in Colorado.

BIOGRAPHICAL/CRITICAL SOURCES:

PERIODICALS

Booklist, June 1, 1999, Vernon Ford, review of *The Heroin Factor,* p. 1800; August, 2000, Vernon Ford, review of *Say Goodnight to the Boys in Blue,* p. 2114.

Kirkus Reviews, December 15, 1995, review of *Tell Me a Tale,* p. 1723.

Publishers Weekly, January 8, 1996, review of *Tell Me a Tale,* p. 59; April 14, 1997, p. 60; August 11, 1997, review of *Farewell to the Mockingbirds,* p. 385; June 21, 1999, review of *The Heroin Factor,* p. 157; August 21, 2000, review of *Say Goodnight to the Boys in Blue,* p. 50.

OTHER

James McEachin's Official Web site, http://www.jamesmceachin.com/ (July 17, 2001).*

*   *   *

McGRATH, Kristina 1950-

PERSONAL: Born March 16, 1950, in Pittsburgh, PA; daughter of William Daniel (a car salesperson and assembly worker) and Eva Ann (a retail sales manager; maiden name, Frombach) McGrath. *Ethnicity:* "White." *Education:* Chatham College, B.A., 1972; Columbia University, M.F.A., 1975. *Avocational interests:* Painting, drawing, sculpture.

ADDRESSES: Home—Louisville, KY. *Agent*—Malaga Baldi Literary Agency, 204 West 84th St., New York, NY 10024.

CAREER: Writer. University of Louisville, Louisville, KY, lecturer, 1996—. Sarabande Books, editorial associate, 1996—. Teacher, New York Poets in the Schools, 1973-84, and California Poets in the Schools, 1986-90.

AWARDS, HONORS: New York Foundation for the Arts, poetry grant, 1977, and fiction grant, 1982; Pushcart Press Prize, 1989, for novel excerpt from *House Work;* *Kenyon Review* Award, 1993, for novel excerpt, "Joshua's Visit"; Kentucky Arts Council professional assistance grants, 1993, 1995, and 1999; *House Work* was named a notable book of 1994 by the *New York Times;* Community Residency Award, National Writer's Voice Project, 1996; grant from Kentucky Foundation for Women, 1997.

WRITINGS:

House Work (novel), Bridge Works (Bridgehampton, NY), 1994.

Contributor to anthologies, including *Catholic Girls,* Penguin Books/New American Library (New York, NY), 1992; *Bless Me Father,* Penguin Books/New

American Library (New York, NY), 1994; *Love Stories for the Rest of Us,* Pushcart Press (Wainscott, NY), 1994; *Tasting Life Twice: Lesbian Fiction by New American Writers,* Avon (New York, NY), 1995; and *A Fine Excess: Contemporary Literature at Play,* Sarabande Books, 2001. Contributing editor, *The American Voice.*

WORK IN PROGRESS: Two novels, *A Scribbler's Life: Being a Faithful Account of Her Days as a Gentleman,* "a story of an eccentric nineteenth-century scribbler, a lyrical evocation of the Victorian age"; and *Last House on January Road,* "a story of an older lesbian in rural Kentucky."

SIDELIGHTS: Kristina McGrath began her writing career as a poet, "but since it was proving to be too restrictive for what I needed to say," she told a *Publishers Weekly* interviewer, "I started a novel." During the long period in which she wrote the novel *House Work,* she also drafted a second novel and wrote poetry, plays, short stories, and books for children. McGrath has received critical acclaim for her fiction, garnering both the 1989 Pushcart Press Prize and a 1993 award for literary excellence from the *Kenyon Review.*

Eventually, McGrath's agent sent the manuscript of her novel to a small press, and *House Work* saw print in 1994, sixteen years after its inception. *House Work* is set in Pittsburgh, Pennsylvania, during the 1950s, and is the story of a mother's heroism in raising her three children alone after the disintegration of her marriage. Defying the dictates of neighborhood priests, she leaves her husband, an alcoholic charmer, and re-establishes a home for herself and her children, at first by taking in ironing and cleaning other people's houses. *House Work* differs from many other novels in its lyricism and circular structure. "The 'house work' of the title," explained Kathleen Norris in the *New York Times Book Review,* "is both the labor of a dedicated 1950s wife and mother, for whom keeping 'a good house' is tantamount to keeping all of life in order, and also the work of a daughter, who uses domestic detail to reveal the family history."

Norris praised *House Work* as "a remarkable achievement" and "a novel bold in accomplishment, yet quiet in tone." The novel was selected by the *New York Times* as a notable book of the year in 1994. David Dodd in *Library Journal* asserted that the book is "startling in its beauty and challenging in its use of poetic language." A *Publishers Weekly* reviewer concluded that McGrath's "carefully wrought debut will linger in readers' minds."

Commenting on her approach to writing, McGrath once told *CA:* "Dramatic event is not paramount to me over language, or over character, voice, interiority. My delight is in language and what it witnesses of beauty, endurance, and joy in the human spirit and in the world of modest incidents."

BIOGRAPHICAL/CRITICAL SOURCES:

PERIODICALS

Library Journal, July, 1994, David Dodd, review of *House Work,* p. 128.
New York Times Book Review, September 25, 1994, Kathleen Norris, review of *House Work,* p. 28.
Publishers Weekly, June 27, 1994, p. 54; September 5, 1994, p. 40.

*   *   *

McKENZIE, John D. 1924-

PERSONAL: Born June 24, 1924, in Los Angeles, CA; son of Henry J. (a business executive) and F. Mildred (a homemaker) McKenzie; married Betty A. Heidbreder (a bookkeeper), September 12, 1947; children: John D., Jr., Anne McKenzie Nickolson. *Ethnicity:* "White Anglo." *Education:* Purdue University, B.S., 1948; University of Pennsylvania, M.B.A., 1950. *Politics:* Republican. *Religion:* Protestant. *Avocational interests:* Reading, photography, travel.

ADDRESSES: Home—332 South Paradise Rd., Golden, CO 80401; fax: 303-526-7877.

CAREER: International Minerals and Chemical Corp., Chicago, IL, director of administration, 1950-72; Industrial Minerals Ventures, Inc., Golden, CO, vice-president for research, development, and marketing, 1973-76; International Medical Corp., Englewood, CO, executive vice president, 1976-79; International Medical Education Corp., Englewood, CO, president, 1976-79; Marketing Communications, Inc., Denver, CO, co-owner and president, 1980-89; writer and independent consultant, 1989—. *Military service:* U.S. Army, 82nd Airborne Division's 456th Parachute Field Artillery Battalion, 1943-45; served in England before Normandy and through VE Day, then in occupation of Berlin; awarded four battle stars and one assault arrow.

MEMBER: National Writers Association, Rocky Mountain Direct Marketing Association, 82nd Airborne Division Association.

AWARDS, HONORS: On Time, On Target was a finalist for the Army History Foundation Book Award, 2000.

WRITINGS:

Uncertain Glory: Lee's Generalship Re-Examined, Hippocrene Books (New York, NY), 1997.
On Time, On Target: The World War II Memoir of a Paratrooper in the 82nd Airborne, Presidio Press (Novato, CA), 2000.

Contributor to periodicals, including *Civil War.*

WORK IN PROGRESS: A novel, *A Wound Unbound* (a search for the truth behind Lincoln's assassination), written with David B. Whitehead; *Little Soldier Man,* a novel about the Civil War exploits of General Philip H. Sheridan.

SIDELIGHTS: John D. McKenzie has written about military history from both a personal and a scholarly perspective. In *Uncertain Glory: Lee's Generalship Re-Examined,* he takes a look at the military career of Robert E. Lee, the Civil War general in charge of the Confederate forces. In *On Time, On Target: The World War II Memoir of a Paratrooper in the 82nd Airborne,* he relates his own experiences in some of the most crucial battles of World War II.

McKenzie's analysis of Robert E. Lee takes a controversial stance. Lee is considered by many to have been a military genius who, despite incredible odds, held off the Northern victory for many months. McKenzie believes that Lee was unable to envision a long-term strategy for the war, failed to adapt to new weaponry, created an inefficient chain of command, and wasted many lives with senseless attacks on Yankee forces. In McKenzie's view, Lee owes his reputation to the failings of certain incompetent Northern generals. Reviewing *Uncertain Glory* for *Library Journal,* Robert A. Curtis commented that it is perhaps too easy to criticize Lee's performance, more than one hundred years later and safe from the stressful conditions in which the general was operating. Curtis admitted, however, that McKenzie "presents his arguments forcefully and well." A reviewer for *Publishers Weekly* praised the "fresh perspective" McKenzie brings to his subject, and concluded that despite some factual errors, the author gives "new and serious insight into a thorny area of Civil War history."

In his personal memoir, *On Time, On Target,* McKenzie recalls his participation during World War II in military actions in Normandy, Holland, Belgium, Germany, and, after the war, occupied Berlin. His book reveals him as having been "a capable, sensitive, observant twenty-year-old," in the opinion of a *Publishers Weekly* writer, and it provides instructive and accurate characterizations of Allied and Axis supporters. McKenzie also reveals the lasting psychological traumas he sustained during his service, including depression, repressed memories, and survivor guilt. "Survivors and fans of the genre alike will appreciate [this book] for its candor and heart," concluded the *Publishers Weekly* reviewer.

McKenzie once told *CA:* "Unless one is extremely lucky, I am convinced that high monetary rewards are not likely to come from any artistic endeavor; this is not my motivation for writing. After forty years in business, in which I did much research and writing, I became convinced that I would enjoy it, and this has proved to be true. I am interested in searching for truth, informing others of original ideas, and leaving a legacy. It helps to have enough experience that both rejection and success are not strangers to me; it also helps to be secure enough that neither of these things overly affects me!

"My parents said I could do anything I wished, but insisted that, whatever I decided to do, I do it well. My father, who took me to Gettysburg in 1939, ignited my interest in the American Civil War. My book *Uncertain Glory* started there, when I questioned the foolishness of Pickett's Charge. It culminated nearly sixty years later, after more visits to Civil War sites and much research.

"After reading about five hundred books on the Civil War, I found I was comfortable with my general knowledge of that subject. In this process, I reached the conclusion that the southern historical and fictional literature that followed Lee's death in 1870 had built a false picture of him as an outstanding commander while, at the same time, denigrating those Union commanders who were superior to Lee in their quality as generals. I felt this was unfair and decided I would try to correct the situation. This was a difficult undertaking. My book is not an attack on Lee himself; it is an attempt to correct the revisions of history made by earlier historians."

Regarding *On Time, On Target*, McKenzie said: "I was a student when I enlisted and went to a paratroop jump school in England. I lost many friends in the eleven months from Normandy to V-E Day, but I was lucky myself. I had lots of near-disasters, including being captured by and escaping from the SS in the Battle of the Bulge, and interesting experiences, like being among the first to enter a re-captured concentration camp. My memoir covers a spectrum of terror, great sadness, sympathy, and lots of humor."

BIOGRAPHICAL/CRITICAL SOURCES:

PERIODICALS

Library Journal, January, 1997, Robert A. Curtis, review of *Uncertain Glory: Lee's Generalship Re-Examined,* p. 120.
Publishers Weekly, January 6, 1997, review of *Uncertain Glory,* p. 57; June 19, 2000, review of *On Time, On Target: The World War II Memoir of a Paratrooper in the 82nd Airborne,* p. 72.

*   *   *

McLEOD, James R(ichard) 1942-

PERSONAL: Born January 8, 1942, in Spokane, WA; married Ellen Gay Brockman, August 1, 1964 (divorced January 2, 1978); married Judith Osterberg Sylte, June, 1982; children: (first marriage) James Brock, Rory Richard; (second marriage; stepchildren) Anne Sylte Bloom, John Christian. *Ethnicity:* "Scot." *Education:* University of Washington, Seattle, B.A., 1966, doctoral study, 1969-70; Eastern Washington State College (now University), M.A., 1969.

ADDRESSES: Home—725 Snowberry Lane, Coupeville, WA 98239. *E-mail*—jrmcleod@nic.edu.

CAREER: Ryther Center for Emotionally Disturbed Children, Seattle, WA, psychiatric group worker, 1961-63; junior high school teacher of English and geography, Spokane, WA, 1966-69; elementary school teacher, Mukilteo, WA, 1969-70; North Idaho Junior College, Coeur d'Alene, instructor in English, 1970-2001, director of creative writing, 1971-82, director of Scottish studies, 1982-90. University of Idaho, visiting professor, 1971, 1974, 1980, and 1982-88; Lewis-Clark State College, visiting professor, 1989-90 and 1994. Co-

leader of adult study tours to Scotland, Greece, and Turkey, 1977-94; Isle of Raasay Heritage Foundation, member. Morningstar Boys' Ranch, counselor, summer, 1966. Coeur d'Alene Citizens Council for the Arts, president, 1971-72; Kootenai County Interagency Council, chair of youth committee, 1972-73. Idaho Writers League State Contest, poetry judge, 1972.

MEMBER: International Society of Cryptozoology, Community College Humanities Association, Associated Clan MacLeod Societies, Gallatin County Historical Society.

AWARDS, HONORS: Recognition award, Kootenai County Centennial Committee and North Idaho College, 1989-90.

WRITINGS:

Theodore Roethke: A Manuscript Checklist, Kent State University Press (Kent, OH), 1971.
Theodore Roethke: A Bibliography, Kent State University Press (Kent, OH), 1973.
Lake Pend Oreille and Its "Monster": Fact and Folklore, Wordcraft (Coeur d'Alene, ID), 1987.

Contributor to books, including *Bibliographic Guide to Midwestern Literature,* University of Iowa Press (Iowa City, IA), 1982; *Deep Down Things: An Anthology of Inland Northwest Poets,* Washington State University Press (Pullman, WA), 1990; and *District Tartans,* Shepherd Walwyn (London, England), 1992. Contributor to periodicals, including *Northwest Review, Mirror Northwest, Connections, Trestle Creek Review, Clan MacLeod, Piping Times,* and *Slackwater Review.*

WORK IN PROGRESS: Drowning with Brock, a collection of poems; *The Highbank MacLeods of Prince Edward Island,* a family history.

SIDELIGHTS: James R. McLeod told *CA:* "My father, an orphan whose Gaelic roots ran deep into the Western Isles of Scotland, and my Scotch-Irish mother, whose family were Kentucky moonshiners, brought me into the world shortly after Pearl Harbor. My mercurial temperament, swinging between depression and elation, probably comes out of this Celtic mix. In other words, writing is in the blood.

"My interest in writing began in high school when a poem I wrote for an assignment received lavish praise. I didn't take writing very seriously, though, until encountering Nelson Bentley at the University of Washington. His poetry course galvanized me, and through him I came to especially appreciate the work of the legendary poet/teacher Theodore Roethke, who had died the previous year. My newfound passion resulted in five years of Roethke research, culminating in the publication of my two-volume master's thesis. Heady with this early success, I began to envision a career devoted to scholarship and teaching.

"By the early 1970s I'd moved to Idaho and begun developing a writing program for North Idaho College. There I first came to know the exceptional Northwest poet/teacher Richard Hugo, who did a number of readings and workshops for our program and became a good friend and powerful mentor. After a long hiatus, I again began to write poetry. The stimulus of working with Dick and many other fine Northwest poets, as well as with students at the college and in the Poets in the Schools program, coupled with the emotional charge of intense personal changes I was going through at the time, sparked a five-year period of profuse poetic output.

"By the 1980s, though, I had begun to crave serenity as much as intensity. I increasingly questioned my wild life as a brooding poet, which sometimes seemed inextricable from loss, pain, and alcohol. My interests turned to Scotland, regional folklore, and family history, including the mystery of my own identity, as well as my teaching and other matters. I continued to write, with some success, but in these new areas—as I still do. In recent years, after another long hiatus, I've begun writing new poems and reworking old ones. These have appeared in regional publications, including the Inland Northwest anthology *Deep Down Things*.

"My poems have been tied to internal landscapes more than local ones. Many have focused on losses and broken relationships. Although I often use stark imagery, I'm a thinly disguised romantic.

"In retrospect, the fact that my interests have always been eclectic has not been conducive to a highly focused career, much less to fame or fortune. Balancing my writing with research, scholarship, and a heavy teaching load has been a challenge. If I have any advice for young writers who aspire to be poets of some stature, it is to be very careful about mixing teaching and writing, common though it may be. Though rewarding in many ways, it's a fiendishly difficult balancing act—unless one relishes a perpetually conflicted life. Often the result is that you become a second-rate teacher or a failed writer—or both.

"Yet, despite all this, I wouldn't likely go back and do it much differently."

BIOGRAPHICAL/CRITICAL SOURCES:

BOOKS

Hunter, James, *A Dance Called America: The Scottish Highlands, the United States, and Canada,* Mainstream Press (Edinburgh, Scotland), 1994.

Hunter, James, *Scottish Highlanders: A People and Their Places,* Mainstream Press (Edinburgh, Scotland), 1992.

Meurger, Michael, and Claude Gagnow, *Lake Monster Traditions: A Cross Cultural Analysis,* Fortean Times (London, England), 1988.

PERIODICALS

American Literature, March, 1972.
American Quarterly Review, March, 1972.
Anomalist, summer, 1997.
Fortean Times, winter, 1987.
Library Journal, December 15, 1971; September 1, 1973.
Reference Services Review, October-December, 1973.
Resources for American Literary Study, autumn, 1973.
Scotsman, February 16, 1991.

*   *   *

McMULLAN, Margaret 1960-

PERSONAL: Born February 19, 1960, in Newton, MS; daughter of James Michael (an investment banker) and Madeleine (a professor of history; maiden name, Engel de Janosi) McMullan; married Patrick O'Connor (a screenwriter), May 29, 1993; children: James O'Connor. *Education:* Grinnell College, B.A., 1982; attended Radcliffe College, 1982; University of Arkansas, M.F.A., 1989. *Politics:* "Mostly Democrat." *Religion:* "Mostly Roman Catholic."

ADDRESSES: Office—Department of English, University of Evansville, 1800 Lincoln Ave., Evansville, IN 47720. *Agent*—Jennie Dunham, Russell & Volkening, 50 West 29th St., Apt. 7E, New York, NY 10001.

CAREER: Botanical Gardens of the Chicago Horticultural Society, Glencoe, IL, gardener, summers, 1975-76; Jamaica Gardens, Libertyville, IL, horticulturalist, summer, 1977; Ravinia Green Country Club, lifeguard, summer, 1978; *Countryside Reminder News,* Barrington, IL, reporter, summers, 1979-81; *Glamour,* New York City, associate entertainment editor, 1982-85; University of Arkansas, Fayetteville, assistant professor of English, 1989-90; University of Evansville, Evansville, IN, assistant professor of English, 1990-96, associate professor of English, 1996—. Gives readings of her works.

MEMBER: PEN West, American Association of University Women, Society of Midland Authors, Authors Guild, Poets and Writers, Associated Writing Programs, Phi Kappa Phi.

AWARDS, HONORS: First Prize, nonfiction, New Press Literary Quarterly and Literary Society, 1993, for "My Right Breast"; fellow of Indiana Arts Commission, 1994-95, 1996-97; finalist for best adult fiction, Society of Midland Authors, 1994, for *When Warhol Was Still Alive;* Best Feature Film, Ft. Lauderdale International Film Festival, 1995, for *Sacred Hearts;* Dean's Teacher of the Year Award, University of Evansville, 1996.

WRITINGS:

When Warhol Was Still Alive (novel), Crossing Press, 1994.

Author of the screenplay *Sacred Hearts* (based on the author's short story "Lifeguarding"). Work represented in anthologies, including *Eating Our Hearts Out: Women and Food,* Crossing Press, 1993; *Catholic Girls and Boys,* Penguin, 1994; *Breaking up Is Hard to Do,* Crossing Press, 1994; *Bless Me Father,* Penguin, 1994; and *Tanzania on Tuesday,* New Rivers Press, 1997. Contributor to magazines and newspapers, including *Boulevard, Brain, Child, Southern Accents, Glamour, Chicago Tribune, Palo Alto Review, New Press, Greensboro Review, New England Living,* and *Clothesline Review.* Member of editorial advisory board, *To Make a Poem,* 1993.

WORK IN PROGRESS: Crook, a novel.

*   *   *

McMULLEN, Sean (Christopher) 1948-

PERSONAL: Born December 21, 1948, in Sale, Victoria, Australia; married Mary Davies, 1973 (divorced, 1978); married Patricia Smyth, 1986; children: one daughter. *Education:* University of Melbourne, B.A. (physics and history), 1974, M.A. (history; with honors), 1984; Canberra CAE, graduate diploma of information science, 1976; Latrobe University, graduate diploma of computer science, 1980; Deakin University, graduate certificate of management, 1999.

ADDRESSES: Home—G.P.O. Box 2653x, Melbourne, Victoria 3001, Australia. *Agent*—Chris Lotts, Ralph Vicinanza Ltd., 111 Eighth Ave., New York, NY 10011.

CAREER: Walter and Eliza Hall Institute, laboratory assistant, 1969-70; Woolworth's, driver, 1970-71; Department of Works, technical clerk, 1972-75; librarian at various libraries, 1975-80; Bureau of Meteorology, computer systems analyst, 1981—. Guest on Radio National programs, including *Faster Than Light Show, Ockham's Razor, Science Fiction Review,* and *Zero G;* speaker to various groups, including National Book Council, United Nations Youth Conference, National Science Fiction Convention, Adelaide Writers Centre, and Australian Space Association.

MEMBER: Science Fiction and Fantasy Writers of America, Melbourne University Karate Club (deputy senior instructor), Melbourne University Fencing Club.

AWARDS, HONORS: Writing prize, World Science Fiction Convention, 1985, for "The Deciad"; Ditmar awards, 1991, for "While the Gate Is Open," 1992, for "Alone in His Chariot," and 1996, for *Mirrorsun Rising;* William Atheling awards for criticism, 1992, 1993, 1996, 1998, and 2000; Aurealis awards, 1999, for *The Centurion's Empire,* and 2001, for *The Miocene Arrow.*

WRITINGS:

Call to the Edge (short stories), Aphelion (North Adelaide, Australia), 1992.

Voices in the Light (novel), Aphelion (North Adelaide, Australia), 1994.

Mirrorsun Rising (novel), Aphelion (North Adelaide, Australia), 1995.

The Centurion's Empire (novel), Tor Books (New York, NY), 1998.

Souls in the Great Machine (novel), Tor Books (New York, NY), 1999.

(With Russell Blackford and Van Ikin) *Strange Constellations: A History of Australian Science Fiction,* Greenwood Press (Westport, CT), 1999.

The Miocene Arrow (novel), Tor Books (New York, NY), 2000.

Eyes of the Calculor (novel), Tor Books (New York, NY), 2001.

Assistant editor, *The MUP Encyclopedia of Australian Science Fiction and Fantasy,* Melbourne University Press (Carlton South, Australia). Contributor to more than a dozen anthologies. Contributor to periodicals, including *Eidolon, Sirius, Aurealis, Analog Science Fiction & Fact, Interzone,* and *Magazine of Fantasy and Science Fiction.*

WORK IN PROGRESS: Voyage of the Shadowmoon, a novel, publication by Tor Books (New York, NY) expected in 2002; *Sorceress, Aged 12,* with Catherine S. McMullen; *Flight of the Stormbird.*

SIDELIGHTS: Sean McMullen is an Australian science fiction writer whose works include the short story collection *Call to the Edge* and several novels, including *Voices in the Light, The Centurion's Empire,* and *The Miocene Arrow.* In his works, McMullen combines hard science with such conventions of the genre as time travel, alternative technology, and visions of a post-apocalyptic civilization. Michael J. Tolley, writing in the *St. James Guide to Science Fiction Writers,* commented, "Sean McMullen's work is that of a fine and natural storyteller. What surprised and delighted the readers of his best-known story, 'The Colours of the Masters,' . . . was not so much its innovative quality . . . as its charm."

McMullen told *CA:* "I have been writing more fantasy lately, because the scope for fantastic technologies, strange people, and general humor is better."

Call to the Edge collects nine of McMullen's short stories. Among the tales, several feature time travel, including "Pax Romana," in which Alfred the Great meets a Roman time-traveler, and "The Dominant Style," in which a time-traveler is sent to alter the past but instead succumbs to its charms. "The Colours of the Masters" describes a "piano-spectrum," an instrument that translates music into colors. "While the Gate Is Open" offers a consideration of life after death. Faren Miller, reviewing *Call to the Edge* in *Locus,* rated it "a fine first collection" and noted that the stories "share certain preoccupations and methods that reveal them as the work of one man. One damn' interesting fellow, in fact."

Voices in the Light is set in a futuristic Australia, 1,696 years after the destruction of our current civilization through a nuclear apocalypse. Establishing a milieu that includes technology that has been devised without electricity, a psychic "Call" that periodically compels people and animals to walk inexplicably toward the sea, a number of squabbling administrative centers, and a library system that preserves the incomprehensible knowledge of past, *Voices in the Light* also introduces a host of characters, including the Highliber (head librarian) Zavora, her aide Lemorel, the mute Darien, the chemist Glasken, and two outsiders who arrive from a land located beyond the known civilized territory. The technological capabilities of the civilization include a communications system that operates using signal towers equipped with mirrors, pedal-and wind-powered trains, and an enormous computer, called the Calculor, that is composed of 2,000 slaves calculating simultaneously using abacus frames. According to Russell Letson in *Locus, Voices in the Light* "is completely satisfying without any overt interest in Big Questions. Instead, it does the *other* science fiction thing, building a complex and appealing world and peopling it with interesting characters."

The Centurion's Empire was McMullen's first novel to be published in the United States. It follows a Roman centurion, Vitellan, through time, from the year 71 A.D. to 2029 A.D. A potent elixir makes it possible for Vitellan to hibernate for centuries, but each time he awakens his body is more ravaged. His extended life takes him around the globe, with stops in England, France, and Australia. Eventually, dark forces become aware of his secret and vie for control of him. "McMullen succeeds admirably at portraying the various eras and locations the Centurion finds himself in," stated Lisa DuMond in a review for *The SF Site.* "A hefty amount of research went into the preparation of this novel. Through Romans, Danes, French revolutionaries and others, the sense of setting holds true. Even the dialects add to the authenticity." Robert Killheffer, a contributor to *Event Horizon,* claimed that *The Centurion's Empire* is the work of "a writer with a fertile imagination and the pure narrative talents to weave engaging stories around his ideas."

Souls in the Great Machine, McMullen's next novel, returns to the low-technology, feudal society of *Voices in the Light* to continue the adventures of Zavora and her companions. A *Publishers Weekly* reviewer praised the author's "dramatic pacing and believable characters" in this "well-wrought, richly imagined multidimensional world," and John Mort in *Booklist* called *Souls in the Great Machine* a "decidedly original, sometimes whimsical, and captivating . . . genuine tour de force." In the sequel, *The Miocene Arrow,* the setting moves to what is left of the United States, now mostly uninhabited due to the ravages of the war and the Call. An alien race, immune to the power of the Call, seeks to infiltrate the small society that struggles to survive in the Rocky Mountain region; their apparent mission is to destroy what remains of human life. "The tale features labyrinthine politics, a large cast of engaging, thorny and occasionally rather cartoonish characters, and many well-depicted scenes of aerial warfare," advised a reviewer for *Publishers Weekly*.

BIOGRAPHICAL/CRITICAL SOURCES:

BOOKS

St. James Guide to Science-Fiction Writers, St. James Press (Detroit, MI), 1996.

PERIODICALS

Booklist, May 15, 1998, Mary Frances Wilkens, review of *The Centurion's Empire,* p. 1604; June 1, 1999, John Mort, review of *Souls in the Great Machine,* p. 1802.
Kirkus Review, June 15, 1998, review of *The Centurion's Empire.*
Library Journal, July, 1998, Jackie Cassada, review of *The Centurion's Empire,* p. 142; August, 2000, Jackie Cassada, review of *The Miocene Arrow,* p. 168.
Locus, June, 1992, Faren Miller, review of *Call to the Edge,* p. 17; November, 1994, Russell Letson, review of *Voices in the Light,* p. 27.
Publishers Weekly, June 22, 1998, review of *The Centurion's Empire,* p. 89; May 24, 1999, review of *Souls in the Great Machine,* p. 73; July 17, 2000, review of *The Miocene Arrow,* p. 179.

OTHER

Ditmar Nominations Page, http://www.vicnet.net (January 7, 1997).
Event Horizon, http://eventhorizon.com/ (October 14, 1998), Robert Killheffer, review of *The Centurion's Empire.*
Sean McMullen Official Web Site, http://www.bdsonline.net/seanmcmullen/ (June 18, 2001).
sfsite.com, http://www.sfsite.com/ (October 9, 2000), Steven H. Silver, review of *The Centurion's Empire.*

The SF Site, http://www.secure.cyberus.ca/sfsite/ (October 9, 2000), Lisa DuMond, review of *The Centurion's Empire.*

*   *   *

McVAUGH, Michael R(ogers) 1938-

PERSONAL: Born December 9, 1938, in Washington, DC; son of Rogers (a botanist) and Ruth (a botanist; maiden name, Beall) McVaugh; married Julia Farrelly (an editor), 1961. *Education:* Harvard University, B.A. (magna cum laude), 1960; Princeton University, M.A., 1962, Ph.D., 1965.

ADDRESSES: Home—379 Tenney Circle, Chapel Hill, NC 27514. *Office*—Department of History, CB 3195, University of North Carolina at Chapel Hill, Chapel Hill, NC 27599-3195.

CAREER: University of North Carolina at Chapel Hill, assistant professor, 1964-70, associate professor, 1970-76, professor, 1976—, William Smith Wells Professor of History, 1996—. Institute for Advanced Study, Princeton, NJ, member of School of Historical Studies, 1968-69; Cambridge University, visiting fellow of Clare Hall, 1994; Wellcome Institute for the History of Medicine, research associate, 1999-2000; Oxford University, visiting fellow of Magdalen College, 2000.

AWARDS, HONORS: National Science Foundation, fellowship, 1968-69, grant, 1974; grants from Wellcome Trust, 1972, and Penrose Fund, American Philosophical Society, 1977; Guggenheim fellow, 1981-82; grant from Spanish Ministry of Education and Science, 1989; William H. Welch Medal from American Association for the History of Medicine, 1994, for *Medicine before the Plague: Practitioners and Their Patients in the Crown of Aragon, 1285-1345.*

WRITINGS:

(Editor with Luis Garcia-Ballester and Juan Antonio Paniagua) *Arnaldi de Villanova Opera Medica Omnia,* Granada (Barcelona, Spain), Volume II (also author): *Aphorismi de gradibus,* 1975, Volume XV, 1981, Volume XVI (also author): *Translatio Libri Galieni de Rigore,* 1981, Volume III (also author): *Tractatus de amore heroico: Epistola de dosi tyriacalium medicinarum,* 1985, Volume IV, 1988, Volume VI, Part 1, 1990, Volume VI, Part 2, 1993.

(With Seymour H. Mauskopf) *The Elusive Science: Origins of Experimental Psychical Research,* Johns Hopkins University Press (Baltimore, MD), 1980.

(With Linda E. Voigts) *A Latin Technical Phlebotomy and Its Middle English Translation,* American Philosophical Society (Philadelphia, PA), 1984.

(With Garcia-Ballester and Agustin Rubio-Vela) *Medical Licensing and Learning in Fourteenth-Century Valencia,* American Philosophical Society (Philadelphia, PA), 1989.

Medicine before the Plague: Practitioners and Their Patients in the Crown of Aragon, 1285-1345, Cambridge University Press (New York, NY), 1993.

Inventarium sive Chirurgia magna Guignos de Caulhiaco (Guy de Chauliac), two volumes, E. J. Brill (Leiden, Netherlands), 1997.

Work represented in anthologies, including *Mathematics and Its Applications to Science and Natural Philosophy in the Middle Ages,* edited by Edward Grant and John Murdoch, [Cambridge], 1987; *Practical Medicine from Salerno to the Black Death,* edited by Garcia-Ballester and others, Cambridge University Press (London, England), 1993; and *Making Medical History: The Life and Times of Henry E. Sigerist,* edited by Elizabeth Fee and Theodore Brown, Johns Hopkins University Press (Baltimore, MD), 1994. Contributor of more than seventy articles and reviews to scholarly journals. Guest editor, *Journal of the Elisha Mitchell Scientific Society,* 1984.

WORK IN PROGRESS: A history of medieval surgery.

*   *   *

MEWS, Siegfried 1933-

PERSONAL: Born September 28, 1933, in Berlin, Germany; son of Ernest and Erna Mews; married Linda Mueller (divorced, 1985); married Marilyn Metzler, 1998; children (first marriage): Randolph. *Education:* Attended University of Halle, 1953-57, and University of Hamburg, Staatsexamen, 1961; Southern Illinois University, M.A., 1963; University of Illinois, Ph.D., 1967.

ADDRESSES: Home—103 Rossburn Way, Chapel Hill, NC 27516. *Office*—Dept. of Germanic Languages and Literatures, 438 Dey Hall, CB #3160, University of North Carolina, Chapel Hill, NC 27599-3160.

CAREER: Centre College, Danville, KY, instructor in German, 1962-63; University of Illinois at Urbana-Champaign, instructor in German, 1966-67; University of North Carolina at Chapel Hill, assistant professor, 1967-71, associate professor, 1971-77, professor of German, 1977—.

MEMBER: International Brecht Society, American Association of Teachers of German, Modern Language Association of America, Heinrich-von Kleist-Gesellschaft, American Association of University Professors, American Comparative Literature Association, South Atlantic Modern Language Association, Delta Phi Alpha.

WRITINGS:

(Editor) *Studies in German Literature of the Nineteenth and Twentieth Centuries: Festschrift for Frederic E. Coenen,* University of North Carolina Press, 1970, 2nd edition, 1972.

Zuckmayer: Der Hauptmann von Koepenick, Diesterweg, 1972, 3rd edition, 1981.

Zuckmayer: Des Teufels General, Diesterweg, 1973, 2nd edition, 1979.

(Editor, with Herbert Knust, and contributor) *Essays on Brecht: Theater and Politics,* University of North Carolina Press, 1974.

Bertolt Brecht: Herr Puntila und sein Knecht Matti, Diesterweg, 1975, 2nd edition, 1985.

(Editor) *Bertolt Brecht, Der Kaukasische Kreidekreis,* Diesterweg, 1980, 2nd edition, 1984.

Carl Zuckmayer, Twayne, 1981.

(Editor and contributor) *"The Fisherman and His Wife": Guenter Grass's "The Flounder" in Critical Perspective,* AMS Press, 1982.

Ulrich Plenzdorf, Beck, 1984.

(Editor) *Critical Essays on Bertolt Brecht,* G. K. Hall, 1989.

(Editor, with James Hardin) *Dictionary of Literary Biography,* Volume 129: *Nineteenth-Century German Writers, 1841-1900,* Gale (Detroit, MI), 1993.

(Editor, with Hardin) *Dictionary of Literary Biography,* Volume 133: *Nineteenth-Century German Writers to 1840,* Gale (Detroit, MI), 1993.

(Editor) *A Bertolt Brecht Reference Companion,* Greenwood Press (Westport, CT), 1997.

Modern Revival of Gnosticismin in Thomas Mann's Doctor Faustus, Camden House (Rochester, NY), 1998.

Contributor of articles and reviews to journals. Editor, *Studies in Germanic Languages and Literature,* 1968-80, and *South Atlantic Review,* 1983—; member of editorial advisory board, *Perspectives on Contemporary Literature,* 1975—, *South Atlantic Review,* 1979-82, and *German Studies Review* and *German Quarterly,* currently.

WORK IN PROGRESS: Guenter Grass and His Critics, for Camden House (Rochester, NY), 2003.

*   *   *

MEYER, Howard N(icholas) 1914-

PERSONAL: Born October 8, 1914, in Brooklyn, NY; son of Richard (a manufacturer) and Minnie (Teitelbaum) Meyer; married Sylvette Engel (an artist), August 30, 1942; children: Andrew, Franklin, Jonathan. *Education:* Columbia University, A.B., 1934, LL.B., 1936. *Politics:* Independent.

ADDRESSES: Home—New York City. *Office*—c/o Da Capo Press, 11 Cambridge Center, Cambridge, MA 02142.

CAREER: Lawyer in private practice, New York City, 1937—. Special assistant to the U.S. attorney general, New York City, 1942-48; Rockville Centre Board of Education, member of advisory committee, 1954-56; panel arbitrator for New York State and New Jersey Boards of Mediation, beginning in 1971; member of Nassau County Public Employment Relations Board.

AWARDS, HONORS: Pulitzer Prize nomination, 1974, for *The Amendment That Refused to Die.*

WRITINGS:

(Editor and author of introduction) T. W. Higginson, *Army Life in a Black Regiment,* Collier Books (New York, NY), 1962.

Let Us Have Peace: A Biography of U. S. Grant, Macmillan (New York, NY), 1965.

(Editor and author of introduction) Angelo Herndon, *Let Me Live,* Arno, 1969.

(Editor) *Integrating America's Heritage,* McGrath (Wilmington, NC), 1970.

Colonel of the Black Regiment: A Biography of Thomas Wentworth Higginson, Norton (New York, NY), 1970.

The Amendment That Refused to Die: Equality and Justice Deferred; The History of the Fourteenth Amendment, Chilton (Radnor, PA), 1973, updated edition, Madison Books (Lanham, MD), 2000.

(Editor) *The Magnificent Activist: The Writings of Thomas Wentworth Higginson (1823-1911),* Da Capo Press (Cambridge, MA), 2000.

Contributor of essays to periodicals, including *Commonweal, Midwest Quarterly, Book Week, Crisis, Negro Digest,* and *New South.* Editor, *Columbia Law Review,* 1934-36.

BIOGRAPHICAL/CRITICAL SOURCES:

PERIODICALS

Publishers Weekly, July 17, 2000, review of *The Magnificent Activist,* p. 189.*

*   *   *

MICKEL, Emanuel J(ohn), Jr. 1937-

PERSONAL: Born October 11, 1937, in Lemont, IL; son of Emanuel J. (a laborer) and Mildred (a homemaker; maiden name, Newton) Mickel; married Kathleen Russell, May 31, 1959; children: Jennifer, Chiara Mickel Gifford, Heather Mickel McMillen. *Ethnicity:* "Scotch-Irish, English, Polish, Czech, German." *Education:* Louisiana State University, B.A., 1959; University of North Carolina, M.A., 1961, Ph.D., 1965. *Religion:* Protestant. *Avocational interests:* Music, painting, travel, sports.

ADDRESSES: Home—3749 Cameron Ave., Bloomington, IN 47401. *Office*—Department of French and Italian, Indiana University—Bloomington, Bloomington, IN 47405. *E-mail*—mickel@indiana.edu.

CAREER: University of Nebraska, Lincoln, assistant professor, 1965-67, associate professor, 1967-68; Indiana University—Bloomington, associate professor, 1968-73, professor of French literature, 1973—, department head, 1984-95, director of Medieval Studies Institute, 1976-91, associate dean, 1976-78. *Military service:* U.S. Army, 1961-63; became captain.

MEMBER: Mediaeval Academy of America, Modern Language Association of America, Societe Rencesvals.

AWARDS, HONORS: Chevalier des Palmes Academiques.

WRITINGS:

The Artificial Paradises in French Literature, Volume I, University of North Carolina Press (Chapel Hill, NC), 1969.

(Coeditor) *Studies in Honor of Alfred G. Engstrom,* University of North Carolina Press (Chapel Hill, NC), 1972.

Marie de France, Twayne (Boston, MA), 1974.

(With Jan Nelson) *The Old French Crusade Cycle,* Volume I: *Naissance du chevalier au cygne,* University of Alabama Press (Tuscaloosa, AL), 1977.

Eugene Fromentin, Twayne (Boston, MA), 1982.

Ganelon, Treason and the "Chanson de Roland," Pennsylvania State University Press (University Park, PA), 1989.

(Translator and author of introduction and notes) Jules Verne, *The Complete "Twenty Thousand Leagues under the Sea": A New Translation of Jules Verne's Science Fiction Classic,* Indiana University Press (Bloomington, IN), 1991.

(Editor) *The Shaping of Text: Style, Imagery, and Structure in French Literature; Essays in Honor of John Porter Houston,* Bucknell University Press (Lewisburg, PA), 1993.

Les enfances Godefroi; [and] Le retour de Cornumarant, University of Alabama Press (Tuscaloosa, AL), 1999.

Contributor of scholarly articles to *Speculum, Romania, Romance Notes, Modern Philology, Modern Language Quarterly, Studi Francesi, Studies in Philology, Romanische Forschungen Zeitschrift für Romanische Philologie,* and other journals.

WORK IN PROGRESS: A book on the *Roman de la rose;* research on nineteenth-century interpretations of classical literature.

SIDELIGHTS: Emanuel J. Mickel, Jr. reads Latin, French, Provencal, German, Spanish, Portuguese, Italian, and Arabic.

BIOGRAPHICAL/CRITICAL SOURCES:

PERIODICALS

Library Journal, June 1, 1991, review of *The Complete "Twenty Thousand Leagues under the Sea,"* p. 202.*

MOGGACH, Deborah 1948-

PERSONAL: Born June 28, 1948, in London, England; daughter of Richard Alexander (a writer) and Charlotte (a writer and illustrator; maiden name, Woodyatt) Hough; married Anthony Austen Moggach (a publisher), November 21, 1971; children: Thomas Alexander, Charlotte Flora. *Education:* University of Bristol, B.A. (with honors), 1970.

ADDRESSES: Home—28 Gloucester Crescent, London N.W.1, England. *Agent*—Curtis Brown Ltd., 162-168 Regent St., London W1R 5TA, England.

CAREER: Oxford University Press, London, England, librarian, 1970-72; freelance writer and teacher in Pakistan, 1972-74; writer, 1978—.

AWARDS, HONORS: Young Journalist Award, Westminster Arts Council, 1975, for "Karachi."

WRITINGS:

You Must Be Sisters, Collins, 1978, St. Martin's, 1979.

Close to Home, Collins, 1979.

A Quiet Drink, Collins, 1980.

Hot Water Man, J. Cape, 1982.

Porky, J. Cape, 1983.

To Have and to Hold, Viking, 1986.

Smile, 1987.

Driving in the Dark, 1988.

Stolen, 1990.

The Stand-In, Little, Brown (Boston, MA), 1991.

The Ex-Wives, 1993.

Changing Babies, and Other Stories, Heinemann (London, England), 1994.

Seesaw, Mandarin (London, England), 1996.

Close Relations, Heinemann (London, England), 1997.

Tulip Fever, Delacorte (New York, NY), 1999.

Contributor to periodicals, including *Cosmopolitan.*

ADAPTATIONS: Tulip Fever was produced as an unabridged audio book by Chivers Audio Books in 2000.

WORK IN PROGRESS: An eight-part television serial.

SIDELIGHTS: Upon completion of her studies the University of Bristol, Deborah Moggach began working as a librarian for Oxford University Press. She stayed there for two years, then embarked for Pakistan, where she worked for two years as a freelance writer and teacher. "Everything I wrote for the local magazines was published simply because the standard was so low," she told *CA*. "I had the rare opportunity of experimenting and developing *in print* rather than simply on the typewriter."

In 1978, four years after returning to England, Moggach published her first book, *You Must Be Sisters,* which concerns a middle-class adolescent and her sister. She recalled to *CA* that she "wanted to show the funnier and more embarrassing side of the struggle into adulthood," and that she "wanted to bridge the generation gap by showing the different viewpoints of parents and children." *New Statesman* reviewer Valentine Cunningham affirmed that the novel reveals "family life most achingly bared." Mary Hope, meanwhile, wrote in *Spectator* that *You Must Be Sisters* is "psychologically pedestrian," but she added that it is "sharp and wry about the unliberated middle-class girl."

Close to Home, Moggach's second novel, chronicles domestic trials and tribulations. She described it to *CA* as a novel "about motherhood, neighbors, and the suffocating, joyful, frustrating world of babyhood and its effects upon marriage." *New Statesman* reviewer Blake Morrison described *Close to Home* as "a funny, affectionate, and unpretentious novel," and he added that it is "always a pleasure to read." A. N. Wilson, though conceding in the *Observer* that he was tired of novels about "marital frustration in London NW3," rated *Close to Home* "quite high." He summarized it as "a collection of hilarious incidents with which one intelligent woman might regale another . . . at the local playgroup."

Moggach followed *Close to Home* with *A Quiet Drink,* a novel about a cosmetics salesman who pitches his product to drugstores. "I had a lot of fun with this book," Moggach revealed to *CA*. She considered the work "a breakthrough" and found it "full of scope."

In 1982 Moggach published *Hot Water Man,* and the next year produced *Porky,* which details the effect of incest on an adolescent girl. Galen Swanson, writing in the *Times Literary Supplement,* acknowledged that the novel conveys "the complexity of the effects of gradually consummated incest, the scope of childish incomprehension, the patchy character of . . . stop-start evolution into fully fledged trauma."

Among Moggach's other novels from the 1980s is *To Have and to Hold,* which explores the relationship of sisters and the complications that ensue when one of them agrees to bear the child of the other's husband. Ellen Feldman wrote in the *New York Times Book Review* of the novel's "brisk pace" and noted that "the characterizations are deft, if one-dimensional." Feldman added that *To Have and to Hold* "is a skillful and occasionally moving novel."

Moggach's ensuing books include *The Stand-In,* which chronicles the sexual intrigues that commence when a middle-aged actress becomes a stand-in for an American movie star. The heroine's lover soon becomes romantically involved with the star. But when the stand-in's career begins to prosper, she begins to plot revenge. A *Publishers Weekly* reviewer summarized *The Stand-In* as "an exciting, deftly executed thriller with considerable psychological intrigue."

Moggach closed the 1990s with *Tulip Fever,* a novel about a young woman who languishes in an unhappy marriage, before finding love with a painter in seventeenth-century Netherlands. A reviewer at the *Pure Fiction* Web site recommended *Tulip Fever* "to anyone who enjoys an intelligent read," and a critic in *Publishers Weekly* deemed the novel "popular fiction created at a high pitch of craft and rapid readability." *Chatelaine* reviewer Buffy Childerhose was less impressed, concluding that the novel "withers in the shadow of its own grand plan," but a *Books on Line* critic found the novel "clever, spry and sad in equal measure." Still another critic, Patty Engelmann, wrote in *Booklist* that *Tulip Fever* is a "lush and sensuously written novel," while Kathy Piehl contended in *Library Journal* that Moggach's novel "plunges readers into 17th-century Amsterdam."

BIOGRAPHICAL/CRITICAL SOURCES:

PERIODICALS

Best Sellers, May, 1979.

Booklist, March 15, 2000, Patty Engelmann, review of *Tulip Fever.*

Chatelaine, May, 2000, Buffy Childerhose, "Going Dutch."

Library Journal, March 1, 2000, Kathy Piehl, review of *Tulip Fever.*

New Statesman, February 17, 1978, Valentine Cunningham, review of *You Must Be Sisters;* March 30, 1979, Blake Morrison, review of *Close to Home.*

New York Times Book Review, March 29, 1987, Ellen Feldman, "Selfless Sex in Britain."

Observer, April 1, 1979, A. N. Wilson, review of *Close to Home.*

Publishers Weekly, June 28, 1991, review of *The Stand-In,* p. 89; February 21, 2000, review of *Tulip Fever.*

Spectator, February 18, 1978, Mary Hope, review of *You Must Be Sisters.*

Times Literary Supplement, February 17, 1978; May 23, 1980; April 30, 1982, June 3, 1983, Galen Swanson, review of *Porky.*

OTHER

Books on Line, http://www.booksonline.co.uk/ (June 7, 2000), review of *Tulip Fever.*

Pure Fiction, http://www.purefiction.co.uk/ (June 7, 2000), review of *Tulip Fever.**

*   *   *

MOORHOUSE, Geoffrey 1931-

PERSONAL: Born November 29, 1931, in Bolton, Lancashire, England; son of William and Gladys (Hoyle) Heald (later Moorhouse); stepson of Richard Moorhouse; married Janet Marion Murray, May 12, 1956 (divorced); married Barbara Jane Woodward, September 23, 1974 (divorced); married Marilyn Isobel Edwards, July 7, 1983 (divorced); children: (first marriage) Ngaire Jane, Andrew Murray, Michael John, Brigid Anne (died, 1981). *Avocational interests:* "Music, gardening, walking in the hill country, looking at buildings, watching cricket and the Bolton Wanderers Football Club."

ADDRESSES: Home—Park House, Gayle, near Hawes, North Yorkshire, DL8 3RT, England. *Agent*—Gillon Aitken, Gillon Aitken Associates, 29 Fernshaw Rd., London SW10 0TG, England.

CAREER: Bolton Evening News, Bolton, Lancashire, England, reporter, 1952-54; *Auckland Star,* Auckland, New Zealand, sub-editor, 1954-57; *News Chronicle,* Manchester, England, sub-editor, 1957-58; *Manchester Guardian,* Manchester, deputy features editor, 1958-63; *Guardian,* London, England, chief features writer, 1963-70; freelance writer, 1970—. *Military service:* Royal Navy, 1950-52.

MEMBER: Fellow of the Royal Society of Literature, Lancashire County Cricket Club.

AWARDS, HONORS: Thomas Cook Travel Book Award, 1984, for *To the Frontier: A Journey to the Khyber Pass;* Cricket Society Award for *The Best-Loved Game: One Summer of English Cricket;* nominated in 1997 for the Booker Prize and for a *Los Angeles Times* Book Prize in history, both for *Sun Dancing.*

WRITINGS:

The Other England, Penguin (London, England), 1964.

The Press, Ward, Lock (London, England), 1964.

Against All Reason, Stein & Day (Briarcliff Manor, NY), 1969.

Calcutta, Weidenfeld & Nicolson (London, England), 1971, Harcourt (New York, NY), 1972, new edition, Phoenix (London, England), 1998.

The Missionaries, Lippincott (Philadelphia, PA), 1973.

The Fearful Void: Across the Implacable Sahara, a Man goes in Search of Himself, Lippincott (Philadelphia, PA), 1974.

The Diplomats: The Foreign Office Today, J. Cape (London, England), 1977.

The Boat and the Town, Little, Brown (Boston, MA), 1979.

The Best-Loved Game: One Summer of English Cricket, Hodder & Stoughton (London, England), 1979.

Prague, Time-Life Books (Alexandria, VA), 1980.

India Britannica, Harper & Row (New York, NY), 1983.

Lord's, Hodder & Stoughton (London, England), 1983.

To the Frontier: A Journey to the Khyber Pass, Hodder & Stoughton (London, England), 1984.

Imperial City: The Rise and Rise of New York, Holt (New York, NY), 1988.

At the George (essays), Hodder & Stoughton (London, England), 1989.

On the Other Side: A Journey to Soviet Central Asia, Holt (New York, NY), 1990, published as *Apples in the Snow: A Journey to Samarkand,* Hodder & Stoughton (London, England), 1990.

Hell's Foundations: A Social History of the Town of Bury in the Aftermath of the Gallipoli Campaign, Holt (New York, NY), 1992, published as *Hell's Foundations: A Town, Its Myths and Gallipoli,* Hodder & Stoughton (London, England), 1992.

Om: An Indian Pilgrimage, Hodder & Stoughton (London, England), 1993.

Sun Dancing: A Vision of Medieval Ireland (fiction), Harcourt (New York, NY), 1997.

Sydney: The Story of a City, Harcourt (New York, NY), 2000.

WORK IN PROGRESS: An account of the rebellion by the northern counties of England against Henry VIII, which was known as the Pilgrimage of Grace; publication expected in 2002.

SIDELIGHTS: British author Geoffrey Moorhouse is best known for his innovative travel writings. An editor and writer affiliated with various English newspapers for nearly two decades, he began publishing book-length accounts of his world travels in the 1960s. His research for *Against All Reason,* an investigation into monastic life, was "broad and unprecedented," according to a *New Yorker* reviewer. The same reviewer said that results of the inquiry into what Catholic and Protestant monks and nuns think and hope were "fascinating and touching, for the struggle of the human to reach the divine is painful, not invariably successful, but—for some, at any rate—inescapably alluring."

The Fearful Void describes Moorhouse's solitary crossing of the Sahara desert—two thousand miles by the most deadly route possible. He describes his travails and setbacks—the worst of which being how he suffered from dehydration—and how, ultimately, he failed to reach his destination at Luxor. However, that he traveled as far as he did was no mean feat. *The Boat and the Town* was the product of a year the author spent working as a deep-sea fisherman out of Gloucester, Massachusetts. Reviewing the book in the *Sunday Telegraph,* Ronald Blythe commented, "His qualities as a writer derive partly from the hard-eyed look he gives to actuality, that direct intention of his to get all that is happening down on paper, and partly from a recognition that both facts and imagination are needed if one is dealing with another man's world. His books are a kind of documentary-plus . . . something more complex than good reporting."

Moorhouse has written several books about the subcontinent of South Asia. Reviewing one of them, *India Britannica,* for the *Washington Post Book World,* Valerie Fitzgerald suggested that "those familiar with Moorhouse's *Calcutta* will know that he has done more than produce just another coffee-table tome. It is, in fact, a compressed but thoroughly enlightened account of the British Raj, written with style and judgment . . . a miracle of considered choice, apt quotation and illuminating incident." Christopher Hicks, writing in *Newsday,* found the book "notable for its deep and exact sense of justice" and called it "a well-judged evocation of past days for our day."

In his 1984 volume *To the Frontier: A Journey to the Khyber Pass,* Moorhouse recounts his trip across Pakistan in 1983. Writing in the *Washington Post Book World,* John Kenneth Galbraith asserted that despite Moorhouse's care with details, his "eye for people and scene," and "a good ear for speech," his report is "an unduly casual introduction to the country, fragmentary and accidental." In the *Los Angeles Times,* Sharon Dirlam noted the author's "unflappable optimism" and "boundless curiosity" in the face of difficult traveling conditions. And Gene Lyons, writing for *Newsweek,* dubbed the travel writer "a diverting companion" and his book "a model of its kind."

Moorhouse moved from the stark drama of Pakistan to an urban stage in *Imperial City: The Rise and Rise of New York,* a collection of his observations on New York City. Wendy Smith wrote in the *Washington Post Book World,* "Perhaps only a foreigner could write about America's most controversial city with such lucid affection." In the London *Times Literary Supplement,* reviewer David Hirson lauded Moorhouse for his "blessedly realistic" treatment, "an amalgam of personal reflections and historical research . . . as toughly critical as it is celebratory." Though Hirson faulted Moorhouse for sometimes being "panoramic at the expense of direction and balance," he acknowledged that the topic of New York City tempts writers generally to "err on the side of trying to do too much" and concluded by pronouncing Moorhouse's *Imperial City* "responsible, engaging, and humane."

Moorhouse again focused on his travels to Asia in *On the Other Side: A Journey to Soviet Central Asia,* published in 1990. According to John Ure in the *Times Literary Supplement,* the book (published in England as *Apples in the Snow: A Journey to Samarkand*) is less a travel narrative than a "series of set-piece essays about the various cities of the [Soviet] plains," blended with historical background on the places where Moorhouse was taken by his official escorts. Ure accorded the author "an honourable place" among the distinguished writers about this part of the world for doing best "the hardest thing of all: he writes with feeling and compassion about the soul of Mother Russia." In a review of *On the Other Side,* John Maxwell Hamilton credited Moorhouse in the *New York Times Book Review* for his ability to "summon up novelty even for those who may think they know a place well." Dirlam, however, believed that the author should have "departed from the apolitical style of the National Geographic Society (which sponsored his trip) long enough to ask more probing questions of the locals" and thus get at the discontent that later erupted in strikes and ethnic rioting in the region.

"[A s]ensitive and vibrant . . . social history of uncanny force" were Paul West's words in the *New York*

Times Book Review regarding *Hell's Foundations,* Moorhouse's 1992 study of the mill town of Bury, Lancashire, after nearly two thousand of the Lancashire Fusiliers died in the ill-conceived attack on Gallipoli, Turkey, in World War I. "Mr. Moorhouse's analysis of myths and mores in postwar Bury," West declared, "develops into a startling, luminous and humane study of how propaganda—elegiac and mesmeric—goes to work on the cannon fodder of the future."

Moorhouse's 1993 book, *Om: An Indian Pilgrimage,* chronicles his journey of enlightenment through southern India. Named for the sacred Hindu incantation, *Om* offers insights into the mystical nature of the Indian nation and further solidifies its author's reputation as a travel writer.

In 1997 Moorhouse produced a combination novel and history entitled *Sun Dancing: A Vision of Medieval Ireland,* which is about the life of medieval monks who once made their homes on the inhospitable Skellig Islands off the coast of Ireland. Always a mysterious location, historians have speculated about why the monks settled on the islands and how they survived unbelievable hardships to preserve their spiritual way of life and propagate the scholarship that they left to western civilization. A *Kirkus Reviews* critic found that "the first half of the book is so intriguing and beautifully written that second [the historical section] . . . pales by comparison." According to the editor of the Commissioners of Irish Lights Web site, however, "The writing is vivid and imaginative, coloured by phrases in Irish and Latin, and quotations from the Psalms. Fiction, to be sure, but fiction constructed from a wealth of historical evidence and tradition."

Moorhouse returned to nonfiction in 2000 with his *Sydney: The Story of a City.* He told an interviewer for the Australian Broadcasting Corporation's "The World Today" that the book was "wholly my idea. And it's because, since I first knew it . . . I just found it immensely attractive and wanted to write about it." He noted that the coming of the Sydney Olympics moved the project along. After meticulous research, he presents a complete picture of this premier Australian city, from its history to its sociology to its flora and fauna. He dwells extensively on the beauty of its harbor. Michael Davie wrote in the *Literary Review* Web site, "[He] seems to have been everywhere, and is thus able to compare [Sydney] with all the famous harbours in the world, concluding that only Istanbul can compete." Although details on present-day Sydney get "short shrift," according to Davie, "few people will read Moorhouse's

Sydney without learning something." Elizabeth Feizkhah noted in *Time International* that Moorhouse's "prevailing mood is enthusiasm" and called the book "serendipitous travelog-history." Brad Hooper, writing in *Booklist,* called Moorhouse a "crackerjack travel writer and storyteller."

Moorhouse told *CA:* "I have never thought of myself as 'a travel writer' so much as a writer who travels a great deal in the course of research, and who from time to time produces a book about a journey I have made (e.g., *The Fearful Void, To the Frontier, Om, Apples in the Snow*) or a place that has fascinated me (*Calcutta, Imperial City, Sydney*). I am, more that most British writers, difficult to categorise because I write in different forms on vastly different topics that are normally tackled by specialists, whereas I am an unreconstructed generalist. But the 'travel books' actually form less than half my total output, which also includes serious and original history (*Hell's Foundations*), socio-political studies (*The Other England, The Diplomats*), religion (*Against All Reason*), sport (*The Best-Loved Game, At the George*), a novel (*The Boat and the Town*), and a book which, in its way, I suppose sums me up as a writer—*Sun Dancing,* which I think of as a novella with elaborate footnotes. Given that the second half of that book consisted of the historical evidence to support the fiction that preceded it, I don't think there was any realistic chance of its winning the Booker Prize, but I was pleased that my publisher nominated it. What I aim for in all my books is simply illumination, created by an imaginative perception of the subject and a sensitive use of the language. I want my reader's first response to be 'Ah, yes, I see . . . ', rather than anything that focuses upon my capacity as a writer."

BIOGRAPHICAL/CRITICAL SOURCES:

PERIODICALS

Atlantic Monthly, October, 1997, review of *Sun Dancing: A Vision of Medieval Ireland,* p. 117.

Booklist, August, 1997, review of *Sun Dancing,* p. 1853; March 15, 2000, Brad Hooper, review of *Sydney: The Story of a City,* p. 1322.

Chicago Tribune, October 18, 1988.

Kirkus Reviews, June 15, 1997, review of *Sun Dancing,* p. 934; April 1, 2000, review of *Sydney.*

Library Journal, September 15, 1997, review of *Sun Dancing,* p. 88.

Los Angeles Times, August 11, 1985, Sharon Dirlam, review of *To the Frontier: A Journey to the Khyber Pass.*

Los Angeles Times Book Review, April 28, 1991.

Newsday, August 7, 1983, Christopher Hicks, review of *India Britannica.*

New Statesman, April 25, 1969.

Newsweek, June 3, 1985, Gene Lyons, review of *To the Frontier,* p. 75.

New Yorker, July 5, 1969, review of *Against All Reason.*

New York Times, February 18, 1972; July 26, 1983.

New York Times Book Review, June 16, 1985; June 9, 1991; June 28, 1992, p. 13; October 18, 1992, p. 52; July 18, 1993, p. 24; November 9, 1997, review of *Sun Dancing,* p. 23.

Observer (London), July 18, 1993, p. 58; September 26, 1993, p. 19; September 11, 1994, p. 25.

Spectator, May 3, 1997, review of *Sun Dancing,* p. 40.

Sunday Telegraph (London), March 25, 1979, Ronald Blythe, review of *The Boat and the Town.*

Time International, July 31, 2000, Elizabeth Feizkhah, review of *Sydney,* p. 46.

Times (London), May 12, 1983; October 20, 1983; April 7, 1988.

Times Literary Supplement, April 15, 1983; June 3, 1988; February 1, 1991; May 8, 1992; August 8, 1997, review of *Sun Dancing,* p. 35.

Washington Post Book World, March 26, 1974; August 14, 1983, p. 4; March 24, 1985; September 11, 1988.

OTHER

ABC News Online, http://abc.net.au/worldtoday/ (October 26, 1999), interview with Moorhouse on *Sydney.*

Commissioners of Irish Lights, http://cil.ie/ (September 21, 2000), review of *Sun Dancing.*

Literary Review, http://www.litreview.com/ (September 21, 2000), Michael Davie, review of *Sydney.*

The Age, http://www.theage.com/ (September 21, 2000), Neil Jillett, review of *Sydney.*

N

NABOKOV, Dmitri 1934-

PERSONAL: Born May 10, 1934, in Berlin, Germany; immigrated to the United States, 1940, naturalized citizen, 1945; son of Vladimir (a writer) and Vera (Slonim) Nabokov. *Education:* Harvard University, A.B. (cum laude), 1955; attended Longe School of Music, 1955-57. *Avocational interests:* Mountaineering, automobile racing, powerboat racing, skiing, tennis, Ferraris.

ADDRESSES: Home—1515 South Flagler Dr., Apt.# 2601, West Palm Beach, FL 33401. *Agent*—Smith/Skolnik, 23 East Tenth St., #712, New York, NY 10003.

CAREER: Translator, 1955—; writer, 1977—; trustee and administrator of Vladimir Nabokov Literary Trust, 1977—, and the PEN/Nabokov Award, 1999—. Operatic bass; performed in opera concert and on radio and television programs in the United States, Europe, and South America; leading actor in an Italian film. Delivered lectures at Harvard and Cornell universities and University of Geneva. *Military service:* U.S. Army, 1957; U.S. Army Reserve, 1957-59.

MEMBER: American Alpine Club, Ferrari Club of Switzerland, Montreux Tennis Club.

AWARDS, HONORS: Won Reggio Emilia International Singing Competition, 1960; won Parma International Opera Competition, 1965; award for Arcophon-Decca recording of music by Carlo Gesualdo; various academic and sports awards.

WRITINGS:

(Translator) Mikhail Lermontov, *Hero in Our Time,* introduction and notes by Vladimir Nabokov, Doubleday (Garden City, NY), 1958.

(Author of commentary) Pia Pera, *Lo's Diary,* translated by Ann Goldstein, Foxrock, 2001.

TRANSLATOR OF WORKS BY FATHER, VLADIMIR NABOKOV

(With V. Nabokov) *Invitation to a Beheading* (novel), Putnam (New York, NY), 1959.

(With V. Nabokov and Michael Scammell) *The Gift* (novel), Putnam, 1963.

(With V. Nabokov) *The Eye* (novel), Phaedra, 1965.

(With V. Nabokov) *The Waltz Invention* (three-act play; produced in Hartford, CT, 1969; produced in New York), Phaedra, 1966.

(With V. Nabokov) *King, Queen, Knave* (novel), McGraw (New York, NY), 1968.

(With V. Nabokov) *Glory* (novel), McGraw, 1971.

(With V. Nabokov and Simon Karlinsky) *A Russian Beauty and Other Stories,* McGraw, 1973.

(With V. Nabokov) *Tyrants Destroyed and Other Stories,* McGraw, 1975.

(And editor) *Cose trasparenti,* Mondadori, 1975.

(And editor) *The Man from the U.S.S.R. and Other Plays,* Harcourt/Bruccoli Clark (New York, NY), 1984.

(And editor) *The Enchanter* (story), Putnam, 1986.

(And editor) *L'Incantatore,* Guanda/Longanesi, 1987.

(And editor with Matthew J. Bruccoli) *Vladimir Nabokov: Selected Letters, 1940-1977,* Harcourt, 1989.

(And editor) *The Stories of Vladimir Nabokov,* Knopf (New York, NY), 1995.

Nabokov's Butterflies: Unpublished and Uncollected Writings, Ballantine (New York, NY), 2000.

Translator of stories, essays, and poems by V. Nabokov that appear in American journals, including the story "The Fight," *New Yorker,* 1985, and the essay "Pushkin;

or, The Real and the Plausible," *New York Review of Books,* 1988. Translator of V. Nabokov's works from Russian and French into English and from Russian and English into Italian. Supervisor of translations of V. Nabokov's works into Russian, Italian, and French, 1977—.

Contributor to anthologies, including *Vladimir Nabokov: A Tribute,* edited by Peter Quennell, 1979, *Nabokov's Fifth Arc,* edited by J. E. Rivers and Charles Nicol, 1982, *The Achievements of Vladimir Nabokov,* 1984, and *Our Private Lives,* edited by Daniel Halpern, 1990. Contributor of book reviews and articles on mountaineering and other subjects to such periodicals as *Antaeus, Encounter,* and *New York Times Book Review.*

WORK IN PROGRESS: A pseudonymous novel; a book of recollections; translating further works of V. Nabokov from Russian into English, including a large collection of poems and a group of short stories, and revising various translations of his works.

SIDELIGHTS: Dmitri Nabokov, the son of Vladimir Nabokov, one of the twentieth century's greatest writers, has translated and edited various volumes of his father's works. According to John Updike in the *New York Times Book Review,* Dmitri was his father's "favorite translator" before Vladimir Nabokov died in 1977. Indeed, his father's death did not dampen Dmitri Nabokov's desire to translate, and in the last decades of the twentieth century a number of Vladimir Nabokov's unpublished essays and scientific writings were brought into print under his son's aegis. *Guardian* correspondent Jay Parini noted that Nabokov "has lavished time and unusual talent on his father's work over several decades."

With Matthew J. Bruccoli, Nabokov compiled a collection of his father's correspondence, *Selected Letters, 1940-1977.* Through the course of this 1989 volume, the writer's life story and the progression of his literary career unfold: from his youth in his native Russia and emigration to Germany and France—where he was hailed as a talented and already controversial writer— through his emigration to the United States, where he struggled to support his family and to become an "American" writer, to his later years spent in Switzerland as a lionized—and some say cantankerous—author. In his letters, Vladimir Nabokov discusses in great detail the publishing histories of his books, *Pnin, Pale Fire,* and his masterpiece, *Lolita,* which, when published in 1958, sparked intense critical and public reaction.

Although Dmitri Nabokov admits in the foreword to the *Letters* that many viewed his father as "austere, cold, somehow inhuman," he maintains, as quoted by Christopher Lehmann-Haupt of the *New York Times,* that "in his real life and daily discourse, Nabokov was the warmest and most humorous of men." Zinovy Zinik, writing in the *Times Literary Supplement,* concurred, noting that "the letters reveal a man who, in spite of the relentless pressure of everyday survival and the demands of a literary vocation, was capable of great kindness to his relatives and loved ones." Other critics, however, were not as convinced of Nabokov's warmth, basically because the correspondence collected in this volume primarily deals with publishers, editors, and literary agents in polite-but-tense business situations. Robert Alter in *Tribune Books* observed, however, that the *Selected Letters* are "intrinsically compelling because of the stylistic brilliance, the habits of precise observation and, above all, the terrific energy of personality with which they are imbued."

Nabokov is the inheritor of his father's literary legacy, and as such, he has faced some challenging custodial situations. In 1999, he went to court to protect Vladimir Nabokov's copyright interests after an Italian author, Pia Pera, wrote a novel called *Lo's Diary* based upon the "Lolita" character; the novel was withheld from publication until an agreement was reached in which Nabokov was allowed to write a commentary that would be published in the book. Also in 1999, he faced a serious decision on the uses to which his father's final, uncompleted novel might be put. The manuscript for Vladimir Nabokov's *The Original of Laura* will be stored at an institute of higher learning, where it will be available to scholars but will remain unpublished for the foreseeable future. Dmitri Nabokov told *Salon.com* that he tries to balance his father's wishes with those of the scholarly community—but that he has never been tempted to finish the famous author's unfinished work, or even amend it in translation. "I translate it as best I can," he said. "I adapt, where I can, [Russian] sentence length to the American and English languages. . . . But I don't ever alter the meaning of the words."

This tenet is put into practice in *Nabokov's Butterflies: Unpublished and Uncollected Writings,* a volume translated by Dmitri Nabokov that contains his father's scientific work and essays on butterflies and moths. A *Publishers Weekly* reviewer styled the work "a volume devotees will delight to browse and scholars will want to own."

Nabokov told *CA:* "My father, Vladimir Nabokov, after having given me a splendid literary apprenticeship, left me the most precious heritage of all when he died: that of inspiration. 'On Revisiting Father's Room,' written shortly after his death, was the first original piece of mine that pleased me, and it led to a gradual shift of priority from singing to writing. My first novel, nearly finished, will be pseudonymous to avoid undeserved fame or blame. Like my father, I despise cruelty, vulgarity, and censorship, whether by a totalitarian state or a fashionable pressure group. Fiction should be original; poetry must have meter. History and biography are academic, not literary matters. Liberty, beauty, and the glory of the human mind should be supreme."

BIOGRAPHICAL/CRITICAL SOURCES:

PERIODICALS

Booklist, March 15, 2000, Donna Seaman, review of *Nabokov's Butterflies: Unpublished and Uncollected Writings,* p. 1304.

Guardian, March 25, 2000, Jay Parini, "The Wings of Desire."

Library Journal, October 15, 1999, Rebecca A. Stuhr, review of *Lo's Diary,* p. 107; March 1, 2000, Ronald Ray Ratliff, review of *Nabokov's Butterflies: Unpublished and Uncollected Writings,* p. 90.

Los Angeles Times, October 24, 1989.

New York Times, October 5, 1989; October 20, 1995, Michiko Kakutani, "Seeing Nabokov Grow over Thirty Years."

New York Times Book Review, October 1, 1989; October 29, 1995, John Updike, "A Jeweler's Eye."

Publishers Weekly, September 4, 1995, review of *The Stories of Vladimir Nabokov,* p. 46; June 21, 1999, Calvin Reid and Judy Quinn, "Rossett, Nabokov Estate Agree on 'Lolita' Retelling," p. 16; October 11, 1999, review of *Lo's Diary,* p. 56; March 13, 2000, review of *Nabokov's Butterflies: Unpublished and Uncollected Writings,* p. 74.

Times Literary Supplement, March 9, 1990.

Tribune Books (Chicago), September 24, 1989.

Washington Post Book World, October 15, 1989.

OTHER

Books Unlimited, http://www.booksunlimited.co.uk/ (November 18, 2000).

CNN, http://www.cgi.cnn.com/books/news/ (June 17, 1999).

Salon.com, http://www.salonmag.com/books/ (April 19, 1999), interview with Dmitri Nabokov.*

NAYLOR, Eric W(oodfin) 1936-

PERSONAL: Born December 6, 1936, in Union City, TN; son of Woodfin J. and Gertrude (Waddell) Naylor. *Education:* University of the South, B.A., 1958; University of Wisconsin, M.A., 1969, Ph.D., 1973. *Religion:* Episcopalian.

ADDRESSES: Office—Department of Spanish, University of the South, Sewanee, TN 37383-1000.

CAREER: University of the South, Sewanee, TN, instructor, 1962-66, assistant professor, 1966-70, associate professor of Spanish, 1970-76, professor, 1976—, currently Keenan Professor of Spanish.

MEMBER: American Association of Teachers of Spanish and Portuguese, American Association of University Professors, Medieval Academy, Phi Beta Kappa.

AWARDS, HONORS: Woodrow Wilson fellowship, 1958-59; Fulbright research fellowship, 1964-65 and 1983-84; National Endowment for the Humanities Old Spanish Dictionary Project, 1976.

WRITINGS:

(With Manuel Criado de Val) *El Libro de buen amor. Texto paleografico,* Consejo Superior de Investigaciones Científicas (Madrid, Spain), 1965, 2nd edition, 1972.

(With Criado) *Glosario de la edicion critica del "Libro de buen amor,"* S.E.R.E.S.A. (Barcelona, Spain), 1972.

(With Criado) *Libro de buen amor. Edicion critica y artistica,* Aguilar (Madrid, Spain), 1976.

(With Criado) *Libro de buen amor. Edicion Facsimil del Manuscrito T[oledo],* 3 volumes, Espasa-Calpe (Madrid, Spain), 1977, reprinted in one volume as *The Artistic Celebration of the Centenary of Espasa-Calpe Publishing House,* 1998.

(Editor, with Thomas D. Spaccarelli) *An Anthology of Spanish Literature to 1700,* 2 volumes, University of the South (Sewanee, TN), 1981.

The Text and Concordances of the Escorial Manuscript h. iii.10 of the "Arcipreste de Talavera" of Alfonso Martinez de Toledo, Seminary of Medieval Spanish Studies (Madison), 1983.

La "Sevillana Medicina" of Juan de Avinon, Seminary of Medieval Spanish Studies (Madison), 1987.

(Editor) *An Anthology of Latin American Literature,* University of the South (Sewanee, TN), 1987.

Pero Lopez de Ayala's Castilian Translation of Boccaccio's "De casibus," Seminary of Medieval Spanish Studies (Madison), 1994.

Co-editor with Robert Benson of a festschrift in honor of Edward B. King, University of the South (Sewanee, TN), 1991.

WORK IN PROGRESS: Translation into English of *El Corbacho,* by Martinez de Toledo, Arcipreste de Talavera; and *La cosomografia de Fernando Colon: Un Estudio y mapa.*

*   *   *

NELSON, Daniel 1941-

PERSONAL: Born August 28, 1941, in Indianapolis, IN; son of Melvin A. and Josephine (Hasfurther) Nelson; married Lorraine May, June 15, 1963; children: Catherine, Debra. *Education:* Ohio Wesleyan University, B.A., 1963; Ohio State University, M.A., 1964; University of Wisconsin—Madison, Ph.D., 1967. *Politics:* Independent. *Religion:* Congregationalist. *Avocational interests:* Environmental action, politics.

ADDRESSES: Home—970 North Hametown Rd., Akron, OH 44333. *Office*—c/o Department of History, University of Akron, Akron, OH 44325. *E-mail*—nelson@ uakron.edu.

CAREER: University of Delaware, Newark, assistant professor of history, 1967-70; worked at Hagley Library, 1967-70; University of Akron, Akron, OH, associate professor, 1970-77, professor of history, 1977-2000, professor emeritus, 2000—, director of graduate studies, 1974-79, department chair, 1995-98. Eleutherian Mills Historical Library, specialist in industrial collections, 1967-69, coordinator of Hagley fellowship program for Eleutherian Mills Hagley Foundation, 1969-70; University of Akron Press, director, 1988-92.

MEMBER: Sierra Club, Portage Trail Group, Medina-Summit Land Conservancy (vice president, 2000—), Phi Beta Kappa.

AWARDS, HONORS: Clarence A. Kulp Award, 1971, for *Unemployment Insurance: The American Experience, 1915-35;* Book Award, Ohio Academy of History,

1989, for *American Rubber Workers and Organized Labor;* "outstanding academic book" citation, *Choice,* 1998, for *Shifting Fortunes: The Rise and Decline of American Labor, from the 1820s to the Present.*

WRITINGS:

Unemployment Insurance: The American Experience, 1915-35, University of Wisconsin Press (Madison, WI), 1969.

Managers and Workers: Origins of the New Factory System, 1880-1920, University of Wisconsin Press (Madison, WI), 1975, revised edition published as *Managers and Workers: Origins of the Twentieth-Century Factory System, 1880-1920,* 1995.

Frederick W. Taylor and the Rise of Scientific Management, University of Wisconsin Press (Madison, WI), 1980.

American Rubber Workers and Organized Labor, 1900-1941, Princeton University Press (Princeton, NJ), 1988.

(Editor) *A Mental Revolution: Scientific Management since Taylor,* Ohio State University Press (Columbus, OH), 1992.

Farm and Factory: Workers in the Midwest, 1880-1990, Indiana University Press (Bloomington, IN), 1995.

Shifting Fortunes: The Rise and Decline of American Labor, from the 1820s to the Present, Ivan R. Dee (Chicago, IL), 1997.

(Editor) Alfred Winslow Jones, *Life, Liberty, and Property,* University of Akron Press (Akron, OH), 1999.

Contributor to books, including *Yankee Enterprise,* edited by Otto Mayr and Robert C. Post, Smithsonian Press (Washington, DC), 1981; *Le Taylorisme,* [Paris, France], 1984; *Masters to Managers,* edited by Sanford Jacoby, Columbia University Press (New York, NY), 1990; and *Industrial Valley,* revised edition, ILR Press (Ithaca, NY), 1992. Some of Nelson's books have been published in Japan.

WORK IN PROGRESS: Northern Landscapes: The Struggle for Wilderness Alaska.

SIDELIGHTS: Daniel Nelson, professor of history emeritus at the University of Akron, is an acknowledged expert in the field of U.S. business and labor history. His published works include subjects such as unemployment insurance, the history of the factory system, a study of efficiency expert Frederick W. Taylor, and a history of the American labor movement. Reviewers have generally praised Nelson's thoroughness, and in spite of his disinterest in social history, his work has been called accessible and perceptive.

In 1975 he produced *Managers and Workers: Origins of the New Factory System, 1880-1920.* This work has become the pre-eminent text on the development of the American factory system. It covers topics such as the relationship between technological and organizational innovation, including the rise of mass production, scientific management, and personnel work, and incorporates important scholarship on these topics from the 1970s through the 1990s.

In a review of the later edition of this work, *Business History* critic Michael Huberman praised the "concise and well-documented" narrative of the first edition and noted that it had stimulated some of the later scholarship that was incorporated into the next edition. Huberman, however, found a lack of "the new literature on the economic history of labour markets" in the book, adding that it "suffers from a lack of international comparisons." Still, he labeled it a standard work in its field, one whose "argument has stood the test of time."

Alex Keyssar, writing in *Industrial and Labor Relations Review,* called Nelson's 1988 work *American Rubber Workers and Organized Labor: 1900-1941* "an important, colorful, and intriguing" story. Using the rubber workers of his native Akron as his base, Nelson presents an account of their organizing efforts and political activities from the era before rubber tires were prevalent to the dramatic, sometimes violent events of the 1930s and 1940s. Keyssar also cited what he called Nelson's narrow focus on "opportunity and response" and on the effects of the business cycle. Keyssar said that the book is an "institutional account" that gives little attention to the social history of rubber workers' lives and spends too much time criticizing Socialists and Communists involved in the rubber workers' labor movement. "[T]he sound of grinding axes is sufficiently loud that it can make a reader uneasy," the reviewer commented. In *Business History Review* Stephen Amberg wrote a much more positive review, noting that Nelson's book "is a generally excellent work that explains unionization by linking it to developments in technology, industrial organization, business strategies, and politics. . . . It will become the definitive study of the unionization of the rubber industry."

In 1980 Nelson published *Frederick Taylor and the Rise of Scientific Management,* an account of Taylor's efforts to transform the factory system in the late nine-

teenth and early twentieth centuries. In 1993 Nelson collected eight essays by different authors that deal with the effects of Taylor's work in a volume titled *A Mental Revolution: Scientific Management since Taylor.* In the *Business History Review,* Hindy Lauer Schachter commented, "This book suggests that a final verdict on whether Taylor was hero or villain cannot emerge from the work of his followers, because his ideas have appealed to people embracing many contradictory programs. The essays contribute to our knowledge of Taylorism's impact by underscoring the diversity of activities and attitudes emanating from scientific management."

Farm and Factory: Workers in the Midwest, 1880-1990 attempts to outline the ways Midwestern industrialization and farm mechanization changed the face of the nation. Dennis Deslippe wrote in *Business History Review* that the book is really "an industrial history of the Midwest" rather than a treatise on the lives of workers. According to Nelson, the Midwest was ripe for industrial development because of its abundant natural resources and its ready pool of labor. The success of the Midwestern economy, he writes, tended to discourage innovation, eventually leading to a decline beginning in the 1950s, when manufacturers started to flee to other areas. Deslippe praised Nelson's "attention to detail" and said that he is "especially effective in emphasizing the importance of technology." Deslippe pointed out a number of questionable assertions in the book, however, and also noted that the book is "not a work about ideology or culture"; "it is never quite clear what place class conflict has" in the narrative. Yet he felt that it thoroughly presented "vast economic, political, and demographic data" and found it useful for academicians in the field.

In 1997 Nelson offered an overview of the history of labor unions in *Shifting Fortunes: The Rise and Decline of American Labor, from the 1820s to the Present.* In this volume he traces labor history from the nineteenth-century mines to the firing of air-traffic controllers by President Reagan in the 1980s, stressing three themes: the increasing autonomy of workers, the benefits of joining labor unions versus the fear of management reprisals, and the condition of the economy at the time he wrote the book. According to Robert Bussel in *Industrial and Labor Relations Review,* Nelson emphasizes "the importance of external factors" on the history of labor unions, "specifically downplaying the importance of ideological and structural concerns." Bussel felt that this approach "tends to underestimate the crucial roles of leadership and human agency"—for example, the importance of union leaders like A. Philip Randolph or

Cesar Chavez. Neither does Nelson, according to Bussel, address recent attempts by unions to increasing their organizing activity. However, "his perceptive, judicious, and unsentimental analysis is a valuable contribution to the renewed discussion about the prospects for union growth."

BIOGRAPHICAL/CRITICAL SOURCES:

PERIODICALS

Business History, July, 1997, Michael Huberman, review of *Managers and Workers: Origins of the New Factory System, 1880-1920,* p. 161.

Business History Review, spring, 1989, Stephen Amberg, review of *American Rubber Workers and Organized Labor, 1900-1941,* pp. 206-209; winter, 1993, Hindy Lauer Schachter, review of *A Mental Revolution: Scientific Management since Taylor,* pp. 655-666; spring, 1997, Dennis Deslippe, review of *Farm and Factory: Workers in the Midwest, 1880-1990,* pp. 127-128.

Industrial and Labor Relations Review, April, 1990, Alex Keyssar, review of *American Rubber Workers and Organized Labor,* pp. 491-492; January, 1999, Robert Bussel, review of *Shifting Fortunes: The Rise and Decline of American Labor, from the 1820s to the Present,* pp. 326-328.

Library Journal, October 15, 1997, Harry Frumerman, review of *Shifting Fortunes,* p. 75.

*   *   *

NEWCOMB, Kerry 1946-
   (Shana Carrol, Peter Gentry, Christina Savage, joint pseudonyms)

PERSONAL: Born December 7, 1946, in Milford, CT; son of Paul Guy (a tool designer) and Anne Marie (Reno) Newcomb; married Patricia Blackwell (a potter), June 14, 1976. *Education:* University of Texas at Arlington, B.A., 1969; Trinity University, San Antonio, TX, M.F.A., 1973. *Politics:* "Populist." *Religion:* Roman Catholic.

ADDRESSES: Home—Ft. Worth, TX. *Agent*—Aaron M. Priest Literary Agency, 708 Third Ave., 23rd Fl., New York, NY 10017.

CAREER: St. Labre Mission School, Ashland, MT, teacher, 1973-74; writer, 1974—. Served in Jesuit Volunteer Corps. Has worked as a singer, entertainer, and director of plays.

AWARDS, HONORS: Greer Garson Award for Achievement in the Theatre from Dallas Theatre Centre, 1972.

WRITINGS:

Feathers (one-act play), first produced in Dallas, TX, at Dallas Theatre Center, March 10, 1972.

Dear Luger (play), first produced at Dallas Theatre Center, January 12, 1973.

(With Frank Schaefer) *Pandora Man,* Morrow (New York, NY), 1979.

(With Schaefer) *The Ghosts of Elkhorn,* Morrow (New York, NY), 1982.

Morning Star, Bantam (New York, NY), 1983.

Sacred Is the Wind, 1990.

Call down Thunder, 1990.

In the Season of the Sun, 1990.

Ride the Panther, 1993.

Jack Iron, Bantam (New York, NY), 1993.

Scorpion, 1995.

The Arrow Keeper's Song, 1995.

The Red Ripper, St. Martin's (New York, NY), 1999.

Mad Morgan, St. Martin's (New York, NY), 2000.

Also contributor to theater magazines.

"ANTHEM" SERIES

Texas Anthem, St. Martin's (New York, NY), 2000.

Texas Born, St. Martin's (New York, NY), 2001.

Shadow Walker, St. Martin's (New York, NY), 2001.

WITH FRANK SCHAEFER, UNDER JOINT PSEUDONYM SHANA CARROL

Paxton Pride, Pyramid (New York, NY), 1976.

Raven, Jove (New York, NY), 1978.

Yellow Rose, Jove (New York, NY), 1982.

WITH FRANK SCHAEFER, UNDER JOINT PSEUDONYM PETER GENTRY

Rafe, Fawcett (New York, NY), 1976.

Titus Gamble, Fawcett (New York, NY), 1978.

Matanza, Fawcett (New York, NY), 1979.

King of the Golden Gate, Fawcett (New York, NY), 1981.

WITH FRANK SCHAEFER, UNDER JOINT PSEUDONYM CHRISTINA SAVAGE

Love's Wildest Fires, Dell (New York, NY), 1977.
Dawn Wind, Dell (New York, NY), 1979.
Tempest, Dell (New York, NY), 1982.

SIDELIGHTS: Kerry Newcomb is the author of historical adventure novels ranging in setting from the American West of the nineteenth century to the days of piracy in the seventeenth century Caribbean. As a *Kirkus Reviews* contributor noted, Newcomb's novels feature "black-hearted villains, lionhearted heroes, and bosomy beauties."

Set in Montana in the early nineteenth century, Newcomb's *In the Season of the Sun* tells of two young brothers who are separated when their party of pioneers is attacked by renegade Shoshoni Indians. Years later the boys confront each other after having been raised in diversely different surroundings and with revenge as their motivating emotion. The critic for *Publishers Weekly* called *In the Season of the Sun* a "workmanlike tale" in which "the Indian lore is handled respectfully and intelligently."

The Red Ripper is a fictionalized retelling of the real-life story of William Wallace, a heroic figure in the history of early Texas and a descendant of Scottish hero William the Braveheart. In Newcomb's tale, Wallace is an expert knife fighter whose adventures take him across Mexico and Texas in search of revenge for his brother's murder, accompanied by an old pirate named Mad Jack, the Butcher of Barbados. Swept up in the Texas Revolution, and infatuated with the beautiful wife of a friend, Wallace joins the men at the ill-fated Alamo in their desperate struggle against the Mexican army. *Publisher's Weekly* quoted Newcomb on his fictional embellishments: "'What isn't true, ought to be.'" The same article noted the novel's "action-filled plot, the broadbrush sagebrush scenes and the romance of the Texas Republic." Budd Arthur in *Booklist* called *The Red Ripper* "an entertaining tale of high adventure and low villains."

In *Mad Morgan* Newcomb bases his story on the life of Henry Morgan, an Englishman who turned to piracy in the seventeenth century and preyed on Spanish treasure ships in the Caribbean. Newcomb's tale finds Morgan sacking the Spanish outpost of Panama City, vying for the attention of his beloved, and eventually sailing back home to England a wealthy man. The critic for *Kirkus Reviews* noted that *Mad Morgan* displayed "flagrant overwriting, derivative plotting: a swashbuckler indeed."

Newcomb has also written a number of novels with Frank Schaefer under various pseudonyms, as well as their real names. The two writers send drafts of their novels back and forth to one another for additions, changes, and input. "We talk of our pseudonyms as individuals," Newcomb told a *Publishers Weekly* interviewer, "because each one has a style that's slightly different from the other. I guess we speak in schizo-sounding language, but it seems to work. . . . The worst part of this pseudonym business is when my wife says to someone she's married to Christina Savage. It gets worse when she says she's also married to Shana Carrol, but then she completes her menage a trois by saying she's married to Peter Gentry too, and so, what the heck?"

In 2000, Newcomb began a series set in Texas in the 1800s. *Texas Anthem, Texas Born,* and *Shadow Walker* tell the saga of the Anthem family, ranchers who must contend with the harshness of the American frontier. In *Texas Born,* John Anthem must abandon the ranch that he struggled to build, to pursue a Mexican bandit who has dealt Anthem's family a devastating blow. In *Shadow Walker,* John Anthem's seventeen year-old son, Cole, restless with life in Texas, strikes out for Arkansas and becomes a bounty hunter. In the town of Teardrop, Cole must hunt down a half breed renegade, the Osage Kid, accused of series of murders. Knowing the Kid is innocent, Cole must team up with the renegade and track the real killer.

BIOGRAPHICAL/CRITICAL SOURCES:

PERIODICALS

Booklist, May 15, 1999, Budd Arthur, review of *The Red Ripper,* p. 1670.
Kirkus Reviews, June 15, 2000, review of *Mad Morgan,* p. 824.
Kliatt, September, 1995, review of *The Arrow Keeper's Song,* p. 13.
Publishers Weekly, May 23, 1980, interview with Kerry Newcomb; January 5, 1990, review of *In the Season of the Sun,* p. 68; May 24, 1999, review of *The Red Ripper,* p. 68.
Roundup, spring, 1993, review of *Ride the Panther,* p. 49; January, 1995, review of *Scorpion,* p. 28.*

O

OLSEN, Jack
See OLSEN, John Edward

*   *   *

OLSEN, John Edward 1925-
(Jack Olsen; Jonathan Rhoades, a pseudonym)

PERSONAL: Born June 7, 1925, in Indianapolis, IN; son of Rudolph O. (in sales) and Florence (Drecksage) Olsen; married Su Peterson, 1966; children: John Robert, Susan Joyce, Jonathan Rhoades, Julia Crispin, Evan Pierce, Barrie Elizabeth, Emily Sara Peterson, Harper Alexander Peterson. *Education:* Attended University of Pennsylvania, 1945-46.

ADDRESSES: Agent—Scott Meredith Literary Agency, 845 Third Ave., New York, NY 10022.

CAREER: San Diego Union Tribune, San Diego, CA, reporter, 1947-48; *San Diego Journal,* San Diego, reporter, 1949-50; *Washington Daily News,* Washington, DC, reporter, 1950-51; WMAL-TV, Washington, DC, television news editor and broadcaster, 1950-51; *New Orleans Item,* New Orleans, LA, reporter, 1952-53; *Chicago Sun-Times,* Chicago, IL, reporter, 1954-55; *Time* magazine, correspondent, 1956-58, chief of Midwest bureau, 1959; *Sports Illustrated,* New York, NY, senior editor, 1960-74. Writer, 1960—. *Military service:* U.S. Army, Office of Strategic Services, 1943-44.

MEMBER: Authors Guild, Authors League of America, Defenders of Wildlife.

AWARDS, HONORS: National Headliner Award, Press Club of Atlantic City; Page One Award, Chicago Newspaper Guild; Washington Governor's Award; Special Edgar Award, Mystery Writers of America; citations from Indiana University and Columbia University; recipient of five Pulitzer Prize nominations.

WRITINGS:

(Under pseudonym Jonathan Rhoades) *Over the Fence Is Out,* Holt (New York, NY), 1961.

UNDER NAME JACK OLSEN

The Mad World of Bridge, Holt (New York, NY), 1960.
The Climb up to Hell, Harper (New York, NY), 1962.
(With Charles Henry Goren) *Bridge Is My Game,* Doubleday (New York, NY), 1965, published as *Bridge Is My Game: Lessons of a Lifetime,* Simon & Schuster (New York, NY), 1986.
Black Is Best: The Riddle of Cassius Clay, Putnam (New York, NY), 1967.
Silence on Monte Sole, Putnam (New York, NY), 1968.
The Black Athlete: A Shameful Story: The Myth of Integration in American Sport, Time-Life (New York, NY), 1968.
Night of the Grizzlies, Putnam (New York, NY), 1969, reprinted, Homestead Publications (Moose, WY), 1996.
(With Fran Tarkenton) *Better Scramble than Lose,* Four Winds Press (New York, NY), 1969.
The Bridge at Chappaquiddick, Little, Brown (Boston, MA), 1970.
Aphrodite: Desperate Mission, Putnam (New York, NY), 1970.
Slaughter the Animals, Poison the Earth, Simon & Schuster (New York, NY), 1971.

The Girls in the Office, Simon & Schuster (New York, NY), 1972.

The Girls on the Campus, Pocket Books (New York, NY), 1974.

Sweet Street: The Autobiography of an American Honkytonk Scene, Ballantine (New York, NY), 1974.

The Man with the Candy: The Story of the Houston Mass Murders, Simon & Schuster (New York, NY), 1974.

Alphabet Jackson (novel), Playboy Press (Chicago, IL), 1974.

Massy's Game, Playboy Press (Chicago, IL), 1975.

The Secret of Fire Five, Random House (New York, NY), 1977.

Night Watch (novel), Times Books (New York, NY), 1979.

Missing Persons, Atheneum (New York, NY), 1981.

Have You Seen My Son?, Atheneum (New York, NY), 1982.

"Son": A Psychopath and His Victims, Atheneum (New York, NY), 1983.

Give a Boy a Gun: A True Story of Law and Disorder in the American West, Delacorte (New York, NY), 1985.

Cold Kill: The True Story of a Murderous Love, Atheneum (New York, NY), 1987.

"Doc": The Rape of the Town of Lovell, Atheneum (New York, NY), 1989.

Predator: Rape, Madness, and Injustice in Seattle, Delacorte (New York, NY), 1991.

The Misbegotten Son: A Serial Killer and His Victims: The True Story of Arthur Shawcross, Delacorte (New York, NY), 1993.

Charmer: A Ladies' Man and His Victims, Morrow (New York, NY), 1994.

Salt of the Earth: One Family's Journey through the Violent American Landscape, St. Martin's (New York, NY), 1996.

Hastened to the Grave: The Gypsy Murder Investigation, St. Martin's (New York, NY), 1998.

Last Man Standing: The Tragedy and Triumph of Geronimo Pratt, Doubleday (New York, NY), 2000.

Contributor to anthologies. Contributor of articles to periodicals, including *Daily Sketch, Fortune, Life, Nouvelle Candide, Reader's Digest, Sports Illustrated, This Week, Time,* and other periodicals.

SIDELIGHTS: A long-time reporter and author of numerous nonfiction works and novels, John Edward "Jack" Olsen is probably best known for his contributions to the "true crime" genre with such works as *The Man with the Candy: The Story of the Houston Mass Murders* and *Give a Boy a Gun: A True Story of Law and Disorder in the American West.* While other books of real-life crimes tend to exploit the lurid aspects of violent actions, Olsen's books avoid focusing on the more prurient elements of criminal cases and instead provide detailed portraits of both the perpetrators and their victims. In *The Man with the Candy,* for example, which investigates the abuse and murders of almost thirty young boys, Olsen "has dissected the sociology of the neighborhood in some depth," noted Dorothy Rabinowitz in the *Saturday Review/World.* "More to the point, his brief sketches of the families from which the murder victims came do much to dispel the unreality that surrounds these boys and their fate."

Reviewers have also commented on Olsen's method of presenting a complete and thorough story while leaving the judgments for his readers to make. In *Give a Boy a Gun,* the account of Claude Dallas, a self-proclaimed "mountain man" who executed two Idaho game wardens and avoided capture for over a year, Olsen "does a very commendable job of refraining from indulging in social commentary and delivering the facts of the case," according to Theodore J. Johnson in *Best Sellers.* The author creates such portraits with a variety of information; *Newsweek* writer Gene Lyons remarked that *Give a Boy a Gun* contains many "virtues," including "a crisp, unambiguous style, a gift for interviewing people in their own terms . . . and an ear for the apposite quote." In *Cold Kill: The Story of a Murderous Love,* Olsen "has another winner," to quote a *Publishers Weekly* reviewer. This study of a woman who convinces her lover to murder her parents "is a somewhat unusual true-crime study," asserted the critic, not because of its topic but for "its searching psychological depiction of the killers."

The study of a young real estate agent who is exposed as a brutal serial rapist, *"Son": A Psychopath and His Victims* is Olsen's best-known work. It is certainly one that intrigued its author, for Olsen spent seventeen months and fifty thousand dollars of his own money researching the crimes. "'This case had all the wonderful elements for a crime book,'" Olsen told *Publishers Weekly* correspondent Lisa See, "'a detective story filled with mystery, human tragedy on the scale of *Hamlet,* revenge, avarice, hatred, terror and irony. Most people have a hobby like collecting stamps or woodworking. [Convicted rapist Fred] Coe's hobbies were looking, peeping, making obscene phone calls and attacking women.'" The case was further complicated after Coe's conviction, when his mother attempted to hire a hit man to kill the presiding judge and prosecutor of the trial.

"Such are the makings of this true story," explained Lowell Cauffiel in the *Detroit News*. "It is bizarre on its own merits, but in the practiced hands of veteran journalist Jack Olsen . . . it becomes a riveting look at the monster lurking beneath a criminal psychopath's polished exterior."

Time contributor J. D. Reed observed that while most true crime narratives are "almost as pernicious as the criminals" in their focus on psychological rationalizations of the criminal's behavior, "Jack Olsen will have none of this. In *Son* he is out to study the evildoer and to finger those who made him go wrong." Other critics, such as *Times Literary Supplement* contributor Clancy Sigal, felt that Olsen focuses too much on the details of the crime and does not do enough to "make interesting links between the multiple rapist's respectable origins and his crimes." Cauffiel, however, believed that these "detailed vignettes shun psychobabble, allowing the reader to speculate for himself." In addition, "Olsen manages to keep the horror of the crimes and subsequent court case before us," stated Carolyn Banks in the *Washington Post*. "He gives us you-are-there accounts by several of the victims, erasing any urge to laugh [at the Coe family's bizarre behavior]." Marty Lieberman concurred, writing in the *Los Angeles Times Book Review* that "Olsen succeeds on all levels," including his "compassionate treatment of rape victims." "The story of the Coe family is a good one on its own," concluded Banks; "because of Jack Olsen's selectivity and skill, it's even better."

In *Salt of the Earth: One Family's Journey through the Violent American Landscape*, Olsen produces a portrait of a family caught in the most horrific of circumstances: Their young daughter has disappeared and is believed to be a murder victim. Rather than focus on the daughter's abduction, however, Olsen portrays the grieving family and their relationships prior to the event and afterwards, delving into their suffering and their brave attempts to carry on with their lives and seek justice for their child. In his *New York Times Book Review* piece, Mark Arax declared: "Through the sheer amount of detail in his reporting, [Olsen] makes their lives and pain count, and he generally succeeds in telling a story of the human spirit's refusal to succumb to incomprehensible tragedy." Christopher Lehmann-Haupt in the *New York Times* commended Olsen for his "painstaking research and wholly objective reporting—with never a scene fictionalized—[that] make you share the agony of the Geres' experience, their hope, their dread, their self-delusion, their rage, their resistance to the truth and, at long last, the awful aftermath of what happened to them."

Hastened to the Grave: The Gypsy Murder Investigation is one of Olsen's most involved projects. Working closely with a San Francisco private investigator named Fay Faron—also known as Rat Dog Dick—Olsen investigates the nefarious activities of a Gypsy family whose various members have conned elderly people out of their wealth and in some cases allegedly murdered them as well. Having been asked to investigate one eighty-two-year-old woman's relationship with a man named Danny Tene—which culminated in the woman's signing over her property to Tene—Faron detected foul play. Faron was convinced that Tene was engaged in criminal activity after the woman unexpectedly died, leaving Tene her entire fortune. *Hastened to the Grave* follows Faron as she almost single-handedly exposes similar cases in San Francisco and builds a case against the extended Tene Bimbo clan. In the *New York Times Book Review*, Judith Newman called the book "a cautionary tale about the perils of loneliness in a society that has ceased to value old age." *Booklist* contributor Mike Tribby deemed the work "masterfully told," adding that "the quintessential story . . . would be funny if it weren't so sad."

Olsen was drawn to the almost incredible tale of Geronimo Pratt after conversing with O. J. Simpson lawyer Johnnie Cochran. A decorated Vietnam War veteran and founding member of the Black Panthers, Pratt was targeted by the Federal Bureau of Investigation and was set up for conviction on a murder he did not commit. *Last Man Standing: The Tragedy and Triumph of Geronimo Pratt* details Pratt's efforts to exonerate himself, with the help of Cochran and other lawyers and clergy who believed in him. "One part Kafka and one part Orwell, the story of Geronimo Pratt's conviction . . . is a textbook case of abuse of the American criminal justice system for political ends," according to a *Publishers Weekly* reviewer. The reviewer further credited Olsen's book as "rigorously researched, skillfully organized, and passionately written." In *Library Journal*, Philip Y. Blue praised *Last Man Standing* as "a classic expose of how an innocent's rights can be swept under the rug of politics and power."

Olsen told *CA:* "I have spent forty years trying to tell it like it is. It hasn't been easy."

BIOGRAPHICAL/CRITICAL SOURCES:

PERIODICALS

Best Sellers, November 15, 1974; March, 1986.
Booklist, May 1, 1998, Mike Tribby, review of *Hastened to the Grave: The Gypsy Murder Investigation*, p. 1483.

Detroit News, March 11, 1984.

Kirkus Reviews, August 15, 2000, review of *Last Man Standing: The Tragedy and Triumph of Geronimo Pratt,* pp. 1174-75.

Library Journal, August, 2000, Philip Y. Blue, review of *Last Man Standing: The Tragedy and Triumph of Geronimo Pratt,* p. 128.

Los Angeles Times Book Review, February 12, 1984.

Newsweek, December 9, 1985.

New York Times, July 21, 1972; May 6, 1996, Christopher Lehmann-Haupt, "An American Family's Journey to Hell and Back."

New York Times Book Review, July 2, 1972; September 27, 1981; February 5, 1984; January 12, 1986; June 16, 1996, Mark Arax, "A Family under Siege"; May 31, 1998, Judith Newman, "No Country for the Old," p. 46.

Publishers Weekly, November 19, 1983; October 2, 1987; April 13, 1998, review of *Hastened to the Grave: The Gypsy Murder Investigation,* p. 62; July 24, 2000, review of *Last Man Standing: The Tragedy and Triumph of Geronimo Pratt,* p. 75.

Saturday Review/World, November 2, 1974.

Time, July 31, 1972, March 19, 1984.

Times Literary Supplement, August 17, 1984.

Washington Post, February 13, 1984.

OTHER

Amazon.com, http://www.amazon.com/ (September 25, 2000), interview with Olsen related to *Hastened to the Grave: The Gypsy Murder Investigation.*

Jack Olsen Home Page, http://www.jackolsen.com/ (September 25, 2000).*

*   *   *

OSBORNE, Milton Edgeworth 1936-

PERSONAL: Born April 17, 1936, in Sydney, Australia; son of George Davenport (a university professor) and Gwynneth J. (Love) Osborne. *Education:* University of Sydney, B.A. (with first class honors), 1958; Cornell University, Ph.D., 1968.

ADDRESSES: Home—42/177 Bellevue Rd., Double Bay, New South Wales 2028, Australia.

CAREER: Australian Diplomatic Service, staff member, 1958-62, member of embassy staff in Phnom Penh, Cambodia, 1959-61; University of Sydney, Sydney, Australia, lecturer, 1962-63; Monash University, Melbourne, Australia, began as senior lecturer, became associate professor of history, 1967-71; American University, Washington, DC, associate professor of history, 1972-74; British Institute in South-East Asia, Singapore, director, 1975-79; Australian National University, Canberra, senior research fellow in international relations, 1979-81; Office of National Assessments, Canberra, Australia, head of Asia Branch, 1982-93; freelance writer and consultant on Asian issues.

MEMBER: Australian Institute of International Affairs, Association for Asian Studies.

WRITINGS:

Singapore and Malaysia, Cornell University Press (Ithaca, NY), 1964.

Strategic Hamlets in South Viet-Nam, Cornell University Press (Ithaca, NY), 1965.

Southeast Asian Reactions to Possible Alternative American Policies in Asia (monograph), Institute of Advanced Studies, Australian National University (Canberra, Australia), 1968.

The French Presence in Cochinchina and Cambodia: Rule and Response (1859-1905), Cornell University Press (Ithaca, NY), 1969.

Region of Revolt: Focus on Southeast Asia, Pergamon (Elmsford, NY), 1970.

Politics and Power in Cambodia, Longman (New York, NY), 1974.

River Road to China: The Mekong River Expedition, 1866-1873, Liveright (New York, NY), 1975.

From Conviction to Anxiety: The French Self-Image in Vietnam (monograph), School of Social Sciences, Flinders University of South Australia (Bedford Park, Australia), 1976.

Southeast Asia: An Introductory History, Allen & Unwin (North Sydney, Australia), 1979, 5th edition, 1990.

Before Kampuchea: Preludes to Tragedy, Allen & Unwin (North Sydney, Australia), 1979.

(Editor) *Ho Chi Minh,* 1982.

Southeast Asia: An Illustrated Introductory History, Allen & Unwin (North Sydney, Australia), 1985.

Fear and Fascination in the Tropics: A Reader's Guide to French Fiction in Indochina, Center for Southeast Asian Studies, University of Wisconsin (Madison, WI), 1986.

Sihanouk: Prince of Light, Prince of Darkness, University of Hawaii Press (Honolulu, HI), 1994.

Strategic Hamlets in South Viet-Nam: A Survey and Comparison, Southeast Asia Program, Department of Asian Studies, Cornell University (Ithaca, NY), 1997.

The Mekong: Turbulent Past, Uncertain Future, Atlantic Monthly Press (New York, NY), 2000.

Contributor to the *New Republic* and a number of scholarly journals.

SIDELIGHTS: Australian author Milton Edgeworth Osborne is an acknowledged expert on Southeast Asia with vast experience in diplomatic circles and in academia. He has produced numerous books on the history, culture, and peoples of the region, culminating in *The Mekong: Turbulent Past, Uncertain Future* in 2000.

The Mekong grew out of Osborne's forty-year personal fascination with the great river that is the lifeblood of China, Burma, Laos, Cambodia, and Vietnam. His ambitious study covers the history of the region from the great Cambodian empire of the ninth century to the coming of western explorers and missionaries, and from the French wars of colonization to the tragedies that preceded and followed the Vietnam war. In addition, he deals extensively with environmental threats to the great river delta. Of particular concern are the many dams already built and those that China plans to build along the river. These dams will bring uncertain effects upon the important fishing industry and other human uses of the river.

In an interview with Robyn Williams for the Australian Broadcasting Corporation that was published on the Internet, Osborne expressed his concerns about the decline in fish catches in recent years and also reviewed the effects of logging, increased agricultural activity, chemical fertilizers, and especially dam building. "What will be the effect of these dams?," he asked. "When all China's dams are in place the Mekong will continue to flow, but it may be a very different river from that which we know today." He added, "Writing about the Mekong more than a hundred years ago, the French explorer Francis Garnier observed that '[w]ithout doubt, no other river, over such a length, has a more singular or remarkable character.' Those who travel on and beside the Mekong today can readily share Garnier's sentiments. Whether they will be able to do so in the future is now open to question."

Reviewers were generally favorable in their assessments of *The Mekong.* Danny Yee on the *Dannyreviews* Web site called the book "episodic and personal, but also readable and informative." *Library Journal* contributor Peggy Spitzer Cristoff called attention to Osborne's "obsession" with the Mekong, begun when he was in the foreign service and continuing through forty years of living and traveling in the region. She felt that Osborne is "not very effective" when he tries to link events in early and modern history but recommended this "very readable book" for most large libraries.

A *Publishers Weekly* reviewer called *The Mekong* a "pathbreaking, ecologically informed chronicle." The critic noted that although the work "is not quite the full-bodied cultural saga the river deserves, his book is a pulsating journey through the heart of Southeast Asia." *Columbus Dispatch* writer John Nance said that the book "provides a broad geographical and historical context in which to view mainland South Asia's past 2,000 years of complex and often violent human history." Nance concluded, "Osborne's book addresses the mighty river with fascination and appreciation. It answers questions about the region's yesterdays and todays, but raises difficult questions for tomorrow. It merits reading."

BIOGRAPHICAL/CRITICAL SOURCES:

PERIODICALS

Columbus Dispatch, July 9, 2000, John Nance, review of *The Mekong: Turbulent Past, Uncertain Future.*

Library Journal, June 1, 2000, Peggy Spitzer Christoff, review of *The Mekong,* p. 154.

Publishers Weekly, April 24, 2000, review of *The Mekong,* p. 69.

OTHER

Australian Broadcasting Corporation, http://www.abc. net/ (August 13, 2000), Robyn Williams, "Ockham's Razor."

DannyReviews.com, http://www.dannyreviews.com/ (September 25, 2000), Danny Yee, review of *The Mekong.*

*   *   *

OSTRIKER, Alicia (Suskin) 1937-

PERSONAL: Born November 11, 1937, in New York, NY; daughter of David (a civil service employee) and Beatrice (Linnick) Suskin; married Jeremiah P. Ostriker (a professor of astrophysics), December, 1958; children:

Alicia Ostriker

Rebecca, Eve, Gabriel. *Education:* Brandeis University, B.A., 1959: University of Wisconsin, M.A., 1961, Ph. D., 1964. *Religion:* Jewish.

ADDRESSES: Home—33 Phillip Dr., Princeton, NJ 08540. *Office*—Department of English, Murray Hall 203B, Rutgers University, New Brunswick, NJ 08903. *E-mail*—ostriker@rci.rutgers.edu.

CAREER: Rutgers University, assistant professor, 1965-68, associate professor, 1968-72, professor of English and creative writing, 1972—. February residency at Villa Serbelloni, Bellagio Study and Conference Center, Italy, 1999.

AWARDS, HONORS: National Council on the Humanities summer grant, 1968; National Endowment for the Arts fellowship, 1976-77; Pushcart Prize, 1979, 2000; New Jersey Arts Council fellowship, 1980-81; Rockefeller Foundation fellowship, 1982; Guggenheim Foundation fellowship, 1984-85; William Carlos Williams Prize, Poetry Society of America, 1986, for *The Imaginary Lover;* Strousse Poetry Prize, *Prairie Schooner,* 1986; Edward Stanley Award, *Prairie Schooner,* 1994;

Anna David Rosenberg Poetry Award, 1994; faculty fellow, Rutgers Center for Historical Analysis, 1995-96; National Book Award finalist, Paterson poetry Award, and San Francisco State Poetry Center Award, all 1996, all for *The Crack in Everything;* National Book Award finalist, and Bookman News Book of the Year, both 1998, and Lenore Marshall Poetry Award finalist, 1999, all for *The Little Space: Poems Selected and New, 1968-1998;* Readers' Choice Award for poems published in *Prairie Schooner,* 1998.

WRITINGS:

POETRY

Songs, Holt (New York, NY), 1969.
Once More out of Darkness, and Other Poems, Smith/Horizon Press (New York, NY), 1971, enlarged edition, Berkeley Poets Cooperative (Berkeley, CA), 1974.
A Dream of Springtime, Smith/Horizon Press (New York, NY), 1979.
The Mother/Child Papers, Momentum (Santa Monica, CA), 1980.
A Woman under the Surface: Poems and Prose Poems, Princeton University Press (Princeton, NJ), 1982.
The Imaginary Lover, University of Pittsburgh Press (Pittsburgh, PA), 1986.
Green Age, University of Pittsburgh Press (Pittsburgh, PA), 1989.
The Crack in Everything, University of Pittsburgh Press (Pittsburgh, PA), 1996.
The Little Space: Poems Selected and New, University of Pittsburgh Press (Pittsburgh, PA), 1998.

OTHER

Vision and Verse in William Blake, University of Wisconsin Press (Madison, WI), 1965.
(Editor) *William Blake: Complete Poems,* Penguin (New York, NY), 1977.
Writing like a Woman, University of Michigan Press (Ann Arbor, MI), 1983.
Stealing the Language: The Emergence of Women Poets in America, Beacon, 1986.
Feminist Revision and the Bible, Blackwell (Cambridge, MA), 1992.
The Nakedness of the Fathers: Biblical Visions and Revisions, Rutgers University Press (New Brunswick, NJ), 1994.

(Author of preface) *The Five Scrolls* (Old Testament Bible), Vintage (New York, NY), 2000.

Dancing at the Devil's Party: Essays on Poetry, Politics, and the Erotic, University of Michigan Press (Ann Arbor, MI), 2000.

Contributor of poems and essays to literary reviews and magazines, including *American Poetry Review, New Yorker, Atlantic Monthly, Paris Review, Nation, Poetry, Signs, Tikkun,* and *New York Times Book Review.* Contributor of poems and essays to anthologies, including *Unsettling America: Race and Ethnicity in Contemporary American Poetry,* edited by Maria Mazziotti Gillan, Viking, 1994; *Out of the Garden: Women Writers on the Bible,* edited by Christina Büchman and Celina Spiegel, Ballantine, 1994; *Our Mothers, Our Selves, Writers and Poets Celebrating Motherhood,* edited by Karen Donnelly and J.B. Bernstein, Bergen and Garvey (Westport, CT), 1996; and *Worlds in Our Words: Contemporary American Women Writers,* edited by Marilyn Kallett and Patricia Clark, Prentice Hall, 1997. Some of Ostriker's poems were included in *Best American Poetry* and *Yearbook of American Poetry,* 1996, and one poem was included in *Pushcart Prize Anthology,* 1999.

Ostriker's poems have been translated into French, Italian, German, Japanese, Hebrew, and Arabic.

WORK IN PROGRESS: The Volcano Sequence, University of Pittsburgh Press, 2002.

SIDELIGHTS: Alicia Ostriker has published nine books of poetry and several works of feminist literary criticism that examine the relationship between gender and literature. In a comment that applies to both Ostriker's poetry and criticism, Amy Williams in *Dictionary of Literary Biography* noted how Ostriker "consistently challenges limitations. For discovery to take place there must be movement, and Ostriker refuses to stand still; each volume tries to uncover anew what must be learned in order to gain wisdom, experience, and identity. She is a poet who breaks down walls." In the *Women's Review of Books,* Adrian Oktenberg wrote: "One of the great pleasures in reading Ostriker is hearing her think out loud; putting her humanity fully on the page is one of her strengths as a writer." Calling Ostriker "America's most fiercely honest poet," *Progressive* contributor Joel Brouwer observed that she "puts the reader to work, and she blenches at nothing that experience offers up." According to Williams, Ostriker's voice is "personal, honest, and strong; her poetry incorporates family experiences, social and political views, and a driving spirit that speaks for growth and, at times, with rage."

In Ostriker's criticism, she argues that literature written by women can be tracked as a tradition. In *Stealing the Language: The Emergence of Women Poets in America,* she asserts that women writers have produced poetry that is "explicitly female in the sense that the writers have chosen to explore experiences central to their sex." Furthermore, in their search to find an aesthetic that accommodates this expression, Ostriker claims that women poets are "challenging and transforming the history of poetry. They constitute a literary movement comparable to romanticism or modernism in our literary past."

These claims have evoked a wide range of response from reviewers. Frieda Gardner, writing in the *Women's Review of Books,* agreed that women have brought new subject matter to American poetry; the "thematic landscape" of literature now includes poems on "women's quests for self-definition, on the uses and treachery of anger, . . . female eroticism and, most impressively, on women poets' sweeping revision of Western mythology," according to Gardner. However, "lots of male poets grew fat on the 'butter and sugar' Ostriker calls peculiarly feminine," Mary Karr pointed out in a *Poetry* review. Reviewers also questioned the notion that poetry by women is unified by the concentrated "drive for power" that Ostriker sees in it. Nonetheless, stated Karr, "those predisposed to feminist criticism will eagerly take up these pages. At the other extreme, certain critics and philosophers will shudder at the very thought of women generating language, a practice they interpret as exclusively masculine."

The Nakedness of the Fathers: Biblical Visions and Revisions (1994) offers "an imaginative and spiritual dialogue with characters and narratives of the Old Testament," wrote Lynn Garrett in *Publishers Weekly.* By exploring both men's and women's stories from the Bible—from Adam and Eve to Job and Job's wife—and speaking through their voices, Ostriker attempts to offer a more humanized and modernized reading of the Bible, and in doing so, she attempts to reconcile the revisionism of feminism with the traditions of Judaism. She presents Esther through the lens of a post-Holocaust family party, and shows Job's wife as a bystander who must accept the "casual brutality of this world," according to Enid Dame in *Belles Lettres.* Ostriker's book is as grand and comprehensive as her subject, offering, noted Dame, "a retelling-with-commentary of Jewish scripture intertwined with a brilliant web of poems, stories, personal memoirs, scholarly observations, and speculative meditations." Ultimately, it is "in the reclamation of the *Shekhina,* or female aspect of God," stated Dame, that Ostriker finds a reconciliation between Judaism and feminism.

Dancing at the Devil's Party: Essays on Poetry, Politics, and the Erotic drew a great deal of praise for its observations on a multitude of poets, from John Milton and William Blake to Maxine Kumin and Lucille Clifton. *Pif Magazine* reviewer Rachel Barenblat maintained that, "for Ostriker, poems are both crucial and relevant. She respects poems, the way one respects magic or religion or anything that smacks of the ineffable." Noting that Ostriker approaches her subject matter with "passion and precision," Barenblat concluded: "Ostriker's criticism is grounded in her impressive knowledge of American literary traditions and their adherents. . . . This is a strong, compelling and beautiful collection of essays. I recommend it highly." In her review of the same title, Oktenberg stated: "As we follow [Ostriker] into her reading, we are more and more illuminated, not only intellectually but with a palpable, physical sense of expansion, and even spirituality. This is the best writing—it gets you at all levels." The critic concluded: "I would . . . recommend this book, and unhesitatingly, as one of the finest I have ever read."

In addition to her reputation as a feminist literary critic, Ostriker is also an accomplished poet. In 1986, the Poetry Society of America awarded her the William Carlos Williams Prize for *The Imaginary Lover,* and two of her works have been finalists for the National Book Award. Ostriker "is at her best when most urbane and ironic" in these poems that look back at marriage from the perspective of mid-life, said *Times Literary Supplement* contributor Clair Wills. "The actions are melodramatic, but the recording consciousness is steady," Patricia Hampl related in the *New York Times Book Review.* Since the poems often reflect on disappointment or loss, they have an elegiac tone. More noticeable, however, "is Mrs. Ostriker's tendency to locate a sustaining force for the rest of life—a force that is both passionate and honorable," Hampl observed. "This is evident in lines from 'Everywoman Her Own Theology,' in which Ostriker declares: 'Ethically, I am looking for / An absolute endorsement of loving-kindness.'" At times, says Hampl, the poems lack music, but they charm the reader with their "candor and thoughtfulness."

Green Age (1989) is a book of poems that blends "personal time, history and politics, and inner spirituality," wrote Williams. As Robyn Selman noted in *Village Voice,* Ostriker's title denotes "the stage in a woman's life—after her children have left home, after the death of her parents—when her sense of herself is clear and muscular: a time of loss, but also of heightened awareness and passion." Ostriker offers love poems, poems which are forceful and persuasive, and poems which, according to a *Publishers Weekly* reviewer, "sympathize

and nurture, affirming life," as when the poet states: "Friend, I could say / I've been alive a half a dozen moments / but that's not true / I've been alive my entire time / on this earth / I've been alive."

The pieces in *The Crack in Everything* are "accomplished poems," declared a *Publishers Weekly* reviewer. To quote Patricia Monaghan in *Booklist,* the poems are "grounded in the details of a woman's daily life and speak with the appeal of an intelligent, sympathetic friend," making the work feel as if it possesses "a quality of being overheard." The topics of some of Ostriker's poems range from the rape of a mentally retarded girl by her high school classmates to the bombing of MOVE in Philadelphia, so that her poems feel, according to a *Publishers Weekly* reviewer, as though "a broad-based politics enters this work routinely, like the morning news." The long sequence, "The Mastectomy Poems," which concludes the collection, movingly address the poet's successful treatment for cancer, "in a frank and liberating clarity," stated Steven Ellis in *Library Journal,* as Ostriker refers to how "cells break down, their membranes crushed / Where the condemned / Beg for forgetfulness."

The Little Space: Poems Selected and New 1968-1998 expresses itself as an autobiography in poetry form, as the volume begins with the birth of Ostriker's child and moves through the changes that age wreaks in relationships between mates, between parents and children, and within the poet's sense of herself. Nominated for a National Book Award, *The Little Space* was described by Judy Clarence in the *Library Journal* as a "lively and moving collection," containing poems that "move into deeper levels of mystery and spirituality." A *Publishers Weekly* contributor maintained that the poems are "simultaneously funny and tragic, intense and conversational, politically charged and personally graphic," and that the book reveals a writer "with a rare intelligence."

Ostriker told *CA:* "All poets have their chosen ancestors and affinities. As an American poet I see myself in the line of Whitman, Williams, and Ginsberg, those great enablers of the inclusive democratic impulse, the corollary of which is formal openness. As a student I wrote in traditional closed forms, as did they—before they discovered the joy and meaning of open forms. To write in open forms is to improvise. Improvisatory verse is like doing a jazz solo: we know what we've just done, and the next line has to be connected to it, has to grow out of it somehow, but there is an essential *unpredictability.* This is an American invention because we act, in America, as if the future is partly shaped by the past, but is not determined by it. We are (a little bit) free. As a poet of the spirit, I have always been inspired by the great heterodox visionaries—Whitman since childhood, Blake since my student days, and H.D. since the 1980's when I discovered that she was not a minor imagist but the exquisite peer and rival of T.S. Eliot and Ezra Pound. Wrestling with the Bible, I am Blake's daughter; trying to imagine the divine Feminine, I am H.D.'s child. I am also in love with the poetry of Lucille Clifton, whom I believe to be the most important spiritual poet writing today. And then there are John Donne, George Herbert, and Gerard Manley Hopkins. As for the women poets who have influenced my poetry and my life, they are probably countless—but among them are Emily Dickinson, Louise Bogan, Edna St. Vincent Millay, Muriel Rukeyser, Adrienne Rich, May Swenson, Sylvia Plath, Anne Sexton, Maxine Kumin, Marge Piercy, June Jordan, Sharon Doubiago, Sharon Olds, Ntozake Shange, Toi Derricotte, and (as said before), H.D., and Lucille Clifton.

"People who do not know my work ask me what I write about. I answer: love, sex, death, violence, family, politics, religion, friendship, painters and painting, the body in sickness and health. Joy and pain.

"I try not to write the same poem over and over. I try to stretch my own envelope, to write what I am afraid to write. Composing an essay, a review or a piece of literary criticism, I know more or less what I am doing and what I want to say. When I write a poem, I am crawling into the dark. Or else I am an aperture. Something needs to be put into language, and it chooses me. I invite such things. 'Not I, not I, but the wind that blows through me,' as D.H. Lawrence says.

"I write as an American, a woman, a Jew, a mother, a wife, a lover of beauty and art, a teacher, an idealist, a skeptic. Critics seem often to remark that I am 'intelligent'—but I see myself also as passionate. Actually, I am a combination of mind, body, and feelings, like everyone else, and I try to get them all into play.

"When I give poetry readings, my hope is to make people in my audience laugh and cry. They often do. The gamble is that my words will reach others, touch their inner lives. When I write literary criticism, I try to see and say clearly what is actually there in the work of other poets. Teaching is extremely important to me, my students are important, I try my best to awaken them to the delight of using their minds. Although clarity is unfashionable, I encourage it. When I teach midrash writ-

ing workshops—midrash is an ancient genre which involves elaborating on Biblical stories and characters—I want people to discover how powerfully the Bible speaks to the issues of our own time: gender roles, family dynamics, social class, freedom and slavery, war and peace, fear of the stranger, and the need to overcome that fear. These are my issues, too."

BIOGRAPHICAL/CRITICAL SOURCES:

BOOKS

Contemporary Authors Autobiography Series, Volume 24, Gale (Detroit, MI), 1996.
Dictionary of Literary Biography, Volume 120: *American Poets since World War II,* third series, Gale (Detroit, MI), 1992.
Jewish American Women Writers, Greenwood Press (Westport, CT), 1994.

PERIODICALS

American Literature, October, 1987, p. 464.
American Poetry Review, July-August, 1981; July, 1986, p. 12.
American Voice, Volume 45, 1997, Gary Pacernik, "Interview with Alicia Ostriker."
Belle Lettres, summer, 1990, p. 30; fall, 1993, p. 56; spring, 1995, p. 44.
Booklist, April 15, 1986, p. 1176; February 15, 1987, p. 871; March, 1988, p. 25; September 1, 1989, p. 29; December 1, 1994, p. 1546; May 1, 1996, p. 1485.
Borderlands: The Texas Poetry Review, spring, 1993, pp. 80-6.
Choice, December, 1986, p. 627; July, 1987, p. 871; March, 1990, p. 1146.
Contemporary Literature, summer, 1988, pp. 305-310.
Criticism, fall, 1989, pp. 505-507.
Georgia Review, fall, 1987, p. 631.
Hiram Poetry Review, fall-winter, 1982, review of *The Mother/Child Papers.*
Hudson Review, autumn, 1985, p. 516; winter, 1997, p. 659+.
Hungry Mind Review, fall, 1996, p. 28.
Iowa Review, spring, 1982, pp. 137-139.
Jerusalem Post, November 27, 1997, Helen Kaye, "Poet with a Punch."
Jewish Bulletin, April 14, 1995, Natalie Weinstein, "Professor Reworks Biblical Stories with Feminist's Eye."

Kliatt Young Adult Paperback Book Guide, fall, 1986, p. 34; April, 1988, p. 26.

Library Journal, May 1, 1986, p. 121; November 15, 1986, p. 100; January 1987, p. 57; September 15, 1989, p. 114; April 1, 1996, p. 87; December, 1998, Judy Clarence, review of *The Little Space: Poems Selected and New, 1968-1998,* p. 112.

Literature and Medicine, Volume 16, number 2, 1997, pp. 273-77.

Literature and Psychology, 1992, pp. 71-83.

Michigan Quarterly Review, spring, 1991, pp. 354-366.

Ms., August, 1986, p. 75.

Nation, May 12, 1997, p. 54, review of *The Crack in Everything.*

National Forum, summer, 1987, p. 45.

New Directions for Women, November-December, 1983, p. 17; January, 1988, p. 17.

New York Times Book Review, July 20, 1986, p. 21; June 7, 1987, p. 15.

Parnassus: Poetry in Review, winter, 2000, pp. 24-30.

Poetry, March, 1983; February, 1987, p. 294; July, 1990, p. 226.

Poets and Writers, November-December, 1989, pp. 16-26.

Prairie Schooner, March, 1984, pp. 82-84.

Progressive, March, 1999, Joel Brouwer, review of *The Little Space: Poems Selected and New, 1968-1998,* p. 43.

Publishers Weekly, October 24, 1984; March 21, 1986, p. 79; October 24, 1986, p. 69; October 6, 1989, p. 94; November 14, 1994, p. 34; April 26, 1996, p. 63; November 2, 1998, review of *The Little Space: Poems Selected and New, 1968-1998,* p. 74.

Religious Studies Review, April, 1989, p. 141.

San Francisco Chronicle, September 6, 1983.

Scientific American, September, 1994, Cory S. Powell, "Profile: Jeremiah and Alicia Ostriker, A Marriage of Science and Art," pp. 28, 31.

Signs, winter, 1984, p. 384; autumn, 1988, p. 220; autumn, 1989, pp. 220-222.

Sojourner, April, 1987, pp. 1-3, review of *The Mother/Child Papers.*

Tikkun, January-February, 1996, pp. 94-96, review of *The Nakedness of the Fathers.*

Times Educational Supplement, August 28, 1987, p. 15.

Times Literary Supplement, July 10, 1987, p. 748.

Tulsa Studies in Women's Literature, fall, 2000.

US, November 18, 1998, Nicole Plett, "A Poet's Dazzling Mind."

USA Today, February 13, 1984.

Village Voice, February 6, 1990, p. 59.

Virginia Quarterly Review, spring, 1990, p. 65; winter, 1997, p. 29.

Wilson Library Bulletin, September, 1986, p. 85.

Women's Review of Books, February, 1984; April, 1987, p. 14; December, 1998; July, 2000, Adrian Oktenberg, "Poetry, Politics, and Passion," pp. 41-42.

World Literature Today, spring, 1987, p. 291; autumn, 1999, p. 745.

OTHER

Pif Magazine, http://www.pifmagazine.com/ (September 5, 2000), Rachel Barenblat, review of *Dancing at the Devil's Party: Essays on Poetry, Politics, and the Erotic.*

Women's Global Perspectives (video), interview with Ostriker by Hazel Staats-Westover, International Center, Princeton University, 1996.

*   *   *

OTIS, Johnny 1921-

PERSONAL: Born December 28, 1921, in Vallejo, CA; son of Alexander (a grocer) and Irene (a homemaker; maiden name, Kiskakis) Veliotes; married Phyllis Walker (a homemaker), May 2, 1941; children: Janice Otis Johnson, Laura Otis Johnson; Johnny "Shuggie", Nicky. *Education:* Attended junior high school. *Avocational interests:* Birds (macaws, cockatoos, pigeons, and pheasants).

ADDRESSES: Home—7105 Baker Lane, Sebastopol, CA 95472.

CAREER: Band leader, musician, composer, and disc jockey. Recording artist; albums include *Creepin' with the Cats: The Legendary Dig Masters,* Ace; *The New Johnny Otis Show with Shuggie Otis,* Alligator; *Spirit of the Black Territory Bands,* Arhoolie; *Johnny Otis Rhythm and Blues Caravan,* three volumes, Atlantic; *Johnny Otis Blues and Swing Party,* Volume I, J & T Records; *Johnny Otis Rhythm and Blues Dance Party,* Volume I, J & T Records; *Cold Shot,* J & T Records; *The Greatest Johnny Otis Show,* Ace; *Johnny Otis—The Capitol Years,* Collectibles; *The Johnny Otis Show Live at Monterey,* Epic; and *Johnny Otis Rock 'n' Roll Hit Parade,* Ace. Nocturne Organic Farm (manufacturers of Johnny Otis Organic Apple Juice), co-owner; presenter of the traveling rhythm and blues music concert "The Johnny Otis Show." University of California, Berkeley, teacher of the history of African American music. Painter and sculptor.

AWARDS, HONORS: Honorary music degree from University of California, Los Angeles, and divinity degree from a California seminary; inducted into Rock and Roll Hall of Fame and Rhythm and Blues Hall of Fame, both 1994; inducted into Blues Hall of Fame, 2000.

WRITINGS:

Listen to the Lambs, Norton (New York, NY), 1966.
Upside Your Head! Rhythm and Blues on Central Avenue, Wesleyan University Press (Middletown, CT), 1994.

Colors and Chords: The Art of Johnny Otis, Pomegranate Publications (Rohnert Park, CA), 1995.
Red Beans and Rice and Other Rock 'n' Roll Recipes, Pomegranate Publications (Rohnert Park, CA), 1997.

BIOGRAPHICAL/CRITICAL SOURCES:

OTHER

Johnny Otis Web Site, http://www.johnnyotisworld.com/ (June 15, 2001).

P

PACKER, J(ames) I(nnell) 1926-

PERSONAL: Born July 22, 1926, in Twyning, Gloucestershire, England; son of James Percy (a clerk) and Dorothy (a teacher; maiden name, Harris) Packer; married Ethel Mullett (a nurse), 1954; children: Ruth, Naomi, Martin. *Education:* Corpus Christi College, Oxford, B.A., 1948, M.A. and D.Phil., both 1954; also attended Wycliffe Hall, Oxford, 1949-52. *Politics:* "Eclectic." *Religion:* Anglican. *Avocational interests:* Music (Western classical and early American jazz), cricket, railroads.

ADDRESSES: Office—Regent College, 5800 University Blvd., Vancouver, British Columbia, Canada V6T 2E4.

CAREER: Anglican clergy; assistant curate in Birmingham, England, 1952-54; Tyndale Hall, Bristol, England, tutor, 1955-61, principal, 1969-71; Latimer House, Oxford, England, librarian, 1961-64, warden, 1964-69; Trinity College, Bristol, England, associate principal, 1971-79; Regent College, Vancouver, British Columbia, Canada, professor of historical and systematic theology, 1979—. Westminster Theological Seminary, visiting professor, 1968; Gordon-Conwell Seminary, adjunct professor, 1975-88; *Christianity Today,* visiting scholar and institute fellow, 1985—.

WRITINGS:

"Fundamentalism" and the Word of God, Eerdmans (Grand Rapids, MI), 1958.

(Editor and translator, with O. R. Johnston) *Luther's Bondage of the Will,* Fleming Revell (Old Tappan, NJ), 1958.

Evangelism and the Sovereignty of God, Inter-Varsity Press (Downers Grove, IL), 1961.

God Has Spoken, Westminster (Philadelphia, PA), 1965, 2nd edition, Inter-Varsity Press (Downers Grove, IL), 1980.

(With A. M. Stibbs) *The Spirit within You,* Hodder & Stoughton, 1967.

Knowing God, Inter-Varsity Press (Downers Grove, IL), 1973.

I Want to Be a Christian, Tyndale House (Wheaton, IL), 1977.

Knowing Man, Cornerstone Press (St. Louis, MO), 1979.

Beyond the Battle for the Bible, Cornerstone Press (St. Louis, MO), 1980.

God's Words, Inter-Varsity Press (Downers Grove, IL), 1982.

Keep in Step with the Spirit, Fleming Revell (Old Tappan, NJ), 1984.

(With Thomas Howard) *Christianity: The True Humanism,* Word Books, 1985.

Your Father Loves You, H. Shaw (Wheaton, IL), 1986.

Hot Tub Religion: Christian Living in a Materialistic World, Tyndale House (Wheaton, IL), 1987.

A Quest for Godliness: The Puritan Vision of the Christian Life, Crossway (Wheaton, IL), 1990.

Rediscovering Holiness, Vine Books (Ann Arbor, MI), 1992.

Concise Theology: A Guide to Historic Christian Beliefs, Tyndale House (Wheaton, IL), 1993.

Growing in Christ, Crossway (Wheaton, IL), 1994.

Knowing Christianity, H. Shaw (Wheaton, IL), 1995.

Knowing and Doing the Will of God, compiled by LaVonne Neff, Vine Books (Ann Arbor, MI), 1995.

A Passion for Faithfulness: Wisdom from the Book of Nehemiah, Crossway (Wheaton, IL), 1995.

Life in the Spirit: A 30-Day Devotional, Crossway (Wheaton, IL), 1996.

Truth and Power: The Place of Scripture in the Christian Life, H. Shaw (Wheaton, IL), 1996.

Great Grace: A 31-Day Devotional, compiled by Beth Nethery Feia, Vine Books (Ann Arbor, MI), 1997.

Great Power: A 31-Day Devotional, compiled by Feia, Vine Books (Ann Arbor, MI), 1997.

A Grief Sanctified: Passing through Grief to Peace and Joy, Vine Books (Ann Arbor, MI), 1997.

Great Joy: A 31-Day Devotional, compiled by Feia, Vine Books (Ann Arbor, MI), 1998.

In God's Presence: Daily Devotions with J. I. Packer, compiled and edited by Jean Watson, H. Shaw (Wheaton, IL), 1998.

The J. I. Packer Collection, edited by Alister McGrath, Inter-Varsity Press (Downers Grove, IL), 1998.

(With Wendy Murray Zoba) *James Innell Packer Answers Questions for Today,* Tyndale House (Wheaton, IL), 2000.

(With Carolyn Nystrom) *Never beyond Hope: How God Touches and Uses Imperfect People,* Inter-Varsity Press (Downers Grove, IL), 2000.

Contributor to books, including *The Kingdom and the Power: Are Healing and the Spiritual Gifts Used by Jesus and the Early Church Meant for the Church Today?,* edited by Gary S. Greig and Kevin N. Springer, Regal Books (Ventura, CA), 1993; and *An Introduction to the Christian Faith,* Lynx (Oxford, England), 1992, published as *Exploring the Christian Faith,* Thomas Nelson (Nashville, TN), 1996. Began as senior editor, became executive editor, *Christianity Today,* 1985—. *Knowing God* has been published in more than twenty languages.

EDITOR

(With Loren Wilkinson) *Alive to God: Studies in Spirituality Presented to James Houston,* Inter-Varsity Press (Downers Grove, IL), 1992.

(With Merrill C. Tenney and William White, Jr.) *Nelson's Illustrated Encyclopedia of Bible Facts,* Thomas Nelson (Nashville, TN), 1995.

(With Tenney) *Illustrated Manners and Customs of the Bible,* Thomas Nelson (Nashville, TN), 1997.

(With Nystrom) *Knowing God Journal,* Inter-Varsity Press (Downers Grove, IL), 2000.

(With Sven K. Soderlund) *The Way of Wisdom: Essays in Honor of Bruce K. Waltke,* Zondervan (Grand Rapids, MI), 2000.

WORK IN PROGRESS: Research on biblical, historical, and systematic theology.

SIDELIGHTS: J. I. Packer has been an important force in the shaping of contemporary Christian evangelicalism. He was ordained in the Church of England and has spent most of his adult life trying to make sure that evangelicals have a place in that church. Enduring much conflict and criticism in England, Packer eventually moved to Regent College in Vancouver, British Columbia, Canada, where he has thrived as a religious leader and author of numerous theological and devotional books.

While at Corpus Christi College, Oxford, Packer experienced a religious conversion. At about the same time, he discovered English Puritan writers such as John Owen and John Bunyan, who had a deep effect on his view of Christianity. Alister McGrath wrote, in the *Christianity Today* article "Knowing Packer: The Lonely Journey of a Passionate Puritan," that Packer began to share his insights with the struggling evangelical minority within the Anglican Church: insights on the "emphasis on God-centeredness, personal discipline, humility and the primacy of the mind." McGrath quoted Packer, "I knew that I had a theology that would stand and that I could deploy. One had to challenge the liberal and vague notions [of Anglicanism] to get them out of the way and clear the way for truth."

Packer decided to seek ordination in the Anglican Church, and in the course of his studies he began an annual forum called the Puritan Studies Conferences, which provided a venue for serious scholarly study of Puritan ideas. In the mid-1950s Packer responded to a resurgence of evangelical fervor in England by producing his first book, *"Fundamentalism" and the Word of God.* In this work, he defends evangelicals against critics who felt that evangelicals were not intellectually rigorous enough in their thinking.

Packer always sought the middle ground between those within Anglicanism who feared the evangelical movement and those evangelicals who favored breaking away from established church. He broke ranks with his friend Martyn Lloyd-Jones, who vociferously opposed the World Council of Churches and advocated a separate evangelical association of congregations.

In 1970 Packer assumed the principalship of Tyndale Hall, a theological school in Bristol. Although he achieved important reforms, he was blocked when the school was merged with two others and he lost his leadership role. As "associate principal," however, he was able to devote more time to travel and writing. In 1973 he published his all-time best-seller, *Knowing God,* which achieved acclaim worldwide, especially in North America.

Tiring of the conflicts with the Anglican hierarchy and within the evangelical movement, in 1979 Packer accepted an invitation to immigrate to British Columbia, where he felt freer to develop a preaching and teaching ministry and to write as he saw fit. With his contribution, Regent College became the largest graduate theological school in its region, placing Packer in a prominent position in most of the important theological discussions in North America. Although some conservative evangelicals have condemned his attempts at rapprochement between Anglicans and Catholics and his alleged dilution of the evangelical message, he has been an important mediating force among evangelicals and mainline churches and among the various factions of evangelicalism.

Since his move to Canada, Packer has produced a prolific succession of books, pamphlets, and articles—from theological treatises, to devotional tracts, to self-help manuals. He interprets religion in lay terms in such works as *Knowing Christianity,* in which he discusses topics such as the nature of God, the Holy Spirit, the Christian response to universalism, the hope of a life to come, and the Christian response to social activism. In *Truth and Power: The Place of Scripture in the Christian Life,* he writes about the authority of the Bible and the ways it has been challenged throughout history, with emphasis on the importance of the Bible to the individual Christian believer.

In 2000 Packer and Carol Nystrom published *Never beyond Hope: How God Touches and Uses Imperfect People,* using the stories of flawed biblical characters to encourage Christians to aspire to serve God despite their human frailties. A *Publishers Weekly* reviewer offered qualified praise for this volume: "Sometimes [the authors] veer into sheer speculation. . . . The text is always readable and often folksy."

Fitting tributes to Packer's career are two works published by McGrath: the full-length biography *J. I. Packer,* and a collection of sixteen essays by Packer titled *The J. I. Packer Collection.* In a *Christianity Today* review of *J. I. Packer,* Wendy Murray Zoba, a friend and collaborator of Packer, noted what Packer's wife once said to her: "[My husband's] devotion to the Lord is the reason for everything he's done. His writing, his preaching, his lecturing, his living are all centered on the Lord." Zoba wrote that Packer "once told me that classical jazz is like the church. . . . [He] meant the church in its truest Reformed sense—a lively, masterful interplay and synergy of members, orchestrated by the Holy Spirit for creating the music of heaven." Packer summarized his own view of the Christian life for McGrath: "I want to see a focused vision of spiritual maturity—the expansion of the soul is the best phrase I can use for it. That is, a renewed sense of the momentousness of being alive, the sheer bigness and awesomeness of being a human being alive in God's world with light, with grace, with wisdom, with responsibility, with biblical truth."

BIOGRAPHICAL/CRITICAL SOURCES:

BOOKS

McGrath, Alister, and Donald Lewis, editors, *Doing Theology for the People of God: Studies in Honor of J. I. Packer,* Inter-Varsity Press (Downers Grove, IL), 1996.

PERIODICALS

Christianity Today, April 6, 1998, Wendy Murray Zoba, "Knowing Packer: The Lonely Journey of a Passionate Puritan," pp. 30-40.
Publishers Weekly, April 24, 2000, review of *Never beyond Hope: How God Touches and Uses Imperfect People,* p. 88.

*   *   *

PANELLA, Vincent 1939-

PERSONAL: Born October 3, 1939, in New York, NY; son of Emilio (a realtor) and Grace (Giaimo) Panella; married Janet Cargill, December 22, 1963 (divorced, 1972); married Susan Sichel (a photographer), May 22, 1977; children: (first marriage) Cassandra, Christina; (second marriage) Marco, Catherine. *Education:* Carnegie-Mellon University, B.S., 1961; Pennsylvania State University, M.A., 1969; University of Iowa, M.F. A., 1971.

ADDRESSES: Home and office—Augur Hale Rd., South Newfare, VT 05351. *Agent*—Sterling Lord Literistic, New York, NY.

CAREER: General Dynamics, Astronautics Division, San Diego, CA, engineer, 1961-62; G. P. Technical Services, New York City, technical writer and editor, 1962-63; Council on Legal Educational Opportunity, instructor in writing, 1970-72; *Dubuque Telegraph-Herald,* Dubuque, Iowa, reporter, 1972-73; Florida State University, Tallahassee, adjunct professor of writing, 1973-76; Vermont Law School, South Royalton, writing specialist, 1988—. *Military service:* U.S. Army, engineer, 1963-65.

WRITINGS:

The Other Side: Growing up Italian in America, Doubleday (New York, NY), 1979.
Cutter's Island: Caesar in Captivity (novel), Academy Chicago Publishers (Chicago, IL), 2000.

Contributor of short stories, articles, and reviews to magazines, including *Mediphors, TV Guide,* and *Country Journal.*

SIDELIGHTS: Vincent Panella, who wrote *The Other Side: Growing up Italian in America* in 1979, produced a very different kind of book in 2000: *Cutter's Island: Caesar in Captivity.* This novel, taking its cue from brief passages from accounts by Roman historians Plutarch and Suetonius of Julius Caesar's youth, is an imaginative look at what might have happened when Caesar, at the age of twenty-five, was briefly taken captive by pirates. Of his captors, Caesar relates in the book, "[I]n my twenty-fifth year I took a trader bound for Greece, and fell into Cutter's hands. Cutter taught in a different kind of school, and this is the story of how I deceived him, and through that deception came to know myself."

The story, according to a *Publishers Weekly* critic, shows a turning point in the young Caesar's life, "complete with swashbuckling action and classical allusions." In the midst of trying to topple the current government of Rome, Caesar is captured by Cilician pirates, who hate the Romans but are fascinated with Caesar despite their open scorn for him. Caesar shows his own leadership ability by negotiating the amount of his own ransom, impressing them with his knowledge, and joining their banquets and athletic events. After his release he vows to assemble a fleet to vanquish his captors.

Reviewers generally found *Cutter's Island* a good fictional introduction to the young Caesar, foreshadowing his later greatness despite his youthful self-doubts. Although a *Kirkus Reviews* critic felt that "Panella stumbles from time to time—into movie dialogue, for example," the critic called the novel "promising as wor-

thy kin of Mary Renault and Steven Pressfield." Noting that the novel is an exciting adventure set against the background of the Roman Republic's impending fall, the *Publishers Weekly* reviewer said that the novel "matches the film *Gladiator* in its vigorous, viscerally affecting depiction of ancient Rome."

Of his earlier work, Panella once told *CA:* "*The Other Side: Growing up Italian in America* is a personal narrative about growing up as a third-generation Italian-American, and central to the book's theme is the question of what cultural losses were accrued by my family in America."

BIOGRAPHICAL/CRITICAL SOURCES:

BOOKS

Panella, Vincent, *Cutter's Island: Caesar in Captivity,* Academy Chicago Publishers (Chicago, IL), 2000.

PERIODICALS

Booklist, August 18, 2000, Brendan Dowling, review of *Cutter's Island,* p. 2.
Kirkus Reviews, August 1, 2000, review of *Cutter's Island: Caesar in Captivity,* p. 1066.
Los Angeles Times, December 4, 2000, Merle Rubin, review of *Cutter's Island.*
Publishers Weekly, August 21, 2000, review of *Cutter's Island,* p. 47.
Seven Days, October 10, 2001, P. P. Vaughan-Hughes, review of *Cutter's Island.*

*   *   *

PARKER, Barbara J.

PERSONAL: Born in Columbia, SC; married; children: Andrea, James. *Education:* Received degree in history from the University of South Florida; received law degree from the University of Miami; Florida International University, M.F.A. (creative writing), 1993.

ADDRESSES: Home—Coral Gables, FL. *Agent*—c/o Dutton, 375 Hudson St., New York, NY 10014-3657.

CAREER: Writer. Became a prosecutor for Dade County State Attorney's Office (Miami, FL), then went into private law practice.

WRITINGS:

MYSTERY NOVELS

Suspicion of Innocence, Dutton (New York, NY), 1994.
Suspicion of Guilt, Dutton (New York, NY), 1995.
Blood Relations, Dutton (New York, NY), 1996.
Criminal Justice, Dutton (New York, NY), 1997.
Suspicion of Deceit, Dutton (New York, NY), 1998.
Suspicion of Betrayal, Dutton (New York, NY), 1999.
Suspicion of Malice, Dutton (New York, NY), 2000.
Suspicion of Vengeance, Penguin (New York, NY), 2001.

SIDELIGHTS: Barbara J. Parker is a former prosecuting attorney who has written several mystery novels. She made her literary debut in 1994 with *Suspicion of Innocence,* the story of a resourceful attorney who must solve the mystery of her sister's death, which had initially been deemed a suicide. The heroine, Gail Connor, is a successful partner at a prominent Miami law firm, but after her sister is found dead, Connor becomes a murder suspect. Connor endeavors to uncover the truth of her sister's demise even as her own family life degenerates: her husband leaves her and their child, and her immediate relatives seem to be behaving rather suspiciously. Connor's investigation into her sister's death takes her into Miami's Cuban community. And while she uncovers evidence of disturbing actions within her own family, she finds solace in a romance with dashing Cuban attorney Anthony Quintana. However, she also finds herself drawn to his equally handsome—but ultimately less endearing—cousin, a real-estate developer. Marvin Lachman, a reviewer for *Armchair Detective,* felt that Parker's "pace seems slow, almost as a function of the warm climate." A reviewer for *Booklist* was more enthusiastic and praised the book's "appealing characters and . . . involving plot."

Gail Connor is also the heroine of Parker's second novel, *Suspicion of Guilt.* In this story, eccentric philanthropist Althea Tillett dies and Connor's former law classmate Patrick Norris, the philanthropist's only living relative, stands to inherit millions. But Tillett has already willed her considerable estate to a variety of Miami charities. Norris disputes the will's validity and engages Connor to represent his legal interests. But when police reveal that Tillett's death was murder, Connor's client is considered the most likely culprit. Connor determines to uncover the killer's identity even as she copes with demanding personal responsibilities, including raising her ten-year-old daughter and main-

taining her relationship with Anthony Quintana, her love interest from the earlier *Suspicion of Innocence.* Christine E. Thompson, in a review for *Armchair Detective,* called the book "an excellent tale that will keep you suspicious of everyone . . . until the heart-throbbing end." A *Publishers Weekly* reviewer felt that the characters were somewhat cliched, but added that "it all fits the steamy Miami setting . . . a breathlessly paced legal thriller with a powerful punch." *Booklist* reviewer Mary Carroll said, "The author deftly shifts puzzle pieces to explore Gail's complex relationships."

In 1996 Parker's third mystery novel, *Blood Relations,* was published. This tale introduces prosecuting attorney Sam Hagan, who is charged with investigating teen model Ali Duncan's allegations that she was gang-raped by prominent Miami authorities and celebrities. Hagan accepts Duncan's accusations as truthful, but his position is complicated when several suspects are found dead. His circumstances are exacerbated still further by his troubled personal life: his marriage seems particularly vulnerable in the wake of his grown son's recent death. And as he works to corroborate Duncan's contentions and stabilize his private life, he uncovers increasing evidence of corruption among Miami's wealthy elite. Reviewing the book for the *Chicago Tribune,* Chris Petrakos wrote, "There aren't many writers who can spin a colorful suspense story while mapping out the near-destruction of a family, but Parker pulls it off in style." "Some of the coincidences and liaisons reach soap-opera proportions, but the pace never flags," wrote one *Publishers Weekly* reviewer. Emily Melton responded to the book similarly in a review for *Booklist,* writing, "The fast paced action should heat up even the coldest mystery buff."

Parker is also the author of *Criminal Justice,* which finds attorney Dan Galindo in dire straits after he has refused to admit a lying witness in a recent trial. Galindo's professional life has since faltered. He has lost his position as a federal prosecutor and alienated an influential federal agent. In addition, his marriage has ended. Galindo seems to find new clients only through the assistance of his former brother-in-law, music producer Rick Robbins. When Galindo's new girlfriend, musician Kelly Dorf, is arrested for striking a police officer, Galindo investigates and discovers ties between Kelly's band mate Martha and former brother-in-law Robbins's covert business partner, suspicious South American Miguel Salazar. Matters are further complicated when Galindo learns that Kelly is helping federal authorities by serving as an informant providing information about Salazar's questionable business practices. After Galindo and Kelly dissolve their romance, she meets with federal authorities and scornfully implicates Galindo in Salazar's operations. In praise of the novel, a *Publishers Weekly* reviewer said that Parker "throws the steak of real experience on the fire of Miami and lets it sizzle."

In *Suspicion of Deceit,* Parker once again features her popular characters Gail Connor and Anthony Quintana. This novel mines the tensions between Yankee and Cuban culture through a high culture vein—opera. Gail, who has started her own firm, is happy to take on the Miami Opera Company; she doesn't realize that Thomas Nolan, its rising young star, has ties to Castro's Cuba that will jeopardize his popularity, and even his safety, in Miami. Anthony Quintana, who is now engaged to Gail, becomes Nolan's escort, but the Opera board fears that Nolan's ties to Castro will be revealed to Quintana's brother-in-law, a "rabble-rousing anti-Castro talk-show host Octavio Reyes," according to a *Kirkus Reviews* writer. Gail becomes aware that Quintana has past connections with the opera board, and to Marxism, having led a number of its members on trip to Nicaragua to support the Sandanistas twenty years before. It was on this trip that a member of the government forces murdered Quintana's former American girlfriend. But suspicions remain that Quintana may have had some responsibility for her killing. And now, members of the board are being murdered.

Reviews of *Suspicion of Deceit* were mixed. *Kirkus Reviews* deemed its climax "too silly for words," and said that "even Parker's fans might put this one down." Elsa Pendleton wrote for *Library Journal* that "the story . . . hovers uneasily between episodes of Gail and Tony's lovemaking and Gail's getting herself into cliched predicaments." Pendleton went on to criticize the *Suspicion* series, saying it degrades female attorneys and Hispanics living in Florida. But Mary Carroll, who reviewed *Deceit* for *Booklist,* called it a "complex, involving tale," and "a satisfying read."

A year later, Parker's *Suspicion of Betrayal* finds Gail secure in her career and her love life: she has established her practice and just bought a beautiful home with husband-to-be Anthony Quintana. Everything seems to be falling into place for Gail until her eleven-year-old daughter, Karen, begins to receive disturbing phone messages from a voice who identifies himself as "Death," as well as letters enclosing scarily altered photos of Gail and Karen. When Karen's kitten is decapitated, Gail puts aside her suspicion of a neighborhood schoolboy and begins to consider other possibilities, including a client's wealthy husband who wants to give

nothing to his wife in their divorce, and her own ex-husband, Dave Metzger, who is suing her for custody of Karen. Even Anthony begins to look suspicious. As Dave and Anthony do battle over how to best protect Karen, the girl is abducted, and Gail's world comes crashing down. Finding Karen alive is all that matters.

Kirkus Reviews compared Parker's work in *Suspicion of Betrayal* to that of the eminent suspense writer Mary Higgins Clark; the review concluded: "All right, the real culprit isn't worth a second shudder. Until the disappointing denouement, though, Parker piles up the menace with all the smooth efficiency of the storied Pedrosas." Conversely, Mary Frances Wilkens wrote for *Booklist* that "although Parker is a little too deliberate in setting up her suspects, the climax and denouement are surprisingly satisfying." And Stacey Reasor, reviewing the novel for the *Library Journal,* wrote that Baker "has written another suspenseful story that keeps the reader guessing until the very end."

Baker's 2000 novel *Suspicion of Malice,* may sadden readers who were rooting for Gail Connor and Anthony Quintana's romance; its outset finds them broken up. But the murder of Roger Creswell, wealthy heir of a yacht-building family, throws them together again as each investigates the case. Gail is brought into the case at the request of Angela Quintana, Anthony's teenage daughter, whose boyfriend, Miami Ballet Company dancer Bobby Gonzalez, is the prime suspect. Angela wants Bobby cleared, but doesn't want her father to know about her involvement with him. Bobby has an alibi: he was smoking marijuana with an esteemed Miami judge at the time of the murder. The judge is a friend of the Quintana family who calls in Anthony to represent him in the case.

Reviewers liked Parker's *Betrayal. Publishers Weekly* called it an "inspired mix of sexy love story, sulky teenagers, family feuds and secrets, . . . and sharp outbreaks of murder and mayhem." And the *Library Journal*'s Stacey Reasor noted one of the hallmarks of good suspense fiction: "Parker keeps you turning the pages."

In 2001 Parker's *Suspicion of Vengeance* appeared in book stores. This recent installment finds Connor and Quintana working on an appeal to free a convicted killer. The case meets strong public resistance as members of the wealthy community where the murder occurred protest the appeal. As Connor and Quintana investigate further they become convinced that their client is the innocent victim of a conspiracy designed to hide the secrets and political motives of prominent citizens in the community.

BIOGRAPHICAL/CRITICAL SOURCES:

PERIODICALS

Armchair Detective, summer, 1994, pp. 305-307; fall, 1995, p. 467.
Booklist, January 1, 1994, p. 807; February 1, 1995, p. 993; February 15, 1996, p. 995; January 1, 1998, Mary Carroll, review of *Suspicion of Deceit,* p. 784; February 1, 1999, Mary Frances Wilkens, review of *Suspicion of Betrayal,* p. 94.
Choice, February/March, 1996, p. 25.
Kirkus Reviews, December 1, 1997, review of *Suspicion of Deceit.*
Library Journal, January, 1998, Elsa Pendleton, review of *Suspicion of Deceit,* p. 143; June 1, 1999, Stacey Reasor, review of *Suspicion of Betrayal,* p. 178; April 15, 2000, Stacey Reasor, review of *Suspicion of Malice,* p. 124.
Publishers Weekly, January 9, 1995, p. 58; January 1, 1996, p. 58; January 6, 1997, p. 66; April 24, 2000, review of *Suspicion of Malice,* p. 64.
Tribune Books (Chicago), December 19, 1993, p. 5; February 18, 1996, p. 6.

OTHER

Barbara Parker Web site, http://www.barbaraparker. com (October 11, 2000).*

*   *   *

PARRY, Richard (Gittings) 1942-

PERSONAL: Born July 6, 1942, in Chicago, IL; son of Norman Gittings (a general surgeon) and Lillian (a registered nurse; maiden name, Koudelka) Parry; married Katherine Sue Peck (a medical technologist), June 12, 1965; children: David, Matthew. *Education:* University of Illinois at Urbana-Champaign, M.D., 1966. *Politics:* Independent. *Religion:* Congregationalist. *Avocational interests:* Painting, sailing.

ADDRESSES: Office—9633 Greenhurst Dr., Sun City, AZ 85351. *Agent*—David Hale Smith, DHS Literary Inc., 2528 Elm St., Suite 350, Dallas, TX 75226. *E-mail*—rparry@earthlink.net.

CAREER: Johns Hopkins University, Baltimore, MD, began as intern in surgery, became junior resident, 1966-68; Boston City Hospital, Boston, MA, resident in surgery, 1968-72; Harvard University, Medical School, Cambridge, MA, resident in plastic and reconstructive surgery, 1974-76; Lahey Clinic, Boston, MA, plastic and reconstructive surgeon, 1976-78; physician in private practice, Fairbanks, AK, 1978-97. *Military service:* U.S. Navy, surgeon, 1972-74; became lieutenant commander.

MEMBER: American Cancer Society (president of Alaska division, 1987-88), Alaska State Medical Association (president, 1983-84), Fairbanks Medical Association (president, 1982-83), Phi Beta Pi, Alpha Omega Alpha.

WRITINGS:

Ice Warrior (novel), Pocket Books (New York, NY), 1991.
Venom Virus, Pocket Books (New York, NY), 1993.
The Winter Wolf: Wyatt Earp in Alaska (first novel of a trilogy), Forge (New York, NY), 1996.
The Wolf's Cub (second novel of a trilogy), Forge (New York, NY), 1997.
The Wolf's Pack (third novel of a trilogy), Forge (New York, NY), 1998.
That Fateful Lightning: A Novel of Ulysses S. Grant, Ballantine (New York, NY), 2000.
Trial by Ice: The True Story of Murder and Survival on the 1871 Polaris Expedition, Ballantine Books (New York, NY), 2001.

Also author of several medical texts. Contributor to professional and medical journals, including *American Journal of Plastic and Reconstructive Surgery* and *Alaska Journal of Medicine.*

SIDELIGHTS: A retired plastic surgeon, Richard Parry lived in Fairbanks in a log home with his wife, Kathie, for twenty years. His first novel, appropriately set in Alaska, is about Rick Benson, a plastic surgeon, former Navy SEAL, and Vietnam veteran who becomes embroiled in a mystery. In the book *Ice Warrior,* Benson's half-Vietnamese daughter, May, is kidnapped by enemies seeking the information encoded in a tattoo behind the girl's ear. In his search for and rescue of May, a search that follows the Iditerod dog-sled race, Benson draws upon his considerable, wide-ranging skills to outwit foreign agents and double agents of the Central Intelligence Agency and also survive the harsh Alaskan environment. Irwin I. Getz described this book in *Kliatt* as a "fast-moving thriller" with "lots of surprising twists." *Ice Warrior* also includes a generous serving of information about Eskimo traditions, Getz noted.

Another of Parry's novels, *The Winter Wolf: Wyatt Earp in Alaska,* launches the author's three-part series, which addresses Wyatt Earp's adventures and life in that state following his departure from Tombstone. Melding fiction with actual events and historical figures, *The Winter Wolf* is based on the fact that the famous ex-marshal and his wife moved to Alaska to seek their fortune during the Gold Rush. This installment, deemed "well-told," and a "good yarn" by Wes Lukowsky in *Booklist,* presents to readers a fictitious son who is unknown to Earp. Born to a former dance-hall girl abandoned by Wyatt, son Nathan sets out at age sixteen to kill his father in order to collect the twenty thousand dollars willed to him a decade earlier by his vengeful mother for this purpose. *The Winter Wolf* details tenderfoot Nathan's adventures as he hooks up with an experienced gunslinger, Newton Jim Riley, who agrees to help in exchange for money and reading lessons. Nathan is befriended along the way, beginning at a Denver orphanage and moving across the Southwest, by other characters he helps rescue. He also fathers a son before finally catching up with Wyatt.

The Winter Wolf also describes how Wyatt—now in his fifties, fallen on hard times, and forced to take on law enforcement jobs—is haunted by the shootout at the O.K. Corral and the knowledge that some old enemies may not be left as far back in his past as he would prefer. A reviewer for *Publishers Weekly* called *The Winter Wolf* a "fast-moving, appealingly offbeat western" and commended Parry's skillful evocation of the era and locale. The eventual encounter between father and son "packs genuine emotional wallop," this reviewer added. "Diverting tall tales told in appropriately mock-heroic fashion" was how a contributor to *Kirkus Reviews* labeled the work, also noting that readers would look forward to Nathan's return in the sequel, which appeared in 1997 under the title *The Wolf's Cub.*

With the 2000 publication *That Fateful Lightning: A Novel of Ulysses S. Grant,* Parry tells the story of Grant's life as he reflects upon his accomplishments and failures during his waning days. Grant, knowing that he is dying of throat cancer, works feverishly to finish his memoirs in the hope that money from the book will help support his family after his death. As he does so, he reviews his failures in business and politics, as well as his successes on the battlefield and bouts with alcoholism. Critics have given the novel mixed reviews, feeling that Parry glossed over some important areas while overemphasizing others. "Parry somewhat overstates Grant's sense of divine mission while understating his alarming tendency to battlefield overconfidence," pointed out John Edwards in *Library Journal.* However, Edwards also averred that the author "successfully captures" the aging Grant's attempts to come to terms with his life. A *Publishers Weekly* contributor concluded, "The author's obvious affection for his subject gives this novel an overly sympathetic bias, but that affection also allows him to illuminate Grant's elusive human side."

Parry blends real-life adventure and murder mystery in his latest book, *Trial by Ice,* an account of the ill-fated 1871 expedition of the ship *Polaris,* led by Captain Charles Francis Hall and commissioned by President Grant and the U.S. Congress to find the North Pole and the Northwest Passage. During a harrowing seven months at sea, conflict brews among the officers and crew until Captain Hall dies suspiciously and the crew is left to suffer through an Arctic winter fighting off starvation and madness. Citing Parry's "extensive research and excellent storytelling skills," *Booklist* reviewer Gavin Quinn also noted that Parry "uses the journals and testimony of the men . . . [to portray] a vivid picture of the loyalties and personal differences among the members." The *Polaris* expedition may have become a little-known event in American history, but as Stanley Itkin observed in *Library Journal,* Parry "has brought the story to light again with this riveting account."

BIOGRAPHICAL/CRITICAL SOURCES:

PERIODICALS

Booklist, October 1, 1996, Wes Lukowsky, review of *The Winter Wolf: Wyatt Earp in Alaska,* p. 323; June 1, 2000, Gilbert Taylor, review of *That Fateful Lightning: A Novel of Ulysees S. Grant,* p. 1853; January 1, 2001, Gavin Quinn, review of *Trial by Ice: The True Story of Murder and Survival on the 1871 Polaris Expedition,* p. 908.

Kirkus Reviews, August 15, 1996, review of *The Winter Wolf,* p. 1180; September 1, 1997, review of *The Wolf's Cub,* p. 1333; September 1, 1998, review of *The Wolf's Pack,* p. 1233.

Kliatt, April, 1991, Irwin I. Getz, review of *Ice Warrior,* p. 12.

Library Journal, May 1, 2000, John Edwards, review of *That Fateful Lightning,* p. 154; February 1, 2001, Stanley L. Itkin, review of *Trial by Ice,* p. 108.

Publishers Weekly, September 9, 1996, review of *The Winter Wolf,* p. 66; September 22, 1997, review of *The Wolf's Cub,* p. 71; September 28, 1998, review of *The Wolf's Pack,* p. 70; May 1, 2000, review of *That Fateful Lightning;* December 11, 2000, review of *Trial by Ice,* p. 74.

Roundup, fall, 1997, p. 29.

*   *   *

PAYNE, (William) David (A.) 1955-

PERSONAL: Born April 13, 1955, in Henderson, NC; married.

ADDRESSES: Agent—Tina Bennett, c/o Janklow & Nesbit, 445 Park Ave., New York, NY 10022-2606.

CAREER: Writer.

AWARDS, HONORS: Houghton Mifflin fellowship, 1984.

WRITINGS:

Confessions of a Taoist on Wall Street: A Chinese American Romance, Houghton (Boston), 1984.
Early from the Dance, Doubleday (New York City), 1989.
Ruin Creek, Doubleday, 1993.
Gravesend Light, Doubleday, 2000.

SIDELIGHTS: David Payne has published four critically acclaimed novels. The essayist for *Contemporary Southern Writers* found that Payne "displays the skills so evident in the finest Southern writers, an ear for colloquial speech, an appreciation of the relationship between characters and place, and a willingness to look for moral realities within the confusion of contemporary life."

Payne made his literary debut in 1984 with the novel *Confessions of a Taoist on Wall Street,* for which he was awarded a Houghton Mifflin fellowship. The story of a Chinese-American Taoist priest who leaves a Chinese monastery to work on the Wall Street stock ex-

change, and in the process searches for his missing father, was received favorably by some critics, and negatively by others. While some critics, notably the *New York Times Book Review*'s Merlin Wexler, found fault with Payne's narrative organization, characterizations, and dialogue, many commentators offered praise for *Confessions,* such as a *Library Journal* reviewer who dubbed the novel "a grand literary romance." D. Keith Mano, in his commentary for *National Review,* chalked up Payne's faults as youthful indiscretions: "*Taoist* . . . lacks concision and self-discipline. . . . Give Payne time and maturing. . . . There is enormous talent here." *Washington Post* contributor Joseph McLellan praised the book's "glorious style and rich profusion of detail. . . . It is, for all its length, a book to be read twice—first to be gulped down in great chunks during sleepless nights; later to be sipped slowly, savoring details, like a well-brewed cup of tea."

In 1989 Payne published *Early from the Dance,* a novel of youthful innocence shattered. The work is set in the late 1960s and early 1970s in the coastal region of North Carolina known as the Outer Banks, where Payne was raised. The plot revolves around two friends, Adam and Cary, who fall in love with the same woman, Jane, and each suffer dire consequences. While Cary commits suicide, Adam lives with unrelenting remorse. Years later, when Adam and Jane meet again, the reader is given glimpses into the former lovers' lives through chapters told in first person that alternate between the two characters. "*Early from the Dance* is a substantial achievement, a book capacious enough to include the dazzlingly obvious and even the false," maintained Richard Dyer, reporter for the *Boston Globe.* Writing for the *Los Angeles Times Book Review,* Gary Marmorstein commented: "The sexually charged tango that Adam and Jane do with two older partners is choreographed with sinewy definition and split-second time. This, the bulk of the book, is David Payne in top form, and it's some of the strongest, most demanding writing to be found in American fiction." "Best of all," concluded Dyer, "Payne has the deepest human sympathy for his characters and knowledge of the heart; everyone in the book comes alive."

Like *Early from the Dance,* Payne's novel *Ruin Creek* treats the theme of loss. It is the chronicle of a dying marriage told from viewpoints that alternate between the husband, wife, and son. Dyer, in his assessment of the novel, declared: "David Payne may not be the most publicized American novelist homing in on 40, but he is certainly the most gifted." According to Tim McLaurin in the *New York Times Book Review,* "Payne knows the hopes, fears and habits of his characters, and weaves a powerful, lyrical story for them that is a joy to read." A *Dallas Morning News* contributor declared: "David Payne is the most gifted American novelist of his generation. Certainly no other young writer has published three more impressive books."

Payne again sets his story in North Carolina in his 2000 novel *Gravesend Light*. A family drama combined with a romantic affair, the novel tells of Joe Madden, a young anthropologist who moves to the fishing community of Little Roanoke to study the local way of life. Madden is interested in the town because little has changed for many years, with the fishermen pursuing their trade in traditional ways. He soon falls in love with Day Shaughnessy, a doctor, and signs on to work on a fishing boat to get first-hand experience of the industry. Day's unplanned pregnancy and a violent storm while Madden is at sea provide tension and suspense to a story of love and family relationships. The *Kirkus Reviews* critic opined: "Payne's portrait of Little Roanoke's fishing community is rich and convincing." GraceAnne A. DeCandido in *Booklist* called *Gravesend Light* "a story rich in color and sentiment, both rip-roaring and romantic."

BIOGRAPHICAL/CRITICAL SOURCES:

BOOKS

Contemporary Southern Writers, St. James Press (Farmington Hills, MI), 1999.

PERIODICALS

Bloomsbury Review, July, 1994, review of *Ruin Creek,* p. 19.
Booklist, October 1, 1993, review of *Ruin Creek,* p. 254; July, 2000, GraceAnne A. DeCandido, review of *Gravesend Light,* p. 2009.
Boston Globe, September 25, 1989, Richard Dyer, review of *Early from the Dance,* p. 61; October 12, 1993, Richard Dyer, review of *Ruin Creek,* p. 30.
Dallas Morning News, October 10, 1993, review of *Ruin Creek.*
Kirkus Reviews, August 1, 1993, review of *Ruin Creek,* p. 962; June 15, 2000, review of *Gravesend Light,* pp. 825-826.
Library Journal, November, 1984, review of *Confessions of a Taoist on Wall Street;* September 15, 1993, review of *Ruin Creek,* p. 106.

Los Angeles Times Book Review, October 22, 1989, Gary Marmorstein, review of *Early from the Dance,* p. 7.
National Review, April 5, 1985, D. Keith Mano, review of *Confessions of a Taoist on Wall Street,* p. 55.
New York Times Book Review, October 21, 1984, Merlin Wexler, review of *Confessions of a Taoist on Wall Street,* p. 30; November 26, 1989, Brock Cole, review of *Early from the Dance,* p. 30; October 24, 1993, Tim McLaurin, review of *Ruin Creek,* p. 18.
People Weekly, October 9, 1989, Susan Toepfer, review of *Early from the Dance,* pp. 36-37.
Publishers Weekly, August 23, 1993, review of *Ruin Creek,* p. 58; June 12, 2000, review of *Gravesend Light,* p. 51.
Washington Post Book World, December 9, 1984, Joseph McLellan, review of *Confessions of a Taoist on Wall Street,* pp. 5-6.

*   *   *

PEARSON, Lon
    See PEARSON, Milo Lorentz

*   *   *

PEARSON, Milo Lorentz 1939-
    (Lon Pearson)

PERSONAL: Born February 13, 1939, in Murray, UT; son of Milo Willard (a laborer) and Gulli Vicktoria (Peterson) Pearson; married Janet Stepan, October 7, 1961; children: Russell, Stephanie, Robert, Richard, Sharon. *Education:* University of Utah, B.A., 1965; University of California, Los Angeles, M.A., 1968, Ph. D., 1973; Johns Hopkins University, postdoctoral study, 1975-76. *Religion:* Church of Jesus Christ of Latter-Day Saints (Mormons).

ADDRESSES: Home—3619 13th Ave., Kearney, NE 68845-8020. *Office*—Department of Modern Languages, University of Nebraska at Kearney, Kearney, NE 68849-1310. *E-mail*—pearsonlon@unk.edu.

CAREER: Church of Jesus Christ of Latter-Day Saints, missionary in Mexico, 1959-61, bishop of Rolla ward, 1986-91, public affairs director for central Nebraska, 1996—; Southeast Builders Supply, Salt Lake City, UT, accountant, 1962-66; University of California, Los Angeles, associate instructor in Spanish, 1969-70; University of Missouri, Rolla, instructor, 1970-73, assistant professor, 1973-77, associate professor, 1977-87, professor of Spanish, 1987-91, inter-varsity soccer coach and assistant coach, 1979-85; University of Nebraska at Kearney, professor of Spanish, 1991—, department chair, 1991-96. Brigham Young University, visiting professor, 1982-83; participant in re-enactment of Mormon Battalion and 1997 Mormon Trail trek. *Military service:* U.S. Army National Guard, 1956-66, and 1977-79; served in Panama and Honduras.

MEMBER: International Institute of Iberoamerican Literature.

AWARDS, HONORS: National Endowment for the Humanities, research fellowship, 1975-76, grant, 1981; Meritorious Service Citation, Phi Kappa Phi, 1981; research grants for South America from University of Missouri and University of Nebraska.

WRITINGS:

(Under name Lon Pearson) *Nicomedes Guzmán: Proletarian Author in Chile's Literary Generation of 1938,* University of Missouri Press (Columbia, MO), 1976.

Editor or translator of other books. Contributor of nearly 100 articles, reviews, and a short story to scholarly journals and newspapers in the United States and South America, including *Southwinds* and *Platte Valley Review. Chasqui: Journal of Latin American Literature,* contributing editor, 1979-93, associate editor and book review editor, 1993—; translator for *American Bee Journal,* 1971-96; editor, *Missouri Foreign Language Journal,* 1973-78; consulting editor, *Studies in Contemporary Satire,* 1994—.

WORK IN PROGRESS: A book on Chilean novelist José Donoso.

BIOGRAPHICAL/CRITICAL SOURCES:

PERIODICALS

La Época, August 16, 1995, "La vigencia de la obra de Nicomedes Guzmán vista desde Estados Unidos: El académico Lon Pearson analiza la novela social como hito literario," p. 26.
Revista del Sabado, June 30, 1973.

                    *   *   *

PERKINS, George (Burton, Jr.) 1930-

PERSONAL: Born August 16, 1930, in Lowell, MA; son of George Burton and Gladys (Jones) Perkins; married Barbara Miller, May 9, 1964; children: Laura, Suzanne, Alison. *Education:* Tufts College (now Tufts University), A.B. (magna cum laude), 1953; Duke University, M.A., 1954; Cornell University, Ph.D., 1960. *Avocational interests:* Travel, tennis, folklore, folk song.

ADDRESSES: Home—1316 King George Blvd., Ann Arbor, MI 48108.

CAREER: Washington University, St. Louis, MO, instructor in English, 1957-60; Baldwin-Wallace College, Berea, Ohio, assistant professor of English, 1960-63; Fairleigh Dickinson University, Rutherford, NJ, assistant professor of English, 1963-66; University of Edinburgh, Edinburgh, Scotland, lecturer in American Literature, 1966-67; Eastern Michigan University, Ypsilanti, associate professor, 1967-70, professor of English, 1970—. Foreign Expert, People's Republic of China, 1989.

MEMBER: Society for the Study of Narrative Literature (founding member), Modern Language Association of America, American Association of University Professors, Phi Kappa Phi.

AWARDS, HONORS: Eastern Michigan University Distinguished Faculty Award for Scholarship, Teaching, and Service; fellow, Institute for Advanced Studies in the Humanities, University of Edinburgh, 1981; Eastern Michigan University Board of Regents commendation; senior Fulbright fellow, University of Newcastle, Australia, 1989; Society for the Study of Narrative Literature created the Perkins Prize in honor of George and Barbara Perkins.

WRITINGS:

Writing Clear Prose, Scott, Foresman, 1964.
(Editor) *Varieties of Prose,* Scott, Foresman, 1966.
(Editor) *The Theory of the American Novel,* Holt, 1970.
(Editor) *Realistic American Short Fiction,* Scott, Foresman, 1972.
(Editor) *American Poetry Theory,* Holt, 1972.
(Contributor) James Vinson, editor, *Contemporary Novelists,* St. Martin's Press (New York, NY), 1972.

(Editor, with Bradley, Beatty, and Long) *The American Tradition in Literature,* 4th edition, Grosset & Dunlap, 1974, 9th edition, with wife, Barbara Perkins, McGraw-Hill, 1999.

(With Northrop Frye and Sheridan Baker) *The Practical Imagination,* Harper & Row, 1980, revised, compact edition, with Frye, Baker, and wife Barbara Perkins, 1987.

(With B. Perkins and Frank McHugh) *Diagnostic and Achievement Tests,* Harper & Row, 1984.

(With Frye, Baker, and B. Perkins) *The Harper Handbook to Literature,* Harper & Row, 1985, 2nd edition, Longman, 1997.

(With B. Perkins) *Contemporary American Literature,* Random House, 1988.

A Season in New South Wales, Commonwealth, 1988.

(With B. Perkins and Phillip Leininger) *Benet's Reader's Encyclopedia of American Literature,* HarperCollins, 1991.

(With B. Perkins) *Kaleidoscope: Stories of the American Experience,* Oxford, 1993.

(With B. Perkins and Robyn Warhol) *Women's Work: An Anthology of American Literature,* McGraw-Hill, 1994.

Advisor and contributor to reference books, including *Contemporary Novelists, Great Writers: Novelists; Great Writers: Poets; and Great Writers: Dramatists.* Contributor of essays, fiction, and reviews to *Nineteenth-Century Fiction, Journal of American Folklore, New England Quarterly, Descant, Choice,* and other journals. General editor, *The Journal of Narrative Techniques,* 1971-92; associate editor, *Narrative,* 1993—.

WORK IN PROGRESS: The American Tradition in Literature Online, Primis/McGraw-Hill, a print-on-demand database for American literature. Also, an academic novel.

*   *   *

PERROTTA, Tom 1961-

PERSONAL: Born August 13, 1961, in Summit, NJ; son of Joseph (a mail carrier) and Suzan (a secretary) Perrotta; married Mary Granfield (a journalist), September 14, 1991; children: Nina, Luke. *Education:* Yale University, B.A., 1983; Syracuse University, M.A., 1988.

ADDRESSES: Home—17 Harding Ave., Belmont, MA 02478. *Agent*—Maria Massie, Witherspoon Associates, 235 East 31st St., New York, NY 10016.

CAREER: Yale University, New Haven, CT, lecturer, 1988-93; Harvard University, Cambridge, MA, preceptor, 1994-98.

WRITINGS:

FICTION

Bad Haircut: Stories of the Seventies, Bridge Works Publishing, 1994.
The Wishbones, Putnam (New York, NY), 1997.
Election, Putnam (New York, NY), 1998.
Joe College, St. Martin's Press (New York, NY), 2000.

ADAPTATIONS: Election was filmed by Paramount in 1999; *The Wishbones* was recorded on audiocassette and is scheduled to be filmed by New Line Cinema.

SIDELIGHTS: In *The Wishbones, Election,* and *Joe College,* Tom Perrotta has written three humorous novels about young people growing up, or failing to grow up, in contemporary America. In *The Wishbones* Perrotta writes of Dave Raymond, a thirty-one-year-old musician in a wedding band who still lives with his parents and dreams of success as a rock star. When the death of a musician friend forces him to confront his life honestly, Dave impulsively proposes to his girlfriend, a move he quickly regrets. A writer for *Kirkus Reviews* called the novel "a series of bittersweet misadventures recounted with irresistible tongue-in-cheek deadpan brio."

Perrotta's second novel, *Election,* takes place in a New Jersey high school where an election for student body president is the focus of everyone's attention. The two main candidates are football player Paul Warren and Tracy Flick, an ambitious beauty who had an affair with one of the school's teachers. When Paul's younger sister decides to enter the race too, a faculty advisor throws the election and loses his job. "This soap opera/comedy is funny, sad, realistic, irreverent, and very readable," claimed Joanna M. Burkhardt in the *Library Journal. New York Times Book Review* critic Peter LaSalle believed that *Election* delivered "exact and telling portraits of the kids" along with "solid plotting."

In *Joe College* Perrotta looks again at contemporary student life, this time delineating the story of Danny, a junior at Yale who drives his father's New Jersey lunch truck during school breaks. Danny has problems with women, including the pregnant girlfriend back home he wants to dump and the Yale girl he secretly desires, and must ward off threats from his father's shady business rivals. According to a critic for *Publishers Weekly, Joe College* shows that Perrotta "is in full control of his quirky comic sensibility."

BIOGRAPHICAL/CRITICAL SOURCES:

PERIODICALS

Booklist, June 1, 1994, review of *Bad Haircut,* p. 1772; May 15, 1997, review of *The Wishbones,* p. 1563; February 1, 1998, Kevin Grandfield, review of *Election,* p. 900.

Christian Science Monitor, July 1, 1994, review of *Bad Haircut,* p. 10.

Kirkus Reviews, March 15, 1994, review of *Bad Haircut,* p. 331; March 15, 1997, review of *The Wishbones,* p. 411; January 15, 1998, review of *Election,* p. 75.

Kliatt, January, 1996, review of *Bad Haircut,* p. 19; January, 1999, review of *Election,* p. 14.

Library Journal, April 15, 1994, review of *Bad Haircut,* p. 116; April 15, 1997, review of *The Wishbones,* p. 120; March 1, 1998, Joanna M. Burkhardt, review of *Election,* p. 128.

Los Angeles Times Book Review, July 24, 1994, review of *Bad Haircut,* p. 6.

New York Times Book Review, August 7, 1994, review of *Bad Haircut,* p. 14; July 27, 1997, review of *The Wishbones,* p. 5; April 19, 1998, Peter LaSalle, review of *Election,* p. 22.

Publishers Weekly, April 11, 1994, review of *Bad Haircut,* p. 53; March 31, 1997, review of *The Wishbones,* p. 61; January 12, 1998, review of *Election,* p. 44; July 17, 2000, review of *Joe College,* p. 174.

*   *   *

PERRY, Paul 1950-

PERSONAL: Born July 8, 1950, in Phoenix, AZ; son of Jewel F. (an insurance agent) and Esther Ida (a home-maker; maiden name, Stanwick) Perry; married Darlene Joy Bennett (a medical librarian), September 30, 1979; children: (first marriage) Paul; (second marriage) Paige-Marie, Reed. *Education:* Arizona State University, B.A., 1972. *Politics:* "Democrat bordering on Libertarian." *Religion:* Protestant.

ADDRESSES: Home and office—6120 East Mountain View Rd., Paradise Valley, AZ 85253-1805. *Agent*—Nat Sobel, Sobel Weber Associates, Inc., 146 East Nineteenth St., New York, NY 10003.

CAREER: Runner's World, Mountain View, CA, managing editor, 1978-80; *Running,* Eugene, OR, editor-in-chief, 1980-83; *American Health,* New York City, executive editor, 1984-88; writer.

AWARDS, HONORS: Gannett Foundation Media Center Scholar.

WRITINGS:

(With Raymond Moody) *The Light Beyond,* Bantam, 1988.

(With Melvin Morse) *Closer to the Light,* Villard, 1990.

(With Herman Hellerstein) *Healing Your Heart,* Simon & Schuster (New York), 1990.

(With Ken Babbs) *On the Bus,* Thunder's Mouth Press, 1990.

(With Raymond Moody) *Coming Back,* Bantam (New York), 1991.

(With Melvin Morse) *Transformed by the Light,* Villard, 1992.

Fear and Loathing: The Strange and Terrible Saga of Hunter S. Thompson, Thunder's Mouth Press, 1992.

(With Raymond Moody) *Reunions: Visionary Encounters with Departed Loved Ones,* American Library Association, 1993.

(With Melvin Morse) *Parting Visions: Uses and Meanings of Pre-Death, Psychic, and Spiritual Experiences,* Villard, 1994.

(With Dannion Brinkley) *Saved by the Light: The True Story of a Man Who Died Twice and the Profound Revelations He Received,* Villard, 1994.

(With Dannion Brinkley) *At Peace in the Light: The Further Adventures of a Reluctant Psychic Who Reveals the Secret of Your Spiritual Powers,* Harper-Collins (New York), 1995.

(With Claude Steiner) *Achieving Emotional Literacy: A Personal Program to Increase Your Emotional Intelligence,* Avon Books (New York), 1997.

(With Hong Liu) *Mastering Miracles: The Healing Art of Qi Gong as Taught by a Master,* Warner Books (New York), 1997.

(With Vern S. Cherewatenko) *The Diabetes Cure: A Medical Approach That Can Slow, Stop, Even Cure Type 2 Diabetes,* Cliff Street Books (New York), 1999.

(With Barry Clifford) *The Black Ship: The Quest to Recover an English Pirate Ship and Its Lost Treasure,* Headline (London), 1999, published as *Expedition Whydah: The Story of the World's First Excavation of a Pirate Treasure Ship and the Man Who Found Her,* Cliff Street Books, 1999.

(With Melvin Morse) *Where God Lives: The Science of the Paranormal and How Our Brains Are Linked to the Universe,* HarperCollins/Cliff Street Books, 2000.

Contributor to periodicals, including *Astronomy, American Way, National Geographic Adventure, Discovery. com, American Health, Reader's Digest,* and *USA Weekend.* Consulting editor to periodicals, including *Outside, Men's Journal,* and *Runner.* Three of Perry's books have appeared on the *New York Times* bestseller list.

SIDELIGHTS: "I write on a wide variety of topics," Paul Perry told *CA,* and a sampling of the author's works proves his point. Frequently collaborating with experts in various fields, Perry has published books that range from preventative medicine (*Healing Your Heart*) to accounts of counterculture heroes such as Ken Kesey and Hunter S. Thompson. A recurring interest for Perry is the topic of temporary death, and he has devoted several books to the subject. *Closer to the Light,* co-authored with Melvin Morse, M.D., placed on the *New York Times* best-seller list for several weeks in late 1990. It recounts the tales of various children who came close to dying, then survived to tell of their unusual experiences. A companion book, also written with Morse, *Transformed by the Light,* followed in 1992. It examines the long-term effects of such experiences. Five more such books followed in quick succession.

On the Bus, which Perry co-wrote in 1990 with Ken Babbs, focuses on the influential bus trip made by novelist Ken Kesey and the Merry Pranksters in the summer of 1964. Using the royalties from his first two novels, *One Flew over the Cuckoo's Nest* and *Sometimes a Great Notion,* Kesey financed a trip from California to New York aboard a bright, multicolored bus. Accompanying Kesey were the Merry Pranksters, a band of likeminded individuals culled from his graduate writing classes. The Prankster's purpose was, ostensibly, to travel America's highways, shoot vast quantities of film, take mind-altering drugs such as LSD, and distill a new medium of literary and artistic expression. The Pranksters' highjinks on the road included dropping acid in the desert, visiting fellow LSD guru Timothy Leary, and meeting up with a Hell's Angels biker gang

for a dangerous night of partying. Perry and Babbs, a member of the Pranksters, use the recollections of the participants, detailed photographs, and news clippings of the times to document Kesey's trek.

The journey of Kesey and the Merry Pranksters, hailed by many as the launch of the hippie era, has already been the subject of various literary works, including Tom Wolfe's popular *Electric Kool-Aid Acid Test* and Kesey's own *Further Inquiry.* "Kesey's book documents those days," noted *New Time*'s Dave Walker, comparing Perry's account with Kesey's. "Paul Perry tries to explain their continuing attraction." Walker added that "Perry tries for the wide angle in [*On the Bus*], and succeeds for all who were merely fellow-travelers 'on the bus' or who first got turned on to the new transportation possibilities revealed in Tom Wolfe's 'electric' book." Charles Bowden, writing in the *Los Angeles Times Book Review,* reported that *On the Bus* provides "a handy history of LSD, and a chronicle of Kesey and the Pranksters after the bus ride—the acid tests, the busts, and the eventual descent of the band into relatively ordinary lives."

Perry investigated another counterculture icon in his 1992 biography *Fear and Loathing: The Strange and Terrible Saga of Hunter S. Thompson.* Thompson gained notoriety in the 1960s as the foremost practitioner of "gonzo journalism." The author's unconventional books and feature articles were highlighted by quirky observations and often focused on his own misadventures while covering the stories. Thompson's writing also dealt with his legendary status as a consumer of drugs and alcohol, with *Fear and Loathing in Las Vegas*—an account of the author's drugged visit to the Nevada gambling mecca—becoming a cult favorite. While Perry's biography further documents Thompson's overindulgence in controlled substances, the book also probes other aspects of his life, including the physical abuse of his wife and his proclivity for threatening people with handguns.

Tom Graves, writing in the *New York Times Book Review,* gave the biography a mixed review. While noting that Perry "comes up woefully short" in documenting Thompson's later career, the critic found that Perry "convincingly recounts Mr. Thompson's troubled youth and his struggles as a journeyman writer." Perry's chronicle of Thompson's life has several competitors: two other biographies, *Hunter: The Strange and Savage Life of Hunter S. Thompson* by E. Jean Carroll and *When the Going Gets Weird: The Twisted Life and Times of Hunter S. Thompson* by Peter O. Whitmer both appeared in 1993. Comparing the three biographies in *Details,* David Streitfeld praised Perry's account, recommending it as "the one to read."

Discussing his biography of Thompson, Perry told *CA:* "This is a traditional biography that traces Hunter's life from childhood. But it is also untraditional in the sense that I write about my own rather bizarre dealings with Hunter. In 1980, as the editor of *Running* magazine, I commissioned Hunter to cover the Honolulu Marathon and spent a considerable amount of time with the self-proclaimed 'doctor of journalism,' pulling the story out of him. Like so many other people who have read the works of Thompson, I thought he over-stated his drug use. But after spending time with him, I realized that he has always understated his amount of pharmaceutical abuse. He calls himself 'the last of the old time drug addicts,' and I can certainly vouch for the fact that he lives up to that reputation.

"Despite the many difficulties in dealing with Hunter, we stayed in touch long after the Honolulu Marathon piece was published in *Running.* In fact, he eventually lengthened the marathon piece and turned it into a book entitled *The Curse of Lono.* We later tried working together again, developing a book idea that would cure Hunter of his addictions to drugs, alcohol, and cigarettes by replacing them with compulsive fitness activities like running and other forms of exercise. The plan was to have him attend the Pritikin Longevity Center and other similar clinics to help him kick his habits. Hunter was fond of the idea, but it was shot down by a publisher at Summit Books who inexplicably felt that involvement in such a healthy endeavor would prove dangerous for Hunter."

In 1993, Perry returned to the paranormal, collaborating with Raymond Moody on *Reunions: Visionary Encounters with Departed Loved Ones.* In this volume, the two authors claim that one does not need a near-death experience to communicate with the dead. Instead, one can use old techniques such as crystal and mirror gazing. Moody and Perry claim that many reunions of the living and the dead have occurred at Moody's Theater of the Mind in Alabama. According to Ilene Cooper in *Booklist,* the book proves that "the desire to contact the departed is as old as life itself. It doesn't take a visionary to know that this book will be very popular."

With Morse, Perry produced another book in the same vein, *Parting Visions: Uses and Meaning of Pre-Death, Psychic, and Spiritual Experiences,* in 1994. This work is a collection of case histories of many who have had premonitions of an imminent death. In the same year, Perry collaborated with Dannion Brinkley in *Saved by the Light: The True Story of a Man Who Died Twice and the Profound Revelations He Received.* Brinkley himself claims to have died as a result of a lightning bolt and then to have been revived nearly thirty minutes later. He feels that his life has been transformed and that he has gained certain psychic powers as a result of the out-of-body experience he had during those minutes. Brinkley describes "Luminous Beings" who engulfed him with "peace and tranquility" in a magnificent lecture hall, where he saw a panoply of historical events yet to occur. In a skeptical critique in the *National Review,* Matthew Scully noted that this book is one in a spate of volumes on the life-after-death phenomenon, beginning with Morse and Perry's *Closer to the Light.* "We are getting our first glimpse of things about which we could once only speculate," wrote Scully. "Rapturous release, dark tunnels, incomparable light, radiant Beings—it's all coming into focus. The veil is being lifted. There is a Heaven! . . . The suspicion is that we are seeing something very much like the current 'angel' mania, with reported sightings of feathery friends throughout the land." Scully concluded, "It is hard to see just how, when we find ourselves being escorted in for the life review, any of us will be better off for having advance knowledge of the examiner's garments or the floorplan of the room."

In *Mastering Miracles: The Healing Art of Qi Gong as Taught by a Master,* Perry worked with Chinese physician Hong Liu to explain Qi Gong, an Eastern practice that attempts to use the patient's own "energy fields" to achieve wellness through a regimen of exercise, diet, and herbal remedies. *Library Journal* contributor Betty Braaksma, while noting that the section describing Liu's quest to become a Qi Gong master is "overly long" for western sensibilities, recommended the book for libraries with a high demand for material on alternative medicine.

Perry went on to collaborate on a book with noted pirate ship hunter Barry Clifford. Published in 1999, *Expedition Whydah: The Story of the World's First Excavation of a Pirate Ship,* took Perry to the east coast where he and his son Reed helped excavate this pirate ship that crashed on the shores of Cape Cod in 1717. The *Wall Street Journal* called this book "the recipe for perfect summer reading, and it's all true," while *National Geographic Adventure* declared that readers "will find themselves exhilarated."

Expedition Whydah led to a Discovery Channel expedition in 2000 that took Perry and Clifford to Madagascar where they searched for the Adventure Galley, the flagship of famed pirate Captain William Kidd. The ship was found and is the subject of a Discovery Channel documentary film. Perry is completing a book about the expedition called *Return to Treasure Island and the Search for Captain Kidd.*

Perry also collaborated with Morse on *Where God Lives: The Science of the Paranormal and How Our Brains Are Linked to the Universe.* In this book, the authors explore the links between science and mysticism, concluding that there is an unseen power that guides human life. The authors contend that the right temporal lobe of the brain is the site of spirituality and self-fulfillment. The book dwells heavily on the experiences of critically ill children, who "feel they can connect with the divine presence they saw when they nearly died." According to a *Publishers Weekly* reviewer, Perry's co-author, "although exuberant in sharing his beliefs, . . . demonstrates the restraint of a veteran man of science, which will help to make [the] claims more convincing to those who consulted [the] earlier works."

BIOGRAPHICAL/CRITICAL SOURCES:

PERIODICALS

Booklist, October 15, 1993, Ilene Cooper, review of *Reunions,* p. 394.
Details, February, 1993, David Streitfeld, review of *Fear and Loathing, Hunter,* and *When the Going Gets Weird,* p. 87.
Library Journal, January, 1997, Betty Braaksma, review of *Mastering Miracles,* p. 136.
Los Angeles Times Book Review, October 21, 1990, Charles Bowden, review of *On the Bus,* pp. 4, 7.
National Review, September 12, 1994, Matthew Scully, review of *Saved by the Light,* pp. 83-86.
New Times, November 28, 1990, Dave Walker, review of *On the Bus,* pp. 22, 34-42.
New York Times Book Review, December 9, 1990; January 17, 1993, p. 24.
Publishers Weekly, July 31, 2000, review of *Where God Lives,* p. 84.
Washington Post Book World, November 18, 1990, p. 1.

*　　*　　*

PROCTOR, William (Gilbert, Jr.) 1941-

PERSONAL: Born October 11, 1941, in Atlanta, GA; son of William Gilbert, Sr. (a controller) and Maud (Moore) Proctor; married Priscilla Moore (a writer), June 17, 1967. *Education:* Harvard University, B.A., 1963, J.D., 1966. *Religion:* Methodist.

ADDRESSES: Home and office—7 Peter Cooper Rd., Apt. 1F, New York, NY 10010. *Agent*—Bill Adler, 1230 Sixth Ave., New York, NY 10020.

CAREER: New York Daily News, New York, NY, writer-reporter, 1969-73; freelance writer, 1973—. Vestry clerk, Calvary/St. George's Episcopal Parish. *Military service:* U.S. Marine Corps, 1966-69; served as judge advocate and military judge; became captain.

MEMBER: Texas Bar Association, Harvard Club of New York, NY.

WRITINGS:

Survival on the Campus: A Handbook for Christian Students, Fleming H. Revell, 1972.
Jews for Jesus, Fleming H. Revell, 1974.
Help Wanted: Faith Required, Fleming H. Revell, 1974.
The Commune Kidnapping, Pyramid Press, 1975.
The Art of Christian Promotion, Fleming H. Revell, 1975.
(Senior contributing author) *Jesus the Living Bread,* Logos Publishing International, 1976.
Women in the Pulpit, Doubleday, 1976.
RX: The Christian Love Treatment, Doubleday, 1976.
PDA: Personal Death Awareness, Prentice-Hall, 1976.
On the Trail of God, Doubleday, 1977.
The Born-again Christian Catalog, M. Evans, 1980.
The Return of the Star of Bethlehem, Doubleday, 1980.
Adventures in Immortality, McGraw, 1982.
(With Larry Burkett) *How to Prosper in the Underground Economy,* Morrow, 1982.
Firm Skin in Ten Minutes a Day, New American Library, 1983.
The Templeton Touch, Doubleday, 1983.
The Preconception Gender Diet, M. Evans, 1983.
The Brain Food Diet for Children, Bobbs-Merrill, 1983.
The Ethical Executive, Simon & Schuster, 1984.
Beyond the Relaxation Response, Times Books, 1984.
Forecast 2000, Morrow, 1984.
Beyond Reason, Morrow, 1984.
(With Paul A. Mickey) *Tough Marriage: How to Make a Difficult Relationship Work,* Morrow, 1986.
(With George Gallup, Jr. and Alec M. Gallup) *The Great American Success Story: Factors That Affect Achievement,* Dow Jones-Irwin (Homewood, IL), 1986.
(With Bradley Bucher) *Winning Them Over: How to Negotiate Successfully with Your Kids,* Times Books, 1987.

(With Herbert Benson) *Your Maximum Mind,* Times Books, 1987.

(With Paul A. Mickey) *Sex with Confidence: How to Achieve Physical and Emotional Intimacy in the New Sexual Age,* Morrow, 1988.

(With Jean Yoder) *The Self-confident Child,* Facts on File (New York, NY), 1988.

(With Archbishop Iakovos) *Faith for a Lifetime: A Spiritual Journey,* Doubleday, 1988.

(With Anne F. Grizzle) *Mother Love, Mother Hate: Breaking Dependent Love Patterns in Family Relationships,* Fawcett Columbine (New York, NY), 1988.

(With Thomas Pike) *Is It Success: Or Is It Addiction?,* T. Nelson, 1988.

(With Sam E. Beller) *The Great Insurance Secret: How to Beat the Insurance Crisis and Get the Coverage You Need Now—For the Right Price,* Morrow, 1988.

(With Sandra Fiebelkorn) *Power Borrowing,* Morrow, 1989.

(With Ralph E. Minear) *Kids Who Have Too Much,* T. Nelson, 1989.

(With Sue Klavans Simring and Steven S. Simring) *The Compatibility Quotient,* Fawcett Columbine, 1990.

(With Mickey) *Twelve Keys to a Better Marriage,* Pyranee Books (Grand Rapids, MI), 1990.

(With Myron Winick) *The Fiber Prescription,* Fawcett Columbine, 1992.

The Terrible Speller: A Quick-and-Easy Guide to Enhancing Your Spelling Ability, Morrow, 1993.

(With Richard N. Podell) *The G-Index Diet: The Missing Link That Makes Permanent Weight Loss Possible,* Warner, 1993.

(With Arthur K. Robertson) *Work a Four-Hour Day: Achieving Business Efficiency on Your Own Terms,* W. Morrow, 1994.

(With R. Theodore Benna) *Escaping the Coming Retirement Crisis: How to Secure Your Financial Future,* Piñon Press (Colorado Springs, CO), 1995.

(With Richard N. Podell) *When Your Doctor Doesn't Know Best,* Simon & Schuster, 1995, reprinted as *Patient Power,* Fireside (New York, NY), 1996.

The Resurrection Report, Broadman & Holman (Nashville, TN), 1998.

The Last Star (novel), T. Nelson (Nashville, TN), 2000.

The Gospel according to the New York Times: How the World's Most Powerful News Organization Shapes Your Mind and Values, Broadman & Holman, 2000.

Contributor to magazines and newspapers.

SIDELIGHTS: After a successful career as a journalist and author of nonfiction books about health, religion, and personal time and money management, William Proctor ventured into fiction with the critically respected novel *The Last Star.* Deemed a "captivating page-turner" by a reviewer for *Publishers Weekly,* the book presents a scenario in which investigators come to believe that a mysterious bright light in the Eastern sky is the Star of Bethlehem. Terrorism, sabotage, and romance ensue as various teams of researchers race to explain the phenomenon. Praising Proctor's well-developed characters and expert plotting, the *Publishers Weekly* contributor ventured that he "shows promise of becoming the Christian Tom Clancy."

Among Proctor's nonfiction titles, which have sold more than twenty million copies, are *Women in the Pulpit, How to Prosper in the Underground Economy, The Ethical Executive, Beyond the Relaxation Response, The Resurrection Report,* and *The Gospel according to the New York Times.* He has served as co-author for several additional titles, including *When Your Doctor Doesn't Know Best,* and has interviewed or collaborated with such prominent individuals as Mother Teresa, Arnold Schwarzenegger, Ronald Reagan, Billy Graham, Charles Colson, Art Linkletter, Willard Scott, Pat Boone, and George Gallup, Jr.

BIOGRAPHICAL/CRITICAL SOURCES:

PERIODICALS

Booklist, August 1992, p. 1986; October 15, 1993, p. 401; March 1, 1994, p. 1170.
Columbia Journalism Review, September, 2000, Mark I. Pinski, review of *The Gospel according to the New York Times,* p. 76.
Christianity Today, September 5, 1986, p. 37.
Library Journal, January 1986, p. 92; February 1, 1988, p. 69; October 1, 1988, p. 91; October 15, 1988, p. 96; March 1, 1989, p. 76; March 4, 1993, p. 98; August 1993, p. 116; November 15, 1994, p. 83; September 14, 1995, p. 78.
Los Angeles Times, May 14, 1982.
National Catholic Reporter, October 12, 1990, p. 17.
New England Journal of Medicine, May 12, 1988, p. 1287.
New York Times Book Review, September 5, 1982.
Publishers Weekly, December 5, 1994, p. 75; November 24, 1997, p. 66; September 4, 2000, p. 85.
West Coast Review of Books, March, 1983.*

*   *   *

PRUNTY, (Eugene) Wyatt 1947-

PERSONAL: Born May 15, 1947, in Humbolt, TN; son of Merle Charles (a geographer) and Eugenia (Wyatt) Prunty; married Barbara Heather Svell, August 14, 1973; children: Heather Carthel, Ian Merle. *Education:*

University of the South, B.A. (with honors), 1969; Johns Hopkins University, M.A., 1973; Louisiana State University, Ph.D., 1979.

ADDRESSES: Home—204 Smithfield Dr., Blacksburg, VA 24060. *Office*—Department of English, Virginia Polytechnic Institute and State University, Blacksburg, VA 24061. *E-mail*—wprunty@seraph1.sewanee.edu.

CAREER: Louisiana State University, Baton Rouge, instructor in English, 1978-79; Virginia Polytechnic Institute and State University, Blacksburg, assistant, associate and full professor of English, 1979-89; University of the South, Carlton Professor of English and founding director of the Sewanee Writers' Conference, 1989—. Visiting writer at Washington and Lee University, 1982-83; visiting associate and professor (Coleman chair) at Johns Hopkins University, 1987-89; visiting teacher at Bread Loaf School of English and Bread Loaf Writers' Conference. Staff associate of Bread Loaf Writers' Conference, 1983. Gives poetry readings. *Military service:* U.S. Navy, deck officer and gunnery officer, 1969-72; became lieutenant.

MEMBER: Modern Language Association of America, Associated Writing Programs, College English Association, English Institute, South Atlantic Modern Language Association.

AWARDS, HONORS: Poetry prize from *Sewanee Review,* 1969, for "Linnet and Leaf"; fellow at Bread Loaf Writers Conference, 1982; recipient of Brown Foundation fellowship.

WRITINGS:

POETRY COLLECTIONS

The Times Between, Johns Hopkins University Press (Baltimore, MD), 1982.
What Women Know, What Men Believe, Johns Hopkins University Press (Baltimore, MD), 1986.
Balance as Belief, Johns Hopkins University Press (Baltimore, MD), 1989.
The Run of the House, Johns Hopkins University Press (Baltimore, MD), 1993.
Since the Noon Mail Stopped, Johns Hopkins University Press (Baltimore, MD), 1997.
Unarmed and Dangerous: New and Selected Poems, Johns Hopkins University Press (Baltimore, MD), 1999.

OTHER

Domestic of the Outer Banks (poetry chapbook), Inland Boat Press, 1980.
Fallen from the Symboled World: Precedents for the New Formalism (literary criticism), Oxford University Press (New York, NY), 1990.
(Editor with Peter Mayer) *Just Let Me Say This about That: A Narrative Poem,* John Bricuth (Sewanee Writers' Series), 1998.
(Editor) *Sewanee Writers on Writing* (Southern Literary Series), Louisiana State University Press (Baton Rouge, LA), 2001.

Work represented in anthologies, including *Pocket Poetry,* Number 1, 1975; *Anthology of Magazine Verse and Yearbook of American Poetry for 1979,* edited by Alan F. Pater, Monitor Books (Beverly Hills, CA), 1980; *Anthology of Magazine Verse and Yearbook of American Poetry for 1980,* edited by Pater, Monitor Book, 1981. Contributor of poems, essays, and reviews to magazines, stateside and abroad, including *Cimarron Review, Colorado Quarterly, Kenyon Review, New Criterion, New Republic, New Yorker, Ploughshares, PN Review, Salmagundi, Southern Review,* and *Yale Review.* Poetry editor, *Sewanee Theological Review;* founding editor, "Sewanee Writers" series (Overlook Press), 1997.

WORK IN PROGRESS: Geography, poems; *Against Time: Shapes and Forms in Recent Poetry,* a study of the disappearance of allegory in recent American poetry; *The Calendar Question,* poems.

SIDELIGHTS: Wyatt Prunty's poetry has generally been associated with the New Formalism movement, although he reportedly attempts to shrug off such labeling as too self-limiting. As detailed on the *Wyatt Prunty June 1998* Web site, "Wyatt Prunty's early memories include weekend field trips taken with his father, Merle Prunty, the geographer. Packed in among graduate students taking notes, a seven-year-old Prunty listened as the landscape ticked by outside the van was summarized inside a day-long monologue delivered from the driver's seat through a haze of unfiltered Lucky Strikes. Prunty's early conviction was that all things were related and between the asking and the next cigarette every question could be answered." The same site noted, "Although Wyatt Prunty's home was located in the college town of Athens, Georgia, during childhood he spent every summer and Christmas on a farm that bordered the small farming community of Newburn, Tennessee, and the patterns found in the landscape of this area still inform some of his writing." This overlay of two radically polarized existences seemed natural to the youthful Prunty. "Now it appears in poems that have their origins in puzzlements over the contrasts between a privileged city life and a raw agricultural existence."

According to William E. Clarkson in *Contemporary Southern Writers,* "Wyatt Prunty's first published poem appeared in the Autumn 1968 issue of the *Sewanee Review* while the poet was still a student at the University of the South. He was taught and encouraged by Allen Tate and Andrew Lytle, who was then editor of the *Review.*" In 1989, after years spent in naval service, graduate study and teaching at other institutions, he returned to the University of the South as a Carlton Professor of English. In the fall of that year, funds received from the estate of Tennessee Williams were used to place into motion plans for the envisioned Sewanee Writers' Conference, and Prunty was appointed its director. He gathered a distinguished group of poets and fiction writers to comprise the faculty for its debut gathering in the summer of 1990. Under the continuing direction of Prunty, the success of its first season has been repeated annually, placing the Sewanee Writers' Conference among the most influential gatherings in American letters.

Despite its inherent formality, Prunty usually eschews structuring his verse upon rigid, historical poetic forms, even when—as several poems in *Since the Noon Mail Stopped* do—they consist of the same traditional, fourteen lines that comprise the form of the sonnet. Most of Prunty's verse is blank, with a loosely metrical basis. His use of rhyme is deft but spare, and while some poems are tightly rhymed throughout, others begin in blank verse and flow so subtly into distant and slant rhyme that the reader may not perceive this transition into a rhymed environment until they reach its final line.

Prunty's verse may be formal, but it is far from repressive or elitist. His work embodies his stated belief that it is not form so much as the poet's "modes of thought, the means of figuration" that are most important. And among the "figurative modes of thought" that interest him, he cites the "New Critical staples of irony, paradox, and ambiguity" as due special attention—staples that his own work enthusiastically embodies.

Perhaps Prunty's most frequently appropriated and celebrated poem is "Learning the Bicycle," the lead-in work of his 1989 collection, *Balance as Belief.* It is a forceful and epigrammatic study in paradox. Its narrator recalls his daughter's struggles and failed attempts to master riding her first bicycle, knowing full well that when she achieves the necessary balance she will ride away, far away from "the place I stop and know / That to teach her I had to follow / And when she learned I had to let her go."

The 1997 collection, *Since the Noon Mail Stopped,* demonstrates Prunty's meditative spirit and wry humor, his deft and imaginative wordplay, the subtle nuances of tone, and the precision and immediacy of his imagery. In "Grown Men at Touch," backyard football players use the shadow of a barn as the demarcation for their goal line. "By four, our shadow-field / Had gone long past the longest pass; / By five, no one could run its length." In "Coach," a poem of four brief stanzas, he turns his attention to expressing the inner life of a family dog, from puppyhood to death. "All trucks were from Hell and deserved my bite, / all children sheep and not to leave the yard . . ." Other poems involve such unlikely subjects as four houseflies, the Zamboni polishing a skating rink, and the inner landscape of a pyromaniac's thoughts.

In discussing *Unarmed and Dangerous: New and Selected Poems,* a *Publishers Weekly* reviewer noted the "Frostian stoicism and precise observation of sad American scenes distinguish the poems of Wyatt Prunty." And in her *New York Times Book Review* assessment, Melanie Rehak stated that "Prunty has spent the last two decades . . . examining the ways in which human experience is made up of small traditions bound together into a larger story—the subset of ritual within narrative, one might say. His language mirrors this relationship; it has a plain-spoken sweep with, every so often, beautiful, intricate phrasing appearing on the horizon." She said, "There is . . . a kind of wistful humor lurking behind the scenes in Prunty's work . . . He has an exquisite hold on life. And in 'Unarmed and Dangerous' he displays an inherent understanding of the fact that comedy and tragedy, both on the page and off, coexist more often than not."

BIOGRAPHICAL/CRITICAL SOURCES:

BOOKS

Contemporary Southern Writers, St. James Press (Detroit, MI), 1999.

PERIODICALS

New York Times Book Review, March 19, 2000, Melanie Rehak, "The Small Stuff."

PN Review, Volume VIII, number 5, 1982; Volume IX, number 2, 1982.
Publishers Weekly, December 6, 1999, "December Collections," review of *Unarmed and Dangerous: New and Selected Poems,* p. 74.
Virginia Quarterly Review, summer, 1982.

OTHER

Wyatt Prunty, June 1998, http://members.aol.com/ poetrynet/month/archive/prunty/(June 11, 2000).*

*　　*　　*

PUZO, Mario 1920-1999

PERSONAL: Born October 15, 1920, in New York, NY; died of heart failure July 2, 1999, in Bay Shore, NY; son of Antonio (a railroad trackman) and Maria (Le Conti) Puzo; married Erika Lina Broske (deceased), 1946; children: Anthony, Joey, Dorothy, Virginia, Eugene. *Education:* Attended New School for Social Research (now New School University) and Columbia University. *Avocational interests:* Gambling, tennis, Italian cuisine, dieting.

CAREER: Novelist. Variously employed as messenger with New York Central Railroad, New York, NY, public relations administrator with U.S. Air Force in Europe, administrative assistant with U.S. Civil Service, New York, NY, and editor-writer with Magazine Management. *Military service:* U.S. Army Air Forces, during World War II; served in Germany; became corporal.

AWARDS, HONORS: Academy Award, American Academy of Motion Picture Arts and Sciences, and Screen Award, Writers Guild of America, West, Inc., for best screenplay adapted from another medium, 1972, for *The Godfather,* and 1974, for *The Godfather: Part II;* Golden Globe Award for best screenplay, Hollywood Foreign Press Association, 1973, for *The Godfather,* and 1990, for *The Godfather: Part III.*

WRITINGS:

The Dark Arena, Random House, 1955, revised edition, Bantam, 1985.
The Fortunate Pilgrim, Atheneum, 1964.

Mario Puzo

The Godfather (also see below), Putnam, 1969.
Fools Die, Putnam, 1978.
The Sicilian, Linden Press/Simon & Schuster, 1984.
The Fourth K, Random House, 1991.
The Last Don: A Novel, Random House, 1996.
Omerta, Random House, 2000.

SCREENPLAYS

(With Francis Ford Coppola) *The Godfather* (based on Puzo's novel of same title), Paramount, 1972.
(With Coppola) *The Godfather: Part II,* Paramount, 1974.
(With George Fox) *Earthquake,* Universal, 1974.
(With David Newman, Leslie Newman, and Robert Benton) *Superman* (based on the comic strip created by Jerry Siegel and Joel Shuster), Warner Bros., 1978.
(With D. Newman and L. Newman) *Superman II,* Warner Bros., 1981.
(With Coppola) *The Godfather: Part III,* Paramount, 1990.

(With John Briley and Cary Bates) *Christopher Columbus: The Discovery,* Warner Bros., 1992.

OTHER

The Runaway Summer of Davie Shaw (juvenile), illustrated by Stewart Sherwood, Platt & Munk, 1966.

(Contributor) Thomas C. Wheeler, editor, *The Immigrant Experience: The Anguish of Becoming an American,* Dial, 1971.

"The Godfather" Papers and Other Confessions, Putnam, 1972.

Inside Las Vegas (nonfiction), photographs by Michael Abramson, Susan Fowler-Gallagher, and John Launois, Grosset, 1977.

Contributor of articles, reviews, and stories to *American Vanguard, New York, Redbook, Holiday, New York Times Magazine,* and other publications.

Manuscript collection is held at Boston University, Boston, MA. *The Godfather* has been translated into Russian.

ADAPTATIONS: A Time to Die, based on a story by Puzo, was adapted for the screen by John Goff, Matt Cimbert, and William Russel, and released by Almi, 1983; *The Cotton Club,* based on a story by Puzo, Coppola, and William Kennedy, was adapted for the screen by Kennedy and directed by Coppola for Orion Pictures, 1984; *The Fortunate Pilgrim* was adapted for television and broadcast as *Mario Puzo's The Fortunate Pilgrim* by NBC, April 3, 1988; *The Sicilian* was adapted for the screen by Steve Shagan and directed by Michael Cimino for Twentieth Century-Fox, 1989; *The Last Don* was adapted for television and broadcast by CBS in May, 1997 and May, 1998.

SIDELIGHTS: Though some critics have dismissed his bestsellers for pandering too much to commercial tastes, novelist and screenwriter Mario Puzo forever changed the way the world thought of the Mafia. His *Godfather* books and the films on which they were based became undisputed classics, garnering both popular and critical acclaim and setting a new standard for the fictional treatment of organized crime. As *Time* writer Karl Taro Greenfeld put it in his 1999 eulogy for the writer, Puzo's work "virtually created the Mafia as literary and cinematic subject."

Yet Puzo's success was a long time coming. The son of immigrants who moved to the Hell's Kitchen area of New York City from their native Italy, Puzo had dreamed of being a writer since high school, but had struggled for years to achieve a footing in the publishing world. After serving in the U.S. Army in World War II, he worked as a freelance writer while attending City College of New York on the G.I. Bill. During this period he completed his first novel, *Dark Arena,* which was published in 1955. A second novel, *The Fortunate Pilgrim,* was published nine years later. Though these books received positive reviews, they were not commercial successes; Puzo earned a mere $6,500 from their combined sales. Struggling to support his wife and five children, Puzo slipped into debt. He told a writer for *Time* that an incident in 1955 convinced him to change his priorities: "It was Christmas Eve and I had a severe gall-bladder attack. I had to take a cab to the Veterans Administration Hospital on 23rd Street, got out and fell into the gutter. There I was, lying there thinking: here I am, a published writer, and I am dying like a dog. That's when I decided I would be rich and famous."

Ten years later, he got his chance. "Late in 1965 a Putnam editor stopped in at Magazine Management's offices, overheard Puzo telling Mafia yarns and offered a $5,000 advance for a book about the Italian underworld," a writer for *Time* reported. The result was *The Godfather,* and "the rest," that writer noted, "is publishing history." In *"The Godfather" Papers and Other Confessions,* Puzo stated that *The Godfather* was written "to make money . . . I was 45 years old and tired of being an artist." Nevertheless, as Robert Lasson of the *Washington Post Book World* contended, "Puzo sat down and produced . . . a novel which . . . had enormous force and kept you turning the pages." *The Godfather* became the best-selling novel of the 1970s, outselling that decade's other blockbusters—*The Exorcist, Love Story,* and *Jaws*—by millions. It remained on the *New York Times* bestseller list for 67 weeks, and was also a bestseller in England, France, Germany.

Puzo's story details the rise of Don Vito Corleone, the fall of his sons Sonny and Michael, the Mafia's peculiar behavior code and honor system, and the violent power struggle among rival "families." To some reviewers, Puzo's tale was a symbolic treatment of the corruption of the American dream. Although not all critics viewed the novel so seriously, most agreed with Polly Anderson in the *Library Journal* that "the book is well written, suspenseful and explodes in a series of dramatic climaxes." *Newsweek's* Pete Axthelm called Puzo "an extremely talented storyteller" and stated that *The Godfather* "moves at breakneck speed without ever losing its balance." And a critic for the *Saturday Review* contended that "Mario Puzo has achieved the definitive novel about a sinister fraternity of crime."

Several reviewers have noted the realism and believ-ability of the book's settings and characters. "He makes his frightening cast of characters seem human and pos-sible," according to a *Saturday Review* critic. And in *Saturday Review,* Vincent Teresa praised the author for portraying the Godfather as a fair and compassionate administrator of justice: "Puzo also showed the com-passion of a don, the fair way Corleone ruled. That's the way most dons are. . . . If you go to a don. . . and you've got a legitimate beef . . . and it proves to be the truth, you'll get justice. That's what makes the dons so important in the mob. They rule fair and square."

Such remarks led some to speculate that Puzo's knowl-edge of the Mafia and its people was first-hand. The au-thor, however, always denied any personal involvement with the Mob. In *"The Godfather" Papers and Other Confessions,* he explains that the book was based on re-search and anecdotes he had heard from his mother and on the streets. Still, the doubts persisted. Real-life un-derworld figures began approaching Puzo, convinced that he had some sort of link to organized crime. "After the book became famous, I was introduced to a few gentlemen related to the material," the author stated in *Time.* "They were flattering. They refused to believe that I had never had the confidence of a don."

While most critics praised *The Godfather's* realism, some objected that Puzo presented his subjects too sympathetically. These critics contended that because Puzo consistently justifies Don Vito's violent actions and solutions, certain readers have found the character and his family worthy of compassion and esteem. "The author has chosen to portray all Godfather's victims as vermin and his henchmen as fairly sympathetic," *Esquire's* Barton Midwood asserted, "and in this way the book manages to glamorize both the murderer him-self and the [imbalanced] economy in which he operates." In *Critical Inquiry,* John G. Cawelti voiced a similar complaint: "Throughout the story, the Corleone family is presented to us in a morally sympathetic light, as basically good and decent people who have had to turn to crime in order to survive and prosper in a cor-rupt and unjust society." Puzo was puzzled by readers' positive response to the Corleones, particularly Vito. As he put it in a *Publishers Weekly* interview with Thomas Weyr: "I was awfully surprised when people loved the Godfather so much. I thought I showed him as a mur-derer, a thief, a villain, a man who threw babies in the oven. . . . So I was astounded when I was attacked for glorifying the Mafia. It's a little tricky. I think it is a novelist's job not to be a moralist but to make you care about the people in the book."

Though *The Godfather* was Puzo's commercial break-through, catapulting him to fame and fortune, he didn't

consider it his best work. "'I wished like hell I'd writ-ten it better,'" *New York Times* obituarist Mel Gussow quoted Puzo as saying. "'I wrote below my gifts in that book.'" According to Gussow, Puzo felt his best book was his second novel, *The Fortunate Pilgrim,* the story of an Italian-American family in New York City that was based on Puzo's own background. Puzo claimed that he had intended to write about himself, but the character of Lucia Santa, based on his mother, became so strong that he made her the novel's focus.

After *The Godfather* and *"The Godfather" Papers and Other Confessions,* Puzo focused his attention on screen-writing, first as co-author of *The Godfather* and *The Godfather: Part II,* then as co-author of *Earth-quake, Superman,* and *Superman II.* Special effects, rather than story or plot, highlight the last three films. Pauline Kael of the *New Yorker* commented: "You go to *Earthquake* to see [Los Angeles] get it, and it really does. . . . *Earthquake* is a marathon of destruction ef-fects, with stock characters spinning through it." A *Time* movie reviewer found that *Superman,* for which Puzo wrote the first draft, is "two hours and fifteen minutes of pure fun, fancy and adventure." Garnering far more serious attention were *The Godfather* movie and its sequels.

The first film covers the period from the mid-1940s to the mid-1950s, when Michael takes command of the "family"; the second film charts the youth and early manhood of the original Godfather, Vito, and contrasts his coming-of-age with Michael's. Vincent Canby of the *New York Times* remarked that "the novel is a kind of first draft—an outline of characters and an inventory of happenings—that has only now been finished as a film." In another *New Yorker* review, Kael deemed *The Godfather* "the greatest gangster picture ever made," and praised the "metaphorical overtones that took it far beyond the gangster genre." Part II, according to Kael, is even more "daring" in that "it enlarges the scope and deepens the meaning of the first film." The critic main-tained that "the second film shows the consequences of the actions of the first; it's all one movie, in two great big pieces, and it comes together in your head while you watch."

Although Puzo was given co-author status for both screenplays, Francis Ford Coppola's direction and inter-pretation are credited with giving the films their "epic" quality. "[Coppola] turns *The Godfather: Part II* into a statement, both highly personal and with an epic reso-nance, on the corruption of the American dream and on the private cost of power," Paul D. Zimmerman wrote in *Newsweek.* Puzo was the first to agree. "'Coppola fought the battle for the integrity of the movies; if it weren't for him, they would have been 30's gangster pictures,'" he told Herbert Mitgang in a *New York Times Book Review* interview. "'*Godfather* is really his movie.'" Yet, Kael noted, "There was a Promethean spark" in Puzo's novel that afforded Coppola "an epic vision of the corruption of America." Kael added, "Much of the material about Don Vito's early life which appears in Part II was in the Mario Puzo book and was left out in the first movie, but the real fecundity of Puzo's mind shows in the way this new film can take his characters further along and can expand . . . the implications of the book."

In October of 1978 Puzo's long-awaited fourth novel, *Fools Die,* was published. The headlines and cover stories surrounding its publication began in June—four months before the first hardcover edition went on sale—when New American Library paid an unprecedented $2.2 million for the paperback rights, plus $350,000 for the reprint rights to *The Godfather.* In spite of the hoopla concerning this record-setting price, or perhaps because of it, critical reaction to *Fools Die* was mixed. "It seems a publishing event rather than a novel," Roger Sale opined in the *New York Review of Books.* In a *New Republic* review, Barbara Grizzuti Harrison offered a similar appraisal, claiming that "it is a publishing event (though hardly a literary one)." And at the *Village Voice,* James Wolcott asked: "In all this commotion, a fundamental question has gone unasked. . . . Has anyone at Putnam actually *read* this book?"

The action of *Fools Die* moves from Las Vegas to New York to Hollywood, purporting to "give us the inside skinny" on gambling, publishing, and movie-making, according to *Washington Post Book World's* William McPherson. Harrison added that "the events loosely strung together in this. . . book are meant to dramatize ambition, power, and corruption. I say *meant* to," she explained, "because Puzo, through the offices of his narrator, John Merlyn, keeps reminding the reader that these are his themes, as if we might otherwise forget." Geoffrey Wolff of *New Times* expressed a corresponding complaint: "Because he won't trust a reader to remember the climaxes of a few pages earlier, he recapitulates the plot, as though *Fools Die* were a serial, or a television series." Wolff suggested that "perhaps Puzo doesn't trust a reader to remember what he has just written because he himself has such trouble remembering what he has just written." The critic went on to detail several contradictory descriptions given throughout the novel concerning characters' appearances, habits, and lifestyles.

Wolcott criticized the novel's structure and syntax as well: "The novel seems to have evolved from manuscript to book without anyone daring . . . to make sorely needed corrections." Wolff attacked the book's "slipshod craftsmanship," and *Newsweek's* Peter S. Prescott stated, "Structurally, *Fools Die* is a mess."

Despite such less-than-favorable reviews, the novel was a popular success (it was the third-highest-selling hardcover novel of 1978), and Prescott and others admitted that *Fools Die* can be entertaining, humorous, and, in some instances, inspired. "I had a fine time reading it," Prescott observed. "Its many stories, developed at varying lengths, are slickly entertaining." A *Time* reviewer commented: "*Fools Die* contains the sort of minidramas and surprises that keep paperback readers flipping pages; a man wins a small fortune at baccarat and blows his brains out; a straightforward love affair turns baroque with kinky sex; an extremely cautious character makes a stupid and fatal error." Moreover, Prescott found: "Puzo here reveals an unsuspected talent for gross comedy. . . . In [the character] Osano, the most famous living American novelist, he has written an inspired caricature of our own dear Norman Mailer."

"'I wrote *Fools Die* for myself,'" the author told Mitgang. "'I wanted to say certain things about gambling, Las Vegas and the country.'" According to David Robinson of the *Times Literary Supplement,* Puzo is quite successful at capturing the flavor and feel of Las Vegas: "The first and best section of *Fools Die* is set in Las Vegas. Puzo's forte is the neo-documentary background; and . . . his portrayal of [that city] has the appearance of authenticity." The *Time* critic agreed: "Puzo's description of Las Vegas, its Strip, showgirls, characters, and the variety of ways one can lose money swiftly and painlessly, are carried off with brio. The green baize world of casino management has never seemed more professional, entertaining and lethal."

In 1984 Puzo returned to the safer ground of Sicily, the Mafia, and the Corleone family with his novel, *The Sicilian,* which Christopher Lehmann-Haupt of the *New York Times* claimed "might more aptly be designated *The Godfather, Part I I/II.*" Based on actual events in the 1950s, it is the story of Salvatore Giuliano, a Robin Hood-style outlaw who, with the support of the church and the Mafia, terrorized the Sicilian aristocracy. *The Sicilian* begins as Michael Corleone is preparing to return to America after a two-year self-imposed exile in Sicily. Shortly before departure, Michael is ordered by his father to find Giuliano and bring him to America before the authorities catch up with him. It is during

Michael's search that Giuliano's history is revealed, along with the history of the Mafia itself. "[*The Sicilian*] gives Mr. Puzo another chance to do what he seems to do best, which is to spin a yarn of treachery, violence, sex, sadism, revenge and bloody justice," wrote Lehmann-Haupt. "But it's also a little sad that [Puzo] has felt it necessary to return to his Italian gangsters. . . . Though *The Sicilian* is fun and compelling, it seems like an admission of defeat in a way."

Author Gay Talese was impressed by the detailed and accurate account of Giuliano's life and the events that made him into a hero. Writing in the *New York Times,* Talese deemed *The Sicilian* "a fine, fast-paced novel about Sicily in the mid-1940s that is historically useful and, given events there in the mid-1980s, hardly out of date." Lehmann-Haupt, too, praised Puzo's well-researched look at the birth and evolution of the Sicilian Mafia. However, he found the characters "a little undernourished" in comparison to the strong personalities that were immortalized in the Godfather movies. "Even the familiar characters seem pale compared with their movie counterparts," he judged.

The Sicilian was released as a film by Twentieth Century-Fox in 1987, having been delayed by production problems and a handful of lawsuits. Though Puzo's novel showed tremendous cinematic potential, the film (adapted by Steve Shagan) was panned by reviewers: Sheila Benson of the *Los Angeles Times* described it as "fuzzy and inert," while the *Washington Post*'s Hal Hinson called the film "unambiguously atrocious . . . [*The Sicilian*] isn't just bad, it's bad in a uniquely emblematic, Hollywood way." Not long after the release of *The Sicilian,* another Puzo novel, *The Fortunate Pilgrim,* was adapted, this time as a television miniseries. "Never has so much tedium been crammed into so little time," lamented a reviewer in *People.* "At only five hours, *The Fortunate Pilgrim* is far from the longest miniseries ever made. It just seems like it."

In 1988, Puzo was once again approached by Coppola, who had developed an idea for continuing the Godfather saga, and less than a year later the screenplay for *The Godfather: Part III* was completed. Picking up twenty years after Part II left off, Part III shows Michael as the head of the tremendously rich and influential Corleone family. However, their influence extends in different directions now, for Michael has taken the Corleone fortune out of gambling and is using it for more legitimate investments. In addition, he has donated hundreds of millions of dollars to the Catholic Church in an attempt to purchase his redemption. Michael, though, is losing control of the family: frail, stricken with diabetes, and reluctant to act against his enemies, he does not command the respect he once did. Eager to replace him as don is Vincent, the illegitimate son of Michael's dead brother, Sonny. Michael struggles to regain his hold on the Corleone family, simultaneously seeking to gain influence within the Vatican; all the while, rival families plot to destroy both him and his investments. The novel culminates with an international banking scandal and the assassination of Pope John Paul I.

When *The Godfather: Part III* was released on Christmas Day, 1990, sixteen years had passed since the last *Godfather* movie—enough time for critics and moviegoers to build almost insurmountable expectations for this newest installment. The *Los Angeles Times*' Michael Wilmington found Part III to be "not quite a fitting climax to a series that ranks among the American cinema's most remarkable sustained achievements." Stuart Klawans observed in *Nation:* "*The Godfather: Part III* turns out to be as good as a post-sequel can be. . . . [It] is less gripping than the first *Godfather* and less interesting as a narrative structure than the second." Yet these flaws become apparent only when Part III is compared to the previous Godfather films; when judged on its own, Klawans pointed out, "it gives and keeps giving and doesn't give out until you're sated with the hero's doom." Wilmington, too, ultimately described *The Godfather: Part III* as "one of the best American movies of the year—a work of high ensemble talent and intelligence, gorgeously mounted and crafted, artistically audacious in ways that most American movies don't even attempt."

Less than a month after the release of *The Godfather: Part III,* Puzo used the increased media attention to promote his political thriller, *The Fourth K.* Set in the first decade of the twenty-first century, it details the events occurring during the presidency of Francis Xavier Kennedy, a distant cousin of John, Robert, and Edward (and the fourth "K" of the novel's title). At the time of FXK's administration, terrorism is out of control: the Pope is assassinated on Easter Sunday by a group of Middle Eastern radicals; when the gunman is captured in New York, the terrorist leader, a man named Yabril, kidnaps and murders the president's daughter. Intended to demonstrate the ineffectiveness of the United States as a world power, these actions instead drive Kennedy to near-madness, prompting him to bomb the capital of Yabril's oil-rich native land. This evokes the wrath of the Socrates Club, a California-based group of billionaire investors with significant oil interests. Meanwhile, a group of ultra left-wing intellectuals detonate a small atomic bomb in Manhattan in an attempt to illustrate the danger of nuclear proliferation. R. Z. Sheppard of *Time* wrote: "The aggressive ways in which FXK handles foreign and domestic threats to his presidency and his life allow Puzo to pull out all the stops." A reviewer in the *West Coast Review of Books* concurred, saying: "Action and intrigue infuse the narrative, and the reader is captivated as the story lines converge in an explosive finale."

Because *The Fourth K* attempts to juggle a number of intricate storylines, it has been accused by several critics of being improbable and unwieldy. "Yes, this is your classic page turner," admitted E. J. Dionne, Jr., in the *Washington Post Book World*. "But it's a page-turner not only for the right reasons but also for the wrong ones. Part of why you want to get to the end is to see how Puzo's Rube Goldberg machine of a plot resolves itself." Frederick Busch, in the *New York Times Book Review*, faulted the novel for a "discordant mix of realities" and "characters [that] are construed from events instead of being built from human traits." Yet Ross Thomas, in the *Los Angeles Times*, proclaimed *The Fourth K* "a witty, sometimes wise, often mordant tale about the American politics of tomorrow. And if [Puzo's] intricately plotted tale offers more insight than hope, it is still fine entertainment, which is more than can be said of today's politics."

With *The Last Don*, written after recovering from quadruple-bypass heart surgery and a protracted convalescence, Puzo produced another crime-family novel, this time introducing a new family—the Clericuzio. R. Z. Sheppard praised the novel in *Time*: "It is headlong entertainment, bubbling over with corruption, betrayals, assassinations, Richter-scale romance and, of course, family values." Set in Long Island, Las Vegas, and Hollywood, the novel relates the aging Don Clericuzio's wish to convert the family's vast criminal empire into legitimate enterprises, including efforts to enter the Hollywood film industry. Puzo's satiric portrayal of Hollywood is especially acerbic—revealing, as several critics noted, the author's lingering resentment over earlier experiences with the studios.

Christopher Lehmann-Haupt, in the *New York Times*, pointed out obvious similarities between *The Godfather* and *The Last Don*: "Like Michael Corleone in *The Godfather*, the protagonist of *The Last Don*, Cross De Lena, tries to escape the criminal workings of his family but ends being drawn into the vortex of its malignity. Like *The Godfather*, *The Last Don* is filled with bloody warfare and shockingly sadistic acts of vengeance." Vincent Patrick wrote in the *New York Times Book Review*, "It is a measure of Mario Puzo's skill that after turning the last page of his rich and ebullient new novel, I was able to remember no fewer than 35 characters and recall clearly their backgrounds, motivations and roles in the convoluted plot and subplots." Patrick added that *The Last Don* is Puzo's "most entertaining read since *The Godfather*." *The Last Don* was also adapted into a television miniseries that aired on CBS in 1997 and 1998.

Omerta, Puzo's final novel, can be seen as a "tying up of loose ends," according to *National Review* writer Victorino Matus. The critic noted that Puzo had told the Associated Press that the book would be "a life-ending book, for me and the Mafia. Then I'll be dead, the Mafia will be dead, and the public will be glad of it. They've had enough of both of us." Indeed, Puzo died shortly after completing the manuscript; *Omerta* was published posthumously in 2000, quickly making bestseller lists and attracting Hollywood attention. The title refers to the Sicilian code of honor that forbids revealing information about crimes that are considered private affairs; the novel, like much of Puzo's late work, shows how this code of honor is no longer respected, particularly among the new generation. The story focuses on the murder of an old don, Raymonde Aprile, whose three adult children have grown up unaware of their father's business. Before Aprile is able to realize his dream to legitimize his operations and retire, he is killed. As his nephew, Astorre, seeks revenge, the FBI is also on the case.

Matus found much of *Omerta* disappointing. He argued that the novel lacks the epic sweep of *The Godfather*, as well as the earlier book's saturation with religious rites and symbols. Yet the novel, in his view, is "far from a failure." Among its merits, he claimed, are its ability to show how the Mafia "is not all that different from other organizations" in its exploration of the generational decline facing the Mob at the end of the twentieth century. *New York Times Book Review* critic Michiko Kakutani also cited the theme of decline, but she had little praise for the novel. Adopting a mock-Mobster voice in her review of *Omerta*, she wrote: "Fact is, the more I think about it, the more this book gives me agita. God forbid that I should criticize the author of the great 'GF,' but I gotta be honest with you: the man has lost his touch."

Time's R. Z. Sheppard, however, was among several critics who praised the novel for its exciting plot and page-turning pace, commenting that it "has more tasty twists than a plate of fusilli." Reviewers for *Booklist*, *Library Journal*, and *Publishers Weekly* also expressed great enthusiasm for the book. And Richard Dyer in the *Boston Globe* opined that, though parts of the novel remain relatively undeveloped and dialogue and narrative voice are not wholly satisfactory, "*Omerta* touches on themes that are bigger than it is and that Puzo didn't have the time or the stamina to realize. But even when he falls back on formula, it's a satisfying formula. After all, he invented it."

Despite the shortcomings that critics have found in Puzo's later work, his contributions to American culture are readily acknowledged. James B. Hall, in *Dictionary of Literary Biography*, argued that Puzo, like the Naturalistic writers of the early twentieth century, excelled at depicting street life and "the underbelly of social institutions." Hall cited Puzo's careful attention to narrative structures and his skill at exploring human nature as evidence of the writer's craft and understanding. Puzo's achievement, Hall concluded, mirrors that of many recent American writers who, despite early critical success, had to resort to commercial formulas to find a large audience. However indirect Puzo's route to literary fame, Hall argued that his place as "an authentic American literary voice" is assured.

BIOGRAPHICAL/CRITICAL SOURCES:

BOOKS

Contemporary Literary Criticism, Gale, Volume 1, 1973, Volume 2, 1974, Volume 6, 1976, Volume 36, 1986.
Green, Rose B., *The Italian-American Novel,* Fairleigh Dickinson University Press, 1974.
Kilber, James E., Jr., editor, *Dictionary of Literary Biography, Volume 6: American Novelists since World War II, Second Series,* Gale, 1980.
Madden, David, editor, *Rediscoveries,* Crown, 1972.
Puzo, Mario, *"The Godfather Papers" and Other Confessions,* Putnam, 1972.
Wheeler, Thomas C., editor, *The Immigrant Experience: The Anguish of Becoming an American,* Dial, 1971.

PERIODICALS

Booklist, April 1, 2000, p. 1413.
Boston Globe, August 24, 2000, p. D6.
Chicago Tribune, June 19, 1981.
Commonweal, May 6, 1955; June 4, 1965.
Critical Inquiry, March, 1975.
Esquire, February, 1971.
Kirkus Reviews, May 15, 1996, p. 711.
Library Journal, April 1, 1969; May 1, 2000, p. 154.
Life, July 10, 1970.
Los Angeles Times, February 14, 1987; October 23, 1987.
Los Angeles Times Book Review, January 13, 1991; July 21, 1996.
Maclean's, March 18, 1991.
McCall's, May, 1971.
Nation, June 16, 1969.
National Review, July 31, 2000.

New Republic, November 18, 1978.
Newsweek, March 10, 1969; December 23, 1974; September 18, 1978; January 1, 1979.
New Times, October 2, 1978.
New York, March 31, 1969; July 10, 2000, p. 52.
New Yorker, December 12, 1974; December 23, 1974; February 11, 1991.
New York Herald Tribune Book Review, March 6, 1955.
New York Review of Books, July 20, 1972; October 26, 1978.
New York Times, February 27, 1955; March 12, 1972; March 16, 1972; June 19, 1981; November 22, 1984; June 5, 1986; May 22, 1987; January 10, 1991; July 25, 1996.
New York Times Book Review, January 31, 1965; February 18, 1979; January 13, 1991; July 28, 1996; June 27, 2000.
New York Times Magazine, January 2, 2000, p. 14.
People, July 3, 1978; July 19, 1999, p. 75.
Publishers Weekly, May 12, 1978; June 10, 1996, p. 83; July 5, 1999, p. 17; July 24, 2000, p. 19; September 4, 2000, p. 42.
Saturday Review, February 26, 1955; January 23, 1965; March 15, 1969; January 20, 1973.
Time, March 13, 1971; December 16, 1974; August 28, 1978; November 27, 1978; January 14, 1991; July 29, 1996; July 17, 2000, p. 75.
Times (London), May 3, 1985.
Times Literary Supplement, December 1, 1978.
Tribune Books (Chicago), January 20, 1991.
TV Guide, August 28, 1999, p. 9.
Village Voice, September 4, 1978.
Wall Street Journal, January 11, 1991.
Washington Post, March 12, 1970; October 23, 1987; October 24, 1987.
Washington Post Book World, March 9, 1969; April 9, 1972; September 24, 1978; January 20, 1991.
World & I, March, 1991.

OTHER

Salon.com, http://www.salon.com/ (October 24, 2000).

OBITUARIES:

PERIODICALS

Entertainment Weekly, July 16, 1999, p. 46.
New York Times, July 3, 1999.
Time, July 12, 1999, p. 21.*

Q-R

QUIRK, Thomas Vaughan 1946-
(Tom Quirk)

PERSONAL: Born December 28, 1946, in Houston, TX; son of Edward L. and Virginia (Carter) Quirk; married, 1970 (divorced); married Catherine Parke (an English professor), 1986; children: (first marriage) Laura Elizabeth; (second marriage) Ann Neal, James Justin. *Ethnicity:* "Caucasian." *Education:* Arizona State University, B.A., 1970; University of New Mexico, M.A., 1972, Ph.D., 1977.

ADDRESSES: Office—Department of English, 107 Tate Hall University of Missouri, Columbia, MO 65211. *E-mail*—QuirkT@missouri.edu.

CAREER: Navajo Community College, Tsaile, AZ, instructor in English, 1974 and 1976; College of Ganado, Ganado, AZ, instructor in English, 1976; University of New Mexico, Gallup, assistant professor, 1978-79; University of Missouri, Columbia, assistant professor, 1979-84, associate professor of English, 1984-89, professor of English, 1989—, Catherine Paine Middlebush Professor of English, 1991-94.

MEMBER: American Literature Association, Melville Society, Mark Twain Circle, Willa Cather Society.

WRITINGS:

UNDER NAME TOM QUIRK

Melville's Confidence Man: From Knave to Knight, University of Missouri Press (Columbia, MO), 1982.

(Editor, with James Barbour) *Romanticism: Critical Essays in American Literature,* Garland Publishing (New York, NY), 1986.

(Editor, with Barbour) *Essays on Puritans and Puritanism,* University of New Mexico Press (Albuquerque, NM), 1986.

(Editor, with Barbour) *The Unfolding of Moby Dick: Seven Essays in Evidence* (monograph), Melville Society, 1987.

(Editor, with Barbour) *Writing the American Classics,* University of North Carolina Press (Chapel Hill, NC), 1990.

Bergson in American Culture: The Worlds of Willa Cather and Wallace Stevens, University of North Carolina Press (Chapel Hill, NC), 1990.

(Author of explanatory notes and commentary) Herman Melville, *Moby Dick,* introduction by Andrew Delbanco, Viking/Penguin Books (New York, NY), 1992.

Coming to Grips with "Huckleberry Finn": Essays on a Book, a Boy, and a Man, University of Missouri Press (Columbia, MO), 1993.

(Editor, with Gary Scharnhorst) *Realism and the Canon: A Collection of Essays,* University of Delaware Press (East Brunswick, NJ), 1994.

(Editor) *Selected Tales, Essays, Speeches, and Sketches of Mark Twain,* Viking/Penguin Books (New York, NY), 1994.

(Editor, with Barbour) *Biographies of Books: The Backgrounds, Genesis, and Composition of Notable American Writings,* University of Missouri Press (Columbia, MO), 1996.

Mark Twain: A Study of the Short Fiction, Twayne (Boston, MA), 1997.

(Editor, with James Nagel) *The Viking Portable American Realism Reader,* Viking/Penguin Books (New York, NY), 1997.

(Editor) *Tales of Soldiers and Civilians and Other Stories by Ambrose Bierce,* Viking/Penguin Books (New York, NY), 2000.

Contributor to books, including *Black Journals of the United States,* edited by Walter Daniel, Greenwood Press (Westport, CT), 1982. Contributor of essays to literature journals. Guest editor, *American Literary Realism,* special issue on canon reformation in the realist era, spring, 1991.

WORK IN PROGRESS: Essays on American Literature: A Mini-Protest; editing *Innocents Abroad,* by Mark Twain, for Penguin Classics; editing *Alexander's Bridge,* by Willa Cather, University of Nebraska Press (Lincoln, NE); editing *Adventures of Huckleberry Finn,* for a documentary series of *Dictionary of Literary Biography,* Bruccoli, Clark, Layman.

SIDELIGHTS: An author who publishes under the name Tom Quirk, Thomas Vaughan Quirk once told *CA:* "Temperamentally and methodologically, I am inclined to study imaginative writing as the resultant effort and genuinely creative act of actual human beings rather than as disembodied linguistic constructs. In my first book I sought to trace the contours of Melville's *The Confidence Man* as they probably developed in the author's creative imagination. In *Bergson in American Culture: The Worlds of Willa Cather and Wallace Stevens* I attempted an 'experiment' in literary history by examining an important transitional period in American culture and by employing an equal mix of intellectual, social, and literary history as a way of framing a discussion of the literary careers of two 'case studies' who were deeply influenced by these cultural changes. I meant to correct by example rather than by polemical argument what I take to be certain deficiencies of both old and 'new' historicism. And in *Coming to Grips with 'Huckleberry Finn': Essays on a Book, a Boy, and a Man,* I examined Twain's novel from a variety of critical angles in order to account for its origins in his imagination and its subsequent effects on several generations of readers. In a word, I am skeptical of postmodern presuppositions about language and literature that, so far as I can see, are not borne out by experience, common sense, history, or philosophy. I have always believed that the human origins of literature are finally more interesting than the sorts of nimble interpretive ventures, no matter how eloquent, that deny or exclude this quality. Most recently, I have spent less time writing and more time pondering the ways that genuinely humanistic values might achieve practical results in the classroom. Higher education, I believe, has suffered too long from what I call the cult of the expert, the cultivation of an arcane sophistication that, ironically, often serves to shore up the exclusionary cultural dominance that its practitioners avowedly wish to dethrone."

BIOGRAPHICAL/CRITICAL SOURCES:

PERIODICALS

Times Literary Supplement, July 15, 1983.

*   *   *

QUIRK, Tom
    See QUIRK, Thomas Vaughan

*   *   *

RAINWATER, (Mary) Catherine 1953-

PERSONAL: Born May 31, 1953, in Corpus Christi, TX; daughter of Louis Ellis and Doris (an artist; maiden name, St. Clair) Rainwater. *Education:* University of Texas at Austin, B.A. (with honors), 1974, Ph.D., 1982; University of California at Irvine, M.A., 1976. *Avocational interests:* Music, painting, and animals.

ADDRESSES: Home—6603 Poncha Pass, Austin, TX 78749. *Office*—School of Humanities, St. Edward's University, Austin, TX 78704.

CAREER: Dabney & Byrn (engineering consultants), San Antonio, TX, technical editor and writer, 1976; *Texas Realtor,* Austin, TX, proofreader and editorial assistant, 1977; English teacher at community school in Austin, TX, 1981-82; Austin Learning Center, Austin, TX, director of special programs, 1983—. Tutor at Del Mar College, 1971; member of faculty at University of Texas at Austin, 1976—, and Austin Community College, 1985; St. Edward's University, adjunct professor, 1985-87, assistant professor of English, 1987-93, associate professor, 1993-2000, professor, 2000—. *Ellen Glasgow Newsletter,* editor.

MEMBER: Ellen Glasgow Society (president).

WRITINGS:

(Editor, with William J. Scheick) *Three Contemporary Women Novelists: Hazzard, Ozick, and Redmon,* University of Texas Press, 1983.

(Editor, with Scheick, and contributor) *Contemporary Women Writers: Narrative Strategies,* University Press of Kentucky, 1985.

Dreams of Fiery Stars: The Transformations of Native American Fiction, University of Pennsylvania Press, 1999.

Contributor to *Dictionary of Literary Biography* and *Twentieth-Century Literary Criticism.* Contributor of articles and reviews to numerous literature journals, including *American Literature, Modern Fiction Studies,* and others.

WORK IN PROGRESS: Uncertain Measures: Ellen Glasgow's Dialogue with Modernity, and another work, a collection of essays on representations of animals in art, co-edited with Mary Pollock.

SIDELIGHTS: "As a teacher," Catherine Rainwater told *CA,* "I am most concerned with showing students how literature and the other arts can become a vital part of their individual lives, and not remain just some branch of specialized knowledge unrelated, say, to their responsibility to evaluate the popular culture and media influences to which they are subjected daily. Ideally, I suppose I would like my students to make the development of their minds, not the mere acquisition of marketable skills, the subject of their primary attention. I try to make students aware of how their knowledge and lack of knowledge shape their present and future lives.

"All of my writing, I think, reveals my fascination with writers' awareness of the literary traditions within which they are working, whether they are reacting against such tradition or acknowledging its inescapable influence. Native American writers, in particular, are especially innovative in their use and transformation of such traditions."

*　　*　　*

RAMSLAND, Katherine 1953-

PERSONAL: Born January 2, 1953, in Ann Arbor, MI; daughter of Henry (an electrical engineer) and Barbara (a homemaker) Johnston; married Steven Ramsland (a mental health agency director), May 26, 1979. *Education:* Northern Arizona University, B.A., 1978; Duquesne University, M.A., 1979; Rutgers University, Ph. D., 1984.

ADDRESSES: Home—646 River Rd., Upper Black Eddy, PA 18972. *Agent*—Lori Perkins, New York, NY.

CAREER: Rutgers University, New Brunswick, NJ, professor, 1980—.

MEMBER: American Philosophical Association, Horror Writers of America, Soren Kierkegaard Society.

WRITINGS:

Engaging the Immediate, Bucknell University Press, 1988.

Prism of the Night, Dutton, 1991.

The Art of Learning, State University of New York Press, 1992.

The Vampire Companion: The Official Guide to Anne Rice's Supernatural Universe, Ballantine (New York, NY), 1993.

The Witches' Companion: The Official Guide to Anne Rice's Lives of the Mayfair Witches, Ballantine (New York, NY), 1994.

The Anne Rice Trivia Book, Ballantine (New York, NY), 1994.

The Roquelaure Reader: A Companion to Anne Rice's Erotica, Plume (New York, NY), 1996.

Dean Koontz: A Writer's Biography, HarperPrism (New York, NY), 1997.

(Editor), *The Anne Rice Reader,* Ballantine (New York, NY), 1997.

(With Steven Ramsland) *Quesadillas: Over 100 Fast, Fresh, and Festive Recipes,* 1997.

Piercing the Darkness: Undercover with Vampires in America Today, HarperPrism (New York, NY), 1998.

Bliss: Writing to Find Your True Self, Walking Stick (Cincinnati, OH), 2000.

The Forensic Science of C.S.I., Boulevard (New York, NY), 2001.

SIDELIGHTS: As the authorized biographer of "Vampire Chronicles" author Anne Rice, Katherine Ramsland is an established expert on Rice's work, as well as on contemporary gothic subculture. After *Prism of the Night: A Biography of Anne Rice,* Ramsland went on to pen several guides to Rice's work, written with Rice's full cooperation. In 1998, Ramsland wrote *Piercing the Darkness,* an account of her investigation of the disappearance of journalist Susan Walsh, who vanished while researching vampire cults in New York City. Trained in clinical psychology and philosophy, Ramsland brought what a *Publishers Weekly* reviewer deemed to be "remarkable empathy" to this project, and which the contributor hailed as "immensely insightful and exciting" and a "model of engaged journalism." Reviewers for *Library Journal* and *Booklist* expressed similar enthusiasm for the book, which presented contemporary vampires as individuals who are sometimes disturbed and frightening, but who are also often misunderstood. Though Ramsland never solved the Walsh mystery, critics pointed out that her speculations as to the journalist's fate were intriguing.

Ramsland has also written a biography of horror writer Dean Koontz. Though *Booklist* reviewer Ray Olson found that "she mostly just synopsizes and biographically interprets [Koontz's] fiction," he appreciated the book's readability and popular appeal.

In *Bliss: Writing to Find Your True Self,* Ramsland guides readers through exercises intended to develop greater personal fulfillment. Central to this approach is journal writing, through which readers can identify and clarify their thinking. A reviewer for *Publishers Weekly* considered it a "nurturing and pragmatic" work which provides a "solid foundation for understanding the concept of bliss" as well as an understanding of the developmental stages associated with its search.

BIOGRAPHICAL/CRITICAL SOURCES:

PERIODICALS

Booklist, February 15, 1997, p. 994; November 15, 1997, p. 537; July 1998, p. 1827.
Library Journal, August 1993, p. 98; November 15, 1997, p. 59; September 15, 1998, p. 97.
Magazine of Fantasy and Science Fiction, may 1998, p. 23.
Playboy, December 1993, p. 36.
Publishers Weekly, June 10, 1996, p. 21; August 17, 1998, p. 54; August 21, 2000, p. 63.

OTHER

Katherine Ramsland Web site, http://www.katherine ramsland.com/ (October 24, 2000).*

*   *   *

RHOADES, Jonathan
    See OLSEN, John Edward

RICH, Frank (Hart) 1949-

PERSONAL: Born June 2, 1949, in Washington, DC; son of Frank Hart Rich (a businessman) and Helene Bernice (an educational consultant; maiden name, Aaronson) Fisher; married Gail Winston, April 25, 1976; married Alexandra Rachelle Witchel, June 9, 1991; children: (first marriage) Nathaniel Howard, Simon Hart. *Education:* Harvard University, A.B., 1971.

ADDRESSES: Office—*New York Times,* 229 West 43rd St, New York, NY, 10036-3959.

CAREER: Richmond Mercury, Richmond, VA, co-editor, 1972-73; *New Times,* New York, NY, senior editor and film critic, 1973-75; *New York Post,* New York, NY, film critic, 1975-77; *Time,* New York, NY, cinema and television critic, 1977-80; *New York Times,* New York, NY, chief drama critic, 1980-93, Op-Ed columnist, 1994—.

WRITINGS:

(With Lisa Aronson) *The Theater Art of Boris Aronson,* Knopf (New York, NY), 1987.
Hot Seat: Theater Criticism for the New York Times, 1980-1993, Random House (New York, NY), 1998.
Ghost Light: A Memoir, Random House (New York, NY), 2000.

Contributor to various anthologies; author of introductions for several works; contributor to periodicals, including *Ms., New Republic,* and *Esquire.*

SIDELIGHTS: Frank Rich, who was nicknamed by his enemies the "Butcher of Broadway" during his long tenure as the *New York Times* drama critic, writes about his childhood infatuation with the theater in the autobiographical *Ghost Light: A Memoir.* Rich's term as drama critic for New York's most powerful newspaper earned him friends and enemies alike. Those theatrical workers whose plays closed early because of a harsh review from Rich often felt that he had been unfair in his assessment of their work. During his career, he suffered their criticisms, including public attacks by such leading Broadway figures as Andrew Lloyd Webber and David Merrick.

Rich reveals in his memoir that, following the divorce of his parents when he was a child, he was drawn to the world of the theater as a means to escape a lonely and troubled home life. *Ghost Light,* remarked Hilma Wolitzer in the *New York Times,* "is a poignant and darkly funny account of a boy's life shaped by difficult circumstances and the consolations of art." James Wolcott of the *New Republic* concluded that Rich's account of his childhood and later life is meant to "watercolor his controversial tenure—the feuds with producers, playwrights, and fellow critics; the accusations of playing favorites and letting power balloon his head—as a fine romance, a tempestuous affair that sometimes got messy. Whatever pain he inflicted as the 'Butcher of Broadway' was rooted in ardent devotion." Reviewing the book for *Variety,* Wendy Smith noted that "Rich's reputation as 'the Butcher of Broadway' has perhaps been overstated. During his 13-year tenure . . . reviews in which he was truly, unfairly nasty were as rare as raves. He seldom offered anything so trivial as a personal response to a production; rather, he instructed readers as to its significance." Dan Wakefield in the *Nation* called Rich's book a "compelling memoir," while James Poniewozik of *Time* noted that *Ghost Light* revealed that "Rich has a heart, and that heart loves the theater passionately and needily."

BIOGRAPHICAL/CRITICAL SOURCES:

PERIODICALS

Back Stage, October 8, 1993, Amy Hersh, "Frank Rich to Exit—But How Powerful Is the *New York Times*?," p. 3.

Boston Magazine, August, 1982, Howie Carr, "The Man Who Would Beat King," p. 82.

Charlotte Observer, November 5, 2000, Christine Dolen, review of *Ghost Light,* p. F7.

Editor & Publisher, December 1, 1990, Ann Marie Kerwin, "War of Words: Broadway Producer David Merrick vs. Two *New Times* Theater Writers," p. 16.

Gentlemen's Quarterly, June, 1990, Chip Brown, "The Most Powerful Man on Broadway," p. 172.

Horizon, March, 1984, Gary Stern, "Rich Criticism: Chief *New York Times* Drama Critic Frank Rich Often Has the First Laugh," p. 44.

House and Garden, October, 1992, "Frank and Alex," p. 128.

Library Journal, September 1, 2000, Carol J. Binkowski, review of *Ghost Light,* p. 213.

Manhattan, Inc., February, 1990, John Heilpern, "He-Devil?," p. 110.

Nation, March 15, 1999, "Tilting at Rumor Mills," p. 10; January 8, 2001, Dan Wakefield, "Speak, Memory!," p. 35.

National Review, February 7, 1994, John O'Sullivan, "Sexual Exceptionalism," p. 10.

New Republic, February 1, 1988, Robert Brustein, review of *The Theater Art of Boris Aronson,* p. 27; March 16, 1992, Robert Brustein, "An Embarrassment of Riches," p. 27; May 11, 1992, Robert Brustein, "Opinions," p. 31; April 26, 1993, Stanley Kauffmann, "Akalaitis Axed," p. 29; February 28, 1994, Robert Wright, "Tonya's Theme," p. 46; March 3, 1997, "Killing Us Softly," p. 10; December 25, 2000, James Wolcott, "The Beltway Boy," p. 28.

Newsweek, December 21, 1987, Walter Clemons, "Boris Aronson's Theatre Art," p. 65.

New York, March 23, 1992, Edwin Diamond, "Two on the Aisle," p. 20; March 14, 1994, Mimi Kramer, "Finally Free of Frank?," p. 46; November 2, 1998, Walter Kirn, review of *Hot Seat,* p. 120.

New York Times, December 8, 1987, Brendan Gill, review of *The Theater Art of Boris Aronson;* February 13, 1994, Frank Rich, "Exit the Critic"; December 6, 1998, Harlow Robinson, review of *Hot Seat;* October 29, 2000, James Shapiro, review of *Ghost Light,* p. 6; October 30, 2000, Hilma Wolitzer, review of *Ghost Light,* p. E8.

New York Times Book Review, December 6, 1998, Harlow Robinson, "Two on the Aisle: Frank Rich Recalls His 13 Years as Chief Drama Critic for the *New York Times,*" p. 44.

Publishers Weekly, October 9, 1987, Genevieve Stuttaford, review of *The Theater Art of Boris Aronson,* p. 74.

Sports Illustrated, December 12, 1994, "Getting Rich," p. 18.

Tikkun, May-June, 1999, Jack Newfield, "An Interview with Frank Rich," p. 56.

Time, December 21, 1987, review of *The Theater Art of Boris Aronson,* p. 66; October 30, 2000, James Poniewozik, "Stages of Development: *Ghost Light* Sketches a Family in Trouble and a Portrait of the Theater Critic as a Young Fan," p. 86.

Variety, May 13, 1987, Richard Hummler, "*Time-Newsweek* Critics Defend Review-Interview Form," p. 127; November 15, 1989, Richard Hummler, "Ruffled Hare Airs Rich Bitch: Writer of El Foldo *Rapture* Lashes out at *N. Y. Times*' Powerful Legit Critic," p. 1; October 11, 1993, Jeremy Gerard, "Rich Ankles Aisle to Write 'Op-Ed' Style," p. 193; July 24, 2000, "Hart Felt," p. 28; December 18, 2000, Wendy Smith, review of *Ghost Light,* p. 37.

Wall Street Journal, December 11, 1989, Meg Cox, "Broadway Is Giving Its Leading Critic Some Nasty Reviews," p. A1; November 6, 1990, Meg Cox, "With Its Romance and Intrigue, It Could Make a First-Rate Farce," p. B1.

RICHARDS, Eric 1940-

PERSONAL: Born August 3, 1940, in Wales; son of William (a manager) and Jessie (a homemaker; maiden name, Pritchard) Richards; married Margaret Pollard (divorced, 1981); married Ngaire Naffine (a professor of law) May 11, 1985; children: Cindy Jane, Louise Jessica, Sally Joan. *Education:* University of Nottingham, B.A., 1963, Ph.D., 1967. *Politics:* "Fabian." *Religion:* "Agnostic." *Avocational interests:* Tennis, music, travel.

ADDRESSES: Home—7 Seaview Terr., Brighton, 5048 South Australia, Australia. *Office*—Department of History, Flinders University, GPO Box 2100, Adelaide 5001, Australia; fax +61-88-201-3350. *E-mail*—Eric. Richards@flinders.edu.au.

CAREER: University of Adelaide, Adelaide, Australia, lecturer in economics, 1964-67; University of Stirling, Stirling, Scotland, lecturer in history, 1967-72; Flinders University, Bedford Park, Australia, professor of history, 1972—. Public speaker on the history of the British in Australia and other historical topics; guest on radio programs.

MEMBER: Royal Historical Society (fellow).

AWARDS, HONORS: Book Award, Scottish Arts Council, 1982, for *A History of the Highland Clearances;* fellow, Australian Academy of the Social Sciences, 1984, and Australian Academy of Humanities, 1986; award from Saltire Society, Scottish history book of the year, 1999, for *Patrick Sellar and the Highland Clearances: Eviction, Homicide, and the Price of Progress.*

WRITINGS:

The Leviathan of Wealth, Routledge & Kegan Paul (London, England), 1973.

The Last Scottish Food Riots, Past and Present Society, 1982.

A History of the Highland Clearances, Croom Helm, Volume 1: *Agrarian Transformation and the Evictions, 1746-1886,* 1982, Volume 2: *Emigration, Protest, Reasons,* 1985.

(Editor) *The Flinders History of South Australia,* Wakefield Press (Netley, Australia), 1986.

(With Monica Clough) *Cromartie: Highland Life, 1650-1914,* Aberdeen University Press (Aberdeen, Scotland), 1989.

(Editor with Richard Reid and David Fitzpatrick) *Visible Immigrants,* Department of History and Centre for Immigration and Multicultural Studies, Research School of Social Sciences, Australian National University (Canberra, Australia), Volume 1: *Neglected Sources for the History of Australian Immigration,* 1989, Volume 2: *Poor Australian Immigrants in the Nineteenth Century,* 1990.

(Editor, with Jacqueline Templeton, and contributor) *The Australian Immigrant in the Twentieth Century,* Research School of Social Sciences, Australian National University (Canberra, Australia), 1998.

Patrick Sellar and the Highland Clearances: Eviction, Homicide, and the Price of Progress, Polygon at Edinburgh University Press (Edinburgh, Scotland), 1999.

The Highland Clearances: People, Landlords, and Rural Turmoil, Birlinn (Edinburgh, Scotland), 2000.

Contributor to books, including *Edward Gibbon Wakefield and the Colonial Dream: A Reconsideration,* GP Publications (Wellington, New Zealand), 1997; *Irish Women in Colonial Australia,* edited by Trevor McClaughlin, Allen & Unwin (Sydney, Australia), 1998; *Myth, Migration, and the Making of Memory: Scotia and Nova Scotia, c. 1700-1990,* John Donald (Edinburgh, Scotland), 1999; *The Australian People,* edited by J. Jupp, 2nd edition, 2000; and *The Wakefield Companion to the History of South Australia,* edited by W. Prest, 2001. Contributor of articles and reviews to British, American, Dutch, and Australian academic journals, including *Scottish Economic and Social History, International Review of Social History, Journal of the Australian Population Association, Northern Studies, Population Studies, Labour History,* and *Stonemason.*

WORK IN PROGRESS: The British Diaspora, 1600-2000; a history of Australian immigration in the twentieth century.

SIDELIGHTS: Eric Richards is a scholar of British history who has written extensively on events of past centuries that helped shape the modern United Kingdom. His early works include such titles as *The Leviathan of Wealth* and *The Last Scottish Food Riots,* but one of his significant contributions to the field has been the two-volume *A History of the Highland Clearances.* Born in Wales, Richards has taught history at an Australian university since the early 1970s. During the 1980s his scholarly interests shifted toward analyzing the role of British Isles immigrants in settling Australia, and the integral role the newcomers have played in forging the destiny of the continent.

Richards's first book, *The Leviathan of Wealth,* is an examination of one of the largest landholders in Scotland in the eighteenth and nineteenth centuries, the Sutherland family. Through marriage and inheritances the Sutherlands controlled almost a million acres of Scottish Highland territory as well as a lucrative shipping canal. Richards's treatise analyzes how these vast holdings were transformed to weather a period of great economic upheaval in Scotland. The bulk of the estate was managed by James Loch, a shrewd administrator who foresaw the economic restructuring that would be caused by the Industrial Revolution and guided the Sutherland trust accordingly. For instance, the Bridgewater Canal in Lancashire was destined to pass from the hands of the direct Sutherland heir, but prior to that its viability was already threatened by the railroad industry. Loch shrewdly invested trust assets into the canal's main competition, the Liverpool and Manchester Railway. Another of Loch's astute transitional moves described by Richards involved the "clearances"— evicting the tenants from the Highlands and subsidizing moves elsewhere, either to the newly created industrial villages in the north of Scotland or abroad. These clearances were enacted due to the realization that the land afforded its tenants a meager existence that was increasingly threatened by population explosion and resulting famine. It was obvious to Loch and the Sutherland family that it was simply more profitable to let sheep graze the land instead. This policy was met with resistance and deep hatred. Richards consulted the historical data extant in the Sutherland papers to show that a great deal of their assets were tied up for years in improving the economic lot of their tenants, first to ameliorate the disastrous Potato Famine of the 1840s and later to resettle the tenants elsewhere, such as Canada and Australia.

The first volume of Richards's *A History of the Highland Clearances,* subtitled *Agrarian Transformation and the Evictions, 1746-1886,* presents a broader view of the type of policies that Loch and the Sutherland family enacted during the course of the century. But, though they were the largest landholders in Scotland, there were many others also engaged in the eviction of families from the Highlands to make room for sheep. Richards points out that this was a widespread movement adopted by the landlords of the era and provides the reasons for it. The work begins with an examination of economic, social, and political changes sweeping through the British Isles and Europe in the mid-eighteenth century, and discusses the various aspects of the landlord-tenant relationship over the generations. Richards also analyzes the changes in economic fortunes that led to the clearances.

The second volume of *A History of the Highland Clearances,* subtitled *Emigration, Protest, Reasons,* examines the economic and social consequences of the evictions and mass immigrations, and the subsequent treatment by historians of the issue in the decades since. The historiographical portion opens the volume, and in it Richards discusses the writings of eighteenth-century economist Adam Smith and the use of Smith's theories to justify the clearance policies. In the section on emigration, Richards demonstrates that the landlords who so favored depopulation as a remedy for overcrowding in the Highlands after only a few years encouraged population increase as a way to supply men for certain industries and a strong military force for the Crown. *Emigration, Protest, Reasons* also examines one of the most notorious enforcers of the clearances, Patrick Sellar, who worked for the Sutherland estate discussed in *The Leviathan of Wealth.* Sellar and his actions were met with extreme resistance, but he was ultimately successful in his career and grew wealthy from it.

Richards once told *CA:* "I have spent much of my time trying to understand the consequences of industrialisation for women and for regions on the periphery of that great transformation such as the Scottish Highlands and Australia. My more recent work on British emigration is a logical extension of this interest. My emigration research tries to connect together these two larger themes."

BIOGRAPHICAL/CRITICAL SOURCES:

PERIODICALS

Times Literary Supplement, May 4, 1973, p. 490; April 2, 1982, p. 390; December 27, 1985, p. 1489.

*   *   *

RICHARDSON, Beth
    See GUTCHEON, Beth R(ichardson)

*   *   *

RIDPATH, Michael 1961-

PERSONAL: Born March 7, 1961, in Devon, England; son of Andrew (a land agent) and Elizabeth (Hind Howell) Ridpath; married Candy Helman (a banker), January 19, 1985 (died, 1992); married Barbara Nunemalzer (a banker), October 1, 1994; children: (first marriage) Julia, Laura; Nicholas. *Education:* Received degree from Merton College, Oxford University, 1982. *Religion:* Church of England.

ADDRESSES: *Home*—Hampstead Garden Suburb, London, England. *Agent*—Carole Blake, Blake Friedmann Literary Agency Ltd., 122 Arlington Rd., Bloomsbury, London WC1E 6HH, England. *E-mail*—comments@ michaelridpath.com.

CAREER: Saudi International Bank, London, England, from credit analyst to bond trader, c. 1982-91; worked for Apax Partners, beginning 1991. Novelist.

MEMBER: Crime Writers Association.

WRITINGS:

Free to Trade, HarperCollins (New York, NY), 1995.
Trading Reality, Heineman/Mandarin (London, England), 1996, HarperCollins (New York, NY), 1997.
The Marketmaker, Michael Joseph (London, England), 1998.
Final Venture, Signet, 2000.

SIDELIGHTS: Michael Ridpath was working in London's financial district, known as the City, when he decided to try his hand at fiction writing during his off hours. Over the course of three years he produced three drafts of what eventually became *Free to Trade,* his first novel, published in 1995. This murder mystery, which features a bond trader as its first-person narrator, initially attracted attention for the large sums it garnered from both British and American publishers. *Free to Trade* was also dubbed the first of a new genre, the "City thriller," by Harry Mount of the *Times Literary Supplement.* Ridpath has since published three more novels in the same vein, *Trading Reality, The Marketmaker,* and *Final Venture.* Critical response to these novels has been mixed, with some reviewers faulting the author for simplistic characterization and faulty plotting, while others have praised his quick pacing and ease in presenting complicated business and technical matters.

In an interview with John Russell in *Books,* Ridpath credited much of the early excitement over his first novel to the inherent interest of the City: "It has a very unnatural feel about it," the author observed, "everyone is wearing suits and walking very fast." The excitement of gambling with huge amounts of other people's money, and the fact that working in the City has become attractive to many young university graduates, who "within a fairly short space of time . . . get the opportunity to play around with quite a lot of responsibility and money," are factors that contribute to an atmosphere Ridpath characterized as ethically murky, if not downright criminal, in his interview with Russell. "I wrote the book for myself and my friends who would know a lot about the world of the City," Ridpath continued. "I didn't attempt to skate over the detail to make it simple for the lay reader. . . . It's much better to include the detail because it's not that difficult and is quite understandable really."

Ridpath has also told *CA:* "My aim is to write novels that entertain. I believe the financial world is a good place to do this. Finance impinges on almost every aspect of modern-day life. It is exciting: the sums of money are large, the pace is fast, and the ethics are difficult—even for the basically honest. It provides a modern backdrop for the classic struggle of good against evil, of youth, courage, and integrity against wealth, power, and greed."

Free to Trade centers on Paul Murray, a former Olympic athlete turned bond trader in the City, whose life takes a decidedly dangerous turn when one of his colleagues is found dead, floating in the Thames. Though the police suspect no foul play, Murray begins to look into the victim's last deals in an attempt to uncover a possible motive for what appears to him a murder. The fraud he discovers sends him to financial centers around the world as he seeks out the mastermind behind the financial crime and the murder.

Aside from Ridpath's protagonist, critics generally found the author's character sketches unsatisfactory: "Individuals are introduced with a trite physical description," remarked Mount, "and thereafter remain fairly insubstantial." But, while both Mount and a reviewer for *Publishers Weekly* expressed disappointment with Ridpath's writing style, the latter asserted: "Ridpath paces matters briskly, conveys the cutthroat ambience of the markets and, along the way, provides a solid seminar in venture capitalism." *Sunday Times* contributor Philip Kerr pointed out, "There is, of course, plenty of authentic detail about what it is like to be a trader and, as you might expect, this is the strongest feature of the book." Kerr added that *Free to Trade* "seems promising rather than accomplished, in the sense that Ridpath promises to do with the City what Dick Francis and John Grisham have done with horse-racing and the law—milk it for all its fictional worth."

After *Free to Trade* was accepted for publication, Ridpath hoped to split his time between trading and writing. However, the writing soon became more important than his work in the City, although he still enjoyed trading thoroughly. He soon delivered another trading-related suspense story called *Trading Reality*. Following the advice of his editor, Ridpath steered away from a plan to form a plot and characters resembling those of *Free to Trade* and tackled a subject in which he had a strong interest, virtual reality businesses. In this second novel, trader Mark Fairfax is submerged in the quickly developing technical field when his brother Richard is killed. Mark takes Richard's place as managing director of a virtual reality company, hoping to keep the business from going bankrupt. However, he risks meeting his brother's fate as he looks for the murderer—who also wants to ruin the company. The key to both the death and plot against the company may lie in the supposedly secret "Project Platform," which promises to put the company far ahead of its competition.

Trading Reality proved to be a strong follow-up to Ridpath's authorial debut. In *Booklist,* Wes Lukowsky admired how "Ridpath carves his complex plot with deft strokes" as well as his "believably consistent" characters and the "witty mix" of the dialogue. Lukowsky also commended the author's ability to digest difficult business and technical details in a way that supported the plot without slowing it down. *Library Journal* reviewer Marylaine Block was also enthusiastic about the business thriller. She called it an "exciting, suspenseful novel" and rated it with "the best of Paul Erdman's financial thrillers." In *Publishers Weekly,* a critic had milder praise for Ridpath, with positive comments on the book's pacing, Scottish setting, and insider knowledge: "The thrills here lie as much in carefully thought out financial and digital tools as in the humans who wield them." The review predicted that readers would not be put off by the "not very original" story.

For his next novel, Ridpath looked to another area of interest that he had been unable to explore as a trader, the emerging bond markets in developing countries. In *The Marketmaker* he chose to focus on trading in Brazil. His protagonist is an academic, Nick Elliot, who tries his hand at trading with the City firm of Dekker Ward. There he meets the high-profile trader Ricardo Ross, a man known as the "marketmaker" because of his dominance in Latin American bonds. A series of events at the company including a firing, a robbery-murder, and the kidnapping of a woman he is interested in romantically convince Nick to look for an underlying problem.

For his subsequent novel, *Final Venture,* Ridpath crafted a story set in Boston, where venture capitalist Simon Ayot has enjoyed a happy life. But things start to fall apart at work and at home. Ayot's colleagues turn down his proposal to give more funds to a company he favors, and when his father-in-law is killed, he becomes a suspect. When even his wife is unsure of his involvement and leaves him, Ayot crosses the country, seeking to clear himself of suspicion.

BIOGRAPHICAL/CRITICAL SOURCES:

PERIODICALS

Booklist, March 15, 1997, Wes Lukowsky, review of *Trading Reality,* p. 1231.
Books, January/February, 1995, pp. 6-7.
Library Journal, January 1997, Marylaine Block, review of *Trading Reality,* p. 150.
Publishers Weekly, September 5, 1994, p. 43; November 7, 1994, p. 65; November 14, 1994, p. 24; December 16, 1996, review of *Trading Reality,* p. 51; July 24, 2000, review of *Final Venture,* p. 74.
Sunday Times (London), January 22, 1995, Section 7, p. 1.
Times Literary Supplement, February 17, 1995, p. 22.

OTHER

Michael Ridpath, http://www.michaelridpath.com/ (June 21, 2001).*

*   *   *

RIFBJERG, Klaus (Thorvald) 1931-

PERSONAL: Born December 15, 1931, in Copenhagen, Denmark; son of Thorvald Rifbjerg and Lilly Nielsen; married Inge Merete Gerner, 1955; children: one son, two daughters. *Education:* Studied at Princeton University and the University of Copenhagen.

ADDRESSES: Office—Gyldendal Publishers, 3 Klareboderne, 1001 Copenhagen, Denmark.

CAREER: Information, Copenhagen, Denmark, literary critic, 1955-57; *Politiken,* Copenhagen, literary critic, 1959-65; *Vindrosen,* editor-in-chief, 1959-63; Gyldendal Publishers, Copenhagen, literary director, 1984-92, board of directors, 1992—; Laererhøjskole, Copenhagen, professor of aesthetics, 1986.

AWARDS, HONORS: Aarestrup Medal, 1964; Danish Critics' Award, 1965; Danish Dramatists, Grant of Honour, 1966; Danish Academy Award, 1966; Golden Laurels, 1967; Soren Gyldendal Award, 1969; Nordic Council Award, 1970; Danish Writers' Guild, Grant of Honour, 1973; P.H. Prize, 1979; Holberg Medal, 1979; H. C. Andersen Prize, 1988; Dr.H.C. (Lund), 1991, (Odense), 1996.

WRITINGS:

NOVELS

Den kroniske uskyld (title means "Chronic Innocence"), Gyldendal, 1958.

(With Jesper Jensen) *Hva' skal vi lave; revykomedie* (title means "What Shall We Do"), Gyldendal, 1963.

Operaelskeren (title means "The Opera Lover"), Gyldendal, 1966.

Arkivet (title means "The Archive"), Gyldendal, 1967.

Lonni og Karl (title means "Lonni and Karl"), Gyldendal, 1968.

Anna (jeg) Anna, Gyldendal, 1969, translation by Alexander Taylor published as *Anna (I) Anna,* Curbstone Press, 1982.

Marts 1970 (title means "March 1970"), Gyldendal, 1970.

Leif den lykkelige junior (title means "Leif the Lucky, Jr."), Gyldendal, 1971.

Lena Jorgensen Klintevej 2650 Hvidovre, Gyldendal, 1971.

Brevet til Gerda (title means "The Letter to Gerda"), Gyldendal, 1972.

R. R., Gyldendal, 1972.

Spinatfuglene (title means "The Culture Vultures"), Gyldendal, 1973.

Dilettanterne (title means "The Amateurs"), Gyldendal, 1973.

Du skal ikke være ked af det, Amalia. En pamflet-roman (title means "Don't Be Upset, Amalia"), Gyldendal, 1974.

En hugorm i solen (title means "A Viper in the Sun"), Gyldendal, 1974.

Vejen ad hvilken (title means "The Road by Which"), Gyldendal, 1975.

Tak for turen (title means "Thanks for the Lift"), Gyldendal, 1975.

Kiks (title means "Biscuits"), Gyldendal, 1976.

Twist, Gyldendal, 1976.

Et bortvendt ansigt (title means "An Averted Face"), Gyldendal, 1977.

Drengene (title means "The Boys"), Gyldendal, 1977.

Tango eller syv osmotiske fortællinger, Gyldendal, 1978.

Dobbeltgænger eller Den korte, inderlige men fuldstændig sande beretning om Klaus Rifbjergs liv (title means "Wraith"), Gyldendal, 1978.

Joker, Gyldendal, 1979.

Voksdugshjertet (title means "The Oilcloth Heart"), Gyldendal, 1979.

Det sorte hul (title means "The Black Hole"), Gyldendal, 1980.

De hellige aber (title means "The Sacred Monkeys"), Gyldendal, 1981, translation by Steven T. Murray published as *Witness to the Future,* Fjord Press, 1987.

Jus, og/eller, Den gyldne middelvej, Gyldendal, 1982.

Hvad sker der i kvarteret (title means "What's Happening in the Area"), Gyldendal, 1983.

En Omvej til klosteret (title means "A Roundabout Way to the Convent"), Vindrose, 1983.

Patience eller Kortene på bordet (title means "Patience or Your Cards on the Table"), Gyldendal, 1983.

Falsk forår (title means "False Spring"), Gyldendal, 1984.

Harlekin skelet: en pantomime roman (title means "Harlequin Skeleton: A Pantomime Novel"), Gyldendal, 1985.

Som man behager (title means "As You Like"), Gyldendal, 1986.

Engel (title means "Angel"), Gyldendal, 1987.

Det ville glæde—: en skjælmeroman (title means "May We Have the Pleasure"), Gyldendal, 1989.

Rapsodi i blåt (title means "Rhapsody in Blue"), Gyldendal, 1991.

Divertimento i mol: roman (title means "Divertimento in the Minor Key"), Gyldendal, 1996.

Billedet: roman (title means "The Picture"), Gyldendal, 1998.

Huset, eller hvad der gjorde størst indtryk på mig i det tyvende århundrede (title means "The House"), Gyldendal, 2000.

POETRY

Under vejr med mig selv (title means "Getting Wind of Myself"), Gyldendal, 1956.

Efterkrig (title means "Post-War"), Gyldendal, 1957.

Konfrontation (title means "Confrontation"), Schønberg, 1960.

Camouflage (title means "Camouflage"), Gyldendal, 1961.

Voliere: et Fuglekor på femogtyve Stemmer (title means "Aviary"), Gyldendal, 1962.

Portræt (title means "Portrait"), Gyldendal, 1963.

Amagerdigte (title means "Amager Poems"), Gyldendal, 1965.

Fædrelandssange (title means "Patriotic Songs"), Gyldendal, 1967.

I skyttens tegn. Digte i udvalg 1956-67 (title means "In the Sign of the Archer"), Gyldendal, 1970.

Mytologi. Digte (title means "Mythology"), Gyldendal, 1970.

Scener fra det daglige liv (title means "Scenes from Everyday Life"), Gyldendal, 1973.

25 desperate digte (title means "25 Desperate Poems"), Gyldendal, 1974.

Stranden (title means "The Beach"), Gyldendal, Forlaget Sommersko, 1974.

Den søndag: digte, Brøndum (Copenhagen), 1975.

Selected Poems, translated by Nadia Christensen and Alexander Taylor, Curbstone Press (Willimantic, CT), 1976.

Spring (in English), Curbstone Press, 1977.

Livsfrisen: Fixérbillede med satyr (title means "The Frieze of Life"), Gyldendal, 1979.

Spansk motiv (title means "Spanish Motif"), Gyldendal, 1981.

Landet Atlantis: digte (title means "The Land of Atlantis"), Gyldendal, 1982.

3 Poems, translated by Taylor, Curbstone Press, 1982.

Det svævende træ (title means "The Hovering Tree"), Gyldendal, 1984.

Udenfor har vinden lagt sig (prose poetry; title means "Outside, the Wind Has Dropped"), Brøndum, 1984.

Digte, H. Reitzel (Copenhagen), 1986.

Byens Tvelys (title means "The City Twilight"), Gyldendal, 1987.

Septembersang (title means "September Song"), Gyldendal, 1988.

Bjerget i himlen (title means "The Mountain in the Sky"), Gyldendal, 1991.

Krigen: en digtcyklus, Gyldendal, 1992, translation by Steven T. Murray and Tiina Nunnally published as *War,* Fjord Press, 1995.

(With Teddy Sørensen and Peter Laugesen) *Tuschrejse* (title means "Indian Ink Journey"), Århus Kunstmuseum, 1994.

Kandestedersuiten: et digt (title means "The Kandesteder Sequence"), Gyldendal, 1994.

Leksikon: digte (title means "Lexicon"), Gyldendal, 1996.

Terrains vagues, Gyldendal, 1998.

PLAYS

(With Jesper Jensen) *Diskret ophold* (title means "Discreet Stop"), Gyldendals teater, 1964.

Udviklinger; et skuespil for fire jazz-musikere, fire skuespillere og lille teater, (title means "Developments"), Gyldendal, 1965.

Hvad en mand har brug for (title means "What a Man Has Need Of"), Gyldendal, 1966.

Voks. Et skuespil i tre akter (title means "Wax"), Gyldendal, 1968.

År. Et sentimentalt panorama i ti billeder fra Danmarks besættelse (title means "Years"), Gyldendal, 1970.

Narrene. Et skuespil i tre akter (title means "The Fools"), Gyldendal, 1971.

Svaret blæser i vinden (title means "The Answer Blows in the Wind"), Gyldendal, 1971.

Sangen om sengen: skuespil i to akter (title means "The Song of the Bed"), Gyldendal, 1982.

Intet nya fra køkkenfronten (title means "All Quiet on the Kitchen Front"), Gyldendal, 1984.

SHORT STORIES

Og andre historier (title means "And Other Stories"), Gyldendal, 1964.

Rejsende (title means "Travellers"), Gyldendal, 1969.

Den syende jomfru og andre noveller eller Ude og hjemme (title means "The Seamstress Maid and Other Stories"), Gyldendal, 1972.

Sommer (title means "Summer"), Gyldendal, 1974.

Det korte af det lange (title means "The Long and Short of It"), Gyldendal, 1976.

Mænd og kvinder (title means "Men and Women"), Gyldendal, 1981.

Borte tit (title means "Often Away"), Gyldendal, 1986.

Det svage køn (title means "The Weaker Sex"), Gyldendal, 1989.

Vi blir jo ældre: noveller (title means "Well, We're Growing Older"), Gyldendal, 1993.

Andre tider (title means "Altered Times"), Gyldendal, 1997.

Kort sagt: egne noveller, Gyldendal, 1999.

CHILDREN'S BOOKS

Kesses krig (title means "Kesse's War"), Gyldendal, 1981.

Linda og baronen (title means "Linda and the Baron"), illustrated by Poul Lange, Gyldendal, 1989.

Da Oscar blev tosset (title means "When Oscar Went Mad"), Gyldendal, 1990.

Det ved jeg da godt! (title means "Well I Know"), Gyldendal, 1990.

Den hemmelige kilde (title means "The Secret Spring"), Gyldendal, 1991.

Hjemve (title means "Homesickness"), Gyldendal, 1993.

CRITICISM, ESSAYS, AND ARTICLES

Rif, Et udvalg af Klaus Rifbjergs journalistik (title means "Rif, A Selection of Klaus Rifbjerg's Media Articles"), Gyldendal, 1967.

Jeg skal nok (title means "Yes, I Will"), Gyldendal, 1984.

Karakterbogen. Et virrehoveds notater (title means "The Report: A Head-shaker's Notes"), Gyldendal, 1992.

Synderegistret: En angergivens betragtninger (title means "The List of Sins: The Reflections of a Repentant"), Gyldendal, 1994.

Facitlisten. En gammel snyders papirer (title means "The Answer Book: An Old Cheat's Papers"), Gyldendal, 1995.

Digtere til tiden: portrætter og præsentationer (title means "Poets Here and Now"), Spektrum (Copenhagen), 1999.

MEMOIRS

Dengang det var før. Syv kronikker (title means "When It Was Before"), Gyldendal, 1971.

Sådan: en livsreportage (title means "Just like That"), Gyldendal, 1999.

TRAVEL AND JOURNALS

(With Georg Oddner) *Til Spanien: ein personlig dokumentation af mødet med landet,* Gyldendal, 1971.

Odysseus fra Amager: på rejse med Klaus Rifbjerg (stories; title means "Odysseus from Amager"), Vindrose, 1981.

(With Georg Oddner) *Japanske klip* (title means "Japanese Clips"), Brøndum, 1987.

En udflugt: dagbog fra 12/4 til 14/5 1990 (title means "An Excursion"), Gyldendal, 1990.

Berlinerdage. Dagbogsimpressioner marts-maj 1995 (title means "Berlin Days: Diary Impressions March-May 1995"), Gyldendal, 1995.

MOVIES, RADIO, AND TELEVISION

(Screenwriter) *Weekend* (in English, also titled *Kosmorama*), Det Danske Film-museum (Copenhagen), 1962.

(With Palle Kjærulff-Schmidt) *Der var engang en krig* (title means "There Was Once a War"), Gyldendal, 1966.

(With Franz Ernst) *Privatlivets fred* (title means "Privacy"), Gyldendal, 1974.

De beskedne: en familiekrønike (title means "The Modest Ones"), Gyldendal, 1976.

Vores år (title means "Our Year"), Gyldendal, 1980.

OTHER

Boi-i-ing 464 (collage; also titled *Den fatastiske virkelighed*) Gyldendal, 1964.

(Editor) *Min yndlingslæsning* (anthology), Stig Vendelkaærs Forlag (Copenhagen), 1965.

Drømmen om København og andre digte fra byen, Gyldendals Bogklub (Copenhagen), 1967.

(With Flemming Arnholm) *Flemming Arnholm,* Rhodos (Copenhagen), 1969.

(With Lilli Friis) *I medgang og modgang. Blide og barske træk af ægteskabets historie i Norden* (title means "In Good Times and Bad"), Gyldendal, 1970.

Værsgo og spis, Gyldendal, 1972.

Deres Majestæt!: åbent brev til Dronning Margrethe II af Danmark fra Klaus Rifbjerg, Corsaren (Copenhagen), 1977.

Livsfrisen: fixerbillede med satyr: et digt, Gyldendal, 1979.

Hvad sker der i kvarteret?: en fabel fra mellemstanden, Gyldendal, 1983.

Intet nyt fra køkkenfronten: skuespil i 2 akter, Gyldendal, 1984.

(With Torben Brostrøm) *På sporet: udvalgte noveller,* Gyldendal, 1987.

150 korte og MEGET korte tekster, Gyldendal, 1991.

Other publications include *Sam, Bum og pølsesnak* (Danish translation of *Sam, Bangs & Moonshine* by Evaline Ness), Gyldendal, 1968; magazine contribution "Before the Mount of Venus, Cuckoo," in *Cimarron Review,* No. 92, 1990. Included in Nordic Poetry Festival anthology, "at three o'clock the dead make" (English translation of excerpt from *Krigen*), Gyldendal, 1993; and catalog text with Keld Zeruneith and Steffen Heiberg, *Hundrede års danse forfatterportrætter,* Frederiksborgmuseet (Hillerød, Denmark), 1994.

SIDELIGHTS: Having had long and varied experience as a poet, novelist, short-story writer, dramatist, screenwriter, critic, and journalist, writer Klaus Rifbjerg has become a prominent if sometimes controversial literary figure in Denmark. His experimental writing style first became noticed in published works of poetry, beginning with the 1956 collection, *Under vejr med mig selv.* His later work as a novelist, including *Anna (jeg) Anna* and *De hellige aber,* expanded on similar themes of psychological analysis. Rifbjerg's fame is also tied to his work as a cultural and literary critic and as a publisher. He has written for the Copenhagen newspapers *Information* and *Politiken,* edited the literary journal *Vindrosen,* and served as director of the Gyldendal Publishing House. In 1967 Rifbjerg was made a member of the Danish Academy.

In a 1975 article for *Books Abroad,* Charlotte Schiander Gray judged that Rifbjerg was "without question the best-known and most influential contemporary writer in Denmark. His modernistic poetry with its rich physical imagery has delineated a literary epoch, and his lyrical novels with their vivid vernacular and superb sense of humor have revitalized the novel." More than twenty years later she expanded on this judgment in the *Encyclopedia of World Literature in the Twentieth Century:* "Because of his vast and varied oeuvre, his technical mastery and topical relevance, [Rifbjerg] has become the most representative and significant author in Denmark during the second half of the twentieth [century]."

Rifbjerg was a student at Princeton before he studied literature at the University of Copenhagen from 1951 to 1955. He went on to become a film instructor from 1955 to 1957, a discipline that would influence his later writings. At about this time, Rifbjerg also received public notice as a poet. His first collection, *Under vejr med mig selv,* was comprised of autobiographical prose poems that explored his childhood and even the preconscious stages of birth and fetal existence. *Efterkrig* offered more of his earliest poetry. However, it was the 1960 collection, *Konfrontation,* that was in Gray's estimation a "modernistic breakthrough." She explained in *Books Abroad* that "the poet feels himself an outsider caught up in an unreal world. He seeks reality through the Now, through the use of all his senses, through concentration on essence, on the concrete." And she described the work as "a modernistic prose poem . . . one in which the reader is confronted, so to speak, with surprising word combinations leading to new insights which, however, are more disruptive than constructive."

The author's breakthrough techniques displayed in *Konfrontation* would be repeated in *Camouflage* and *Portræt.* The first of these two collections is a lyrical, highly personal exploration of the subconscious. Gray commented in *Books Abroad* that the poems were difficult to interpret because of "their seemingly incomplete development and their frequently overly personal nature." *Portræt* is notable for its use of cinematic techniques. However, it also marked the end of a phase in Rifbjerg's writing. Gray commented, "*Portræt* signaled a state of crisis. Rifbjerg had for the time being reached the end of his modernistic experiment."

The subsequent collection, *Amagerdigte,* proved to be a turning point in the writer's poetic development. Here he used simple realism in describing everyday life in the middle-class Copenhagen suburb of Amager. In her *Books Abroad* article, Gray described it as "a work of memory and nostalgia, an attempt to reach the Now through the past." Rifbjerg would not return to complex, metaphorical forms of poetry until *Livsfrisen: Fixérbillede med satyr.*

Among Rifbjerg's later poetry, the 1992 collection *Krigen* stands out as one of his few volumes translated into English. In a review of the original work for *World Literature Today,* Niels Ingwersen described *Krigen,* saying, "Rifbjerg invokes war in all ages—a phenomenon that may never disappear—and as a state of mind." The poet describes all of the stages of war, including its anticipation and after-effects, as well as its influence on ordinary life. Thus the tone ranges widely from anger to sadness to joy. Ingwersen concluded, "Rifbjerg's project is an ambitious one; consequently, not all the texts are equally effective but many are—very much so." In a *Choice* review of the English version, entitled *War,* J. G. Holland admired the translation of Rifbjerg's presentation of "the insidiousness of war." Holland commented, "Realism and surrealism become absurdly real, playing off against each other with sympathy and wit."

Rifbjerg has also had a long career as a writer of fiction. According to Gray in *Books Abroad,* the major themes found in all of Rifbjerg's writing are represented in his novels as well. "The basic subject for Rifbjerg's investigation is inevitably the identity problem—the origin of the human being, his formative stages and his further development into adulthood," declared Gray.

Rifbjerg's first novel was *Den kroniske uskyld,* a story about the necessity of losing childhood innocence. The tale involves two friends, Tore and Janus, and Tore's girlfriend Helle. While the story is told through Janus, the events are dominated by the actions of Tore and Helle. Tore wants to have sex with Helle, but is prevented by her overbearing mother, who seduces the sexually frustrated boy. The double betrayal leads Helle to commit suicide, while Tore becomes mentally unstable. As Gray explained, however, the story is really about Janus and his own problematic relationship with a girl. "The other characters can be seen as projections of Janus's own psyche; and when Janus does not succeed in integrating his split world, Helle and Tore are destroyed," averred Gray in *Books Abroad.* The critic also described the book as being well known for its use of vernacular, having become "a classic novel of puberty in Danish literature."

In *Operaelskeren,* Rifbjerg explores the belated "puberty" of a middle-aged science professor who is having an affair with an opera singer. Written as his diary, it shows how Helmer Franck remains immature while having repressed his irrational impulses. These subconscious feelings are represented in the outgoing, emotional Mira, his lover. Gray found that when viewed as "an identity search, the book ends with Helmer's failure to integrate his 'anima.'"

Lack of self-knowledge is also the subject of *Arkivet,* a deceptively realistic portrayal of office workers in an archive. Gray described the work as being "very different from the preceding lyrical, emotional novels. The author pretends to have no more insight than the characters." Rifbjerg shows two young men working in an archive, doing easy, insignificant work. The peace and repetition are disturbed by an explosion. As Gray noted, "The irrational had been overlooked in this 'well-known' ordinary world."

One of Rifbjerg's best-known novels is *Anna (jeg) Anna,* which has been praised for its sensitivity toward women's psychological issues. The story centers on the middle-aged wife of the Danish ambassador to Pakistan. She is traveling to Denmark to seek the help of a psychiatrist because she has become obsessed with the thought of killing her four-year-old daughter. The root of this obsession is her guilt over having abandoned an integral part of her unconscious self, her lower-class roots and sympathies, during her rise into the privileged classes. On the plane trip home she meets a criminal named Jorgen, and she helps him escape from the authorities. The two become lovers and travel back to Denmark. In the process, they steal a car, shoot a policeman, and Anna is raped by American soldiers.

Reviews of the novel have included praise for its social commentary and innovation. Gray found an important development in the writer's focus: "The personal problem cannot be separated from the social one. There is no doubt that Rifbjerg is moving from his earlier exis-

tentialism toward greater social and political involvement." Writing in *Scandinavian Studies,* Timothy R. Tangherlini found that the novel was significant as a postmodernist "(re)Definition" of the feminine. Tangherlini asserted that Rifbjerg was "able to break through male-dominated modes of expression, write among them, and shatter the male projection of the feminine which holds the women imprisoned both in society and in the text itself."

The publication of *Anna (I) Anna* marked the first of Rifbjerg's novels to be translated into English. In *Library Journal* Ulla Sweedler remarked that Rifbjerg's novel showed "his stylistic virtuosity," and she added that "the many themes explored . . . are well integrated and the symbolism is never obtrusive." However, a *Publishers Weekly* reviewer deemed that "there is no real resolution to this story, which becomes disjointed, increasingly alienating and ultimately pointless."

Rifbjerg's next novel to be translated into English would be *De hellige aber,* which was published in 1987 as *Witness to the Future.* The science-fiction story begins in 1941, while Denmark is under Nazi occupation. Two boys, Mik and Niels, are exploring a cave, but when they exit into the familiar fields surrounding it they discover they are now in the year 1988. The modern cars and highways, technical innovations, and inflated prices surprise them. They meet a boy their age and try to comprehend his confusing, slang answers to their questions about who won World War II. The boy, called Shadow, is addicted to dope and has to steal in order to eat. It is gradually revealed that these events are taking place on the eve of a nuclear holocaust.

A reviewer for *Publishers Weekly* called the novel "an allegory of the chaos and emptiness of modern times that conveys admiration for a simpler past." In a review for *Scandinavian Studies,* Gray reflected that the plot resembles that of the film *Back to the Future,* noting that "where period descriptions and plot mainly serve entertainment purposes in the movie, they are part of the major theme in Rifbjerg's book, in which the description of a stressed and inhuman society functions as a warning."

In 1997 Rifbjerg produced a collection of short fiction entitled *Andre tider.* As in some of his earlier works, the stories focus on everyday life, describing its common, more unremarkable qualities as well as its surprises and gradual developments. In a review for *World Literature Today,* Gray judged that within the collection of twenty-three stories, "each . . . consists of a brief description of a situation, an episode, a stage of life, a person, or a couple; the unity of the stories is created through atmosphere, not plot." Gray found that "the originality lies in the rendition of 'manners,' sensation, and atmosphere, the limitation in a basically unchanging and unsurprising subject."

Among Rifbjerg's nonfiction writing is the 1994 essay, *Synderegistret: En angergivens betragtninger.* In her review of the book in *World Literature Today,* Gray called the book "a good introduction to and summary of Rifbjerg's oeuvre and thinking in general." The author reviews his life and beliefs by looking at various topics, events, and localities. And though the title may lead the reader to expect a confession of guilt, Gray found that "Rifbjerg is not a repentant," at least not in the traditional religious sense. "He reserves the right to rebel against stultifying norms and irrational prejudices. . . . [And] pokes fun at so-called serious and one-dimensional people," she explained. At the same time, she concluded, "His essay is also a hymn to . . . ordinary middle-class people."

BIOGRAPHICAL/CRITICAL SOURCES:

BOOKS

Encyclopedia of World Literature in the Twentieth Century, St. James Press (Detroit), Volume 3, pp. 670-671.

PERIODICALS

Books Abroad, winter, 1975, Charlotte Schiander Gray, "Klaus Rifbjerg: A Contemporary Danish Writer," pp. 25-28.
Choice, November, 1995, J. G. Holland, review of *War,* p. 470.
Library Journal, November 1, 1982, Ulla Sweedler, review of *Anna (I) Anna,* p. 2110.
Publishers Weekly, July 30, 1982, review of *Anna (I) Anna,* p. 73; June, 26, 1987, review of *Witness to the Future,* p. 67.
Scandinavian Studies, spring, 1990, Charlotte Schiander Gray, review of *Witness to the Future,* p. 259; summer, 1995, Timothy R. Tangherlini, "Uncertain Centers, Uncentered Selves: Postmodernism and the (re)Definition of Feminine in *Anna (jeg) Anna* and *Baby,*" pp. 306-329.

World Literature Today, autumn, 1994, Charlotte Schiander Gray, review of *Synderegistret: En angergivens betragtninger,* p. 826; winter, 1994, Niels Ingwersen, review of *Krigen,* p. 143; autumn, 1998, Gray, review of *Andre tider,* p. 849.

*   *   *

RILKE, Rainer Maria 1875-1926

PERSONAL: Born Rene Karl Wilhelm Johann Josef Maria Rilke December 4, 1875, in Prague, Austria (now the Czech Republic); changed his name to Rainer Maria Rilke, 1897; died of leukemia, December 29, 1926, in Montreaux, Switzerland; son of Josef (a railway official) and Sophie Entz Rilke; married Clara Westhoff (a sculptress), 1901 (separated, 1902); children: Ruth. *Education:* Attended Handelsakademie, Linz, Austria, 1891-92, and University of Prague, 1895-96. *Religion:* Raised Roman Catholic.

CAREER: Poet, novelist, short story writer, and translator. Traveled extensively throughout Europe. Joined the Worpswede artists' colony, 1900-02; worked as a secretary for sculptor Auguste Rodin in Paris, France, 1905-06. *Military service:* Austro-Hungary Army, First Infantry Regiment; served in the War Department, 1916.

WRITINGS:

Leben und Lieder: Bilder und Tagebuchblaetter (poems; main title means "Life and Songs"), Kattentidt, 1894.
Larenopfer (poems; title means "Offering to the Lares"), Dominicus (Prague), 1896.
Todtentaenze: Zwielicht-Skizzen aus unseren Tagen, Loewit & Lamberg (Prague), 1896.
Traumgekroent: Neue Gedichte (title means "Crowned with Dreams: New Poems"), Friesenhahn (Leipzig), 1896.
Wegwarten (poems), Selbstverlag (Prague), 1896.
In Fruehfrost: Ein Stueck Daemmerung, Drei Vorgaenge (play), Theaterverlag O. R. Eirich (Vienna), 1897.
Advent (poems), Friesenhahn, 1898.
Ohne Gegenwart: Drama in zwei Akten, Entsch (Berlin), 1898.
Am Leben hin: Novellen und Skizzen, Bonz (Stuttgart), 1898.
Zwei Prager Geschichten, Bonz, 1899, translation by Angela Esterhammer published as *Two Stories of Prague,* University Press of New England, 1994.

Rainer Maria Rilke

Mir zur Feier: Gedichte (poems), Meyer (Berlin), 1899, reprinted as *Die fruehen Gedichte,* Insel (Germany), 1909, Ungar, 1943.

Vom lieben Gott und Anderes: An Grosse für Kinder erzaehlt (short stories), Schuster & Loeffler, 1900, published as *Geschichten vom lieben Gott,* Insel, 1904, Ungar, 1942, translation by Nora Purtscher-Wydenbruck and M. D. Herter Norton published as *Stories of God,* Norton, 1932, revised edition, 1963.

Das taegliche Leben: Drama in zwei Akten (play; first produced in Berlin at the Residenz Theater, December, 1901), Langen (Munich), 1902.

Zur Einweihung der Kunsthalle am 15. Februar 1902: Festspielszene, [Bremen], 1902.

Buch der Bilder (poems), Juncker (Berlin), 1902, enlarged edition, 1906, Ungar, 1943.

Die Letzten, Juncker, 1902.

Worpswede: Fritz Mackenses, Otto Modersohn, Fritz Overbeck, Hans am Ende, Heinrich Vogeler, Velhagen & Klasing, 1903.

Auguste Rodin (biography), Bard (Berlin), 1903, translation by Jesse Lemont and Hans Trausil published as *Auguste Rodin,* Sunwise Turn (New York City), 1919, published as *Rodin,* Haskell Booksellers, 1974.

Das Stundenbuch enthaltend die drei Bücher: Vom mönchischen Leben; Von der Pilgerschaft; Von der Armuth und vom Tode (poems), Insel, 1905, translation by Babette Deutsch published as *Poems from the Book of Hours,* New Directions, 1941, reprinted, 1975, translation by A. L. Peck published as *The Book of Hours; Comprising the Three Books: Of the Monastic Life, Of Pilgrimage, Of Poverty and Death,* Hogarth, 1961, published as *Rilke's Book of Hours: Love Poems to God,* Riverhead Books, 1996.

Die Weise von Liebe und Tod des Cornets Christoph Rilke (prose poem), Juncker, 1906, translation by B. J. Morse published as *The Story of the Love and Death of Cornet Christopher Rilke,* Osnabrueck, 1927, translation by Herter Norton published as *The Tale of the Love and Death of Cornet Christopher Rilke,* Norton, 1932, translation by Stephen Mitchell published as *The Lay of the Love and Death of Cornet Christopher Rilke,* Arion, 1983, new edition, Graywolf Press, 1985.

Neue Gedichte (poems), two volumes, Insel, 1907-08, translation by J. B. Leishman published as *New Poems,* New Directions, 1964, translation by Edward Snow, North Point Press, Volume 1: *New Poems (1907),* 1984, Volume 2: *New Poems: The Other Part (1908),* 1987.

Requiem (poems), Insel, 1909.

Die Aufzeichnungen des Malte Laurids Brigge (novel), Insel, 1910, translation by John Linton published as *The Journal of My Other Self,* Norton, 1930, translation by Norton published as *The Notebooks of Malte Laurids Brigge,* Norton, 1964, translation by Mitchell published as *The Notebooks of Malte Laurids Brigge,* Random House, 1983.

Erste Gedichten, Insel, 1913, Ungar, 1947.

Das Marien-Leben, Insel, 1913, translation by R. G. L. Barrett published as *The Life of the Virgin Mary,* Triltsch (Würzburg), 1921, translation by Stephen Spender published as *The Life of the Virgin Mary,* Philosophical Library, 1951.

Poems, translation by Lemont, Wright, 1918.

Aus der Fruehzeit Rainer Maria Rilke: Vers, Prosa, Drama (1894-1899), edited by Fritz Adolf Huenich, Bibliophilenabend (Leipzig), 1921.

Mitsou: Quarante images par Baltusz, Rotapfel, 1921.

Puppen, Hyperion (Munich), 1921.

Duineser Elegien (poems; also see below), Insel, 1923, Ungar, 1944, translation by V. Sackville-West and Edward Sackville-West published as *Duineser Elegien: Elegies from the Castle of Duino,* Hogarth, 1931, translation by Leishman and Spender published as *Duino Elegies,* Norton, 1939, translation by Robert Hunter and Gary Miranda published as

Duino Elegies, Breitenbush, 1981, translated by Stephen Cohn, preface by Peter Porter, Northwestern University Press (Evanston, IL), 1998, translated by John Waterfield, E. Mellen Press (Lewiston, NY), 1999.

Die Sonette an Orpheus: Geschrieben als ein Grab-Mal fuer Wera Ouckama Knoop (poems; also see below), Insel, 1923, Ungar, 1945, translation by Leishman published as *Sonnets to Orpheus, Written as a Monument for Wera Ouckama Knoop,* Hogarth, 1936, translation by Norton published as *Sonnets to Orpheus,* Norton, 1942, translation by Mitchell published as *The Sonnets to Orpheus,* Simon & Schuster, 1986, published as *Os Sonetos a Orfeu,* Quetzal Editores, 1994.

Vergers suivi des Quatrains Valaisans, Editions de la Nouvelle Revue Francaise (Paris), 1926, translation by Alfred Poulin, Jr., published as *Orchards,* Graywolf Press (Port Townsend, Wash.), 1982.

Gesammelte Werke, six volumes, Insel, 1927.

Les Fenetres: Dix Poemes, Officina Sanctandreana (Paris), 1927, translation by Poulin published as *The Windows* in *The Roses and the Windows,* Graywolf Press, 1979.

Les Roses, Stols (Bussum, Netherlands), 1927, translation by Poulin published as *The Roses* in *The Roses and the Windows,* Graywolf Press, 1979.

Erzaehlungen und Skizzen aus der Fruehzeit, Insel, 1928.

Ewald Tragy: Erzaehlung, Heller (Munich), 1929, Johannespresse (New York City), 1944, translation by Lola Gruenthal published as *Ewald Tragy,* Twayne, 1958.

Verse und Prosa aus dem Nachlass, Gesellschaft der Freunde der Deutschen Buecherei (Leipzig), 1929.

Gesammelte Gedichte, four volumes, Insel, 1930-33.

Ueber den jungen Dichter, [Hamburg], 1931.

Gedichte, edited by Katharina Kippenberg, Insel, 1931, Ungar, 1947.

Rainer Maria Rilke auf Capri: Gespraeche, edited by Leopold von Schloezer, Jess (Dresden), 1931.

Spaete Gedichte, Insel, 1934.

Bücher, Theater, Kunst, edited by Richard von Mises, Jahoda & Siegel (Vienna), 1934.

Der ausgewaehlten Gedichten anderer Teil, edited by Kippenberg, Insel, 1935.

Ausgewaehlte Werke, two volumes, edited by Ruth Sieber-Rilke, Carl Sieber, and Ernst Zinn, Insel, 1938.

Translations from the Poetry of Rainer Maria Rilke, translation by Norton, Norton, 1938, reprinted, 1962.

Fifty Selected Poems with English Translations, translation by C. F. MacIntyre, University of California Press, 1940.

Selected Poems, translation by Leishman, Hogarth, 1941.

Tagebücher aus der Fruehzeit, edited by Sieber-Rilke, Insel, 1942, translation by Snow and Michael Winkler published as *Diaries of a Young Poet,* Norton, 1997.

Briefe, Verse und Prosa aus dem Jahre 1896, two volumes, Johannespresse, 1946.

Thirty-one Poems, translation by Ludwig Lewisohn, Ackerman, 1946.

Freundschaft mit Rainer Maria Rilke: Begegnungen, Gespraeche, Briefe und Aufzeichnungen mitgeteilt durch Elga Maria Nevar, Zuest (Buempliz), 1946.

Five Prose Pieces, translation by Carl Niemeyer, Cummington Press (Cummington, MA), 1947.

Gedichte, edited by Hermann Kunisch, Vandenhoeck & Ruprecht (Goettingen), 1947.

Gedichte in franzoesicher Sprache, edited by Thankmar von Muenchhausen, Insel, 1949.

Aus Rainer Maria Rilkes Nachlass, four volumes, Insel, 1950, Volume 1: *Aus dem Nachlass des Grafen C. W.,* translation by Leishman as *From the Remains of Count C. W.,* Hogarth, 1952.

Werke: Auswahl in zwei Baenden, two volumes, Insel, 1953.

Gedichte, 1909-26: Sammlung der verstreuten und nachgelassenen Gedichte aus den mittleren und spaeteren Jahren, translation, with additions, by Leishman published as *Poems 1906 to 1926,* Laughlin (Norfolk, CT), 1953, reprinted, Knopf, 1996.

Selected Works, two volumes, translation by G. Craig Houston and Leishman, Hogarth, 1954, New Directions, 1960.

Saemtliche Werke, six volumes, edited by Zinn, Insel, 1955-66.

Angel Songs/Engellieder (bilingual), translation by Rhoda Coghill, Dolmen Press (Dublin), 1958.

Die Turnstunde und andere Novellen (novella collection), edited by Fritz Froehling, Hyperion, 1959.

Selected Works: Prose and Poetry, two volumes, 1960.

Poems, edited by G. W. McKay, Oxford University Press, 1965.

Werke in drei Baenden, three volumes, Insel, 1966.

Gedichte: Eine Auswahl, Reclam (Stuttgart), 1966.

Visions of Christ: A Posthumous Cycle of Poems, translation by Aaron Kramer, edited by Siegfried Mandel, University of Colorado Press, 1967.

Das Testament, edited by Zinn, Insel, 1975.

Holding Out: Poems, translation by Rika Lesser, Abbatoir Editions (Omaha, NE), 1975.

Possibility of Being: A Selection of Poems, translation by Leishman, New Directions, 1977.

The Voices, translation by Robert Bly, Ally Press, 1977.

Duino Elegies [and] *The Sonnets to Orpheus,* translation by Poulin, Houghton Mifflin, 1977.

Werke: In 3 Baenden, three volumes, edited by Horst Nalewski, Insel, 1978.

Where Silence Reigns: Selected Prose, New Directions, 1978.

Nine Plays, translation by Klaus Phillips and John Locke, Ungar, 1979.

I Am Too Alone in the World: Ten Poems, translation by Bly, Silver Hands Press, 1980.

Selected Poems of Rainer Maria Rilke, translation by Bly, Harper, 1980.

Requiem for a Woman, and Selected Lyric Poems, translation by Andy Gaus, Threshold Books (Putney, Vt.), 1981.

An Unofficial Rilke: Poems 1912-1926, edited and with translation by Michael Hamburger, Anvil Press, 1981.

Selected Poetry of Rainer Maria Rilke, edited and with translation by Mitchell, Random House, 1982.

The Astonishment of Origins: French Sequences, translation from the French by Poulin, Graywolf Press, 1982.

Selected Poems, translation by A. E. Flemming, Golden Smith (St. Petersburg, Fla.), 1983.

The Unknown Rilke: Selected Poems, translation by Franz Wright, Oberlin College, 1983.

The Migration of Powers: French Poems, translation by Poulin, Graywolf Press, 1984.

Between Roots: Selected Poems, translation by Lesser, Princeton University Press, 1986.

The Complete French Poems of Rainer Maria Rilke, translation by Poulin, Graywolf Press, 1986.

Die Briefe en Karl und Elisabeth von der Heydt (letters), Insel, 1986.

Rodin and Other Prose Pieces, translation by G. Craig Houston, Salem House, 1987.

Shadows on the Sundial (selected poems), edited by Stanley H. Barkan, translation by Norbert Krapf, Cross-Cultural Communications, 1989.

The Best of Rilke, translation by Walter Arndt, University Press of New England, 1989.

The Book of Images (selected poems), translation by Snow, North Point, 1991.

Rilke: Poisia-Coisa, edited by Augusto de Campos, Imago, 1994.

Selected Poems of Rainer Maria Rilke: The Book of Fresh Beginnings, translated by David Young, Oberlin College, 1994.

Two Stories of Prague: "King Bohush" and "The Siblings," translation by Angela Estherhammer, University Press of New England, 1994.

Uncollected Poems, translated by Snow, North Point Press, 1995.

Ahead of All Parting: The Selected Poetry and Prose of Rainer Maria Rilke, edited by Mitchell, Modern Library, 1995.

The Duino Elegies: A Critical Presentation, introduction, translation, and commentary by Jeno Platthy, Federation of International Poetry Associatons (Evansville, IN), 1999.

The Essential Rilke, selected and translated by Galway Kinnell and Hannah Liebmann, Ecco Press (Hopewell, NJ), 1999.

The Duino Elegies: Bilingual Edition, translated by Snow, North Point Press, 2000.

TRANSLATOR

Elizabeth Barrett Browning, *Sonette nach dem Portugiesischen,* Insel, 1908.

Maurice de Guerin, *Der Kentaur,* Insel, 1911.

Die Liebe der Magdalena: Ein franzoesischer Sermon, gezogen durch den Abbe Joseph Bonnet aus dem Ms. Q I 14 der Kaiserlichen Bibliothek zu St. Petersburg, Insel, 1912.

Marianna Alcoforado, *Portugiesische Briefe,* Insel, 1913.

Andre Gide, *Die Rueckkehr des verlorenen Sohnes,* Insel, 1914.

Die vierundzwanzig Sonette der Louise Labe, Lyoneserin, 1555, Insel, 1918.

Paul Valery, *Gedichte,* Insel, 1925.

Valery, *Eupalinos oder Ueber die Architektur,* Insel, 1927.

Uebertragungen, Insel, 1927.

Dichtungen des Michelangelo, Insel, 1936.

Gedichte aus fremden Sprachen, Ungar, 1947.

Maurice Maeterlinck, *Die sieben Jungfrauen von Orlamuende,* Dynamo (Liege), 1967.

LETTERS

Briefe an Auguste Rodin, Insel, 1928.

Briefe aus den Jahren 1902 bis 1906, edited by Sieber-Rilke and Sieber, Insel, 1929.

Briefe an einen jungen Dichter, Insel, 1929, translation by Norton published as *Letters to a Young Poet,* Norton, 1934, translation by K. W. Maurer published as *Letters to a Young Poet,* Langley (London), 1943, revised edition, Norton, 1963, translation by Mitchell, Random House, 1984, translation by Joan J. Burnham, foreword by Kent Nerburn, New World Library (Novato, CA), 2000.

Briefe an eine junge Frau, Insel, 1930, translation by Maurer published as *Letters to a Young Woman,* Langley, 1945.

Briefe aus den Jahren 1906 bis 1907, edited by Sieber-Rilke and Sieber, Insel, 1930.

Briefe und Tagebuecher aus der Fruehzeit, edited by Sieber-Rilke and Sieber, Insel, 1931.

Briefe aus den Jahren 1907 bis 1914, edited by Sieber-Rilke and Sieber, Insel, 1933.

Ueber Gott: Zwei Briefe, Insel, 1933.

Briefe an seinen Verleger 1906 bis 1926, edited by Sieber-Rilke and Sieber, Insel, 1934.

Briefe aus Muzot 1921 bis 1926, edited by Sieber-Rilke and Sieber, Insel, 1935.

Gesammelte Briefe, six volumes, edited by Sieber-Rilke and Sieber, Insel, 1936-39.

Lettres a une Amie Venitienne, Asmus, 1941.

Briefe an eine Freundin, edited by Herbert Steiner, Wells College Press, 1944.

Briefe, Oltener Buecherfreunde (Olten), 1945.

Briefe an Baronesse von Oe, edited by von Mises, Johannespresse, 1945.

Letters of Rainer Maria Rilke, translation by Jane Bannard Greene and Norton, Norton, Volume 1: *1892-1910,* 1945, reprinted, 1969, Volume 2: *1910-1926,* 1948, reprinted, 1969.

Briefe an eine Reisegefaehrtin: Eine Begegnung mit Rainer Maria Rilke, Ibach (Vienna), 1947.

Briefe an das Ehepaar S. Fischer, edited by Hedwig Fischer, Classen (Zurich), 1947.

La derniere amitie de Rainer Maria Rilke: Lettres inedites de Rilke a Madame Eloui Bey, edited by Edmond Jaloux, Laffont (Paris), 1949, translation by William H. Kennedy published as *Rainer Maria Rilke: His Last Friendship; Unpublished Letters to Mrs. Eloui Bey,* Philosophical Library, 1952.

"So lass ich mich zu traeumen gehen," Mader, 1949, translation by Heinz Norden published as *Letters to Benvenuta,* Philosophical Library, 1951.

Briefe an seinen Verleger, two volumes, edited by Sieber-Rilke and Sieber, Insel, 1949.

Briefe, two volumes, edited by Sieber-Rilke and Karl Altheim, Insel, 1950.

Die Briefe an Graefin Sizzo, 1921 bis 1926, Insel, 1950, enlarged edition, edited by Ingeborg Schnack, Insel, 1977.

Briefwechsel in Gedichten mit Erika Mitterer 1924 bis 1926, Insel, 1950, translation by N. K. Cruickshank published as *Correspondence in Verse with Erika Mitterer,* Hogarth, 1953.

Lettres francaise a Merline 1919-1922, du Seuil (Paris), 1950, translation by Violet M. Macdonald published as *Letters to Merline, 1919-1922,* Methuen, 1951.

Rainer Maria Rilke/Marie von Thurn und Taxis: Briefwechsel, two volumes, edited by Zinn, Niehans & Rokitansky (Zurich), 1951, translation by Nora Wydenbruck published as *The Letters of Rainer Maria Rilke and Princess Marie von Thurn and Taxis,* New Directions, 1958.

Rainer Maria Rilke/Lou Andreas-Salome, Briefwechsel, edited by Ernst Pfeiffer, Insel, 1952, revised and enlarged edition, 1975.

Rainer Maria Rilke/Andre Gide: Correspondance 1909-1926, edited by Renee Lang, Correa (Paris), 1952.

Briefe über Cezanne, edited by Clara Rilke, Insel, 1952, translation by Joel Agee published as *Letters on Cezanne,* Fromm, 1985.

Die Briefe an Frau Gudi Noelke aus Rilkes Schweizer Jahren, edited by Paul Obermueller, Insel, 1953, translation by Macdonald published as *Letters to Frau Gudi Noelke during His Life in Switzerland,* Hogarth, 1955.

Rainer Maria Rilke/Katharina Kippenberg: Briefwechsel, edited by Bettina von Bomhard, Insel, 1954.

Briefwechsel mit Benvenuta, edited by Kurt Leonhard, Bechtle (Esslingen), 1954, translation by Agee published as *Rilke and Benvenuta: An Intimate Correspondence,* Fromm, 1987.

Rainer Maria Rilke et Merline: Correspondance 1920-1926, edited by Dieter Basserman, Niehans (Zurich), 1954, reprinted, Paragon House, 1988.

Lettres milanaises 1921-1926, edited by Lang, Plon (Paris), 1956.

Rainer Maria Rilke/Inge Junghanns: Briefwechsel, edited by Wolfgang Herwig, Insel, 1959.

Selected Letters, edited by Harry T. Moore, Doubleday, 1960.

Wartime Letters of Rainer Maria Rilke, 1914-1921, translation by Norton, Norton, 1964.

Briefe an Sidonie Nadherny von Borutin, edited by Bernhard Blume, Insel, 1973.

Über Dichtung und Kunst, edited by Hartmut Engelhardt, Suhrkamp (Frankfurt), 1974.

Rainer Maria Rilke on Love and Other Difficulties: Translations and Considerations, edited by John J. L. Mood, Norton, 1975.

Rainer Maria Rilke/Helene von Nostitz: Briefwechsel, edited by Oswalt von Nostitz, Insel, 1976.

Briefe an Nanny Wunderly-Volkart, two volumes, edited by Niklaus Bigler and Raetus Luck, Insel, 1977.

Lettres autour d'un jardin, La Delirante (Paris), 1977.

Hugo von Hofmannsthal/Rainer Maria Rilke: Briefwechsel, edited by Rudolph Hirsch and Schnack, Suhrkamp, 1978.

Briefe an Axel Juncker, edited by Renate Scharffenberg, Insel, 1979.

Briefwechsel mit Rolf Freiherrn von Ungern-Sternberg, edited by Knorad Kratzsch, Insel Verlag Anton Kippenberg (Leipzig), 1980.

Rainer Maria Rilke/Anita Forrer: Briefwechsel, edited by Magda Kerenyi, Leipzig (Frankfurt am Main), 1982.

Rainer Maria Rilke/Marina Zwetajewa/Boris Pasternak: Briefwechsel, edited by Jewgenij Pasternak, Jelena Pasternak, and Konstantin M. Asadowski, Insel, 1983, translation by Margaret Wettlin and Walter Arndt published as *Letters Summer 1926,* Harcourt, 1985.

Rainer Maria Rilke: Briefe an Ernst Norlind, edited by Paul Astroem, Paul Astroems Forlag (Partille), 1986.

Rilke und Russland: Briefe, Erinnerungen, Gedichte, edited by Asadowski, Russian text translation by Ulrike Hirschberg, Insel, 1986.

Rainer Maria Rilke: Briefwechsel mit Regina Ullman und Ellen Delp, edited by Walter Simon, Insel, 1987.

Rainer Maria Rilke/Stefan Zweig: Briefe und Dokumente, edited by Donald Prater, Insel, 1987.

Briefe an Schweizer Freunde, Insel, 1994.

Briefwechsel mit Anton Kippenberg 1906 bis 1926, edited by Ingeorg Schnack and Renate Scharffenberg, Insel, 1995.

SIDELIGHTS: Of the poetry composed by the three major German poets writing during the early twentieth century—Stefan George, Hugo von Hofmannsthal, and Rainer Maria Rilke—the lyrical intensity of Rilke's verses is generally considered to represent the highest artistic achievement. Rilke was unique in his efforts to expand the realm of poetry through new uses of syntax and imagery and in the philosophy that his poems explored. With regard to the former, W. H. Auden declared in *New Republic,* "Rilke's most immediate and obvious influence has been upon diction and imagery." Rilke expressed ideas with "physical rather than intellectual symbols. While Shakespeare, for example, thought of the non-human world in terms of the human, Rilke thinks of the human in terms of the non-human, of what he calls Things (Dinge)." Besides this technique, the other important aspect of Rilke's writings was the evolution of his philosophy, which reached a climax in *Duineser Elegien* (*Duino Elegies*) and *Die Sonette an Orpheus* (*Sonnets to Orpheus*). Rejecting the Catholic beliefs of his parents as well as Christianity in general, the poet strove throughout his life to reconcile beauty and suffering, life and death, into one philosophy. As C. M. Bowra observed in *Rainer Maria Rilke: Aspects of His Mind and Poetry,* "Where others have found a unifying principle for themselves in religion or morality or the search for truth, Rilke found his in the search for impressions and the hope these could be turned into poetry. . . . For him Art was what mattered most in life."

Rilke was the only child of a German-speaking family in Prague, then part of the Austro-Hungarian empire. His father was a retired officer in the Austrian army who worked as a railroad official; his mother, a socially ambitious and possessive woman. At age eleven Rilke began his formal schooling at a military boarding academy, and in 1891, less than a year after transferring to a secondary military school, he was discharged due to health problems, from which he would suffer throughout his life. He immediately returned to Prague, to find that his parents had divorced in his absence. Shortly thereafter he began receiving private instruction toward passing the entrance exams for Prague's Charles-Ferdinand University. In 1894 his first book of verse, *Leben und Lieder: Bilder und Tagebuchblatter,* was published.

By 1895 Rilke had enrolled in the philosophy program at Charles-Ferdinand University, but soon became disenchanted with his studies and left Prague for Munich, ostensibly to study art. In Munich Rilke mingled in the city's literary circles, had several of his plays produced, published his poetry collections, *Larenopfer* and *Traumgelkront,* and was introduced to the work of Danish writer Jens Peter Jacobsen, who was a decisive influence during Rilke's formative years. Visiting Venice in 1897, Rilke met Lou Andreas-Salome, a married woman fifteen years his senior, who was also a strong influence on Rilke. After spending the summer of 1897 with her in the Bavarian Alps, Rilke accompanied Salome and her husband to Berlin in late 1897 and to Italy the following year.

Rilke's early verse, short stories, and plays are characterized by their romanticism. His poems of this period show the influence of the German folk song tradition and have been compared to the lyrical work of Heinrich Heine. The most popular poetry collections of Rilke's during this period were *Vom lieben Gott und Anderes* (*Stories of God*) and the romantic cycle *Die Weise von Liebe und Tod des Cornets Christoph Rilke* (*The Story of the Love and Death of Cornet Christoph Rilke*), which remained the poet's most widely recognized book during his lifetime. *Dictionary of Literary Biography* contributor George C. Schoolfield called Rilke's first poetry collection, *Leben und Lieder* ("Life and Songs"), "unbearably sentimental," but thought later works such as *Larenopfer* ("Offering to the Lares") and *Traumgekroent* ("Crowned with Dreams") demonstrated "considerably better proof of his lyric talent." Although none of Rilke's plays are considered major works, and his short stories, according to Schoolfield, demonstrate the author's immaturity, the latter do show "his awareness of language and a certain psychological refinement," as well as "flashes of brilliant satiric gift" and "evidence of a keen insight into human relations." Schoolfield also observed that "some of Rilke's best tales are autobiographical," such as "Pierre Dumont," which features a young boy saying goodbye to his mother at the gates to a military school, and "Ewald Tragy," a two-part story about a boy who leaves his family and hometown of Prague for Munich, where he fights loneliness but enjoys a new sense of freedom.

In 1899 Rilke made the first of two pivotal trips to Russia with Salome, discovering what he termed his "spiritual fatherland" in both the people and the landscape. There Rilke met Leo Tolstoy, L. O. Pasternak (father of Boris Pasternak), and the peasant poet Spiridon Droschin, whose works Rilke translated into German. These trips provided Rilke with the poetic material and inspiration essential to his developing philosophy of existential materialism and art as religion. Inspired by the lives of the Russian people, whom the poet considered more devoutly spiritual than other Europeans, Rilke's work during this period often featured traditional Christian imagery and concepts, but presented art as the sole redeemer of humanity. Soon after his return from Russia in 1900, he began writing *Das Stundenbuch enthaltend die drei Bücher: Vom moenchischen Leben; Von der Pilgerschaft; Von der Armuth und vom Tode,* a collection that "marked for him the end of an epoch," according to Bowra and others. This book, translated as *The Book of Hours; Comprising the Three Books: Of the Monastic Life, Of Pilgrimage, Of Poverty and Death,* consists of a series of prayers about the search for God. Because of this concern, *Hound and Horn* critic Hester Pickman noted that the book "might have fallen out of the writings of Christian contemplatives," except that "the essential pattern is an inversion of theirs. God is not light but darkness—not a father, but a son, not the creator but the created. He and not man is our neighbor for men are infinitely far from each other. They must seek God, not where one or two are gathered in His name, but alone."

Whenever Rilke writes about God, however, he is not referring to the deity in the traditional sense, but rather uses the term to refer to the life force, or nature, or an all-embodying, pantheistic consciousness that is only slowly coming to realize its existence. "Extending the idea of evolution," Eudo C. Mason explained in an introduction to *The Book of Hours,* "and inspired probably also in some measure by Nietzsche's idea of the Superman, Rilke arrives at the paradoxical conception of God as the final result instead of the first cause of the cosmic process." Holding in contempt "all other more traditional forms of devoutness, which . . . merely

'accept God as a given fact,'" Rilke did not deny God's existence, but insisted that all possibilities about the nature of life be given equal consideration.

The real theme of *The Book of Hours,* concluded Mason, is the poet's "own inner life," his struggles toward comprehension, and, "above all . . . his perils *as a poet.*" The second major concept in *The Book of Hours* is Rilke's apotheosis of art. "'Religion is the art of those who are uncreative,'" Mason quoted Rilke as having said; the poet's work is often concerned with the artist's role in society and with his inner doubts about his belief in poetry's superiority. Because of the firm establishment of these two themes in *The Book of Hours,* the collection "is essential to the understanding of what comes afterwards" in Rilke's writing, attested Pickman. *The Book of Hours* was also another of the poet's most popular works, second only to *The Story of the Love and Death of Cornet Christoph Rilke* during his lifetime. But despite being a "very beautiful" book, it also "remains too constantly abstract. It lacks the solid reality of great poetry," according to Pickman.

Rilke fixed his verse more firmly in reality in his next major poetry collection, *Neue Gedichte (New Poems).* The major influence behind this work was Rilke's association with the famous French sculptor, Auguste Rodin. Working as Rodin's secretary from 1905 to 1906, Rilke gained a greater appreciation of the work ethic. More importantly, however, the poet's verses became objective, evolving from an impressionistic, personal vision to the representation of this vision with impersonal symbolism. He referred to this type of poetry as *Dinggedichte* (thing poems). These verses employed a simple vocabulary to describe concrete subjects experienced in everyday life. Having learned the skill of perceptive observation from Rodin and, later, from the French painter Paul Cezanne, Rilke "sustained for a little while the ability to write without inspiration, to transform his observations—indeed his whole life—into art," according to Nancy Willard, author of *Testimony of the Invisible Man.* The "'thingness' of these poems," explained Erich Heller in *The Artist's Journey into the Interior and Other Essays,* "reflects not the harmony in which an inner self lives with its 'objects'; it reflects a troubled inner self immersing itself in 'the things.'" But although this objective approach innovatively addressed subjects never before recognized by other poets and created "dazzling poems," Rilke realized, according to Willard, that it "did not really open the secret of living things."

By this point in his career, Rilke was reaching a crisis in his art that revealed itself both in *New Poems* and his only major prose work, the novel *Die Aufzeichnungen des Malte Laurids Brigge* (*The Notebooks of Malte Laurids Brigge*). These works express the poet's growing doubts about whether anything existed that was superior to mankind and his world. This, in turn, brought into question Rilke's very reason for writing poetry: the search for deeper meaning in life through art. In her book, *Rainer Maria Rilke,* E. M. Butler averred that "*The Notebooks of Malte Laurids Brigge*" marks a crisis in Rilke's attitude to God, a crisis which might be hailed as the loss of a delusion, or deplored as the loss of an ideal. . . . [His concept of the] future artist-god had never been more than a sublime hypothesis, deriving from Rilke's belief in the creative and transforming powers of art." Having failed, in his mind, to accurately represent God in his poetry, Rilke attempted to "transform life into art" in his *New Poems.* "What he learnt," Butler continued, "is what every artist has to face sooner or later, the realisation that life is much more creative than art. So that his mythological dream, the apotheosis of art, appeared to be founded on delusion. Either art was not as creative as he had thought, or he was not such a great artist. Both these doubts were paralyzing, and quite sufficient to account for the terrible apprehension present in every line of *Malte Laurids Brigge.* For this skepticism struck at the roots of his reason and justification for existence. Either he was the prophet of a new religion, or he was nobody."

Some critics, however, felt that Butler's interpretation overanalyzed Rilke's novel. In *Rainer Maria Rilke: The Ring of Forms,* for example, author Frank Wood granted that Butler had devised an "ingenious theory," but added that her interpretation "does less than justice to its artistic importance. Though no one would claim the *Notebooks* to be a completely achieved work of art, Malte's story nonetheless provides a valuable commentary on [Rilke's] Paris poetry and that yet to come, interpreting and enlarging still nuclear ideas. More than that, Malte allows us an inside view, as the poetry itself rarely does, into the poetic mind in process, with all its variety and even confusion."

"*The Notebooks of Malte Laurids Brigge* were supposed to be the coherent formulation of the insights which were formulated disjointly in the *New Poems,*" wrote Norbert Fuerst, author of *Phases of Rilke.* The book is a loosely autobiographical novel about a student who is the last descendant of a noble Danish family (Rilke believed, erroneously according to his biographers, that he was distantly related to Carinthian nobility), and follows his life from his birth to a grim, poverty-stricken life as a student in Paris. Images of death and decay (especially in the Paris scenes) and Malte's fear of death are a continuous presence through-

out the narrative. The novel concludes with a retelling of the story of the Prodigal Son that represents, according to a number of critics like Schoolfield, "Rilke's long search for the freedom that would enable him to apply his artistic will to the fullest."

Because Rilke never finished *The Notebooks of Malte Laurids Brigge* (in one of his letters, the author told a friend he ended the book "'out of exhaustion,'" reported Schoolfield) Malte's ultimate fate is left ambiguous. Ronald Gray commented in his *The German Tradition in Literature: 1871-1945:* "Malte seems to have come to terms with suffering not so much by enduring it as by cutting himself off from contact with all others. But does Rilke present this as an ideal or as a deplored end? His own comments . . . are inconclusive, and in part this was due to his own uncertainty as to the extent to which Malte's life could be identified with his own." In one of Rilke's letters translated in *Letters of Rainer Maria Rilke: 1910-1926,* the author remarked that the most significant question in *The Notebooks of Malte Laurids Brigge* is: "[How] is it possible to live when after all the elements of this life are utterly incomprehensible to us?" Some authorities, summarized Wood, concluded that the answer to this question is that it is not possible to live; therefore, Malte is doomed. Others believed that Malte's answer lies in finding God. Wood, however, held that both these interpretations are too extreme. The solution, he proposed, can instead be found in Rilke's poetry collection, *Requiem,* which was written about the same time as his novel and "emphasizes that not victory but surviving is everything." As William Rose determined in *Rainer Maria Rilke: Aspects of His Mind and Poetry, The Notebooks of Malte Laurids Brigge* actually was kind of a catharsis for the author in which "Rilke gave full vent . . . to the fears which haunted him." "Without the *Notebooks* behind him," Wood concluded, "the poet would hardly have ventured" to write the *Duino Elegies* in 1912.

Duino Elegies "might well be called the greatest set of poems of modern times," claimed Colin Wilson, author of *Religion and the Rebel.* Wilson averred, "They have had as much influence in German-speaking countries as [T. S. Eliot's] *The Waste Land* has in England and America." Having discovered a dead end in the objective poetry with which he experimented in *New Poems,* Rilke once again turned to his own personal vision to find solutions to questions about the purpose of human life and the poet's role in society. *Duino Elegies* finally resolved these puzzles to Rilke's own satisfaction. Called *Duino Elegies* because Rilke began writing them in 1912 while staying at Duino Castle on the Italian Adriatic coast, the collection took ten years to complete, due to an inspiration-stifling depression the poet suffered during and after World War I. When his inspiration returned, however, the poet wrote a total of eleven lengthy poems for the book; later this was edited down to ten poems.

The unifying poetic image that Rilke employs throughout *Duino Elegies* is that of angels, which carry many meanings, albeit not the usual Christian connotations. The angels represent a higher force in life, both beautiful and terrible, completely indifferent to mankind; they represent the power of poetic vision, as well as Rilke's personal struggle to reconcile art and life. Butler elaborated: "[The] Duino angels are truly a poetical creation to be completely susceptible of rational interpretation, and too complex to stand for any one idea. Rilke's idolatry of art as the supreme creative power became incarnate in them; a more mysterious and less ambiguous piece of symbolism than his previous use of the word God to represent an emergent aesthetic creator." The Duino angels thus allowed Rilke to objectify abstract ideas as he had done in *New Poems,* while not limiting him to the mundane materialism that was incapable of thoroughly illustrating philosophical issues.

Duino Elegies, according to E. L. Stahl, a contributor to *Rainer Maria Rilke: Aspects of His Mind and Poetry,* "begin with lament, but end with praise." Beginning in the first elegy with what Butler called "a bitter confession of poetical and emotional bankruptcy," Rilke steadily develops his reasons for lamenting our existence, until the seventh elegy, where the discovery of a means to solving life's puzzles first turns lament into praise. The "lesson of the seventh elegy," wrote Butler, is "that the only real world is within us, and that life is one long transformation. Rilke had at last found the formula for his cosmic mission and a connecting link between himself and the angel." However, it is not until the ninth elegy that this formula is used. "We exist," said Stahl in his clarification of Rilke's revelation, "because existence is in itself of value and because everything which exists apparently appeals to us and depends on us for its future existence, though in this world we are the most fleeting creatures of all. . . . The purpose of our existence is to praise and extol the simple things of existence."

This conclusion allowed Rilke to accept life's suffering and death because he realized the purpose of life was not to avoid these destructive forces in favor of happiness. Instead, as the poet explains in the tenth elegy, the "principle of the whole of our life, in this world and the next, is sorrow." Having reconciled himself to the belief that man's existence by necessity involves suffering, Rilke concluded, according to Stahl, that the poet's function is to project "the world into the angel, where it becomes invisible." "Then the angels," Butler finished, "who can only apprehend what is invisible, will marvel at this hymn of praise to humble, simple things. They will receive them and rescue them from oblivion." This complex explanation of life's purpose, which Rilke developed slowly over many years, is not one that lends itself to a "rational explanation," Stahl pointed out. "It is a matter of Rilke's personal belief."

The revolutionary poetic philosophy that Rilke proposed in *Duino Elegies* is considered significant to many literary scholars. "No poet before him had been brave enough to accept the *whole* of [the dark side of the] world, as if it were unquestionably valid and potentially universal," asserted Conrad Aiken in his *Collected Criticism.* Like the German philosopher Friedrich Nietzsche, who lived about the same time as Rilke, the poet determined his objective to be "[praise] and celebration in the face of and in full consciousness of the facts that had caused other minds to assume an attitude of negativity," wrote *Emergence from Chaos* author Stuart Holroyd. But even though the final purpose of *Duino Elegies* is to praise existence, the "predominant note . . . is one of lament." By overcoming his quandaries in this collection, Rilke was completely free to devote his poetry to praise in *Sonnets to Orpheus.*

"The *Sonnets* are the songs of his victory," affirmed Bowra in *The Heritage of Symbolism.* "In the *Sonnets,*" Bowra wrote, "Rilke shows what poetry meant to him, what he got from it and what he hoped for it. The dominating mood is joy. It is a complement to the distress and anxiety of the *Elegies,* and in Rilke's whole performance the two books must be taken together." Aiken similarly commented that the "*Sonnets to Orpheus . . .* is, with the *Elegies,* Rilke's finest work—the two books really belong together, shine the better for each other's presence."

In the last few years of his life, Rilke was inspired by such French poets as Paul Valery and Jean Cocteau, and wrote most of his last verses in French. Always a sickly man, the poet succumbed to leukemia in 1926 while staying at the Valmont sanatorium near Lake Geneva. On his deathbed, he remained true to his anti-Christian beliefs and refused the company of a priest. Hermann Hesse summed up Rilke's evolution as a poet in his book, *My Belief: Essays on Life and Art:* "Remarkable, this journey from the youthful music of Bohemian folk poetry . . . to *Orpheus,* remarkable how . . . his mastery of form increases, penetrates deeper and deeper into his problems! And at each stage now and again the miracle occurs, his delicate, hesitant, anxiety-prone person withdraws, and through him resounds the music of the universe; like the basin of a fountain he becomes at once instrument and ear." Without his parents' religious ideals to comfort him, Rilke found peace in his art. As Holroyd concluded, the "poetry which Rilke wrote to express and extend his experience . . . is one of the most successful attempts a modern man has made to orientate himself within his chaotic world."

Rilke is among the most widely translated of modern poets, a distinction that promotes varied interpretations of his poetry resulting from the disparate readings of various translators. Among the poet's notable translators are Walter Arndt, Stephen Mitchell, and David Young. Arndt's version of a selection of Rilke's poems in his 1989 publication, *The Best of Rilke,* attempts to translate the poet's unique idiom into English while simultaneously attempting to maintain the original rhythm and rhyme scheme of the poet's verse. While recognized as an ambitious and difficult endeavor, the translation received mixed reviews. Mitchell, considered the most popular of Rilke's English translators, produced a version of the *Elegies* that *New Republic* contributor Brian Phillips considered "functional, accessible, prosaic, and drastically oversimplified, constantly threatening to transform Rilke, in Christopher Benfey's words, into 'a sort of gemutlich Kahlil Gibran.'"

Edward Snow, in the opinion of many poets and critics, has emerged as the best contemporary translator of Rilke into English. His version of Rilke's *Uncollected Poems* received high praise from several critics, including Michael Dirda of *Washington Post Book World,* who hailed Snow as "among the most trustworthy and exhilarating of Rilke's contemporary translators." While noted for the quality of the English translation, the volume is also significant in its presentation of some of Rilke's lesser-known verse, which, some argue, has been overshadowed by the *Duino Elegies.* Writing in *Nation,* William H. Gass commented: "Snow's splendid selection supports his contention that these late poems—as occasional as lit matches in a crowd, and so different, in their quick responsive character, from the vatic seriousness of the *Elegies* and *Sonnets*—have their own high value and importance."

The *Duino Elegies* alone have been translated into English some twenty times; in 2000 three new English versions of the *Elegies* attracted critical attention. William Gass's translation, aimed at debunking some of the myths Phillips claims have been inadvertently perpetuated by the poet's translators, is accompanied by an extended prose essay on the problems of translation. Nicole Kraus in the *Boston Review* found Gass's criticism more pointed and interesting than his translation. "Gass is not a poet," she observed. "His *Elegies* borrow generously from existing translations, and though he sometimes smoothes over other translators' rough patches, his lines often suffer from a wordiness that chokes them of air." Phillips, commenting that "Gass plays shockingly fast and loose with the German," deemed his *Elegies* "a travesty of translation" that is marred by excess, vulgarity, and "blustery confusion." Poet Galway Kinnell's version of the *Elegies,* included in his *The Essential Rilke,* is, according to Phillips, an improvement over Gass's but only a "modest success," because it fails to enliven Rilke's poetry and "does little that has not been done before." In Phillips's view, Edward Snow's translation of the *Elegies* is indisputably the best version in English. Indeed, the critic suggests that "Snow may be the best translator that Rilke has ever had." Noting that Snow's earlier translation of *Uncollected Poems* "did more than any other work to correct the myth that Rilke lived—as Rilke himself seemed sorrowfully to believe—through almost unendurable periods of creative drought in between his lightning-blasts of inspiration," Phillips adds that "now [Snow's] new version of the *Elegies* shows Rilke not as a mythic visionary retreading for the benefit of others the revealed path to salvation, but as a human poet who struggled with fear and doubt and pain, an individual who acted cruelly not solely out of a consuming commitment to his art, but also out of uncertainty and loneliness."

BIOGRAPHICAL/CRITICAL SOURCES:

BOOKS

Aiken, Conrad, *Collected Criticism,* Oxford University Press, 1968.

Baron, Frank, Ernst S. Dick, and Warren R. Maurer, editors, *Rainer Maria Rilke: The Alchemy of Alienation,* Regents Press of Kansas, 1980.

Borkowska, Ewa, *From Donne to Celan: Logo(theo)logical Patterns in Poetry.* Uniwersytet Slnaskiego, 1994.

Bowra, C. M., *The Heritage of Symbolism,* Macmillan, 1943.

Burnshaw, Stanley, editor, *The Poem Itself,* Holt, 1960.

Butler, E. M., *Rainer Maria Rilke,* Macmillan, 1941.

Casey, Timothy J., *Rainer Maria Rilke: A Centenary Essay,* Macmillan, 1976.

Dictionary of Literary Biography, Volume 81: *Austrian Fiction Writers, 1874-1913,* Gale, 1989.

Feste-McCormack, Diana, *The City as Catalyst: A Study of Ten Novels,* Fairleigh Dickinson University Press, 1979.

Freedman, Ralph, *Life of a Poet: A Biography of Rainer Maria Rilke,* Farrar, Straus, 1995.

Fuerst, Norbert, *Phases of Rilke,* Indiana University Press, 1958.

Gass, William, *Reading Rilke: Reflections on the Problems of Translation,* Knopf, 2000.

Graff, W. L., *Rainer Maria Rilke: Creative Anguish of a Modern Poet,* Princeton University Press, 1956.

Gray, Ronald, *The German Tradition in Literature: 1971-1945,* Cambridge at the University Press, 1965.

Guardini, Romano, *Rilke's "Duino Elegies": An Interpretation,* translated by K. G. Knight, Henry Regnery, 1961.

Heep, Hartmut, *A Different Poem: Rainer Maria Rilke's American Translators Randall Jarrell, Robert Lowell, and Robert Bly,* P. Lang, 1996.

Heller, Erich, *The Artist's Journey into the Interior and Other Essays,* Random House, 1965.

Hesse, Hermann, *My Belief: Essays on Life and Art,* Farrar, Straus, 1974.

Holyroyd, Stuart, *Emergence from Chaos,* Houghton Mifflin, 1957.

Komar, Kathleen L., *Transcending Angels: Rainer Maria Rilke's "Duino Elegies,"* University of Nebraska Press, 1987.

Lewisohn, Ludwig, *Cities and Men,* Harper & Brothers, 1927.

Mandel, Siegfried, *Rainer Maria Rilke: The Poetic Instinct,* edited by Harry T. Moore, Southern Illinois University Press, 1965.

Olivero, Federico, *Rainer Maria Rilke: A Study in Poetry and Mysticism,* W. Heffer & Sons, 1931.

Peters, H. F., *Rainer Maria Rilke: Masks and the Man,* University of Washington Press, 1960.

Poetry Criticism: Volume 2, Gale, 1991.

Pollard, Percival, *Masks and Minstrels of New Germany,* Johw W. Luce and Company, 1911.

Prater, Donald, *A Ringing Glass: The Life of Rainer Maria Rilke,* Clarendon Press, 1986.

Rilke, Rainer Maria, *Letters of Rainer Maria Rilke: 1910-1926,* Volume 2, Norton, 1948.

Rilke, Rainer Maria, *The Book of Hours: Comprising the Three Books, Of the Monastic Life, Of Pilgrimage, Of Poverty and Death,* Hogarth Press, 1961.

Rilke, Rainer Maria, *Nine Plays,* Ungar, 1979.

Rilke, Rainer Maria, *The Notebooks of Malte Laurids Brigge,* Vintage Books, 1985.

Rose, William, and G. Craig Houston, editors, *Rainer Maria Rilke: Aspects of His Mind and His Poetry,* Gordian, 1970.

Sword, Helen, *Engendering Inspiration: Visionary Strategies in Rilke, Lawrence, and H. D.,* University of Michigan Press, 1995.

Tavis, Anna A., *Rilke's Russia: A Cultural Encounter,* Northwestern University Press, 1994.

Twentieth-Century Literary Criticism, Gale, Volume 1, 1978, Volume 6, 1982, Volume 19, 1986.

Van Heerikhuizen, F. W., *Rainer Maria Rilke: His Life and Work,* translated by Fernand G. Renier and Anne Cliff, Routledge and Kegan Paul, 1951.

Willard, Nancy, *Testimony of the Invisible Man,* University of Missouri Press, 1970.

Wilson, Colin, *Religion and the Rebel,* Houghton Mifflin, 1957.

Wood, Frank, *Rainer Maria Rilke: The Ring of Forms,* University of Minnesota Press, 1958.

Ziolkowski, Theodore, *Dimensions of the Modern Novel: German Texts and European Contexts,* Princeton University Press, 1969.

PERIODICALS

Booklist, April 15, 1994, p. 1516.

Boston Review, summer 2000, pp. 58-59.

Choice, November, 1989, p. 490.

Commonweal, March 9, 1990, pp. 153-154.

Comparative Literature, summer, 1983, pp. 215-246.

Hound and Horn, April-June, 1931.

Library Journal, June 15, 1991, p. 81; April 1, 1994, p. 136.

Listener, December 18, 1975.

Modern Austrian Literature, Volume 15, nos. 3 and 4, 1982, pp. 71-90; Volume 15, nos. 3 and 4, 1982, pp. 291-316.

Modern Language Notes, January, 1991, p. 255.

Modern Language Review, April, 1979.

Nation, December 17, 1930; September 26, 1987, pp. 316-318; April 1, 1996, p. 27.

New Criterion, January 2000, p. 17.

New Republic, September 6, 1939; January 3, 1994, p. 31; July 1, 1996, p. 32; May 8, 2000, p. 38.

New Yorker, September 9, 1991, pp. 96-97.

New York Herald Tribune Books, December 14, 1930.

New York Times Book Review, January 17, 1988, p. 15; April 28, 1996, p. 16.

PMLA, October, 1974.

Publishers Weekly, February 28, 1994, p. 73; January 10, 2000, p. 60.

Small Press, February, 1990, p. 51.

Times Literary Supplement, December 12, 1975; July 27-28, 1988, p. 795; May 29, 1992, p. 23.
University of Dayton Review, spring, 1981.
Washington Post Book World, March 31, 1996, p. 5.
World Literature Today, winter, 1988, p. 122.*

*   *   *

ROBINSON, Peter (Mark) 1957-

PERSONAL: Born April 18, 1957, in Binghamton, NY; son of Theodore H. (an artist) and Alice (an artist; maiden name, Booth) Robinson; married Edita Piedra (a homemaker), September 9, 1990; children: Edita Maria, Peter Nicolas Theodore. *Education:* Dartmouth College, A.B. (summa cum laude; English), 1979; Stanford Graduate School of Business, M.B.A, 1990. *Politics:* "Contentious." *Religion:* Roman Catholic.

ADDRESSES: Office—Hoover Institution, Stanford, CA 94305-6010. *Agent*—Richard S. Pine, 250 West 57th St., New York, NY 10019.

CAREER: The White House, Washington, DC, chief speech writer to Vice President George Bush, 1982-83, special assistant and speech writer to President Ronald Reagan, 1983-88; The News Corporation, Ltd., New York City, assistant and political counsel to Rupert Murdoch, Gulf War commentator, and producer of news segments for Fox television affiliates, 1990-91; Securities and Exchange Commission, Washington, DC, director of the office of public affairs, policy evaluation, and research, 1991-93; Hoover Institution (public policy research center), Stanford, CA, fellow, 1993—. Assistant to William F. Buckley, Jr., in Gstaad, Switzerland, for two months in 1988. Political commentator for Fox television during 1992 presidential campaign; composer of storyboards for Ronald Reagan Presidential Library; speech writer for David Rockefeller.

MEMBER: Leander Club (Henley-on-Thames, England), Phi Beta Kappa.

AWARDS, HONORS: Honorary degree, Oxford University, 1981.

WRITINGS:

Snapshots from Hell: The Making of an MBA, Warner Books (New York, NY), 1994.
It's My Party: A Republican's Messy Love Affair with the GOP, Warner Books (New York, NY), 2000.

Former editor of *The Dartmouth* (daily newspaper); contributor of articles to periodicals, including the *New York Times, Boston Herald, San Francisco Chronicle,* and *Forbes.*

SIDELIGHTS: Peter Robinson was a speech writer in the Reagan White House from 1982 until 1988, when he entered Stanford Graduate School of Business in pursuit of an M.B.A. degree. Business school, he soon discovered, was much different from what he had envisioned, with most of the students, and even the instructors, lacking any real passion for business. The degree itself, not the knowledge leading to it, seemed to be the goal of most of his fellow classmates. In addition to his idealistic expectations, Robinson had to overcome his being a "poet," the business school nickname for a student from a liberal arts background.

In his book *Snapshots from Hell: The Making of an MBA,* Robinson chronicles his first year, sharing humorous observations of various students and instructors and describing some of the tedious lectures he was required to endure. In a *New York Times* excerpt of *Snapshots from Hell,* Robinson offered this insight on why he was compelled to write his book: "I discovered that business school would be a far more turbulent and, as they say in California, awesome experience than I had expected. And so I offer these notes, a record of my first year, as a simple act of decency. Like going back to the last calm bend in the river and nailing up a sign saying, 'Waterfall Ahead.'"

Although Robinson earned his degree, his career in business was short lived. He worked for a time for one of Rupert Murdoch's organizations but soon found himself unemployed, along with a number of others, due to corporate downsizing. Nevertheless, his degree has paid off through the production of his book, which was well-received. For instance, reviewer Joe Queenan, writing in *American Spectator,* approved Robinson's move to the Hoover Institution after leaving Murdoch, predicting, "He will not regret that move: He is a talented writer, but he would have made a dud businessman, and the United States doesn't need any more dud businessmen. On the evidence of *Snapshots from Hell,* Robinson knows it." *National Review* contributor Neal B. Freeman also appreciated *Snapshots from Hell,* writing, "*Snapshots* takes a curious, comprehensive walk through the academic year, pausing to collect perspectives from odd angles. And given the author's tour as a phrase-maker for the Great Communicator, it's not surprising to find the tale told in crisp, post-collegiate prose."

In 2000 Robinson published *It's My Party: A Republican's Messy Love Affair with the GOP. It's My Party* "provides an interesting look at the Republican Party," noted Vanessa Bush in *Booklist,* "one that will evoke cheers from true believers and occasional scorn from Democrats and Independents." The work attempts to answer the question: What does it mean to be a Republican? To answer this, Robinson, basing his work on a journal he kept while traveling around the United States talking with Republicans, discusses the history of the party, divisions and differences within the party, and the party's current demographics, among other topics.

"Robinson is a Reaganite . . . and this makes his assessment of the party somewhat predictable," said a critic in *Publishers Weekly.* "However, he also displays what has become a rare quality: healthy partisanship." Although *Library Journal* reviewer Jill Ortner called the work "superficial and largely uncritical," Christopher Buckley, writing in *Washington Monthly,* lauded the work as "sprightly and amusing." Buckley praised Robinson's "honest, uncomplicated, almost naive prose style."

BIOGRAPHICAL/CRITICAL SOURCES:

PERIODICALS

American Spectator, September, 1994, Joe Queenan, review of *Snapshots from Hell,* pp. 70-71.
Booklist, August, 2000, Vanessa Bush, review of *It's My Party,* p. 2086.
Business Week, June 20, 1994, p. 21.
Library Journal, August, 2000, Jill Ortner, review of *It's My Party,* p. 131.
National Review, September 12, 1994, Neal B. Freeman, review of *Snapshots from Hell,* pp. 82-83.
New York Times, October 2, 1994, Section 3, p. 9.
New York Times Book Review, May 8, 1994, p. 6.
Publishers Weekly, April 18, 1994, p. 56; July 10, 2000, review of *It's My Party,* p. 57.
Washington Monthly, July, 2000, Christopher Buckley, review of *It's My Party,* p. 50.*

*   *   *

ROGERS, Jane 1952-

PERSONAL: Born July 21, 1952, in London, England; daughter of Andrew W. (a professor) and Margaret (a nurse; maiden name, Farmer) Rogers; married Michael Harris (a writer and teacher), March, 1981; children: two. *Education:* New Hall, Cambridge, B.A. (with honors), 1974; Leicester University, postgraduate certificate of education, 1976.

ADDRESSES: Home—Lancashire, England. *Agent*—Peters, Fraser & Dunlop Group LTD., Drury House, 34-43 Russell St., London WC2B 5HA, England.

CAREER: Glossop Comprehensive School, Derbyshire, England, English teacher, 1976-79; Hachney College of Further Education, London, England, English teacher, 1979-80; Peel Sixth Form College, Bury, Lancashire, England, English teacher, 1980-83; Worker's Educational Association, Manchester, England, creative writing teacher, 1983—; College of Adult Education, Manchester, creative writing teacher, 1983—. Fiction reviewer for a local newspaper. Has also worked at a mental hospital, for a housing association, and at homes for children.

MEMBER: Royal Society of Literature (fellow).

AWARDS, HONORS: Northwest Arts Grant for Writers, Arts Council of Great Britain, 1983; Somerset Maugham Award, 1984, for *Her Living Image;* Samuel Beckett Award, 1990, for *Dawn and the Candidate;* Writers Guild Best Fiction Award, 1996, for *Promised Lands.*

WRITINGS:

NOVELS

Separate Tracks, Faber & Faber (London, England), 1983.
Her Living Image, Faber & Faber (London, England), 1984, Doubleday (Garden City, NY), 1986.
The Ice Is Singing, Faber & Faber (London, England), 1987.
Mr. Wroe's Virgins (historical), Faber & Faber (London, England), 1992.
Promised Lands, Faber & Faber (London, England), 1995.
Island, Overlook Press (Woodstock, NY), 2000.

OTHER

Author of television dramas *Dawn and the Candidate* and *Mr. Wroe's Virgins* (adapted from Rogers' novel of the same title). Has also adapted works by other authors for radio.

WORK IN PROGRESS: Editing a *Readers' Guide to Fiction,* Oxford University Press.

SIDELIGHTS: Jane Rogers is a critically acclaimed English author and educator. Known primarily for her novels, including *Separate Tracks, Her Living Image, The Ice Is Singing,* and *Islands,* Rogers is also the author of an award-winning teleplay, *Dawn and the Candidate.* She lives in Lancashire with her husband and two children.

Separate Tracks, Rogers' first novel, traces the lives of Emma, a middle-class woman from a broken home, and Anthony, a child abandoned to an institution while still an infant. They meet when Emma accepts a temporary position at the foster home where Anthony lives, and eventually Anthony becomes a prevailing influence upon her emotions and her political beliefs. *Times Literary Supplement* writer John Melmoth called the book "an impeccable piece of social realism," while praising Roger's "considerable narrative versatility and command of nuance." Rogers once told *CA,* "Although I had been writing for years, *Separate Tracks* was the first manuscript I ever sent to a publisher or agent, and I was lucky enough to have it accepted within a week."

Rogers' *Mr. Wroe's Virgins,* published in 1992, is the story of John Wroe, a charismatic, self-proclaimed prophet who claims that God has instructed him to take seven virgins into his home. Based on actual events, the story follows Wroe and the seven women who live with him for a period of nine months. "Part morality tale, part history; packed with accurate details of early 19th-century life, the stories of Leah, Joanna, Hannah and Martha unfold as they cope with the hypocrisy, blind beliefs and idealism of the sexually threatening prophet," noted a critic in *Publishers Weekly.* Steffanie Brown wrote in *Booklist,* "Gracefully written and immensely powerful, this imaginative reconstruction of what nine months with a peculiar patriarch might have been like is also an insightful exploration of the interplay between faith, passion, and betrayal."

Rogers' *Promised Lands* combines two main narrative threads. The first story revolves around William Dawes, a member of the first British settlement in Australia. The second story is that of Stephen Beech, a modern-day author writing about Dawes, whose wife, Olla, believes their child, a crippled boy named Daniel, is the world's savior. Critics were enthusiastic in their response to *Promised Lands.* "Intensely atmospheric, structurally sophisticated and deeply political, this is a challenging and hypnotic work," wrote a critic for *Publishers Weekly. Booklist* reviewer Eric Robbins called the work "an engrossing meditation on illusions and reality. . . . Themes within the story constantly echo

and reverberate in this extremely satisfying work." Joshua Cohen also lauded the work in *Library Journal,* concluding: "Rogers's superbly crafted narrative immerses the reader in the harsh choices and conditions of colonial life."

Rogers' 2000 work, *Island,* is the story of Nikki Black, a young woman whose mother abandoned her nearly thirty years before by leaving her on the steps of a London post office. Nikki travels to the Scottish Hebrides to find her mother and exact her revenge. Nikki's plan to murder her mother is complicated, however, by the existence of Calum, her innocent half-brother. Calling the novel a "brooding, furiously powerful tale," a *Kirkus Reviews* critic concluded, "This tale of a madness . . . is also a complex rendering of the art of storytelling, where history and invention seem to purposefully converge, each to transform the other."

BIOGRAPHICAL/CRITICAL SOURCES:

PERIODICALS

Booklist, April 15, 1997, Eric Robbins, review of *Promised Lands,* p. 1386; June 1, 1999, Steffanie Brown, review of *Mr. Wroe's Virgins,* p. 1795.
Financial Times, February 19, 1983.
Harper's and Queen, February, 1983.
Kirkus Reviews, August 15, 2000, review of *Island,* p. 1139.
Library Journal, April 1, 1997, Joshua Cohen, review of *Promised Lands,* p. 131.
New Society, February 3, 1983.
New Statesman & Society, September 1, 1995, Judy Cooke, review of *Promised Lands,* p. 32.
New York Times Book Review, August 17, 1986, Barbara Tritel, review of *Her Living Image,* p. 22; September 21, 1997, David Willis McCullough, review of *Promised Lands,* p. 20; August 22, 1999, Kathryn Harrison, review of *Mr. Wroe's Virgins,* p. 10.
Publishers Weekly, April 25, 1986, Sybil Steinberg, review of *Her Living Image,* p. 65; March 10, 1997, review of *Promised Lands,* p. 49; April 12, 1999, review of *Mr. Wroe's Virgins,* p. 51.
Times Literary Supplement, February 11, 1983; October, 1983; October 19, 1984.

OTHER

MetroActive, http://www.metroactive.com/ (October 5, 2000).*

RUBINSTEIN, Amnon 1931-

PERSONAL: Born September 5, 1931, in Tel Aviv, Palestine (now Israel); son of Aaron and Rachel (Vilozny) Rubinstein; married Ronny Havatseleth (a lawyer), 1958; children: Tal (daughter), Nir (son). *Education:* Hebrew University of Jerusalem, LL.M. and B.A., 1956; London School of Economics and Political Science, Ph. D., 1961. *Religion:* Jewish.

ADDRESSES: Office—Knesset, Jerusalem 91950, Israel.

CAREER: Hebrew University of Jerusalem, Tel Aviv, Israel, lecturer, 1961-64, senior lecturer in constitutional law, 1964-68; Tel Aviv University, Ramat Aviv, Israel, senior lecturer, 1968-70, associate professor, 1970-74, professor of law, 1974-75, dean of Faculty of Law, 1969-75. Shinui (Centre) Party, founder, 1974, chairperson, beginning in 1975; Meretz Party, member, beginning in 1978; Knesset, member, 1977—, member of committees on foreign affairs and defense, 1977-81, economy, 1981-84, constitution, law, and justice, 1984-88, internal affairs and environment and ethics, 1984-88, and house committee, 1988-92; National Unity Government, minister of communications, 1984-88; State of Israel, minister of education, culture, and sports.

WRITINGS:

Jurisdiction and Illegality: A Study in Public Law, Oxford University Press (Oxford, England), 1965.

The Constitutional Law of Israel, Schocken (Tel Aviv, Israel), 1968, 3rd edition, 1980.

Here, Now, Schocken (Tel Aviv, Israel), 1969.

(Contributor) Yoram Dinstein, editor, *Israel Yearbook on Human Rights,* Israel Press, Volume II, 1972, Volume III, 1973.

The Enforcement of Morality in a Permissive Society, Schocken (Tel Aviv, Israel), 1974.

To Be a Free People, Schocken (Tel Aviv, Israel), 1977.

From Herzl to Gush Emunim, Schocken (Tel Aviv, Israel), 1980.

Ha-Mishpat ha-konstitutsyoni shel Medinat Yi'sra'el, two volumes, Shoken (Jerusalem, Israel), 1991.

(With Ra'anan Har-Zahav) *Hok-yesod: Ha-Kneset,* [Jerusalem], 1993.

Me-Hertsel 'ad Rabin ve-hal'ah: Me'ah shenot Tsiyonut, Shoken, 1997, translation published as *From Herzl to Rabin: The Changing Image of Zionism,* Holmes & Meier (New York, NY), 2000.

Also author of *The Zionist Dream Revisited,* 1984, and of published lectures. Contributor to periodicals in the United States, Canada, England, and Israel. Member of editorial board, *Israel Yearbook on Human Rights* and *Ha'aretz* (Israeli independent daily newspaper).

BIOGRAPHICAL/CRITICAL SOURCES:

PERIODICALS

Kirkus Reviews, August 15, 2000, review of *From Herzl to Rabin,* p. 1179.*

S

SALAMUN, Tomaz 1941-

PERSONAL: Born July 4, 1941, in Zagreb, Croatia; son of Branko (a pediatrician) and Misa (an art historian; maiden name Gulic); married Marusa Krese (a painter) April, 1969 (divorced, 1975); married Metka Krasovec (a painter), April 11, 1979; children: Ana and David. *Ethnicity:* "Slovenian." *Education:* University of Ljubljana, Slovenia, M.A. (art history and history), 1965; attended University of Iowa, 1971-73; studied art history in Krakow, Pisa and Paris.

ADDRESSES: Home—Dalmatinova 11, 1000 Ljubljana, Slovenia; 321 East 14th St., Apt. 4B, New York, NY 10003. *Office*—Consulate General of Slovenia, 600 Third Ave., 21st Floor, New York, NY 10003.

CAREER: Poet. Modern Gallery, Ljubljana, Slovenia, assistant curator, 1968-70; Academy of Fine Arts, Ljubljana, assistant professor, 1970-73; University of Tennessee, Chattanooga, workshop class, 1987-88, 1996; Vermont College, visiting writer, 1988; Consul, Slovenian Cultural Attaché, New York City, 1996-97; writer-in-residence at Yaddo, Saratoga Springs, NY, 1973-74, 1979, 1986, 1989, MacDowell Colony, Peterborough, NH, 1986, Karoly Foundation, Vence, France, 1987, Maisons des escrivains etrangers, Saint-Nazaire, France, 1996, and Civitella Ranieri, Umbertide, Italy, 1997. *Military service:* Yugoslav Army, 1966-67; became private.

MEMBER: PEN, Writer's Union in Slovenia.

AWARDS, HONORS: Fulbright grant, 1986-87; Preseren Fünf Prize; Mladost Prize; Pushcart Prize; Jenko Prize; Fulbright fellow; Yaddo fellow; McDowell fellow.

WRITINGS:

Poker, Samizdat (Ljubljana, Slovenia), 1966.

Namen Pelerine (title means "The Intention of the Pelerine"), Samizdat (Ljubljana, Slovenia), 1968.

Romanje za Marusko (title means "Pilgrimage for Maruska"), Cankarjeva Zalozba, 1971.

Bela Itaka (title means "White Ithaca"), Drzavna Zalozba Slovenije (Ljubljana, Slovenia), 1972.

Amerika, Obzorja (Maribor) 1973.

Arena, Lipa (Koper), 1973.

Turbines: Twenty-one Poems, translated by Tomaz Salamun, Anselm Hollo, and Elliott Anderson, Windover Press University of Iowa (Iowa City, IA), 1973.

Snow, translated by Anselm Hollo, Bob Perelman, Michael Waltuch, and others, Toothpaste Press (West Branch, IA), 1973.

Sokol (title means "Falcon"), Mladinska Knjiga (Ljubljana, Slovenia), 1974.

Imre, Drzavna Zalozba Slovenije (Ljubljana, Slovenia), 1975.

Druidi (title means "Druids"), Lipa (Koper), 1975.

Praznik (title means "Holiday"), Cankarjeva Zalozba (Ljubljana, Slovenia), 1976.

Zvezde (title means "Stars"), Drzavna Zalozba Slovenije (Ljubljana, Slovenia), 1977.

Metoda Angela (title means "Angel's Method"), Mladinska Knjiga (Ljubljana, Slovenia), 1978.

Po Sledeh Divjadi (title means "On the Track Game"), Lipa (Koper), 1979.

Zgodovina Svetlobe je Oranzna (title means "The History of Sight Is Orange"), Obzorja (Maribor), 1979.

(With Svetlana Makarovic and Niko Grafenauer) *Pesmi* (title means "Poems"), Mladinska Knjiga (Ljubljana, Slovenia), 1979.

Maske (title means "Masks"), Mladinska Knjiga (Ljubljana, Slovenia), 1980.

Balada za Metko Krasovec, Drzavna Zalozba Slovenije (Ljubljana, Slovenia), 1981, translated as *A Ballad for Metka Krasovec,* Twisted Spoon Press, 2001.

Analogije Svetlobe (title means "Analogies of Light"), Cankarjeva Zalozba (Ljubljana, Slovenia), 1982.

Glas (title means "Voice"), Obzorja (Maribor), 1983.

Sonet o Mleku (title means "Sonnet on Milk"), Mladinska Knjiga (Ljubljana, Slovenia), 1984.

Soy Realidad (title means "I Am Reality"), Lipa (Kroper), 1985.

Ljubljanska Pomlad (title means "Ljubljana Spring"), Drzavna Zalozba Slovenije (Ljubljana, Slovenia), 1986.

Mera Casa, Cankarjeva Zalozba (Ljubljana, Slovenia), 1987.

Ziva Rana, Zivi Sok (title means "Living Wound, Living Sap"), Obzorja (Maribor), 1988.

The Selected Poems of Tomaz Salamun, edited and translated by Charles Simic and others, Ecco Press (New York, NY), 1988.

Otrok in Jelen (title means "Child and Stag"), Weiser (Salzburg, Germany), 1990.

Painted Desert: Poems, translated by Michael Biggins, Bob Perelman, and Salamun, edited by Richard Seehus, Poetry Miscellany (Chattanooga, TN), 1991.

The Shepherd, The Hunter, Pedernal (Santa Fe, NM), 1992.

Ambra, Mihelac (Ljubljana, Slovenia),1995.

The Four Questions of Melancholy: New and Selected Poems, edited by Christopher Merrill, White Pine Press (Fredonia, NY), 1997.

Crni labod (title means "Black Swan"), Mihelac (Ljubljana, Slovenia), 1997.

Knjiga za mojega brata (title means "The Book for My Brother"), Mladinska Knjiga (Ljubljana, Slovenia), 1997.

Morje, Nova Revija (Ljubljana, Slovenia), 1999.

Feast, translated by Joshua Beckman and others, edited by Charles Simic, Harcourt (New York, NY), 2000.

Also author of *Riva.* Contributor of poems and articles to periodicals, including *Grand Street, Paris Review, Antaeus, Agni, Ploughshares, Boulevard, Partisan Review, Trafika, Chelsea, New American Review, Third Coast, Harvard Review, New Republic, Mississippi Review, Chicago Review, Cimarron Review, Esprit,* and *Akzente.* Contributor of poems to anthologies, including *New Writing in Yugoslavia,* Penguin (New York, NY), 1971; *East European Poetry,* Ardis (Dana Point, CA), 1983; and *Child of Europe,* Penguin (New York, NY), 1991.

Also translator of works, including (with David Senar) *Dvajset let pzneje,* by Alexandré Dumas, Obzorja (Maribor), 1969; (with others) *Spisi, pisma, govori, 1920-1967,* by Ho Chi Minh, Cankarjeva Zalozba (Ljubljana, Slovenia), 1969; and *Mandarini,* by Simone de Beauvoir, Cankarjeva Zalozba (Ljubljana, Slovenia), 1971.

WORK IN PROGRESS: Writing poetry.

SIDELIGHTS: Considered Slovenia's greatest living poet, Tomaz Salamun attracted critical notice with his first collection, *Poker,* published when he was only twenty-five. Henry R. Cooper, Jr. wrote in *World Literature Today* that it was "a fundamental turning point in Slovene literature, the initiation of avant-garde writing." As Michael Biggins explained in *Dictionary of Literary Biography,* Salamun's poetry signaled an abrupt shift away from conventional Slovenian themes and styles, nothing less than a "Copernican revolution" that set "new boundaries, or antiboundaries, of what would follow [in Slovenian poetry] over the next three decades." Salamun's work, according to Biggins, "cut loose from meaning completely" and, at its best, is characterized by "rebelliousness, antic wit, willful opacity, and perfect timing."

After publishing two more collections of poems, Salamun left for the United States, where he had been invited to join the University of Iowa's International Writing Program. There he studied with Anselm Hollo, a Finnish American poet who later became one of Salamun's English translators. Critics pointed out that this exposure to American life and literature influenced Salamun's subsequent work. His fourth collection, *Amerika,* features longer narrative poems and what Biggins described as "a new, winningly naïve and amiably seductive dimension to the poetic self." According to Biggins, "Salamun's polyphonic voice reached maturation in the early 1970s."

The extent to which North America captured Salamun's interest can be seen in the abundant references in his work to Mexico and the United States. In *A Ballad for Metka Krasovec,* Salamun sets his poems in American cities, including New York and Minneapolis, as well as in Mexican towns. English is occasionally inserted in a word or line, and Salamun's themes include travel, sex, and aging. Cooper emphasized that Slovenia is "a touchstone for all his experiences," and that Salamun's family and extended family "are the source of much of the humor of the collection."

Cooper noted in the same review that the poems of *Analogije Svetlobe,* which Salamun wrote while in Paris and Crete, are "far less personal. . . . Only the next to last poem of the collection, 'Tell the People,' picks up (predicts?) the narrative mode."

Cooper pointed out in another *World Literature Today* review that in *Soy Realidad,* Salamun writes in his often-used mix of Slovene, English, Latin, and French and also includes a trio of poems in Spanish. Settings include the Sierra Nevada and Belize. "Metka Krasovec, his wife and editor, is mentioned often and longingly," wrote Cooper, who called *Soy Realidad* "an interesting but not startlingly new example of a maturing Salamun."

Again in *World Literature Today,* Cooper said that *Ljubljanska Pomlad,* is "full of strange images, bizarre juxtapositions of languages, nonsense rhymes, and engaging rhythms." Cooper declared that a native speaker could detect "subtle references," but he found the text "baffling," and called it "difficult reading."

Cooper reviewed *Ziva Rana, Zivi Sok,* noting that in Salamun's poems "love, with all its attendant delights and miseries, still seems to be alive," but that "its object . . . remains for me a mystery." Cooper said it was no longer the poet's wife, but a "thou" who is "male, inarticulate, and well traveled," and concluded that the author's work appears "to grow both more daring in theme and expression and more obscure in meaning."

Cooper compared another Salamun work, *Otrok in Jelen,* to the author's first work, *Poker,* commenting that in *Otrok in Jelen,* "poetic structure of a sort makes an appearance," and concluding that "all in all it would seem to be vintage Salamun: not very clear but fun to read."

Several major collections of Salamun's works have been translated into English. The first, *English Turbines: Twenty-one Poems,* was published in 1977. The second, *The Selected Poems of Tomaz Salamun,* published in 1988, was described by Ales Debeljak in *World Literature Today* as offering "a very good display of some of the author's most poignant and remarkable accomplishments. Salamun exposes lyric intimacy as well as existentialist angst with ironic wit and converts many unquestionable truths . . . into . . . his joyful . . . 'transvaluation of all values.'"

Library Journal reviewer Robert Hudzik called *Selected Poems* "an imaginatively daring, and liberating, book." According to Richard Jackson in the *Georgia Review,* "Salamun's is a remarkably expansive poetry, ready to take the world in with all its contradictions rather than risk missing any of it." Jackon referred to Salamun's work as "mythic." "Salamun understands the role of the body and the spirit in the poetics of Eastern Europe, and the elemental processes of imagination and art in liberating each," wrote Jonas Zdanys in the *Yale Review,* concluding, "this is a wonderful book."

The Four Questions of Melancholy: New and Selected Poems, published in 1997, is a collection of poems from twenty-five volumes published from 1964 to 1994. "The earliest work is primarily surreal and makes use of lullaby repetition, but the recognizable subject matter, drawn from everyday life in Central Europe, is common and recognizable," wrote a *Publishers Weekly* reviewer. A *New Yorker* reviewer concluded that the poems "affirm Salamun's status as a major Central European poet." Reviewing *The Four Questions of Melancholy* in the *Artful Dodge,* Andrew Zawacki noted that "Salamun's poetry is indeed of the world, and he has been informed by international poetry in the most comprehensive sense." Zawacki stated that the work "concludes with some of Salamun's most intense, poignant and understated poems to date." Matthew Zapruder in *Verse* wrote that "one of the first things that is obvious about *The Four Questions of Melancholy* is the brilliance of the early poems, which immediately introduce the boldness and strengths that have stayed with Salamun for his entire career."

In a *Chicago Review* article, Matthew Rohrer suggested that Salamun's focus on the surreal, which critics sometimes find difficult, is a way of tapping into our collective imagination. "If his poems seem obtuse or cut adrift from our planet's surface," Rohrer wrote, "this is because they are utterances of a different kind from what we might expect of contemporary poetry." Conventional notions of what is "real," the critic noted, do not engage Salamun; rather, "The real situation of Salamun's poetry is that things are said about the world that may or may not be true, but if that is your great concern, to know which of these is the case, then you have not understood the usefulness of his poetry."

Feast, a collection published in 2000 that editor Charles Simic culled from Salamun's entire oeuvre, includes sixty-five poems rendered into English by seven translators. A *Publishers Weekly* reviewer commented that the volume is "by turns brutal and coy, gnomic and blunt," and "insistently dismembers the world, only to slyly recreate and celebrate it." Daniel L. Guillory in *Library Journal* hailed it as a daring, "arresting and often outrageous collection" that will "transform" readers used to more conventional poetic fare.

In an interview with Jeffrey Young in *Trafika,* Salamun stated that "poetry is a parallel process to spiritual development. As in religion, you are trained how not to be scared. As in the cabala or in dervish dances, you are trained how to be with the world as long as you can endure it. Language takes you forward, and you endure as long as you can endure. But still, there is this constant fear of being too diabolic, that you will be punished for what you are doing, because when you write you compare with God."

BIOGRAPHICAL/CRITICAL SOURCES:

BOOKS

Chevalier, Tracy, editor, *Contemporary World Writers,* St. James Press (Detroit, MI), 1993.
Dictionary of Literary Biography: Volume 181: *South Slavic Writers since World War II,* Gale (Detroit, MI), 1997.
Pibernek, France, *Med modernizmom in avantgardo,* Slovenska matica (Ljubljana, Slovenia), 1981.

PERIODICALS

Artful Dodge, Number 32-33, 1998, pp. 138-149.
Chicago Review, summer 1998, p. 58.
Denver Quarterly, summer, 1990, pp. 110-120.
Georgia Review, winter, 1988, pp. 863-866.
Library Journal, August, 1988, p. 162; August 2000, p. 110.
Literatura, Number 9, 1990, pp. 47-65.
New Yorker, July 14, 1997, p. 80.
New York Press, November 12-19, 1997.
Poetry Miscellany, Number 20, 1988, pp. 7-9.
Publishers Weekly, April 28, 1997, p. 70; August 14, 2000, review of *Feast;* April 23, 2001, review of *A Ballad for Metka Krasovec,* p. 74.
Slovene Studies, Volume 7, number 1-2, 1985, pp. 13-22.
Trafika, Number 5, 1997, pp. 104-107.
Verse, fall, 1998, pp. 140-153.
World Literature Today, winter, 1983, pp. 136-137; summer, 1986, p. 492; autumn, 1987, p. 656; autumn, 1989, p. 710; winter, 1990, p. 156; winter, 1992, p. 166.
Yale Review, spring, 1990, pp. 477-478.*

*   *   *

SALEM, James M. 1937-

PERSONAL: Born November 15, 1937, in Portage, WI; son of Carleton A. and Blanche (Cross) Salem; married Donna McLernon, December 27, 1958; children: Timothy, Betsy, Jennifer, Jon. *Ethnicity:* "Caucasian." *Education:* Wisconsin State University—La Crosse (now University of Wisconsin—La Crosse), B.S., 1961; Kent State University, graduate study, 1961-62; Louisiana State University, Ph.D., 1965. *Politics:* Liberal. *Religion:* "Unorganized."

ADDRESSES: Home—50 Southmont Dr., Tuscaloosa, AL 35401. *Office*—Department of American Studies, University of Alabama, Tuscaloosa, AL 35487-0214; fax 205-348-9766. *E-mail*—jsalem@tenhoor.as.ua.edu.

CAREER: Kent State University, Kent, OH, assistant professor of English, 1965-67; University of Alabama, Tuscaloosa, assistant professor, 1967-68, associate professor of English, 1968-74, professor of American studies, 1974—, director of American Studies Program, 1968-84, department chair, 1984—. Producer of record albums, including (with John Fletcher) *Oakley Hill: Live from the Tomb,* American Pie (Tuscaloosa, AL), 1980. *Military service:* U.S. Army, active duty, 1956. U.S. Army Reserve, 1959-64.

MEMBER: International Association for the Study of Popular Music, American Studies Association, American Culture Association, Society for American Music, Southeastern American Studies Association.

AWARDS, HONORS: Citation for outstanding reference work, American Library Association, 1970, for *Drury's Guide to Best Plays,* 2nd edition; certificate of excellence for distinguished achievement in the communicating arts, Chicago '77 Vision Exhibition, 1977, for the article "Teenage Suicide: A Permanent Answer to a Temporary Problem."

WRITINGS:

A Guide to Critical Reviews, Scarecrow (Metuchen, NJ), Part I: *American Drama from O'Neill to Albee,* 1966, 2nd edition published as *American*

Drama, 1909-1982, 1973, Part II: *The Musical from Rodgers and Hart to Lerner and Loewe,* 1967, 3rd edition published as *The Musical, 1909-1989,* 1991, Part III: *British and Continental Drama from Ibsen to Pinter,* 1968, 2nd edition published as *Foreign Drama, 1909-1977,* 1979, Part IV: *The Screenplay from "The Jazz Singer" to "Dr. Strangelove,"* two volumes, 1971, Part IV: *The Screenplay, Supplement One, 1963-1980,* 1982.

Drury's Guide to Best Plays, Scarecrow (Metuchen, NJ), revised 2nd edition, 1969, 4th edition, 1987.

A New Generation of Essays, with instructor's manual, W. C. Brown (Dubuque, IA), 1972.

The Late Great Johnny Ace and the Transition from R&B to Rock 'n' Roll, University of Illinois Press (Urbana, IL), 1999.

Contributor to encyclopedias. Contributor to *American Music, Prospects: Annual of American Cultural Studies, Serif, Renascence, Shaw Review, Nutshell, Graduate,* and other periodicals. Songwriter, including coauthor of the songs "It's Gettin' Too Deep," "(I Ain't Ever Been to Texas) But I Sure Do Like to Swing," "Gerald," and "The Changes Are Coming So Fast," all Rocker Music (Nashville, TN), 1978; and "Angelina," "Alabama Honky Tonk," and "Alabama Outlaws," all American Pie Music (Tuscaloosa, AL), 1980.

SCRIPTS

Them Whirligig of Life (one-act play), Dramatic Publishing (Chicago, IL), 1968.

(With wife, Donna Salem) *April and the Fools* (one-act play), published in *Instructor,* 1969.

The Courtmartial of Billy Budd (one-act play), Dramatic Publishing (Chicago, IL), 1969.

The Love Life of Herbert Packenstacker (one-act play), Pioneer Drama Service (Cody, WY), 1969.

Beauty and the Beast (television play), Alabama Public Television, 1970.

The Prince Who Wouldn't Grow (television play), Alabama Public Television, 1970.

Beatlemania: A Catalyst for Change (television documentary), Alabama Public Television, 1984.

WORK IN PROGRESS: A book about the 1950s.

SIDELIGHTS: James M. Salem once told *CA* that he undertook *A Guide to Critical Reviews* because no reference book existed to help him locate reviews of American plays for his doctoral dissertation; he started the volume on American drama as soon as he received his Ph.D., and added that the "other parts grew out of that book's popularity."

Salem later commented: "In 1987 I was writing the 'middle' chapter of my book on the 1950s—a chapter about Johnny Ace, the rhythm and blues singer whose posthumous 'Pledging My Love' may be the first rock 'n' roll record—when I recovered the 'lost' official Harris County, Texas, inquest proceedings of Ace's death that had been stored in a Houston warehouse for decades. The chapter turned longer and longer, especially when I discovered that almost every written account of Ace's life and career was flawed and misinformed. In addition, over the years he had clearly been 'colonized' by white rock writers. Finally I abandoned the general book on the 1950s and concentrated on researching the life and career of Johnny Ace. Several journal articles and *The Late Great Johnny Ace and the Transition from R&B to Rock 'n' Roll* came out of that experience."

*　　*　　*

SASSOON, Rosemary 1931-

PERSONAL: Born February 19, 1931, in London, England; daughter of Frank Raphael and Olga (Wilenkin) Waley; married John Philip Sassoon (an educationist and writer), March 31, 1958; children: Caroline, Joanna Sassoon Whitten, Kathryn Sassoon Cameron. *Education:* Attended Tunbridge Wells Art School, 1946-48; studied under textile master scribe M. C. Oliver. *Religion:* Jewish.

ADDRESSES: Home—34 Witches Lane, Sevenoaks, Kent TN13 2AX, England. *E-mail*—sassoon@centrenet. co.uk.

CAREER: Lettering, packaging, and textile designer, 1948—; teacher of calligraphy, 1975—; researcher, lecturer, and consultant in handwriting problems, 1980—; type designer, 1985—.

MEMBER: Internationale, Graphonomics Association, Association Typographique Internationale, The Letter Exchange.

AWARDS, HONORS: Honorary doctorate in philosophy, University of Reading, 1988.

WRITINGS:

The Practical Guide to Calligraphy, Thames & Hudson (London, England), 1982.

The Practical Guide to Children's Handwriting, Thames & Hudson (London, England), 1983, new edition, 1995.

(With G. S. E. Briem) *Teach Yourself Handwriting,* Hodder & Stoughton (London, England), 1984, new edition published as *Teach Yourself Better Handwriting,* 1993.

The Practical Guide to Lettering, Thames & Hudson (London, England), 1985.

Helping Your Handwriting, with teacher's edition, Arnold-Wheaton/Nelson, 1986, new edition published as *Helping with Handwriting,* John Murray, 1994.

Handwriting: The Way to Teach It, Stanley Thornes (Cheltenham, England), 1990, new edition, Leopard Learning, 1995.

Handwriting: A New Perspective, Stanley Thornes (Cheltenham, England), 1990.

(With P. Lovett) *Creating Letterforms: Calligraphy and Lettering for Beginners,* Thames & Hudson (New York, NY), 1992.

Computers and Typography, Intellect, 1993.

The Art and Science of Handwriting, Intellect, 1993.

The Acquisition of a Second Writing System, Intellect, 1995.

(With A. Gaur) *Signs, Symbols, and Icons,* Intellect, 1997.

Handwriting of the Twentieth Century, Routledge (London, England), 1999.

Computers and Typography 2, Intellect, in press.

Contributor to periodicals, including *Times Educational Supplement.*

SIDELIGHTS: A lettering designer turned educator and author, Rosemary Sassoon told Helen Mason in a London *Times* interview that at one time she believed that "beautiful lettering was the most important thing." Yet when asked by an education official to create a remedial handwriting course she changed that emphasis; Sassoon was stunned by the extent of the difficulties experienced by children who lacked proper handwriting instruction. "Beauty in writing will emerge as a result of doing things properly," Sassoon amended.

Sassoon's *Practical Guide to Children's Handwriting* is a manual for teachers and parents on how to teach handwriting. Concentrating on a relaxed grip, flowing movement, correctly formed letters, and repetitive patterns that program the mind and hand, the Sassoon method also encourages a personal, creative hand once legibility and speed have been attained. "I don't expect everyone to agree with the book, but I hope it will make people think," Sassoon stated. Mason remarked, "It is difficult to imagine any teacher resisting the lucidity and joy of writing, the logic and flexibility of the manual she has produced."

Sassoon once told *CA:* "Being one of the last to enjoy a traditional training in lettering, I felt that there was an obligation to pass this on. A request to run remedial handwriting courses showed the need in this area and led to a shift in career emphasis—finally pointing to a research degree and a more scientific approach to this neglected subject."

Sassoon later added: "I have been involved in letterforms all my life. My early training and work was that of a scribe and a designer, before I turned to methods of teaching calligraphy. I became involved in handwriting problems in the late 1970s and have specialized in the educational and medical aspects of handwriting. I lecture and research worldwide on various aspects of handwriting as well as other letterform issues. My handwriting research interests include the causes and remediation of writer's cramp and the acquisition of a second writing system, as well as the detailed history of the teaching of handwriting during the past century.

"The other side of my work concerns type design in relation to children's reading. In the mid-1980s I discovered that there had been no proper research with children to discover their preferences in typefaces—what features of letters and what spacing best suited young children. This led to the design of 'Sassoon Primary,' a typeface originally aimed at educational publishers. With the advent of computers in schools, this became recognized as a benefit to education. It is increasingly installed in British school computers and is spreading around the world. To date there are over a dozen typefaces in the family for different educational purposes—for teaching handwriting as well as reading. My interests have extended to the design of educational software and research on how typographical design factors can influence the assimilation of knowledge from the screen. These views are reflected in several of my recent publications.

"Work in progress, in quite a different area, includes a book on different perspectives on strokes. Having myself suffered a stroke in 1998, I have become aware of the necessity to change many of the entrenched attitudes to this condition."

BIOGRAPHICAL/CRITICAL SOURCES:

PERIODICALS

Times (London), September 30, 1983, Helen Mason, interview with Rosemary Sassoon.

*   *   *

SAVAGE, Christina
  See NEWCOMB, Kerry

*   *   *

SAYLOR, Steven 1956-
  (Aaron Travis)

PERSONAL: Born March 23, 1956, in Port Lavaca, TX; son of Lyman Harrison Saylor and Lucy Lee (Reeves) Saylor; became registered domestic partner of Richard K. Solomon, March 15, 1991. *Education:* University of Texas at Austin, B.A., 1978. *Avocational interests:* Furniture making, bicycling, exploring the American West, the classical world.

ADDRESSES: Home—1711 Addison St., Berkeley, CA 94703. *Agent*—Alan Nevins, Renaissance Agency, 8523 Sunset Blvd., Los Angeles, CA 90069.

CAREER: Writer.

MEMBER: Mystery Writers of America.

AWARDS, HONORS: Robert L. Fish Memorial Award for best debut short story in the mystery genre, Mystery Writers of America, 1993, for "A Will Is a Way"; Lambda Literary award for gay men's mystery, 1994; Critics' Choice Award, 1995.

WRITINGS:

MYSTERY NOVELS; "ROMA SUB ROSA" SERIES

Roman Blood, St. Martin's (New York, NY), 1991.
Arms of Nemesis, St. Martin's (New York, NY), 1992.
Catilina's Riddle, St. Martin's (New York, NY), 1993.
The Venus Throw, St. Martin's (New York, NY), 1995.

A Murder on the Appian Way, St. Martin's (New York, NY), 1996.
The House of the Vestals (short stories), St. Martin's (New York, NY), 1997.
Rubicon, St. Martin's (New York, NY), 1998.
Last Seen in Massilia, St. Martin's (New York, NY), 2000.

UNDER PSEUDONYM AARON TRAVIS

Big Shots, Masquerade (New York, NY), 1993.
Beast of Burden, Masquerade (New York, NY), 1993.
Slaves of the Empire, Masquerade (New York, NY), 1996.

OTHER

A Twist at the End: A Novel of O. Henry, Simon and Schuster (New York, NY), 2000.

Also author, under the pseudonym Aaron Travis, of short stories anthologized in *Flesh and the Word,* edited by John Preston, for Dutton. Contributor, under his real name, to books, including *Hometowns,* 1991, *A Member of the Family,* and *Friends and Lovers,* all edited by Preston, for Dutton, and to *The Year's Best Mystery and Suspense Stories 1993,* edited by Edward Hoch, for Walker & Co. Contributor of short stories and essays to periodicals, including *Ellery Queen's Mystery Magazine, Threepenny Review, San Francisco Review of Books,* and *Frontiers.* Former fiction editor, *Drummer.*

Saylor's work has been translated into German, Spanish, and Dutch.

SIDELIGHTS: Steven Saylor once told *CA:* "In my twenties my muse was overwhelmingly erotic, and I wrote a great deal of fiction under the pen name Aaron Travis; stories under that pen name have been reprinted in John Preston's *Flesh and the Word* anthologies for Dutton, and almost all of the Aaron Travis oeuvre is currently being brought back into print as mass market paperbacks from Masquerade Books (New York). During the same period that I was producing stories as Aaron Travis in the 1980s, I also served for a couple of years as fiction editor of the decidedly subcultural magazine, *Drummer.*

"My first trip to Rome in the late 1980s reignited my collegiate interest in the classical world; at the same time my muse began to take a turn toward the genres of mystery and intrigue. The result was my first novel under my own name, *Roman Blood,* a historical whodunit set in the Roman Republic. It is narrated by an invented sleuth, Gordianus the Finder, and based on Roman orator and philosopher Marcus Tullius Cicero's first murder trial and the defense oration that made him famous. The next novel in the series, *Arms of Nemesis,* takes Gordianus to the Bay of Naples at the time of the Spartacus slave revolt. The third novel of the series, *Catilina's Riddle,* examines the famous conspiracy of Roman politician Lucius Sergius Catilina at the time of Cicero's consulship.

"Together these novels are part of my 'Roma Sub Rosa' series portraying the last decades of the Roman Republic before it became ruled by the Caesars. To draw exact parallels to our own time would be fatuous, but I will say that delving into the unremitting nastiness of Roman politics does provide an uneasy insight into the continuing and worsening plight of our own republic. Somehow, immersing myself in a milieu even more nakedly greedy and unscrupulous than our own gives me a curious comfort, and I sometimes think that writing *Roman Blood* was the only way I kept my sanity during the degrading spectacle of the George Bush-Michael Dukakis presidential campaign. The cruel absurdities of the Bush presidency provided more inspiration, specifically for *Catilina's Riddle,* which I hope will be my absolute last word on the subject of politics; exposing Cicero's chicanery and hypocrisy over the course of a 500-page novel was a grueling experience.

"The 'Roma Sub Rosa' series has become something of a family saga, with the books set several years apart and the characters growing older and experiencing various changes. To fill in the years between the novels, and to use specific historical material that lends itself to fiction, I also write short stories in the series, in which Gordianus solves minor mysteries and in which I can explore various byways of ancient Roman life. These stories have been published in *Ellery Queen's Mystery Magazine* and in the *Armchair Detective.* The first, 'A Will Is a Way,' won the 1993 Robert L. Fish Memorial Award given by the Mystery Writers of America for the best debut short story in the genre and was also selected for *The Year's Best Mystery and Suspense Stories 1993,* edited by Edward Hoch.

"In the last few years I have been writing a series of autobiographical essays for John Preston's anthology series for Dutton, including *Hometowns: Gay Men Talk about Where They Belong; A Member of the Family: Gay Men Write about Their Families;* and the forthcoming *Friends and Lovers.* Any reader who is really curious about intimate details about the author may consult these essays."

"Steven Saylor has so effectively created an alternative fictional universe in his *Roma Sub Rosa* series . . . that fans of his novels may be tempted to imagine that every day the author wakes, dons a toga, opens dense historical texts about ancient Rome in the original Latin, and plucks from them those little nuggets of believability . . . that he uses to transport readers to the scene of the crime," wrote Clay Smith in an *Austin Chronicle* feature on the popular mystery author. Hailed by a *Publishers Weekly* contributor as "one of today's finest historical mystery series," the seven novels and one story collection that comprise the series have drawn both rave reviews and an enthusiastic popular readership. To quote *St. James Guide to Crime and Mystery Writers* contributor Robin H. Smiley, each of Saylor's books "is firmly grounded in the classical sources of the late Roman Republic's chaotic history, a time that led to the fall of the republic and the beginnings of the Roman Empire. Saylor has an affinity not only for the politics of Rome, but for its social and cultural milieu. He is so much at home in Ancient Rome he seems to have lived there."

The seven novels form a chronological series that begins when protagonist Gordianus the Finder is thirty years old, and continues episodically through his adulthood until his children are grown and entering their own careers. The stories combine real historical detail with fictitious plot devices involving Gordianus and his wife and children. A central character in several of the books is the famed lawyer Cicero, who often engages Gordianus to do some sleuthing in reference to prominent court cases. Gordianus thus finds himself in the political hot seat to the point that his life is threatened. Sexual intrigue enters the series too, especially in *The Venus Throw,* which a *Publishers Weekly* reviewer described as "a talky, absorbing brew of Rome's decay."

In a *Publishers Weekly* piece on *A Murder on the Appian Way,* the critic noted that Gordianus "is put in the delicate position of having to solve a crime and keep his own counsel amid the scheming and duplicitous rulers of Rome." Helped by his "unusual and morally sturdy character," Gordianus mingles with such historic notables as Pompey, Caesar, and Mark Antony without ever losing his integrity or focus. The *Publishers Weekly* reviewer concluded that *A Murder on the Appian Way* is "a sophisticated political thriller that also brings [Saylor's] readers up to speed on their Roman history."

Times Literary Supplement reviewer Mary Beard also appreciated Saylor's historical perspective, noting that *A Murder on the Appian Way* "offers a devastating expose of Cicero himself" and "is a good instance of the novelist doing the historian's dirty work." Though Beard felt that Saylor's insistence on accuracy sometimes adds a tedious quality to his novels, she enjoyed his "compelling" plots and his "striking talent for historical reconstruction."

New York Times Book Review correspondent David Dawson commented that Saylor's "skill and wry confidence" contribute to the authenticity of his Roman settings. Saylor's work, the critic concluded, "represents the best of two genres: a faithful and breezy historical novel and a compulsively entertaining whodunit." Smiley observed: "The details of Gordianus's personal life add a great deal to *Roma Sub Rosa*. With each book, there are changes and growth in the character; there is also a strong sense of the passage of time. This continuity gives the series a resonance and a growing richness, but it also poses a potential problem. Shortly, Gordianus will be simply too old to withstand the physical demands of his profession. Nevertheless, these . . . novels are so fine that, taken by themselves, they place Saylor in the forefront of the American historical mystery novelists of his generation."

Though *The House of the Vestals* is a volume in the "Roma Sub Rosa" series, it is not a novel but a collection of short stories, each based on a historical mystery. Critic Alan Massie observed in the *Times Literary Supplement* that the short form poses problems for mystery writers because it doesn't allow "sufficient complication, too often inviting an ending that is neat and contrived rather than convincing." Saylor doesn't entirely avoid this difficulty, Massie wrote, but "although the stories collected in *The House of the Vestals* are less satisfying than [his] full-length novels, they are agreeable, entertaining tales which provide glimpses of a slice of life that is both authentic and . . . unusual."

Last Seen in Massilia, based on the 49 B.C.E. siege of Massilia (now Marseilles) during the civil war between Pompey and Julius Caesar, finds Gordianus trapped in the plague-ridden city, which he had secretly entered to get information about the fate of his son, Meto. There, Gordianus witnesses a death that may have been a murder. As he investigates, he unearths various treacheries, and battles for his own survival. This is "one of the best" in the "Roma Sub Rosa" series, exclaimed Connie Fletcher in *Booklist.* "Saylor presents a vivid tableau of an ancient city under siege and an empire riven by internecine strife," wrote a *Publishers Weekly* contributor.

Saylor risked another departure from his successful Roman mysteries with *A Twist at the End,* a historical mystery featuring the writer O. Henry as its protagonist. Based loosely on a series of unsolved axe murders in 1880s Austin, Texas, the novel reveals some unsavory details about O. Henry while also providing, according to a *Publishers Weekly* contributor, "a hard look at racial bigotry and politico-economic deceit." The reviewer, hailing the book as both "cracking good historical entertainment" and an "effective morality play," predicted that it could be Saylor's "breakout" novel. *Texas Monthly* contributor Anne Dingus, however, expressed a different view, finding the novel unconvincing and "uninspired." Though Liam Callanan in the *New York Times Book Review* also leveled some criticism at the novel, suggesting that the story is almost overwhelmed with detail and that the protagonist "is the story's least convincing aspect," the critic found the book ultimately "fascinating and provocative."

BIOGRAPHICAL/CRITICAL SOURCES:

BOOKS

St. James Guide to Crime and Mystery Writers, fourth edition, St. James (Detroit, MI), 1996.

PERIODICALS

Booklist, April 15, 1999, p. 1484; September 1, 2000, Connie Fletcher, review of *A Twist at the End,* p. 7.
Library Journal, April 15, 1999, p. 146.
New York Times Book Review, October 18, 1992; July 30, 2000.
Publishers Weekly, September 6, 1993, p. 86; February 27, 1995, p. 89; April 8, 1996, pp. 58-59; April 28, 1997, p. 53; April 12, 1999, p. 57; March 27, 2000, p. 54; August 14, 2000, p. 332.
Texas Monthly, April 2000, Anne Dingus, review of *A Twist at the End,* p. 30.
Times Literary Supplement, May 8, 1998, p. 23; September 10, 1999, p. 33; December 10, 1999, p. 22.

OTHER

Austin Chronicle, http://www.auschron.com/issues/vol18/issue44/ (November 3, 2000), Clay Smith, "Author Literatus."*

SCHMIDT, Warren H(arry) 1920-

PERSONAL: Born November 10, 1920, in Detroit, MI; son of Henry W. (in business) and Lillian (Kath) Schmidt; married Amanda Regelean, September 25, 1945; children: Jacqueline Ann, Barbara Jean, Nancy Marie, Ronald Henry. *Education:* Wayne University (now Wayne State University), B.A., 1942; Concordia Theological Seminary, B.D., 1945; Washington University, St. Louis, MO, Ph.D., 1950. *Politics:* Democrat.

ADDRESSES: Home—9238 Petit Ave., North Hills, CA 91343-3530.

CAREER: Ordained Lutheran minister, 1945; pastor in Glendale, MO, 1945-47; Washington University, St. Louis, MO, instructor in psychology, 1948-49; University of Missouri, Columbia, instructor in psychology, 1949-50; Union College, Schenectady, NY, assistant professor of psychology, 1950-51; Springfield College, Springfield, MA, assistant professor of psychology, 1951-53; Adult Education Association of the U.S.A., Washington, DC, project coordinator, 1953-55; University of California, Los Angeles, lecturer in psychology, 1955-59, lecturer, 1965-68, senior lecturer in behavioral sciences, 1969-77, professor emeritus, 1976—, director of statewide conferences and community services, 1959-61, director of M.B.A. program, 1965-68, assistant dean for executive education, 1969-73; University of Southern California, Los Angeles, professor of public administration, 1976-91, professor emeritus, 1991—. Leadership Resources, Inc., Washington, DC, senior vice president, 1960-68; Chrysalis, Inc. (management training and consulting company), president, c. 2000. Consultant to airlines, National Council of Churches, and other organizations, business firms, government agencies, and film production companies.

MEMBER: International Association of Applied Social Scientists, American Psychological Association, Academy of Management, Western Academy of Management, California Psychological Association, Sigma Xi, Beta Gamma Sigma.

AWARDS, HONORS: Academy Award for best animated short subject, Academy of Motion Picture Arts and Sciences, 1970, for film script, *Is It Always Right to Be Right?*

WRITINGS:

Techniques That Produce Teamwork, Croft Educational, 1954.
Looking into Leadership, Leadership Resources (Washington, DC), 1962.

Organizational Frontiers and Human Values, Wadsworth (Belmont, CA), 1970.
Is It Always Right to Be Right? (adapted from film script of same title), Wadsworth (Belmont, CA), 1970, published as *Is It Always Right to Be Right? A Tale of Transforming Workplace Conflict into Creativity and Collaboration,* AMACOM (New York, NY), 2001.
(With Barry Z. Posner) *Managerial Values and Expectations: The Silent Personal and Organizational Life,* American Management Associations (New York, NY), c. 1982.
(With Barry Z. Posner) *Managerial Values in Perspective,* American Management Associations (New York, NY), c. 1983.
(With Jerome P. Finnigan) *The Race without a Finish Line: America's Quest for Quality,* Jossey-Bass (San Francisco, CA), c. 1992.
(With Jerome P. Finnigan) *TQManager: A Practical Guide for Managing in a Total Quality Organization,* Jossey-Bass (San Francisco, CA), 1993.
(With B. J. Hateley) *A Peacock in the Land of Penguins: A Tale of Diversity and Discovery,* illustrated by Sam Weiss, foreword by Ken Blanchard, Berrett-Koehler (San Francisco, CA), 1995.
(With Hateley) *Pigeonholed in the Land of Penguins: A Tale of Seeing beyond Stereotypes,* American Management Associations (New York, NY), 2000.

Contributor to adult education, business, and management journals.

ANIMATED FILM SCRIPTS

Freedom River, Stephen Bosustow Productions, 1971.
The Hand-off, Salenger Educational Media, 1979.
Creative Problem Solving, CRM, 1979.

Also associated with the animated film *Is It Always Right to Be Right?*

WORK IN PROGRESS: Caretakers of Culture, a series of television documentaries about World Heritage sites.

SIDELIGHTS: In addition to being the author of several books and scripts on managerial practices and the president of a management training and consulting company, Warren H. Schmidt is also an ordained minister and has worked as a college educator since the late 1940s. He has drawn notice from critics for both conventional analytical business studies and for illustrated parable-style advice for managers.

Schmidt wrote *The Race without a Finish Line: America's Quest for Quality* with Jerome P. Finnigan. The book looks at current American management practices known as Total Quality Management (TQM). Using twelve case studies, the authors compare its application by companies that have won the Malcolm Baldrige National Quality Award with its use by selected government agencies. The book includes sections titled "Planning for Change" and "Laying the Foundation through Leadership Commitment," and lays out five key strategies for implementing TQM practices.

In a review for *Business Horizons,* G. Ronald Gilbert described *The Race without a Finish Line* as a valuable text for readers with a background in management theory, including educators. The critic also judged the book to be better suited to the needs of large organizations than to smaller businesses. He praised the book's introduction to the TQM concept as being "written in common language and easy to grasp" and admired the fact that "coverage is both broad in scope and incisive in real-world recommendations concerning implementation." Gilbert further described the book as "an excellent explanation of TQM," with the reservation that it did not address cases where TQM had failed to keep businesses from financial difficulties, naming IBM and Florida Power and Light as examples.

Two of Schmidt's books that use a very different approach to guiding business managers are *A Peacock in the Land of Penguins: A Tale of Diversity and Discovery* and *Pigeonholed in the Land of Penguins.* These illustrated corporate parables, written with B. J. Hateley, share a humorous approach to describing the ways that businesses can unwittingly limit their potential and that of their employees. The authors wrote *A Peacock in the Land of Penguins* to show how a corporate culture that rewards conformity can stifle communication. The experiences of Perry the Peacock, one of a number of non-penguin birds who live in the Land of Penguins, reveal the difficulty of being different from others. The story is largely based on the work experiences of author Hateley at a Fortune 500 company. This book has been translated into more than a dozen languages.

In *Pigeonholed in the Land of Penguins* the authors return to the same fictional territory to explore the plight of Paula Pigeon. The dominant penguins are unable to understand the strange contents of a box that has been discovered. It is the under-appreciated Paula who provides a creative way to solve the puzzle—that the parts will make a helicopter and give the birds a vehicle for exploring "The Sea of Organizations." Thus the authors show how stereotyping individuals by background, gender, race, or other status can hurt an organization. Following the story is a section that includes twenty tips on avoiding stereotyping and questionnaires for managers to determine if they are in fact "pigeonholing" people by appearance or occupation. A *Publishers Weekly* reviewer enjoyed the book's illustrations but suggested that "those looking to make major changes in management style should look elsewhere." The book was recommended to readers who had valued earlier books, seminars, and videotapes using the "Land of Penguins" theme.

BIOGRAPHICAL/CRITICAL SOURCES:

PERIODICALS

Business Horizons, September-October, 1993, G. Ronald Gilbert, review of *The Race without a Finish Line: America's Quest for Quality,* p. 89.
Publishers Weekly, March 20, 2000, review of *Pigeonholed in the Land of Penguins,* p. 80.

*   *   *

SEIDEL, Frederick (Lewis) 1936-

PERSONAL: Born February 19, 1936, in St. Louis, MO; son of Jerome Jay (a business executive) and Thelma (Cartun) Seidel; married Phyllis Munro Ferguson, June 7, 1960 (divorced, 1969); children: Felicity, Samuel. *Education:* Harvard University, A.B., 1957.

ADDRESSES: Home—251 West 92nd St., New York, NY 10028.

CAREER: Poet, c. 1963—. Occasional lecturer, Rutgers University, 1964—.

AWARDS, HONORS: Lamont Poetry Prize, Academy of American Poets, 1980, for *Sunrise;* book award for poetry, National Book Critics Circle, 1981, for *Sunrise;* poetry prize, *American Poetry Review,* for *Sunrise;* Guggenheim Foundation fellow, 1993; *Going Fast* was a finalist for the 1999 Pulitzer Prize in poetry.

WRITINGS:

POEMS

Final Solutions, Random House (New York, NY), 1963.

Sunrise: Poems, Viking (New York, NY), 1979.

Men and Woman: New and Selected Poems, Chatto & Windus (London, England), 1984.

Poems, 1959-1979, Knopf (New York, NY), 1989.

These Days: New Poems, Knopf (New York, NY), 1989.

My Tokyo: Poems, Farrar, Straus (New York, NY), 1993.

Going Fast: Poems, Farrar, Straus (New York, NY), 1998.

The Cosmos Poems, pictures by Anselm Kiefer, Farrar, Straus (New York, NY), 2000.

Life on Earth, Farrar, Straus (New York, NY), 2001.

Paris Review, Paris editor, 1960-61, advisory editor, 1962—; author of screenplay for the film *Afraid of the Dark.*

SIDELIGHTS: Rarely has a poet's first book created as much controversy as Frederick Seidel's *Final Solutions.* As William Jay Smith noted in *Harper's,* "Mr. Seidel's first collection has already caused quite a stir, largely because it was banned even before publication, a distinction that few poets achieve." The book was awarded a literary prize, but the prize was withdrawn when the poems were judged to be libelous. Seidel, according to Smith, "attempts the grotesque on a grand scale . . . and at times he succeeds. . . . [But] the failure of much of Mr. Seidel's book for me lies . . . in the lack of . . . adequate images, in a too heavy reliance on Robert Lowell's meters, and a theatricality that . . . does not ultimately ring true."

Several reviewers have commented on the similarity of Seidel's poetry to Robert Lowell's, especially in regards to style and meter. "In Frederick Seidel's case," James Dickey wrote in the *New York Times Book Review,* "his relationship to the poetry of Robert Lowell amounts not so much to influence as to slavery. The diction is the same as Lowell's, as are the historical references, and the inflated, hortatory style." In a review of *Final Solutions,* Dickey concluded: "Imitation and shock tactics are no substitute for personal creativity. . . . Mr. Seidel's talents are by no means imposing." In a review of the same collection for *Book World,* Charles Berger found that "Seidel seems to have been testing the premises and the ordinary language of poetry. . . . The result is an extremely savvy book of poems, reminiscent

of Lowell as social prophet, but without the latter's deep moral affiliations." And Denis Donoghue, reviewing *Sunrise* for the *New York Review of Books,* believed Seidel is "loyal to his first book, as well he may be. Even then he had a gift of style, though in some poems it seemed mostly a gift of Robert Lowell's style. . . . A remarkably gifted and serious poet, [Seidel] gives me the impression, in some poems, of having lost or given up his confidence in the official forms seriousness has been supposed to take. . . . Despite that, *Sunrise* is an even stronger book than *Final Solutions.* Seidel's voice is now securely his own. . . . 'The Soul Mate' is the most beautiful poem in the book, a love poem as touching as anything I have read in years."

Despite the influence of Lowell, Seidel speaks with a unique voice. His poetry is intense and pessimistic, born of a "sensibility made raw by experience, uneasy by history," William Logan wrote in *Library Journal.* Reviewing *Sunrise,* Logan commented, "Beyond the small tragedies of personal life he finds the mocking disasters of the great, from Vietnam to our assassinated presidents, and with an ear for the flux of literature and politics he exploits their varied mythologies." In a review of *Final Solutions* for the *New Yorker,* Louise Bogan stated: "Seidel is angry, and his anger, ultimately, is directed less against evils apparent in this or that person or society than against the basic stupidities and depravities of mankind itself. . . . The terrifying aspects of the experiences he describes are outlined with clinical precision. . . . Whether or not Seidel's talent will come into the full power it now suggests it is impossible to predict. But how extraordinary if it should." Stephen Stepanchev, in a *New York Herald Tribune Books* article on *Final Solutions,* felt that in Seidel's poetry "the world seems a place of predicaments of cruelty and madness. . . . But the structure of the poems is relatively weak and tends to disintegrate in the 'meaninglessness' that is at the center of the poet's vision." And Jerome Mazzaro said of Seidel in a review of *Sunrise* for the *Hudson Review:* "Writers know the power of words, and . . . Seidel is not beyond painting a desert to get his effects. Readers have only to turn to '1968,' 'Men and Women,' 'Wanting to Live in Harlem,' and the title poem to recognize the importance of Seidel's concerns and talent and be reassured that, although not now venturous enough, Seidel has the power to be an important visionary."

Seidel's *Sunrise* was accorded some impressive literary honors, including the 1981 National Book Critics Circle award for poetry. He continued to publish just a few volumes every decade, continuing with *Men and Woman: New and Selected Poems* from 1984. In 1989, two collections came forth: *Poems, 1959-1979,* an assemblage of previously published work, and *These Days.* Don Stap reviewed the latter, which contained new work, for the *New York Times Book Review* and found it consistent with Seidel's poetic style of previous works, featuring "social prophecy and private anguish in highly literate, formal, often enigmatic poems." In *These Days,* the poet uses modern history for inspiration, touching upon such events as the death of the Shah of Iran from cancer or the Russian civil war of the 1920s. Stap termed some of the later poems in the volume unsuccessful, however. He described them as delivered by a voice "suffocating in a private malaise . . . [that] can only record confusion and distress." The final poems, noted the critic, "have no weight, no center, nothing to hold onto."

Seidel published another collection, *My Tokyo,* in 1993, and ended the decade with *Going Fast,* which appeared in 1998. In the latter, the poems are nostalgic, and their creator pines for the Manhattan of the 1950s, lyricizing vintage objects like steakhouses and damask. Again, famous names crop up, among them assassinated Israeli leader Yitzhak Rabin, and recent events, like France's controversial decision to begin nuclear testing in the South Pacific in the mid-1990s. He imagines space, and an astronaut out on a walk whose tether is cut when his companions must suddenly abort their mission. "To a great extent, 'Going Fast' is concerned with endings and mourning for a less technocratic world," noted *New York Times* critic Melanie Rehak, and commented elsewhere that Seidel's Gotham "becomes 'an onion-domed metropolis' on a winter night, the city evoking church towers and snow globes at once—a miniature of preserved perfection and devotion." Rehak found some poems in *Going Fast* less successful in conveying the poet's trademark cynical ire; at other moments he rhapsodized about shoes made by hand in Paris and a vintage Italian motorcycle. "But when he aims well, Seidel is nervy and dark," Rehak wrote. David Wojahn reviewed it for *Poetry,* and stated: "In the best poems of *Going Fast* Seidel has created a sort of anxious elegy for this century which evokes the cinematic visions of [Italian director Bernardo] Bertolucci and the early [French New Wave films from Jean-Luc] Godard." Wojahn contended that "Seidel has over the years grown increasingly mordant, dyspeptic, and misanthropic, even as his accomplishment has deepened," and declared him "among the finest poets at work today."

Seidel's place in contemporary American poetry was honored by an invitation from the American Museum of Natural History to contribute verse for a limited edition volume to commemorate the opening of its new planetarium in 2000. *The Cosmos Poems,* at a cost of $100, also included full-color lithographs by German artist Anselm Kiefer complementing thirty-three of Seidel's new poems. All are paeans to the universe, science, and the wonder of nature. A *Kirkus Reviews* writer singled out poems like "Supersymmetry" and others "that express childish delight and awe at the marvelous workings of the universe."

In 2001, Seidel published *Life on Earth,* the second in a planned trilogy that began with *The Cosmos Poems.* In the thirty-three poems contained in the book, Seidel spans history and touches on subjects from Joan of Arc, to the Nazis, to Hollywood, and to spaceships. In *Library Journal,* Fred Muratori wrote, "He populates his tersely metered . . . images taken from Geography, history, pop culture and, most importantly, the body itself." In *Booklist,* Donna Seaman felt that Seidel's poems reach, "Into the realms of whales, spaceships, and, the greatest mystery of them all, the human heart."

BIOGRAPHICAL/CRITICAL SOURCES:

BOOKS

Contemporary Literary Criticism, Volume 18, Gale (Detroit, MI), 1981.

PERIODICALS

Book World, July 6, 1980.
Booklist, April, 1998, Donna Seaman, review of *Going Fast,* p. 1295; March 15, 2001, Donna Seaman, review of *Life on Earth.*
Harper's, September, 1963.
Hudson Review, autumn, 1980.
Kirkus Reviews, February 15, 2000, review of *The Cosmos Poems,* p. 209.
Library Journal, March 1, 1980; March 1, 1998, Rochelle Ratner, review of *Going Fast,* p. 92: February 15, 2001, Fred Muratori, review of *Life on Earth.*
Lingua Franca, May, 2000, "Unsung Poets."
New Criterion, June, 1998, William Logan, "Soiled Desires," p. 61.
New York Herald Tribune Books, August 11, 1963.
New York Review of Books, August 14, 1980, Denis Donoghue, review of *Sunrise.*
New York Times, July 19, 1998, Melanie Rehak, "Our City of Light."

New York Times Book Review, September 1, 1963, James Dickey, review of *Final Solutions;* September 21, 1980; October 14, 1990, Don Stap, "Screams beneath the Snow," p. 20.

New Yorker, October 12, 1963.

Poetry, July, 1999, David Wojahn, review of *Going Fast,* p. 219.

Publishers Weekly, February 23, 1998, review of *Going Fast,* p. 68; January 10, 2000, review of *The Cosmos Poems,* p. 60.*

*   *   *

SHAPIRO, Alan 1952-

PERSONAL: Born February 18, 1952, in Boston, MA; son of Harold (a salesman) and Marilyn (a secretary; maiden name, Katz) Shapiro; married Della Pollock (a professor), September 7, 1984. *Education:* Brandeis University, B.A., 1974.

ADDRESSES: Office—Department of English, Greenlaw Hall, CB #3520, University of North Carolina, Chapel Hill, NC 27599-3520.

CAREER: Stanford University, Stanford, CA, Stegner fellow in poetry, 1975, lecturer in creative writing, 1976-79; Northwestern University, Evanston, IL, lecturer, 1979-85, associate professor of English, beginning 1985; University of North Carolina, Chapel Hill, currently professor of English and creative writing.

AWARDS, HONORS: Fellow of National Endowment for the Arts, 1984; Guggenheim fellow, 1986; received nomination for National Book Critics Circle award, 1987, for *Happy Hour;* Lila Wallace/*Reader's Digest* Award, 1991; *Los Angeles Times* award for poetry, 1996, for *Mixed Company;* received nomination for National Book Critics Circle award, 1996, for *The Last Happy Occasion;* recipient of a writing fellowship from the Open Society Institute of New York.

WRITINGS:

POETRY

After the Digging, Elpenor Books, 1981, with a new afterword, University of Chicago Press (Chicago, IL), 1998.

The Courtesy, University of Chicago Press (Chicago, IL), 1983.

Happy Hour, University of Chicago Press (Chicago, IL), 1987.

Covenant, University of Chicago Press (Chicago, IL), 1991.

Mixed Company, University of Chicago Press (Chicago, IL), 1996.

The Dead Alive and Busy, University of Chicago Press (Chicago, IL), 2000.

Song and Dance, Houghton Mifflin, 2002.

OTHER

In Praise of the Impure: Poetry and the Ethical Imagination: Essays, 1980-1991, Triquarterly Books (Evanston, IL), 1993.

The Last Happy Occasion (memoir), University of Chicago Press (Chicago, IL), 1996.

Vigil (memoir), University of Chicago Press (Chicago, IL), 1997.

Shapiro's poems have been published in the *Christian Science Monitor.*

SIDELIGHTS: Alan Shapiro told *CA:* "When I was writing the poems in my first two books, *After the Digging* and *The Courtesy,* most American poetry was committed to free verse lyric of some kind, and most poets and critics of poetry assumed that formal verse was old-fashioned and mechanical, incapable of responding to the urgencies of the contemporary world. Poets as different as Allen Ginsberg, Robert Duncan, Galway Kinnell, and Adrienne Rich claimed that only free verse and its improvised rhythms could render faithfully the contours of immediate experience, and that the business of the poet was not to traffic in ideas or statements but to present and juxtapose images and feelings with as much concreteness and intensity as possible. There was, moreover, almost exclusive attention to the poem as self-expression, and to form as the transparent medium of personality. Although my first two books differ greatly in style and subject, they share the ambition to go against the grain of many of these assumptions and tendencies and to attempt to win back some of the territory given up to prose.

"*After the Digging* comprises two suites of historical narratives, one devoted to the potato famine in Ireland in the mid-nineteenth century, and the other to the seventeenth-century American Puritans. My intention was to enter into lives foreign to my own as imaginatively and accurately as I could, so as to better understand the historical and cultural circumstances out of which arose the Irish famine on the one hand, and the Salem witch trials on the other.

"*The Courtesy* deals with more contemporary experience: the problems of familial and religious continuities in a secular and mobile culture, and the tensions between desire and circumstance in the context of love. Most of these poems are in rhyme and meter, yet the style is plain and idiomatic. Although *The Courtesy* is primarily a book of lyric poems concerned with personal experience, I am less interested in autobiography or confessional self-exposure than in distilling from personal experience some sort of understanding that can clarify, if not resolve, emotional and psychological complexity.

"In a way . . . *Happy Hour,* attempts to combine the best qualities of *After the Digging* and *The Courtesy*. All these poems are grounded in contemporary life, yet most of them are narrative, not lyrics, and are therefore only indirectly personal. I am still working in a plain style but there is greater attention to circumstance and detail, not quite so much exposition, and there is also a wider range of forms—a variety of free verse lines as well as some traditional measures. The concerns of *Happy Hour* are similar to those of *The Courtesy,* but in the best poems they are treated more inclusively, more dramatically.

"It is difficult to say exactly where my new work is going. One proceeds intuitively, from line to line, and poem to poem, and it is only in retrospect that one can see how the work developed. What I hope is that the poems I am writing now continue to cultivate the same inclusive tendency begun in *Happy Hour.* I want to write poems that can speak to individual experience without restricting themselves to private mood and feeling, the staples of the lyric mode.

"During the late 1970s and early 1980s I began to write essays and reviews on contemporary poetry, and since then criticism has become a vital aspect of my intellectual and artistic life. The criticism, however, is very much a poet's, not a scholar's. It is highly polemical, preoccupied with principles of judgment and evaluation, and eager to challenge the assumptions many poets of my generation have uncritically accepted, assumptions that I believe have a limiting effect on the practice and understanding of the art. Perhaps a less

fancy way of putting this would be to say that like all poet-critics, I write criticism to create an audience for the poetry I am struggling to write and the poetry by others I admire. I want to stress, too, that the criticism follows from the poetry, not the other way around. My conception of what poetry is or can be changes as my own work develops and evolves. Thus, just as I find it difficult to forecast the poems I may go on to write, so also I find it difficult to say what direction my criticism will take in the future."

The critical essays of which Shapiro spoke were collected for a 1993 volume, *In Praise of the Impure: Poetry and the Ethical Imagination: Essays, 1980-1991*. He then wrote two acclaimed volumes of memoirs. *The Last Happy Occasion* was nominated for a 1996 National Book Critics Circle award and recounts incidents in his life—skipping synagogue services in order attend an automobile show, the Woodstock music festival, a girlfriend and their contentious relationship, the birth of his son—and anchors each with a poem from another writer, among them Philip Larkin, Thom Gunn, and Elizabeth Bishop. "Shapiro uses poetry and its 'transformative power' as the basis for his fascinating perceptions about a relatively ordinary life," remarked a *Publishers Weekly* writer, who designated it a book of unusual interest and merit. *New York Times Book Review* critic Emily Barton also commended Shapiro's effort, calling it "touching and intelligent, emotionally satisfying and eloquent testimony to the power of poetry to instruct, heal and inspire."

A tragic family loss incited Shapiro to pen his second volume of memoir, 1997's *Vigil*. It recounts the period of time he spent at the bedside of his sister, Beth, at a hospice in Texas, before her death of breast cancer at the age of forty-nine. Shapiro's chapters chronicle more than her final moments, however: Beth was a radical who been a founding member of the famous Students for a Democratic Society (SDS) in the 1960s. She married an African-American man, and there were some years of strife in the family that only her illness would heal. *Progressive* writer Anne-Marie Cusac called *Vigil* "an elegiac book—celebratory and grieving. Shapiro lets us see his passionate sister and her rich life. . . . And, with Shapiro and the other family members who make their awkward, tender amends, we watch Beth die." Steven Harvey, who reviewed it for *Brightleaf,* also praised Shapiro's effort. "At times the book is lyrical, especially passages about the ugliness of dying," he observed. "There is the description of the last time Beth walked—it is to go to the bathroom. In the struggle to do so on her own, she summons her last reserves of modesty and dignity." Harvey praised the literary gift that Shapiro brought to such a wrenching topic. "The poet is in control, too, when, near the end of the ordeal, Shapiro has a surreal vision of his sister's soul escaping from her body. He imagines her as a Rockette with a Cheshire cat smile." A *Publishers Weekly* reviewer also commended his talents: "Once again, Shapiro's perfect pitch lacks sentimentality but brims with the truest of emotions and observations."

Shapiro has continued to publish other volumes of poetry after *Happy Hour,* which a 1987 *New York Times Book Review* from J.D. McClatchy extolled for its new direction. "Shapiro has cultivated a new generosity of detail and insight," noted McClatchy, and found some of the longer works "more like versified short stories than poems, but their skill and force are moving." Volumes following this include *Covenant,* published in 1991, and *Mixed Company,* which appeared in 1996. In *The Dead Alive and Busy,* published in 2000, the death of his sister continues to preoccupy Shapiro and his work. The aging of his parents also shapes some of the verse, such as "The Bath," about helping his father. "His poetry is a theater of disease; it makes illness hold stage center and demands an unflinching audience," noted a *Kirkus Reviews* contributor of this volume. Classical and biblical themes concerning insurmountable tasks or misery—particularly the figures of Sisyphus and Job—crop up throughout the volume. Its title refers to Shapiro's conviction that the dead continue to be a presence for the living. *New York Times* writer Michael Hainey likened Shapiro to a medium whose poetry traverses both worlds, the dead and the undead, "and, in the process, gives those of us on this side of the great divide a new way of seeing. His unblinking gaze yields unforgettable images."

In 2002, Shapiro published *Song and Dance,* a volume of poems centered around the tragic loss of his brother, David, to brain cancer. This occurred only three years after his sister's death from breast cancer. The poems celebrate his brother's life, as well as the emotions surrounding his sickness during his last painful months.

Shapiro, who left Northwestern University to accept a professorship at the University of North Carolina, has read his work at the White House as a guest of the Clintons and Poet Laureate of the Library of Congress, Robert Pinsky. On that occasion, he delivered "On Men Weeping," about Michael Jordan and one of his National Basketball Association championships.

BIOGRAPHICAL/CRITICAL SOURCES:

PERIODICALS

Booklist, September 1, 1997, review of *Vigil,* p. 42.
Brightleaf: A Southern Review of Books, January-February, 1998, Steven Harvey, review of *Vigil.*
Kirkus Reviews, February 15, 2000, review of *The Dead Alive and Busy,* p. 210.
Library Journal, October 1, 1996, review of *The Last Happy Occasion,* p. 77; August, 1997, Joshua Cohen, review of *Vigil,* p. 89; February 1, 2000, Rochelle Ratner, review of *The Dead Alive and Busy,* p. 90.
New York Times, April 9, 2000, Michael Hainey, review of *The Dead Alive and Busy.*
New York Times Book Review, July 26, 1987, J.D. McClatchy, "Catching the World," p. 9; October 27, 1996, Emily Barton, review of *The Last Happy Occasion.*
Progressive, December, 1998, Anne-Marie Cusac, review of *Vigil,* p. 42.
Publishers Weekly, August 26, 1996, review of *The Last Happy Occasion,* p. 82; September 15, 1997, review of *Vigil,* p. 58.*

*   *   *

SHIELDS, David 1956-

PERSONAL: Born July 22, 1956, in Los Angeles, CA; son of Milton (a journalist) and Hannah (a journalist; maiden name, Bloom) Shields. *Education:* Brown University, B.A., 1978; University of Iowa, M.F.A. (with honors), 1980.

ADDRESSES: Home—1902 North 46th St., Seattle, WA 98103. *Office*—English Department, University of Washington, Seattle, WA 98195. *E-mail*—dshields@u.washington.edu.

CAREER: University of Iowa, Iowa City, research assistant, 1978-79, teaching assistant in literature, 1979-80, instructor in creative writing and literature, 1980; researcher and writer for former California governor, Pat Brown, 1984; visiting lecturer in creative writing at University of California, Los Angeles, 1985; St. Lawrence University, Canton, NY, visiting assistant professor, 1985-86, 1987-88; University of Washington,

David Shields

Seattle, assistant professor, 1988-92, associate professor, 1992-97, professor of English, 1997—, director of creative writing program, 1999-2000. Faculty member, Warren Wilson College, Asheville, NC, 1996—. Guest instructor, Bread Loaf Writers' Conference, 2001, Bay Area Writers Conference, 1992, Napa Valley Writers Conference, 1994 and 1995, Third Coast Writers Conference, 1996, Heartland of America Writers Conference, 1996, Iowa Writers' Workshop, 1996 and 1999, and University of Idaho, 2000. Juror for numerous fiction competitions, 1989-94, including Drue Heinz Award, University of Pittsburgh Press, 1992, and Barnard College undergraduate fiction writing competition, 1993. Has appeared on television and radio, including National Public Radio (NPR) and C-Span.

MEMBER: International PEN, Authors Guild, Writers Guild of America, Modern Language Association of America, Poets and Writers, Associated Writing Programs, Phi Beta Kappa.

AWARDS, HONORS: James Michener fellowship, Iowa Writers' Workshop, 1980-82; James D. Phelan Award Literary Award, San Francisco Foundation, 1981; National Endowment for the Arts fellowship in fiction, 1982 and 1991; Residency fellowships at Corporation of Yaddo, MacDowell Colony, Virginia Center for the Creative Arts, Ragdale Foundation, Millay Colony, Cummington Community of the Arts, Centrum, 1982-91; Authors League Fund grant, 1983; PEN Writers Fund grant, 1983, 1986, and 1987; Ingram-Merrill Foundation award, 1983; Carnegie Fund for Authors grant, 1984 and 1987; Change Inc. grant, 1985; winner of PEN Syndicated Fiction Project Competition, 1985 and 1988; Faculty Research grant, St. Lawrence University, 1986 and 1988; Ludwig Vogelstein Foundation grant, 1986; William Sloane Fellowship in Prose, Bread Loaf Writers' Conference, 1986; Pushcart Prize nomination, 1987, 1988, 1989, 1992, and 1993; New York Foundation for the Arts fellowship, 1988; Graduate School Research Fund grant, University of Washington, 1989; "Audrey" chosen one of "Ten Best" stories, PEN Syndicated Fiction Project, 1989; Silver Medal, Commonwealth Club of California Book Awards, 1989, and Washington State Governor's Writers Award, 1990, both for *Dead Languages;* Artist Trust Fellowship for Literature, 1991; PEN/Revson Foundation fellowship, 1992; King County Arts Commission Independent Artist New Works award, 1992; Seattle Arts Commission fellowship, 1992; Distinguished Author's Award, Brandeis University National Women's Committee (Seattle chapter), 1993; Graduate School Research Fund grant, University of Washington, 1994; Royal Research Fund fellowship, University of Washington, 1997; Artist Trust GAP grant, 1997; first prize, *Web Del Sol* creative nonfiction contest, 1999; finalist, PEN West Award in creative nonfiction, and finalist, National Book Critics Circle Award in criticism, both 2000.

WRITINGS:

Heroes (novel), Simon & Schuster (New York, NY), 1984.

Dead Languages (novel), Knopf (New York, NY), 1989, reprinted, Graywolf Press (Minneapolis, MN), 1998.

(Contributor) *Vital Lines: Contemporary Fiction about Medicine,* St. Martin's Press (New York, NY), 1990.

A Handbook for Drowning (stories), Knopf (New York, NY), 1992.

(Contributor) *Listening to Ourselves: More Stories from "The Sound of Writing," As Heard on National Public Radio,* Anchor (New York, NY), 1994.

(Contributor) *Infant Tongues: The Voice of the Child in Literature,* Wayne State University Press (Detroit, MI), 1994.

Remote, Knopf (New York, NY), 1996.

(Contributor) *Listen with Your Heart,* Friends Publications, 1998.

Black Planet: Facing Race during an NBA Season, Crown (New York, NY), 1999.

(Contributor) *In Brief: Short Takes on the Personal,* Norton (New York, NY), 1999.

(Contributor) *The Workshop: Seven Decades of the Iowa Writers' Workshop,* Hyperion (New York, NY), 1999.

(Contributor) *Taking Sport Seriously: Social Issues in Canadian Sport,* Thompson Educational, 2000.

Contributor of articles and stories to numerous periodicals, including *Harper's, Village Voice, Utne Reader, Threepenny Review, Story, Witness, New York Times Magazine, Details,* and *Conjunctions; Dead Languages* has been translated to Dutch.

SIDELIGHTS: A professor of English at the University of Washington, David Shields has earned a growing reputation as a keen observer of life in a media-saturated society. Shields's fiction is informed by his personal experiences, especially his childhood stuttering. His nonfiction explores contemporary American alienation, racism, and worship of celebrity. In the *New York Review of Books,* Robert Towers called Shields "an enviably talented writer, a stylist with a strong metaphoric gift and the ability to stage scenes of almost excruciating intensity." A *Publishers Weekly* reviewer said Shields was a "gifted writer capable of surprising perceptions and considerable wit."

The son of two left-wing journalists, Shields grew up in California and was educated at Brown University and the prestigious Iowa Writers' Workshop, from which he graduated with honors. Throughout his childhood and youth he struggled with stuttering, finally overcoming the difficulty when he reached his mid-twenties. This painful aspect of his formative years has become a frequent theme in his writing. As Michiko Kakutani put it in the *New York Times,* stuttering for Shields becomes "a kind of metaphor for the difficulties of communication and the limitations of language itself." Shields himself told the *Seattle Post-Intelligencer:* "What makes me a stutterer is what also makes me a writer—I have a violent relationship to language."

In his first novel, *Heroes,* Shields writes about "those two great American preoccupations, Lost Innocence and Sports," according to James Marcus in the *Philadelphia Inquirer.* The story dramatizes the mid-life crisis and ultimate self-realization of a fictitious Midwestern sportswriter named Al Biederman. A former college basketball star whose career is prematurely ended by an injury sustained on the court, Biederman turns to journalism when he can no longer participate physically in the game. While reporting on basketball for a small-town newspaper in Iowa, he discovers a talented college athlete who reminds the middle-aged Biederman of his now-diminished athletic prowess. Clinging to a romanticized vision of the past, Biederman sees the young transfer student, Belvyn Menkus, as the epitome of everything the unsuccessful sportswriter once hoped to become. Ironically, however, Menkus is entangled in some illegal recruiting practices. The admiring Biederman is torn between exposing the wrongdoing—possibly thereby gaining a more prestigious post on a big city paper—and turning away, thus sacrificing personal attainment for the good of the game. Complicating Biederman's decision-making are several other conflicts, such as resentment for his wife's success, intolerance for his son's frail health, and an affair with an enamored journalism student.

Heroes garnered favorable reviews from a number of critics. Marcus deemed the book a celebration of "the subtler brand of heroism." It "makes a particular virtue of showing how . . . ideals run aground, but nonetheless survive intact," he added. A critic for the *Chicago Tribune* called Shields "a keen observer of humanity," and in a later Chicago *Tribune Books* review of *Heroes,* Clarence Petersen stated that the questions Shields raises "are important and eternal and have almost nothing to do with any game." Diana L. Smith, writing in the *Fort Worth Star Telegram,* opined that Shields "has an engaging way of incorporating important events . . . with a pleasant mix of hilarity and pathos." Noting that the clarity of the characters and scenes is "excellent," she concluded that *Heroes* "is a thoroughly enjoyable book."

Shields' acclaimed second novel, *Dead Languages,* concerns young Jeremy Zorn, a stutterer who lives with his domineering mother and manic-depressive father, and his efforts to overcome his disability. Eva Hoffman, writing in the *New York Times,* observed that much of the novel "consists of inventive, often lyrical reflections on how language can become a diversion from communication rather than a means to it." *Boston Review* contributor Pagan Kennedy noted: "*Dead Languages* is a novel-long stutter, hemming and hesitating, titillating with its titubation. The language of the book is not just decoration, it is part of the plot."

Evelyn Toynton in the *New York Times Book Review* found *Dead Languages* intelligent and humorous. "Mr. Shields's own language is wonderfully fluent—colloquial and elegiac by turns," Toynton stated, "—and when his sense of the ridiculous comes to the fore, as it does in deadpan descriptions of Jeremy's stint as a teacher's aide in a summer school program for black children and his romance with a cheerful illiterate druggy, his character's dilemma seems both touching and wryly comic." In the *Los Angeles Daily News,* Danielle Roter admitted that Jeremy "may be a prickly and morbidly self-absorbed character, but he is rooted in truth. And that makes him irresistible." Matthew Gilbert of the *Boston Globe* stated: "As he narrates his history, with a wry good humor that belies his constant pain, Jeremy transforms his lifelong antagonism with language into a universal plight: the failure to be understood."

Needless to say, some reviewers were interested to know how closely *Dead Languages* corresponded to Shields's own life. The author told the *Seattle Weekly* that the work was a "huge exaggeration" of his experiences. He added, however: "My passion for the subject is legitimate. That's not to say that good writing should be confessional or weepy of self-absorbed . . . but it seems to me the great work comes from writers willing to pin themselves to the page." In her *New York Times* review of the novel, Eva Hoffman declared that stuttering "becomes an analogue for all the collected vulnerability, loneliness and anguish of childhood and adolescence." Hoffman added: "Mr. Shields is a talented writer, and in 'Dead Languages' he explores fertile themes with intelligence and verbal energy. One has confidence that a wider vision will follow."

A Handbook for Drowning, Shields's first story collection, is a work of inter-linked pieces focusing on Walter Jaffe, a young man struggling to come to terms with his family neuroses as well as the complexities of his own life. Like Jeremy Zorn in *Dead Languages,* Walter grows up under the shadow of a strong, activist mother and an ineffectual father who obsesses about the Ethel and Julius Rosenberg trial. In the *New York Times,* Michiko Kakutani noticed the similarities between the books, stating: "Mr. Shields works a variation on the material in *Dead Languages,* stripping away the more symbolic aspects of the story to focus on the coming of age of a young man. . . . Mr. Shields again demonstrates his ability to conjure up the past using lyrical, rhythmic language to relate ordinary domestic events. He possesses a gift for taking a seemingly mundane moment . . . and investing it with layers of psychological resonance."

Commenting on *A Handbook for Drowning*'s unorthodox narrative style, Robert Taylor wrote in the *Boston Globe:* "A structure of connecting through nonchrono-

logical stories dispenses with the yoke of time. It also abolishes the drudgery of detailed exposition and character development in a conventional cause-and-effect manner; instead, juxtaposition provides contrast and sudden flashes of insight reveal an extensive landscape of feeling." In *Newsday,* Dan Cryer noted that Shields "has the latitude not to flesh out a character's background or fill in plot lines or aim toward an identifiable climax. The short-story format permits, even luxuriates in, a pointillist mysteriousness regarding all these elements." Cryer later commented: "Even if some of the stories by themselves are rather slight, their cumulative effect is powerful." "*A Handbook for Drowning* is sometimes excessively sensitive," remarked Rhoda Koenig in her *New York* review, "but it does chronicle painfully, accurately the endemic disease of our time: the difficulty of feeling."

It was with *Remote* in 1996 that Shields began to earn a reputation for social commentary. Presented as a series of fifty-two short pieces, the book finds Shields musing on popular culture, from talk show hosts to bumper stickers, as well as on his own adolescent and mid-life angst. *Philadelphia Inquirer* correspondent Steven Rea felt that, in *Remote,* Shields "assembles a self-portrait shaped as much by the world around him as anything dredged up from personal history. . . . In *Remote,* in chapters where the poet Wallace Stevens and the porn star Seka are cited in virtually the same breath, Shields holds a mirror to society and sees himself. He holds a mirror to himself and sees society. And it is always a fun-house mirror—warped by irony and goofy insight." In the *Houston Chronicle,* Brad Tyer likewise found *Remote* "a fractured self-portrait of the artist as some guy who wishes, almost guiltily, but always with a certain detached bemusement, that he were more famous than he is."

Washington Post contributor Carolyn See deemed *Remote* a "series of postmodern moments." She praised the work as "very funny, and it tells us more than we want to know about the American life." Describing the book as "a species of search in which the seeker, a product of a media society, discovers truths about his own particular identity," *Boston Globe* reviewer Robert Taylor added that it "approaches contemporary autobiography in an engagingly non-alienated manner, and its wit is welcome." In *Gentlemen's Quarterly (GQ),* Thomas Mallon wrote, "Make no mistake: Shields is on to something that's happening in the world. . . . In its odd, creepy way, Shields's book forces one to feel the insidious power of that desire to be connected to what everyone else is doing. He forces thought about the absurd little kinks in one's own responses to mass entertainment." *Newsday* contributor A. O. Scott felt that *Remote* "should, in retrospect, be seen as one of the definitive texts of the 1990s."

Shields's social observations continue in *Black Planet: Facing Race during an NBA Season.* When he did not receive full journalist's credentials to report upon the Seattle Sonics' 1994-95 basketball season, Shields chose to write about basketball from a fan's perspective. What emerges in the book is a rumination about the relationship between professional basketball's white, middle class observers and its black superstars. According to Robert Lipsyte in the *New York Times,* "instead of another piece of reportage, made bitter or ingratiating by how the reporter was treated, we get serious reflection." Shields assesses the acrimony between players and coaches, the sometimes erotic envy of aging white men for the superbly conditioned black athletes, and the manner in which professional basketball serves as a counterpoint to American society at large, because in basketball the black men wield all the power. As A.O. Scott saw it in his review of *Black Planet* in *Newsday,* Shields "approaches his beat not as a reporter but as a literary critic poring over texts and contexts in search of hidden connections and guiding metaphors."

The critical response to *Black Planet* was once again favorable. Scott declared that Shields "has produced one of the best books ever written on the subject of sport in America, which is to say a book that is about a great deal more than sport." In the online magazine *Salon,* Sallie Tisdale commented: "There is doubling here, tripling and more—layers of identity not only defined by race, gender, class and physical skill but between the lines of the book. These are the layers between all the lines writers write and readers read. They are the layers, disguises and ghosts that form the territory of literature itself." *Booklist* correspondent Dennis Dodge perhaps put it most succinctly when he characterized *Black Planet* as "a provocative and thought-provoking treatment of a central issue in American society."

BIOGRAPHICAL/CRITICAL SOURCES:

PERIODICALS

Bloomsbury Review, June, 1992.

Booklist, September 15, 1997, Molly McQuade, "Rewriting Clichés with David Shields," p. 198; September 1, 1999, Dennis Dodge, review of *Black Planet: Facing Race during an NBA Season,* p. 63.

Boston Globe, May 24, 1989, Matthew Gilbert, "The Bittersweet Story of a Young Stutterer"; January 22, 1992, Robert Taylor, "Shields' Fresh Stories of an American Coming of Age"; March 14, 1996, Robert Taylor, "An Autobiography in 52 Tasty Sound Bites."

Boston Review, August, 1989.

Chicago Tribune, January 20, 1985; January 28, 1985; May 1, 1989; December 26, 1991, Joseph Coates, "Seven Years Later, a First Novel."

Cleveland Plain Dealer, July 30, 1989; January 12, 1992.

Fort Worth Star-Telegram, December 16, 1984.

Gentlemen's Quarterly (GQ), March, 1996, Thomas Mallon, "Distant Replay," pp. 109-110.

Houston Chronicle, August 20, 1989; July 21, 1996, Brad Tyer, "'Remote' Pursues Cult of Celebrity with Detached Bemusement."

Iowa City Press-Citizen, April 3, 1985; November 14, 1988.

Kirkus Reviews, December 15, 1995, review of *Remote,* p. 1756.

Lake Effect, fall, 1989.

Los Angeles Daily News, August 20, 1989.

Los Angeles Times, May 26, 1989.

Los Angeles Times Book Review, June 25, 1989.

Newsday, April 22, 1990; January 20, 1992; November 7, 1999, A.O. Scott, "Hoop Daydreams."

New York, January 13, 1992, p. 62.

New Yorker, July 3, 1989.

New York Review of Books, July 20, 1989, Robert Towers, "The Raw and the Cooked," p. 30.

New York Times, April 26, 1989, Eva Hoffman, "Long Shadow of Mother's Tongue"; December 27, 1991, Michiko Kakutani, "Tales of a Man Young and Old, Snapshots of a Life"; February 16, 1996, Michiko Kakutani, "Surfing along to Keep Life Distant"; June 6, 1999, Robert Lipsyte, "The Real Knicks Team, and the One That We Fantasize About," p. SP13.

New York Times Book Review, February 3, 1985; April 26, 1989; June 18, 1989; July 9, 1982; April 15, 1990; January 19, 1992.

Philadelphia Inquirer, December 8, 1984; February 25, 1996, Steven Rea, "Portrait of a Writer Shaped by His Times and by Pop Culture," p. D5.

Pittsburgh Press, July 23, 1989.

Publishers Weekly, November 27, 1991, review of *A Handbook for Drowning;* February 5, 1996, review of *Remote,* p. 75.

Review of Contemporary Fiction, spring, 1992.

San Francisco Chronicle, June 11, 1989.

San Francisco Review of Books, March-April, 1995, pp. 17-19.

San Mateo Times, August 22, 1984.

Santa Monica Evening Outlook, May 7, 1985.

Seattle Post-Intelligencer, January 14, 1992, John Marshall, "Stutter Pushed David Shields toward Writing."

Seattle Times/Seattle Post-Intelligencer, May 14, 1989; December 31, 1989.

Seattle Weekly, November 1, 1989, Bruce Barcott, "Breaking the Sound Barrier: David Shields Talks about the Lost Language of Pains."

Tribune Books (Chicago), November 27, 1988, p. 7.

Washington Post, February 23, 1996, Carolyn See, "Snippets on the Folly of Fame."

Writing, October, 1989.

OTHER

David Shields Web site, http://www.davidshields.com (July 16, 2001).

Salon, http://www.salon.com/ (December 7, 1999), Sallie Tisdale, "Blackballed: A White Sports Fan Wrestles with Basketball's Racial Taboos."

*   *   *

SHIELDS, John M(ackie) 1954-

PERSONAL: Born October 9, 1954, in Windsor, Ontario, Canada; son of John Mackie (a steelworker and foreman) and Jessie Florence (a homemaker; maiden name, Cote) Shields; married Hawley Lynn Neuert (a teacher), June 19, 1976; children: Raya Naomi. *Education:* University of Windsor, B.A. (with honors), 1978, M.A., 1980; University of British Columbia, Ph.D., 1989. *Politics:* "Democratic Socialist." *Religion:* "Nil." *Avocational interests:* Music, running.

ADDRESSES: Home—27 Mapleview Ave., Toronto, Ontario, Canada M6S 38A. *Office*—Department of Politics, Ryerson Polytechnic University, 350 Victoria St., Toronto, Ontario, Canada M5B 2K3; fax 416-979-5289. *E-mail*—jshields@acs.ryerson.ca.

CAREER: University of Windsor, Windsor, Ontario, Canada, research officer for Canadian National Election Study, 1981; University of British Columbia, Vancouver, labor archival researcher, 1982; University of Saskatchewan, Saskatoon, lecturer in politics, 1985-87; Ryerson Polytechnic University, Toronto, Ontario, Canada, professor of politics, 1988—, research professor, 1994. Simon Fraser University, member of Centre for Governance Studies; member of Canadian Centre for Policy Alternatives and Joint Centre of Excellence for Research on Immigration and Settlement; Ontario Ministry of Labour, policy advisor, 1993-94; labor research consultant.

MEMBER: Canadian Political Science Association, Society for Socialist Studies, Ryerson Faculty Association (member of executive committee, 1992-93 and 1996-98).

AWARDS, HONORS: Teaching Award from Continuing Education Students Association of Ryerson Polytechnic University, 1990-91.

WRITINGS:

(Editor, with Stephen McBride and Larry Haiven, and contributor) *Regulating Labour: The State, Neo-Conservatism, and Industrial Relations,* Garamond Press (Toronto, Ontario, Canada), 1991.

(With McBride) *Dismantling a Nation: Canada and the New World Order,* Fernwood Publishing (Halifax, Nova Scotia, Canada), 1993, 2nd edition published as *Dismantling a Nation: The Transition to Corporate Rule in Canada,* 1997.

(With B. Mitchell Evans) *Shrinking the State: Globalization and the "Reform" of Public Administration,* Fernwood Publishing (Halifax, Nova Scotia, Canada), 1998.

(Editor, with Mike Burke and Colin Mooers, and contributor) *Restructuring and Resistance: Canadian Public Policy in an Age of Global Capitalism,* Fernwood Publishing (Halifax, Nova Scotia, Canada), 2000.

Understanding the Canadian Nonprofit Sector: Civil Society, Social Capital, and the Challenge of Neoliberalism, Fernwood Publishing (Halifax, Nova Scotia, Canada), 2001.

Contributor to books, including *Power and Resistance: Thinking Critically about Canadian Social Issues,* edited by Les Samuelson, Fernwood Publishing (Halifax, Nova Scotia, Canada), 1994; *Health, Illness, and Health Care in Canada,* edited by B. Singh Bolaria and Harley D. Dickinson, Harcourt (Toronto, Ontario, Canada), 1994; *Continuities and Discontinuities: The Political Economy of Social Welfare and Labour Market Policy in Canada,* University of Toronto Press (Toronto, Ontario, Canada), 1994; *The Training Trap: Ideology, Training, and the Labour Market,* Garamond Press

(Toronto, Ontario, Canada), 1996; and *Power in a Global Era,* Macmillan (London, England), 2000. Contributor to academic journals.

WORK IN PROGRESS: Research on "the assault on the social security state by forces on the political right."

* * *

SHUSTERMAN, Neal 1962-

PERSONAL: Born November 12, 1962, in New York, NY; son of Milton and Charlotte (Altman) Shusterman; married Elaine Jones (a teacher and photographer), January 31, 1987; children: Brendan, Jarrod, Joelle, Erin. *Education:* University of California, Irvine, B.A. (psychology and drama), 1985. *Politics:* "No." *Religion:* "Yes."

ADDRESSES: Home—7 Columbine, Dove Canyon, CA 92679. *Office*—P.O. Box 18516, Irvine, CA 92623-8516. *E-mail*—Nstoryman@aol.com.

CAREER: Screenwriter, playwright, and novelist.

MEMBER: PEN, Society of Children's Book Writers and Illustrators, Writers Guild of America (West).

AWARDS, HONORS: Children's Choice Award, International Reading Association, 1988, and Volunteer State Book Award, Tennessee Library Association, 1990, both for *The Shadow Club;* American Library Association (ALA) Best Book, 1992, Children's Choice Award, International Reading Association, 1992, Outstanding Fiction for Young Adults Award, 1992, Young Adult Choice Award, International Reading Association, 1993, and Oklahoma Sequoyah Award, 1994, all for *What Daddy Did;* C.I.N.E. Golden Eagle Awards, 1992 and 1994, for writing and directing educational films *Heart on a Chain* and *What about the Sisters?;* New York Public Library Best Book for the Teen Age list, 1992, and California Young Reader Medal nomination, 1995-96, both for *Speeding Bullet;* Best Books for Reluctant Readers, ALA, 1993, for *The Eyes of Kid Midas;* ALA Best Book for Young Adults and Quick Pick list nominations, 1996, and New York Public Library Best Book for the Teen Age list, 1997, for *Scorpion Shards;* Best Books for Reluctant Readers, ALA, 1997, for *MindQuakes: Stories to Shatter Your Brain;* ALA Quick Pick Top Ten List and Best Book for Young Adults, both 1998, Outstanding Book of the Year, Southern California Council

on Literature for Children and Young People, 1999, and state award lists in California, New York, Maine, South Carolina, Oklahoma, Texas, Utah, Indiana, Illinois, and Nebraska, 2000, all for *The Dark Side of Nowhere; Downsiders* was a Texas Lone Star Award Book, 2000-01.

WRITINGS:

FOR YOUNG ADULTS

It's Okay to Say No to Cigarettes and Alcohol (nonfiction), TOR Books, 1988.

The Shadow Club (novel), Little, Brown, 1988.

Dissidents (novel), Little, Brown, 1989.

(With Cherie Currie) *Neon Angel: The Cherie Currie Story,* Price, Stern, 1989.

Speeding Bullet (novel), Little, Brown, 1990.

What Daddy Did (novel), Little, Brown, 1990.

Kid Heroes: True Stories of Rescuers, Survivors, and Achievers, TOR Books, 1991.

The Eyes of Kid Midas (fantasy), Little, Brown, 1992.

Darkness Creeping: Tales to Trouble Your Sleep (horror), illustrated by Michael Coy, Lowell House, 1993.

Piggyback Ninja (fiction), illustrated by Joe Boddy, Lowell House, 1994.

Scorpion Shards (fiction), Forge, 1995.

Darkness Creeping II: More Tales to Trouble Your Sleep (horror), Lowell House, 1995.

The Dark Side of Nowhere (novel), Little, Brown, 1996.

MindQuakes: Stories to Shatter Your Brain, TOR Books, 1996.

MindStorms: Stories to Blow Your Mind, TOR Books, 1996.

MindTwisters: Stories to Play with Your Head, TOR Books, 1997.

The Thief of Souls (fiction; sequel to *Scorpion Shards*), TOR Books, 1999.

Downsiders (fiction), Simon & Schuster, 1999.

MindBenders: Stories to Warp Your Brain, TOR Books, 2000.

Also author of novel *Shattered Sky,* St. Martin's Press, as well as of television adaptations, including *Night of the Living Dummy III* and *The Werewolf of Fever Swamp* for R. L. Stine's "Goosebumps" series; staffwriter for *Animorphs* television series; author of educational films for the Learning Corporation of America, including *Heart on a Chain* and *What about the Sisters?* Creator of "How to Host a Mystery" and "How to Host a Murder" games.

SIDELIGHTS: "Writers are a lot like vampires," noted author Neal Shusterman on his Web site. "A vampire will never come into your house, unless invited—and once you invite one in, he'll grab you by the throat, and won't let go. A writer is much the same." Shusterman, an award-winning author of books for young adults, screenplays, stage plays, music, and games, works in genres ranging from biographies and realistic fiction to fantastic mysteries, science fiction, and thrillers. Following the publication of *Dissidents,* Shusterman's third book, *Bulletin of the Center for Children's Books* critic Roger Sutton called the author "a strong storyteller and a significant new voice in YA fiction." Lyle Blake, writing in *School Library Journal,* found *The Eyes of Kid Midas* to be "inspired and hypnotically readable." In his many books for young readers Shusterman acts the part of benevolent vampire, "feeding on your turmoil, as well as feeding on your peace," as he put it on his Web site.

It was this power of books to not only entertain and inform but to totally captivate that Shusterman himself experienced as a young reader. "Books played an important part in my life when I was growing up," Shusterman noted. "I always loved reading. I remember there was this trick I would play for my friends. They'd blindfold me, then shove a book under my nose, and I could tell them the name of the publisher by the smell of the paper and ink." At age ten, Shusterman, who was born and raised in Brooklyn, went off to summer camp. One particular book, *Jonathan Livingston Seagull* by Richard Bach, which he discovered in the rafters of one of the cabins, swept him away in time and place, as did Roald Dahl's *Charlie and the Chocolate Factory* not long after. "I remember wishing that I could create something as imaginative as *Charlie and the Chocolate Factory,* and as meaningful as *Jonathan Livingston Seagull,*" Shusterman said. Writing his own stories came soon thereafter; inspired by the movie *Jaws,* he wrote the scenario of a similarly beleaguered small town, substituting giant sand worms for the shark.

Shusterman moved with his family to Mexico City, where he finished high school, and then went on to the University of California, Irvine, where he earned degrees in drama and psychology and set out to write his own novels. Returning to the same summer camp he had attended as a boy—now as a counselor—he tried out his stories on youthful ears and left another copy of *Jonathan Livingston Seagull* in the rafters for some other imaginative youth to discover. At age twenty-two he became the youngest syndicated columnist in the country when his humor column was picked up by Syndicated Writer's Group.

Shusterman first gained larger recognition for his first novel *The Shadow Club,* published in 1988. It tells the story of seven junior high school friends who grow tired of living in the shadows of their rivals. Each one is second-best at something, and they form a secret club in order to get back at the students who are number one. At first they restrict their activities to harmless practical jokes like putting a snake in an actress's thermos or filling a trumpet player's horn with green slime. Before long, however, their pranks become more destructive and violent. The mystery involves whether the members of the club have unleashed "a power that feeds on a previously hidden cruel or evil side of their personalities," as David Gale wrote in *School Library Journal,* or whether another student has been responsible for the more dangerous actions. In *Voice of Youth Advocates,* Lesa M. Holstine predicted that the book would be popular with young adults, since it would likely resemble their own experience with "rivalries and constantly changing friendships."

Dissidents, Shusterman's next novel, tells the story of Derek, a rebellious fifteen-year-old who is shipped off to Moscow to live with his disinterested mother, who is the U.S. ambassador to Russia, after his father dies in a car accident. Derek misses his father, hates all the restrictions of his new life, has trouble making friends at school, and acts out his frustrations in wild behavior. He soon becomes fascinated with Anna, the daughter of an exiled Soviet dissident, after he sees her in a television interview. Anna's mother is dying, and Derek comes up with a scheme to reunite her with her father. Although a *Publishers Weekly* contributor found Shusterman's portrayal of U.S.-Soviet relations "simplistic," the reviewer went on to praise the book as "a briskly paced, intriguing" adventure. Kristiana Gregory, writing in the *Los Angeles Times Book Review,* called the novel "an excellent glimpse of life on the other side of the globe."

Horn Book reviewer Ellen Fader called 1990's *Speeding Bullet* a "gritty, fast-paced, and, at times, funny novel." Nick is an angst-ridden tenth grader who does poorly in school and has no luck with girls. His life changes dramatically one day when, without thinking, he puts himself in danger to rescue a little girl who is about to be hit by a subway train. He becomes a hero and is thanked personally by the mayor of New York City. Nick then decides to make saving people his mission in life, and before long he also rescues an old man from a burning building. His newfound celebrity status gets the attention of Linda, the beautiful but deceitful daughter of a wealthy developer, and the two begin dating. Nick continues rescuing people, but he soon discovers that Linda has set up the situations and paid actors to portray people in distress. His next real rescue attempt results in Nick being shot, but he recovers and ends up with a better outlook on life. In *School Library Journal*, Lucinda Snyder Whitehurst called Shusterman's book "a complex, multilayered novel" that would provide young adults with "much material for contemplation," while a writer for *Publishers Weekly* found it to be "a fast-paced modern parable with compelling characters and true-to-life dialogue." Shusterman followed this fictional story with a 1991 book about real heroes called *Kid Heroes: True Stories of Rescuers, Survivors, and Achievers.*

Shusterman's next novel, *What Daddy Did,* is based on a true story. It is presented as the diary of fourteen-year-old Preston, whose father killed his mother during a heated argument. It details Preston's complex emotions as he deals with the tragedy, learns to live without his parents, and then struggles with his father's release from prison. Preston finally comes to forgive his father, and even serves as best man when his father remarries. Dorothy M. Broderick, writing in *Voice of Youth Advocates,* called *What Daddy Did* "a compelling, spellbinding story of a family gone wrong," adding that it might inspire young adults to "actually stop and think about their own relationship with their parents." Though Gerry Larson commented in *School Library Journal* that "too many issues are not sufficiently resolved" in the book, Rita M. Fontinha wrote in *Kliatt* that it "is an important book for many reasons: violence, love, faith, growth, denial, forgiveness are all explored and resolved."

In *The Eyes of Kid Midas* Shusterman takes an amusing fantasy situation and shows the frightening consequences as it spins out of control. Kevin Midas, the smallest kid in the seventh grade, is continually picked on by class bullies and annoyed by his family at home. Then he climbs to the top of a mysterious hill on a school trip and finds a magical pair of sunglasses that make all his wishes come true. At first, he uses the sunglasses for simple things such as making an ice cream cone appear in his hand or making a bully jump into a lake. Over time he becomes addicted to the power, even though he realizes that his wishes can be dangerous and irreversible. When even his dreams start turning into reality and no one seems to notice that anything is out of the ordinary besides him, Kevin must find a way to return things to normal before it is too late. *Voice of Youth Advocates* contributor Judith A. Sheriff stated that events in the novel "provide much for thought and discussion, yet do not get in the way of a well-told and intriguing story." Writing in *Wilson Library Bulletin*, Frances Bradburn noted that "Shusterman has written a

powerful fantasy based on every adolescent's desire to control his or her life," while a contributor for *Publishers Weekly* called "this fable for the 90s" both "imaginative and witty," and one that "convincingly proves the dangers of the narcissistic ethos of having it all."

For his next novel, *Scorpion Shards,* Shusterman took special powers once step beyond, enlisting the science-fiction/fantasy genre and the realms of the supernatural for a projected three-part series. A *Publishers Weekly* reviewer noted that in this novel "Shusterman takes on an outlandish comic-book concept and, through the sheer audacity and breadth if his imagination, makes it stunningly believable." Six teenagers are outcasts because of the usual afflictions of the age, such as acne, obesity, and the fear of being different. But the exaggerated sense of their problems is also accompanied by something special: supernatural powers. Tory's acne makes/enables her to taint everything she touches; Travis likes to break things and subsequently destroys several homes in a landslide. Soon these six divide into those who want to get rid of such powers and those who wish to cultivate them. "This is a classic story about the battle between [good] and evil made especially gripping as the teenagers struggle with opposing forces literally within themselves," wrote *Kliatt* reviewer Donna L. Scanlon. *Booklist* critic Bill Ott felt that "with all the symbols, metaphors, archetypes—so much meaning—clanging around in this book, it's hard for the characters to draw a breath." However, Ott went on to note that "the horror story is suspenseful and compelling."

The second novel in the proposed trilogy, *Thief of Souls,* appeared in 1999. It follows five of the teenagers who have discovered the origins of their superhuman powers yet attempt to live normal lives. Now, drawn to San Simeon, California, by the sixth, Dillon, they are enlisted to become "misguided miracle workers," according to a reviewer for *Publishers Weekly,* by the mysterious and "Mephistophelean" Okoya. "Echoes of classical and Christian mythology reverberate throughout this tale of fallible messiahs and fallen creatures," noted the reviewer, "giving it an uncommonly solid subtext." Jackie Cassada, reviewing the novel in *Library Journal,* commented, "The author's economy of style and bare-bones characterization propel his tale to its climax with few distractions."

Shusterman further explored the supernatural with the short stories in the "MindQuakes" series, including *MindQuakes, Mind Twisters, MindStorms,* and *Mind-Benders,* stories guaranteed to "snare even reluctant readers," according to a contributor for *Publishers Weekly.* Reviewing the second installment in the series, *MindStorms,* Scanlon noted that "these stories range from humorous to poignant and capture the reader's imagination," while in their "quirky, off-the-wall" style they resemble the *Twilight Zone* in "tone." A contributor to *Voice of Youth Advocates,* writing about *Mind-Twisters,* warned readers to "prepare to have your mind twisted and your reality warped by this exciting collection of weird tales."

The Dark Side of Nowhere is a science fiction thriller in which teenager Jason feels trapped in his small town until he discovers an awful secret about himself. He undergoes an identity crisis and a crucial choice after discovering that he is the son of aliens who stayed on earth following an unsuccessful invasion. *Booklist* critic Carolyn Phelan noted that "Shusterman tells a fast-paced story, giving Jason many vivid, original turns of phrase, letting the plot get weird enough to keep readers enthralled, then coming back to the human emotions at the heart of it all." A writer for *Kirkus Reviews* felt that "Shusterman delivers a tense thriller that doesn't duck larger issues," and "seamlessly combines gritty, heart-stopping plotting with a wealth of complex issues." *School Library Journal* contributor Bruce Anne Shook concluded, "This is great science fiction."

With his 1999 title *Downsiders,* Shusterman built another tale skirting the boundaries between reality and science-fiction/fantasy. Talon is a young New Yorker—with a difference. His people live underground—the "Downsiders" of the title—in the sewers and subways beneath the city. His people never mix with "Topsiders" until Talon falls for Lindsay. But their fragile romance is threatened when Lindsay's father, a city engineer, is working on an underground aqueduct and one of Talon's friends denounces him for his collaboration with the Topsiders. "Facts . . . are blended with fantasy until it is difficult to tell where truth stops and fiction begins," wrote Shook in a *School Library Journal* review of the book. Shook went on to note, "Overall . . . this is an exciting and entertaining story that will please fans of adventure, science fiction, and fantasy." Janice M. Del Negro, reviewing the same title for *Bulletin of the Center for Children's Books,* commented specifically on the "quick and suspenseful" pace of the novel and on the "believable underground culture" that Shusterman created. "Shusterman twines suspense and satire through this ingenious tale of a secret community living deep beneath the streets of New York," wrote a contributor for *Kirkus Reviews.* The same reviewer concluded, "Urban readers, at least, will be checking the storm drains for peering faces in the wake of this cleverly envisioned romp."

Shusterman has also written for television and film, as well as directed educational short films. In all of his ventures, he takes the creative process and its responsibilities to heart. "I often think about the power of the written word," he explained on his Web site. "Being a writer is like being entrusted with . . . or, more accurately stealing the power of flames, and then sling-shotting it into the air to see who catches fire. I think writers have a responsibility not to launch those fireballs indiscriminately, although occasionally we do. Still, what a power to find yourself responsible for, because words can change the world. I've always felt that stories aimed at adolescents and teens are the most important stories that can be written, because it is adolescence that defines who we are going to be."

BIOGRAPHICAL/CRITICAL SOURCES:

PERIODICALS

Booklist, March 15, 1993, p. 1346; February 1, 1996, Bill Ott, review of *Scorpion Shards,* p. 926; April 1, 1997, Carolyn Phelan, review of *The Dark Side of Nowhere,* p. 1322; March 15, 1998, pp. 1218, 1226; March 15, 1999, p. 1293.

Bulletin of the Center for Children's Books, May, 1988, p. 188; June, 1989, Roger Sutton, review of *Dissidents,* p. 264; May, 1991, p. 227; January, 1993, p. 157; September, 1999, Janice M. Del Negro, review of *Downsiders,* p. 31.

Children's Book Review Service, July, 1999, p. 155.

Horn Book, May-June, 1991, Ellen Fader, review of *Speeding Bullet,* p. 340; July-August, 1997, p. 463.

Kirkus Reviews, December 1, 1992, p. 1508; March 15, 1997, review of *The Dark Side of Nowhere,* p. 468; June 1, 1999, review of *Downsiders,* p. 889.

Kliatt, May, 1993, Rita M. Fontinha, review of *What Daddy Did,* p. 10; July, 1994, p. 18; January, 1997, Donna L. Scanlon, review of *Scorpion Shards,* pp. 10-11, and *MindStorms,* p. 16; May, 1999, p. 13.

Library Journal, March 15, 1999, Jackie Cassada, review of *Thief of Souls,* p. 113.

Los Angeles Times Book Review, July 23, 1989, Kristiana Gregory, review of *Dissidents,* p. 11.

Publishers Weekly, May 12, 1989, review of *Dissidents,* p. 296; December 14, 1990, review of *Speeding Bullet,* p. 67; November 16, 1992, review of *The Eyes of Kid Midas,* p. 65; March 28, 1994, p. 98; December 4, 1995, review of *Scorpion Shards,* p. 63; May 27, 1996, review of *MindQuakes,* p. 79; November 18, 1996, p. 78; February 8, 1999, review of *Thief of Souls,* p. 199; June 28, 1999, p. 80.

School Library Journal, May, 1988, David Gale, review of *The Shadow Club*, p. 113; October, 1989, p. 137; February, 1991, Lucinda Snyder Whitehurst, review of *Speeding Bullet*, p. 94; June, 1991, Gerry Larson, review of *What Daddy Did*, p. 128; December, 1992, Lyle Blake, review of *The Eyes of Kid Midas*, p. 133; March, 1996, p. 221; July, 1997, Bruce Anne Shook, review of *The Dark Side of Nowhere*, p. 9; November, 1997, p. 123; May, 1998, p. 51; July, 1999, Bruce Anne Shook, review of *Downsiders*, p. 100.

Voice of Youth Advocates, June, 1988, Lesa M. Holstine, review of *The Shadow Club*, p. 90; February, 1991, p. 358; June, 1991, Dorothy M. Broderick, review of *What Daddy Did*, p. 103; February, 1993, Judith A. Sheriff, review of *The Eyes of Kid Midas*, p. 358; April, 1998, review of *MindTwisters*, p. 14; July-August, 1997, p. 463; October, 1997, p. 254; December, 1997, p. 328; June, 1998, p. 103; August, 1999, p. 196.

Wilson Library Bulletin, March, 1993, Frances Bradburn, review of *The Eyes of Kid Midas*, p. 85.

OTHER

Neal Shusterman Homepage, http://www.storyman.com/ (October 26, 2000).

*   *   *

SKIMIN, Robert (Elwayne) 1929-

PERSONAL: Born July 30, 1929, in Belden, OH; son of Ellwyn W. and Mildred L. (Summerton) Skimin. *Education:* Attended Monmouth Junior College, 1948-49, University of Georgia, 1957-58, South Dakota School of Technology, 1959-60, and Cornish School of Allied Arts, 1967-68. *Avocational interests:* Golf, bridge, history, art, museums, "witty people."

ADDRESSES: Home and office—804 River Elms, El Paso, TX 79922. *Agent*—Jacques de Spoelberch, 9 Shagbark Rd., Norwalk, CT 06854. *E-mail*—rskimin@aol.com.

CAREER: U.S. Army, aviator and paratrooper, 1947-67, fourth youngest commissioned officer in the Army, 1949, artillery forward observer with 187 Airborne RCT in Korea, served in Germany, 1954-57, 1961-63, first aviator attached to Green Berets, 1955-57, numerous stateside assignments, retired as major; 1967. Commercial and fine artist; Owner of Abode Apartment Locators, 1972-82; Director of West Texas Council on Alcoholism, 1972-74.

MEMBER: Retired Officers Association, El Paso Historical Society, Order of Daedalius, National Society of Arts and Letters (El Paso chapter president, 1996-97), University of Texas at El Paso Friends Advisory Board (president, 2001—).

AWARDS, HONORS: Military: Purple Heart, Bronze Star, Army Commendation Medal with Oak Leaf Cluster; El Paso Writers Hall of Fame; Ohiana Book Award, 1984, for *Chikara!*

WRITINGS:

Rob's Guide to El Paso and Juarez (self-illustrated), privately printed, 1973.

Rob's San Antonio Bit (self-illustrated), privately printed, 1974.

The Booze Game: What You Don't Know about Alcoholism! Newfoundland Outdoors Publishing, 1976.

The Rhodesian Sellout, Libra, 1977.

Trojan in Iran, Zebra Books (New York, NY), 1981.

Zulu Blood, Zebra Books (New York, NY), 1981.

U.N. Sabotage, Zebra Books (New York, NY), 1981.

Bloodletting, Zebra Books (New York, NY), 1982.

Chikara! (a saga), St. Martin's (New York, NY), 1983.

Gray Victory, St. Martin's (New York, NY), 1988.

(With Ferdie Pacheco) *Renegade Lightning*, Lyford Books (Novato, CA), 1992.

Apache Autumn, St. Martin's (New York, NY), 1993.

Ulysses: A Biographical Novel of U.S. Grant, St. Martin's (New York, NY), 1994, published in paperback edition as *Ulysses S. Grant: A Novel*, Herodias (New York, NY), 1999.

The River and the Horsemen: A Novel of the Little Bighorn, Herodias, 1999.

(With William E. Moody) *Custer's Luck*, Herodias, 2000.

Stage play adaption of *Ulysses*. Film scripts include: *Sargeant Jake* and *Suzi Q.* Also contributor to regional magazines.

ADAPTATIONS: Gray Victory has been optioned as a feature film, with Skimin as co-producer and co-writer.

WORK IN PROGRESS: Derzava, a novel of twentieth-century Russia.

SIDELIGHTS: Historical events, in particular those involving military exploits, feature prominently in Robert Skimin's fiction. His *Soldier for Hire* series, which includes the novels *Trojan in Iran, Zulu Blood, U.N. Sabotage,* and *Bloodletting,* made the best-seller lists, as did *Gray Victory,* an alternative history in which the South wins the Civil War.

Skimin's two novels about General George Armstrong Custer, leader of the disastrous campaign against the Sioux at the Little Big Horn River, drew significant attention. *The River and the Horsemen* is a straightforward historical novel, showing Custer as contemporary accounts revealed him: arrogant and flawed, yet compelling. Paul Kaplan, in *Library Journal,* judged the book a "fine historical novel" and particularly noted Skimin's skillful use of detail and insightful portrait of Custer's nemesis, Sitting Bull. *Texas Monthly* reviewer Anne Dingus also praised Skimin's realistic characterizations, commenting that Skimin "knows what he's doing." *Custer's Luck* presents a very different story. Deemed "a fascinating what-if historical fantasy" by *Booklist* contributor Budd Arthur, the novel tells what would have happened if Custer had won the battle at the Little Big Horn. So popular does the general become that he is elected president of the United States. "The author makes us believe that it could all have happened," enthused Arthur.

Among Skimin's other critically acclaimed novels are *Chikara!,* the saga of an immigrant family from Hiroshima, which won the Ohiana Book Award, and *Apache Autumn,* in which a New Mexican bride is captured by a band of Apaches and forced to become the wife of their chief, whose son she bears before making her escape. A contributor to *Publishers Weekly* found *Apache Autumn* a "dramatic narrative solidly buttressed by historical details," and particularly noted the "understanding and empathy" with which Skimin writes about Apache society.

Renegade Lightning, a military thriller set in World War II, which Skimin co-wrote with Ferdie Pacheco, was hailed as a "well-told tale" in *Publishers Weekly. Ulysses,* a novel based on the life of Ulysses S. Grant, also received respectful reviews.

Skimin once told *CA:* "I feel so fortunate that I can write, particularly about history. When I can adapt, through fiction, to the reality of actual people and events, I feel I can *touch* them—be there. It's a great turn-on for me. And since a writer owes his audience a rich palette of authenticity, the sometimes staggering research (as in my Japanese saga, *Chikara!,* and Civil War works) is an adventure equal to that of the writing itself. And as difficult as writing books that dare to recreate history can be, the labor remains a definite adventure. Why else would we persist? And thank God for libraries and those marvelous creatures who run them!"

BIOGRAPHICAL/CRITICAL SOURCES:

PERIODICALS

Booklist, March 1, 1992, p. 1198; November 15, 1992, p. 580; September 15, 2000, Budd Arthur, review of *Custer's Luck,* p. 219.
Library Journal, Marcy 1, 1988, p. 79; February 15, 1992, p. 198; December 1992, p. 189; May 1, 2000, Paul Kaplan, review of *The River and the Horsemen,* p. 180.
Publishers Weekly, April 20, 1984, p. 82; January 22, 1988, p. 105; January 13, 1992, review of *Renegade Lightning,* p. 47; November 30, 1992, review of *Apache Autumn,* p. 37; September 12, 1994, p. 84.
Texas Monthly, November 1999, Anne Dingus, review of *The River and the Horsemen,* p. 30.

OTHER

Robert Skimin, http://www.robertskimin.com/ (November 5, 2000).*

*   *   *

SLOAN, Kay 1951-

PERSONAL: Born April 11, 1951, in Hattiesburg, MS; daughter of Andrew G. and LaVerne (Davidge) Sloan. *Education:* Attended Millsaps College, 1969-71; University of California at Santa Cruz, B.A., 1974; University of Texas, M.A., 1979, Ph.D., 1984.

ADDRESSES: Office—Department of English, Miami University, Oxford, OH 45056.

CAREER: Institute for Policy Studies, Washington, DC, research associate, 1977-78; University of Texas, Austin, instructor in American studies, 1979—; currently professor, English Dept., Miami University.

MEMBER: American Studies Association.

AWARDS, HONORS: Nominated for Pushcart Prize from *Southern Exposure,* 1981, for "The First Glaciers"; Ohioana Award for Best Fiction, 1992, for *Worry Beads;* nominated for the Pushcart Prize for Poetry and Fiction.

WRITINGS:

(With William H. Goetzmann) *Looking Far North: The Harriman Expedition to Alaska, 1899,* Viking, 1982.
The Loud Silents: Origins of the Social Problem Film (cultural history), University of Illinois Press, 1988.
Worry Beads (novel), Louisiana State University Press, 1991.
Elvis Rising: Stories of the King, Morrow, 1993.

Author of script for "Suffragettes in the Silent Cinema" (a documentary for educational use), 1981. Fiction, poetry, and essays, published in *Paris Review, Southern Review, Michigan Quarterly Review, Room of One's Own, The Journal, Indiana Review, Western Humanities Review,* and elsewhere. Scholarly articles published in *American Quarterly, American Heritage, New Orleans Review, Cineaste,* and elsewhere.

WORK IN PROGRESS: A book on images of marriage in Hollywood films; research on film and popular culture.

SIDELIGHTS: In 1899, fifty-one-year-old Edward H. Harriman, a powerful railroad magnate, planned a scientific expedition to Alaska after being encouraged by his doctor to take a long vacation. The expedition, which began on May 23, 1899, is the subject of *Looking Far North: The Harriman Expedition to Alaska, 1899,* by Kay Sloan and William H. Goetzmann. According to Richard Martin, who reviewed the book for the *Wall Street Journal,* Harriman hoped the trip would "restore his vigor, add substantially to the body of scientific knowledge, bring him a new image as a philanthropist and help promote tourism and rail travel in the West."

In addition to fourteen Harriman family members and servants, the expedition included eighty-two crew members, an assortment of animals, and "the latest scientific paraphernalia." During the two-month trip, expedition members collected "fossils, mollusks, bird, mammal and geologic specimens that would take years to sort and classify," as well as "sealskins, walrus tusks, Eskimo artifacts and most of an Indian village, even its totem poles."

Sloan and Goetzmann used diaries, letters, transcribed conversations of expedition members, and photographs from a souvenir album of the expedition to compile a book that, according to Martin, "makes for pleasant summer reading."

Sloan told *CA:* "The story-telling traditions of the Deep South were still strong when I was growing up in Mississippi during the 1950s and 1960s. My writing—whether poetry, fiction, or history—is still the telling of a story that speaks to human experience and social change. Part of my interest in the Harriman Alaska expedition lay in its marvelous cast of characters, who virtually delivered the narrative themselves. Writing social history is a special challenge: it should entertain as well as inform, and certainly always raise the question of how we can create a more compassionate world."

BIOGRAPHICAL/CRITICAL SOURCES:

PERIODICALS

Wall Street Journal, July 23, 1982.
Washington Post Book World, August 15, 1982.

*   *   *

SMITH, April 1949-

PERSONAL: Born in 1949 in Bronx, NY; daughter of a physician and a special education teacher; married Douglas Brayfield; children: two. *Education:* Boston University, received degree (English literature; cum laude); Stanford University, M.A. (creative writing).

ADDRESSES: Home—Los Angeles, CA. *Agent*—c/o Aaron Priest Literary Agency, 708 Third Ave., 23rd Floor, New York, NY, 10017.

CAREER: During early career was founding city editor of *The Cambridge Phoenix* (an alternative weekly newspaper), and an advertising copywriter for Patrick Nugent and Company; executive story editor for television series *Lou Grant,* CBS, 1979-82; television producer for CBS, including *Cagney and Lacey,* 1982, and co-producer of *Chicago Hope,* 2000. Editorial board member of Boston University's *The BU News,* for four years. Has also worked as a medical and legal typist.

AWARDS, HONORS: MacDowell Colony fellowship; co-winner, Hatch Award, for radio campaign "Dial an Oxford Pickle Joke"; Emmy nomination and Writers Guild Award nomination, both for teleplay *Ernie Kovacs: Between the Laughter;* two other Emmy nominations; one other Writers Guild Award.

WRITINGS:

James at 15 (adaptation of television special), Dell (New York, NY), 1977.
Friends, 1978.
North of Montana (novel), Knopf (New York, NY), 1994.
Be the One (novel), Knopf (New York, NY), 2000.

TELEPLAYS

(And co-producer) *Best Kept Secrets,* first broadcast on ABC, March 26, 1984.
Ernie Kovacs: Between the Laughter, first broadcast on ABC, May 14, 1984.
Love Lives On, first broadcast on ABC, 1985.
(With Winston Beard) *Queenie* (two-part miniseries; based on novel by Michael Korda), first broadcast on ABC, May 10, 1987.
Taking Back My Life: The Nancy Ziegenmeyer Story, first broadcast on CBS, March 15, 1992.
The Taking of Pelham One Two Three (adapted from novel by John Godey), first broadcast on ABC, February 1, 1998.
Black and Blue (adapted from the novel by Anna Quindlen), first broadcast on CBS, November 17, 1999.

Also author of television show episodes, including for *Upstairs, Downstairs* and *Letting Go,* on *Chicago Hope,* CBS, 2000. Contributor of articles to periodicals, including *Fusion.* Contributor of stories to periodicals, including *Atlantic Monthly.*

SIDELIGHTS: April Smith is a television producer and story editor, who has also written novels. Her first two books balance thriller stories with modern women's issues. *North of Montana* is set in southern California and depicts the escapades of FBI agent Ana Grey as she attempts to determine who is responsible for the murder of Violeta Alvarado, who was possibly Grey's cousin. Alvarado was also employed by a physician who is accused by film star Jayne Mason of causing her addic-tion to prescription drugs. Coincidentally, Grey has been assigned to investigate Mason's case. The novel delineates both Grey's investigation of the case and her self-discovery as she unearths a number of suppressed memories from her childhood and reflects on her own desires and motivations. A reviewer for *Kirkus Reviews* offered high praise for the novel, asserting that it "transcends all conventions," and a *Publishers Weekly* contributor applauded *North of Montana* for "an unflagging pace, authoritative use of detail and an appealing heroine."

Whereas the story of *North of Montana* uses Dodger Stadium on opening day just as a setting for the novel's beginning, Smith's second novel, *Be the One,* surrounds itself with the world of professional baseball. Smith was given "broad access to the Dodger organization for the five years it took to research and write [*Be the One,*]" as the author informed readers in a Random House online interview discussing her 2000 novel. Smith tells of a female baseball scout caught "in a classic triangle of deception and greed in which boundaries become blurred until you can't rely on your most basic perceptions." In the plot of her thriller, a baseball player named Alberto Cruz and an L.A. developer named Joe Galinis are both receiving blackmail notes. Joe is the lover of Cassidy Sanderson, a baseball scout who is brutally attacked. The riddle is to find out what these three characters have in common and who is out to get them. Cassidy soon becomes "caught between the man she loves and the boy she believes in," according to the author. The story is not only a thriller, but a portrayal of the hardships a woman faces when she tries to break into a male-dominated field such as sports. A *Publishers Weekly* critic felt that this "ambitious novel" does a good job of portraying the hardships of a woman who has to work and live "in a man's world."

BIOGRAPHICAL/CRITICAL SOURCES:

PERIODICALS

Kirkus Reviews, review of *North of Montana,* July 15, 1994, p. 945.
Publishers Weekly, review of *North of Montana,* July 4, 1994, p. 52; review of *Be the One,* June 5, 2000, p. 70.
School Library Journal, January, 1978, p. 98.

OTHER

April Smith, http://www.aprilsmith.net/ (June 30, 2000).
Random House, http://www.randomhouse.com/ (June 30, 2000).*

SMITH, John David 1949-

PERSONAL: Born October 14, 1949, in Brooklyn, NY; son of Leonard Calgut (in business) and Doris (Woronock) Smith. *Education:* Baldwin-Wallace College, A.B. (cum laude; history), 1971; University of Kentucky, A.M. (American history), 1973, Ph.D. (southern history), 1977.

ADDRESSES: Office—Department of History, North Carolina State University, Box 8108, Raleigh, NC 27695-8108. *E-mail*—smith_jd@unity.ncsu.edu.

CAREER: Louis A. Warren Lincoln Library and Museum, Fort Wayne, IN, curator, 1977-79; Indiana University-Purdue University, Fort Wayne, associate faculty member, 1978-79; University of South Carolina, lecturer, 1979-80; Historic Columbia Foundation, Columbia, SC, executive director, 1979-80; Southeast Missouri State University, Cape Girardeau, instructor, 1980-81, assistant professor of history, 1981-82; North Carolina State University, Raleigh, assistant professor, 1982-87, director of the M.A. in public history program, beginning 1982, associate professor, 1987-91, professor of history, 1991-92, Graduate Alumni Distinguished Professor of History, 1992—. Visiting assistant professor, University of Kentucky, summer, 1981; visiting assistant professor, School of Library Science, University of North Carolina at Chapel Hill, 1986-88; Fulbright Professor of American Studies, Amerika-Institut, Ludwig-Maximilians-Universitaet, Munich, Germany, 1998-99. Friends of the North Carolina State Archives, member of board of directors, 1983-86, vice president, 1986-88, president, 1988-90; member of International Council on Archives Committee on Professional Training and Education, 1986—; member of board of directors, Society of North Carolina Archivists, 1988-89; member of board of directors, Historic Stagville Foundation, 1995—; member of advisory council, Lincoln Prize at Gettysburg College, 1995—; member of Historian Advisory Committee, African American Civil War Memorial Foundation, Washington, D.C., 1996—. Lecturer.

MEMBER: American Historical Association, Organization of American Historians, Society of American Archivists, Southern Historical Association, African American Civil War Memorial Foundation (historian advisory committee, 1996—).

AWARDS, HONORS: Cornelius D. Penner History Award, Baldwin-Wallace College, 1970; Albert D. Kirwan Prize, University of Kentucky, 1976; research fellow, Southern Studies Program, University of South Carolina, 1980; American Council of Learned Societies fellowship, 1981-82; James Still Fellowship, Andrew W. Mellon Foundation, summer 1982; fellowship, Project '87 Seminar on "Race and Slavery in the American Constitutional System," Stanford University, summer 1983; Albert J. Beveridge Travel Grant, American Historical Association, 1983, 1987; Outstanding Academic Book award, American Library Association, 1983, for *Black Slavery in the Americas: An Interdisciplinary Bibliography, 1865-1980;* National Endowment for the Humanities grant, 1986; *The Dictionary of Afro-American Slavery* selected as Best Reference Book by *Library Journal,* 1988, Outstanding Academic Book by *Choice,* 1989, and Outstanding Reference Book by American Library Association, 1989; Richard H. Collins Prize, Kentucky Historical Society, 1989; Hilbert T. Ficken Memorial Award, Baldwin-Wallace College, 1994; Distinguished American Speaker, United States Information Service, Melbourne, Australia, summer 1994; Myers Center Award for the Study of Human Rights in North America, Myers Center for the Study of Intolerance in the United States, University of Arkansas, 1996, for *Anti-Black Thought, 1863-1925;* Mayflower Society Award for Nonfiction, 2000, for *Black Judas: William Hannibal Thomas and "The American Negro";* National Book Award and Pulitzer Prize for Biography nominations, both 2000, both for *Black Judas: William Hannibal Thomas and "The American Negro."*

WRITINGS:

An Old Creed for the New South: Proslavery Ideology and Historiography, 1865-1918, Greenwood (Westport, CT), 1985, Brown Thrasher edition, University of Georgia Press (Athens), 1991.

Black Voices from Reconstruction: 1865-1877, Millbrook (Brookfield, CT), 1996, revised edition, University Press of Florida (Gainesville), 1997.

Slavery, Race, and American History: Historical Conflict, Trends, and Method, 1866-1953 (essays), M. E. Sharpe (Armonk, NY), 1999.

Black Judas: William Hannibal Thomas and "The American Negro," University of Georgia Press, 2000.

Emancipation in the American South, Routledge (London), in press.

EDITOR, EXCEPT AS NOTED

(With William Cooper, Jr.) *Window on the War: Frances Dallam Peter's Lexington Civil War Diary,* Fayette County Historic Commission (Lexington, KY),

1976, second edition, 1992, revised edition, University Press of Kentucky (Lexington), 1997, revised edition published as *A Union Woman in Civil War Kentucky: The Diary of Frances Peter,* University Press of Kentucky, 2000.

(Compiler) *Black Slavery in the Americas: An Interdisciplinary Bibliography, 1865-1980,* two volumes, foreword by Stanley L. Engerman, Greenwood, 1982.

(With Randall M. Miller) *The Dictionary of Afro-American Slavery,* Greenwood, 1988, updated, with a new introduction and bibliography, Praeger (New York City), 1997.

(With John C. Inscoe) *Ulrich Bonnell Phillips: A Southern Historian and His Critics,* Greenwood, 1990, Brown Thrasher edition, University of Georgia Press, 1993.

(And author of introduction) *Anti-Black Thought 1863-1925: "The Negro Problem" An Eleven-Volume Anthology of Racist Writings,* Volume 1: *Anti-Abolition Tracts and Anti-Black Stereotypes,* Volume 2: *Racist Southern Paternalism,* Volume 3: *Van Evrie's White Supremacy and Negro Subordination,* Volume 4: *The "Benefits" of Slavery,* Volume 5: *The "Ariel" Controversy,* Volume 6: *The Biblical and "Scientific" Defense of Slavery,* Volume 7: *Racial Determinism and the Fear of Miscegenation* (part one), Volume 8: *Racial Determinism and the Fear of Miscegenation, Post-1900,* Volume 9: *Disfranchisement Proposals and the Ku Klux Klan,* Volume 10: *The American Colonization Society and Emigration,* Volume 11: *Emigration and Migration Proposals,* Garland (New York City), 1993.

John Brown: A Biography by W. E. B. Du Bois: A New Edition with Primary Documents and Introduction, M. E. Sharpe, 1997.

(With Thomas H. Appleton, Jr.) *A Mythic Land Apart: Reassessing Southerners and Their History,* Greenwood, 1997.

(With Julie A. Doyle and Richard M. McMurry) *This Wilderness of War: The Civil War Letters of George W. Squier, Hoosier Volunteer,* University of Tennessee Press (Knoxville), 1998.

Black Soldiers in Blue: African-American Troops in the Civil War Era, University of North Carolina Press (Chapel Hill), in press.

Frederick Douglass, *My Bondage and My Freedom,* Penguin (New York City), in press.

When Did Segregation Begin in the American South?, Bedford (Boston), in press.

Also series editor of *Studies in Historiography,* Greenwood/Praeger, 1990—; advisory editor, *Reconstructing America,* Fordham University Press, 1997—;

and series editor of *New Perspectives on the History of the South,* University Press of Florida, 1997—. Member of editorial board, *North Carolina Historical Review,* 1989-94, *Plantation Society in the Americas,* 1998—; contributing editor, *American Historical Association Perspectives,* 1995-98.

OTHER

Author of pamphlets published by Louis A. Warren Lincoln Library and Museum (Fort Wayne, IN), including *Lincoln in Portrait, Print, and Statuary,* 1978; *Abraham Lincoln: A Most Unlikely Military Man,* 1979; *Lincoln's Cabinet of All Factions,* 1979; and *A. Lincoln: Commander in Chief,* 1979. Contributor to books, including *A Man for the Ages: Tributes to Abraham Lincoln,* compiled by Louis A. Warren, Louis A. Warren Lincoln Library and Museum (Fort Wayne, IN), 1978; *Our Kentucky: A Study of the Bluegrass State,* edited by James C. Klotter, University Press of Kentucky, 1992; *Encyclopedia of the Confederacy,* four volumes, edited by Richard N. Current, Simon & Schuster (New York City), 1993; and *The Moment of Decision: Biographical Essays on American Character and Regional Identity,* edited by Randall M. Miller and John R. McKivigan, Greenwood, 1994.

Author of introduction/foreword to books, including *Are We Losing Our Past? Records Preservation in the North Carolina State Archives,* by David J. Olson, The Friends of the Archives (Raleigh), 1989; *Louisiana Sugar Plantations during the Civil War,* by Charles P. Roland, Louisiana State University Press (Baton Rouge), 1997; *The Diary of James T. Ayers, Civil War Recruiter,* edited by John Hope Franklin, Louisiana State University Press, 1999; and *The Collapse of the Confederacy* by Charles H. Wesley, University of South Carolina Press (Columbia), in press.

Contributor of more than fifty scholarly articles to journals, including *American Archivist, Carolina Comments, Civil War History, Georgia Historical Quarterly, Journal of Folklore Research, Journal of Negro History, Military History of the West, Phylon,* and *South Atlantic Quarterly.* Contributor of book reviews to magazines and newspapers, including *Times Literary Supplement* (London), *Choice,* and *Civil War Book Review;* contributor to journals, including *American Historical Review, Historian, Journal of American History, Journal of Southern History, North Carolina Historical Review,* and *Religious Studies Review.* Contributor to encyclopedias and other reference books, including *Dictionary of*

Literary Biography, Biographical Dictionary of Social Welfare in America, Historical Encyclopedia of World Slavery, and *Macmillan Encyclopedia of World Slavery.*

SIDELIGHTS: Historian John David Smith has researched, lectured, and produced numerous works on the Civil War, American slavery, and life in the American South. In addition to contributing to scholarly journals, reference books, and various other publications, Smith has written and edited many books, among them a series of eleven volumes released in 1993 as *Anti-Black Thought 1863-1925: "The Negro Problem" An Eleven-Volume Anthology of Racist Writings.* Smith's efforts in writing *Black Voices from Reconstruction: 1865-1877,* a 1996 publication, will benefit researchers, particularly junior high and high school classrooms, according to Hazel Rochman in *Booklist.* When reviewing *Black Voices from Reconstruction* in *Choice,* T. F. Armstrong wrote that "rarely . . . does one find a text designed for younger readers, yet so rich in summary insight." *Booklist* contributor Nora Harris stated that people researching slavery should begin with Smith's *The Dictionary of Afro-American Slavery,* a 1988 release that was later updated in 1997.

More recently, Smith published *Black Judas: William Hannibal Thomas and "The American Negro,"* a product of fifteen years of investigative research and the recipient of the Mayflower Society Award for Nonfiction for 2000. William Hannibal Thomas, an Ohio mulatto who served with distinction in the U.S. Colored Troops during the Civil War, was a self-professed and nationally known critic of his own race. *Black Judas* tells the story of Thomas's transformation from a critical but optimistic black nationalist to a cynical black Negrophobe as the twentieth century dawned. This radical change erupted in Thomas's 1901 publication of *The American Negro,* a scandalous, blatantly insulting attack on African Americans that located "the Negro problem" in the black community and grossly characterized the entire race as inherently backward and inferior.

In his writings and actions, Thomas distanced himself from his race, recommending that Negroes model themselves after "notable" mulattoes, persons like himself. In doing so Thomas projected on African Americans his own complicated emotional and physical problems. In his book, Smith examines Thomas's dramatic behavioral and ideological shifts. Smith contextualizes them within Thomas's many years of subjection to white racism and his emotional and physical traumas that resulted from severe pain due to the amputation of his right arm during the Civil War. *Black Judas,* the first biography of Thomas, traces his life-long pattern of self-destruction in the wake of repeated professional successes. Using research in such areas as military medicine and psychoanalytic theory, Smith not only shows how this former preacher, lawyer, teacher, journalist, and state legislator destroyed himself, but also analyzes the influence of *The American Negro* on both black and white Americans in the racially tense era of Jim Crow.

Writing in the *Chronicle of Higher Education,* Smith explained, "I was drawn to Thomas because of my long interest in proslavery thought after emancipation. When I first read *The American Negro,* I thought that the author was just another white supremacist; when I discovered who he was, I became intrigued." Though some scholars have questioned Smith about why he devoted so much time to Thomas, critics have praised Smith's objective presentation of a complicated historical figure. Calling *Black Judas* "an engrossing, wonderfully narrated story," Stephen W. Angell of *Georgia Historical Quarterly* wrote that Smith "has provided us with a meticulously researched, beautifully written, and scrupulously fair biography of Thomas. The methodologically imaginative book makes innovative use of psychology, medical history, and numerous other subdisciplines of history." Nell Irvin Painter, writing in Raleigh's *News and Observer,* considered the book "a compelling portrait," and Charles E. Walker of *North Carolina Historical Review* praised, "Smith's analysis of William Hannibal Thomas's career is jargon-free and not psychologically reductive. . . . Smith has taken a difficult subject and handled it splendidly." *Black Judas* was nominated for both the National Book Award and the Pulitzer Prize for Biography for 2000.

BIOGRAPHICAL/CRITICAL SOURCES:

PERIODICALS

Booklist, November 1, 1996, Hazel Rochman, review of *Black Voices from Reconstruction,* p. 485; February 15, 1999, Nora Harris, review of *Dictionary of Afro-American Slavery,* p. 1087; December 1, 1999, Vanessa Bush, review of *Black Judas,* p. 663.

Choice, April, 1997, T. F. Armstrong, review of *Black Voices from Reconstruction,* p. 1407.

Chronicle of Higher Education, March 31, 2000, John David Smith, "How the 'Black Judas' Can Help to Reveal African-American History," p. B9.

Georgia Historical Quarterly, June, 2000, Stephen W. Angell, review of *Black Judas.*

Herald-Sun (Durham, NC), February 27, 2000, Sharon A. Hill, "*Black Judas* Details Life of Complex, Twisted Man," p. G5.

Library Journal, November 1, 1999, John Carver Edwards, review of *Black Judas,* p. 96.

News and Observer (Raleigh, NC), February 6, 2000, Nell Irvin Painter, "Betrayal."

North Carolina Historical Review, July, 2000, Clarence E. Walker, review of *Black Judas,* pp. 383-384.

School Library Journal, February, 1997, Marilyn Fairbanks, review of *Black Voices from Reconstruction,* p. 126.

OTHER

North Carolina State University, http://www.ncsu.edu/chass/history/ (June 21, 2001).

*   *   *

STANLEY, Jerry 1941-

PERSONAL: Born July 18, 1941, in Highland Park, MI; son of Hurschel (a musician) and Beatrice (a health care worker; maiden name, Kula) Stanley; married Dorothy Bushman (a math professor); children: Mark Thomas, Sara Ellen. *Education:* Yuba Community College, A.A. (with honors), 1965; Chico State College (now California State University, Chico), B.A. (cum laude), 1967; University of Arizona, M.A., 1969, Ph.D., 1973. *Avocational interests:* Fishing, observing nature.

ADDRESSES: Home—3504 Robinwood, Bakersfield, CA 93309. *E-mail*—jdstanle@pacbell.net.

CAREER: California State University, Bakersfield, assistant professor, 1973-77, associate professor, 1977-81, professor of history, 1981-98. Freelance writer. *Military service:* U.S. Air Force, 1959-63.

MEMBER: American Historical Association, Organization of American Historians, Western Writers of America, Phi Beta Kappa, Phi Kappa Phi, Phi Alpha Theta.

AWARDS, HONORS: Orbis Pictus Award from National Council of Teachers of English, Spur Award from Western Writers of America, Beatty Award from California Library Association, Focal Award from Los Angeles Public Library, Jefferson Cup from Virginia Library Association, and best book citations from *School Library Journal* and *Hornbook Fanfare,* all 1993, and citation for "100 noteworthy children's books," Library of Congress and the New York Public Library, all for *Children of the Dust Bowl: The True Story of the School at Weedpatch Camp;* finalist for National Book Award, 2000, for *Hurry Freedom: African Americans in Gold Rush California.*

WRITINGS:

Children of the Dust Bowl: The True Story of the School at Weedpatch Camp, Crown (New York, NY), 1992.

I Am an American: A True Story of Japanese Internment, Crown (New York, NY), 1994.

Big Annie of Calumet: A True Story of the Industrial Revolution, Crown (New York, NY), 1996.

Digger: The Tragic Fate of the California Indian from the Missions to the Gold Rush, Crown (New York, NY), 1997.

Frontier Merchants: Lionel and Barron Jacobs and the Jewish Pioneers Who Settled the West, Crown (New York, NY), 1998.

Hurry Freedom: African Americans in Gold Rush California, Crown (New York, NY), 2000.

Contributor to periodicals.

WORK IN PROGRESS: A nonfiction book on the cowboy.

SIDELIGHTS: Jerry Stanley's books deal with a basic human theme: people overcoming adversity against great odds. His award-winning *Children of the Dust Bowl: The True Story of the School at Weedpatch Camp* tells the story of children from Oklahoma persevering in California during the Great Depression; *I Am an American: A True Story of Japanese Internment* details the trials of Nisei—people of Japanese ancestry born in the United States—during World War II.

Stanley once told *CA:* "The last thing in the world I thought I would be when I grew up was a writer. I never liked to read when I was young. I liked my girl friend, my gang, and my car, and when I was expelled from high school at the age of seventeen, I had passed two units, one in wood shop and one in gym. I suppose the subjects I choose to write about reflect how I became a writer. It was a long hard struggle for me to get an education, to get a teaching position, and finally to become a freelance writer."

Stanley joined the Air Force in 1959 after leaving school, leaving his native Michigan to be stationed at Beale Air Force Base near Sacramento, California. Recalling what happened following his stint in the military, Stanley commented, "I guess the turning point in my life would be getting on my own. When I was about twenty or twenty-one and ready to get out of the service, a friend of mine talked me into trying some college classes. By that time I figured there had to be a better way to earn a living than operating heavy machinery as I had been doing, so I took a battery of tests at a local junior college and was accepted." Stanley graduated with honors from the junior college and then went on to Chico State where he majored in history, relying on the musicianship nurtured by his father—a saxophone player for the Lionel Hampton band—to fund his education. "I drummed my way through college," Stanley recalled. "I played for jazz bands, rock bands, country western bands, you name it." Following his graduation from Chico State, Stanley went to Tucson where he attended the University of Arizona. "I didn't even know what a Ph.D. was when my counselor asked if that was my goal. I was the first person in my family to get any degree from college, and for me, every degree was a terminal one. Then I decided to just keep going to school until there were no more degrees to earn."

By the early 1970s Stanley was an assistant professor of history at California State University, Bakersfield, where he specialized in California, western, and Native American history. He began writing professional articles during this period, and in 1975 he "stumbled on" the story of the Weedpatch School that was opened during the Depression for the children of migrant workers. This research eventually led to the publication of his first book, *Children of the Dust Bowl.* In 1976 Stanley published n historical account of the grassroots development of the Weedpatch School in the *California Courier,* a publication of the California Historical Society. In the mid-1980s, Stanley rewrote the story for a general audience and sold it to *American West.* A film producer from Hollywood read the article in a dentist's office and contacted Stanley to discuss a movie option on the story. A nationwide news feature on the Weedpatch School brought more interest; more than a dozen movie producers eventually sought to option the story. In the late 1980s, Stanley decided to turn his research into a historical story for children.

"Being a historian, I already had a good working knowledge of the Depression," Stanley explained. "So I sat down and wrote a few generic chapters about the dust bowl in Oklahoma and the failure of the crops and how the people there lost their homes." The story takes place in California, echoing the setting that author John Steinbeck covers in his famous novel *The Grapes of Wrath.* Like Steinbeck, Stanley focused on the story of one group of people in the midst of a larger story.

Publication of *Children of the Dust Bowl* brought enthusiastic responses from many quarters. Writing in *Horn Book,* Margaret A. Bush called the book "a fascinating account of the cruelty society heaps on its underdogs as well as an inspiring lesson for adults." Joyce Adams Burner, in the *School Library Journal,* found it "a well-researched, highly readable portrait [and] an informative and inspirational bit of American history." Newspaper reviewers agreed. Evelyn C. White in the *San Francisco Chronicle,* described it as "a moving historical account [that is] a testament to the power of love and compassion," while Henry Mayer, writing in the *New York Times Book Review,* called the book "a powerful account of a desperate time."

This initial success convinced Stanley to pursue a career in writing for children in addition to his academic duties. His second book, *I Am an American,* was another case of simply stumbling onto a subject. On a camping trip with his wife, Stanley visited the site of the Japanese-American internment camp at Manzanar. This period in California history had long interested him, and he had taught a class on it at California State University. While visiting a nearby museum he was introduced to a memoir written by one of the Nisei interned there during World War II; the man's story became the centerpiece of *I Am an American.*

Typically, Stanley spends up to six months researching the time period about which he is writing, taking copious notes. "In the end, I may only use five per cent of the research in the book," Stanley said, "but the reader *feels* the other ninety-five per cent."

"I think good writing is the hardest thing in the world to do," Stanley commented. "Good writing requires good thinking and good thinking requires good reading. Good thinking is the hardest thing in the world to do, and it's only done after reading, reading, reading."

"Because I'm a historian, nonfiction writing has always been more interesting to me than fiction, and because of my background, I am drawn to topics where people overcome adversity against great odds. I must have an emotional attachment to a story or I can't write it. The children of Weedpatch Camp were kicked out of school, built their own school, got an education, and went on to do great things with their lives. If they can do it, anyone can do it. If I can do it, anyone can do it. I remember my own youth; how I hated those books that had no life to them. Now I feel a commitment to my discipline of history. I want to present history to young readers as what it should be: dramatic story-telling."

BIOGRAPHICAL/CRITICAL SOURCES:

PERIODICALS

Booklist, September 1, 1992, p. 55; January 15, 1993, p. 845; March 15, 1993, p. 1338.
Bulletin of the Center for Children's Books, October, 1992, p. 55.
Five Owls, September-October, 1992, pp. 17-18.
Horn Book, January-February, 1993, Margaret A. Bush, review of *Children of the Dust Bowl: The True Story of the School at Weedpatch Camp,* p. 100.
Kirkus Reviews, September 1, 1992, p. 1134.
New York Times Book Review, January 17, 1993, Henry Mayer, review of *Children of the Dust Bowl,* p. 27.
San Francisco Chronicle, January 3, 1993, Evelyn C. White, review of *Children of the Dust Bowl,* sec. R, p. 10.
School Library Journal, November, 1992, Joyce Adams Burner, review of *Children of the Dust Bowl,* p. 132.

*   *   *

STANSBERRY, Domenic (Joseph) 1952-

PERSONAL: Born March 15, 1952, in Washington, DC; son of Chadwick Leroy (an aerospace engineer) and Teresa (Mussolino) Stansberry; married Gillian Conoley (a writer), March 22, 1986. *Education:* Attended University of California at Santa Cruz, 1970-72; Portland State University, B.A., 1977; Colorado State University, M.A., 1980; University of Massachusetts, M.F.A., 1984.

ADDRESSES: Home—Box 657, Corte Madera, CA 94976-0657. *Agent*—Fred Hill, 1842 Union St., San Francisco, CA.

CAREER: Freelance journalist. University of New Orleans, New Orleans, LA, instructor in composition and creative writing, 1984-87; Tulane University, visiting lecturer, 1985-86; Eastern Washington University, Spo-

kane, editor and writer of public relations and marketing material, beginning 1987; California State University at Hayward, instructor in writing, 1990-92; Stansberry Communications, dialogue writer and media consultant, 1992—. *Daily Hampshire Gazette,* feature writer, 1981-83; Black River Publishing, cofounder and coeditor. Designer and writer for artificial intelligence engines.

AWARDS, HONORS: Edgar Allan Poe Award nomination, Mystery Writers of America, 1988, for *The Spoiler,* and 1999, for *The Last Days of Il Duce;* Dashiell Hammett Award nomination, for *The Last Days of Il Duce;* Film Arts Foundation Award, for work in documentary video; grants from National Endowment for the Humanities and Pioneer Fund.

WRITINGS:

The Spoiler (novel), Atlantic Monthly Press (Boston, MA), 1988.
Exit Paradise: Stories, Lynx House Press (Amherst, MA), 1992.
The Last Days of Il Duce (novel), Permanent Press (Sag Harbor, NY), 1998.
Labyrinths—The Art of Interactive Writing and Design: Content Development for New Media, Wadsworth (Belmont, CA), 1998.
Manifesto for the Dead (novel), Permanent Press (Sag Harbor, NY), 2000.

SIDELIGHTS: Domenic Stansberry has published several novels that have garnered critical praise and several awards. His tales of crime and murder "are as raw and unadulterated as any in the genre," noted Bill Ott in *Booklist.* Stansberry worked his way through the creative writing program at the University of Massachusetts as a freelance journalist. One of his assignments was to do a piece on the Millers, a minor league baseball team in the nearby town of Holyoke. In the process, he became fascinated by the small stadium where the team played, and the run-down, arson-riddled, neighborhood in which it stood. These elements stayed with him and later formed the atmosphere of his first novel, *The Spoiler.*

The Spoiler was billed by Tom Shea in the *Springfield Union-News* as "a story of baseball and murder" centered on a reporter assigned to cover the minor-league Holyoke Redwings. In the process, the reporter uncovers an arson-for-insurance scheme, a murder, and political corruption. He also becomes involved with the mistress of one of the team's owners. Stansberry's novel was generally well received, with critics praising its well developed sense of setting and character. *Los Angeles Times Book Review* contributor Michael J. Carroll heralded *The Spoiler* as "less of a thriller than a moving chronicle of humanity—disquietingly black and totally absorbing." In the *New York Times Book Review* Newgate Callendar assessed that the author "knows his baseball, and obviously is in love with the game." *Willamette Week* writer D. K. Holm compared *The Spoiler* quite favorably with other fiction about baseball, noting that the book "is suffused with the quality of William Kennedy's paeans to losers beating the pavement all day and night. Stansberry has a sympathetic but realistic appraisal of life's peripheral people, hanging on the edges."

The Last Days of Il Duce is an urban murder mystery about racial tensions and hidden political secrets. It concerns Niccolo Jones, a San Francisco ex-lawyer who is in love with his brother's wife. When his brother turns up murdered, Niccolo tracks down the killer in a neighborhood where native Italians are being driven out by Chinese immigrants. The ethnic tension between the two groups hampers Niccolo's investigation, which leads him to uncover dangerous fascist secrets from World War II among members of the city's Italian community. Ott called the book a "gut-wrenching tale of doomed lovers." A critic for *Publishers Weekly* believed that Stansberry offers "an intriguing picture of Italian fascist activity in San Francisco."

In *Manifesto for the Dead* Stansberry writes a fictionalized story in which real-life mystery writer Jim Thompson—famous for his gritty novels of low-life criminality—finds himself framed for a Hollywood murder. Writing in a manner similar to Thompson's, Stansberry creates "an eerie echo of a dead man's style," wrote a *New York Times Book Review* critic. A *Publishers Weekly* reviewer likewise noted Stansberry's "uncanny recreations of Thompson's writing." Ott found that "Stansberry manages to make the pain [of his story] palpable while also constructing an airtight plot that feeds on itself." The story, the *New York Times Book Review* critic concluded, "would make Thompson's own skin crawl."

Speaking about his first novel, Stansberry told *CA:* "I was attracted to sports not so much for their own sake, though that's part of it, but because of what they tell us about human aspiration, about our striving for success, and the inevitability, in many ways, of failure. There is a certain glory in failure, particularly anonymous failure, and that small bit of glory, 'the beauty in the ruins,' remains the subject of my fiction, even now that I've gone on to other subject matter."

BIOGRAPHICAL/CRITICAL SOURCES:

PERIODICALS

Booklist, January 1, 1998, Bill Ott, review of *The Last Days of Il Duce,* p. 785; November 15, 1999, Bill Ott, review of *Manifesto for the Dead,* p. 607.

Library Journal, June 1, 1998, Thom Gillespie, review of *Labyrinths,* p. 144.

Los Angeles Times Book Review, October 18, 1987, Michael J. Carroll, review of *The Spoiler,* p. 4.

New York Times Book Review, November 8, 1987, Newgate Callendar, review of *The Spoiler,* p. 62; January 9, 2000, review of *Manifesto for the Dead,* p. 24.

Publishers Weekly, August 7, 1987, review of *The Spoiler,* p. 435; November 24, 1997, review of *The Last Days of Il Duce,* p. 55; December 13, 1999, review of *Manifesto for the Dead,* p. 65.

Springfield Union-News, November 10, 1987, Tom Shea, review of *The Spoiler.*

Willamette Week, December 17, 1987, D. K. Holm, review of *The Spoiler.*

*   *   *

STEEL, Danielle (Fernande) 1947-

PERSONAL: Born August 14, 1947, in New York, NY; daughter of John and Norma (Stone) Schuelein-Steel; married Thomas Perkins, 1998; children: (first marriage) one daughter; (third marriage) two stepsons, four daughters, two sons. *Education:* Educated in France; attended Parsons School of Design, 1963, and New York University, 1963-67. *Religion:* Catholic.

ADDRESSES: Home—P.O. Box 1637, New York, NY 10156-1637. *Agent*—Janklow & Nesbit Associates, Inc., 445 Park Ave., New York, NY 10022.

CAREER: Writer. Supergirls, Ltd. (public relations firm), New York City, vice president of public relations, 1968-71; Grey Advertising, San Francisco, CA, copywriter, 1973-74; has worked at other positions in public relations and advertising; taught creative writing in En-

Danielle Steel

glish, 1975-76. National chair of the American Library Association. Founder of Nick Traina Foundation to benefit mental health.

WRITINGS:

NOVELS

Going Home, Pocket Books (New York, NY), 1973.
Passion's Promise, Dell (New York, NY), 1977.
The Promise (based on a screenplay by Garry Michael White), Dell (New York, NY), 1978.
Now and Forever, Dell (New York, NY), 1978.
Season of Passion, Dell (New York, NY), 1979.
Summer's End, Dell (New York, NY), 1979.
The Ring, Delacorte (New York, NY), 1980.
Loving, Dell (New York, NY), 1980.
Remembrance, Delacorte (New York, NY), 1981.
Palomino, Dell (New York, NY), 1981.
To Love Again, Dell (New York, NY), 1981.
Crossings, Delacorte (New York, NY), 1982.
Once in a Lifetime, Dell (New York, NY), 1982.

A Perfect Stranger, Dell (New York, NY), 1982.
Changes, Delacorte (New York, NY), 1983.
Thurston House, Dell (New York, NY), 1983.
Full Circle, Delacorte (New York, NY), 1984.
Secrets, Delacorte (New York, NY), 1985.
Family Album, Delacorte (New York, NY), 1985.
Wanderlust, Delacorte (New York, NY), 1986.
Fine Things, Delacorte (New York, NY), 1987.
Kaleidoscope, Delacorte (New York, NY), 1987.
Zoya, Delacorte (New York, NY), 1988.
Star, Delacorte (New York, NY), 1989.
Daddy, Delacorte (New York, NY), 1989.
Message from 'Nam, Delacorte (New York, NY), 1990.
Heartbeat, Delacorte (New York, NY), 1991.
No Greater Love, Delacorte (New York, NY), 1991.
Mixed Blessings, Delacorte (New York, NY), 1992.
Jewels, Delacorte (New York, NY), 1992.
Vanished, Delacorte (New York, NY), 1993.
The Gift, Delacorte (New York, NY), 1994, Spanish-language version with Maria Jose Rodellar published as *El Regalo,* 1994.
Accident, Delacorte (New York, NY), 1994.
Wings, Delacorte (New York, NY), 1994.
Five Days in Paris, Delacorte (New York, NY), 1995.
Lightning, Delacorte (New York, NY), 1995.
Malice, Delacorte (New York, NY), 1996.
Silent Honor, Delacorte (New York, NY), 1996.
The Ranch, Delacorte (New York, NY), 1997.
Special Delivery, Delacorte (New York, NY), 1997.
The Ghost, Delacorte (New York, NY), 1997.
The Long Road Home, Delacorte (New York, NY), 1998.
The Klone and I: A High-Tech Love Story, Delacorte (New York, NY), 1998.
Mirror Image, Delacorte (New York, NY), 1998.
Now and Forever, Delacorte (New York, NY), 1998.
Bittersweet, Delacorte (New York, NY), 1999.
Granny Dan, Delacorte (New York, NY), 1999.
Irresistible Forces: A Novel, Delacorte (New York, NY), 1999.
The House on Hope Street, Delacorte (New York, NY), 2000.
The Wedding, Delacorte (New York, NY), 2000.
Journey, Delacorte (New York, NY), 2000.
Leap of Faith, Delacorte (New York, NY), 2001.
Lone Eagle, Delacorte (New York, NY), 2001.
The Kiss, Delacorte (New York, NY), 2001.

JUVENILE

Amando, Lectorum Publications, 1985.
Martha's Best Friend, Delacorte (New York, NY), 1989.
Martha's New Daddy, Delacorte (New York, NY), 1989.

Martha's New School, Delacorte (New York, NY), 1989.

Max and the Baby-Sitter, Delacorte (New York, NY), 1989.

Max's Daddy Goes to the Hospital, Delacorte (New York, NY), 1989.

Max's New Baby, Delacorte (New York, NY), 1989.

Martha's New Puppy, Delacorte (New York, NY), 1990.

Max Runs Away, Delacorte (New York, NY), 1990.

Max and Grandma and Grandpa Winky, Delacorte (New York, NY), 1991.

Martha and Hilary and the Stranger, Delacorte (New York, NY), 1991.

Freddie's Trip, Dell (New York, NY), 1992.

Freddie's First Night Away, Dell (New York, NY), 1992.

Freddie's Accident, Dell (New York, NY), 1992.

Freddie and the Doctor, Dell (New York, NY), 1992.

OTHER

Love Poems: Danielle Steel (poetry), Dell (New York, NY), 1981, abridged edition, Delacorte (New York, NY), 1984.

(Coauthor) *Having a Baby* (nonfiction), Dell (New York, NY), 1984.

His Bright Light: The Story of Nick Traina (biography/memoir), Delacorte (New York, NY), 1998.

Contributor to *The Fabergé Case: From the Private Collection of Traina,* by John Traina. Contributor of articles and poetry to numerous periodicals, including *Good Housekeeping, McCall's, Ladies' Home Journal,* and *Cosmopolitan.*

WORK IN PROGRESS: Johnny Angel, for Delacorte; more novels.

ADAPTATIONS: Twenty-one of Steel's works have been adapted for film or television: *Now and Forever,* adapted into a movie and released by Inter Planetary Pictures, 1983; *Crossings,* made into an ABC-TV miniseries, 1986; *Kaleidoscope* and *Fine Things,* made into NBC television movies, 1990; *Changes, Daddy,* and *Palomino,* aired by NBC, 1991; *Jewels,* adapted as a four-hour miniseries, 1992; *Secrets,* 1992; *Heartbeat, Star,* and *Message from Nam,* 1993; *Once in a Lifetime, A Perfect Stranger,* and *Family Album,* 1994; *Mixed Blessings,* 1995; *Danielle Steel's "Zoya,"* made into a miniseries, 1996; and *No Greater Love, The Ring, Full Circle,* and *Remembrance,* 1996. Several of Steel's other novels, including *Wanderlust* and *Thurston House,* have also been optioned for television films and miniseries. *The Ranch* has been recorded and released by Bantam Books Audio, 1997.

SIDELIGHTS: After producing a score of bestselling novels, Danielle Steel has distinguished herself as nothing less than "a publishing phenomenon," Jacqueline Briskin reported in the *Los Angeles Times Book Review.* Since the publication of her first hardcover in 1980, Steel has consistently hit both hardback and paperback bestseller lists; there are reportedly over 450 million of her books in print. Her popularity has also spilled over into television, where twenty-one film versions of her books have been produced and garnered good ratings.

Steel's fiction is peopled by women in powerful or glamorous positions; often they are forced to choose the priorities in their lives. Thus, in *Changes* a New York anchorwoman who weds a Beverly Hills surgeon must decide whether her career means more to her than her long-distance marriage does. *Jewels* tells of the struggles of an American-born noblewoman, the Duchess of Whitfield, to find peace and raise her children in pre-World War II Europe. And while reviewers seldom express admiration for the style of romantic novelists in general—*Chicago Tribune Book World* critic L. J. Davis claimed that *Changes* is written in "the sort of basilisk prose that makes it impossible to tear your eyes from the page even as your brain is slowly [turning] to stone"—some reviewers, such as a *Detroit News* writer, found that the author's "flair for spinning colorful and textured plots out of raw material . . . is fun reading. The topic [of *Changes*] is timely and socially relevant." Toronto *Globe & Mail* contributor Peggy Hill similarly concluded about 1988's *Zoya:* "Steel has the ability to give such formula writing enough strength to not collapse into an exhausted state of cliché. *Zoya* is a fine example of that achievement."

In addition to her contemporary fiction, Steel also confronts serious issues in her books. *Mixed Blessings* looks at issues of infertility in a work that a *Rapport* reviewer called "not only well written but extremely well researched." "On the whole," the reviewer concluded, "*Mixed Blessings* is definitely one of Steel's all-time best books." *Vanished* confronts the problem of kidnapped children in a story "set mainly in 1930's Manhattan," declared a *Kirkus Reviews* contributor. "The questions Steel raises about the tug-of-wars between guilt and responsibility . . . are anything but simple," stated Stuart Whitwell in *Booklist.* "The author of *Mixed Blessings* keeps her secrets well," stated a *Publishers Weekly* reviewer, "and . . . presents a strong portrait of a tormented young woman moving toward stability."

In *Accident* Steel offers a story about the stresses placed on a family after a serious car accident puts a couple's teenaged daughter in the hospital for a brain injury. Romance reenters protagonist Page Clark's life when she falls for the Norwegian divorced father of her daughter's friend—this after having learned that her husband has been having an affair with another woman. "Steel's good intentions—to show the resilience of the human spirit in the face of insurmountable odds—are obscured by her prose," stated Joyce R. Slater in the *Chicago Tribune*. "The ending is predictable but pleasant," declared a *Publishers Weekly* contributor, "bound to delight Steel's fans."

Malice is the story of Grace Adams's attempts to deal with her self-defense murder of her abusive father, while *The Gift* tells how a 1950s family slowly comes to accept the death of their youngest daughter and welcomes an unmarried expectant mother into their fold. "The narrative," stated a critic in a *Publishers Weekly* review of *The Gift*, has "well-meaning characters, uplifting sentiments and a few moments that could make a stone weep." A *Rapport* reviewer asserted that the most significant part of the story is "the affirmation of the grand design of tragedy and its transcendent message of purpose."

In 1998 Steel produced *The Klone and I: A High-Tech Love Story*. "While sticking to the typical Steel plot . . . this time around, she throws a bit of humor and weird sexual fantasy into the mix," commented Kathleen Hughes in *Booklist*. The story revolves around Stephanie, who, having been left by her husband, meets a new man, Peter, on a trip to Paris. Stephanie soon learns that Peter has cloned himself and Stephanie must decide between the two of them. Critics were largely positive in their assessment of *The Klone and I*. "Give Steel points for turning from her usual tearjerkers . . . and trying her hand at a playful romantic comedy with a twist," wrote a critic for *Kirkus Reviews*. A *Publishers Weekly* critic argued that although "the SF element is minimal (approximately one part Ray Bradbury to 35 parts Steel), Steel's speculative whimsy spices her romantic concoction to produce a light but charming read."

In 2000, the prolific Steel published three new novels, *House on Hope Street*, *The Wedding*, and *Journey*. Critics generally felt these novels gave Steel's fans exactly what they were looking for. In a *Booklist* review of *The Wedding*, for example, Patty Engelmann wrote, "All the key elements are here: a glamorous Hollywood setting along with the beautiful people and all their

insecurities." Engelmann called the work "a good old-fashioned love story," claiming Steel is in "peak form." Engelmann felt similarly about *The House on Hope Street*: "Standard Steel fare and an excellent beach book, this will definitely please her readers." *Journey* received a similar reaction from critics. "Steel has her formula down pat, and she executes her story with her usual smooth pacing," concluded a critic for *Publishers Weekly*.

In addition to her novels, juvenile fiction, and poetry, Steel ventured into biographical memoir in 1998 with *His Bright Light: The Story of Nick Traina*. The intensely personal memoir recounts the nineteen turbulent years of Steel's son's life—a life of manic depression, drugs, and ultimately suicide. Susan McCaffrey wrote in *Library Journal* that while Steel "is at times melodramatic and the pace is sometimes hampered by the inclusion of lengthy letters and poems, this is a compelling and surprisingly objective portrait of the devastating effects of mental illness." Steel founded the Nick Traina Foundation after her son's death to benefit mental health and other children's causes. Proceeds from *His Bright Light* went directly to the foundation.

Steel once told *CA:* "I want to give [readers] entertainment and something to think about."

BIOGRAPHICAL/CRITICAL SOURCES:

BOOKS

Almanac of Famous People, sixth edition, Gale (Detroit, MI), 1998.
Bane, Vickie L. (with Lorenzo Benet), *The Lives of Danielle Steel: The Unauthorized Biography of America's #1 Best-Selling Author,* St. Martin's Press (New York, NY), 1994.
Bestsellers 89, Issue 1, Gale (Detroit, MI), 1989.
Bestsellers 90, Issue 4, Gale (Detroit, MI), 1991.
Contemporary Popular Writers, St. James Press (Detroit, MI), 1997.
Encyclopedia of World Biography, second edition, seventeen volumes, Gale (Detroit, MI), 1998.
Newsmakers, issue two, Gale (Detroit, MI), 1999.
Twentieth-Century Romance and Historical Writers, third edition, St. James Press (Detroit, MI), 1994.

PERIODICALS

Booklist, April 1, 1992, p. 1413; October 15, 1992, p. 380; June 1 & 15, 1993, p. 1735; October 15, 1994, pp. 372-373; April 15, 1995, p. 1453; October 15, 1995, p. 364; March 1, 1996, p. 1077; February 1, 1998, Kathleen Hughes, review of *The Long Road Home*, p. 877; April, 1998, Kathleen Hughes, review of *The Klone and I*, p. 1278; October 15, 1998, Kathleen Hughes, review of *Mirror Image*, p. 371; March 1, 1999, Melanie Duncan, review of *Bittersweet*, p. 1104; February 1, 2000, Patty Engelmann, review of *The Wedding*, p. 997; March 15, 2000, Patty Engelmann, review of *The House on Hope Street*, p. 1294; August, 2000, Whitney Scott, review of *Journey*, p. 2076.

Books, July, 1992, p. 18.

Chicago Tribune, September 26, 1993, pp. 6-7; March 27, 1994, p. 4.

Chicago Tribune Book World, August 28, 1983, L. J. Davis, review of *Changes*.

Detroit Free Press, December 1, 1989.

Detroit News, September 11, 1983, review of *Changes*.

Globe & Mail (Toronto), July 9, 1988, Peggy Hill, review of *Zoya*.

Kirkus Reviews, October 1, 1992, p. 1212; June 1, 1993, p. 685; January 1, 1994, p. 16; April 15, 1994, p. 504; September 15, 1994, p. 1225; April 1, 1995, p. 422; October 1, 1995, pp. 1377-1378; March 1, 1996, pp. 328-329; April 1, 1998, review of *The Klone and I*; August 15, 2000, review of *Journey*, p. 1141.

Library Journal, September 1, 1993; October 15, 1993; October 15, 1994, p. 89; June 1, 1998, Kathy Ingels Helmond, review of *The Klone and I*, p. 161; December, 1998, Susan McCaffrey, review of *His Bright Light*, p. 172.

Los Angeles Times, January 6, 1988.

Los Angeles Times Book Review, April 14, 1985.

New York Times Book Review, September 11, 1983; August 19, 1984; March 3, 1985; July 9, 1995, p. 21.

People Weekly, October 3, 1994, p. 43.

Publishers Weekly, March 30, 1992, p. 88; October 26, 1992, pp. 55-56; June 7, 1993, p. 52; January 10, 1994, p. 41; May 23, 1994, p. 76; October 10, 1994, p. 60; December 12, 1994, p. 17; February 13, 1995, p. 21; May 1, 1995, p. 41; October 16, 1995, p. 44; March 25, 1996, p. 63; February 2, 1998, review of *The Long Road Home*, p. 78; April 20, 1998, review of *The Klone and I*, p. 44; June 1, 1998, review of *The Klone and I*, p. 34; October 26, 1998, review of *Mirror Image*, p. 45; March 15, 1999, review of *Bittersweet*, p. 46; May 24, 1999, review of *Granny Dan*, p. 65; February 14, 2000, review of *The Wedding*, p. 171; April 17, 2000, review of *The House on Hope Street*, p. 46; August 28, 2000, review of *Journey*, p. 50; March 5, 2001, review of *Lone Eagle*, p. 61; May 21, 2001, review of *Leap of Faith*, p. 82.

Rapport, Volume 17, number 3, 1993, p. 23; Volume 18, number 1, 1994, p. 26; Volume 18, number 3, 1994, p. 23.

Saturday Evening Post, January, 1999, Patrick Perry, review of *His Bright Light*, p. 65.

Time, November 25, 1985.

Washington Post Book World, July 3, 1983; March 3, 1985.

OTHER

Danielle Steel Web site, http://www.randomhouse.com/ (June 27, 2001).

* * *

STEPHENS, Reed
    See DONALDSON, Stephen R(eeder)

* * *

STERN, Guy 1922-

PERSONAL: Born January 14, 1922, in Hildesheim, Germany; came to United States in 1937, naturalized in 1943; son of Julius and Hedwig (Silberberg) Stern; married Margith Langweiler, 1948 (divorced, 1977); children: Mark. *Education:* Attended St. Louis University, 1940-42; Hofstra College (now Hofstra University), B.A., 1948; Columbia University, M.A. (with honors), 1950, Ph.D. (with honors), 1953.

ADDRESSES: Home—6197 Forest Grove, West Bloomfield, MI 48322. *Office*—Wayne State University, 409 Manoogian Hall, Detroit, MI 48202.

CAREER: Columbia University, New York, NY, lecturer, 1948-49, instructor in German, 1950-55, summer instructor, 1955-61; Denison University, Granville, OH, assistant professor, 1955-58, associate professor of German, 1958-63; University of Cincinnati, Cincinnati, OH, professor of German literature and head of department of Germanic languages and literatures, 1963-73, dean of university, 1973-76; University of Maryland, College Park, professor of German and chair of department, 1976-78; Wayne State University, Detroit, MI, vice-president and provost, 1978-81, distinguished professor, 1981—. Leo Baeck Institute, New York, fellow, 1964—, member of board of directors, 1967—; guest professor, Goethe Institute, Munich, summers, 1963-66;

guest professor, Universities of Freiburg, Frankfurt, Leipzig, Potsdam, and Munich, 1963-66. Advisory editor for languages and linguistics, Dover Publications, Inc., 1957—. *Military service:* U.S. Army, Military Intelligence, 1942-45; received Bronze Star.

MEMBER: American Association of Teachers of German (president, 1970-72), American Council for German Studies (national secretary), Modern Language Association of America, American Association of University Professors, South Atlantic Modern Language Association, Lessing Society, Brecht Society, and German Studies Association.

AWARDS, HONORS: Fulbright grant for research at University of Munich, 1961-63; Bollingen Foundation research fellow, 1962-63; U.S. Office of Education grants for work-study in Hamburg, 1967; research awards from DRRD, Thyssen Foundation.

WRITINGS:

Brierlich Erzaehlt, Norton, 1956.

Listen and Learn German, Dover, 1957.

Say It in German, Dover, 1958.

Uebung macht den Meister, Norton, 1958.

An Invitation to German Poetry, Dover, 1960.

Hints on Speaking German, Dover, 1961.

Quick Change Pattern Drills, Regents Publishing, Volume I, 1962, Volume II, 1963.

(Editor) *Konstellationen: Die grossen Novellen des "Neuen Merkur,"* Deutsche Verlags Anstalt, 1964.

Efraim Frisch: Zum Verstaendnis des Geistigen, Lambert Schneider Verlag, 1964.

Hoer zu und Rat mit, McGraw, 1964.

(With Gustave Mathieu) *In Briefen erzaehlt,* Max Hueber Verlag, 1965.

(Editor) *Nelly Sachs Ausgewaehlte Gedichte,* Harcourt, 1968.

War, Weimar, and Literature: The Story of the Neue Merkur, Pennsylvania State University Press, 1971.

(Compiler, with Mathieu) *German Poetry: A Selection,* Dover, 1971.

(With Everett F. Bleiler) *Essential German Grammar,* Teach Yourself Books, 1975.

Literarische Kultur im Exil, Dresden University Press, 1997.

(Editor, with Helmut Loos) *Kurt Weill-Auf dem Weg zum: Weg der Verheissung,* Rombach Litterae (Freiburg), 2000.

Also contributor to *Revolte und Experiment, Die Literatur der Sechziger Jahre in Ost und West,* edited by Wolfgang Paulsen, 1971; *Exil und inhere Emigration II,* edited by Peter Hohendahl and Egon Schwarz, 1972; *Der deutsche Roman und seine historischen und politischen Bedingungen,* edited by Paulse; (with Dorothy Wartenberg) *Gegenwartsliteratur und Drittes Reich: Deutsche Autoren in der Auseinandersetzung mit der Vergangenheit,* edited by Hans Wagner; *The Companion to Jewish Writing and Thought in German Culture, 1096-1996,* edited by Gilman and Zipes, Yale University Press, 1997; *Für ein Kind war das anders,* edited by Bauer and Strickhausen, Metropole (Berlin), 1999; *Literatur und Geschichte: Festschrift fuer Wulf Koepke zum 70. Geburtstag,* edited by Menges, Rodopi (Amsterdam), 1998; *The New Europe at the Crossroads,* edited by Beitter, Peter Lang (New York); and *Zweimal verjagt: Die Deutschsprachigt Emigranten und der Fluchtwegs Frankreich-Lateinamerika 1933-1945,* edited by Saint Sauveur-Henn, Metropol (Berlin), 1998. Contributor of articles and reviews to language journals. Associate editor and editor, *Lessing Yearbook.*

*   *   *

STEVENS, Greg
   See COOK, Glen (Charles)

*   *   *

STILLMAN, (John) Whit(ney) 1952-

PERSONAL: Born 1952, in Washington, DC; son of John Sterling (in politics) and Margaret (in politics) Stillman; married Irene Perez Porro (a television journalist), 1980; children: two daughters. *Education:* Harvard University, B.A., 1973. *Religion:* Protestant.

ADDRESSES: Agent—William Morris Agency, 151 El Camino Drive, Beverly Hills, CA 90212.

CAREER: Screenwriter and director. Doubleday, New York City, editorial assistant and first reader, 1974-78; Access News Summary, 1979-81; foreign sales agent for Spanish films, Barcelona, Spain, 1981-85; Riley Illustration (cartoonist agency), New York City, owner and operator, 1984-91; director and producer of motion picture *Metropolitan,* 1990; director of motion pictures *Barcelona,* 1994, and *The Last Days of Disco,* 1998. Has appeared in several Spanish motion pictures, including *Sal Gorda,* 1982, and *La linea del cielo,* 1984.

Whit Stillman

MEMBER: Directors Guild of America, Writers Guild of America, Academy of Motion Picture Arts and Sciences.

AWARDS, HONORS: Academy Award nomination, best screenplay, 1991, for *Metropolitan*.

WRITINGS:

SCREENPLAYS

Metropolitan (also known as *Metropolitan: Doomed. Bourgeois. In Love*), New Line Cinema, 1990, published in *Barcelona and Metropolitan: Tales of Two Cities,* Faber & Faber, 1995.

Barcelona, Castle Rock/Fine Line, 1994, published in *Barcelona and Metropolitan: Tales of Two Cities,* Faber & Faber, 1995.

The Last Days of Disco (see also below), Castle Rock/ Westerly Films, 1998.

Contributor to the screenplay of the film *Skyline,* 1984.

OTHER

The Last Days of Disco: With Cocktails at Petrossian Afterwards (novel based on Stillman's screenplay *The Last Days of Disco*), Farrar, Straus (New York, NY), 2000.

Contributor to periodicals, including *Harper's, Village Voice,* the *Guardian* (London), and *El Pais* (Barcelona).

SIDELIGHTS: Whit Stillman is an American screenwriter and director of three critically acclaimed independent films, *Metropolitan, Barcelona,* and *The Last Days of Disco.* After establishing himself on the independent circuit with *Metropolitan,* funded in part by the sale of Stillman's Manhattan apartment, the director firmly established himself as a unique voice in contemporary independent cinema with the follow-ups *Barcelona* and *The Last Days of Disco.* He later adapted *The Last Days of Disco* as a novel in 2000.

Metropolitan, a romantic comedy of manners with roots in the works of F. Scott Fitzgerald, Jane Austen, and Philip Barry (the screenwriter of such 1940s class comedies as *Holiday* and *The Philadelphia Story*), is a semiautobiographical look at New York City's upper crust (Urban Haute Bourgeoisie, or UHB, as Stillman has dubbed them). According to *New York* magazine contributor David Denby, Stillman stated that he was inspired to create *Metropolitan* because there is "an absence in American cinema of accurate portraits of the American upper class." The result, wrote London *Times* contributor John Marriot, is "a warmly critical essay on New York's debutante set. With a fresh, eager eye which lifts the urban movie beyond the grasp of usual tired imagery, [Stillman] homes in on the Upper East Side and . . . outlines the strengths, foibles and anxieties of a disappearing class."

Metropolitan, which is subtitled *Doomed. Bourgeois. In Love,* focuses on a group of debutantes and their male friends—escorts in class-speak—who call themselves the Sally Fowler Rat Pack. Told in short, episodic segments, the film follows the characters from balls to after parties filled with earnest discussions of philosophy, class burdens (one fatalistic character is obsessed with falling from upper class grace), and politics. Tom Townsend, whose parents' divorce, socialist leanings, and reduced economic circumstances have made him a bit of an outsider, falls in with the group when an "escort shortage" makes him sought-after for the Christmas season's debutante balls. These details of Tom's circumstances parallel that of a young Stillman, who, according to *New York Times* reviewer Alessandra Stanley, serves up *Metropolitan* with "an edge of gentle irony." As Stillman told *Washington Post* interviewer Martha Sherrill, "I like to like the people I'm approaching satirically. And a lot of the stuff in the film is really just my own attitudes of 15 or 20 years ago. And so it would be masochistic to be too brutal about it."

Stillman also directed and produced *Metropolitan*, which was made on a very low budget by Hollywood standards (under three hundred thousand dollars) and sported a cast of unknown, inexperienced actors. He wrote the script over four years, whenever he had time out from his work as an agent for cartoonists and illustrators, and admits that he was still reading "how-to-direct-a-movie" books when filming began.

Despite Stillman's lack of experience, the film generated considerable word-of-mouth interest at the prestigious Sundance and Cannes film festivals and received glowing reviews from a number of respected critics. According to *Los Angeles Times* reviewer Sheila Benson, "Stillman's gift for quiet, scrupulous observation grows on you. . . . [He] understands caste, class and deportment as perfectly as . . . Jane Austen and by the time he's through, so do we." Calling the work "immensely likable," Denby also likened Stillman's class acuity to Austen and proclaimed that, despite an occasional weakness, "most of *Metropolitan* is funny and graceful. That such a film exists at all is almost a miracle." *Nation* writer Stuart Klawans professed to having "thoroughly enjoyed" Stillman's film. Klawans stated that the writer/director's accomplishment with *Metropolitan* was "so satisfying that nothing more could be wanted." Some critics, however, saw Stillman's portrayal of the UHB world as too esoteric for mass consumption; *Washington Post* contributor Desson Howe remarked that "true appreciation for this movie may be restricted to those with firsthand experience in this kind of world, or a certain upper-haute stamina."

Stillman's second film, *Barcelona*, retains much of *Metropolitan*'s episodic nature, but the film uses these narrative flashes in the service of a larger, more distinct plot. As the screenwriter explained in an interview with *Film Comment* contributor Donald Lyons, he wrote *Metropolitan* with the idea that "life is essentially an eventless affair and to make a movie full of plot and incident would be a false and inauthentic repetition of genre movie clichés. In the interval between the two scripts I changed my mind: life does have melodramatic turns."

Barcelona, set in the Spanish city of the title, concerns Ted, a sales representative for an American company, and his cousin Fred, a U.S. Navy lieutenant who is the advance man for a visit by the U.S. Sixth Fleet. Ugly American Fred arrives in Barcelona unannounced and makes himself at home in his relative's apartment, upending Ted's precariously ordered life. Ted, who expresses a Puritan sensibility, reads motivational books, and studies the Bible while dancing to Glenn Miller music, offers a marked contrast to Fred's uncensored opinions, egotistical confidence, and deep patriotism. The men find a small patch of common ground in their appreciation for and romantic involvement with the Spanish women working at a trade fair. The cousins' odd-couple antics and romantic escapades take a serious turn when Fred's outspoken politics and aloof manner lead him to be mistaken as a CIA agent; Barcelona's anti-American fervor leads to an act of violence against the Naval officer. The event leads Ted to a reassessment of his feelings toward his cousin, his job, his ideals of womanhood, and ultimately his life. As James Bowman commented in the *American Spectator,* "all the way through, the expected things do not happen and unexpected ones do, prejudices are upended and firm opinions proven wrong, including the two cousins' opinions of each other."

Barcelona garnered some very enthusiastic reviews, although the overall response was mixed. *New Yorker* contributor Terrence Rafferty noted that although the film "begins promisingly, its charm peters out fast: it's all attitude, no story." *National Review* critic John Simon registered a similar complaint, remarking, "What Mr. Stillman has is a good situation, but no story." Bowman, however, praised *Barcelona*'s "freshness and wit." The critic stated further that it "takes someone like Whit Stillman, from outside the film culture, to make a film that is not burdened with that culture's simple-minded view of America." *New Republic* critic Stanley Kauffmann commented that "*Barcelona* makes *Metropolitan* look retrospectively like a warm-up. . . . It is immediately apparent that [Stillman's] sheer cinematic fluency has taken a great leap forward." Lyons also compared *Barcelona* favorably to Stillman's first film: "The brilliant *Barcelona* shows, in its greater richness than that of *Metropolitan,* the kind of growth we always hope for in a major artist."

Positioned between *Metropolitan* and *Barcelona* is the third installment of Stillman's semi-autobiographical trilogy, *The Last Days of Disco*. Set in the early 1980s, *The Last Days of Disco* follows a group of young adults as they "converge on the hottest disco in New York, no doubt intended to closely resemble Studio 54," noted

Todd McCarthy in *Variety.* "Much is made of the characters' anxieties about getting past the velvet ropes and into the club. . . . But if you're beautiful and well dressed and female, you have no trouble being ushered into the inner sanctum," summarized McCarthy. "At the disco, an after-hours bar, on the streets, these kids blatantly humiliate each other, subtly switch their romantic allegiances, as everyone in their early twenties is wont to do, and talk talk talk," commented Graham Fuller in *Interview.* The film, according to Fuller, idolizes the last days of disco as "something it wasn't, which is what nostalgia always does. . . . Some of them [the characters] changed and some of them didn't but for all of them the electrifying, demoralizing last days of disco, if not quite a metaphor, were the last days of the best years before the rest of their lives."

Critical reaction to the movie was mixed but largely positive. David Ansen in *Newsweek* lauded Stillman's capturing of "what it feels like to start your adult life in a big city; to find yourself roommates with people you don't really like; to rush into relationships without quite knowing why." A *People Weekly* critic claimed it "takes time to sort out *Disco*'s many characters and relationships, but once you do—just like disco—the beat takes over and you're in the flow." *Entertainment Weekly* reviewer Lisa Schwarzbaum argued that Stillman "employs his story in the service of something deeper and much less trendy: a thoughtful study of decency and sin, loyalty and sex, friendship and socioeconomics, as manifested by articulate, attractive WASPs much like himself. But it's no tedious sermon." McCarthy, on the other hand, found the glib conversation among the characters "brittle" and "bizarrely out of context when taking place against the backdrop of the hedonistic, anything-goes disco scene." Stuart Klawans, however, concluded in *Nation,* "There are plenty of improbably memorable conversations (such as a debate on the moral ambiguities of Lady and the Tramp), plenty of ironies (all of them earned), and plenty of bass-heavy hits from the cocaine-and-herpes era. Whatever you may have thought of disco itself, *The Last Days of Disco* is a pleasure."

In 2000 Stillman adapted *The Last Days of Disco* as the novel *The Last Days of Disco: With Cocktails at Petrossian Afterwards.* "The premise is preciously, playfully postmodern," wrote a *Publishers Weekly* critic. In the book, Jimmy Steinway substitutes for Stillman as he writes a novelization of his disco film. "Steinway relates the events of the film from his own perspective," the *Publishers Weekly* critic continued, "clueing readers in to the way things 'really' happened." Critics were largely enthusiastic in their assessment of the novel.

Booklist contributor Kristine Huntley called the work a "witty and engaging novel," adding that "Stillman's characters are as alive on the page as they are on screen." However, Peter Khoury, writing in the *New York Times Book Review,* found the book, in light of the existence of the movie, "superfluous." Wilda Williams, on the other hand, concluded in *Library Journal,* "Stillman's tale is a wry, perspective portrait of urban young people and their mating rituals. Both fans of the film and sophisticated readers will enjoy."

BIOGRAPHICAL/CRITICAL SOURCES:

PERIODICALS

American Spectator, October, 1994, James Bowman, review of *Barcelona,* pp. 67-68.

Booklist, August, 2000, Kristine Huntley, review of *The Last Days of Disco* (novel), p. 2117.

Entertainment Weekly, June 5, 1998, Lisa Schwarzbaum, review of *The Last Days of Disco* (film), p. 46.

Film Comment, July-August, 1994, pp. 82-83, 85.

Forbes, July 6, 1998, Ben Pappas, review of *The Last Days of Disco* (film), p. 288.

Interview, May, 1998, Graham Fuller, review of *The Last Days of Disco* (film), p. 54.

Library Journal, July, 2000, Wilda Williams, review of *The Last Days of Disco* (novel), p. 143.

Los Angeles Times, August 10, 1990, Sheila Benson, review of *Metropolitan.*

Nation, August 13-20, 1990, pp. 178-180; June 15, 1998, Stuart Klawans, review of *The Last Days of Disco* (film), p. 32.

National Review, September 12, 1994, John Simon, review of *Barcelona,* pp. 87-88.

New Republic, August 15, 1994, Stanley Kauffmann, review of *Barcelona,* pp. 30-31.

Newsweek, June 8, 1998, David Ansen, review of *The Last Days of Disco* (film), p. 66.

New York, August 13, 1990, David Denby, review of *Metropolitan,* pp. 64-65.

New Yorker, August 15, 1994, Terrence Rafferty, review of *Barcelona,* p. 77.

New York Times, July 29, 1990; January 20, 1991, pp. 13, 18.

New York Times Book Review, September 10, 2000, Peter Khoury, review of *The Last Days of Disco* (novel).

People Weekly, June 8, 1998, review of *The Last Days of Disco* (film), p. 37.

Psychology Today, May-June, 1998, "The Soul of Whit Stillman," p. 28.

Publishers Weekly, July 31, 2000, review of *The Last Days of Disco* (novel), p. 73.

Times (London), November 22, 1990, John Marriot, review of *Metropolitan.*

Variety, May 25, 1998, Todd McCarthy, review of *The Last Days of Disco* (film), p. 55.

Washington Post, September 14, 1990, pp. C1, C9.

OTHER

Roughcut, http://www.roughcut.com/ (September 27, 2000).

Salon, http://www.salonmag.com/ (September 27, 2000).*

*   *   *

STRUVE, Walter 1935-

PERSONAL: Born May 6, 1935, in Somers Point, NJ; son of Louis W. (a college instructor) and Mary Laforge (a school administrator; maiden name, Russell) Struve; married Cynthia R. Rivers, February 21, 1959; children: Adam, Derick (deceased). *Education:* Lafayette College, A.B., 1955; University of Kiel, graduate study, 1955-56; Yale University, M.A., 1957, Ph.D., 1963; Free University of Berlin, graduate study, 1960-61. *Religion:* Unitarian-Universalist.

ADDRESSES: Home—New York City. *Office*—Department of History, City College of the City University of New York, 138th St. and Convent Ave., New York, NY 10031.

CAREER: Princeton University, Princeton, NJ, instructor in history, 1961-64; City College of the City University of New York, New York City, instructor, 1964-65, assistant professor, 1965-73, professor of history, 1974—, Rifkind fellow, 1998. Graduate Center of the City University of New York, professor of Germanic languages and literatures, 1997—. Public speaker in Germany and the United States.

MEMBER: American Historical Association, Conference Group on Central European History.

AWARDS, HONORS: Fulbright grants for Germany, 1955-56, 1978-79, and 1990; grants from German Academic Exchange Service, 1960-61 and 1978, American Philosophical Society, 1968-69, and Fritz Thyssen Foundation, 1979-80.

WRITINGS:

Elites against Democracy: Leadership Ideals in Bourgeois Political Thought in Germany, 1890-1933, Princeton University Press (Princeton, NJ), 1973.

Die Republik Texas, Bremen, und das Hildesheimische: Ein Beitrag zur Geschichte von Auswanderung, Handel, und gesellschaftlichem Wandel im 19. Jahrhundert, Verlag August Lax (Hildesheim, Germany), 1983, translation published as *Germans and Texans: Commerce, Migration, and Culture in the Days of the Lone-Star Republic,* University of Texas Press (Austin, TX), 1996.

Aufstieg und Herrschaft des Nationalsozialismus in einer industriellen Kleinstadt: Osterode am Harz, 1918-1945 (title means "The Rise and Rule of Nazism in the Small Industrial Town: Osterode am Harz, 1918-1945"), Klartext Verlag (Essen, Germany), 1992.

Contributor to books published in German. Contributor of articles and reviews to periodicals, including *Current History, American Historical Review, Journal of the German-Texan Heritage Society,* and *German Studies Review.*

WORK IN PROGRESS: Research for a book, *The Demise of an Ethnic Group: German Americans since 1914;* research for a book on the development and disintegration of the political culture of white-collar workers in Germany since 1880.

BIOGRAPHICAL/CRITICAL SOURCES:

PERIODICALS

American Historical Review, October, 1984, Leo Schelbert, review of *Die Republik Texas, Bremen, und das Hildesheimische,* p. 1155; April, 1998, Johnpeter Horst Grill, review of *Aufstieg und Herrschaft des Nationalsozialismus in einer industriellen Kleinstadt,* p. 542.

Journal of American History, March, 1985, La Vern J. Rippley, review of *Die Republik Texas, Bremen, und das Hildesheimische,* p. 866; September, 1997, Andreas Reichstein, review of *Germans and Texans,* p. 649.

Journal of Southern History, November, 1997, Lauren Ann Kattner, review of *Germans and Texans,* p. 869.

OTHER

Graduate Center of the City University of New York,
http://web.gc.cuny.edu/ (September 27, 2000).
University of Texas Press, http://www.utexas.edu/
(September 27, 2000).*

* * *

SWANSON, Doug J. 1953-

PERSONAL: Born in 1953.

ADDRESSES: Home—Dallas, TX, and Palo Alto, CA.
Office—c/o HarperCollins, 10 East 53rd St., New York,
NY 10022-5299.

CAREER: Dallas Morning News, Dallas, TX, staff
writer, 1982—, New York, NY, bureau chief, 1986-91,
currently Palo Alto, CA, bureau chief. Stanford University, John S. Knight fellow in journalism, 1998-99.

AWARDS, HONORS: John Creasey Award, British
Crime Writers Association, Edgar Award nomination,
Mystery Writers of America, and Anthony Award nomination, all for *Big Town;* Golden Dagger Award, British
Crime Writers Association; Pulitzer Prize nomination
for journalism; Star Reporter of the Years Award, Headliners Club of Texas.

WRITINGS:

"*JACK FLIPPO*" *MYSTERY NOVELS*

Big Town, HarperCollins (New York, NY), 1994.
Dreamboat, HarperCollins (New York, NY), 1995.
96 Tears, HarperCollins (New York, NY), 1996.
Umbrella Man, Putnam (New York, NY), 1999.
House of Corrections, Putnam (New York, NY), 2000.

SIDELIGHTS: Doug J. Swanson is the author of mystery novels featuring Jack Flippo, a private investigator
working in the Dallas, Texas, area. A *Publishers Weekly*
critic explained, "In the small but distinct subgenre of
the private eye as likable loser, Swanson's Jack Flippo
looms large." "Anyone who enjoys an antihero loser as
their sleuth will flip over Jack Flippo," wrote Harriet
Klausner in *BookBrowser.*

In Swanson's first novel, *Big Town,* Flippo loses his job
at the district attorney's office after he is discovered
having sexual relations with the wife of a prominent
drug dealer. After finding work with an uncouth lawyer,
Flippo is assigned the task of covertly photographing
Buddy George, a popular motivational speaker. Paula,
Flippo's client, is soon assaulted by George. After
Flippo intervenes, he finds himself sexually involved
with Paula, whose activities escalate from blackmail to
murder. Upon publication in 1994, *Big Town* revealed
Swanson to be a compelling and accomplished newcomer to the mystery genre. A reviewer from *Books*
found the novel "a very promising debut" and Emily
Melton, writing in *Booklist,* complimented Swanson for
"a wonderfully offbeat story that's darkly sinister, terrifically funny, and oddly touching."

In *Dreamboat,* Swanson's second novel, Flippo is a private investigator working insurance-fraud cases. When
the co-owner of a sordid bar suddenly drowns in a boating mishap, partner Rex Echols stands to recover half a
million dollars from the insurance policy. Flippo is sent
to investigate and soon realizes that the local authorities
are not prepared to cooperate. He nonetheless obtains
the aid of fetching bartender Sally Danvers, an employee at Echols's bar. In the course of pursuing the
truth about the victim's demise, Flippo uncovers other
murders and becomes endangered as well. Marilyn Stasio commented in the *New York Times Book Review*
that "you don't so much follow the plot as trot alongside, giggling in horror."

In *96 Tears,* Swanson's third Jack Flippo mystery,
Flippo is hired by stripper Sherri Plunkett to detect who
is secretly tracking Plunkett's daughter, Sandra, a beautiful actress seemingly unconcerned with her stalker.
Flippo, considerably impressed with Sandra's beauty,
discovers that her former lover is an old acquaintance
of his who was once an arsonist. In fathoming the identity and motivation of Sandra's stalker, Flippo also becomes familiar with a deadly duo of thugs, one of whom
is exceedingly violent. Melton remarked in *Booklist* that
she would be hard pressed to "find a funnier, flakier,
more entertaining mystery this side of Carl Hiassen." A
reviewer for *Publishers Weekly* stated, "Swanson proves
that the spectacle of really stupid people trying to live
by their wits makes for highly entertaining, hyperbolic
comedy."

Jack Flippo is drawn into the world of crackpot conspiracies in *Umbrella Man,* a novel in which he is asked
to locate a rumored segment of missing film showing
that there was a second gunman at the John F. Kennedy

assassination in Dallas. His investigation leads Flippo to "an assortment of sinister nut cases, from a homicidal con artist to an oxygen-deprived hit man," as Wes Lukowsky noted in *Booklist.* "The liveliest moments," a *Publishers Weekly* critic believed, "come when Jack plunges into the touristy cesspool spawned by JFK-assassination-mania (a tour in a 1963 Lincoln called the Grassy Knoll Experience, for example)." Lukowsky called *Umbrella Man* "a comic caper . . . with a uniquely Texas twist."

House of Corrections finds Flippo helping out old lawyer buddy, Wesley Joy, when he is arrested in a small town on a drug charge. Jack is soon helping Wesley locate his unreliable wife, Angelique. Then Wesley breaks out of jail, and everyone is looking for a stash of drug money that has gone missing. The *Publishers Weekly* critic found that "Swanson's mix of crudity and wit, humor and crime, sex and murder works to keep the smiles coming and the pages turning."

BIOGRAPHICAL/CRITICAL SOURCES:

PERIODICALS

Armchair Detective, winter, 1997, review of *96 Tears,* p. 114.
Booklist, February 15, 1994, Emily Melton, review of *Big Town,* p. 1064; February 1, 1995, p. 103; October 15, 1996, Emily Melton, review of *96 Tears,* p. 407; May 15, 1999, Wes Lukowsky, review of *Umbrella Man,* p. 1674.
Books, July-August, 1994, review of *Big Town,* p. 26.
Kirkus Reviews, December 1, 1993, review of *Big Town,* p. 1486; December 15, 1994, review of *Dreamboat,* p. 1526; September 1, 1996, review of *96 Tears,* p. 1279; June 15, 1999, review of *Umbrella Man,* p. 925.
Library Journal, February 1, 1995, review of *Dreamboat,* p. 103.
New York Times Book Review, March 5, 1995, Marilyn Stasio, review of *Dreamboat,* p. 20; February 2, 1997, review of *96 Tears,* p. 22.
Publishers Weekly, November 29, 1993, review of *Big Town,* p. 56; January 9, 1995, review of *Dreamboat,* pp. 57-58; September 2, 1996, review of *96 Tears,* p. 116; June 7, 1999, review of *Umbrella Man,* p. 77.

OTHER

BookBrowser, http://www.bookbrowser.com/ (June 22, 1999), Harriet Klausner, review of *Umbrella Man.**

**SWANSON, Logan
See MATHESON, Richard Burton**

*   *   *

SWEET, Leonard Ira 1947-

PERSONAL: Born May 14, 1947, in Gloversville, NY; married Karen Elizabeth Rennie. *Education:* Attended Roberts Wesleyan College, 1965-66; University of Richmond, B.A. (with honors), 1969; Colgate Rochester Divinity School, M.Div., 1972; University of Rochester, Ph.D., 1974.

ADDRESSES: Office—SpiritVentures Ministries, 86 South St., Suite C1, Morristown, NJ 07960. *E-mail*—LenISweet@aol.com.

CAREER: Ordained United Methodist minister; associate pastor of Methodist church in Rochester, NY, 1972-74; Geneseo United Methodist Church, Geneseo, NY, pastor, beginning 1974; University of Rochester, teacher, 1973-74, 1976, 1978, 1979; Colgate Rochester Divinity School, teacher, 1977-78, adjunct associate professor, beginning 1979, provost until 1985; Drew University, Madison, NJ, former professor of postmodern Christianity, vice president of academic affairs and dean of theological school, currently E. Stanley Jones Professor of Evangelism. United Theological Seminary, Dayton, OH, served as president and professor of church history; Wesley Foundation of Geneseo, served as director; Geneseo Campus United Ministries, vice president, 1976-77, president, beginning 1977.

MEMBER: American Historical Association, Organization of American Historians, American Society of Church History (past member of council), American Studies Association, American Academy of Religion, Phi Beta Kappa.

WRITINGS:

Black Images of America, 1784-1870, Norton (New York, NY), 1976.
New Life in the Spirit, 1982.
The Minister's Wife: Her Role in Nineteenth-Century American Evangelism, 1984.
The Evangelical Tradition in America, 1985.
ChartNotes, 1993.
FaithQuakes, Abingdon Press (Nashville, TN), 1994.

Health and Medicine in the Evangelical Tradition, 1994.

Communication and Change in American Religious History, 1994.

Strong in the Broken Places, 1995.

The Jesus Prescription for a Healthy Life, Abingdon Press (Nashville, TN), 1996.

A Cup of Coffee at the SoulCafe, Broadman & Holman, 1998.

Eleven Genetic Gateways to Spiritual Awakening, 1998.

SoulTsunami, Sink or Swim in the New Millennium Culture: 10 Life Rings for You and Your Church, Zondervan (Grand Rapids, MI), 1999.

AquaChurch: Essential Leadership Arts for Piloting Your Church in Today's Fluid Culture, Group Publishing, 1999.

SoulSalsa: 17 Surprising Steps for Godly Living in the 21st Century, Zondervan (Grand Rapids, MI), 2000.

Post-Modern Pilgrims: First Century Passion for the 21st-Century Church, Broadman & Holman, 2000.

The Dawn Mistaken for Dusk: If God So Loved the World, Why Can't We? (online book), 2000.

Carpe Manana: Is Your Church Ready to Seize Tomorrow?, Zondervan (Grand Rapids, MI), 2001.

Author (with Rick Warren) of audio seminar *The Tides of Change*, 1995, the video resource *AquaChurch*, 2000, and hundreds of published sermons; contributor to the Internet preaching resource *PreachingPlus.com*. Columnist, *Vital Ministry*, 1997—. Contributor of numerous articles and reviews to theology and history journals. Member of editorial council, *Theology Today;* editor, *Sweet's SoulCafe* (newsletter), 1995—.

WORK IN PROGRESS: *A Pilgrim's Primer; Nuts: Let Jesus Drive You Crazy; Forget the Vision Thing: The Power of Voice; Giving Blood: The Art of Abductive Preaching;* a biography of Phoebe Palmer; *Futuribles,* a game.

SIDELIGHTS: Leonard Sweet, a Methodist minister and scholar of church history, argues in his writings for a "postmodern" Christianity embracing the computer age and using its technological potential to spread the Gospel. Sweet's books include *SoulTsunami, Sink or Swim in the New Millennium Culture: 10 Life Rings for You and Your Church* and *AquaChurch: Essential Leadership Arts for Piloting Your Church in Today's Fluid Culture.*

In *SoulTsunami, Sink or Swim in the New Millennium Culture,* the title comes from the Japanese word for a massive tidal wave. Here Sweet presents his case that the church must adapt its message to the fast-moving technology of the time. "The present postmodern culture," explained the critic for *Publishers Weekly,* "is advancing on churches, as it has on business, education and other areas of life, with comparable great force and speed." The exponential growth of information is overwhelming Americans, Sweet argues, Americans who need to be reminded of the church's traditional values as a counterbalance to the confusion of modern society. The public must be reached with this message through the new technology. "I'm trying to move the church from fishing nets to the Internet," Sweet told Dori Perrucci in *Publishers Weekly.* Writing in *New Voice News,* Andrew R. Johnson remarked that Sweet "expresses himself in *SoulTsunami* with remarkable ease, clarity and entertaining candor."

Sweet's *AquaChurch* uses the metaphor of water to describe the societal environment in which churches operate today. He recommends specific skills that ministers can use to increase their effectiveness in this climate. "*AquaChurch,*" wrote Chad Canipe in *Next Wave,* "neither waters down the gospel nor suffers from being too hip. . . . Sweet demonstrates a well rounded set of skills that are indispensable." According to Michael Maudlin in *Christianity Today, SoulTsunami* and *AquaChurch* "flesh out [Sweet's] case for why we need to see the world and our mission in it with new glasses. . . . [Sweet] deepens and sharpens and opens us to seeing God in a newer, grander way."

Speaking with Ron Pratt of *Lifeway Christian Resources,* Sweet explains the change in approach he believes the contemporary church must undergo: "The modern world was a book culture, and we Protestants embraced the book. Look all around us in our sanctuary. All around us are books—hymn books, prayer books, Bible books, programs, bulletins, etc. This is an image culture, not a print culture. To communicate the Gospel in an image culture, one now needs screens, and in a few short years or decades, we'll need holograms, 3-D moving pictures. The real issue for our churches is do they want to be in ministry to the world, or don't they?"

BIOGRAPHICAL/CRITICAL SOURCES:

PERIODICALS

Christian Century, May 15, 1985, review of *The Evangelical Tradition in America,* p. 514; March 16, 1994, review of *Communication and Change in*

American Religious History, p. 289; May 11, 1994, Jeffrey H. Mahan, review of *Communication and Change in American Religious History,* p. 506; August 9, 1999, Michael Maudlin, "Leonard Sweet: A Postmodern Ezekiel."

Christian History, December, 1997, review of *Strong in the Broken Places,* p. 858.

Insight on the News, September 28, 1998, Laura R. Vanderkam, review of *A Cup of Coffee at the Soul-Cafe,* p. 41.

Journal of American History, December, 1983, Joan Jacobs Brumberg, review of *The Minister's Wife: Her Role in Nineteenth-Century American Evangelism,* p. 663.

Journal of Religion, April, 1998, review of *Strong in the Broken Places,* p. 282.

Library Journal, April 15, 1982, review of *New Life in the Spirit,* p. 818; March 1, 1999, Graham Christian, review of *SoulTsunami, Sink or Swim in the New Millennium Culture: 10 Life Rings for You and Your Church,* p. 93.

Publishers Weekly, March 23, 1998, review of *A Cup of Coffee at the SoulCafe,* p. 94; November 16, 1998, Dori Perrucci, "Leonard Sweet," p. S29; February 15, 1999, review of *SoulTsunami, Sink or Swim in the New Millennium Culture,* p. 101; April 12, 1999, review of *SoulTsunami, Sink or Swim in the New Millennium Culture,* p. 33; April 24, 2000, review of *SoulSalsa: 17 Surprising Steps for Godly Living in the 21st Century,* p. 87; June 12, 2000, review of *Post-Modern Pilgrims: First Century Passion for the 21st-Century Church,* p. 66.

Religious Studies Review, April, 1993, review of *Health and Medicine in the Evangelical Tradition,* p. 103.

Theology Today, January, 1994, review of *FaithQuakes,* p. 654.

OTHER

Leonard Sweet's Home Page, http://www.Leonardsweet.com/ (April, 2001).

Lifeway Christian Resources, http://chat.lifeway.com/ (January 13, 2000), Ron Pratt, "Dialogue with Leonard Sweet."

New Voice News, http://www.newvoicenews.com/ (November, 1999), Andrew R. Johnson, review of *SoulTsunami, Sink or Swim in the New Millennium Culture.*

Next Wave, http://www/next-wave.org/ (September, 1999), Chad Canipe, "*AquaChurch:* Will the Gospel 'Ship' Sail off the Edge of the Earth?"

Servant Evangelism, http://www.servantevangelism.com/ (April, 2001), Tom Brown, "An Introduction to Leonard Sweet."

Zondervan Church Source, http://www.zondervanchurchsource.com/ (April, 2001), "Interview with Leonard Sweet."

T

TALBERT, Charles H(arold) 1934-

PERSONAL: Born March 19, 1934, in Jackson, MS; son of Carl E. (a minister) and Audrey (Hale) Talbert; married Betty Weaver, June 30, 1961; children: Caroline O'Neil, Charles Richard. *Ethnicity:* "Scott-Irish-German." *Education:* Howard College (now Samford University), B.A., 1956; Southern Baptist Theological Seminary, B.D., 1959; Vanderbilt University, Ph.D., 1963. *Politics:* Democrat. *Religion:* Baptist.

ADDRESSES: Home—9602 Old Farm Road, Waco, TX 76712. *Office*—Box 97284, Baylor University, Waco, TX 76798-7284; fax: 817-755-3740. *E-mail*—charles_talbert@baylor.edu.

CAREER: Wake Forest University, Winston-Salem, NC, assistant professor, 1963-68, associate professor, 1969-74, professor of religion, 1974-89, Wake Forest Professor of Religion, 1989-96; Baylor University, Waco, TX, distinguished professor of religion, 1996—.

MEMBER: Catholic Bible Association, National Association of Baptist Professors of Religion, Society of Biblical Literature, Studiorum Novi Testamenti Societas, Phi Beta Kappa, Phi Kappa Phi, Omicron Delta Kappa.

AWARDS, HONORS: Cooperative Program in Humanities fellowship, 1968-69; Society for Religion in Higher Education fellowship, 1971-72; Reynolds Research leaves, 1979, 1986, and 1991; Doctor of Letters (honorary), Samford University, 1990; Catholic Biblical Association Visiting Professor, Pontifical Biblical Institute, Rome, 2001.

WRITINGS:

Luke and the Gnostics, Abingdon (Nashville, TN), 1966.
Reimarus: Fragments, Fortress (Philadelphia, PA), 1970, Scholars Press, 1985.
Literary Patterns, Theological Themes, and the Genre of Luke-Acts, Scholars Press, 1974.
What Is a Gospel?, Fortress, 1977.
The Certainty of the Gospel, Stetson, 1982.
Reading Luke, Crossroad Publishing (New York, NY), 1982.
Acts: Knox Preaching Guides, John Knox (Louisville, KY), 1984.
Reading Corinthians, Crossroad Publishing (New York, NY), 1987.
Learning through Suffering, Michael Glazier (Wilmington, DE), 1990.
Reading John, Crossroad Publishing (New York, NY), 1992.
The Apocalypse, Westminster/John Knox (Louisville, KY), 1994.
Reading Acts: A Literary and Theological Commentary on the Acts of the Apostles, Crossroad Publishing (New York, NY), 1997.
(With Earl J. Richard) *Reading 1 Peter, Jude, and 2 Peter: A Literary and Theological Commentary ("Reading the New Testament" series),* Smyth & Helwys, 2000.

Literary Patterns, Theological Themes, and the Genre of Luke-Acts has been translated into Japanese.

EDITOR

Perspectives on Luke-Acts, Association of Baptist Professors of Religion, 1978.

Luke-Acts: New Perspectives from the Society of Biblical Literature Seminar, Crossroad Publishing (New York, NY), 1983.

Perspectives on the New Testament, Mercer (Macon, GA), 1985.

Perspectives on I Peter, Mercer (Macon, GA), 1986.

OTHER

Also editor of *Perspectives on New Testament Interpretation,* Mercer (Macon, GA). Member of editorial board, *Journal of Biblical Literature,* 1981-83. Editor of dissertation series, National Association of Baptist Professors of Religion, 1981-83, and Society of Biblical Literature, 1984-89; associate editor, *Catholic Biblical Quarterly,* 1991-98.

WORK IN PROGRESS: A book on the Sermon on the Mount; a commentary on Paul's letter to the Romans.

SIDELIGHTS: Charles H. Talbert told *CA* that he is competent in Hebrew, Greek, Latin, French, German, and Italian.

*   *   *

TANENBAUM, Robert K.

PERSONAL: Born in Brooklyn, NY; son of a lawyer and teacher; married Patti Tyre; children: three. *Education:* University of California, Berkeley, B.A., 1965, law degree, 1968.

ADDRESSES: *Home*—Beverly Hills, CA. *Office*—c/o HarperCollins Publishers, 10 East 53rd. St., New York, NY 10022.

CAREER: Freelance writer. New York District Attorney's Office, New York, NY, assistant district attorney, 1968-73, chief of homicide division, 1973-76; Congressional Committee on Investigations, Washington, DC, deputy chief counsel, 1976-78; private law practice in Beverly Hills, CA, 1978-81; California State Attorney General's Office, special counsel, 1981; Beverly Hills, CA, member of city council, 1986-88; mayor, 1988-96. Deputy chief counsel for the Congressional committee investigating the assassinations of President John F. Kennedy and Dr. Martin Luther King, Jr.; special prosecution consultant in the Hillside Strangler case, 1981; guest lecturer, Boalt Hall School of Law, University of California, Berkeley, 1999.

WRITINGS:

NOVELS

No Lesser Plea, F. Watts (New York, NY), 1987.

Depraved Indifference, New American Library (New York, NY), 1989.

Immoral Certainty, Dutton (New York, NY), 1991.

Reversible Error, Dutton (New York, NY), 1992.

Material Witness, Dutton (New York, NY), 1993.

Justice Denied, Dutton (New York, NY), 1994.

Corruption of Blood, Dutton (New York, NY), 1995.

Falsely Accused, Dutton (New York, NY), 1996.

Irresistible Impulse, Dutton (New York, NY), 1997.

Act of Revenge, HarperCollins (New York, NY), 1999.

Reckless Endangerment, Signet (New York, NY), 1999.

True Justice, Pocket Books (New York, NY), 2000.

Enemy Within, Pocket Books (New York, NY), 2001.

OTHER

(With Philip Rosenberg) *Badge of the Assassin,* Dutton (New York, NY), 1979.

(With Peter S. Greenberg) *The Piano Teacher: The True Story of a Psychotic Killer,* New American Library (New York, NY), 1988.

ADAPTATIONS: *Badge of the Assassin* was adapted as a television movie.

SIDELIGHTS: A writer of courtroom dramas whose work has gone from mass-market paperback to hardcover bestseller, Robert K. Tanenbaum draws on his own experience as a lawyer and New York assistant district attorney to create tales of moral justice. "Of the lawyers who turned novelist in the 1980s and 1990s," wrote Jon L. Breen in the *St. James Guide to Crime and Mystery Writers,* "Robert K. Tanenbaum is among the most professionally accomplished as well as the most fictionally capable." Tanenbaum's novels have sold more than seven million copies worldwide.

Tanenbaum's novels feature New York City district attorney Butch Karp, who is, explained Lisa See in *Publishers Weekly,* "a fictionalized version of [Tanenbaum]. . . . Like Tanenbaum, Karp is a former college basketball player whose career was sidetracked by a serious knee injury. Working in the New York District Attorney's Office, he's surrounded by attorneys, cops and killers who talk and act as they do in real life." Besides Karp himself, lawyer Marlene Ciampi plays an important role in the series, first as Karp's friend, then lover, and finally his wife. The relationship between the two—both career-driven—is often stormy. When Marlene gives birth to the couple's first child, it is when killers are storming the door of her apartment. In another adventure, the child is almost killed. Breen noted that the marriage between Karp and Marlene is "one of the most exasperatingly rocky, sporadically communicative marriages in mystery fiction annals." The early books are set in the 1970s, but move forward in time as the series progresses. As time goes on, Butch and Marlene's daughter Lucy grows up and the couple advance in their respective careers. According to J. D. Reed in *People Weekly,* Tanenbaum's novels about Butch and Marlene form a "richly plotted, tough and funny crime series."

Tanenbaum's ability to capture the milieu of the New York City justice system is widely praised. Breen commented: "Throughout the series, Karp's personal and professional relationships and the depiction of the politics of the New York legal system, bolstered by insider details, engage the reader's attention." A *Publishers Weekly* critic explained that, though "Tanenbaum moved to Beverly Hills long ago, his New York is still as fresh as today's police blotter." Reviewing the novel *Corruption of Blood* for *Entertainment Weekly,* Richard North Patterson found that, even if the novel is not set in New York City, "as a portrait of prosecutors at work, it pulses with authenticity."

At their best, the novels featuring Butch and Marlene mix authenticity with a high degree of suspense, witty dialogue, and strong narrative pace. Speaking of *Act of Revenge,* the critic for *Publishers Weekly* found that "Tanenbaum has crafted a believably twisted gem of a gangster tale with visceral action and smooth comic relief." Reviewing the same novel, the *Kirkus Reviews* writer noted: "As usual, Tanenbaum pulls off a hundred effective scenes in a dozen different tones." A reviewer for *Publishers Weekly* summed up: "For those who prefer their legal thrillers with plenty of spice and a high IQ, Tanenbaum remains an essential addiction."

BIOGRAPHICAL/CRITICAL SOURCES:

BOOKS

St. James Guide to Crime and Mystery Writers, 4th edition, St. James Press (Detroit, MI), 1996.

PERIODICALS

Armchair Detective, winter, 1993, review of *Reversible Error,* p. 117; spring, 1995, review of *Justice Denied,* p. 186; summer, 1996, review of *Material Witness,* p. 338; winter, 1997, review of *Falsely Accused,* p. 71.

Best Sellers, July, 1979, p. 140.

Booklist, November 15, 1990, p. 603; August, 1994, review of *Justice Denied,* p. 2029; November 1, 1995, review of *Corruption of Blood,* p. 458; September 1, 1996, review of *Falsely Accused,* p. 69; October 15, 1997, review of *Irresistible Impulse,* p. 392; April 15, 1998, Mary Carroll, review of *Reckless Endangerment,* p. 1395; May 15, 1999, Budd Arthur, review of *Act of Revenge,* p. 1674.

Book World, July 12, 1998, review of *Reckless Endangerment,* p. 8.

Entertainment Weekly, July 18, 1997, Richard North Patterson, review of *Corruption of Blood,* p. 76.

Kirkus Reviews, November 15, 1990, p. 1566; April 1, 1993, review of *Material Witness,* p. 406; June 15, 1994, review of *Justice Denied,* p. 802; September 1, 1995, review of *Corruption of Blood,* p. 1217; July 15, 1996, review of *Falsely Accused,* p. 1001; August 1, 1997, review of *Irresistible Impulse,* p. 1149; May 1, 1999, review of *Act of Revenge,* p. 662; June 15, 2000, review of *True Justice,* pp. 828-829.

Kliatt, April 1, 1993, review of *Material Witness,* p. 16; September, 1993, review of *Reversible Error,* p. 14.

Library Journal, April 1, 1979, p. 846; November 15, 1990, p. 94; July, 1994, review of *Justice Denied,* p. 130.

Los Angeles Times, February 9, 1988.

Los Angeles Times Book Review, December 23, 1990, p. 10; April 21, 1991, p. 7.

New York Times, July 12, 1979.

New York Times Book Review, July 8, 1979, p. 11; December 16, 1990, p. 32; January 28, 1996, review of *Corruption of Blood,* p. 21.

People Weekly, June 22, 1998, J. D. Reed, review of *Reckless Endangerment,* p. 39.

Publishers Weekly, October 26, 1990, p. 65; April 19, 1993, review of *Material Witness,* p. 48; June 20, 1994, p. 103; July 11, 1994, review of *Justice Denied,* p. 62; September 12, 1994, p. 71; July 10, 1995, p. 55; September 25, 1995, p. 42; August 5, 1996, review of *Falsely Accused,* p. 430; September 29, 1997, review of *Irresistible Impulse,* p. 65; April 13, 1998, review of *Reckless Endangerment,* p. 50; April 26, 1999, review of *Act of Revenge,* p. 57; June 12, 2000, review of *True Justice,* p. 50.

Rapport, Volume 17, number 5, 1993, review of *Material Witness,* p. 30.

Tribune Books (Chicago), June 20, 1993, review of *Material Witness,* p. 7; July 24, 1994, p. 2; August 21, 1994, review of *Justice Denied,* p. 7; November 19, 1995, review of *Corruption of Blood,* p. 6.*

* * *

TERRY, Saralee
See KAYE, Marvin (Nathan)

* * *

THOMAS, Evan (III) 1951-

PERSONAL: Born April 25, 1951, in Huntington, NY; son of Evan II and Anne (Robins) Thomas; married Osceola Freear; children: two daughters. *Education:* Harvard University, B.A., 1973; University of Virginia, J.D., 1977.

ADDRESSES: Office—c/o *Newsweek,* 1750 Pennsylvania Ave. NW, Suite 1220, Washington, DC 20006. *Agent*—c/o Alice Mayhew, Simon & Schuster, 1230 Avenue of the Americas, New York, NY 10020.

CAREER: Time, New York, NY, writer, 1978-86; *Newsweek,* Washington, DC, assistant managing editor, 1986—.

AWARDS, HONORS: Harry S Truman Book Award, 1988, for *The Wise Men: Six Friends and the World They Made;* National Magazine Award, 1998, for coverage of events related to President Bill Clinton and Monica Lewinsky; "best in the business" citation from *American Journalism Review,* for political coverage.

WRITINGS:

(With Walter Isaacson) *The Wise Men: Six Friends and the World They Made,* Simon & Schuster (New York, NY), 1986.

The Man to SEE: Edward Bennett Williams, the Ultimate Insider; Legendary Trial Lawyer, Simon & Schuster (New York, NY), 1991.

The Very Best Men: Four Who Dared; The Early Years of the CIA, Simon & Schuster (New York, NY), 1995.

(With others) *Back from the Dead: How Clinton Survived the Republican Revolution,* Atlantic Monthly Press (New York, NY), 1997.

Robert Kennedy: His Life, Simon & Schuster (New York, NY), 2000.

SIDELIGHTS: As assistant managing editor of *Newsweek* magazine, Evan Thomas has had a privileged position as an observer of national politics. A single theme joins his book-length biographical works: Washington power brokers after World War II. Thomas's first book, *The Wise Men: Six Friends and the World They Made,* looks at six powerful men who formulated post-World War II foreign policy in the United States. Washington lobbyist and lawyer Edward Bennett Williams was the subject of Thomas's second book, *The Man to SEE: Edward Bennett Williams, the Ultimate Insider; Legendary Trial Lawyer.* Then, in the perhaps somewhat ironically titled *The Very Best Men: Four Who Dared; The Early Years of the CIA,* Thomas focused on a set of upperclass players in the Central Intelligence Agency (CIA) during the 1950s and early 1960s. *Robert Kennedy: His Life* seeks to demythologize the former attorney general and presidential candidate whose life was cut short by assassination.

Thomas's first book, *The Wise Men,* was written with Walter Isaacson, national editor at *Time.* During the year of publication, Thomas moved from a staff writer job at *Time* to become an editor at *Newsweek.* Reflecting both authors' backgrounds in popular magazine writing, *The Wise Men* tended toward anecdote and quotation rather than in-depth scholarly analysis. Nonetheless, in the book's 853 pages, a fairly thorough picture emerges of the subjects: Averell Harriman, Dean Acheson, Charles Bohlen, George Kennan, Robert Lovett and John McCloy. These six men were members of an elite "think tank" during the years of the Cold War. Committed to an anti-Soviet policy, they offered early support for President Lyndon Johnson's commitment to hostilities during the Vietnam War, but eventually they became disenchanted with the war and lost their influence as a result. A reviewer for *Time* characterized the book as being full of "vigor and style."

The Wise Men was generally well received. Godfrey Hodgson, writing in the *New Republic,* asserted that the authors had painted their setting "with a very sure touch." While leaving some historical questions to be further explored, Hodgson maintained that Thomas and Isaacson were "owed admiration for a superbly realized collective biography."

The Man to SEE: Edward Bennett Williams, the Ultimate Insider; Legendary Trial Lawyer, is a biography of lawyer/lobbyist Edward Bennett Williams, who died of cancer in 1988. The book was authorized by Williams's widow and friends. Thomas's portrait of Williams depicts a man of accomplishments but also one with significant personal and professional weaknesses. Williams argued a string of important constitutional cases against the government before the Supreme Court during the 1950s and 1960s, and made an enemy of J. Edgar Hoover. *The Man to See* also recounts Williams's use of character assassination to further his causes, as well as his representation of parties whose interests conflicted; in general, engaging in acts that would likely constitute ethical violations by today's standards of legal conduct. Jill Abramson, reviewing the book for the *New Republic,* declared that Thomas, in recording his subject's efforts to become the ultimate Washington insider, was "rather too impressed by Williams's grasping and clawing." Attorney and *New York Times Book Review* contributor Alan M. Dershowitz contended: "There is something unfair, it seems to me, about disclosing Williams's heretofore unknown underside so shortly after his death. . . . Writing critically of a man who so recently died is, in effect, a denial of literary due process and of the right to confront one's accuser." Dershowitz concluded: "Mr. Thomas's book is thorough and creditable, but Williams has too many friends to allow this biography to become the standard reference."

In *The Very Best Men: Four Who Dared; The Early Years of the CIA,* Thomas examines the lives of a set of well-educated, upperclass men, of the ilk depicted in his first book, *The Wise Men.* Once again the setting is the Cold War era, but the power players in this volume are Central Intelligence Agency planners Tracy Barnes, Richard Bissell, Desmond FitzGerald, and Frank Wisner. While he was the CIA's chief of operations, Frank Wisner recruited Barnes, Bissell, and FitzGerald, and together they fashioned what became known as the CIA's "department of dirty tricks." Optimism, arrogance, and zealous anti-communism were said to have characterized the work of the men depicted in *The Very Best Men.* Certainly some of their efforts, such as the Bay of Pigs invasion of Cuba, were recognized as disasters from the start. David Wise, commenting in the *Washington Post Book World,* deemed this "a jewel of a book." *The Very Best Men* offers a more vivid portrait of CIA covert activities, its rationales and failings—at least in the Cuba arena—than previously available, largely because the author was granted access to CIA confidential records unavailable to others.

Thomas's *Robert Kennedy: His Life* joins a wealth of biographies on the tragic political figure who endured first his brother's assassination and then was himself killed while running for president. Where Thomas's differs from other books is in its author's distance from his subject: Thomas did not know Kennedy, is not a left-wing idealist, and did not seek to expose more prurient details about Kennedy's private life. According to Michael Lind in the *New York Times Book Review,* this practical detachment—as well as Thomas's use of newly available information—has produced a "judicious and thorough book . . . likely to be the most comprehensive and balanced study of the life and career of Robert F. Kennedy for a long time to come." Lind added: "Despite his measured approach, or rather because of it, Thomas, who is clearly sympathetic to Robert Kennedy, demolishes the myth of Bobby the liberal icon far more effectively than any exercise in debunking has done."

BIOGRAPHICAL/CRITICAL SOURCES:

PERIODICALS

National Review, February 13, 1987, pp. 50-52.

New Republic, February 9, 1987, Godfrey Hodgson, review of *The Wise Men: Six Friends and the World They Made,* pp. 40-44; November 25, 1991, Jill Abramson, review of *The Man to SEE: Edward Bennett Williams, the Ultimate Insider; Legendary Trial Lawyer,* pp. 38-42.

Newsweek, November 3, 1986, pp. 74-75.

New Yorker, January 27, 1992, p. 84.

New York Times, October 4, 1995, p. C19.

New York Times Book Review, December 15, 1991, Alan M. Dershowitz, review of *The Man to See,* p. 14; November 12, 1995, p. 55; September 10, 2000, Michael Lind, "The Candidate."

Publishers Weekly, September 13, 1991, p. 71; August 21, 1995, p. 55.

Time, October 27, 1986, review of *The Wise Men,* p. 98.

Washington Post Book World, October 8, 1995, David Wise, review of *The Very Best Men: Four Who Dared; The Early Years of the CIA,* p. 4.

*   *   *

TRAGER, James 1925-

PERSONAL: Born May 27, 1925, in White Plains, NY; son of J. Garfield and Helen (Mosbacher) Trager; married Olivia A. Hirsch, October 1, 1955 (divorced, August, 1967); married Chie Nishio, August 28, 1972; children: (first marriage) Oliver R., Amanda M., James B. *Education:* Harvard University, A.B., 1946; Columbia University, graduate study. *Avocational interests:* Photography, history, the environment, population problems.

ADDRESSES: Home—117 West 58th St., New York, NY 10019.

CAREER: Gimbels (department store), New York, NY, advertising copywriter, 1947-48; C. J. LaRoche & Co. (advertising agency), New York, NY, copywriter, 1948-59; Warwick & Legler, Inc. (advertising agency), New York, NY, copywriter, 1959-64; Benton & Bowles, Inc. (advertising agency), New York, NY, copywriter, 1964-66; freelance writer, 1966—. New School for Social Research (New School University), teacher, 1973-74. U.S. Senate Select Committee on Nutrition and Human Needs, member of Popular Nutrition Education Panel, 1974.

AWARDS, HONORS: Julia Child Award for best reference book on food, 1995, for *The Food Chronology;* Literati Club Award for Excellence, 1992, for *The People's Chronology.*

WRITINGS:

The Enriched, Fortified, Concentrated, Country-fresh, Lip-smacking, Finger-licking, International, Unexpurgated Foodbook, Grossman, 1970.

The Big, Fertile, Rumbling, Cast-Iron, Growling, Aching, Unbuttoned Bellybook, Grossman, 1972.

Amber Waves of Grain: The Secret Russian Wheat Sales That Sent American Food Prices Soaring, Dutton (New York, NY), 1973, revised edition published as *The Great Grain Robbery,* Ballantine (New York, NY), 1975.

The People's Chronology: A Year-by-Year Record of Human Events from Prehistory to the Present, Holt (New York, NY), 1979, revised edition, 1993.

Letters from Sachiko: A Japanese Woman's View of Life in the Land of the Economic Miracle, Atheneum (New York, NY), 1982.

West of Fifth: The Rise and Fall and Rise of Manhattan's West Side, Atheneum (New York, NY), 1987.

Park Avenue: Street of Dreams, Atheneum (New York, NY), 1990.

The Women's Chronology: A Year-by-Year Record from Prehistory to the Present, Holt (New York, NY), 1994.

The Food Chronology: A Food-Lover's Compendium of Events and Anecdotes from Prehistory to the Present, Holt (New York, NY), 1995.

Contributor to magazines and newspapers, including *Medical Tribune* and *New York Times.* Former editor, *Harvard Crimson.*

ADAPTATIONS: The People's Chronology was included in the *Microsoft Bookshelf CD-ROM,* 1994-97.

SIDELIGHTS: Ad-man turned writer James Trager specializes in well-researched nonfiction books that are "massive in size, readable in style and panoramic in scope," according to *Washington Post* reporter Joseph McLellan. His first publication, *The Enriched, Fortified, Concentrated, Country-fresh, Lip-smacking, Finger-licking, International, Unexpurgated Foodbook,* is an education book laced with anecdote and humor. "This is no Betty Crocker Bake-off," wrote the *Harper's* magazine critic, "but an entirely serious history of food, in its infinite variety, cultivation, and preparation, which [Trager] deftly relates to anthropology, archaeology, biology, ecology, sociology, mythology, etc." *Washington Post Book World* contributor Joel Sayre, who described the book as being "carefully planned and beautifully executed," believed that "Trager, as a first-rate professional writer, knew that without plenty of leavening and livening the text would smother the reader to death. . . . So he brightened it up wherever he could and the results are immensely successful."

Trager returned to food history with *The Food Chronology: A Food-Lover's Compendium of Events and Anecdotes from Prehistory to the Present,* a massive gathering of facts about food throughout human history. "Trager has done an excellent job," Jan Lewis wrote in *Booklist,* "in verifying obscure facts." Among those facts are the first official serving of sherbet in Europe (to King Richard the Lion-Hearted in 1191), the first appearance of brandy (1300, in France), and the real-life source for the Mother Goose nursery rhyme involving blackbirds baked in a pie (1454). George W. Hunt in *America* described *The Food Chronology* as "a wonderful, endlessly fascinating book."

The People's Chronology: A Year-by-Year Record of Human Events from Prehistory to the Present is a historical encyclopedia that stresses human events rather than political accomplishments. Trager spent ten years researching what the *New York Times Book Review* calls "the striking events and anecdotes that have customarily been left out of serious history." McLellan believes that "besides being a handy and impressive compilation of facts, 'The People's Chronology' is enormous fun to read, at least for those who are gifted with random and voracious curiosity."

The Women's Chronology: A Year-by-Year Record from Prehistory to the Present follows the same pattern developed in *The People's Chronology,* this time noting the achievements of women throughout the ages. Beginning with the female fossil known as "Lucy," the earliest known example of human remains, Trager traces women's accomplishments on a year-by-year basis up to the present time. Some 3,500 women and 13,000 events are included in what the *Booklist* contributor described as an "attractive and readable" volume.

BIOGRAPHICAL/CRITICAL SOURCES:

PERIODICALS

America, February 24, 1996, George W. Hunt, review of *The Food Chronology: A Food-Lover's Compendium of Events and Anecdotes from Prehistory to the Present*, p. 2.

American History, April, 1995, review of *The Women's Chronology: A Year-by-Year Record from Prehistory to the Present*, p. 24.

American Spectator, July, 1990, Richard Brookhiser, review of *Park Avenue: Street of Dreams*, p. 45.

Booklist, May 15, 1992, review of *The People's Chronology: A Year-by-Year Record of Human Events from Prehistory to the Present*, p. 1717; October 15, 1994, review of *The Women's Chronology*, p. 453; January 1, 1996, review of *The Food Chronology*, p. 882.

Harper's, January, 1971, review of *The Enriched, Fortified, Concentrated, Country-fresh, Lip-smacking, Finger-licking, International, Unexpurgated Foodbook.*

Library Journal, April 15, 1980, review of *The People's Chronology*, p. 923; January, 1990, Susan Hamburger, review of *Park Avenue*, p. 132; March 1, 1992, Kenneth F. Kister, review of *The People's Chronology*, p. 86; August, 1994, Patricia A. Beaber, review of *The Women's Chronology*, p. 76; January, 1996, Wendy Miller, review of *The Food Chronology*, p. 92.

New York Times, October 10, 1970; October 25, 1982; February 17, 1987.

New York Times Book Review, December 6, 1970; November 12, 1972; September 9, 1973; October 28, 1979; March 1, 1987, David W. Dunlap, review of *West of Fifth: The Rise and Fall and Rise of Manhattan's West Side*, p. 21; July 29, 1990, Richard F. Shepard, review of *Park Avenue*, p. 21; May 3, 1992, David Walton, review of *The People's Chronology*, p. 20.

Penthouse, January, 1980, Robert Stephen Spitz, review of *The People's Chronology*, p. 64.

Publishers Weekly, December 15, 1989, Genevieve Stuttaford, review of *Park Avenue*, p. 54.

School Library Journal, August, 1992, Barbara Hawkins, review of *The People's Chronology*, p. 192; February, 1995, Maureen Connelly, review of *The Women's Chronology*, p. 133; June, 1996, Martha Ray, review of *The Food Chronology*, p. 170.

Smithsonian, March, 1983, Randy Sue Coburn, review of *Letters from Sachiko: A Japanese Woman's View of Life in the Land of the Economic Miracle*, p. 176.

Washington Post, September 10, 1979.

Washington Post Book World, March 7, 1971, Joel Sayre, review of *The Enriched, Fortified, Concentrated, Country-fresh, Lip-smacking, Finger-licking, International, Unexpurgated Foodbook;* February 8, 1987.

Wilson Library Bulletin, September, 1992, James Rettig, review of *The People's Chronology*, p. 121; January, 1995, James Rettig, review of *The Women's Chronology*, p. 74.

*   *   *

TRAVIS, Aaron
See SAYLOR, Steven

*   *   *

TUCKER, Paul Hayes 1950-

PERSONAL: Born July 7, 1950, in New York, NY; son of William Duane (an attorney) and Mary Elizabeth (Hayes) Tucker; married Maggie Moss (a teacher), November 17, 1973; children: Jonathan Moss. *Education:* Williams College, B.A., 1972; Yale University, M.A., Ph.D., 1979.

ADDRESSES: Home—21 Monument Sq., Charlestown, MA 02129. *Office*—Department of Art, University of Massachusetts, 100 Morrissey Blvd., Boston, MA 02125.

CAREER: University of Massachusetts, Boston, assistant through full professor of art, 1978—; also serves on the faculties of the Institute of Fine Arts (Boston), and Williams College.

MEMBER: College Art Association of America, Charlestown Preservation Society.

AWARDS, HONORS: Distinguished Scholarship Award, University of Massachusetts at Boston, 2000; creation of the Paul Hayes Tucker Endowed Chair for the Arts at the University of Massachusetts at Boston, 2000; Governor's Award, Yale University; recipient of grants from the Florence Gould Arts Foundation.

WRITINGS:

Monet at Argenteuil, Yale University Press (New Haven, CT), 1982.

Monet in the '90s: The Series Paintings, Museum of Fine Arts (Boston, MA)/Yale University Press (New Haven, CT), 1989.

Richard Upton and the Rhetoric of Landscape, c. 1991, also published as *Richard Upton: The Italian Landscapes: Grey Art Gallery and Study Center, New York, New York, Paysage demoralisé—Landscape at the End of the Century . . .,* c. 1991.

(Editor, with Jeanne Clegg) *The Dominion of Daedalus: Papers from the Ruskin Workshop Held in Pisa and Lucca, 13-14 May 1993,* Brentham Press (St. Albans), 1994.

Claude Monet: Life and Art, Yale University Press (New Haven, CT), 1995.

(Editor) *Manet's Le déjeuner sur l'herbe,* Cambridge University Press (Cambridge, England), 1998.

Monet in the Twentieth Century (catalogue), Yale University Press (New Haven, CT), 1998.

The Impressionists at Argenteuil (catalogue), National Gallery of Art (Washington, DC)/Wadsworth Atheneum Museum of Art (Hartford, CT), 2000.

(Translator) Maria Michela Sassi and Geoffrey Lloyd, *The Science of Man in Ancient Greece,* University of Chicago Press (Chicago, IL), 2001.

Contributor to exhibition catalogues, including *Guggenheim Museum Thannhauser Collection,* foreword by Thomas Krens, Solomon R. Guggenheim Museum/Rizzoli (New York), 1992, 3rd revised edition 2001; *Monet, a Retrospective,* Chunichi Shinbunsha, 1994; and *Monet: Late Paintings of Giverny from the Musée Marmottan,* Abrams, 1994, and to periodicals such as *Art Bulletin* and *Modernism and Modernity.*

SIDELIGHTS: French impressionist painter Claude Monet resided in the town of Argenteuil from 1871 to 1878. In his study of Monet's paintings from this time period, entitled *Monet at Argenteuil,* Paul Tucker argues that Monet displayed an inability to accept the conflicts he saw between nature and the newly industrialized French society. Although *Los Angeles Times Book Review* writer Suzanne Muchnic did not ultimately agree with

Tucker's analysis of the Argenteuil paintings, she acknowledged that his "thesis is absorbing and his context rewarding." Muchnic further observed that while *Monet at Argenteuil* is of particular interest to art scholars, more generalized readers will also benefit from Tucker's "easily comprehensible volume."

Monet at Argenteuil was followed by a score of other books and exhibition catalogues, most focusing on Monet and his milieu. In *Monet in the Twentieth Century,* Tucker focuses on the last twenty-five years of the artist's life, when he had already become a national treasure in the world of modern art. The author points to Monet's continuing growth as an artist, as well as the effects of the modern world on the artist, including World War I and the Dreyfus affair. The second half of the book reproduces the art of the period under discussion, including the famous water lilies series. "Tucker has made a thought-provoking and important contribution," Ellen Bates contended in *Library Journal.* Like *Monet in the Twentieth Century, The Impressionists at Argenteuil* is an exhibition catalogue combining critical essays and reproductions of the paintings. Here, Tucker expands the view of his *Monet at Argenteuil* by including commentary on the other artist-denizens of 1870s Argenteuil, the small town credited with the birth of Impressionism, such as Boudin, Caillebotte, Manet, Renoir, and Sisley.

BIOGRAPHICAL/CRITICAL SOURCES:

PERIODICALS

ARTnews, May, 1990, Nancy Stapen, "Paul Hayes Tucker: Monet in a New Light," p. 139.

BM, July, 1999, review of *Manet's Le dejeuner sur l'herbe,* p. 427.

Choice, March, 1999, review of *Monet in the Twentieth Century,* p. 1257.

Chronicle of Higher Education, April 25, 1990, Zoe Ingalls, "The Quest to Reunite Monet's Famous Series Paintings," p. B7.

Library Journal, April 15, 1990, Lynell A. Morr, review of *Monet in the '90s: The Series Paintings,* p. 92; November 15, 1998, Ellen Bates, review of *Monet in the Twentieth Century,* p. 65.

Los Angeles Times Book Review, May 9, 1982, Suzanne Muchnic, review of *Monet at Argenteuil.*

New York Times Book Review, December 5, 1982; December 17, 1995, Mignon Nixon, review of *Monet in the '90s: The Series Paintings,* p. 11.*

V

Van WINCKEL, Nance 1951-

PERSONAL: Born October 24, 1951, in Roanoke, VA; daughter of Winford Hilton (in sales) and Mary Lee (a banker; maiden name, Penn) Van Winckel; married Robert Fredrik Nelson (an artist), 1985. *Education:* University of Wisconsin—Milwaukee, B.A., 1973; University of Denver, M.A., 1976.

ADDRESSES: Home—12506 South Gardner, Cheney, WA 99004. *Office*—Graduate Creative Writing Program, Eastern Washington University, Spokane. *E-mail*—nancev@sisnd.com.

CAREER: Milwaukee Journal, Milwaukee, WI, journalist, 1974; Marymount College, Salina, KS, instructor in English, 1976-79; Lake Forest College, Lake Forest, IL, associate professor of English and director of writing program, 1979-90; Eastern Washington University, Spokane, associate professor of English, beginning 1990, currently professor in graduate creative writing program. Vermont College, faculty member in M.F.A. program, 2000—.

AWARDS, HONORS: Fellow of Illinois Arts Council, 1983, 1985, 1987, and 1989; fellowships from National Endowment for the Arts, 1988 and 2001; poetry award from Society of Midland Authors, 1989, for *Bad Girl, with Hawk;* Gordon Barber Award, Poetry Society of America, 1989; grants from Northwest Institute, 1991, 1993, and 1994; Paterson Fiction Prize, 1998; Washington State Artists Trust Literary Award in fiction, 1998; Washington State Governor's Award for literature, 1999.

WRITINGS:

The Twenty-four Doors: Advent Calendar Poems, Bieler Press (St. Paul, MN), 1985.

Bad Girl, with Hawk (poems), University of Illinois Press (Champaign, IL), 1988.
Limited Lifetime Warranty (stories), University of Missouri Press (Columbia, MO), 1994.
The Dirt (poems), Miami University Press (Oxford, OH), 1994.
Quake (stories), University of Missouri Press (Columbia, MO), 1997.
After a Spell (poems), Miami University Press (Oxford, OH), 1998.
Curtain Creek Farm (stories), Persea Books (New York, NY), 2000.

Contributor of poems to magazines, including *American Poetry Review, Georgia Review, Ploughshares, Grand Street, Prairie Schooner, Paris Review, Ohio Review, North American Review, Poetry Northwest,* and *Antioch Review.* Associate editor, *Denver Quarterly,* 1976, and *Ark River Review,* 1979-81; editor, *Willow Springs,* 1990—.

SIDELIGHTS: Nance Van Winckel is a poet and short-story writer who has won wide acclaim for her work. Among her published books are the poetry collections *Bad Girl, with Hawk* and *The Dirt,* and the story collections *Limited Lifetime Warranty, Quake,* and *Curtain Creek Farm.*

Speaking of her poetry, a critic for *Contemporary Poets* noted: "Van Winckel is a versatile and talented writer. The strong voices that compel her poems, coupled with her studious attention to craft, have served to elevate her work and establish her as a significant American poet."

In her collection *Limited Lifetime Warranty* Van Winckel interweaves sixteen related stories, all narrated by a young girl named Martha. Each of the stories focuses on a moment when Martha learns one of life's lessons—how to accept tragedy, for example—as she grows into adulthood and a career as a veterinarian. "Over and over," noted Jeanne Schinto in *Belles Lettres,* "Martha and the other characters experience tragedy and somehow, instead of being crumpled are fortified by it." While the critic for *Publishers Weekly* found that "Van Winckel has assembled a set of striking characters," he also observed that "Martha's own rich life deserves more expansive treatment." But Schinto concluded that *Limited Lifetime Warranty* "presents as hopeful a view of life as I have read anywhere in a long time."

Van Winckel again links her stories in the collection *Quake,* this time by making an earthquake figure into each story. Recurring characters include Sarah, a divorced woman who is struck by lightning, an extended gypsy family, some of whom are involved in helping draft dodgers, and a young artist who uses scavenged materials to create his art. A reviewer for *Publishers Weekly* found that Van Winckel's "writing is crisp, marked by dry humor and the uncommon ability to make a narrator's voice convincing while letting the reader in on ironies lost to the speaker." A critic for *Kirkus Reviews* noted that "Van Winckel demands and deserves a careful reading."

Curtain Creek Farm centers on a rural commune founded in the 1960s and still thriving. The stories range over wide terrain, from how the community deals with a prowling cougar, to their decision to create their own Web site, to the romantic relationships between members. "Life on the farm can be of considerable interest," noted a *Kirkus Reviews* critic. According to a *Publishers Weekly* reviewer, Van Winckel's collection "tenderly and honestly describes the joys, compromises, dreams and hard realities of the farm." Writing in the *Seattle Times,* Bob Papinchak praised "the overall rich sense of community that the reader feels about this group of intensely committed females."

Van Winckel once told *CA* that her interests include American folklore and folk life. She added: "I like writing dramatic monologues. I am interested in reaching an intersection between narrative and lyric voices."

BIOGRAPHICAL/CRITICAL SOURCES:

BOOKS

Contemporary Poets, 6th edition, St. James Press (Detroit, MI), 1996.

PERIODICALS

Another Chicago, spring, 1997, review of *Limited Lifetime Warranty,* p. 325.
Belles Lettres, fall, 1994, Jeanne Schinto, review of *Limited Lifetime Warranty,* p. 29.
Georgia Review, fall, 1994, review of *Limited Lifetime Warranty,* p. 618.
Kirkus Reviews, March 15, 1994, review of *Limited Lifetime Warranty,* p. 339; February 15, 1997, review of *Quake,* p. 254; July 1, 200, review of *Curtain Creek Farm,* p. 917.
Library Journal, May 1, 1994, review of *Limited Lifetime Warranty,* p. 141.
Publishers Weekly, May 2, 1994, review of *Limited Lifetime Warranty,* p. 286; March 17, 1997, review of *Quake,* p. 78; July 10, 2000, review of *Curtain Creek,* p. 44.
Seattle Times, August 20, 2000, Bob Papinchak, review of *Curtain Creek Farm,* p. M8.

*   *   *

VELIE, Alan R. 1937-

PERSONAL: Born November 16, 1937, in New York, NY; son of Lester (a writer) and Frances (Rockmore) Velie; married Sue Thompson (a teacher), June 23, 1962; children: Jonathan Thompson, William Place. *Education:* Harvard University, B.A., 1959; Stanford University, M.A. and Ph.D., 1969. *Politics:* Democrat.

ADDRESSES: Home—1022 Kings Rd., Merrymen Green, Norman, OK 73072. *Office*—Department of English, University of Oklahoma, Norman, OK 73019.

CAREER: University of Oklahoma, Norman, member of faculty teaching English and Native American literature, 1967—, chair of English department, 1978—. *Military service:* U.S. Marine Corps, 1959-62; became first lieutenant.

AWARDS, HONORS: National Endowment for the Humanities fellowship, 1973.

WRITINGS:

Shakespeare's Repentance Plays, Fairleigh Dickinson University Press, 1972.
Blood and Knavery, Fairleigh Dickinson University Press, 1973.

Man and Nature in Literature, Goodyear Publishing, 1974.

American Indian Literature: An Anthology, University of Oklahoma Press, 1979, revised edition, 1991.

The Lightning Within, University of Nebraska Press, 1991.

Native American Perspectives on Literature and History, University of Oklahoma Press, 1995.

Also author of *Four American Indian Literary Masters: N. Scott Momaday, James Welch, Leslie Marmon Silko, and Gerald Visenor.*

*   *   *

VINCENT, Gabrielle
[A pseudonym]

PERSONAL: Born in Brussels, Belgium.

ADDRESSES: Home—Brussels, Belgium. *Agent*—c/o Front Street, 20 Battery Park Ave., No. 403, Asheville, NC 28801-2734.

CAREER: Illustrator and author of children's books, 1980—.

AWARDS, HONORS: Notable Book designation, American Library Association, 1982, for *Ernest and Celestine, Ernest and Celestine's Picnic,* and *Smile, Ernest and Celestine;* Best Illustrated Children's Book of the Year designation, *New York Times,* 1982, for *Smile, Ernest and Celestine;* Children's Books of the Year selections, Child Study Association, 1986, for *Breakfast Time, Ernest and Celestine* and *Ernest and Celestine's Patchwork Quilt.*

WRITINGS:

FOR CHILDREN; SELF-ILLUSTRATED

Ernest and Celestine, Greenwillow (New York, NY), 1982.

Bravo, Ernest and Celestine!, Greenwillow (New York, NY), 1982.

Ernest and Celestine's Picnic, Greenwillow (New York, NY), 1982.

Smile, Ernest and Celestine, Greenwillow (New York, NY), 1982, published as *Smile Please, Ernest and Celestine,* Picture Lions (London, England), 1986.

Merry Christmas, Ernest and Celestine, Greenwillow (New York, NY), 1984.

Ernest and Celestine's Patchwork Quilt, Greenwillow (New York, NY), 1985.

Breakfast Time, Ernest and Celestine, Greenwillow (New York, NY), 1985.

Where Are You, Ernest and Celestine?, Greenwillow (New York, NY), 1986.

Mimi und Brumm in museum, Sauerlaunder, 1986.

Feel Better, Ernest!, Greenwillow (New York, NY), 1988, published as *Get Better, Ernest,* Julia MacRae (London, England), 1988.

Ernest and Celestine at the Circus, Greenwillow (New York, NY), 1989.

Mr. Bingley's Bears, Hutchinson (London, England), 1993.

a day, a dog, Front Street (Asheville, NC), 2000.

ILLUSTRATOR

Christophe Gallaz, *Threadbear,* translated by Martin Sokolinsky, Creative Education (Mankato, MN), 1993.

Charlotte Pomerantz, *Halfway to Your House* (poems), Greenwillow (New York, NY), 1993.

ADAPTATIONS: Ernest and Celestine's Picnic was adapted into a filmstrip with cassette by Weston Woods, 1984; *Ernest and Celestine* was adapted into a filmstrip by Weston Woods and is available in a Braille edition.

SIDELIGHTS: Painter, illustrator, and author Gabrielle Vincent is the creator of the popular children's book characters Ernest and Celestine, a stalwart bear and young mouse, respectively. In a series of warmhearted adventures, the two friends celebrate holidays, travel together, and serve as close companions in times of trouble. With their simple texts originally written in French, Vincent's stories have proved universal, appealing to children around the world as much for their text as for the author's gentle sepia ink and watercolor artistry. Commenting on the illustrations for *Breakfast Time, Ernest and Celestine, School Library Journal* contributor Susan McCord noted that Vincent's "soft pastel watercolors shine with a joy of simple life" while "wonderful expression in the simple faces make up for the lack of words." Linda Boyles echoed such praise by noting in her *School Library Journal* review that the series' popularity is based on "the display of gentleness and warmth between Ernest, the grown-up; and Celestine, the child." In *Junior Bookshelf* a critic hailed Vincent's text in *Get Better, Ernest!* (published in the United States as *Feel Better, Ernest!*) as "a model of its kind, not a word too many and all to the point."

Born and raised in Belgium, Vincent made the decision to become an artist when she was a child. Unfortunately, as often happens, life got in the way and it wasn't until 1980 that she was able to fully devote herself to drawing, painting, and writing. In 1981, Vincent's popular Ernest and Celestine characters first appeared, presented at the Bologna Book Fair shortly before making their way to bookstore shelves. The bear and mouse have continued to be popular throughout Europe as well as in the United States, and Vincent's books have been translated into several other languages.

In *Ernest and Celestine,* readers meet the bear and mouse for the first time as tiny Celestine is in a tizzy over the loss of her toy duck. With only a few days to go before the Christmas holidays, she can count on reliable Ernest to help her in her hour of need in a story that a *Publishers Weekly* contributor dubbed effective at illustrating a "loving relationship." *Merry Christmas, Ernest and Celestine* finds the friends throwing a holiday party in a book that *New York Times Book Review* contributor Molly Ivins hailed as "world-class adorable." In a *Kirkus Reviews* article, a critic found *Merry Christmas, Ernest and Celestine* "buoyant and poignant . . . with the perennial appeal of Christmas from scraps."

In *Ernest and Celestine at the Circus,* readers follow the pair under the Big Top, Ernest donning the clown outfit he once wore in his younger days and Celestine embarrassed at the way her companion is attracting attention. After Ernest wins a round of applause in center ring, the young mouse's embarrassment changes to pride in her friend. *School Library Journal* contributor Linda Boyles called the story "a warm and gentle vignette from the daily life of two caring friends." On the move again in *Where Are You, Ernest and Celestine?,* the bear and mouse travel to the Louvre in Paris, where Ernest wants to find a job. While he is turned down because of his condition that he be allowed to bring young Celestine with him to work everyday, Ernest nonetheless enjoys the museum with his tiny companion, although at one point she fears she has lost her guide. The two are once again close to home in *Feel Better, Ernest!,* as Celestine becomes caretaker of her older companion. While finding this installment in the series less effective than other books, Denise Wilms maintained in a *Booklist* critique that *Feel Better, Ernest!* shows Vincent's writing to be "as fluid as ever, and the sketches . . . very apt."

BIOGRAPHICAL/CRITICAL SOURCES:

BOOKS

Children's Literature Review, Volume 13, Gale (Detroit, MI), 1987.
St. James Guide to Children's Writers, fifth edition, St. James (Detroit, MI), 1999.

PERIODICALS

Booklist, January 1, 1985, Denise Wilms, review of *Merry Christmas, Ernest and Celestine,* p. 644; September 15, 1985, Denise Wilms, review of *Breakfast Time, Ernest and Celestine* and *Ernest and Celestine's Patchwork Quilt,* p. 141; November 15, 1988, Denise Wilms, review of *Feel Better Ernest!,* p. 588; August, 1989, Denise Wilms, review of *Ernest and Celestine at the Circus,* p. 1982.
Books for Keeps, May, 1986, Jill Bennett, review of *Smile Please, Ernest and Celestine,* p. 19.
Bulletin of the Center for Children's Books, January, 1986, Zena Sutherland, review of *Breakfast Time, Ernest and Celestine,* p. 98; February, 1986, Zena Sutherland, review of *Ernest and Celestine's Patchwork Quilt,* p. 119.
Horn Book, November, 1987, review of *Merry Christmas, Ernest and Celestine,* p. 763.
Junior Bookshelf, October, 1988, review of *Get Better, Ernest!,* p. 230; April, 1994, review of *Mr. Bingley's Bears,* p. 52.
Kirkus Reviews, November 1, 1984, review of *Merry Christmas, Ernest and Celestine,* p. 92; July 1, 1989, review of *Ernest and Celestine at the Circus,* p. 998.
New York Times Book Review, November 11, 1984, Molly Ivins, review of *Merry Christmas, Ernest and Celestine,* p. 58; October 6, 1985, review of *Breakfast Time, Ernest and Celestine,* p. 41; March 30, 1986, Arthur Yorinks, review of *Where Are You, Ernest and Celestine?,* p. 23; February 12, 1989, review of *Feel Better, Ernest!,* p. 25; April 10, 1994, Cynthia Zarin, review of *Halfway to Your House,* p. 35.
Publishers Weekly, October 31, 1986, review of *Ernest and Celestine,* p. 74.
School Librarian, November, 1988, Maisie Roberts, review of *Get Better, Ernest!,* p. 133; May, 1994, Janet Sims, review of *Mr. Bingley's Bears,* p. 56.
School Library Journal, May, 1985, Susan McCord, review of *Breakfast Time, Ernest and Celestine,* p. 78; November, 1985, Susan McCord, review of *Ernest*

and Celestine's Patchwork Quilt, p. 78; May, 1986, Cathy Woodward, review of *Where Are You, Ernest and Celestine?,* p. 85; December, 1988, Gratia Banta, review of *Feel Better, Ernest!,* p. 94; October, 1989, Linda Boyles, review of *Ernest and Celestine at the Circus,* p. 97.*

*   *   *

VONDRA, J. Gert
   See VONDRA, Josef (Gert)

*   *   *

VONDRA, Josef (Gert) 1941-
   (J. Gert Vondra)

PERSONAL: Born June 11, 1941, in Vienna, Austria; son of Josef Vondra (an architect) and Theresa Knoll Horvath (an actress); married Janet (a journalist), August 18, 1975 (divorced); children: Alexandra (Ally). *Education:* Attended De La Salle College, 1952-59; attended University of Melbourne, 1960-63. *Religion:* Pantheist. *Avocational interests:* Swimming.

ADDRESSES: Home and office—27 Waverley Ave., Lorne, Victoria 3232 Australia. *E-mail*—jvondra@ crimus.com.au.

CAREER: Sun-New Pictorial, Melbourne, Victoria, Australia, cadet journalist, 1960-63; Radio Australia, reporter, 1964-67; freelance writer, 1967—.

AWARDS, HONORS: Senior Writer's fellowship, Australian government, 1974.

WRITINGS:

(Under name J. Gert Vondra) *Timor Journey,* Lansdowne (Melbourne, Victoria, Australia), 1968.
The Other China, Lansdowne (Melbourne, Victoria, Australia), 1968.
(Under name J. Gert Vondra) *Hong Kong: City without a Country,* Lansdowne (Melbourne, Victoria, Australia), 1970.
A Guide to Australian Cheese, Lansdowne (Melbourne, Victoria, Australia), 1971, 4th edition published as *A Guide to Australian Cheese: A Complete Guide,* Cavalier Press (South Yarra, Victoria, Australia), 1992.

Paul Zwilling (novel), Wren (Melbourne, Victoria, Australia), 1974, published as *For the Prime Minister: The Paul Zwilling Papers,* David & Charles (London, England), 1975.
Hellas Australia/Ellada Australia, Greek translation by George Psaros, Widescope (Melbourne, Victoria, Australia), 1979.
German-speaking Settlers in Australia, Cavalier (South Yarra, Victoria, Australia), 1981.
No-Name Bird (young adult), Puffin (Ringwood, Victoria, Australia), 2000.

WORK IN PROGRESS: A novel on the Lorne, Australia Blue Water Swim Classic "Pier-to-Pub" race, and a young adult novel about dolphins. Researching a young adult novel on Guillet-Barre Syndrome.

SIDELIGHTS: Journalist Josef Vondra once commented: "Coming from an Australian mainstream journalistic professional background, I have always tried to write about what I know, rather than what I have made up. In writing fiction, however, the straight putting down of facts is often not suitable and therefore I try to separate the emotion from the fact. A story can be pure fiction, though the thoughts and feelings expressed are personal. This is especially helpful in writing for children as they have keen senses on what is real and what is not.

"I started off writing for adults—travel books, a biographical novel, two historical works and a guide to cheese—but since the publication of my novel, *No-Name Bird,* I have been drawn to writing more for young adults. There is a strong link between the very young and the mature—a child is the most truthful of human beings. As you grow, you learn to lie, cheat, and to acquire all the other characteristics that make up an adult. With age, however, you tend to know who and what you are and life does become simpler and more truthful, certainly more honest.

"I live in Lorne, a seaside resort town on the southwestern coast of Victoria and the place does inspire me to write. Not so much the peace and quiet, but rather the companionship of a small community. It's hard to be lonely (and writing is a lonely occupation) in a place like this. Most of my work is done in the morning, from 6:30 a.m. to about 2 p.m. Often, I work the day through. Lorne has inspired at least one work—a novel about the town's "Pier-to-Pub" swim over a 1.2 km distance. About 3,500 swimmers aged between fourteen and eighty swim the distance each year. It is the biggest "Blue Water Classic" in the world.

"For recreation, I swim at a pool at least twice a week at Colac, a country town about a forty minutes' drive from Lorne. I used to swim competitively and swimming still gives me enormous joy."

*   *   *

VOS, Ida 1931-

PERSONAL: Born December 13, 1931, in Gröningen, Netherlands; daughter of Joseph (a commercial agent) and Bertha (Blok) Gudema; married Henk Vos (an insurance broker), April 3, 1956; children: Josephine, Karel, Bert. *Education:* Kweekschool Voorbereidend Ondervijs Training College, teaching certificates, 1950, 1952.

ADDRESSES: Home—Dr. Wibautlaan 6G, Rijswijk, Holland 2285XY, Netherlands; c/o Terese Edelstein, 1342 Devonshire, Grosse Pointe Park, MI 48230.

CAREER: Writer. Teacher in Den Haag, Rijswijk, Holland, Netherlands.

MEMBER: Dutch Writers Association, Women's Club.

AWARDS, HONORS: Has received numerous Dutch awards for writing.

WRITINGS:

Vijvendertig tranen (poetry; title means "Thirty-five Tears"), [Holland], 1975.
Schiereiland (poetry; title means "Peninsula"), Nijgh & van Ditmar (Netherlands), 1979.
Miniaturen (poetry; title means "Miniature"), Nijgh & van Ditmar (Netherlands), 1980.
Wie niet weg is wordt Gezien, Leopold (Netherlands), 1981, translated by Terese Edelstein and Inez Smidt as *Hide and Seek,* Houghton (Boston, MA), 1991.
Anna is er nog, Leopold (Netherlands), 1986, translated by Terese Edelstein and Inez Smidt as *Anna Is Still There,* Houghton (Boston, MA), 1993.
Dansen op de brig van Avignon, Leopold (Netherlands), 1989, translated by Terese Edelstein and Inez Smidt as *Dancing on the Bridge at Avignon,* Houghton (Boston, MA), 1995.
The Key Is Lost, translated by Terese Edelstein, Morrow (New York, NY), 2000.

Also author of *Witte zwanen zwarte zwanen,* 1992. Author of radio play *De bevrijding van Rosa Davidson* (title means "The Liberation of Rosa Davidson"), first broadcast, 1984. Contributor of articles and short fiction to periodicals.

SIDELIGHTS: In her homeland of the Netherlands, Ida Vos is well known as the author of several books, numerous short stories and poems, and many articles focusing on her experiences growing up during World War II. Four of Vos's book-length works have been translated into English, allowing readers and critics in the United States to appreciate the author. Her most widely read work, the 1981 novel translated in 1991 as *Hide and Seek,* has become one of the classic works of fiction relating to the Holocaust. Praising Vos's novel *Dancing on the Bridge at Avignon, School Library Journal* contributor Ann W. Moore commented that Vos's "short, episodic chapters are well crafted; her writing is poignant in its understatement."

Born in Gröningen, Netherlands, in 1931 and raised in a traditional Jewish family, Vos and her family moved to Rotterdam when she was five years old. "In 1940, Germany started the war with Holland and my life changed totally," Vos once recalled. "The big bombardment of Rotterdam on May 14, 1940, made a deep impression on me. Seeing the Germans enter our city shocked me terribly. All my books are connected with World War II."

Vos was a novice reader by the time she was four years old and spent much of her time trying to make sense of the books and newspapers she discovered in her home. "My parents felt unhappy about my reading habits," she recalled. "I could read for hours. They thought that a child of my age should play outside instead of reading all the time. My books brought me to places I never visited. By reading I could fly from reality and forget the terrible world around me." Writing quickly followed, and by the age of eight Vos was composing poems, letters, and short stories. "Unfortunately nothing has been kept," she explained. "The Nazis stole everything from our home."

Following the bombing of Rotterdam in 1940, Vos, her sister, Esther, and the girls' parents relocated to Rijswijk, a small city near the Hague. Although she was immediately enrolled at the local elementary school, Vos was soon forced to change schools due to increasing measures taken against Jews. "We were forbidden a lot of things," the author recalled: "Entering a park, visiting a cinema, library, or swimming pool. We were not allowed to travel by train, enter restaurants, etc." Like the character in *Hide and Seek,* Vos had to wear a large yellow star of David inscribed with the word "Jew" on her clothing.

Gradually the Voses became aware of friends and family members being gathered up and sent to German concentration camps; they decided it was time for the family to go into hiding. With help from friends in the Dutch resistance movement, they went underground, hiding with first one family, then another, to avoid capture. "We had to move so many times that I really don't remember all the people that helped us," Vos commented. "I owe a lot to all of them. They risked their lives and that of their families in order to save us." At first the family managed to stay together, but eventually Vos and her sister were separated from their parents. "As a child of eleven, I had to play the role of older and wiser sister," Vos recalled, remembering her efforts to calm her younger sister through stories and games while never revealing her own fear. In 1945, when Europe was liberated from German control, Vos and her family were reunited. "But I couldn't feel happiness," Vos explained. "The counting had started— counting all our relatives and friends who didn't come back from the concentration camps, being murdered— gassed—by the invading Nazis."

The following year Vos returned to school, a thirteen-year-old enrolling in the fifth grade. "I had forgotten many of the things I learned before the war," Vos admitted. "I felt stupid sitting between younger children." She quickly got up to speed with her studies, and moved to the appropriate grade in high school. After graduation, Vos entered a teacher's training college, where she earned teaching certifications in 1950 and 1952. By 1956 she had married Henk Vos, with whom she would have three children. Vos suffered an emotional breakdown in the early 1970s. "All the grief of the war came back to me," she explained. "I wanted to stay in bed all the time. I wept the whole day and didn't see any future." She eventually checked into a psychiatric clinic for war victims, where she underwent therapy for three months. "I was never fully cured but I could endure life again," she once admitted.

It was during her stay at the psychiatric clinic that Vos began putting her memories and feelings about the war down on paper. "Poems flew out of my pen and I couldn't stop. The poems were printed and I got enthusiastic reviews. Now the author Ida Vos was born. . . . I also wrote several short stories. . . . An editor, read-

ing some of them, asked me to write a book about my life during World War II. First I refused, thinking that I was not able to stand it, being also afraid that I would again break down mentally." It was an article she discovered in a local newspaper—an article explaining that there were people claiming that the Holocaust never really happened; that it was an invention of the Jewish people—that inspired her to put pen to paper. "I was terribly shocked and it made me change my mind. Now I wanted to tell the truth. People should know what really happened." Vos's contribution to telling the truth began with *Hide and Seek.*

Reviewers have praised *Hide and Seek* for its compelling portrayal of the experiences of a young Jewish girl during the Nazi invasion of Holland. In Vos's novel, eight-year-old Rachel Hartog's life is suddenly turned upside down during World War II. The invading Nazis force Rachel to wear a yellow star to indicate her Jewish heritage and to attend a school for Jewish children only, and they forbid Rachel to enter the local parks or use the neighborhood swimming pool. Rachel cannot understand these injustices and wrestles with the many intense emotions she feels as she and her family struggle to survive. A reviewer for *Publishers Weekly* remarked of *Hide and Seek* that Vos "fills the narrative with understated but painfully realistic moments . . . [Her] novel deserves special attention for its sensitive and deeply affecting consideration of life after liberation." Equally laudatory, *Booklist* contributor Hazel Rochman added that "any number of the vignettes—wearing the star for the first time, hiding with the Dutch underground, Rachel's parting from her parents . . .—would make a gripping book-talk/read-aloud that will move children to imagine 'What if it happened to me?'"

Vos followed *Hide and Seek* with several other books. The next to appear in U.S. bookstores was a 1986 novel translated in 1993 as *Anna Is Still Here.* In this story, which serves as a sequel to *Hide and Seek* in that it continues to parallel the author's own experiences, Anna survives the war by hiding with her family, but must learn to readjust to a normal life. Forced to attend school with younger children because her education has lapsed, and reacquainting herself with her parents and other family members, thirteen-year-old Anna begins to learn about the horror of the concentration camps—a horror that had taken the life of at least one of her former friends. "Vos conveys Anna's heartbreaking and heroic efforts with exemplary economy," noted a *Publishers Weekly* contributor, adding that the author's answers to the questions her novel raises are "hard-won and profoundly stirring." Praising the simplicity of the "terse" translation by Terese Edelstein and Inez Smidt, *School*

Library Journal contributor Susan Kaminow added that *Anna Is Still Here* "is a stark reminder that the effects of the Holocaust did not end with the end of the war."

Dancing on the Bridge at Avignon, published in English translation in 1995, breaks even more into fictional territory than Vos's earlier works. In this story ten-year-old Rosa de Jong and her little sister, Sylvie, try to escape from the fear and tension caused by the Nazi occupation of their home town by keeping to their normal routines, which include playing the violin, getting into trouble, starting up an informal school, and making the Nazi edicts into quiz games; all the while the girls' parents live in quiet fear and plan for an escape that, tragically, does not happen in time. Noting the novel's "dark lyricism," a *Publishers Weekly* critic maintained that *Dancing on the Bridge at Avignon* contains a message likely to be "haunting and inescapable" to both adult and teen readers. Similar praise was given *The Key Is Lost,* which describes life for two Jewish sisters as they are moved from house to house while in hiding from the Nazis. "The precariousness of the hiding places, the dangers of moving from one to another and the girls' unnatural existence within them are thrown into sharp relief as Vos distills each scene to its most telling moments," noted a *Publishers Weekly* contributor.

In addition to writing, Vos speaks at libraries, schools, and other gatherings around the world, describing her memories of being a Jew in Holland in World War II.

"Children are very interested," she explained. "I have received many letters and paintings from them. I am very happy about my contacts with youth. Through my lectures I am able to warn them against war, discrimination, and fascism."

BIOGRAPHICAL/CRITICAL SOURCES:

PERIODICALS

Booklist, March 15, 1991, Hazel Rochman, review of *Hide and Seek,* p. 1504; April 15, 1993, Hazel Rochman, review of *Anna Is Still Here,* p. 1513; October 15, 1995, Hazel Rochman, review of *Dancing on the Bridge at Avignon,* p. 405; April 1, 2000, Hazel Rochman, review of *The Key Is Lost,* p. 1478.

Horn Book, January-February, 1996, Hanna B. Zeiger, review of *Dancing on the Bridge at Avignon,* p. 75.

Publishers Weekly, February 15, 1991, review of *Hide and Seek,* p. 90; April 19, 1993, review of *Anna Is Still Here,* p. 62; November 13, 1995, review of *Dancing on the Bridge at Avignon,* p. 62; June 5, 2000, review of *The Key Is Lost,* p. 95.

School Library Journal, May, 1993, Susan Kaminow, review of *Anna Is Still Here,* p. 110; October, 1995, Ann W. Moore, review of *Dancing on the Bridge at Avignon,* p. 141; July, 2000, Jack Forman, review of *The Key Is Lost,* p. 112.*

W-Z

WALLERSTEIN, Judith (Hannah) S(aretsky) 1921-

PERSONAL: Born December 27, 1921, in New York, NY; daughter of Samuel and Augusta (Tucker) Saretsky; married Robert S. Wallerstein, January 26, 1947; children: Michael Jonathan, Nina Beth, Amy Lisa. *Education:* Hunter College (now of the City University of New York), B.A. (cum laude), 1943; Columbia University, M.S.W., 1946; further graduate study at Topeka Institute for Psychoanalysis, 1955-61.

ADDRESSES: Office—c/o Hyperion Books, 77 West 66th St., 11th Floor, New York, NY 10023.

CAREER: Community Service Society, New York, NY, assistant director of Residential Treatment Center, 1945-47; Menninger Foundation, Topeka, KS, senior psychiatric social worker and child therapist, 1949-57; University of Kansas, Lawrence, instructor in social work, 1965-66; University of California, Berkeley, lecturer in social welfare, beginning in 1966. Founder, Judith Wallerstein Center for the Family in Transition. Lecturer at University of Amsterdam, 1967, and Paul Baerwald School of Social Welfare, Jerusalem, Israel, 1970. Member of board of directors of Homewood Terrace Adolescent Treatment Center, San Francisco, CA, 1971-73; senior consultant to Marin County Community Mental Health Center.

MEMBER: Association for Child Psychoanalysis, American Orthopsychiatric Association, National Association of Social Workers.

AWARDS, HONORS: Koshland Award in Social Welfare, 1975.

WRITINGS:

(With Joan Berlin Kelly) *Surviving the Breakup: How Children and Parents Cope with Divorce,* Basic Books (New York, NY), 1980.

(With Sandra Blakeslee) *Second Chances: Men, Women, and Children a Decade after Divorce,* Ticknor & Fields (New York, NY), 1989.

(With Blakeslee) *The Good Marriage: How and Why Love Lasts,* Houghton Mifflin (Boston, MA), 1995.

(With Blakeslee and Julia Lewis) *The Unexpected Legacy of Divorce: A Twenty-five Year Study,* Hyperion (New York, NY), 2000.

Contributor to magazines.

SIDELIGHTS: Dr. Judith S. Wallerstein is considered one of the nation's foremost authorities on the effects of divorce on children and adults. In 1971 Wallerstein began a small study that charted the emotional responses of a select group of children to their parents' divorces. Wallerstein conducted extensive interviews with the 131 children and their parents and followed up with more interviews five years later, ten years later, and ultimately twenty-five years later. She published her findings in *Surviving the Breakup: How Children and Parents Cope qith Divorce, Second Chances: Men, Women, and Children a Decade after Divorce,* and *The Unexpected Legacy of Divorce: A Twenty-five Year Study.* While her statistical sample was small, Wallerstein was nevertheless able to come to the conclusion that divorce has a major negative impact on many children, and that this impact can be felt even as the children mature into adulthood. As Margaret Talbot noted of Wallerstein in a *New York Times Book Review,* "She, more than anyone else, has made us face the truth that a divorce can free one or both parents to start a new and more hopeful life and still hurt their children." This is not to say that Wallerstein advocates keeping bad marriages intact, but according to Talbot, "she has urged parents and policy makers alike to think seriously about the impact of divorce on children, while acknowledging its necessity as an escape route for couples yoked miserably together."

Almost from the outset of what was then called the California Children of Divorce Study, Wallerstein discovered that widely held notions of children's resiliency in the face of divorce were false. In a *New York Times Book Review* piece on *Second Chances,* Carol Tavris wrote: "[Wallerstein's] research findings, clinical interpretations and interviews are interwoven beautifully. The case studies are believable and compelling. . . . *Second Chances* portrays the complexities and nuances of the emotional aftermath of divorce from all participants' perspectives, but it is the findings on children that are the most haunting." *New York Times* correspondent Caryn James declared of the same book: "Dr. Wallerstein's study is important because it shows that divorce is not a temporary crisis or a disease that has a cure but an enduring problematic condition we know far too little about." James added: "Her statistics have already been questioned by other psychologists, but no one can deny that the children she describes were profoundly altered by divorce." Tavris likewise observed that Wallerstein's work is "a slender study whose 60 atypical families do not support the weight of all its conclusions." The critic nonetheless concluded: "As a work of clinical observation, *[Second Chances]* is a beautiful piece of writing, full of insights that will prove indispensable to people contemplating divorce as a necessary evil, idealizing divorce as a cure-all for their woes, or living in its muddy aftermath."

Subsequent larger demographic studies confirmed many of Wallerstein's theories about children of divorce. Her conclusions were strongly reinforced as well by the return interviews she conducted after the children had entered adulthood. Her subjects described difficulties with intimacy and trust, significant levels of anxiety and depression, and the feeling that they lacked knowledge about how to craft a functional family. These are some of the issues she addresses in *The Unexpected Legacy of Divorce.* In *Publishers Weekly,* Bridget Kinsella wrote: "*The Unexpected Legacy of Divorce* is not anti divorce, but barring an abusive environment, it shows that by and large most children of divorce face more economic and emotional challenges into their adult lives than their counterparts from 'good-enough' intact families. In terms of having their own relationships,

children of divorce, it says, do not have a template with which to gauge their choices."

Wallerstein and her co-author Sandra Blakeslee are also authors of *The Good Marriage: How and Why Love Lasts,* a study of fifty couples who have been able to sustain their marriages. Wallerstein told *Mother Jones* magazine that the purpose of this book "was really to learn what goes into a happy family, a happy marriage." She added: "I really think of it as a pilot study. We have everything to learn about how to make a good marriage in contemporary society." *Atlantic Monthly* reviewer Barbara Dafoe Whitehead found *The Good Marriage* to be "a remarkably sunny and affecting portrait of marriage and its satisfactions. What we learn is that a good marriage falls into the art of the possible." Dafoe added: "One of the nice things about *The Good Marriage* is its modesty. It doesn't pretend to offer a philosophy or even a lecture on marriage. It takes no position on the ideologically charged issues of women's marital roles and status. . . . *The Good Marriage* offers powerful evidence in support of a model for relationships that are based not on theories of exchange or self-interest but on notions of sacrifice and altruism."

BIOGRAPHICAL/CRITICAL SOURCES:

PERIODICALS

Atlantic Monthly, September, 1995, Barbara Dafoe Whitehead, review of *The Good Marriage: How and Why Love Lasts,* p. 114.
Booklist, July, 2000, Mary Carroll, review of *The Unexpected Legacy of Divorce: A Twenty-five Year Landmark Study,* p. 1971.
Elementary School Guidance Counselor, October, 1984.
Mother Jones, July-August, 1995, Mary Ann Hogan, "The Good Marriage?," p. 18.
New York Times, February 11, 1989, Caryn James, "Sins of the Fathers and Mothers," p. A16.
New York Times Book Review, February 26, 1989, Carol Tavris, "A Remedy but Not a Cure," p. 13; October 1, 2000, Margaret Talbot, "The Price of Divorce."
Publishers Weekly, August 14, 2000, Bridget Kinsella, "Parents Split: The Kids Can't Commit," p. 201.
Spectator, December 13, 1980.

OTHER

Prism: America's Alternative Evangelical Voice, http://www.esa-online.org/ (November-December, 1998), Terry Cooper, "A Big, Big, Unmet Need: The PRISM Interview with Dr. Judith S. Wallerstein."

Split-up: Helping People Deal with Divorce, http:// www.split-up.com/advisors/ (October 1, 2000), "Board of Advisors—Dr. Judith S. Wallerstein."*

*   *   *

WARD, Andrew (Spencer) 1946-

PERSONAL: Born January 7, 1946, in Chicago, IL; son of Fredrick Champion (an educator) and Duira (in social services; maiden name, Baldinger) Ward; married Deborah Huntington (a nurse practitioner), July 27, 1969; children: Jacob Champion. *Education:* Attended Oberlin College, 1964-66, and Rhode Island School of Design, 1966-68.

ADDRESSES: Home—Seattle, WA. *Office*—c/o Farrar, Straus and Giroux, 19 Union Sq. W., New York, NY 10003. *E-mail*—asward@sprynet.com.

CAREER: Writer. Worked as photographer for Ford Foundation in New Delhi, India, 1968-70; freelance writer and photographer, 1970-72; Marvelwood School, Cornwall, CT, art teacher, 1972-74. Former commentator for National Public Radio program *All Things Considered.*

AWARDS, HONORS: Atlantic grant from *Atlantic,* 1977, for *Fits and Starts;* Washington Governor's Award for *Our Bones Are Scattered.*

WRITINGS:

Fits and Starts: The Premature Memoirs of Andrew Ward, Little, Brown (Boston, MA), 1978.
Bits and Pieces (essays and parodies), Little, Brown (Boston, MA), 1980.
Baby Bear and the Long Sleep, Little, Brown (Boston, MA), 1980.
The Blood Seed: A Novel of India, Viking (New York, NY), 1985.
A Cry of Absence: The True Story of a Father's Search for His Kidnapped Children, Viking (New York, NY), 1988.
Out Here: A Newcomer's Notes from the Great Northwest, Viking (New York, NY), 1991.
Our Bones Are Scattered: The Cawnpore Massacres and the Indian Mutiny of 1857, Holt (New York, NY), 1996.

Dark Midnight When I Rise: The Story of the Jubilee Singers Who Introduced the World to the Music of Black America, Farrar, Straus (New York, NY), 2000.

Also author of television documentary on the Jubilee Singers for WGBH. Work anthologized in *Best American Short Stories of 1973,* edited by Martha Foley. Contributor to magazines and newspapers, including *Redbook, Fantasy and Science Fiction, Horizon, American Heritage,* and *Inquiry.* Contributing editor of *Atlantic Monthly;* former columnist, *Washington Post.*

SIDELIGHTS: In his book *Dark Midnight When I Rise: The Story of the Jubilee Singers Who Introduced the World to the Music of Black America,* Andrew Ward tells the story of the nineteenth-century group of singers who toured the United States and Europe singing Negro spirituals. A fund-raising effort of the all-black Fisk University in Tennessee, the Jubilee Singers raised much-needed money for the financially challenged school. They also were instrumental in introducing Negro music of the time to a white audience. Based on Ward's extensive research in the archives of Fisk University, *Dark Midnight When I Rise* records the history of a forgotten group of early black artists. "They introduced the Negro spiritual as one of the great, indigenous American art forms," noted David Herbert Donald in the *New York Times Book Review,* "which had incalculable effect on all subsequent music." A reviewer for *Kirkus Reviews* found Ward's account to be "a bittersweet and movingly told story" as well as a "readable history." In his interview on the *Amazon.com* Web site, Ward explained, "the Jubilee Singers project has been the most moving and satisfying of my career." He added, "I hope that the publication of *Dark Midnight When I Rise . . .* will remind the country of the extraordinary contributions of the emancipated generation of African Americans to our culture."

Ward once told *CA:* "I consider myself a humorist, a designation which performs the function of forcing my intentions out into the open. My work must pass a simple test; if it fails to get a laugh or raise a smile from my readers (meaning my wife and brother) then it fails to justify itself. This may not seem a particularly lofty test, but I'm not a very lofty fellow, and believe that laughter, at least the laughter that comes with recognition, is our surest barometer of truth. Besides, being a humorist beats being a puzzle cutter, a soda jerk, a machinist, a janitor, a teacher, a photographer, or any of the other professions I've given a try."

BIOGRAPHICAL/CRITICAL SOURCES:

PERIODICALS

Booklist, April 15, 1996, Roland Green, review of *Our Bones Are Scattered,* p. 1419.

Christian Science Monitor, January 30, 1997, review of *Our Bones Are Scattered,* p. B1.

Kirkus Reviews, January 15, 1996, review of *Our Bones Are Scattered,* p. 126; March 15, 2000, review of *Dark Midnight When I Rise,* p. 368.

Library Journal, September 1, 1985, Ellen Kaye Stoppel, review of *The Blood Seed,* p. 214; February 15, 1991, review of *Out Here,* p. 212; March 1, 1996, Daniel Liestman, review of *Our Bones Are Scattered,* p. 92.

New Haven Register, June 5, 1978.

New York Times Book Review, December 22, 1985, Sheila Solomon Klass, review of *The Blood Seed,* p. 18; May 12, 1996, Karl E. Meyer, review of *Our Bones Are Scattered,* p. 25; July 23, 2000, David Herbert Donald, review of *Dark Midnight When I Rise.*

Observer, August 25, 1996, review of *Our Bones Are Scattered,* p. 15.

Publishers Weekly, March 28, 1980, review of *Baby Bear and the Long Sleep,* p. 49; May 27, 1988, Genevieve Stuttaford, review of *A Cry of Absence,* p. 47; January 11, 1991, review of *Out Here,* p. 87; February 12, 1996, review of *Our Bones Are Scattered,* p. 67.

School Library Journal, August, 1980, Mary B. Nickerson, review of *Baby Bear and the Long Sleep,* p. 58.

Stamford Advocate, August 13, 1978.

Times Literary Supplement, January 10, 1997, review of *Our Bones Are Scattered,* p. 11.

OTHER

Amazon.com, http://www.amazon.com/ (September 4, 2000), "Amazon.com Talks to Andrew Ward."*

*   *   *

WARNER, Sharon Oard 1952-

PERSONAL: Born July 16, 1952, in Dallas, TX; daughter of Eugene Edwin Oard (an engineer and business owner) and Ann (Curtis) Horne; married Teddy Dean Warner (a psychologist), August 19, 1978; children: Carey Dean, Devi Alan. *Education:* University of Texas at Austin, B.A. (with honors), 1977; University of Kansas, M.A., 1984. *Politics:* Democrat.

ADDRESSES: Home—4800 Snapdragon Rd., NW, Albuquerque, NM 87120-2758. *Office*—Department of English Language and Literature, Humanities Building 217, University of New Mexico, Albuquerque, NM, 87131-1106. *Agent*—Kimberly Witherspoon & Associates, 235 East 31st St., New York, NY 10016.

CAREER: Oaks Treatment Center, Austin, TX, educational activities coordinator at short term adolescent center, 1977-79; Lawrence Community Center, Lawrence, KS, creative writing instructor, 1980; University of Kansas, Lawrence, instructor, 1980-84, lecturer in English, 1984-85; Northeast Louisiana University, Monroe, instructor in English, 1985-87; Lawrence Arts Center, Lawrence, creative writing instructor, 1983; Iowa State University, Ames, instructor in English, 1987-88; Drake University, Des Moines, IA, visiting assistant professor of English, 1988-93; Iowa State University, Ames, IA, instructor in creative writing, 1993; Des Moines Area Community College, Ancien, IA, instructor in composition and literature, 1993-94; University of New Mexico, Albuquerque, NM, assistant professor in English, 1994-2000, associate professor, 2000—, director of creative writing program, 1998—. Spectrum/Focus on Deaf Artists, writer and grants coordinator, 1978-79; member of board of directors, *Iowa Woman,* 1991; University of Iowa Summer Writing Festival, instructor in short fiction writing, novel writing, and book reviewing, summers, 1993-98, 2000; University of New Mexico, Taos Summer Writer's Conference, founding director, 1998—; gives readings from her works.

MEMBER: American Association of University Professors, Associated Writing Programs, Iowa Council of Teachers of English, PEN.

AWARDS, HONORS: Bread Loaf Writers' Conference scholar, 1977; first prize in annual fiction competition, *Sonora Review,* 1983; Universal Press Syndicate fellow at Longboat Key Writers' Conference, 1985; winner of Tenth Anniversary Contest, Cleveland State University, 1990; fiction winner, Minnesota Voices Project, 1990; Iowa humanities scholar, Iowa Humanities Board, 1991-92; Squaw Valley Community of Writers Screenwriting Workshops scholar, 1991; support award for writing the novel, *Deep in the Heart,* Iowa Arts Council, 1993; Margaret Bridgmam Fellow in Fiction, Bread Loaf Writers' Conference, 1993; Keleher Faculty Award for Outstanding Assistant Professor, University of New Mexico, 1997; short-listed for O'Henry Award, *Prize Stories,* 1999, for "The Object Lesson"; Gunter Starkey Teaching Award, College of Arts and Sciences, University of New Mexico, 2000.

WRITINGS:

(Editor with Melanie Farley) *Nineteen Stories: Contemporary Fiction by Kansas Writers,* Cottonwood Review Press, 1982.

Learning to Dance and Other Stories, New Rivers Press, 1992.

(Editor) *The Way We Write Now: Short Stories from the AIDS Crisis,* Carol Publishing Group (Secaucus, NJ), 1995.

Deep in the Heart (novel), Dial (New York, NY), 2000.

Work represented in anthologies, including *Everlasting Earth: Contemporary Writing from the Rural Midwest,* University of Minnesota Press, 1993. Contributor of stories, articles, and reviews to periodicals, including *Other Voices, Green Mountains Review, Texas Woman, Maverick, Gamut,* and *Vanderbilt Review.* Assistant editor and fiction editor, *Cottonwood Review,* 1981-85.

ADAPTATIONS: Warner has adapted her novel *Deep in the Heart* for a screenplay of the same name, written in collaboration with Hilary Gilford and Campbell Scott, 1999.

SIDELIGHTS: Sharon Oard Warner told *CA:* "Social issues, particularly those that relate to children and families, have a real impact on my work. A number of the stories in *Learning to Dance* deal with characters who have to cope with disabilities and do so admirably. I am also inspired by visual artists, especially Andrew Wyeth and Mary Cassatt. I have written stories based on paintings, including Wyeth's *Christina's World.*"

For her first novel, *Deep in the Heart,* Warner chose to focus on one of the most contentious public health issues in the late twentieth century: abortion. In a revolving narrative that gives voice to four characters, two on each side of the issue, *Deep in the Heart* demonstrates the pro-life and abortion rights positions from the inside. Hannah Solace, a high school assistant principal, finds herself pregnant for the first time at age forty, and against her husband's wishes decides to have an abortion. Across town, twenty-three-year-old Penny Reed has been raised by her Christian fundamentalist grandmother to follow the preaching of Dr. Bill, an anti-abortion activist. The four meet up at the abortion clinic where Hannah's grieving husband becomes a target for Dr. Bill's protesters, Penny among them. A reviewer for *Beliefnet* states that "*Deep in the Heart* will disappoint both sides in the abortion debate" due to the

difficult nature of the subject matter it handles. Similarly, a reviewer for the *Chicago Tribune* notes that the novel is one that "honors complexity and humanity." Writing for the *Women's Review of Books,* Annie David noted that Warner tackles a "big ideological" issue in this work, which she handles with a "writer's heart and a social scientist's brain." *Library Journal* reviewer Kimberly G. Allen contends that "the author depicts the controversial subject of choice in a manner that is highly effective." And though a reviewer for *Publishers Weekly* complains that Warner's plot is too "symmetrical," this critic also praised the author's "gift for detailed, evocative writing and careful characterizations."

Warner has also edited the collection *The Way We Write Now: Short Stories from the AIDS Crisis.*

BIOGRAPHICAL/CRITICAL SOURCES:

PERIODICALS

Chicago Tribune, July 30, 2000, Lynna Williams, "When the Political Is Personal," section 14, p. 3.

Kirkus Reviews, March 1, 2000, review of *Deep in the Heart,* p. 266.

Newsday, May 7, 2000, Beth Gutcheon, "Colliding Choices."

Publishers Weekly, January 10, 2000, Heather Vogel Frederick, review of *Deep in the Heart,* pp. 28-29.

Women's Review of Books, November, 2000, Annie David, "True Believers."

OTHER

Beliefnet, http://www.beliefnet.com (June 2000), review of *Deep in the Heart.*

*   *   *

WATT-EVANS, Lawrence 1954-

PERSONAL: Born July 26, 1954, in Arlington, MA; son of Gordon Goodwin (a professor of chemistry) and Doletha (a secretary; maiden name, Watt) Evans; married Julie Frances McKenna (a chemist), August 30, 1977; children: Kyrith Amanda, Julian Samuel Goodwin. *Education:* Attended Princeton University, 1972-74, 1975-77. *Avocational interests:* Comic book collecting.

ADDRESSES: Agent—Russell Galen, Scoville Chichak Galen, 381 Park Ave. S., 11th Floor, New York, NY 10016.

CAREER: Novelist. Purty Save-Mor supermarket, Bedford, MA, sacker, 1971; Griffith Ladder, Bedford, worker, 1973; Arby's, Pittsburgh, PA, counterman and cook, 1974; Student Hoagie Agency, Princeton, NJ, occasional salesman, 1974-76; Mellon Institute of Science, Pittsburgh, bottle washer, 1976; freelance writer, 1977—.

MEMBER: Science Fiction and Fantasy Writers of America, Horror Writers of America.

AWARDS, HONORS: Hugo Award, World Science Fiction Society, Nebula Award nomination, Science Fiction Writers of America, and reader's poll award, *Isaac Asimov's Science Fiction Magazine,* all 1988, all for short story "Why I Left Harry's All-Night Hamburgers"; reader's poll award, *Isaac Asimov's Science Fiction Magazine,* 1990, for "Windwagon Smith and the Martians."

WRITINGS:

"THE LORDS OF DUS" SERIES; FANTASY

The Lure of the Basilisk, Del Rey (New York, NY), 1980.
The Seven Altars of Dusarra, Del Rey (New York, NY), 1981.
The Sword of Bheleu, Del Rey (New York, NY), 1983.
The Book of Silence, Del Rey (New York, NY), 1984.

"WAR SURPLUS" SERIES; SCIENCE FICTION

The Cyborg and the Sorcerer, Del Rey (New York, NY), 1982.
The Wizard and the War Machine, Del Rey (New York, NY), 1987.

"LEGENDS OF ETHSHAR" SERIES; FANTASY

The Misenchanted Sword, Del Rey (New York, NY), 1985.
With a Single Spell, Del Rey (New York, NY), 1987.

The Unwilling Warlord, Del Rey (New York, NY), 1989.
The Blood of a Dragon, Del Rey (New York, NY), 1991.
Taking Flight, Del Rey (New York, NY), 1993.
The Spell of the Black Dagger, Del Rey (New York, NY), 1993.

"THREE WORLDS" TRILOGY; FANTASY

Out of This World, Del Rey (New York, NY), 1993.
In the Empire of Shadow, Del Rey (New York, NY), 1995.
The Reign of the Brown Magician, Del Rey (New York, NY), 1996.

FANTASY NOVELS

(With Esther M. Friesner) *Split Heirs* (humorous fantasy), Tor (New York, NY), 1993.
Touched by the Gods, Tor (New York, NY), 1997.
Dragon Weather, Tor (New York, NY), 1999.
Night of Madness, Tor (New York, NY), 2000.

OTHER

The Chromosomal Code, Avon (New York, NY), 1984.
Shining Steel, Avon (New York, NY), 1986.
Denner's Wreck, Avon (New York, NY), 1988.
Nightside City, Del Rey (New York, NY), 1989.
The Nightmare People, New American Library (New York, NY), 1990.
(Editor and contributor) *Newer York,* New American Library (New York, NY), 1990.
The Rebirth of Wonder, Wildside Press, 1992, bound with *The Final Folly of Captain Dancy,* Tor (New York, NY), 1992.
Crosstime Traffic (short stories), Del Rey (New York, NY), 1992.

Author of e-books, published by Alexandria Digital Entertainment, including *The Final Challenge, Foxy Lady, The Murderer,* and *Spirit Dump,* all 1998, and *Efficiency,* 1999. Work represented in anthologies, including *One Hundred Great Fantasy Short Short Stories,* edited by Isaac Asimov, Terry Carr, and Martin H. Greenberg, Doubleday, 1984; *"Why I Left Harry's All-Night Hamburgers" and Other Stories from Isaac Asimov's Science Fiction Magazine,* edited by Dehlia Williams and Charles Ardai, Delacorte, 1990; *Dead End,* edited by

Paul F. Olson and David B. Silva, St. Martin's Press, 1991; and *Prom Night*, edited by Nancy Springer, DAW, 1999. Contributor to game *Tales of Talislanta*, Wizards of the Coast, 1992.

Also author of column "Rayguns, Elves, and Skin-tight Suits" for *Comics Buyers Guide*, 1983-87, and of comic book scripts and stories for Marvel Comics and Eclipse Comics. Contributor of short stories, articles, poems, and reviews to periodicals, including *Amazing*, Louisville *Courier-Journal*, *Bedford Patriot*, *Dragon*, *Late Knocking*, *Movie Collector's World*, *Sagebrush Journal*, *Space Gamer*, and *Starlog*.

SIDELIGHTS: Working primarily in the fantasy and science-fiction genres, Lawrence Watt-Evans has produced a number of novels, poems, and short stories that feature both intricate plots and a sense of fun. Watt-Evans once commented: "My parents both read science fiction—and lots of other things—so I grew up in a house filled with books and magazines, many of them with bright, splashy covers showing spaceships and monsters and people firing rayguns. I loved it all." School seemed dull by comparison, and as Watt-Evans admitted, "I would sneak in books and comic books and read them in class; fortunately, I had tolerant teachers, and as long as I kept up with the class work they didn't object."

"I wasn't clear on the distinction between children's books and grown-up books (I'm still not always)," the author admitted, "so at age seven I started borrowing my mother's books as soon as she was done reading them—I figured if she liked them, I would too. So in second grade, while the other kids read 'Dick and Jane,' I read Ray Bradbury, and fell in love with words and stories. And I never got over it."

After graduating from high school, Watt-Evans enrolled at Princeton University in 1972, but eventually ended his college studies to devote his time to writing. His first novel, *The Lure of the Basilisk*, was published in 1980; it would be the first in a four-part series called "The Lords of Dus." Other novels and other series have followed, among them the "War Surplus" series of science-fiction novels, the "Legends of Ethshar" fantasy series, and the "Three Worlds" trilogy, which Watt-Evans published between 1993 and 1996.

Beginning with *Out of This World*, the "Three Worlds" trilogy introduces readers to life in the parallel universes of the raygun-toting Galactic Empire and Faery.

Maryland lawyer Pel Brown and his client, Amy Jewell, have their everyday lives disrupted by elves and robed medieval-looking figures, as well as futuristic forces drawn right from 1950s pulp sci-fi, all claiming to be from other worlds and engaged in a classic battle of good against evil. Calling the first installment in the "Three Worlds" trilogy "well-told" but not altogether "believable," *Voice of Youth Advocates* contributor Larry Condit praised the work as being of interest to "fantasy and imaginative fiction readers." Sally Estes dubbed the novel a "playful spoof" of the science fiction and fantasy genres in her *Booklist* review, while a *Publishers Weekly* critic noted that Watt-Evans "initially displays a fine wit and intelligence" despite the novel's somewhat disjointed cast of characters. *Out of This World* was followed in 1995 by *In the Empire of Shadow*. In this book Pel and friends continue their battle against the evil "Shadow" in an unfamiliar, war-torn land. "Light-hearted moments contrast with dark undertones" to create an "uncomfortable ambiance," noted a critic for *Library Journal*, who nonetheless recommended the series. In *Booklist* Carl Hays commended Watt-Evans for "blend[ing] just the right touch of whimsy into his well-told action adventure." The battle concludes with *The Reign of the Brown Magician*, which was published in 1996.

In addition to book series, Watt-Evans has authored numerous stand-alone volumes, many of them in the fantasy genre. *Dragon Weather* finds an eleven-year-old boy named Arlian trapped in his basement after his home is destroyed by a dragon attack. During his imprisonment Arlian is transformed into a "dragonheart" by an accidental infusion of dragon blood. After being rescued, he eventually becomes a slave of the dragon overlord and is forced to work in the mines for many years. This treatment does not endear Arlian to dragons. Ultimately he frees himself, determined to avenge the death of his grandfather as well as the loss of his village. "Remarkably inventive" was the description given the novel by a *Kirkus Reviews* writer, who went on to call the plot of *Dragon Weather* "commendably well organized."

In the 1997 novel *Touched by the Gods*, Watt-Evans also focuses his story on a young boy. Malledd, a blacksmith's son living in the Domdur empire, is proclaimed to be the champion of the gods of his world at his birth, but he has tried long and hard to ignore his fate and lead a normal life. Unfortunately, an evil magician puts his world into peril, causing Malledd's abilities to be put to the test in a novel that a *Library Journal* contributor deemed "gracefully present[ed] by its author." On a more humorous note, Watt-Evans teamed up with co-author Esther M. Friesner to write *Split Heirs,* the story of a twisted family tree, mistaken identities, secret multiple births, painful puns, and muddled magic. A *Publishers Weekly* reviewer praised it as an "often funny, frequently precious" fantasy. And the author's 1992 book *Crosstime Traffic* collects nineteen short stories that feature parallel worlds, resulting in a work of "great entertainment with an occasional jolt into serious thought," according to *Kliatt* reviewer Sister Avila Lamb.

BIOGRAPHICAL/CRITICAL SOURCES:

BOOKS

St. James Guide to Fantasy Writers, St. James Press, 1996.
St. James Guide to Science Fiction Writers, fourth edition, St. James Press, 1996.

PERIODICALS

Booklist, July, 1993, review of *Split Heirs,* p. 1953; February 1, 1994, Sally Estes, review of *Out of This World,* p. 1000; February, 1995, Carl Hays, review of *In the Empire of Shadow,* p. 993; November 1, 2000, Roland Green, review of *Night of Madness,* p. 522.
Kirkus Reviews, September 1, 1999, review of *Dragon Weather,* p. 1355.
Kliatt, January, 1993, Sister Avila Lamb, review of *Crosstime Traffic,* p. 20.
Library Journal, February 15, 1995, review of *In the Empire of Shadow,* p. 186; November 15, 1997, review of *Touched by the Gods,* p. 79; November 15, 2000, Jackie Cassada, review of *Night of Madness,* p. 101.
Publishers Weekly, June 21, 1993, review of *Split Heirs,* p. 90; December 20, 1993, review of *Out of This World,* p. 54; September 27, 1999, review of *Dragon Weather,* p. 79; November 6, 2000, review of *Night of Madness,* p. 75.
Voice of Youth Advocates, April, 1994, review of *Split Heirs,* p. 8; August, 1994, Larry Condit, review of *Out of This World,* p. 161.*

*　　　*　　　*

WAYNE, Donald
See DODD, Wayne (Donald)

WEBER, Robert J(ohn) 1936-

PERSONAL: Born June 6, 1936, in Detroit, MI; son of Clarence (a carpenter) and Edith Weber; married Gloria Valencia (a professor of law), December 28, 1959; children: Mark, Karen. *Education:* Attended Phoenix College, 1955-57; Arizona State University, B.S., 1959; Princeton University, Ph.D., 1962.

ADDRESSES: Agent—c/o W. W. Norton & Co., 500 Fifth Ave., New York, NY 10110.

CAREER: Long Island University, C. W. Post Center, Greenvale, NY, assistant professor of psychology, 1963-64; Kenyon College, Gambier, OH, assistant professor of psychology, 1964-67; Oklahoma State University, Stillwater, began as associate professor, became professor of psychology, 1967. University of New Mexico, visiting professor, 1992-93.

MEMBER: American Psychological Association, American Association of University Professors.

WRITINGS:

(Editor, with David N. Perkins) *Inventive Minds: Creativity in Technology,* Oxford University Press (New York, NY), 1992.
Forks, Phonographs, and Hot Air Balloons: A Field Guide to Inventive Thinking, Oxford University Press (New York, NY), 1993.
The Created Self: Reinventing Body, Persona, and Spirit, Norton (New York, NY), 2000.

Contributor of about fifty articles to psychology journals.

SIDELIGHTS: Robert J. Weber once told *CA:* "I have spent most of my academic career studying mental imagery, the ability to imagine scenes or sounds. Early on, I made some measurements of the peak rate at which those processes take place.

"During 1984 and 1985, I was on sabbatical at Harvard University, where it became clear to me that I was running out of ideas on imagery. On a lark, I went to the Boston Public Library to look up patents on imaging devices (like radar and medical scanners) to see if I could get some new insights on the imagery system that humans use. During a number of visits in the patent section of the library, I found myself ever less interested in imagery as such, and ever more interested in the wonderful ideas embodied in the patents that I was reading. When I returned to Oklahoma, I continued my interest in invention, but I found a new viewpoint: instead of high technology invention, I looked at simple crafts like sewing and simple devices like knives. A standard question became: Where could that idea have come from? If you ask that question often enough, it soon takes you very far back in time. Mental time travel to study inventions has its bad and good sides. The bad part is that the inventions of prehistory do not come with lab notebooks or user manuals; the good part is that they are often so simple and transparent that principles of their formation just jump out at you. It is these simple inventions and the hidden intelligence that underlies them that provided the inspiration for one of my books, *Forks, Phonographs, and Hot Air Balloons: A Field Guide to Inventive Thinking.* In this book I analyze simple inventions and technologies, because it is easy to extract the powerful mental principles behind them. Along the way, I try to systematize some of the more transparent procedures of inventive thinking.

"The principles of simple inventions also manifest themselves in more complex inventions and technologies. That story is told in *Inventive Minds: Creativity in Technology.* What David N. Perkins and I did here was to gather important contemporary inventors, historians of invention, to represent the great minds of the past, and cognitive psychologists to try to understand the inventive thinking process. The result is an account of some important inventions that have shaped history and contemporary life: the electron microscope, ultrasound applied to clinical problems, Kevlar, the telephone, and the airplane.

"What I hope to achieve in my work is an appreciation and understanding of the mental principles and intelligence behind invention. We tend to think of human creativity in terms of the arts or the sciences. Yet hidden creative acts are all around us, embodied in the intelligence that underlies the artifacts of our everyday world, a record that goes back two million years. When we seek out that intelligence, it gives us a new way of looking at the world and at our own thinking processes. Like Lewis Carroll's Alice, when we step into the looking glass, we enter an invented place: a world of our own making."

Weber's *The Created Self: Reinventing Body, Persona, and Spirit* is a work aimed at general readers, which explores personal transformation, from the most profound (such as changes in religious faith) to the most ordinary (such as decisions to get tattoos or body piercings). The author delineates three major components of the self: body, persona, and soul, and he shows how self-awareness affects each of these three components. One of Weber's concerns is personal decisions that run against strict evolutionary biology—for instance, a person's decision to concentrate on a career in lieu of having children. A *Publishers Weekly* reviewer noted: "Weber's account of the self is certainly provocative, exploring phenomena such as body piercing in an effort to show some of the ways that selfhood extends behavior beyond the ends prefigured by our genetic endowment." According to Mary Carroll in *Booklist,* Weber's book "won't solve an identity crisis, but readers will be able to better understand such crises' universality and to pursue some interesting theories about their roots and purposes."

BIOGRAPHICAL/CRITICAL SOURCES:

PERIODICALS

Booklist, January, 2000, Mary Carroll, review of *The Created Self: Reinventing Body, Persona, and Spirit,* p. 836.

Publishers Weekly, December 13, 1999, review of *The Created Self: Reinventing Body, Persona, and Mind,* p. 75.*

*   *   *

WEISMAN, John 1942-

PERSONAL: Born August 1, 1942, in New York, NY; son of Abner I. (a physician) and Syde (a schoolteacher; maiden name, Lubowe) Weisman; married Susan Povenmire (a government employee), February 12, 1983. *Education:* Bard College, A.B., 1964. *Religion:* Jewish. *Avocational interests:* Skeet shooting, hunting.

ADDRESSES: Home—Bluemont, VA. *Agent*—Jay Acton, East Egg Ent., 55 Fifth Ave., New York, NY 10003. *E-mail*—jweisman@ix.netcom.com.

CAREER: Coast (magazine), Los Angeles, CA, managing editor, 1969-70; *Rolling Stone,* staff member, 1970-71; *Detroit Free Press,* Detroit, MI, staff writer, 1971-73; *TV Guide,* Radnor, PA, associate editor and bureau chief in Washington, DC, 1973-89; freelance writer, 1989—. LOTI Group, coproducer of the videotape *Red Cell.*

MEMBER: Authors League, International Defence Pistol Association, Association of Former Intelligence Officers, Cosmos Club (Washington, DC), Naval and Military Club (London, England).

AWARDS, HONORS: Annenberg senior fellow, Northwestern University, 1989-91.

WRITINGS:

Guerrilla Theater, Doubleday (New York, NY), 1973.
Evidence, Viking (New York, NY), 1980.
Watchdogs, Viking (New York, NY), 1983.
Blood Cries, Viking (New York, NY), 1987.
(With Felix Rodriguez) *Shadow Warrior,* Simon & Schuster (New York, NY), 1989.

Also author of *Seal Team Six* (interactive compact disc), Magnet Interactive Studios, and *Unusual Suspects,* edited by James Grady, Vintage. Work represented in anthologies, including *Best American Mystery Stories, 1997,* edited by Robert B. Parker, Houghton (Boston, MA), 1998. Contributor to *Columbia Journalism Review* and *Soldier of Fortune.*

"ROGUE WARRIOR" SERIES; WITH RICHARD MARCINKO

Rogue Warrior, Pocket Books (New York, NY), 1991.
Red Cell, Pocket Books (New York, NY), 1994.
Green Team, Pocket Books (New York, NY), 1995.
Task Force Blue, Pocket Books (New York, NY), 1996.
Designation Gold, Pocket Books (New York, NY), 1997.
Seal Force Alpha, Pocket Books (New York, NY), 1998.
Option Delta, Pocket Books (New York, NY), 1999.
Echo Platoon, Pocket Books (New York, NY), 2000.
Detachment Bravo, Pocket Books (New York, NY), 2001.

ADAPTATIONS: Simon & Schuster Audio has recorded the "Rogue Warrior" books on audio cassette.

SIDELIGHTS: John Weisman conceived and developed the "Rogue Warrior" series, which features Marcinko, a former Navy SEAL and specialist in counter-terrorism, as the protagonist and narrator of the fictional adventures. Roland Green of *Booklist* described the series as "the purist kind of thriller around, with action, pacing, and hardware galore." Weisman also wrote the

best-selling *Shadow Warrior* with Felix Rodriguez; it is a nonfiction account of Rodriguez's career in the Central Intelligence Agency and his role in capturing communist guerrilla leader Che Guevara.

The "Rogue Warrior" books feature Marcinko and a cast of dependable co-warriors—with such colorful names as Boomerang, Pick, Duck Foot, and Half-Pint—who together go on death-defying missions to thwart the schemes of America's enemies. Each story, according to a *Publishers Weekly* critic, includes "pit-stops for humor, Rogueish philosophy and patriotic speechifying." A *Kirkus Reviews* contributor explained that a typical "Rogue Warrior" title contains "rip-snorting action sequences and acronyms aplenty, plus a glossary for the confused," along with "the customary blend of heroics and politically incorrect commentary."

In the course of conducting their duties, the Rogue Warrior team confronts Japanese right-wingers intent on obtaining an American nuclear weapon, Russian-Iranian plotters trying to destabilize the newly-independent Moslem countries of the former Soviet Union, and an ambitious billionaire hoping to seize the American presidency by stirring up terrorist trouble and then promoting a dictatorial solution to the chaos.

Recounted in Marcinko's salty language, and filled with plenty of straight-shooting violence, each "Rogue Warrior" novel is fast-paced and grounded in actual Navy SEAL tactics. Sometimes the series draws criticism for its tough approach. A *Publishers Weekly* reviewer referred to the series' characters as the "merry band of violence-loving Rogue Warriors," for example. And Green admitted that "new readers must, of course, make allowances for the f-word." But the "Rogue Warrior" series enjoys best-selling sales and a loyal audience who appreciate high-octane adventure tales. In his review of *Task Force Blue,* Green noted that, "as usual for a Rogue Warrior yarn, this one is a gripping hard-boiled thriller."

BIOGRAPHICAL/CRITICAL SOURCES:

PERIODICALS

Booklist, March 1, 1994, Roland Green, review of *Red Cell,* p. 1181; March 1, 1995, Roland Green, review of *Green Team,* p. 179; February 1, 1996, Roland Green, review of *Task Force Blue,* p. 917;

January 1, 1999, Roland Green, review of *Option Delta;* March 15, 2000, Roland Green, review of *Echo Platoon,* p. 1293.

Kirkus Reviews, January 1, 1994, review of *Red Cell;* March 15, 2000, review of *Echo Platoon,* p. 334.

Library Journal, April 1, 1993, James Dudley, review of *Rogue Warrior;* April 15, 1994, Michael T. Fein, review of *Red Cell,* p. 130.

New York Times Book Review, May 22, 1983, Elisabeth Jakab, review of *Watchdogs,* p. 43; April 24, 1994, Newgate Callendar, review of *Red Cell,* p. 23; March 26, 1995, Newgate Callendar, review of *Green Team,* p. 27.

Playboy, April, 1994, Digby Diehl, review of *Red Cell,* p. 32; April, 1995, Digby Diehl, review of *Green Team,* p. 34.

Publishers Weekly, February 6, 1995, review of *Green Team,* p. 77; January 15, 1996, review of *Task Force Blue,* p. 443; February 10, 1997, review of *Designation Gold,* p. 68; January 12, 1998, review of *Seal Force Alpha,* p. 46; December 21, 1998, review of *Option Delta,* p. 57.

*   *   *

WEISS, Daniel Evan 1953-

PERSONAL: Born October 11, 1953, in New York, NY; son of Malcolm Arthur (a scientific research director) and Carol (a sociology professor; maiden name, Hirschon) Weiss; married Katharine Keiffer (a chef), November 28, 1992. *Education:* Harvard University, B.A. (magna cum laude), 1976. *Religion:* Jewish.

ADDRESSES: Home—New York, NY. *Agent*—Joy Harris, Lantz-Harris Literary Agency, 156 Fifth Ave., Suite 617, New York, NY 10010. *E-mail*—deweiss@panix. com.

CAREER: Writer.

WRITINGS:

100% American, illustrated by Patrick McDonnell, Poseidon Press (New York, NY), 1988.

Unnatural Selection (novel), Black Swan, 1990, published as *The Roaches Have No King,* Serpent's Tail (New York, NY), 1994.

The Great Divide: How Females and Males Really Differ, Poseidon Press (New York, NY), 1991.

Hell on Wheels (novel), Black Swan, 1991.

The Swine's Wedding (novel), Serpent's Tail (New York, NY), 1996.

Honk If You Love Aphrodite (novel), Serpent's Tail (New York, NY), 1999.

Contributor to home improvement, travel, medical, and history books published by *Reader's Digest.* Weiss's novels have been translated into French, German, and Italian.

SIDELIGHTS: In 1994 the dark but comedic novel *The Roaches Have No King* by Daniel Evan Weiss appeared in American bookstores (it was originally published in the United Kingdom in 1990 under the title *Unnatural Selection).* The book tells of Ira Fishblatt, a philanthropist who lives in an urban apartment which is overrun by cockroaches. By day, Ira works as an attorney for Legal Aid, then comes home to his lover, known as "The Gypsy," and the insects. The Gypsy is an unapologetic slob whom the roaches love, because she frequently leaves food out in the apartment. When the relationship dissolves, Ira becomes involved with Ruth Grubstein, who is obsessively neat. Ira decides to remodel the kitchen to please his new girlfriend, a decision which throws his household into an uproar.

The prospect of renovation is extremely upsetting to the roaches, and their displeasure is documented in the pages of *The Roaches Have No King.* They make up a small, very literate, and very loquacious nation in Ira's quarters, and refer to one another by names derived from books, products, and labels they have read—Kotex, Julia Child, Bismarck, and others. When their leader, Numbers, suggests that they should begin hoarding food in preparation for the remodeling, Bismarck dismisses the idea, asserting that "Ants do that. They're so obsessed with protecting themselves against a bad day that they never have a good one. That's not living." Numbers devises another strategy that involves luring a cocaine dealer named Rufus into the web of deceit; the plan's ultimate goal is to get rid of Ruth and have Ira get together with his married neighbor. *New York Times Book Review* contributor Lewis Burke Frumkes described Weiss's novel as "an appealing, often mordant satire" that manages to be "dark and erotic in addition to being clever and charming."

Weiss is also the author of nonfiction works. His first published volume, *100% American,* is a compendium of statistics that provide a snapshot of American habits, beliefs, and eccentricities. Arranged in numerical order from one to 100 percent, Weiss reports such tidbits as sixty-seven percent of U.S. citizens think that secret dossiers have been compiled about them. Weiss continues to present statistics in his 1991 book *The Great Divide: How Females and Males Really Differ,* spending eighteen months researching data to uncover some unusual dissimilarities between the sexes. One thing he unearthed concerns the Caldecott Medal, a prestigious award annually given to illustrators of children's books. Inside the pages of the winning books over the years, "ten boys are pictured for every girl," Weiss told *Atlanta Journal/Constitution* writer Don O'Briant, and remarked, "I'm not sure how that group is going to explain that." Another statistic reports that "fifty-two percent of executive women and four percent of executive men are single or divorced."

Weiss once told *CA:* "I am alarmed at the indifference of the modern world to anything more ancient than last week."

BIOGRAPHICAL/CRITICAL SOURCES:

BOOKS

Weiss, Daniel Evan, *100&pcnt; American,* illustrated by Patrick McDonnell, Poseidon Press (New York, NY), 1988.
Weiss, Daniel Evan, *The Roaches Have No King,* Serpent's Tail (New York, NY), 1994.

PERIODICALS

Atlanta Journal/Constitution, March 27, 1991, article by Don O'Briant, p. D4.
Los Angeles Times Book Review, September 25, 1988, p. 4.
Modern Language Review, July, 1989, p. 687.
New York Times, June 29, 1994, p. C21.
New York Times Book Review, May 29, 1994, Lewis Burke Frumkes, review of *The Roaches Have No King,* p. 11.

*   *   *

WEISS, Thomas G. 1946-

PERSONAL: Born February 26, 1946, in Detroit, MI; son of Franklin G. and Doris May (Lennon) Weiss; married Priscilla Read; children: Hannah, Rebeccah. *Education:* Harvard University, B.A., 1964; Princeton University, M.P.A., 1971, Ph.D., 1974; attended Institut Universitaire de Hautes Etudes Internationales, Geneva, 1971-72.

ADDRESSES: Home—57 Barnes St., Providence, RI 02906. *Office*—Thomas J. Watson, Jr., Institute for International Studies, Brown University, Box 1970, Providence, RI 02912.

CAREER: International Labor Organization, Geneva, Switzerland, research associate, 1971; Institute for World Order, New York, NY, assistant director of University Program, 1972-73; United Nations Institute for Training and Research, New York, NY, research associate, 1974-75; United Nations Conference on Trade and Development, Geneva, senior economic affairs officer, 1975-85; Office of the United Nations Commissioner for Namibia, New York, NY, senior aid coordinator, 1978; International Peace Academy, New York, NY, executive director, 1985-89; Brown University, Providence, RI, associate director of Thomas J. Watson, Jr., Institute for International Studies, 1990—, associate dean of faculty for international faculty affairs, 1992—. Academic Council on the United Nations System, executive director, 1992—. Visiting professor at Colgate University and Princeton University; part-time instructor at New School for Social Research, 1974-84.

MEMBER: International Institute for Strategic Studies, International Studies Association, Council on Foreign Relations.

WRITINGS:

International Bureaucracy, Heath, 1975.
(With Robert S. Jordan) *The World Food Conference and Global Problem Solving,* Praeger, 1976.
(Editor, with Anthony Jennings) *The Challenge of Development in the Eighties,* Pergamon, 1982.
(With Jennings) *More for the Least?: Prospects for the Poorest Countries in the Eighties,* Heath, 1983.
(Editor, with David Pitt) *The Nature of the United Nations Bureaucracies,* Croom Helm, 1986.
Multilateral Development Diplomacy in UNCTAD: The Lessons of Group Negotiations, 1964-1984, Macmillan (New York, NY), 1986.
(Editor) *American, Soviet, and Third World Perceptions of Regional Conflicts,* IPA, 1989.
(Editor) *The United Nations in Conflict Management: American, Soviet, and Third World Views,* IPA, 1990.
(Editor) *Humanitarian Emergencies and Military Help in Africa,* Macmillan (New York, NY), 1990.
(With Augustus R. Norton) *UN Peacekeepers: Soldiers with a Difference,* Foreign Policy Association, 1990.

(With Larry Minear and others) *Humanitarianism under Siege,* Red Sea Press, 1991.

(Editor, with Leon Gordenker) *Peacekeepers, Soldiers, and Disasters,* Macmillan (New York, NY), 1991.

(Editor, with Meryl A. Kessler) *Third World Security in the Post-Cold War Era,* Lynne Rienner, 1991.

(Editor, with James G. Blight) *The Suffering Grass: Superpowers and Regional Conflict in Southern Africa and the Caribbean,* Lynne Rienner, 1992.

(Editor) *Collective Security in a Changing World,* Lynne Rienner, 1993.

(With Minear) *Humanitarian Action in Times of War: A Handbook for Practitioners,* Lynne Rienner, 1993.

(Editor, with Minear) *Humanitarianism across Borders: Sustaining Civilians in Times of War,* Lynne Rienner, 1993.

(With David P. Forsythe and Roger A. Coate) *The United Nations and Changing World Politics,* Westview (Boulder, CO), 1994, 2nd edition, 1997.

(Co-author) *Humanitarian Politics,* Foreign Policy Association, 1995.

(Editor) *The United Nations and Civil Wars,* Lynne Reinner, 1995.

(Co-author) *Mercy under Fire: War and the Global Humanitarian Community,* Westview, 1996.

(Editor, with Robert I. Rotberg) *From Massacres to Genocide: The Media, Public Policy, and Humanitarian Crises,* Brookings Institution, 1996.

(Co-editor) *Volunteers against Conflict,* UN University Press, 1996.

(Co-editor) *NGOs, the UN, and Global Governance,* Lynne Reinner, 1996.

(With Minear and Colin Scott) *The News Media, Civil War, and Humanitarian Action,* Lynne Reinner, 1996.

(Co-author) *Humanitarian Challenges and Intervention: World Politics and the Dilemmas of Help,* Westview (Boulder, CO), 1996.

Military-Civilian Interactions: Intervening in Humanitarian Crises, Rowman, 1999.

(With Louis Emmerij, Richard Jolly and Kofi Annan) *Ahead of the Curve: UN Ideas and Global Challenges (United Nations Intellectual History),* Indiana University Press, 2001.

Also author of *American Economic Development in Historical Perspective.* Member of editorial board, *Washington Quarterly,* 1993—, and *Global Governance,* 1994—. Contributor to periodicals, including *Foreign Policy, Ethics and International Affairs, Security Studies, World Policy Journal, Survival, Third World Quarterly, World Politics,* and *International Affairs.*

SIDELIGHTS: Much of Thomas G. Weiss's writing focuses on the question of introducing international mili-

tary forces into local disturbances. In particular, humanitarian reasons are often examined as reasonable arguments for such military intervention. In such books as *From Massacres to Genocide: The Media, Public Policy and Humanitarian Causes, The News Media, Civil War, and Humanitarian Action,* and *Military-Civilian Interactions: Intervening in Humanitarian Crises,* Weiss has presented a case for the United Nations or other international bodies becoming involved in local or even internal conflicts.

Both *From Massacres to Genocide* and *The News Media, Civil War, and Humanitarian Action* examine the role played by the media, especially television, in shaping the views of the American public about foreign crises. In *From Massacres to Genocide,* for example, the American intervention in Somalia is contrasted with the lack of action taken in the neighboring country of Sudan, where war and famine had also caused widespread suffering. Weiss and co-editor Robert I. Rotberg argue that American television played a large role in creating public pressure for action in Somalia and not in Sudan by distorting coverage of the two situations. *The News Media, Civil War, and Humanitarian Action* argues for a closer cooperation between the news media, government, and non-governmental organizations so that humanitarian crises can be objectively evaluated.

In *Military-Civilian Interactions,* Weiss analyzes five recent cases where American intervention occurred in crisis situations abroad. In each case, Weiss argues that American military presence was tentative and unwilling or unable to address the underlying causes of the local problem. A. C. Tuttle, writing in *Choice,* called *Military-Civilian Interactions* a "well-researched book" and "a valuable text in undergraduate and graduate national security and foreign policy classes."

BIOGRAPHICAL/CRITICAL SOURCES:

PERIODICALS

Choice, November, 1999, A. C. Tuttle, review of *Military-Civilian Interactions,* p. 618.

Current History, May, 1997, Emily Shartin, review of *Humanitarian Challenges and Intervention,* p. 236.

Economic Development and Cultural Change, April, 1988, Richard J. Ward, review of *Multilateral Development Diplomacy in UNCTAD,* p. 597.

Foreign Affairs, September-October, 1995, Francis Fukuyama, review of *The United Nations and Civil Wars,* p. 162; May-June, 1996, Francis Fukuyama, review of *From Massacres to Genocide,* p. 134; November-December, 1996, Francis Fukuyama, review of *The News Media, Civil War, and Humanitarian Action,* p. 145.

Journal of American History, March, 1995, Stuart Bruchey, review of *American Economic Development in Historical Perspective,* p. 1703.

Journal of Developing Areas, October, 1992, Jerry L. Weaver, review of *Humanitarian Emergencies and Military Help in Africa,* p. 106.

Journal of Development Studies, October, 1992, James Derrick Sidaway, review of *The Suffering Grass,* p. 183.

Public Administration, spring, 1987, Mark Imber, review of *The Nature of the United Nations Bureaucracies,* p. 121.*

*   *   *

WHEELER, Douglas L. 1937-

PERSONAL: Born July 19, 1937, in St. Louis, MO; son of Russell Charles (a dentist) and Lucille (a teacher and homemaker; maiden name, Wengler) Wheeler; married Katherine Wells (a state senator), June 13, 1964; children: Katherine Gladney, Lucille Lanphier Wheeler Goodrum. *Ethnicity:* "White." *Education:* Dartmouth College, A.B. (with distinction), 1959; Boston University, M.A., 1960, Ph.D., 1963. *Politics:* Democrat. *Religion:* United Church of Christ. *Avocational interests:* Reading, walking, tennis, theater (including locally produced, amateur theatricals).

ADDRESSES: Home—27 Mill Rd., Durham, NH 03824-3098. *Office*—Department of History, University of New Hampshire, Durham, NH 038243586; fax 603-868-6935. *E-mail*—dwheeler@christa.unh.edu.

CAREER: Morgan State College, Baltimore, MD, part-time lecturer in history, 1965; University of New Hampshire, Durham, assistant professor, 1965-69, associate professor, 1969-75, professor of history, 1975—, Prince Henry the Navigator Professor of Portuguese History, 1995—. Harvard University, Richard Welch fellow in history of intelligence at Center for International Affairs, 1984-85; Boston University, visiting assistant professor, 1969, visiting associate professor, 1972. Professional consultant to U.S. Department of State on Portugal and Africa, 1974, 1976. Missouri Historical Society, assistant to the curator, 1960. *Military service:* U.S. Army Reserve, active duty in Army Intelligence, 1963-65; became first lieutenant.

MEMBER: International Conference Group on Portugal, Historical Society, Society for Spanish and Portuguese Historical Studies, American Portuguese Society.

AWARDS, HONORS: Gulbenkian Foundation grants for Portugal; Fulbright grant for Portugal, 1961-62; grants from Camoes Institute and Luso-American Development Foundation, Lisbon.

WRITINGS:

(With M. Rene Pelissier) *Angola,* Praeger (New York, NY), 1971.

Republican Portugal, University of Wisconsin Press (Madison, WI), 1978.

(Editor with L. Graham) *In Search of Modern Portugal,* University of Wisconsin Press (Madison, WI), 1983.

A ditadura militar portuguesa, Europa-America (Lisbon, Portugal), 1988.

Historical Dictionary of Portugal, Scarecrow (Metuchen, NJ), 1993.

'Fifty-nine Remembers: A "Fifties" Tribute to Dartmouth College, Peter Randall (Portsmouth, NH), 1999.

Contributor of articles and reviews on African history to periodicals, including *Armed Forces and Society, USA Today, Journal of Modern African Studies, Journal of Military History, Africa Report, Foreign Affairs,* and *Christian Science Monitor;* translator of Portuguese articles.

WORK IN PROGRESS: Research on the history of the modern Portuguese empire (Africa, America, Asia), 1822-1975, and on the history of espionage since 1890.

SIDELIGHTS: Douglas L. Wheeler told *CA:* "Since April, 1961, when I published my first (relatively) scholarly article, I have been interested in two regions in particular: tropical Africa and Iberia, especially Portugal. My direction in research and writing was initially influenced by my dissertation research years spent in Lisbon, Portugal, 1961-62, an experience which changed my life in many ways. First I concentrated on colonial African history, to the mid-1970s, and then, increasingly, I concentrated on the history of Portugal and her empire.

"I have enjoyed writing for a wide variety of different kinds of publications, in part because such work assisted my development as a nonfiction writer. Writing for encyclopedias, for example, was a more useful exercise than I had originally imagined it would be."

Wheeler speaks Spanish in addition to Portuguese, and reads French.

BIOGRAPHICAL/CRITICAL SOURCES:

PERIODICALS

History Today, March, 1995, Tom Gallagher, review of *Historical Dictionary of Portugal,* p. 53.

*   *   *

WHIM-WHAM
   See CURNOW, (Thomas) Allen (Monro)

*   *   *

WHITE, James P(atrick) 1940-

PERSONAL: Born September 28, 1940, in Wichita Falls, TX; son of Joseph and Minnie (Mann) White; married Janice Lou Turner, September 11, 1961; children: Christopher Jules. *Education:* University of Texas, B.A. (with honors), 1961; Vanderbilt University, M.A. (history), 1967; graduate study at Texas Christian University, 1969-71; Brown University, M.A. (creative writing), 1973.

ADDRESSES: Home—P.O. Box 428, Montrose, AL 36559. *Office*—Department of Creative Writing, University of South Alabama, Mobile, AL 36688. *Agent*—Joan Raines, Raines & Raines, 71 Park Ave., New York, NY 10016. *E-mail*—james@americanartists.org.

CAREER: Blue Mountain College, Blue Mountain, MS, associate professor of history, 1964-66; freelance writer in Europe and the United States, 1967-70; University of Texas of the Permian Basin, Odessa, assistant professor, 1973-74, associate professor of creative writing and department chair, 1974-76; Texas Center for Writers, Dallas, founder and director, 1976-77; University of Texas at Dallas, visiting university professor, 1977-78; University of Southern California, Los Angeles, director of master of arts program in professional writing, 1979-83; University of South Alabama, Mobile, professor and director of creative writing, 1983—. Texas Joint English Committee for Schools and Colleges, member of state executive committee, 1973-74; Dallas Theater Center, chair of advisory board for Down Center Stage, 1978-79.

MEMBER: American Literary Translators Association (member of international editorial board, 1978—), Associated Writing Programs (member of national editorial board, 1973-75), Conference of College Teachers of English (state chair of creative writing section, 1975-76), Modern Language Association of America (South Central section), Texas Association of College Creative Writing Teachers (founding president, 1973-74), Gulf Coast Association of College Creative Writing Teachers (founding president, 1993), Theta Xi, Phi Delta Phi, Phi Alpha Theta, Phi Eta Sigma.

AWARDS, HONORS: Marston fellow, 1971; Guggenheim fellow, 1988-89; Fulbright fellow, 1991; Shubert grant.

WRITINGS:

Broadside (three-act play), first produced in Cleveland, OH, at Muse Theater, 1969.
Family Circle (three-act play), first produced in Providence, RI, at Brown University, 1973.
(Editor) *Bicentennial Collection of Texas Short Stories,* Texas Center for Writers Press, 1974.
(Editor) *New and Experimental Literature,* Texas Center for Writers Press, 1975.
(Editor) *William King's Southwest,* 1975.
Birdsong (novel), Copper Beech Press (Providence, RI), 1977, 4th edition, Texas Center for Writers Press, 1999.
Poems, Calliope Press (North Hollywood, CA), 1978.
(With Anne Reed Rooth) *The Ninth Car* (novel), Putnam (New York, NY), 1978.
(Editor, with W. McDonald) *Texas Stories and Poems,* 1978.
(Editor, with J. White) *Poetry Dallas,* 1978.
(With wife, Janice L. White) *Clarity: A Text on Writing,* Paul Hanson, 1981.
The Persian Oven (novella), Imperial Press, 1983, published with *California Exit,* Methuen (New York, NY), 1987.
(Editor, with Don Bachardy) *Where Joy Resides: A Christopher Isherwood Reader,* Farrar, Straus (New York, NY), 1989.
(Editor) *Gulf Coast Collection of Stories and Poems,* Texas Center for Writers Press, 1992.
Clara's Call (novel), Texas Center for Writers Press, 1994.

Contributor of articles, poems, and short stories to more than forty periodicals, including *Kansas Quarterly, Quartet, Texas Quarterly, Arizona Quarterly, Arts and*

Letters, Mundus Artium, Contemporary Literary Scene, Journal of African History, Markham Review, and *New Writers.* Editor, *Texas Writer's Newsletter,* 1973-76, and *Sand,* 1976—; founding editor and publisher, *Texas Books in Review,* 1975-78.

SIDELIGHTS: "I think that the most important thing about writing," James P. White once told *CA,* "is obviously the work itself—enjoying, developing, and caring about it and the writing of others. I've been involved in a lot of literary activities and have run several writing programs. What matters is a person's work. I particularly admire Christopher Isherwood and Thomas Williams and Susan Fromberg Schaeffer. Building a literary career is difficult; much of it adds up to nothing. But what really matters is continuing to learn about writing and caring about writing well."

*   *   *

WHITE, John K(enneth) 1952-

PERSONAL: Born October 20, 1952, in Providence, RI; son of Harold A. (an accountant) and Margaret (a librarian; maiden name, Morrissey) White. *Education:* University of Rhode Island, B.A. (summa cum laude), 1975; University of Connecticut, M.A., 1976, Ph.D., 1980. *Religion:* Roman Catholic.

ADDRESSES: Home—9619 Duffer Way, Gaithersburg, MD 20879. *Office*—Department of Politics, Catholic University of America, Washington, DC 20064. *E-mail*—white@cua.edu.

CAREER: Southern Connecticut State College, New Haven, instructor in government, 1978-79; State University of New York College at Potsdam, visiting assistant professor, 1980-81, assistant professor, 1981-86, associate professor of political science, 1986-88; Catholic University of America, Washington, DC, associate professor in department of politics, 1988—. Lecturer, University of Massachusetts at Amherst, Rhode Island College, and Providence Heritage Commission. Committee for Party Renewal, executive director.

MEMBER: American Political Science Association, New England Political Science Association, Northeastern Political Science Association, New York State Political Science Association (member of executive board, 1982-88), National Capital Area Political Science Association (member of executive board, 1989-92), Pi Sigma Alpha, Phi Kappa Phi.

WRITINGS:

The Fractured Electorate: Political Parties and Social Change in Southern New England, University Press of New England (Hanover, NH), 1983.

The New Politics of Old Values, University Press of New England (Hanover, NH), 1988, third edition, University Press of America (Lanham, MD), 1998.

(Editor, with Peter W. Colby, and contributor) *New York State Today: Government, Politics, and Public Policy,* State University of New York Press (Albany, NY), 1989, third edition, with Colby and Jeffrey M. Stonecash, published as *Governing New York State,* 1994.

(Editor, with Jerome M. Mileur, and contributor) *Challenges to Party Government,* Southern Illinois University Press (Carbondale, IL), 1992.

(Editor, with John C. Green) *The Politics of Ideas: Intellectual Challenges to the Party after 1992,* Rowman & Littlefield Publishers (Lanham, MD), 1995, new edition published as *The Politics of Ideas,* State University of New York Press (Albany, NY), 2001.

Still Seeing Red: How the Old Cold War Shapes the New American Politics, Westview Press (Boulder, CO), 1997, revised edition, 1998.

(Editor, with Philip John Davies) *Political Parties and the Collapse of the Old Orders,* State University of New York Press (Albany, NY), 1998.

(With Daniel M. Shea) *New Party Politics: From Jefferson and Hamilton to the Information Age,* St. Martin's Press (New York, NY), 2000.

Contributor to books, including *New England Political Parties,* edited by Josephine F. Milburn and William Doyle, Schenkman, 1983. Contributor to periodicals. Editor of *Party Line,* 1984-86.

WORK IN PROGRESS: The Two Nations: American Values in a Time of Transition, for Chatham House Publishers, 2002.

SIDELIGHTS: In *New Party Politics: From Jefferson to Hamilton to the Information Age* John K. White and co-author Daniel M. Shea present "a thorough overview of the history, organization, and influence of parties in elections and governments," explained Thomas J. Baldino in *Library Journal. New Party Politics* begins by tracing the origins of America's political parties to the 1790s, when Thomas Jefferson's idea of local government first clashed with Alexander Hamilton's conception of a centralized government. White and Shea detail the growth and development of political parties from these beginnings to their peak of strength at the beginning of the twentieth century to their relative weakness today. In addition, the authors speculate on future electoral developments spurred by the growth of computer use and the Internet. A reviewer for *Kirkus Reviews* found *New Party Politics* to be "a model book of practical political science" containing "a light touch and many illustrative anecdotes."

White once told *CA:* "For too long, American writers have examined our nation's politics in unidimensional terms. Too often, we have viewed U.S. politics on one giant canvas—forgetting that our federal system created fifty separate (and unique) mosaics.

"*The Fractured Electorate: Political Parties and Social Change in Southern New England* attempts to arrange the jigsaw pieces of the puzzle of politics in southern New England into a composite picture—something that hadn't been done for nearly twenty-five years. Massachusetts, Connecticut, and Rhode Island are very different. Yet, by using these states as 'laboratories' for analysis, political scientists can test hypotheses and explore their meaning for the nation as a whole."

White later told *CA:* "In subsequent books, I have continued to explore the relationships between the American voter and the political parties. *The New Politics of Old Values* describes how Ronald Reagan used American values to forge a deep and long-lasting relationship with the American electorate. Reagan's successors have attempted to emulate his success with mixed results. *Still Seeing Red* explores how the Cold War reshaped American politics to produce its own unique party system whose effects persist long after the Cold War is over. *The Two Nations: American Values in a Time of Transition* returns to the subject of values once more. Since Reagan's presidency ended in 1981, there has been an enormous demographic, cultural, and values shift in the United States. Democrats and Republicans have attempted to cope with this transformation, albeit mostly unsuccessfully.

"In all of my work, I have asked two fundamental questions: 1) What makes the voters tick? and 2) What does it mean to be an American? These themes have dominated my writing about American politics. William Shakespeare best posed the issue in *King Henry IV,* Part I. One of the characters boasts that 'I can call spirits from the vasty deep' only to hear the rejoinder: 'Why so can I, or so can any man; but will they come when you do call for them?' What ultimately moves the 'spirits of the vasty deep' remains, for me, a lifelong academic inquiry."

BIOGRAPHICAL/CRITICAL SOURCES:

PERIODICALS

American Political Science Review, September, 1998, review of *Still Seeing Red: How the Old Cold War Shapes the New American Politics,* p. 720.

Booklist, July, 2000, Mary Carroll, review of *New Party Politics: From Jefferson and Hamilton to the Information Age,* p. 1982.

Choice, May, 1998, review of *Still Seeing Red,* p. 1609; November, 1999, review of *Political Parties and the Collapse of the Old Orders,* p. 614.

Kirkus Reviews, July 1, 1997, review of *Still Seeing Red,* p. 1021; June 15, 2000, review of *New Party Politics,* p. 873.

Library Journal, September 1, 1997, Edward Goedeken, review of *Still Seeing Red,* p. 202; July, 2000, Thomas J. Baldino, review of *New Party Politics.*

Political Science Quarterly, fall, 1998, review of *Still Seeing Red,* p. 521.

Research and Reference Book News, February, 1999, review of *The New Politics of Old Values,* p. 44; May, 1999, review of *Still Seeing Red,* p. 126.

University Press Book Notes, December, 1992, review of *Challenges to Party Government,* p. 18.

OTHER

History Net, http://www.historynet.com/ (June, 1999), review of *Still Seeing Red.*

*　　*　　*

WIESNER, Merry E. 1952-

PERSONAL: Born November 24, 1952, in Charleston, SC; daughter of H. B. (in management) and Bette Lou (an artist; maiden name, Nelson) Wiesner; married Neil Hanks (a paddle sports consultant), August 9, 1986; children: Kai, Tyr. *Education:* Grinnell College, B.A., 1973; University of Wisconsin—Madison, M.A., 1975, Ph.D., 1979. *Politics:* "Democrat of the old DFL type." *Avocational interests:* Gardening, sweater design, canoeing.

ADDRESSES: Home—12455 North Wauwatosa Rd., Mequon, WI 53097-2711. *Office*—Department of History, University of Wisconsin—Milwaukee, Milwaukee, WI 53201. *E-mail*—merrywh@uwm.edu.

CAREER: Augustana College, Rock Island, IL, assistant professor of history, 1979-85; University of Wisconsin—Milwaukee, assistant professor, 1985-87, associate professor, 1987-94, professor of history, 1994—, director of Center for Women's Studies, 1992-96, department chair, 1998—. Stanford University, visiting associate professor, 1988; Marquette University, holder of women's chair in humanistic studies, 1996-97; lecturer at Albion College, Hartwick College, University of Minnesota—Twin Cities, University of Cincinnati, Duke University, Carroll College, Morningside College, Washington University, St. Louis, MO, University of Chicago, University of Akron, Michigan State University, Northern Illinois University, and University of Kassel.

MEMBER: Sixteenth Century Studies Council (vice president, 1992-93; president, 1993-94), American Historical Association, Society for Reformation Research, Social Science History Association, Berkshire Women's History Conference.

AWARDS, HONORS: Fulbright fellow, 1973-74; grants from Deutscher Akademischer Austauschdienst, 1987, and American Council of Learned Societies, 1987 and 1994-95; Guggenheim fellow, 1997-98.

WRITINGS:

Working Women in Renaissance Germany, Rutgers University Press (New Brunswick, NJ), 1986.
(With Julius Ruff and Bruce Wheeler) *Discovering the Western Past: A Look at the Evidence,* Volumes I-II, Houghton (Boston, MA), 1988, 2nd edition, 1993.
Women and Gender in Early Modern Europe, Cambridge University Press (New York, NY), 1993.
Discovering the World's Past, Houghton (Boston, MA), 1996.
(Editor) *Encyclopedia of the Reformation,* Oxford University Press (New York, NY), 1996.
Christianity and the Regulation of Sexuality, Routledge & Kegan Paul (London, England), 2000.
(With Lisa Di Caprio) *Lives and Voices: Sources on Women in European History,* Houghton (Boston, MA), 2000.

Contributor to books, including *The Art of Midwifery: Early Modern Midwives in Europe,* edited by Hilary Marland, Routledge & Kegan Paul (London, England), 1993; *Chloe: Beihefte zum Daphnis,* Volume XIX: *The*

Graph of Sex and the German Text: Gendered Culture in Early Modern Germany, 1500-1700, edited by Lynne Tatlock, Rodopi (Amsterdam, Netherlands), 1994; and *Handbook of European History in the Later Middle Ages, Renaissance, and Reformation, 1400-1600,* edited by Thomas A. Brady, Jr., Heiko A. Oberman, and James Tracy, E. J. Brill (Leiden, Netherlands), 1994. Contributor of articles and reviews to history and women's studies journals. Coeditor, *Archiv für Reformationsgeschichte;* member of editorial board, *Sixteenth Century Journal* and *Journal of Women's History.*

SIDELIGHTS: Merry E. Wiesner once told *CA:* "My career as a writer (or better said, as a published historian) began rather dismally, with my first article going through seven rejections. Ah, the great joy (and slight feeling of smugness) when early efforts are reprinted, translated, and cited! Probably nothing I've done since then has received as much careful editing as that article, for nearly everything has been written according to publishers' deadlines. My central piece of advice to other writers, or at least to other historians hoping to be writers, is to meet those deadlines. Doing this will cause people to ask you to write more and bigger projects, a spiral that only goes upward until you realize you will never have to market another book or article. People will come to you, not for your brilliance, but for your punctuality. A sad fact, perhaps, but it means you can spend more time writing.

"My only other word of advice is to learn what audience you most enjoy writing for, and don't be ashamed of it. I've found, to my surprise, that I most enjoy writing about things that are new to me, not my specialties. Overarching surveys are great fun, as are comparative studies that leap centuries and continents. This may stem from the fact that even when I *am* writing or speaking about what I know best (women in Germany in the sixteenth century), I'm usually addressing people for whom one of those things (women, Germany, or the sixteenth century) is a mystery. I have been well trained to explain new things, and I like it.

"Like all feminist historians, I want the lives of women to be part of any consideration of the past. I feel especially strongly about this in terms of textbooks. If we as feminists won't make sure that 'the past' includes women, who will?"

*   *   *

WILSON, Barbara Ker
See KER WILSON, Barbara

WOODIWISS, Kathleen E(rin) 1939-

PERSONAL: Born June 3, 1939, in Alexandria, LA; daughter of Charles Wingrove, Sr., and Gladys (Coker) Hogg; married Ross Eugene Woodiwiss (a U.S. Air Force major), July 20, 1956 (divorced); children: Sean Alan, Dorren James, Heath Alexander. *Education:* Attended schools in Alexandria, LA. *Politics:* Republican.

ADDRESSES: Home—Princeton, MN. *Office*—c/o Avon Books, 1350 Avenue of the Americas, New York, NY 10019.

CAREER: Writer. Worked as a model in fashion shows in Tokyo, Japan.

WRITINGS:

The Flame and the Flower, Avon (New York, NY), 1972.
The Wolf and the Dove, Avon (New York, NY), 1974.
Shanna, Avon (New York, NY), 1977.
Ashes in the Wind, Avon (New York, NY), 1979.
A Rose in Winter, Avon (New York, NY), 1982.
Come Love a Stranger, Avon (New York, NY), 1984.
So Worthy My Love, Avon (New York, NY), 1989.
Forever in Your Embrace, Avon (New York, NY), 1992, author's preferred edition, 1999.
(With others) *Three Weddings and a Kiss* (anthology), Avon (New York, NY), 1995.
(Editor and contributor) *Married at Midnight,* Avon (New York, NY), 1996.
Petals on the River, Avon (New York, NY), 1997.
A Season beyond a Kiss, Avon (New York, NY), 2000.

ADAPTATIONS: The Flame and the Flower, So Worthy My Love, Petals on the River, and *A Season beyond a Kiss* have been recorded on audio cassette.

SIDELIGHTS: A pioneering writer of romance fiction, Kathleen E. Woodiwiss's first novel is generally credited with creating the subgenre known as "erotic historical" romance. When *The Flame and the Flower* was published in 1972, the field of romance writing was dominated by "contemporary gothics" produced by writers such as Mary Stewart, Victoria Holt, and Phyllis Whitney. *The Flame and the Flower* differed from its predecessors in that it was substantially longer, but also because it contained lengthy, often detailed passages describing the sexual encounters of the hero and

heroine. The immediate success of *The Flame and the Flower* cleared the way for writers like Rosemary Rogers and Laura McBain, authors who, along with Woodiwiss, have helped make the historical romance an enormously popular form. *The Flame and the Flower* has gone through eighty printings and has sold over four million copies.

The novels following *The Flame and the Flower* continued to be ground-breakers and assured Woodiwiss a large and loyal readership. *Shanna,* Woodiwiss's third book, made publishing history by becoming the first historical romance released in a trade paperback edition, and it went on to sell over three million copies and spend a full year on the *New York Times* bestseller list. In 1979 Avon published *Ashes in the Wind* with a first printing of one-and-a-half million copies; the publisher backed the book with a huge promotional campaign, including full-page advertisements in national women's magazines and commercials on network television. The publicity paid off almost immediately as *Ashes in the Wind* sold over two million copies and went into a third printing within a month of its release. The 2000 release *A Season beyond a Kiss* was launched with a first printing of seven hundred thousand copies and was the first romance novel to top the *Publishers Weekly* paperback bestseller list. In total, some thirty-six million copies of Woodiwiss's books have been sold worldwide.

Historical romances vary in some respects but share fundamental similarities. Settings are typically exotic and frequently change from continent to continent. Heroes are characteristically handsome and commanding, while heroines are beautiful and sensitive. Often innocent, the heroine is usually introduced to the hero with whom she falls in love. *The Flame and the Flower* clearly embodies the traditions of its genre. The heroine, Heather, is a teenager throughout the narrative, which begins in England around 1800 and eventually moves to the American Carolinas. A beautiful and decorous girl who becomes the ward of a cruel aunt, Heather is mistaken for a harlot by an attractive Yankee who, in turn, is forced to marry her. After many adventures, the pair work out their initial hatred for each other and fall in love. *The Flame and the Flower* also maintains the traditional structural relationship of males as dominant to and protective of females.

Where *The Flame and the Flower* and other Woodiwiss novels break with tradition is in their frank depiction of the sexual relationship between the hero and the heroine. While her books contain occasional sexual passages, Woodiwiss objects to charges that her books are "erotic." "I'm insulted when my books are called erotic," she maintained in a *Cosmopolitan* interview. "I don't think people who say that have read my books. I believe I write love stories. With a little spice. Some of the other current romances are a bit savage, though. They make sex dirty. It's embarrassing to read them. But women are looking for the love story. I get a lot of fan mail, and they tell me that." Janice Radway, writing in *Twentieth-Century Romance and Historical Writers,* saw the erotic passages in Woodiwiss's novels as being integral parts of "complex plots which all focus on the *gradual* development of love between the two principal characters. Unlike many writers of this subgenre who keep the heroine and the hero apart until the final pages of the novel, Woodiwiss brings them into contact early in the tale. Having established their initial attraction for each other, she then shows how love develops between two extraordinary individuals, emphasizes that the relationship must be cultivated carefully, and demonstrates that compromise, tenderness, and generosity are necessary to maintain it."

Just such a relationship is presented in Woodiwiss's 1979 novel, *Ashes in the Wind.* This tale features the heroine Alaina MacGaren, a seventeen-year-old orphan who must leave her home in central Louisiana for New Orleans when a rumor is started that she is a traitor. In order to keep her identity a secret, Alaina assumes a number of disguises, including that of a street urchin, a penniless widow, and a hospital volunteer. In the midst of these many identities, the life of surgeon Captain Cole Lattimer becomes entangled with Alaina's, and the two overcome adversity to find a deep and lasting love. Although *Washington Post Book World* contributor Maude McDaniel found *Ashes in the Wind* to be filled with silly characters, a formulaic plot, and awful writing, she went on to conclude, "Actually, I rather enjoyed" the novel. And a *Publishers Weekly* contributor maintained that Woodiwiss "has fashioned her heroine in a picaresque tradition. Readers will find Alaina's spunky ingenuity refreshing."

In Woodiwiss's 1989 romance, *So Worthy My Love,* Maxim Seymour, another alleged traitor, this time to Queen Elizabeth, is thought to be dead. The young man, hated by the noble Radborne family, is actually hiding in Germany, desperately wanting his beloved, Arabella Radborne, to be with him. Sending his men to kidnap her, Maxim is surprised when they bring back Arabella's beautiful cousin Elise by mistake. Unable to let Elise go, the two battle each other defiantly until they realize that they are actually in love. Woodiwiss "provides ripe descriptions" in *So Worthy My Love,* stated a *Publishers*

Weekly contributor, adding, "This long romance by a veteran of the genre delivers well-paced, well-structured diversion."

In 1998 Woodiwiss wrote a long-awaited sequel to her first novel, *The Flame and the Flower,* titled *The Elusive Flame.* Picking up the story with Heather and Brandon Birmingham's son, Beauregard, who is a sea captain, the novel tells of Beau's romance with the orphan Cerynise, their tempestuous relationship, their troubles with London scoundrels who have stolen Cerynise's rightful inheritance, and their eventual triumph over all ordeals during a "melodramatic climax in a storm-buffeted house," as a *Publishers Weekly* critic put it. Melanie Duncan, writing in *Booklist,* stated, "Woodiwiss set the standard for excellence in romance novels with *The Flame and the Flower* . . . a standard that current authors still try to meet, and fans have waited 25 years for this wonderful sequel." *The Elusive Flame* enjoyed a first printing of 800,000 copies.

A Season beyond a Kiss, published in 2000, brought back the Birmingham family for the third time. Brandon's younger brother, Jeffrey, has just wed beautiful Raelynn Barrett. Their marriage, however, hits upon rocky times almost immediately when Jeff is accused of getting a young girl pregnant. Despite Jeff's claims of innocence, Raelynn, who wants to believe him, is not sure if he can be trusted. When the young girl in question is murdered, Jeff is found in possession of the murder weapon. He must now try to prove his innocence while going up against a mysterious conspiracy and a vicious murderer.

Although Woodiwiss's novels are enormously successful with the public, they are generally ignored by "serious" reviewers. This situation does not seem to bother Woodiwiss, however, nor does it make her wish to change her approach to writing. "I never started out to win any prizes for my writing," she related in her interview with Judy Klemesrud in the *New York Times Book Review.* "I wanted to appease a hunger for romantic novels, and that is what I shall continue to do." Woodiwiss similarly pointed out to *CA* that her books are only an attempt to give readers "enjoyment. Escape. I would like to be able to give the reader a time period of relaxation and pleasure, a time of being able to put the worries and everything aside and just enjoy and relax." She told Giovanna Breu in *People* that her books "are fairy tales. They are an escape for the reader, like an Errol Flynn movie."

For an interview with Woodiwiss, See *Contemporary Authors New Revisions,* Volume 23.

BIOGRAPHICAL/CRITICAL SOURCES:

BOOKS

Falk, Kathryn, *Love's Leading Ladies,* Pinnacle, 1982.
Twentieth-Century Romance and Historical Writers, second edition, St. James (Detroit, MI), 1990.

PERIODICALS

Booklist, September 15, 1998, Melanie Duncan, review of *The Elusive Flame,* p. 214; July, 2000, Mary McCay, review of audio cassette version of *A Season beyond a Kiss,* p. 2054.
Cosmopolitan, February, 1978, interview with Kathleen E. Woodiwiss.
Library Journal, May 15, 1974, p. 1410; February 15, 1995, p. 198.
New York Times Book Review, November 4, 1979, Judy Klemesrud, interview with Kathleen E. Woodiwiss.
People, February 7, 1983, Giovanna Breu, "Romance Writer Kathleen Woodiwiss Is Passionate about Horses—and Happy Endings," p. 75.
Publishers Weekly, January 21, 1974, p. 88; January 31, 1977; May 30, 1977; September 3, 1979, review of *Ashes in the Wind,* p. 94; October 22, 1982, p. 51; August 25, 1989, review of *So Worthy My Love,* p. 57; August 24, 1998, Daisy Maryles, "Fanning the Flames," p. 19; August 31, 1998, review of *The Elusive Flame,* p. 50; March 20, 2000, Daisy Maryles and Dick Donahue, "The Flame 28 Years Later," p. 21.
Romance Reader, August 28, 1998, review of *The Elusive Flame.*
Village Voice, May 9, 1977.
Washington Post Book World, April 9, 1972, p. 9; October 7, 1979, Maude McDaniel, review of *Ashes in the Wind,* pp. 9, 14.
West Coast Review of Books, January, 1983, p. 42.*

*   *   *

WOODS, Lawrence T(imothy) 1960-

PERSONAL: Born May 11, 1960, in Vancouver, British Columbia, Canada; son of Thomas H. and Helen M. (Kessel) Woods; married Joan E. Buchanan (a writer, storyteller, and teacher), June 23, 1984; children: Elizabeth M. B. *Education:* Attended McGill University, 1978-80; University of British Columbia, B.A. (with honors), 1983; Queen's University, Kingston, Ontario, Canada, M.A., 1984; Australian National University, Ph.D., 1989. *Avocational interests:* Family, sports, travel, political novels.

ADDRESSES: Home—169 South Ridge Dr., Salt Spring Island, British Columbia, Canada V8K 1Y9. *Office*—International Studies Program, University of Northern British Columbia, 3333 University Way, Prince George, British Columbia, Canada V2N 4Z9; fax 250-960-5544. *E-mail*—woods@unbc.ca.

CAREER: Substitute teacher at a high school in Vernon, British Columbia, Canada, 1984-85; Oakangan College, Vernon, instructor in Continuing Education Division, 1985; Bishop's University, Lennoxville, Quebec, Canada, assistant professor of political studies, 1988-93, head men's soccer coach, 1989; University of Northern British Columbia, Prince George, associate professor of international studies, 1993—, acting director of Office of International Programs, 1993-94. McGill University, guest lecturer, 1990; Simon Fraser University, guest lecturer, 1993; University of British Columbia, honorary research associate at Institute of International Relations, 1993, visiting professor at Institute of Asian Research, 1998-99; University of Victoria, visiting professor at Centre for Asia Pacific Initiatives, 1998-99. Asia-Pacific Roundtable, member of Canadian delegation to Kuala Lumpur, 1994; Canadian Consortium on Asia Pacific Security, member of board of directors, 1997, co-chair, 1998-2001, vice president, 1998-2000, president, 2000-01; Canada-Asia Pacific Resource Network, member. Prince George Public Interest Research Group, convenor of East Timor Action Group, 1999; Prince George Immigration and Multicultural Services Society, member of board of directors, 2000—. Workshop leader; public speaker; guest on television and radio programs.

MEMBER: International Studies Association, Canadian Political Science Association (departmental liaison for Trust Fund, 1990-93), Academic Council on the United Nations System, Japan Studies Association of Canada (president, 1998-99), Association for Asian Studies, British Columbia Political Studies Association (northern representative, 1998-99).

AWARDS, HONORS: Commonwealth scholar in Australia, 1985-88; prize from Max Bell Business-Government Studies Program Essay Contest, York University, 1987, for "The Business of Canada's Pacific Relations"; fellow of American Society of International Law and Academic Council on the United Nations System, 1992; grant from Asia Pacific Foundation of Canada, 1993; *Asia-Pacific Diplomacy: Nongovernmental Organizations and International Relations* was named an outstanding academic book of 1993 by *Choice;* grants from Waseda University, 1994 and 1996, and Rockefeller University, 1994; travel grant for Nankai University, British Columbia Scholars to China, 1996; grants from British Columbia Council for International Education and Human Resources and Development Canada, both 1997, Canadian Centre for Foreign Policy Development, 1998, Japan Foundation, 1998 and 1999, and Shastri Indo-Canadian Institute, 1999; travel grant from Carnegie Council on Ethics and International Affairs, 1999; grant from Japanese Ministry of Education; travel grants for Japan and China, University of Northern British Columbia.

WRITINGS:

Asia-Pacific Diplomacy: Nongovernmental Organizations and International Relations, University of British Columbia Press (Vancouver, British Columbia, Canada), 1993.

(Editor, and author of preface and introduction) E. Herbert Norman, *Japan's Emergence as a Modern State: Sixtieth Anniversary Edition,* University of British Columbia Press (Vancouver, British Columbia, Canada), 2000.

(Editor, with Paul Bowles, and author of introduction) *Japan after the Economic Miracle: In Search of New Directions,* Kluwer Academic Publishers (Dordrecht, Netherlands), 2000.

Contributor to books, including *Human Rights and International Relations in the Asia-Pacific Region,* edited by James T. H. Tang, Pinter (London, England), 1995; *Asia-Pacific in the New World Order,* edited by Anthony McGrew and Christopher Brook, Routledge (London, England), 1998; *The North Pacific Triangle: The United States, Japan, and Canada at the End of the Century,* edited by Michael Fry, Mitsuru Kurosawa, and John Kirton, University of Toronto Press (Toronto, Ontario, Canada), 1998; *Politics in the Twentieth Century: Where We've Been and Where We're Going,* edited by Mary Louise McAllister, Michael Howlett, and Patrick Smith, Simon Fraser University (Burnaby, British Columbia, Canada), 1998; and *Crosscurrents: International Relations in the Post-Cold War Era,* 2nd edition, ITP Nelson (Scarborough, Ontario, Canada), 1999. Contributor of more than fifty articles and reviews to academic journals and newspapers, including *Canadian*

Foreign Policy, Journal of Shibusawa Studies, Asian Perspective, Pacific Review, Journal of Developing Societies, Australian Journal of International Affairs, and *Asian Culture Quarterly.* Area editor and member of editorial board, *Current Politics and Economics of Japan,* 1990-93; member of editorial board, *Pacific Affairs,* 2000—.

WORK IN PROGRESS: A biography of John Nelson, a founding member of the Institute of Pacific Relations; editing (with Brian L. Job) and writing contributions to *Understanding Japan in the Twenty-first Century: Essays Inspired by Frank Langdon.*

*   *   *

WRIGHT, Robert (Alan) 1957-

PERSONAL: Born January 25, 1957, in Lawton, OK; son of Raymond Jay (an army officer) and Margie (a homemaker; maiden name, Brooks) Wright; married Elizabeth O'Neill (a teacher), October 1, 1988. *Education:* Princeton University, B.A., 1979.

ADDRESSES: Home—1616 18th St. NW, Apt. 806, Washington, DC 20009. *Office*—c/o New Republic, 1220 19th St. NW, Ste. 600, Washington, DC 20036.

CAREER: Sciences, New York, NY, senior editor, 1984-87; *New Republic,* Washington, DC, senior editor, 1988—; writer.

AWARDS, HONORS: National Book Critics Circle Award for biography and autobiography, 1988, for *Three Scientists and Their Gods.*

WRITINGS:

Three Scientists and Their Gods: Looking for Meaning in an Age of Information, Times Books (New York, NY), 1988.
The Moral Animal, Pantheon (New York, NY), 1994.
Nonzero: The Logic of Human Destiny, Pantheon (New York, NY), 2000.

SIDELIGHTS: Robin Wright is a magazine editor and writer who won a National Book Critics Circle Award for his 1988 publication *Three Scientists and Their Gods: Looking for Meaning in an Age of Information.*

Wright was born in Lawton, Oklahoma in 1957, and graduated from Princeton University in 1979. He served as a senior editor at *Sciences* from 1984 to 1987. The next year, he assumed the same position at *New Republic.* During that same period, he also published *Three Scientists and Their Gods,* which earned the National Book Critics Circle Award in the category of biography and autobiography.

Wright followed *Three Scientists and Their Gods* with *The Moral Animal.* A *Business Week* writer later recalled *The Moral Animal* as an "acclaimed" publication, and a *Publishers Weekly* critic remembered it as a "much-praised" volume.

In 2000, Wright produced *Nonzero: The Logic of Human Destiny,* in which he perceives the course of human existence as what Gilbert Taylor, writing in *Booklist,* called "an ineluctable path to betterment, material if not moral." In the book, Wright appropriates the notion of non-zero-sum gaming, in which all competitors—as opposed to one player, or one team—may prosper. Wright contends that the course of evolution is akin to non-zero-sum gaming, and he declares that the future, as a *Publishers Weekly* critic related, is "a world of increasing human cooperation where greed and hatred have outlived their usefulness."

Nonzero has been praised as an informed and compelling study. A *Business Week* reviewer deemed it "erudite and optimistic" and noted Wright's "graceful writing." H. James Birx, wrote in *Library Journal* that Wright's book is "informative and insightful," and Gilbert Taylor affirmed in *Booklist* that *Nonzero* provides an "opinionated big-picture history." Writing in *National Catholic Reporter,* Michael J. Farrell was less impressed. "There is an immense thrill in the prospect that Wright is right and we stand on another threshold for another quantum leap," Farrell wrote. "But to what shall we leap?" He concluded, "One can see why religion still appeals to so many, hinting unrealistically at something more sublime than even non-zero-sum can offer." But a *Publishers Weekly* reviewer concluded that the book "sends an important message that . . . history, in its broadest outlines, is getting better all the time."

BIOGRAPHICAL/CRITICAL SOURCES:

PERIODICALS

Booklist, January 1, 2000, Gilbert Taylor, review of *Nonzero: The Logic of Human Destiny.*

Business Week, February 28, 2000, "Is Humanity Getting Better All the Time?"
Library Journal, February 15, 2000, H. James Birx, review of *Nonzero: The Logic of Human Destiny.*
National Catholic Reporter, February 4, 2000, Michael J. Farrell, "New Book Says We Stand on a Threshold."
Publishers Weekly, January 24, 2000, review of *Nonzero: The Logic of Human Destiny.*
Los Angeles Times, August 10, 1988.*

*   *   *

ZOHAR, Danah 1944-

PERSONAL: Married Ian Marshall; children: two. *Education:* Massachusetts Institute of Technology, B.Sc. (physics), 1966; studied philosophy, religion, and psychology at Harvard University, 1966-69.

ADDRESSES: Home—57 Bainton Rd., Oxford OX2 7AG, England. *Agent*—(speaking engagements) Royce Carlton, Inc., 866 United Nations Plaza, New York, NY 10017. *E-mail*—dzohar@dzohar.com.

CAREER: Freelance writer and lecturer. Hebrew University, graduate research fellow, 1969-71; Cranfield School of Management, visiting fellow; Oxford Brookes University and Templeton College, Oxford, teacher; Cambridge Management Consultants, associate member. Has given lectures at colleges and for businesses and government organizations, including Massachusetts Institute of Technology, University of Arizona, Motorola University, World Business Academy, and European Cultural Foundation.

WRITINGS:

Up My Mother's Flagpole (autobiography), Stein & Day (New York, NY), 1974.
Israel: The Land and Its People, Macdonald Educational, 1977.
Through the Time Barrier: A Study in Precognition and Modern Physics, Heinemann (London, England), 1982, Academy Chicago, 1984.
(With husband, Ian Marshall) *The Quantum Self: Human Nature and Consciousness Defined by the New Physics,* Morrow (New York, NY), 1990.
(With Ian Marshall) *The Quantum Society: Mind, Physics, and a New Social Vision,* Morrow (New York, NY), 1994.

Who's Afraid of Schrodinger's Cat?: A Dictionary of the New Scientific Ideas, Bloomsbury (London, England), 1997.

Rewiring the Corporate Brain: Using the New Science to Rethink How We Structure and Lead, Berrett Koehler, 1997.

(With Ian Marshall) *SQ: Spiritual Intelligence, the Ultimate Intelligence,* Bloomsbury (London, England), 1999.

SIDELIGHTS: Danah Zohar has written several books about the impact that the discoveries and concepts of quantum physics will have on the larger society. In *The Quantum Self: Human Nature and Consciousness Defined by the New Physics, The Quantum Society: Mind, Physics, and a New Social Vision,* and *SQ: Connecting with Our Spiritual Intelligence,* Zohar has speculated upon the possible changes that quantum physics may have on such varied topics as government structure, religious belief, and human psychology.

In *The Quantum Self* Zohar and her co-author husband, Ian Marshall, discuss the quantum nature of the human mind, presenting an argument that the mind has the "capacity to conceive of many possibilities simultaneously," as Christopher Lehmann-Haupt explained in the *New York Times Book Review.* Lehmann-Haupt judged that Zohar writes with "considerable clarity, even growing lyrical at times." Zohar developed her ideas about the relevance of quantum physics to modern society in *The Quantum Society,* also co-authored with Marshall. In this title, the pair argue that societies of the past have been too "mechanistic" in their thinking. Quantum thinking, which goes beyond the either/or approach of the mechanistic to a multi-optional way of viewing the world, is what Zohar and Marshall recommend. According to Karen G. Evans in *Public Administration Review,* the authors "invite us to visualize a plural society, rich with diversity." While Stuart Whitwell in *Booklist* found that *The Quantum Society*'s argument "would appear weak even in an undergraduate class in philosophy," Evans believed that the book "provides considerable food for thought." A critic for *Kirkus Reviews* concluded that the authors "offer the general reader a better introduction to contemporary science than to social philosophy."

In *SQ: Connecting with Our Spiritual Intelligence,* Zohar and Marshall present their case for the existence of what they define as Spiritual Intelligence. Similar to IQ, which measures intelligence, and EQ, which measures emotional levels, SQ measures a spiritual dimension Zohar and Marshall maintain is essential to a successful life. The authors speculate that certain neural oscilla-

tions discovered in the brain may be signs of the hypothetical spiritual intelligence. *SQ* was described as an "engrossing and inevitably controversial book" by a critic for *Publishers Weekly,* while John Cornwell in the London *Times* found that Zohar and Marshall's "attempt to escape from what they call eliminative materialism, the soulless reductionism of much of cognitive science, is laudable."

BIOGRAPHICAL/CRITICAL SOURCES:

PERIODICALS

Booklist, April 15, 1994, Stuart Whitwell, review of *The Quantum Society,* p. 1493; March 15, 1997, Gilbert Taylor, review of *Who's Afraid of Schrodinger's Cat?,* p. 1211.

BookWatch, May, 1994, review of *The Quantum Society,* p. 7.

Choice, December, 1994, review of *The Quantum Society,* p. 637; November, 1995, review of *The Quantum Self,* p. 411; May, 1998, review of *Rewiring the Corporate Brain,* p. 1575.

Kirkus Reviews, February 15, 1994, review of *The Quantum Society,* p. 217; November 15, 1999, review of *SQ: Connecting with Our Spiritual Intelligence,* p. 1800.

Library Journal, March 1, 1997, Bruce Slutsky, review of *Who's Afraid of Schrodinger's Cat?,* p. 96; March 15, 1998, review of *Rewiring the Corporate Brain,* p. 39; January, 2000, review of *SQ: Connecting with Our Spiritual Intelligence,* p. 124.

New Statesman & Society, January 19, 1990, Robert Walgate, review of *The Quantum Self,* p. 38.

New York Times Book Review, March 1, 1990, Christopher Lehmann-Haupt, review of *The Quantum Self.*

Observer, October 10, 1993, review of *The Quantum Society,* p. 18.

People Management, February 17, 2000, review of *SQ: Connecting with Our Spiritual Intelligence,* p. 55.

Public Administration Review, September-October, 1996, Karen G. Evans, review of *The Quantum Society,* p. 491.

Publishers Weekly, December 22, 1989, Genevieve Stuttaford, review of *The Quantum Self,* p. 50; November 22, 1999, review of *SQ: Connecting with Our Spiritual Intelligence,* p. 48.

Spectator, December 4, 1993, review of *The Quantum Society,* p. 42.

Times (London), January 23, 2000, John Cornwell, review of *SQ: Connecting with Our Spiritual Intelligence,* Culture Section, p. 41

OTHER

Danah Zohar's Web page, http://www.dzohar.com/ (September 4, 2000).*